World Almanac of Islamism
2017 Edition

American Foreign Policy Council

ROWMAN & LITTLEFIELD
Lanham • Boulder • New York • London

Published in association with the American Foreign Policy Council

Published by Rowman & Littlefield
A wholly owned subsidiary of The Rowman & Littlefield Publishing Group, Inc.
4501 Forbes Boulevard, Suite 200, Lanham, Maryland 20706
www.rowman.com

Unit A, Whitacre Mews, 26-34 Stannary Street, London SE11 4AB

Copyright © 2017 by Rowman & Littlefield

All rights reserved. No part of this book may be reproduced in any form or by any electronic or mechanical means, including information storage and retrieval systems, without written permission from the publisher, except by a reviewer who may quote passages in a review.

British Library Cataloguing in Publication Information Available

Library of Congress Cataloging-in-Publication Data Available

ISBN: 978-1-4422-7344-3 (cloth : alk. paper)
ISBN: 978-1-4422-7345-0 (electronic)

∞™ The paper used in this publication meets the minimum requirements of American National Standard for Information Sciences—Permanence of Paper for Printed Library Materials, ANSI/NISO Z39.48-1992.

Printed in the United States of America

The World Almanac of Islamism
2017 Edition

TABLE OF CONTENTS

Preface 1

North America 4
Canada 5
United States 23

Latin America 44
Argentina 45
Bolivia 58
Brazil 70
Nicaragua 81
Venezuela 88

Middle East and North Africa 97
Algeria 98
Bahrain 110
Egypt 133
Iraq 152
Iran, Islamic Republic of 169
Israel 185
Jordan 201
Kuwait 212
Lebanon 228
Libya 248
Morocco 263
The Palestinian Territories 277
Qatar 297
Saudi Arabia 314
Syria 333
Tunisia 362
United Arab Emirates 378

Yemen 398

Sub-Saharan Africa 417
Ethiopia 418
Mali 429
Nigeria. 444
Somalia 456
South Africa 472
Tanzania 482

Europe. 496
Albania. 497
Denmark. 515
France 526
Germany. 538
Italy 559
Kosovo. 570
Macedonia. 586
Netherlands 603
Spain. 622
United Kingdom. 638

Eurasia 655
Azerbaijan 656
Kazakhstan. 666
Kyrgyzstan. 680
Russian Federation. 687
Tajikistan 705
Turkey 715
Turkmenistan 742
Uzbekistan. 751

South Asia. 764
Afghanistan 765
Bangladesh. 782
India. 796
Maldives 817

Pakistan 833

East Asia 855
Australia 856
China 875
Indonesia 889
Malaysia 908
Philippines 921
Thailand 934

Global Movements 942
Al-Qaeda 943
Boko Haram 956
Fetullah Gülen Movement 969
Hezbollah 987
Hizb ut-Tahrir 1005
Islamic State 1016
Lashkar-e Taiba 1040
Muslim Brotherhood 1058
Tablighi Jamaa't 1072
Tabilan 1087

Contributors 1109

Preface

Welcome to the 2017 edition of the American Foreign Policy Council's *World Almanac of Islamism*. The *Almanac* is a unique compilation designed to examine the current status of the political phenomenon of Islamism worldwide. It is intended to provide a snapshot of contemporary Islamism, as well as of the movements it motivates and the governments it impacts.

For the purposes of this collection, the term Islamist is used to describe movements, groups, and individuals which harness religious values and ideals in the service of a political agenda aimed at spreading or imposing Islamic law, either locally, regionally, or internationally. While it showcases a broad spectrum of Islamist thought and ideology, and touches more briefly upon more moderate Muslim movements, the Almanac does not—and is not meant to—provide a comprehensive chronicle of the full range of Islamic political thought.

Since the *Almanac* was last published in 2014, the complexion of Islamism has changed considerably. In North America, the United States has been impacted by several terrorist incidents inspired by the ideology of the Islamic State, while both the U.S. and Canada remain mired in debate over the proper response to migrants fleeing violence in the Middle East. In Latin America, Islamic activism continues to rise, propelled by the ongoing conflict in the Middle East, as well as quiet efforts to establish a regional presence by groups such as the Islamic State. Iranian activity is likewise increasing in the Americas, as the Islamic Republic—now unfettered from international sanctions as a result of its 2015 nuclear deal with the West (formally known as the Joint Comprehensive Plan of Action)—has begun reengaging wit the region in earnest, strengthening its trade and strategic relationships with various Latin American countries.

In the Middle East, Syria's civil war has become a new front for global *jihad*, as well as a crucible for future terrorism. Foreign fighters from throughout the Middle East, Europe and Asia have flocked to Syria by the thousands to fight against the regime of Bashar al-Assad, while a smaller but still significant number of "volunteers" has been recruited by Iran to enter the conflict on the side of the Syrian regime. The resulting conflict has the potential to destabilize multiple regions in the years ahead, as its "alumni" return to their home countries and foment local instability in those places.

Africa, too, has emerged as a significant locus of Islamist violence. In Libya, once ruled by the regime of Col. Muammar Gadhafi, the Islamic State and other assorted militants have gained a foothold, aided by the political chaos of two warring governments. Further south, two major Islamist movements—Somalia's al-Shabaab and Nigeria's Boko Haram—continue to thrive, as well as to expand their international connections.

Like North America, Europe has experienced its share of terrorist incidents in recent years, among them a series of coordinated attacks in Paris in November 2015 a December 2016 attack in Berlin, and a March 2017 attack on the British Parliament. These "lone wolf" style attacks have intensified Europe's ongoing debate over the fate of migrants and refugees from the Middle East and Africa.

Eurasia, meanwhile, has seen a significant mobilization of Islamists, with militants from Russia and several Central Asian nations migrating to the Middle East to join the ranks of the Islamic State in comparatively large numbers. Extremist activity has also intensified at home throughout the "post-Soviet space," propelled by a variety of causes (from official repression to Russia's ongoing involvement in the Syrian civil war).

Islamist extremism continues to represent a significant threat to nations of Asia as well. Afghanistan's government still struggles to contain the militant Taliban movement—a challenge now made more difficult by the presence of the Islamic State in that country. China, for its part, continues to engage in an extensive policy of repression against its indigenous Uighur Muslim minority, propelled by fears of rising militancy and growing extremist influence on this segment of the population from beyond its borders.

Islamist tactics and behavior are changing as well. As the world becomes increasingly globalized, Islamist movements are in increasing competition with one another for both resources and recruits. But that are also in greater communication than ever before, a dynamic evident in the growing sophistication of extremist media and messaging. Likewise, with the lion's share of international counterterrorism efforts being directed against the Islamic State, its main ideological competitor, al-Qaeda, has been afforded relative freedom of action—something the Bin Laden network has used to great effect, solidifying its territorial presence throughout the greater Middle East and honing a more inclusive, though equally subversive, Islamist message.

Islamist thought, as well as the operations and objectives of Islamist groups themselves, continues to change and evolve at a rapid pace. The Almanac represents our attempt to track and codify those changes as a way of assisting policymakers in the United States and elsewhere to develop better, more comprehensive approaches to that changing challenge.

It is, by its nature, a massive undertaking, and this edition of the Almanac simply would not have been possible without the help of a number of talented and dedicated researchers: Liam Bobyak, John Burke, Brian Carpowich, Cory Driver, Tzara Geraghty, Katelyn Johnson, Garret Lynch, Alexis Mrachek, Amir Sanatkar, Jennifer Schneider, and Hannah Wallace. We are deeply grateful to all of them for their help and assistance. Special thanks also go to AFPC Vice President of Operations and Director of Defense Technology Programs Rich Harrison, for his continued support, and to AFPC President Herman Pirchner, Jr., whose guidance and vision have been indispensable throughout this undertaking.

Ilan Berman, Executive Editor
Chloe Thompson, Managing Editor

Washington, DC
March 2017

NORTH AMERICA

COUNTRIES
Canada
United States

CANADA

Quick Facts

Population: 35,362,905 (July 2016 est.)

Area: 9,984,670 sq km

Ethnic Groups: Canadian 32.2%, English 19.8%, French 15.5%, Scottish 14.4%, Irish 13.8%, German 9.8%, Italian 4.5%, Chinese 4.5%, North American Indian 4.2%, other 50.9%

Religions: Catholic 39% (includes Roman Catholic 38.8%, other Catholic .2%), Protestant 20.3% (includes United Church 6.1%, Anglican 5%, Baptist 1.9%, Lutheran 1.5%, Pentecostal 1.5%, Presbyterian 1.4%, other Protestant 2.9%), Orthodox 1.6%, other Christian 6.3%, Muslim 3.2%, Hindu 1.5%, Sikh 1.4%, Buddhist 1.1%, Jewish 1%, other 0.6%, none 23.9%

Government Type: Federal parliamentary democracy (Parliament of Canada) under a constitutional monarchy; a Commonwealth realm

GDP (official exchange rate): $1.532 trillion (2015 est.)

Map and Quick Facts courtesy of the CIA World Factbook (January 12, 2017)

Overview

Canada is a free and peaceful society, with a large and generally successful immigration program. Newcomers to Canada tend to learn the local language (English or French), integrate into the economy, adopt Canadian values, and develop a positive Canadian identity. Muslims are no exception, and most Muslim communities in Canada are better integrated than their European counterparts. That said, Canada has also earned the unsavory reputation of being a terrorist haven, thanks to decades of political inaction and a weak legal framework to stop terrorist activities. A succession of terrorist groups flocked to Canada in the decades prior to 9/11. Following the 2001 attacks, Canada finally enacted stricter anti-terrorism laws. Islamist, jihadist and other terrorist groups have, nevertheless, been able to hide amid Canada's immigrant communities – including its Muslim population of just over 1 million.[1] Persistent and subversive Islamist groups have penetrated this community and established terrorist cells, fundraising operations, communal organizations, mosques, and schools across Canada. The Canadian government once again strengthened its response to these developments through legislation (including the 2015 Anti-Terrorism Act, known as Bill C51) which has provided new tools for the Canadian government to fight terrorism and the ideology responsible for it.

ISLAMIST ACTIVITY

Exploiting the lack of anti-terrorism legislation that existed prior 2001, terrorist groups traditionally used Canada's immigrant communities as safe havens and, occasionally, as bases of operations. These groups included, among others, the Armenian Secret Army for the Liberation of Armenia (ASALA),[2] Sri Lanka's Liberation Tigers of Tamil Eelam (LTTE),[3] and Sikh extremists.[4] More recently, these organizations and groups have been joined and outpaced by radical Islamist elements of various political and ideological stripes.

Canada's Islamist terrorists fall into three broad camps: (1) *Salafist*, including the new and enthusiastic supporters of the Islamic State, (2) Shi'ite, and (3) Palestinian. *Salafists* in Canada belong primarily to al-Qaeda, the Islamic State, and Armed Islamic Group (GIA) – an Algerian group striving to turn Algeria into a theocratic Islamic state.

According to the Canadian Security Intelligence Service (CSIS), there are three primary ways in which terrorism threatens Canadian safety and security:[5] 1) terrorists continue to plot direct attacks against Canada and its allies, at home and abroad, with the intent of causing death, disruption and fear; 2) terrorists conduct activities in Canada to support terrorist activity globally, namely fundraising to support attacks and military groups; and 3) terrorists use social media to reach and radicalize individual Canadians, who are then convinced to travel abroad to join a terrorist army and commit attacks, or to receive training on terrorist methods.

Al-Qaeda

Al-Qaeda has a persistent presence in Canada, and al-Qaeda extremists continue to pose a threat to Canada's national security. While Al-Qaeda has experienced international decline over the past five years, it continues to command the loyalty, and, according to CSIS, continues to constitute a serious threat to Canada's security.[6]

Al-Qaeda has a history of organizing and raising funds in Canada. One of the most prominent ties linking Canada to al-Qaeda has been the Khadr family. Ahmed Said Khadr, the patriarch of the family, moved to Montreal in 1975, and began raising extensive funds for al-Qaeda. At one point, he was the highest-ranking member of the group in Canada. He died in a 2003 confrontation with the Pakistani military,[7] but his Islamist legacy lives on through his children. Two sons, Omar and Abdul Rahman, fought for the Taliban and were sent to Guantanamo. Omar infamously killed an American medic, Spt. 1st Class Christopher J. Speer, during a gun battle in Afghanistan in July 2002. He was then arrested and sent to Guantanamo Bay. Abdul Rahman was released in 2002, and returned back to Canada.[8]

Omar Khadr pleaded guilty to murder in violation of the laws of war, attempted murder in violation of the laws of war, conspiracy, two counts of providing material support for terrorism, and spying in the United States.[9] In exchange for his guilty plea, the military tribunal sentenced him to eight years in prison and promised to repatriate him to Canada after he had served the first year of his sentence at Guantanamo. The U.S. finally repatriated Omar Khadr to Canada on September 29, 2012.[10] He was then released on bail from an Edmonton prison and put on "house arrest" in May 2015. Since this time, Khadr has had his bail conditions relaxed to include visiting his still-radicalized family members in Toronto, he become engaged to a Palestinian activist, and he filed a $20 million lawsuit against the Canadian government.[11]

The Khadr's may be Canada's most infamous al-Qaeda-linked operatives, but they are certainly not alone in Canada. Fateh Kamel headed another al-Qaeda-GIA cell in Canada. Kamel fought with *mujahideen* in Afghanistan in the 1980s[12] and Bosnia in the 1990s. In 1996, he became a liaison between al-Qaeda and the GIA.[13] He applied for a Canadian passport in 2005, and while his request was denied, citing national security threats, in response, Kamel sued.[14] The Canadian federal judge initially declared the restriction unconstitutional, that decision was overturned upon appeal and Kamel was denied citizenship.[15]

Two Canadians also participated in the In Amenas hostage crisis in January 2013. An al-Qaeda-linked terrorist group took over 800 hostages at a gas facility in In Amenas, Algeria, and, ultimately, at least 38 civilians and 29 terrorists died during the siege.[16] Two of the terrorists, Ali Medlej and Xristos Katsiroubas, were Canadian men and high school classmates from London South Collegiate Institute in London, Ontario. Both of these men were killed in the attack.[17] Mauritanian authorities had previously arrested a third classmate, Aaron Yoon, who was convicted in July 2012 of having ties to al-Qaeda and of posing a danger to national security. He was sentenced to two years in prison,[18] following which, Yoon was transferred back to London, Canada in July 2013.[19]

In recent years, al-Qaeda cells in Canada have graduated from planning attacks in Canada, to be carried out overseas, to planning attacks against Canada. In 2006, the Royal Canadian Mounted Police (RCMP) arrested eighteen men plotting to bomb the Toronto Stock Exchange, the Toronto offices of CSIS, and a nearby military base.[20] They also intended to storm the Canadian Broadcasting Corporation

(CBC) and Canadian Parliament, take hostages, and decapitate the leaders of each party, including the Prime Minister. They planned to demand that Canada withdraw her troops from Afghanistan.[21]

These terrorists' efforts were thwarted thanks to an undercover effort by the RCMP. Of the 18 men arrested, eleven have been convicted of terrorism offences and two have been sentenced to life in prison.[22] The ring-leader, Zakaria Amara pled guilty, received a life sentence and was stripped of his Canadian citizenship under a new law brought in by the government of Canada's former Prime Minister Stephen Harper. Harper's successor, current Prime Minister Justin Trudeau, has pledge to reverse this law and overhaul the government's ability to strip citizenship from foreign-born dual citizens convicted on terrorism charges.

Another al-Qaeda connected plot was thwarted on April 22, 2013, after an eight-month investigation. The RCMP arrested Tunisian-born Chiheb Esseghaier and Raed Jaser, a Palestinian from the United Arab Emirates, for plotting to derail a VIA Rail passenger train near Toronto. Police claim that the pair received guidance from members of al-Qaeda living in Iran.[23]

A final example of an al-Qaeda connected terrorist cell was that headed up by Hiva Mohammad Alizadeh in Ottawa. The Iranian-born Kurdish refugee to Canada, considered the ringleader of an Ottawa al-Qaeda cell, pled guilty to a terror plot in 2014 and was sentenced to 24 years in a federal prison.[24] Alizadeh admitted that he spent two months in an al-Qaeda terrorist training camp in Afghanistan in 2009, where he received training on using firearms and assembling improvised explosive devices, and smuggled 56 circuit boards, capable of triggering remote bombs, back to Canada.[25]

The Islamic State
The Islamic State has garnered appeal in Canada since its emergence in 2014. Dozens of Canadians have left their homes to fight in the Islamic State's *caliphate* in Iraq and Syria, and there have been at least two attacks, using lone wolf tactics, carried out by Canadian men who had sworn allegiance to the Islamic State.

The first attack was carried out by Canadian-born Martin Couture-Rouleau, who, on October 20, 2014, intentionally rammed his car into a pair of Canadian Forces soldiers in a shopping mall parking lot in Saint-Jean-sur-Richelieu, Quebec, killing one of them. Couture-Rouleau converted from Christianity to Islam in 2013, and began regularly posting pro-Islamic State and anti-Semitic messages on his Facebook page.[26] Just two days later, a second Islamist attack took place on Parliament Hill in Ottawa. Islamist terrorist Michael Zehaf-Bibeau shot and killed Corporal Nathan Cirillo, who was standing ceremonially on guard at the Canadian War Memorial. After the shooting, Zehaf-Bibeau reportedly raises his gun in the air and shouted

"For Iraq." He then stormed the Centre Block building of the Canadian Parliament, shot a security guard and made his way towards the Library of Parliament before being fatally shot by parliamentary security guards. Both Prime Minister Stephen Harper and Leader of Her Majesty's Royal Opposition Thomas Mulcair were in adjacent rooms when the terrorist was killed.[27]

On top of these attacks at home, a sizeable number of young Canadians have taken up arms to fight alongside Islamic State militants in Iraq, Syria and beyond. A 2016 report from the Canadian department of public safety highlighted that at least 180 individuals with a connection to Canada are currently overseas fighting alongside Islamist terrorist organizations, primarily the Islamic State.[28] There are also at least 60 known returned foreign fighters in Canada, most of them living freely.[29] According to Larry Brooks, a former CSIS counter-terrorism official, it's nearly impossible to prove to a Canadian judge, in a Canadian court, that an individual has participated in terrorist activities overseas.[30]

Hezbollah

Canada remains an important source of financing and operational organizing for Hezbollah, and despite being banned in 2002 as a terrorist entity,[31] the Iranian-backed Lebanese Shi'ite militia continues to raise funds, procure equipment, and hide wanted terrorists in Canada.[32]

The case of Mohammad Hussein al Husseini, a Hezbollah operative deported from Canada in 1994, helped shine light on the organizations strong position in Canada. During interviews with CSIS, al Husseini provided insight into the network of members, supporters, and operatives and their activities in cities across Canada.

Years later, Mohammad Hassan Dbouk began to run the Canadian portion of Hezbollah's funding and procurement network, under the command of Haj Hassan Hilu Laqis, then Hezbollah's chief military procurement officer.[33] After seeking refugee status in Canada in 1998, Dbouk raised cash through credit card and banking scams, as well as cigarette smuggling, and used the proceeds to purchase high-tech military supplies used in Lebanon. Dbouk became an important asset for Hezbollah, and he was rejected five times for suicide missions because he was too valuable in Canada.[34] CSIS agents began monitoring his activates, and Dbouk was indicted by a U.S. federal court in 2001.[35]

In June 2002, Israeli authorities arrested Fawzi Ayoub, a 39-year-old Lebanese-born Canadian, who used a fake American passport to enter Israel. Israel accused him of being a Hezbollah fighter and of training Palestinian militants in the West Bank in Hezbollah bomb-making techniques.[36]

Hezbollah was also known to hide terrorists wanted by other countries in Canada. Hani Abd al-Rahim al-Sayegh, a leader of Saudi Hezbollah involved in the 1996 Khobar Towers bombing that killed nineteen American Air Force personnel, made a refugee claim in Canada using a false name and settled in Ottawa, where he was arrested a year later.[37]

Hezbollah was listed as a banned terrorist entity in Canada in 2002, following a federal court case brought forward by Jewish organization B'nai Brith.[38] Although officially banned, Hezbollah continues its subversive reach into Canada. In 2011, the US Treasury Department identified the Lebanese Canadian Bank SAL, along with its subsidiaries, as a "financial institution of primary money laundering concern under Section 311 of the USA PATRIOT Act for the bank's role in facilitating the money laundering activities of an international narcotics trafficking and money laundering network.[39] This bank's network facilitated the movement of illegal narcotics from Latin America to Europe and the Middle East, and laundered hundreds of millions monthly. This was done through bank accounts and other assets, including U.S. used car dealerships, according to the U.S. Treasury.[40] The U.S. government found that Hezbollah derived direct "financial support from the criminal activities of [this] network."[41]

The Lebanese Canadian Bank (LCB) was headquartered in Beirut, and had a representative office in Montreal, Quebec. Originally established in 1960, LCB operated as a subsidiary of the Royal Bank of Canada in the Middle East from 1968 to 1988, before becoming a privately-owned bank. In 2009, LCB's total assets were worth more than $5 billion.[42]

The Iranian embassy in Ottawa also had a history of funding and aiding a controversial cultural center with ties to Hezbollah, and was increasingly considered an outpost for espionage and subversion by the Iranian regime. The Iran embassy regularly hosted and funded conferences for Iranian Canadians and invited guests only. These events sought to reach sympathetic members of the Muslim community – to recruit, persuade, and intimidate them to join the Islamic Republic's network.[43] In 2012, the Canadian government posted a notice on the Iranian embassy door ordering all Iranian officials to leave the country within five days. The government also closed Canada's embassy in Tehran, recalling all Canadian diplomats, cutting diplomatic ties with Iran, and officially listing Iran as a state sponsor of terrorism.

Canada went further by amending the *State Immunity Act* and adopting the *Justice for the Victims of Terrorism Act*, both of which allowed the families and victims of terrorism to take legal action and seek damages from the perpetrators of terrorism and those who support them, including the government of Iran. This effectively eliminated the legal distinction between terrorist groups and the states that bankroll them, extinguishing the sovereign immunity protection typically granted to governments. To assist victims in identifying and locating Iran's state assets, the government released a list of known Iranian state-owned property in Canada. In 2014, an Ontario judge ordered the seizure of more than $7 million in bank accounts and property belonging to Iran. The historic ruling validated the Harper government's legal changes. Currently over 90 Canadian victims of terrorism have launched claims in Ontario's Superior Court seeking compensation from Iran for its role in training, arming, and financing Islamic terror networks.[44]

Palestinian Islamists

Hamas, the most influential Palestinian Islamist group, has a history of using Canada as a fundraising base, even after the government designated it a terrorist organization in November 2002.[45] A May 2000 Privy Council Office memo to Prime Minister Jean Chrétien identified the Jerusalem Fund for Human Services (Jerusalem Fund) as a fundraising entity for Hamas.[46]

The Canadian Coalition for Democracies alleges that the Jerusalem Fund responded to the flagging by merely changing its name to the International Relief Fund for the Afflicted and Needy (IRFAN) in 2001-2002. The Canadian Jewish News discovered that the Jerusalem Fund and IRFAN shared a mailing address in Mississauga, as well as a fax number.[47]

In 2004, IFRAN came under scrutiny from the Canada Revenue Agency and its auditors over fundraising links to Hamas, but was able to keep its charitable status by signing an agreement stating it would not fund any organization linked to Hamas.[48] A later audit found that, between 2004 and 2009, IFRAN had "openly supported and provided funding to Hamas" while also engaging in "deceptive and misleading fundraising."[49] A Charities Branch document highlights how IFRAN sent almost $15 million to Hamas and related agencies during this period, leading to the government's decision to strip IFRAN of its charity status in 2011, and, in 2014, to add IFRAN to Canada's official list of terrorist groups.[50]

Hamas also has raised hundreds of thousands of dollars in Canada through the Texas-headquartered Holy Land Foundation (HLF).[51] The U.S., which designated Hamas a terrorist organization in 1995, shut down HLF in 2008 and, in 2009, sentenced five of its leaders to prison terms ranging from 15 to 65 years.[52]

Additionally, Hamas is known to have recruited Canadians to commit attacks within Canada. In 2003, for instance, Israel arrested a Canadian man in Gaza who pled guilty to conspiracy and illegal military training for planning attacks against Jews in Canada and the U.S.[53] Hamas denied recruiting him, claiming that they limit their attacks to Middle Eastern targets.[54]

The smaller Palestinian Islamic Jihad (PIJ) has also tried to penetrate Canada – albeit on a much more modest scale. The group is known to have long collected and laundered money in Canada, and even attempted to acquire a fraudulent visa so that its treasurer, Muhammed Tasir Hassan Al-Khatib, could visit Canada.[55] Additional details of PIJ activity inside Canada remain spotty, but the country's intelligence service has warned that the group could expand its current, minimal activity in the years ahead; a confidential 2003 CSIS report notes that the discovery of a PIJ fundraising network in Florida "raises the possibility of PIJ elements crossing the border to develop a similar infrastructure in Canada."[56] To date, however, here is no evidence that the PIJ has done so. Like Hamas, PIJ was designated a foreign terrorist organization by the Canadian government in November 2002, and its activities seem to have waned in Canada since this designation.[57]

Islamist community organizations

Though it is not the norm for the Canadian Muslim community, a number of Islamic community organizations that have been infiltrated with radical extremists. The most prominent example was the Canadian Islamic Congress (CIC), which called itself "Canada's largest national non-profit and wholly independent Islamic organization."[58] After a number of controversies, the CIC finally closed its doors in 2014, and is now defunct. The CIC had a history of demonizing Israel, fabricating lies about opponents, and apologizing for hardline Islamist groups,[59] including by inciting anti-Semitism and justifying violence committed by Islamist groups against Israel. The CIC's leadership has further validated terrorism by denouncing the Canadian government's decision to designate Hamas and Hezbollah as terrorist groups, calling it an "unconscionable act of hypocrisy and a mockery of justice."[60]

The Islamist Muslim Students' Association (MSA) has chapters at many Canadian universities. Muslim Brotherhood activists founded the MSA in 1963 at the University of Illinois Urbana-Champaign[61] to help Muslims "practice Islam as a complete way of life."[62] Chapters of the MSA have raised funds for the Hamas-linked Holy Land Foundation,[63] as well as the Benevolence International Foundation and the Global Relief Foundation (both of which were later outlawed by the U.S. government for their links to al-Qaeda).[64]

Radicalism can be found in Canadian places of worship as well, with some mosques and Islamic schools indoctrinating their parishioners and students. The Salaheddin Islamic Center and the Al-Rahman Islamic Centre, both in Toronto, are examples of this trend. The Khadr family frequented the former, and six of the terrorists in the cell that planned to storm parliament and decapitate the Prime Minister prayed at the latter.[65] The Salaheddin Islamic Center's imam, Aly Hindy, refused to join 120 other Canadian imams in condemning the London Tube Bombings in

2004, and he later defended members of the Toronto 18 terror cell.[66] He also directs his parishioners not to cooperate with Canadian authorities, and officiates at illegal polygamous weddings.[67]

ISLAMISM AND SOCIETY

Canada's 2011 census, the most recent data available from the Government of Canada, recorded 1.05 million Muslims in the country, equaling 3.2 percent of the total population.[68] Sixty-eight percent of Canada's Muslims are immigrants, and more than 387,000 Muslims have entered Canada since 2001. A majority of Canada's Muslims live in the province of Ontario (581,950) and most of those are located in the city of Toronto (424,930). The province of Quebec hosts the second largest Muslim community (243,430), 221,040 of whom live in Montreal, and it is home to many immigrants from the former French colonies of Algeria and Lebanon. Sizeable Muslim populations also reside in the provinces of Alberta (113,445) and British Columbia (79,310).

Continued immigration and a high birth rate are rapidly increasing those numbers, making Islam Canada's fastest growing religion. Between 2001 and 2011, for example, Muslims grew from 2% of the population to 3.2%.[69] The community is very ethnically diverse. It was recorded in 2001 that 36.7 percent were South Asian, 21.1 percent were Arab, 14.0 percent were West Asian, and 14.2 percent belonged to other groups.[70] This Muslim population tends to underperform compared to the larger Canadian public on a number of measures. As of 2001, for example, the Muslim community suffered a 14.4 percent unemployment rate, almost double the national rate of 7.4 percent.[71] An updated analysis based on the 2011 Statistics Canada National Household Survey similarly found that 13.9 percent of Muslims in Canada were unemployed, as compared to a 7.8 percent national unemployment rate in Canada.[72]

However, despite the disproportionately high unemployment rate, according to a 2007 Environics poll, 81 percent of Canadian Muslims "felt satisfied with the way things were going in their country."[73] Unfortunately, the same Environics poll highlighted a troubling propensity for radicalism among respondents, with about 12 percent of Canadian Muslims polled saying that the terrorist plot to storm Parliament and behead the Prime Minister was justified.[74]

Perhaps that often-vocal minority explains why a 2010 Leger Marketing poll found that 55 percent of Canadians disagreed when asked whether "Muslims share our values."[75] A subsequent 2009 Angus Reid Strategies poll uncovered similar opinions, with only 28 percent of Canadians polled viewing Islam favorably, compared with 72 percent approval for Christianity and 53 percent approval for Judaism.[76]

The updated 2016 Environics report on Muslims in Canada found similarly mixed results. On the one hand, it found that 83 percent of Muslims polled were "very proud to be Canadian," compared to 73 percent of non-Muslims in Canada. However, when it comes to social views, on issues such as acceptance of homosexuals in society, and the dominance of men in the household, for instance, Muslims and non-Muslims have very diverging opinions. While 80 percent of Canadians believe that homosexuality should be accepted by society, only 36 percent of Muslims agree with that statement.[77]

Nevertheless, Islamic law has made at least a limited mark in certain locales and sectors of Canadian society. When first passed, Ontario's *Arbitration Act of 1991* permitted people to submit civil disputes to arbitration panels whose decisions, if the parties consented, could deviate from Canadian civil law as long as they did not breach the criminal code.[78] Controversy erupted in 2003 when the Islamic Institute for Civil Justice broadcast its intention to establish panels that would use *sharia*. The fierceness of the debate prompted Ontario's government to ask Marion Boyd, a former attorney general of Ontario, to study the proposal for sharia-influenced arbitration panels. Although Boyd concluded that the *Arbitration Act* should remain in force so long as several new safeguards were added,[79] Ontario's Premier, Dalton McGuinty, ultimately decided to scrap the arbitration panels altogether. In 2006, Ontario's legislature amended the *Arbitration Act* to require that arbitration be "conducted exclusively in accordance with the law of Ontario or another Canadian jurisdiction."[80]

This precedent-setting decision to prevent Sharia law in Canada was reached, in part, thanks to protests and coordinated efforts led by prominent moderate Muslim figures in Canada, including Tarek Fatah, founder of the Muslim Canadian Congress who called it "a Saudi-funded cancer spreading across the world," and Raheel Raza, a leading liberal Muslim activist, author and documentary filmmaker who created the film "Honor Diaries."[81]

ISLAMISM AND THE STATE

Canada passed its first anti-terrorism legislation, the *Canadian Anti-Terrorism Act* (Bill C-36), in the wake of the September 11th terrorist attacks on the United States. Before the *Anti-Terrorism Act* received the Royal Assent on December 18, 2001, the Canadian criminal code did not formally define "terrorist activity." The *Anti-Terrorism Act* rectified this deficiency, providing a definition of both "terrorist activity" and "terrorist group,"[82] and authorizing the Governor in Council, on the recommendation of the Solicitor General, to designate an entity as a terrorist group.[83]

The *Anti-Terrorism Act*'s prohibition of providing financial services to terrorist groups represented Canada's first measure aimed at curbing terrorist financing. Before the *Act*, people could legally raise money for terrorist groups in Canada and the government could only prosecute people for directly funding a terrorist attack. However, as a practical matter, because of the opaque manner in which terrorist groups use banks and financial markets, it had proven to be almost impossible to connect donors to attacks.[84]

The *Anti-Terrorism Act* equipped authorities with several new tools to fight terrorism, including investigative hearings, preventive arrests, and new rules concerning information disclosure and rescinding a group's charity status. The *Act* amended the *Proceeds of Crime (Money Laundering) Act* to provide authorities with a scheme for monitoring suspicious financial transactions that could be tied to terrorism. The *Act* also established a mechanism for rescinding organizations' charitable status if there are reasonable grounds to believe that it has or will fund a terrorist group.[85]

However, in the wake of the 2013 Boston Marathon Bombing, Liberals and Conservatives united to pass the *Combating Terrorism Act*. The bill revives the investigative hearing and preventive detention practices discontinued in 2007. Authorities may compel someone to submit to interrogation if he or she is suspected of having knowledge of a terrorist act, and they may imprison anyone who refuse to cooperate for up to twelve months. Authorities may also detain someone for up to three days and impose probationary conditions for up to a year on anyone suspected of engaging in terrorist activity.[86]

In the wake of the two Islamist terrorist attacks that resulted in the death of two members of the Canadian Forces in October, 2014 the Harper government introduced updates to the *Anti-Terrorism Act* in January 2015, through Bill C-51. The bill—an Act to enact the *Security of Canada Information Sharing Act* and the *Secure Air Travel Act*, to amend the *Criminal Code*, the *Canadian Security Intelligence Service Act* and the *Immigration and Refugee Protection Act* and to make related and consequential amendments to other Acts—sought to broaden the mandate of CSIS and to allow various Canadian government agencies to share information more easily, with the goal of proactively thwarting attacks before they happen.[87] While Bill C-51 sparked some controversy, it was passed and received royal assent in June 2015. During the 2015 Canadian election campaign, current Prime Minister Justin Trudeau pledged to amend the bill in order to strike a greater balance between promoting security and respecting civil liberties. Despite this pledge, the Trudeau government has not taken steps to amend the *Act* since forming government in late 2015.[88]

Prime Minister Trudeau, much like former U.S. President Barack Obama, is reluctant to discuss the threat posed by Islamists in Canada, and avoids using the term Islamist terrorism. In September 2016, Trudeau visited a gender-segregated mosque, the Ottawa Muslim Association, whose *imam* is a member of a group considered by some to be a terrorist organization. Trudeau met with Samy Metwally, who is a member of the International Union for Muslim Scholars (IUMS), which was founded by Yusuf al-Qaradawi, the Muslim Brotherhood's leading ideological figure. In 2014, the United Arab Emirates listed IUMS on its list of designated terrorist organizations.[89]

Trudeau's candidate selection and subsequent members of the Liberal caucus also raise concerns about his apparent lack of concern toward individuals with connections with Islamists in Canada and abroad. Two members of his Liberal caucus, MPs Ali Ehassi and Majid Jowhari, are also Iranian nationals, and have been lobbying to re-open diplomatic ties with Iran. The two men hosted an invitation-only roundtable event in Toronto in November 2016 to discuss Canadian-Iranian relations. The event was criticized for being stacked with pro-regime voices and not discussing Iran's human rights violations.[90]

Possibly even more concerning is Mississauga Liberal MP Omar Alghabra, who Trudeau appointed as the Parliamentary Secretary to the Minister of Foreign Affairs. The Saudi-born Syrian Alghabra is the former president of the Canadian Arab Federation, an organization that was defunded by the Canadian government in 2009 over its participating in a conference with Hamas and Hezbollah delegates and for comparing Israelis to Nazis. In 2014, a Federal Court ruling upheld the decision, citing evidence that included a sign threatening to murder a Jewish child, and because of a CAF-sponsored essay contest on the topic of "ethnic cleansing" in Israel. Alghabra once wrote an open letter calling Israel "a country that is conducting a brutal and the longest contemporary occupation in the world."[91]

While Canada has the unfortunate reputation, particularly in the United States, for not taking national security and terrorism seriously, this stereotype is not accurate. Canada has made significant stride and marked legal progress in investigating and combating terrorism, and the silent majority of Canadians support measures to boost immigration security and protect the safety of Canadians. While terrorism and the broader threat of Islamist infiltration remains a threat to Canada, Canadians and Canadian security officials remain vigilant against the various threats of Islamist organizations and terrorist groups.

ENDNOTES

[1] Statistics Canada, "2011 National Household Survey: Data tables," http://www12.statcan.gc.ca/nhs-enm/2011/dp-pd/dt-td/Rp-eng.cfm?LANG=E&APATH=3&DETAIL=0&DIM=0&FL=A&FREE=0&GC=0&GID=0&GK=0&GRP=0&PID=105399&PRID=0&PTYPE=105277&S=0&SHOWALL=0&SUB=0&Temporal=2013&THEME=95&VID=0&VNAMEE=&VNAMEF=.

[2] Andrew Millie and Dilip K. Das, Contemporary Issues in Law Enforcement and Policing (Boca Raton: CRC Press, 2008), 88.

[3] Stewart Bell, Cold Terror: How Canada Nurtures and Exports Terrorism Around the World (Ontario: Wiley, 2005), 42.

[4] "In Depth: Air India, The Victims," CBC News, March 16, 2005, http://www.cbc.ca/news/background/airindia/victims.html.

[5] Canadian Security Intelligence Service, Public Report, 2013-2014, February 2015. https://www.csis.gc.ca/pblctns/nnlrprt/2013-2014/2013-2014_Public_Report_Inside_ENG.pdf.
[6] Ibid.
[7] "Khadr Family," Global Jihad, September 15, 2010, http://www.globaljihad.net/view_page.asp?id=902.
[8] Anti-Defamation League, "Canada And Terrorism," January 2004, http://www.adl.org/terror/tu/tu_0401_canada.asp.
[9] "Youngest Guantanamo Detainee Pleads Guilty," CNN, October 25, 2010, http://www.cnn.com/2010/US/10/25/khadr.plea/.
[10] Michelle Shephard, "Omar Khadr Repatriated to Canada," Toronto Star, September 29, 2012, http://www.thestar.com/news/2012/09/29/omar_khadr_repatriated_to_canada.html
[11] Colin Perkel, "Omar Khadr wins right to expand $20M suit vs. Canadian government," The Canadian Press. October 23, 2014. http://www.cbc.ca/news/politics/omar-khadr-wins-right-to-to-expand-20m-suit-vs-canadian-government-1.2811226.
[12] Stewart Bell, Cold Terror: How Canada Nurtures and Exports Terrorism Around the World (Ontario: Wiley, 2005), 140.
[13] "Fateh Kamel," Global Jihad, September 15, 2010, http://www.globaljihad.net/view_page.asp?id=294.
[14] Stewart Bell, "Montreal man with terror-related convictions denied passport," National Post, September 15, 2011, http://news.nationalpost.com/news/canada/montreal-man-with-terror-related-convictions-denied-passport.
[15] "Court Restores Rule that Denied Terrorist a Passport," Toronto Star, January 29, 2009, http://www.thestar.com/news/canada/2009/01/29/court_restores_rule_that_denied_terrorist_a_passport.html.
[16] Angelique Chrisafis, Julian Borger, Justin McCurry, and Terry Macalister, "In Amenas: Timeline of Four-Day Siege in Algeria," Guardian (London), January 25, 2013, https://www.theguardian.com/world/2013/jan/25/in-amenas-timeline-siege-algeria.
[17] Tonda MacCharles, "'Clear leader of raid on Algerian plant was Ali Medlej, Canadian officials believe," Toronto Star, September 19, 2013, https://www.thestar.com/news/canada/2013/09/19/clear_leader_of_raid_on_algerian_plant_was_ali_medlej_canadian_officials_believe.html.
[18] Tonda MacCharles, "Mauritania Jailed Canadian Aaron Yoon for Al Qaeda Ties, Says Amnesty," Toronto Star, April 5, 2013, http://www.thestar.com/news/canada/2013/04/05/aaron_yoon_serving_twoyear_sentence_in_mauritania_for_al_qaeda_ties_amnesty_international.html.
[19] "Aaron Yoon trying to readjust to life in London after time in Mauritanian prison," CTV London, September 18, 2013, http://london.ctvnews.ca/aaron-yoon-trying-to-readjust-to-life-in-london-after-time-in-mauritanian-prison-1.1460730.

[20] "Toronto 18 Bomb Plot Chief' Jailed," Al-Jazeera (Doha), September 28, 2010, http://english.aljazeera.net/news/americas/2010/01/201011935438946391.html

[21] "Another 'Toronto 18' Member Pleads Guilty," CBC News, September 28, 2010, http://www.cbc.ca/canada/toronto/story/2010/01/20/toronto-18-plea941.html.

[22] Christie Blatchford, "'Toronto 18' Case Our First Sign that 'Good Canadian Boys' are being Radicalized Too," National Post, April 2, 2013, http://fullcomment.nationalpost.com/2013/04/02/christie-blatchford-toronto-18-case-our-first-sign-that-good-canadian-boys-are-being-radicalized-too/.

[23] Megan O'Toole, Stewart Bell and Adrian Humphreys, "I Don't Want a Book Written By Humans: VIA Terror Plot Accused again Rejects Criminal Code," National Post, May 23, 2013, http://news.nationalpost.com/2013/05/23/i-dont-want-a-book-written-by-humans-via-terror-plot-accused-again-rejects-criminal-code/.

[24] Robert Bostelaar, "Hiva Alizadeh pleads guilty to terror plot," Ottawa Citizen, September 18, 2014, http://ottawacitizen.com/news/local-news/hiva-alizadeh-pleads-guilty-to-terror-plot.

[25] "Hiva Alizadeh pleads guilty in Ottawa terrorism trial" CBC News, September 17, 2014, http://www.cbc.ca/beta/news/canada/ottawa/hiva-alizadeh-pleads-guilty-in-ottawa-terrorism-trial-1.2768944.

[26] Erika Tucker, "Who is Quebec terror-linked suspect Martin Rouleau?" Global News, November 30, 2014, http://globalnews.ca/news/1626457/who-is-quebec-terror-linked-suspect-martin-rouleau/.

[27] Evan Solomon, "Ottawa shooting: The face-to-face encounter that ended the attack on Parliament," CBC News, October 24, 2014, http://www.cbc.ca/news/politics/ottawa-shooting-the-face-to-face-encounter-that-ended-the-attack-on-parliament-1.2812802.

[28] Department of Public Safety, Government of Canada. "2016 Public Report on the Terrorist Threat to Canada," August 25, 2016. https://www.publicsafety.gc.ca/cnt/rsrcs/pblctns/2016-pblc-rpr-trrrst-thrt/index-en.aspx.

[29] Ibid

[30] Stewart Bell, "About 180 'individuals with a nexus to Canada' suspected of participating in terrorist activities oversea," National Post, August 25, 2016, http://news.nationalpost.com/news/canada/canada-a-target-of-direct-threats-from-isil-and-other-extremists-government-says-in-overdue-report

[31] Stewart Bell, "Canada pushed EU to add Hezbollah to list of banned terrorist organizations, officials says," July 24, 2013, http://news.nationalpost.com/news/canada-pushed-eu-to-add-hezbollah-to-list-of-banned-terrorist-organizations-official-says

[32] Matthew Levitt, "Another path to Martydom," National Post, August 28, 2013, http://news.nationalpost.com/full-comment/matthew-levitt-another-path-to-martyrdom.

[33] Ibid.
[34] Ibid.
[35] Ibid.
[36] Anti-Defamation League, "Canada and Terrorism."
[37] Bell, Cold Terror, 107.
[38] "Group goes to court to get Hezbollah banned," CBC News, November 29, 2002, http://www.cbc.ca/news/canada/group-goes-to-court-to-get-hezbollah-banned-1.326366
[39] U.S. Department of the Treasury, "Treasury Identifies Lebanese Canadian Bank Sal as a 'Primary Money Laundering Concern,'" February 10, 2011, https://www.treasury.gov/press-center/press-releases/Pages/tg1057.aspx.
[40] Ibid.
[41] Ibid.
[42] Ibid.
[43] Michael Petrou, "Iran's long reach into Canada," Macleans, June 20, 2012, http://www.macleans.ca/authors/michael-petrou/irans-long-reach-into-canada/.
[44] Candice Malcolm "A hawk among doves," C2C Journal, March 1, 2016, http://www.c2cjournal.ca/2016/03/a-hawk-among-doves/.
[45] Department of Public Safety, Government of Canada, "Currently Listed Entities," October 20, 2010 http://www.publicsafety.gc.ca/prg/ns/le/cle-eng.aspx - Hamas.
[46] Paul Lungen, "Group Claims Hamas Raising Funds in Canada," Canadian Jewish News, November 22, 2004, http://www.cjnews.com/index.php?option=com_content&task=view&id=5971&Itemid=86.
[47] Bell, Cold Terror, 107.
[48] Stewart Bell, "Muslim group appealing Ottawa's 'unreasonable' and 'unconstitutional' decision to list it as a terrorist entity," National Post, May 4, 2014, http://news.nationalpost.com/news/canada/muslim-non-profit-appealing-ottawas-unreasonable-and-unconstitutional-decision-to-list-it-as-a-terrorist-group.
[49] Ibid.
[50] Ibid.
[51] Anti-Defamation League, "Canada And Terrorism."
[52] Anti-Defamation League, "Backgrounder: The Holy Land Foundation for Relief And Development," May 28, 2009, http://www.adl.org/main_Terrorism/backgrounder_holyland.htm.
[53] "Canadian Pleads Guilty In Plot To Kill Jews," CBC News, November 24, 2004, http://www.cbc.ca/world/story/2004/11/24/akkal-israel041124.html.
[54] Rami Amichai, "Israel Remands Canadian In Alleged Attack Plot," The Age (Melbourne), December 16, 2003, http://www.theage.com.au/articles/2003/12/15/1071336890251.html.

[55] Stewart Bell, "The Holy War Comes To Canada," National Post, October 23, 2003, http://archive.frontpagemag.com/readArticle.aspx?ARTID=15775.
[56] Ibid.
[57] Department of Public Safety, Government of Canada, "Listed Terrorist Entities," https://www.publicsafety.gc.ca/cnt/ntnl-scrt/cntr-trrrsm/lstd-ntts/index-en.aspx.
[58] Canadian Islamic Congress, "Facts About the CIC," September 10, 2010, http://www.canadianislamiccongress.com/cicfacts.php.
[59] Wahida Valiante, "The New Syndrome - F.e.a.r. -- Fear Everything Anxiety Reaction," Friday Magazine 9, iss. 60 (2006), http://www.canadianislamiccongress.com/opeds/article.php?id=2840; Canadian Islamic Congress, "Islamic Congress And Arab Federation Call On All Canadians To Condemn Continuing Israeli War Crimes In Gaza," January 21, 2008, http://www.canadianislamiccongress.com/mc/media_communique.php?id=985.
[60] Canadian Islamic Congress, "Islamic Congress Urges Government to Take Hezbollah And Hamas Off Terrorist' List," August 22, 2006, http://www.canadianislamiccongress.com/mc/media_communique.php?id=814.
[61] The Investigative Project on Terrorism, "Muslim Student's Association," January 1, 2008, http://www.investigativeproject.org/profile/166.
[62] Muslim Student's Association, "Constitution/Bylaws," October 25, 2010, http://www.msanational.org/about/constitution.
[63] Jonathan Dowd-Gailey, "Islamism's Campus Club: The Muslim Students' Association," Middle East Quarterly 11, no. 1 (2004), 63-72.
[64] Ibid.
[65] Anthony DePalma, "Six of 17 Arrested In Canada's Antiterror Sweep Have Ties To Mosque Near Toronto," New York Times, June 5, 2006.
[66] "Mohammed Adam, Fundamentalist And Proud Of It," Ottawa Citizen, August 13, 2005, http://www.truthandgrace.com/clericscarborough.htm.
[67] Noor Javed, "GTA's Secret World of Polygamy," Toronto Star, May 24, 2008, http://www.thestar.com/News/GTA/article/429490.
[68] Statistics Canada, "2011 National Household Survey: Data tables," http://www12.statcan.gc.ca/nhs-enm/2011/dp-pd/dt-td/Rp-eng.cfm?LANG=E&APATH=3&DETAIL=0&DIM=0&FL=A&FREE=0&GC=0&GID=0&GK=0&GRP=0&PID=105399&PRID=0&PTYPE=105277&S=0&SHOWALL=0&SUB=0&Temporal=2013&THEME=95&VID=0&VNAMEE=&VNAMEF=..
[69] Statistics Canada, "2001 Census: Selected Religions, For Canada, Provinces And Territories," n.d., http://www12.statcan.ca/english/census01/products/highlight/Religion/Page.cfm?Lang=E&Geo=PR&View=1a&Code=01&Table=1&StartRec=1&Sort=2&B1=Canada&B2=1.
[70] Jennifer Selby, "Islam In Canada," EuroIslam.info, September 21, 2010, http://www.euro-islam.info/country-profiles/canada/.

[71] Statistics Canada, "2001 Census: Selected Cultural And Labour Force Characteristics (58), Selected Religions (35A), Age Groups (5A) And Sex (3) For Population 15 Years And Over, For Canada, Provinces, Territories And Census Metropolitan Areas," n.d., http://www12.statcan.ca/english/census01/products/standard/themes/RetrieveProductTable.cfm?Temporal=2001&PID=67773&APATH=3&GID=517770&METH=1&PTYPE=55496&THEME=56&FOCUS=0&AID=0&PLACENAME=0&PROVINCE=0&SEARCH=0&GC=0&GK=0&VID=0&VNAMEE=&VNAMEF=&FL=0&RL=0&FREE.

[72] "Canadian Muslims face high unemployment," IQRA.ca March 31, 2015, http://iqra.ca/2015/canadian-muslims-face-high-unemployment/.

[73] "Canada's Muslims: An International Comparison," CBC News, February 13, 2007, http://www.cbc.ca/news/background/islam/muslim-survey.html.

[74] David B. Harris, "Is Canada Losing The Balance Between Liberty And Security?" in Alexander Moens and Martin Collacott, eds., Immigration Policy and the Terrorist Threat in Canada and the United States (Vancouver: Fraser Institute, 2008), 137.

[75] Elizabeth Thompson, "Canadians Don't Believe That Muslims Share Their Values," National Post, September 10, 2010, http://www.nationalpost.com/Canadians+believe+Muslims+share+their+values+poll/3508281/story.html.

[76] John Geddes, "What Canadians Think Of Sikhs, Jews, Christians, Muslims," Maclean's, April 28, 2009, http://www2.macleans.ca/2009/04/28/what-canadians-think-of-sikhs-jews-christians-muslims/.

[77] Environics, "Survey of Muslims in Canada, 2016," http://www.environicsinstitute.org/uploads/institute-projects/survey%20of%20muslims%20in%20canada%202016%20-%20final%20report.pdf.

[78] Anthony Bradney, Law and Faith in a Skeptical Age (New York: Routledge, 2009), 49.

[79] Marion Boyd, "Dispute Resolution In Family Law: Protecting Choice, Promoting Inclusion," December 20, 2004, http://www.attorneygeneral.jus.gov.on.ca/english/about/pubs/boyd/.

[80] Arbitration Act, 1991, S.O. 1991, c. 17 (version in force between 22 June 2006 and 29 April 2007), http://www.canlii.org/en/on/laws/stat/so-1991-c-17/1917/so-1991-c-17.html - history.

[81] Dana Kennedy, "Canada's Growing Jihadi Cancer," Daily Beast, December 13, 2015, http://www.thedailybeast.com/articles/2015/12/14/canada-s-growing-jihadist-cancer.html

[82] Department of Justice, Government of Canada, "About the Anti-terrorism Act," http://www.justice.gc.ca/eng/cj-jp/ns-sn/act-loi.html.

[83] Ibid.

[84] Bell, Cold Terror, 97.

[85] Department of Justice, Government of Canada, "About the Anti-terrorism Act," http://www.justice.gc.ca/eng/cj-jp/ns-sn/act-loi.html.

[86] "Controversial Anti-terrorism Tools Revived as Bill Passes," CBC News, April 24, 2013, http://www.cbc.ca/news/politics/controversial-anti-terrorism-tools-revived-as-bill-passes-1.1414767.

[87] Parliament of Canada, Statutes of Canada 2015, Chapter 20, Second Session, Forty-first Parliament, http://www.parl.gc.ca/HousePublications/Publication.aspx?Language=E&Mode=1&DocId=8056977&File=4.

[88] Chris Hall, "Trudeau tracker: Promised changes to anti-terrorism law C-51 still months away," CBC News, May 17, 2016, http://www.cbc.ca/news/politics/trudeau-tracker-anti-terrorism-bill-1.3586337.

[89] Anthony Furey, "Trudeau visits mosque with terror connections," Toronto Sun, September 12, 2016, http://www.torontosun.com/2016/09/12/trudeau-visits-mosque-with-terror-connections.

[90] Michael Petrou, "Liberal MPs defend invitation list for Stephane Dion roundtable on Iran," CBC News, November 4, 2016, http://www.cbc.ca/news/politics/iran-canada-dion-engagement-1.3834592.

[91] Ari Yashar, "Is Trudeau's new Foreign Minister Secretary a Hamas backer?" Israel National News, April 12, 2016, http://www.israelnationalnews.com/News/News.aspx/204406

UNITED STATES

QUICK FACTS

Population: 323,995,528 (July 2016)

Area: 9,826,675 sq km

Ethnic Groups: white 79.96%, black 12.85%, Asian 4.43%, Amerindian and Alaska native 0.97%, native Hawaiian and other Pacific islander 0.18%, two or more races 1.61%

Religions: Protestant 46.5%, Roman Catholic 20.8%, Mormon 1.6%, Jehovah's Witness 0.8%, other Christian 0.9%, Jewish 1.9%, Muslim 0.9%, Buddhist 0.7%, Hindu 0.7%, other 1.8%, unaffiliated 22.8%, don't know/refused 0.6%

Government Type: Constitutional Federal Republic

GDP (official exchange rate): $18.56 trillion (estimated 2015)

Map and Quick Facts courtesy of the CIA World Factbook (January 2017)

OVERVIEW

Over the years and with the help of modern technologies, the nature, faces, methods, and organizational structure of threats posed by militant Islamists to the security of United States has evolved significantly. With the rise of the Islamic State in 2014, as in the wake of the 9/11 attacks, the public conversation on Islam has focused on militant Islamism, specifically on the question The Atlantic *magazine asked in a cover article a few months after the San Bernardino shooting: "Is America Any Safer?"[1] The competition over the answer to that question is not simply political or tactical—it encompasses the law enforcement and national security communities, and includes tensions over data, vocabulary, and constitutionally protected civil liberties.*

The threat from militant Islamists and terrorists networks like the Islamic State remains a challenge. In 2015, Federal Bureau of Investigations (FBI) Director James Comey told the Senate Judiciary Committee that the Islamic State remains committed to motivating people in the United States to become killers on their behalf, as well as to sending people to the United States to launch attacks.[2] Addressing these threats requires a collaborative effort among a variety of stakeholders, including the United States government and Muslim civil society and community organizations, as well as inter-faith groups and organizations from across the American political spectrum.

ISLAMIST ACTIVITY

Contemporary Islamist activity in the United States can be understood in the context of five loose conceptual groupings:

The Ikhwan-Jama'at duopoly[3]

The *Ikhwan-Jama'at* duopoly is the largest and most influential grouping of organized Islamist activism in the United States. In the 1950s and 1960s, Muslim Brotherhood activists fled repression in Egypt and sought refuge in Saudi Arabia. Wahhabi[4] authorities took advantage of their organizational experience, placing them in key positions at major Islamic NGOs. With Saudi backing, these Brotherhood activists, joined by *Jama'at-e Islami*[5] cadres, propagated Islamist thought and institutions all over the world, including the United States and the wider Western world.[6]

The structure of the U.S.-based *Ikhwan-Jama'at* duopoly can be understood on three levels: 1) a covert vanguard, 2) professional activist organizations with formalized membership schemes, and 3) the related grassroots they seek to mobilize. The vanguard consists of Brotherhood and *Jama'at* leaders in North America who hold key leadership positions in a network of overlapping activist organizations. These activist organizations are the most prominent Islamic groups in American civil society. They are influential in local, state, and national politics and have established relationships with editorial boards and news producers at media outlets throughout the country.

Internal U.S. Brotherhood records released as evidence in the terrorism financing trial of the Holy Land Foundation for Relief and Development (HLF) reveal that a covert vanguard of Muslim Brotherhood activists founded and directed the most influential Muslim-American civil society groups in the United States, including the Muslim Students' Association (MSA)[7] the Islamic Society of North America (ISNA), the North American Islamic Trust (NAIT), the International Institute of Islamic Thought (IIIT), the Council on American-Islamic Relations (CAIR) and the Muslim American Society (MAS). The Islamic Circle of North America (ICNA) similarly has been identified as a "front" for *Jama'at-i-Islami*.[8] The public faces of these groups are professionally-led activist organizations that are concerned with civil rights, religious education, political awareness, grass-roots organization, and other seemingly benign activities.[9] However, internal Brotherhood documents reveal another use for these organizations: promoting "the main goal of Islamic activism," which is "establishing the nation of Islam, the rule of God in the lives of humans, making people worship their Creator and cleansing the earth from the tyrants who assault God's sovereignty, the abominators in His earth and the suppressors of His creation."[10] Brotherhood officials have done so by promoting the creation of civic organizations with a covert—and occasionally an overt—political agenda, an activity described by one Brotherhood official in the 1980s as "energizing political work fronts."[11] Such groups include:

The Muslim Student Association (MSA)

Founded in 1963 by Brotherhood activists at the University of Illinois Urbana-Champaign, the MSA, or MSA National, served as a coordinating committee for Brotherhood activities during the organization's formative years in the United States. During this early era, all Brotherhood activists in the U.S. had to be active in the MSA.[12] Now a national organization, the MSA has about 150 affiliated university chapters in the United States and Canada, including numerous Ivy League affiliations.[13] In the U.S., the MSA is divided into East Zone, Central Zone, and West Zone. It is a 501(c)4 tax exempt organization, and claims to refuse foreign funding.[14]

Like all member organizations of the *Ikhwan-Jama'at* duopoly, the MSA proclaims "moderation," but public statements by MSA activists reveal an Islamist agenda and ideology. For instance, MSA officials have espoused the desire "to restore Islam to the leadership of society" and to be working toward "the reestablishment of the Islamic form of government."[15] They have likewise emphasized the importance of *dawah* (propagation of faith) as a vehicle for the spread of Islam in the United States, with the ultimate goal of making America "a Muslim country."[16]

The North American Islamic Trust (NAIT)

NAIT was founded in 1973 as a *waqf* (trust) for the MSA and other Islamic institutions, including the Islamic Society of North America (ISNA).[17] NAIT is a nonprofit 501(c)3 organization and holds the titles to hundreds of Islamic institutions—including mosques and schools—across the U.S., making it, according to some analysts, a holding company and financial hub for various Muslim Brotherhood-tied groups in North America.[18] It also manages the Iman Fund, a no-load mutual fund, and runs American Trust Publications (which publishes Islamic literature, including the works of Brotherhood luminary Yusuf al Qaradawi[19]) and the Islamic Book Service.[20] A 1987 FBI investigation of NAIT concluded that the organization supported the "Islamic Revolution." "Their support of JIHAD (a holy war) in the U.S. has been evidenced by the financial and organizational support provided through NAIT from Middle East countries to Muslims residing in the U.S. and Canada," it continued. The countries named as providing this support were Iran, Libya, Kuwait, and Saudi Arabia. "The organizational support provided by NAIT includes planning, organizing, and funding anti-U.S. and anti-Israel demonstrations, pro-PLO demonstrations and the distribution of political propaganda against U.S. policies in the Middle East and in support of the Islamic Revolution as advocated by the [Government of Iran]. NAIT also supports the recruitment, training and funding of black Muslims in the U.S. who support the Islamic Revolution."[21]

The Islamic Society of North America (ISNA)

ISNA, which emerged out of the MSA in 1981, was named as an unindicted co-conspirator in the Hamas financing trial against the Holy Land Foundation.[22] Like NAIT, ISNA is included among the "individuals/entities who are and/or were members of the US Muslim Brotherhood."[23] There is no evidence that ISNA currently provides material support to terrorist organizations. However, to this day, key U.S. Brotherhood activists hold leadership positions in ISNA. ISNA's nineteen member board of directors includes the chairman of NAIT, the president of the MSA, and the heads of ISNA's other "constituent organizations:" the Association of Muslim Scientists and Engineers, the Islamic Medical Association of North America, the Canadian Islamic Trust, Muslim Youth of North America, and the Council of Islamic Schools of North America—some of which are explicitly named as Brotherhood-allied groups in internal Brotherhood documents.[24]

The Islamic Circle of North America (ICNA)

ICNA is the successor to the Pakistani-American organization *Halaqa Ahbabe Islami*, which sought to recruit "Islamic movement oriented Urdu speaking Muslims and to strengthen the Jama'at-e-Islami Pakistan."[25] In 1977, *Halaqa Ahbabe Islami* formally changed its name to ICNA.[26] Today, ICNA holds conferences throughout the U.S. and states that "by focusing on self-development, education, outreach and social services, ICNA has cemented its place as a leading grassroots organization in the American Muslim community."[27]

The Council on American-Islamic Relations (CAIR)

The idea for CAIR emerged out of a 1993 meeting in Philadelphia of the Muslim Brotherhood's Palestine Committee in the United States. Participants spoke of the need for a lobbying and public affairs group to promote the Islamist point of view in the U.S. The short-term goal was to serve as a spoiler for the Oslo Accords, but the long-term goal was to manipulate the public discourse in America on issues related to Islam and the Muslim world.[28] Three IAP officials founded CAIR several months later. CAIR portrays itself as a civil rights group, and has since become the most influential and pervasive Muslim civil society group in the United States.[29] They have been heavily involved in "sensitivity training" and other briefings on Islam and the Muslim community for U.S. law enforcement officers. However, in 2008, CAIR came under both suspicion and scrutiny as a result of the Holy Land Foundation case, in which Ghassan Elashi, the chairman of the Holy Land Foundation charity in Dallas and a board member of the Texas chapter of CAIR, was found guilty of conspiring to funnel funds to Hamas.[30] As a result of the revelations of the 2009 trial of the Holy Land

Foundation, the FBI ceased its cooperation with CAIR.[31] Instead, the FBI has turned to ISNA, which has taken up the mantle of a larger role in advising and training U.S. government and military officials.[32]

The Muslim American Society (MAS)

The Northern Virginia-based MAS was founded in 1993. Among its founding members was Ahmed Elkadi, who supposedly led the Brotherhood in the U.S. from 1984 to 1994.[33] Mohammad Mehdi Akef, the Supreme Guide of the global Muslim Brotherhood in Egypt from 2004 to 2010, claims to have played a role in founding MAS in a push for more "openness" in the Brotherhood's activities in the U.S.[34] MAS is open about its lineage in the U.S., lauding older Brotherhood-affiliated groups such as MSA, ISNA, and NAIT.[35]

MAS claims to promote understanding between Muslims and non-Muslims, and its mission is "to move people to strive for God consciousness, liberty, and justice, and to convey Islam with utmost clarity."[36] The MAS Freedom Foundation is perhaps the most active and public part of the organization. It engages in and coordinates grassroots activism, including voter registration, civil rights work, lobbying Congress, and protesting.[37] Other departments include the Council of Imams (coordinated with ICNA), the National Council of Islamic Centers (also coordinated with ICNA), the Tarbiyya (religious educational) program, the dawah (propagation) program, Islamic American University, and the Muslim Youth Program.[38]

The International Institute of Islamic Thought (IIIT)

Conceived at a 1977 Islamic conference in Lugano, Switzerland, IIIT was founded four years later in Pennsylvania as "a private, non-profit, academic, cultural and educational institution, concerned with general issues of Islamic thought and education."[39] It is now based in Herndon, Virginia. IIIT ostensibly "promotes academic research on the methodology and philosophy of various disciplines, and gives special emphasis to the development of Islamic scholarship in contemporary social sciences."[40] However, IIIT has been accused by the U.S. government of contributing funds to the World and Islam Studies Enterprise (WISE), which was founded to support the Palestinian Islamic Jihad terrorist organization.[41] IIIT is a part of a network of companies and not-for-profit organizations based in Northern Virginia known as the SAAR Network or the Safa Group, which has been under investigation by the U.S. Justice Department since at least 2003.[42] In May 2009, Ishaq Farhan, a trustee of IIIT, was chosen to head the Islamic Action Front—the political party of the Jordanian Muslim Brotherhood—a post he had held before.[43] Farhan had long been associated with the IAF and is said to be one of the key figures behind its formation.[44] (Since then, Farhan has been replaced as head of the IAF by Hamza Mansour.[45] Ostensibly, however, Farhan still retains an affiliation—and a position of prominence—with the organization.)

Jamaat al Fuqra

Jama'at al Fuqra (JF, Arabic for "Community of the Impoverished") was founded in New York in 1980 by the Pakistani religious leader Sheikh Mubarak Ali Gilani.[46] JF has been described as a splinter group of *Jaish-e-Mohammad* (JeM).[47] Daniel Pearl, the late *Wall Street Journal* reporter, was on his way to interview Gilani in 2002 when he was kidnapped in Pakistan and subsequently beheaded.

In the U.S., JF is a loosely structured movement primarily composed of African-American converts to Islam. JF functions officially through Muslims of the Americas, a non-profit organization, and the International Quranic Open University.[48] JF also operates a news publication called *The Islamic Post*.[49] JF runs a network of rural compounds in New York, Maryland, Pennsylvania, Arizona, Oregon, South Carolina, California and Colorado. Members of the group were involved in a wave of violent crime and fraud—including murder and arson—in the 1980s and 1990s.[50] Some members have also been known to attack Hindu places of worship.[51] Over the past decade, the group has been fairly quiet in the U.S. It received some attention in 2008 and 2009 as a result of a documentary on the group produced by the controversial Christian Action Network entitled "Homegrown Jihad."[52]

Hizb ut-Tahrir

Hizb ut-Tahrir in America (HTA) has been led by Middle Eastern activists who moved to the U.S. in the 1980s. For most of its history, it has met with little success in expanding its native activist base. This has been attributed to competition from other Islamist groups (mainly the Brotherhood); the limited ability of an older leadership to connect with the younger generation; and a level of paranoia and secrecy among the leadership that have limited outreach efforts, hindered online interaction, and may have turned off potential recruits.[53]

The HTA website states that the organization's aim is "to resume the Islamic way of life and to convey the Islamic da'wah to the world."[54] HTA is currently well-networked and connected with the larger global presence of HuT. Their three-stage methodology for taking power is the same as that promoted by the global movement:

> The First Stage: The stage of culturing to produce people who believe in the idea and the method of the Party, so that they form the Party group.
>
> The Second Stage: The stage of interaction with the Ummah (global Muslim community), to let the Ummah embrace and carry Islam, so that the Ummah takes it up as its issue, and thus works to establish it in the affairs of life.

> The Third Stage: The stage of establishing government, implementing Islam generally and comprehensively, and carrying it as a message to the world.[55]

In the West, HuT seeks to foster a mass movement toward revolution, while in Muslim-majority countries it attempts to recruit members of the military for the purpose of carrying out a military coup.[56] According to one specialist, HTA "counts well-educated professionals who are influential in their communities among their members" and in recent years the group has expanded beyond their main hubs of activity in New York, Orange County (California), Chicago, and Milwaukee.[57]

The jihadist-activist milieu

There are a number of small U.S.-based formal and informal groups and networks that support violent *jihad* in America and elsewhere, but do not necessarily engage in it themselves. Most of their activities are political and social in nature, consisting of provocative public statements and demonstrations. Two particularly prominent groups deserve mention in this regard.

Revolution Muslim was a New York-based *jihadist*-activist group. Founded in 2007 "to invite people to proper Islam… and command the good… while forbidding the falsehood," RM's mission "is to one day see the Muslims united under one Khalifah and under the commands of Allah."[58] RM maintained an active blog and website, which serves as a forum for a dissemination of its views, proselytization, condemnation of U.S. policies, and even support for violence. In April 2014, Revolution Muslim co-founder Yousef al-Khattab was sentenced to two-and-a-half years in prison for advocating violence against the Chabad Jewish organization's headquarters in Brooklyn.[59] Khattab posted a photograph of the building, along with a map, to Revolution Muslim's website, and pointed out that "the man temple was always full at prayer times." In the past, he had told his readers to "deal with" prominent Jewish leaders "directly at their homes."[60]

One of Revolution Muslim's other co-founders was Jesse Morton. Morton was arrested in 2011 after one of his associates published the home addresses of the writers of *South Park*, after an episode of the cartoon show mocked the Prophet Muhammad. Before that time, Morton was one of the most prolific recruiters for al-Qaeda in the United States.[61] After his arrest, Morton worked as informant for the Federal Bureau of Investigation (FBI) and made contact with several of his former recruits.[62] In September 2016, Morton began a job as a researcher at George Washington University's Program on Extremism.[63] This affiliation, however, proved to be short-lived; Morton's affiliation with the University was severed after he was arrested in late 2016 on drug possession and solicitation of prostitution charges.[64]

Homegrown jihadist cells and networks

A number of Islamist terrorist plots in the U.S. have been thwarted or uncovered in recent years. Many of these were planned by cells of Muslims who were either born in the U.S. or lived there for many years. There were also episodes of Americans planning attacks against U.S. interests abroad and/or going to fight with foreign Islamist movements. These included:

- In May 2009, James Cromitie, David Williams, Onta Williams, and Laguerre Payen were arrested in New York and charged with conspiring to bomb synagogues in the Bronx and shoot down military aircraft at the New York Air National Guard Base at Stewart Airport in Newburgh, New York with a surface-to-air missile.[65]

- David Coleman Headley (AKA Daood Gilani) of Chicago was accused of providing crucial assistance for the 2008 *Laskhar-e-Taiba* (LeT) attack in Mumbai, India. Headley allegedly attended LeT training camps in 2002 and 2003. Beginning in 2006, Headley allegedly carried out extensive surveillance of possible targets in Mumbai on behalf of LeT. He was charged with aiding and abetting the murders of six U.S. citizens who were killed in the Mumbai attack. Headley was also accused of conspiring with LeT members and Ilyas Kashmiri, the head of the Kashmiri militant group *Harakat ul Jihad al Islami* (HUJI), to carry out attacks in Denmark against *Jyllands Posten*, the newspaper that published the Mohammad cartoons that led to the 2006 Danish Cartoon Crisis. Headley allegedly carried out surveillance in Denmark for that planned attack.[66] Headley was ultimately sentenced to 35 years in prison, a relatively lenient punishment, due to his cooperation in providing intelligence on terrorist networks.[67]

- Najibullah Zazi, who drove an airport shuttle bus in Denver and, before that, lived in Queens, New York, was accused of conspiring to use explosives in an attack thought to have been planned for New York City in 2009. Zazi was born in Afghanistan and raised in Pakistan. He is thought to have travelled to the Federally Administered Tribal Areas in Pakistan, where he received training from al-Qaeda.[68] Zazi pled guilty in 2010.[69]

- Bryant Neal Vinas, an American convert to Islam, was charged with participating in and supporting terrorist attacks against U.S. persons and facilities in Afghanistan in 2008. He was accused of firing rockets at a U.S. military base in Afghanistan and providing "expert advice and assistance" to al-Qaeda about the New York transit system and Long Island Railroad.[70] He pled guilty to all charges in 2009.[71]

- Daniel P. Boyd, an American convert to Islam, was accused in 2009 of heading a seven-man North Carolina-based cell that allegedly planned to provide material support to al-Qaeda, murder, kidnap, maim and injure persons in Israel and elsewhere, and kill U.S. military personnel stationed at Quantico, Virginia.[72] Boyd pleaded guilty to conspiracy to commit murder and conspiracy to provide material support to terrorists in U.S. District Court in February 2011, and subsequently cooperated with the government, providing testimony at trial against several of his co-conspirators, who were convicted that October.[73]

- Hosam Maher Husein Smadi, a Jordanian national, was found guilty of planning to blow up the Fountain Place office complex in downtown Dallas with a vehicle bomb in 2009, and in 2010 was sentenced to twenty-four years in prison.[74] He also reportedly considered attacking a National Guard Armory and the Dallas Airport.[75]

- In August 2013, a U.S. citizen and a foreign national were charged in a Miami court with providing financing and recruits to al-Qaeda and two other designated other foreign terrorist organizations. Gufran Ahmed Kauser Mohammed, a naturalized U.S. citizen born in India, and Mohamed Hussein Said, a Kenyan, were brought up on a fifteen count indictment after being arrested in Saudi Arabia and transferred to the U.S. The two men allegedly wired a total of $96,000 to an al-Qaeda affiliate in Syria, the *al Nusra Front*, and to the militant group *al Shabaab* in Somalia.[76]

- There was also a "lone wolf" Islamist terrorist attack launched at Fort Hood, Texas on November 5, 2011 by Major Nidal Malik Hasan, a U.S. Army psychiatrist, who had been in regular contact with Anwar al-Awlaki, an American-born imam of Yemeni descent who served as one of al-Qaeda's main ideologues before his death in September 2011 as a result of an American drone strike. Hasan opened fire on base, killing thirteen people and wounding 31 others. Hasan was shot multiple times, but survived.[77] In August 2013, Hasan was unanimously convicted by a jury of army officers.[78] Hasan's defense lawyer asked the judge to spare Hasan's life, but the request was denied and Hasan is to die by lethal injection (although a date for his execution has not been set).[79] The Department of Defense and White House have declined to classify Hasan as a terrorist, however, instead labeling the Fort Hood incident as a case of workplace violence.[80] Numerous Members of Congress have objected to this description, asserting that the attack was clearly one of "homegrown terror[ism]" and urging the U.S. government to recognize this fact.[81]

- In April 2013, brothers Dzhokar Tsarnaev and Tamerlane Tsarnaev planted bombs at the annual Boston Marathon road race. The resulting explosion killed three and injured more than 170.[82] Dzhorkar was captured by police, and Tamerlane died after being shot several times and being run over by Dzhorkar in his attempt to escape.[83] After his capture, the surviving Tsarnaev claimed that he and his brother were motivated by extremist Islamic beliefs, but that they were not connected to any militant group in particular. He also claimed they learned to build bombs through the website of the al-Qaeda affiliate in Yemen.[84] In May 2015, a federal jury sentenced Tsarnaev to death.[85]

- In December 2015, married couple Syed Rizwan Farook and Tashfeen Malik killed 14 people and injured 22 in San Bernardino, California. The couple was killed in a shootout with police that afternoon.[86] The Islamic State later released a statement claiming responsibility for the attack, referring to Farook and Malik as "'soldiers of the caliphate,'" a term used to describe its soldiers.[87]

- In June 2016, Omar Mateen killed 49 people in a gay nightclub in Orlando, Florida. Mateen himself was shot and killed by Orlando police.[88] During the massacre, Mateen called 911. In the recording, he identified himself, claimed responsibility for the shootings, and pledged allegiance to "Abu Bakr al-Baghdadi of the Islamic State."[89] Mateen also called Orlando news station News 13 and claimed his actions had been motivated by loyalty to the Islamic State.[90]

- In November 2016, Abdul Razak Ali Artan injured 11 people at Ohio State University before being shot by a police officer. Artan rammed a car into a crowd on campus and then stabbed several people with a butcher knife. Shortly before the attack, Artan posted angrily on Facebook about American interference in Muslim countries, referencing radical cleric Anwar al-Awlaki and lone wolf attacks.[91]

ISLAMISM AND SOCIETY

The U.S. has the most diverse Muslim population in the Western world. In 2016, the Pew Research Center estimated that 3.3 million Muslims live in the United States, equaling about 1 percent of the U.S. population.[92] Sixty-five percent of U.S. Muslims identify themselves as Sunnis, 11 percent as Shi'a, and 24 percent as having no specific affiliation (describing themselves as "just a Muslim").[93] A large proportion of Muslims in the U.S. are first generation immigrants (63 percent), and 37 percent are native-born, with 15 percent being second generation.[94] Foreign-born Muslim Americans have come from at least 77 different countries. Twenty-six percent of Muslim immigrants to the United States come from the Arab world (Middle East and North Africa), nine percent from Pakistan, seven percent from other South Asian countries (including Pakistan, India, Bangladesh and Afghanistan), three percent come from Iran, five percent come from Europe, and seven percent come from Sub-Saharan Africa. One-third of all Muslim immigrants came to the U.S. during the 1990s and 40 percent have come after 2000. Over three-quarters (81 percent) of all Muslim-Americans are U.S. citizens.[95] At 30 percent, whites make up the largest proportion of Muslims in America.[96] Muslims in America, as a group, are younger than other major religious groups in the U.S.[97]

Seventy percent of Muslim Americans hold very unfavorable views of al-Qaeda, and 81 percent of Muslims in the United States say that violence against civilians and suicide bombings are never justified. Furthermore, 21 percent of American Muslims believe there is either a great deal or a fair amount of support for extremism within their community. Forty-eight percent say that Muslim leaders are not doing enough to challenge extremists.[98]

The fact that the most influential and well-resourced Muslim-American civil society groups are, in a very concrete sense, affiliated with the Muslim Brotherhood and *Jama'at-e-Islami* is not widely held knowledge. This is partially because Islamist organizations have successfully framed themselves as "moderate," "mainstream," and representative American Muslim religious and civil rights organizations. This has allowed them to avoid widespread public distrust and frame criticism of them as Islamophobia targeting the Muslim-American community rather than criticism of the organizations themselves.

ISLAMISM AND THE STATE

Since 2001, the U.S. government has spent more than $1 trillion in the fight against threats like the Islamic State and al-Qaeda.[99] These efforts, which include dismantling terrorist cells, countering terror financing, disrupting online networks, and preventing access to critical infrastructure, have helped secure the country, while also altering the nature of the threats faced.

This change is partly due to the success of global counterterrorism efforts and victories on the battlefield, which have made it more difficult, though not impossible, for violent extremists to perpetrate elaborate coordinated attacks. The shift is also attributable to innovations in technology that have facilitated communication between *jihadists* and potential violent extremists, as well as a shift in extremist messaging—from encouraging other violent extremist fighters to join the battle in Syria and Iraq, to directing them to perpetrate attacks in fighters' home countries.[100]

In recent years, the overwhelming focus of the U.S. government's counterterrorism efforts has been the Islamic State. The Obama administration initially responded dismissively to the rise of the terrorist group in Iraq and Syria in 2013-2014. In an ill-fated interview with the *New Yorker's* David Remnick in late 2013, President Obama famously referred to the organization as a "jayvee team" of terrorists.[101] However, the Islamic State's rapid expansion and consolidation of power—and its declaration of a "caliphate" in June 2014[102]—prompted the White House to assume a more hands-on approach. In November 2014, the Administration rolled out a new counterterrorism strategy encompassing nine "lines of effort" against the Islamic State, encompassing:

1. Supporting Effective Governance in Iraq
2. Denying the Islamic State Safe-Haven
3. Building Partner Capacity
4. Enhancing Intelligence Collection on ISIL
5. Disrupting ISIL's Finances
6. Exposing ISIL's True Nature
7. Disrupting the Flow of Foreign Fighters
8. Protecting the Homeland
9. Humanitarian Support[103]

Yet, with the notable exception of the so-called "line five" effort targeting the organization's finances, the Obama administration's strategy produced few tangible results, at least initially.[104] Over time, however, military operation by the U.S.-led "global coalition" against the Islamic State have succeeded in producing significant results, including the constriction of territory under ISIS control by as much as one-quarter[105] and slashing its revenues by as much as one-half.[106]

Nevertheless, as of this writing, the Islamic State remains a resilient threat. An October 2016 study by the U.S. House of Representatives Committee on Homeland Security detailed that the group's extensive revenue stream, which relies on black market oil and natural gas, black market commodities, antiquities, extortion, taxation, and robbery, kidnappings for ransom support from nation states in the Gulf, and emerging fundraising tactics like fraudulent financial activities, "continue to strain the U.S. Government's ability to disrupt the group's financial flows."[107] Additionally, the organization retains the capability to strike globally. A June 2016 report by the Congressional Research Service noted that, in addition to independent cells inspired by the group's ideology and message, the Islamic State has succeeded in fielding at least six functioning "armies" in Libya, Egypt, Nigeria, Saudi Arabia, Yemen and Afghanistan.[108]

The election of Donald J. Trump to the U.S. presidency in November 2016 is likely to usher in a significant change in U.S. counterterrorism policy. While still on the campaign trail, Mr. Trump spoke extensively about the need for greater military investments in the fight against the Islamic State, as well as a broader offensive against Islamic radicalism. Since taking office in January 2017, he has reiterated this commitment—most prominently in address to a joint session of Congress in February

2017.[109] His administration has also issued a series of measures designed to protect the U.S. homeland and American citizens from terrorism, including an Executive Order temporarily prohibiting entry to individuals from Iran, Iraq, Libya, Somalia, Sudan, and Yemen,[110] as well as tighter Transportation Security Administration regulations governing travel from ten separate foreign destinations to the United States.[111] (Notably, some of these measures—most prominently the Executive Order on Muslim immigration—have generated widespread opposition, and their constitutionality has been challenged.[112]) As of this writing, however, the Trump administration has not publicly unveiled a comprehensive strategy to counter the Islamic State, or to respond to the broader problem of radical Islamic ideology globally.

ENDNOTES

[1] Steven Brill, "Is America Any Safer?" The Atlantic, September 2016, https://www.theatlantic.com/magazine/archive/2016/09/are-we-any-safer/492761/

[2] "FBI says it is refocused on movement of Islamic State into the US," Los Angeles Times, December 9, 2015, http://www.latimes.com/world/middleeast/la-fg-foreign-fighters-20151208-story.html

[3] This term was coined in Kalim Siddiqui, Stages of Islamic Revolution (London: The Open Press, 1996). It refers to groups tied to the Muslim Brotherhood (Al-Ikhwan al-Muslimeen) and the Pakistani Islamist party, Jama'at al-Islami.

[4] Wahhabi here is understood as the Saudi brand of Salafism, which is a movement within Islam that seeks to practice Islam in the fashion of the pious ancestors – namely the Prophet Muhammad and his Companions. Wahhabism derives from Muhammad ibn abd al Wahhab, who introduced a form of Salafism to the Arabian Peninsula in alliance with the House of Saud in the early 20th Century.

[5] Jama'at-e Islami is a Pakistani Islamist party founded in 1941 by Syed Abul A'ala Maududi, who was perhaps the most influential Islamist thinker of the 20th Century.

[6] Giles Kepel, The War for Muslim Minds: Islam and the West (Cambridge, MA: Belknap Press, 2006); Lorenzo Vidino, The New Western Brothers (New York: Columbia University Press, forthcoming 2010); Lorenzo Vidino, "Aims and Methods of Europe's Muslim Brotherhood," Current Trends in Islamist Ideology 4 (2006); Allison Pargeter, The New Frontiers of Jihad: Radical Islam in Europe (Philadelphia: University of Pennsylvania Press, 2008), 20.

[7] "Elbarasse Search 1," U.S. v. Holy Land Foundation et al, 3:04-CR-240-G (Northern District TX, 2008), http://www.txnd.uscourts.gov/judges/hlf2/09-25-08/Elbarasse Search 1.pdf; "Elbarasse Search 3," U.S. v. Holy Land Foundation et al, http://www.txnd.uscourts.gov/judges/hlf2/09-25-08/Elbarasse Search 3.pdf; "Elbarasse Search 19," U.S. v. Holy Land Foundation et al, http://www.txnd.uscourts.gov/judges/hlf2/09-29-08/Elbarasse Search 19.pdf; "Elbarasse Search 2," U.S. v. Holy Land Foundation et al, http://www.txnd.uscourts.gov/judges/hlf2/09-25-08/Elbarasse Search 2.pdf; Esam Omeish, Letter to the Washington Post, September 16, 2004, http://www.unitedstatesaction.com/documents/omeish/www-masnet-org_pressroom_release-asp_nycmexs4.pdf; Noreen S. Ahmed-Ullah et al., "A Rare Look at the Secretive Brotherhood in America," Chicago Tribune, September 19, 2004, http://www.chicagotribune.com/news/watchdog/chi-0409190261sep19,0,3008717.story.

[8] Stephen P. Cohen, The Idea of Pakistan (Washington, DC: Brookings Institution, 2004), 348, n. 7; Vali Reza Nasr, The Vanguard of the Islamic Revolution: The Jama'at-I Islami of Pakistan (Berkeley: University of California Press, 1994).

[9] See, for example: Esam Omeish, "MAS President Letter to the Washington Post," Muslim American Society Website, September 16, 2004, http://www.unitedstatesaction.com/documents/omeish/www-masnet-org_pressroom_release-asp_nycmexs4.pdf

[10] "Exhibit 0003918-0003919," (Letter from "The Political Office" re: the founding of the Islamic Association for Palestine by "the Group"), U.S. v. Holy Land Foundation et al., 5.

[11] Zeid al-Noman, as quoted in "Elbarasse Search 2," U.S. v. Holy Land Foundation et al.

[12] "Elbarasse Search 2," U.S. v. Holy Land Foundation et al.

[13] "Yale Muslim Students Association," http://yalemsa.org/. "University of Pennsylvania Muslim Students Assocaition," http://www.upennmsa.org//"Columbia Muslim Students Association," http://columbiamsa.org/"Dartmouth Muslim Students Association," http://www.dartmouthmsa.org/

[14] "Frequently Asked Questions About the MSA of the US & Canada," MSA National Website, n.d., http://muslimamericansociety.org/main/content/frequently-asked-questions-about-mas

[15] Ahmed Shama, Speech before the 7th Annual MSA West Conference, University of Southern California, January 2005.

[16] Shah Imam, Speech before the MSA 2006 East Zone Conference, University of Maryland, March 2006

[17] North American Islamic Trust Website, http://www.nait.net/.

[18] "The North American Islamic Trust – NAIT," North American Islamic Trust Website, n.d., http://www.nait.net/NAIT_about_ us.htm; See also John Mintz and Douglas Farah, "In Search of Friends Among the Foes," Washington Post, September 11, 2004, http://www.washingtonpost.com/wp-dyn/articles/A12823-2004Sep10.html; Zeyno Baran, "The Muslim Brotherhood's U.S. Network," Current Trends in Islamist Ideology 6 (2008); Steven Merley, "The Muslim Brotherhood in the United States," Hudson Institute Research Monographs on the Muslim World Series no. 2, paper no. 3, April 2009.

[19] Qaradawi is often described as the spiritual leader of the Muslim Brotherhood. He is based in Doha, Qatar and hosts the popular Al-Jazeera television show 'Ash-Shariah wal-Hayat' (Islamic Law and Life). For more, see Husam Tammam, "Yusuf al-Qaradawi and the Muslim Brothers: The Nature of a Special Relationship," in Jakob Skovgaard-Petersen and Bettina Graf, eds., Global Mufti: The Phenomenon of Yusuf al-Qaradawi (London: Hurst & Co, 2009), 55-84.

[20] Ibid.

[21] Federal Bureau of Investigation, Indianapolis, Indiana, "North American Islamic Trust (NAIT)," December 15, 1987, http://www.investigativeproject.org/documents/misc/148.pdf

[22] "List of Unindicted Co-Conspirators and Joint Venturers," U.S. v. Holy Land Foundation et al, http://www.investigativeproject.org/documents/case_docs/423.pdf

[23] Ibid.

[24] "ISNA Board of Directors (Majlis Ash-Shura)," ISNA Website, n.d., http://www.isna.net/board-of-directors.html; "Elbarasse Search 3," U.S. v. Holy Land Foundation et al.

[25] Zaheer Uddin, "ICNA: A Successful Journey and a Promising Road Ahead." The Message International 23, no. 8 (1999), 24.

[26] Ibid.

[27] "About ICNA", ICNA Website, n.d., http://www.icna.org/about-icna/

[28] See, for example, "Government's Trial Brief," U.S. v. Holy Land Foundation et al; Excerpts of the FBI transcripts of this meeting are available at http://www.investigativeproject.org/documents/case_docs/836.pdf and http://www.investigativeproject.org/documents/case_docs/720.pdf

[29] "Our Vision, Mission, and Core Principles," CAIR Website, n.d., http://www.cair.com/about-us.html

[30] Gretel C. Kovach, "Five Convicted in Terrorism Financing Trial," New York Times, November 24, 2008, http://www.nytimes.com/2008/11/25/us/25charity.html

[31] See, for example, James E. Finch, letter to MCOP Invitee, October 8, 2008, http://www.investigativeproject.org/documents/misc/238.pdf; "Congressman 'Deeply Disappointed' By FBI's Lack of Answers on CAIR's Questionable Ties," FoxNews.com, March 11, 2009, http://www.foxnews.com/politics/2009/03/11/congressman-deeply-disappointed-fbis-lack-answers-cairs-questionable-ties/; Charles Schumer, Tom Coburn, and Jon Kyl, letter to Robert Mueller, February 24, 2009, http://www.investigativeproject.org/documents/misc/242.pdf

[32] See, for example, Erick Stakelbeck, "Controversial Islamic Speaker Welcomed at Ft. Hood," CBN, December 9, 2009, http://www.cbn.com/cbnnews/us/2009/December/Controversial-Speaker-Welcomed-at-Ft-Hood/. The paucity of sources that have reported on this issue reflect the extent to which basic information about Islamist groups in the U.S. outside mainstream discourse. The outlets that have addressed Louay Safi's work at Fort Hood include the Christian Broadcasting Network, the website Jihad Watch, the Investigative Project on Terrorism, a series of right-wing blogs, and other similar organizations.

[33] Ahmed-Ullah, Roe and Cohen, "A rare look at secretive Brotherhood in America."

[34] Ibid.

[35] "About MAS," MAS Website, n.d, http://www.muslimamericansociety.org/main/content/about-us

[36] Ibid.

[37] "MAS Freedom," MAS Website, n.d., http://muslimamericansociety.org/main/content/mas-freedom

[38] "Departments," MAS Website, n.d., http://muslimamericansociety.org/main/.

[39] "About IIIT," IIIT Website, n.d., http://www.iiit.org/AboutUs/AboutIIIT/tabid/66/Default.aspx

[40] Ibid.

[41] "Affidavit of SA David Kane," In the Matter Involving 555 Grove Street, Herndon, Virginia, and Related Locations, 02-MG-114 (ED VA, March 2002), 49–50. (Hereinafter Kane Affidavit).

[42] Kane Affidavit.

[43] Mintz and Farah, "In Search Of Friends Among The Foes"; "Jordan's Islamic Action Front picks up New Leadership," Deutsche Presse-Agentur, May 31, 2009.

[44] Syed Saleem Shahzad, "Jordan's Islamic Front rallies Muslims," Asia Times Online, March 7, 2003, http://www.atimes.com/atimes/Middle_East/EC07Ak01.html.

[45] See, for example, Jamal Halaby, "Jordan Islamists to Step up Anti-Election Campaign," Associated Press, January 15, 2013, http://news.yahoo.com/jordan-islamists-step-anti-election-campaign-114524529.html.

[46] "Jamaat ul-Fuqra," South Asia Terrorism Portal (SATP), n.d., http://www.satp.org/satporgtp/countries/pakistan/terroristoutfits/jamaat-ul-fuqra.htm

[47] Richard Sale, "Pakistan ISI link to Pearl kidnap probed," United Press International, January 29, 2002, http://www.upi.com/Business_News/Security-Industry/2002/01/29/Pakistan-ISI-link-to-Pearl-kidnap-probed/UPI-22581012351784/. JeM is designated as a Foreign Terrorist Organization by the U.S. government. JeM seeks to liberate Kashmir and reunite it with Pakistan.

[48] "Welcome to the International Quranic Open University," International Quranic Open University Website, n.d., http://www.iqou-moa.org/.

[49] The online edition of The Islamic Post can be accessed at http://islamicpostonline.com/.

[50] Colorado Attorney General Press Release, "Attorney General Salazar announces 69 Year Sentence for 'Fuqra' defendant convicted of racketeering and conspiracy to commit murder," March 16, 2001.

[51] "United States: The Jamaat al-Fuqra Threat," Stratfor, June 2, 2005, http://www.stratfor.com/memberships/61912/united_states_jamaat_al_fuqra_threat.

[52] "'Homegrown Jihad: The Terrorist Camps Around U.S.' Hits Cable TV," Christian Action Network Website, n.d., http://www.christianaction.org/homegrown-jihad/.

[53] Madeleine Gruen, "Hizb ut Tahrir's Activities in the United States," Jamestown Foundation Terrorism Monitor 5, no. 16, August 22, 2007, http://www.jamestown.org/single/?no_cache=1&tx_ttnews%5Btt_news%5D=4377

[54] "Hizb ut Tahrir," Hizb ut Tahrir America Website, n.d., http://www.hizb-america.org/index.php/aboutus/hizbuttahrir.

[55] Ibid.

[56] Houriya Ahmed and Hannah Stuart, Hizb ut Tahrir: Ideology and Strategy (London: Centre for Social Cohesion, 2009).

[57] Gruen, "Hizb ut Tahrir's Activities in the United States."

[58] "Mission Statement," Revolution Muslim Website, n.d., http://www.revolutionmuslim.com/index.php?option=com_content&view=article&id=3&Itemid=17

[59] Matt Zapotosky, "New Jersey man sentenced to prison for extremist Islamic Web posts," Washington Post, April 25, 2014, https://www.washingtonpost.com/local/crime/new-jersey-man-to-be-sentenced-for-extremist-islamic-web-posts/2014/04/24/406e65a8-cbc4-11e3-93eb-6c0037dde2ad_story.html?utm_term=.95898084ffe5

[60] Ibid.

[61] Rukmini Callimachi, "Once a Qaeda Recruiter, Now a Voice Against Jihad," New York Times, August 29, 2016, https://www.nytimes.com/2016/08/30/us/al-qaeda-islamic-state-jihad-fbi.html?_r=0.

[62] Matt Zapotosky, "The feds billed him as a threat to American freedom. Now they're paying him for help," Washington Post, February 5, 2016, https://www.washingtonpost.com/local/public-safety/the-feds-billed-him-as-a-threat-to-american-freedom-now-theyre-paying-him-for-help/2016/02/04/32be460a-c6c5-11e5-a4aa-f25866ba0dc6_story.html?utm_term=.f1f753576d06.

[63] Callimachi, "Once a Qaeda Recruiter, Now a Voice Against Jihad."

[64] Rachel Weiner, "Man Who Turned Away from Radical Islam Arrested on Drug, Prostitution Charges," Washington Post, January 25, 2017, https://www.washingtonpost.com/local/public-safety/man-who-turned-away-from-radical-islam-arrested-on-drug-prostitution-charges/2017/01/25/70a9627e-de7a-11e6-ad42-f3375f271c9c_story.html?utm_term=.1e354de7fed0.

[65] "Sealed Complaint," U.S. v. Cromitie et al, (SD NY, May 19, 2009).

[66] "Indictment," U.S. v. Headley, 09-CR-830 (ED IL, December 7, 2009).

[67] Michael Tarm and Sophia Tareen, "David Coleman Headley Sentencing: American Mumbai Attack Plotter Sentenced To 35 Years," Huffington Post, January 24, 2013, http://www.huffingtonpost.com/2013/01/24/david-coleman-headley-sen_n_2541782.html

[68] "Indictment," U.S. v. Najibullah Zazi, 09-CR-663 (ED NY, September 24, 2009); "Memorandum of Law in Support of the Government's Motion for a Permanent Order of Detention," U.S. v. Najibullah Zazi; U.S. Department of Justice Press Release, "Three Arrested in Ongoing Terror Investigation," September 20, 2009, http://www.justice.gov/opa/pr/2009/September/09-nsd-1002.html

[69] Phil Hirschkorn, "Would-Be Subway Suicide Bomber Najibullah Zazi Speaks," CBS News, April 19, 2012, http://www.cbsnews.com/8301-201_162-57416351/would-be-subway-suicide-bomber-najibullah-zazi-speaks/

[70] "Superseding Information," U.S. v Bryan Neal Vinas, 08-823 (ED NY, July 22, 2009).

[71] William K. Rashbaun and Souad Mekhennet, "L.I. Man Helped Qaeda, Then Informed," New York Times, July 22, 2009, http://www.nytimes.com/2009/07/23/nyregion/23terror.html

[72] U.S. Department of Justice Press Release, "Seven Charged with Terrorism Violations in North Carolina," July 27, 2009; U.S. Department of Justice Press Release, "Superseding Indictment in Boyd Matter Charges Defendants with Conspiring to Murder U.S. Military Personnel, Weapons Violations," September 24, 2009.

[73] U.S. Attorney's Office, Eastern District of North Carolina, "North Carolina Resident Daniel Patrick Boyd Sentenced for Terrorism Violations," August 24, 2012, http://www.fbi.gov/charlotte/press-releases/2012/north-carolina-resident-daniel-patrick-boyd-sentenced-for-terrorism-violations

[74] United States Department of Justice, "Man Sentenced to 24 Years in Prison for Attempting to Use a Weapon of Mass Destruction to Bomb Skyscraper in Downtown Dallas," October 19, 2010, http://www.justice.gov/opa/pr/2010/October/10-nsd-1170.html.

[75] "Criminal Complaint," U.S. v. Smadi, 3:09-MT-286 (ND TX, September 24, 2009).

[76] Zachary Fagenson, "Two men charged in Miami with financing foreign terrorist groups," Reuters, August 13, 2013, http://www.reuters.com/article/2013/08/13/us-usa-florida-suspects-idUSBRE97C0ZL20130813.

[77] Philip Sherwell and Alex Spillius, "Fort Hood Shooting: Texas Army Killer Linked to September 11 Terrorists," Telegraph (London), November 7, 2009.

[78] "Judge Denies Defense Lawyers' Request in Fort Hood Case," New York Times, August 27, 2013, http://www.nytimes.com/2013/08/28/us/judge-denies-defense-lawyers-request-in-fort-hood-case.html.

[79] "Death Penalty for Rampage at Fort Hood," New York Times, August 28, 2013, http://www.nytimes.com/2013/08/29/us/jury-weighs-sentence-for-fort-hood-shooting.html?pagewanted=all

[80] See, for example, "Pentagon Will Not Classify Fort Hood Shootings as Terrorism -- or Anything Else," CNS News, October 22, 2012, http://cnsnews.com/news/article/pentagon-will-not-classify-fort-hood-shootings-terrorism-or-anything-else - sthash.YWjerBq9.dpuf.

[81] "Lawmakers Call Ft. Hood Shootings 'Terrorism,'" New York Times, November 19, 2009, http://www.nytimes.com/2009/11/20/us/politics/20hood.html.

[82] Katherine Q. Seelye, William K. Rashbaum, and Michael Cooper, "2nd Bombing Suspect Caught After Frenzied Hunt Paralyzes Boston," New York Times, April 19, 2013, http://www.nytimes.com/2013/04/20/us/boston-marathon-bombings.html?hp.

[83] Ibid.

[84] Michael Cooper, Michael S. Schmidt, and Eric Schmidt, "Boston Suspects Are Seen as Self-Taught and Fueled by Web," New York Times, April 23, 2013, http://www.nytimes.com/2013/04/24/us/boston-marathon-bombing-developments.html?hp&pagewanted=all.

[85] Ann O'Neill, Aaron Cooper and Ray Sanchez, "Boston Marathon bombing Dzhokar Tsarnaev sentenced to death," CNN, May 17, 2015, http://www.cnn.com/2015/05/15/us/boston-bombing-tsarnaev-sentence/.

[86] Joe Mozingo, "'The worst thing imaginable:' Bodies and blood everywhere after San Bernardino terrorist attack, DOJ report shows," Los Angeles Times, September 9, 2016, http://www.latimes.com/local/lanow/la-me-san-bernardino-terror--20160909-snap-story.html.

[87] Rukmini Callimachi, "Islamic State Says 'Soldiers of Caliphate' Attacked in San Bernardino," New York Times, December 5, 2015, https://www.nytimes.com/2015/12/06/world/middleeast/islamic-state-san-bernardino-massacre.html.

[88] AnneClaire Stapleton and Ralph Ellis, "Timeline of Orlando nightclub shooting," CNN, June 17, 2016, http://www.cnn.com/2016/06/12/us/orlando-shooting-timeline/.

[89] United States Department of Justice, Office of Public Affairs, "Joint Statement From the Justice Department and FBI Regarding Transcript Related to Orlando Terror Attack," June 20, 2016, https://www.justice.gov/opa/pr/joint-statement-justice-department-and-fbi-regarding-transcript-related-orlando-terror-attack.

[90] Scott Fais, "Mateen to News 13 producer: 'I'm the shooter. It's me,'" News 13, June 15, 2016, http://www.mynews13.com/content/news/cfnews13/news/article.html/content/news/articles/cfn/2016/6/14/orlando_shooting_oma.html.

[91] Pete Williams, Tom Winter, Andrew Blankstein and Tracy Connor, "Suspect Identified in Ohio State Attack as Abdul Razak Ali Artan," NBC News, November 28, 2016, http://www.nbcnews.com/news/us-news/suspect-dead-after-ohio-state-university-car-knife-attack-n689076.

[92] Besheer Mohamed, "A new estimate of the U.S. Muslim population," Pew Research Center, January 6, 2016, http://www.pewresearch.org/fact-tank/2016/01/06/a-new-estimate-of-the-u-s-muslim-population/.

[93] Michael Lipka, "Muslims and Islam: Key findings in the U.S. and around the world," Pew Research Center, February 27, 2017, http://www.pewresearch.org/fact-tank/2017/02/27/muslims-and-islam-key-findings-in-the-u-s-and-around-the-world/.

[94] Pew Research Center, "Muslim Americans: No Signs of Growth in Alienation or Support for Extremism," August 30, 2011, http://people-press.org/files/2011/08/muslim-american-report.pdf

[95] Ibid.

[96] Ibidem.

[97] Ibidem.

[98] Ibidem.

[99] Brill, "Is America Any Safer?"

[100] House Committee on Homeland Security, "December Terror Threat Snapshot," December 2016, https://homeland.house.gov/press/chairman-mccaul-releases-december-terror-threat-snapshot-2/

[101] As cited in David Remnick, "Going the Distance," New Yorker, January 27, 2014, http://www.newyorker.com/magazine/2014/01/27/going-the-distance-david-remnick.

[102] "Sunni Rebels Declare New 'Islamic Caliphate,'" Al Jazeera (Doha), June 30, 2014, http://www.aljazeera.com/news/middleeast/2014/06/isil-declares-new-islamic-caliphate-201462917326669749.html.

[103] White House, Office of the Press Secretary, "FACT SHEET: The Administration's Strategy to Counter the Islamic State of Iraq and the Levant (ISIL) and the Updated FY 2015 Overseas Contingency Operations Request," November 7, 2014, https://obamawhitehouse.archives.gov/the-press-office/2014/11/07/fact-sheet-administration-s-strategy-counter-islamic-state-iraq-and-leva.

[104] James S. Robbins, "Fighting the Islamic State: The U.S. Scorecard," The Journal of International Affairs no. 30, Winter 2016, http://www.securityaffairs.org/issues/number-30/fighting-islamic-state-us-scorecard#7.

[105] "Islamic State Lost A Quarter Of Its Iraq, Syria Territory In 18 Months: IHS," Reuters, July 10, 2016, http://www.reuters.com/article/us-mideast-crisis-iraq-syria-idUSKCN0ZQ0FW.

[106] See, for example, Jose Ragliery, "ISIS Cuts its Fighters' Salaries by 50%," CNN Money, January 19, 2016, http://money.cnn.com/2016/01/19/news/world/isis-salary-cuts/.

[107] U.S. House of Representatives, Committee on Homeland Security, Cash to Chaos: Dismantling ISIS' Financial Infrastructure, October 2016,https://homeland.house.gov/wp-content/uploads/2016/10/Dismantling-ISIS-Financial-Infrastructure.pdf.

[108] Rowan Scarborough, "Islamic State Expands Beyond Iraq-Syria Base with Six Armies on Three World Regions," Washington Times, June 20, 2016,http://www.washingtontimes.com/news/2016/jun/20/isis-expands-beyond-iraq-syria-base-with-six-armie/.

[109] See, for example, "Trump's Address to Joint Session of Congress, Annotated," NPR, February 28, 2017, http://www.npr.org/2017/02/28/516717981/watch-live-trump-addresses-joint-session-of-congress.

[110] The White House, Office of the Press Secretary, "EXECUTIVE ORDER: PROTECTING THE NATION FROM FOREIGN TERRORIST ENTRY INTO THE UNITED STATES," January 27, 2017, https://www.whitehouse.gov/the-press-office/2017/01/27/executive-order-protecting-nation-foreign-terrorist-entry-united-states.

[111] Ron Nixon, Adam Goldman and Eric Schmitt, "Devices Banned on Flights From 10 Countries over ISIS Fears," New York Times, March 21, 2017, https://www.nytimes.com/2017/03/21/us/politics/tsa-ban-electronics-laptops-cabin.html?_r=0.

[112] "Challenges to Trump's immigration orders spread to more U.S. states," Reuters, February 1, 2017, http://www.reuters.com/article/us-usa-trump-immigration-sanfrancisco-idUSKBN15F2B1.

Latin America

COUNTRIES
Argentina
Bolivia
Brazil
Nicaragua
Venezuela

Argentina

> **Quick Facts**
>
> Population: 43,886,748 (July 2016 est.)
>
> Area: 2,780,400 sq km
>
> Ethnic Groups: white (mostly Spanish and Italian) 97%, mestizo (mixed white and Amerindian ancestry), Amerindian, or other non-white groups 3%
>
> Religions: nominally Roman Catholic 92% (less than 20% practicing), Protestant 2%, Jewish 2%, other 4%
>
> Government Type: presidential republic
>
> GDP (official exchange rate): $541.7 billion (2015 est.)
>
> *Map and Quick Facts courtesy of the CIA World Factbook (Last Updated January 2017)*

Overview

Argentina is home to one of the largest Muslim populations in Latin America.[1] A growing percentage of the community is made up of Argentine converts to Islam, many of whom have been recruited and radicalized by Islamist operatives working throughout the country.

The Argentine Muslim community has gone largely unnoticed since its establishment in the 19th century, but national scandals such as Carlos Menem's controversial administration and bombings in Buenos Aires in the early 1990s—the largest terror attacks in the region at the time—brought it into the national spotlight. Since then, the community has been stigmatized for its connection to radical Islamist networks tied to Iran and its proxy, Hezbollah. Through use of these networks, Iran has used intelligence operatives to infiltrate Muslim society and recruit members from a community that shows signs of increasing radicalization.

These networks pose significant danger to Argentina, whose policy towards Iran and other Arab states has often been ambivalent and inconsistent. Moreover, Argentina's failing economy and its strained relationships with Western allies during the Fernández de Kirchner made it even more vulnerable to Iranian advances and activities in the region.

ISLAMIST ACTIVITY

Radical Islamist activity has been growing throughout Argentina since at least the early 1980s, when the Iranian Revolution was "exported" to the Americas.[2] Iran has maintained a presence in the hemisphere since the 1850s, when it first sought U.S. assistance in keeping European powers at bay and later built diplomatic relationships with other countries in the region such as Argentina, Brazil, and Mexico.[3] However, Iran's political objectives changed with the 1979 Revolution, resulting in a break in ties with the United States and an eventual shift toward Latin America, particularly toward countries antagonistic to "American imperialism."[4]

According to Alberto Nisman, the special prosecutor for the AMIA attack, Iran and Hezbollah saw Argentina as a land of opportunity[5] for spreading radical Islam due to the large number of Muslim communities in the region, particularly the Tri-Border Area at the crossroads of Argentina, Brazil, and Paraguay.[6] Nisman cited documents seized from Iranian operatives identifying high-density areas of Muslim population to be used "as centers of penetration of Islam" throughout South America.[7] Since then, Argentina in particular has served as one of the main hubs through which radical Islamists have developed an extensive network of terrorists, clergymen and recruiters, money launderers, and other operatives all dedicated to "exporting the revolution" throughout the region.[8]

The result of this growing network was the execution of Latin America's most notorious Islamist terrorist attack—the July 18, 1994 bombing in Buenos Aires, Argentina of the *Asociación Mutual Israelita Argentina* (AMIA) that killed 85 civilians and injured hundreds more. Two years earlier, on March 17, 1992, a similar attack had been carried out against Israel's embassy in Buenos Aires, murdering 29 people and injuring over two hundred.[9] These twin attacks awoke Argentina to the real threat of Islamist activity within and around its borders.

According to Nisman, Iran's Islamist terrorist network in Argentina was first established in 1983 with the arrival of Iranian operative Mohsen Rabbani. Originally sent to Argentina ostensibly as a commercial representative of the Iranian meat industry,[10] Rabbani quickly established himself as a leader within the country's Shi'ite Muslim community and began leading prayers at the At-Tauhid mosque in the Floresta neighborhood of Buenos Aires.[11] In his role as a prayer leader, he was able to address believers at will, inserting radical political rhetoric into his sermons and developing relationships with young "disciples" who would later become operatives within his evolving terror network.

The network Rabbani established throughout the Shi'ite Muslim community in Buenos Aires grew to include more than 40 Islamic associations, including schools, media outlets, and charity organizations that are used today as backdoor channels through which the Islamic Republic and Hezbollah perform intelligence and covert operations.[12] It spans across state borders, allowing Iran and its proxies to pursue various terror operations in the region as a part of their political expansion. The most well-known of these operations is the 1994 AMIA attack in Buenos Aires, of which Nisman identified Rabbani as "the mastermind."[13] Though Rabbani escaped justice in Argentina by leaving the country in 1997, Interpol has since placed him on a "red alert" list, barring his travel to the region. However, the Islamist terror network he established continues to grow under the supervision of his many radical disciples.

According to a recent report by the Center for a Secure Free Society (SFS), Rabbani's Argentine disciples can be broken down into three different types of actors: shadow facilitators, "super fixers," and "fixers."[14] While prohibited from entering Argentina, Rabbani still acts as a shadow facilitator from Iran, providing guidance and funding to various Islamist activities in Argentina.[15] His disciples act as "super fixers," moving across countries throughout Latin America and acting as point persons for the "fixers," or local Argentine agents who have access to or knowledge of targeted communities in the country. Perhaps the two most infamous Rabbani disciples and "super fixers" are Abdul Karim Paz and Edgardo Ruben "Suhail" Assad. According to Nisman, Karim Paz is Rabbani's first convert and has been described as his "right-hand man" and immediate successor as the Imam of the At-Tauhid mosque.[16] Similarly, Suhail Assad is known as a prominent leader in the local Shi'a community, with strong connections to the government of former Argentine president Cristina Fernández de Kirchner.[17] Some of these connections come from Suhail Assad's cousin, Jorge Alejandro "Yussuf" Khalil, who was accused by Nisman of conspiring with the Fernández de Kirchner regime to cover up Iran's involvement in the AMIA attack through a controversial agreement signed between both countries in 2013. Yussuf Khalil is currently the General Secretary of the At-Tauhid Mosque.[18]

Together, Yussuf Khalil, Abdul Karim Paz and Suhail Assad serve as Iran's "informal ambassadors" in Argentina, continuing to recruit and radicalize Islamic communities to join the revolution.[19] Under their supervision, the radical Islamist network in Argentina grows stronger and more expansive behind its façade of Muslim community and religious centers, cultural associations, and seemingly innocuous development of diplomatic and trade relations with Argentine leaders. So does its influence on the local Muslim population, susceptible to radicalization and recruitment to Islamic extremism through proselytizing in mosques, schools, and cultural events in Argentine society.

Rabbani and his disciples have paved the way for other extremist groups to target Argentina, most notably the Islamic State. In September of 2016, Secretary of National Security Eugenio Burzaco mentioned the possibility of ISIS operatives in Corrientes.

While he later announced that national security forces had investigated and found no evidence of an ISIS cell in the region, he maintained that the Argentine government remained worried that Argentines who travelled to Syria and Iraq to join ISIS might return to form terrorist cells within Argentina.[20] President Mauricio Macri has also received threats from individuals possibly linked to ISIS, implying that Argentina is under threat of imminent attack.[21] While these individuals may be acting independently and the threats have so far not materialized, they nonetheless reflect an alarming degree of infiltration and activism by Islamist elements—a level of activity influenced and encouraged by the inroads created by Mohsen Rabbani and his network.

ISLAMISM AND SOCIETY

The date of Islam's first appearance in Argentina is unknown, as the first Argentine censuses regarded Muslims as "other" rather than specifically categorizing them, as was done with Jews and Catholics. Some believe the first Muslims to arrive in Argentina were descendants from the Moors who came to the Americas with the Spanish conquistadors, though this theory has not been verified.[22] However, the first official data on Arab/Islamic migration to Argentina indicates a wave of Syrian and Lebanese immigrants arriving in the mid- to late-19th century. This population continued to grow through the 20th century to an estimated 700,000 Muslims, mainly of Arab descent.[23] In 2010, the Pew Forum estimated Argentina's Muslim community to have grown to almost 1 million people, a total of 2.5 percent of the country's population of approximately 41 million.[24,25] Approximately 70% of the population is Sunni, with the Shiite community making up the remaining 30%.[26] However, within the Muslim community, the Arab population is starting to shrink as immigration from Arab countries like Syria and Lebanon is replaced by increasing immigration from West Africa.[27] Furthermore, the current growth of Islam in Argentina owes less to immigration from Arab states and more to converts from within Argentina itself,[28] thus changing the cultural demographic of the country's Muslim community from primarily Arab to a more diverse group.

Islam's spread to populations beyond the Arab community can be credited to the proliferation of Islamic centers and schools established since the late 20th century. Though the Arab immigrant community originally established organizations and centers focused on preserving cultural rather than religious identity (Jews and Christians of Arab origin also participated in these groups), certain centers devoted exclusively to "preserving the religious legacy" also were established. The foundation of the *Centro de Estudios Islámicos* (Center of Islamic Studies), headed by Imam Mahmoud Hussein, initiated the process of "diffusion of Islam" in 1973 and began to attract converts of non-Arab origin.[29] Since then, several mosques and Islamic centers have emerged throughout Argentina, though the Islamic community remains overwhelmingly concentrated in Buenos Aires.

One such mosque is the King Fahd mosque in Palermo, the largest mosque and Muslim cultural center in Latin America. Inaugurated in 2000, the mosque is notable for the fact that the approximately $15 million in building costs were paid for by King Fahd himself, and the land, formerly property of the Argentine state, was donated to King Fahd in the mid-1990s by ex-President Carlos Menem.[30][31] Despite the presence of multiple mosques and Muslim cultural centers in Buenos Aires, the Argentine Congress passed a bill approving the construction of the mosque, which drew criticism from members of the community who cited it as an example of Menem's tendency to favor pro-Arab or pro-Muslim ventures in Argentina, while failing to support other faiths with donations in cash or land.

Despite its size and international connections, until Menem's election as president in 1989, the Muslim population went largely unnoticed by the rest of Argentine society. Though Menem maintained his identity as a Catholic convert, his Arab background and family's continued ties to Islam brought the Muslim community into the public eye. As Menem raised the Muslim community to political prominence by adding members of the community, including his own family, to high-ranking positions within his cabinet, scandal and controversy also dominated his administration, resulting in a rejection of the Muslim community by certain sectors of Argentine society.[32]

After the bombings in Buenos Aires in the early 1990s, anti-Arab and anti-Muslim sentiment within Argentine society intensified. Argentina, which had until then considered itself safe from international terrorism, turned against the Islamic population.[33] Muslims and Arabs were stigmatized for their community's ties to the perpetrators of the AMIA attack,[34] most notably the leader of the Shi'ite Muslim community in Argentina, Mohsen Rabbani. Muslims in Argentina also faced considerable public discrimination following the September 11, 2001 attacks, according to Alexis El-Sayer of the *Centro Islámico de la República Argentina* (CIRA).[35] At that time, Muslims often hesitated to identify themselves publicly, though by 2012 the community had largely "overcome" this challenge and continued to practice Islam in peace, despite widespread ignorance about the Islamic faith and community in Argentina.[36]

Though the Islamic community remains a small minority within larger Argentine society, the Arab community continues to grow and is now the third largest community in Argentina after Italians and Spaniards. Islamic leaders hope that the proliferation of Islamic/Arab cultural centers and increased Islamic influence on society, particularly in Buenos Aires, will help "create a new bond between Islam and Latin America"[37] and help spread a positive, unbiased image of Islam.

The Argentine government also makes an effort to help the Muslim community feel like a part of Argentine society. The Argentine Secretariat of Worship under the Office of Foreign Affairs maintains a close relationship with leaders of the Islamic community and seeks to promote religious harmony by sending government officials to religious celebrations of all faiths.[38] The Islamic community has seen the attendance of government officials, including ex-President Cristina Fernández de Kirchner, at Muslim celebrations and events as "recognition… of our existence within Argentine society."[39]

The familiarity with which the Fernández de Kirchner administration treated the Muslim community can be attributed to the presence of a major cultural organization known as the *Federación de Entidades Árabes*, or FEARAB. Originally founded in 1972 to represent Muslim immigrant communities in Latin America,[40] the organization has offices throughout the region and its leaders maintain strong relationships with local governments. In Argentina especially, FEARAB leadership was successful in developing relationships with the federal government during the Fernández de Kirchner era.[41] This access to high-ranking Argentine officials allowed FEARAB to supersede its original social and cultural spheres and become a political entity. This ascent is cause for concern because at least some of the leaders of FEARAB, the ranks of which include Abdul Karim Paz and Yussuf Khalil, maintain connections with Mohsen Rabbani's Islamist network.[42] A series of Argentine government wiretaps reveal that these individuals took advantage of the organization's access to top Argentine officials to implement Iran's political agenda and further extend Iranian influence in Argentine politics—resulting in the Kirchner government's introduction of a controversial Memorandum of Understanding in 2013, under which the two countries agreed to work together to investigate the perpetrators of the 1994 AMIA attack.[43]

ISLAMISM AND THE STATE

Argentina's policy towards Arab or Middle East states has historically been rather ambivalent, particularly on controversial issues such as the Israel/Palestine conflict. As early as 1947, Argentina showed itself unwillingly to pick a side in the conflict, choosing to abstain from voting on the UN resolution that would partition Palestine into a Jewish and Arab state. This decision was most likely motivated by a desire to balance the interests of Jewish and Arab populations within the country and maintain Argentina's position in international systems at the time. This was also seen in later policies in favor of Palestine in order to avoid oil embargos from OPEC nations and the subsequent adoption of more moderate positions toward Israel after public outcry from the Argentine Jewish community. Since, Argentina has typically sought to balance every gesture of support for Palestine with the same for Israel.[44]

This duality of Argentina's stance toward Arab/Muslim and Jewish/Western issues became even more pronounced during the presidency of Carlos Menem, who offered to mediate the Arab-Israeli conflict and extended links to Israel by becoming the first Argentine president to visit the country,[45] despite his ties to the Arab/Muslim community both in Argentina and abroad. Official attitudes toward Arab and Islamic elements were further confused by the revelation that Libyan leader Muammar Ghadafi had contributed $4 million to Menem's electoral campaign[46] and the president's "donation" of state property, valued at $10 million, to the Saudi Arabian Islamic Affairs Department for the construction of what is today the Fahd center in Buenos Aires.[47] Meanwhile, Menem had terminated Argentina's cooperation with Iran's nuclear program in 1992,[48] the same year that the Israeli embassy in Buenos Aires was bombed by a group linked to Iran and Hezbollah[49] and two years before the 1994 AMIA attack that led to a break in diplomatic ties between Argentina and Iran.

Argentina's relationship with Iran is one of the longest-standing in the region, beginning in 1902, but the 1992 and 1994 terror attacks in Buenos Aires resulted in a cooling of diplomatic relations between the two countries as Argentina sought extradition of the high-ranking Iranian officials linked to the attacks.[50] With the advent of the Kirchner government (2007-2015), however, Argentine policy shifted dramatically, abandoning its traditional pro-Western, pro-United States orientation in favor of warmer ties with anti-US regional governments such as Cuba, Venezuela and other "Bolivarian" states, as well as with Iran.

Energy deficits and mounting debt alienated Argentina from its formerly friendly Western allies, nudging the Kirchner administration toward "friendlier" governments in Venezuela and Cuba. The Chávez administration in particular served as a new political ally and source of economic support to Argentina and provided further incentive for Fernández de Kirchner to distance herself from the U.S.[51]

Iran took this shift as an opportunity to re-open relations with Argentina. In 2007, then-Iranian President Mahmoud Ahmedinejad allegedly asked Venezuela's Hugo Chávez to reach out to Kirchner with the aim of "changing Argentine policy and allowing Iran access to Argentine nuclear technology."[52] The result was a gradual re-establishment of diplomatic ties between Argentina and Iran, a development that allowed Iran to increase its trade opportunities in the region and further strengthen its proxy terrorist network in the country.[53]

As part of this process, then-Foreign Minister Héctor Timerman broke with the Argentine Jewish community in 2012 in order to pursue ties with Iran,[54] and Fernández de Kirchner offered to freeze the longstanding federal investigation into the AMIA bombing in exchange for expanded bilateral trade with the Islamic Republic.[55] This move was partly motivated by Argentina's increasing political and economic desperation, and its growing dependence on alternative sources of trade.[56] It had the effect of making Argentina one of Iran's largest trade partners in the hemisphere, providing the Islamic Republic with long sought-after agricultural commodities.[57] Meanwhile, Argentina's dependence on oil and gas, which make up 90 percent of the country's primary energy sources, intensified its dependence on imports from Iran.[58] This warming of ties culminated with the announcement of the 2013 Memorandum of Understanding between Argentina and Iran,[59] which further normalized relations between the two countries.

This normalization proved to be short lived, however. Just half a year later, Argentina voted against Iran at the UN Human Rights Council,[60] and in 2014 Fernández de Kirchner announced the abrogation of the Memorandum due to lack of progress and internal opposition. A series of back and forth maneuvers followed, with Kirchner alternately courting the country's Jewish community and contesting a decision by the country's Federal Criminal Appeals Court that declared the MOU unconstitutional.[61] This inconsistent attitude toward Iran remained in place until the end of her tenure in 2015.

Meanwhile, Argentina continued to develop relationships with other anti-Western Arab nations. In 2010, Syrian President Bashar Al-Assad visited Buenos Aires and was warmly received by the President, who never acknowledged him as a dictator.[62] In the years following, Foreign Minister Timerman would make various trips to Aleppo to meet with Syrian officials, arranged by pro-Iran Ambassador to Syria Roberto Ahuad. This rapprochement and Argentina's reluctance to denounce the Syrian Civil War in late 2012 demonstrated an effort to maintain a positive relationship with a Syrian government closely allied to Iran.[63]

The election of Mauricio Macri to the Argentine presidency in late 2015 signaled yet another change in Argentina's rather disjointed policy toward Iran. Macri expressed disgust at Iran's involvement in the AMIA case and the relationship Fernández de Kirchner's administration had developed with the Islamic Republic.[64] In the first weeks of his presidency, he ordered the withdrawal of the appeal filed by his predecessor's government regarding the federal ruling of the MOU's unconstitutionality.[65] Additionally, Macri called for the use of Mercosur's Democracy Clause to expel Venezuela from the economic bloc for its human rights abuses, thus striking another blow to Iranian influence in the region.[66] This signified a clear break from the previous administration's policies towards Iran and its anti-Western allies and set a precedent for Argentina's realignment with the United States, Europe, and Israel.

However, Macri's attitude towards other Middle Eastern and Arab states, particularly the Gulf States, has not been as clear. In the year since Macri took office in late 2015, the most notable of his actions toward the Middle East have included the signing of a controversial commercial treaty with Qatar, aimed at encouraging and protecting bilateral investment,[67] and the announcement that Argentina would accept at least 3,000 Syrian refugees in cooperation with the European Union.[68]

This announcement did not indicate any intention to divert from the previous administration's policy toward the Syrian conflict. In fact, it built upon the creation of *Program Siria* (Syria Program) by the previous administration, in which Syrians affected or displaced by the country's civil war were granted residency in Argentina for up to two years.[69] Palestinian nationals that had been residing in Syria were also eligible to participate in this program.[70] Under Macri's administration, the refugee acceptance program has been augmented by the creation of the *Gabinete Nacional del Programa Siria* (National Cabinet for the Syria Program), an inter-departmental entity whose main goal is establishing guidelines for the country's reception of refugees and facilitating their social integration.[71]

Like his predecessors, Macri has demonstrated a certain level of ambivalence in his policies toward Arab and Muslim nations, attempting to balance criticism of one with support for another. His decision to accept Syrian refugees into Argentina is a continuation of that of the administration before him, which tended to favor the interests of its Arab and Muslim communities. The knowledge that Iranian terror agents have been operating within these communities and have used them to gain access to government officials, radicalize and recruit members, and raise funds puts Macri's decision in the spotlight as a potential security risk. However, his condemnation of Iran's influence and activity under the Fernández de Kirchner administration and his efforts to lessen the Islamic Republic's presence in Argentina since his election are cause for hope. Argentina is not yet free from the threat of radical Islamist terrorism, nor are its Arab and Muslim communities rid of the terror network still operating in their midst today, but Macri's reversal of a pro-Iran agenda and his rapprochement with Israel and Western allies is a step in the right direction.

ENDNOTES

[1] The Argentine national census does not record religious data, so statistics vary by source, with some reports citing Argentina as home to the largest Muslim population in Latin America (1,000,000 members) and others citing Brazil (35,000 to 1.5 million members). For more information, see the US Department of State International Religious Freedom Report for 2015, accessed October 27, 2016, http://www.state.gov/j/drl/rls/irf/religiousfreedom/index.htm#wrapper.

[2] As described in the 2013 Nisman Dictum, the "export of the revolution" is Iran's official policy of extending its political-religious view beyond its borders. Alberto Nisman, Report on Terrorist Networks in Latin America, pg. 10, May 2013, accessed October 12, 2016, http://albertonisman.org/nisman-report-dictamina-on-sleeper-cells-full-text/.

[3] Stephen Johnson, Iran's Influence in the Americas (Center for Strategic and International Studies, February 2012), accessed October 27, 2016, http://csis.org/files/publication/120223_Johnson_IranInfluence_ExecSumm_Web.pdf.

[4] Ibid.

[5] Alberto Nisman, 2013 Dictum, op cit., p. 59, 72, 180-181.

[6] Marcelo Martinez Burgos and Alberto Nisman, Office of Criminal Investigations: AMIA CASE; Investigations Unit of the Office of the Attorney General (Argentina), October 25, 2006, accessed October 27, 2016, http://www.peaceandtolerance.org/docs/nismanindict.pdf.

[7] Matthew Levitt, "Exporting Terror in America's Backyard," Foreign Policy, June 14, 2013, accessed October 27, 2016, http://foreignpolicy.com/2013/06/14/exporting-terror-in-americas-backyard/.

[8] Ibid.

[9] US Department of State. "Patterns of Global Terrorism: 1992," accessed October 27, 2016, http://fas.org/irp/threat/terror_92/chron.html.

[10] Nisman's report indicates that this role was merely a front; Rabbani was already a member of Iran's intelligence bureau upon his arrival in Argentina.

[11] Alberto Nisman, 2013 Dictum, op cit., p. 56, 58-59.

[12] Douglas Farah, Back to the Future: Argentina Unravels (Inter-American Institute for Democracy, 2013), 75.

[13] Alberto Nisman, 2013 Dictum, op. cit.

[14] Douglas Farah, Fixers, Super Fixers and Shadow Facilitators: How Networks Connect, (International Assessment and Strategy Center, April 23, 2012), accessed October 16, 2016, http://www.strategycenter.net/docLib/20120423_Farah_FixersSuperFixersShadow.pdf.

[15] Joseph Humire, After Nisman: How the death of a prosecutor revealed Iran's growing influence in the Americas, (Center for a Secure Free Society, 2016), 17.

[16] Alberto Nisman, Complaint of Criminal Plot, p. 96, 2015, accessed October 27, 2016, http://albertonisman.org/nisman-complaint-denuncia/.

[17] Humire, op cit., p. 19-20.

[18] Ibid, 17.

[19] Ibid.

[20] El Día. "Eugenio Burzaco descartó presencia demiembros de Isis en Argentina," September 11, 2016, accessed October 27, 2016, http://www.eldia.com/el-pais/el-gobierno-detecto-argentinos-formados-por-el-estado-islamico-164431.

[21] Jerry Nelson, "ISIS to Argentina: We're Coming to See You," Huffington Post, accessed October 27, 2016, http://www.huffingtonpost.com/entry/isis-to-argentina-were-coming-to-see-you_us_57dfb7d0e4b0d5920b5b3054.

[22] Pedro Brieger, "Muslims in Argentina," ISIM Newsletter 06/00: 33, accessed October 27, 2016, https://openaccess.leidenuniv.nl/bitstream/handle/1887/17433/ISIM_6_Muslims_in_Argentina.pdf?sequence=1.

[23] Chris Moss, "Latin America's First Mega-Mosque," Hispanic Muslims, accessed May 16, 2016, accessed October 27, 2016, http://hispanicmuslims.com/articles/other/openseyes.html.

[24] "Table: Muslim Population by Country," (The Pew Center, January 27, 2011), accessed May 16, 2016, http://www.pewforum.org/2011/01/27/table-muslim-population-by-country/?utm_expid=53098246-2.Lly4CFS-VQG2lphsg-KopIg.0.

[25] The World Bank cites Argentina's population at 41,222,875 people in 2010. For more information, please see World Bank population data, accessed December 9, 2016, http://data.worldbank.org/indicator/SP.POP.TOTL?end=2010&locations=AR&start=2010&view=bar.

[26] "International Religious Freedom Report—Argentina," (The United States Department of State, November 17, 2010), accessed October 11, 2016, http://www.state.gov/j/drl/rls/irf/2010/148731.htm.

[27] The Argentina Independent. "Ramadan Mubarak: Observing the Month-Long Fast in Buenos Aires," July 20, 2012, accessed May 16, 2016, http://www.argentinaindependent.com/life-style/ramadan-mubarak-observing-the-month-long-fast-in-buenos-aires/.

[28] Rosemary Pennington, "Is there Islam in Latin America?," Muslim Voices, accessed May 16, 2016, http://muslimvoices.org/islam-latin-america/.

[29] Brieger, op.cit., 33.

[30] Moss, op.cit.

[31] Clarín. "Se inaugura la mezquita más grande de Sudamérica," September 9, 2000, accessed December 9, 2016, http://edant.clarin.com/diario/2000/09/25/s-03801.htm.

[32] Brieger, op.cit., 33.

[33] Moss, op.cit.

[34] Brieger, op.cit., 33.

[35] The Argentina Independent, op.cit.

[36] Ibid.

[37] Moss, op.cit.

[38] "Argentina," International Religious Freedom Report 2010 (U.S. Department of State Bureau of Democracy, Human Rights, and Labor, November 27, 2010), accessed May 16, 2016, http://www.state.gov/j/drl/rls/irf/2010/148731.htm.

[39] The Argentina Independent, op.cit.

[40] Jose R. Cardenas and Roger Noriega, The Mounting Hezbollah Threat in Latin America (American Enterprise Institute, October 6, 2011), accessed October 27, 2016, http://www.aei.org/publication/the-mounting-hezbollah-threat-in-latin-america/.

[41] For more information on the FEARAB relationship with the Argentine government, see Humire's special report After Nisman, op. cit.

[42] Ibid.

[43] Ibid., 24.

[44] Cecilia Baeza, "América Latina y la cuestión palestina (1947-2012)," Araucaria Revista Iberoamericana de Filosofia, Política y Humanidades 14/28 (2012): 111-131.

[45] Ibid.

[46] Brieger, "Muslims in America," 33.

[47] Moss, "Latin America's First Mega-Mosque."

[48] Noriega, op.cit.

[49] The United States Department of State, "The Year in Review," Patterns of Global Terrorism: 1992, April 30, 1993, accessed October 11, 2016, https://fas.org/irp/threat/terror_92/review.html.

[50] Ilan Berman and Joseph M. Humire, Iran's Strategic Penetration of Latin America (London: Lexington Books, 2014), 35, 81.

[51] Berman and Humire, op.cit., 82.

[52] Roger F. Noriega, Argentina's Secret Deal with Iran?, (American Enterprise Institute), accessed May 16, 2016, https://www.aei.org/publication/argentinas-secret-deal-with-iran/.

[53] Berman and Humire, op.cit., 86.

[54] Ilan Berman, "The Dangerous Iran Flirtation," The Washington Times, accessed May 16, 2016, http://www.washingtontimes.com/news/2012/sep/27/at-first-blush-argentina-seems-like-an-odd-choice-/.

[55] Jaime Darenblum, "How Argentina and Brazil Help Iran," The Weekly Standard, accessed May 16, 2016, http://www.weeklystandard.com/article/how-argentina-and-brazil-help-iran/659920.

[56] Berman and Humire, op.cit., 82.

[57] Johnson, op.cit.

[58] Berman and Humire, op.cit., 82.

[59] Ibid.

[60] Buenos Aires Herald. "Argentina votes against Irán at UN Human Rights Council," accessed May 16, 2016, http://www.buenosairesherald.com/article/127012/argentina-votes-against-irán-at-un-human-rights-council.

[61] Buenos Aires Herald. "Appeals Court declares unconstitutional deal with Iran on AMIA attack probe," accessed October 10, 2016, http://www.buenosairesherald.com/article/159604/appeals-court-declares-unconstitutional-deal-with-iran-on-amia-attack-probe-.

[62] Pepe Eliaschev, "El Gobierno negocia un pacto secreto con Irán para 'olvidar' los atentados," Perfil, accessed May 16, 2016, http://www.perfil.com/politica/El-Gobierno-negocia-un-pacto-secreto-con-Iran-para-olvidar-los-atentados-20110326-0004.html.

[63] Ibid.

[64] Dana Chocron, "Argentina: A New Foreign Policy?," Young Diplomats, accessed October 10, 2016, http://www.young-diplomats.com/argentinas-promised-foreign-policy/.

[65] Uki Goñi and Jonathan Watts, "Argentina president-elect pledges radical policy changes in shift to right," The Guardian, accessed October 10, 2016, https://www.theguardian.com/world/2015/nov/23/argentina-president-elect-mauricio-macri-iran-venezuela.

[66] Eamonn MacDonagh, "Analysis: Macri Victory in Argentina Marks Setback for Iranian Ambitions in Latin America," The Tower, accessed October 10, 2016, http://www.thetower.org/2600-macri-victory-in-argentina-election-marks-setback-for-iranian-ambitions-in-latin-america/.

[67] Ramón Indart, "Qué dice el polémico memorándum que firmó el gobierno de Macri con Qatar," Perfil, November 17, 2016, accessed January 16, 2017, http://www.perfil.com/politica/que-dice-el-polemico-memorandum-que-firmo-el-gobierno-de-macri-con-qatar.phtml.

[68] Amanda Blohm, "Argentina will accept 3,000 Syrian refugees," PanAm Post, July 7, 2016, accessed January 5, 2017, https://panampost.com/amanda-blohm/2016/07/07/argentina-will-receive-3000-syrian-refugees/.

[69] La Nación. "La Argentina también recibirá refugiados sirios," October 22, 2014, accessed January 5, 2017, http://www.lanacion.com.ar/1737801-la-argentina-tambien-recibira-refugiados-sirios.

[70] Ibid.

[71] Telam. "El gobierno creará un gabinete para atender a las necesidades de los refugiados sirios," September 22, 2016, accessed January 5, 2017, http://www.telam.com.ar/notas/201609/164023-gabinete-nacional-programa-siria-refugiados.html.

Bolivia

> **Quick Facts**
>
> Population: 10,969,649 (July 2016 est.)
>
> Area: 1,098,581 sq km
>
> Ethnic Groups: mestizo (mixed white and Amerindian ancestry) 68%, indigenous 20%, white 5%, cholo/chola 2%, black 1%, other 1%, unspecified 3% ; 44% of respondents indicated feeling part of some indigenous group, predominantly Quechua or Aymara
>
> Religions: Roman Catholic 76.8%, Evangelical and Pentecostal 8.1%, Protestant 7.9%, other 1.7%, none 5.5%
>
> Government Type: presidential republic
>
> GDP (official exchange rate): $35.7 billion (2015 est.)
>
> *Map and Quick Facts courtesy of the CIA World Factbook (Last Updated January 2017)*

Overview

Bolivia, a country of over 10.6 million people, has a Muslim population of approximately 2,000. But while the practice of the religion in Bolivia remains small and dispersed, the election of President Evo Morales in 2005 brought about a more amiable relationship with Islamic countries in the Middle East, and significantly opened Bolivia's official policy towards Islam in the years since.[1]

Bolivia's Muslim population counts among its members' descendants from Bangladesh, Pakistan, Egypt, the Palestinian territories, Iran, Syria, and Lebanon. These communities are generally spread out between the major cities of La Paz and Santa Cruz, with a smaller presence in Sucre, Cochabamba, and Oruro and other remote cities throughout the country. There are at least nine different Islamic organizations, both Shi'a and Sunni, operating within Bolivia, funded primarily by either Saudi Arabia or the Islamic Republic of Iran.

Since opening an embassy in La Paz in 2008, Iran has been a driving force in increasing the Islamic presence in Bolivia, within both society and the state. Iran has proposed several bilateral agreements with Bolivia, ranging from economic development projects to military-to-military exchanges. In return, Bolivia has lifted visa restrictions for Iranian citizens, and has facilitated the increased presence of Iranian officials in this Andean nation.

ISLAMIST ACTIVITY

Islamic proselytization (*da'wah*) began in Bolivia in the early 1970s, during the economic boom that integrated Santa Cruz into national and international markets. Over the ensuing years, Santa Cruz became the financial hub of Bolivia and in the 1990s the department's local economy was greatly bolstered by the capitalization of the country's petroleum and gas industry. This spurred a mass wave of immigration that flooded Santa Cruz, of which an initial influx of Islamic immigrants was also a part. Today, this shift has ended, and economic investment by the state is focused on the western highlands of Bolivia. As a result, Islamic communities, particularly those that are Shi'a, have begun to populate this western region, and many Islamist elements have followed.

In La Paz, the capital of Bolivia, a prominent local Islamist is known to boast ties to the Islamic Republic of Iran and its proxies. The leader of the Association of the Islamic Community of Bolivia (ACIB) *Ahlul Bait*, and of the Bolivian Shi'a community writ large, is Roberto Chambi Calle, a Bolivian lawyer who converted to Islam in 1996. Chambi also goes by the name of Yousef, and simultaneously runs another Shi'a organization—the Bolivia Islamic Cultural Foundation (FCIB in its Spanish acronym). Also based in La Paz, the FCIB was founded in August 2007 with the support of the Iranian government.

Chambi and his wife, Sdenka Saavedra Alfaro, actively promote an Islamist message through seminars and small meetings that they organize. They have invited *imams* from other Latin American countries, such as Argentina and Brazil, to these gatherings, and have a longstanding relationship with Shi'a spiritual leader Sheikh Abdul Karim Paz from Buenos Aires. Karim Paz is a direct disciple of Iranian intelligence operative Mohsen Rabbani, and was his successor at the At *Tawhid* mosque in Buenos Aires after Rabbani left Argentina following his involvement in the 1994 bombing of the Argentine-Jewish Mutual Association (AMIA) building.[2]

The Bolivian couple currently resides in Qom, Iran, alongside Rabbani, but continues to actively help in the spread of an Islamist message to the indigenous peoples of Bolivia. The Iran government, meanwhile, has further enhanced these effort via its work with state-owned media. In 2008, for instance, the Iranian government attempted to build a television station in Bolivia's coca-growing region of Chapare.[3] Although that project did not materialize, Iran did succeed in launching a broader, Spanish language television network in 2011. Known as HispanTV, it is owned and operated by the Islamic Republic of Iran Broadcasting (IRIB) conglomerate and is based out of Tehran.[4] HispanTV currently broadcasts Islamist-leaning programming 24 hours a day in several countries throughout Latin America and the Caribbean. The channel's local Bolivian correspondent is an Argentine journalist, Andrés Sal-lari, who used to work for Bolivia's state-owned Canal 7.[5]

Andrés Sal-lari is also a reporter for a new state-owned media outlet believed to be financed by the Iranian government to the tune of approximately $3 million. In 2012, President Evo Morales reportedly received a gift from his then-Iranian counterpart, Mahmud Ahmadinejad, to launch *Abya Yala*, a new multimedia network. Financed through one of Morales' foundations, the *Abya Yala* network has benefited from large amounts of government advertising and preferential contracts with various government agencies, notably the national tax service and the hydrocarbons agency, among other public entities. As of 2015, *Abya Yala* had 135 hours of national coverage a week through a major telecommunications firm, and in the eastern cities of La Paz and El Alto broadcast 24-hour coverage through an open signal on channel 41.

According to Bolivian journalist Amalia Pando, the *Abya Yala* network's rapid expansion raises at least some suspicion: "here are two immoralities, first that the president receives three million dollars from a foreign power to launch a TV channel, then that the channel, which does not have a significant audience, receives such large amounts of public contracts and advertising."[6] *Abya Yala*'s meteoric rise in Bolivia is due, in part, to its integrated programming with Venezuela's state-owned Telesur network, Russia Today, and the Iranian-owned HispanTV. In the case of Iran, *Abya Yala* provides an authentic way to reach Bolivia's largely indigenous population to propagate an Islamist message.

For instance, in July 2015, the *Abya Yala* network broadcast the opening of a new Iranian-funded hemodialysis center, The Red Crescent Society, in the city of Cochabamba. Nevertheless, the broadcast omitted the fact that the women working at The Red Crescent Society were forced to wear *hijabs*, to the displeasure of many Bolivians. Lourdes Millares, the deputy for an opposition party in Bolivia, subsequently called this Iranian demand an "assault on the dignity of women…" and excoriated President Morales for, "…submission to the rules of another government."[7]

ISLAMISM AND SOCIETY

Bolivia has a small Islamic community, numbering between one and three thousand, most of whose members are Sunni, with a smaller number of Shi'a followers. Altogether, Muslims in Bolivia account for less than 0.1% of the total population. However, they are increasingly active.

Most of the established members of the Islamic community in Bolivia were born in the country and converted, or are the descendants of Palestinian or Lebanese immigrants who have lived in Bolivia for decades. The traditional Islamic community in Bolivia is primarily Sunni, and typically adheres to the local Bolivian style of dress and culture. They do not practice fundamentalist Islamic traditions, nor do they actively proselytize. Nevertheless, there has been a recent influx of Pakistanis and Iranians that follow a more fundamentalist line, and are actively recruiting and proselytizing among Bolivian youth and women, causing some friction with the established Muslim community in Bolivia.[8]

Bolivia's Islamic community began its Islamic proselytization (*da'wah*) in 1974, when Mahmud Amer Abusharar arrived from the Palestinian territories. Almost immediately after arriving, Amer started gathering Muslims from around Bolivia and inviting them to his home for prayer. He quickly became the leader of the small but emerging Islamic community in Bolivia, particularly in Santa Cruz, and in 1986 registered the first Bolivian Islamic organization—which was officially recognized by Bolivia's Ministry of Foreign Affairs Office of Religion three years later, in 1989.[9]

This organization, the Bolivian Islamic Center (CIB is its Spanish acronym), based in the country's commercial capital, Santa Cruz, claims to have founded Bolivia's first fully operational mosque in 1994, serving some 300 congregants. The CIB claims to support "open-mindedness and peace," but does appear to espouse an anti-U.S. political position closely aligned with that of the Bolivian government.[10]

On May 14, 2011, Mahmud Amer Abusharar died of natural causes. One of his disciples, Isa Amer Quevedo, has since stepped in to serve as Director of the CIB. Quevedo has a degree in Islamic jurisprudence from the University of Medina in Saudi Arabia, and used to be the CIB's administrative director and translator. Anecdotal evidence suggests that Quevedo supports his predecessor's anti-U.S. stance, as he offered criticism of the United States on the CIB website immediately after the September 11th attacks.[11]

The CIB has grown over the years to become Bolivia's largest Islamic organization, and is known to receive support from the Saudi-based Islamic Organization for Latin America and the Muslim World League. The Egyptian Embassy in Bolivia and the Gulf Cooperation Council both also have helped to fund the CIB's first mosque. Moreover, the CIB has an affiliation with the World Assembly of Muslim Youth, acting as this organization's headquarters in Bolivia.

Also, connected with the Muslim World League is the Bolivian Muslim Cultural Association (ACBM is its Spanish acronym), located in Sucre, the constitutional capital of Bolivia. A Palestinian doctor and lawyer, Fayez Rajab Khedeer Kannan, runs this organization. Kannan espouses an extreme worldview, and has, among other things, openly praised the late Libyan leader Muammar al-Qadhafi.[12] In 1998, he received a 30-year grant from the Sucre city council to use five acres of land in the *Los Liberta-*

dores neighborhood to construct an educational center and clinic, with additional funding for the effort coming from the Muslim World League and the Islamic Development Bank. By 2003, ACBM had built a private Islamic school, which led to some legal disputes over a revoked title transfer (disputes which were finally resolved in 2006, in favor of ACBM). It is not clear whether this school is still active.

More recently, in 2016, an Indian couple, Ghalib Ataul and Nayara Zafar, built a new mosque in the Paititi district of Warnes, a small town outside the city of Santa Cruz de la Sierra. The mosque adheres to the creed of the Ahmadiyya, a small sect of Islam from the late 19th century in northern India, and, according to Ghalib Ataul, will serve all faiths, both Muslim and non-Muslim. The mosque, however, has generated some negative reaction, as noted by Bolivian journalist Magali Sánchez: "As long as they respect our customs and our creed, no problem. But do not try to change us. They should not think that the women of Warnes want to wear hijabs and burkas."[13] The new mosque in Warnes is emblematic of the small but notable growth of Islamic communities within remote eastern regions of Bolivia, including in San Borja and Riberalta, Beni, where there are practicing Muslims.

Moving north along the Andean ridge, in La Paz, is the Association of the Islamic Community of Bolivia (ACIB is its Spanish acronym). It is believed that the origin of Islam in La Paz dates to 1995, when Moumin Candia, a Bolivian trained in an Argentine mosque, brought Islam to the city. A Bolivian convert and the former president of ACIB, Gerardo Cutipa Trigo is educated as an engineer, and was an atheist through most of his college years in Bolivia, assuming leadership roles in leftist student unions. It wasn't until the late 1990s that Cutipa converted to Islam while working in Spain, where he first was exposed to the religion. The ACIB is now led by Ahmad Ali, who claims to informally represent a community of approximately 300 Muslims, of which around 70 regularly attend service at the ACIB's mosque, called *Masjidum Jbelannur*.[14]

In 2006, a more fundamentalist mosque was opened in La Paz by a group of Pakistanis that had arrived in Bolivia three years earlier. This small Pakistani community, known as the Islamic Association of Bolivia, operates the *Masjid As-Salam* mosque, and has offered prayer services to other Muslims, including many Bolivian-born Muslim converts in La Paz. The *imam* of the *Masjid As-Salam* mosque was Mahmud Ali Teheran, a Peruvian-born son of Iranian immigrants who converted to Sunni Islam. Prior to this, Ali Teheran lead the *Babu Ul-Islam* mosque in Tacna, Peru and as of 2008 has left Bolivia to lead the Islamic community in Uruguay.[15]

La Paz is also a hub for a small but growing Shi'a community, which is much smaller than its Sunni counterparts. This small influx of Shi'a Muslims is primarily due to the newfound Iranian presence in Bolivia, as the more visible Shi'a organizations have ties to the Iranian Embassy in La Paz.

The oldest Shi'a organization has a name like the Sunni ACIB; however, it adds the suffix "*Ahlul Bait*" which literally means "family of the House." This has an important distinction for Shi'a Muslims because the term refers to the family of the Islamic prophet Muhammad, and is generally where Shi'a Muslims derive their *hadiths*. It is unclear how this organization was founded, but it appears to have been operational since 2000. For at least some time, however, it seems to have operated under a different name (Shi'a Islamic Community of Bolivia), until resurfacing with its original name in 2006.

During the brief time that the ACIB *Ahlul Bait* was organized under a different name, it was run by a licensed psychologist named Tommy Nelson Salgueiro Criales, a former Jesuit who converted to Islam in the mid-1990s while living in Australia. ACIB *Ahlul Bait* is known for its publications and translations of Islamic text into Spanish, and was the first to introduce Islamic literature to the 15th annual international book fair in 2010, where they presented Bolivian Vice President Alvaro Garcia Linera with their own in-house publication, "*La Revolución de la Mano de Dios*," written by resident Islamic scholar Sergio Grover Dueñas Calle.

ACIB *Ahlul Bait* has an associated mosque purchased with the help of the Iranian government. The first Shi'a mosque in Bolivia, *As-Salam*, is a three-story building in the heart of La Paz with a large prayer hall that was inaugurated in 2006. The mosque is meant to serve a growing Shi'a community in La Paz, and other smaller Islamic communities nearby.

Many of the organizations mentioned above have created their own websites, radio broadcasts, and/or social media outlets. Social media plays a significant part in spreading the Islamic message throughout Bolivia, as many communities have a virtual presence on Facebook, Twitter and YouTube. Roberto Chambi and his colleagues at ACIB *Ahlul Bait* are arguably the most active in both mainstream and social media, establishing a local radio program, "*Al-Islam*," that broadcasts every weekday morning on 107.3 FM. Chambi is also a regular on HispanTV's local broadcasts and is featured in ACIB's web portal *Islam en Bolivia* (www.islam.org.bo). This portal is frequently updated, largely with articles claiming Israeli atrocities against Palestinians, and recently launched an effort to proselytize in *Aymara*, one of Bolivia's mayor indigenous languages and culture. It currently offers a translation of the tract "What is Islam?" in the Aymara language.[16]

In 2014, according to an interview with Ahmad Ali, an American student researching Islam in Bolivia discovered that Aymara and Quechua Indians had begun converting to Islam.[17] This represents an important advance for the Islamic community, because *Aymara* indigenous groups hold important political currency with the current government and society. Establishing a footprint with this group would help advance Islam (and, potentially, Islamism) to a significant degree within Bolivian society.

ISLAMISM AND THE STATE

The growing political and strategic ties between La Paz and Tehran dominate Bolivia's contemporary relationship with Islam. Bolivian President Evo Morales first met former Iranian President Mahmoud Ahmadinejad at the inauguration of Ecuadorian President Rafael Correa in mid-January 2007. At the time, the two leaders showed unprecedented interest in bringing their respective countries closer together politically, culturally, and economically. Ahmadinejad focused on agriculture, gas, and oil, referring to "academic potentials" in Iran for "improving the technical knowledge of Bolivia experts... in accordance with our Islamic teachings and duties."[18]

Months later, in September 2007, Bolivia's Foreign Minister, David Choquehuanca, visited Tehran to meet with his then-counterpart, Manuchehr Mottaki, to build upon the January meeting with firm commitments outlined in a strategic agreement to broaden political and economic relations. Later in the month, the first bilateral agreement was drafted. It provided a strategic framework for future collaborative ventures in the hydrocarbons, extractive, agriculture, oil and gas industries, as well as science, culture and technology. There were also several side agreements made to implement the importation and installation of six Iranian milk-processing plants in Bolivia. But the larger strategic agreement was the focus of the effort, and was announced on September 27, 2007 during Ahmadinejad's first official visit to Bolivia. At the time, Morales noted: "we are interested in broadening relations with Iran, starting in the trade area with a view to continuing and consolidating relations of friendship, understanding and diplomacy."[19]

However, the agreement was not ratified by the Bolivian Congress until three years later, in 2010. Nevertheless, this did not stop the two countries from continuing to foster their diplomatic relationship, and the first Embassy of the Islamic Republic of Iran was inaugurated in La Paz in February 2008. Evo Morales announced later that year that Bolivia would move its only embassy in the Middle East from Cairo to Tehran (such a move, however, never happened, likely due to a lack of resources on Bolivia's part).

By March 2008, Iran's relationship with Bolivia had developed an economic facet as well. News sources out of Tehran reported that Iran had signed several joint projects with Bolivia worth some $1 billion in total.[20]

Morales finally reciprocated Ahmadinejad's Bolivian visit when he arrived in Tehran on September 1, 2008. Brief meetings with the Iranian president and the country's Minister of Mining and Industry punctuated his short stay in the Islamic Republic, where he focused on persuading Ahmadinejad to accelerate payments under Iran's promise to invest $1 billion in Bolivia.

By the end of September 2008, Bolivia and Iran had exchanged technical delegations, with one Hojatollah Soltani emerging as Iran's business attaché to Bolivia. Soltani pledged that, apart from the promised investment of $1 billion, Iran would also invest some $230 million in a cement factory and another $3 million to build dairy farms.[21] A month later, Soltani announced that Iran would use Bolivia as the base for a planned Red Crescent health clinic expansion across Latin America.[22] The announcement coincided with Bolivia signing a credit agreement with Venezuela and Iran for $115 million, reportedly to cooperate in mineral exploration in Coroma, a mineral rich region in southern Bolivia. This cooperation created suspicion of a dual-use effort, because—according to a retired Bolivian mining engineer—Coroma covers more than 100,000 hectares where there are uranium and other dispersed minerals.[23]

By February 2009, pledges from Iran to invest in economic development projects had yet to materialize, but the milk processing plants were already under construction. Some Iranian funding had found its way to Bolivia, but much of what was promised had not yet been delivered. This gap between rhetoric and action, however, did not appear to dampen relations between the two countries. In July 2009, Bolivia announced that it would receive a $280 million loan from the Islamic Republic. Iran's top diplomat in Bolivia, Masoud Edrisi, stated at the time that the money was to be used as President Morales saw fit.[24] The loan was part of the $1 billion originally promised when Ahmadinejad first met Morales in 2007. Later in 2009, a new Iranian-funded maternal care health clinic was opened in the poor municipality of El Alto, on the outskirts of La Paz. The health clinic reportedly cost $2.5 million and filled a gap in community healthcare despite some controversy over a requirement that female nurses wear *hijabs*, or head covering.[25]

In 2010, some of the original financial promises made by Iran began to materialize, albeit quite slowly and extremely inconsistently. By the middle of that year, more agreements were signed, particularly in the extractive industry, as Iran began to look at Bolivia's strategic resource wealth. Bolivia is one of Latin America's most resource-rich countries, and possesses some of the world's largest reserves of lithium chloride. Knowing this, Iran made a move to become Bolivia's co-developer of this resource, to include the production of lithium batteries. This resource exploitation project, in turn, has prompted speculation that other strategic minerals, namely uranium, would be exploited. To date, however, there is no evidence that Iran has effectively received any uranium ore from Bolivia.[26]

This is not to say, however, that Iran is not exploring or exploiting other strategic resources from Bolivia. In 2010, the Bolivian government awarded six new oil and gas exploration blocks to Iran and later signed an agreement to train Bolivian technicians in petroleum drilling and petrochemical operations. By July 2011, 26 Bolivian technicians had completed their first petrochemical training in Iran.[27] While the Islamic Republic was training Bolivian engineers, and exploring the country's strategic mineral deposits, a more nefarious relationship began to form through military-to-military exchanges between both countries. This bilateral military relationship was highlighted when Bolivia's Defense Ministry invited then-Iranian Minister of Defense, Ahmad Vahidi, one of the accused masterminds of the bombings of the AMIA community center in Buenos Aires in 1994, to attend the inauguration of a new regional defense school for the Bolivarian Alliance of the Americas (ALBA in its Spanish acronym). Iran reportedly helped finance this regional defense school to the tune of approximately $1.8 million. Argentine foreign minister Hector Timmerman immediately sent a complaint to his Bolivian counterpart, and Vahidi had to make a hasty exit from the country, leaving President Morales to do damage control by apologizing to Argentina for the fiasco.[28]

Vahidi's trip sparked many questions as to what type of military relationship exists between the two countries, and it was subsequently discovered that Bolivia had bought a package of military equipment from Iran just a year earlier, in October 2010. The items procured included a FAJR-3 piston trainer, an S-68 turboprop trainer, and the Iran-140 light transport (a licensed version of the Russia Antonov An-140 light transport).[29]

Once the aftermath and embarrassment of Vahidi's trip to Bolivia had subsided, the Bolivian government re-established military ties with Iran. On June 20, 2012, during Ahmadinejad's third official visit to Bolivia, an anti-narco trafficking accord was signed to help Bolivia in its "fight" against drug trafficking. This accord created the political and legal groundwork for Iran to have a military footprint in Bolivia, and the Islamic Republic is currently rumored to be helping Bolivia set up a new unit within one of their military special operations wing.[30]

A few months prior to Ahaminejad's visit, on April 2, 2012, news surfaced that a Bolivian-flagged vessel had been seized by Somali pirates off the coast of Maldives. After learning that the vessel, the *MV Eglantine*, belonged to Iran, it was freed by the pirates and continued its route to deliver sugar to Brazil. The incident sparked speculation that the Bolivian government maybe violating international sanctions then in effect against Iran by helping its sanctioned ships sail through strategic ports using a Bolivian flag.[31] Later that month, Reuters reported that 15 vessels linked to IRISL, the UN-sanctioned Iranian shipping conglomerate, carried the Bolivian flag. The Bolivian government responded by saying that it would revoke the Bolivian flag license and remove these Iranian vessels from its shipping register, but it was never confirmed that this took place.

Bolivia has become one of Iran's most important strategic partners in Latin America. This relationship has fostered and enhanced a greater Islamic presence in this plurinational state—one that is unprecedented in size and scope. Growing alongside this presence is the size of Iran's official mission in the country—which has been linked to the propagation of an increasingly active Islamist element there. The Spanish daily *El Pais* reported in 2012 that Bolivia has at least 145 registered Iranian diplomats in country.[32] By comparison, Spain has only ten. On the surface, Bolivia appears to be the beneficiary of this relationship, but upon closer examination one can determine that for every Iranian investment or action into this Andean nation, there is a reciprocal action by Bolivia.

Some analysts speculated that this strategic relationship had been prompted by aggressive outreach of the Ahmadinejad regime, and would dissipate with Ahmadinejad's departure from power in 2013. However, more recent Iranian activity suggests otherwise. For example, on August 25, 2016, Iranian Foreign Minister Mohammed Javad Zarif arrived in Santa Cruz, Bolivia along with a delegation of at least 70 executives of Iranian state-owned firms for a series of events with prominent Bolivian businessman. Against the backdrop of Iran's 2015 nuclear deal with the West, known as the Joint Comprehensive Plan of Action (JCPOA), Zarif's visit was a clear signal that Iran is back in business in Bolivia. In a concrete demonstration of his government's commitment to Iran, Bolivian President Evo Morales flew from La Paz to Santa Cruz to meet with Zarif and decorated him with the Order of the Condor of the Andes, a state medal awarded for exceptional merit to Bolivians or foreign nationals.[33]

ENDNOTES

[1] Pew Research Center, "Global Muslim Population: A Report on the Size and Distribution of the World's Muslim Population," October 2009.

[2] "Bolivia – Key Muslim Converts Assert Local Peril, Ally with Zealots Abroad," Open Source Center Report, May 12, 2009, https://fas.org/irp/dni/osc/bolivia.pdf.

[3] "Iran's Bolivian TV venture to 'interface' with Venezuela's Telesur," Fars (Tehran), March 19, 2008.

[4] Adam Housley, "Iran moving in on Latin American television market," Fox News Latino, March 20, 2012, http://latino.foxnews.com/latino/news/2012/03/20/iran-moving-in-on-latin-american-television-market/.

[5] Andrés Sal-lari has his own blog (http://andressallari.blogspot.com/) where he posts interviews and media appearances for both the Iranian-owned HispanTV and the Bolivian-controlled National Corporation for Bolivian Television (ENTVB), which operates the Canal 7 television station.

[6] Amalia Pando, "El Canal de TV de Evo Morales ganó más de Bs 2,1 milliones con la propaganda del Estado," Cabildeo (La Paz, Bolivia), March 17, 2016, http://www.amaliapandocabildeo.com/2016/03/el-canal-de-tv-de-evo-morales-gano-mas.html

[7] Ann "Babe" Huggett, "Iran Demands Nurses in Bolivia Wear Hijabs," Red State, Dec. 3, 2009, http://www.redstate.com/diary/annbabehuggett/2009/12/03/iran-demands-nurses-in-bolivia-wear-hijabs/

[8] U.S. Ambassador Phillip Goldberg, "Bolivia's Tiny Muslim Community," WikiLeaks cable 08LAPAZ872 dated April 16, 2008, http://wikileaks.org/cable/2008/04/08LAPAZ872.html.

[9] Rinat Sueiro-Phillips, "El Centro Islámico Boliviano busca promover la realidad del Islam," El Mundo (Santa Cruz), July 10, 2011, http://www.elmundo.com.bo/Secundaria.asp?edicion=10/07/2011&Tipo=Comunidad&Cod=15149.

[10] The CIB was reported on by the Open Source Center (OSC) of the Office of the Directorate of National Intelligence (ODNI) in the U.S., and the Federation of American Scientists released the official report in 2009. "Bolivia – Key Muslim Converts Assert Local Peril, Ally with Zealots Abroad."

[11] Ibid., 3.

[12] Ibidem, 4.

[13] Quote taken from an interview with El Deber newspaper in Santa Cruz, Bolivia published on Aug. 9, 2015. Online link is no longer active, however, the article has been reposted on Eju.tv: http://eju.tv/2015/08/ahmadies-quieren-aportar-en-la-construccion-de-una-bolivia-mas-multicultural/

[14] Goldberg, WikiLeaks cable 08LAPAZ872.

[15] Victor Rodriguez, "La voz de Islam' llego a Durazno," El Pais (Uruguay), October 24, 2008, http://historico.elpais.com.uy/08/10/24/pciuda_377459.asp.

[16] Diana Rojas, "El Islam de los Aymaras en Bolivia," Islamico.org, April 12, 2012.

[17] This statement is from Ahmad Ali, when giving an interview on April 20, 2014, to Andrea Estéfany Caballero for Erbol, a digital platform in Bolivia. Ahmad Ali is the president of the Asociación de la Comunidad Islámica de Bolivia. See here: http://www.erbol.com.bo/noticia/indigenas/20042014/hay_aymaras_y_quechuas_que_se_convierten_al_islam

[18] "President of Iran, Bolivia ask for Higher Level Ties," IRNA (Tehran), January 16, 2007.

[19] "President Makes Agreement with Iran Official," La Razón (La Paz), September 9, 2007.

[20] At the time, Morales announced that Bolivia would remove visa restrictions for Iranian nationals traveling to Bolivia. See John Kiriakou, "Iran's Latin America Push: As the U.S. ignores its neighbors to the south, Tehran has been making friends and influencing nations," Los Angeles Times, November 18, 2008.

[21] Faramarz Asghari, "Iran-Bolivia Strategic Interaction," Siyasat-e Ruz (Tehran), September 1, 2008.

[22] "Iran to open two clinics in Bolivia," Moj News Agency (Tehran), October 11, 2008, http://www.presstv.com/Detail.aspx?id=71865&sectionid=351020706.

[23] "Detectaron uranio en la zona que controlan Irán y Venezuela en Bolivia," Infobae, Aug. 30, 2010, http://www.infobae.com/2010/08/30/534064-detectaron-uranio-la-zona-que-controlan-iran-y-venezuela-bolivia/

[24] "Iran Approves US$280 Million Loan for Bolivia," Associated Press, July 29, 2009.

[25] "Iran to open two clinics in Bolivia."

[26] Stephen Johnson, Iran's Influence in the Americas (Washington, DC: Center for Strategic & International Studies, March 2012).

[27] Ibid., 67.

[28] Ilan Berman, "Iran Woos Bolivia for Influence in Latin America," Newsweek/Daily Beast, May 20, 2012, http://www.thedailybeast.com/articles/2012/05/20/iran-woos-bolivia-for-influence-in-latin-america.html.

[29] Johnson, Iran's Influence in the Americas.

[30] Author's interviews with retired military officials in Bolivia, October 2012.

[31] Daniel Fineren, "Exclusive: Bolivia says may de-flag Iranian ships," Reuters, Apr. 18, 2012, http://www.reuters.com/article/us-iran-ships-bolivia-idUSBRE83H10H20120418

[32] Jorge Marirrodriga, "Irán se lanza a la conquista de Latinoamérica" El Pais (Spain), June 23, 2012, http://internacional.elpais.com/internacional/2012/06/23/actualidad/1340465739_921466.html.

[33] "Zarif recibe la medulla más prestigiosa del Gobierno de Bolivia," HispanTV, Aug. 26, 2016, http://www.hispantv.com/noticias/diplomacia/286074/iran-zarif-bolivia-medalla-prestigiosa-morales

Brazil

Quick Facts

Population: 205,823,665 (estimated 2016)

Area: 8,514,877 sq km

Ethnic Groups: white 47.7%, mulatto (mixed white and black) 43.1%, black 7.6%, Asian 1.1%, indigenous 0.4%

Religions: Roman Roman Catholic 64.6%, other Catholic 0.4%, Protestant 22.2% (includes Adventist 6.5%, Assembly of God 2.0%, Christian Congregation of Brazil 1.2%, Universal Kingdom of God 1.0%, other Protestant 11.5%), other Christian 0.7%, Spiritist 2.2%, other 1.4%, none 8%, unspecified 0.4%

Government Type: Federal Republic

GDP (official exchange rate): $1.77 trillion (estimated 2015)

Map and Quick Facts courtesy of the CIA World Factbook (January 2017)

Overview

The Federative Republic of Brazil is Latin America's largest country, both in geographical size and in terms of population, and subsequently has the largest Islamic population in the region, hovering at around one million.[1] A growing portion of this population is made up of converts to Islam, as da'wah (Islamic proselytization activities) is in full effect in most major cities within Brazil.

With antecedents going back 500 years to the founding of the state of Brazil, Islam is generally accepted within society, and there are many successful Muslim entrepreneurs who have assimilated into Brazilian culture. Unfortunately, however, a radical element is forming within the larger Muslim population, fueled by ties to Islamist terrorist networks from the Middle East. Iran and Hezbollah have historically been major propagators of these networks in Brazil. However, recent years have seen a rise in followers and sympathizers of the Islamic State terrorist group within the country.

In March 2016, Brazil enacted its first piece of national antiterrorism legislation, one that provides the government legal authority to surveil, apprehend, and arrest members of Islamist terrorist organizations. Four months later, the Brazilian Federal Police foiled a major terrorist plot by ISIS affiliate Ansar al-Khilafah *targeting the 2016 Summer Olympic Games in Rio de Janeiro.*[2] *These arrests stopped what would have been the worst Islamic terrorist attack in Latin America in the last twenty years.*

ISLAMIST ACTIVITY

Since the mid-1980s, an Islamist movement has been steadily growing within Brazil. This movement consists of radical clergymen, terrorists, influence peddlers and money laundering "fixers" who use the country as a logistics hub for many of their regional operations, which stretch from the Southern Cone to the Andes. The most prominent of these operations was the 1994 bombing of the *Asociación Mutual Israelita Argentina* (AMIA) Jewish community center in Buenos Aires, Argentina, which in part was supported by radical Islamist elements in Brazil and the Triple Frontier, or Tri-Border Area (TBA) where Argentina, Paraguay and Brazil meet.[3]

According to the late Argentine prosecutor of the AMIA case, Alberto Nisman, Iran's intelligence apparatus first engaged Brazil in 1984 by sending operative Mohammad Tabataei Einaki to its capital, Brasilia. Some years later, Einaki was expelled for his involvement in political activities incompatible with the role he had declared to perform. Nevertheless, Iranian intelligence continued to operate through the early 1990s from the Embassy of the Islamic Republic in Brasilia via a Civil Attaché, Jaffar Saadat Ahmad-Nia. To local authorities, Jaffar Saadat was known as a "fixer" for regional logistical problems. This would come to light when he was implicated in the 1992 bombing of the Israeli Embassy in Argentina, which preceded the larger attack on AMIA a couple of years later.[4]

Part of the reason Iranian intelligence targeted Brazil as an area of support for regional operations is because of the heavy Islamic presence in the southern city of Foz do Iguaçu (state of Paraná). Historically, Foz do Iguaçu, which is within the TBA, has one of the largest Lebanese enclaves in Latin America, and is in close proximity, across the Parana River, to the largest free trade zone in South America—Ciudad del Este, Paraguay. Combined, these conditions provide a permissive environment for recruitment, proselytizing, fundraising and other terrorist operations by a variety of Islamist terrorist groups.

Most notable is Iranian terror proxy Hezbollah, which has had a presence in the TBA since the mid-1980s, at the height of the Lebanese civil war.[5] Hezbollah's decision to establish its presence in the TBA, and Foz do Iquaço in particular, turned out to be a lucrative one, reportedly funneling between $15 million and $150 million annually to Lebanon through a variety of illicit activities, including drugs and arms trafficking as well as counterfeit and contraband operations.[6] Hezbollah, however, is not the only Islamist terrorist group operating in Foz do Iquaço. The presence of Egypt's *Al-Gama'a al-Islamiyya* (Islamic Group) and *Al-Jihad* (Islamic Jihad), as well as Hamas, has also been noted.[7]

Al-Qaeda likewise has an interest and presence in the TBA. Both Osama bin Laden and 9/11 mastermind Khaled Sheikh Mohammed (KSM) reportedly visited Foz do Iguaço in 1995 to attend meetings at the local mosque there.[8] KSM returned to this mosque three years later in 1998 to connect with other radical elements throughout Brazil. The Islamist presence in Brazil originated in the TBA but began to spread north into major cities, such as Sao Paulo, in the 21st century. In 2011, reports resurfaced of al-Qaeda cells on the move in western Brazil, when a Lebanese man, Khaled Hussein Ali, was discovered to be running an Internet Café in Sao Paulo, Brazil's largest city. According to *Veja*, the prominent newsweekly that ran this story, the Internet café controlled an online communications arm of al-Qaeda called Jihad Media Battalion.[9]

These terrorist groups have planned several operations over the years, most of which have been foiled by authorities. Yet some have succeeded, such as the infamous AMIA attack, in which one of the mobile phones used by the suspects was purchased in Foz do Iguaço. Coincidentally, a Colombian citizen of Lebanese descent, Samuel Salman El Reda, had residence in Foz do Iguaço, and was accused of coordinating the logistics of the attacks from Brazil. He later fled to Lebanon to escape detention for his role in the AMIA attack.[10]

A more recent terrorist plot was foiled this past summer, when 12 Brazilian Islamists were arrested on suspicion of being linked to ISIS and planning terrorist attacks during the 2016 Summer Olympic Games in Rio de Janeiro.[11] These arrests, heralded as a success, are the first high-profile use of Brazil's new anti-terrorism law passed earlier in 2016.[12] Brazilian Justice Minister Alexandre de Moraes hailed the new law as an important tool that empowered Brazilian authorities to coordinate effectively across nine Brazilian states to neutralize the terrorist plot against the Olympic games.[13]

Appropriate anti-terrorism laws are a strong step in addressing the counterterrorism challenge in Brazil. The country's porous borders, weak institutions, and recent influx of Syrian refugees, however, present additional challenges. Due to these conditions, over the years Brazil has become a hub for Islamism in South America. This challenge is compounded by high levels of public and private corruption and organized crime, which have catalyzed a growing crime-terror nexus that facilitates increased arms, drugs, and human trafficking, along with new avenues for terror finance and immigration fraud.

The most notable example of the criminal-terrorist convergence in Brazil is the infamous Barakat brothers, who lead a Lebanese clan prevalent in the Tri-Border Area (TBA) and prominent within Hezbollah. Assad Ahmad Barakat has been identified by the U.S. Treasury Department as one of Hezbollah's most prominent members, raising some $50 million for the terrorist organization from the TBA.[14] In 2004, he was arrested and extradited to Paraguay for tax evasion. A decade later, in 2014, Brazilian police arrested Assad's brother, Hamze Ahmad Barakat, and convicted him of embezzling money from fellow Lebanese immigrants, and creating false documents to create companies to cover for trafficking in arms and drugs.[15] Reportedly, the proceeds from these illicit activities went to Hezbollah, which contacted a well-known Brazilian criminal gang "First Capital Command" to establish an arms-for-drugs pipeline in Brazil.[16] Today, the Barakat brothers have been released from prison and are back on the streets of Brazil.

Hezbollah remains the most active foreign terrorist organization in South America. However, recent years have seen an uptick in Islamic State followers and sympathizers within Brazil's borders. The use of social media and modern pop culture provides increased avenues for Islamists to attract Brazilian youth. For instance, the following of Saudi extremist Muhammad Al Arifi, who is banned from 30 countries in Europe, has grown exponentially over the years to include some Brazilian youth appearing in ISIS propaganda videos. According to Brazilian intelligence, the most active Brazilian Islamist propagandist on the web is Ismail Abdul-Jabbar al-Brazili, aka "the Brazilian." Believed to have been recruited by Abu-Khalid Al-Amriki, an American ISIS fighter who died in Syria, al-Brazili's virtual profile is responsible for providing Portuguese content on social media in support of ISIS using the hashtags: #EstadoIslâmico (Islamic State) and #CalifadoPT (Caliphate PT).[17]

The increase in Islamist social media in Brazil led to the creation of an encrypted channel on the messaging app Telegram called *Ansar al-Khilafah*, which officially pledged allegiance to ISIS in 2016. One message on this channel read: "If the French police cannot stop attacks on its territory, training given to the Brazilian police will not do anything."[18] *Ansar al-Khilafah* was created in response to a call from an ISIS-linked Telegram account named Online Dawah Operations, which requested its supporters with Spanish or Portuguese skills to contact a local Brazilian militant and join its ranks. This call to action sparked an internal discussion within Brazilian intelligence on handling ISIS recruitment in Brazil, resulting in a report on the phenomenon entitled "Islamic State: Reflections for Brazil."[19] The findings of the report led to more aggressive surveillance by Brazilian authorities and subsequently more arrests of Islamists in Brazil prior to the Rio 2016 Olympic Games. In July 2016, authorities uncovered a terrorist plot targeting the Olympic Games through potential small arms attacks at various locations, emulating the 2015 Paris attacks carried out by ISIS.[20] For the period that the Olympics took place, more than 110 intelligence agencies from around the world were installed in Rio de Janeiro to augment the 85,000 security personnel employed by the Brazilian government as force protection for the Games.[21] Empowered by recently enacted antiterrorism legislation, Brazilian authorities thwarted what could have been the worst Islamist terrorist attack in its history.

Argentine intelligence has been monitoring Brazil since the Buenos Aires bombings in the 1990s, and has determined that pro-Iranian Shi'ite groups, such as the Islamic Jihad and Lebanese Hezbollah, which normally work separately from orthodox Sunni groups, have been collaborating and cooperating within Brazil. This Sunni-Shi'ite collaboration is embodied in the work of Khaled Taki Eldyn, formerly from the Al Murabitun Mosque in Guarulhos, Sao Paulo. Taki Eldyn is a Sunni of Egyptian origin who was the Director of Islamic Affairs of the Brazilian Muslim Associations Federation. He is believed to be a member of the Egyptian Islamic Jihad, and to have coordinated the visit of Bin Laden and KSM to Foz do Iquaço in the mid-1990s. Although Taki Eldyn is believed to be an al-Qaeda sympathizer, he has maintained a longstanding relationship with, and even received support from, Mohsen Rabbani, the Iranian Shi'ite cleric labeled the mastermind of the AMIA attack.[22]

This Sunni-Shi'ite nexus is even more pronounced when dissecting the money-laundering network of the Barakat brothers, who laundered millions of dollars for both Osama bin Laden of al-Qaeda and Imad Mughniyah of Hezbollah through a construction company with offices in Ciudad del Este and Beirut.[23] There are unconfirmed reports that Barakat organized a "terrorist summit" in 2002 in the TBA, with high-level officials from al-Qaeda and Hezbollah in attendance to discuss cooperation in casing U.S. and Israeli targets throughout the Western Hemisphere.

Since the mid-1980s, this Islamist mobilization has intruded into Brazilian society through an array of mosques, Islamic cultural centers and commercial endeavors. Its stealthy presence provides its members with the ability to move freely within Brazil, and to continue their attempts to unify and radicalize other Muslim populations throughout the country. As one prominent former Brazilian official, has described it: "Without anyone noticing, a generation of Islamic extremists is emerging in Brazil."[24]

Islamism and Society

Islam in Brazil has been present since the founding of the country over 500 years ago, and was first practiced by African slaves who led the largest urban slave revolt in Latin America. This uprising in Bahia, known as the Malé Revolt of 1835, involved 300 African slaves who stormed the streets of Salvador, Bahia and confronted soldiers and Brazilian authorities. Although the revolt was short-lived (spanning just a few hours), its implications would impact Islamic propagation in Brazil in future years, when authorities began to monitor the *malê* people and made efforts to force them to convert to Catholicism.[25]

The Islamic community, however, was not erased and the *da'wah* in Brazil continued into the late 19th century, when an *imam*, born in Baghdad and educated in Damascus, arrived in Rio de Janeiro. This *imam*, Al-Baghdadi al-Dimachqi, would connect with small Islamic communities in Salvador, Bahia and later was invited to Recife to continue his proselytization work. There are conflicting reports as to when the first mosque in Brazil was built, but around the same time Al-Baghdadi al-Dimachqi moved to Recife, the Brazilian government passed a resolution to allow for temples other than Catholic churches to be built. More than a century later, Brazil's first contemporary mosque, the so-called *Mesquita Brasil* (Brazil Mosque) was built on Avenida Do Estado in Sao Paulo.[26] It remains one of Brazil's largest mosques, but as Sao Paulo continued to grow, it became more difficult for congregants to attend. Thus, smaller mosques were built in surrounding neighborhoods.

Today, there are over 100 active mosques, cultural centers and Islamic associations in the country, and it is estimated that there are close to 100,000 Muslim converts living in Brazil.[27] Moreover, Islam is increasingly noticeable in Brazilian society, not only through the presence of mosques, but also Islamic libraries, newspapers, schools. But it wasn't until a *telenovela* (soap opera) called "The Clone" was launched in 2001 that Islam hit the Brazilian mainstream. This soap opera centered around showing the difference between Islam and the Western world and was such a success that *Globo*, the most prominent TV channel in Brazil, dedicated a half-hour weekly show to talk about a variety of Muslim issues.[28]

Islam has experienced comparatively rapid growth in recent years in Brazil, relative to other countries in Latin America, even though Muslims still make up a small percentage of the overall population.

The majority of the Muslim community in Brazil is Sunni, and most have assimilated into Brazilian society.[29] There are smaller and more reclusive Shi'ite communities, which remain somewhat insular, located in Sao Paulo, Curitiba and Foz do Iguaço. The Sunnis, however, have been able to accumulate wealth, which has allowed them to organize and represent their political interests in Brasilia. For instance, in the first half of 2013, legislation was proposed in the Brazilian parliament to create a "national day of Islam" as a federal holiday in Brazil. Although the legislative proposal failed, it highlights that an Islamic lobby of sorts is active in Brasilia.

Brazil already has a major problem with drug trafficking/consumption and organized crime, and the addition of Islamist terror networks to this mix would dramatically complicate the country's security environment. Unfortunately, the radical Islamist movement described in the previous section is all too aware of these conditions, and has begun outreach to disenfranchised communities within Brazil in order to proselytize and radicalize them. The goal is not to assimilate into Brazilian society and culture, but rather to assimilate Brazil into the global *jihadist* movement.

ISLAMISM AND THE STATE

Under President Luiz Inácio Lula da Silva of the Workers' Party (*Partido de Trabajadores*, PT), Brazil engaged in a new foreign policy paradigm known as the "South-South Strategy." This paradigm was part of Lula's vision to align African and Middle Eastern nations to Brazil, and his successor, Dilma Rousseff, largely continued his pursuit of a multi-polar world.[30]

Emblematic of Brazil's growing support for Islamic nations in the Middle East and North Africa (MENA) was Lula's controversial intervention in the Iranian nuclear dispute in May 2010. To help Iran avoid further UN Security Council sanctions, in April 2010 Lula attempted to negotiate an agreement between Iran and the P5+1 countries (the U.S., UK, France, China, Russia and Germany) to swap low-enriched uranium for higher-enriched uranium. The deal, however, eventually broke down, and the UN Security Council adopted another resolution calling on Iran to suspend all enrichment activity that could be used to support their nuclear program.[31] While this activism shocked some in the U.S. foreign policy community, Brazil's political ties to the Middle East and North Africa had grown stronger under Lula's tenure.

Dilma Rousseff built on Lula's foreign policy paradigm while prioritizing social spending during her term as president. Under the control of the PT for over a decade, the state expanded massive welfare programs and crowded out private enterprise. The concurrent Lula and Rousseff governments imposed burdensome regulations on businesses that made it nearly impossible to create companies or fire under-performing employees. The result was Brazil's private sector struggled, while the state rewarded crooked businessmen and created a culture of corruption within the government.

This reached a boiling point in 2014, when the largest corruption scandal in Brazil's history erupted after known money launderer (and the son of Lebanese immigrants), Alberto Youssef, implicated the state-run energy giant Petrobras in a massive public corruption scheme. Upwards of $5 billion was believed to have changed hands between corrupt public and private actors as kickbacks and bribes. In 2015, this scandal implicated top politicians in Brazil including the former president Lula da Silva. Throughout the year, massive public protests spread throughout Brazil calling for Rousseff's impeachment or resignation. By December, the Brazilian Parliament answered the protestors' call to action by filing for the impeachment of President Rousseff.[32] On August 31, 2016, the Brazilian Senate voted by a 61-20 margin to remove Rousseff from office, finding her guilty of breaking budgetary laws.[33] Acting President Michel Temer, who took office after Rousseff's impeachment, appears committed to establishing fiscal discipline but is also realigning Brazil's foreign policy priorities.

One of the last governmental initiatives of the Rousseff regime was to begin talks with Germany, the European Union, and the United Nations to consider taking in additional Syrian refugees. As of March 2016, Brazil had agreed to accept 8,474 Syrian refugees with humanitarian visas, and had already granted 2,250 Syrians full asylum. Following calls from various sectors of society for the Brazilian government to welcome additional Syrian refugees, Rousseff responded. Shortly before leaving his post in May, Eugenio Aragao, the former justice minister, said the country could welcome "up to 100,000 Syrians, in groups of 20,000 per year." Following the suspension—and later impeachment—of Rousseff as Brazil's president, the new Temer government has decided to abandon discussions of taking in more Syrian refugees, citing security concerns.

The decision to abandon talks over Syrian refugees is symbolic of a wider pivot in foreign policy being taken by the interim President Temer and his foreign minister, Jose Serra. In his first act as minister, Serra set out a list of policy directives recalibrating Brazil's foreign policy priorities. Chief among them is an emphasis to strengthen Brazil's relationships with its traditional economic and trade partners: Europe, the U.S., and Japan. This was a significant shift from the previous governments' engagement with Middle Eastern and Islamic countries. In practical terms, this shift resulted in Brazil withdrawing its vote in support of a UNESCO resolution describing Israel as an "occupying power."[34] While marginal in its effect, the decision to realign foreign relations closer to Israel broke Brazil's longstanding supportive attitude toward the Palestinian Authority. Under Rousseff, Brazil had become home to the first Palestinian Authority embassy in the Western Hemisphere, which was inaugurated in early 2016 in Brasilia.[35]

Brazil's future is uncertain, as acting President Michel Temer is also facing potential corruption charges. Elections in 2018 will define the leadership of the country and renew Brazil's foreign policy priorities. The critical issue of Syrian refugees and large public corruption scandals have highlighted the importance of paying attention to the rise of Islamism in Brazil, a phenomenon still largely misunderstood in Brazil, Latin America, and the world writ large.

Endnotes

[1] The Brazilian Census of 2010 puts the number of Muslims in Brazil at 35,207, while religious authorities speak of far higher numbers: between one and two million. Based on the scope of Islamic activities in Brazil, the number of one million seems a more plausible estimate.

[2] Julia Corthian, "Brazilian Police Arrest 10 Suspected of Plotting Olympics Terror Attack" TIME magazine, July 21, 2016, http://time.com/4417762/rio-olympics-brazil-terror-plot/

[3] Marcelo Martinez Burgos and Alberto Nisman, Office of Criminal Investigations: AMIA CASE; Investigations Unit of the Office of the Attorney General (Argentina), October 25, 2006, http://www.peaceandtolerance.org/docs/nismanindict.pdf

[4] Alberto Nisman released a special follow-on 502-page report on May 29, 2013 that discussed Iran's clandestine intelligence structure in Latin America. An English translation of this report can be found at www.albertonisman.org (http://albertonisman.org/nisman-report-dictamina-on-sleeper-cells-full-text/)

[5] Rex Hudson, Terrorist and Organized Crime Groups in the Tri-Border Area (TBA) of South America (Congressional Research Service, July 2003 (revised December 2010)), http://www.loc.gov/rr/frd/pdf-files/TerrOrgCrime_TBA.pdf.

[6] Ibid, 5.

[7] Ibid., 20.

[8] Ibidem, 25.

[9] Leonardo Coutiñho, "A Rede do Terror Finca Bases no Brasil," VEJA (Brazil), April 6, 2011.

[10] Burgos & Nisman, Office of Criminal Investigations: AMIA CASE, 64 .

[11] Holly Yan, Julia Jones, and Shasta Darlington, "Brazilian police arrest 12 suspected of planning terrorist acts during Olympics," CNN World, July 25, 2016, http://www.cnn.com/2016/07/21/americas/brazil-olympics-terror-arrests/index.html

[12] "Brazil: New Anti-Terrorism Law Enacted," Global Legal Monitor, Library of Congress, Apr. 15, 2016; http://www.loc.gov/law/foreign-news/article/brazil-new-anti-terrorism-law-enacted/

[13] For more information on the ISIS terrorist plot in Brazil, please see the Situation Report (SITREP) from the Center for a Secure Free Society (SFS) published on August 2016.

[14] Press Release, "Treasury Targets Hizballah Fundraising Network in the Triple Frontier of Argentina, Brazil, and Paraguay," Dec. 6, 2006, https://www.treasury.gov/press-center/press-releases/Pages/hp190.aspx

[15] Simon Romero, "Businessman Linked by U.S. to Hezbollah Is Arrested in Brazil in a Fraud Scheme," The New York Times, May 20, 2013, http://www.nytimes.com/2013/05/21/world/americas/man-linked-by-us-to-hezbollah-is-arrested-in-brazil.html

[16] "Hezbollah has ties to Brazil's largest criminal gang; group also found active in Peru," Fox News World, November 11, 2014, http://www.foxnews.com/world/2014/11/11/hezbollah-has-ties-to-brazil-largest-criminal-gang-group-also-found-active-in.html

[17] Jack Moore, "ISIS Calls for Recruitment of Portuguese 'Brothers' Ahead of Rio Olympics," Newsweek, June 21, 2016, http://www.newsweek.com/isis-calls-recruitment-portuguese-brothers-ahead-rio-olympics-472649

[18] Christine Williams, "Jihadists pledge loyalty to Islamic State in first public declaration in South America," Jihad Watch, July 19, 2016, https://www.jihadwatch.org/2016/07/jihadists-pledge-loyalty-to-islamic-state-in-first-public-declaration-in-south-america-weeks-before-olympics

[19] This report is in the author's possession. For more information please see the SFS SITREP from August 2016.

[20] "Ten People Arrested on Suspicion of Terrorism," Global Legal Monitor, Library of Congress, July 26, 2016; http://www.loc.gov/law/foreign-news/article/brazil-ten-people-arrested-on-suspicion-of-terrorism/

[21] Robert Windrem and William Arkin, "More than 1,000 U.S. Spies Protecting Rio Olympics," NBC News, Aug. 5, 2016, http://www.nbcnews.com/storyline/2016-rio-summer-olympics/more-1-000-u-s-spies-brazil-protecting-rio-olympics-n623186

[22] Jose R. Cardenas, Roger F. Noriega, "The mounting Hezbollah threat in Latin America," American Enterprise Institute, October 6, 2011, https://www.aei.org/publication/the-mounting-hezbollah-threat-in-latin-america/

[23] Cyrus Miryekta, "Hezbollah in the Tri-Border Area of South America," Small Wars Journal, September 10, 2010, http://usacac.army.mil/cac2/call/docs/11-15/ch_11.asp.

[24] Robin Yapp, "Brazil Latest Base for Islamic Extremists," Telegraph (London), April 3, 2011, http://www.telegraph.co.uk/news/worldnews/southamerica/brazil/8424929/Brazil-latest-base-for-Islamic-extremists.html.

[25] Cristina Maria de Castro, The Construction of Muslim Identities in Contemporary Brazil (Lanham, MD: Lexington Books, 2013).

[26] Ibid., 17.

[27] Paulo G. Pinto, Muslim Identities in Brazil: Shared Traditions and Cultural Creativity in the Making of Islamic Communities (Florida International University Applied Research Center, April 2010), http://strategicculture.fiu.edu/LinkClick.aspx?fileticket=jDk1ZPpNivg%3D&tabid=89.

[28] Robert Plummer, "Giving Brazil a taste of Arabia," BBC, December 11, 2005, http://news.bbc.co.uk/2/hi/business/4468070.stm.

[29] Pinto, pg. 46

[30] Jaime Darenblum, "How Argentina and Brazil help Iran," Weekly Standard, November 1, 2012, http://www.weeklystandard.com/blogs/how-argentina-and-brazil-help-iran_659920.html.

[31] Jackson Diehl, "Has Brazil's Lula Become Iran's Useful Idiot?" Washington Post, May 6, 2010, http://voices.washingtonpost.com/postpartisan/2010/05/has_brazils_lula_become_irans.html.

[32] Helio Bicudo, Miguel Reale Jr, Janaína Paschoal (lawyers) (15 October 2015). "Pedido de impeachment da presidente Dilma Rousseff" [Impeachment request of President Dilma Rousseff] (PDF) (in Portuguese). p. 11. Retrieved 13 May 2016.

[33] CNN, Catherine E. Shoichet and Euan McKirdy. "Brazil's Senate ousts Rousseff in impeachment vote". CNN. Retrieved 31 August 2016. http://www.cnn.com/2016/08/31/americas/brazil-rousseff-impeachment-vote/index.html

[34] Raphael Ahren, "Support for UNESCO Temple Mount resolution was 'error,' Brazil says, The Times of Israel, June 13, 2016; http://www.timesofisrael.com/support-for-unesco-temple-mount-resolution-was-error-brazil-says/

[35] JTA, "Palestinians Open Embassy in Brazil, First in Western Hemisphere," Forward, Feb. 4, 2016; http://forward.com/news/world/332909/palestinians-open-embassy-in-brazil-first-in-western-hemisphere/

NICARAGUA

QUICK FACTS

Population: 5,966,798 (July 2016 est.)

Area: 130,370 sq km

Ethnic Groups: mestizo (mixed Amerindian and white) 69%, white 17%, black 9%, Amerindian 5%

Religions: Roman Catholic 58.5%, Protestant 23.2% (Evangelical 21.6%, Moravian 1.6%), Jehovah's Witnesses 0.9%, other 1.6%, none 15.7%

Government Type: presidential republic

GDP (official exchange rate): $13.41 billion (2015 est.)

Map and Quick Facts courtesy of the CIA World Factbook (January 2017)

OVERVIEW

Islam has had a presence in Nicaragua since the late 19th century, when Muslims from the territories of what was then known as Palestine placed a particular focus on Central America as an emigration destination. According to one estimate, as many as 40 families from Palestine settled in Nicaragua during this period.[1] However, this first wave of Muslim immigration, and a subsequent second wave that took place in the 1960s, did little to establish Islam in Nicaragua. The most recent group of immigrants arrived in the early 1990s, however, and this group helped establish what is today a small but thriving Islamic community.

Nicaragua's Islamic community consists of Muslim descendants of Arab emigrants from the territory of Palestine and Lebanon. There are likewise a relatively small number of Nicaraguan nationals who have converted to the Muslim faith. According to 2007 statistics released by the U.S. State Department, there were between 1,200 and 1,500 Muslims, mostly Sunnis, who are either resident aliens or naturalized citizens in Nicaragua. A 2009 Pew Forum on Religion and Public Life claimed 1,000

Muslims in the country, while a local Imam placed the number closer to 500. Most Nicaraguan Muslims originated from Palestine, Libya, and Iran, or are natural-born Nicaraguan citizens born into one or more of those groups. While this is a relatively low number, it nonetheless has resulted in notable religious activity, with prayer centers established in private residences around the country, including in Masaya, Leon and Granada.[2]

The first mosque that was built in Nicaragua was constructed in 1999 with local funding, as well as the assistance of Panamanian Muslims. Construction on a second mosque began in 2009. In January 2007, then-Iranian President Mahmoud Ahmadinejad visited the country's first mosque, signaling a growing international recognition of Nicaragua's Islamic community. The resumption of power by Daniel Ortega in 2006 brought with it a positive change in the relationship between Nicaragua's Muslim community and the government, including considerably better treatment than under past regimes, when Muslims were forced into hiding or made to convert to Christianity.

ISLAMIST ACTIVITY

Native Islamist activity in Nicaragua has been limited. The Muslim community in Nicaragua is small and generally moderate. Nicaragua's Islamic Cultural Association in Managua serves as the focal point of the country's Muslim population. Run by Fahmi Hassan and his staff, the center also operates the country's first mosque. Apart from traditional prayer activities, the center maintains an office, a library, a children's area, and a school, and offers the use of its basketball and soccer field to local residents. Religious seminars are available for men and women and Spanish-language literature is made available for the community and visitors.

Hassan arrived in Nicaragua in 1960 and has remained in the country since, with one exception. During the Sandinista Revolution, he lived in Saudi Arabia and Jordan, but as he explains in an interview, he left for business reasons.[3]

In 2007, the Cultural Center of Nicaraguan Islam opened in Managua with the purpose of spreading Islamic teachings.[4] Founded by Carlos Arana, a Palestinian descendant, the center was set up to organize seminars and to maintain a library and website. There is no indication at this point that the Cultural Center is used for anything other than non-radical Islamic teaching.

ISLAMISM AND SOCIETY

Throughout much of Nicaragua's history, Muslim citizens have been victims, off-and-on, of government repression, largely due to rejection by the country's dominant Catholic society. The peak of this repression occurred just before the beginning of the

Sandinista Revolution in the late 1970s. During the Revolution, however, Nicaragua's government treated the Muslim community exceptionally well, especially Palestinian Arabs. Most men and women who immigrate to Nicaragua from the Middle East choose to settle in the country, and leave only when they are old because they would prefer to die in their homeland.[5] This trend suggests a high level of acceptance of Islam within Nicaraguan society.

Another indication of Islamic acceptance is Managua's Arabic business district. All along a road known as *Casa de los Encajes*, in the *Ciudad Jardin* section of the capital, there is concentration of Arabic stores, most of them owned by Palestinians who sell Arabic rugs, home decoration, clothing, and fabrics. Mr. Hassan owns a rug store located in this small district, which by 2003 had been in place for "many years."[6] More recently, historical pressures have all but disappeared as President Daniel Ortega has focused on bringing the Central American country closer to Middle Eastern states, especially Iran. While there has been no significant presence of ISIS or other radical cells reported to be operating in Nicaragua over the past year, an Afghan man with terrorist ties was caught in 2016 after passing through Nicaragua en route to the U.S.[7]

ISLAMISM AND THE STATE

The Islamist activity that does occur in Nicaragua tends to occur in political spheres, rather than in grassroots organizations or local communities. The two main instances of Islamism in Nicaragua are the connection between the revolutionary Sandinista party and the Palestine Liberation Organization (PLO), and Iran's growing interest and interference in Nicaraguan affairs.

Current President Daniel Ortega led the Sandinistas to power in 1979. The relationship between the Sandinistas and the PLO was already well established at that point, as PLO fighters had trained Sandinista guerrillas before the Sandinista Revolution. Once the Sandinistas seized power, the PLO sent a 25-man team to train Sandinista soldiers in the use of Eastern-bloc weapons, and provided a loan of $12 million.[8] Yasser Arafat, then head of the PLO, visited Managua in 1980. And by 1982, some 70 high-ranking PLO officers were assisting with special infantry training for the Nicaraguan army.[9] In return, Ortega and the Sandinistas granted the PLO full diplomatic status. The Sandinista regime, from the time it came into power, has considered Israel an enemy. For its part, the Israeli government shipped weapons to the Contras in 1983, to aid the U.S.-backed resistance fighters in their fight against the Soviet-backed Sandinistas.[10]

In 1989, Ortega visited Europe and the Middle East in search of support, with stops in Qatar, Kuwait, and Bahrain. During a layover in Newfoundland, he announced that he had secured significant financing and aid for his country, presumably from patrons in the Middle East.[11] When Ortega unexpectedly lost the historic elections of 1990 to Violeta Chamorro, the Nicaraguan attitude toward the Islamic world changed dramatically. One of the first things Chamorro's administration did was close the Iranian embassy in Managua as well as the Nicaraguan embassy in Tehran. In addition, Chamorro renewed relations with Israel and significantly reduced the presence of the PLO and Libya in Nicaragua.

However, Chamorro's acquiescence to entreaties from the international community for reconciliation ended up allowing a number of Sandinista holdovers to serve in her government. *The Economist* magazine noted the result of this decision in June 1998:

> ...One relic of Nicaragua's 11 years under far-left government remains—more exactly, at least 1,000 relics: sympathisers, militants, actual terrorists of half-a-dozen extremist movements who found a welcome and have extended it, despite the election of right-wing governments in 1990 and later. Beside sundry Latin Americans, they include left-overs of Germany's Baader-Meinhof gang, Italy's Red Brigades, Basque separatists, Islamic fundamentalists, Palestinian extremists and others. They have been able to stay because the Sandinistas, in their last weeks of power, gave them Nicaraguan passports.[12]

Support in the form of providing government documents and identification to enable unfettered travel to radical Islamists continued throughout the 1990s. When Saddam Hussein's troops retreated from Kuwait in 1991, they also left a cache of Nicaraguan passports behind, and the terrorists who set off a bomb under the World Trade Center in 1993 were found to have five Nicaraguan passports in their possession.[13]

Chamorro's policy of refocusing Nicaraguan attention on Latin America and the United States continued until Ortega's reelection in November 2006. During his second tenure as president, Daniel Ortega welcomed Islam into Nicaragua through increasingly close ties with Iran. One of Ortega's first official acts was to reestablish diplomatic ties with Iran, waiving visa requirements for Iranian travelers and authorizing Iran to reopen its embassy in Managua. In a sign of this growing warmth, then-Iranian President Mahmoud Ahmadinejad attended Ortega's inauguration ceremony in January 2007 before visiting the country's mosque. President Ortega has also visited Iran, where on June 10, 2007 he met with Supreme Leader Ali Khamenei to mutually criticize "American imperialism" and secure Iranian support for a raft of foreign direct investment projects. While in Tehran, Ortega declared that the Iranian revolution and Nicaragua's Sandinista revolution were "practically twins" because they shared not only the same birth year (1979) but the same goals of "justice, self-determination and the struggle against imperialism."[14] The meeting yielded concrete dividends. In August of that year, Iran's Deputy Minister of Energy, Hamid Chitchian, visited Nicaragua with a delegation of 21 businessmen. Ortega presented the delegation with a long list of discussed projects: a deep-water port, a wharf at Port Corinto and Monkey Point, a 70-kilometer highway on the Caribbean coast, improvements to Managua's drinking water system, six hydraulic plants, a plan for the mechanization of the country's agricultural sector, assembly plants for tractors and other agricultural machinery, five milk processing plants, ten milk storage centers, and a health clinic in Managua. In exchange, Ortega offered meat, plantains, and coffee exports to Iran.[15]

Since then, Iran has moved forward on studies for a $350 million deep-water port in Nicaragua, but as of this writing construction on the project has yet to begin. And of the six hydroelectric plants, Iran has agreed to assist with four, but had the funding to invest only in one. Construction on the $120 million hydroelectric plant remains delayed.[16]

In the wake of the April 2013 death of Venezuelan strongman Hugo Chavez, many speculated that Ortega would attempt to fill the resulting regional leadership void, possibly through closer ties to the Iranian regime. Contacts between Managua and Tehran, however, remain largely unchanged, with hardly a mention of unfulfilled agreements between the two nations during subsequent diplomatic visits.

In a March 2015 congressional hearing on Iran and Hezbollah in the Western Hemisphere, it was noted that "the Central America four-border control agreement originally signed in 2006 permits the free movement of citizens from El Salvador, Guatemala, Honduras, and Nicaragua without any restrictions, similar to the Schengen agreement in Europe," signaling a continuing concern among security officials of operatives infiltrating via a permeable southern border.[17]

Earlier rumors of Iran operating the largest embassy in Central America in Managua have proven untrue.[18] And while Iran will not pardon Nicaragua's $160 million dollar debt, the country has indeed followed through with some initial investments.[19] At least 1,000 of the 10,000 promised "social housing" units have been slated for construction, according to an agreement signed between President Ortega and Iranian Deputy Energy Minister Hamid Chitchian.[20]

Nicaragua, however, opened an embassy office in Tehran, and sent Mario Antonio Barquero Baltadano to serve as ambassador in 2015. Through President Ortega's efforts, the Central American country continues to be an international partner for the Iranian regime. By contrast, Nicaragua's contacts with Lebanon, Libya, and the Palestinian Territories—where most of the country's Muslim population retains some connection—are limited.

In August 2016, Iranian Foreign Minister Mohammad Javad Zarif made a trip to Nicaragua with a high-ranking "politico-economic delegation" that consisted of 120 businessmen and financial executives from the Iranian government and private sectors. Zarif indicated that Iran "greatly values its relationship with Latin American nations, including Nicaragua."[21]

Although there was no reported discussion of unfulfilled previous commitments, Zarif stated that: "Cooperation between Iran and Nicaragua can include collaboration in the construction of the [Grand] Interoceanic Canal to the areas of agriculture, energy production, petrochemistry, banking, credit, transportation, food and pharmaceutical industries, and science and technology." [22] The Interoceanic Canal has long been touted by the Nicaraguan government to compete with the Panama Canal, but it has mostly been promoted in fits and starts. As of December 2014, the government had broken ground on the project, but has since claimed to be awaiting environmental impact studies in order to continue construction. It has issued some ancillary concessions based on where the proposed canal would be placed, though even these have caused controversy, creating growing doubt about the country's ability to see the project through to completion.[23]

The Joint Comprehensive Plan of Action (JCPOA, or the Iran nuclear deal), signed between the five permanent members of the United Nations Security Council—China, France, Russia, United Kingdom, United States—plus Germany) and the European Union in July 2015, has received plaudits by Nicaraguan officials. Edwin Castro, head of the Sandinista bloc and co-chair of the Iran-Nicaragua Friendship group in the Nicaraguan parliament, said that the Nicaraguan government welcomed lifting the "unfair" sanctions imposed on Iran "in contravention of international law."[24] However, though Iran has seen an infusion of cash since the JCPOA was signed, it has not significantly increased its economic investment with Nicaragua nor made overtures toward completing earlier trade and construction commitments.

ENDNOTES

[1] Roberto Marín Guzmán, A Century of Palestinian Immigration into Central America: A Study of Their Economic and Cultural Contributions (Editorial Universidad de C.R., 2000), 49–59.

[2] Roberto Tottoli (editor), Routledge Handbook of Islam in the West, (Routledge, 2015), p. 166.

[3] Edwin Sanchez, "El Ramadan de un musulman en El Oriental," El Nuevo Diario, October 9, 2005, http://impreso.elnuevodiario.com.ni/2005/10/09/nacionales/2967

[4] Doren Roa, "Inaguran Centro Cultrual Islámico," El Nuevo Diario, September 15, 2007, http://tinyurl.com/yeqmsnu

[5] Sanchez, "El Ramadan de un musulman en El Oriental."

[6] Eduardo Tercero Marenco, "La defensa de Irak es obligatoria y necesaria," La Prensa, April 6, 2003, http://tinyurl.com/yzjhlp3

[7] "Smuggling network guided illegals from Middle East terror hotbeds to U.S. border," The Washington Times, June 2, 2016, http://www.washingtontimes.com/news/2016/jun/2/smuggling-network-guided-illegal-immigrants-from-m/

[8] Robert Fisk, "Long link with Middle East / Nicaraguan involvement in US-Iran arms deal," Times of London, November 28, 1986.

[9] George Gedda, "Administration Worried About Sandinista Ties to Middle East 'Radicals,'" Associated Press, July 10, 1985.

[10] Robert Fisk, "Long link with Middle East / Nicaraguan involvement in US-Iran arms deal," Times of London, November 28, 1986.

[11] "Nicaragua Ortega on results of Middle East tour," Voz de Nicaragua, October 20, 1989.

[12] "Nicaragua: Rest Home for Revolutionaries," The Economist, June 18, 1998, http://www.economist.com/node/136402

[13] Larry Rohter, "New Passports Being Issued By Nicaragua to Curb Fraud," New York Times, January 28, 1996.

[14] "Nicaragua e Iran: 'Union Invencible,'" BBC Mundo.com, June 11, 2007, http://news.bbc.co.uk/hi/spanish/latin_america/newsid_6741000/6741829.stm

[15] Revista Envio, Nicaragua Briefs 313, August 2007, http://www.envio.org.ni/articulo/3628

[16] "Latin America warms to Iran amid anti-U.S. sentiment," Reuters, August 29, 2007, https://www.gpo.gov/fdsys/pkg/CHRG-114hhrg93819/html/CHRG-114hhrg93819.htm

[17] Congressman Jeff Duncan (R-SC-3rd), Opening Statement at joint hearing of the House of Representatives Committee on Foreign Affairs Subcommittee on the Western Hemisphere and Subcommittee on the Middle East and North Africa and Subcommittee entitled "Iran and Hezbollah in the Western Hemisphere," March 18, 2015, https://www.gpo.gov/fdsys/pkg/CHRG-114hhrg93819/html/CHRG-114hhrg93819.htm

[18] Anne-Marie O'Connor and Mary Beth Sheridan, "Iran's Invisible Nicaraguan Embassy," Washington Post, July 13, 2009, http://tinyurl.com/knfpyt

[19] Ludwin Lopez Loaisiga, "Iran sin perdonar US$160 millones," La Prensa, February 7, 2009, http://tinyurl.com/yj79tcr.

[20] Ludwin Loaisiga Lopez, "Iran hace promesas de ayudas millonarias," La Prensa, August 2007, http://eldiarioexterior.com/iran-hace-promesas-de-ayudas-15621.htm

[21] "Iran Greatly Values Latin America Ties: Zarif In Nicaragua," Press TV, August 24, 2016, http://www.caribflame.com/2016/08/iran-greatly-values-latin-america-ties-zarif-in-nicaragua/.

[22] Ibid.

[23] Edwin Nieves, "The Canal Stuck in a Quagmire," Council On Hemispheric Affairs, April 25, 2016, http://www.coha.org/the-canal-stuck-in-a-quagmire/

[24] "Nicaraguan MP: Latin American states welcome JCPOA," IRNA, August 24, 2016, https://www3.irna.ir/en/News/82201646/

VENEZUELA

QUICK FACTS

Population: 30,912,302 (July 2016 est.)

Area: 912,050 sq km

Ethnic Groups: Spanish, Italian, Portuguese, Arab, German, African, indigenous people

Religions: nominally Roman Catholic 96%, Protestant 2%, other 2%

Government Type: Federal Presidential Republic

GDP (official exchange rate): $333.7 billion (2015 est.)

Map and Quick Facts courtesy of the CIA World Factbook (Last Updated January 2017)

OVERVIEW

Nicolas Maduro, has continued his predecessor's welcoming stance toward the propaganda, recruitment, and fundraising of groups, including Islamist ones, that fit into the anti-US and anti-semitic worldview inherent in the anti-globalist anti-US "Bolivarian" ideology of Venezuela. He continues to provide them with assistance and safe haven for a range of their financial activities,.

The roots of this institutional affinity stretch back to Chavez's years as a revolutionary in the 4-F guerilla group, during which time the future Venezuelan president fell under the sway of individuals with a sympathetic view of a variety of "non-aligned" Middle Eastern rogues. Members of that group included now-embattled Syrian despot Bashar al-Assad, the late Libyan dictator Muammar Qadhafi, former Iraqi strongman Saddam Hussein, and the leaders of the Iranian Revolution.[1] These early lessons provided the basis of the foreign policy that Chavez pursued from the time of his assumption of power in 1998—a foreign policy that has made his country a close ally of the Islamic Republic of Iran and an array of radical Islamist groups, chief among them Hezbollah.

Islamist Activity

Venezuela is an attractive way station for Islamist groups, which have a quiet but longstanding and profitable presence there that includes fundraising, smuggling, money laundering, and training. The U.S. Southern Command (SOUTHCOM) estimates that "Islamist terrorist groups raise between three hundred million and five hundred million dollars per year in the Triple Frontier and the duty-free zones of Iquique, Colon, Maicao, and Margarita Island, Venezuela."[2]

There is a special relationship between the Venezuelan government and Iran's chief terrorist proxy, Hezbollah. Venezuela provides political, diplomatic, material and logistical support to Hezbollah. As it is in most of Latin America, Hezbollah is the primary Islamist force in Venezuela. Capitalizing on the network of enterprising Lebanese Shi'a merchants throughout the country's larger cities, the group uses the South American country for fundraising and various forms of money-laundering, smuggling, and fraud. The basic model is a simple "pay to play" system, in which local Lebanese Shi'a merchants are persuaded by Hezbollah agents and financiers, through varying degrees of coercion, to "tithe" to Hezbollah.[3] Most worrisome, however, is the network of underworld connections that Hezbollah is building throughout the hemisphere from its base in Venezuela. According to former Assistant Secretary of State for Western Hemisphere Affairs Roger Noriega, Hezbollah operatives are collaborating with sophisticated and high level drug-smugglers and guerrillas in the region. In 2013, Noriega outlined two such schemes—Walid Makled García's "Lebanese Cartel" (Cártel Libanés) and Ayman Jouma's cocaine smuggling and money-laundering scheme—in testimony to the House Committee on Foreign Affairs.[4] In recognition of this and related Iranian/Hezbollah activity in the region, the U.S. Congress passed the "Countering Iran in the Western Hemisphere Act of 2012" which mandated the Secretary of State to develop a strategy that should include:

> within Latin American countries, a multiagency action plan, in coordination with United States allies and partners in the region, that includes the development of strong rule-of-law institutions to provided security in such countries and a counterterrorism and counter-radicalization plan to isolate Iran, the IRGC, its Qods Force, Hezbollah, and other terrorist organizations linked to Iran that may be present in the Western Hemisphere from their sources of financial support and counter their facilitation of terrorist activity.[5]

There has been much speculation that the financial assets freed by the Joint Comprehensive Plan of Action (JCPOA) between the P5+1 nations, the European Union, and Iran would be funneled into Latin America. While Iran has shown an increased interest in deepening relations with several Latin American countries, including Venezuela,[6] there is no concrete evidence at this time to suggest that increased interest has been matched by increased investment.

ISLAMISM AND SOCIETY

Venezuela's Muslim population is small but influential. According to the U.S. State Department's conservative estimate in the 2015 *International Religious Freedom Report*, there are more than 100,000 Muslims in Venezuela, primarily of Lebanese and Syrian descent, and concentrated in Nueva Esparta and Caracas.[7] While Margarita Island's Muslim population is almost entirely Lebanese Shi'a, there are Sunni Muslims elsewhere in the country, and Caracas has a largely Sunni population of 15,000 that is served by the largest mosque in Latin America, built by the Saudis as a sister mosque to the Sheikh Ibrahim Al-Ibrahim mosque in Gibraltar.[8] There are other mosques in the major cities of Maracaibo, Valencia, Vargas, Punto Fijo, and Bolivar. Local cable television outlets in Margarita carry *al-Jazeera* and the Lebanese Hezbollah outlet LBC, while on the mainland the Saudi Channel is available via satellite as well.[9]

The picture of Islamism and society in Venezuela resembles that of much of Latin America. While there is a vague anti-globalist sense that pervades society, actual friendship with Islamist aims is at the political, rather than the religious, level.[10] While the Latin American left at times can sound Islamist in its politics and its understanding of who the "enemy" is, apart from one-off episodes, there is no conversion to Islam taking place in Venezuela—or, indeed, in the region as a whole. This is not to say that efforts have not been made, especially among indigenous and Creole groups whose Christianity has never been especially solid. To the contrary, in the past 150 years of immigration from the Middle East to the New World, the opposite trend has held sway. A large number of prominent *turcos* (immigrants and their descendants from the Middle East) originally were Muslim, but have been genuine *conversos* (converts to Christianity) for generations.

Thus, the presence in Caracas of the largest mosque in the New World may give Muslim proselytizers the right to say they have penetrated Latin America, but it reflects Venezuela's cosmopolitan self-image more than it serves as evidence of an Islamist trajectory. Nonetheless, one should not dismiss the larger fact that Islam does play a significant—if not central—role in Venezuela's anti-globalist and anti-hegemonic culture, which post-colonial critic Robert Young notes incarnates a "tricontinental counter-modernity" that combines diaspora and local cultural elements, and blends Arab, Islamic, black and Hispanic factors to generate "a revolutionary black, Asian and Hispanic globalization, with its own dynamic counter-modernity... constructed in order to fight global imperialism."[11]

However, there has been an instance of a radical Islamist group that was based in Venezuela and seemingly concerned with Venezuelan social issues. The group advertised itself as *Hezbollah en América Latina* ("Hezbollah in Latin America.") Though it was largely eclipsed in the news media by the U.S. 2006 mid-term elections, *Hezbollah en América Latina's* failed attempt in October 2006 to bomb the U.S. (and perhaps the Israeli) embassy in Caracas was a significant event. The group, based within the country's Wayuu Indian population, boasts of activity in Argentina, Chile, Colombia, El Salvador and Mexico on their website,[12] which is written in Spanish and Chapateka (a combination of the Wayuu language and Spanish). However, the backbone of the organization is located in Venezuela on the country's western border with Colombia. The members of this group are locals and not Muslim in origin, despite their tenuous claim to be Shi'ite supporters of Hezbollah and Iran.[13]

In its manifesto, the organization asserted that Venezuelan society, with its interest in sex, money, industry and commerce, has become a "swamp of immorality and corruption."[14] It claimed that political movements and parties could not provide an answer to these challenges because they were also part of the problem. Thus, only "a theocratic, Political-Islamic force can liberate society from this situation."[15] By contrast, *Hezbollah en América Latina* "respect[ed] the Venezuelan revolutionary process, and support[ed] its social policies as well as its anti-Zionism and anti-Americanism," even as it rejected socialism in favor of an Islamic order. Tellingly, the group urged everyone to vote for and support Chavez.[16]

It is not coincidental that this phenomenon occurred at a time when Hugo Chavez and Iranian President Mahmoud Ahmedinejad had become close allies, which is further discussed below. It points to an alarming possibility: that Hezbollah and radical Islamist groups need not import Islamists from the Muslim world to Latin America. Rather, they can be homegrown in the region, because the social and emotional conditions provide fertile ground. Furthermore, this new available human capital does not need previous connection to Islam; it can be converted, because Islamism is not merely a religion but also a political movement.

This principle helps to explain the near-perfect symbiosis of the "Bolivarian" Revolution promoted by Chavez with the aims of Hezbollah: "Hezbollah Latin America respects the Venezuelan revolutionary process and supports the policies of this process that have to do with social benefits for the poor, as well as the anti-Zionist and anti-imperialist policies of the revolution. It does not, however, support the socialist ideology. This is not because we are opposed to it but because we are theocrats and we obey a divine prerogative."[17]

ISLAMISM AND THE STATE

Ever since Hugo Chavez took his first trip to Iran in 2001, close relations with the Islamic Republic have been a cardinal tenet of Venezuelan foreign policy. During Iran's 2009 elections, Chavez offered "total solidarity" to Iranian president Mahmoud Ahmadinejad, equating attacks on him as an assault by "global capitalism,"[18] and con-doned the brutal tactics of Iran's domestic militia, the basij, in their crackdown on opposition protesters.[19] Iran reciprocated these friendly feelings. When he decorated Hugo Chávez with the Higher Medal of the Islamic Republic of Iran in 2008, Mahmoud Ahmadinejad called Chávez "my brother… a friend of the Iranian nation and the people seeking freedom around the world. He works perpetually against the dominant system. He is a worker of God and servant of the people."[20] Ahmedinijad even risked a public embrace of Chavez's grieving mother at the *caudillo's* funeral, a move which scandalized the mullahs back home.

This relationship manifested itself in a series of agreements over the years. Venezuela announced the agreement to purchase Unmanned Aerial Vehicles (UAVs) from Iran in 2007. But this drone cooperation, troubling enough in itself, may mask still more sinister cooperation. There was speculation, never corroborated, that Venezuela and Iran signed an agreement to construct a joint missile base in Venezuela and co-develop ballistic missiles.[21] The State Department claimed that it had "no evidence to support this claim and therefore no reason to believe the assertions made in the article are credible."[22]

In November 2008, Iranian and Venezuelan officials signed a secret "science and technology" agreement formalizing cooperation "in the field of nuclear technology."[23] As part of that outreach, Iranian Minister of Science, Research and Technology Mohammad-Mehdi Zahedi led a delegation to hold talks with Venezuelan high-ranking officials in Caracas. The delegation visited the Venezuelan Foundation for Seismological Research, Caracas Central University, the Simon Bolivar University, and the Venezuelan Institute for Scientific Research.[24] During the visit, Chavez promised to provide the Islamic Republic with 20,000 barrels of petrol a day, despite the sanctions on Iran's economy being contemplated by much of the world and in spite of Venezuela's own problems in supplying its domestic markets with fuel.[25]

In April 2009, the two countries launched a bi-national bank with $200 million of initial capital—with each country contributing half—and a final goal of $1.2 billion.[26] The bank is supposed to finance projects of mutual benefit to the two countries. Based in Venezuela, it will offer a convenient channel for Iran to sidestep U.S.-led sanctions along with the several branches of Iran's Saderat Bank already open there.[27] Furthermore, U.S. State Department cables, published by Wikileaks, reveal an Iranian shipment of *Mohajer*-2 unmanned aerial vehicles in violation of UNSC 1747 bound for Venezuela sometime before May 2009.[28] Subsequently, a visit to Iran by Chavez in September 2009 yielded a new deal on nuclear cooperation.[29] The agreement was an addition to a rapidly growing list of bilateral pacts between Caracas and Tehran. Despite U.S. sanctions, in November 2011, the first *Mohajer* was spotted at El Libertador airbase in Ochoa. In the summer of 2012, a Spanish news source, ABC.es, broke a story about U.S. investigations into the program and Chavez admitted and shared pictures of the UAVs, according to a Reuters report.[30]

The relationship between Iran and Venezuela has persisted four years now beyond the individual affinities of the late president Chavez and the former president Ahmedinijad. Iran sees its Venezuelan connection as an important means to render international sanctions impotent. The joint ventures erected between Caracas and Tehran, and the purchase of Venezuelan enterprises, allow Iran to do business with U.S. companies and even within the United States itself. Because of the direct connection between Caracas and Tehran, efforts to contain trade with Iran are futile without cutting off the billions of dollars of legitimate U.S. trade with Venezuela, according to Manhattan District Attorney Robert Morganthau.[31] In June of 2015, Iran and Venezuela signed a series of agreements, complete with a $500 million line of credit. Included along with drugs and surgical equipment in the scope of the agreement was joint nanotechnology research.[32]

Just as Iran's Foreign Minister Javad Zarif was touring Venezuela in August 2016, the Brazilian press obtained a 2009 document in which the late Chavez approved the release of funds designated for the import of equipment for a gunpowder factory and the development of production plants for nitroglycerin and nitrocellulose.[33] These two elements are used in rocket propulsion.[34] This document sheds light on the fact that less than a year later, in October 2010, Chavez announced an initial study of nuclear capacity for his country, a move analysts believe could be largely one of cover for Iran's program which Venezuela has been supporting for several years.[35]

Nor is all of this limited to Venezuela. Iran is interested in Latin America generally, as they perceive it in some strategic sense as our soft underbelly. It will be important to watch, over the longer term, for this sort of cultural and ideological solidarity at the popular level between the traditional leftist, anti-globalist, and anti-Semitic forces of Venezuela and elsewhere in both the "Bolivarian" and the more status quo countries of Latin America with the radical Islamists of the Middle East. After all, the phenomenon of apparent confluence of interests and ideals is one that is not limited to Venezuela but could be – and no doubt is being – worked into a narrative of natural partnership between Latin Americanism and the Iranian face of Islamism. One thing is certain, if America allows itself to be seen as an adversary of Latin America, the more currency this narrative will have, in Venezuela and beyond. And the greater currency this narrative has, the more Venezuela's government can be expected to continue to be sympathetic to Islamist groups, and provide them with assistance and safe haven for their financial, narco-trafficking, and training activities in America's near abroad.

Endnotes

[1] Alberto Garrido, Las Guerras de Chavez (Rayuela: Taller de Ediciones, 2006), 17.

[2] Paul D. Taylor, ed., "Latin American Security Challenges: A Collaborative Inquiry from North and South," Naval War College Newport Paper no. 21, 2004.

[3] U.S. Department of the Treasury, Office of Public Affairs, "Treasury Designates Islamic Extremist, Two Companies Supporting Hezbollah in Triborder Area," June 10, 2004, http://www.treas.gov/press/releases/js1720.htm.

[4] Roger F. Noriega, Testimony before the U.S. House of Representatives Committee on Foreign Affairs Subcommittee on Terrorism, Nonproliferation, and Trade, March 20, 2013, http://www.aei.org/files/2013/03/20/-hezbollahs-strategic-shift-a-global-terrorist-threat_134945797264.pdf.

[5] "Countering Iran in the Western Hemisphere Act of 2012," H.R. 3783 (112th Congress, 2012), Sec 5-B-6.

[6] Arash Karami, "Post-nuclear deal, Iran looks to expand ties with Latin America," Al-Monitor, August 18, 2016, http://www.al-monitor.com/pulse/originals/2016/08/zarif-latin-america-cuba-venezuela-iran-economy.html.

[7] "Venezuela" in U.S. Department of State, Bureau of Democracy, Human Rights and Labor, 2011 Report on International Religious Freedom, September 2011, http://www.state.gov/j/drl/rls/irf/2011/index.htm.

[8] Ibid.

[9] Ibidem.

[10] For evidence of this claim, one only need look at a few of the overwhelmingly negative comments on Hezbollah Venezuela's website: http://hezboallahpartidoislamico.blogspot.es/1149260280/hezboallah-grupo-islamico-venezolano/ (in Spanish).

[11] Robert Young, Postcolonialism: An Historical Introduction (London: Blackwell Publishers, 2001), 2.

[12] The organization's website was previously located at http://groups.msn.com/AutonomiaIslamicaWayuu. It currently appears to be housed at http://autonomiaislamicawayuu.blogspot.com/.

[13] Manuel Torres Soriano, "La Fascinación por el éxito: Hezbollah en América Latina," Jihad Monitor, October 17, 2006.

[14] Ibid, 2.

[15] Gustavo Coronel, "Chávez Joins the Terrorists: His Path to Martyrdom," Venezuela Today, September 2, 2006.

[16] Gustavo Coronel, "The Hezbollah Venezuelan Metastasis," Venezuela Today, September 4, 2006, 3.

[17] Ibid; See also Hezbollah Venezuela, "Comunicado De Hezbollah Venezuela a Centro Simón," August 22, 2006, http://comunicadohezbollahacentrosimon.blogspot.com/2006/08/comunicado-de-hezbollah-latino-amrica.html.

[18] "Iran-Venezuela Ties Serve Strategic Aims," United Press International, August 14, 2009, http://www.upi.com/Top_News/Special/2009/08/14/Iran-Venezuela-ties-serve-strategic-aims/UPI-91201250266165.

[19] Ibid.
[20] "Chávez decorated in Iran; initials cooperation pacts," El Universal (Caracas), July 31, 2006, http://english.eluniversal.com/2006/07/31/en_pol_art_31A756133.shtml.
[21] Von C. Wergin and H. Stausberg, "Iran plant Bau einer Raketenstellung in Venezuela," Die Welt (Hamburg), November 25, 2010, http://www.welt.de/politik/ausland/article11219574/Iran-plant-Bau-einer-Raketenstellung-in-Venezuela.html; Von Clemens Wergin, "Iranische Raketenbasis in Venezuela in Planungsphase" Die Welt (Hamburg), May 15, 2011, http://www.welt.de/politik/ausland/article13366204/Iranische-Raketenbasis-in-Venezuela-in-Planungsphase.html.
[22] CNN Wire Staff, "U.S. knocks down report of Iran, Venezuela missile base," CNN, March 21, 2011, http://www.cnn.com/2011/WORLD/americas/05/21/venezuela.iran.missiles/.
[23] Roger F. Noriega, "Chávez's Secret Nuclear Program" Foreign Policy, October 5, 2010, http://www.foreignpolicy.com/files/fp_uploaded_documents/101004_0_Acuerdos_Ciencia_y_Tecnologia.pdf.
[24] "Iranian Delegation In Venezuela," Mathaba (London), November 17, 2008, http://mathaba.net/news/?x=611701.
[25] Robert M. Morgenthau, "The Emerging Axis Of Iran And Venezuela," Wall Street Journal, September 8, 2009, http://online.wsj.com/article/SB10001424052970203440104574400792835972018.html.
[26] Ibid.
[27] "Iran Raises Profile In Latin America," Washington Post, November 22, 2008.
[28] "Shipment of UAVs from Iran to Venezuela," State Department cable dated March 24, 2009, http://www.wikileaks.ch/cable/2009/03/09STATE28302.html; "Additional information on Shipment of UAVs from Iran to Venezuela," State Department cable dated April 14, 2009, http://wikileaks.org/cable/2009/04/09STATE36825.html.
[29] "Venezuela's President Wants to Marshal the Forces of Anti-Imperialism," The Economist, September 15, 2009, http://www.economist.com/displayStory.cfm?story_id=14444403.
[30] Brian Ellsworth, "Venezuela says Building Drones with Iran's Help", Reuters, June 14, 2012, http://www.reuters.com/article/2012/06/14/us-venezuela-iran-drone-idUSBRE85D14N20120614.
[31] Robert M. Morgenthau, "The Link between Iran and Venezuela: A Crisis in the Making?" Briefing before the Brookings Institution, Washington, DC, September 8, 2009.
[32] Aditya Tejas, "Venezuela, Iran Sign Economic Cooperation Deals; Venezuela Signs $500M Credit Line With Iran," International Business Times, June 2015, http://www.ibtimes.com/venezuela-iran-sign-economic-cooperation-deals-venezuela-signs-500m-credit-line-iran-1986665.

[33] "Chávez ajudou o Irã a burlar sanções da ONU, mostra document," Veja (Sao Paulo), http://veja.abril.com.br/mundo/chavez-ajudou-o-ira-a-burlar-sancoes-da-onu-mostra-documento/.

[34] Lisa Daftari, "New evidence Iran evaded sanctions, continued nuclear weapons development with Venezuela," The Foreign Desk, August 2016, http://www.foreigndesknews.com/breaking-news/new-evidence-iran-evaded-sanctions-continued-nuclear-weapons-development-venezuela/.

[35] Noreiga, "Chávez's Secret Nuclear Program."

Middle East and North Africa

COUNTRIES
Algeria
Bahrain
Egypt
Iraq
Islamic Republic of Iran
Israel
Jordan
Kuwait
Lebanon
Libya
Morocco
Palestinian Territories
Qatar
Saudi Arabia
Syria
Tunisia
United Arab Emirates
Yemen

ALGERIA

QUICK FACTS

Population: 40,263,711 (estimated July 2016)

Area: 2,381,741 sq km

Ethnic Groups: Arab-Berber 99%, European less than 1%

Religions: Muslim (official; predominantly Sunni) 99%, other (includes Christian and Jewish) <1%.

Government Type: Presidential Republic

GDP (official exchange rate): $168.3 billion (estimated 2015)

Map and Quick Facts courtesy of the CIA World Factbook (January 2017)

OVERVIEW

Algeria declared its independence from France in 1962. Since then, Islamist parties and armed groups have made up the major opposition to successive Algerian governments. Between 1991 and 1999, civil strife between violent Islamist extremists and security forces plagued Algeria and claimed over 150,000 lives. The majority of those killed were civilians. Despite the brutality of that conflict, however, Islamism still holds appeal for many in Algeria. The Algerian government's attempts at reconciliation in 1999 and again in 2005 have aided the decline of violent extremist groups, but have simultaneously legitimated and empowered political Islamism. Recent years have seen Islamism rise in the Algerian political sphere; Islamist parties multiplied and gained parliamentary seats in national elections. While these parties have of late diminished in stature and appeal, evidenced by their declining power and dismal electoral results, Islamist ideas and underlying social conservatism nonetheless remain widespread in Algeria.

Islamist Activity

The exact numbers of Islamist militants operating in any country are generally hard to discern. Algeria is no different, and estimates vary from around 300 and 1,000.[1] Many of these militants shift their affiliation between more established groups and splinter groups in the region—of which al-Qaeda in the Islamic Maghreb (AQIM) is one of the most significant.

GSPC/AQIM

The Salafist Group for Preaching and Combat (GSPC) in Algeria was a militant organization that focused on waging *jihad* against the Algerian government and trying to implement *sharia* there.[2] In 2006, the GSPC merged with al-Qaeda and in 2007 it renamed itself al-Qaeda in the Islamic Maghreb (AQIM). AQIM follows GSPC's basic tenet of resisting the Algerian government, but now as a part of al-Qaeda's global network rather than a solely domestic organization.[3] Since the rise of the Islamic State in 2013, AQIM has had to compete with it for influence in the Maghreb-Sahel region.

AQIM is primarily concentrated in the ethnically Kabylie region in eastern Algeria (where the GSPC originally established its headquarters), and in the Algerian desert along the Sahara-Sahel in northern Mali. However, the Algerian government's successful attacks in the Kabylie region have compelled AQIM to move into Algeria's southern territory and beyond its borders (northern Mali). Counterterrorism operations carried out by Algerian security forces have greatly reduced the number of fighters in the north of the country. However, AQIM's sporadic attacks have not abated.[4] In January 2013, AQIM militants attacked the In Amenas gas plant in southern Algeria. The attack resulted in the death of 40 staff members (mostly foreigners) of the gas plant and at least 29 militants.[5] AQIM assassinations of police and military officers likewise have been ongoing.[6]

By 2013, the number of victims of terrorism from disparate armed groups had decreased substantially, with 30 to 40 a month–a considerable drop from the so-called "black decade" (1992-1999), when the number had reached 1,000 per month.[7] In 2014, Algeria witnessed the second largest reduction in deaths caused by terrorism around the world (the lowest since 1993, when only 7 deaths occurred.)[8] In 2015, a total of 62 terrorist attacks took place, resulting in a couple dozen victims.[9] Security forces were quite successful in 2016 as they neutralized 350 terrorists, of whom 125 were killed and 225 arrested.[10] In February 2017 alone, the Armed Forces killed 19 extremist fighters and arrested nine.[11] Generally, Algerian security forces do not reveal the names of the groups that carry out these terrorists attacks; both AQIM and the so-called Islamic State have claimed responsibility for some of their operations. Other, smaller armed groups also claim responsibility for the sporadic attacks, but it is not clear how realistic the existence of these groups is. With the exception of AQIM, the current extremist groups operating in Algeria have limited means, no popular support, and little impact.

The income of AQIM comes mostly from smuggling, credit-card fraud, and car theft.[12] Kidnapping foreigners has also been used to finance AQIM's activities, since many countries, such as Switzerland, Austria, Germany, and Canada, France, Spain, and Italy, have agreed to pay ransoms for the release of their citizens. Algeria itself has had a consistent policy of not negotiating with terrorists, and has been pushing for international legislation to criminalize the payment of ransoms. Algeria has lobbied in the African Union, the United Nations, and in the Global Counterterrorism Forum (GCFT) to criminalize the payment of ransoms. In 2009, it managed to get the African Union to pass a resolution this matter which "strongly condemns the payment of ransoms to terrorist groups for hostages to be freed."[13] In fact, the country has strived to persuade the UN to adopt an analogous resolution on the payment of ransoms. Although not as strong as the AU's, UN Security Council

Resolution 1904 of 2009 contains provisions criminalizing such payments.[14] The lobbying at the UN for the passing of more constraining resolutions;[15] Algeria's activism on the question has been more successful at the GCTF.[16] In January 2014, the UN Security Council adopted "Resolution 2133 (2014), Calling upon States to Keep Ransom Payments, Political Concessions from Benefiting Terrorist."[17]

Both the Movement for the Oneness and Jihad in West Africa (MUJAO) and AQIM also are known to receive considerable amounts of money from drug trafficking.[18] Both groups have sought various sources of funding in order to purchase weapons and to invest in some lucrative sectors, and established links with drug traffickers as a way of increasing their revenues. Thus, although AQIM does not traffic drugs directly, it provides safe passage for smugglers through the desert. It also provides protection to the drug traffickers in exchange for large sums of money. AQIM has also provided storage facilities for drugs in exchange for payment.[19]

The Algerian state has initiated a relatively effective crackdown against AQIM in recent years.[20] The crackdown has relied on support from the local population, which has helped thwart kidnappings and has demonstrated a growing mobilization against AQIM's operations in certain parts of the country. State security operations have continued to this day, with notable results. In 2012, for instance, state security forces neutralized more than 400 militants, killing nearly 200 of them, including a few emirs (leaders), and arresting the rest. Others surrendered the same year.[21] These successes are attributable to greater intelligence now possessed by the state (amassed from Islamists who surrendered or repented, advanced databases, and so forth), as well as to the population's collaboration with the security forces; villagers denounce suspicious movements of individuals believed to be terrorists, thus prompting the deployment of soldiers in the suspected area, a trend that has continued into 2017. In February 2017, security forces launched important antiterrorist operations following information the villagers had provided.

Meanwhile, the presence in Algeria of al-Qaeda's main competitor, the Islamic State, is minimal, in spite of IS's repeated attempts to establish cells in the country. Algerian security forces eliminated the most important IS cell, *Jund al Khalifah* group, an AQIM splinter faction that pledged allegiance to IS in September 2014. Security forces have also attempted to destroy another cell, likewise an AQIM splinter faction based in the eastern city of Skikda that pledged allegiance to IS in spring 2015. A lesser-known group, the *al-Ghuraba Brigade*, which operates near the eastern city of Constantine (yet another splinter group from AQIM), has also allied with IS, also poses a security risk. Al-Ansar Brigade and Humat al-Dawa are believed to have joined IS, but security forces prevented them from launching any attacks. In spite of the media attention they elicit, these cells are very small and their attacks have not been lethal. The latest illustration is the failed suicide attack on 27 February 2017 against a police station in the eastern city of Constantine, an attack for which IS claimed responsibility.[22] In sum, the terrorist groups in Algeria are very small for the most part and their influence among the population is insignificant, unlike what occurred throughout the 1990s.

Political Parties: FIS, MSP, Nahda, MRN, and the Small Islamist Formations

The emergence of Islamist political parties in Algeria is a comparatively recent phenomenon.[23] Religious political parties only became legal after the regime consented to political liberalization, prompted by bloody riots in October 1988. Most of the Islamist parties born in the period between 1989 and 1991 emerged out of a heterogeneous Islamist movement that took root in the 1960s. The most powerful and radical of them was the Islamic Salvation Front (FIS), which was banned in March 1992 following its overwhelming victory in the first round of the legislative elections the previous December. Notwithstanding FIS' popularity (it won overwhelming victories in the 1990 municipal elections and in the 1991 legislative elections), its impressive organization, and its capacity to mobilize large segments of society, the authorities banned the group because of its radical ideology and the threat it purportedly posed to the state and society. Although the FIS is defunct today, its influence has not vanished. Some of its members joined the still-legal Islamist parties and/or voted for them during elections, while others joined the multitude of armed groups that have fought the state since the 1990s.

Today, numerous legal Islamist parties remain active on the political scene: the Movement for Society and Peace (MSP), the Movement for Islamic Renaissance (*Nahda*), and its offshoot, the Movement for National Reform (MRN), and the recent ones legalized before the May 2012 legislative elections, namely, the Party for Liberty and Justice (PLJ), the Front for Justice and Development (FJD - *El Adala*), the Front for

New Algeria (FAN), and the Front for Change (FC).[24] All endorse the eventual application of *sharia* law. But, unlike the FIS, which wished to immediately implement it, these parties (the MSP in particular) seek a gradual implementation of Islamic principles.

The MSP, the largest legal Islamist party in Algeria, was created in 1990 as the Movement for Islamic Society/HAMAS, but changed its name to conform to the 1996 constitution, which forbids religious political expression. The group belonged to the "presidential alliance," a conservative mixture of nationalist, Islamist, and technocratic parties. In early January 2012, the MSP withdrew from the presidential alliance, without however pulling its four ministers out of the government. In March 2012, the MSP, with El Islah and Ennahda, formed the Green Alliance. The three parties ran on the same ticket in the country's subsequent legislative election. However, the Green Alliance did quite poorly in the 2012 legislature, garnering only 48 seats out of an expanded field of 462.

Nahda split in 1999 when its charismatic founding leader, Abdallah Djaballah, created yet another party, the Movement for National Reform (MRN or *Islah*). The MRN did very well in the 2002 local elections, coming in ahead of both the MSP and *Nahda*, after which it demanded a ban on the import of alcoholic beverages in 2004. However, Djaballah did quite poorly in the 2004 presidential election, receiving only 5 percent of the votes.[25] The party has undergone further crises, and it is not clear what influence either *Nahda* or MSN now have—for, like most Algerian political parties, the fate of the parties is often linked to the individual that founded them. In the 2007 legislative election, the two parties garnered only five and three parliamentary seats, respectively. It is doubtful whether these parties will gain many votes in the upcoming legislative election in May 2017. For now, Islamist parties are contemplating the possibility of building an opposition bloc in the hope of doing better than in the previous election in 2012.

The three older parties had worked with the Algerian government, and abided by its constraints on political participation. In 2009, all three endorsed the candidacy of sitting President Abdelaziz Bouteflika for a third term in office.[26] That cooperation was a product of the comparative decline in popularity experienced by Islamist political parties in recent years, as well as their internal turmoil. For example, the MSP split into two factions in 2009 due to the loss of popularity of its president, Aboudjera Soltani, who served as a minister under various governments. Many members of the party did not agree with Soltani's unconditional support for President Abdelaziz Bouteflika, and in June 2009 orchestrated a revolt inside the MSP. Following the dissensions and eventual split of the party, the MSP is no longer the force it represented. Algerian Islamist parties have lost their appeal.[27]

However, the electoral decline of Algeria's Islamist political parties should not be interpreted as a decline of Islamism in the country writ large. To the contrary, social conservatism has grown, making it possible to countenance a revival of support for these factions. And radical parties, such as the Front of the Salafist Islamic Sahwah [Renaissance] propagate extremist ideas.

ISLAMISM AND SOCIETY

Islam in Algeria is not simply the main religion of the population; it constitutes the primary foundation of identity and culture. Islamic beliefs and practices regulate social behavior and, to a large extent, govern social relations. While the socioeconomic failure of the 1980s provided a trigger for the emergence of Islamism in Algerian society, its doctrinal aspects derive at least in part from the crisis of identity generated by 132 years of colonial rule. France's brutal colonialism served to undermine the principal local religious institutions: mosques and religious schools were turned into churches or even bars, religious lands were expropriated, and Islamic culture was openly held up to be inferior to Christian/Western civilization. Because French colonialists treated the native population and values with contempt, Algerians as a whole turned to Islam to establish their cultural identity. The country's nationalist movement used Arab-Islamic values as symbols for popular mobilization against colonialism. Contemporary Islamists often claim that they are the legitimate offspring of that effort.

Today, Islamism is still prevalent in Algeria. However, the overwhelming majority of Algerians do not support armed groups, as many did in the early and mid-1990s. The brutal massacres that armed groups committed in 1996-1999 alienated large segments of the population, and authorities continue to progressively dismantle the small number of die-hard support groups. Currently, only a few marginalized youths are attracted to groups like AQIM or the Islamic State. Rather, Islamism today has become a form of social conservativism with no institutional or partisan attachment.[28]

Islamist parties did rather poorly in the 2007 legislative elections and even worse in the legislative election in May 2012. The municipal elections held on November 29, 2012, confirmed the regression of Islamist parties in Algeria.[29] This decline was already perceptible in the April 2009 presidential election, during which the Islamist candidates were marginalized, with the *Nahda* candidate Djahid Younsi garnering a mere 1.3 percent of the votes and others even less. Based on this analysis, and the recent results at the polls, it is possible to conclude that Islamism, at least in its political form, is appealing to, at most, two percent of the electorate.[30]

Therefore, while it is hard to gauge the present popularity of Islamism as a social and political movement, what is certain is that the institutional parties as well as the armed groups have lost the appeal that they had throughout the 1990s and even in the early 2000s. One can advance four reasons for such decline: 1) the legacy of the civil strife which left more than 150,000 dead, mostly innocent civilians, 2) the relative loss of legitimacy on the part of armed groups like AQIM, which resorted to barbaric methods to impose their will upon the population; the methods were criticized by the leadership of Al-Qaida central itself because their use could alienate the population and lose its support 3) the relative success of the 2005 National Reconciliation, which led to the surrender of thousands of armed militants and the extension of amnesty to numerous Islamists, and 4) general disappointment with Islamist political parties, which are perceived as opportunistic and self-serving.

ISLAMISM AND THE STATE

In 1989, Algerian authorities, in violation of a constitution that forbade the existence of parties based on religion, legalized the radical Islamist party, the Islamic Salvation Front (FIS). A front made up of a variety of forces, including Arab alumni of the Afghan *jihad*, the FIS eventually became one of the most potent armed groups against the state. In June 1990, the government organized nationwide municipal elections, the first pluralist elections in the country, and then cancelled them when it appeared that the FIS would win. It cancelled the election on the grounds that the victory of the FIS would have put an end to the democratic process altogether. The government banned the FIS shortly thereafter—and imprisoned its leaders— which resulted in a crisis of the state. The civil strife that ensued not only pitted the security forces against armed groups but also spilled over to ravage the civilian population, notably in the horrible collective massacres of 1997 and 1998.

The intensity of the armed Islamist insurrection in the 1990s took Algeria's security forces by surprise. The authorities never envisioned the remarkable degree of organization among the *jihadist* groups, or the significant resources available to them. The level of unrestrained destruction that the armed groups inflicted upon the state structures, personnel, intellectuals, journalists, moderate Islamists, and the various strata of society was intense, such that some spoke of the demise of the Algerian state.[31]

Aware of the near-collapse of the state and its institutions, civilian and military authorities took measures to safeguard the state. The first action was to remove elected Islamist officials from the municipalities and replace them with state-appointed officials. Armed Islamists eventually assassinated many of those replacements. The state also decided to arm thousands of people, many of them unemployed youths, throughout the country to serve as auxiliary forces for regular troops. These security agents, known as *gardes communaux*, played a critical role in fighting Islamist insurgents.

To protect public infrastructures, the authorities forced companies to create specially trained security services (known as the services *de sûreté interne d'établissements*) within those organizations. According to Algerian officials, within one year of their creation, the existence of such services reduced the number of acts of sabotage against social and economic structures by 75 percent.[32] The state also created the *détachements de protection et de sûreté*, brigades entrusted with the protection of industrial plants. Because *jihadists* targeted isolated villages and the suburbs of most cities, the authorities also set up the *groupes de légitime défense* (GLDs), which, though sometime deficient, did much to reduce terrorist attacks on innocent civilians.

Moreover, the government increased the size of the police force and provided new recruits with more efficient antiterrorist training, both in Algeria and abroad.[33] The police force acquired some adapted equipment imported from the former Soviet bloc, South Africa, and elsewhere. The state also took measures to thwart the financing of the insurgency. It incorporated a series of decisions, notably "*La lutte contre le blanchiment* (LAB) *et contre le financement du terrorisme* (CFT)," into the 2003 Finance Act (Loi de Finance)[34] to combat the funding of terrorist groups and money laundering. These laws allow authorities to trace the financial sources of the terrorist networks through numerous methods, from the freezing of suspicious assets and to the use of intelligence procedures to prevent suspicious financial operations.[35]

The 2005 Law on National Reconciliation offered clemency measures and/or pardon for those Islamist fighters who surrendered to the state. In October 2010, authorities declared that 7,500 armed insurgents had surrendered.[36] The law was relatively successful. However, it did not provide provision through which to seek justice against Islamists or members of security forces who committed crimes in the bloody decade of the 1990s. As the fates of thousands of people who were disappeared during the conflict are still unknown, this lack of closure rankles many in the population.

The Algerian government cooperates closely with the governments of countries in the Sahel, such as Mali and Niger in its counterterrorism efforts. The most noteworthy pursuit is its participation in the U.S.-led Trans-Saharan Counter-Terrorism Partnership to fight terrorism in the Maghreb-Sahel region.[37] Algeria has also sought to create a quasi-collective security community with the Sahel states, namely, Mali, Mauritania, and Niger, the so called "core countries," in order to counter the terrorist threat in the region. Unfortunately, the fragility of those states undermined the potential for a General Staff Joint-Operations Committee (CEMOC) and the Algiers-based Joint-Intelligence Centre (CRC).[38] But, like other initiatives in the region, CEMOC is a moribund alliance due to the lack of trust among the members, as well as foreign interference.

A war has been ongoing in northern Mali since January 2013, and Algeria has played a small but significant role. It has allowed French warplanes to overfly its territory to dislodge AQIM, the MUJAO and other groups, such as the Tuareg *Ansar el Dine*, from the cities they had occupied. It likewise has closed its long border with Mali, to prevent *jihadists* from fleeing the conflict and seeking refuge on Algerian territory. Algeria has also helped broker a deal between the various Tuareg factions and between those factions and the central government in Bamako.[39] In July 2015, the Tuareg factions and Bamako signed a peace deal; the deal so far has been unsuccessful. Peace has not been restored and the groups continue their in the persistent absence of the state in the north of the country.[40] Furthermore, Algeria is helping Tunisia protect its borders against assaults from IS and has deployed thousands of troops along both its Tunisian and Libya borders. Algeria has thereby become a key player in the war on terrorism.

Endnotes

[1] Author's interview with Algerian military officers, Algiers, January and September 2016. See also, Hebba Selim, "Des chiffres très précis sur le nombre de terroristes en Algérie: 304 dont 73 à Jund Al-Khilafa (Journal)," HuffPost Algérie, May 3, 2016, http://www.huffpostmaghreb.com/2016/05/03/terrorisme-effectifs-aqmi-jound-al-khilafa_n_9826062.html

[2] Zachary Laub and Jonathan Masters, "Al-Qaeda in the Islamic Maghreb (AQIM)," Council on Foreign Relations, March 27, 2015, http://www.cfr.org/terrorist-organizations-and-networks/al-qaeda-islamic-maghreb-aqim/p12717.

[3] Zachary Laub and Jonathan Masters, "Al-Qaeda in the Islamic Maghreb (AQIM)," Council on Foreign Relations, March 27, 2015, http://www.cfr.org/terrorist-organizations-and-networks/al-qaeda-islamic-maghreb-aqim/p12717.

[4] Djallil Lounnas and Yahia H. Zoubir, "L'Algérie face à l'arc des menaces: Quelle stratégie?" Stratégie et Sécurité (forthcoming16); Stefano Maria Torelli, "Jihadism and Counterterrorism Policy in Algeria: New Responses to New Challenges," Terrorism Monitor, Volume 11, Issue 19, October 7, 2013, https://jamestown.org/program/jihadism-and-counterterrorism-policy-in-algeria-new-responses-to-new-challenges/.

[5] "In Amenas inquest: British victims of Algeria attack," BBC News, November 28, 2014, http://www.bbc.com/news/uk-29127935.

[6] R.P., "Deux militaires et un civil tués--L'inquiétant faux barrage de Aïn Defla," El-Watan, November 16, 2016, http://www.elwatan.com/actualite/l-inquietant-faux-barrage-de-ain-defla-16-11-2016-332966_109.php.

[7] A.F., "Me Merouane Azzi à propos du dossier Réconciliation Nationale: 'Le nombre de victimes du terrorisme décroît,'" Liberté (Algiers), March 4, 2013, http://www.liberte-algerie.com/actualite/le-nombre-de-victimes-du-terrorisme-decroit-120259 .

[8] "Global Terrorism Index 2015—Measuring and Understanding Terrorism," Global Terrorism Index (Sidney, Australia: Institute for Economics and Peace, 2016), p. 19, http://economicsandpeace.org/wp-content/uploads/2015/11/Global-Terrorism-Index-2015.pdf.

[9] "Country Reports on Terrorism 2015," United States Department of State, June 2016, http://www.state.gov/documents/organization/258249.pdf.

[10] [10] El-Djeich, No. 641, December 2016, p. 20, available at: http://www.mdn.dz/site_principal/sommaire/revue/images/EldjeichDec2016Fr.pdf.

[11] Hakima Hadjam, "Lutte antiterroriste : 19 terroristes abattus et 9 autres arrêtés en février," 13 March 2017, http://www.tsa-algerie.com/20170313/lutte-antitteroriste-19-terroristes-abattus-9-autres-arretes-fevrier/.

[12] Author's interviews with security officials, Algiers, Algeria, September 2010, October 2011, and January 2016.

[13] African Union, "Decisions and Declarations – Assembly of the African Union Thirteenth Ordinary Session 1–3 July 2009 Sirte," Great Socialist People's Libyan Arab Jamahiriya Assembly/AU/Dec. 243–267 (XIII) Rev.1 Assembly/AU/Decl.1– 5(XIII). https://au.int/web/sites/default/files/decisions/9560-assembly_en_1_3_july_2009_auc_thirteenth_ordinary_session_decisions_declarations_message_congratulations_motion_0.pdf

[14] Security Council, SC/9825. Security Council Amends United Nations Al-Qaida/Taliban Sanctions Regime, Authorizes Appointment of Ombudsperson to Handle Delisting Issues, 17 December 2009, available at http://www.un.org/News/Press/docs/2009/sc9825.doc.htm

[15] A.B. S., "L'Algérie s'oppose aux paiements des rançons," Algérie-Focus, September 29, 2012, http://www.algerie-focus.com/2012/09/lalgerie-soppose-aux-paiements-des-rancons/

[16] Global Counterterrorism Forum, https://www.thegctf.org/Cross-Cutting-Initiatives/Kidnapping-for-Ransom

[17] https://www.un.org/press/en/2014/sc11262.doc.htm

[18] Mohamed Mokeddem. Al-Qaïda au Maghreb islamique-Contrebande au nom de l'islam (Algiers: Casbah Editions, 2010), esp. 37-68.

[19] Brisard, "Terrorism Financing in North Africa," op. cit.; "Al-Qaeda in the Islamic Maghreb and the Africa-to-Europe Narco-Trafficking Connection," Jamestown Foundation Terrorism Monitor 8, iss. 43, November 24, 2010, http://www.jamestown.org/single/?no_cache=1&tx_ttnews[tt_news]=37207.

[20] In 2009, AQIM ambushes led to a death toll of 120 among security forces, who began carrying out major and effective counter-offensives against AQIM troops and support networks, leading to a reduction of AQIM attacks.

[21] Brahim Takheroubt, "L'ANP fait saigner Al Qaîda," L'Expression (Algiers), January 3, 2013, http://www.lexpressiondz.com/actualite/166638-l-anp-fait-saigner-al-qaida.html.

[22] Zineb Hamdi, Daech revendique la tentative d'attentat kamikaze déjoué à Constantine, TSA-Tout Sur L'Algérie, 27 February 2017, http://www.tsa-algerie.com/20170227/daech-revendique-tentative-dattentat-kamikaze-dejoue-a-constantine/

[23] Yahia H. Zoubir, "Islamist Political Parties in Contemporary Algeria," in Ibrahim M. Abu-Rabi', ed., The Contemporary Arab Reader on Political Islam (London: Pluto Press/University of Alberta Press, 2010).

[24] Ahmed Aghrout and Yahia H. Zoubir, "Algeria: Reforms without change?" In, Yahia H. Zoubir and Gregory White, North African Politics: Change and Continuity (London & New York: Routledge, 2016), pp. 145-155..

[25] For a detailed analysis, see Yahia H. Zoubir and Louisa Dris-Aït-Hamadouche, "L'islamisme en Algérie: institutionnalisation du politique et déclin du militaire," Maghreb-Machrek no. 188 (Summer 2006), 63-86.

[26] Louisa Aït-Hamadouche and Yahia H. Zoubir, "The Fate of Political Islam in Algeria," in Bruce Maddy-Weitzman and Daniel Zisenwine, eds., The Maghrib in the New Century-Identity, Religion, and Politics (Gainesville: University of Florida Press, 2007), 103-131.

[27] Saïd Boucetta, "Après L'abdication des Tunisiens, l'effacement des Marocains et la dérive des Turcsles islamistes algériens dans la galère," L'Expression (Algiers), November 5, 2016, http://www.lexpressiondz.com/actualite/253382-les-islamistes-algeriens-dans-la-galere.html

[28] Rachid Tlemçani, "Les islamistes échappent aujourd'hui à tout contrôle institutionnel ou partisan," El Watan (Algiers), April, 23, 2009 , http://www.elwatan.com/Les-islamistes-echappent-aujourd.

[29] The results are available in "Elections locales : le ministère algérien de l'Intérieur rend public les résultats de chaque parti," SIWEL, December 1, 2012, http://www.siwel.info/Elections-locales-le-ministere-algerien-de-l-Interieur-rend-public-les-resultats-de-chaque-parti_a4325.html.

[30] See Louisa Dris-Aït-Hamadouche, "Régime et islamistes en Algérie: un échange politique asymétrique?" Maghreb-Machrek (Paris) no. 200 (Summer 2009), 43.

[31] Graham Fuller, Algeria: The Next Fundamentalist State? (Santa Barbara: RAND, 1996).

[32] Yahia H. Zoubir and Louisa Aït-Hamadouche, "Penal Reform in Algeria," in Chris Ferguson and Jeffrey O. Isima, eds., Providing Security for People: Enhancing Security through Police, Justice and Intelligence Reform in Africa (London: Global Facilitation Network for Security Sector Reform, 2004), 75-84.

[33] Ibid.

[34] Abbas Aït-Hamlat, "Terrorisme au Maghreb-Al-Qaîda menace et l'UE resserre l'étau, " L'Expression (Algiers), September 24, 2008, http://www.lexpressiondz.com/article/2/2008-09-24/56544.html.

[35] See "Lutte contre le financement du terrorisme et le blanchiment d'argent. La fin du secret bancaire pour l'argent suspect," Le Quotidien d'Oran, January 8, 2003; See also Algeria's National Report, "Mise en œuvre de la Résolution 1373 (2001) Adoptée par le Conseil de Sécurité des Nations-Unies le 28 septembre 2001," which describes at length the actions taken by the Algerian government to implement UN Resolution 1373 on terrorism. See also Yazid F. "Algérie: Le Gouvernement durcit la législation sur les changes, " Ministère de l'Economie et des Finances, Cellule nationale du traitement des informations financières, September 13, 2010, http://www.centif.ci/news.php?id_news=67.

[36] Souhil B. "Bilan de la réconciliation nationale-7500 terroristes ont bénéficié des dispositions de la charte, " El Watan (Algiers), October 4, 2010, http://www.elwatan.com/actualite/7500-terroristes-ont-beneficie-des-dispositions-de-la-charte-04-10-2010-93047_109.php.

[37] Yahia H. Zoubir, "The United States and Maghreb-Sahel Security," International Affairs 85, no. 5 (Fall 2009), 977-995.

[38] Yahia H. Zoubir, "The Sahara-Sahel Quagmire: Regional and International Ramifications," Mediterranean Politics, 17:3 (November 2012), 452-458.

[39] See, "Accord pour la paix et la réconciliation au Mali issu du processus d'Alger," http://photos.state.gov/libraries/mali/328671/peace-accord-translations/1-accord-paix-et-reconciliation-francais.pdf. See also, Benjamin Roger, "Accord d'Alger pour la paix au Mali : le plus dur reste à faire," Jeune Afrique, 1 July 2015, http://www.jeuneafrique.com/mag/241413/politique/accord-dalger-pour-la-paix-mali-le-plus-dur-reste-a-faire/

[40] Selma Mihoubi, "Mali: un an après la signature de l'Accord d'Alger, quel avenir pour le Nord?" Jeune Afrique, 20 juin 2016, http://www.jeuneafrique.com/334516/politique/mali-paix-ans-apres-signature-de-laccord-dalger/

BAHRAIN

QUICK FACTS

Population: 1,378,904 (estimated WHEN)

Area: 760 sq km

Ethnic Groups: Bahraini 46%, non-Bahraini 54%

Religions: Muslim (Sunni and Shi'a) 70.3%, Christian 14.5%, other 15.2%

Government Type: Constitutional Monarchy

GDP (official exchange rate): $31.82 billion (estimated 2015)

Quick Facts courtesy of the CIA World Factbook (January 2017)

OVERVIEW

Bahrain has traditionally been something of an anomaly among the Arab states of the Persian Gulf. While its ruling al-Khalifa family and as much as 30 percent of its population are Sunni Muslims, a substantial majority of its citizens are Shi'ites. One of the first major oil exporters in the region, it was also the first of the Gulf "oil sheikhdoms" to face significant depletion of its petroleum reserves and the need to develop a non-resource-based economy. Further, although it has never been close to qualifying as a truly free country, Bahrain stands apart from other Gulf states in its relatively high degree of social and cultural openness: the sale and consumption of alcohol are permitted; discos, movie theaters, and labor unions are allowed; freedom of worship is respected; the press was, until recently, somewhat free; the NGO sector is active (albeit regulated and constrained); and, at times, there has even been a significant—albeit limited—degree of democracy. However, freedom of the press, latitude for NGOs to operate, and what elements of democracy existed in the past are all currently under threat.[1]

While political parties are officially banned in Bahrain, an assortment of "political societies," most of them sectarian and Islamist, field slates of candidates for legislative elections, and in general function as political parties in all but name. The royal family has attempted to preserve Bahrain's stability (and their rule) by pitting Shi'ites against Sunnis and Islamists against secularists, and until the onset of the "Arab Spring" this strategy generally worked rather well.

Islamism in Bahrain has traditionally maintained an almost exclusively domestic focus, largely directed at confronting economic and morality issues through political action rather than violence. There are indications, however, that this relatively peaceful type of Islamism may be giving way, at least in part, to more violent forms: while in the past only a few Bahrainis traveled overseas to join in jihad, *and some others were involved in providing financial or logistical support for al-Qaeda, there are now accusations that Bahrainis have joined ISIS, received combat training, and attempted to form local terrorist cells.[2] Shi'ite attacks on Bahraini security forces also show signs of increasing sophistication.[3] While the presence of the U.S. Fifth Fleet in Bahrain would appear to make the country an attractive target for anti-American terrorism, neither Bahrain's government nor its traditional Islamists appear ready to condone or facilitate such attacks. However, if ISIS succeeds in creating a local infrastructure in Bahrain, U.S. facilities and personnel could find themselves at risk.*

Sadly, since the "Arab Spring" protests began in February 2011, Bahrain has become less of a happy exception and more of a typical example of Middle Eastern despotism. The Bahraini government's response to the protests often consisted of brutal repression, coupled with occasional promises of a reconciliation dialogue that became less and less convincing over the succeeding years.[4,5] As of late 2016, Bahrain seems locked in an uneasy stasis, with attitudes among both Sunni and Shi'ite residents hardened to such an extent that it is difficult to imagine how the country can resume even the semblance of a functioning democracy. Bahrain's domestic impasse, along with events in nearby countries, will strengthen the appeal and extremism of both Sunni and Shi'a Islamist forces. And despite the country's tiny size, the failure of major powers and international organizations to exert effective pressure on the Bahraini government to reform has had significant regional implications.

Islamist Activity

Bahrain's majority Shi'ite population is significantly poorer than its Sunni minority counterpart, and complains of discrimination in employment (particularly with regard to senior-level government and security-service jobs—a significant issue given the government's dominant status as an employer, not to mention the importance such jobs have in influencing the nature of life in Bahrain), housing, immigration policy, and government services. Accordingly, the Shi'ite opposition—which is almost entirely Islamist in character—has an agenda largely based around the attempt to redress these inequalities, in addition to more traditional Islamist goals such as the imposition of *sharia* law. The political and economic goals of the Shi'ite opposition include:

- Genuine democracy, in which the Shi'ite community, as the majority population, would have a much greater say in legislating and setting policy. This would necessitate the rewriting of Bahrain's constitution, as well as revising an electoral-district system that favors Sunni candidates.[6]

- The dismantling, or at least a substantial weakening, of Bahrain's internal-security apparatus, and the release of political prisoners.

- Economic justice, including equality of opportunity in employment and equal provision of government services.

- Equal access to positions of authority in the government bureaucracy and the military/security services.

- An end to Bahrain's policy of facilitating Sunni immigration, which is perceived as a governmental effort to reduce or eliminate the Shi'ite demographic advantage. (Participants in the February 2011 demonstrations noted that many of the security personnel confronting them were immigrants from other Arab countries, and even Urdu-speaking Pakistanis, who had been granted Bahraini citizenship as an inducement to serve in the Bahraini security services.)[7]

- Traditional Islamist moral and social issues, such as the elimination of alcohol, prostitution, and other evils from the kingdom, the application of *sharia* law, etc.

It is worth noting that most Bahraini Shi'ites are adherents of the *Akhbari* school of Twelver Shi'ism, as opposed to Iranian Shi'ites (and most Iraqi Shi'ites), who are members of the more common *Usuli* Twelver faction. Among other differences, *Akhbaris* believe that while clerics can and should advise political leaders, they should not seek or be given direct political power. As *Akhbaris*, Bahraini Shi'ites traditionally claimed that they were loyal to the state and to its ruling family, seeking change within the system rather than wanting to overthrow it.[8] The Bahraini Shi'ite community does not have its own *marja* ("source of emulation") or any other religious figure of sufficient stature to constitute a Khomeini-style threat to the Bahraini establishment. However, the Bahraini government's heavy-handed response to Shi'ite protests and political activism has significantly radicalized Shi'ite political discourse, to the extent that overt calls for the overthrow of the monarchy are now common.[9]

Despite the Shi'ite community's past assertions of loyalty to Bahrain and its governing family (if not to its Constitution, which provides some semblance of democracy but effectively leaves the monarchy and the Sunni minority in firm control of the country), many Bahraini Sunnis have long accused the Shi'ites of being suspiciously close, culturally and politically, to Iran; the fact that Bahraini Shi'ite clerics are often trained in Iran adds some credibility to this accusation. Shi'ites have often responded by pointing out that many Bahraini Sunnis have just as much cultural connection to Iran, and that quite a few of these Sunnis in fact speak Farsi, rather than Arabic, at home. The ongoing government repression of Bahraini Shi'ites, as well as Bahrain's participation in the Saudi-led campaign against the Shi'ite Houthi in Yemen, have increased the community's identification with Iran, as well as Iranians' feelings of solidarity with Bahraini Shi'ites.[10]

The Bahraini government and others in the Sunni elite, as well as outside commentators concerned about Iranian influence in the region, have repeatedly claimed that Shi'ite unrest in Bahrain is the product of Iranian scheming, aided by allies and proxies such as Syria and Hezbollah. At first glance, such accusations are plausible: Iran is certainly not averse to meddling in other countries' affairs, and Iranian officials occasionally reassert their country's historical claim on Bahrain as Iranian territory.[11] However, little to no concrete, convincing evidence has ever been produced to back these claims of Iranian interference; and neutral observers have pointed out that Shi'ite unrest can be quite adequately explained by the genuine grievances of Bahraini Shi'ites.[12] The protests that began in February 2011 did not strengthen the case for an Iranian conspiracy to destabilize Bahrain; nothing in the protestors' goals, capabilities, or tactics at that time was inconsistent with what would be expected from an entirely domestic movement.[13] The use of more sophisticated explosives in recent Shi'ite attacks does, however, strengthen the case for Iranian involvement, if not instigation.[14]

Ultimately, as long as Bahrain's Shi'ites are kept relatively powerless, there is no way to validate their claims of loyalty to the country and its al-Khalifa rulers; and no matter how enthusiastically Shi'ite demonstrators wave Bahraini flags, many Bahraini Sunnis will continue to believe that the country's Shi'ites are, at best, a potential pro-Iranian fifth column. Even if Bahrain's Shi'ites are sincere in their expressions of patriotism, there is no question that, should they achieve significant political power, Iran will view Bahrain as "low-hanging fruit" and likely attempt to gain their allegiance;[15] In any case, the Bahraini government seems intent on doing everything in its power to destroy whatever loyalty the country's Shi'ites still have to the ruling regime.

Shi'ite Organizations

The most prominent Bahraini Shi'ite political "society" is the *al-Wefaq* National Islamic Society (*Jam'iyat al-Wifāq al-Watanī al-Islāmīyah*, also known as the Islamic National Accord Association), led by Qom-educated cleric Sheikh Ali Salman, with at least 1,500 active members.[16] (Salman himself is considered a "mid-level" cleric. Bahrain's most prominent Shi'a cleric, Ayatollah Isa Qassim, himself a disciple of Iraqi Grand Ayatollah Ali al-Sistani, is generally considered *al-Wefaq's* spiritual leader, although this is not an official position; in 2005 he publicly endorsed the group's decision to register as a "political society" and enter the Council of Representatives.[17]) After boycotting the 2002 elections to protest the new constitution's failure to provide a fully democratic constitutional monarchy, *al-Wefaq* decided to compete in the 2006 elections, and scored a resounding success: out of 17 candidates fielded by the group, 16 won their districts outright in the first round of voting (and the 17th candidate won his seat in a second-round run-off), making *al-Wefaq* by far the largest bloc in the Council of Representatives.[18] The group repeated this success in the 2010 elections, winning all 18 seats it contested; and were the Bahraini electoral system not gerrymandered to favor Sunni candidates, there is little question that, given the country's demographics, *al-Wefaq* would have easily won a commanding majority of the Council's 40 seats.[19]

Until the 2011 Arab Spring protests and the government's violent response to them, *al-Wefaq* had consistently positioned itself as a loyal opposition, working to achieve equality for Bahraini Shi'ites while maintaining allegiance to Bahrain and its monarchy, if not to the current Constitution and Cabinet. This stance has since largely evaporated. All 18 *al-Wefaq* members of the Council of Representatives resigned in protest in early 2011, and the group's leaders initially refused to enter a dialogue with the government until Prime Minister Khalifa al-Khalifa, perceived to be the primary driving force behind the marginalization of Bahraini Shi'ites, was replaced.[20] *Al-Wefaq*, partly in response to American and British persuasion, did agree to participate in a government-organized "national consensus dialogue" that began in July 2011; but the group's representatives walked out about a week later, frustrated at the allocation of only 25 out of 300 seats to the opposition, and the failure of the "dialogue" effectively to address Shi'ite grievances.[21]

Al-Wefaq, along with the rest of the opposition, boycotted the September-October 2011 by-election called to fill the seats it had vacated.[22] Protests were violently suppressed,[23] and, despite government claims backed by some rather odd mathematics,[24] the vast majority of Shi'ite voters obeyed calls to boycott the vote.[25] With no opposition representation, the Council of Representatives could no longer claim to provide even a skewed representation of the citizens of Bahrain. Matters did not improve with the next elections in 2014, when *Al-Wefaq*, along with other opposition groups, boycotted the vote.[26]

In 2016, the government significantly escalated its conflict with *al-Wefaq*, first suspending its activities and freezing its funds, and then in July ordering the organization dissolved and its assets turned over to the national treasury.[27] Ayatollah Isa Qassim was accused of financial misdeeds[28] and stripped of his citizenship,[29] and Sheikh Ali Salman and other leaders of the group were imprisoned.[30] Most recently, Salman's prison sentence (which had previously been increased from four to nine years—the charge being "inciting hatred, promoting disobedience and insulting public institutions"[31]) was overturned, and he will face retrial for "inciting hatred and calling for forceful regime change."[32] The U.S. and other Western powers condemned the suppression of *al-Wefaq*, but Bahraini authorities were unmoved.[33]

Al-Wefaq's main competition for the loyalty of Bahraini Shi'ites is the *Haq* Movement for Liberty and Democracy, founded in 2005 by a group consisting mostly of *al-Wefaq's* more radical leaders, who objected to *al-Wefaq's* decision to participate in the 2006 elections and thus grant an appearance of legitimacy to Bahrain's quasi-democratic constitution. *Haq's* agenda is more specifically targeted at achieving full democracy, and the group is less identified with morality issues and Shi'ite sectarianism than its parent movement; in fact, one of *Haq's* leaders, Sheikh Isa Abdullah Al Jowder (who died in September 2011), was a Sunni cleric, and another founder (who eventually left the movement[34]), Ali Qasim Rabea, is a secular leftist-nationalist.[35] Nonetheless, *Haq* is generally thought of as both Shi'a and Islamist, even though its leader, Hasan Mushaima, is a layman and the group is not endorsed by any senior Bahraini Shi'ite cleric.[36]

Haq has unquestionably benefited from the breakdown in the relationship between the Bahraini government and Bahraini Shi'ites, since—unlike *al-Wefaq*—Haq never invested its credibility in a political process that it perceived (and loudly denounced) as inherently unfair and dishonest. (In fact, *Haq* has consistently refused even to register as an official "political society,"[37] even though its rejectionist record is not absolute: Mushaima met with King Hamad in London in March, 2008.[38]) While *al-Wefaq* spent four years in the Council of Representatives ineffectually working for the Shi'ite community's interests, *Haq* (or, at least, groups of young Shi'ites apparently inspired by low-level *Haq* activists) was out on the streets throwing rocks at the police,[39] and *Haq* itself was submitting petitions to the United Nations and the United States calling for condemnation of the Bahraini government.[40] While the rocks and petitions accomplished no more at the time than did *al-Wefaq's* political maneuvering, they established *Haq* as a genuine "fighting opposition"—one respected by Shi'ites and feared (and persecuted) by the Bahraini government. The fact that *Haq* leaders Hasan Mushaima and Abdeljalil al-Singace were among the opposition leaders imprisoned by the government in the aftermath of the 2011 protests only reinforced the movement's credibility.[41]

As part of the Bahraini government's efforts to confront *Haq*, officials have accused the organization's leaders of being in the pay of Iran, either directly or through Hezbollah intermediaries. While it is very difficult to prove that such a relationship does not exist, and many in the Sunni community take it as an article of faith that Bahraini Shi'ites are more loyal to Iran than to Bahrain, disinterested observers, including the U.S. Embassy in Bahrain, have pointed out that no convincing evidence has ever been produced to back these accusations.[42]

Haq Secretary General Hasan Mushaima (one of the founders of *al-Wefaq*, who left that group to co-found *Haq*) returned to Bahrain from Great Britain in late February 2011 to a "rapturous" welcome; he had previously been charged and tried in absentia for conspiring against the government, but the charges against him were dropped as part of a package of government concessions aimed at establishing a dialogue with the Bahraini opposition.[43] Upon his return, Mushaima attempted, together with other opposition leaders, to formulate a unified platform of demands and expectations.[44] As the government crackdown continued, Mushaima was again brought to trial and imprisoned, along with many other protest leaders.[45]

A third Shi'ite opposition movement, *Wafa'* ("Loyalty"), was founded in early 2009 by Abdulwahab Hussain, a cleric who had been a leading Shi'a activist in the 1990s and a co-founder of *al-Wefaq*. Unlike *Haq*, *Wafa'* enjoys the open backing of senior cleric (and rival of Ayatollah Isa Qassim) Sheikh Abduljalil al-Maqdad. And unlike *al-Wefaq*, *Wafa'* has consistently and firmly opposed participation in Bahrain's quasi-democratic constitutional government.

The period when *Haq* leader Hasan Mushaima was in a brief self-imposed exile should have presented something of an opportunity for *Wafa'* to attract support from Shi'a rejectionists. However, despite the fact that *Wafa'* has the clerical backing *Haq* lacks and has credible, experienced leadership, it does not appear so far to have gained much traction among Bahraini Shi'ites. Now that Hasan Mushaima has returned to Bahrain (and is unlikely to be able to leave any time soon) and *al-Wefaq* has quit the Council of Representatives, *Wafa'* is likely to have a great deal of difficulty finding a meaningful niche for itself in Bahraini Shi'ite politics.[46]

Yet another rejectionist Shi'ite Islamist "political society" is Amal (the "Islamic Action Society," *Jam'iyyat al-Amal al-Islami*, also referred to by Bahrainis as "the Shirazi faction"). This group is "the non-violent heir to the defunct Islamic Front for the Liberation of Bahrain, which launched a failed uprising in 1981 inspired by Iran's Islamic revolution."[47] *Amal* refused to register as a "legal" faction before the 2002 election, did not win any seats in the 2006 election,[48] and decided not to participate in the 2010 election. The society's Secretary General, Sheikh Mohammed al-Mahfoodh, justified this decision by citing the usual objections to Bahrain's political system, claiming that "[W]e don't want to just be employees... the members of parliament are just employees who get a big salary."[49] (It is not entirely clear, however, if Sheikh al-Mahfoodh's feelings would have been the same had there been a significant likelihood of his actually becoming one of these "employees.") *Amal* was apparently considered enough of a threat to the Bahraini government that the movement was effectively shut down in July 2012.[50]

The challenge for the official organized Shi'ite opposition (both legal and illegal), as well as for leaders of the young, self-organizing protestors (known for using Twitter and social media) and the leftist secular organizations that have joined the anti-government protests, was to agree on a set of demands that were ambitious enough to maintain the enthusiasm of the protestors (and, of course, to offer a realistic hope of solving the genuine problems facing Bahraini Shi'ites) but could also be palatable to Bahrain's ruling family and its Sunni allies.[51] This challenge has only become more intractable as the conflict has drawn on.

Sunni Organizations

Unlike the majority Shi'ites, Bahrain's Sunni community is not overwhelmingly Islamist in its beliefs. This means that Sunni Islamist "political societies" must compete with secular groups and independent candidates for voter support. Further, Sunni Islamist groups are constrained in their ambitions by Bahrain's demographic and economic situation: because Sunnis are a relatively wealthy, privileged minority, Sunni Islamists do not join their Shi'ite colleagues in calling for genuine democratic reform (which would effectively disempower Sunni politicians and their supporters), and[52]—while they may aspire to "increase the standard of living for Bahrainis; strengthen political, social and economic stability; and enhance financial and administrative oversight of the government and industry"—they quite understandably do not agitate for fully equal opportunity for Bahrain's Shi'ites. Because the American military presence contributes to Bahrain's economy and provides a bulwark against supposed Iranian designs on their country, the mainstream Sunni Islamist groups do not oppose the presence of the infidels on Bahrain's territory.

In short, Bahrain's organized Sunni Islamist "societies" have traditionally been seen as basically pro-government parties, working at times for incremental modifications to the status quo but not advocating full democracy or other large-scale, disruptive changes. Further, as the ongoing protests assumed an increasingly sectarian character, what goodwill and cooperation there was between Sunni and Shi'ite Islamists largely disappeared,[53] and the government used Sunni Islamists as a counter to Shi'ite agitation.

More recently, however, it appears that the relationship between local Sunni Islamists and Bahrain's government may be becoming slightly less cozy, largely as a result of outside pressure. The Muslim Brotherhood, which has a branch in Bahrain, is increasingly seen by *status quo* Sunni-dominated states as an antagonist; and given its substantial dependency on Saudi and Emirati support, official Bahrain policy has little to no choice but to toe the line, or at least create some anti-Brotherhood atmospherics.[54]

There are two principal Sunni Islamist "political societies" in Bahrain. The first is the *al-Menbar* National Islamic Society (*al-Minbar al-Islami*), the political wing of the al-Eslah Society, which is generally seen as Bahrain's branch of the Muslim Brotherhood. The second is the al-Asala Political Society, which in turn is the political wing of the Islamic Education Society (*al-Tarbiya al-Islamiya*), a conservative Salafist organization. *Al-Menbar* is the more liberal of the two Sunni Islamist parties, and has, for example, taken positions in favor of women's rights.[55] However, this liberalism has its limits: in 2006 the group's Council of Representatives members formed part of a bloc that prevented Bahrain from ratifying the government's signature on the International Covenant on Civil and Political Rights, on the basis that the Covenant would mean "that Muslims could convert to another religion, something against the Islamic law, since those who do so should be beheaded."[56] *Al-Menbar* had promised to field several female candidates for the 2006 election, but as part of an electoral pact with *al-Asala*, which does not approve of women's standing for political office, this pledge was dropped. Further, *al-Menbar's* parent organization (with "support" from the Islamic Education Society) held a 2008 workshop opposing government efforts to promote gender equality.[57]

Its association with al-Eslah, which runs a network of mosques, gives *al-Menbar* a solid social support base among Bahraini Sunnis. Furthermore, al-Eslah (and, by extension, al-Menbar) benefits from the official patronage of the Bahraini royal family (its President is Sheikh Isa bin Mohammed al-Khalifa), as well as from some of Bahrain's largest businesses.[58] While charitable contributions to *al-Eslah* do not necessarily provide direct support for *al-Menbar's* political activity, they unquestionably contribute to al-Eslah's standing in society, and thus to al-Menbar's credibility.

Al-Asala takes a harder line than *al-Menbar* on various issues. As noted above, *al-Asala* does not approve of fielding female candidates, and the group is, in general, opposed to Bahrain's comparatively modern, freewheeling character. It has also taken positions opposed to U.S. military action in Iraq. Despite their differences, however, *al-Menbar* and *al-Asala* have often cooperated; and, like *al-Menbar*, *al-Asala* cannot be accurately described as an opposition "society" even though it dissents from some Bahraini government policies.

In the 2006 elections, *al-Menbar* and *al-Asala* agreed to divide the Sunni electoral districts between them in order not to compete with each other and split the Sunni Islamist vote.[59] This strategy worked well, with the two groups winning seven seats each.[60] In 2010, however, they failed to organize a similar arrangement. As a result, the two "societies" ran against each other in many districts, and the consequence was the loss of most of their seats. *Al-Menbar* won only two seats in the Council of Representatives, and *al-Asala* received just three.[61] Furthermore, the Sunni Islamist "societies" lost two seats in the 2014 election, perhaps in part as a result of government redistricting.[62]

Unsurprisingly, Sunni Islamist organizations have not participated in the anti-government demonstrations in Bahrain; if anything, they may have been one of the forces behind several pro-government rallies that took place while Bahrain's Shi'ites were protesting against government policies.[63] While these pro-government rallies were not openly acknowledged as *al-Menbar* or *al-Asala* events, there is no question that Bahrain's Sunnis consider Shi'ite protests to be a threat to their privileged situation, and Sunni "societies," like all political parties, need to be seen as promoting the interests of their constituents. Beyond any such cynical calculations, Sunni Islamists would be justifiably concerned that a Shi'ite-Islamist-governed Bahrain would be much less hospitable to Sunni practices and beliefs than a relatively liberal Sunni-dominated Bahrain—despite the latter's tolerance of various social vices. (It is also worth noting that these pro-government rallies may not have been quite the "spontaneous outpouring of affection" that they appeared to be; Bangladeshi expatriate workers claimed that they had been forced to participate.[64])

Traditionally, then, Sunni Islamists were seen as a "loyal opposition" to the al-Khalifa rulers of Bahrain, if they were properly considered an opposition at all; any more militant expressions of Sunni extremism were directed outward. There is now concern that Bahrainis drawn to fight for ISIS and other Sunni extremist groups in Syria may return to their country radicalized not only against Shi'ites, but also against the *status quo* in Bahrain.[65] The al-Khalifa regime is far enough from *sharia* compliance that it is easily classified as *kafir* (infidel) and thus in need of overthrow; it has been further pointed out that the government's policy of recruiting foreign Sunnis to join the security forces and receive Bahraini citizenship could ultimately backfire, as some of these recruits may be easily (or already) radicalized, and they are likely to lack any personal feelings of loyalty to the al-Khalifa family.[66] One irony in this situation is that while Bahrain is officially part of the international coalition fighting ISIS, those native-born Bahrainis joining the organization are typically from social strata close to the al-Khalifa monarchy.[67] To date, at least 24 Bahrainis have been accused of joining ISIS, and have been sentenced to prison and, in many cases, to loss of Bahraini citizenship;[68] but at the same time, the Bahraini government has failed to demonstrate consistent attitudes and policies to counter Sunni radicalization, apparently preferring to attempt to use it against Shi'ites while preventing it from becoming too much of a threat to the monarchy.[69]

ISLAMISM AND SOCIETY

In addition to political activities, many of the established Islamist groups in Bahrain engage in conventional charitable and outreach work: supporting widows, orphans, and other poor people, operating mosques and providing religious education, and proselytizing for their particular brand of Islam. *Al-Eslah*, in particular, runs a large charitable enterprise, supported by corporate zakat as well as private contributions. Notably, *al-Eslah* has also made a number of prominent humanitarian contributions to the Gaza Strip, including funding construction of a building at the Islamic University there in 2005 and sending five ambulances to Gaza in 2009.[70] The particular affinity of *al-Eslah* for aid to Gaza is explained by the fact that both *al-Eslah* and Hamas are offshoots of the Muslim Brotherhood; Hamas has ruled the Gaza Strip since 2007, and the Islamic University there has been associated with Hamas since its founding. (In fact, the university was founded by Sheikh Ahmed Yassin, ten years before he founded Hamas.)

As bitter rivals for political and economic power, Shi'ite and Sunni Islamists in Bahrain are not particularly comfortable cooperating, even when they agree. However, some issues are uncontroversial enough (at least within Islamist circles) that Shi'ite and Sunni leaders have joined forces to fight for their shared ideals, or at least have managed not to interfere with each others' efforts:

- While they have not been successful in completely banning the sale and consumption of alcohol in Bahrain, Islamists have done what they can to impose limits on drinking in the kingdom. Islamist organizations supported a government move to close bars in cheap hotels in 2009.[71]

- Horrified by reports that Manama had been ranked as one of the top ten "vice cities" in the world, Islamists have attempted to eliminate prostitution—either by banning female entertainers in cheap hotels or by attempting to prevent the issuance of visas to women from Russia, Thailand, Ethiopia, and China. (The latter measure, proposed by the *Salafist al-Asala* "society," fell flat; even other Islamists in the Council of Representatives pointed out that it would cause diplomatic damage if passed, and probably not be very effective in any case.)[72]

- In 2007, Islamist parliamentarians condemned a performance by Lebanese composer/oudist Marcel Khalife and Bahraini poet Qassim Haddad that was presented as part of a government-sponsored culture festival, complaining that it included "sleazy dance moves" that would "encourage debauchery." It appears the show went ahead as planned.[73] A year later, the same Council members united again to attempt to ban a show by provocative Lebanese singer Haifa Wehbe; this show also went ahead, although Wehbe did tone down her act a bit in response.[74]

- In late 2012, between 50 and 100 "hardline" Islamists protested U.S. celebrity Kim Kardashian's visit to Bahrain to open a milkshake shop. Among the signs at the protest was one asserting that "[n]one of our customs and traditions allow us to receive stars of porn movies." The government responded with tear gas.[75] (In fact, it is unclear whether the protesters in this case were Sunni or Shi'ite, or both. At the very least, one can say that there were no reports of Islamist pro-Kardashian demonstrations.)

Traditionally, Bahraini Sunnis and Shi'ites lived and worked together with minimal friction. However, the recent Shi'a protests and the Sunni government's response to them (including, in at least some cases, Sunni vigilante participation)[76] have done a great deal to damage the relationship between the two communities. Within a week of the February 14, 2011 onset of Shi'ite protests, Sunnis had begun to mount counter-demonstrations,[77] and as the crisis continued, confrontations between Sunni and Shi'ite groups became more frequent and more violent. Some Sunni groups explicitly came out against government-Shi'ite dialogue, apparently preferring the *status quo* to a resolution they felt would favor Shi'ites over their own community.[78] Even assuming that a political settlement is someday reached between Bahrain's government and the organizations representing the Shi'ite majority, it is difficult to imagine that Bahrain's social atmosphere will quickly return to the comfortable *status quo ante*.

Islamism and the State

After a turbulent period during the 1990s, the country's new king, Hamad bin Isa al-Khalifa, restored constitutional government in 2002. From then until January 2011, Bahrain's government was largely successful in channeling the energies of the country's Islamists into non-violent political activity rather than terrorism or major civil unrest. In accordance with the 2002 constitution, elections with universal suffrage are held every four years (most recently in November 2014) for the lower chamber of the National Assembly, the Council of Representatives (*Majlis an-nuwab*); all members of the upper chamber, the Consultative Council (*Majlis al-shura*), are appointed by the King. Both chambers must approve any legislation, giving each one effective veto power over proposed laws. As a result, since the one national body that is democratically elected has such limited ability to accomplish anything against the wishes of the ruling establishment, Bahrain's version of democracy has never been entirely satisfactory to the majority of the country's citizens. Still, for a few years, even this limited form of democracy provided the people of Bahrain with a voice and hope for future improvement.

Nevertheless, Bahrain has retained most of the essential characteristics of traditional Gulf emirate governance. Real power is concentrated in the ruling al-Khalifa family, members of which occupy the most important governmental positions, including 20 of the country's 25 Cabinet seats.[79] The Prime Minister, Prince Khalifa ibn Sulman al-Khalifa, has held office since the country was granted independence in 1971, and is currently the world's longest-serving Prime Minister. He is the uncle of King Hamad, and is also thought to be one of the wealthiest people in Bahrain.[80] Even the Council of Representatives' ability to block legislation is not really much of a constraint on royal power; under the Constitution, the King retains the right to rule by royal decree, bypassing the legislature entirely.[81]

While the ongoing Shi'ite unrest in Bahrain has eclipsed most other news about Bahraini Islamism, earlier news stories paint a more complex picture of a government quite willing to work with Islamists to achieve its goals, but equally willing to take strong measures to limit the actions and influence of Islamist forces. The Bahraini government is generally perceived as working against Islamism (or at least working to limit Islamists to minor victories while preserving Bahrain's modern, relatively open character). However, it is not above using Sunni Islamists as weapons against the Shi'ite community. In a 2006 report, the Gulf Centre for Democratic Development detailed a government effort led by Sheikh Ahmed bin Ateyatalla al-Khalifa to "manipulate the results of… elections, maintain sectarian distrust and division, and to ensure that Bahrain's Shi'as remain oppressed and disenfranchised." The initiative reportedly involved government payments to a number of individuals and NGOs, including both *al-Eslah/al-Menbar* and the Islamic Education Society/*al-Asala*. Among the tasks to be achieved by the various participants in this scheme were "running websites and Internet forums which foment sectarian hatred" and running "Sunni Conversion" and "Sectarian Switch" projects.[82]

The foreign-policy implications of Islamism can sometimes create problems for the Bahraini government. *Al-Eslah's* affinity for the Gaza Strip has already been mentioned, and is harmless enough when it involves sending ambulances and other forms of aid there. But when, in late 2009, *al-Eslah* leader Sheikh Fareed Hadi gave a sermon condemning the Egyptian government for building a steel barricade across the Egypt-Gaza Strip border, Bahrain's government, not wishing to ruffle feathers, stepped in and suspended him from delivering further sermons. The eloquently-named "Bahraini Society to Resist Normalization with the Zionist Enemy" promptly objected, reminding Bahrain's government and citizens of "the dangers of Zionism and its drive to infiltrate Arab and Islamic societies and influence them."[83] Anti-Zionism continues to serve as one of the few factors uniting Bahraini Sunnis and Shi'ites: in the midst of the government's dissolution of *al-Wefaq*, the Shi'ite organization's Deputy Secretary General, Sheikh Hussein al-Daihi, found time to condemn the government's permission for an Israeli delegation to attend an international conference of the world soccer association FIFA to be held in Manama in May 2017.[84]

Nevertheless, Bahrain is not usually considered a major source of *mujahideen*, terrorists, or financial/logistical support for overseas *jihad* in its various forms. Much of this is probably due to the fact that Sunni Bahrainis are neither especially impoverished nor exposed to the more radical forms of *Wahhabi* Islamic fundamentalism—and, of course, they are also not very numerous. Still, a number of Bahrainis have traveled abroad to participate in *jihad*. One, Khalil Janahi, was arrested by Saudi authorities in the course of his religious studies in Riyadh, and was accused of being one of a group of 172 al-Qaeda militants planning "to storm Saudi prisons to free militants and attack oil refineries and public figures."[85] Another was royal family member Sheikh Salman Ebrahim Mohamed Ali al-Khalifa, who was captured near the Pakistan-Afghanistan border and held by the United States in Guantanamo Bay, Cuba as a Taliban/al-Qaeda supporter before eventually being released to return to Bahrain.[86] The Bahraini government is actively concerned about the trend toward increasing Sunni radicalization through participation in fighting abroad, as well as radicalization through the internet.

Inside Bahrain itself, the government has acted against individuals providing funding or other support to al-Qaeda, ISIS, and other radical Sunni organizations. For example, two men associated with a small *Salafist* movement known as "National Justice" were arrested in June 2008 for sending money to al-Qaeda; one was released shortly afterwards for lack of evidence,[87] and the other was among a group of prisoners officially pardoned in mid-2009.[88] Some other Bahrainis have been implicated in plots to support or engage in terrorism,[89] but until recently, the Bahraini government had far more serious problems dealing with domestic Shi'ite popular unrest than it does with the global jihad.

In the months leading up to the country's 2010 elections, Bahrain's government instituted a crackdown on many political organizations and news outlets, and vigorously suppressed demonstrations and civil unrest.[90] The ostensible justification was that Shi'ite opposition leaders were planning to lead a revolt against the government. In February 2011, Bahrain experienced a new and significant round of demonstrations and rioting by Shi'ite citizens, triggered by this apparent rollback of democratic reforms, and by the revolutions in Tunisia and Egypt. The beginning of the mass demonstrations also coincided with the February 14th anniversary of the restoration of constitutional government in 2002 and the referendum in 2001 that approved the new constitution.[91]

The government's initial reaction to these demonstrations was an indecisive and unproductive vacillation between brutal suppression and attempts at conciliation. But after seven demonstrators had been killed and many more injured, Bahrain's rulers decided to back down from lethal confrontation, and on February 19th began a concerted effort, led by Crown Prince Salman bin Hamad al-Khalifa, to de-escalate the crisis and promote a "national dialogue" to iron out a solution.[92] At first, it appeared likely that such a dialogue would soon take place.[93] But Shi'ite leaders demanded substantial concessions before talks could begin, and when a dialogue was eventually begun in July 2011, its mechanism—apparently dictated by the hardline faction of the royal family—was clearly not intended to facilitate a genuine airing and resolution of Bahrain's problems, and ended with no accomplishments.[94] Calls for dialogue continued to be made, but some six years after the beginning of the "Arab Spring," it still seems impossible for the faction-ridden royal family, the disparate opposition, and loyalist groups to agree on conditions that would enable a meaningful and productive dialogue to take place.[95]

Clearly, even once negotiations begin, they will be difficult; after years of protests, repression, torture,[96] mass dismissal of Shi'ites from their jobs,[97] revocation of citizenship,[98] and demolition of Shi'ite mosques,[99] there is very little good will or mutual trust between Bahrain's Shi'ites and their government.[100]

The Bahraini government has a number of factors in its favor as it attempts to maintain the *status quo*:

- It appears to have solid support from almost all members of the country's Sunni minority, which holds most economic power and controls all of Bahrain's security forces.

- It enjoys substantial outside support from neighboring Sunni states—particularly Saudi Arabia, which is concerned about the possibility of unrest or even rebellion by its own large Shi'ite minority and has a history of intervention to preserve Bahrain's Sunni regime. In March of 2012, a 1,500-strong force of Gulf Cooperation Council troops and policemen (which may in fact have been as large as 5000 or more men),[101] headed by Saudi Arabia, entered Bahrain to assist government forces in restoring order. In all likelihood, the Saudis will quickly return at any time they (or the al-Khalifas) feel that the existing order is threatened.

- It is backed by the United States. Although the U.S. has been critical of the Bahraini government's more extreme measures to confront unrest, and has called for more democratic rule and better protection of human rights, Bahrain's importance as a naval base and the dangers a regime collapse would pose to other Persian Gulf governments give Washington little real maneuvering room.[102] In the words of one anonymous U.S. official, Bahrain is "just too important to fail."[103]

Nonetheless, it is clear that the Bahraini government has done tremendous damage to its own perceived legitimacy, both at home and abroad. While it would appear unlikely that the regime faces any real danger of being overthrown in the near future, it is equally true that unless it can find some way to regain the trust of the country's Shi'ite community, Bahrain's ruling class will have a difficult time maintaining long-term stability in an era of increasing democratization and rising expectations. Lastly, as the regional Sunni-Shi'a conflict has intensified, Bahrain's rulers face challenges even assuring the loyalty of their Sunni subjects.

ENDNOTES

[1] Freedom House, "Bahrain", 2016, https://freedomhouse.org/report/freedom-world/2016/bahrain; Amnesty International, "Bahrain 2015/2016", https://www.amnesty.org/en/countries/middle-east-and-north-africa/bahrain/report-bahrain/.

[2] "Bahrain jails 24 for forming ISIS cell," The Daily Star (Lebanon), June 23, 2016, http://www.dailystar.com.lb/News/Middle-East/2016/Jun-23/358553-bahrain-jails-24-for-forming-isis-cell.ashx.

[3] U.S. Department of State, "Bahrain 2016 Crime & Safety Report," n.d., https://www.osac.gov/pages/ContentReportDetails.aspx?cid=19255.

[4] Andrew Hammond, "Bahrain Says Will Hold Dialogue to End Crisis Soon," Reuters, March 10, 2012, http://www.reuters.com/article/2012/03/10/us-bahrain-protest-talks-idUSBRE8290A420120310.

[5] Bill Law, "Time running out as Bahrain tries to revive national dialogue", BBC, January 30, 2014, http://www.bbc.com/news/world-middle-east-25918628.

[6] Mahjoob Zweiri and Mohammed Zahid, "The victory of Al Wefaq: The rise of Shiite politics in Bahrain," Research Institute for European and American Studies (RIEAS) Research Paper no. 108, April 2007, 10-11, http://rieas.gr/images/rieas108.pdf; Al Wefaq National Islamic Society, "Bahrain Split by Electoral Boundaries," June 9, 2010, http://alwefaq.net/-alwefaq/index.php?show=news&action=article&id=4723; "Bahrain Opposition Representation: Was it a Silent Majority or is it now a Loud Minority?" n.p., n.d., http://www.scribd.com/doc/49888133/Bahrain-Opposition-Representation.

[7] Robert Fisk, "Abolish Bahrain's Monarchy, Chant Shia Muslims," New Zealand Herald, February 21, 2011, http://www.nzherald.co.nz/democracy/news/article.cfm?c_id=171&objectid=10707688; "Several Hurt as Sunnis. Shiites Clash in Bahrain," Reuters, March 4, 2011, http://tribune.com.pk/story/127573/several-hurt-as-sunnis-shiites-clash-in-bahrain/.

[8] "Bahrain Shiites Eye Easing of Sunni Grip," Agence France Presse, October 23, 2010, http://www.arabtimesonline.com/NewsDetails/tabid/96/smid/414/ArticleID/161106/reftab/73/t/Bahrain-Shiites-eye-easing-of-Sunni-grip/Default.aspx.

[9] Joost Hiltermann and Toby Matthiesen, "Bahrain Burning," New York Review of Books, August 18, 2011, http://www.tobymatthiesen.com/wp/newspaper_articles/bahrain-burning/.

[10] Imran Khan, "Inside Friday prayer in Tehran," Al Jazeera (Doha), May 18, 2012, http://blogs.aljazeera.com/blog/middle-east/inside-friday-prayer-tehran.

[11] "Bahrain WikiLeaks Cables: Bahrain as 'Iran's Fourteenth Province,'" Telegraph (London), February 18, 2011, http://www.telegraph.co.uk/news/wikileaks-files/bahrain-wikileaks-cables/8334785/GENERAL-PETRAEUS-VISIT-TO-BAHRAIN.html.

[12] Christopher Hope, "WikiLeaks: Bahrain Opposition 'Received Training from Hezbollah,'" Telegraph (London), February 18, 2011, http://www.telegraph.co.uk/news/worldnews/wikileaks/8333686/WikiLeaks-Bahrain-opposition-received-training-from-Hizbollah.html; "US Embassy Cables: Bahrainis Trained by Hezbollah, Claims King Hamad," Guardian (London), February 15, 2011, http://www.guardian.co.uk/world/us-embassy-cables-documents/165861.

[13] Report of the Bahrain Independent Commission of Inquiry, paragraphs 1584 and 1585, 387, http://www.bici.org.bh/BICIreportEN.pdf.

[14] U.S. Department of State, "Bahrain 2016 Crime & Safety Report."

[15] Jonathan Spyer, "Gulf Regimes: The Real Game – Saudi Arabia," Jerusalem Post, March 11, 2011, http://www.jpost.com/Features/FrontLines/Article.aspx?id=211679. According to Spyer, "Iran… is adept, however, at turning political chaos into gain… If the Gulf regimes fail to effectively navigate the current unrest, Iran is fair set to begin to apply these practices in this area."

[16] Zweiri and Zahid, "The Victory of Al Wefaq," 9.

[17] "US Embassy Cables: Guide to Bahrain's Politics," Guardian (London), February 15, 2011, http://www.guardian.co.uk/world/us-embassy-cables-documents/168471; "Bahrain WikiLeaks Cables: Wafa': A New Shia Rejectionist Movement," Telegraph (London), February 18, 2011, http://www.telegraph.co.uk/news/wikileaks-files/bahrain-wikileaks-cables/8334607/WAFA-A-NEW-SHIA-REJECTIONIST-MOVEMENT.html.

[18] Zweiri and Zahid, "The Victory of Al Wefaq," 11.

[19] Al Wefaq National Islamic Society, "Bahrain Split by Electoral Boundaries." Note that in addition to having district lines that separate Sunni and Shi'a populations in order to create Sunni-majority districts, the population size of the districts drawn varies widely: some Sunni-majority districts have as few as 1,000 voters, while some Shi'ite-majority districts have as many as 15,000 voters.

[20] "MPs Urge Al Wefaq to Rethink Resignation," Gulf Daily News, March 9, 2011, http://www.gulf-daily-news.com/NewsDetails.aspx?storyid=301425; Adrian Bloomfield, "Bahrain King under Pressure to Sack Prime Minister Uncle," Telegraph (London), February 20, 2011, http://www.telegraph.co.uk/news/worldnews/middleeast/bahrain/8336934/Bahrain-king-under-pressure-to-sack-prime-minister-uncle.html.

[21] Sara Sorcher, "What's The State of Play In Bahrain's Protests?" National Journal, July 18, 2011, http://www.nationaljournal.com/nationalsecurity/what-s-the-state-of-play-in-bahrain-s-protests--20110718; Hiltermann and Matthiesen, "Bahrain Burning."

[22] Reuters, "Bahrain holds vote to fill seats vacated during unrest," AhramOnline, September 24, 2011, http://english.ahram.org.eg/~/NewsContent/2/8/22324/World/Region/Bahrain-holds-vote-to-fill-seats-vacated-during-un.aspx.

[23] Ethan Bronner, "Bahrain Vote Erupts in Violence," New York Times, September 24, 2011, http://www.nytimes.com/2011/09/25/world/middleeast/bahrain-protesters-and-police-clash-during-election.html.

[24] Mohammed A'Ali, "Thousands defy threats and flock to the polls," Gulf Daily News, September 25, 2011, http://www.gulf-daily-news.com/NewsDetails.aspx?storyid=314082.

[25] Andrew Hammond, "UPDATE 1-Fewer than 1 in 5 vote in Bahrain by-elections," Reuters, September 25, 2011, http://www.reuters.com/article/2011/09/25/bahrain-vote-results-idUSL5E7KP13G20110925.

[26] "Bahrain opposition groups announce elections boycott", BBC, October 11, 2014, http://www.bbc.com/news/world-middle-east-29583378.

[27] Associated Press, "Bahrain court orders Shia opposition group to be dissolved", The Guardian, July 17, 2016, https://www.theguardian.com/world/2016/jul/17/bahrain-al-wefaq-shia-opposition-group-sunni; "Bahrain regime to auction Al-Wefaq's seized assets", Al Masdar News, October 22, 2016, https://www.almasdarnews.com/article/bahrain-regime-auction-al-wefaqs-seized-assets/.

[28] "Bahrain's leading Shia cleric charged with corruption", Middle East Eye, July 18, 2016, http://www.middleeasteye.net/news/bahrain-s-leading-shias-religious-leader-charged-corruption-1212082735.

[29] "Bahrain strips Sheikh Isa Qassim of nationality," Al Jazeera, June 21, 2016, http://www.aljazeera.com/news/2016/06/bahrain-strips-religious-leader-nationality-160620122338238.html.

[30] "Bahrain court orders Shia opposition group to be dissolved."

[31] Kate Kizer & Michael Payne, "Bahrain's five-year plan of repression", Middle East Eye, February 14, 2016, http://www.middleeasteye.net/columns/bahrain-s-five-year-plan-repression-1903103504.

[32] "Bahrain court overturns jail term of opposition chief," Middle East Eye, October 17, 2016, http://www.middleeasteye.net/news/bahrain-court-overturns-jail-term-opposition-chief-215996772.

[33] U.S. Department of State, "Closure of Opposition Political Society Al-Wefaq in Bahrain," June 14, 2016, http://www.state.gov/r/pa/prs/ps/2016/06/258464.htm; "Bahrain snubs Western allies' condemnation of opposition ban", Middle East Eye, July 19, 2016, http://www.middleeasteye.net/news/bahrain-rejects-us-and-uk-condemnation-opposition-ban-517968328.

[34] "Bahrain WikiLeaks Cables: Wafa': A New Shia Rejectionist Movement."

[35] "Shaikh Isa Al Jowder and the Haq Movement," Chan'ad Bahraini blog, May 31, 2006, http://chanad.weblogs.us/?p=487.

[36] "Bahrain WikiLeaks Cables: Wafa': A New Shia Rejectionist Movement."

[37] "US Embassy Cables: Guide to Bahrain's Politics."

[38] "Bahrain WikiLeaks Cables: Wafa': A New Shia Rejectionist Movement."

[39] "Bahrain – Political Parties," globalsecurity.org, n.d., http://www.globalsecurity.org/military/world/gulf/bahrain-politics-parties.htm.

[40] "US Embassy Cables: Guide to Bahrain's Politics."

[41] "Bahrain Appeal Court Upholds Activists' Convictions," BBC, September 4, 2012, http://www.bbc.co.uk/news/world-middle-east-19474026.

[42] "US Embassy Cables: Guide to Bahrain's Politics".

[43] "Bahrain Unrest: Shia Dissident Hassan Mushaima Returns," BBC, February 26, 2011, http://www.bbc.co.uk/news/world-middle-east-12587902.

[44] "Bahraini Shia Groups Seek to Unify Demands," Financial Times, February 27, 2011, http://www.ft.com/cms/s/0/a5766674-429e-11e0-8b34-00144feabdc0.html.

[45] "Bahrain Appeal Court Upholds Activists' Convictions."

[46] "Bahrain WikiLeaks Cables: Wafa': A New Shia Rejectionist Movement"; "Wafa' ('loyalty')," globalsecurity.org, n.d., http://www.globalsecurity.org/military/world/gulf/bahrain-politics-parties-wafa.htm.

[47] "US Embassy Cables: Guide to Bahrain's Politics."

[48] Ibid.

[49] Zoi Constantine, "Opposition Party Votes against Bahrain Election," The National (UAE), August 26, 2010, http://www.thenational.ae/news/worldwide/middle-east/opposition-party-votes-against-bahrain-election.

[50] "The Opposition Parties: The Decision to Dissolve Amal Society is a Deliberate Attack on Political Activity in Bahrain," Al Wefaq, July 12, 2012, http://alwefaq.net/index.php?show=news&action=article&id=6664.

[51] Joe Parkinson, "Bahrain is Roiled by Return of Shiite," Wall Street Journal, February 28, 2011, http://online.wsj.com/article/SB10001424052748704430304576170661773277324.html; Joe Parkinson and Nour Malas, "Bahrain Opposition Steps Up Pressure," Wall Street Journal, March 7, 2011, http://online.wsj.com/article/SB10001424052748704504404576183972416733938.html?mod=WSJEurope_hpp_LEFTTopStories.

[52] "US Embassy Cables: Guide to Bahrain's Politics."

[53] Hussein Ibish, "The Bahrain Stalemate," The Atlantic, July 18, 2011, http://www.theatlantic.com/international/archive/2011/07/the-bahrain-stalemate/242086/.

[54] Alex MacDonald, "Sunni Islamists could face uphill struggle in Bahrain elections", Middle East Eye, February 13, 2015, http://www.middleeasteye.net/in-depth/features/sunni-islamists-could-face-uphill-struggle-bahrain-elections-1404489268.

[55] Zweiri and Zahid, "The Victory of Al Wefaq," 7.

[56] Ibid.

[57] Suad Hamada, "Anti-Gender Equality Campaign Starts," womangateway.com, August 4, 2008, http://www.womengateway.com/NR/exeres/7A81C4CA-5539-4C3D-9F97-38EB79F2A735.htm.

[58] National Bank of Bahrain, "Social Responsibility," n.d., http://www.nbbonline.com/default.asp?action=category&id=6; "Sakana Contributes Zakat to Al Eslah Society," sakanaonline.com, October 7, 2010, http://www.sakanaonline.com/en/press-releases/sakana-zakat-al-eslah-society.html.

[59] "Bahrain: The Political Structure, Reform and Human Rights," Eurasia Review, February 28, 2011, http://www.eurasiareview.com/analysis/bahrain-the-political-structure-reform-and-human-rights-28022011/.

[60] Ibid.

[61] Ibidem; Habib Toumi, "Al Asala, Islamic Menbar Join Forces in Bahrain," Gulf News, October 29, 2010, http://gulfnews.com/news/gulf/bahrain/al-asala-islamic-menbar-join-forces-in-bahrain-1.703600.

[62] Habib Toumi, "Bahrain's political societies lose big in polls", Gulf News, November 30, 2014, http://gulfnews.com/news/gulf/bahrain/bahrain-s-political-societies-lose-big-in-polls-1.1420042.

[63] Michael Slackman and Nadim Audi, "Protests in Bahrain Become Test of Wills," New York Times, February 22, 2011, http://www.nytimes.com/2011/02/23/world/middleeast/23bahrain.html; Nancy Youssef, "Huge Bahraini Counter-Protest Reflects Rising Sectarian Strife," McClatchy, February 21, 2011, http://www.mcclatchydc.com/2011/02/21/109155/huge-bahraini-counter-protest.html.

[64] "Bangladeshis Say Being Forced to take Part in Bahrain Pro Government Rally," ANI, March 18, 2011, http://www.sify.com/news/bangladeshis-say-being-forced-to-take-part-in-bahrain-pro-government-rally-news-international-ldsrkjcfgba.html.

[65] Husain Marhoon, "Bahraini Salafists in Spotlight," Al-Monitor, June 18, 2013, http://www.al-monitor.com/pulse/originals/2013/06/bahrain-jihadists-syria-salafism.html.

[66] Bill Law, "Bahrain: The Islamic State threat within," Middle East Eye, October 14, 2014, http://www.middleeasteye.net/columns/bahrain-islamic-state-threat-within-884335108.

[67] Sayed Ahmed Alwadaei, "The Islamic State's Bahraini Backers," New York Times, November 25, 2015, http://www.nytimes.com/2015/11/26/opinion/the-islamic-states-bahraini-backers.html.

[68] Obaid al-Suhaymi, "Bahrain Revokes Nationality of 13 ISIS Members, Postpones Session to Dissolve Wefaq Islamic Society", Asharq al-Awsat, June 24, 2016, http://english.aawsat.com/2016/06/article55353290/bahrain-revokes-nationality-13-isis-members-postpones-session-dissolve-wefaq-islamic-society ; Bahrain Mirror, "Appeals Court Adjourns Case of Bahrain ISIS cell until Jan. 12", January 3, 2017, http://mirror.no-ip.org/en/news/35796.html.

[69] Giorgio Cafiero and Daniel Wagner, "Bahrain's Daesh Dilemma", The World Post, January 15 / March 17 2015, http://www.huffingtonpost.com/giorgio-cafiero/bahrains-daesh-dilemma_b_6462998.html .

[70] Aniqa Haider, "Society Sends Five Ambulances," Gulf Daily News, January 15, 2009, http://www.gulf-daily-news.com/NewsDetails.aspx?storyid=240214.

[71] Habib Toumi, "Bahraini Islamist Societies Press for Closure of Bars, Discos," Gulf News, April 22, 2009, http://gulfnews.com/news/gulf/bahrain/bahrain-islamist-societies-press-for-closure-of-bars-discos-1.1880.

[72] Habib Toumi, "Bahraini Islamist Societies Press for Closure of Bars, Discos"; Alexandra Sandels, "BAHRAIN: Islamists Seeking to Curb Prostitution Fail in Bid to Ban Women From 4 Countries," Los Angeles Times Babylon & Beyond blog, December 15, 2009, http://latimesblogs.latimes.com/babylon-beyond/2009/12/bahrain-conservatives-seeking-to-curb-prostitution-fail-in-bid-to-ban-visas-for-women-from-russia-thailand-ethiopia-and-china.html.

[73] "Marcel Khalife and Qassim Haddad Cause Fury in Bahrain's Parliament," FREEMUSE, March 27, 2007, http://www.freemuse.org/sw18500.asp.

[74] "Haifa Wehbe Sings in Bahrain," Middle East Online, May 2, 2008, http://www.middle-east-online.com/english/?id=25672.

[75] "Bahrain Police Deploy Teargas at anti-Kim Kardashian Protest," USA Today, December 1, 2012, http://www.usatoday.com/story/life/people/2012/12/01/bahrain-kardashian-protest/1739609/; Robert Mackey, "Bahrain's Embrace of Kim Kardashian," New York Times, December 3, 2012, http://thelede.blogs.nytimes.com/2012/12/03/bahrains-embrace-of-kim-kardashian/.

[76] "Bahrain Protesters March on Palace as Gates Visits," Associated Press, March 12, 2011, http://www.washingtonpost.com/wp-dyn/content/article/2011/03/12/AR2011031201563.html.

[77] Youssef, "Huge Bahraini Counter-Protest Reflects Rising Sectarian Strife."

[78] "Bahrain's Sunni party rejects dialogue, calls for end to street violence," Global Times (China), December 27, 2012, http://www.globaltimes.cn/content/752643.shtml; Justin Gengler, "Look Who's Boycotting Dialogue Now," Religion and Politics in Bahrain, March 25, 2012, http://bahrainipolitics.blogspot.co.il/2012/03/look-whos-boycotting-dialogue-now.html.

[79] "Factsheet: Bahrain Protests Feb. 2011," Canadians for Justice and Peace in the Middle East CJPME Factsheet Series no. 114, February 22, 2011, http://www.cjpme.org/fs_114.

[80] Bloomfield, "Bahrain King under Pressure to Sack Prime Minister Uncle."

[81] "Bahrain Opposition Representation."

[82] "'Al Bander Report': Demographic Engineering in Bahrain and Mechanisms of Exclusion," Bahrain Center for Human Rights, September 30, 2006, http://www.bahrainrights.org/node/528.

[83] Habib Toumi, "Call to Reinstate Imam Who Criticised Egypt's Steel Fence," Gulf News, December 25, 2009, http://gulfnews.com/news/gulf/bahrain/call-to-reinstate-imam-who-criticised-egypt-s-steel-fence-1.557927.

[84] "Al-Wefaq: Bahrain will always support Palestine", Press TV, October 19, 2016, http://presstv.ir/Detail/2016/10/19/489831/wefaq-bahrain-fifa-israeli.

[85] Sandeep Singh Grewal, "UAE Releases Suspected Al Qaeda Militant of Bahraini Origin," NewsBlaze, June 12, 2009, http://newsblaze.com/story/20090612184137sand.nb/topstory.html.

[86] "The Guantanamo Docket: Sheikh Salman Ebrahim Mohamed Ali al Khalifa," New York Times, n.d., http://projects.nytimes.com/guantanamo/detainees/246-sheikh-salman-ebrahim-mohamed-ali-al-khalifa/documents/2/pages/1781.

[87] Bahrain Freedom Movement, "Two Men Accused of Funding al-Qaeda Groups," June 25, 2008, http://www.vob.org/en/index.php?show=news&action=article&id=324.

[88] Grewal, "UAE Releases Suspected Al Qaeda Militant of Bahraini Origin."

[89] Ibid.

[90] See, for example, Jon Marks, "Bahrain returns to the bad old days," Guardian (London), September 13, 2010, http://www.guardian.co.uk/commentisfree/2010/sep/13/bahrain-opposition-protests.

[91] Canadians for Justice and Peace in the Middle East, "Factsheet: Bahrain Protests Feb. 2011"; Simeon Kerr, Robin Wigglesworth and Abigail Fielding-Smith, "Arab Regimes Brace for 'Days of Rage,'" Financial Times, February 3, 2011, http://www.ft.com/cms/s/0/63ce290c-2ef1-11e0-88ec-00144feabdc0.html#axzz1G7GakJjJ.

[92] "Bahrain King Orders Release of Political Prisoners," Associated Press, February 22, 2011, http://www.independent.co.uk/news/world/middle-east/bahrain-king-orders-release-of-political-prisoners-2222371.html.

[93] "Bahrain's Shiite Opposition Set to Talk to Rulers," Associated Press, March 3, 2011, http://www.cbsnews.com/stories/2011/03/03/ap/world/main20038661.shtml.

[94] See Note 22.

[95] Shahira Salloum, "Bahrain: A Return to Dialogue?" Al-Akhbar, December 14, 2012, http://english.al-akhbar.com/node/14375; Bill Law, "Bahrain Minister Plays Down Dialogue Calls," BBC, December 17, 2012, http://www.bbc.co.uk/news/world-middle-east-20757862.

[96] Kristen Chick, "Bahrain Rights Activist's Wife Details Torture, Unfair Trial," Christian Science Monitor, May 16, 2011, http://www.csmonitor.com/World/Middle-East/2011/0516/Bahrain-rights-activist-s-wife-details-torture-unfair-trial.

[97] Kristen Chick, "Amid Unrest, Bahrain Companies Fire Hundreds of Shiites," Christian Science Monitor, April 7, 2011, http://www.csmonitor.com/World/Middle-East/2011/0407/Amid-unrest-Bahrain-companies-fire-hundreds-of-Shiites.

[98] Human Rights Watch, "Bahrain – Events of 2015", n.d., https://www.hrw.org/world-report/2016/country-chapters/bahrain. See also Amnesty International, "Bahrain 2015/2016," n.d., https://www.amnesty.org/en/countries/middle-east-and-north-africa/bahrain/report-bahrain/.

[99] "Mosques Under Construction Re-Demolished by Authorities in Bahrain," Bahrain Center for Human Rights, December 9, 2012, http://www.bahrainrights.org/en/node/5550.

[100] Roy Gutman, "U.S. Warns Bahrain's Society 'Could Break Apart,'" McClatchy, November 20, 2012, http://www.mcclatchydc.com/2012/11/20/175207/us-warns-bahrains-society-could.html.

[101] "Gulf State Troops to Remain in Bahrain in 2011," World Tribune, May 13, 2011, http://www.worldtribune.com/worldtribune/WTARC/2011/me_gulf0577_05_13.asp.

[102] Thomas Fuller, "Bahrainis Fear the U.S. Isn't Behind Their Fight for Democracy," New York Times, March 5, 2011, http://www.nytimes.com/2011/03/05/world/middleeast/05bahrain.html.

[103] Adam Entous and Julian E. Barnes, "U.S. Wavers on 'Regime Change,'" Wall Street Journal, March 5, 2011, http://online.wsj.com/article/SB10001424052748703580004576180522653787198.html?mod=WSJEUROPE_hpp_MIDDLETopNews.

EGYPT

QUICK FACTS

Population: 94,666,993 (July 2016 est.)

Area: 1,001,450 sq km

Ethnic Groups: Egyptian 99.6%, other 0.4%

Religions: Muslim (predominantly Sunni) 90%, Christian (majority Coptic Orthodox, other Christians include Armenian Apostolic, Catholic, Maronite, Orthodox, and Anglican) 10%

Government Type: presidential republic

GDP (official exchange rate): $342.8 billion (2015 est.)

Map and Quick Facts courtesy of the CIA World Factbook (Last Updated January 2017)

OVERVIEW

Egypt has played a central role in the history and the development of Islamism. In 1928, an Egyptian teacher named Hassan al-Banna founded the Muslim Brotherhood, the world's first modern Islamist movement, and the most prominent Islamist force in Egypt. The Brotherhood soon conceived an ideological framework that would go on to inspire most contemporary Islamists, and eventually became the main political opposition force against successive governments in Egypt. From the time of President Gamal Abdel Nasser through the era of President Hosni Mubarak, the Muslim Brotherhood was outlawed but tolerated to varying extents.

Following the 1952 Free Officers Revolution in Egypt, during which a small group of military officers ousted King Farouk, the Brotherhood and the military-led government enjoyed a short period of cooperation. This ended with an attempt on Nasser's life in 1954, whereupon the organization was outlawed and a number of prominent Brotherhood members were imprisoned, including Hassan al-Banna's ideological descendant

Sayyid Qutb. In the late 1970s, the Muslim Brothers officially renounced violence at the insistence of President Anwar Sadat, temporarily easing their relationship with Egyptian authorities. The movement was granted enough space to expand its influence on civil society through social services and other outreach activities. This distinguished the Brotherhood at the time from jihadist groups, such Islamic Jihad (Al-Jihad), whose members assassinated President Sadat in 1981, bringing Hosni Mubarak to power. Mubarak cracked down on more radical Islamist currents such as the Islamic Jihad, and rhetorically justified the slow pace of democratic reforms by pointing to the security threat posed by extremists. The Muslim Brotherhood remained tolerated by the Mubarak regime (though still illegal), as Mubarak viewed the organization as a useful counter to the spread of those more radical ideologies.

Mubarak's ouster in 2011 marked a turning point for Islamists, with many Islamist groups establishing legal political parties to participate in post-uprising politics. In the parliamentary elections held between November 2011 and January 2012, Islamists won nearly three-quarters of all seats in the new Egyptian parliament. A Muslim Brotherhood leader, Mohammed Morsi, was elected Egypt's president on June 30, 2012, in the country's first democratic presidential election. However, in the wake of mass protests against Morsi's increasingly authoritarian and incompetent government in late June and early July of 2013, the Egyptian military ousted Morsi and replaced him with an interim government tasked with drafting a new constitution, which was approved in a popular referendum in January 2014. Meanwhile, the government severely repressed the Muslim Brotherhood, imprisoning tens of thousands of its leaders and members. Since Morsi's overthrow, Egypt has contended with an upsurge of jihadist violence in the Sinai Peninsula, where the main militant group swore allegiance to the Islamic State terrorist group in November 2014.

ISLAMIST ACTIVITY

Egyptian Islamism has always spanned a diverse ideological and operational spectrum, the entirety of which is reflected in the post-Mubarak era.

The most prominent Egyptian Islamist movement is the Muslim Brotherhood (*Al-Ikhwan al-Muslimun*), founded in 1928 by Hassan al-Banna. Its ideology states that a true "Islamic society" is one in which state institutions and the government follow the principles of the Qur'an, and in which laws follow *sharia*, or "Islamic law."[1] Al-Banna, a teacher from a modest background, was heavily influenced by Syrian-Egyptian thinker Mohammed Rashid Rida, who believed that a return to the Islam of the 7th and 8th century was the only way for Muslim societies to regain strength and to escape Western colonialism and cultural hegemony.[2] Al-Banna viewed Islam as an "all-embracing concept," meant to govern every aspect of life, and he constructed the Muslim Brotherhood to advance this totalitarian interpretation within Egypt from the grassroots up. Specifically, he sought to "reform" the individual through the Brotherhood's multi-year indoctrination process, those individuals would then form families, and the families would then spread the message within Egyptian society. Once Egyptian society was "Islamized," an Islamic state would emerge, and once this happened throughout the Muslim world, the states would unify under a new caliphate.

Muslim Brotherhood cells spread rapidly throughout Egypt in the 1920s and 1930s. Amid episodic government crackdowns, the Brotherhood formed a violent "secret apparatus," which was implicated in multiple assassinations and terrorist attacks. Al-Banna was assassinated in February 1949, and while the Brotherhood initially cooperated with Egypt's military following the July 1952 Free Officers' revolution, the new regime cracked down on it severely following an attempt on President Gamal Abdel Nasser's life. During this period, the Brotherhood's chief ideologue, Sayyid Qutb, authored the famous Islamist manifesto *Milestones Along The Way* (*Ma'alim fi-l-Tariq*) while in prison in 1964. In *Milestones*, Qutb claims that all non-Muslim societies, and indeed those societies that are only Muslim in name but not in practice, are in a state of "ignorance" (*jahiliyya*). *Jahili* societies are those that do not strictly follow revelation, and Qutb called on Muslims to wage offensive *jihad* against *jahiliyya* until they established a united Islamic community worldwide. This was interpreted as a call to arms against the Egyptian state, and Qutb was executed in 1966.[3]

Following Nasser's death in 1970, his successor, Anwar al-Sadat, lifted restrictions on Islamist activism, viewing Islamists as useful counters to the leftists who challenged his authority. During this period, a wide variety of Islamist groups emerged on Egyptian campuses, and as the Egyptian government liberated Brotherhood leaders during the 1970s, the Brotherhood integrated many of these young Islamists as the organization rebuilt itself. The Brotherhood ultimately renounced violence, thereby distinguishing itself from other Islamist movements, such as the Islamic Group (*Al-Gama'a al-Islamiyya*), which recruited on university campuses, in Egyptian prisons, and in the country's poor urban and rural areas.

The Islamic Group was involved in a series of attacks during the 1980s and 1990s aimed at deposing Egypt's secular, autocratic government and replacing it with an Islamic theocracy. These attacks included the 1997 killing of Western tourists in Luxor, the attempted assassination of President Hosni Mubarak in Ethiopia in 1995, the Cairo bombings of 1993, and several other armed operations against Egyptian intellectuals and Coptic Christians. The movement's spiritual leader, Umar Abd al-Rahman, was connected to Ramzi Yusuf, the perpetrator of the first World Trade Center bombing in 1993.[4] Rahman and nine followers were subsequently arrested and convicted of plotting to blow up the United Nations headquarters in New York, the New York Federal Reserve Building, the George Washington Bridge, and the Holland and Lincoln Tunnels. In 1999, the Islamic Group declared a unilateral ceasefire in its longstanding struggle against Cairo. This declaration marked a major ideological shift and was accompanied by a steady drift away from the use of violence, which was completed in 2002. The Islamic Group's members have not claimed responsibility for any armed attack since.[5] Subsequent moves to diminish radicalism within the party drove a faction of the Islamic Group's more violent adherents to join al-Qaeda in 2006.[6] In the 2011-2012 parliamentary elections, the Islamic Group ran under the Building and Development Party and won thirteen seats in the lower house.[7] Members of the Islamic group have protested the Egyptian military's deposing of Morsi and the dissolution of his government, but in February 2014 the organization announced it was ready to engage with the interim government to end Egypt's political impasse.[8]

The third Islamist group that has played a major role in recent Egyptian history is the Islamic Jihad (*Al-Jihad*). Active since the 1970s, it was officially formed in 1980 as a result of the merger of two Islamist cells led by Karam Zuhdi and Muhammad Abd al-Salam Faraj. Faraj's famous manifesto, *The Absent Duty* (*Al-Farida al-Ghaiba*), outlined the new movement's ideology.[9] Like those affiliated with the Islamic Group, members of the Islamic Jihad represent a relative minority within Egypt's Islamist spectrum and are mostly former members of the Brotherhood. Some are believed to have fought alongside the Afghan *mujahideen* in the 1980s against the Soviet Union. The organization's stated objective was to overthrow the Egyptian "infidel" regime and establish an Islamic government in its place. The Islamic Jihad also sought to attack U.S. and Israeli interests in Egypt and abroad. The group is infamous for assassinating President Anwar Sadat in 1981 and for additional attacks on Egyptian government officials in the early 1990s. It is also believed to have attacked Egypt's embassy in Pakistan in 1995 and to have been involved in planning bombings against U.S. embassies in Kenya and Tanzania in 1998. In June 2001, the group merged with al-Qaeda to form a new entity, called *Gama'a Qa'idat al-Jihad*, headed by Osama bin Laden's second-in-command, Ayman al-Zawahiri.

Over time, Egypt's Islamist landscape has evolved considerably. While the ideology of Egyptian Islamist groups remains radical and anti-democratic in nature, many of them have changed their tactics, favoring elections rather than revolution and/or violence as a means for achieving power.

In this vein, during the late 1970s and early 1980s, the Muslim Brotherhood increasingly disavowed *jihad* in favor of political participation. The process began with the release of a text entitled *Preachers, Not Judges* in 1969, which was likely written by multiple individuals but has been attributed to supreme guide Hassan al-Hudaybi. In this tract, al-Hudaybi developed a series of theological counterarguments to Qutb's radical views.[10] Under the influence of al-Hudaybi and his successor, Umar al-Tilmisani, the Brotherhood gradually distanced itself from armed action, gave an oath to Sadat not to use violence against his regime, and even named him a "martyr" after he was killed in 1981. Under Mubarak, the Brotherhood participated in most parliamentary elections, sometimes in partnership with legal parties, including non-

Islamist ones. However, it remained an illegal organization, and the government used its illegality as a pretext for cracking down on it whenever it appeared to be gaining strength, such as during the run-up to the 1995 elections and following the Brotherhood's success in the 2005 elections, when it won 88 of 444 contested seats.

The Brotherhood's ideological shift drew condemnation from other Islamist groups, most notably the Islamic Jihad and its commander Ayman al-Zawahiri, who severely criticized the Brotherhood's reorientation in a book entitled *The Bitter Harvest: The Muslim Brotherhood in Sixty Years* (*Al-Hasad al-Murr: Al-Ikhwan al-Muslimun fi Sittin 'Aman*).[11] In it, al-Zawahiri condemned the Brotherhood's good relations with King Farouk and Presidents Nasser, Sadat, and Mubarak:

> The Muslim Brotherhood, by recognizing the tyrants' legitimacy and sharing constitutional legitimacy with them, has become a tool in the tyrants' hands to strike *jihadist* groups in the name of [fighting] extremism and disobeying *sharia* [Islamic law]. There should be no doubt that we are proud to be outside of this "legitimacy of disbelief," which the Muslim Brotherhood has accepted and approved.

The Egyptian government's success in combating *jihadist* trends during the 1990s compelled some of these groups to offer theological arguments against political violence. One of the most prominent instances of this trend occurred within the Islamic Group. In July 1997, during a military tribunal, one of the group's activists, Muhammad al-Amin Abd al-Alim, read a statement signed by six other Islamist leaders that called on their affiliates to cease all armed operations in Egypt and abroad.[12] While it elicited considerable controversy within the movement, the statement heralded the beginning of the group's renunciation of violence. In March 1999, the group's leadership launched an "Initiative for Ceasing Violence" and declared a unilateral ceasefire. Ideologues and leaders were mostly successful in convincing their base to renounce armed struggle and support a non-violent approach by authoring a series of texts to provide the ideological justification for their rejection of violence. Leaders published four books in January 2002 under the title of *Correcting Conceptions* (*Silsilat Tashih al-Mafahim*), addressing the reasons behind the Islamic Group's ideological reorientation and explaining why jihad in Egypt had failed. Twelve other books followed, developing a critique of al-Qaeda's extreme ideology.[13]

In addition to ideological revisionism within these groups, the increasing interactions of radical Islamists with non-violent ones, as well as with non-Islamists, helped the process of embracing politics over violence to take root. This, surprisingly, occurred within Egypt's prison facilities, where inmates discussed their beliefs and tactics. The Muslim Brothers were the first to undergo such a process following the execution of Sayyid Qutb in 1966. Members of the movement began questioning the relevance of *jihad* as a way to combat the government, and many chose to reject violence. Another notable example of this dynamic was the interaction between the Islamic Group and the smaller, more radical Islamic Jihad that began in the 1990s and culminated in 2007, when the latter embraced non-violence to some degree. These efforts were led by the movement's former leader Sayyid Imam al-Sharif—also known as Abd al-Qadir Ibn Abd al-Aziz, or "Dr. Fadl." His *Document for the Right Guidance of Jihad in Egypt and the World* (*Tarshid al-'Amal al-Jihadi fi Misr wa-l-'Alam*) had an enormous impact within prisons and led numerous inmates to reject violent *jihad*.[14]

The state's use of repression and positive incentives vis-à-vis *jihadist* groups escalated following the September 11, 2001 terrorist attacks. In the case of the Islamic Group, the regime provided fighters with pensions, and the Interior Ministry offered other incentives such as business grants to reformed *jihadists*.[15] In addition, the heavy-handed approach of Egyptian security forces to radical movements encouraged the view that armed resistance was no longer a promising method for these elements to achieve their goals.

To be sure, these efforts to dissuade violence did not always resonate with group members. The case of Islamic Jihad, for which deradicalization has only been partially successful, illustrates this point. While the group's leaders have publicly abandoned violence, some affiliated factions continue to advocate *jihad*, sometimes even leaving the movement to join other groups more closely aligned with their beliefs. One cell of Islamic Jihad, for example, joined al-Qaeda in the early 2000s and was likely involved in the wave of attacks that hit Egypt after 2003. The Islamic Group faced similar difficulties. In a 2010 interview, Nagih Ibrahim, one of its former ideologues, emphasized that although the group's formal rejection of violence had obviously helped limit the spread of violent Islamism in Egypt, such ideological revisions had had less impact on the younger generations, especially those sympathetic toward or active within hardline *jihadist* groups such as al-Qaeda.[16]

By the same token, the Brotherhood's renunciation of violence was limited to the domestic sphere. The organization otherwise continued to praise terrorist acts conducted by its Palestinian off-shoot Hamas, as well as by the Iranian-backed Shi'ite militia Hezbollah. Several little-known violent groups, like the *jihadist* "Abdallah Azzam Brigades in Egypt" or the "Holy Warriors of Egypt,"[17] also emerged in the 2000s, spreading radical and extremist ideologies, conducting anti-regime activity, and accusing society and state institutions of "apostasy."[18] Another group calling itself "Monotheism and Holy War" (*Tawhid wa-l-Jihad*), which was connected to al-Qaeda, emerged during that period in the Sinai. It targeted the country's tourism sector in a wave of bombings that first hit the town of Taba in 2004 and then the resort towns of Sharm al-Sheikh and Dahab in 2005 and 2006.

The Sinai Peninsula, in particular, has been a hotbed for Islamic extremism for years. The Peninsula has been largely neglected by the state for decades, and clauses in the 1979 Egypt-Israel peace treaty restrict Egyptian security operations in the Sinai, though the two sides negotiated massive Egyptian deployments to combat *jihadists* in recent years under one of the treaty's annexes. During the 2000s, however, the mix of state neglect and insufficient security control enabled groups to develop smuggling networks, plan attacks, and develop local support, and a number of militant groups have expressed the goal of creating an independent Islamic Emirate in the Peninsula.

When Mubarak was ousted following Egypt's 2011 "Arab Spring" uprising, Islamic extremist activities there took on a new intensity. On multiple occasions, armed fighters attacked Egyptian security forces, police stations, and the al Arish-Ashkelon pipeline exporting natural gas to Israel and Jordan. Other operations targeted Israeli patrols and soldiers.[19] New *jihadist* groups emerged, such as the "Supporters of Holy War" (*Ansar al-Jihad*),[20] while other existing groups like "Excommunication and Exodus" (*Takfir wa-l-Hijra*), established in 1965 by Muslim Brother Shukri Mustafa, have been reconstituted.[21] After the military ousted President Mohammed Morsi on July 3, 2013, violence has surged, mostly propelled by relatively small insurgent groups, the most prominent of which was *Ansar Beit al-Maqdis*, which swore allegiance to the Islamic State in November 2014 and renamed itself *Wilayat Sinai* (Sinai Province).[22] On August 7, 2013, the army launched an operation into the Sinai and killed sixty suspected terrorists, losing thirty from their own ranks, and it remains engaged against these groups at the time of this writing.[23] Overall, the Sinai region with its mountainous terrain, particularly in the areas of Rafah and Sheikh Zuwaid, provides vast hideouts for *jihadist* networks and has become increasingly unstable since the July 3 2013 coup. The Egyptian government's tight control over news regarding its operations in the Sinai make it difficult to assess the military's performance, though the continuation of attacks within the Sinai reflect the military's failure to restore security in the Peninsula thus far.

ISLAMISM AND SOCIETY

Since the 1950s, failures in governance, economic stagnation, and political exclusion have provided opportunities for reactionary Islamists to expand their influence in Egyptian society. Islamists have used their politicized interpretation of Islam as a source of legitimacy, and they have set up a number of informal institutions (charities, educational organizations, health services) to advance their ideology within various sectors.[24] While some extremist groups started to renounce violence in the 1970s, this rejection almost always catalyzed the emergence of violent groups that rejected the renunciations. As a result, radical discourse perpetuated within Islamist circles even when groups were technically non-violent. For example, the Brotherhood continued to read and teach Sayyid Qutb's works even while claiming to have disavowed them.

Meanwhile, political stagnation and poor economic conditions under Mubarak generated sympathy for the Muslim Brotherhood and Salafist groups, which offered social services, religious education, and preaching.[25] Salafists inherit their name from the Arabic term "*al-salaf al-salih*," meaning the "righteous ancestors," a phrase referring to the first generations of Muslims after the Prophet Mohammed's death who sought to emulate his practices and maintained a literalist reading of the Qur'an and the *hadith* (the sayings of the Prophet). Salafists regard deviations from this literalist approach as *bida'a* (innovation), and therefore tantamount to *kufr* (apostasy). Under Mubarak, Salafists were strictly prohibited from political activities – in stark contrast to the Brotherhood, which was at times tolerated within formal politics and at other times repressed. Salafists therefore focused almost exclusively on social work and spiritual development, and were permitted to launch television networks dedicated to preaching. At the same time, the most prominent Salafist groups such as Salafist Call (*al-Dawa al-Salfiyya*) encouraged allegiance to the state, including at the height of the 2011 uprising, though some (typically younger) Salafists rejected this and joined the protests.

The presence of Salafists in Egypt began in the early 20th century. The first Salafist association, the "Sharia Assembly," was created in 1912, even before the formation of the Muslim Brotherhood. Another group, named the "Supporters of the Sunna" (*Ansar Al-Sunna*), was founded by Sheikh Mohammed Hamid al-Fiqi in 1926. Its members were focused on protecting monotheism and fighting un-Islamic practices and beliefs.

Salafism became more visible in Egypt during the 1970s and 1980s, for two reasons. First, as previously mentioned, President Sadat permitted Islamists greater freedom during this period to counter the leftists domestically. Second, Egyptians working abroad in Saudi Arabia and other Persian Gulf states returned home to Egypt. It was during this period that the organization "Salafist Call" was established. The Salafist Call is the preeminent Salafist organization in Egypt, and in the past has focused primarily on preaching and social service, but recently has shifted to focus on politics. In 1980, the Salafists institutionalized their activities, and the Salafist Call became active in education and charity. Yet the Egyptian state soon outlawed the movement, and regularly arrested its members.

Although few Egyptians openly identified as Salafists under the Mubarak regime, there were signs that their puritanical interpretation of Islam was gaining ground among the general public. This was, for instance, evidenced by the growing number of women wearing the *niqab*, (full veil) and men growing their beards. Beyond the traditional role of radical *imams* in mosques, satellite television channels also started to adopt explicitly Salafist rhetoric, and widened their audience in the process.[26] The phenomenon was worrisome to a number of secular Egyptians, especially as it related to the protection of women's and minority rights, which most Salafists reject.

Radical Islamists have openly targeted religious minorities for years in an attempt to provoke sectarian warfare in Egypt. Coptic Christians, a community that represents 10 percent of the population, has been a special target of Salafist bigotry, though anti-Christian (and anti-Semitic) ideas also pervade Brotherhood teachings. Militant Salafists commonly portray Christians as "infidels" who conspire against Islam, and have regularly called for violent attacks on them.[27] The rise of Islamists following Mubarak's ouster brought these attitudes to the fore, as radical preachers called minorities "heretics" and threatened to expel them if they did not pay the *jizya*, a tax levied on non-Muslims, in certain instances.[28]

Since the 2011 uprising, Salafists have engaged in a massive anti-Coptic hate campaign. As a result, many Egyptian Christians left the country during this period, fearing for their future under Islamist rule.[29] In 2012, several Salafists accused Copts of being "traitors" for voting against Islamists in the presidential polls.[30] Then following Morsi's ouster in July 2013, dozens of churches were torched nationwide. Unfortunately, these types of attacks have continued under the rule of President Abdel Fattah al-Sisi, despite the fact that he is not an Islamist and the Coptic Orthodox Church's close official relations with him.

Salafists have also targeted other sects of Islam, such as the Shi'a, Baha'i and Sufis, viewing them as un-Islamic because of their beliefs.[31] Before 2011, Salafists managed to ban the *dhikr* (a devotional act of Sufi orders) and continued to call for the prohibition of all Sufi ceremonies. In addition to labeling Sufis as "infidels," Salafists accuse them of encouraging sin and debauchery by mixing the sexes at shrines and during their rituals—a practice that Salafists consider improper. They have, for example, regularly pointed to the mosque of Ahmad al-Badawi in Tanta—where the founder of the Sufi *Ahmadiyya* order is buried—which does not enforce segregation between men and women, except during prayers, as one instance of un-Islamic behavior. Salafists also view ancient Egyptian monuments as idolatrous, and various Salafist groups threatened to cover the pyramids in wax following Mubarak's overthrow, when these groups appeared to be on the threshold of power.[32]

Finally, Salafists have increasingly targeted Egyptian women. Egyptian law requires that at least one candidate from each party be a woman. The Salafist Al-Nour party responded by running female candidates, but replacing their pictures with either a rose or a logo. On multiple occasions, Salafist leaders who have appeared on political talk shows insist either that they be separated from female hosts by a screen, or that the female hosts wear the veil. In 2011, the spokesman of the Salafist Daawa party, Abdel Moneim Alshahat, requested that host Iman al-Israf wear a headscarf during their interview. Al-Ishraf consented. After the interview he told her that she should: "wear the veil now voluntarily before you have to wear it by force."[33]

ISLAMISM AND THE STATE

From the 1970s until the overthrow of Mubarak, the Egyptian state actively fought violent Islamists who acted locally, but tolerated other Islamist groups at certain points while repressing them at others. The Muslim Brotherhood in particular used moments of tolerance to build its nationwide organization and win parliamentary seats, and it frequently generated public sympathy when the regime then cracked down on it.

The Brotherhood's greatest political success during these years came in 2005, when it fielded approximately 150 candidates in the parliamentary elections and won 88 of 444 contested seats, making it the largest opposition bloc. The regime viewed these gains as threatening, and it responded with a series of constitutional amendments in 2007 that limited the political participation of religious groups. The following year, these restrictions resulted in the rejection of more than 800 Muslim Brothers as candidates for local council elections. Additional constitutional changes further extended the "temporary" emergency law enforced after the assassination of President Anwar Sadat in 1981. And the adoption of a new anti-terrorism law (Article 179) gave security forces extensive powers to crack down on Islamists. During the November 2010 parliamentary elections, the repression worsened: hundreds of Muslim Brothers were arrested, and the organization's parliamentary candidates lost the most forged elections in Egypt's contemporary history.[34]

While the fraudulence of the late 2010 parliamentary elections contributed to the January 2011 uprising, the Brotherhood and Salafist groups largely stayed on the sidelines during its earliest days. Salafist groups largely preached fealty to the state, while the Brotherhood feared that its participation in the protests would catalyze an even more severe crackdown. (Indeed, the Mubarak regime warned the Brotherhood prior to the protests that it would decapitate the organization if it got involved.) Moreover, the Brotherhood's leaders were skeptical of the mostly non-Islamist youth activists who called for the protests.[35] After massive protests on January 25, 2011, however, the Brotherhood endorsed the pivotal January 28th "Friday of Rage" protests, during which protesters overwhelmed the police and forced the military to take control of the streets. The Brotherhood attempted to negotiate with the regime on at least two occasions during the uprising, but faced criticism from its youth members and revolutionary groups for doing so, and ultimately called for Mubarak's overthrow on February 7, 2011, four days before Mubarak was forced from power.[36]

Following Mubarak's overthrow and the collapse of his ruling National Democratic Party, Egypt's Islamist groups were the only political forces capable of mobilizing their members nationwide. Non-Islamist groups, by contrast, had been weakened after decades of mostly working within the regime's legal constraints. So when the Supreme Council of the Armed Forces (SCAF) took control of the country on February 11, 2011 and opened Egypt's political arena, many of these Islamist groups quickly established legal political parties. In this vein, the Brotherhood announced in late April 2011 the creation of its "Freedom and Justice Party" (FJP), stating that its policies would be grounded in Islamic principles, but that the party would be non-confessional and tolerant, including both women and Christians in its ranks. In June 2011, the FJP received official recognition as a political party, enabling it to run candidates in the 2011-2012 parliamentary elections.

In a surprising and unexpected move,[37] the Salafist Call too entered party politics, establishing the "Light Party" (*Hizb al-Nour*), led by Imad Abd al-Ghaffour, as did the Islamic Group with its "Building and Development Party" (*Hizb al-Bina' wa-l-Tanmia*). The new Salafist end of the political spectrum also included smaller movements such as the ultraconservative "*Al-Asala* Party" in Cairo, founded by Adil Abd al-Maqsoud Afifi. This marked a considerable historical departure for Salafist groups, which had always been apolitical. Members of the groups generally refused to work with un-Islamic state institutions, dismissing the concept of democracy as "alien."[38] But under the guidance of charismatic preachers, Salafist movements opted for participation because they saw it as an opportunity to implement *sharia* and feared that their failure to participate would lead to Egypt's secularization.[39] Salafists also sought to provide ideological justification for their entry into politics. One important concern for leaders was to make sure that its members did not view the decision to enter the political arena as an abandonment of religious principles. Their arguments hinged on pointing to the duty incumbent on Muslims to try and implement *sharia* law wherever possible. Given the contested political environment of post-Mubarak Egypt, this duty was now achievable, and the alternative (namely, a secular regime) would constitute negligence of that duty.

Non-Islamist political parties, some of which had only recently been established and others whose growth was stunted during Mubarak's rule, fared poorly in the parliamentary elections of late 2011 and early 2012. By contrast, Islamists did extremely well: the FJP-led Democratic Alliance for Egypt won 47 percent of the seats, while the Light Part-dominated Islamic Bloc, which included the Islamic Group's Building and Development Party, won 24 percent. The Wasat Party, an offshoot of the Brotherhood, won another two percent of the parliament.[40] The Salafists' electoral gains were by far the most unanticipated development of the election.[41]

The most critical issue before the resulting parliament was selecting the members of the Constituent Assembly, as that body would draft Egypt's new constitution. Muslim Brotherhood leader Saad al-Katatny was appointed parliamentary speaker, Muslim Brothers became either the chairman or deputy chairman of 18 out of 19 total committees, and Salafist Ministers of Parliament had the chairmanships of three committees.[42] Though the Brotherhood and the Salafists certainly had their differences, both wanted a Constituent Assembly that was as Islamist as possible. The two groups collaborated to produce an Assembly that was roughly 65 percent Islamist. Non-Islamist Assembly members were alarmed by this turn of events, and responded by boycotting the Assembly. A court disbanded the Assembly just two weeks after it had been formed.

However, the Assembly was not the Brotherhood's last attempt to use its dominance in parliament to its advantage. The group did its best to undermine the SCAF's political legitimacy, including trying to use the parliament to declare no confidence in the SCAF-backed government. In response, the SCAF issued a statement that tacitly threatened with a major crackdown.[43]

In 2011, just before the collapse of Mubarak's regime, the Muslim Brotherhood had promised not to run a presidential candidate. The simmering tensions between the military and the Brotherhood, combined with the threat of a new crackdown, propelled the group into breaking that promise. Furthermore, former Muslim Brotherhood leader Abdel Moneim Abouel Fotouh had emerged as a dominant candidate in the presidential elections of May/June 2012. The Brotherhood had banished Abouel Fotouh from its ranks for declaring his intention to run for president, despite the group's orders not to do so. The Brotherhood was concerned that if it did not run its own approved candidate, its members would vote for a disgraced former member and cause chaos in the ranks.[44]

The Brotherhood's initial candidate was disqualified due to his incarceration during the Mubarak regime, as were several other leading candidates, for a variety of reasons.[45] The Brotherhood nominated FJP chairman Mohammed Morsi. The final list of candidates included thirteen people, including members of former governments. Hamdeen Sabbahi was a member of parliament during Nasser's time, Ahmed Shafiq was Mubarak's Prime Minister, and Amr Moussa was a former Foreign Minister. Morsi won with 24 percent of the vote,[46] and then won the run-off election against Shafik with 51.7 percent of the vote.

In June of 2012, a court disbanded the FJP-controlled parliament on the grounds that its election was unconstitutional, because the electoral format did not give political independents an equal opportunity to win. Also in June, the SCAF issued a constitutional declaration that protected the military from the president's oversight and granted itself legislative authority, to prevent Morsi from gaining power. In response, the Brotherhood and its allies occupied Cairo's Tahrir Square and threatened mass protests if Morsi did not become Egypt's president.

The constitutional declaration had significant impact. When Morsi was sworn in on June 30th, 2012, there was no parliament and no new constitution, and his exact powers were poorly defined.[47] On August 12, however, Morsi used a major attack in the Sinai that had taken place the previous week as a pretext for firing the SCAF's leaders, promoting director of military intelligence Abdel Fatah al-Sisi to defense minister, and issuing a new constitutional declaration granting himself legislative power until a new parliament was sworn in.[48]

This made Morsi Egypt's undisputed power holder, at least legally. But in November 2012, it appeared as though a second Constituent Assembly, which parliament had appointed before it was disbanded in June, was going to be nullified by the courts much as the first one had been. Morsi responded by issuing another constitutional declaration that protected the Constituent Assembly from the courts, but also placed his own edicts above any judicial oversight. It was effectively a total power grab, and when mass protests broke out, Morsi used the ensuing political crisis to ram a theocratic constitution through to ratification.[49]

While the new constitution passed by 64 percent through referendum,[50] the political crisis persisted for months, with increasingly violent protests against Morsi erupting with greater regularity. Meanwhile, the economy plummeted, lines for gas extended around city blocks, and power shortages created outages lasting many hours on end.[51] As a result, on June 30, 2013, millions of Egyptians took to the streets to demand Morsi's ouster. When Morsi refused to compromise, the military responded by ousting Morsi on July 3, 2013.

In the wake of the coup, the Brotherhood gathered is members and allies in northern Cairo's Rabaa al-Adawiya Square and Giza's al-Nahda Square. Protesters denounced the interim government installed to replace Morsi as illegitimate. After negotiations between the new government and the Brotherhood broke down, security forces violently cleared these protests on August 14, 2013, killing at least 800 civilians, according to Human Rights Watch.[52]

After the clearing of Rabaa, the government arrested tens of thousands of Brotherhood leaders and supporters. Then, following a massive terrorist incident in al-Mansoura in December 2013, the government labeled the Muslim Brotherhood as a terrorist group.[53] Ultimately the government's crackdown on the Brotherhood appears to have been successful: with its leaders in prison, exile, or hiding, the organization has been decapitated, rendering it incapable of executing a nationwide strategy within Egypt. Meanwhile, the Brotherhood faces a significant internal crisis pitting younger members, who want to fight the current government with violence, against older leaders, who fear that Brotherhood violence will legitimate the regime's crackdown. The Brotherhood youth's wing appears to have won internal elections that were held in 2014, which explains the Brotherhood's January 2015 statement calling for *jihad* and martyrdom in fighting the regime. But the "old guard" has rejected these elections, creating a rift that has not been resolved at the time of this writing. While deputy supreme guide Mahmoud Ezzat, who heads the group's "old guard" faction, called for reunifying the organization (presumably under his leadership), the Brotherhood's youth-oriented "revolutionary" faction appeared to consolidate its power with new elections in late 2015, after which some of its older members resigned from their leadership posts.[54]

Due to these internal disagreements as well as the Egyptian government's repression, the Brotherhood no longer represents a significant threat to the current regime. The regime has sought to prevent the Brotherhood's possible reemergence by shutting down its social services and implementing strict restrictions on mosque preaching. In this vein, in mid-2016, the Egyptian government mandated that *imams* read government-approved sermons in Friday prayers. This edict was also intended to constrain Salafist preachers, despite the fact that the leading Salafist party – the Light Party – supported Morsi's overthrow and is the only Islamist group still participating in Egyptian politics.

In the Brotherhood's absence, however, other Islamist groups have emerged. Islamist youths who appear to have been affiliated with the Brotherhood have formed a variety of low-level insurgency groups, such as the Molotov Movement and Revolutionary Punishment, which focus their attacks on state infrastructure and security forces. At the same time, Sinai-based *jihadists* used the coup as a pretext for escalating their attacks on security forces. These groups also benefitted from the regional environment: state breakdown in Libya made weapons more available and therefore cheaper to acquire. These groups also aligned to varying extents with groups in Gaza, such as Hamas, in trying to destabilize the Egyptian government.

The most significant *jihadist* group is Ansar Bayt al-Maqdis, (Supporters of Jerusalem). Ansar Bayt al-Maqdis started its violent operations immediately following Mubarak's ouster in 2011, targeting Israel and Israeli interests in Egypt, such as the al Arish-Ashkelon natural gas pipeline, which has been bombed repeatedly since 2011. Since the 2013 coup, however, the Egyptian military has been the organization's primary target and, as previously mentioned, the Egyptian military has been actively fighting ABM since September 2013.[55] Another *jihadist* group is Ajnad Misr ("Soldiers of Egypt"), which emerged in late January 2014, saying that it was targeting "criminal" elements of the regime. As of early February 2014, the group has claimed responsibility for seven attacks in Cairo.[56] Ansar Bayt al-Maqdis has referred to Ajnad Misr as "brothers" and suggested that the two organizations have cooperated on attacks in the past, but neither the extent nor the nature of the collaboration is currently known. Meanwhile, Brotherhood sympathizers have formed smaller militant organizations, such as Revolutionary Punishment and *Hasm*, which have orchestrated numerous attacks against security forces.[57]

While the rise of *jihadist* groups within Egypt since Morsi's ouster bodes ill for the country's long-term stability, Islamists overall exert less influence in Egypt today than they have in nearly five decades. The Brotherhood's rapid failure in power, combined with a broad anti-Brotherhood media campaign within Egypt, badly damaged the organization's image. And despite the attempts of some Brotherhood leaders to exert influence from exile in Istanbul, London, and elsewhere, they are increasingly detached from events on the ground. Moreover, the government's severe repression of the organization has deterred other Islamist organizations from escalating their activities, and many of the Brotherhood's initial allies in the "Coalition for Legitimacy" have either been imprisoned or resigned from the coalition. For this reason, those Islamists who have not joined *jihadist* movements have deferred their political ambitions until the current regime falls, whenever that might be.

Endnotes

[1] For an overview of the Muslim Brotherhood's formative ideology, see Hassan al-Banna's writings and memoirs, among which the Letter To A Muslim Student posits the core principles of the movement. For the English translation, see http://www.jannah.org/articles/letter.html.

[2] For a detailed biography, see "Muhammad Rashid Rida," Encyclopedia Britannica online, n.d., http://www.britannica.com/EBchecked/topic/491703/Rashid-Rida.

[3] Sayyid Qutb, Milestones (Kazi Publications, 2007).

[4] "The Trial Of Omar Abdel Rahman," New York Times, October 3, 1995, http://www.nytimes.com/1995/10/03/opinion/the-trial-of-omar-abdel-rahman.html.

[5] Holly Fletcher, "Jamaat al-Islamiyya," Council on Foreign Relations (CFR) Backgrounder, May 30, 2008, http://www.cfr.org/publication/9156/jamaat_alislamiyya.html.

[6] Dana J Suster, "Egyptian political party wants off U.S. terrorist list," Foreign Policy, May 14, 2013, http://blog.foreignpolicy.com/posts/2013/05/14/egyptian_political_party_wants_off_us_terrorist_list.

[7] "Egypt: 2011/2012 People's Assembly elections results," Electoral Institute for Sustainable Democracy in Africa, January 2013, http://www.eisa.org.za/WEP/egy2012results1.htm.

[8] Kamel Kamel and Ramy Nawar, "Gamaa Islamiyya seeking political solution to current crisis," The Cairo Post, February 20, 2014, http://thecairopost.com/news/92346/news/gamaa-islamiyya-seeking-political-solution-to-current-crisis.

[9] Youssef H. Aboul-Enein, "Al-Ikhwan Al-Muslimeen: the Muslim Brotherhood," Military Review, July-August 2003, 26-31, http://www.ikhwanweb.com/print.php?id=5617.

[10] Barbara Zollner, The Muslim Brotherhood: Hasan al-Hudaybi and Ideology (London: Routledge, 2008).

[11] This book was first published in 1991 and attacked the Brotherhood for its "betrayal" after "recognizing the legitimacy of secular institutions" in Egypt and "helping the Tyrants [the government]" repress jihadists. Ayman al-Zawahiri, The Bitter Harvest: The Muslim Brotherhood in Sixty Years, trans. Nadia Masid, (Egypt: n.p., 1991).

[12] Omar Ashour, "Lions tamed? An inquiry into the causes of de-radicalization of armed Islamist movements: the case of the Egyptian Islamic Group," Middle East Journal 61, no. 4, 2007, 596-597; Rohan Gunaratna and Mohamed Bin Ali, "De-Radicalization Initiatives in Egypt: A Preliminary Insight," Studies in Conflict & Terrorism 32, no. 4, 2009, 277-291.

[13] Among these are Karam Zuhdi, The Strategy and the Bombings of Al-Qaeda: Mistakes and Dangers (Istratijiyyat wa Tajjirat al-Qa'ida: Al-Akhta' wa-l-Akhtar) (Cairo: Al-Turath al-Islami, 2002); Nagih Ibrahim and Ali al-Sharif, Banning Extremism in Religion and the Excommunication of Muslims (Hurmat al-Ghuluw fi-I-Din wa Takfir al-Muslimin) (Cairo: Al-Turath al-Islami, 2002).

[14] On this interactional process, see Omar Ashour, "De-Radicalization of Jihad? The Impact of Egyptian Islamist Revisionists on Al-Qaeda," Perspectives on Terrorism II, no. 5, 2008, http://www.terrorismanalysts.com/pt/index.php?option=com_rokzine&view=article&id=39&Itemid=54. See also Lawrence Wright, "The Rebellion Within: An Al Qaeda mastermind questions terrorism," The New Yorker, June 2, 2008, http://www.newyorker.com/reporting/2008/06/02/080602fa_fact_wright?currentPage=all.

[15] Ashour, "Lions tamed?"

[16] Mohammad Mahmoud, "Islamic Group theorist: al-Qaeda's ideology in a state of decline," Al-Shorfa.com, August 2, 2010, http://www.al-shorfa.com/cocoon/meii/xhtml/en_GB/features/meii/features/main/2010/08/02/feature-01.

[17] "Who are the Abdullah Azzam Brigades?" Reuters, August 4, 2010, http://uk.reuters.com/article/idUKTRE6733QJ20100804; Hugh Roberts, "Egypt's Sinai Problem," The Independent (London), April 26, 2006, http://www.crisisgroup.org/en/regions/middle-east-north-africa/egypt-syria-lebanon/egypt/egypts-sinai-problem.aspx.

[18] See "Another Salafi-Jihadi Cell Arrested In Egypt," Middle East Media Research Institute MEMRI TV no. 5017, January 4, 2010, http://www.memritv.org/report/en/4193.htm.

[19] "Egypt army dispatches team to Sinai following Eilat attack," Ahram Online (Cairo), April 17, 2013, http://english.ahram.org.eg/News/69484.aspx; Jodi Rudoren, "Sinai Attack Tests New Egyptian President's Relationship With Israel," New York Times, August 6, 2012, http://www.nytimes.com/2012/08/07/world/middleeast/sinai-attack-a-test-for-israel-egypt-and-gaza.html; "Pipeline Supplying Israel Is Attacked," Agence France Presse, February 4, 2012, http://www.nytimes.com/2012/02/05/world/middleeast/egyptian-pipeline-supplying-israel-is-attacked.html?_r=0.

[20] See Bill Roggio, "Ansar al Jihad swears allegiance to al Qaeda's emir," Long War Journal, January 24, 2012, http://www.longwarjournal.org/archives/2012/01/ansar_al_jihad_swear.php.

[21] See Abigail Hauslohner, "What Scares the Sinai Bedouin: the Rise of the Radical Islamists," Time, August 10, 2011, http://www.time.com/time/world/article/0,8599,2087797,00.html.

[22] Abigail Hauslohner, "In Egypt's Sinai, insurgency taking root," Washington Post, July 28, 2013, http://www.washingtonpost.com/world/insurgency-takes-root-in-egypts-sinai/2013/07/28/2e3e01da-f7a4-11e2-a954-358d90d5d72d_story.html; Stephanie McCrummen, "Car bombs hit military site in Egypt's Volatile Sinai Peninsula," Washington Post, September 11, 2013, http://www.washingtonpost.com/world/middle_east/car-bombs-hit-military-sites-in-egypts-volatile-sinai-peninsula/2013/09/11/53f6d30e-1ae3-11e3-80ac-96205cacb45a_story.html.

[23] "Egypt since Mohammed Morsi was ousted: timeline" ABC News, August 15, 2013, http://www.abc.net.au/news/2013-08-15/egypt-since-mohammed-morsi-was-ousted3a-timeline/4887986.

[24] See Samir Amin, "Egypt: Muslim Brotherhood - Revolutionary or Anti-Revolutionary?" Pambazuka News, July 4, 2012, http://www.pambazuka.org/en/category/features/83202.

[25] On the rise and spread of Salafism in Egyptian society, see Nathan Field and Ahmed Hamem, "Egypt: Salafism Making Inroads," Carnegie Endowment for International Peace Arab Reform Bulletin, March 9, 2009, http://www.carnegieendowment.org/arb/?fa=show&article=22823; Saif Nasrawi, "Egypt's Salafis: When My Enemy's Foe Isn't My Friend," Al-Masry al-Youm (Cairo), April 27, 2010, http://www.egyptindependent.com/news/egypt%E2%80%99s-salafis-when-my-enemy%E2%80%99s-foe-isn%E2%80%99t-my-friend.

[26] On the media dimension, see Nathan Field and Ahmed Hamam, "Salafi Satellite TV In Egypt," Arab Media & Society no. 8, Spring 2009, http://www.arabmediasociety.com/?article=712.

[27] See "Salafi Violence against Copts," Islamopedia online, n.d., http://www.islamopediaonline.org/country-profile/egypt/salafists/salafi-violence-against-copts.

[28] See "Coptic (Catholic) priest: We will resist reimposition of jizya to the point of martyrdom," Jihad Watch, January 2, 2012, http://www.jihadwatch.org/2012/01/coptic-priest-we-will-resist-reimposition-of-jizya-to-the-point-of-martyrdom.html.

[29] André Aciman, "After Egypt's Revolution, Christians Are Living in Fear," New York Times, November 19, 2011, http://www.nytimes.com/2011/11/20/opinion/sunday/after-egypts-revolution-christians-are-living-in-fear.html?pagewanted=all.

[30] "Islamists in Egypt Blame Christians for Voting," Assyrian International News Agency (AINA), May 29, 2012, http://www.aina.org/news/20120528191505.htm.

[31] See Baher Ibrahim, "Salafi Intolerance Threatens Sufis," The Guardian (London), May 10, 2010, http://www.guardian.co.uk/commentisfree/belief/2010/may/10/islam-sufi-salafi-egypt-religion.

[32] See Sarah Sheffer, "Salafi group reaffirms call to set Egypt's Pharaonic relics in wax," bikyarmasr.com, December 6, 2011, http://www.masress.com/en/bikyamasr/50394; Raymond Ibrahim, "Calls to Destroy Egypt's Great Pyramids Begin," Counter Jihad Report, July 10, 2012, http://counterjihadreport.com/2012/07/10/calls-to-destroy-egypts-great-pyramids-begin/.

[33] Mohammad Abdel Rahman, "Effacing Women in Salafi Campaign Bid," Al-Akhbar, November 15, 2011, http://english.al-akhbar.com/node/1505.

[34] Yasmine Fathi, "Another Round of MB Arrests," Ahram Online (27 Nov. 2010): <http://english.ahram.org.eg/NewsContent/1/5/677/Egypt/Egypt-Elections-/Another-round-of-MB-arrests.aspx>.

[35] "Egyptian Elections Watch: Al-Nour Party,", Ahram Online (Cairo), December 4, 2011, http://english.ahram.org.eg/NewsContentPrint/33/0/26693/Elections-/0/AlNour-Party.aspx.

[36] Eric Trager, Arab Fall: How the Muslim Brotherhood Won and Lost Egypt in 891 Days (Washington: Georgetown University Press, 2016) 32-25.

[37] See Omar Ashour, "The unexpected rise of Salafists has complicated Egyptian politics," Daily Star, January 6, 2012, http://www.dailystar.com.lb/Opinion/Commentary/2012/Jan-06/159027-the-unexpected-rise-of-salafists-has-complicated-egyptian-politics.ashx#ixzz1iz2mHPKa.

[38] The Islamic Group declared: "We believe that the suffering we endured during the past years was due to neglecting religion and putting those who don't fear [God] in power (...) Islam can contain everyone and respects the freedom of followers of other religions to refer to their own Sharia in private affairs." See "Al-Gamaa Al-Islamiya calls for unity, says minority rights guaranteed," Daily News Egypt, September 1, 2011, http://www.dailynewsegypt.com/2011/09/01/al-gamaa-al-islamiya-calls-for-unity-says-minority-rights-guaranteed/.

[39] Salafist cleric Yasser Burhami, who was instrumental in the establishment of the al-Nour party, declared that, "Islam must become involved of all aspects of life, even the political, and the Islamic movement must unite." See Hani Nasira, "The Salafist movement in Egypt" (Al-Salafiyya fi Misr), Al-Ahram Center for Political and Strategic Studies Strategic Note no. 46, 2011.

[40] Jasmine Coleman, "Egypt election results show firm win for Islamists," The Guardian (London), January 21, 2012, http://www.theguardian.com/world/2012/jan/21/egypt-election-clear-islamist-victory.

[41] Yolande Knell, "What will Salafists' election success mean for Egypt?" BBC News, December 12, 2011, http://www.bbc.co.uk/news/world-middle-east-16112833.

[42] Sherif Tarek, "El-Katatni: From prisoner to speaker of parliament," Ahram Online (Cairo), January 24, 2012, http://english.ahram.org.eg/NewsContent/1/0/32600/Egypt//ElKatatni-from-prisoner-to-speaker-of-parliament.aspx.

[43] Trager (2016) 122-124.

[44] Trager (2016) 129-130.

[45] Muslim Brotherhood and Salafists excluded from presidential poll," Asia News, April 16, 2012, http://www.asianews.it/news-en/Muslim-Brotherhood-and-Salafists-excluded-from-presidential-poll-24512.html.

[46] Although some contest the electoral results. See Borzou Daragahi, "Egypt nervously awaits election results," Financial Times, June 22, 2012, http://www.ft.com/cms/s/0/a17de564-bc5b-11e1-a470-00144feabdc0.html#axzz21WobfdCf.

[47] Trager (2016) 145.

[48] Trager (2016) 157-160.

[49] Trager (2016) 175-177.

[50] Trager (2016) 186-187.

[51] Trager (2016) 209.

[52] Ali Omar, "Muslim Brotherhood responds to NCHR Rabaa report," Daily News Egypt, March 8, 2014, http://www.dailynewsegypt.com/2014/03/08/muslim-brotherhood-responds-nchr-rabaa-report/.

[53] Salma Abdelaziz and Steve Almasy, "Egypt's interim Cabinet officially labels Muslim Brotherhood a terrorist group," CNN, December 25, 2013, http://www.cnn.com/2013/12/25/world/africa/egypt-muslim-brotherhood-terrorism/.

[54] Amr Darrag, "Statement of My Retirement from Political Work," Facebook December 22, 2016, https://www.facebook.com/amr.darrag.9/posts/1188793107837161.

[55] "Profile: Egypt's militant Ansar Beit al-Maqdis group," BBC News, January 24, 2014, http://www.bbc.com/news/world-middle-east-25882504.

[56] David Barnett, "Ajnad Misr claims 7th Cairo area attack, 6 wounded," The Long War Journal, February 7, 2014, http://www.longwarjournal.org/threat-matrix/archives/2014/02/ajnad_misr_claims_7th_cairo_ar.php.

[57] See for example, "Deadliest attack in months on Egypt's Security forces," CBS News December 9, 2016, http://www.cbsnews.com/news/egypt-cairo-explosion-police-killed-likely-bomb-attack-pyramids-road-giza.

IRAQ

> **QUICK FACTS**
>
> Population: 38,146,025 (July 2016 est.)
>
> Area: 438,317 sq km
>
> Ethnic Groups: Arab 75%-80%, Kurdish 15%-20%, Turkoman, Assyrian, other 5%
>
> Religions: Muslim (official) 99% (Shia 60%-65%, Sunni 32%-37%), Christian 0.8%, Hindu <0.1, Buddhist <0.1, Jewish <0.1, folk religion <0.1, unafilliated 0.1, other <0.1
>
> Government Type: federal parliamentary republic
>
> GDP (official exchange rate): $156.3 billion (2015 est.)
>
> *Map and Quick Facts courtesy of the CIA World Factbook (January 2017)*

OVERVIEW

Iraq's history contains both secular and Islamist currents. Shi'a and Sunni Islamist movements formed in Iraq in response to Saddam Hussein's secular nationalist Ba'athist regime, and as part of the political Islam movement sweeping the region in general. Most of these Islamist parties existed in exile or in hiding for much of 1980s and 1990s and emerged in Iraq only after the fall of Saddam in 2003. Since that time, both Sunni and Shi'a Islamist parties have played an important role in Iraq's political system. Although the 2010 parliamentary election saw the rise of secular political coalitions, rising sectarianism gave new life to Islamist currents. An extreme example was the Islamic State, which took Iraqi towns and cities in early 2014, as well as certain Shi'a paramilitary groups in the Popular Mobilization Units (PMU), which were formed as a response to the Islamic State. Both Sunni and Shi'a Islamist militant groups are active in Iraq and have fueled sectarian violence. In 2015, the Iraqi Security Forces, supported by the PMUs, began re-taking territory from the Islamic State. The question of Shi'a militant groups, however, remains more uncertain as some of these groups have sought a more prominent role in Iraqi society yet remain unwilling to integrate into the state apparatus. As Iraq's nascent democratic system evolves, secular and Islamist forces will continue to vie for influence and power.

Islamist Activity

Islamist activity in Iraq today takes three distinct forms. Given that the Shi'a population of Iraq is significantly larger than that of Iraq's Sunnis, there exists a wider array of Shi'a militant groups. However, Sunni groups, especially the Islamic State, pose a significant threat to the Iraq state. Among the Kurdish population, Islamic activity exists but is relatively minimal.

Shi'a Groups

The main Shi'a political factions in Iraq are the Ḥizb al-Daʿwa al-Islamiyya (the Islamic Dawa Party), al-Tayyar al-Sadri (the Sadrist Trend), and al-Majlis al-A'ala al-Islami al-Iraqi, (the Islamic Supreme Council of Iraq, or ISCI). The main Shia military factions fall under the al-hashd al-shaabi (the Popular Mobilization Units, or PMU), including the Badr Organization, Asaib ahl al-Haq, Kataib Hezbollah, and others. Many of these paramilitaries have their own political identities. Smaller Islamist groups include the National Reform Trend (led by former Prime Minister Ibrahim al-Jaafari) and the Fadhila (Islamic Virtue) Party.

The Islamic Dawa Party

The Dawa Party is the oldest Shi'a Islamist party in Iraq. It emerged in the late 1950s in response to the spread of socialist and communist movements in Iraq.[1] Grand Ayatollah Mohammed Baqir al-Sadr, a distinguished Shi'a scholar, is widely credited as Dawa's founder.[2] Dawa emphasized the promotion of Islamic values and ethics and believed the right to govern was distinct from the juridical function of religious authorities. It believed that both should be subsumed under constitutional mechanisms.[3]

In the 1980s, Sadr split from Dawa due to tensions with the *hawza* (Shi'a seminary) in Najaf, where Grand Ayatollah Abu al-Qasim al-Khoei remained wary of Sadrists. Dawa remained the leading Shi'a Islamist opposition party of the 1970s and 1980s, and therefore suffered fierce persecution from Saddam Hussein's Ba'athist regime. During this time, its members remained active and hid in either Iraq or exile. The main exiled Dawa branches existed in Iran, Syria, and the United Kingdom.

Following the 2003 Iraq war and the establishment of the Coalition Provisional Authority (CPA), Dawa emerged as one of the main Shi'a political groups in Iraq. The CPA was a transitional government for Iraq that lasted from March 2003 to April 2004. Since the handover of power, all of Iraq's Prime Ministers have been members of Dawa, including Prime Minister Nouri al-Maliki (2006-2014).

Initially, Maliki was selected in 2006 as a compromise candidate because of his reputation for weakness. Until 2008, he relied heavily on other Shi'a factions, such as ISCI and the Sadrists for political support. However, with U.S. support in the form of a "surge" of military personnel, he was able to launch a political and military campaign against both Sunni (AQI) and Shi'a (the Sadrist Trend's Jaysh al-Mahdi, or JAM) militant groups, thus solidifying his leadership and the political supremacy of Dawa. Maliki then formed the State of Law Coalition (*Dawlat al-Qanoon*), which has remained the umbrella organization for Dawa. Maliki became the single most powerful political actor in Iraq during his second term as premier (2010-2014), when he centralized power and weakened Sunni and Shia political opponents.[4]

The emergence of the Islamic State, however, caused Maliki to step down and allow another compromise candidate, Haider al-Abadi, to emerge to the premiership. Although they come from the same party, Abadi and Maliki are political rivals. Due to this schism, and despite continuing to be the strongest party, Dawa has split into two factions.

The Sadrist Trend

The Sadrist Trend is a nationalist religious movement founded by Shi'a cleric Mohammed Sadeq al-Sadr (the son of Mohammad Baqir al-Sadr) in the 1990s. Across southern Iraq and in Baghdad, the movement gained widespread support from poor Shi'a communities that were drawn to its emphasis on economic and social relief, along with its focus on traditional Islamic law and customs.[5] The Sadrists believe that religious leaders should take an active role in political and social affairs— a position that is aligned with the current Iranian regime, but distinguished by their desire for technocratic ministers.[6] Sadrists oppose the interference of any external actor (including both the United States and Iran) in Iraqi domestic affairs.

In 1999, Saddam Hussein ordered the assassination of Sadeq al-Sadr and his two oldest sons, causing much of the movement's leadership to go into hiding. After the 2003 invasion of Iraq, the Sadrist Trend re-emerged under the leadership of his youngest son, Muqtada al-Sadr. The Sadrists vehemently opposed the presence of U.S. forces in Iraq. They also opposed Baghdad's new elite of exiled returnees who had spent decades away from the country – referring to these leaders as "foreigner Iraqis."[7] Muqtada al-Sadr was able to derive considerable legitimacy on the street by making the claim that he was the only leader who had lived in Iraq under the Saddam Hussein dictatorship. The Sadrist Trend and its *Jaysh al-Mahdi* (JAM) militia were a powerful force during the height of sectarian violence in Iraq from 2004 to 2007.

The movement lost significant influence as U.S. and Iraqi forces degraded the JAM during security offensives in 2007 and 2008. Nouri al-Maliki's *Saulat al-Fursan* (Operation Knights Charge) effectively drove out Sadr, who disbanded the JAM and went into exile in Iran.[9]

In 2011, Sadr returned from exile. His time in Iran had turned his sympathies back toward Iraq, and his public discourse reflected this change in sentiment. He restructured the movement to emphasize political and social programs and a need to combat ineffective governance.[8] Sadr has also presented himself as cross-sectarian – he worked with Kurdistan Region President Massoud Barzani and secular leader

Ayad Allawi (who represented Iraq's Sunnis) in an effort to depose Maliki in 2012. His emphasis on combatting corruption and calling for a change to the political system of *muhasasa*, which grants power based on identity, has won Sadr significant support with the population. The Sadrist political wing, *al-Ahrar*, is competitive in local and national elections.

Moreover, in 2016, Sadr inspired a protest movement that saw millions take to the street of Baghdad's Tahrir Square.[9] In March 2016, Sadr trespassed into Baghdad's Green Zone, which houses most of the international embassies in the city. Rather than reprimanding or arresting Sadr for trespassing, the Iraqi general in command greeted him respectfully.[10] The Sadrists continue to maintain a militant wing, called Sarayat al-Salam (the Peace Brigades), which has less sectarian connotations than the previous JAM. The Peace Brigades have fought alongside Sunni tribes in Anbar, and remain skeptical of the better-funded, Iranian-backed Shi'a paramilitaries – particularly Asaib ahl al-Haq and Kataib Hezbollah.

The Islamic Supreme Council of Iraq

The third significant Islamist political actor is the Islamic Supreme Council of Iraq (ISCI), previously known as the Supreme Council for the Islamic Revolution in Iraq (SCIRI). SCIRI was originally founded in Iran in 1982, following Saddam Hussein's crackdown on *Dawa*, and worked closely with the Iran government during the Iran-Iraq War to support Shi'a activism against the Saddam regime. It had a militia called the Badr Corps.

Following the 2003 U.S.-led invasion, SCIRI became a dominant political force in the post-CPA government, while maintaining its close relationship with Iran. In the mid 2000s, many Badr members were incorporated into the Iraqi Security Forces, where they retained their fighting status.[11]

As time went on, Iran only increased its interference in Iraq. In an effort to distance itself from Iran, SCIRI changed its name to ISCI in 2007.[12] In addition, the group began to focus more heavily on Iraqi nationalism. It also shifted its primary religious allegiance away from Iran's Supreme Leader, the Ayatollah Khamenei, to Grand Ayatollah Ali Sistani, who believes religious leaders should not be involved in the administration of the state. Sistani is the head of the Najaf *hawza* (seminary) and as such is the head of the *marjai'ya* (Shia religious establishment).

ISCI, however, remains only the third most-influential Shia party. Its inability to broaden its political base and the continued perception that it maintains close and historical ties with the Iranian regime have proved to be significant stumbling blocks in the group's development. Furthermore, leadership personality has affected the group's standing. After the death of ISCI leader Abd al-Aziz al-Hakim in August 2009, his son, Ammar al-Hakim, assumed control of the movement.[13] Hakim has a reputation of being unwilling to take a stance and working from the shadows. As such, he has not been able to become a dominant figure in Iraqi politics.

In March 2012, ISCI split from the Badr Organization. The split was partly due to leadership squabbles in the wake of poor performance in the 2010 parliamentary elections.[14] More importantly, the two organizations disagreed over whether to support the incumbent prime minister, Maliki. The Badr organization, under the leadership of Hadi al-Ameri, split off to continue supporting the prime minister. Hakim, however, was wary of Maliki's consolidation of power and hesitant to support his bid for a second term as premier.

Under the auspices of the PMU ISCI maintains a military wing, which is active in the fight against the Islamic State. Its militias include the Ashura Brigades and the Supporters of the Faith brigades. These groups receive funding and weapons from the prime minister's office, and abide by the central government's policy decisions. They often fight alongside the Iraqi Security Forces.

The ideological concept of *wilayat al-faqih* (leadership of clerics) divides ISCI from Dawa and the Sadrists. ISCI maintains its belief that clergy should lead society. By contrast, Dawa and the Sadrists, stemming from the influence of Mohammad Baqir al-Sadr, believe that the community should be dominant in society (*wilayat al-umma*).

The various Shi'a political parties differ in their views of the role of federalism in Iraq. In 2008, there was an important shift in Iraqi politics away from Islamist and sectarian movements. In the 2009 provincial elections, Shi'a parties sought to style themselves as nationalist, secular, cross-sectarian movements in response to growing popular sentiment and a rejection of the sectarian violence that fueled Iraq's civil war in 2006 and 2007.[15] This was particularly evident during the formation of electoral coalitions in the run-up to the country's 2010 parliamentary election. Notably, Prime Minister Maliki's *Dawa* Party abstained from joining the main Shi'a coalition, the Iraqi National Alliance, and instead created a separate electoral list, the State of Law Coalition.[16] This move was against Iran's will. The victory of the al-Iraqiyya coalition, which was a secular nationalist list comprised of a number of Sunni political parties but led by a secular Shi'a politician, exemplified this trend.

However, there has been a reversal of this anti-sectarian trend in recent years, and following 2010 Shi'a parties returned to identifying as Shi'a in order to stop the emergence of al-Iraqiyya. Since that time, sectarian identity and Shi'a Islamism have manifested a renewed and important role in Iraqi politics.

Like *Dawa*, the Sadrist Trend supports a strong central Iraqi government, but opposes an American or Iranian presence in Iraq. They also oppose the current elite, which they believe are corrupt and unrepresentative of the people.

The Popular Mobilization Units (PMU)

Following the emergence of the Islamic State, which began taking over Iraqi towns and cities in early 2014, Maliki established the PMU, which was later further legitimized by Sistani's *fatwa*, which called on Iraqis to volunteer to fight against the group. The PMU is not a single organization; rather, it consists of some 50 militias, some of which are loyal to Sistani, but the most powerful and formidable PMUs are loyal to and backed by Iran. Those groups tend to be better-funded and better-equipped than their wholly Iraqi counterparts.

Hadi al-Ameri's Badr Organization, Abu Muhandis' *Kataib Hezbollah* (KH), and Qais Khazali's *Asaib ahl al-Haq* (AAH) are all groups that are fighting in direct coordination with Iran. They are known to receive extensive support from the Qods Force paramilitary unit of Iran's Revolutionary Guard Corps (IRGC-QF), including training, funding, and supplies. They share strong relations with the IRGC-QF's leader Qassem Solaimani.[17]

KH emerged in 2007, and since that time has conducted numerous attacks on U.S. and Iraqi forces.[18] KH has used advanced tactics and systems, including Improvised Rocket-Assisted Mortars (IRAMs).[19] The group has remained active following the withdrawal of U.S. forces from Iraq in 2011.[20] It has reportedly conducted attacks against the camps of the *Mujahedeen-e-Khalq*, an Iranian dissident group with elements based in Iraq. KH fighters are also fighting in Syria at the behest of the Iranian and Assad regimes.[21]

AAH is an offshoot of JAM and was formed following the split between Muqtada al-Sadr and Qais Khazali.[22] Khazali, who was captured by Coalition forces in March 2007 but subsequently released as part of a prisoner exchange in January 2010, is the leader of AAH.19 Since the departure of U.S. forces in December 2011, AAH has expressed its desire to participate in Iraqi politics and rebranded itself as a nationalist organization also dedicated to Islamic resistance. It has established political offices throughout the country and has instituted religious and social outreach programs.[23] AAH's turn towards politics has heightened its competition with the Sadrist Trend. Sadr and Khazali have publicly traded accusations and the tensions have even resulted in violent clashes.[24] Maliki cultivated strong ties with AAH as a counterbalance to the Sadrists and other opponents. The second group includes paramilitaries closer to Sistani. The Ali al-Akbar Brigades and the Abbadiyah Brigades are part of this group.

The third group is made up of militias that represent wings of political parties. For instance, the above-mentioned ISCI militias, or *Sadr's Sarayat al-Salam*, fall into this category.[25]

Sunni Groups

The Sunni political landscape has shifted dramatically in post-2003 Iraq. The major ideological debate among the Sunni Islamist community has been over the question of cooperating with Baghdad.[26] During the civil war (2006-2007) and then again following the emergence of the Islamic State in Mosul and elsewhere (2014-present), many Sunni Islamists have chosen to reject the central government, which they perceive to be a Shi'a-Iranian dictatorship. However, during the Anwar Awakening and subsequent period of comparatively good governance in Iraq (2008-2010), Sunni Islamists participated in the political process.

The Iraqi Islamic Party

The only Sunni Islamist political party in Iraq has been the Iraqi Islamic Party (IIP) – although it is not a unified organization and lacks the institutional capacities of most political parties. It is currently led by Ayad al-Samarraie.

The IIP has its earliest roots in the mid-1940s or early 1950s, when Mohammed al-Sawwaf, an Iraqi studying in Egypt, met Muslim Brotherhood founder Hassan al-Banna.[27] Upon his return to Iraq, al-Sawwaf and another activist, Amjad al-Zahawi Mahmood, founded an Iraqi organization modeled on the Muslim Brotherhood, known as the Islamic Brotherhood Society.[28] Later, in 1960, the Iraqi Islamic Party was formally established after Abdul-Karim Qassem's government allowed political parties to form in Iraq.[29] Following the overthrow of Qassem's government by the Ba'ath Party in 1963, the IIP was violently suppressed but continued its operations clandestinely and in exile.[30] Ayad al-Samarraie, who had been the Secretary General of the IIP since 1970, fled Iraq in 1980.[31]

Following the fall of Saddam Hussein's Ba'athist regime in 2003, many IIP leaders, including al-Samarraie, returned to Iraq and the party re-emerged. In the December 2005 parliamentary election, the IIP ran as a party of a Sunni coalition known as *Tawafuq* (Iraqi Accord Front), which won 44 seats in the 275-member parliament. From 2005 to early 2009, *Tawafuq* was the dominant Sunni political presence in the parliament, though it was seen by many Sunni Iraqis as an exile party that did not represent their interests. By early 2009, *Tawafuq* began to disintegrate as its constituent parties left the coalition during the debate over the selection of the parliamentary speaker.[32]

In recent years, the influence of the IIP has waned as a variety of other Sunni political groups and leaders have emerged. Today, IIP is a divided group, with some of its leaders sharing close relationships with Shia leaders. For instance, parliamentary speaker Salim Jabouri hails from IIP and shares a close relationship with Maliki. Others in the IIP, however, blame Maliki for the breakdown of Iraqi governance.

In 2009 and 2010, the IIP lost a considerable portion of its electorate to the secular nationalist coalition of former Prime Minister *Allawi's al-Iraqiyya*, also called the Iraqiyah list. By the 2010 parliamentary election, the vast number of Sunni political entities joined the Iraqiyah List. Even IIP leader Tariq al-Hashimi left the group to join al-Iraqiyya. IPP was the only party to run under the *Tawafuq* banner in 2010, and consequently, the total number of seats held by *Tawafuq* shrank from 44 to just 6.

The Association of Muslim Scholars

The Association of Muslim Scholars (*Hay'at al-'Ulama' al-Muslimeen*) formed immediately after the U.S.-led invasion in April of 2003. The group is not a political party, but rather a group of influential Sunni clerics and scholars seeking to represent the Sunni voice in a Shi'a-dominated Baghdad. It was initially led by Harith al-Dhari, a cleric who called on Iraqis to boycott the U.S.-led attempts to rebuild the Iraqi government in a *fatwa* that also called for a "national insurgency."[33] Such sentiments, along with the Iraqi people's fear of retaliation if they participated in the political process, combined to significantly depress voter turnout. For example, Anbar Province, which is 90% Sunni[34] and has often suffered from violence and high levels of insurgency, had a voter turnout of just 1% in the January parliamentary interim elections of 2005.[35] However, by the December 2005 elections for a permanent government, national voter turnout rose to 77%.[36] The group was an important driving force of Sunni insurgency in 2006. However, the group came into conflict with AQI and its leader, Abu Musab al-Zarqawi, particularly on the question as to the type and scope of acceptable violence. Following Harith's death, his son, Muthanna, has taken over the organization, which continues to claim to speak on behalf of disenfranchised Sunnis. It also relies on rousing a sense of Iraqi nationalism.

The Islamic State (formerly al-Qaeda in Iraq - AQI)

The Islamic State initially grew out of an al-Qaeda offshoot, al-Qaeda in Iraq (AQI). AQI members included native Sunni Iraqis, members of the Kurdish Islamist group Ansar Al-Islam, and some foreigners, including its Jordanian-born leader, Abu Musab al-Zarqawi.[37] AQI was responsible for some of the deadliest car bombs and suicide bomb attacks in Iraq, as well as a surge in sectarian violence. AQI lost many of its strongholds in northern and western Iraq following the security offensives that began in 2007; however, it continued to operate in areas of northern Iraq, especially the city of Mosul, and in areas of Diyala, Salah ad-Din, Anbar, Baghdad, and its surrounding areas. Though AQI leaders pledged their allegiance to al-Qaeda in 2004, the group lost the affiliation and was no longer able to retain operational links with al-Qaeda leaders based in the tribal areas of Pakistan.[38]

The group subsequently transformed into the Islamic State in Iraq and the Levant (ISIL). Back in Iraq, the group maintained a largely passive presence, but as Maliki began suppressing and attacking Iraqi Sunnis, the Islamic State grew in numbers. Finally, in early 2014, it began taking over Iraqi territory, beginning in Fallujah and leading to Mosul, Iraq's second largest city, which was taken in June 2014. Following this, ISIL formally declared a Caliphate and changed its name to the Islamic State. The group's leader is currently Abu Bakr al-Baghdadi. In 2016, the group has suffered defeats at the hands of the Iraqi security forces, the PMU, and the Kurdish *peshmerga*, reversing a trend of steady territorial gains and political growth. As of this writing, it has lost Ramadi, Fallujah, and Tikrit. To maintain legitimacy, it has altered its tactics, reverting to the AQI-style guerilla warfare and attacks on civilians in Baghdad and other major cities that took place a decade ago.

The Army of the Men of the Naqshbandi Order (JRTN)

The Army of the Men of the Naqshbandi Order (*Jaysh Rajal al-Tariqah al-Naqshbandia*, or JRTN) is a Sunni Sufi militant group that was founded in December 2006 in response to the execution of Saddam Hussein.[39] JRTN is linked to former Iraqi Ba'athist officials, including Izzat Ibrahim al-Duri, one of Saddam's closest deputies.[40] A main goal of the group is the return of the Ba'ath Party in Iraq.[41] JRTN operates primarily in the northern Iraqi provinces of Ninewah, Kirkuk, Salah ad-Din, and Diyala, where it conducts attacks.

Kurdish Groups

Political Islam has also developed extensively in Iraqi Kurdistan, also called the Kurdistan Region, an autonomous region in northern Iraq run by the Kurdistan Regional Government (KRG). It is particularly strong in the city of Halabja, but occurs in other major areas as well. The largest Kurdish Islamist political groups are the Kurdistan Islamic Union (KIU) and the Kurdistan Islamic Group (KIG).[42]

The Kurdistan Islamic Union

The KIU, also known as Yekgirtu, was established in 1994. Principally an adherent to Sunni Islam, the group was closely aligned with the Muslim Brotherhood. The group describes itself as "an Islamic reformative political party that strives to solve all political, social, economic and cultural matters of the people in Kurdistan from an Islamic perspective which can achieve the rights, general freedom, and social justice."[43] It is currently led by Secretary General Sheikh Salah ad-Din Muhammad Baha-al-Din. The KIU has no armed forces of its own, and is most active in charity work.

The Kurdistan Islamic Group

The KIG was established in 2001 as a splinter faction of the KIU. It is led by Mala Ali Bapir. The KIG is believed to have close ties with extremist Islamist armed groups, such as *Ansar al-Islam*, which has been involved in attacks against leaders of the predominant political parties in Kurdistan, the Kurdistan Democratic Party (KDP) and the Patriotic Union of Kurdistan (PUK).[44] Bapir, however, claims his group has abandoned violence.

Nevertheless, the political influence of the KIU and KIG cannot compete with that of the KDP, PUK, and Change List (*Gorran*), which dominate Kurdish political and social life. Of the 111 seats in the Kurdish parliament, the KIU and KIG have only four.[45] At the national level, the influence of Kurdish Islamist parties is even further diminished. The KIU has 4 seats in the 325-seat Iraqi parliament, while the KIG has only 2 seats. The emergence of Gorran shifted the balance of power and gave the KIU and KIG another ally in the Kurdish Regional Government parliament with which to challenge the dominant Kurdish parties. However, Kurdish Islamist parties remain only marginal actors in Iraqi political life.

ISLAMISM AND SOCIETY

97 percent of the Iraqi population is Muslim, and of that group, 60-65 percent are Shi'a Muslims.[46] Iraqi Shi'a primarily live in central and southern Iraq, though there are Shi'a communities in the north. 32-37 percent of Iraqi Muslims are Sunnis, and they are concentrated mainly in central and northern Iraq.[47] Of Iraq's more than 30 million citizens, 75-80 percent are Arabs; 15-20 percent are Kurds; and Turkmen, Chaldean, Assyrian, Armenians, and other minority groups comprise the remaining 5 percent.[48] Religious minorities, such as Christians, Mandeans, and Yazidis, comprise the remaining three percent of Iraq's population; however, these non-dominant ethnic and religious populations have declined significantly since 2003.[49]

According to the U.S. military, more than 77,000 Iraqis were killed during the height of sectarian violence from 2004 to 2008; Iraqi government statistics put that number at over 85,000.[50] According to the UN, the emergence of the Islamic State in Iraq led to "staggering violence" with some 18,800 killed between January 1, 2014 and October 31, 2015.[51] Fortunately, the death toll has since abated. The United Nations Assistance Mission to Iraq estimated that approximately 6,878 Iraqi civilians were killed in 2016 in total, primarily by the Islamic State.[52]

Following the fall of Saddam Hussein's secular regime in 2003, both Sunni and Shi'a Iraqis were able to openly express their Islamic faith in ways that they had not been able in decades. This was especially true for Shi'a Iraqis, who for the first time in decades could take part in the religious pilgrimages to the holy cities of Najaf and Karbala in southern Iraq. Exiled Sunni and Shi'a Islamist parties and movements returned to Iraq, where they played key roles in shaping Iraq's emerging political system. Iraqi politics, after 2003, became defined by identities – making political Islam an important tool for legitimacy.

Parts in the north of Iraq have, during various periods, fallen under strict Salafi-Jihadi rule. From 2004 to 2007 and from 2014 to the present day, as the security situation has deteriorated and the Iraqi state proved itself unable to capably govern, Sunni Islamist militant groups (namely, AQI then the Islamic State) have grown in strength and violently imposed their strict interpretations of Islamic law. They established strongholds in the predominantly Sunni areas of northern and western Iraq, such as the Anbar or Ninewah province. There, they brutally enforced harsh rules, including the banning of smoking and singing, prohibiting men from shaving their beards, forcing marriages and raping local women, such as Yezidi women, forcing minorities to flee their homes, enforcing the wearing of strict Islamic dress by women, and maiming or killing anyone caught violating their radical laws.[53]

In the south, Shi'a militia groups have also at times enforced strict rules in the areas of Baghdad and southern Iraq that were under their control. During the 2005-2007 civil war, sectarian violence soared, as Shi'a militia groups violently attacked mixed areas of Baghdad.

At other times, however, sectarianism has been rejected. In 2008, Iraqis of all sects and ethnicities grew frustrated with the years of strife, under which Islamist parties and militias dominated. Sunni tribal leaders in Anbar province rejected AQI rule and took arms against Sunni extremists, in a movement that became known as the Anbar Awakening. Awakening movements spread across Sunni areas from 2007 to 2008.[54] This, coupled with the U.S.-led security offensive that cleared first Baghdad and later the provinces surrounding the capital, significantly degraded AQI's capabilities and networks. During the Surge, Iraqi forces supported by the U.S. also targeted Shi'a militia groups in Baghdad and throughout central and southern Iraq. This culminated in the Iraqi-led operations in Basra and Baghdad, which dealt a significant blow to JAM and culminated in Sadr's announcement to disband his once-fearsome militia.[55] By mid-2008, when the last of the Surge forces left Iraq, violence had plummeted by more than 60 percent.[56]

The 2009 and 2010 elections saw the reorientation of Iraqi politics away from Islamism in a manner that reflected changes in society. As discussed above, Islamist exile parties like ISCI and the IIP lost considerable influence.[57] New political realities emerged in Iraq, and there was widespread anti-incumbent sentiment and a growing demand for secular, nationalist, and technocratic government that could preserve security, provide essential services, and reduce corruption.[58] These themes played an important role in the provincial and parliamentary elections.

Nonetheless, Iraqi society remains heavily fragmented and sectarian divisions still exist, providing an opening for the re-emergence of the Islamic State.[59] Iraq's leading Shi'a parties, *Dawa* and the Sadrist Trend, retain their Islamist character and have emphasized this identity to shore up support.

ISLAMISM AND THE STATE

Iraq is a parliamentary democracy and not a theocratic republic like its neighbor, Iran. The Iraqi Constitution guarantees the democratic rights of all Iraqi citizens as well as "full religious rights to freedom of religious belief and practice of all individuals."[60] Yet the Iraqi Constitution stipulates Islam as the official religion of the state and makes clear that no law may be enacted that contradicts the establish provisions of Islam. The ambiguities inherent in these provisions have led to challenges in interpretation and meaning. In some areas of Iraq, local governments have adopted stricter interpretations of Islamic law. The provincial councils in Basra and Najaf, for instance, have banned the consumption, sales, or transit of alcohol.[61] In November

2010, the Baghdad provincial council used a resolution from 1996 to similarly ban the sale of alcohol.[62] There have been occasional violent raids or attacks on venues believed to be selling alcohol.[63]

The Iraqi government's response to Islamist militant groups has varied. Islamist parties dominated provincial and national governments from 2004 to 2008. During that time, the state was both unwilling and unable to challenge the Islamist militant groups that threatened the state's legitimacy. Shi'a militia groups penetrated elements of the Iraqi Security Forces, and certain paramilitary and police units were accused of perpetrating brutal sectarian violence.[64] The threat from extremist groups ultimately jeopardized the functioning of the Iraqi state by late 2006. Several months later, in early 2007, U.S. forces announced a change of strategy in Iraq and the deployment of 20,000 additional troops, in what became known as the Surge. As the counterinsurgency offensives of the Surge unfolded, the Iraqi state also became more willing and able to challenge Sunni and Shi'a extremist groups as their influence and capability waned.[65] U.S. support during this time was critical in giving the Iraqi Security Forces, and even Iraq's political leadership, the confidence to move against extremist groups as well as in preventing the manipulation of the security forces for political ends. U.S. and Iraqi leaders also worked to professionalize the Iraqi Security Forces, expand their capabilities, and root out corrupt or sectarian elements.[66] U.S. and Iraqi operations from 2007 to the present significantly degraded both Sunni and Shi'a extremist groups and reduced violence, doing so by over 90 percent.[67]

Today, the Iraqi forces continue to robustly target the Islamic State in Iraq. Despite the growing influence of the PMU, which Amnesty International and Human Rights Watch have both criticized for committing war crimes, the government has decided not to act against Shi'a militant groups. Given the weakness of the central government, it is unclear whether the Iraqi state can maintain the will or muster the ability to sufficiently check Shi'a militant groups (some of which continue to receive Iranian assistance) or whether political interests will enable such groups to expand.

ENDNOTES

[1] Vali Nasr, The Shia Revival: How Conflicts within Islam will Shape the Future (New York: Norton, 2006), 117.

[2] Patrick Cockburn, Muqtada (New York: Scribner, 2008), 31; Faleh Jabar, The Shi'ite Movement in

[3] Jabar, The Shi'ite Movement in Iraq, 78-80; Islamic Dawa Party, "Party History," n.d., http://www.islamicdawaparty.com/?module=home&fname=history.php&active=7&show=1.

[4] Jabar, Malik, "Maliki and the Rest: A Crisis within a Crisis", IIST Iraq Crisis Report – 2012, June 2012, http://iraqstudies.com/books/featured3.pdf

[5] Jabar, The Shi'ite Movement in Iraq, 272-273.

[6] Marisa Cochrane Sullivan, "The Fragmentation of the Sadrist Movement," Institute for the Study of War Iraq Report 12, January 2009, http://www.understandingwar.org/files/Iraq%20Report%2012.pdf.

[7] Makiya, Kanan. The Rope (New York : Pantheon Books, 2016).

[8] Ibid.

[9] Mansour, Renad and Clark, Michael, "Is Muqtada Al-Sadr Good For Iraq?", War on the Rocks, May 2016, http://warontherocks.com/2016/05/is-muqtada-al-sadr-good-for-iraq/

[10] "Iraqi cleric Muqtada al-Sadr starts Green Zone sit-in," Al Jazeera March 28, 2016, http://www.aljazeera.com/news/2016/03/iraqi-cleric-muqtada-al-sadr-starts-green-zone-sit-160328040820897.html.

[11] Ibid.

[12] "Shiite Politics in Iraq: The Role of the Supreme Council," International Crisis Group Middle East Report Number 70, November 15, 2007.

[13] Ma'ad Fayad, "Ammar al-Hakim Appointed New Leader of Supreme Islamic Iraqi Council," Ash-Sharq al-Awsat (London), September 1, 2009, http://www.aawsat.com/english/news.asp?section=1&id=17965.

[14] "URGENT...SIIC, Badr Organization announce their official split," All Iraq News, March 11, 2012,http://www.alliraqnews.com/en/index.php?option=com_content&view=article&id=5847:urgentsiic-badr-organization-announce-their-official-split&catid=35:political&Itemid=2.

[15] Marisa Cochrane Sullivan, "Iraq's Parliamentary Election," Institute for the Study of War Backgrounder, October 20, 2009, http://www.understandingwar.org/files/IraqsParliamentaryElection.pdf.

[16] Rahma al-Salim, "Al Maliki Announces Break With Iraqi National Alliance," Ash-Sharq al-Awsat (London), September 25. 2009, http://www.aawsat.com/english/news.asp?section=1&id=18246.

[17] Sullivan, "The Fragmentation of the Sadrist Movement."

[18] Yusif Salman: "Leading Figure in the Al-Sadr Trend to Al-Mashriq: Al-Sadr Met Asa'ib Ahl al-Haq Leader in Qom," Al-Mashriq (Iraq), January 18 , 2010; Martin Chulov, "Qais al-Khazali: from Kidnapper and Prisoner to Potential Leader,"Guardian (London), December 31, 2009, http://www.guardian.co.uk/world/2009/dec/31/iran-hostages-qais-al-khazali.

[19] U.S. Department of the Treasury, "Treasury Designates Individual, Entity Posing Threat to Stability in Iraq."

[20] Ashish Kumar Sen, "Dissidents Blame Camp Attack on Iraq," Washington Times, February 18, 2013,http://www.washingtontimes.com/news/2013/feb/18/dissidents-blame-camp-attack-on-iraq/?page=all.

[21] Michael Gordon and Steven Lee Myers, "Iran and Hezbollah Support for Syria Complicates Peace-Talk Strategy,"New York Times, May 21, 2013, http://www.nytimes.com/2013/05/22/world/middleeast/iran-and-hezbollahs-support-for-syria-complicates-us-strategy-on-peace-talks.html?pagewanted=all; Will Fulton, Joseph Holliday, and Sam Wyer, "Iranian Strategy in Syria," A Joint Report by AEI's Critical Threats Project and the Institute for the Study of War, May 2013, 23-25, http://www.understandingwar.org/sites/default/files/IranianStrategyinSyria-1MAY.pdf.

[22] Karin Bruilliard, "Ex-Sadr Aide Held in American Deaths," Washington Post, March 23, 2007,http://www.washingtonpost.com/wp-dyn/content/article/2007/03/22/AR2007032200261.html; Felter and Fishman, "Iranian Strategy in Iraq: Politics and 'Other Means,'" 35; Sullivan, "The Fragmentation of the Sadrist Movement."

[23] For a detailed analysis of AAH's political activities, see Sam Wyer, "The Resurgence of Asa'ib Ahl al-Haq," Institute for the Study of War Middle East Security Report 7, December 2012,http://www.understandingwar.org/sites/default/files/ResurgenceofAAH.pdf.

[24] Ibid. 22-25.

[25] Habib, Mustafa, "Taming The Beast: Can Iraq Ever Control Its Controversial Volunteer Militias?", Niqash, http://www.niqash.org/en/articles/security/5323/

[26] Mansoure, Renad, "The Sunni Predicament in Iraq", Carnegie Endowment for International Peace, March 2016, http://carnegieendowment.org/2016/03/03/sunni-predicament-in-iraq-pub-62924

[27] Basim Al-Azami, "The Muslim Brotherhood: Genesis and Development," in Faleh A. Jabar, ed., Ayatollahs, Sufis and Ideologues: State, Religion and Social Movements in Iraq (London: Saqi, 2002), 164.

[28] Ibid.; Graham Fuller and Rend Rahim Francke, The Arab Shi'a: The Forgotten Muslims (Basingstoke, UK: Palgrave Macmillan, 2000); "Iraqi Islamic Party," globalsecurity.org, n.d., http://www.globalsecurity.org/military/world/iraq/iip.htm; Iraqi Islamist Party, "History," n.d., http://www.iraqiparty.com/page/who-are-we/.

[29] Thabit Abdullah, A Short History of Iraq: From 636 to the Present (London: Longman, 2003).

[30] "Iraqi Islamic Party"; Iraqi Islamic Party, "History."

[31] Ibid.

[32] Domergue and Sullivan, "Balancing Maliki."

[33] Meijer, Roel, "The Association of Muslim Scholars in Iraq", Middle East Research and Information, http://www.merip.org/mer/mer237/association-muslim-scholars-iraq

[34] "Irakische Streitkräfte starten Rückeroberung Ramadis". Deutsche Welle, May 26, 2015, http://www.dw.com/de/irakische-streitkr%C3%A4fte-starten-r%C3%BCckeroberung-ramadis/a-18477575.

[35] Wong, Edward, "Turnout in the Iraqi Election is Reported at 70 Percent", The New York Times, December 2005, http://www.nytimes.com/2005/12/22/world/middleeast/turnout-in-the-iraqi-election-is-reported-at-70-percent.html

[36] Anthony H. Cordesman, Iraq's Evolving Insurgency and the Risk of Civil War, Center for Strategic and International Studies, 2006, pg, 8, http://reliefweb.int/sites/reliefweb.int/files/resources/1B26E4C64879415AC125715D002C49E3-csis-irq-26apr.pdf.

[37] United States Forces-Iraq, "The Insurgency," July 31, 2009, http://www.usf-iraq.com/?option=com_content&task=view&id=729&Itemid=45.

[38] Kenneth Katzman, "Al Qaeda in Iraq: Assessment and Outside Links," Congressional Research Service Report for Congress, August 15, 2008, http://www.fas.org/sgp/crs/terror/RL32217.pdf; DoD News Briefing with Commander, U.S. Forces-Iraq Gen. Raymond Odierno from the Pentagon, June 4, 2010.

[39] United States Forces-Iraq, "The Insurgency"; Geoff Ziezulewicz, "Insurgent Group Looks to Future Without U.S.: Former Saddam Loyalists Work to Return Baath Party to Power," Stars and Stripes, April 3, 2009.

[40] Ziezulewicz, "Insurgent Group Looks to Future Without U.S."

[41] Ibid.

[42] Rafid Fadhil Ali, "Kurdish Islamist Groups in Northern Iraq," Jamestown Foundation Terrorism Monitor 6, iss. 22, November 25. 2008, http://www.jamestown.org/single/?no_cache=1&tx_ttnews[tt_news]=34176.

[43] Qassim Khidhir Hamad, "Kurdish Election Lists," Niqash (Baghdad), June 30, 2009.

[44] Kathleen Ridolfo, "A Survey of Armed Groups in Iraq," Radio Free Europe/Radio Liberty Iraq Report 7, no. 20, June 4, 2004.

[45] "The Kurdistan Parliament," Kurdistan Regional Government website, accessible athttp://www.krg.org/articles/detail.asp?rnr=160&lngnr=12&smap=04070000&anr=15057; "The Members of the Parliament for Third Term 2009," Kurdistan Parliament website, accessible at http://www.perleman.org/Default.aspx?page=Parliamentmembers&c=PresidencyMember2009&group=40.

[46] Ibid.

[47] Ibidem.

[48] "Iraq," CIA World Factbook, updated April 6, 2011, https://www.cia.gov/library/publications/the-world-factbook/geos/iz.html; "Background Note: Iraq," U.S. Department of State, September 17, 2010,http://www.state.gov/r/pa/ei/bgn/6804.htm.

[49] Ibidem.

[50] "US military says 77,000 Iraqis killed over 5 years," Associated Press, October 15, 2010, http://www.post-journal.com/page/content.detail/id/120540/US-military-says-77-000-Iraqis-killed-over-5-years-.html?isap=1&nav=5030.

[51] BBC Middle East, "Iraq Conflict: Civilians suffering 'staggering' violence – UN", BBC News, January 2015, http://www.bbc.com/news/world-middle-east-35349861

[52] Bethan McKernan, "Scale of Iraqi civilian casualties inflicted by Isis revealed by UN," The Independent, January 3, 2017, http://www.independent.co.uk/news/world/middle-east/iraq-isis-casualties-civilian-islamic-state-un-figures-united-nations-middle-east-mosul-a7507526.html.

[53] Rod Nordland, "Despite Gains, Petraeus Cautious About Iraq," Newsweek, August 21, 2008,http://www.newsweek.com/2008/08/20/avoiding-the-v-word.html; "Marriages split al Qaeda alliance," Washington Times, August 31, 2007, http://www.washingtontimes.com/news/2007/aug/31/marriages-split-al-qaeda-alliance/?page=all#pagebreak; "Severe Islamic law which banned 'suggestive' cucumbers cost Al Qaeda public support in Iraq,"Daily Mail (UK), August 10, 2008, http://www.dailymail.co.uk/news/worldnews/article-1043409/Severe-Islamic-law-banned-suggestive-cucumbers-cost-Al-Qaeda-public-support-Iraq.html.

[54] John A. McCary, "The Anbar Awakening: An Alliance of Incentives," The Washington Quarterly, January 2009,http://www.twq.com/09winter/docs/09jan_mccary.pdf.

[55] Marisa Cochrane Sullivan, "The Fragmentation of the Sadrist Movement," Institute for the Study of War Iraq Report12, January 2009, 37-38, http://www.understandingwar.org/files/Iraq%20Report%2012.pdf.

[56] Viola Gienger, "Iraq Civilian Deaths Drop for Third Year as Toll Eases After U.S. Drawdown," Bloomberg, December 29, 2010, http://www.bloomberg.com/news/2010-12-30/iraq-civilian-deaths-drop-for-third-year-as-toll-eases-after-u-s-drawdown.html.

[57] Iraqi High Electoral Commission, "Iraqi CoR Election Results," n.d., http://ihec-iq.com/en/results.html.

[58] Sullivan, "Iraq's Parliamentary Election."

[59] Marisa Cochrane Sullivan and James Danly, "Iraq on the Eve of Elections," Institute for the Study of WarBackgrounder, March 3, 2010, http://www.understandingwar.org/files/IraqEveofElections.pdf.

[60] Iraqi Constitution, Section One, Article Two.

[61] "Alcohol Banned in Iraq holy Shiite City of Najaf," Middle East Online, October 11, 2009, http://www.middle-east-online.com/english/?id=34869.

[62] John Leland, "Baghdad Raids on Alcohol Sellers Stir Fears," New York Times, January 15, 2011,http://www.nytimes.com/2011/01/16/world/middleeast/16iraq.html.

[63] Ibid.; "Kurdish Club Scene Booming as Baghdad Bans Alcohol," Associated Press, January 11, 2011.

[64] Lionel Beehner, "Shiite Militias and Iraq's Security Forces," Council on Foreign Relations Backgrounder, November 30, 2005, http://www.cfr.org/iraq/shiite-militias-iraqs-security-forces/p9316; "Iraq 'death squad caught in act,'" BBC, February 16, 2006, http://news.bbc.co.uk/2/hi/middle_east/4719252.stm; Steve Inskeep, "Riding Herd on the Iraqi Police's Dirty 'Wolf Brigade,'" National Public Radio, March 28, 2007, http://www.npr.org/templates/story/story.php?storyId=9170738.

[65] Marisa Cochrane Sullivan, "The Fragmentation of the Sadrist Movement," Institute for the Study of War Iraq Report12, January 2009, 22, http://www.understandingwar.org/files/Iraq%20Report%2012.pdf.

[66] For more information on the growth and professionalization of the Iraqi Security Forces during the Surge, see LTG James Dubik, "Building Security Forces and Ministerial Capacity: Iraq as a Primer," Institute for the Study of War Best Practices in Counterinsurgency Report 1, August 2009, http://www.csmonitor.com/World/Middle-East/2011/0208/US-reports-20-percent-drop-in-Iraq-violence.

[67] Scott Peterson, "US reports 20 percent drop in Iraq violence," Christian Science Monitor, February 8, 2011,http://www.csmonitor.com/World/Middle-East/2011/0208/US-reports-20-percent-drop-in-Iraq-violence.

IRAN, ISLAMIC REPUBLIC OF

> **QUICK FACTS**
>
> Population: 82,801,633 (July 2016 est.)
>
> Area: 1,648,195 sq km
>
> Ethnic Groups: Persian, Azeri, Kurd, Lur, Baloch, Arab, Turkmen and Turkic tribes
>
> Religions: Muslim (official) 99.4% (Shia 90-95%, Sunni 5-10%), other (includes Zoroastrian, Jewish, and Christian) 0.3%, unspecified 0.4%
>
> Government Type: theocratic republic
>
> GDP (official exchange rate): $412.3 billion (2015 est.)
>
> *Map and Quick Facts courtesy of the CIA World Factbook (January 2017)*

OVERVIEW

Since its founding in February of 1979, the Islamic Republic of Iran has consistently ranked as the world's most active state sponsor of terrorism, according to the estimates of the United States government. Iran's support for terrorism is both pervasive and ideological, encompassing a vast array of official and quasi-official institutions, individuals and policies. It finds its roots in the ideas of the Ayatollah Ruhollah Khomeini, the founder of the Islamic Revolution, who espoused the need to "export" Iran's successful religious model the world over. Nearly three decades after Khomeini's death, that priority continues to animate Iran's leaders and guide their sponsorship of instability, both in Iran's immediate geographic neighborhood and far beyond.

Today, Iran's capabilities to do so are expanding significantly. In the decade between 2003 and 2013, the Iranian regime's persistent pursuit of a nuclear capability engendered escalating pressure from the United States and international community in the form of economic sanctions and diplomatic isolation. Over time, these measures took their toll, progressively isolating the Islamic Republic and severely impacting its eco-

nomic fortunes. However, the successful conclusion of a nuclear deal between Iran and the P5+1 powers in July of 2015 has fundamentally altered this dynamic. As a result of that agreement, formally known as the Joint Comprehensive Plan of Action (JCPOA), the Iranian regime has received massive direct economic relief totaling upwards of $100 billion.[1] The agreement has likewise commenced a protracted process of economic rehabilitation, with the Iranian regime engaging with—and benefiting from—an array of new, post-sanctions trade. This has served to greatly expand the resources available to the Islamic Republic to support terror proxies in the region and beyond, and breathed new life into Tehran's longstanding efforts to reshape the global order in its own image.

Islamist Activity

The Iranian regime's support for international terrorism predates the establishment of the Islamic Republic itself. In the 1960s and 1970s, while in exile in Iraq and in France, the Ayatollah Ruhollah Khomeini formulated his ideas about the need for a radical Islamic transformation in his home country, Iran, and of subsequently "exporting" this system of government throughout the Middle East and beyond.[2] In keeping with this thinking, Khomeini's political manifesto, *Islamic Government*, extolled the virtues of "a victorious and triumphant Islamic political revolution" that would go on "to unite the Moslem nation, [and] to liberate [all] its lands."[3]

When the Ayatollah and his followers subsequently swept to power in Tehran in the spring of 1979, this principle became a cardinal regime priority. The preamble of the country's formative constitution, adopted in October 1979, outlines that the country's military would henceforth "be responsible not only for guarding and preserving the frontiers of the country, but also for fulfilling the ideological mission of jihad in God's way; that is, extending the sovereignty of God's law throughout the world."[4] These words were backed by concrete regime action, with Khomeini consolidating the country's various radical religious militias into an ideological army known as the Islamic Revolutionary Guard Corps (IRGC, or *Pasdaran*), tasked with promoting his revolutionary message abroad, with violence if necessary.

The three-plus decades since have seen a consistent regime commitment to international terrorism. In the early years of the Islamic Republic, Iran is known to have ordered, orchestrated or facilitated a series of terrorist attacks in the Middle East, among them the 1983 U.S. Embassy and Marine Barracks bombings in Beirut, Lebanon, as well as abortive coup attempts and bombings in Bahrain, the United Arab Emirates and Kuwait.[5] These activities, and the rationale behind them, were reinforced by the outcome of the country's bloody eight-year war with Iraq, which strengthened the Iranian government's belief that radical proxies could serve as an attractive, low-cost substitute for direct military action. As a result, the principle of "exporting the revolution" remained a vibrant element of regime policy after the death of Khomeini in 1989. In the decade that followed, the Islamic Republic continued to bankroll assassinations and terrorist acts on foreign soil, aided the infiltration of countries in Europe, Africa and Latin America by radical Islamic groups, and assisted irregulars in various international conflict zones.[6]

In the aftermath of the September 11, 2001 terrorist attacks, the Islamic Republic chose to dramatically strengthen its links to international terrorism, redoubling its support for Lebanon's Hezbollah militia and Palestinian rejectionist groups, expanding its footprint in the Palestinian territories, maintaining at least low-level links to the al-Qaeda network, and becoming heavily involved in the bankrolling of radical Shi'ite militias and activities aimed at hindering the U.S.-led Coalition in post-Saddam Iraq.

This support for terrorism, while ideologically driven, was and remains rooted in pragmatism. While Khomeini's Islamic Revolution was a distinctly Shi'a one, in the nearly four decades since its establishment, the Islamic Republic has embraced a more universalist conception of its international role, aspiring to serve as the vanguard of Islamic revolution worldwide.[7] The Iranian regime today funds a broad range of both Sunni and Shi'a groups throughout the greater Middle East and beyond. The critical determinant appears to be the degree to which these movements and organizations can reinforce Iran's leading role in the "Shi'a revival" now taking place in the Muslim world, and their shared animosity toward the West, most directly Israel and the United States.

The scope of Iran's support of violent Islamism is global in nature, and so is its reach. In the decade that followed the 9/11 attacks, it encompassed: ongoing support for Hezbollah in Lebanon and a reconstitution of the Shi'ite militia's strategic capabilities;[8] extensive involvement in post-Saddam Iraq, first through the provision of arms and materiel to the country's various Shi'a militias and later through political and strategic support of various forces both inside and outside of the government of Iraqi Prime Minister Nouri al-Maliki;[9] the provision of significant military and operational assistance to the insurgency in Afghanistan, increasing the lethality of forces arrayed against the government of President Hamid Karzai and Coalition authorities there;[10] exerting influence in the Palestinian arena through financial aid and support to Palestinian rejectionist groups, chief among them Hamas and the Palestinian Islamic Jihad[11] and; bankrolling terrorist and subversive activities in various countries, including Egypt.[12]

The onset of the Arab Spring in early 2011 marked a turning point for Iranian activities—and for its regional standing. In the early stages of the "Spring," Iranian officials sought to take credit for the anti-regime sentiment sweeping the region, depicting it as the belated product of the Ayatollah Khomeini's successful Islamic revolution in 1979 and heralding an "Islamic awakening" in which Iran would inevitably play a leading role.[13] Iran's stance was not simply rhetorical; the Islamic Republic became a political supporter of various regional insurgent causes, from protests by Bahrain's majority-Shi'ite population against the country's ruling al-Khalifa family[14] to the successful struggle by Yemen's al-Houthi rebellion against the central government in Sana'a.[15]

Iran's most conspicuous initiative, however, was to assume the role of a lifeline for the regime of Syrian dictator Bashar al-Assad. Shortly after the eruption of anti-regime unrest in Syria in March 2011, Iran took on a major role in bolstering and strengthening Assad's hold on power. It did so through extensive financial assistance, as well as the provision of forces to augment Syria's military in its fight against the country's disparate opposition elements. This has included the deployment of a large IRGC contingent to the Syrian battlefield, including hundreds of trained snipers who have helped to reinforce Syrian forces and increase their lethality against Syria's opposition.[16] Together with its Lebanese proxy Hezbollah, it has also played a key role in organizing pro-Assad militias among the country's Alawite and Shi'a communities, as well as coordinating pro-regime foreign fighters from Iraq, Yemen, Lebanon and Afghanistan.[17] While more modest than the migration of Sunni *jihadists* to join the ranks of the Islamic State, this secondary flow is nonetheless significant; as of January 2017, Iran is estimated to have recruited and deployed as many as 20,000 fighters to augment Syrian forces.[18]

Iran's objectives in this effort are two-fold. Most immediately, Iran's aid is intended to shore up the stability of the Assad regime, its most important regional partner. More broadly, however, Iran sees its involvement in Syria as a direct blow against the "Great Satan," the United States. "Since Syria was and continues to be part of the Islamic resistance front and the Islamic Revolution, it provokes the anger of the Americans," IRGC commander Mohammad Ali Jafari explained on Iranian television in April of 2014.[19]

Broadly construed, Iran's regional efforts have been singularly successful. The Iranian regime can now be said to control four regional capitals in the Middle East. The first is Damascus, where Iranian (as well as Russian) support has been instrumental to keeping the Assad regime in power to date. The second is Baghdad, where Iran simultaneously wields extensive influence among the country's political elites and supports an extensive network of powerful Shi'a militias. The third is Lebanon where—in addition to the pervasive influence of Hezbollah—Michel Aoun, a long-time political ally of Tehran, was elected to the Presidency in October of 2016.[20] The fourth is Sana'a, where Iranian-supported rebels have effectively taken over the national government since the spring of 2015.[21]

The financial scope of these activities is enormous. In the past, U.S. officials have estimated that the Islamic Republic boasts "a nine-digit line item in its budget for support to terrorist organizations."[22] More recently, in the summer of 2015, in the aftermath of the conclusion of the JCPOA, the Congressional Research Service estimated that the Islamic Republic was spending between $3.5 billion and $16 billion annually on support for terrorism and insurgency worldwide.[23] That estimate encompassed:

- Extensive aid to the regime of Syrian dictator Bashar al-Assad (estimated at some $6 billion annually);
- Material and economic assistance to the Shi'a Houthi rebels in Yemen;
- Support for various Shi'a militias in Iraq;
- The entire operating budget of the Palestinian Islamic Jihad terrorist organization;
- Renewed aid (previously estimated at between $20-25 million monthly) to the Hamas terrorist group; and
- Between $100 and $200 million annually in financial support for Lebanon's Hezbollah militia.

Notably, however, this figure now has the potential to expand significantly. White House officials have admitted that at least some of Iran's JCPOA-related economic windfall is likely to go to terrorist groups and extremist causes.[24] Indeed, given the scope of sanctions relief inherent in the JCPOA, the investment of even a fraction of those funds in this fashion could double or even triple the Islamic Republic's current spending on terror sponsorship.

ISLAMISM AND SOCIETY

While "exporting the revolution" was and remains a persistent regime objective, involvement and investment on the part of the Iranian population in this pursuit is far from universal. There is little empirical data to suggest that ordinary Iranians share the depth of their regime's commitment to the exportation of radical Islam. To the contrary, terrorism funding in Iran remains an elite—rather than popular—undertaking, directed through state institutions rather than non-governmental organizations, and overseen at an official, not a grassroots, level.

At times, Iran's involvement in the support of radical groups abroad has served as a significant bone of contention between the Iranian regime and its population. In the wake of Hezbollah's summer 2006 war with Israel, for example, Iran's extensive financial support for Lebanon's Shi'ites became a domestic flashpoint, with ordinary Iranians publicly questioning—and condemning—their government's skewed strategic priorities.[25]

Support for radical Islamic causes is eroded by Iran's complex ethno/religious composition. Although the country is overwhelmingly (98 percent) Muslim and predominantly (89 percent) Shi'a, as of 2013 ethnic Persians were estimated to hold only a modest majority (61 percent) in Iran's population of almost 80 million. The remainder is Azeri (16 percent), Kurdish (10 percent), Baloch (2 percent), Arab (2 percent), and a range of other minorities,[26] many of which are systematically discriminated against by the Islamic Republic and feel little or limited allegiance to it. The base of support for Islamic radicalism—and other governmental priorities—in Iranian society is further weakened by the regime's persecution of religious minorities, which, according to the U.S. State Department, has created "a threatening atmosphere for nearly all non-Shi'a religious groups" in the Islamic Republic.[27]

Social and economic malaise has historically served to dilute identification with regime ideals and principles. The Islamic Republic was severely impacted by the 2008-2009 global economic crisis, and thereafter was burdened by unsustainable federal spending and ruinous fiscal policies adopted by the government of President Mahmoud Ahmadinejad. These trends—coupled with growing pressure applied by the West over the Islamic Republic's nuclear program—resulted in worsening economic conditions (such as rising inflation and unemployment) as well as a variety of social ills, from widespread drug addiction to rampant prostitution to high levels of poverty.[28]

Discontent over the country's political direction and socio-economic conditions found its expression in dramatic fashion in the summer of 2009, in the largest episode of unrest in the Islamic Republic's history. The mass protests were catalyzed by the appearance of blatant institutional fraud in the re-election of Mahmoud Ahmadinejad in the country's June 2009 presidential election. In the weeks after the election, opposition to the Iranian regime gathered momentum, growing to encompass significant cracks in the previously-sound ideological consensus among Iran's clerical elites regarding the institutions and policies of Khomeini's Islamic Republic.

The Iranian regime responded with a major campaign to dominate the domestic media, intimidate regime opponents, and purge ideological dissent. These efforts included: tightening of already-strict controls over the Internet;[29] targeting of opposition leaders, both secular and religious;[30] and intimidation of Iranian opposition activists living abroad.[31] This crackdown, and the lack of action by the West to support democratic forces within the Islamic Republic, resulted in the marginalization of Iran's opposition forces. Despite sporadic signs of life,[32] the Green Movement has become a marginal actor, largely irrelevant in Iranian politics. This was confirmed in the run-up to the country's June 2013 presidential election; pro-democracy activists remained largely dormant until just days before the June 14th poll. When they did finally emerge, it was not in the form of a political game-changer, but as a bit player, focusing their internal deliberations on whether or not to boycott the election entirely.

Reformist opposition to clerical rule has been further weakened by the Iranian regime's nuclear rapprochement with the West. While growing economic malaise in 2011-2013 as a result of widening Western sanctions did have an adverse political effect on regime stability and prosperity, the election of Hassan Rouhani, a bureaucrat, to the Iranian presidency in June of 2013, and his subsequent initiation of nuclear negotiations with the international community, has effectively neutered political alternatives to the ruling regime. The results of those negotiations, at least for a time, were widely perceived within Iran as being advantageous to the country, strengthening support for the current regime and further diminishing movement toward meaning political change in Tehran.

However, there is now evidence to suggest that public opinion in Iran is progressively souring on the nuclear deal. A January 2017 survey conducted by the University of Maryland's Center for International Security Studies, for example, found declining enthusiasm for the agreement among Iranians, and growing dissatisfaction with its lack of tangible dividends.[33] This, in turn, has created a political challenge to Hassan Rouhani's continued tenure in office.[34]

ISLAMISM AND THE STATE

Iran's support for Islamism is channeled through an elaborate infrastructure of institutions and governmental bodies tasked with the promotion of radical Islamic thought and action. These include:

The Islamic Revolutionary Guard Corps (IRGC, or Pasdaran)

At home, the IRGC, in addition to its professional military duties, has become the guardian of the regime's ballistic missile and weapons of mass destruction programs.[35] The agenda of Iran's ideological army, however, is global in scope, and so is its reach. Over the past three-and-a-half decades, the IRGC has emerged as the shock troops of Iran's Islamic Revolution, training terrorist organizations both within Iran and in specialized training camps in places like Lebanon and Sudan, as well as providing assistance to radical movements and terrorist proxies throughout the Middle East, Africa, Europe and Asia via specialized paramilitary units.[36] The most notorious of these is the Quds Force, a crack military battalion formed in 1990 and dedicated to carrying out "extra-regional operations of the Islamic Revolutionary Guard Corps"—namely, terrorism and insurgency in the name of the Islamic Republic.[37] Since the 2003 ouster of Saddam Hussein, this unit has played a leading role in Iraq as part of what analysts have characterized as an "open-ended, resilient, and well-funded" covert effort on the part of the Iranian regime to extend its influence into the former Ba'athist state.[38] More recently, the IRGC has become a principal player in the Iranian government's ongoing assistance to Syrian dictator Bashar al-Assad.[39]

The IRGC also boasts a dedicated intelligence service, the Protection and Intelligence Department, or *Hefazat va Ettelaat-e Sepah-e Pasdaran*. Founded in 1980, it encompasses three main functions: intelligence in support of IRGC military operations; political operations at home and abroad; and support to the foreign terrorist operations of the Quds Force.[40]

Ministry of Intelligence and Security (MOIS)

Controlled directly by Supreme Leader Ali Khamenei, the MOIS is used by Iran's ruling clergy to quash domestic opposition and carry out espionage against suspect members of the Iranian government.[41] Abroad, the MOIS plays a key role in planning and carrying out terrorist operations on foreign soil, using Iranian embassies and diplomatic missions as cover.[42] MOIS operatives are also known to operate abroad under unofficial identities—for example, as employees of Iran Air, Iran's official airline.[43] The MOIS conducts a variety of activities in support of the operations of Tehran's terrorist surrogates, ranging from financing actual operations to intelligence collection on potential targets. The Ministry also carries out independent operations, primarily against dissidents of the current regime in Tehran living in foreign countries, at the direction of senior Iranian officials.[44]

Ministry of Foreign Affairs

Iran's Foreign Ministry serves as an important enabler of the Iranian regime's international terrorist presence. Agents of the IRGC and MOIS often operate out of Iranian missions abroad, where they are stationed under diplomatic cover, complete with blanket diplomatic immunity. These agents—and through them Iranian foreign proxies—use the Ministry's auspices to untraceably obtain financing, weapons and intelligence from Tehran (for example, via diplomatic pouch).[45]

Cultural Affairs Ministry

Supplementing the role of the Foreign Affairs Ministry in exporting terrorism is Iran's Ministry of Culture and Guidance. Tasked with overseeing the cultural sections of Iranian foreign missions, as well as free-standing Iranian cultural centers, it facilitates IRGC infiltration of—and terrorist recruitment within—local Muslim populations in foreign nations.[46] The Ministry is particularly influential among majority Muslim countries like the former Soviet Republics, many of which share substantial cultural, religious and ideological bonds with Tehran. Between 1982 and 1992, the official in charge of the Ministry—and of its role in support of Iranian terror abroad—was Mohammed Khatami, Iran's subsequent "reformist" president.

Basij

Formed during the early days of the Islamic Republic and trained by the Pasdaran, this militia represents the Iranian regime's premier tool of domestic terror. During the eight years of the Iran-Iraq war, the organization's cadres were the Islamic Republic's cannon fodder, selected to clear minefields and launch "human wave" attacks against Iraqi forces.[47] With the end of the conflict with Iraq, the role of the Basij was reoriented, and the organization became the watchdog of Iranian society. Today, it is used by the ayatollahs to quell domestic anti-regime protests and eradicate "un-Islamic" behavior. Their role ranges from enforcing modest dress to gathering intelligence on university students, which is handed over to the regime's undercover police.[48] The

Basij played a significant role in suppressing domestic dissent through violence and intimidation in the aftermath of the fraudulent reelection of Mahmoud Ahmadinejad to the Iranian presidency in June of 2009.[49]

There are reported to be as many as 10 million registered Basij members, though not all are on active service.[50] The Basij also plays an important supporting role in Iran's state sponsorship of terror. It is known to be active in training anti-Israeli forces, including carrying out maneuvers designed to ready Hezbollah and assorted Palestinian militants for guerrilla warfare.

Domestic paramilitaries (guruh-I fishar)

Supplementing the role of the Basij are the numerous vigilante or "pressure" groups that are harnessed by the Iranian government. Though officially independent, these gangs actually operate under the patronage of government officials, the IRGC or the MOIS, and target internal opposition to the clerical regime.[51] The most famous is the *Ansar-i Hezbollah*, which was responsible for fomenting the July 1999 crisis at Tehran University that led to the bloody governmental crackdown on student opposition forces.

Bonyads

These sprawling socio-religious foundations, which are overseen only by Iran's Supreme Leader, serve as conduits for the Islamic Republic's cause of choice. Arguably the most important is the *Bonyad-e Mostazafan* (Foundation of the Oppressed), a sprawling network of an estimated 1,200 firms created in 1979 with seed money from the Shah's coffers.[52] Another is the *Bonyad-e Shahid* (Martyrs' Foundation), an enormous conglomerate of industrial, agricultural, construction and commercial companies with some 350 offices and tens of thousands of employees.[53] The sums controlled by these organs are enormous: more than 30 percent of Iran's national GDP, and as much as two-thirds of the country's non-oil GDP.[54] And while many of their functions are legitimate, they are also used by Iran's religious leaders to funnel money to their pet causes, from financing domestic repression to arming radical groups abroad.

Notably, even as Iran remains complicit in the pervasive sponsorship of international terrorism, it is itself the target of violent activity by two separate and distinct groups. The first is the *Mujahideen e-Khalq* (MeK or MKO), also known as the People's Mujahideen Organization of Iran, or PMOI. The MeK is the most prominent and well-organized opposition group to the ruling Iranian government in existence today.[55] A guerrilla group of radical Marxist-Islamist ideology, the MeK was established in the 1960s in opposition to the government of Shah Mohammed Reza Pahlavi.[56] Following the overthrow of the Shah, however, the MeK found itself shut out of the Iranian regime's power structures. By the early 1980s, the organization moved into opposition, and became an active target of the Iranian security forces. As a result, it relocated to neighboring Iraq, which subsequently became its principal source of financial and political support, as well as the organization's major base of operations in its periodic attacks against the Iranian regime.[57] According to the U.S. Department of State, the MeK also assumed a domestic role, assisting the Iraqi government in "suppressing the Shia and Kurdish uprisings in northern and southern Iraq" in 1991 and thereafter playing a part in Iraq's internal security services.[58] In exchange, the regime of Saddam Hussein became the source of all of the MeK's military assistance, and the bulk of its economic revenue—a situation that would endure until the overthrow of the Iraqi regime by Coalition forces in the spring of 2003.[59] During the 1990s, this support was estimated to be some $7 million monthly.[60] The extent of this support was made public in January 2004, when the Iraqi daily *Al-Mada* published a list of 270 beneficiaries of oil allocations from the regime of Saddam Hussein.[61] That list revealed that the MeK had been a major recipient of oil vouchers from the Iraqi government.[62] All told, the MeK is believed to have received more than 38 million barrels of oil from the Iraqi government in the four years before the U.S.-led invasion of Iraq—theoretically generating profits of more than $16 million.[63]

The organization maintains a sizeable base of supporters and members in Europe, most directly in France, where the organization's political head, Maryam Rajavi, is believed to reside. Members of the MeK are also resident in Iraq, where several thousand were held for years at Camp Ashraf in Iraq's Diyala province pursuant to a 2004 grant of "protected persons" status by the U.S. military[64] and a subsequent arrangement struck between the U.S.-led Coalition and the government of Iraqi Prime Minister Nouri al-Maliki. In the fall of 2012, then-Secretary of State Hillary Clinton formally removed the MeK from the U.S. government's Foreign Terrorist Organizations (FTO) list, reversing the designation made by President Bill Clinton in 1997.[65]

Iran has consistently sought to persecute the MeK and individuals thought to be affiliated with it, including through the arrest and detention of family members of those resident in Camp Ashraf.[66] With the withdrawal of U.S. forces from Iraq at the end of 2012, this pressure steadily increased, with Iranian officials actively lobbying the Iraqi government to oust the group from the country. As of the Spring of 2016, Iranian officials claimed that the remainder of the group would be expelled from Iraq "soon."[67] Politically, meanwhile, the conclusion of the JCPOA between Iran and the P5+1 powers has translated into a more *laissez faire* attitude toward the group on the part of the Obama administration—and incentivized the Iranian regime to undertake greater efforts to dismantle it. It is as yet unclear what stance the new Trump administration will assume toward the MeK.

The second, smaller group is the Free Life Party of Kurdistan, or PJAK. Led by Iranian-born German national Abdul Rahman Haji Ahmadi, PJAK is a violent Kurdish nationalist group that has carried out attacks on Iran from strongholds in neighboring Iraq since its formation in 2004. PJAK, which maintains an affiliation with Turkey's larger Kurdistan Workers Party (PKK), claims to seek "democratic change" and characterizes its actions as a "defense" against Iranian state repression of its Kurdish minority.[68]

Iranian regime forces clashed repeatedly with members of PJAK between 2008 and 2011, successfully arresting and killing numerous group members as part of ongoing counterterrorism operations.[69] A major counterterrorism campaign against the group by Iranian security forces followed in the fall of 2011, culminating in a ceasefire between the two parties.[70] This ceasefire held until 2013, when clashes between the group and Tehran began anew,[71] and have continued sporadically until the present day. As above, it is unclear as of this writing what stance the new administration in Washington will take toward Kurdish militias in general, and PJAK in particular.

ENDNOTES

[1] See, for example, Guy Taylor, "Iran is Banking Billions More Than Expected Thanks to Obama's Deal," Washington Times, February 3, 2016, http://www.washingtontimes.com/news/2016/feb/3/iran-claims-100-billion-windfall-from-sanctions-re/.

[2] Emmanuel Sivan, Radical Islam: Medieval Theology and Modern Politics (New Haven: Yale University Press, 1985), 188–207.

[3] Ruhollah Khomeini, Islamic Government (New York: Manor Books, 1979).

[4] Preamble of the Constitution of the Islamic Republic of Iran, http://www.oefre.unibe.ch/law/icl/ir00000_.html.

[5] Robin Wright, Sacred Rage: The Wrath of Militant Islam (New York: Simon & Schuster, 1986), 111–21.

[6] "Iranian Terrorism in Bosnia and Croatia," Iran Brief, March 3, 1997, http://www.lexis-nexis.com; Mike O'Connor, "Spies for Iranians Are Said to Gain a Hold in Bosnia," New York Times, November 28, 1997, 1.

[7] Vali Nasr, The Shi'a Revival: How Conflicts within Islam will Shape the Future (New York: W.W. Norton & Company, 2006), 137.

[8] "Hezbollah has 50,000 Rockets: Report," Agence France Presse, December 7, 2010, http://www.spacewar.com/reports/Hezbollah_has_50000_rockets_report_999.html.

[9] Joseph Felter and Brian Fishman, "Iranian Strategy in Iraq: Politics and 'Other Means,'" Combating Terrorism Center at West Point Occasional Paper, October 13, 2008, http://ctc.usma.edu/Iran_Iraq/CTC_Iran_Iraq_Final.pdf; Ned Parker, "Ten Years After Iraq War Began, Iran Reaps the Gains," Los Angeles Times, March 28, 2013, http://articles.latimes.com/2013/mar/28/world/la-fg-iraq-iran-influence-20130329.

[10] "Chapter 3. State Sponsors of Terrorism," in Country Reports on Terrorism 2012 (Washington, DC: U.S. Department of State, May 2013), http://www.state.gov/j/ct/rls/crt/2012/209985.htm.

[11] Ibid.

[12] The historically tense relations between Iran and Egypt deteriorated precipitously during 2008-2010, spurred in large part by Egyptian fears of Iranian internal meddling. These worries were showcased in spring of 2009, when Egyptian authorities arrested a total of twenty-six individuals suspected of

carrying out espionage for Hezbollah, and of plotting to carry out terrorist attacks within Egypt. The suspects were subsequently formally charged with plotting subversion against the Egyptian state. "Egypt Charges 26 'Hizbullah Spies,'" Jerusalem Post, July 26, 2009, http://www.jpost.com/servlet/Satellite cid=1248277893866&pagename=JPost%2FJPArticle%2FShowFull.

[13] See, for example, "Lawmaker: Uprisings in Region Promising Birth of Islamic Middle-East," Fars News Agency (Tehran), February 5, 2011, http://english.farsnews.com/newstext.php?nn=8911161168.

[14] "Iran's Support for Bahrain Protesters Fuels Regional Tensions," Deutsche Welle, April 15, 2011, http://www.dw.de/irans-support-for-bahrain-protesters-fuels-regional-tensions/a-6504403-1.

[15] See, for example, Eric Schmitt, and Robert F. Worth, "With Arms for Yemen Rebels, Iran Seeks Wider Mideast Role," New York Times, March 15, 2012, http://www.nytimes.com/2012/03/15/world/middleeast/aiding-yemen-rebels-iran-seeks-wider-mideast-role.html.

[16] Luke McKenna, "Syria is Importing Iranian Snipers to Murder Anti-Government Protesters," Business Insider, January 27, 2012, http://www.businessinsider.com/syria-is-importing-iranian-snipers-to-murder-anti-government-protesters-2012-1.

[17] See, for example, Farnaz Fassihi, "Iran Recruiting Afghan Refugees to Fight for Regime in Syria," Wall Street Journal, May 15, 2014, http://online.wsj.com/news/articles/SB10001424052702304908304579564161508613846?mg=reno64-wsj&url=http%3A%2F%2Fonline.wsj.com%2Farticle%2FSB10001424052702304908304579564161508613846.html.

[18] See, for example, Ahmad Majidyar, "Iran Recruits and Trains Large Numbers of Afghan and Pakistani Shiites," Middle East Institute, January 18, 2017, http://www.mei.edu/content/article/io/iran-s-recruitment-afghan-pakistani-shiites-further-destabilizes-south-asia.

[19] "Iranian Revolutionary Guard Corps Commander Jafari: We Support Resistance to U.S. and Israel in Syria and Elsewhere in the Region," Middle East Media Research Institute Clip no. 4272, April 21, 2014, http://www.memritv.org/clip/en/4272.htm.

[20] Martin Chulov, "Iranian Ally Michel Aoun Elected as President of Lebanon," Guardian (London), October 31, 2016, https://www.theguardian.com/world/2016/oct/31/michel-aoun-elected-president-lebanon-iran-tehran-saudi-arabia.

[21] "Yemen's Houthis Form Own Government in Sanaa," Al-Jazeera (Doha), February 6, 2015, http://www.aljazeera.com/news/middleeast/2015/02/yemen-houthi-rebels-announce-presidential-council-150206122736448.html.

[22] Under Secretary of the Treasury for Terrorism and Financial Intelligence Stuart Levey, Remarks before the 5th Annual Conference on Trade, Treasury, and Cash Management in the Middle East, Abu Dhabi, United Arab Emirates, March 7, 2007,

http://uae.usembassy.gov/remarks_of_stuart_levey_.html.

[23] Carla Humud, Christopher Blanchard, Jeremy Sharp and Jim Zanotti, "Iranian Assistance to Groups in Yemen, Iraq, Syria, and the Palestinian Territories," Congressional Research Service Memorandum, July 31, 2015, http://www.kirk.senate.gov/images/PDF/Iran%20Financial%20Support%20 to%20Terrorists%20and%20Militants.pdf.

[24] See, for example, Matthew Lee, "Kerry: Some Iran Sanctions Relief Likely to Go to Terrorists," Associated Press, January 21, 2016, http://bigstory. ap.org/article/9ab669cada3b47cfaa3e6793a3ca6faa/kerry-rejects-iranian-criticism-us-sanctions.

[25] See, for example, Azadeh Moaveni, "The Backlash against Iran's Role in Lebanon," Time, August 31, 2006, http://www.time.com/time/world/article/0,8599,1515755,00.html.

[26] U.S. Central Intelligence Agency, "Iran," World Factbook, August 13, 2013, https://www.cia.gov/library/publications/resources/the-world-factbook/geos/ir.html.

[27] U.S. Department of State, Bureau of Democracy, Human Rights and Labor, International Religious Freedom Report 2008, n.d., http://www.state.gov/g/drl/rls/irf/2008/108482.htm.

[28] Karl Vick, "Opiates of the Iranian People," Washington Post, September 23, 2005, A01; "US to Reverse Afghan Opium Strategy," Al-Jazeera (Doha), June 28, 2009, http://english.aljazeera.net/news/asia/2009/06/200962815525664398.html; Nazila Fathi, "To Regulate Prostitution, Iran Ponders Brothels," New York Times, August 28, 2002, http://query.nytimes.com/gst/fullpage.html?res=9404E0DE1F3CF93BA1575BC0 A9649C8B63; United Nations Childrens' Fund, "At a Glance: Iran, Islamic Republic Of," n.d., http://www.unicef.org/infobycountry/iran.html.

[29] Iran to Monitor Cyberspace to Fight Offenses," Press TV (Tehran), July 20, 2009, http://edition.presstv.ir/detail/101138.html.

[30] See, for example, Human Rights Watch, "Iran: Stop 'Framing' Government Critics," July 21, 2009, http://www.hrw.org/en/news/2009/07/21/iran-stop-framing-government-critics.

[31] Farnaz Fassihi, "Iran's Crackdown Goes Global," Wall Street Journal, December 3, 2009, http://online.wsj.com/article/SB125978649644673331.html.

[32] In the summer of 2011, for example, Iran's opposition crafted a "green manifesto" intended to articulate organizing principles around which the country's various anti-regime elements could coalesce. See, for example, Genieve Abdo, "Iran's Opposition Launches New Manifesto," Al-Jazeera (Doha), July 22, 2011, http://www.aljazeera.com/indepth/opinion/2011/07/2011722104456488653.html. However, this initiative failed to generate new momentum for—or greater coherence in—the Green Movement.

[33] "Iranian Attitudes on Iranian-U.S. Relations in the Trump Era," Center for International & Security Studies at Maryland, January 2017, http://www.cissm.umd.edu/publications/iranian-attitudes-iranian-us-relations-trump-era.

[34] See, for example, Ilan Berman, "The JCPOA Helps Iran's Elites and Hurts Rouhani," Foreign Affairs, March 29, 2017, https://www.foreignaffairs.com/articles/iran/2017-03-29/jcpoa-helps-irans-elites-and-hurts-rouhani?cid=int-lea&pgtype=hpg.

[35] Mohammad Mohaddessin, Islamic Fundamentalism: The New Global Threat (Washington: Seven Locks Press, 1993), 132-136.

[36] See, for example, Michael Eisenstadt, Iranian Military Power: Capabilities and Intentions (Washington: Washington Institute for Near East Policy, 1996), 70-72.

[37] Mohaddessin, Islamic Fundamentalism, 102.

[38] Michael Knights, "Iran's Ongoing Proxy War in Iraq," Washington Institute for Near East Policy Policywatch 1492, March 16, 2009, http://www.washingtoninstitute.org/templateC05.php?CID=3029.

[39] See, for example, Amir Toumaj, "IRGC Special Officer's Death Highlights Involvement in Syria," Long War Journal, October 1, 2016, http://www.longwarjournal.org/archives/2016/10/irgc-special-forces-officers-death-highlights-involvement-in-syria.php.

[40] "Rev. Guards Intelligence," Iran Brief, January 6, 1997, http://www.lexis-nexis.com.

[41] "Ministry of Intelligence and Security [MOIS]: Vezarat-e Ettela'at va Amniat-e Keshvar VEVAK," globalsecurity.org, February 19, 2006, http://www.globalsecurity.org/intell/world/iran/vevak.htm.

[42] [Eisenstadt, Iranian Military Power, 70.

[43] Federation of American Scientists, "Ministry of Intelligence and Security [MOIS]: Organization," n.d., http://www.fas.org/irp/world/iran/vevak/org.htm.

[44] See, for example, "Khamene'i Ordered Khobar Towers Bombing, Defector Says," Iran Brief, August 3, 1998, http://www.lexis-nexis.com; American intelligence officials have long maintained that Iranian terrorism is authorized at the highest official levels. See, for example, CIA Director R. James Woolsey, "Challenges to Peace in the Middle East," remarks before the Washington Institute for Near East Policy's Wye Plantation Conference, Queenstown, Maryland, September 23, 1994, http://www.washingtoninstitute.org/templateC07.php?CID=66.

[45] Eisenstadt, Iranian Military Power, 71.

[46] Ibid.; Mohaddessin, Islamic Fundamentalism, 101-102.

[47] Drew Middleton, "5 Years of Iran-Iraq War: Toll May Be Near a Million," New York Times, September 23, 1985, 4.

[48] Geneive Abdo, "Islam's Warriors Scent Blood," Observer (London), July 18, 1999, 26.

[49] "Basij Commander Admits Forces Shot at 2009 Protesters," International Campaign for Human Rights in Iran, January 6, 2014, https://www.iranhumanrights.org/2014/01/basij-shot/.

[50] Angus McDowall, "Tehran Deploys Islamic Vigilantes to Attack Protesters," Independent (London), July 11, 2003, 12.

[51] For more on the guruh-i fishar, see Michael Rubin, Into the Shadows: Radical Vigilantes in Khatami's Iran (Washington: Washington Institute for Near East Policy, 2001).

[52] Robert D. Kaplan, "A Bazaari's World," Atlantic Monthly 277, iss. 3 (1996), 28.

[53] Wilfried Buchta, Who Rules Iran? The Structure of Power in the Islamic Republic (Washington: Washington Institute for Near East Policy – Konrad Adenauer Stiftung, 2000), 75.

[54] Ibid.; See also Kenneth Katzman, Statement before the Joint Economic Committee of the United States Congress, July 25, 2006.

[55] In October 1997, pursuant to the Anti-Terrorism and Effective Death Penalty Act of 1996, the MeK was designated Foreign Terrorist Organization under U.S. law—a status it held until September of 2012, when the organization was delisted by the U.S. Department of State.

[56] International Policy Institute for Counterterrorism, "Mujahedin-e Khalq Organization (MEK or MKO)," n.d. Available online at http://www.ict.org.il/.

[57] United States Department of State, Office of the Coordinator for Counterterrorism, Patterns of Global Terrorism 2003 (Washington, DC: U.S. Department of State, June 2004), 129.

[58] United States Department of State, Office of the Coordinator for Counterterrorism, Patterns of Global Terrorism 2001 (Washington, DC: U.S. Department of State, May 2002), 101. The MeK has publicly denied these charges.

[59] U.S. Department of State, Office of the Coordinator for Counterterrorism, Country Reports on Terrorism 2004 (Washington, DC: U.S. Department of State, April 2005), 105.

[60] Cited in Charles Recknagel, "Iran: Washington Says Iranian Opposition Helping with Iraqi Security Operations," Radio Free Europe/Radio Liberty, May 23, 2002, http://www.rferl.org/features/2002/05/23052002084552.asp.

[61] Al-Mada (Baghdad), as cited in "The Beneficiaries of Saddam's Oil Vouchers: The List of 270," Middle East Media Research Institute Inquiry and Analysis no. 160, January 29, 2004, http://memri.org/bin/articles.cgi?Page=countries&Area=iraq&ID=IA16004.

[62] Ibid.

[63] Ibidem.

[64] Scott Peterson, "Why the US Granted 'Protected' Status to Iranian Terrorists," Christian Science Monitor, July 29, 2004, 7.

[65] Scott Shane, "Iranian Dissidents Convince U.S. to Drop Terror Label," New York Times, September 21, 2012, http://www.nytimes.com/2012/09/22/world/middleeast/iranian-opposition-group-mek-wins-removal-from-us-terrorist-list.html?pagewanted=all.

[66] Amnesty International, "Iran: Arbitrary Arrests, Torture and Executions Continue," May 20, 2011, http://www.amnesty.org/en/library/asset/MDE13/051/2011/en/ad9b1ffd-7c9f-475c-9ace-c1e712a29f60/mde130512011en.html.

[67] "Rest of MEK to be Epelled from Iraq Soon, Claims Iran Diplomat," Rudaw, April 8, 2016, http://rudaw.net/english/middleeast/iraq/04082016.

[68] "Tehran Faces Growing Kurdish Opposition," Washington Times, April 3, 2006, http://www.washingtontimes.com/news/2006/apr/3/20060403-125601-8453r/.

[69] See, for example, "4 Members of PJAK Terrorist Group Arrested in Iran," Fars News Agency (Tehran), November 30, 2010, http://english.farsnews.com/newstext.php?nn=8909091200; See also "Iranian Troops Attack Kurdish PJAK Rebel Bases in Iraq," BBC (London), July 18, 2011, http://www.bbc.co.uk/news/world-middle-east-14189313.

[70] "Iran Deploying Troops, Tanks to Kurdistan Border," World Tribune, July 19, 2013, http://www.worldtribune.com/2013/07/19/iran-deploying-troops-tanks-to-kurdistan-border/.

[71] "Five IRGC Soldiers Killed in Clash with 'Terrorists' in Western Iran," Xinhua, October 11, 2013, http://news.xinhuanet.com/english/world/2013-10/11/c_125510936.htm

ISRAEL

QUICK FACTS

Population: 8,174,527 (July 2016 est.)

Area: 20,770 sq km

Ethnic Groups: Jewish 74.8% (of which Israel-born 75.6%, Europe/America/Oceania-born 16.6%, Africa-born 4.9%, Asia-born 2.9%), non-Jewish 25.2%

Religions: Jewish 74.8%, Muslim 17.6%, Christian 2%, Druze 1.6%, other 4%

Government Type: parliamentary democracy

GDP (official exchange rate): $311.7 billion (2015 est.)

Map and Quick Facts courtesy of the CIA World Factbook (January 2017)

OVERVIEW

Although there was a strong Islamist current in the Palestinian national movement of the British Mandate Period, the Israeli War of Independence (1947-49) and subsequent policies adopted by the Israeli government kept Islamism largely at bay until the 1970s. Islamism regained popularity in the wake of Iran's 1979 Islamic Revolution, spreading to the Palestinian Territories and even into Israel itself as Israeli Arabs have shown increasing identification with their Palestinian cousins in the West Bank and Gaza Strip in recent years. Israeli preoccupation with secular Arab nationalist groups in the 1970s and 80s enabled Islamism to metastasize unfettered. Today, the phenomenon is manifested most concretely in the Islamic Movement of Israel. Increasingly, Israeli Islamists collaborate with secular Arab Israeli nationalists to undermine the security of the State of Israel and erode its Jewish identity.

ISLAMIST ACTIVITY

Hamas

The Islamist group known by the acronym HAMAS is the premier Islamist faction in the Palestinian Territories, and the principal extremist threat to the state of Israel. Its precursor was an Islamist group known as *Mujama al-Islamiya*. In the 1970s, over the objections of moderate Palestinians,[1] the Israeli government permitted Sheikh Ahmed Yassin, the leader of the Muslim Brotherhood in the Gaza Strip, to register *Mujama al-Islamiya*, first as a charity and then, in 1979, as an association.[2] At first, the group devoted itself primarily to building schools, clinics, and libraries. *Mujama al-Islamiya* refrained from anti-Israel violence in its early years, but when the first *intifada* erupted in December of 1987, Yassin and some of his *Mujama al-Islamiya* colleagues founded Hamas. Hamas (the "Islamic resistance movement" in Arabic) promotes the following of fundamentalist Islamic norms, such as requiring women to wear the *hijab* and allowing polygamous unions, Furthermore, Hamas has committed itself, to waging an armed struggle to obliterate Israel and to establish an Islamic state governed by *sharia* law "from the Jordan River to the Mediterranean Sea."[3]

Hamas, despite being a Sunni movement, benefits significantly from Iranian support. Iran has provided financial and military assistance to Hamas since the early 1990s. It has also provided both rhetorical and logistical support to the group in its operations. In one well known incident in 2002, Israel captured the *Karine A*, a ship destined for the Gaza Strip and carrying 50 tons of advanced weaponry on board. The ship had been stocked in Iranian waters.[4]

Iran has also provided substantial financial aid to Hamas. In January 1995, former Central Intelligence Agency (CIA) Director James Woolsey testified before the Senate Intelligence Committee that Iran had provided more than $100 million to Hamas, though he did not specify a timeframe.[5] In December 2006, Hamas reported on its website that Iran had provided the organization with $250 million.[6] After Operation Cast Lead in 2008-2009, Iran provided Hamas with a variety of weapons, including Grad rockets with range of 20-40 KM, anti-tank missiles and others. Along with the military aid, Iran has provided advanced training for Hamas operatives with instructors from the Iranian Revolutionary Guards, as well as propaganda support.[7]

The Syrian civil war initially proved detrimental to the relationship between Hamas and Iran. Hamas refused to support Syrian dictator Bashar al-Assad, one of Iran's key allies.[8] In response to this refusal, Tehran cut off Hamas's funding, which amounted to about $23 million per month.[9] This move forced Hamas to seek out alternative sources of funding, including from wealthy Sunni states such as Qatar,[10] and Saudi Arabia. However, Hamas and Iran eventually reconciled, and in 2015 Iran began supplying Hamas with military technology, helping it repair tunnels destroyed in the 2014 conflict with Israel, and hosting Hamas delegations in Iran.[11]

Like many militant groups, Hamas has secured popular support among Palestinians and pursued recruitment through community service and engagement. Hamas provides schools, hospitals, and other necessary social services. Hamas guarantees economic assistance to the surviving family of its suicide bombers, including providing education and healthcare, and covering funeral expenses. This financial support—especially in impoverished communities—serves as a continuing recruitment driver.[12]

Though Hamas is more active and powerful in Palestinian communities, Israeli-Arabs have also been involved with the organization. In May 2011, the Haifa District Court sentenced an Israeli Arab to five years in prison for conspiring with his brother-in-law to gather an arms cache in Israel for Hamas.[13] The same year, Israeli authorities arrested two Arab residents of East Jerusalem holding Israeli citizenship who were planning to attack Jerusalem's Teddy Stadium during a Premier League soccer match. Authorities divulged that the two men had longstanding ties with Hamas.[14]

Islamic Movement in Israel

The Islamic Movement in Israel is a Sunni group that advocates for the vital role of Islam in public life in Israel. Abdullah Darwish founded the movement. Much like Hamas, The Islamic Movement courts favor from local populations through providing social services. During the first *intifada*, the Islamic Movement established the "Islamic Relief Committee," the stated purpose of which was to provide assistance to injured Palestinians. In 1993, it split in response to internal discord over the Oslo Accords. Darwish supported accepting the Accords, while more hardline members, such as Sheikh Ra'ed Salah and Sheikh Kemal Khatib, did not support the agreement. The hardline faction became known as the "Northern Branch" (as the majority of its leaders came from Northern Israel.)[15] Darwish led the more moderate Southern Branch. The Northern Branch played a part in inciting the second *intifada* in 2000. Specifically, incitement by the group helped instigate clashes between Israeli-Arabs and police in the Wadi Ara region in October 2000—clashes that left 13 protesters dead.[16]

Most of the Islamic Movement's support within Israel comes from the Bedouin community (discussed further below). In November 2015, the Israeli government designated the Northern Branch of the Islamic Movement and its 17 affiliated charities illegal, and jailed its leader, Ra'ed Salah. Yet, despite (or perhaps because of) these measures, the organization remains popular among Israeli Arabs.[17]

Palestinian Islamic Jihad

The Palestinian Islamic Jihad (PIJ) was founded in 1979 as a branch of the Egyptian Muslim Brotherhood[18] by Fathi Shaqaqi and Abd al-Aziz Awda, Until the killing of the Egyptian President, Anwar Sadat, the PIJ operated from Egypt, then its leadership was exiled to Gaza. In 1987 when exiled from Gaza to Lebanon, and in 1989 Shaqaqi decided to relocate the official command to Damascus.[19] According to the U.S. State Department, PIJ's high-ranking leadership is located in Syria while some leaders live in Lebanon, though most of its affiliates live in Gaza.[20]

After Shaqaqi was killed in 1995, Ramadan Shallah, previously a professor at the University of South Florida, became the head of the organization.[21] PIJ is much smaller than Hamas and consist of around 1,000 members[22] (although in 2011, the organization was reported to have at least 8,000 fighters in Gaza).[23] The PIJ, like Hamas, is ardently committed to the violent destruction of Israel,[24] but in contrast spends little time on social services for Palestinians in the Gaza and the West Bank, where it is active today. The organizations' armed wing is called the "al-Quds Brigades," and is responsible for many suicide attacks during the Second Intifada (2000-2005). In recent years, the organization intensified its rocket launching from Gaza to Israel.[25]

PIJ has a degree of support from Israeli-Arabs. In August 2008, Israeli authorities arrested a five-man PIJ cell, which included two Israeli-Arabs, accused of planning an attack on an army checkpoint near Ramallah and of planning to assassinate Israeli pilots, scientists and university professors.[26] Then, in January 2013, Israeli police detained three members of a PIJ cell at the Eyal Junction in the Sharon region. The men, including two Palestinians from Jenin and an Israeli-Arab from Tira, planned to kidnap an Israeli soldier and trade him for the release of incarcerated Palestinian terrorists.[27]

Though the group is Sunni, PIJ is nonetheless strongly influenced by the model of Islamic political activism embodied by Iran's 1979 Revolution.[28] As a result, Iran has historically provided extensive support to the group via funding, as well as military equipment and training. In 1998 it was revealed that Iran had allocated 2 million dollars to PIJ annual budget. Since then, the Iranian support to the PIJ has been much higher. In 2013 PIJ sources stated that they received from Iran around $3 million per month.[29] According to Ali Nourizadeh, director of the Center for Iranian Studies in London, Iran transferred to the organization $100-150 million every year.[30]

However, in 2015, tensions between the group and Iran began to appear, due to PIJ's refusal to condemn the Sunni Gulf state attacks, led by Saudi Arabia, against the Houthi rebels in Yemen.[31] In 2015, a senior leader at PIJ acknowledged that the organization is suffering from the worst financial catastrophe since its foundation, among other things since Iran had cut back its financial support.[32] According to different reports from 2016, Iran cut its support for the organization by 90 percent.[33] However, a report revealed that Iran is planning to restart its financing of PIJ.[34]

Hezbollah

Hezbollah is a Shia Muslim organization that maintains a terrorist wing and a political/social-welfare wing.[35] The organization was founded in 1982 during the destructive Lebanese Civil War, with significant support from the Iranian Revolutionary Guard Corps (IRGC).[36] In its founding statement,[37] in 1985 expressed its loyalty to Iran's supreme leader, Ayatollah Ruhollah Khomeini; called for the establishment of an Islamic regime; and called for the removal of the U.S, France and Israel from Lebanon in addition to the annihilation of Israel.[38] Iran regards Hezbollah as a way to achieve its aims indirectly and spread its influence through the region. The Islamic Republic provides financial support, training, and advanced weaponry to Hezbollah.[39] In total, Iran's support is estimated at $100-200 million per year, including weaponry, training, and logistics support. Since 2002, Iran has established training camps for different terrorist organizations, including Hezbollah, Hamas and PIJ. These camps are run by the IRGC. In addition, Iran funds Hezbollah's propaganda mechanisms including its television channel *Al-Manar*. The station reported that it receives most of its funding from Iran, approximately $15 million annually.[40]

In 1982, Israel invaded Lebanon in Operation Peace for Galilee.[41] In 1985, the Israeli Defense Force (IDF) withdrew to the "security belt" in southern Lebanon, and subsequently withdrew out of Lebanon completely in 2000. After the IDF withdrew, Hezbollah quickly became a dominant actor in the region.[42] Hezbollah officially entered politics in the 1992 parliamentary elections. It has continued to grow in influence and power, and now constitutes a major part of the Lebanese parliament.[43]

According to Israeli Security Agency (ISA) assessments, following Israel's withdrawal from Lebanon in 2000, Hezbollah began to focus on penetrating the Israeli-Arab population. Hezbollah sees Israeli-Arabs as advantageous operatives because they have the advantage of being Israeli citizens who enjoy freedom of movement and accessibility to targets.[44] While the majority of its activities are affiliated with Fatah's *Al Aqsa Martyrs* Brigades, Hezbollah also cooperates with Hamas, the PIJ, and the Popular Front for the Liberation of Palestine (PFLP).[45] Hezbollah uses its global infrastructure to recruit Israeli-Arabs when they travel outside of Israel.[46]

Hezbollah is known for its cross-border operations in addition to extensive terrorist activities abroad, such as the attacks in Argentina against the Israeli embassy in Buenos Aires in 1992 and the Jewish Community Center in 1994,[47] as well as the attack against the Israeli tourist bus in Burgas, Bulgaria in 2012. Hezbollah maintains a large presence of supporters and operatives all around the world, including North and South America, Africa, Asia and Europe.[48] Some of the attacks carried out by the organization were initiated and directed by Iran, such as the Khobar Towers bombing in Saudi Arabia in 1996 and the attacks in Argentina.[49]

In 2006, Hezbollah operatives killed eight Israeli soldiers and captured two more, Israel and Hezbollah entered a 33-day war.[50] During the conflict, Hezbollah launched thousands of rockets into Israel.[51] The war ended in a stalemate,[52] but given Israel's overwhelming victory in the majority of the military conflicts between it and Arab state, a stalemate was a significant victory in and of itself for Hezbollah. Since 2006, the northern border has seen relatively little terrorist activity.[53] In February 2017, Hezbollah leader Hassan Nasrallah threatened to attack Israel's nuclear reactor in Dimona, and has previously threatened to attack ammonia supplies in Haifa.[54]

Syria has historically been a key supporter for Hezbollah and a vital ally of Iran's. When the Arab Spring threatened the stability of the Assad dictatorship, both Iran and Hezbollah intervened to support the regime. Hezbollah involved itself gradually. At first, its help was covert and only in advisory capacity. However, the group eventually began sending its own fighters and leaders into battle. The war in Syria has killed a significant number of Hezbollah's fighters. Estimates range from 5,000 to 8,000 death, from a total of 45,000 full and part-time fighters.[55] Before its involvement in the Syrian civil war, Hezbollah was very popular throughout the Shia community in

Lebanon, Kuwait, Jordan, and Egypt.[56] Furthermore, Hezbollah's involvement in the Syrian conflict is impacting the group significantly, especially as its commitment to the Syrian conflict has pulled it away from its traditional role of focusing on Israel and domestic Lebanese politics.[57]

Al-Qaeda and the Islamic State

Al-Qaeda formed during the later half of the Afghan-Soviet War.[58] Al-Qaeda's first *emir* was Osama bin Laden, who founded the group based on *Salafi* ideology and believed that *jihad* is a personal obligation for all Muslims.[59] Bin Laden was captured and killed by U.S. forces in May 2011. The current leader of al-Qaeda is his deputy Ayman al-Zawahiri.[60] Currently, al-Qaeda is embroiled in an ideological battle with the Islamic State. In some ways, the Islamic State has taken over al-Qaeda's role as the "premier" terrorist group of the world, not least in terms of social media and recruitment, and this has prompted self-reflection and rebranding on the part of al-Qaeda.

Israel has more often been a rhetorical target of al-Qaeda, rather than a literal one.[61] In almost every one of his public statements between 1990 and 2011, bin Laden referenced the Palestinian issue. A 2001 Treasury Department report reveals that Zarqawi had received more than $35,000 for training Jordanian and Palestinian operatives in Afghanistan and enabling their travel to the Levant, with assurances that he would receive more funding for attacks against Israel.[62] However, nothing came of these attacks, and in general, "al Qaeda's plotting against Israel has never matched its anti-Israel propaganda."[63]

However, there are some exceptions indicating that rhetoric is translated into actions against Israel in the past years. In 2010, four Israeli-Arabs were among those charged by Israeli authorities with establishing a terror cell and killing a taxi driver.[64] Two of the plaintiffs had trained at an al-Qaeda camp in Somalia.[65] More recently, in January 2014 Israeli officials revealed an al-Qaeda plot in Israel with a direct involvement of senior leaders of the organization. According to the reports, an al-Qaeda operative in Gaza run by Zawahiri recruited three men (two from East Jerusalem and one from the West Bank) through Skype and Facebook. All four operators were arrested.[66]

Another threat to Israel has recently emerged in the form of the Islamic State (ISIS). The Islamic State emerged from a branch of al-Qaeda, al-Qaeda in Iraq.[67] Since 2014, ISIS has managed to occupy vast areas in the region of Iraq and Syria and to take control over the population in its territory. However, in recent months, the organization has started losing control in Syria and Iraq due to Coalition efforts, forcing the organization to expand into secondary territories, such as in Libya and the Sinai.[68]

The affiliate that proves most dangerous for Israel is the affiliate formerly known as *Ansar Bayt al-Maqdis*. The organization is located in the Sheikh Zweid area in the northern Sinai Peninsula, near the border with Israel,[69] with an estimation of several dozen fighters.[70] Now known as the Sinai Province of the Islamic State," the group pledged allegiance to ISIS on November 2014 with an emphasis on the importance of fighting the Jews:

> After decades...Allah ordered the flag of jihad to be raised in our land and gave us the honor of being the soldiers [Allah] chose to fight the nation's most bitter enemies...the Jews....Our swords will be extended against them until Allah is victorious.[71]

The Sinai Province has launched several attacks against Israel over the past few years, including a combined attack that was carried out against a bus in Eilat in August 2011, several rocket attacks on Eilat, and attacks against the gas pipeline between Egypt and Israel in north Sinai.[72] Israeli-Arabs have not proven immune to ISIS' appeal. According to Israeli Security Agency report, during 2015, 32 Israeli-Arabs left to fight with ISIS in Syria. Also, since the beginning of 2015, 41 Israeli citizens were arrested for supporting ISIS, a number of ISIS networks were exposed in Israel, as well as a number of terror attacks of ISIS supporters in Israel were prevented. In June 2015, the Israeli Security Agency uncovered six Hura residents in the Negev spreading ISIS' ideology in the Israeli school system (since some were teachers) and well as planning to join ISIS in Syria.[73]

ISLAMISM AND SOCIETY

Israel's population numbers nearly 8.2 million people, 74.8 percent of which is Jewish, and 17.6 percent is Muslim.[74] Within this body politic, however, deep divisions exist over the future of the state. According to a study conducted by Pew Research Center in 2015, 76 percent of Israeli-Jews believe that Israel can simultaneously be a Jewish state and a democracy, whereas only 27 percent of Israeli-Arabs agree with this sentiment. Furthermore, belief in the two-state solution (that of Israel and an independent Palestinian state living side by side) appears to be declining, at least among Israeli Arabs; according to the Pew poll, approximately half of Israeli-Arab respondents believed that the two state solution was viable, down from 74 percent in 2013.

The tension between Israel and its Arab citizens is also evident in the traditionally nomadic Bedouin community. Official Israeli neglect of the Bedouin communities in the Negev, and the difficulty transitioning from a nomadic to a sedentary lifestyle, has spawned increasing alienation from the state among that community—an alienation that the Northern Branch of the Islamic Movement is exploiting. Thus, when the military planned a parade through Rahat, Israel's largest Bedouin town, to celebrate Israel's 63rd independence day in 2011, the town's mayor, Faiz Abu Sahiban, who belongs to the Islamic Movement, objected, preferring to commemorate the 1948 exodus of the Palestinian refugees instead.[75] This came in the wake of violent resistance to the Israeli government demolishing a mosque built illegally on public land in 2010 by the Northern Branch of the Islamic Movement.[76]

Concerns that Bedouin alienation might breed violence increased when two Bedouin from the Negev, Mahmoud Abu Quider, aged 24, and his 21-year-old brother Samah, confessed in January 2013 to planning to fire rockets, mount a suicide bombing at the Beer Sheba Central Bus Station, and launch other attacks. Before their arrest, the brothers built several explosive devices and traded drugs for an IDF soldier's rifle.[77] In another incident in 2015, Bedouin teachers from the South were suspected of promoting the ideology of the Islamic State in a local school.[78] The perpetrator of a deadly terrorist attack in Beer Sheba in October 2015 attended the same school.[79]

The Northern Branch is increasingly penetrating the Negev and successfully discouraging Bedouin from joining the Israeli Defense Forces (IDF), where a high percentage of Bedouins have historically served, mainly in scouting or tracking capacities. Furthermore, as the Islamic Movement has gained control of more town councils in Bedouin areas, they have been able to use their authority to obstruct the hiring of Bedouin who serve in the military.[80]

In a related concern, there has been a public debate over whether young Israeli-Arabs citizens should be required to join the civilian or military national service. In this case, opinions are significantly divided between Jews and Arab respondents; the majority of the Jews polled support this requirement (74.1%) while the majority of Arabs oppose it (71.8%).[81] The Israeli government has long hoped that Islamist tendencies among Israeli-Arabs would be mitigated by the liberal-democratic culture of the state. Today, that assumption is being sorely tested, as Israeli-Arabs become increasingly receptive to—and involved in—Islamist activities within Israel.

ISLAMISM AND THE STATE

Israel has struggled with Islamism and Islamist sentiment both internally and externally. Officially, Israel sees the issue of the political-legal status of Israeli-Arabs as a purely domestic matter without strategic implications. At the same time, however, it has traditionally refused to recognize Israeli-Arabs as a national minority possessing collective rights apart from specific cases (such as in the education system and family law, each religious community being subject to its own clerical elite). This opening in the education system has enabled Israeli-Arabs to cultivate a separate national identity—and created an ideological space in which Islamism can increasingly take root.

The education system in Israel has emerged as a notable ideological battleground in this regard. The country's Education Ministry has attempted to counter Islamism by banning the teaching of the *Nakba* ("catastrophe," the common Arabic reference for the establishment of Israel in 1948) in schools, by forcing students to sing *Hatikva* (the Israeli national anthem) and by encouraging military and national service as a criterion for rewarding schools and staff. Israeli-Arab leaders have voiced opposition to the campaign to promote Israeli-Arab participation in national service, terming it a veiled attempt by the government to erode the community's sense of unity.[82]

Externally, Israel's national security was deeply and negatively impacted by the Arab Spring in 2011. First and foremost, the overthrow of the Mubarak regime in Egypt in February 2011 undermined law and order in the Sinai Peninsula, enabling Al-Qaeda to develop a base there. As of May 2011, senior Egyptian security officials estimated that over 400 Al-Qaeda militants were then operating in the Sinai Peninsula.[83] The growing Islamist presence in the Sinai has coincided with increasing terrorism originating from the territory. In August 2011, a cross border attack by militants belonging to the "Mujahideen Shoura Council from the Environs of Jerusalem", an Al-Qaeda affiliate founded in 2011 and operational in Gaza and Sinai, killed eight Israelis. The "Mujahideen Shoura Council" has since launched rocket attacks on Sderot in August 2012[84] and March 2013, during President Obama's visit to Israel,[85] as well as to Eilat in April 2013.[86] However, today, the main threat to Israel from its southern border is Sinai Province.

Islamist militants have also attacked key infrastructure that lies outside Israel's borders. As of April 2012, Islamic militants have carried out at least fourteen attacks on the Egyptian pipeline passing through the Sinai that previously provided Israel with 40 percent of its natural gas.[87] From the end of the Mubarak regime until June 2012, there was a significant increase in the number of attacks against the gas pipelines in the region and terrorist infiltration to Israel.[88] *Salafi-Jihadists* see the pipelines as an instance of an Islamic resource sold to the Zionist enemy.[89]

Smuggling is another issue of concern to the Israeli security forces. Israel's withdrawal from the Gaza Strip significantly increased the smuggling of weapons, food and fuel to Gaza.[90] This was much intensified after Hamas takeover of Gaza in 2007.[91] Alongside the smuggling, the organization created an extensive network of tunnels contributing to the Gazan economy 230 million dollars per month.[92] During Operation Protective Edge in 2014, one of the operation's goals was to terminate cross border tunnels, which were widely used for smuggling arms and people. The IDF destroyed of 32 tunnels. Unfortunately, Israel has not yet fully succeeded in developing technology to deal with the tunnels.[93] IDF officials and residents leaving near the Gazan border, have expressed worries that Hamas is reconstructing its destroyed tunnels from 2014.[94]

The Israeli-Egyptian border (around 230 kilometers in length), is also characterized by extensive smuggling of people, drugs, weapons and goods. After the Israeli disengagement, the Israeli-Egyptian border has also become a transit point of two types of terrorists: specialists in the manufacture of weapons and terrorists on their way to attack Israel.[95] Indeed the Sinai Peninsula has become a main global *jihad* front vis-à-vis Israel.[96]

ENDNOTES

[1] Anat Kurz and Nahman Tal, "Hamas: Radical Islam in a National Struggle," Tel Aviv University Jaffee Center for Strategic Studies Memorandum no. 48, July 1997.

[2] Andrew Higgins, "How Israel Helped to Spawn Hamas," Wall Street Journal, January 24, 2009, http://online.wsj.com/article/SB123275572295011847.html.

[3] Khaled Mash'al, "We Will Not Relinquish an Inch of Palestine, from the River to the Sea," (speech, Al-Aqsa TV, December 7, 2012,) Middle East Media Research Institute, https://www.memri.org/tv/hamas-leader-khaled-mashal-we-will-not-relinquish-inch-palestine-river-sea/transcript.

[4] Rachel Brandenburg, "Iran and the Palestinians", United States Institute of Peace - The Iran Primer, updated 2016, http://iranprimer.usip.org/resource/iran-and-palestinians (updated by Cameron Glenn and Garrett Nada in January 2016).

[5] Meyrav Wurmser, "The Iran-Hamas Alliance," Jewish Policy Center, 2007, https://www.jewishpolicycenter.org/2007/08/31/the-iran-hamas-alliance/.

[6] Intelligence and Terrorism Information Center at the Israel Intelligence Heritage & Commemoration Center (IICC), "Iranian Support of Hamas", January 12, 2008, http://www.terrorism-info.org.il/data/pdf/PDF_09_019_2.pdf.

[7] Intelligence and Terrorism Information Center at the Israel Intelligence Heritage & Commemoration Center (IICC), "Iranian Support of Hamas", January 12, 2008, http://www.terrorism-info.org.il/data/pdf/PDF_09_019_2.pdf

[8] Matthew Levitt, " Iran's Support for Terrorism Under the JCPOA", The Washington Institute, July 8, 2016, http://www.washingtoninstitute.org/policy-analysis/view/irans-support-for-terrorism-under-the-jcpoa.

[9] Harriet Sherwood, "Hamas and Iran rebuild ties three years after falling out over Syria," The Guardian, January 9, 2014, https://www.theguardian.com/world/2014/jan/09/hamas-iran-rebuild-ties-falling-out-syria.

[10] Rachel Brandenburg, "Iran and the Palestinians", United States Institute of Peace - The Iran Primer, 2010, http://iranprimer.usip.org/resource/iran-and-palestinians (updated by Cameron Glenn and Garrett Nada in January 2016).

[11] Matthew Levitt, " Iran's Support for Terrorism Under the JCPOA", The Washington Institute, July 8, 2016, http://www.washingtoninstitute.org/policy-analysis/view/irans-support-for-terrorism-under-the-jcpoa.

[12] Israeli Security Agency, ""Dawa" – Hamas' Civilian Infrastructure and its Role in Terror Financing", https://www.shabak.gov.il/English/EnTerrorData/Reviews/Pages/Dawa%E2%80%93Hamas-report.aspx

[13] "Israeli Arab Gets 5 Years for Hamas Plot," UPI, May 11, 2011, http://www.upi.com/Top_News/World-News/2011/05/11/Israeli-Arab-gets-5-years-for-Hamas-plot/UPI-54921305125753/.

[14] Ibid.

[15] Hillel Frisch, "Israel and Its Arab Citizens," in Israeli Democracy at the Crossroads (New York: Routledge, 2005), 216.

[16] Jonathan Lis, "Salah Calls for 'Intifada' against Temple Mount Excavation," Ha'aretz (Tel Aviv), March 7, 2007.

[17] Ariel Ben Solomon, "Israel's Islamic Movement: Overcoming Obstacles", The Jerusalem Post, May 15, 2016, http://www.jpost.com/Arab-Israeli-Conflict/Israels-Islamic-Movement-Overcoming-obstacles-453861

[18] "Palestinian Islamic Jihad," The Counter Extremism Project, 2017, https://www.counterextremism.com/threat/palestinian-islamic-jihad.

[19] Holly Fletcher, "Palestinian Islamic Jihad", Council on Foreign Relations, April 10, 2008, http://www.cfr.org/israel/palestinian-islamic-jihad/p15984.

[20] "Country Reports on Terrorism 2013: Chapter 6. Foreign Terrorist Organizations," U.S. Department of State, April 30, 2014, http://www.state.gov/j/ct/rls/crt/2013/224829.htm.

[21] Susan Aschoff, "Jihad Leader Emerged from Shadows of USF," St. Petersburg Times, February 21, 2003, http://www.sptimes.com/2003/02/21/TampaBay/Jihad_leader_emerged_.shtml.

[22] Holly Fletcher, "Palestinian Islamic Jihad", Council on Foreign Relations, April 10, 2008, http://www.cfr.org/israel/palestinian-islamic-jihad/p15984.

[23] https://www.counterextremism.com/threat/palestinian-islamic-jihad#overview

[24] The Meir Amit Intelligence and Terrorism Information Center, "The Palestinian Islamic Jihad", http://www.terrorism-info.org.il/he/%D7%94%D7%92%60%D7%94%D7%90%D7%93_%D7%94%D7%90%D7%A1%D7%9C%D7%90%D7%9E%D7%99_%D7%91%D7%A4%D7%9C%D7%A1%D7%98%D7%99%D7%9F?page=8

[25] http://almanac.afpc.org/palestinian-territories

[26] Jack Khoury and Yuval Azoulay, "Two Israeli Arabs Arrested over Suspected Jihad Plot to Kill Pilots, Scientists," Ha'aretz (Tel Aviv), August 28, 2008, http://www.haaretz.com/news/2-israeli-arabs-arrested-over-suspected-jihad-plot-to-kill-pilots-scientists-1.252814.

[27] Yaniv Kubovich and Gili Cohen, "Shin Bet Nabs Islamic Jihad Cell Plotting to Kidnap Israelis," Ha'aretz (Tel Aviv), February 3, 2013. http://www.haaretz.com/news/diplomacy-defense/shin-bet-nabs-islamic-jihad-cell-plotting-to-kidnap-israelis-1.501107.

[28] Fletcher, "Palestinian Islamic Jihad."

[29] Hazem Balousha, "Islamic Jihad May Respond If Israel Enters Syria War," Al-Monitor, September 2, 2013, http://www.al-monitor.com/pulse/originals/2013/09/islamic-jihad-syria-us-strike.html.

[30] "Expert: Hamas Received $2 Billion from Iran; Islamic Jihad Gets $150 Million Annually," Algemeiner, February 11, 2014, http://www.algemeiner.com/2014/02/11/expert-hamas-received-2-billion-from-iran-islamic-jihad-gets-150-million-annually/.

[31] Rachel Brandenburg, "Iran and the Palestinians", United States Institute of Peace - The Iran Primer, 2010, http://iranprimer.usip.org/resource/iran-and-palestinians (updated by Cameron Glenn and Garrett Nada in January 2016).

[32] Hazem Balousha, "Islamic Jihad's coffers run dry," Al-Monitor, June 2, 2015, http://www.al-monitor.com/pulse/originals/2015/06/palestine-islamic-jihad-financial-crisis-money-iran-hezbolla.html.

[33] "Iran cuts 90% of support for Palestinian Islamic Jihad," Middle East Monitor, January 11, 2016,

[34] Maayan Groisman, "Iran to Renew Financial Support for Islamic Jihad After Two-Year Hiatus," Jerusalem Post, May 25, 2016, http://www.jpost.com/Middle-East/Reembracing-Islamic-Jihad-Iran-to-renew-financial-aid-for-Palestinian-terror-group-454968

[35] Matthew Levitt, "Hezbollah Finances: Funding the Party of God", the Washington Institute, February 2005, http://www.washingtoninstitute.org/policy-analysis/view/hezbollah-finances-funding-the-party-of-god

[36] Matthew Levitt, "Hezbollah Finances: Funding the Party of God", the Washington Institute, February 2005, http://www.washingtoninstitute.org/policy-analysis/view/hezbollah-finances-funding-the-party-of-god

[37] http://www.cfr.org/terrorist-organizations-and-networks/open-letter-hizballah-program/p30967

[38] http://www.cfr.org/lebanon/hezbollah-k-hizbollah-hizbullah/p9155

[39] "Hezbollah," The Counter Extremism Project, 2017, https://www.counterextremism.com/threat/hezbollah#overview.

[40] Matthew Levitt, "Hezbollah Finances: Funding the Party of God", the Washington Institute, February 2005, http://www.washingtoninstitute.org/policy-analysis/view/hezbollah-finances-funding-the-party-of-god

[41] "1982 Lebanon invasion," BBC News, May 6, 2008, http://news.bbc.co.uk/2/hi/middle_east/7381364.stm.

[42] http://www.terrorism-info.org.il/en/Hezbollah

[43] http://www.terrorism-info.org.il/en/Hezbollah

[44] Israel Security Agency, "Terror Dana and Trends: Hizballa Activity involving Israeli Arabs", http://www.shabak.gov.il/ENGLISH/ENTERRORDATA/REVIEWS/Pages/HizballaActivity.aspx

[45] The Knesset Research and Information Center, "Terrorist Organizations fighting Israel", July 2004, https://www.knesset.gov.il/mmm/data/pdf/m01057.pdf (in Hebrew)

[46] Shabak Web site, Hizballah Recruiting Activity of Israeli-Arabs, https://www.shabak.gov.il/English/EnTerrorData/Reviews/Pages/Hizbal-

lahRecruitingActivityofIsraeli-Arabs.aspx

[47] http://www.terrorism-info.org.il/en/Hezbollah

[48] http://almanac.afpc.org/Hezbollah

[49] Matthew Levitt, "Hezbollah Finances: Funding the Party of God", the Washington Institute, February 2005, http://www.washingtoninstitute.org/policy-analysis/view/hezbollah-finances-funding-the-party-of-god

[50] "2006: Lebanon war," BBC News, May 6, 2008, http://news.bbc.co.uk/2/hi/middle_east/7381389.stm.

[51] Dov Leiber, " Hezbollah chief threatens Israel's Dimona nuclear reactor," The Times of Israel, February 2017, http://www.timesofisrael.com/hezbollah-chief-threatens-israels-dimona-nuclear-reactor/.

[52] "2006: Lebanon war," BBC News, May 6, 2008, http://news.bbc.co.uk/2/hi/middle_east/7381389.stm.

[53] http://www.terrorism-info.org.il/en/Hezbollah

[54] Dov Leiber, " Hezbollah chief threatens Israel's Dimona nuclear reactor", The Times of Israel, February 2017, http://www.timesofisrael.com/hezbollah-chief-threatens-israels-dimona-nuclear-reactor/

[55] Nadav Pollak, "The Transformation of Hezbollah by Its Involvement in Syria", The Washington Institute, August 2016, http://www.washingtoninstitute.org/uploads/Documents/pubs/ResearchNote35-Pollak-2.pdf

[56] Nadav Pollak, "The Transformation of Hezbollah by Its Involvement in Syria", The Washington Institute, August 2016, http://www.washingtoninstitute.org/uploads/Documents/pubs/ResearchNote35-Pollak-2.pdf

[57] Matthew Levitt, "Hezbollah," The World Almanac of Islamism, 2017, http://almanac.afpc.org/Hezbollah.

[58] Daveed Gartenstein-Ross, "Al-Qaeda," The World Almanac of Islamism, 2017, http://almanac.afpc.org/al-qaeda.

[59] Information on The Global Jihad/ Al-Qaeda, TerrorismInfo,org, 2017, http://www.terrorism-info.org.il/en/The_Global_Jihad_/_Al-Qaeda.

[60] Information on The Global Jihad/ Al-Qaeda, TerrorismInfo,org, 2017, http://www.terrorism-info.org.il/en/The_Global_Jihad_/_Al-Qaeda.

[61] Matthew Levitt, "Zawahiri Aims at Israel", Foreign Affairs, February 3, 2014,https://www.foreignaffairs.com/articles/israel/2014-02-03/zawahiri-aims-israel

[62] Matthew Levitt, "Zawahiri Aims at Israel", Foreign Affairs, February 3, 2014,https://www.foreignaffairs.com/articles/israel/2014-02-03/zawahiri-aims-israel

[63] Matthew Levitt, "Zawahiri Aims at Israel", Foreign Affairs, February 3, 2014,https://www.foreignaffairs.com/articles/israel/2014-02-03/zawahiri-aims-israel.

[64] "Israeli Arabs 'Inspired by Global Jihad' Charged with Taxi Driver Murder," Ha'aretz (Tel Aviv), June 28, 2010.

[65] "Shin Bet Arrests Eight Israeli Arabs for Illicit Arms Trading," Ha'aretz (Tel Aviv), July 15, 2010.

[66] Matthew Levitt, "Zawahiri Aims at Israel", Foreign Affairs, February 3, 2014, https://www.foreignaffairs.com/articles/israel/2014-02-03/zawahiri-aims-israel

[67] Alberto Fernandez, "Islamic State," The World Almanac of Islamism, 2017, http://almanac.afpc.org/islamic-state.

[68] Dr. Eitan Azani, Col. (Res.) Jonathan Fighel and Lorena Atiyas Lvovsky, "The Islamic State's Threat to Israel", The International Institute for Counter-Terrorism (ICT), February 17, 2016, https://www.ict.org.il/Article/1612/The-Islamic-States-Threat-to-Israel

[69] Borzou Daragahi, "Sinai jihadi group emerges at forefront of Egypt violence", Financial Times, January 31, 2014. http://www.ft.com/cms/s/0/b5ad40d0-8a7b-11e3-9c29-00144feab7de.html#axzz3RfJCfft2

[70] Khalil al-Anani, "The Resurgence of Militant Islamists in Egypt", Middle East Institute, February 14, 2014, http://www.mei.edu/content/resurgence-militant-islamists-egypt

[71] The Meir Amit Intelligence and Terrorism Information Center (ITIC), "ISIS: Portrait of a Jihadi Terrorist Organization", November 2016, http://www.terrorism-info.org.il/Data/articles/Art_20733/101_14_Ef_1329270214.pdf

[72] Middle East Institute, "A History of Terrorism in Egypt's Sinai, http://www.mei.edu/sinai-terrorism

[73] Israeli Security Agency, "2015 Annual Summary Terrorism and CT Activity Data and Trends" March 2016, http://www.shabak.gov.il/English/EnTerrorData/Archive/Annual/Pages/2015AnnualSummary.aspx

[74] "Israel," The CIA World Factbook, January 12, 2017, https://www.cia.gov/library/publications/the-world-factbook/geos/is.html.

[75] Ilana Curiel, "Rahat objects to IDF Independence Day exhibit," Yediot Ahronot (Tel Aviv), May 9, 2011, http://www.ynetnews.com/articles/0,7340,L-4066563,00.html.

[76] Yaakov Lappin, "Israel Lands Authority demolishes Illegal Rahat Mosque," Jerusalem Post, November 7, 2010, http://www.jpost.com/Israel/Article.aspx?id=194375.

[77] Yoav Zitun, "2 Bedouins Confess to Plotting Terror Attacks," Yediot Ahronot (Tel Aviv), January 20, 2013, http://www.ynetnews.com/articles/0,7340,L-4334793,00.html.

[78] The Knesset Committee on Education, Culture and Sport, "Promoting the "Islamic State" ideology in the educational system", November 10, 2015, http://main.knesset.gov.il/Activity/committees/Education/Conclusion/161115.pdf#search=%D7%91%D7%93%D7%95%D7%90%D7%99%D7%9D

[79] The Knesset Committee on Education, Culture and Sport, "Promoting the "Islamic State" ideology in the educational system", November 10, 2015,

http://main.knesset.gov.il/Activity/committees/Education/Conclusion/161115.pdf#search=%D7%91%D7%93%D7%95%D7%90%D7%99%D7%9D

[80] Donna Rosenthal, The Israelis: Ordinary People in an Extraordinary Land 2nd ed. (New York: Free Press, 2008), 300.

[81] The Israel Democracy Institute, "The Israeli Democracy Index 2015", http://en.idi.org.il/analysis/idi-press/publications/english-books/the-israeli-democracy-index-2015/

[82] "Israeli Arab Volunteers Rising," JTA, August 27, 2009, http://www.jta.org/news/article/2009/08/27/1007492/israeli-arab-volunteers-rising.

[83] Ilan Berman, "Al-Qaeda's Newest Outpost," Forbes, December 29, 2011,http://www.forbes.com/sites/ilanberman/2011/12/29/al-qaedas-newest-outpost/.

[84] Elad Benari, "Salafi Terrorists: Jihad Against Criminal Jews is a Duty," Israel National News, August 27, 2012,http://www.israelnationalnews.com/News/News.aspx/159309#.UXOET4VHqkB.

[85] Yaakov Lappin, "IDF Decreases Gazan Fishing Zone after Rockets," Jerusalem Post, March 21, 2013,http://www.jpost.com/National-News/Two-rockets-slam-into-Sderot-during-Obama-visit-307212.

[86] Aaron Kalman, "Gazan Salafist Vows to Keep Attacking Israel," Times of Israel, April 18, 2013,http://www.timesofisrael.com/gazan-salafist-vows-to-keep-attacking-israel/

[87] "Egypt Scraps Israel Gas Supply Deal," BBC, April 23, 2012, http://www.bbc.co.uk/news/world-middle-east-17808954.

[88] Middle East Institute, "A History of Terrorism in Egypt's Sinai", http://www.mei.edu/sinai-terrorism

[89] International Center for Counter-Terrorism, "Security in the Sinai: Present and Future", March 2014, http://www.icct.nl/download/file/ICCT-Gold-Security-In-The-Sinai-March-2014.pdf

[90] Zack Gold, "Sinai Security: Opportunities for Unlikely Cooperation Among Egypt, Israel, and Hamas", The Saban Center at Brookings, Analysis Paper Number 30, October 2013, http://www.brookings.edu/-/media/research/files/papers/2013/10/22%20sinai%20egypt%20israel%20hamas%20gold/22%20sinai%20hamas%20egypt%20israel%20gold.pdf

[91] Middle East Institute, "A History of Terrorism in Egypt's Sinai", http://www.mei.edu/sinai-terrorism

[92] Zachary Laub, "Egypt's Sinai Peninsula and Security", Council of Foreign Relations, December 12, 2013, http://www.cfr.org/egypt/egypts-sinai-peninsula-security/p32055

[93] Prof. Efraim Inbar, "The Gaza Tunnels Get Too Much Attention", BESA Center Perspectives Paper No. 369, October 6, 2016, https://besacenter.org/wp-content/uploads/2016/10/Inbar-Efraim-Gaza-Tunnels-Get-Too-Much-Attention-PP-369-6-Oct-2016a.pdf

[94] "Netanyahu Threatens to Eclipse 2014 War to Destroy Gaza Tunnels," Times of Israel, January 31, 2016, http:// www.timesofisrael.com/netanyahu-threatens-to-eclipse-2014-war-to-destroy-gaza-tunnels/.

[95] The Knesset Research and Information Center, "Smuggling through Israel-Egypt border", 2006, https://www.knesset.gov.il/mmm/data/pdf/m01667.pdf (in Hebrew).

[96] Dr. Eitan Azani, Col (Res.) Jonathan Fighel and Lorena Atiyas Lvovsky, "The Islamic State's Thereat to Israel", The Internationall Institute for Counter-Terrorism (ICT), January 2016, https://www.ict.org.il/UserFiles/ICT-IS-Threat-to-Israel.pdf.

Jordan

Quick Facts

Population: 8,185,384 (estimated July 2016)

Area: 89,342 sq km

Ethnic Groups: Arab 98%, Circassian 1%, Armenian 1%

Religions: Muslim 97.2% (official; predominantly Sunni), Christian 2.2% (majority Greek Orthodox, but some Greek and Roman Catholics, Syrian Orthodox, Coptic Orthodox, Armenian Orthodox, and Protestant denominations), Buddhist 0.4%, Hindu 0.1%, Jewish <0.1, folk religionist <0.1, unaffiliated <0.1, other <0.1 (2010 est.)

Government Type: parliamentary constitutional monarchy

GDP (official exchange rate): $39.45 billion (2015 est.)

Map and Quick Facts courtesy of the CIA World Factbook (Last updated January 2017)

Overview

Five years into the Arab Spring, the threats facing the Hashemite Kingdom, both from within the country and from outside it, continue to mount. Jordan is the most vulnerable of the monarchies affected by the currents of the Arab Spring, and in recent years has faced a growing challenge to its stability from extreme, violent and political Islamist groups. On the other hand, Jordan has weathered the collapse of both Syria and Iraq, and the takeover by jihadist groups of parts of their territory. These developments have been accompanied by large-scale refugee flows which have upset the Kingdom's demographic balance, and which could in the future destabilize its social structure and invite external interference.

For its part, the Jordanian regime has long waged a wide-ranging and determined ideological struggle against radical Islamic organizations on its soil. In this contest, the Kingdom has sought to de-legitimize Salafi jihadi ideology while disseminating a brand of moderate traditional Islam as a religious "vaccine" against it. The large and easily radi-

calized Palestinian component of the country's population, the combined influence of the Muslim Brotherhood offshoot in Jordan, and Salafi jihadi trends from Iraq and Syria, all pose real and imminent threat to the stability of the Kingdom.

Islamist Activity

Islam has been a part of the political life of Jordan for entire history. In 1921, the British crafted the Emirate of Transjordan, with King Abdallah I becoming the new nation's king. Abdallah's Islamic identity, as well as the Hashemite family's connections to the Prophet Muhammad's tribe, was and continues to be a central source of legitimacy for the monarchy. Abdallah and his grandson Hussein presented themselves as deeply religious Muslims, publicly praying and taking part in rituals, as well as performing the *Hajj*. In 1952, the Jordanian constitution made Islam the kingdom's official religion and stipulated that the king could only be a Muslim, born of Muslim parents. The constitution also establishes *sharia* as a key legal framework of the kingdom. However, unlike other Muslim countries, *sharia* was never considered the sole source of legal legitimacy.[1]

The radical Islamic camp in Jordan is composed of two separate—though frequently overlapping—wings. The first is the main body of Jordanian Islamists, which identifies with the Muslim Brotherhood (MB) movement that originated in Egypt. The second is the radical *jihadi-Salafi* movement, which has been traditionally embodied by al-Qaeda and its ideological fellow travelers within Jordan, and more recently also by supporters of ISIS who were either Jordanian or arrived as refugees from Syria.

The radical Islamic camp in Jordan largely draws its strength from a diverse array of sources and circumstances within Jordanian society. Foremost among them are: its own organizational and ideological infrastructure inside the country; the indirect influence and public sympathy from the wider activities of the MB, which has deep roots among the Jordanian public (both Trans-Jordanian and Palestinian); the inflammatory influence of the war in Iraq and Syria; the ongoing Arab conflict with Israel; and the rise of Islamism across the region following the Arab Spring. Confronting all of these factors is a weak official religious establishment that lacks popular support and is incapable of mobilizing those with religious authority to defend the regime's views.

The Muslim Brotherhood

The Muslim Brotherhood is deeply rooted in Jordan and boasts a presence in the country's political arena through the Islamic Action Front (IAF) party and parliamentary faction, as well as in civil society (in mosques, schools, labor and trade unions and universities). Since the birth of the Jordanian MB in the 1940s, internal struggles have taken place between a "dovish", "moderate" faction that aspires to co-exist and maintain sound relations with the regime, and a "hawkish", "extremist" wing that draws its ideology from the *takfiri* doctrine of Egyptian MB leader Sayyid Qutb, and as a result attempts to confront the regime both politically and ideologically.

The Palestinian issue ranks high on the agenda of Jordan's Islamist groups, in particular the MB and its political arm, the IAF; this for a number of reasons, including that a sizable portion of the Jordanian MB's leaders are themselves Palestinian. Furthermore, the MB views Jordan's Palestinian population, which traditionally has been estimated to constitute about half of the country's entire population, as its primary constituency. The Jordanian MB also has traditional organizational ties with its counterpart in the Palestinian Territories, Hamas.[2]

Throughout most of the MB's history in Jordan, the Trans-Jordanian faction led it, and tended to work in cooperation with the regime. This cooperation made the MB the only organized political force in the country and allowed it to establish a broad *da'wah* network of civil society organizations and charities.[3] The extremist wing of the group has usually been affiliated with leaders of Palestinian origin, whose identification with the Hashemite regime was weaker than that of their Trans-Jordanian compatriots.[4]

In the past, this latter, extremist wing was relatively marginal in the overall operations of the MB in Jordan. In the 1980s and 1990s, it devoted most of its energies to the *jihad* in Afghanistan, and subsequently in Chechnya, Bosnia and other places. Since the early 2000s, however, this more extreme faction has gained in strength and daring, as reflected by the results of the internal leadership elections carried out by the MB in early 2006, and manifested particularly in the composition of the IAF. The MB's religious rulings, or *fatwa*, express its identification with the *Salafi* worldview, identifying with the *jihadi* struggles in Iraq and Syria, and in Israel/Palestine. The top figures of this faction have also been founding members of the Global Anti-Aggression Campaign (GAAC), an international *Salafi*-led international umbrella organization that brings under its wings *Salafi*, *Salafi-Jihadi*, Muslim Brotherhood and Hamas leaders, aiming to coordinate anti-Western strategies under the perception that the West it at war with Islam. At least seven leading GAAC figures and/or their organizations have been designated as terrorists by the United States, the EU, and/or the United Nations for their support of Al-Qaeda and related groups.[5]

Serious disputes between the two factions continue to this day, and are expected to do so as long as in the post Arab Spring period Islamism advances in the Middle East—and as Hamas continues to gain power in the Palestinian arena. As of late 2016, Dr. Hamanm Sa'id, a member of the 'hawkish' faction, serves as the MB's Inspector General, and Zaki Bani Irsheid, another 'hawkish' faction member, serves as his deputy.

The rapid political rise and fall of the MB in the Middle East—especially the Egyptian mother movement, has had a great effect on the Jordanian MB as well. Internally, the Jordanian Brotherhood now seems to be divided more than ever. In October

2012, members of the "dovish" faction came up with the Zam Zam Initiative, an "Islamist nationalist framework" of national reconstruction that aspired to return to working more closely with the national establishment. Zam Zam aimed for methodical and systematic change through five phases, which included the recruitment of new cadres and membership, including youth, male and female; launching a manifesto and laying down internal laws; the launch of a new political project and the seeking of participation in national institutions and partnership with the government.[6] In April 2014, three leading members who led the Initiative were expelled from the ranks of the movement, accused of aspiring to establish a new party to compete with the MB,[7] and subsequently took part in the 2016 elections, winning three seats in the parliament.[8]

Another split occurred after Abdul Majid Thneibat, another "hawkish" leader, re-registered the Muslim Brotherhood Society / Association in 2015 as a Jordanian entity with no affiliation with the Egyptian mother movement. Altogether, more than 400 members left the Brotherhood during 2015 to join these and other splinter groups.[9]

In February 2016, the Jordanian MB formally cut its ties with its parent movement in Egypt.[10] This tactic of separation is not uncommon among Middle Eastern offshoots of the Muslim Brotherhood, as an attempt to regain credibility and avoid their own governments' ire. However, in all likelihood the split was only a cosmetic move, and the links between Muslim Brotherhood offshoots and affiliates remain.

Salafi jihadism

The Muslim Brotherhood in general, and its "hawkish" faction in particular, have played a pivotal role in the dissemination and acceptance of the *Salafi-jihadi* message in Jordanian society, especially among the younger generation of citizens. Outbreaks of violence between Israel and the Palestinians, particularly in the Gaza Strip, and the wars in Iraq, Syria and Afghanistan, likewise have served to strengthen *Salafi* sentiment in Jordan.

The ebb and flow of *jihadist* activity in Iraq profoundly affected Islamist organizations in Jordan. The 2006 killing of Abu Musab al-Zarqawi, the leader of al-Qaeda in Iraq (which subsequently became the Islamic State in Iraq, which turned into ISIS), and coalition successes against the group thereafter (as a result of the "surge" strategy adopted by the Bush administration), along with local Jordanian pressure, all served to create fissures in the Jordanian *jihadist* movement. The result was the emergence and rise of a more "pragmatic" wing of the movement, led by the prominent Salafi cleric Abu Muhammad al-Maqdisi. Since his release from Jordanian prison in 2008, and again in 2014, al-Maqdisi has consistently criticized the school of thought epitomized by al-Zarqawi and more recently by Abu Bakr Al-Baghdadi's ISIS, which sanctions intra-Muslim conflict due to ideological and political differences. Al-Maqdisi did not change the principles of *takfir*, the declaration of Muslims as heretics or apostates. However, he made a case against *jihadist* attacks inside Jordan, thus revising his own views about the permissibility of collateral casualties among Muslims (or even their direct targeting) if necessary in order to kill "infidels".[11]

In the past few years, many *Salafi-Jihadi* Jordanians joined the ranks of Al-Qaeda and its affiliated *Jabhat Fath Al-Sham* (formerly known as *Jabhat Al-Nusra*).[12] In early 2015 it was even claimed that Jordanians "have enjoyed the lion's share of power" in *Jabhat Al-Nusra*'s chain of command.[13] More recently however, it seems that ISIS is also gradually gaining more popularity within *Salafi-Jihadi* ranks.[14] Towards the end of 2015, Jordan came in fourth in the list of countries of origin of ISIS fighters in Iraq and Syria with an official number of more than 2000.[15] In addition concerns were raised that among the many Syrian refugees who entered the country there were also ISIS sleeper cells.

Jordan has been a member in the U.S.-led Coalition to battle the Islamic State, and fierce criticism of the group has proliferated, particularly after the capture and burning alive of Jordanian pilot Mu'ath Safi Yousef al-Kaseasbeh, whose plane went down over the city of Raqqa in Syria in December 2014. In the Spring of 2015 it was found in a poll that 94 percent of the wider Jordanian population viewed ISIS negatively.[16]

ISLAMISM AND SOCIETY

The Jordanian population is 98 percent Arab, with Circassians and Armenians each accounting for 1 percent of the population.[17] 97.2 percent of the population is Muslim, and the majority of that population is Sunni, and 2.2 percent of the population is Christian.[18] Strict Islamic codes enjoy a broad popular base among both the country's Trans-Jordanian and Palestinian populace. In recent years, Islamic dress—particularly for women—has become more and more ubiquitous. Islamic bookstores selling radical tracts can now be found near almost any mosque in Amman. Pew polls found that support in Jordan for the enactment of *sharia* law was widespread. 58 percent of those polled even said *sharia* law should be extended to apply to all citizens, including non-Muslim, while 67 percent of respondents favored stoning for the crime of adultery and 82 percent approved capital punishment for apostates.[19]

In recent years, support for *Salafi-jihadi* groups among the wider population are declining. This is true both in the case of ISIS as already demonstrated, as well as in the case of Al-Qaeda, which in 2014 was only supported by 13 percent.[20] Nevertheless, *Salafi-jihadi* attitudes have multiple outlets in Jordanian society. Those outlets include popular mosques not under the regime's supervision, and bookstands that propagate a radical, exclusionary religious worldview. The many websites of global *jihadist* groups provide a means for mass dissemination of this ideology. *Jihadist* activists arrested by authorities have been found to be indoctrinated via these outlets. A prominent example is Abed Shahadeh, nicknamed Abu Muhammad al-Tahawi, who was imprisoned for three years in 2005 and has been arrested several times since.

The Palestinian issue is a perennial interest in Jordan's politics, and of major concern to the public. The MB, as discussed previously, shares and capitalizes upon this focus. As one official with the group has explained, the MB "has a religious and national obligation to support the Palestinians and their problem."[21] The current Inspector General, Hamam Sa'id, has gone further, stating that the MB's involvement in the Palestinian arena serves to provide "the Palestinians [with] *jihadist* assistance and support."[22] Like the Palestinian issue generally, the MB's relationship with Hamas remains an important element of Islamist expression in Jordan.

In spite of the decline in the MB's popularity, which also affected its political power in the syndicates, demonstrations were held during October 2016, led by the Teachers' Union against reforms and changes in school textbooks in the Kingdom, which toned down their Islamic content and started showing women without headscarves. This act had been perceived as a threat to Islamist dominance of the education system.[23]

ISLAMISM AND THE STATE

Salafi jihadi organizations in Jordan remain under intense pressure from the Jordanian government, which has succeeded in disrupting numerous attempted terrorist attacks inside the Kingdom in recent years. It has done so through the imprisonment of large numbers of *jihadist* activists and sympathizers, in the process wreaking havoc on their respective organizations and restricting their activities. A high point was the January 2009 trial of twelve members of a *Salafi-jihadi* group charged with attacks on a Christian church and cemetery, and with involvement in the shooting of a group of Lebanese musicians performing in downtown Amman.[24]

Also notable was the December 2009 trial of twenty-four Islamists on criminal charges stemming from their management of the Islamic Centre Society (ICS), which had been dissolved three years prior. Before its dissolution, the ICS had served as the MB's financial arm, administering assets worth over a billion dollars, running scores of schools, health establishments and social centers. In 2006, at the height of internal tensions between the MB and the IAF, the government of former Prime Minister Marouf Bakhit dissolved the ICS. The government at that time charged ICS officials with corrupt practices, but Brotherhood leaders contended that the step was designed to deprive the Islamic Movement of its financial backing. The move was widely believed to have been one of the key reasons behind the IAF's downturn in the November 2007 elections.[25]

The real challenge facing the MB, "hawks" and "doves" alike, appears to be the far-reaching reforms of the internal political system announced by King Abdullah II in late November 2009. The MB in particular has had doubts about the regime's intention to implement the genuine political reform it promised the public. From the MB's point of view, the implementation of a thorough political reform that would introduce the principle of "one person, one vote" and pledge to hold "honest and fair elections" is a basic condition for translating their potential electoral power into a significant quota of parliamentary seats, and subsequently making political and public gains. The Brotherhood has accused the regime of not holding fair and transparent elections. Leading figures also referred to the political triumph and rise in power of Islamist movements across the region following the Arab Spring as an issue which could be translated into political leverage at home: "We use the results in the other Arab countries to say to our government: look, when the elections are fair, the Islamists win."[26]

The Arab Spring has deeply impacted the debate surrounding governance within Jordan. Initially, the revolutionary currents did not seriously undermine the Jordanian regime. The vanguard of protests in Jordan appeared to be more the *Salafi jihadi* movement than the MB itself. The violence also exposed divisions between this faction and the larger *Salafi* movement. However, the fall of the Egyptian and Tunisian regimes and the continued, unsettled situation in other countries (such as Iraq and Syria) encouraged the Jordanian MB to increase its pressure on the regime. The regime, for its part, accused the protestors of receiving orders from the original movement in Egypt and elsewhere. It has also animated the normally quiescent East-Jordanian political leadership; according to various reports, tribal leaders have warned the King that they would not tolerate a light hand in dealing with the threat, which they perceived as a Palestinian attempt to topple the Hashemite government.[27] This was expressed in demonstrations under increasingly radicalized slogans, along with the classic demands for an end to corruption and the abrogation of the peace treaty with Israel. These demonstrations escalated in March 2011, resulting in a number of casualties (though far less than in other Arab countries).

The MB boycotted the January 2013 elections, and continued to demand the implementations of "reforms" and the limiting of the King's power. In April 2013, the MB issued a warning letter to the King and the national intelligence services, accusing the regime of corruption and calling on him to change his current policies.[28]

King Abdullah II, like his counterparts in the Gulf States, has expressed concern over the emerging Egypt-Turkey-Qatar "axis" that has materialized from the Arab Spring, and which has promoted Muslim Brotherhood influence throughout the region.[29] The MB, for its part, has pushed back against these concerns, claiming new discrimination. The Kingdom began with a crackdown on the MB which included taking over various social charities, the removal of MB sheikhs from the traditional roles they hold in mosques and more.[30] Irsheid, the MB's Deputy Head, was even imprisoned for several months in 2014-2015 for insulting the UAE.

In a June 2016 interview with the Islamist portal *Middle East Eye*, IAF Spokesman Murad Adaileh maintained that the levels of democracy have receded in the country while critiquing the lack of adequate political reform. Adaileh added that the new constitutional amendments granted King Abdallah dramatically more power over the security forces. He also noted that the government has continued arresting activists, most notably for criticizing Jordan's war against the Islamic State, which has intensified the Brotherhood's distrust of the government.[31] Nevertheless, the Brotherhood's deteriorating situation caused the IAF to end its elections boycott in 2016. The Brotherhood's decision was welcomed by Queen Rania[32] and the Brotherhood replied that this was a "positive" step.[33]

The IAF joined a wider alliance, the National Coalition for Reform (NCR), which included candidates from various backgrounds, in the September 2016 elections. This coalition gained 16 seats in parliament, 10 of which were won by members of the group and the remaining were won by their allies.[34] In January 2017, the IAF announced it will try to repeat this experience by forming coalitions towards the forthcoming municipal elections as well.[35]

ENDNOTES

[1] See Shmuel Bar, "The Muslim Brotherhood in Jordan," Moshe Dayan Center for Middle Eastern and African Studies Data and Analysis, June 1998, http://www.dayan.tau.ac.il/d&a-jordan-bar.pdf.

[2] According to a senior source in the Muslim Brotherhood, the Brotherhood's Inspector General, Hamam Sa'id, and two members of the Brotherhood's Executive Bureau are also members of the Hamas Shura Council and participate in its debates.

[3] These were widely referred to and named in Ibrahim Gharaybah, Jamaat Al-Ikhwan Al-Muslimin fi-l-Urdun 1946-1996 (Amman: Markaz al-Urdun al-Jadid lil-Dirasat: Dar Sindibad lil-Nashr, 1997), 169-185; Quintan Wiktorowicz, The Management of Islamic Activism (State University of New York Press, 2001), 83-92

[4] Bar, "The Muslim Brotherhood in Jordan, 50-52.

[5] Steven Merley, "The Global Anti-Aggression Campaign 2003-2016 A Global Muslim Brotherhood, Salafi and Jihadi Alliance Against The West", 2017. https://www.globalmbresearch.com/wp-content/uploads/2017/02/Global_Anti-Aggression_Campaign_2003-2016.pdf

[6] Larbi Sadiki, "Jordan: Arab Spring Washout?" Al-Jazeera, January 12, 2013. http://www.aljazeera.com/indepth/opinion/2013/01/201319134753750165.html

[7] Tamer Al-Samadi, 'Zamzam' Reveals Divisions in Jordan's Muslim Brotherhood, Al-Monitor, December 5, 2012. http://www.al-monitor.com/pulse/politics/2012/12/divisions-hit-jordanian-muslim-brotherhood.html

[8] Taylor Luck, "Muslim Brotherhood expels three over the 'Zamzam' incident," Jordan Times, April 21, 2014. http://www.jordantimes.com/news/local/muslim-brotherhood-expels-three-over-zamzam%E2%80%99-initiative

[9] Khetum Malkawi, "Muslim Brotherhood ends link with Egyptian mother group," Jordan Times, February 14, 2016. http://www.jordantimes.com/news/local/muslim-brotherhood-ends-link-egyptian-mother-group

[10] "Jordanian Muslim Brotherhood split from Egyptian parent group," The New Arab, February 16, 2016, https://www.alaraby.co.uk/english/news/2016/2/16/jordanian-muslim-brotherhood-split-from-egyptian-parent-group

[11] See al-Maqdisi's website, http://www.tawhed.ws/, and the subsequent debate with other jihadi authorities such as Ma'asari. For a summary of these debates, see Joas Wagemakers, "Reflections on Maqdisi's Arrest," Jihadica, October 2, 2010, http://www.jihadica.com/reflections-on-al-maqdisis-arrest/.

[12] See for example https://www.youtube.com/watch?v=vtUPfPbrokY

[13] Suhaib Anjarini, How Jordanians Came to Dominate al-Nusra Front, January 16, 2015. http://english.al-akhbar.com/node/23238

[14] See for example a demonstration in support of ISIS, June 2014. http://www.jordanews.com/jordan/27280.html

[15] FOREIGN FIGHTERS: THE SOUFAN GROUP, December 2015, An Updated Assessment of the Flow of Foreign Fighters into Syria and Iraq. http://soufangroup.com/wp-content/uploads/2015/12/TSG_ForeignFightersUpdate3.pdf

[16] Jacob Foushter, In nations with significant Muslim populations, much disdain for ISIS, December 17, 2015. http://www.pewresearch.org/fact-tank/2015/11/17/in-nations-with-significant-muslim-populations-much-disdain-for-isis/

[17] "Jordan," The CIA World Factbook, November, 2016, https://www.cia.gov/library/publications/the-world-factbook/geos/jo.html.

[18] Ibid.

[19] The World's Muslims: Religion, Politics and Society, April 30, 2013. http://www.pewforum.org/2013/04/30/the-worlds-muslims-religion-politics-society-beliefs-about-sharia/

[20] Jacob Poushter, Support for al Qaeda was low before (and after) Osama bin Laden's death, May 12 2014. http://www.pewresearch.org/fact-tank/2014/05/02/support-for-al-qaeda-was-low-before-and-after-osama-bin-ladens-death/

[21] "Two Dozen Islamists Go on Trial on Corruption Charges," Deutsche Press-Agentur, December 24, 2009. http://monstersandcritics.com/news/middleeast/news/article_1521391.php/Two-dozen-Islamists-go-on-trial-on-corruption-charages.

[22] Al-Kifah al-Arabi (Beirut), December 21, 2009.

[23] Dia Hadid, "Jordan Tones Down Tetbooks' Islamic Content, and Tempers Rise," The New York Times, October 14, 2016, http://www.nytimes.com/2016/10/15/world/middleeast/jordan-tones-down-textbooks-islamic-content-and-tempers-rise.html?_r=0.

[24] "Two Dozen Islamists Go on Trial on Corruption Charges," Deutsche Press-Agentur, December 24, 2009. http://monstersandcritics.com/news/middleeast/news/article_1521391.php/Two-dozen-Islamists-go-on-trial-on-corruption-charages.

[25] Jacob Amis, "The Jordanian Brotherhood in the Arab Spring," Hudson Institute Current Trends in Islamist Ideology 14 (January 2013), 43.

[26] Ibid., 42.

[27] "Thousands of protesters demanding the 'downfall of the regime' in Jordan," BBC, http://www.bbc.co.uk/arabic/middleeast/2012/11/121116_jordan_protest_king.shtml.

[28] See, for example, Tim Lister, "Jordanian Tribal Figures Criticize Queen, Demand Reform," CNN, February 6, 2011, http://articles.cnn.com/2011-02-06/world/jordan.monarchy_1_jordanians-king-abdullah-ii-tribal-leaders?_s=PM:WORLD.

[29] "Qatari political money in Jordan starts with the support of Islamic Associations and ends with the production of the drama," Al-Sharq (Saudi Arabia), December 15, 2012, http://www.alsharq.net.sa/2012/12/15/626813.

[30] Tareq Al Naimat, "The Jordanian regime and the Muslim Brotherhood: a tug of war," Woodrow Wilson Center Viewpoints no. 58 (July 2014). https://www.wilsoncenter.org/sites/default/files/jordanian_regime_muslim_brotherhood_tug_of_war.pdf

[31] Aaron Magid, "Analysis: Jordan's Muslim Brotherhood comes in from the cold," Middle East Eye (London), June 21, 2016. http://www.middleeasteye.net/news/analysis-jordan-s-muslim-brotherhood-ends-election-boycott-1119065410

[32] "'Jordan's Islamists': What are the expectations after their return to Parliament?" BBC Arabic, September 22, 2016. http://www.bbc.com/arabic/interactivity/2016/09/160922_comments_jordan_elections

[33] "'Spinning political' between brothers Jordan and Queen Rania," RT Arabic, September 22, 2016. https://arabic.rt.com/news/842076-%D8%BA%D8%B2%D9%84-%D8%A8%D9%8A%D9%86-%D8%A5%D8%AE%D9%88%D8%A7%D9%86-%D8%A7%D9%84%D8%A7%D8%B1%D8%AF%D9%86-%D9%88%D8%A7%D9%84%D9%85%D9%84%D9%83%D8%A9-%D8%B1%D8%A7%D9%86%D9%8A%D8%A7/

[34] Hassan Abu Haniya, "Has the Muslim Brotherhood in Jordan overcome the danger of fragmentation and danger?" Middle East Monitor (London), October 4, 2016. https://www.middleeastmonitor.com/20161004-has-the-muslim-brotherhood-in-jordan-overcome-the-danger-of-fragmentation-and-danger/

[35] Sawsan Tabazah, Islamic Action Front mulls coalitions as it prepares for local elections, January 17, 2014. http://jordantimes.com/news/local/islamic-action-front-mulls-coalitions-it-prepares-local-elections

KUWAIT

> **QUICK FACTS**
>
> Population: 2,832,776 (estimated July 2016)
>
> Area: 17,818 sq km
>
> Ethnic Groups: Kuwaiti 31.3%, other Arab 27.9%, Asian 37.8%, African 1.9%, other 1.1% (includes European, North American, South American, and Australian)
>
> Religions: Muslim (official) 76.7%, Christian 17.3%, other and unspecified 5.9%
>
> Government Type: Constitutional Emirate
>
> GDP (official exchange rate): $110.5 billion (estimated 2015)
>
> *Quick Facts courtesy of the CIA World Factbook (January 2017)*

OVERVIEW

Kuwaiti soldiers, civilians, and U.S. forces have all been the targets of sporadic attacks by radical religious elements in recent years. However, the phenomenon of global jihad is less prevalent in Kuwait than in many of its Gulf neighbors, despite the June 2015 suicide bombing that killed 27 people in a Shia mosque in Kuwait City.[1] Najd Province, an Islamic State affiliate, claimed responsibility for that attack.[2] Nevertheless, ISIS and other terrorist groups more commonly use Kuwaiti soil for logistical activities, such as the recruitment of fighters for arenas of jihad (Iraq, Afghanistan, Syria and so on), and as a hub through which funds, operatives and equipment are transferred to other countries. While counterterrorism measures have been successful in preventing fatal attacks in Kuwait itself, efforts against facilitation networks serving the global jihad have so far been lacking.

In the political arena, Kuwait preserves a delicate balance: permitting Islamists a presence in the nation's parliament but vesting power in the nation's Emir to dissolve parliament, a power that he exercises whenever Islamist ideas and criticism cross political red lines. Kuwait's Islamists, for their part, have exhibited a subtle approach, working to gradually expand the role of sharia law within the day-to-day life of Kuwaitis while remaining loyal to the country's constitution.

ISLAMIST ACTIVITY

While not a primary target for al-Qaeda, ISIS, and other terror groups, Kuwait does have a place on the global *jihadi* agenda, for two main reasons. First, its long-standing relationship with the United States, especially since the first Gulf War, symbolizes to a great extent the "imperialist presence" that Washington allegedly represents on the Arabian Peninsula. Even with cutbacks following the 2011 withdrawal of troops from Iraq, Kuwait currently hosts an extensive American military presence (encompassing some 16 active and 6 inactive bases, and tens of thousands of soldiers) on its soil,[3] which serves as a natural target for organized terror groups and individual extremists driven by Salafi *jihadist* ideology. Islamists also consider the Kuwaiti regime a target as well, as they perceive it to be pro-U.S. and to an extent "apostate" (not adhering completely to the Islamic, or *sharia*, law). Second, and perhaps more important, Kuwait serves as a transit country for money, equipment and operatives into countries in which "Holy War" is being waged—mainly Iraq, Pakistan and Afghanistan, but also Syria since 2012.

There is little known about the organized Islamist presence in Kuwait.[4] However, Kuwaiti security forces occasionally respond to terror attacks and expose plots inside the small Gulf country. Notably, however, they failed to predict or prevent the June 2015 ISIS attack perpetrated by a Saudi citizen working with a local support network in Kuwait. In September 2015, a criminal court in Kuwait convicted fifteen out of 29 suspects in the bombing, acquitting the other fourteen. The fifteen convictions included seven death sentences, of which five were handed down in *absentia*, as two of the suspects were believed to be fighting for ISIS in Iraq and two others were Saudi citizens arrested in Saudi Arabia.[5]

Al-Qaeda is believed to operate in Kuwait in a clandestine manner. Geographically, al-Qaeda's activity in Kuwait is supposedly subordinate to "al-Qaeda in the Arabian Peninsula" (AQAP), the official al-Qaeda franchise in the region. AQAP is mainly based in Saudi Arabia and Yemen, and there is little known regarding its actual operational control over *jihadist* activity in Kuwait. Nonetheless, AQAP's agenda strongly suggests that the organization's reach includes the entire Gulf region. Given the rise in attention garnered by AQAP since 2009, especially in Yemen, it is likely that the organization will be slower to expand its reach to the smaller countries under its supposed authority, including Kuwait.

AQAP's focus on Saudi Arabia and Yemen has opened the door for other actors to take part in planning attacks against Western targets in Kuwait. Such players are often elements with historical ties to core al-Qaeda leaders in Afghanistan and Pakistan, who for years have been operating independently, carrying out sporadic attacks in the country. In this regard, one should remember that the most senior operational figures of al-Qaeda have Kuwaiti connections. The conspirators behind the infamous "Bojinka" plot, Abd al Karim Murad, Ramzi Yousef, and above all Khalid Sheikh Mohamed (who would later masterminded the September 11 attacks), were all Kuwaiti residents, and their large families still live in the country. Abu Ahmed al-Kuwaiti, a Kuwait-born Pakistani national, was Osama bin Laden's courier and confidante and was killed with him in the Navy SEAL raid on the Abbottabad compound in May 2011.[6] In the years since September 11th, although there have been few and relatively infrequent terror incidents in Kuwait, most of those that have occurred are generally attributed to al-Qaeda (though not always proven to be so).

- In October 2002, one U.S. Marine was killed and a second wounded after two Kuwaiti Muslim extremists opened fire on soldiers in Faylaka Island, about 10 miles off the coast of Kuwait City.[7] Both attackers, one of whom had allegedly pledged allegiance to Osama bin Laden, were killed during the altercation. In an audiotape that surfaced the following month, bin Laden praised the attack as the work of "zealous sons of Islam in defense of their religion."[8] Khalid Sheikh Mohamed, al-Qaeda's former chief of external operations, claimed full responsibility for the attack in his military court hearing.[9]

- In January 2003, two civilian contractors working for the U.S. military in Kuwait were attacked in an ambush a few miles from "Camp Doha," a U.S. military base. One was killed and the other injured.[10]

- In a series of raids conducted in early 2005, Kuwaiti authorities arrested about 30 operatives belonging to a global *jihadi* cell in the country. Among those arrested were many nationalities: Kuwaiti, Saudi, Jordanian, and Yemeni. While it is likely these activists were at least al-Qaeda-affiliated, several other names were associated with the group, among them "The Brigades of the Two Shrines [Mecca and Medina] in Kuwait," "Sharia Falcons Squadrons" and "Peninsula Lion Brigades." The arrests followed other incidents during the same period in which Kuwaiti army officers plotted to attack American targets after they were allegedly inspired by anti-U.S. propaganda.[11]

- In August 2009, Kuwaiti authorities arrested six members of a terrorist network linked to al-Qaeda, who were planning to attack the "Camp Arifjan" U.S. military base. At the time, the heavily protected camp housed 15,000 U.S. soldiers and was used as a logistics base for troops serving in Iraq. The six arrested operatives were of Kuwaiti origin and had also planned to attack the headquarters of Kuwait's internal security agency.[12]

Aside from the aforementioned attacks directed against Western and government targets, the Kuwaiti arena is used for the benefit of other *jihadi* theaters.

First and foremost, Kuwait is an important transit point for the transfer of funds, equipment and operatives from the Gulf countries to Pakistan and Afghanistan.[13] This route, only sparsely monitored by Kuwaiti authorities, is a significant pipeline that feeds insurgent and terror groups in the Afghan-Pakistan arenas. Through a network of smugglers and document forgers, Kuwait is used to support these organizations financially and militarily. Operatives of Kuwaiti origin consequently have grown into significant actors within the core al-Qaeda organization in Pakistan, playing both logistical and operational roles.[14]

Similarly, Kuwait served as a source of fighters and suicide bombers for the al-Qaeda franchise in Iraq (al-Qaeda in Iraq or AQI), the precursor to today's Islamic State terrorist group.[15] Kuwaiti youth were recruited and sent to Iraq, usually through Syria, to perform their "*jihadi* duty" by fighting Coalition forces. According to one local AQI commander in Iraq, dozens of Kuwaiti nationals were operating in his area of command as of 2008.[16] Although the participation of Kuwaiti nationals in the Iraqi insurgency declined in tandem with the winding down and 2011 withdrawal of U.S. forces from Iraq, the escalation of the civil war in Syria in 2012-13 offered Kuwaitis (along with other foreign nationals) a new platform to engage in *jihadist* activity, incidentally also boosting the Sunni-led opposition in Iraq to Prime Minister Maliki.[17]

One of the greatest threats to Kuwait's national security stems from veteran *jihadists* of Kuwaiti nationality who have completed their "duty" in Afghanistan or Iraq, and wish to put to use the lessons they learned there against targets in their homeland. These experienced fighters, who have widespread contacts with other militants and the necessary know-how in guerilla fighting and the construction of bombs, can significantly increase the threat to Western and Kuwait government targets in the country. According to some reports, there have been past attempts to use Kuwaiti veterans in attacks, and senior al-Qaeda officials in Pakistan are known to have entrusted Kuwaiti recruits with secret missions to be conducted in Kuwait.[18] However, so long as more attractive *jihad* arenas exist (such as Iraq, Afghanistan, Somalia, Syria etc.), the phenomenon of experienced Kuwaiti *jihadists* launching attacks on Kuwaiti soil will remain limited.

Terrorism finance is another critical issue in Kuwait. While the source of the problem mainly lies in neighboring Saudi Arabia, there are also several terror supporters known to be operating in Kuwait, providing global *jihadists* in the Middle East and Asia with the funds necessary to carry out their terror activities. As official awareness of this phenomenon has grown, more effort has been put into interdicting and stopping illegal financial transfers. Similar initiatives have also been implemented by the UN Security Council's Sanctions Committee that are designed to freeze financial assets and restrict the travel and arms trade of such operatives. The committee's effectiveness, however, is questionable.[19] Moreover, the efficiency and comprehensiveness of Kuwait's own counterterror efforts are hampered by the fact that it has no specific legal framework criminalizing terrorist financing and other terrorist-related activities.[20] Thus the prosecution of any such crimes must take place through alternative statutes.

Since 2012, credible reports have suggested that Kuwait-based actors play a pivotal role in the channeling of funds to rebel groups fighting the Assad regime in Syria. An in-depth investigation by *The National* newspaper in Abu Dhabi found that Kuwait "has emerged as a central fund-raising hub for direct financial support to insurgents" fighting in Syria, compounding the tens of millions of dollars in humanitarian aid raised by private or individual means.[21] Kuwait also hosted a UN donor conference on Syria on January 30, 2013. This resulted in pledges totaling more than $1.5 billion, of which $300 million was promised by the Kuwaiti government.[22] In addition to these official and unofficial funding channels, prominent Sunni Islamist politicians and clerics have openly campaigned to arm rebel fighters in Syria. A conservative Islamist former MP, Waleed al-Tabtabie, posted photographs of himself on Twitter wearing combat gear in Syria.[23]

The rapid growth of ISIS and its capture of a swathe of territory linking eastern Syria and western Iraq in 2014 heightened concerns among U.S. policymakers about the extent of illicit funding flowing from Kuwait to the organization. Former U.S. Treasury Undersecretary David Cohen stated bluntly in March 2014 that Kuwait had become "the epicenter of fundraising for terror groups in Syria" and noted more generally that a new financial tracking unit set up by the Kuwaiti government to investigate suspicious financial transactions and money laundering was still not operational. The Treasury Department expressed particular concern over the "dual nature" of alleged funding flows, in which organizations "to some extent channel money to blankets and bread and schools, and then money also to supporting terrorist activities."[24] Moreover, Kuwait's Justice and Endowments Minister, Nayef al-Ajmi, resigned in May 2014 after being named by Cohen as having a history of "promoting terrorism," and with his ministry coming under suspicion for allowing non-profit organizations and charities to collect donations for the Syrian people at Kuwaiti mosques, which Cohen argued was "a measure we believe can be easily exploited by Kuwait-based terrorist fundraisers."[25]

A suicide bombing at a Shi'a mosque in Kuwait City on June 26, 2015 that left 27 dead and 227 wounded highlighted Kuwait's vulnerability both to the general surge in sectarian tension across the region and to the particular threat posed by the Islamic State. The attack was the worst act of terrorism in Kuwait in more than thirty years, since the coordinated December 12, 1983 bombings that targeted the United States and French Embassies in Kuwait and the headquarters of the Kuwait Petroleum Corporation.[26] The bombing of the Imam al-Sadiq mosque was designed to cause maximum damage to intercommunal relations in Kuwait. The blast, carried out by Fahad

Suleiman al-Gabbaa, a Saudi citizen, targeted the center of the *Hasawi* community of Kuwaiti Shi'a. Also known as *Sheikhis*, the *Hasawi* originally emigrated from the al-Hasa region of Saudi Arabia's Eastern Province in the late-nineteenth and early-twentieth centuries, in part to escape endemic marginalization and discrimination.[27]

The final element of Islamist activity in Kuwait lies in the role of fundamentalist religious scholars. Such figures play a critical role in the education and indoctrination of Kuwaiti *Salafis*—especially those that join the armed *jihadist* struggle.[28] The most famous among them is Hamid al-Ali, a *Salafi* cleric known for his considerable following. Al-Ali, previously a professor of Islamic studies at Kuwait University, has been officially designated by the U.S. government as a global terrorism financier and supporter. His views—at times radical and supportive of al-Qaeda (for instance, issuing fatwas approving of crashing planes into buildings as a form of attack) and at others more aligned with the moderate approach imposed upon him by the regime—reach many young Muslims through the sermons and articles he publishes online.[29] Another important radical religious figure is Suleiman Abu Gheith, a former high school religion teacher in Kuwait City who became a leading figure within al-Qaeda. After joining the group in 2000, Abu Gheith was a member of the al-Qaeda quasi-legislative and consultative committee (*Majles al Shura*). He headed the organization's media committee responsible for propaganda and was one of Osama bin Laden's top aides as well as his son-in-law. Abu Gheith departed for Iran as part of a group of al-Qaeda senior leaders in 2003.[30] Ten years later, in March 2013, he was seized by U.S. Special Forces in Jordan and extradited to the U.S., where he appeared in a federal court in New York and pleaded not guilty to charges of conspiracy to kill Americans ahead of his trial in 2014, which sentenced him to life imprisonment.[31]

In its fight against radicalization and as a part of the global effort against al-Qaeda and ISIS, the Kuwaiti regime is implementing policies to control and prevent radical Islamists from engaging in terrorism—although, as previously discussed, not always doing so sufficiently. In addition to outright arrests and the targeting of Islamist financial flows, the Kuwaiti government has also initiated a number of other counter-terrorism measures, including a wide-scale educational program aimed at countering the influence of unchecked radicalism. In addition, Kuwaiti imams are sporadically taken to court by the government, which accuses them of "activities contrary to the function of the Ministry of Islamic Affairs and the mosque."[32]

ISLAMISM AND SOCIETY

Approximately 85 percent of Kuwait's total population of 3.4 million is Muslim, but Kuwaiti citizens (which comprise only 1 million of that total) are nearly all Muslims. While the national census does not distinguish between Sunnis and Shi'ites, approximately 70-75 percent of citizens, including the ruling family, belong to the Sunni branch of Islam. The remainder, with the exception of about 100-200 Christians and a few Baha'is, are Shi'ites.[33]

Despite the sectarian violence in neighboring Iraq, Kuwait manages to maintain a relatively stable sectarian environment, although tensions have risen sharply since 2012 as hardline Sunni and Shi'ite politicians have publicly favored differing sides in the Syrian civil war. Generally speaking, Shi'ites in Kuwait are less organized politically than the Sunnis. Their most notable point of contention is their desire to redress longstanding inequalities and obtain an apology for accusations that they constitute a "fifth column" for Iran (an allegation that surfaced during the 1980-1988 Iran-Iraq War, but which abated as Shi'ites demonstrated their loyalty during the Iraqi invasion of Kuwait in August 1990).

The general level of public support in Kuwait for Islamist activity and radicalism is hard to determine. Electoral preferences provide only limited insight, as over two-thirds of Kuwait's population consists of non-citizens who lack the right to vote, and organized political parties are banned. As in many other Arab countries, September 11th and the subsequent U.S. invasions of Afghanistan and Iraq ignited and exposed latent feelings of suspicion and hatred in certain quarters towards the West and the U.S. in particular, irrespective of relatively fruitful cooperation at the governmental level. Nevertheless, the U.S.-led invasion of Iraq in 2003 was less controversial in Kuwait than elsewhere in the Arab world, due to the legacy of Kuwaitis suffering at the hands of Saddam Hussein's dictatorship.

Kuwait manages a delicate balance with regard to Islamic devotion. The society remains traditionally Muslim in many ways, although there are no *mutawwa* (religious police) as in Saudi Arabia, nor are the five daily prayer times strictly observed. The Kuwaiti public, however, generally supports Islamic traditions; alcohol, gambling, mixed dancing, and other such "Western symbols" are relatively rare. More extreme anti-Western voices are largely censored out of the country's otherwise fairly free press. However, they are still easily available to the public on the Internet or in pan-Arabian media.

A 2007 Pew poll suggested that there is a significant fringe element inside Kuwait that actively supports or sympathizes with more extremist views and activities. According to the survey, 20 percent of Kuwaitis believed that suicide bombings "in defense of Islam" were sometimes justified, and 13 percent expressed "some confidence" in Osama bin Laden, al-Qaeda's founder and general chief.[34] Since 2011, despite comparative polling evidence, the conflict in Syria has brought extremist voices closer to the surface in support of *jihadist* groups. Even though these views are a minority in Kuwait, they persist under the protective umbrella of some Islamist spokesmen, among them the aforementioned Sheikh Hamid al-Ali.

ISLAMISM AND THE STATE

Kuwait is a constitutional hereditary emirate.[35] The *Emir* Sabah al-Ahmad al-Jaber Al-Sabah is the head of state, and has the power to appoint the prime minister, dissolve the parliament and even suspend certain parts of the constitution, as occurred between 1976 and 1981 and between 1986 and 1992. Kuwait's constitution, which was approved in 1962, states that "the religion of the state is Islam and the *Sharia* shall be a main source of legislation." Thus, though driven by Islamic belief, the government is less strict in the enforcement of Islamic law. *Sharia*, according to the constitution, is a "guideline" rather than the formal state law. Notably, the first action of the Islamist-dominated parliament elected in February 2012 was to call for an amendment to the constitution to make *sharia* "the" rather than "a" source of legislation.[36]

The ruling elite has put considerable effort into maintaining order, and is committed to achieving the right balance between emphasizing the importance of Islam to its citizens and ensuring stability by blunting the rise of extremism. The Kuwaiti government exercises direct control over Sunni religious institutions and appoints Sunni *imams*, monitors their Friday sermons, and pays the salaries of mosque staff. It also finances the building of new Sunni mosques.[37]

The overall number of mosques in Kuwait exceeds 1,100. Only six of them are Shi'ite, while the rest are Sunni.[38] There are no official reports delineating the number of mosques open to a radical interpretation of Islam, but several hints can be found on Kuwaiti Internet websites, which suggest the number is derived from the external involvement and financial support of radical elements (mainly from Saudi Arabia).[39]

As no formal political parties are permitted in Kuwait, the 50 seats in the Kuwaiti parliament are occupied by quasi-political societies of Bedouins, merchants, moderate Sunni and Shi'ite activists, secular liberals, and nationalists. Parliament members either conform to these unofficial national and religiously affiliated blocs or sit as independents.

The Islamist bloc, which functions as a *de facto* political party, is the most influential group in the Kuwaiti Parliament. It consists mainly of Sunni *Salafis* and members of *Hadas* (the Kuwaiti Islamic Constitutional Movement). Its principal long-term goal is to impose *sharia* law in Kuwait. However, the Islamist bloc operates conservatively in the short-term, attempting to wield influence within parliament in order to pass legislation that conforms to Islamic law. The bloc is composed of devoted Islamists, but not necessarily extremists.

The most prominent Islamic movement in Kuwait remains *Al-Haraka al-Dostooriya al-Islamiya*, or *Hadas*, also known as the Islamic Constitutional Movement (ICM).[40] The ICM was established in 1991, following the liberation of Kuwait from Iraqi control in the first Gulf War. The ICM serves as the political front of the Muslim Brotherhood in Kuwait, though in recent years the ICM has grown away from its parent organization. The ICM broke ties with the international Muslim Brotherhood after the latter backed the Iraqi invasion in 1990 and failed to provide sufficient support for the liberation of Kuwait.[41] Neither the ICM nor the Muslim Brotherhood retains any legal status within the country. Instead, the movement's main legally recognized manifestation is the Social Reform Society, a charitable nongovernmental organization.

Salafis are another important Islamist factor in the Kuwaiti political system. Since its founding in the early 1960s, the Salafi movement in Kuwait has focused on *dawa* ("religious call," or proselytization) and has been active in charities, heritage, relief work, and building schools, universities, mosques, orphanages, and hospitals. In parliament, the movement is represented by two main groups: the Islamic Salafi Grouping (*al-Tajamu al-Islami al-Salafi*) and the *Salafi* Movement (*al-Haraka al-Salafiyya*), an offshoot of the former. Both signify a more extreme—yet far less organized—opposition to the regime. Many other *Salafi* MPs are independent Islamists. A growth in their numbers, and especially the establishment of a wide and organized political movement for the *Salafis* to work from, might serve as a prelude for the country's movement down a more fundamentalist path in the future.

Any initiative pursued by Islamists in parliament can be easily blocked, as the *Emir's* approval is required for all constitutional amendments. For instance, Islamists have long called for an amendment to Article 2 of the constitution, which states that *sharia* is "a main source of legislation," and to have the article rephrased to read that *sharia* is "the source of legislation." The amendment passed in parliament, only to be vetoed by the *Emir* in 2006. It was attempted anew, again without success, in 2012.[42] A similar change requested by the Islamist bloc relates to Article 79, which states that: "No law may be promulgated unless it has been passed by the National Assembly and sanctioned by the *Emir*." To this the Islamists sought to add "and according to the *Sharia* [sic]."[43] This measure was also rejected by the *Emir* in May 2012.[44]

The number of parliamentary seats in the Islamist bloc typically fluctuates between 15 and 24 members. Elections have become a common occurrence in recent years, as the parliament was dissolved by the Kuwaiti *Emir* four times in seven years, most recently due to protests over election laws and allegations of fraud. In addition to repeated dissolution by the *Emir*, the Constitutional Court also stepped in to annul the two parliaments elected in February and December 2012, owing to technical irregularities in the conduct of the two elections.[45] In the May 2009 elections, Sunni Islamists won only 13 seats (a sharp decrease compared to their rise in power over the previous decade), while Shi'ite Islamists won six seats and independents, mostly associated with the government, won 21—a significant portion of the total 50 seats of the parliament.[46]

The 2009 elections were likewise significant because they saw the election of four women MPs for the first time in the country's history.[47] Prior to that year, men had filled the seats of Kuwait's parliament exclusively for nearly five decades, and it was only in 2005 that the country granted women the right to vote and run for office.[48] This phenomenon, along with the loss of seats by Islamists, was taken in 2009 to signify a more moderate and liberal approach emerging in already relatively modernized Kuwait, and although no women were elected in the February 2012 election, three subsequently won seats in the December 2012 parliament and two in the July 2013 vote. To further exemplify the trend, Kuwait's highest court judged in 2009 that female MPs are not obliged to wear headscarves, striking yet another blow to Muslim fundamentalists.[49] Though the majority of Kuwaiti women do wear the *hijab*, it is not compulsory according to the country's law, as it is in the ultra-conservative neighboring Saudi Arabia.

However, relations between the government and the parliament elected in 2009 deteriorated sharply after the start of the Arab Spring in early 2011. Youth movements associated with the Kuwaiti branch of the Muslim Brotherhood as well as with liberal blocs called for the resignation of the unpopular Prime Minister, Sheikh Nasser al-Mohammed Al-Sabah, a nephew of the *Emir*. In autumn 2011, popular mobilization intersected with the disclosure of a large political corruption scandal, which implicated 16 of the 50 MPs in having allegedly received government payments in return for votes. The resulting anger culminated in the November 2011 storming of the National Assembly building by demonstrators and the subsequent resignation of the Prime Minister a fortnight later.[50]

During 2012, Kuwait witnessed two controversial elections that left the country—and its society—deeply polarized. Elections in February 2012 resulted in an opposition landslide as conservative tribal and Islamist MPs won 35 out of the 50 seats. At least 21 MPs were Sunni Islamists, including four MPs each from the Islamic *Salafi* Alliance and the ICM. A further five pro-government Sunni politicians and seven Shi'ites were elected, reinforcing the strongly Islamist character of the parliament. During a turbulent four-month tenure before its annulment by the Constitutional Court in June 2012, Islamist MPs called for the introduction of the death penalty for blasphemy, a move that was particularly significant in the context of the attempt earlier that year to make *sharia* the sole basis of the constitution.[51]

Sunni Islamists then joined with tribal groups to boycott the December 2012 election. This occurred in protest of a decree issued by the *Emir* that October amending the electoral law to reduce the number of votes each Kuwaiti could cast from four to one. A series of mass public demonstrations—the largest in Kuwait's history—were organized by the opposition, which argued that only elected parliamentarians and not the *Emir* could change the electoral law, while the boycott movement was joined by liberal societies in an unlikely alignment of interests. An informal Opposition Coalition formed, consisting of the ICM, the Popular Action Bloc, trade unions, and student groups, which then proceeded to demand an elected government and an end to Al-Sabah control of the executive. Musallim al-Barrak emerged as the charismatic figurehead of the opposition; of Sunni tribal origin, his views are populist rather than ideological or Islamist in nature.[52]

With the opposition boycotting, the December vote resulted in the emergence of a new political class. An unprecedented seventeen Shi'ite MPs—more than double their usual number—were elected, spread across four ideological groupings. In response, the Islamist and tribal opposition migrated away from the parliamentary chamber toward street politics. This constituted a destabilizing development that signaled a worrying loss of faith in Kuwait's existing political system. Most of the Islamist groups, including the ICM, also boycotted the subsequent election in July 2013, although the Islamic *Salafi* Alliance broke ranks and gained two parliamentary seats.

Ahead of the next parliamentary election, which must take place by July 2017 at the latest, the ICM has announced that it will abandon its political boycott and take part in the vote. The decision to return to electoral participation reflects the weakening of the oppositional coalition and a judgment that there is more to gain by taking part in the political process than by standing aside. However, an amendment to the electoral law that prohibits people from standing for election if they have been convicted of slandering the Emir is likely to rule out many potential candidates from ICM and other groups from the opposition, including al-Barrak, who remains in prison serving his two-year sentence for criticizing the *Emir*.[53]

The ICM traditionally holds only between two and six seats, yet their influence within the Islamist bloc is significant. It is the most popular and powerful—and also by far the best funded and most highly organized—entity of the Islamist movements. The ICM, through the clandestine activity of the Kuwaiti Muslim Brotherhood and through the Social Reform Society, is involved in various social, charitable, educational and economic activities. It recruits its members from mosques and university campuses, adding many doctors and other highly educated academics to its ranks.[54]

The ICM formally seeks the implementation of *sharia* law and the protection of a fairly conservative vision of Kuwaiti traditions and values. In addition to leading and supporting the amendments mentioned above, the movement has occasionally introduced legislation that aims to implement various *sharia* provisions, such as a law mandating payment of zakat, a religious tax. It is, however, interested in operating within the Kuwaiti constitutional order rather than overturning it.[55] Relative to other national and trans-national affiliates of the Muslim Brotherhood, the ICM maintains a mild position toward the United States (though not toward Israel) and it has not criticized the security relationship between Kuwait and Washington, DC.[56]

If able to unite with other Islamists, the ICM's electoral power could help the movement achieve its goal of expanding the role of Islamic law in the day-to-day life of

Kuwaitis. Kuwaiti political history, however, is reason enough for skepticism on that score, as the opposition has never been able to maintain a united front for long, and the Kuwaiti government has tools at its disposal to easily disperse and even exclude dissenters.[57]

The ICM's gradual success is attributed largely to its discretion in picking its battles with the government and the ruling family. The ICM has strived to position itself simultaneously as an opposition movement and as a party accepting gradualism and the limitations of the Kuwaiti political system.[58] However, many of the occasions on which the *Emir* dissolved the parliament were precipitated by political disputes with the ICM. Moreover, ties between the ICM and the Kuwaiti government soured after Kuwait extended financial and political support to the military-led interim regime in Egypt that overthrew the democratically elected Muslim Brotherhood-led government of Mohammed Morsi in July 2013.[59]

It is also worth mentioning that, regardless of its relative success, the ICM suffers criticism on multiple fronts. Some critique it for being insufficiently dedicated to the cause of political opposition. A different line of criticism claims the ICM is masking its true, radical sentiments.[60]

Endnotes

[1] "Kuwait Shia mosque blast death toll 'rises to 27'" BBC, June 25, 2015, http://www.bbc.com/news/world-middle-east-33287136.

[2] Scott Neuman, "ISIS Claims Responsibility For Suicide Attack At Kuwait Mosque," National Public Radio, June 26, 2015, http://www.npr.org/sections/thetwo-way/2015/06/26/417708840/isis-claims-responsibility-for-suicide-attack-at-kuwait-mosque

[3] See, for example, "Kuwait Facilities," globalsecurity.org, n.d., http://www.globalsecurity.org/military/facility/kuwait.htm.

[4] No comprehensive and reliable database for jihadists in Kuwait exists. The figures provided represent best assessments by the author, based on material relating to arrests and plots that has appeared in the open source.

[5] "Seven Sentenced to Death over Kuwait Mosque Bombing." Al Jazeera (Doha), September 15, 2015, http://www.aljazeera.com/news/2015/09/sentenced-death-kuwait-mosque-bombing-150915064024530.html.

[6] Mark Memmott, "Bin Laden's Courier, Abu Ahmed al-Kuwaiti, Had Several Responsibilities," National Public Radio, May 4, 2011, http://www.npr.org/sections/thetwo-way/2011/05/06/135994650/bin-ladens-courier-abu-ahmed-al-kuwaiti-had-several-responsibilities

[7] Andrew Buncombe, "American Marine On Maneuvers In Kuwait Is Killed By Terrorist Attack," Independent (London), October 9, 2002, http://www.independent.co.uk/news/world/middle-east/american-marine-on-manoeuvres-in-kuwait-is-killed-by-terrorist-attack-5359632.html

[8] "Al-Jazirah: Usama Bin Ladin Hails Recent Operations In Bali," Al-Jazeera (Doha), November 12, 2002. See full coverage of Bin Laden's statements, as transcribed by FBIS, at http://www.fas.org/irp/world/para/ubl-fbis.pdf.

[9] Verbatim transcript of combatant status review tribunal hearing for ISN 10024, March 10, 2007, 18, http://www.defense.gov/news/transcript_isn10024.pdf.

[10] "Camera May Have Recorded Kuwait Killing," CNN, January 21, 2003, http://edition.cnn.com/2003/WORLD/meast/01/21/kuwait.american/

[11] Stephen Ulph, "Terrorism Accelerates in Kuwait," Jamestown Foundation Terrorism Focus 2, iss. 3, February 2, 2005, http://www.jamestown.org/programs/gta/single/?tx_ttnews%5Btt_news%5D=27494&tx_ttnews%5BbackPid%5D=238&no_cache=1.

[12] "Kuwait 'Foils US Army Base Plot,'" BBC, August 11, 2009, http://news.bbc.co.uk/2/hi/middle_east/8195401.stm.

[13] "Walking the Talk: Forum Members Travel to Afghanistan and Iraq (Part 1)," Jihadica.org, June 30, 2008, http://www.jihadica.com/walking-the-talk-forum-members-travel-to-afghanistan-and-iraq-part-1/; "Walking the Talk: Forum Members Travel to Afghanistan and Iraq (Part 2)," Jihadica.org, July 2, 2008, http://www.jihadica.com/walking-the-talk-forum-members-travel-to-afghanistan-and-iraq-pt-2/

[14] For example, Abu Obeida Tawari al-Obeidi and Abu Adel al-Kuwaiti, who were killed in Waziristan in early 2009. "Terrorism: Three Al-Qaeda Leaders Killed in US Attack," AKI (Rome), February 5, 2009, http://www.adnkronos.com/AKI/English/Security/?id=1.0.1845929971

[15] "Video Of Former Gitmo Detainee-Turned-Al-Qaida Suicide Bomber In Iraq," NEFA Foundation, January 2009, http://www.nefafoundation.org/multimedia-prop.html

[16] "Abu Islam the Iraqi: Kuwaiti Young Men Are Being Manipulated, 25 Of Them Fought With Al-Qaeda in Diyala," Al-Watan (Kuwait), July 16, 2008, http://www.elaph.com/ElaphWeb/NewsPapers/2008/7/348810.htm.

[17] Daniel DePetris, "Kuwait's Hidden Hand in Syria," The National Interest, July 16, 2013, http://nationalinterest.org/commentary/kuwaits-hidden-hand-syria-8729

[18] Walking the Talk: Forum Members Travel to Afghanistan and Iraq."

[19] David Pollock and Michael Jacobson, "Blacklisting Terrorism Supporters in Kuwait," Washington Institute for Near East Policy Policywatch 1333, January 25, 2008, http://www.washingtoninstitute.org/templateC05.php?CID=2709.

[20] U.S. Department of State, "Kuwait," Country Reports on Terrorism 2012, May 30, 2013, http://www.refworld.org/docid/51a86e8216.html

[21] Elizabeth Dickinson, "Kuwait, 'the back office of logistical support' for Syria's Rebels," The National, February 5, 2013, http://www.thenational.ae/news/world/middle-east/kuwait-the-back-office-of-logistical-support-for-syrias-rebels

[22] Kristian Coates Ulrichsen, "The Gulf States and Syria," Open Democracy, February 11, 2013, https://www.opendemocracy.net/opensecurity/kristian-coates-ulrichsen/gulf-states-and-syria

[23] Sylvia Westall and Mahmoud Harby, "Insight: Kuwaitis Campaign Privately to Arm Syrian Rebels," Reuters, June 27, 2013, http://www.reuters.com/article/us-syria-kuwait-insight-idUSBRE95P0TG20130627

[24] Kuwait, a U.S. Ally on Syria, Is Also the Leading Funder of Extremist Rebels,' Washington Post, April 25, 2014, https://www.washingtonpost.com/world/national-security/kuwait-top-ally-on-syria-is-also-the-leading-funder-of-extremist-rebels/2014/04/25/10142b9a-ca48-11e3-a75e-463587891b57_story.html?utm_term=.92c750d6cf28

[25] Habib Toumi, "Kuwait Justice Minister's Resignation Accepted," Gulf News, May 12, 2014. http://gulfnews.com/news/gulf/kuwait/kuwaiti-justice-minister-s-resignation-accepted-1.1331524

[26] "Kuwait Attack: Islamic State Suicide Bombing at Shia Mosque Kills 27," Daily Telegraph, June 26, 2015, http://www.telegraph.co.uk/news/worldnews/middleeast/kuwait/11701322/Kuwait-attack-Islamic-State-suicide-bombing-at-Shia-mosque-kills-13-live.html

[27] '27 Killed in ISIS Attack on Kuwait Mosque,' Al Arabiya (Riyadh), June 26, 2015, http://english.alarabiya.net/en/News/middle-east/2015/06/26/Explosion-hits-mosque-in-Kuwait-during-Friday-prayers-.html

[28] Chris Heffelfinger, "Kuwaiti Cleric Hamid al-Ali: The Bridge between Ideology and Action," Jamestown Foundation Terrorism Monitor 5, iss. 8, April 26, 2007, http://www.jamestown.org/single/?no_cache=1&tx_ttnews%5Btt_news%5D=4112.

[29] "Treasury Designations Target Terrorist Facilitators," U.S. Department of the Treasury, December 7, 2006, https://www.treasury.gov/press-center/press-releases/Pages/hp191.aspx

[30] Al-Qaeda Spokesman 'In Iran,'" BBC, July 17, 2003, http://news.bbc.co.uk/2/hi/middle_east/3074785.stm.

[31] "Abu Ghaith Trial is Proof For Some that Federal Courts Can Better Handle Terror Cases," Washington Post, April 1, 2014, https://www.washingtonpost.com/world/national-security/abu-ghaith-trial-is-proof-for-some-that-federal-courts-can-better-handle-terror-cases/2014/04/01/d15ee8f6-b906-11e3-96ae-f2c36d2b1245_story.html?utm_term=.0f07627cbf8c

[32] Ulph, "Terrorism Accelerates in Kuwait."

[33] U.S. Department of State, Bureau of Public Affairs, "Background Notes: Kuwait," February 2009, http://www.state.gov/r/pa/ei/bgn/35876.htm.

[34] Pollock and Jacobson, "Blacklisting Terrorism Supporters in Kuwait."

[35] U.S. Department of State, "Background Notes: Kuwait."

[36] Sylvia Westall, "Kuwait's Ruler Blocks Parliament's Proposal to Make All Laws Comply with Sharia," Al Arabiya (Riyadh), May 17, 2012. http://english.alarabiya.net/articles/2012/05/17/214673.html

[37] "Kuwait," in U.S. Department of State, Bureau of Democracy, Human Rights and Labor, International Religious Freedom Report 2009, October 26, 2009, http://www.state.gov/g/drl/rls/irf/2009/127351.htm

[38] Ibid

[39] See, for example, "Limadha al-Masajed? [Why The Multiplicity Of Mosques?]" Al-Jarida (Kuwait), March 15, 2009, http://www.aljarida.com/aljarida/Article.aspx?id=101363

[40] See ICM's website at http://www.icmkw.org/.

[41] Scheherezade Faramarzi, "Kuwait's Muslim Brotherhood," Jadaliyya, April 18, 2012, http://www.jadaliyya.com/pages/index/5116/kuwaits-muslim-brotherhood

[42] Nathan J. Brown, "Pushing Toward Party Politics? Kuwait's Islamic Constitutional Movement," Carnegie Endowment Carnegie Papers no. 79, January 2007, 10.

[43] Wendy Kristianasen, "Kuwait's Islamists, Officially Unofficial," Le Monde Diplomatique (Paris), June 2002, http://mondediplo.com/2002/06/04kuwait.

[44] Sylvia Westall, "Kuwait's Ruler Blocks MP's Islamic law proposal," Reuters, May 17, 2012, http://uk.reuters.com/article/2012/05/17/uk-kuwait-sharia-idUKBRE84G0G42...

[45] Kristian Coates Ulrichsen, "Kuwait Votes, Again," Foreign Policy, July 25, 2013, http://foreignpolicy.com/2013/07/25/kuwait-votes-again/

[46] [46] Michael Herb, "Kuwait Politics Database (in Arabic)," n.d., http://www2.gsu.edu/~polmfh/database/database.htm; "Kuwait Parliamentary Election, 2009,"

[47] Robert F. Worth, "First Women Win Seats In Kuwait Parliament," New York Times, May 17, 2009, http://www.nytimes.com/2009/05/18/world/middleeast/18kuwait.html

[48] "Woman Elected In Kuwait Says Gender In Politics Is 'History,'" CNN, May 17, 2009, http://edition.cnn.com/2009/WORLD/meast/05/17/kuwait.women.elections/.

[49] "Kuwait: Headscarf Not A Must For Female Lawmakers," Associated Press, October 28, 2009, http://gulfnews.com/news/gulf/kuwait/headscarf-not-a-must-for-female-lawmakers-in-kuwait-1.520316

[50] Kristin Smith Diwan, "Kuwait's Constitutional Showdown," Foreign Policy, November 17, 2011, http://foreignpolicy.com/2011/11/17/kuwaits-constitutional-showdown/

[51] Kristian Coates Ulrichsen, "Political Showdown in Kuwait," Foreign Policy, June 20, 2012, http://foreignpolicy.com/2012/06/20/political-showdown-in-kuwait/

[52] Kristin Smith Diwan, "The Politics of Transgression in Kuwait," Foreign Policy, April 19, 2013, http://foreignpolicy.com/2013/04/19/the-politics-of-transgression-in-kuwait/

[53] Kristin Smith Diwan, 'Parliamentary Boycotts in Kuwait and Bahrain Cost Opposition,' Arab Gulf States Institute in Washington, July 16, 2016, http://www.agsiw.org/parliamentary-boycotts-in-kuwait-and-bahrain-cost-opposition/

[54] Brown, "Pushing toward Party Politics? Kuwait's Islamic Constitutional Movement," 7.

[55] Ibid., 11.

[56] Scheherezade Faramarzi, "Kuwait's Muslim Brotherhood," Jadaliyya, April 18, 2012, http://www.jadaliyya.com/pages/index/5116/kuwaits-muslim-brotherhood.

[57] Brown, "Pushing toward Party Politics? Kuwait's Islamic Constitutional Movement," 4.

[58] Ibid., 5.

[59] Lori Plotkin Boghardt, "Kuwait's Elections: It's Not What Happens Now, but What Happens Next," Washington Institute for Near East Policy Policy Watch 2109, July 26, 2013, http://www.washingtoninstitute.org/policy-analysis/view/kuwaits-elections-its-not-what-happens-now-but-what-happens-next; Faramarzi, "Kuwait's Muslim Brotherhood."

[60] Brown, "Pushing toward Party Politics? Kuwait's Islamic Constitutional Movement," 16

LEBANON

Quick Facts

Population: 6,237,738 (July 2016 est.)

Area: 10,400 sq km

Ethnic Groups: Arab 95%, Armenian 4%, other 1%

Religions: Muslim 54% (27% Sunni, 27% Shia), Christian 40.5% (includes 21% Maronite Catholic, 8% Greek Orthodox, 5% Greek Catholic, 6.5% other Christian), Druze 5.6%, very small numbers of Jews, Baha'is, Buddhists, Hindus, and Mormons

Government Type: parliamentary republic

GDP (official exchange rate): $51.82 billion (2015 est.)

Map and Quick Facts courtesy of the CIA World Factbook (January 2017)

Overview

Islamism in Lebanon is sui generis in a multitude of important respects. The cohabitation of large Sunni Muslim and Shi'a Muslim populations in relatively close proximity, with neither constituting a national majority (and alongside a comparably sized multidenominational Christian community and smaller minority groups) has meant that few Islamists of either sectarian persuasion have aggressively pursued the establishment of a theocratic state in Lebanon, or even sought the wholesale downfall of the existing political order. Rather, Islamists have typically sought to advance transnational aims of, and secure patronage from, powerful co-religionists abroad, often at the expense of Lebanese stability.

Hezbollah, the dominant Shi'a Islamist group in Lebanon, has carved out a heavily armed state-within-a-state in Shi'a-inhabited areas of southern Lebanon, the eastern Beqaa Valley, and suburban Beirut, while commanding sufficient electoral strength to block encroachment by the central government. Though once revered across the predominantly Sunni

Arab world for its armed "resistance" to Israel, its blind obedience to Iran and willingness to turn its guns on other Muslims in recent years have increasingly made it a pariah outside of its own constituency.

Sunni Islamist groups are more numerous and ideologically varied, far more politically marginalized, and surprisingly unwilling to work with one another in pursuit of common objectives. Radicalization in impoverished Sunni areas of northern Lebanon has been growing steadily for years, but has not been effectively channeled by Islamist leaders.

The start of the civil war in neighboring Syria in 2011 has progressively drawn both Shi'a and Sunni Lebanese Islamists into direct combat with each other across the border, and increasingly at home, while instigating an influx of 1.2 million mostly Sunni Syrian refugees into Lebanon.

Notwithstanding the troubling proliferation of terror attacks in Lebanon by local branches of the **Nusra Front** *and the Islamic State group—and the first ever Lebanese-on-Lebanese suicide bombing of civilian targets—a renewed regional and international commitment to support the Lebanese Army appears likely to prevent the country from collapsing further into civil war.*

ISLAMIST ACTIVITY

Established in 1920 by the French mandatory authorities after the collapse of the Ottoman Empire, Lebanon gained full independence in 1943. The new state combined the predominantly Maronite Christian and Druze Mount Lebanon region with the largely Sunni coastal cities of Beirut, Sidon, and Tripoli, as well as the predominantly Shi'a hinterland to the south and east. Under the terms of the 1943 National Pact between Muslim and Christian leaders and subsequent formal and informal adjustments, fixed shares of political power are distributed by sect, with a Maronite Christian as president, a Sunni as prime minister, a Shi'a as speaker of the National Assembly, and other specific offices falling to various smaller sects. Fixed shares of legislative power are divided among the various groups. While Lebanon's sectarian system *(al-nizam al-ta'ifiyya)* provided for a modicum of democracy and political stability in the decades following independence, it also impeded the development of a shared national identity, limited the power of the state, and facilitated intervention by outside parties sharing ethnic, religious, and cultural ties to particular sectarian groups.

The growth of Islamism in Lebanon is partly rooted in the same regional crisis conditions that fueled its growth throughout the Middle East—the humiliating Arab defeat in the 1967 war with Israel, severe political oppression by autocratic governments, poor economic growth, and gross wealth disparities. Shi'a Islamism and Sunni

Islamism both emerged as a challenge to the existing political order and to secular leftist and nationalist ideologies then prevalent in opposition circles. However, they have followed very different trajectories.

Shi'a Islamism

Shi'a Islamism began emerging as a strong socio-political force in Lebanon during the 1970s, under the influence of Lebanese clerics who were radicalized studying in the religious seminaries of Najaf, Iraq (alongside many Iranian students who would play leading roles in their country's 1979 revolution). The most prominent Shi'a leader at the time was Sayyid Musa al-Sadr, the Iranian-born child of a prominent Lebanese family that had produced many religious scholars over the years. Upon settling in Lebanon during the 1960s, Sadr assumed leadership of the state-sanctioned Supreme Islamic Shi'ite Council and created a political movement called the Movement of the Dispossessed, which preached a form of moderate Islamism focused mainly on the pursuit of Shi'ite socio-economic advancement and modest reform of Lebanon's constitution.

With the onset of civil war in 1975 and Sadr's disappearance (and presumed murder) three years later while on a trip to Muammar Qadhafi's Libya, the Sadrist movement was corrupted (and noticeably secularized) by the need to arm itself and accept Syrian patronage, so much so that it has since been popularly known as *Amal*, the Arabic acronym for the name of its wartime militia.

A more revolutionary wave of Islamism centered around Muhammad Hussein Fadlallah, a distinguished Najaf-trained cleric who called on Shi'a to fight not for their own communal advancement but on behalf of all Muslims against Israel. Though Fadlallah himself did not embrace Iranian Ayatollah Ruhollah Khomeini's revolutionary doctrine of *velayat-e faqih* (Guardianship of the Jurisconsult), which forms the basis for Iran's post-1979 Islamic Republic, many younger clerics who followed his guidance did, whether out of genuine conviction or in pursuit of Iranian patronage.

In the early 1980s, Iran saw Lebanon as a vehicle through which to increase its regional influence. Tehran consequently deployed its Iranian Revolutionary Guard Corps (IRGC, or *Pasdaran*) to train and indoctrinate local Shi'a. Syrian President Hafez al-Assad, whose army maintained a considerable troop presence in eastern Lebanon, facilitated the infiltration, as he was eager to prevent Lebanon from falling under the orbit of Israel (which had invaded Lebanon in 1982 to eliminate the threat from Palestinian terrorists dominating southern Lebanon) and the West.

Radical Shi'a fundamentalists from the Beqaa Valley, the south of Lebanon and the Beirut suburb of Dahiyeh flocked to the emerging network, among them a breakaway faction of *Amal* led by Hussein Mussawi. Using aliases such as the Islamic Jihad Organization and the Organization of the Oppressed on Earth, from 1983 to 1985 they carried out a series of deadly suicide bomb attacks against Israeli forces and the Western Multinational Force in Lebanon (MFL) later deployed to assist President

Amine Gemayel in restoring government authority in Beirut. Both had incurred the animosity of most Shi'a and both subsequently withdrew from the capital under the weight of the assault.

In 1985, these disparate underground groups united and issued a manifesto, calling itself Hezbollah (Part of God) and calling for the establishment of an Islamic state in Lebanon.[1] In practice, however, they were concerned first and foremost with advancing more immediate Iranian interests. During the mid-1980s, militants affiliated with Hezbollah kidnapped dozens of Americans and Europeans, allowing Tehran to extract concessions from Western government bargaining for their release. In 1985, they hijacked TWA flight 847. Though the Iranian government denied responsibility, considerable circumstantial evidence pointed to involvement by high-ranking members of the regime in Tehran.[2] Lavish Iranian financing also enabled Hezbollah to build an extensive social welfare network to provide for civilians living in towns and urban neighborhoods under its control.

Under the 1989 Taif Accord that brought most of the Civil War fighting to an end, the Lebanese constitution was amended to equalize Muslim and Christian representation in parliament and transfer most executive authority to the Sunni prime minister. In return for accepting the Taif Accord, Hezbollah was allowed by Damascus to remain armed, unlike other wartime militias, ostensibly for the purpose of "liberating" the border strip in south Lebanon occupied by Israeli forces. Hezbollah also acted as a conduit for Iranian supplies, finance, and training to Palestinian Sunni Islamist groups fighting Israel, notably Hamas and Islamic Jihad.[3]

Hezbollah participated in the electoral process and sent representatives to parliament. In sharp contrast to Sunni Islamists, however, it made only modest efforts to push Islamist socio-political causes in Lebanon and dismissed the viability of an Islamic state,[4] preferring instead a secular appeal for national unity and resistance to oppression that appealed to non-Shi'a. The withdrawal of Israeli troops from Lebanon in 2000 left Hezbollah enormously popular in Lebanon and the broader Arab world. Although Arab leaders bemoaned what Jordan's King Abdullah famously called a "Shi'a crescent" extending from Iran through Iraq and Syria to Lebanon,[5] this kind of sect baiting failed to strike a chord with most Sunnis.

Hezbollah's involvement in the February 2005 car bombing that killed former Lebanese Prime Minister Rafiq Hariri, a Saudi-backed Sunni billionaire widely expected to challenge allies of Syrian-backed President Emile Lahoud in that year's parliamentary elections, marked a major watershed for the group. So pristine was Hezbollah's reputation as a selfless "resistance" movement that even its fiercest critics had not imagined that four of its operatives helped carry out the killing, as alleged (convincingly) in the 2011 indictments released by the Special Tribunal for Lebanon (STL), a special court tasked by the Security Council with prosecuting those responsible for the bombing.[6]

Thereafter, Syria's 2005 withdrawal from Lebanon touched off a struggle for control of the state, with the March 14 coalition of Saad Hariri attempting to leverage strong Western support in effecting Hezbollah's disarmament (see below). Hezbollah's self-proclaimed "divine victory" in the 2006 Israel-Lebanon war appealed broadly to Sunnis in Lebanon and across the Arab world.[7] As recently as March 2008, polling showed Nasrallah to be overwhelmingly the most popular public figure throughout the Arab world. This changed in May 2008, when Hezbollah responded to an attempt by Prime Minister Siniora to close its private telecommunications network by briefly seizing control of predominantly Sunni West Beirut.

Though initially reluctant to get involved in Syria's ongoing civil war, strategic necessity forced Nasrallah's hand. A rebel victory in Syria would cut off Iran's ability to resupply the group with weapons (which are flown to Damascus and driven overland across the Syrian-Lebanese border), leaving it vulnerable to Israeli attack and eventually crippling its capacity to resist the Lebanese Army. When the fortunes of war began turning against the Assad regime in 2012, Hezbollah deployed its forces to help retake territory captured by the rebels and to man defenses in important sites such as the Sayyida Zeinab shrine near Damascus or Shi'a villages east of the Beqaa valley. Importantly, Hezbollah proved vital in the retaking of Qusair, a major point of entry for supplies heading to Syrian rebels.

Hezbollah's engagement is Syria has only deepened since. The group has sent thousands of fighters, who have frequently played a key role on the battlefield, often leading military operations. Hezbollah saw the need to support Syria both to ensure its logistical base, but also out of a recognition that the Islamist violence against the Assad regime would almost certainly strike the Lebanese Shia as well. Current deployments are estimated to be between 6,000 and 8,000 total. Hezbollah's total forces are believed to be 30,000 to 50,000, with about of them half full-time fighters. The other half are believed to be reservists and village guard members.[8]

During the conflict in Syria, Hezbollah's conflict with Israel has, on the whole, been dormant. In January 2015, Israel killed a group of Hezbollah leaders on the Golan Heights. Later that month, Hezbollah fired on IDF troops near the Israeli-Lebanese border, killing two soldiers. But, preoccupied in Syria, Hezbollah has had little energy to confront its primary adversaries. Nonetheless, Israeli strategists are concerned of the potential future effects of Hezbollah's involvement in Syria, since the group has obtained enormous battlefield experience in Syria and has become a mentor to a panoply of Shi'a militias throughout the greater Middle East.[9]

Sunni Islamism

Broadly speaking, Sunni Islamists in Lebanon fall into two categories. The first consists of various offshoots of the Muslim Brotherhood. The second consists of *Salafis*.

Political Islamists

Although Sunni Islamic revivalist movements in Lebanon date back to the 1920s, they were largely focused on renewing religious faith through educational, cultural, and social activities, while operating squarely within the existing political system.

The first Islamic group to directly challenge the country's political order was *al-Jama'a al-Islamiyah* (Islamic Association), the Lebanese chapter of the Muslim Brotherhood. Established in Tripoli in 1964 by Fathi Yakan and Faysal Mawlawi, *al-Jama'a* called for the establishment of an Islamic state through peaceful means.

After the outbreak of the Lebanese Civil War, *al-Jama'a* took up arms alongside the leftist National Movement against the Maronite Christians. Following the entry of Syrian troops into Lebanon in the summer of 1976, Yakan and most other *al-Jama'a* leaders reached an accommodation with the Assad regime, and later with the Iranians. In the early 1980s, *al-Jama'a* founded a new armed force in Sidon, known as *Quwat Fajr* (the Fajr Brigades), to fight against Israeli forces in Lebanon. Yakan's pro-Syrian sympathies went so far that he recommended Lebanon merge with Syria as a solution to its confessional problems.[10]

In contrast, breakaway factions of *al-Jama'a* in the predominantly Sunni northern port of Tripoli, a deeply conservative city home to numerous exiled Syrian Muslim Brotherhood fighters, defied the Syrian occupiers. Most of these merged in 1982 to form *Harakat al-Tawhid al-Islami* (the Islamic Unification Movement). Led by the popular preacher Said Sha'ban, *Tawhid* imposed *sharia* law there and enforced strict Islamic behavior in the city, regardless of sect. Christian women were forced to wear the veil, while liquor stores, clubs, and churches were vandalized or bombed. In the fall of 1985, the Syrian army entered Tripoli and crushed *Tawhid*. Sha'ban and most *Tawhid* commanders reached an accommodation the Syrians; those who didn't were hunted down and killed or imprisoned in Damascus.

Thereafter, *al-Jama'a* and *Tawhid* both operated squarely within the Iranian-Syrian orbit. Though barred from directly fighting the Israelis after the war ended, they embraced Hezbollah's vision of a society of resistance.[11] *Al-Jama'a* supported Lebanon's post-Taif political system and participated in municipal and parliamentary elections, with modest success.

After the withdrawal of Syria forces in 2005, *al-Jama'a* split over political loyalties. Mawlawi and most of its leaders favored the March 14 coalition, while Yakan remained loyal to Syria. After the 2006 war, Yakan resigned and, together with *Tawhid* leaders Hashem Minqara and Bilal Sha'ban (the son of its late founder) and other pro-Syrian Sunni Islamists, formed *Jabhat al-Amal al-Islami* (the Islamic Action Front, IAF). In its founding statement, the IAF described its mission as "an affirmation of Islamic and national unity, protecting the Resistance and defending the unity of Lebanon... confronting sectarian and ethnic strife... and rejecting Western and American threats to Arab and Muslim countries."[12] In contrast, *Al-Jama'a* was rewarded for its allegiance by inclusion in the March 14 electoral coalition for the 2009 elections, which netted the group one seat in parliament. Now led by Ibrahim Masri, it has avoided entanglement in the Syrian Civil War and maintains only a limited armed presence in Lebanon.

IAF factions, on the other hand, have established a significant armed presence in Tripoli, with money and arms provided by Hezbollah. They are closely aligned with the militias of pro-Syrian Sunni clans in Tripoli (especially the Mouri family)[13] and of the small Alawite community in the Jabal Mohsen neighborhood,[14] altogether about 1,500-strong. The Sha'ban wing of *Tawhid* is said to be financed by Iran, while the Minqara wing is closer to Syria.[15]

During the Syrian civil war, the Assad regime's Islamist allies have been linked to a number of attacks against its enemies in north Lebanon. In August 2013, two major *Salafi* mosques in Tripoli that supported Syrian rebels were bombed, killing 48 worshippers. Lebanese investigators linked the bombings to Ahmad Gharib, a key Minqara aide close to Syrian intelligence.[16] At least two IAF-affiliated clerics have been assassinated to date: *Tawhid* preacher Abdul-Razzaq al-Asmar in October 2012, and Saadedine Ghiyyeh, a leading cleric in the IAF, in November 2013.[17]

Al-Ahbash

The Association of Islamic Philanthropic Projects (*Jam'iyyat al-Mashari' al-Khairiyya al-Islamiyya*) is a comparatively moderate Sufi movement long supported by Syria as a counterweight to radical Islamist forces in Lebanon, and very much corrupted in the process. The movement devoutly follows the teachings of its founder Abdallah al-Harari, popularly known as Abdallah al-Habashi.[18] His school of thought emphasizes Islam's pluralistic nature and mixes elements of Sunni and Shi'a theological doctrines with Sufi spiritualism. It opposes the use of violence against the ruling authorities and accepts the legitimacy of many Shi'a and Sufi beliefs typically condemned by Islamists as heresies.[19] During the Syrian occupation, however, the movement adopted thuggish tactics to intimidate opponents.[20] Its influence has sharply diminished since the withdrawal of Syrian forces.

Hizb ut-Tahrir (Party of Liberation)

Hizb ut-Tahrir, a non-denominational Islamist movement founded in Jordan in the early 1950s, has had an active branch in Lebanon since 1959. Although sharing with hardline *Salafis* (see below) the goal of restoring an Islamic caliphate across the Muslim world, it believes this can be achieved through non-violent persuasion, and its activities in Lebanon (and elsewhere in the Arab world) have been largely peaceful and apolitical. Nevertheless, the group's rhetoric is deeply unsettling to many non-Sunni Lebanese and Westerners alike,[21] and members of the group have gone on to become involved in al-Qaeda-linked *jihadist* organizations.[22] Judging from the number of attendees at the party's annual conferences and public demonstrations, *Hizb ut-Tahrir* in Lebanon appears to have several hundred active members.

Traditional Salafis

Salafism is an ultra-orthodox Sunni Islamist current that preaches literal interpretation of the Koran, a return to early Islamic traditions, and the rejection of "innovations" (*bidaa*) that have taken root in the centuries since—particularly those practiced by non-Sunni Muslims and Sufis, who are viewed as heretics. In sharp contrast to the Muslim Brotherhood and its offshoots, *Salafis* have traditionally avoided involvement in politics, focusing instead on missionary work (*da'wa*) to convert Muslim societies to their way of thinking.

Salafism spread rapidly among poor Sunni communities during the 1990s, due in part to the influx of funding from Islamic charities in the Arab Gulf. One of Salem al-Shahal's sons, Dai al-Islam, was the primary recipient of this largesse, notably from the Al-Haramain Islamic Foundation,[23] a Saudi charity later linked to al-Qaeda[24] and closed under American pressure, and Kuwait's *Jama'iyat Ihya' Al-Turath Al-Islami* (Revival of Islamic Heritage Society, RIHS). Dai al-Islam al-Shahal's charity, *Jama'iyat al-Hidaya wa al-Ihsan al-Islami* (Islamic Guidance and Charity Association), funded *Salafi* mosques, schools, and social welfare institutions throughout the country.

Although Shahal does not appear to have explicitly advocated violence during this period, many of the *jihadists* who ran afoul of authorities during the Syrian occupation (see below) were educated and indoctrinated within his circle. These links led RIHS to cut off most funding to Shahal. In 2000, Lebanese authorities closed his charity and arrested many of his followers, forcing Shahal to flee the country for Saudi Arabia. After this, RIHS directed funding to more quietist Lebanese Salafis, notably Safwan al-Zu'bi, Hassan al-Shahal (a cousin of Dai al-Islam), and Saad al-Din al-Kibbi.

Following the withdrawal of Syrian forces from Lebanon in 2005, Dai-Islam al-Shahal returned to Lebanon, as did other notable Islamists. Selim al-Rafei, a Salafi preacher who has eclipsed Shahal in influence, returned to Lebanon for the first time since the fall of Tripoli to Syrian forces in 1985.

The *Salafi* movement became involved in politics following the 2005 Hariri assassination and the subsequent withdrawal of Syrian forces. While *al-Jama'a* boycotted the May/June 2005 parliamentary elections, *Salafi* preachers in Tripoli roundly endorsed Saad Hariri's Future Movement and its allies, which proved critical to their defeat of Michel Aoun's Free Patriotic Movement (FPM) in mixed Sunni-Christian districts of north Lebanon. Now controlling a parliamentary majority, Hariri designated his father's former finance minister, Fouad Siniora, to head the new government.

In the wake of Hezbollah's May 2008 seizure of West Beirut and widespread disillusionment with Saad Hariri,[25] the *Salafi* movement has grown more radical. Abu Bakr al-Shahal (another son of Salem al-Shahal) said that *jihad* is permissible "under the banner of legitimate defense" and that "a reenactment of the May 7 events could certainly prompt a new *jihad*."[26]

By 2013, a number of *Salafi* preachers were calling for Lebanese citizens to go fight in Syria. Echoing the views of his peers, Dai al-Islam al-Shahhal told the BBC that people must "sacrifice money and life" to confront what he described as a Shi'a plan to take over the Middle East. "They will move on to besiege Saudi Arabia and other countries in the Gulf, to control the sacred places and the riches of that region, to rule the Islamic world, if they can, and become a world superpower."[27] The most notable exception to this trend is Imama, who has urged his followers to support the rebels by donating money and sheltering their families, but not by going to fight there.[28] A number of *Salafi* figures have gone further, however, and sent their sons to fight in Syria. Shahhal's son Zayed fought with the rebels, later bragging to the BBC about killing captured Hezbollah fighters.[29]

Salafi-jihadis

While traditional *Salafis* have eschewed violence (with the exception of that aimed at Syria), a more radical *Salafi* current identifying with al-Qaeda's global *jihad* has operated in under-developed and poor Sunni areas there,[30] drawing members from among Lebanese Sunnis, Palestinian refugees, and various Arab expatriates resident in the country. The return home of Arab *mujahideen* who fought the Soviet occupation of Afghanistan (1979-1989) was the critical catalyst for the development of this trend.

The first of these groups, *Isbat al-Ansar* (Band of Partisans), emerged in the Palestinian refugee camp of Ain al-Hilweh near the southern city of Sidon. Led by Muhammad Abd al-Karim al-Saadi (aka Abu Muhjin), *Isbat al-Ansar* initially gained notoriety for carrying out a number of attacks on Christian religious targets and liquor stores. In 1995, members of the group assassinated *Al-Ahbash* leader Nizar al-Halabi. Lebanese authorities publicly executed three members of the group for their participation in the plot. In June 1999, the group took revenge by assassinating three Lebanese judges and the chief prosecutor for southern Lebanon at the Justice Palace in Sidon. Following the 2003 U.S.-led occupation of Iraq, several members of the group took part in the jihad against coalition forces there.[31] The group is estimated to command the loyalty of between 100 and 300 fighters.[32] An offshoot of *Isbat al-Ansar* known as *Jund al-Sham* also operates in the camp.[33] The Palestinian groups in Ain al-Hilweh have continued to clash both within the camps and without. In May 2015, a Hezbollah member was killed in the refugee camp. In the end of 2016 there were clashes between *Isbat al-Ansar* and other Palestinian factions that left several dead. *Hamas* brokered a ceasefire.[34]

In 2006, Shaker al-Absi, a Jordanian-Palestinian best known for organizing the 2002 assassination of U.S. diplomat Lawrence Foley in Amman, infiltrated Lebanon and raised a force of Lebanese, Palestinian, and other Arab fighters who had returned from *jihad* in Iraq. In November of that year, they seized control of the Palestinian Nahr al-Bared refugee camp near Tripoli and declared the establishment of *Fatah al-Islam* (Conquest of Islam). The Lebanese government subsequently linked the group to deadly bus bombings in Ain Alaq that killed three people in February 2007. In May 2007, Lebanese troops stationed outside of Nahr al-Bared were ambushed in retaliation for a police raid against suspects in a bank robbery. The Army laid siege to the camp. The fighting lasted until September and claimed the lives of over 160 Lebanese soldiers.

The Abdullah Azzam Brigades, a *jihadist* terrorist group with branches in Lebanon, Saudi Arabia and Pakistan, has been active since 2009-2010, initially claiming responsibility for sporadic acts of violence against the United Nations Interim Force in Lebanon (UNIFIL) and firing Katyusha rocket attacks into Israel.[35] Since the outbreak of the Syrian Civil War, its operations in Lebanon have focused on Hezbollah and Iranian targets. The group claimed responsibility for the November 2013 double suicide bombing outside the Iranian embassy that left 22 dead and a February 2014 attack on the Iranian Cultural Center in suburban Beirut that killed 11, both ostensibly in retaliation for Iran's support for the Assad regime. Its *emir*, Sirajeddine Zureiqat, has called for open war against Hezbollah inside Lebanon and urged Sunni soldiers to desert the military.[36]

Syria's two leading *Salafi-jihadist* groups, Abu Bakr al-Baghdadi's Islamic State (formerly known as the Islamic State in Iraq and Syria, ISIS) and *Jabhat al-Nusra*, have both built networks of operatives in Lebanon to ferry supplies and men across the border. Two young militia leaders in Tripoli, Shadi al-Mawlawi and Osama Abu Mansour (the nephew and son, respectively, of local *Salafi* preachers) have pledged loyalty to ISIS. Both were indicted by a military judge for their involvement in an August 2014 bombing that wounded 11 people.[37] ISIS also claimed responsibility for an earlier January 2014 bombing that killed four people outside a Hezbollah office in Beirut. The bomber was believed to be the first Lebanese Sunni to carry out a suicide bombing against fellow Lebanese civilians.[38] That same month, *Al-Nusra* claimed responsibility for two suicide bombings in the predominantly Shi'ite border town of Hermel that left eight people dead.[39] In addition, *ISIS* and *al-Nusra* have been recruiting in Lebanon, particularly in the Palestinian and Syrian refugee camps.[40]

As the Syrian Civil War has continued and Hezbollah's involvement has deepened, Syrian *Salafists* have continued to target Hezbollah in its home territory. On September 20, 2014, an *al-Nusra* suicide bomber struck a Hezbollah checkpoint in the Beqaa, killing three along with the bomber. In Tripoli, in Lebanon's Sunni heartland, a pair of suicide bombers struck a café in the predominantly Alawite neighborhood of Jabal Mohsen, killing nine (including the two bombers) and wounding 36, on January 10, 2015. *Al-Nusra* claimed responsibility, calling it retaliation for the August 2013 bombings against Sunni mosques in Tripoli (see above) that were attributed to the Syrian regime, which is predominantly Alawite. Later that month, full-blown fighting broke out between the Lebanese Army and the Islamic State on the Syrian-Lebanese border in the Beqaa Valley.

Lebanon was relatively quiet for the rest of 2015, until November 12, when a pair of suicide bombers struck the predominantly Shi'a neighborhood (and Hezbollah stronghold) of Burj al-Barahneh in Beirut. Over 200 were wounded and forty were killed in the attack. The Islamic State claimed credit, stating that it was undertaken in revenge for Hezbollah's actions in Syria. Although there have been several smaller scale attacks, including a series of suicide bombings in June 2016 targeting a Christian village near the Syrian border that killed five, Lebanon was spared continuing spillover violence from the Syrian Civil War.[41]

Islamism and Society

Shi'a and Sunni Islamist movements in Lebanon, as elsewhere, have been fueled by acute socio-economic, political, and sectarian grievances. But the success or failure of Islamist movements in channeling grievances into action in the Lebanese arena has depended on a range of factors, including availability of outside financing, the strength of secular rivals, and doctrinal flexibility.

The Shi'a

Though Lebanon's Shi'a community had grown to become the country's largest sect by the early 1970s, it was by far the most impoverished and the most politically disenfranchised when the country descended into civil war in 1976. Barred from the nation's two highest political offices and apportioned less than a fifth of parliamentary seats, most Shi'a came to view the confessional system as fundamentally unfair to Muslims in general, and Shi'a in particular.

The 1989 Taif Accord slightly amended this imbalance by modestly expanding the speaker's powers and increasing Shi'a parliamentary representation to 21 percent of the seats. But Sunnis gained the most from the Saudi-brokered accord through a strengthened premiership, and Shi'a arguably gained the least from the Beirut-centered *laissez-faire* post-war economic order,[42] which neglected the agricultural sector in which most Shi'a still worked, invited an influx of unregulated Syrian labor, and spawned systemic corruption. So brazen was the state's failure that former Hezbollah Secretary-General Subji Toufaili broke with his compatriots and launched an ill-fated "revolution of the hungry" in the late 1990s.

State failure made Hezbollah's Shi'a constituency easier to co-opt. With Iran providing around $200 million to the group annually,[43] Hezbollah built an expansive social welfare network to provide the country's Shi'a with education, healthcare, low-interest loans, and myriad other benefits. In a country where it is often impossible to secure government services without paying a bribe, Hezbollah came to be seen by most Shi'a (and many non-Shi'a) as having "clean hands." The fact that most Shi'a continued to support Hezbollah's "resistance" to Israel even after the latter withdrew from Lebanon, and despite having no major territorial disputes with the Jewish state, is a measure of how secure Hezbollah's stature as communal guardian had become.

Hezbollah's political hegemony within the Shi'a community was at its peak when Syrian troops departed Lebanon in 2005, and it remained unshaken throughout the bruising battle with the March 14 forces for control of government. With the dramatic upsurge in Sunni Islamist violence against Shi'a in Iraq, Pakistan and Afghanistan during the mid-2000s, even many secular Shi'a came to think it unwise to surrender their community's one point of leverage when the future was so uncertain. The horrific sectarian violence-taking place in Syria and Iraq today only reinforces the view that Hezbollah was wise to remain armed.

The Sunnis

Tragically, Hezbollah's path to Shi'a empowerment was part and parcel of Syria's brutal subjugation of Lebanon, which in many respects was felt most acutely by Sunnis.

The pre-war years were not a time of prosperity for all Sunnis, the vast majority of whom inhabited one of the country's three largest cities: Beirut, Tripoli, and Sidon. The latter two declined in prosperity relative to Beirut after the establishment of an independent Lebanon severed their trade routes to the Syrian interior.

Moreover, the Sunni community was dominated politically and economically by a handful of powerful families.[44] The latter also unduly influenced the Sunni religious establishment, known as *Dar al-Fatwa*, and its vast network of mosques, schools, and other institutions by manipulating its internal elections.

Efforts by *Al-Jama'a* and various secular Sunni opposition groups to channel growing public resentment of the above into effective political mobilization during the 1960s and 1970s were greatly impeded by demography. Though comprising 25-30 percent of the population, Sunnis are concentrated in three noncontiguous urban centers, with substantial cultural and socio-economic differences among them.[45]

No Sunni political party has ever developed strong public support in all three of these areas. Even when the power of traditional elites was broken during the 1976-1990 civil war, each city fell under the sway of Sunni militias with little or no national reach (e.g. the Murabitoun in Beirut, the Popular Nasserite Organization in Sidon).[46] The Syrian occupation created a new sectarian underclass in Lebanon, this time among Sunni Palestinian and Lebanese constituencies.

Most impoverished are the 350-400,000 Palestinian refugees in Lebanon, primarily Sunnis, who live in squalid, overcrowded camps and are barred by law from owning property and working in many professions.[47] For decades, Lebanese authorities have, with few exceptions, declined to enter the camps, for fear of enflaming sectarian tensions. It is no surprise that the *Salafi-jihadist* current took root there first.

Outside of the camps, the most underprivileged areas are Tripoli and the nearby Akkar region. According to one widely cited study, about 36 percent of the population in the North was living below the poverty line in 2012, more than double the poverty rate in Beirut; more than 20 percent in Mount Lebanon and Nabatieh; about 38 percent in the Beqaa; and 31 percent in the South.[48] Those Sunnis who have risked life and limb fighting the Assad regime in Syria or punishing its supporters in Lebanon come disproportionately from such poor urban neighborhoods and underdeveloped rural areas.

But the proliferation of *Salafi* networks in recent years masks extraordinary divisions. Sunni Islam lacks the rigid hierarchies linking followers to the clerical establishment that are prevalent in Shi'ism, a major factor accounting for Hezbollah's internal cohesion and public legitimation. In fact, *Salafis* loathe organizational hierarchies, viewing them as "innovations" (*bidaa*) that encourage loyalty to the group, rather than to God. "Almost without exception, *Salafi* groups lack sophisticated organizational strategies," notes scholar Zoltan Pall. "Members are connected to each other through informal networks, and there is no clear, formal hierarchy between them."[49]

The result is that *Salafi* organizations tend to work at cross-purposes. Some want to convert other Sunnis to their austere doctrines, while others focus their attention on discrediting Shi'ism and other heterodox beliefs. Among the activist (*haraki*) wing of the *jihadists*, some think that focusing on the conflict in Syria is the right path, while others want to shake up the system in Lebanon. The former are themselves divided over how to help the rebels (e.g. whether to actively recruit Lebanese volunteers), the latter over whether the Army or just Hezbollah is the enemy.

This same phenomenon was often evident among *Salafi-jihadist* groups sharing similar aspirations during the 2000s. *Isbat al-Ansar*, for example, handed over to the Army a Dinniyeh Group fugitive who fled into Ain al-Hilweh in July 2002 and openly disavowed the 2007 *Fatah al-Islam* uprising (*Jund al-Sham* expressed support for the latter, but did not join in). *Tawhid*, though not properly *Salafi*, succumbed in Tripoli during the mid-1980s in part due to the failure of local "emirs" to consolidate their forces.

Even if Islamist groups in Tripoli were to unite under one banner, it's unlikely that they could build a substantial base of popular support in north Lebanon, let alone in Beirut and the south. "Few Sunnis of any other class or region would join their ranks or accept their leadership," notes scholar Yezid Sayigh.[50]

ISLAMISM AND THE STATE

Although nearly all Islamist movements in Lebanon advocate the abolition of the state's confessional system in principle, in practice they have all accommodated it in one way or another. However, Shi'a and Sunni Islamist movements have had very different experiences interacting with the Lebanese state.

Hezbollah's fortuitous choice of patrons during the 1975-1990 Civil War translated into effective immunity from government interference for the next fifteen years. Year after year of continuous hostilities against Israeli forces in south Lebanon transformed its wartime militia units into an elite fighting force stronger in nearly every respect than the national army. Syrian vetting of appointments to the military-security apparatus ensured that it enjoyed cooperative relations with Hezbollah.

Hezbollah was obliged by the Syrians to maintain rough parity with *Amal* in parliamentary representation, civil service appointments, and other political spoils and pointedly did not join any of the coalition governments that ruled from 1990 to 2005. However, this bolstered Hezbollah's image as rising above partisanship for the good of the nation.

Hezbollah has not found it difficult to preserve these prerogatives since the withdrawal of Syrian forces in 2005. Its electoral clout alone was sufficient to fend off most challenges to its sprawling paramilitary apparatus. Recognizing that Shi'a votes would likely decide the outcome of the 2005 legislative elections in several important mixed districts, both the Aounists and Saad Hariri's Future Movement gave Nasrallah assurances that they would not seek Hezbollah's disarmament.

Under the Lebanese constitution, a "one-third-plus-one" or "blocking" minority of seats in the cabinet and parliament is sufficient to veto decisions by the majority (either by not showing up to vote or resigning, preventing the necessary two-thirds quorum). Hezbollah's effective monopolization of Shi'a representation in parliament (since the Syrian withdrawal, *Amal* deputies are squarely subordinate to Nasrallah) and its durable alliance with the FPM and assorted pro-Syrian groups is more than sufficient to veto the formation of any government. This leverage which enables it to demand a blocking cabinet minority up front.

Moreover, the parliamentary and cabinet representation of Hezbollah and its allies enabled them to prevent the Siniora administration from reforming the security apparatus; the Army and military intelligence are still dominated by personnel who rose through their ranks during the Syrian occupation. Hariri and his allies took over (and still hold) key posts in the Internal Security Force (ISF), especially its intelligence branch.[51] Reclaiming these assets is a high priority for Hezbollah leaders.

Hezbollah's May 2008 seizure of West Beirut was necessary only because shifting alliances had left it without a blocking minority in the cabinet—an unusual circumstance that is unlikely to repeat itself now that post-occupation alignments have solidified. Druze leader Walid Jumblatt and his parliamentary bloc gravitated away from March 14 after this, leaving neither Hezbollah nor Nasrallah with reliable majority support in parliament.

In sharp contrast to Hezbollah, Sunni Islamist groups have not come anywhere near exerting decisive influence over the state. Distrusted by both the Syrians and Sunni political elites, and lacking a state sponsor committed to their empowerment, they had little opportunity during the Syrian occupation to gain representation in government or substantially influence its policies.

Since the outbreak of the Syrian civil war, Lebanon's chronic political deadlock has gotten steadily worse. In January 2011, the Hezbollah-led March 8 coalition pulled its ministers out of government when Prime Minister Hariri refused to disavow the "special tribunal" ahead of its expected indictment of Hezbollah operatives. Hariri was replaced by Najib Miqati, a wealthy Sunni businessman friendly to Hezbollah. In March 2013, Hezbollah forced Miqati's resignation to prevent the extension of the term of Major General Ashra Rifi, a close Hariri ally, as head of the ISF.[52]

Lebanon was without a functioning government from March 2013 to February 2014 because the opposing sides could not agree on the composition of Prime Minister-designate Tammam Salam's cabinet. Unable to agree on an electoral law, lawmakers postponed the 2013 legislative elections until 2014 and then postponed them again. They are currently set for May 2017.[53] Although President Michel Suleiman's term in office came to an end in May 2014, because the Lebanese factions could not agree on his successor, Michel Aoun was only chosen as president in late 2016.[54]

The shocking regional advances of ISIS in 2013 and 2014 led to a strong regional and international consensus in favor of bolstering the Lebanese security forces. American and European states have increased aid and provided unprecedented intelligence cooperation with Lebanese security agencies.[55] In December 2013, Saudi Arabia pledged to give the Lebanese Army $3 billion over five years.[56] But Saudi Arabia has become concerned about increasingly close relations between the Lebanese government and Hezbollah (and its Iranian masters). When Lebanon did not condemn an Iranian mob sacking the Saudi Embassy in Tehran in January 2016, the Saudis froze payments.[57]

In late 2013, the Army deployed in force in Tripoli to halt the three-year old intermittent clashes in the city between fighters in the Sunni Bab al-Tabbaneh neighborhood and the adjacent, predominantly Alawi Jabal Mohsen neighborhood. The city was declared a "military zone," making all security personnel subordinate to the Army.[58] Scores of combatants were arrested.

In February 2014, Hariri addressed his followers by video link on the ninth anniversary of his father's death and vowed to "confront incitement and dubious calls to drag Lebanese, particularly the Sunnis, into crazy wars with no use other than to pull Lebanon into a sectarian holocaust."[59] Along with the long awaited formation of a new government, this gave the Army the political cover it needed to crack down more forcefully in April, when it arrested the heads of warring militias on both sides for the first time.

Notwithstanding the shocking seizure of Arsal by *Nusra* and ISIS in August 2014, expanded Army operations in the north appear to have averted the kind of worst-case scenarios many feared were on the horizon a year earlier. While the suicide bombings in Lebanese cities have been devastating, so far the country has avoided becoming a full-scale battleground in the multi-pronged war in Syria. But despite the appointment of a government in late 2016, Lebanon has been locked into a chronic political stalemate that has undercut any hope of implementing the kinds of political and economic reforms that will undercut its appeal in the long term.

Endnotes

[1] See the text of the open letter by Hezbollah to the oppressed in Lebanon and the world of February 16, 1985, as reprinted in Joseph Alagha, The Shifts in Hizbullah's Ideology: Religious Ideology, Political Ideology, and Political Program (Amsterdam: Amsterdam University Press, 2006), 223-238.

[2] For more on this episode, see Augustus Richard Norton, "Walking between Raindrops: Hizballah in Lebanon," Mediterranean Politics 3, no. 1 (Summer 1998), and Magnus Ranstorp, Hizb'allah in Lebanon: The Politics of the Western Hostage Crisis (New York: St. Martin's Press, 1997).

[3] Gary C. Gambill, "Islamist Groups in Lebanon," Middle East Review of International Affairs 11, no. 4, December 2007.

[4] "We believe the requirement for an Islamic state is to have an overwhelming popular desire, and we're not talking about fifty percent plus one, but a large majority. And this is not available in Lebanon and probably never will be," said Nasrallah in 2004. As cited in Adam Shatz, "In Search of Hezbollah," New York Review of Books, April 29, 2004.

[5] See Ian Black, "Fear of a Shia full moon," Guardian (London), January 26, 2007.

[6] "U.N. court indicts Hezbollah members in 2005 assassination in Lebanon," Washington Post, August 17, 2011.

[7] University of Maryland, "2008 Annual Arab Public Opinion Poll," April 2008, https://www.brookings.edu/wp-content/uploads/2012/04/0414_middle_east_telhami.pdf

[8] Nadav Pollack, "The Transformation of Hezbollah by Its Involvement in Syria," Washington Institute for Near East Policy Research Notes no. 35, August 2016, http://www.washingtoninstitute.org/uploads/Documents/pubs/ResearchNote35-Pollak-2.pdf

[9] Ibid.

[10] Fathi Yakan, al-Masa'la al-Lubnaniyah min Manthur Islami [The Lebanese Question from an Islamic Perspective] (Beirut: Mu'assassat al-Risalah, 1979), 126-128.

[11] For ideological and political details on Fathi Yakan, see Robert G. Rabil, Religion, National Identity, and Confessional Politics in Lebanon: The Challenge of Islamism (New York: Palgrave Macmillan, 2011).

[12] For details on the founding of the Islamic Action Front, including a list of its members, see "Tashkil Jabhat al-Amal al-Islami" (Forming of the Islamic Action Front), al-Mustaqbal (Beirut), August 3, 2006.

[13] "The curious case of the Mouri family," Nowlebanon (Beirut), March 8, 2012. https://now.mmedia.me/lb/en/reportsfeatures/the_curious_case_of_the_mouri_family

[14] Raphaël Lefèvre, "Tripoli's Fragmented Sunni Islamists," Carnegie Endowment for International Peace, March 13, 2014, http://carnegieendowment.org/syriaincrisis/?fa=54920.

[15] "Behind the scenes in Tripoli," Nowlebanon, September 10, 2008, https://now.mmedia.me/lb/en/commentaryanalysis/behind_the_scenes_in_tripoli

[16] "Pro-Assad sheikh detained over Tripoli blasts," Daily Star (Beirut), August 30, 2013.

[17] "Tripoli Sheikh Shot Down Inciting Peace," Al-Akhbar, October 23, 2012. http://english.al-akhbar.com/node/13080; "Lebanon: Assassination of pro-Hezbollah sheikh pushes Tripoli to the brink," Asharq al-Awsat (London), November 13, 2013, http://www.aawsat.net/2013/11/article55322284.

[18] Habashi literally means "the Abyssinian." Harari migrated to Beirut from Ethiopia in the 1950s and became a lecturer at al-Azhar University's Lebanese campus.

[19] A. Nizar Hamzeh and R. Hrair Dekmejian, "A Sufi Response to Political Islamism," International Journal of Middle East Studies 28 (1996), 217-229.

[20] See Daniel Nassif, "Al-Ahbash," Middle East Intelligence Bulletin 3, no. 4, April 2001, http://www.meforum.org/meib/articles/0104_ld1.htm.

[21] At the party's annual conference in 2009, its leader, Sheikh Adnan Mizyan, proclaimed that, "In light of the fact that many countries of Muslims are today under occupation, including Palestine, Iraq, Cyprus, the Balkans, the Caucasus, Afghanistan, and Kashmir, the Islamic Ummah must take Jihad measures in order to free them." As quoted in "Speaker at Hizb al-Tahrir Conference in Lebanon Calls for Jihad in Cyprus, Balkans, Caucasus," as-Safir (Beirut), July 20, 2009, http://www.thememriblog.org/blog_personal/en/18360.htm.

[22] In 2005, Lebanese authorities indicted members of the group in absentia for their role in planning terror attacks in Iraq. See "Khamsat Kawader fi Hizb al-Tahrir al-Islami Yuhadirun li-Hajamat fi al-Iraq bil-Tansiq Ma'a Isbat al-Ansar" [Five Cadres from Hizb al-Tahrir Plan in Coordination with Isbat al-Ansar Attacks in Iraq], al-Mustaqbal (Beirut), August 27, 2005.

[23] Zoltan Pall, Salafism in Lebanon: Local and Transnational Resources, Ph.D dissertation, Utrecht University, January 14, 2014, 117, http://dspace.library.uu.nl/handle/1874/289260.

[24] U.S. Department of the Treasury, "U.S.-Based Branch of Al Haramain Foundation Linked to Terror: Treasury Designates U.S. Branch, Director," September 9, 2004, http://www.treasury.gov/press-center/press-releases/Pages/js1895.aspx.

[25] "We have been insulted by what Hizbullah did in Beirut, but much more by what Al-Hariri did not do," said Hassan al-Shahal. "He has done nothing to defend ahl al-Sunna [the Sunnis]." As cited in Omayma Abdel-Latif, "Alliance in question," Al-Ahram Weekly (Cairo), June 12-18, 2008, http://weekly.ahram.org.eg/2008/901/re1.htm.

[26] Mona Alami, "Radical Islam Comes to Town" Inter Press Service, July 14, 2008, http://www.ipsnews.net/2008/07/lebanon-radical-islam-comes-to-town/

[27] "Lebanese families drawn into Syrian conflict," BBC, June 18, 2013, http://www.bbc.com/news/world-middle-east-22938132.

[28] Nada, "Lebanon's Sheikhs Take on Assad and Hezbollah."

[29] "Lebanese families," BBC.

[30] Fida' 'Itani, Al-Jihadiyun fi Lubnan: Min Quwat Fajr ila Fath al-Islam [The Jihadists in Lebanon: From Fajr Brigades to Fath al-Islam] (Beirut: Dar al-Saqi, 2008); See also Bilal Y. Saab and Magnus Ranstorp, "Securing Lebanon from the Threat of Salafist Jihadism," Studies in Conflict and Terrorism 30 (2007).

[31] See Thair Abbas, "Al-Qaeda in Lebanon," Asharq al-Awsat (London), March 19, 2006.

[32] U.S. Department of State, Office of the Coordinator for Counterterrorism, Country Reports on Terrorism 2009 (Washington, DC: U.S. Department of State, August 2010), 244.

[33] Adnan Abu Amer, "Hamas working to lower tensions in Lebanese camps," Al-Monitor, June 15, 2015, http://www.al-monitor.com/pulse/originals/2015/06/palestinian-refugee-camps-lebanon-hamas-tension.html

[34] Mohammad Zaatar, "Palestinian factions announce cease-fire in south Lebanon camp," The Daily Star, December 22, 2016, http://www.dailystar.com.lb/News/Lebanon-News/2016/Dec-22/386357-tensions-mar-south-lebanon-camp.ashx

[35] Ali Hashem, "Al Qaeda-affiliated emir arrested in Lebanon," Al-Monitor, January 1, 2014, http://www.al-monitor.com/pulse/originals/2013/12/abdullah-azzam-emir-custody-hashem.html

[36] "Abdullah Azzam Brigades urges attacks against Hezbollah, not the Army," Daily Star (Beirut), October 13, 2014. https://www.dailystar.com.lb/News/Lebanon-News/2014/Oct-13/273917-abdullah-azzam-brigades-urges-attacks-against-hezbollah-not-the-army.ashx

[37] "Tripoli's terror duo: Mawlawi and Mansour," Daily Star (Beirut), October 3, 2014, http://www.dailystar.com.lb/News/Lebanon-News/2014/Oct-03/272834-tripolis-terror-duo-mawlawi-and-mansour.ashx

[38] "The Syria effect: Lebanese Sunnis begin to strap on bombs," Christian Science Monitor, January 7, 2014.

[39] Bill Roggio, "Al Nusrah Front launches another suicide attack in Lebanon," Long War Journal, February 2, 2014, http://www.longwarjournal.org/archives/2014/02/al_nusrah_front_laun_2.php

[40] Mark Townsend, "Isis paying smugglers' fees in recruitment drive among child refugees," The Guardian, February 4, 2017, https://www.theguardian.com/world/2017/feb/05/isis-recruitment-drive-child-refugees

[41] National Consortium for the Study of Terrorism and Responses to Terrorism (START). (2016). Global Terrorism Database [Data file]. Retrieved from https://www.start.umd.edu/gtd.

[42] Gary C. Gambill, "Lebanese Farmers and the Syrian Occupation," Middle East Intelligence Bulletin, October 2003, http://www.meforum.org/meib/articles/0310_l1.htm.

[43] See Matthew Levitt, Hezbollah: The Global Footprint of Lebanon's Party of God (Washington, DC: Georgetown University Press, 2013).

[44] Four prominent Sunni families (Solh, Karameh, Yafi, and Salam) held the post of prime minister in forty of the fifty-three cabinets that served from 1943 to 1982. Samir Khalaf, Lebanon's Predicament (New York: Columbia University Press, 1987), 106.

[45] The World Factbook 2013-14. (Washington, DC: Central Intelligence Agency, 2013),https://www.cia.gov/library/publications/the-world-factbook/index.html

[46] Yezid Sayigh, "Shadow War, Not Civil War, in Lebanon," Al-Hayat, December 12, 2013, http://carnegie-mec.org/2013/12/12/shadow-war-not-civil-war-in-lebanon/gw09.

[47] See Are Knudsen, "The Law, the Loss and the Lives of Palestinian Refugees in Lebanon," Chr. Michelson Institute, Bergen, Norway (2007), https://www.cmi.no/publications/2607-the-law-the-loss-and-the-lives-of-palestinian

[48] "Snapshot of Poverty and Labor Market Outcomes in Lebanon based on Household Budget Survey 2011/2012," Central Administration for Statistics and World Bank, May 25, 2016, http://documents.worldbank.org/curated/en/279901468191356701/pdf/102819-REVISED-PUBLIC-Snapshot-of-Poverty-and-Labor-Market-in-Lebanon-10.pdf.

[49] Pall, Salafism in Lebanon: Local and Transnational Resources, 39.

[50] Sayigh, "Shadow War, Not Civil War, in Lebanon."

[51] Bilal Y. Saab, "Why Lebanon's Najib Mikati Resigned," Foreign Affairs, March 25, 2013, https://www.foreignaffairs.com/articles/lebanon/2013-03-25/why-lebanons-najib-mikati-resigned

[52] Ahmad K. Majidyar, "Is Deepening Shi'ite-Sunni Tension Plunging Lebanon into a New Civil War?" American Enterprise Institute, March 6, 2014, https://www.aei.org/publication/is-deepening-shiite-sunni-tension-plunging-lebanon-into-a-new-civil-war/

[53] "Interior Minister launches preparations for 2017 parliamentary elections," The Daily Star, January 19, 2017, http://www.dailystar.com.lb/News/Lebanon-News/2017/Jan-19/390140-interior-minister-launches-preparations-for-2017-parliamentary-elections.ashx

[54] Thanassis Cambanis, "Michel Aoun Rises to Lebanese Presidency, Ending Power Vacuum," The New York Times, October 31, 2016, https://www.nytimes.com/2016/11/01/world/middleeast/michel-aoun-lebanon-president.html?rref=collection%2Ftimestopic%2FLebanon&action=click&contentCollection=world&region=stream&module=stream_unit&version=latest&contentPlacement=8&pgtype=collection

[55] Nicholas Noe, "The Islamic State effect: Lebanon's new security symbiosis," European Council on Foreign Relations (ECFR), August 28, 2014, http://www.ecfr.eu/article/commentary_the_islamic_state_effect_lebanons_new_security_symbiosis302

[56] "Saudis Pledge $3 Billion to Support Lebanon's Army," Wall Street Journal, December 28, 2013.

[57] Ben Hubbard, "Saudis Cut Off Funding for Military Aid to Lebanon," The New York Times, February 19, 2016, https://www.nytimes.com/2016/02/20/world/middleeast/saudis-cut-off-funding-for-military-aid-to-lebanon.html?_r=1

[58] Militias battle anew in Lebanon's Tripoli, army arrests 21 fighters," Reuters, December 3, 2013; Raphaël Lefèvre, "The Roots of Crisis in Northern Lebanon," Carnegie Middle East Center, April 2014, 20, http://carnegieendowment.org/files/crisis_northern_lebanon.pdf.

[59] "Lebanon's Hariri vows to confront Sunni radicals," Reuters, February 15 2014, http://www.reuters.com/article/us-lebanon-hariri-idUSBRE-A1E06P20140215

LIBYA

> **QUICK FACTS**
>
> Population: 6,541,948 (July 2015 est.)
>
> Area: 1,759,540 sq km
>
> Ethnic Groups: Berber and Arab 97%, other 3% (includes Greeks, Maltese, Italians, Egyptians, Pakistanis, Turks, Indians, and Tunisians)
>
> Religions: Muslim (official; virtually all Sunni) 96.6%, Christian 2.7%
>
> Government Type: In transition
>
> GDP (official exchange rate): $39.39 billion (2015 est.)
>
> *Map and Quick Facts courtesy of the CIA World Factbook (January 2017)*

OVERVIEW

Since the ouster of longtime dictator Muammar Qaddafi in 2011, small contingents of local jihadists, militias, renegade generals, and secular forces have been battling for control of Libya. On the whole, Libyans have rejected extreme ideologies. In the country's 2014 parliamentary elections, a coalition of moderate parties emerged victorious while the Libyan Muslim Brotherhood had a poor showing compared to its brethren in Egypt and Tunisia. Further, candidates from the Libyan Islamic Fighting Group (LIFG), which took part in the election, did not garner any popular support. It is likely, though, that as public debate—which was completely snuffed out by Qaddafi's repressive policies—opens further in Libya, Islamists will have an opportunity to gain more of a following. Several jihadist groups, including Ansar al-Sharia in Libya *(ASL) and the Islamic State in Iraq and Syria (ISIS/ISIL) have contributed to the violence and instability in Libya, as the country's civil war continues. Despite a U.S. air campaign and the successes of pro-government militias, these Islamist groups remain formidable destabilizing forces in the country.*

ISLAMIST ACTIVITY

Libya declared itself a constitutional monarchy under King Idris in 1951, after it won its independence from Italy in the aftermath of World War II. In September 1969, Colonel Muammar al-Qaddafi staged a military *coup d'état,* after which he established an Arab nationalist regime that adhered to an ideology of "Islamic socialism." Before long, Qaddafi's authoritarian regime began to generate resentment among Islamist groups, leading to an Islamist revival beginning in the late 1970s. Yet the Qaddafi regime also supported terrorist activities abroad that included the downing of two airliners and a discotheque bombing in Berlin.

When the Arab Spring began in several Middle Eastern and North African countries in late 2010 (reaching Libyan cities in 2011), Qaddafi responded with a brutal crackdown on protesters. The response from the populace ignited a fierce civil war that lasted until mid-2011, when the Qaddafi regime was toppled. The resulting power vacuum invited chronic instability as various groups, both Islamist and secular, vied for power and influence, with no single group able to exert full control. In the interim, Libya's government struggled to maintain order and rebuild state institutions, witnessing a rise in the presence and power of militias and other non-state actors.

In February 2014, retired General Khalifa Haftar, a former Qaddafi loyalist, began "Operation Dignity" with a sizable military force, attacking Islamist militant groups and targeting terrorists. To counter Haftar's movement, an alliance of Islamist militias launched "Operation Dawn" in August 2014, seizing the Tripoli airport and other parts of the capital. Since then, outside actors such as the United Arab Emirates have thrown their support behind Haftar in the form of airstrikes.

The Muslim Brotherhood

The origins of the Muslim Brotherhood date back to Egypt in the 1920s, but the organization would not make its first appearance in Libya until 1949, when a number of its members fled political persecution in Cairo and were granted refuge in Benghazi by King Idris.[1] The Libyan Muslim Brotherhood (LMB) thus began as a branch of the original Egyptian organization. The LMB was founded by Egyptian cleric Ezadine Ibrahim Mustafa and several other refugees. Under King Idris, the group and its leaders were allowed relative freedom to spread their ideology. The LMB attracted local adherents and continued to gain support via other Egyptian leaders working in Libya.

This changed when Colonel Muammar Qaddafi came to power in 1969. Viewing the Brotherhood as a potential source of opposition, Qaddafi promptly arrested a number of the Brothers and repatriated them back to Egypt.[2] The crackdown continued until 1973, when members of the Libyan Muslim Brotherhood were arrested by security services and, under torture, agreed to dissolve the organization -- effectively silencing themselves for the remainder of the 1970s.

However, in the early 1980s, the Brotherhood (which by then had renamed itself the "Libyan Islamic Group" or *al-Jama'a al-Islamiya al-Libiyya*) revived its aspirations to replace the existing secular regime with sharia law through peaceful means. Once again, it began accumulating popular support, including from Libyan students who returned from the UK and U.S. after making contact with LMB members who had fled earlier repression. Through these contacts, the new generation was exposed to a plethora of Islamist ideas. The students took an active role in helping to spread the Brotherhood's ideology, joining the movement's covertly operated groups of interlinked cells active throughout the country.[3]

The group drew much of its popular appeal through the charitable and welfare work of its members. These programs were particularly successful at attracting members of Libya's middle class to join the LMB. The group's programs were particularly strong in the eastern area of Benghazi, where the main tribes had traditionally opposed Qaddafi's rule.[4] The regime, however, continued to take an uncompromising stance toward the LMB, persecuting most of its members, and publicly executing some. By the mid-1980s, the majority of LMB members who remained in Libya were either imprisoned or executed.[5]

The Libyan Muslim Brotherhood returned to the scene in 1999 through dialogue with the Qaddafi regime. The talks gained momentum in 2005-2006 when Muammar Qaddafi's son, Sayf al-Islam, personally worked to advance the dialogue in an effort to co-opt and neutralize opposition groups. These efforts focused in particular on Islamist groups, such as the Brotherhood. By the eve of the Libyan uprising in the spring of 2011, it was estimated that the Libyan Muslim Brotherhood had roughly one thousand members within Libya, and two hundred more in exile.[6]

The Libyan Muslim Brotherhood has lost popularity in recent years. This decline first manifested itself after a poor showing in the 2012 parliamentary elections that followed Qaddafi's ouster, which is especially noteworthy considering the political success of its counterparts in Egypt and Tunisia during the same timeframe.[7] The setbacks suffered by the Egyptian Muslim Brotherhood after its electoral success, including the deposing of the Brotherhood-backed president, Mohamed Morsi, in 2013, seems to have encouraged rather than placated anti-Brotherhood activists in Libya. The downward trend continued in the 2014 parliamentary elections, with the Muslim Brotherhood only able to secure 25 of the 200 available seats in the country's legislature.[8] The outright rejection of the movement might be seen as part of the legacy of Qaddafi's opposition to, and demonization of, the party. In some cases, resentment toward the Brotherhood stems from perceptions that it is inherently antidemocratic, or due to associations between the Brotherhood and more radical groups like al-Qaeda or *Ansar al-Sharia*.[9]

Tablighi Jama'at

The number of *Tablighi* supporters in Libya today is relatively small, and there is only one known *Tablighi* center in the country.[10] The *Tablighi Jama'at*, however, distanced itself from politics after many of the organization's members were arrested in the 1980s, and were subsequently co-opted by the regime.[11] However, *Tablighi Jama'at* is pursuing active *dawa* (proselytization) campaigns in Libya, which receive significant communal support. In a lecture hosted on *Tablighi Jama'at's* official website, Muhammad Jihani, also known as Sheikh Jihani, gave a short lecture, posted in June of 2016, in which he described traveling to Libya. He claimed that all Libyans knew of *Tablighi Jama'at's* efforts at *dawa* in the United Kingdom, and that the minister of religion invited Jihani to his ministry, and offered Jihani any and all help that he might need.[12]

The Libyan Islamic Fighting Group

The roots of the Libyan Islamic Fighting Group can be found in an underground *jihadi* movement formed in 1982 by Iwad al-Zawawi. However, the LIFG did not officially announce its formation until 1995.[13] Unlike the Muslim Brotherhood, the LIFG advocated for military operations against the regime, seeking to overthrow Qaddafi and plotting attacks against other senior figures in the government. After failed attempts to overthrow the regime in 1986, 1987, and 1989, authorities arrested many of its rebels, including al-Zawawi himself.[14] Many of those who were not captured fled to Afghanistan and Pakistan.

Many LIFG members seized the opportunity to fight the Soviets in Afghanistan during the 1980s. There, they and other Libyans set up their own military training camps. At times, LIFG members received instruction from members of al-Qaeda.[15] In addition to military training, the Libyan recruits were indoctrinated by influential *jihadi* clerics such as Abdullah Azzam.[16] While in exile in Pakistan and Afghanistan, the movement began to form into an identifiable organization.

Following the anti-Soviet Afghan *jihad*, Libyan LIFG members either returned home to establish cells, moved to Sudan to establish a base of operations to plan the overthrow of the Qaddafi regime, or moved to London to obtain logistical and financial support. Contrary to popular belief, however, the LIFG's interlude in Sudan was not predicated on the plans of Osama bin Laden and al-Qaeda. According to Noman Benotman, a senior leader and member of the group's *shura* council, the LIFG staked out Sudan as a potential base following the Afghan *jihad* in 1988-1989, deciding it was appropriate to move closer to the Libyan front in 1993.[17] It was from Sudan that they sent delegations to Algeria to continue training.

Under the leadership of Commander Abu Abdullah al-Sadek, the LIFG worked to establish its structure and develop the leadership skills of cell leaders throughout the country.[18] LIFG leaders were forced to accelerate their plan in 1995 due to poor operational security. When members of the LIFG extracted one of their comrades from a hospital in Benghazi, Libyan security became aware of the operation and quickly moved to suppress the group. As a result, the LIFG was compelled to officially announce itself for the first time in October 1995.[19]

After the incident at the hospital, the Qaddafi regime asked, and eventually convinced, the Sudanese regime to eject the LIFG from Sudan. As a result, many LIFG members returned to Libya, while others escaped to London. Once the LIFG was exposed, the group sprang into action and throughout the 1990s conducted military operations against the Libyan regime, including several failed attempts to assassinate Qaddafi himself. The Libyan regime fought relentlessly against the LIFG, killing Salah Fathi bin Sulayman (a.k.a. Abu 'Abd al-Rahman al-Khattab), one of the group's founding fathers, in a battle with Libyan soldiers near Darnah in September 1997.[20]

By 1998, the LIFG's insurgency and terrorist campaign within Libya had, by all measurable standards, come to a halt. However, the group did not declare an official ceasefire until 2000.[21] Following the campaign, many members were imprisoned in Libya. Many of those who escaped returned to Afghanistan. Among those who fled were the LIFG's *emir*, Abu 'Abd Allah al-Sadiq, chief religious official Abu al-Mundhir al-Sa'idi, and Abu Anas al-Libi, who had been recently implicated in the 1998 Embassy bombings.[22]

By 2005, the Libyan regime began a reconciliation and de-radicalization process at the prompting of Qaddafi's son, Sayf al-Islam.[23] After years of negotiations, in September 2009 LIFG leaders in Libya released a new "code" for *jihad* in the form of a 417-page religious document titled "Corrective Studies."[24] The new code viewed the armed struggle against Qaddafi's regime as illegal under Islamic law, and set down new guidelines for when and how *jihad* should be fought. However, it also stated that *jihad* would be permissible if Muslim lands were invaded, citing Afghanistan, Iraq and the Palestinian Territories as examples.[25] Many leaders and members of the LIFG were eventually released from prison in March 2010.[26] However, others such as Abd al-Wahab Qa'id were not released until after the uprising against the Qaddafi regime began in March 2011.[27]

The LIFG went on to play a prominent role in challenging the Qaddafi regime during the events of Arab Spring. Following the overthrow of Qaddafi, many leaders and members have created political parties and have opted to participate in the new Libyan political system. Furthermore, LIFG has shifted its efforts toward providing social services and youth activities. In an attempt to change the group's image, the LIFG even changed its name to the Libyan Islamic Movement for Change.

Ansar al-Sharia in Libya

When the LIFG ended its military operations and joined the political process in the post-Qaddafi era, new jihadi groups began to emerge in its absence. Most prominent among these has been *Katibat Ansar al-Sharia* in Benghazi (ASB), which first announced itself in February 2012.[28] The organization is led by Muhammad al-Zahawi, a former inmate of Qaddafi's infamous Abu Salim prison, who remains the primary suspect in the 2012 attack on the U.S. consulate in Benghazi.[29] ASB has since changed its name to *Ansar al-Sharia in Libya* (ASL) - a move that signifies its desire to be perceived as a national movement, rather than a rebel fighting force.[30]

ASL should not be confused with *Ansar al-Sharia in Derna* (ASD), despite some crossover in membership and political goals. ASD operates under the leadership of former Guantanamo Bay inmate Abu Sufyan bin Qumu, and, as the name suggests, is based out of Derna.[31] ASD also shares the similar objective of establishing sharia law in Libya. However, there are no known direct ties between the two *Ansar al-Sharia* organizations.[32]

ASL has been able to expand in size and popularity through its violent *da'wa* campaign at home and abroad.[33] ASL has also involved itself in the training of *jihadis*, preparing them to conflicts in Syria, Mali, and North Africa as foreign fighters.[34] This has further cemented ASL's role as a cog in the facilitation and logistics network within the global *jihadi* movement. However, ASL's most successful method to advance its agenda has been through the provision of social services.[35]

ASL has provided local services similar to those historically provided by other Islamist organizations, such as the Muslim Brotherhood in Egypt, including infrastructure repair and development projects, the provision of security, and general aid.[36] One of the group's most successful projects has been its anti-drug campaign, which was orchestrated in cooperation with the Rehab Clinic at the Psychiatric Hospital of Benghazi, the Ahli Club (soccer team) the Libya Company (telecom and technology company) and the Technical Company.[37]

In late November 2014, the UN placed both ASB and ASD on its blacklist, adding them to the list of terror organizations associated with al-Qaeda. This designation targets the groups for arms embargos, global travel bans, and asset freezes.[38]

ASL has known ties to several smaller *Salafi-jihadi katibas* (battalions) in Libya, including *Katibat Abu 'Ubaydah al-Jarah and Saraya Raf Allah al-Sahati*. Many of these *katibas*, among others, participated in ASL's first "annual conference" held on June 6, 2012.[39] Based on photos from the event, as many as a thousand individuals attended. At that time, it was believed that ASL had only a few hundred members.[40] ASL has made use of the chaos and instability in Libya to strengthen its presence in Libyan communities, including optimizing its social service and community activity as *dawa*.[41]

When retired Libyan Army General Khalifa Haftar initiated his self-declared "Operation Dignity" in May 2014, ASL became one of the key targets of his campaign.[42] Although General Haftar has made progress toward his goal of expelling Islamist forces from Benghazi, the Operation's successes have come at a great cost. In response to "Operation Dignity," ASL launched a violent counteroffensive that killed scores of civilians, as well as soldiers fighting under General Haftar.[43] In fact, the group has made headlines throughout the duration of the Operation. On July 24, 2014, ASL overran Camp 319 and 36th Battalion bases in Benghazi, seizing howitzers, a 2K12 Kub mobile air defense system, Strela-2 MANPADs, ammunition, and military vehicles.[44] Days later, on July 30, ASL declared the city of Benghazi an "Islamic Emirate."[45] Although General Haftar openly declared victory against the Islamist militants in November 2016, ASL remains active in various Benghazi communities.[46]

Islamic State (ISIS/ISIL)

The Islamic State's aspirations for a Libyan province began in 2013, when Abu Bakr al-Baghdadi deployed an emissary to the eastern city of Derna to examine to possibility of expanding the organization's global reach.[47] Derna has been particularly hospitable to Islamist militants for at least a decade, and ISIS leadership understood that establishing ties to the city could provide a necessary fallback option if the group were to be pushed out of the Levant.[48] Shortly after the Islamic State declared the establishment of its Caliphate in Iraq and Syria, affiliates of the organization began to appear in different countries. By late 2014, Libyan militias and ideologues with ties to Iraq and Syria began pledging their allegiance to the Islamic State, seeking legitimacy through affiliation with the group's brutal brand of Islamism.[49] The establishment of Islamic State provinces in Libya, in turn, provided the terrorist group with a space where it could operate without the burden of government intervention, while taking advantage the country's strategic proximity to Europe.

Derna was among the group's most important strongholds, as demonstrated by al-Baghdadi's decision to deploy senior leadership from Iraq and Syria to oversee the new affiliate's activities. The Islamic State was simultaneously developing outposts elsewhere in Libya, including Sirte and Sabratha, alongside various neighborhoods seized in Benghazi.

It is difficult to evaluate the size of the Islamic State's forces in Libya, and assessments vary significantly in their estimates. In February 2015, United States Africa Command (AFRICOM) One estimate put the Islamic State in Libya's forces at 1,000 to 3,000 in Libya as of February 2015.[50] Nonetheless, the Islamic State's Libyan affiliate appears to maintain a much smaller fighting force than its counterpart in Iraq and Syria.[51] In June 2016, the National Bureau of Economic Research estimated that approximately 30,000 fighters have joined the Islamic State in Iraq and Syria. The number of native fighters in the group is currently unknown.

In May 2014, French Special Forces assisted General Khalifa Haftar in his self-initiated "Operation Dignity," driving the Islamic State from its posts in Benghazi. At the same time, American airstrikes supported an offensive that eradicated the Islamic State's foothold in Sabratha. These operations greatly diminished the group's presence in Libya, leaving Sirte as the Islamic State's primary stronghold, apart from other small towns nearby.

The Libya affiliate also embraced the gruesome nature of ISIS propaganda. For example, an April 2015 video portrayed the executions of Egyptian Coptic Christians who were abducted by the group, as well as African migrants bound for Europe. (Libya has served as a key stopping-point for migrants, who would eventually cross the Mediterranean via boats and rafts.) The 29-minute video showed a dozen Egyptian men in orange jumpsuits kneeling on a beach, with the Mediterranean in the background. ISIS fighters beheaded the men, and the video showed their blood spilling into the water. The video's second execution scene was filmed in the Libyan desert, with ISIS executioners shooting another 16 prisoners.[52]

The video was heavily scrutinized by experts, with some claiming that it had been altered[53]—raising speculation about the presence of a green screen during the filming process, something that would indicate an advanced propaganda machine, paralleling the propaganda of the Islamic State in Syria.

The Islamic State's extreme ideology and brutal methods, however, were largely unpopular with other *jihadi* organizations in Derna, provoking a violent backlash from these groups. In June 2015, various Derna-based *jihadists* launched an anti-ISIS campaign in coordination with the *Shura Council of Mujahideen in Derna*, another *Islamist* militia. This successful operation ultimately forced the Islamic State to withdraw from Derna in a move that was a major setback to the group's aspirations.[54]

Despite these territorial losses, however, the Libyan branch of ISIS remains a potent threat. In June 2016, then-CIA Director John Brennan told the Senate Select Committee on Intelligence that ISIS' Libya affiliate was the group's most dangerous and developed branch.[55] In his remarks, Brennan warned that the group's influence in Africa posed a significant risk, and that it was capable of staging attacks throughout the region, as well as Europe.

Experts estimate that ISIS has maintained approximately 3,000 fighters in Sirte, although U.S. intelligence reports claimed that, as of late last year, 6,000 fighters occupied the city.[56] In 2016, the group suffered significant territorial losses, with pro-government militias successfully seizing ISIS-held territories within the city of Sirte.[57] These losses were compounded by U.S. aerial operations, which continued through early 2017 and resulted in significant loss of life among ISIS fighters.[58] Nevertheless, this affiliate remains a major threat to Libya's national security.

ISLAMISM AND SOCIETY

Libya has over six and a half million citizens, roughly ninety-seven percent of whom are Sunni Muslim. The remaining three percent includes a mix of Christians, Buddhists, Hindus, and Jews.[59] The dominant school of Sunni thought in Libya is the Maliki school, often considered the most moderate of the four traditional schools of Islamic jurisprudence.[60] Non-Sunni Muslims in Libya are primarily native Ibadi Muslims or foreigners from other countries.

For the majority of Libyans, Islam permeates everyday life. In all public schools, alongside the private schools that admit citizens, religious instruction in Islam is compulsory. *Sharia* governs family matters such as inheritance, divorce, and the right to own property.[61]

The dominant role that Islam plays in Libyan society is highlighted by its legal authority as the official state religion, as dictated by the country's interim constitution. *Sharia* law provides the principal source of legislation. However, the constitution offers protections for non-Muslims, who are granted the freedom to practice their own beliefs. Some laws that were enacted during the Qaddafi regime, such as those restricting religious freedom, remain in place, although they are rarely enforced.[62]

The Qaddafi regime was staunchly opposed to Islamism, although the ideology traditionally found few followers inside Libya. However, following Qaddafi's ouster in 2011, Libyans responded enthusiastically to Islamist political parties because they promoted a sense of identity and pledged to maintain order.[63] On the other hand, while Libyans continue to grasp for a political identity, many remain skeptical of Islamist extremism.[64] Nonetheless, almost six years have passed since Qaddafi was removed from power, and the failed political transition has emboldened various Islamist factions and militias.

In the absence of strong political and social institutions, many Islamic organizations have filled the void by providing valuable social and governmental services. By providing services such as health care, youth activity planning, and religious organization, groups like ASL and the LIFG have gradually moved away from their image as global *jihadi* organizations, and gained favorability with domestic populations.

ISLAMISM AND THE STATE

When Qaddafi took power in 1969, he implemented a new political system, entitled the *Jamahiriyah*, meaning the "state of the masses." Under this system, he engaged in a series of repressive reforms that outlawed political parties and refused to tolerate any organized political dissent.[65]

Nevertheless, the Muslim Brotherhood began to organize in the 1980s with a plan to change the existing regime, albeit via peaceful means. When great socio-economic problems struck Libya in the 1990s, however, the Muslim Brotherhood opted for a more violent path to promote its platform. By 1998, the Qaddafi regime had overcome the Islamic opposition within the country and by the early 2000s, it only small pockets of *jihadist* resistance remained.[66]

After 2005, Qaddafi's son and political advisor, Sayf al Islam, entered negotiations with Islamists to free those imprisoned under the Qaddafi regime in exchange for the recognition of the legitimacy of the government, the renunciation of violence, and formal revisions of their Islamist doctrines. As a result of these negotiations, more than one hundred members of the Muslim Brotherhood were released in 2006, as well as hundreds of members of the Libyan Islamic Fighting Group by 2008.[67]

When Arab Spring reached Libya in February 2011, the country plunged into civil war. The war ended later that year when Qaddafi's regime was toppled with the assistance of Western airstrikes and the former dictator was assassinated. After Qaddafi's death, the country began a turbulent transition to democracy. Parliamentary elections were held in 2012 in which the LMB-affiliated Justice and Construction Party (JCP) and the National Forces Alliance ran in opposition to one another.[68]

At the time, Mohammed Sawan led the JCP, overseeing electoral victories in 17 of 80 seats available to parties within the 200-seat parliament.[69] Meanwhile, the National Forces Alliance won 39 of the 80 seats. To the JCP's dismay, the party did not achieve the same electoral successes as Egypt's Freedom and Justice Party, the JCP's model and inspiration.

Also following Qaddafi's fall, the LIFG split into two political factions - the *Hizb al-Watan* (HW) and *Hizb al-Umma al-Wasat* (HUW) - both of which took part in the legislative elections in 2012. The HW ran as a broad-based moderate party while the HUW ran as a more conservative Islamic party. The HUW claimed the rest of the LIFG members, and operated under the leadership of Sami al-Sa'adi.[70] To their dismay, the HW did not win any seats in the election, while HUW garnered just one seat. The HUW's lone seat was allocated to Abdul Wahhab al-Qa'id, brother of the late Abu Yahya al-Libi, a senior al-Qaeda figure. Other small Islamist parties also failed to make a political showing. The *Salafi* party *al-Asala* failed to win a single seat while the *Hizb al-Islah wa-l-Tanmiyya*, led by former member of the Muslim Brotherhood Khaled al-Werchefani, similarly garnered very little support.

Libya's legislative elections in June 2014 showed improved support for Islamist parties, with 30 of the 80 parliamentary seats available going to Islamist factions or candidates. However, due to political hostilities between secular forces and Islamist militants, the results of the election proved highly contentious.[71]

In May 2014, retired general Khalifa Haftar began "Operation Dignity," a campaign to drive Islamist militants out of Benghazi and eastern Libya.[72] The Operation has been somewhat controversial within the Libyan community, and several senior military officers have refused to enter the campaign.[73] The House of Representatives (HoR) made Haftar the commander of its armed forces in March 2015.[74] Haftar's force, the Libyan National Army (LNA), is a combination of military units, armed regional factions, and tribal groups, and "is not recognized as a proper army by all military personnel across the east or west of Libya."[75] The LNA maintains varying levels of control in central and eastern Libya.[76]

As of early 2017, Libya has three centers of power, two based in Tripoli, and one based in Tobruk and al-Bayda. The most recent is the United Nations-backed Presidential Council (PC), which has been based in Tripoli since March 30, 2016.[77] The PC oversees the Government of National Accord (GNA), which is meant to be the unity government that brings together the warring HoR and the Government of National Salvation, the alternative government proposed by the General National Congress (GNC). The United Nation's peace plan provided that the HoR would become the legislative branch to the GNA's executive branch, while the GNC would become a State Council that would advise the HoR. However, the HoR has twice refused to ratify the agreement, and the GNC has backed away from its original promise to comply with the plan.[78] Elections were meant to be held within six months of the initial agreement in March 2016, then postponed repeatedly.[79] The HoR has called for elections in February 2018.[80] Whether the UN-backed unity government will endure remains to be seen.

Endnotes

[1] Omar Ashour, "Libyan Islamists Unpacked: Rise, Transformation, and Future," Brookings Institution Policy Briefing, May 2012, http://www.brookings.edu/~/media/research/files/papers/2012/5/02%20libya%20ashour/omar%20ashour%20policy%20briefing%20english.pdf.

[2] Allison Pargeter, "Political Islam in Libya," Jamestown Foundation Terrorism Monitor 3, iss. 6, May 5, 2005, http://www.jamestown.org/single/?no_cache=1&tx_ttnews[tt_news]=306

[3] Ibid.

[4] Ibidem.

[5] Omar Ashour, "Libya's Muslim Brotherhood faces the future," Foreign Policy, March 9, 2012, http://mideast.foreignpolicy.com/posts/2012/03/09/libya_s_muslim_brotherhood_faces_the_future.

[6] Ibid.

[7] Aaron Y. Zelin, "Jihadism's Foothold in Libya," Washington Institute for Near East Policy PolicyWatch no. 1980, September 12, 2012, http://www.washingtoninstitute.org/policy-analysis/view/jihadisms-foothold-in-libya.

[8] Cameron Glenn, "Libya's Islamists: Who They Are - And What They Want." Wilson Center, August 27, 2015, https://www.wilsoncenter.org/libyas-islamists-who-they-are-and-what-they-want.

[9] Mary Fitzgerald, "Libya's Muslim Brotherhood Struggles to Grow," Foreign Policy, May 1, 2014, http://www.foreignpolicy.com/articles/2014/05/01/the_rise_of_libyas_muslim_brotherhood_justice_and_construction_party.

[10] The facility is part of a comprehensive list of Tabligh facilities worldwide that is available at http://adressmarkazjemaahtabligh.blogspot.com.

[11] Pargeter, "Political Islam in Libya."

[12] Sheikh Jihani, "Dawah—The Life Blood," The Hanafi Fiqh Channel, September 16, 2016, http://www.tablighijamaat.org/dawah-the-life-blood-sheikh-jihani-libya/.

[13] Ibid.

[14] Camille Tawil, Brothers in Arms: The Story of al-Qa'ida and the Arab Jihadists (London: Saqi Books, 2010), 33.

[15] Evan F. Kohlmann, "Dossier: Libyan Islamic Fighting Group," NEFA Foundation, October 2007, 3, http://www.nefafoundation.org/miscellaneous/nefalifg1007.pdf.
[16] Ibid., 4.
[17] Tawil, Brothers in Arms, 93-94.
[18] Kohlmann, "Dossier: Libyan Islamic Fighting Group," 8.
[19] Tawil, Brothers in Arms, 65.
[20] Kohlmann, "Dossier: Libyan Islamic Fighting Group," 8-11.
[21] Tawil, Brothers in Arms, 140.
[22] Ibid., 179.
[23] Omar Ashour, "Post-Jihadism: Libya and the Global Transformations of Armed Islamist Movements," Studies in Conflict and Terrorism 23, iss. 3, 2011, 384.
[24] Ibid., 385. According to Ashour, there were a few bumps in the road: "the six leaders in Abu Selim Prison wanted the decision to be unanimous so as to maximize the impact on the middle-ranks, the grassroots, and the sympathizers, and thus guarantee successful organizational de-radicalization. They thus demanded the involvement of the LIFG leaders abroad in the dialogue with the regime. Those leaders included two Shura Council members (Abu Layth al-Libi and 'Urwa al-Libi) and two influential members of the LIFG's legitimate (theological) committee: Abu Yahya al-Libi, currently believed to be the third person in al-Qaida, and Abdullah Sa'id, who was killed in December 2009 by a U.S. drone strike in Pakistan. All four rejected the offer."
[25] Ibidem, 388.
[26] Ibidem, 384.
[27] David D. Kirkpatrick, "Political Islam and the Fate of Two Libyan Brothers," New York Times, October 6, 2012, http://www.nytimes.com/2012/10/07/world/africa/political-islam-and-the-fate-of-two-libyan-brothers.html?pagewanted=all.
[28] Aaron Y. Zelin, "Know Your Ansar al-Sharia," Foreign Policy, September 21, 2012, http://www.washingtoninstitute.org/policy-analysis/view/know-your-ansar-al-sharia.
[29] Mary Fitzgerald, "It Wasn't Us," Foreign Policy, September 18, 2012, http://www.foreignpolicy.com/articles/2012/09/18/it_wasn_t_us.
[30] Aaron Y. Zelin, "Libya Beyond Benghazi," Journal of International Security Affairs no. 25, Fall/Winter 2013, http://www.securityaffairs.org/sites/default/files/issues/archives/fw2013covertocover_small.pdf.
[31] Zelin, "Know Your Ansar al-Sharia."
[32] Zelin, "Libya Beyond Benghazi."
[33] Ibid.

[34] Aaron Y. Zelin, Testimony before the House of Representatives Committee on Foreign Affairs, Subcommittee on Terrorism, Nonproliferation, and Trade and Subcommittee the Middle East and North Africa, July 10, 2013, https://www.washingtoninstitute.org/uploads/Documents/testimony/ZelinTestimony20130710-v2.pdf

[35] Zelin, "Libya Beyond Benghazi."

[36] Zelin, "Know Your Ansar al-Sharia."

[37] Zelin, "Libya Beyond Benghazi."

[38] "U.N. Blacklists Libya's Ansar al-Sharia, Involved in Benghazi Attack," Reuters, November 19, 2014, http://www.reuters.com/article/2014/11/19/us-libya-security-un-idUSKCN0J32KX20141119

[39] The others that were at the conference included, the Islamic Foundation for Da'wa and Islah, The Supreme Commission for the Protection of Revolution of February 17, Liwa Dara' Libya, Katibat Shuhada Libya al-Hurrah, Katibat Faruq (Misrata), Katibat Thuwar Sirte, Katibat Shuhada al-Khalij al-Nawfaliya, Katibat Ansar al-Huriyya, Katibat Shuhada al-Qawarsha, Katibat al-Shahid Muhammad al-Hami, Katibat al-Jabal, Katibat al-Nur, Katibat Shuhada Abu Salim, Katibat Shuhada Benghazi, the Preventative Security Apparatus, Katibat al-Shahid Salih al-Nas, and other brigades from Darnah, Sabratha, Janzur, and Ajdabiya. Pictures of the conference can be accessed at https://www.facebook.com/media/set/?set=a.373188266078865.86838.156312127766481&type=1

[40] Zelin, "Know Your Ansar al-Sharia."

[41] Aaron Zelin, "Libya's jihadists beyond Benghazi," Foreign Policy, August 12, 2013, http://foreignpolicy.com/2013/08/12/libyas-jihadists-beyond-benghazi/.

[42] "Profile: Libya's military strongman Khalifa Haftar." BBC, September 15, 2016, http://www.bbc.com/news/world-africa-27492354.

[43] "Ansar al-Sharia in Libya (ASL)," Counter Extremism Project, n.d., https://www.counterextremism.com/threat/ansar-al-sharia-libya-asl.

[44] Ibid.

[45] Ibidem.

[46] "Haftar forces claim 'great victory' in Libya's Benghazi," Alaraby, November 18, 2016, https://www.alaraby.co.uk/english/news/2016/11/18/haftar-forces-claim-great-victory-in-libyas-benghazi.

[47] Geoff D. Porter, "How Realistic Is Libya as an Islamic State "Fallback"?" Combating Terrorism Center at West Point, March 16, 2016, https://www.ctc.usma.edu/posts/how-realistic-is-libya-as-an-islamic-state-fallback.

[48] Ibid.

[49] Tarek Kahlaoui, "The rise of ISIS in Libya, explained," Newsweek, May 29, 2016, http://www.newsweek.com/understanding-rise-islamic-state-isis-libya-437931

[50] Kate Brannen, Keith Johnson, "The Islamic State of Libya Isn't Much of a State," Foreign Policy, February 17, 2015, http://foreignpolicy.com/2015/02/17/the-islamic-state-of-libya-isnt-much-of-a-state/.

[51] Les Picker, "Where are ISIS's Foreign Fighters Coming From?" The National Bureau of Economic Research, June 2016, http://www.nber.org/digest/jun16/w22190.html.

[52] David D. Kirkpatrick and Rukhmini Callimachi. "Islamic State Video Shows Beheadings of Egyptian Christians in Libya," New York Times, February 15, 2015, https://www.nytimes.com/2015/02/16/world/middleeast/islamic-state-video-beheadings-of-21-egyptian-christians.html?_r=0.

[53] Malia Zimmerman, "ISIS' army of 7-footers? Experts say video of Copt beheadings manipulated," Fox News, February 21, 2015, http://www.foxnews.com/world/2015/02/21/isis-army-7-footers-experts-say-video-copt-beheadings-manipulated.html.

[54] Porter, "How Realistic Is Libya as an Islamic State "Fallback"?"

[55] John Brennan, Statement before the Senate Select Committee on Intelligence, June 16, 2016, https://www.cia.gov/news-information/speeches-testimony/2016-speeches-testimony/statement-by-director-brennan-as-prepared-for-delivery-before-ssci.html

[56] Patrick Wintour, "Isis loses control of Libyan city of Sirte." Guardian (London). December 5, 2016, https://www.theguardian.com/world/2016/dec/05/isis-loses-control-of-libyan-city-of-sirte.

[57] Patrick Wintour, "Isis loses control of Libyan city of Sirte." Guardian (London). December 5, 2016, https://www.theguardian.com/world/2016/dec/05/isis-loses-control-of-libyan-city-of-sirte.

[58] Patrick Wintour, "Isis loses control of Libyan city of Sirte." Guardian (London). December 5, 2016, https://www.theguardian.com/world/2016/dec/05/isis-loses-control-of-libyan-city-of-sirte.

[59] U.S. Department of State, Bureau of Democracy, Human Rights and Labor, International Religious Freedom Report for 2013, n.d., http://www.state.gov/j/drl/rls/irf/religiousfreedom/index.htm?year=2013&dlid=222303#sthash.IH9pgQVJ.dpuf. "Libya," Central Intelligence Agency World Factbook, January 12, 2017, https://www.cia.gov/library/publications/the-world-factbook/geos/ly.html

[60] Manal Omar, "The Islamists are Coming," Woodrow Wilson International Center for Scholars, n.d., http://www.wilsoncenter.org/islamists/libya-rebuilding-scratch

[61] U.S. Department of State, International Religious Freedom Report for 2013.

[62] Ibid.

[63] Omar, "The Islamists are Coming."

[64] Mohamed Eljarh, "In Post-Qaddafi Libya, It's Stay Silent or Die," Foreign Policy, September 24, 2014, http://transitions.foreignpolicy.com/posts/2014/09/24/in_post_qaddafi_libya_its_stay_silent_or_die

[65] Pargeter, "Political Islam in Libya."

[66] Ibid.

[67] Manal Omar, "Libya: Rebuilding From Scratch," Woodrow Wilson International Center for Scholars, n.d., https://www.wilsoncenter.org/libya-rebuilding-scratch.

[68] Ashour, "Libya's Muslim Brotherhood faces the future."

[69] Mary Fitzgerald, "A Current of Faith," Foreign Policy, July 6, 2012, http://www.foreignpolicy.com/articles/2012/07/06/a_current_of_faith.

[70] Camille Tawil, "Tripoli's Islamist Militia Leader Turns to Politics in the New Libya," Jamestown Foundation Terrorism Monitor 10, iss. 11, June 1, 2012, http://www.jamestown.org/single/?no_cache=1&tx_ttnews%5Btt_news%5D=39450.

[71] "Libya Publishes Parliamentary Election Results," The Journal of Turkish Weekly, July 22, 2014, http://www.turkishweekly.net/news/169449/-libya-publishes-parliamentary-election-results.html.

[72] "Profile: Libya's military strongman Khalifa Haftar," BBC, September 15, 2016, http://www.bbc.com/news/world-africa-27492354.

[73] Mary Fitzgerald, A Quick Guide to Libya's Main Players: Armed Groups, Council on Foreign Relations, December 2016, http://www.ecfr.eu/mena/mapping_libya_conflict#.

[74] "Profile: Libya's military strongman Khalifa Haftar," BBC, September 15, 2016, http://www.bbc.com/news/world-africa-27492354.

[75] Mary Fitzgerald, A Quick Guide to Libya's Main Players: Armed Groups, Council on Foreign Relations, December 2016, http://www.ecfr.eu/mena/mapping_libya_conflict#.

[76] Ibid.

[77] Ibidem.

[78] John Pike, "Libya - Politics." Global Security, October 17, 2016. http://www.globalsecurity.org/military/world/libya/politics.htm.

[79] Ibid.

[80] "HoR calls for presidential and parliamentary elections in Libya in early 2018," Libyan Express, March 9, 2017, http://www.libyanexpress.com/hor-calls-for-presidential-and-parliamentary-elections-in-libya-in-early-2018/.

Morocco

Quick Facts

Population: Morocco: 33,655,786 (July 2016 est., CIA World Factbook); Morocco and Western Sahara: 34,242,806.

Area: 446,550 sq km; Morocco and Western Sahara: 712,550

Ethnic Groups: Arab-Berber 99%, other 1%

Religions: Muslim 99%, Christian 1%, Jewish about 6,000

Government Type: Parliamentary constitutional monarchy

GDP (official exchange rate): $103.1 billion (2015 est.)

Map and Quick Facts courtesy of the CIA World Factbook (December 2016)

Overview

Unlike many other Arab and majority-Muslim states, Morocco has integrated Islamist political movements that oppose violence and support the constitutional order into its political process, while relentlessly prosecuting adherents to Salafist *and other extremist ideologies. Not surprisingly, the U.S. State Department's most recent report on global terrorism trends went out of its way to laud the country's "comprehensive counter-terrorism strategy that includes vigilant security measures, regional and international cooperation, and counter-radicalization policies."[1] While the reformist course charted by King Mohammed VI has enabled Moroccans to avoid both the revolutionary tumult and violent repression which have characterized their neighbors' attempts to come to terms with the so-called Arab Spring, the North African kingdom nevertheless has been subjected to jihadist attacks and still confronts an Islamist movement that openly calls for the overthrow of the monarchy and creation of an Islamic state, as well as an Algerian-backed separatist group that, while previously secular, has increasingly been linked to al-Qaeda's regional affili-*

ate. Thus, it remains to be seen whether the "Moroccan exception" is ultimately sustainable and, if so, what implications this might have for the region and the wider Arab and Muslim world.

ISLAMIST ACTIVITY

A number of Islamist groups and movements, either indigenous or foreign, are currently active in Morocco. Unlike in many other Arab or majority-Muslim nations, however, Islamism in Morocco is quite fragmented.

Ash-Shabiba al-Islamiyya ("Islamic Youth")

Founded in 1969, the Association of Islamic Youth (*Shabiba*, sometimes known by the French acronym AJI) was the first organization in the Maghreb region established with the explicit objective of advancing Islamist politics.[2] The group also opposed the political leftism then in vogue in many Arab countries. Led by Abdelkarim Mouti, a former education ministry inspector, the group attracted support among university and high school students for whom it ran vacation camps where they received training in propaganda and protest techniques. *Shabiba* also cultivated ties with clandestine Algerian organizations in the early 1970s.

Mouti fled into exile in 1975 following the murder of two prominent leftist political figures, journalist and Socialist Union of the Forces of Progress (USFP) party official Omar Benjelloun and Party for Progress and Socialism (PPS) secretariat member Abderrahim Meniaoui, which authorities blamed on Shabiba. The investigation of the assassinations revealed that *Shabiba* had built up a secretive military arm, the *al-Mujahidun al-Maghariba* ("Moroccan Holy Warriors"), which was headed by a onetime law student named Abdelaziz Naamani. Sentenced to death *in abstentia*, Mouti spent time in both Saudi Arabia and Libya, but settled in Belgium where he continued to agitate against the Moroccan government, for a while publishing a small magazine, *Al-Mujahid* ("The Holy Warrior") and garnering a few followers among the immigrant communities in Europe.

Meanwhile, back in Morocco, following the discovery in 1985 of arms caches near the Algerian border and the subsequent arrest, trial, and conviction of more than two dozen militants, including a number who admitted to *Shabiba* membership, authorities set in motion a crackdown that, for all intents and purposes, shut down the group.

Al-Islah wa't-Tajdid ("Reform and Renewal") / At-Tawhid wa'l-Islah ("Unity and Reform")

The Movement for Reform and Renewal was created in 1992 by former *Shabiba* members who came to reject the group's embrace of violence and sought instead for a way to advance their objectives within Morocco's existing political system; in 1996, they changed the organization's name to the Association for Unity and Reform (at-Tawhid).[3] While King Hassan II tolerated *at-Tawhid*, he did not accord it legal recognition. Consequently, Abdelilah Benkirane and other *at-Tawhid* leaders negotiated an arrangement with a longstanding, but minor, political party, the Democratic Constitutional Movement, that enabled them to participate in elections under the aegis of the latter. The merger took place in 1997, and the new political party changed its name the following year to the Justice and Development Party (generally known by its French acronym, PJD).[4] (A full description of PJD follows below)

Al-Adl Wal-Ihsan ("Justice and Charity")

The Justice and Charity Organization (*al-Adl*, or JCO), formed in 1988, has been the most virulent Islamist political and religious movement in Morocco. Considered illegitimate and barely tolerated by the Moroccan government, JCO has gained adherents through its role as the sole indigenous Islamist movement challenging the king's political and religious roles and through its extensive social and charitable organizational network. The Moroccan government refuses to recognize JCO as a political party.[5]

JCO advocates a restoration of Islamic law (*sharia*), but asserts allegiance to democratic principles in order to differentiate itself as a political movement that opposes what it considers to be Morocco's authoritarian political system. Since the 1970s, its leader and founder, Sheikh Abdessalam Yassine, has openly challenged the legitimacy of the Moroccan monarchy. For that stance, he was tried in 1984 and sentenced to house arrest—a sentence that remained in force until 1989.[6] The following year, JCO was officially outlawed pursuant to a ban that would endure until modified by the current king, Mohammed VI, in 2004. Sheikh Yassine's daughter, Nadia Yassine, increasing emerged as movement's chief political organizational leader as her father slipped into his dotage (he died in 2012).

Openly critical of the monarchy and in almost constant conflict with the Moroccan government, JCO is committed to the dissolution of the country's current constitutional system and its replacement by an Islamic republic. Nevertheless, at least publicly JCO has renounced the use of violence and armed struggle, relying instead on protests and occasional civil disobedience to advance its goals. The scope of support for JCO is a closely guarded secret, both by the organization itself and by the Moroccan government, although some observers consider its support substantial given its extensive charitable and social network.[7]

Given the Moroccan government's intense opposition to JCO internally, the group's leadership decided to export their movement to Europe, beginning roughly in 1996, through the creation of the Muslim Participation and Spirituality (MPS) Association.[8] MPS has established chapters in various European cities, headed by JCO Islamist activists who have fled Morocco. The goal of MPS is to generate opposition to Morocco's king and government through political activities with the goal of winning legal status for the JCO inside Morocco.⁹ The French and Belgian MPS branches often organize demonstrations against Morocco. Nadia Yassine also visits Europe regularly to denounce the repression of JCO, and, in 2006, she created the "New Europe-Morocco Friendship"—an association based in Belgium which convened a conference on the theme "Human Rights Flouted in Morocco."¹⁰

The Party of Justice and Development (PJD)

In order to co-opt Islamist movements in Morocco, King Hassan II permitted the emergence of new political movements that incorporated Islamist orientations—the most significant being the Justice and Development Party (PJD), which draws on Islamic values and inspiration from Turkey's Justice and Development Party (AKP), although there is no official connection between the two.

As previously discussed, the Islamist-inspired *at-Tawhid* entered a decline and fused with the Constitutional Democratic Popular Movement, emerging as the PJD. The merged group brought together a coalition of small, moderate Islamist organizations, including conservative Islamist pro-monarchial political figures. In contrast to JCO, the PJD is a political party that has competed in Morocco's parliamentary elections since 1997. In the following elections, in 2002, the PJD emerged as the country's leading opposition party, winning 42 of the 325 seats in Morocco's parliament, making it the third-largest group in the national legislature. In the subsequent poll, in 2007, the PJD won the largest percentage of popular vote (10.9 percent on the local and 13.4 percent on the national lists) garnered by any single party.¹¹

Unlike JCO, the PJD is non-revolutionary and does call for the overthrow of the monarchy, and, consequently, does not directly challenge Morocco's constitutional system. Nor does it advocate the creation of an Islamist state, or caliphate, in Morocco. Indeed, PJD intentionally downplays any religious agenda. Nevertheless, it views itself as the guardian of Morocco's Muslim identity and conservative religious traditions, and opposes any effort that would compromise Morocco's Islamic character. Thus it opposes further westernization of Moroccan society, but it pragmatically recognizes the importance of Morocco's ties to the West. The PJD also regards itself as a bulwark against radical Islamic groups such as JCO.

Since 1997, the PJD has gradually gained popular support throughout Morocco, and has become quite entrenched in Morocco's political process—balancing its participation in legislative affairs with its adherence to an Islamic political agenda. PJD legislators have won plaudits for focusing their attention on ameliorating Morocco's significant social and economic challenges—of course, once they became the governing party (see below), their failure to deliver to deliver on those promises also led to a resurgence of other parties to whom dissatisfied voters turned. Nevertheless, during its period in opposition, the party's ability to influence actual policy is limited, with only marginal ability to translate its agenda into meaningful programs that would obtain greater popular support.

The PJD's agenda in parliament has occasionally taken it into pure *sharia* territory—calling for prohibition against alcohol distribution and consumption, and challenging media that it views as defacing Islamic principles. On other occasions, however, PJD has trended in the opposite direction. In 2004 for example, the party actively participated in the adoption of a new, more liberal version of the country's code regulating marriage and family life, known as the *Moudawana*.[12] The revision of the *Moudawana* greatly improved the social status of women in Morocco, and was ridiculed by more conservative Islamists. PJD's leader at the time, Saad Eddine el-Othmani, defended his party's approval of the code's revision, asserting in 2006 that it had been approved by religious leaders, aided families, and was consistent with Islamic traditions.[13]

In the November 25, 2011 elections—the first held under the new constitution proposed by King Mohammed VI and approved by plebiscite earlier that year—the PJD won 27.1 percent of the vote and came away with 107 seats, making it by far the single largest party in the new legislature. Since the new charter stipulates that the monarch should appoint the prime minister from the largest party in parliament, the mandate to form a government was given to the PJD's Benkirane, who formed a coalition government with support from the venerable conservative nationalist Independence Party (*Istiqlal*) and two left-leaning parties. The new government was sworn in on January 3, 2012, with the PJD holding eleven of thirty ministerial portfolios.[14]

Five years later, in the October 7, 2016 parliamentary elections, the PJD again emerged as the largest single party in parliament, with 125 seats, after winning a slightly higher proportion of the overall vote at 27.88 percent. However, widespread dissatisfaction with the PJD's management of the government also manifested itself in an even stronger rally behind the Party of Authenticity and Modernity (PAM) which surged from a fourth-place finish in the previous election to second place with 20.95 percent of the vote and thus winning 102 seats in the legislature (up from the 47 it had). As of the end of 2016, the PJD had yet to be able to garner enough parliamentary support from other parties to form a new coalition government.[15]

Salafist Jihadism

Morocco has "numerous small 'grassroots' extremist groups"[16] that collectively adhere to *Salafi-jihadi* ideology. Indeed, Spanish anti-terror judge Baltazar Garzon has stated that "Morocco is the worst terrorist threat to Europe."[17] He estimated that al-Qaeda-linked cells in Morocco number more than 100 and that at least 1,000 terrorists are now being actively sought by Moroccan authorities.[18] Al-Qaeda's regional offshoot, al-Qaeda in the Islamic Maghreb (AQIM), has made recent efforts to bring these disparate groups (which number less than 50 members per grouping, on average) under its umbrella.

AQIM, like its counterpart al-Qaeda in the Arabian Peninsula (AQAP), constitutes a potent regional terrorist threat not only to Morocco but to Algeria, Mauritania, Mali and Tunisia. Formed when the Salafist Group for Preaching and Combat (GSPC) reconstituted itself into AQIM in early 2007, its goal has been to integrate all of the North African radical movements, including the small Moroccan Islamic Combatant Group (GICM). On September 11, 2013, AQIM released an unprecedented 41-minute video "documentary" attacking Moroccan domestic and foreign policy, especially its counterterrorism efforts. Analysts believe that the production was the result of the terrorist organization's frustration that, while it had recruited some Moroccans, it had largely failed to target the country successfully, much less compromise its institutions.[19]

Salafist jihadis as a whole remain a significant threat to Morocco and the West. Scores of young Moroccans traveled to Iraq and Afghanistan to fight Americans and there are continuing arrests of extremists.[20] *Salafis* also represent a challenge to the Moroccan state, as a number of incidents have underscored. On May 16, 2003, terrorists claiming to be members of the GICM launched a series of five coordinated suicide attacks in Casablanca, killing more than 40 people and wounding more than 100. In April 2007, a series of suicide bomb attacks occurred in central Casablanca, one taking place near the U.S. Consulate and one near the American Language Center. In February 2008, Moroccan authorities arrested nearly 40 members of an alleged terrorist network, led by Abdelkader Belliraj, a Belgian-Moroccan suspected of committing multiple assassinations in addition to arms smuggling and money laundering for al-Qaeda.[21] Belliraj was subsequently convicted and sentenced to life in prison. Press reports have at times asserted that more than 100 al-Qaeda-linked cells exist in Morocco, and that Moroccan police have either imprisoned or placed under house arrest/police surveillance over 1,000 *Salafist jihadists* either openly sympathetic to AQIM or part of other hard-core underground Islamist movements.[22]

On April 28, 2011, the bombing of a popular tourist café in Marrakech left seventeen people dead and at least twenty wounded. Among those killed were eight French nationals, a Briton, an Israeli-Canadian, a Swiss, and a Portuguese. The government accused AQIM of the attack.

In recent years, Islamist activity has generated scores of arrests. In July 2008, Moroccan security services arrested 35 members of an alleged terrorist network specializing in the recruitment of volunteers for Iraq.[23] In August of the same year, another 15-person network calling itself "Fath al-Andalus" was reportedly disbanded in Layoune, the capital of the Western Sahara, for planning attacks on the UN peacekeeping force there.[24] There also have been reports of considerable numbers of Moroccans traveling to Mali and Algeria to receive training from AQIM elements.[25] In more recent years, Moroccans have also traveled to Syria and Iraq—and, more recently,

Libya—to join the Islamic State (ISIS). It is estimated that, as of the end of 2015, approximately 1,500 Moroccans had joined the ISIS. If European citizens of Moroccan descent are included, the number rises to between 2,000 and 2,500.[26]

Although Morocco has so far fortunately not seen a successful assault on its soil by ISIS, since 2013, authorities have dismantled more than three dozen cells plotting attacks both within the kingdom and abroad. In July 2016, fifty-two people were arrested and various armaments seized. According to authorities, the militants were planning a string of attacks to inaugurate a "province" (*wilayat*) of the Islamic State in the country.[27]

The impoverished slums in Morocco's inner cities and northern regions have produced many of these extremists, and many of the Moroccan extremist groupings are composed of family members and friends from the same towns and villages. Indeed, the north of Morocco has become an especially fertile ground for *Salafists* who favored *Wahhabism* and other extremist creeds over Morocco's more tolerant version of Islam.

ISLAMISM AND SOCIETY

Under Moroccan law, the monarch is revered as the "Commander of the Faithful" and traces his lineage back to the Prophet Mohammad. Consequently, the majority of Moroccans take great pride in their nation's embrace of moderate, tolerant Islam. It is worth noting that the reformed Moroccan constitution of 2011, unique in the Arab world, explicitly acknowledges that the country's national culture is "enriched and nourished by African, Andalusian, Hebrew, and Mediterranean influences."[28]

Social and economic conditions, however, play a role in Islamist sentiment. Given Morocco's high unemployment rate, year after year thousands of Moroccans risk their lives attempting to illegally immigrate to Europe across the Straits of Gibraltar.[29] Many, however, are left behind, transforming cities like Tangier, Tetouan, or Al Houcema into smuggling centers feeding criminal elements and opponents of the regime. Despite the current king's efforts to promote a legislative agenda to modernize Islamic laws governing civil society in Morocco (detailed below), the continued growth of political parties such as the PJD and continued political activities by JCO, both inside Morocco and in Europe, point to the fractures in Morocco's society between those who favor a more moderate, tolerant Islam and significant elements of Morocco's populace which prefer stronger Islamic control over the nation's society and its political system.

Morocco's urban slums and rural north continue to be fertile ground for extremism and its recruiters to AQIM. Indeed, hundreds of Moroccans have volunteered to fight in Iraq and Afghanistan against the United States.[30] Morocco's north, especially cities such as Tetouan and the surrounding Rif Mountain villages have at times been centers of *jihadist* agitation. It is in Morocco's north that such sentiment has most successfully taken root, as a result of institutional neglect. Following a Berber rebellion against his rule in the early 1980s, King Hassan II largely abandoned the northern tier of Morocco to its own devices. The King rarely visited the north during his reign. Consequently, government services were severely cut, and Islamists filled the void with a social and charitable network offering food and medical treatment to the population. While King Mohammed has reversed his father's policy of abandonment of the north (and even conducted an ancient traditional ceremony of mutual allegiance there[31]), the region is still relatively underdeveloped and deeply dependent on charitable networks, some with extremist links, for services not provided by the government.

ISLAMISM AND THE STATE

Following the 2003 Casablanca bombings, the Moroccan government focused increasing attention on modernizing Islamic teaching and Islamic infrastructure and adopted laws liberalizing civil marriage and the role of women in Morocco's society. The Ministry of Endowments and Islamic Affairs was provided with new funding and authority to train more moderate Islamic clerics and to expand its programs in Morocco's educational system.

In 2004, King Mohammed VI pushed through a reform of the family code (*Moudawana*), overcoming conservative opposition and mass demonstrations in part by invoking his religious authority as Commander of the Faithful. Among other provisions, the legislation significantly advanced women's rights by elevating the minimum age of marriage to 18, limiting polygamy, granting couples joint rights over their children, and permitting women to initiate divorce proceedings.[32]

One incident in particular points to Morocco's more aggressive stance against ultraconservative Muslim clerics who oppose the government's efforts to modernize Morocco's Islamic infrastructure and its religious teachings. In September 2008, Sheikh Mohamed Ben Abderrahman Al Maghraoui issued a highly provocative *fatwa* legitimizing the marriage of underage women as young as nine years old.[33] The Moroccan government sought to discredit the *fatwa* and ordered the immediate closure of 60 Koranic schools under his control. The government also launched an inquiry into Sheikh Al Maghraoui's competence as an Islamic scholar, and the public prosecutor's office initiated a criminal case against him for encouraging pedophilia.[34]

Following the incident, King Mohammed unveiled his "proximity strategy," which represented a modernization program for Islamic institutions in Morocco. Under the program, 3,180 mosques were designated to be "modernized," (essentially a wholesale replacement of *imams* deemed by the regime to be opponents of moderate Islamic principles). Thirty-three thousand new *imams* were to be trained and the number of regional *ulama* councils (charged with overseeing Islamic teaching and the competency of *imams*) was increased from 30 to 70. Exceptionally for the Arab world, women also have a place in Morocco's official religious establishment with *mourchidates*, or female religious guides, trained alongside more traditional male *imams*.[35]

To counter violent Islamist extremist ideologies, Morocco has developed a national strategy to reaffirm and further institutionalize Moroccans' historically widespread adherence to Sunni Islam's Maliki school of jurisprudence and its Ashari theology, as well as to the mystical spirituality of Sufism.

The aborted terrorist plot in 2007 and the continuing threat of *jihadi* sentiment in the country's north only briefly the pace of King Mohammed's reform agenda with respect to rights of women and the judiciary, including enacting legislation in 2014 to end the use of military tribunals to try civilians.

Unlike his father, the King has largely refrained from playing an activist role in Middle East diplomacy, focusing his diplomatic efforts closer to home in Africa, which the monarch has repeatedly characterized as the "top priority" of his country's foreign policy, emphasizing that "this multi-dimensional relationship puts Morocco in the center of Africa" and "Africa holds a special place in the heart of Moroccans."[36] In addition to extensive partnerships with African countries on a variety of political and economic issues, Morocco's influence is increasingly seen in its efforts to train religious leaders and preachers from across the continent—and, indeed, even some from Europe and beyond—in the kingdom's moderate form of Islam. The Mohammed VI Institute for the Training of Imams, Morchidines, and Morchidates, established in 2015, has enrolled hundreds of students from Mali, Tunisia, Guinea, Côte d'Ivoire, and France.[37]

For many years, Morocco has permitted mainstream Islamic political parties that do not condone extremism and violence to exist and indeed, to participate in elections, although it continues to deny legal status to the JCO. Since the Casablanca bombings in 2003, Moroccan authorities have maintained a vigilant and aggressive stance against any *jihadist* movement. Moroccan authorities currently have almost 1,000 prisoners considered to be Islamic radicals in jail.[38] And in July 2007, Moroccan authorities jailed six Islamist politicians who were accused of complicity in a major terrorist plot.[39] On the other hand, the Moroccan government has rewarded Islamist parties that have embraced more moderate Islamic principles, such as the PJD. Notwithstanding the ever-present scourge of *jihadi* operatives in Morocco, the Moroccan government has demonstrated ingenuity in its "divide and conquer" strategy against Islamists who challenge the state. In addition to adopting the above-referenced "proximity strategy" to replace recalcitrant *imams*, authorities have established a grassroots police operation to report on any suspicious activities by Islamists.[40]

The Moroccan government has also implemented a concerted social development program, the National Initiative for Human Development (INDH), a multibillion-dollar undertaking aimed at generating employment, fighting poverty, and improving infrastructure in both rural areas as well as the sprawling slums on the outskirts of urban centers that have been susceptible to Islamist-oriented charities nurturing radicalism. In the largest "bidonvilles" (shantytowns) in Morocco's cities, significant social welfare, health and education programs have been instituted and many families have been relocated to new affordable housing units.[41] Overall, the U.S. State Department has applauded Morocco for having "a comprehensive strategy for countering violent extremism that prioritizes economic and human development goals in addition to tight control of the religious sphere and messaging."[42]

Amid the reforms that have been adopted in recent years,[43] even the historically touchy issue of Moroccan sovereignty over the former Spanish Sahara has seen forward movement.[44] In 2007, the government advanced a proposal to break the longstanding impasse over the issue by offering generous autonomy to the area (including not only an elected local administration but also ideas about education and justice and the promise of financial support). Under the plan, the only matters that would remain in Rabat's control would be defense and foreign affairs, as well as the currency. The regional authority, meanwhile, would have broad powers over local administration, the economy, infrastructure, social and cultural affairs, and the environment. Then-Secretary of State Hillary Rodham Clinton described the autonomy proposal as "serious, credible, and realistic."[45]

Nevertheless, now well into its fourth decade, the "question of Western Sahara," as it is termed in the nomenclature of the United Nations, is one of those challenges which, defying multiple efforts by the international community to facilitate its "solution," despite increasingly dire warnings, recently reiterated by UN Secretary-General Ban Ki-moon and others, that "the rise of instability and insecurity in and around the Sahel" and the risk of "spillover" from the fighting in Mali requires "an urgent settlement" of this "ticking time bomb."[46]

Supported by Algeria, the *Frente Popular de Liberación de Saguía el Hamra y Río de Oro* ("Popular Front for the Liberation of Saqiet al-Hamra and Río del Oro," commonly known as the Polisario Front) continues to demand the complete independence of the territory, even though the armed conflict of the late 1970s and early 1980s left Morocco in control of more than 85 percent of it. The construction by the Moroccan government of a "sand berm," (a defensive shield consisting of a series of barriers of sand and stone completed in 1987) and subsequent deployment of a UN monitoring force has largely confined the Polisario Front to a small zone around Tindouf in southwestern Algeria where it has sequestered tens of thousands of Sahrawi refugees in the squalid camps which have recently been the object of UN Secretary-General Ban Ki-Moon's concerns about conflict spillover.[47]

While for most of its history the Polisario Front has been avowedly secular and, indeed, leftist in its political orientations—many of its leaders studied in the Soviet bloc and fighters received training in Cuba well into the 1990s—there are worrisome indications of growing linkages with AQIM[48] and other Islamist groups in the Maghreb and the Sahel, including providing AQIM's allies in northern Mali with both fighters and, in one notorious case, Western hostages to trade for ransom.[49] Should this trend continue, it would not only heighten the challenge of Islamist violence for Morocco, but also exacerbate an already volatile security situation for the entire region.

ENDNOTES

[1] U.S. Department of State, Office of the Coordinator for Counterterrorism, "Country Reports: Middle East and North Africa Overview," in *Country Reports on Terrorism 2015*, June 2, 2016, https://www.state.gov/j/ct/rls/crt/2015/257517.htm.

[2] John P. Entelis, "Political Islam in the Maghreb," in John P. Entelis, ed., *Islam, Democracy, and the State in North Africa* (Bloomington: Indiana University Press, 1997), 52-53.

[3] Amr Hamzawy, "Party for Justice and Development in Morocco: Participation and Its Discontents," Carnegie Endowment for International Peace *Carnegie Paper* no. 93, July 2008, 7-8, http://www.carnegieendowment.org/publications/index.cfm?fa=view&id=20314.

[4] Ibid., 8.

[5] Samir Amghar, "Political Islam in Morocco," Center for European Policy Studies *CEPS Working Document* No. 269, June 2007.

[6] Ibid.

[7] National Democratic Institute, *Final Report on the Moroccan Legislative Elections*, September 7, 2007.

[8] Amghar, "Political Islam in Morocco."

[9] Ibid.

[10] Ibid.

[11] Daniel Williams, "Morocco Parliament May be Controlled by Islamic Party," Bloomberg, December 30, 2009, http://www.bloomberg.com/apps/news?pid=newsarchive&sid=aLXRR7EuJeEo.

[12] Hamzawy, "Party for Justice and Development in Morocco: Participation and Its Discontents."

[13] See Mona Yacoubian, "Engaging Islamists and Promoting Democracy: A Preliminary Assessment," in Daniel Brumberg and Dina Shehata (eds.), *Conflict, Identity and Reform in the Muslim World: Challenges for U.S. Engagement* (Washington: U.S. Institute of Peace Press, 2009), 420.

[14] "Morocco: Islamist Party Takes over New Government," *Al Bawaba*, January 3, 2012, http://www.albawaba.com/news/morocco-islamist-party-takes-over-new-government-407621.

[15] "Benkirane: 3 Parties Agreed to Form Moroccan Government," *Middle East Monitor*, November 30, 2016, https://www.middleeastmonitor.com/20161130-benkirane-3-parties-agreed-to-form-moroccan-government/.
[16] U.S. Department of State, Office of the Coordinator for Counterterrorism, *Country Reports on Terrorism 2008* (Washington, DC: U.S. Department of State, April 2009), 130, http://www.state.gov/documents/organization/122599.pdf.
[17] Olivier Guitta, "Morocco Under Fire," *Weekly Standard*, March 29, 2007, http://www.weeklystandard.com/Content/Public/Articles/000/000/013/470ucfqo.asp.
[18] Ibid.
[19] Mawassi Lahcen, "AQIM Lashes Out at Morocco," Magharebia, September 16, 2013, http://magharebia.com/en_GB/articles/awi/features/2013/09/16/feature-01.
[20] Mustapha Tossa, "Morocco's Fight Against Terrorism," Common Ground News Service, September 2, 2008, http://commongroundnews.org/article.php?id=23883&lan=en&sid=1&sp=0.
[21] U.S. Department of State, *Country Reports on Terrorism 2008*.
[22] Stephen Erlanger and Souad Mekhennet, "Islamic Radicalism Slows Moroccan Reforms," *New York Times*, August 26, 2009, http://www.nytimes.com/2009/08/27/world/africa/27morocco.html.
[23] U.S. Department of State, *Country Reports on Terrorism 2008*.
[24] Ibidem.
[25] Ibidem.
[26] Mohammed Masbah, *Moroccan Foreign Fighters*, German Institute for International and Security Affairs (SWP) Comments, no. 46 (October 2016), https://www.swp-berlin.org/fileadmin/contents/products/comments/2015C46_msb.pdf.
[27] "Morocco Foils Terrorist Attacks, Arrests 52 Militants," *Asharq al-Awsat English*, July 27, 2016, http://english.aawsat.com/2016/07/article55355229/morocco-foils-terrorist-attacks-arrests-52-militants.
[28] Moroccan Constitution of 2011, Preamble, http://www.al-bab.com/arab/docs/morocco/constitution_2011.htm.
[29] See, for example, Moha Ennaji, "Illegal Migration From Morocco To Europe," Paper presented before the 7th international Metropolis conference, Oslo, Norway, September 10, 2002, http://international.metropolis.net/events/Metromed/Ennaji_e.pdf.
[30] Andrea Elliott, "Where Boys Grow Up To Be Jihadis," *New York Times Magazine*, November 25, 2007, 16.
[31] Erlanger and Mekhennet, "Islamic Radicalism Slows Moroccan Reforms."
[32] Francesco Cavatorta and Emanuela Dalmasso, "Liberal Outcomes through Undemocratic Means: The Reform of the *Code du statut personnel* in Morocco," *Journal of Modern African Studies* 47, no. 4 (2009), 487-506.

[33] U.S. Department of State, *Country Reports on Terrorism 2008*.

[34] Ibid.

[35] Fatima Zahra Salhi, Ilham Chafik, and Nezha Nassi, "The Mourchidates of Morocco," in Maureen E. Fiedler, ed., *Breaking through the Stained Glass Ceiling: Women Religious Leaders in Their Own Words* (New York: Seabury Press, 2010), 28-30.

[36] "S.M. le Roi adresse un discours à la Nation à l'occasion du 63ème anniversaire de la Révolution du Roi et du Peuple, " Maghreb Arabe Presse, August 2016, http://www.mapnews.ma/fr/activites-royales/sm-le-roi-adresse-un-discours-la-nation-loccasion-du-63-eme-anniversaire-de-la-rev.

[37] Kamailoudini Tagba, "Morocco Sets Up New Foundation for African Ulemas," North Africa Post, June 8, 2016, http://northafricapost.com/12452-morocco-sets-new-foundation-african-ulemas.html.

[38] Erlanger and Mekhennet, "Islamic Radicalism Slows Moroccan Reforms."

[39] Ibid.

[40] Tossa, "Morocco's Fight Against Terrorism."

[41] Ibid.

[42] U.S. Department of State, *Country Reports on Terrorism 2015*.

[43] See J. Peter Pham, "Morocco's Momentum," *The Journal of International Security Affairs* 22 (Spring 2012), 13-20.

[44] See J. Peter Pham, "Not Another Failed State: Towards a Realistic Solution of the Western Sahara," *Journal of the Middle East and Africa* 1, no. 1 (Spring 2010), 1-24.

[45] Secretary of State Hillary Rodham Clinton, Remarks with Moroccan Foreign Minister Taieb Fassi Fihri, March 23, 2011, archived at http://www.state.gov/secretary/rm/2011/03/158895.htm.

[46] United Nations Secretary-General Ban Ki-moon, quoted in Tim Witcher, "Ban says Western Sahara Risks being Drawn into Mali War," Agence France-Presse, April 9, 2013, http://www.google.com/hostednews/afp/article/ALeqM5iOnupKvBuc8I_WTR3J5BnNCFnmEw?docId=CNG.566cbe22180951c72bc8d9c6ad6fd9d1.d1.

[47] Ibid.

[48] See J. Peter Pham, "The Dangerous 'Pragmatism' of Al-Qaeda in the Islamic Maghreb," *Journal of the Middle East and Africa* 2, no. 1 (January-June 2011), 15-29.

[49] Three aid workers, one Italian and two Spaniards, were kidnapped from a Polisario-controlled camp in southern Algeria in October 2011 and eventually transferred to the control of the Movement for Unity and Jihad in West Africa (MUJAO), which extorted a ransom of €15 million for their release in July 2012. See "Rebels: $18.4 Million Paid for Hostage Release," Associated Press, July 20, 2012, http://bigstory.ap.org/article/rebels-184-million-paid-hostage-release.

The Palestinian Territories

Quick Facts

Population: West Bank: 2,697,687 Gaza Strip: 1,753,327

Area: West Bank: 5,860sq km Gaza Strip: 360 sq km

Ethnic Groups: West Bank: Palestinian Arab and others 83%, Jewish 17% Gaza Strip: Palestinian Arab

Religions: West Bank: Muslim 80-85% (predominately Sunni), Jewish 12-14%, Christian 1--2.5% (mainly Greek Orthodox), other, unaffiliated, unspecified <1% Gaza Strip: Muslim (predominately Sunni) 98-99%, Christian <1%, other, unaffiliated, unspecified <1%

Government Type: PLO/Fatah (contested)

GDP (official exchange rate): West Bank: $9.828 billion Gaza Strip: $2.983 billion

Map and Quick Facts courtesy of the CIA World Factbook (Last Updated January 2017)

Overview

The Palestinian National Authority (PA or PNA) was created in accordance with the 1993 Oslo Accords. Under the subsequent "Oslo Process," the PA assumed the responsibilities of Israeli military administration in parts of the West Bank and Gaza Strip ("Area A"), and was expected to expand that territory through final status negotiations. The PA includes a Palestinian Legislative Council (PLC), a legislative body with 132 seats elected from Gaza and the West Bank. As a result of the last Palestinian legislative elections, held in 2006, Hamas became the largest faction in the PLC, with 72 seats. However, the rival Fatah faction, backed by Western governments, blocked Hamas from forming a government. After more than a year of tension, Hamas forcibly seized control of Gaza in 2007. The two territories remained under separate rule for seven years. In June 2014, Hamas and Fatah forged an interim unity government, with the aim of holding elections to formally re-unify. But soon thereafter, conflict between Gaza and Israel erupted. It became clear that

Hamas remained in full control of the territory, and commanded a formidable rocket arsenal that had the capacity to reach deep into Israeli territory. Hamas remains the true power broker in Gaza, while Fatah maintains an iron grip on the West Bank. Moreover, Hamas remains the most influential Islamist movement in the Gaza Strip, but other Islamist groups have also gained support from the Palestinian public.

ISLAMIST ACTIVITY

Hamas

"Hamas" means "zeal" in Arabic, and is an Arabic acronym for *Ḥarakat al-Muqāwamah al-'Islāmiyyah* (the Islamic Resistance Movement). The group is primarily concentrated in the Gaza Strip, but does have support in pockets of the West Bank. The group was founded as a splinter group of the Muslim Brotherhood in December 1987, during the early days of the *intifada* (uprising) against Israel. The Brotherhood refused to engage in violence against Israel, but Hamas' founders believed that it was a duty to engage in "resistance." According to one insider's account, the secretive organization's founders included Sheikh Ahmad Yassin, Hassan Yousef, Ayman Abu Taha, Jamil Hamami, Mahmud Muslih, Muhammed Jamal al-Natsah, and Jamal Mansour.[1]

In addition to its immediate goal of destroying the State of Israel, Hamas' 1988 *mithaq* (founding charter) illustrates the organization's commitment to universal Islamist principles. This is demonstrated by its slogan: "Allah is its goal [theocratic rule], the Prophet is its model [importance of the Sunna], the Qur'an its Constitution [*sharia*], *Jihad* [violence] is its path and death for the sake of Allah is the loftiest of its wishes."[2] While most Hamas members are Palestinian Sunni Arabs, the charter welcomes all Muslims who: "embraces its faith, ideology, follows its program, keeps its secrets, and wants to belong to its ranks and carry out the duty."[3]

The Hamas charter also conveys the conviction that Palestine is *waqf*, or land endowed to Muslims by Allah because it was "conquered by the companions of the Prophet."[4] Hamas also clearly defines nationalism as "part of the religious creed,"[5] thereby universalizing the notion of "nationalism" to include the entire Muslim *umma* (community).[6]

To achieve its immediate goal of an Islamic Palestinian state, Hamas has steadfastly denounced the 1993 Oslo Accords, the 2007 Annapolis conference, and all other diplomatic efforts to establish a lasting peace in the region as a "contradiction to the principles of the Islamic Resistance Movement."[7] However, when addressing Western audiences, Hamas leaders such as Gaza-based Ismail Haniyeh and politburo chief Khaled Meshal have stated that they are willing to recognize Israel along pre-1967 borders.[8] Yet, other senior Hamas officials, such as Mahmoud al Zahar, bluntly state that there are no leaders within Hamas willing to acknowledge the pre-1967 borders or live at peace with Israel.[9]

Hamas gained the support of a significant portion of the Palestinian people by providing social and welfare services and by presenting itself as Israel's implacable foe, as well as a pious opponent of the more corrupt and ossified Fatah faction, whose officials also comprise most of the leadership of the Palestine Liberation Organization (PLO) and the PA. Since its violent takeover of Gaza in 2007, Hamas has taken steps to Islamize the society. However, there are indications that this may have only served to undermine the movement's authority.[10] Additionally, press reports indicate that Hamas has been losing popularity as a result of its inability to deal with Gaza's festering economic problems, among other issues.[11]

Following the attacks of September 11, 2001, the United States made efforts to cut the flow of cash to countless terror groups, including Hamas. Funds from Saudi Arabia, long identified as a top sponsor of Hamas, slowed following the Kingdom's decision to cut back on funding *jihadi* groups in 2004, after suffering attacks by a local al-Qaeda affiliate.[12] However, Iran, the world's leading state sponsor of terrorism, filled the void.

Iran soon became Hamas' primary state sponsor, with hundreds of millions of dollars pledged and delivered.[13] Iranian largesse was an important source of income for Hamas, and that revenue stream was significantly and adversely impacted over time as U.S.-led sanctions sapped the Islamic Republic's cash reserves. Thereafter, Tehran cut most, if not all, financial assistance when tension arose between it and Hamas over attitudes toward the Assad regime in Syria. The Iranians strongly supported the embattled Syrian leader, even as he slaughtered Sunnis and Palestinians in the country's ongoing civil war. Hamas, however, did not. As a result, it vacated its headquarters in Damascus, where it had been based, and reportedly turned to new patrons, including Qatar and Turkey.[14] Recent press reports indicate that, following the decline of the Muslim Brotherhood regionally in 2013, Hamas and Iran may now be seeking to restore their ties.[15]

Hamas augments its funds from state sponsors with donations from private charities (the most notorious being the Texas-based Holy Land Foundation, now defunct, which channeled $12 million to the organization before it was proscribed[16]), as well as deep-pocketed donors around the world. For more than a decade Hamas also extracted significant tax revenues from the subterranean tunnels connecting the Gaza Strip to the Sinai Peninsula, through which a great many products, including weapons, flowed. However, since the overthrow of the Muslim Brotherhood-affiliated government of Mohammed Morsi in July 2013, Egyptian authorities have shut down hundreds of smuggling tunnels along the Egypt-Gaza border. According to officials in Gaza, the closure of these tunnels is currently causing the Gaza economy to suffer monthly losses of approximately $230 million.[17]

Hamas, along with other like-minded violent factions, has fired more than 15,000 rockets and mortars into Israel since 2001.[18] The group draws a distinction between its political activities and its paramilitary attacks. However, this is a false distinction, as all of the movement's component parts contribute to "resistance" activities.[19] According to Hamas founder Sheikh Ahmad Yassin, "We cannot separate the wing from the body. If we do so, the body will not be able to fly."[20] Since 1993, the military wing of Hamas, the Izz ad-Din al-Qassam Brigades, is believed to have killed over five hundred people in more than 350 separate terrorist attacks, many of them suicide bombings.[21]

Although attacks against Israel from Gaza slowed in 2013, Israeli authorities foiled numerous Hamas terror plots in the West Bank.[22] Israeli officials identified Gaza-based Hamas official Fathi Hamad[23] as well as Turkey-based Hamas leader Saleh al-Aruri[24] as key catalysts for many of these plots.[25] Meanwhile, the rocket war of July 2014 revealed that Hamas maintains a significant arsenal, primarily via Iran, which gives the faction the ability to fire deep into Israeli territory.

After the 2014 war, Hamas continued to build tunnels into Israel and attempt to replenish its rocket supply.[26] Hamas regularly uses items meant for humanitarian aid to construct rockets.[27] The group has also carried out attacks across the West Bank, such as the fatal shooting of an Israeli couple in October of 2015.[28] The group has also planned attacks against Palestinian Authority leader Mahmoud Abbas, one of which was foiled by the Israeli Defense Forces (IDF).[29] Meanwhile, Hamas' cooperation with the ISIS affiliate group in Sinai has escalated tensions with the Egyptian government.[30] Hamas regularly trains and treats Islamic State fighters before sending them back into the Sinai Peninsula.[31]

Hamas has also tried to rally public support for a third *intifada*, or uprising. Since the start of the wave of terror that hit Israel from late-2015 into mid-2016, Hamas has either celebrated terrorists killed in attacks against Israelis or claimed attackers as members of the group. After three Israeli soldiers were wounded in an attack in February 2016, Hamas held a rally in Gaza.[32] A similar rally was held in April 2016 after a member of Hamas blew up a bus in Jerusalem. That attack wounded 21 Israelis.[33] In September 2016, the international NGO World Vision halted funding to Gaza projects after Israel alleged one of its employees, Mohammad el-Halabi, was funneling the foreign funds to Hamas.[34] In December 2016, the Israeli Shin Bet uncovered a 20-member Hamas cell in the West Bank that was plotting suicide bombings in major Israeli cities.[35]

Palestinian Islamic Jihad (PIJ)

Harakat al-Jihād al-Islāmi fi Filastīn (Palestinian Islamic Jihad, or PIJ) was founded sometime between 1979 and 1981 by several Muslim Brotherhood members who, like Hamas, felt that the Brotherhood was too moderate and not fully committed to the principle of *jihad* and the establishment of a Palestinian state governed according to sharia. In addition, the founding members were also inspired by the 1979 Iranian Revolution.[36] Founders Fathi Shikaki and Abd al-Aziz Awda forged an organization whose ultimate aim was to destroy Israel through *jihad*. Unlike Hamas, which is amenable to a *hudna* (tactical truce) with Israel, PIJ explicitly rejects any and all forms of recognition of the Jewish State.[37]

The exact size of PIJ, a highly secretive organization, is unknown. Most estimates suggest that membership ranges from a few hundred to a few thousand.[38] The ethnic make-up of the group is overwhelmingly Palestinian Sunni, though there have been reports of increasing Shi'ite presence, a direct result of Iranian support.[39]

While PIJ was known for its suicide bombing attacks during the Second Intifada (2000-2005), in recent years the group has primarily focused on rocket and sniper attacks from the Gaza Strip. The IDF has tried to thin PIJ's ranks through targeted killings and arrests in recent years. The effectiveness of these actions is as yet unclear.

In January 2014, the U.S. State Department designated Ziyad al Nakhalah, the Deputy Secretary General of Palestinian Islamic Jihad (PIJ), as a Specially Designated Global Terrorist (SDGT).[40] Other leaders of the group have yet to be designated. Like Hamas, PIJ's activity against Israel from Gaza declined in 2013. However, it continued to plot and carry out attacks from the West Bank.[41] It subsequently played a significant role in the rocket war of July 2014, firing Iranian-made or Iranian-furnished rockets deep into Israeli territory.

PIJ has also been a strong supporter of the third *intifada* which is now sweeping across Israel. In November 2015, PIJ and Hamas announced "new methods of resistance" against Israel.[42] In May of 2016 it was revealed that Iran would renew its financial support to PIJ after nearly two years.[43] In Tehran, PIJ leader Ramadan Shallah praised Iran for its support of the "Palestinian *intifada*."[44] When municipal elections were initially announced in the West Bank and Gaza in August 2016, PIJ boycotted the elections and instead urged Palestinians to escalate the *intifada*.[45]

Popular Resistance Committees

The Popular Resistance Committees (PRC) is made up of "former armed activists of different factions,"[46] and is likely the third largest violent group in the Palestinian territories, after Hamas and PIJ. According to the IDF, the PRC often "acts as a sub-contractor" for Iran, and is heavily influenced by Hezbollah.[47]

Since its founding in 2000, through its military wing known as the Al-Nasser Salah al-Din Brigades, the PRC has taken responsibility for a number of terror attacks against Israel,[48] and an attack on U.S. personnel in Gaza in 2003.[49] Some of the group's operations have been conducted jointly with Hamas.[50] It has also reportedly worked with Salafi jihadist groups operating in the Sinai Peninsula abutting Gaza.[51]

In February 2014, the Israeli Air Force targeted a PRC operative who was known to work with the Sinai-based *jihadist* group Ansar Bayt al Maqdis.[52] In recent years, the group has become increasingly Salafi in outlook, as conveyed through Sunni *jihadist* forums online.[53] In 2006, Israeli officials warned that the PRC's leadership was in contact with "Global Jihad sources in North Africa and the Sinai."[54]

In light of Hamas' attempts to prevent unauthorized rocket attacks against Israel, the group has at times found itself at odds with Hamas. In July 2013, for example, the PRC issued a communiqué that demanded that Hamas stop its arrest of the *mujahideen* in the Gaza Strip.[55] The PRC maintained a low profile during the 2014 rocket war.

Al Aqsa Martyrs Brigades

The Al Aqsa Martyrs Brigades is the military wing of the secular Fatah faction,[56] which has adopted Islamist symbols and slogans that stand in stark contrast to those of the secular Fatah faction. The group was formally designated as a Foreign Terrorist Organization by the United States in March 2002, largely for its actions inside Israel and the West Bank, where it carried out suicide bombings and small arms attacks against Israel during the second *Intifada*.[57]

Over the past few years, the group has not been terribly active. The group has primarily operated out of the Gaza Strip, with handful of operations in the West Bank.[58] According to the U.S. Department of State, "Iran has exploited al-Aqsa's lack of resources and formal leadership by providing funds and guidance, mostly through Hezbollah facilitators."[59]

The primary acts of violence carried out by the group in recent years have been rocket attacks from Gaza into southern Israel.[60] Press reports, however, have suggested that the group may seek a comeback in the West Bank.[61]

Indeed, in March 2016, thirteen Palestinians were injured in firefights between the Palestinian Authority and members of the Aqsa Martyrs in Nablus.[62] As clashes heated up again in Nablus in August 2016, the PA arrested a local leader of the Brigades, Ahmed Izz Halawa, and beat him to death.[63] Halawa's death sparked mass protests in the West Bank.[64]

Jaysh al-Islam (JI)

Jaysh al-Islam (JI), or "Army of Islam," is closely linked to the Dughmush clan of Gaza, and is believed to have several hundred members.[65] The Salafi group was founded in 2005, and similar to other Palestinian Islamist splinter groups, it has global *jihadist* objectives and is believed to have ties to al-Qaeda.[66]

The group's most notable action was the March 2007 kidnapping of BBC journalist Alan Johnston in order to negotiate the release of al-Qaeda-affiliated Islamist militant Abu Qatada, who was then jailed in the United Kingdom.[67] The Johnston kidnapping, as well as an attack that killed five senior Hamas officials, led to a clash with Hamas in August 2008 that is said to have weakened the group significantly.[68]

The group's affinity for al-Qaeda has been widely documented. Days after the death of Osama bin Laden in May 2011, the group released a eulogy for the fallen al-Qaeda leader.[69] In May 2011, the group was designated as a terrorist group by the U.S. Department of State. The accompanying press release noted that the group "worked with Hamas and is attempting to develop closer al Qaeda contacts."[70] In 2006, the group sent a letter to senior al-Qaeda leaders, asking whether it was permissible to accept money from other groups in Gaza that did not share their ideology, specifically nationalists or Iranian-backed factions.[71] Israeli officials also noted in 2006, "alleged efforts by Mumtaz Dughmush to make contact with Global Jihad sources, possibly to include those responsible for the bombing of the USS Cole."[72]

During Operation Pillar of Defense in November 2012, the Mujahideen Shura Council in the Environs of Jerusalem, a consolidation of Salafi jihadist groups in Gaza, and JI conducted joint rocket attacks against Israel.[73] According to Israeli officials, JI current operates training camps in Gaza for jihadists who subsequently go to fight in Yemen, Syria, and Egypt's Sinai Peninsula, among other locations.[74] Hamas allows these camps to operate in Gaza.[75]

Jaysh al-Ummah (JU)

Ideologically affiliated with al-Qaeda, Jaysh al-Ummah (JU), or the "Army of the Nation," believes that "the sons of Zion are occupiers and they must be uprooted completely… We will fight them as we are ordered by God and the Prophet Mohammad."[76] The Salafi *jihadist* group was formed in either 2006[77] or 2007,[78] and is led by Abu Hafs al-Maqdisi. While the group's membership number is kept secret, it lacks the capability to strike targets outside of Gaza, suggesting it is small in size.[79]

JU has been very critical of Hamas since its inception. Most notably, it has criticized Hamas for arresting its members as they were attempting to carry out terrorist operations.[80] Hamas does appear to allow the group to conduct *dawa*-related activity in the Gaza Strip, however.[81]

JU has warned against the increasing influence of Iran and its proxy Palestinian Islamic Jihad in the Gaza Strip. While the group has denied an operational connection to al-Qaeda, it has a similar ideological outlook.[82] We are "connected to our brothers in Al Qaeda by our beliefs, we and they are following the great Prophet. Osama bin Laden is our brother and we appreciate him very much," a JU official stated.[83]

Since 2013, the group has issued a number of statements and videos that belie its Salafi beliefs. In January 2013, the *jihadist* group issued a video urging "all the *mujahideen* all over Earth to target Iranian interests everywhere."[84] In a separate message released in January 2013, JU called for greater support for *jihadists* in Mali: "[W]e will support and be loyal and aid our mujahideen monotheist brothers in Mali without limits."[85] In August 2013, Abu Hafs al Maqdisi, JU's leader, called on Egyptians to wage *jihad* against Egyptian army chief General Abdel Fattah el-Sisi.[86] And, in November 2013, the group issued a eulogy for Hakeemullah Mehsud, the former emir of the Movement of the Taliban in Pakistan.[87]

Hizb-ut-Tahrir (HuT)

The Palestinian "Party of Liberation" is a local affiliate of the larger HuT movement, which has a presence in some 45 countries. The group's immediate aim is to establish a caliphate and implement *sharia* throughout the Muslim world.[88]

Despite HuT's well-documented enmity toward Israel, the group does not directly engage in terrorism, nor do its branches maintain an armed wing. Rather, HuT seeks to "agitate and educate."[89] While no reliable figures can be found regarding HuT's membership in the Palestinian Territories, it is widely considered to be small, despite its organic base of support.

To voice opposition to the PLO's participation in the 2007 Annapolis peace summit, HuT organized a demonstration with over 2,500 attendees in Hebron, culminating in the killing of one protestor by PA police.[90] Soon after, over 10,000 HuT supporters gathered in Al-Bireh under the slogan: "the caliphate is the rising force."[91] In July 2010, PA security forces arrested thousands of HuT supporters at a rally in Ramallah, which was banned by the PA.[92]

In 2011, PA forces disrupted one of the group's rallies in the West Bank.[93] This was followed by reports of a campaign of arrests of HuT members by the Palestinian Authority.[94] In August 2011, the group slammed Palestinian Authority President Mahmoud Abbas, when he suggested that NATO may have a presence in a future Palestinian state.[95]

Despite intermittent crackdowns by Palestinian security forces in the West Bank, the Islamist movement has continued to hold events there.[96] Most recently, in February 2014, HuT accused Palestinian Authority security forces in the West Bank of arresting its members for criticizing President Abbas.[97] The group had a significant presence (flags, mainly) during the unrest in the Jerusalem neighborhood of Shuafat, following the murder of a Palestinian teenager by Israeli extremists.

Mujahideen Shura Council in the Environs of Jerusalem (MSC)

The MSC, a Salafi *jihadist* group, was formed in the Gaza Strip in 2012. The group is a consolidation of Ansar al Sunnah and the Tawhid and Jihad Group in Jerusalem.[98] In November 2012, one of the group's leaders stated that the MSC aims to "fight the Jews for the return of Islam's rule, not only in Palestine, but throughout the world."[99]

While the exact size of the group is unknown, it has taken responsibility for a number of rocket attacks against Israel,[100] some of which have been carried out with Jaysh al Islam.[101] In addition, MSC took responsibility for a June 2012 bombing and shooting attack that killed one Israeli civilian.[102] According to a video released by the MSC, the June attack was "a gift to our brothers in Qaedat al Jihad [al-Qaeda] and Sheikh [Ayman al-] Zawahiri" and a retaliation for the killing of former al-Qaeda emir Osama bin Laden.[103]

Several Israeli air strikes targeted MSC operatives in 2012. After those attacks, *jihadi* groups such as al-Qaeda in the Arabian Peninsula (AQAP) and leaders like al-Qaeda head Ayman al-Zawahiri posted eulogies online.

The MSC was one of several Salafi *jihadi* groups that took part in the November 2012 conflict with Israel. Following the ceasefire, the group said that "[W]e truly are not a party to the signing of this truce between the Palestinian factions and the

Jews."[104] Throughout 2013, the MSC, through the Ibn Taymiyyah Media Center, its media wing, promoted the *jihad* in Syria as well as the efforts of the Sinai-based *jihadist* group Ansar Bayt al Maqdis.[105]

Harakat as-Sabirin Nasran li-Filastin

Harakat as-Sabirin Nasran li-Filastin (as-Sabirin), or "The Movement of the Patient Ones for the Liberation of Palestine" is a new, Iran-sponsored terror group in Gaza.[106] Founded in early 2014, the group burst onto the scene when one of its fighters, Nizar Saeed Issa, died in a mysterious explosion in the Gaza refugee camp of Jabalya.[107] Since then, *As-Sabirin* has lost two fighters, Ahmad Sharif as-Sarhi and Mus'ab al-Khayr al-Sakafi, in apparent clashes with Israel.

As-Sabirin is Shi'a group in a predominantly Sunni territory. Its flag and logo are derived from those of Hezbollah, and its fighters are pulled from another Iranian proxy: Palestinian Islamic Jihad. Its charter states that "*jihad* is the way of Allah to open doors to paradise…and in particular our journey faces the might enemies of the racist Zionist body and on its head America the great Satan."[108]

As-Sabirin is headed by Hisham Salem. Formerly a commander in PIJ, Salem hails from a prominent family in the Beit Lahia neighborhood in Gaza.[109] Salem was jailed in 1996 by the Palestinian Authority for organizing suicide attacks in Israel and during the second *intifada* was placed on Israel's most wanted terrorist list.[110] He has run several charities in the Gaza Strip, one of which, al-Baqiyat al-Salihat, was shut down by Hamas for spreading Shi'ism.[111]

The Iranian proxy group receives approximately $10 million per year from Tehran, which is typically smuggled through tunnels into Gaza.[112] Local reports suggest fighters in the group receive a salary of 250 to 300 U.S. dollars per month, while senior officials make up to 700 dollars a month.[113]

In February 2016, the Palestinian Authority broke up an *as-Sabirin* cell in Bethlehem.[114] According to PA security officials, the group was attempting to convert families in the West Bank to Shi'ism.[115]

ISLAMISM AND SOCIETY

Evidence suggests that Hamas was, in recent years, more popular among Palestinians than its secular rival, Fatah. This was true even before Hamas' unexpected victory in the PA's 2006 legislative election, and this trend continued since the organization's abrupt seizure of power in Gaza in June 2007.

Some analysts contend that such support is attributable more to a rejection of Fatah's alleged corruption than sincere support for Hamas' Islamism and militancy.[116] However, it may also be tied to the lack of popular support for the PLO's peace negotiations with Israel. One recent poll from the Palestinian Center for Policy and Survey Research found that more than 54 percent of Palestinians in Gaza oppose the idea of a two-state-solution.[117] Furthermore, data collected in 2013 by the Pew Research Center found that 62 percent of Muslims in the Palestinian Territories believe suicide bombings can be often or sometimes justified.[118] However, since Hamas' takeover of Gaza in 2007, anecdotal evidence suggests that the daily challenges of governance have eroded some of the popular support Hamas garnered through its resistance of Israel.[119] In other words, it is hard to maintain popular support as a revolutionary movement when saddled with mundane problems, such as electricity and garbage collection.

Under both Hamas rule in Gaza and PLO rule in the West Bank, evidence suggests that Christian minorities in both territories suffer discrimination and persecution, including religiously-motivated attacks on churches, destruction of crosses and altars, and the kidnapping and forced conversion of Christian girls.[120] Admittedly, Christians live with significantly more freedom in the West Bank since Hamas took control of Gaza, where Christians reportedly "feel increasingly unwelcome."[121]

ISLAMISM AND THE STATE

The active role of violent Islamist groups in the West Bank has dropped precipitously since the 2007 Palestinian civil war. Fearing a Hamas takeover in the West Bank, the United States and Israel have been furnishing the Palestinian Authority government in the West Bank with military training, weaponry, financing, and intelligence in order to more efficiently battle Hamas and other factions. The results have yielded some victories. According to a 2009 study by the Israel Security Agency (*Shin Bet* or *Shabak*), joint patrols were a key factor in reducing the number of terrorist attacks in the West Bank.[122] However, attacks in the West Bank in 2013 doubled compared to 2012.[123]

Since the end of Operation Pillar of Defense in November 2012, rocket fire from the Gaza Strip has been significantly reduced. In fact, the number of rockets fired in 2013 from Gaza towards Israel was the lowest in about a decade. Nonetheless, concerns persist that the ceasefire can easily be broken, by Hamas or by other groups.[124]

With Hamas firmly entrenched in Gaza, it appears unlikely that Israel will be able to neutralize the group with military power alone. This was made clear again during the 2014 conflict; even as Israel pounded hundreds of Hamas targets, long-range rockets continued to strike deep into Israeli territory. This has prompted some to propose that Israel should enter into negotiations with its long-time foe. Others contend that since Hamas is at one of its weakest points, both economically and politically, since its founding, now may be the time to cripple the group. Yet, the question of who would control Gaza after Hamas has prompted the Israelis to tread carefully, at least so far.

ENDNOTES

[1] Mosab Hassan Yousef and Ron Brackin, Son of Hamas: A Gripping Account of Terror, Betrayal, Political Intrigue, and Unthinkable Choices (Carol Stream: Tyndale House, 2010), 253-255.

[2] "Hamas Covenant 1988," The Avalon Project, n.d., http://avalon.law.yale.edu/20th_century/hamas.asp.

[3] Ibid.

[4] Ibidem.

[5] Ibidem.

[6] See, for example, "Hamas MP and Cleric Yunis Al-Astal: The Jews Were Brought to Palestine for the "Great Massacre" Through Which Allah Will "Relieve Humanity of Their Evil"," Middle East Media Research Institute, May 11, 2011, http://www.memri.org/clip/en/0/0/0/0/0/0/2934.htm.

[7] "Hamas Covenant 1988."

[8] Amira Hass, "Haniyeh: Hamas Willing To Accept Palestinian State With 1967 Borders," Ha'aretz, September 11, 2008, http://www.haaretz.com/news/haniyeh-hamas-willing-to-accept-palestinian-state-with-1967-borders-1.256915; "Meshal: Hamas Seeks Palestinian State Based on 1967 Borders," Ha'aretz, May 5, 2009, http://www.haaretz.com/news/meshal-hamas-seeks-palestinian-state-based-on-1967-borders-1.275412.

[9] Shlomi Eldar, "Hamas Official Says 'Abbas Doesn't Represent Anyone'," Al Monitor, February 20, 2014, http://www.al-monitor.com/pulse/originals/2014/02/mahmoud-al-zahar-hamas-recognizing-israel-mahmoud-abbas.html.

[10] Jonathan Schanzer, "The Talibanization of Gaza: A Liability for the Muslim Brotherhood," Hudson Institute Current Trends in Islamist Ideology 9, August 19, 2009, http://www.currenttrends.org/research/detail/the-talibanization-of-gaza-a-liability-for-the-muslim-brotherhood; Abeer Ayyoub, "Hamas Pushes Islamization of Gaza," Al Monitor, February 4, 2013, http://www.al-monitor.com/pulse/originals/2013/02/hamas-islamization-gaza.html.

[11] Rasha Abou Jalal, "Hamas Sinks in Polls After Cutting Salaries to Public Servants," Al Monitor, February 20, 2014, http://www.al-monitor.com/pulse/originals/2014/02/hamas-gaza-salaries-payments-siege.html.

[12] Matthew Levitt, "A Hamas Headquarters in Saudi Arabia," Washington Institute for Near East Policy Policy Watch 521, September 28, 2005, http://www.washingtoninstitute.org/policy-analysis/view/a-hamas-headquarters-in-saudi-arabia.

[13] Nidal al-Mughrabi, "Hamas Gaza Leader Heads for Iran," Reuters, January 30, 2012, http://uk.reuters.com/article/2012/01/30/uk-palestinians-hamas-iran-idUKTRE80T14P20120130.

[14] Jonathan Schanzer, "Hamas Rising," Foreign Policy, July 25, 2012, http://www.foreignpolicy.com/articles/2012/07/25/hamas_rising.

[15] Harriet Sherwood, "Hamas and Iran Rebuild Ties Three Years After Falling Out Over Syria," Guardian (London), January 9, 2014, http://www.theguardian.com/world/2014/jan/09/hamas-iran-rebuild-ties-falling-out-syria.

[16] "Five US Men Jailed for Allegedly Funding Hamas," Ma'an News Agency (Ramallah), May 28, 2009, http://maannews.net/eng/ViewDetails.aspx?ID=210849.

[17] "Tunnel Closure 'Costs Gaza $230 Million Monthly,'" Agence France Presse, October 27, 2013, http://www.google.com/hostednews/afp/article/ALeqM5gj2-72tPr4jJFBW_e52ASHwGfy8g?docId=aa97be5f-8a83-45b7-9fdd-cf4bc0ec6d74.

[18] "Rocket Attacks on Israel From Gaza," IDF Blog, n.d, http://www.idfblog.com/facts-figures/rocket-attacks-toward-israel/; "2010 Annual Summary," Israel Security Agency, n.d., http://www.shabak.gov.il/SiteCollectionImages/english/TerrorInfo/reports/2010summary2-en.pdf.

[19] Matthew Levitt, Hamas: Politics, Charity and Terrorism in the Service of Jihad (New Haven: Yale University Press, 2006).

[20] U.S. Department of the Treasury, "U.S. Designates Five Charities Funding Hamas and Six Senior Hamas Leaders as Terrorist Entities," August 22, 2003, http://www.treasury.gov/press-center/press-releases/Pages/js672.aspx.

[21] Bryony Jones, "Q&A: What is Hamas?" CNN, November 24, 2012, http://www.cnn.com/2012/11/16/world/meast/hamas-explainer/.

[22] See, for example: David Barnett, "Hamas Terror Plot Targeting Jerusalem Mall Foiled," Long War Journal – Threat Matrix, September 1, 2013, http://www.longwarjournal.org/threat-matrix/archives/2013/09/hamas_terror_plot_targeting_je.php.

[23] David Barnett, "Hamas Interior Minister Behind Terror Group's Activities in West Bank," Long War Journal – Threat Matrix, March 13, 2013, http://www.longwarjournal.org/threat-matrix/archives/2013/03/hamas_interior_minister_behind.php.

[24] Amos Harel, "Hamas is Alive and Kicking in the West Bank – But in Remote Control," Ha'aretz (Tel Aviv), December 21, 2013, http://www.haaretz.com/weekend/week-s-end/.premium-1.564568.

[25] Israel Security Agency, "2013 Annual Summary," n.d., http://www.shabak.gov.il/English/EnTerrorData/Reports/Pages/2013AnnualSummary.aspx.

[26] "Hamas Says it Continues to Build Tunnels to Attack Israel," Huffington Post, January 29, 2016. (http://www.huffingtonpost.com/huffwires/20160129/ml-gaza-tunnels/?utm_hp_ref=world&ir=world)

[27] "Israel Intercepts Materials for Building Tunnels, Rockets on their Way to Hamas," The Tower, May 27, 2016, http://www.thetower.org/3430oc-israel-intercepts-materials-for-building-tunnels-rockets-on-their-way-to-hamas/.

[28] "5-Man Hamas Cell that Killed Naama and Eitam Henkin Arrested," Times of Israel, October 5, 2015, http://www.timesofisrael.com/shin-bet-terror-cell-behind-henkin-murders-arrested/.

[29] Mitch Ginsburg, "Abbas Orders Probe into Hamas Coup Plot Revealed by Israel," Times of Israel, August 19, 2014, http://www.timesofisrael.com/abbas-orders-investigation-into-hamas-coup-plot-revealed-by-israel/.

[30] Ehud Yaari, "Hamas and the Islamic State: Growing Cooperation in the Sinai," Washington Institute for Near East Policy Policywatch 2533, December 15, 2015, http://www.washingtoninstitute.org/policy-analysis/view/hamas-and-the-islamic-state-growing-cooperation-in-the-sinai.

[31] "IDF General: IS Fighters Training with Hamas in Gaza," Times of Israel, May 13, 2016, http://www.timesofisrael.com/idf-general-is-fighters-entered-gaza-to-train-with-hamas/.

[32] "Islamic Jihad, Hamas Officials Rally in Gaza to Support West Bank Shooting," Ma'an News Agency (Ramallah), February 1, 2016, http://www.maannews.com/Content.aspx?id=770075.

[33] Jack Moore, "Hamas Says Jerusalem Bus Bomb Shows Commitment to Third Intifada," Newsweek, April 29, 2016, http://www.newsweek.com/hamas-says-jerusalem-bus-bomb-shows-commitment-third-intifada-453845.

[34] "World Vision Halts Gaza Projects and Cuts Jobs Amid Claims Funds Sent to Hamas," The Guardian, September 9, 2016, https://www.theguardian.com/world/2016/sep/10/world-vision-halts-gaza-projects-and-cuts-jobs-amid-claims-funds-sent-to-hamas.

[35] Ilan Ben Zion, "Israel Busts Hamas Cell Planning Suicide Bombings in Jerusalem, Haifa," The Times of Israel, December 22, 2016, http://www.timesofisrael.com/israel-busts-hamas-cell-planning-suicide-bombings-in-jerusalem-haifa/.

[36] Asmaa al-Ghoul, "Palestinian Islamic Jihad: Iran Supplies All Weapons in Gaza," Al Monitor, May 14, 2013, http://www.al-monitor.com/pulse/originals/2013/05/gaza-islamic-jihad-and-iranian-arms.html.

[37] Holly Fletcher, "Palestinian Islamic Jihad," Council on Foreign Relations, April 10, 2008, http://www.cfr.org/israel/palestinian-islamic-jihad/p15984.

[38] "Chapter 6. Foreign Terrorist Organizations," in U.S. Department of State, Country Reports on Terrorism 2011, July 31, 2012, http://www.state.gov/j/ct/rls/crt/2011/195553.htm; Abeer Ayyoub, "Iran Top Backer of Palestinian Islamic Jihad," Al Monitor, January 9, 2013, http://www.al-monitor.com/pulse/originals/2013/01/palestinian-islamic-jihad.html; Crispian Balmer and Nidal al-Mughrabi, "Single-Minded Islamic Jihad Grows in Gaza's Shadows," Reuters, November 12, 2013, http://www.reuters.com/article/2013/11/12/us-palestinians-islamicjihad-idUSBRE9AB08720131112.

[39] Avi Issacharoff, "Hamas Brutally Assaults Shi'ite Worshippers in Gaza." Ha'aretz (Tel Aviv), January 17, 2012, http://www.haaretz.com/news/middle-east/hamas-brutally-assaults-shi-ite-worshippers-in-gaza-1.407688.

[40] David Barnett, "US Designates Deputy Secretary-General of Palestinian Islamic Jihad," Long War Journal, January 23, 2014, http://www.longwarjournal.org/archives/2014/01/us_designates_deputy.php.

[41] See, for example, David Barnett, "Palestinian Islamic Jihad Operatives Behind Recent Bus Bombing Near Tel Aviv," Long War Journal – Threat Matrix, January 3, 2014, http://www.longwarjournal.org/threat-matrix/archives/2014/01/palestinian_islamic_jihad_oper.php.

[42] "Hamas, Islamic Jihad Warn of 'New Methods of Resistance'," Ma'an News Agency, November 4, 2015. (http://www.maannews.com/Content.aspx?id=768645)

[43] Maayan Groisman, "Iran to Renew Financial Support for Islamic Jihad After Two-Year Hiatus," Jerusalem Post, May 25, 2016, http://www.jpost.com/Middle-East/Reembracing-Islamic-Jihad-Iran-to-renew-financial-aid-for-Palestinian-terror-group-454968.

[44] Ibid.

[45] Adam Rasgon, "Islamic Jihad Calls to Escalate Intifada and Boycott Palestinian Elections," The Jerusalem Post, August 9, 2016, http://www.jpost.com/Arab-Israeli-Conflict/Islamic-Jihad-calls-to-escalate-intifada-as-it-boycotts-Palestinian-elections-463651.

[46] "Who is the Palestinian Group Blamed for the Attacks?" Reuters, August 19, 2011, http://www.haaretz.com/news/diplomacy-defense/who-is-the-palestinian-group-blamed-for-the-attacks-1.379509.

[47] "What Is The Popular Resistance Committee?" IDF Blog, March 10, 2012, http://www.idfblog.com/2012/03/10/popular-resistance-committee/; "Who is Organizing the PRC," Walla, June 28, 2006, http://news.walla.co.il/?w=//931483.

[48] See, for example, Jack Khoury, "Palestinians Release Video Showing Gaza Anti-Tank Missile Hitting IDF Jeep,"Ha'aretz (Tel Aviv), November 13, 2012, http://www.haaretz.com/news/diplomacy-defense/palestinians-release-video-showing-gaza-anti-tank-missile-hitting-idf-jeep.premium-1.477488.

[49] "Palestinians Bomb US Convoy," Guardian (London), October 16, 2003, http://www.guardian.co.uk/world/2003/oct/16/israel.

[50] "Who is the Palestinian Group Blamed for the Attacks?"

[51] David Barnett, "Israeli Intelligence: Sinai is The 'Home of An Independent Jihadist Network,'" Long War Journal, October 3, 2012, http://www.longwarjournal.org/archives/2012/10/israeli_intelligence.php; Eli Lake, "Al Qaeda Linked to Israeli Bus Ambush," Washington Times, August 22, 2011, http://www.washingtontimes.com/news/2011/aug/22/al-qaeda-linked-to-israeli-bus-ambush/.

[52] David Barnett, "Israel Targets Gaza Terror Operative Linked to Sinai-Based Ansar Jerusalem," Long War Journal – Threat Matrix, February 9, 2014, http://www.longwarjournal.org/threat-matrix/archives/2014/02/israel_targets_gaza_terror_ope.php.

[53] "Category Archives: Nāṣir Ṣalāḥ ad-Dīn Brigades (PRC)," Jihadology, n.d., http://jihadology.net/category/na%E1%B9%A3ir-%E1%B9%A3ala%E1%B8%A5-ad-din-brigades-prc/.

[54] Wikileaks, "Frances Townsend's November 12 Meeting With ISA," November 24, 2006, http://wikileaks.org/cable/2006/11/06TELAVIV4603.html.

[55] David Barnett, "Popular Resistance Committees Calls on Hamas to Stop Arrests of 'Mujahideen,'" Long War Journal – Threat Matrix, July 22, 2013, http://www.longwarjournal.org/threat-matrix/archives/2013/07/popular_resistance_committees.php.

[56] Israel Ministry of Foreign Affairs, "The Involvement of Arafat, PA Senior Officials and Apparatuses in Terrorism against Israel: Corruption and Crime," May 6, 2002, http://www.mfa.gov.il/MFA/MFAArchive/2000_2009/2002/5/The+Involvement+of+Arafat-+PA+Senior+Officials+and.htm.

[57] Holly Fletcher, "Al-Aqsa Martyrs Brigade," Council on Foreign Relations, April 2, 2008, http://www.cfr.org/israel/al-aqsa-martyrs-brigade/p9127.

[58] See, for example, Ethan Bronner, "Israeli Military Kills 6 Palestinians," New York Times, December 26, 2009, http://www.nytimes.com/2009/12/27/world/middleeast/27mideast.html.

[59] "Chapter 6. Foreign Terrorist Organizations."

[60] See, for example: "Militant Group Claims Responsibility for Projectile," Ma'an News Agency (Ramallah), December 28, 2011, http://www.maannews.net/eng/ViewDetails.aspx?ID=448358.

[61] "In Photos: Al-Aqsa Brigades Hold Military Parade in Qalandiam," Ma'an News Agency (Ramallah), November 17, 2013, http://www.maannews.net/eng/ViewDetails.aspx?ID=648178; Naela Khalil, "Is Fatah's Armed Wing Making Comeback?," Al Monitor, September 25, 2013, http://www.al-monitor.com/pulse/originals/2013/09/hebron-israeli-soldiers-killed-fatah-intifada.html.

[62] Daniel Douek, "13 Injured as Palestinian Police Clash with Gunmen in Nablus," Times of Israel, March 29, 2016, http://www.timesofisrael.com/13-injured-as-palestinian-police-clash-with-gunmen-in-nablus/.

[63] Adam Rasgon, "PA Official: Top Suspect in Killing of Two PA Officers Arrested and Beaten to Death," Jerusalem Post, August 23, 2016, http://www.jpost.com/Arab-Israeli-Conflict/Top-suspect-in-killing-of-two-PA-officers-arrested-and-beaten-to-death-464841.

[64] "Mass Protests in West Bank City After Palestinian Detainee Dies," Reuters, August 23, 2016, http://uk.reuters.com/article/uk-palestinians-nablus-death-idUKKCN10Y1FM.

[65] "Chapter 6. Foreign Terrorist Organizations."

[66] Jonathan Dahoah Halevi, "Al Qaeda Affiliate Jaish al-Islam Receives Formal Sanctuary In Hamas-Ruled Gaza," Jerusalem Center for Public Affairs Jerusalem Issue Briefs 8, no. 7, August 20, 2008, http://jcpa.org/article/al-qaeda-affiliate-jaish-al-islam-receives-formal-sanctuary-in-hamas-ruled-gaz/.

[67] Ibid.

[68] Ibidem.

[69] Bill Roggio, "US Designates Palestinian Salafist Group as a Foreign Terrorist Organization," Long War Journal, May 19, 2011, http://www.longwarjournal.org/archives/2011/05/us_designates_palest.php.
[70] Ibid.
[71] "SOCOM-2012-0000008," Combating Terrorism Center, n.d., http://www.ctc.usma.edu/posts/socom-2012-0000008-english.
[72] Wikileaks, "Frances Townsend's November 12 Meeting With Isa Chief Diskin Focuses On The Palestinians," November 24, 2006, http://wikileaks.org/cable/2006/11/06TELAVIV4603.html.
[73] David Barnett, "Gaza-Based Salafi Jihadists Conduct Joint Rocket Attacks, Sinai Jihadists Suppressed," Long War Journal – Threat Matrix, November 22, 2012, http://www.longwarjournal.org/threat-matrix/archives/2012/11/salafi-jihadist_groups_in_gaza.php.
[74] David Barnett, "Report Provides Insight on Israeli View of Salafi Jihadists in Sinai," Long War Journal, August 20, 2013, http://www.longwarjournal.org/archives/2013/08/report_provides_insi.php.
[75] Barak Ravid, "Shin Bet Forms New Unit to Thwart Attacks on Israel by Sinai Jihadists," Ha'aretz (Tel Aviv), August 20, 2013, http://www.haaretz.com/news/diplomacy-defense/.premium-1.542417.
[76] "Pro Al-Qaeda Fighters Train in Gaza Strip," Reuters, September 1, 2008, http://www.alarabiya.net/articles/2008/09/01/55828.html.
[77] Yoram Cohen, Matthew Levitt, and Becca Wasser, Deterred but Determined: Salafi-Jihadi Groups in the Palestinian Arena (Washington, DC: Washington Institute for Near East Policy, January 2010), http://www.washingtoninstitute.org/uploads/Documents/pubs/PolicyFocus%2099.pdf.
[78] "Radical Islam in Gaza," International Crisis Group, March 29, 2011, http://www.crisisgroup.org/~/media/Files/Middle%20East%20North%20Africa/Israel%20Palestine/104%20Radical%20Islam%20in%20Gaza.ashx.
[79] Jaysh Al-Ummah Official: Expect Military Operation In South Lebanon Directed At Israel," NOW Lebanon, April 11, 2010, https://now.mmedia.me/lb/en/nownews/jaysh_al-ummah_official_expect_military_operation_in_south_lebanon_directed_at_israel.
[80] "Jaish Al Ummah To Hamas: 'Whose Side Are You On?'" CBS News, May 27, 2009, http://www.cbsnews.com/news/jaish-al-ummah-to-hamas-whose-side-are-you-on/.
[81] "Al-Rāyyah Foundation for Media Presents New Pictures From Jaysh al-Ummah: 'The Arrival of Goodness #3'," Jihadology, October 13, 2013, http://jihadology.net/2013/10/13/al-rayyah-foundation-for-media-presents-new-pictures-from-jaysh-al-ummah-the-arrival-of-goodness-3/.
[82] "Jaysh Al-Ummah Official: Expect Military Operation In South Lebanon Directed At Israel."

[83] "Al Qaeda Conducted Attack Against Israel from Gaza," Ma'ariv (Tel Aviv), September 2, 2008, http://www.nrg.co.il/online/1/ART1/781/681.html.

[84] "Palestinian Faction Urges Help to Sunnis in Ahvaz, Iran, in Audio," SITE Intelligence Group, January 17, 2013, https://news.siteintelgroup.com/index.php/19-jihadist-news/2658-palestinian-faction-urges-help-to-sunnis-in-ahvaz-iran-in-audio.

[85] "Palestinian Faction Supports Malian Jihadists, Calls for Attacks on West," SITE Intelligence Group, January 22, 2013, http://news.siteintelgroup.com/index.php/19-jihadist-news/2678-palestinian-faction-supports-malian-jihadists-calls-for-attacks-on-west.

[86] David Barnett, "Gaza Jihadists Call for 'Jihad' Against Egypt's El Sisi," Long War Journal, August 15, 2013, http://www.longwarjournal.org/archives/2013/08/gaza_jihadists_call.php.

[87] David Barnett, "Gaza-Based Jaish al Ummah Praises Hakeemullah Mehsud," Long War Journal – Threat Matrix, November 13, 2013, http://www.longwarjournal.org/threat-matrix/archives/2013/11/gaza-based_jaish_al_ummah_prai.php.

[88] "About Us," Hizb Ut Tahrir, n.d., http://english.hizbuttahrir.org/index.php/about-us.

[89] Jonathan Spyer, "Hizb ut-Tahrir: A Rising Force In Palestinian Territories," Global Politician, December 14, 2007, https://web.archive.org/web/20120202204241/http://globalpolitician.com/23871-palestine.

[90] Isabel Kershner, "Palestinian Is Killed in Hebron as Police Disperse Protest Over Mideast Peace Talks," New York Times, November 27, 2007, http://www.nytimes.com/2007/11/28/world/middleeast/28palestinians.html.

[91] Jonathan Spyer, "A 'Rising Force,'" Ha'aretz (Tel Aviv), June 12, 2007, http://www.haaretz.com/hasen/spages/932087.html.

[92] "Hizb Ut-Tahrir: PA Attempts Arrest Of Member," Ma'an News Agency (Ramallah), December 17, 2009, http://www.maannews.net/eng/ViewDetails.aspx?ID=247723; "Hizb Ut-Tahrir: PA Arrests Thousands," Ma'an News Agency (Ramallah), July 17, 2010, http://www.maannews.net/eng/ViewDetails.aspx?ID=300222.

[93] "PA Forces Disperse Hizb ut-Tahrir Rally in Ramallah," Ma'an News Agency (Ramallah), July 2, 2011, http://www.maannews.net/eng/ViewDetails.aspx?ID=401698.

[94] "PA Arrests 13 Islamists in Crackdown," Ma'an News Agency (Ramallah), July 15, 2011, http://www.maannews.net/eng/ViewDetails.aspx?ID=405427.

[95] "Hizb ut-Tahrir Accuses PLO of Betrayal," Ma'an News Agency (Ramallah), August 13, 2011, http://www.maannews.net/eng/ViewDetails.aspx?ID=412772.

[96] Khaled Abu Toameh, "Radical Islam Arrives in Ramallah," Gatestone Institute, June 5, 2013, http://www.gatestoneinstitute.org/3751/radical-islam-ramallah; "Hizb al-Tahrir Holds West Bank Festival," Ma'an News Agency (Ramallah), June 17, 2012, http://www.maannews.net/eng/ViewDetails.aspx?ID=496157.

[97] "Group Says PA Arrested Dozens of Its Members Over Abbas Criticism," Ma'an News Agency (Ramallah), February 9, 2014, http://www.maannews.net/eng/ViewDetails.aspx?ID=672063.

[98] David Barnett, "Mujahideen Shura Council is Consolidation of Salafi-Jihadist Groups in Gaza: Sources," Long War Journal, October 14, 2012, http://www.longwarjournal.org/archives/2012/10/mujahideen_shura_cou.php.

[99] David Barnett, "Mujahideen Shura Council Leader Slams Hamas, Calls for Public Dialogue," Long War Journal – Threat Matrix, November 9, 2012, http://www.longwarjournal.org/threat-matrix/archives/2012/11/mujahideen_shura_council_leade.php.

[100] Ibid.

[101] David Barnett, "Gaza-Based Salafi Jihadists Conduct Joint Rocket Attacks, Sinai Jihadists Suppressed," Long War Journal – Threat Matrix, November 22, 2012, http://www.longwarjournal.org/threat-matrix/archives/2012/11/salafi-jihadist_groups_in_gaza.php.

[102] Thomas Joscelyn, "Al Qaeda-Linked Group Claims Responsibility for Attack in Israel," Long War Journal, June 19, 2012, http://www.longwarjournal.org/archives/2012/06/al_qaeda-linked_grou.php.

[103] Bill Roggio, "Mujahideen Shura Council Calls Attack in Israel a 'Gift' to Zawahiri and Al Qaeda 'Brothers,'" Long War Journal, July 30, 2012, http://www.longwarjournal.org/archives/2012/07/egyptian_jihadist_gr.php.

[104] David Barnett, "Mujahideen Shura Council: We Are Not Truly a Party to the Ceasefire with Israel," Long War Journal, November 27, 2012, http://www.longwarjournal.org/archives/2012/11/mujahideen_shura_cou_2.php.

[105] David Barnett, "Jihadist Media Unit Urges Fighters to Strike Egyptian Army," Long War Journal – Threat Matrix, September 23, 2013, http://www.longwarjournal.org/archives/2013/09/jihadist_media_unit.php; David Barnett, "Jihadist Media Unit Releases Posters for Palestinian Fighters Killed in Syria," Long War Journal – Threat Matrix, October 1, 2013, http://www.longwarjournal.org/threat-matrix/archives/2013/10/jihadist_media_unit_releases_p.php.

[106] Jonathan Schanzer & Grant Rumley, "Iran Spawns New Jihadist Group in Gaza," Long War Journal, June 18, 2014, http://www.longwarjournal.org/archives/2014/06/by_jonathan_schanzer.php.

[107] "Gaza Militant Dies in Apparent Explosives Accident," Times of Israel, May 26, 2014, http://www.timesofisrael.com/gaza-militant-dies-in-apparent-explosives-accident/.

[108] Al-Sabireen, "Our Charter," n.d., http://alsabireen.ps/ar/page/4/%D9%87%D9%88%D9%8A%D8%AA%D9%86%D8%A7

[109] Ehud Yaari, "Replacing Hamas," Foreign Affairs, September 28, 2015, https://www.foreignaffairs.com/articles/palestinian-authority/2015-09-28/replacing-hamas.

[110] Ehud Yaari, "Replacing Hamas," Foreign Affairs, September 28, 2015, https://www.foreignaffairs.com/articles/palestinian-authority/2015-09-28/replacing-hamas.

[111] Adnan Abu Amer, "Why Hamas Closed Down Iranian Charity in Gaza," Al Monitor, March 22, 2016, http://www.al-monitor.com/pulse/originals/2016/03/gaza-hamas-shut-down-iran-affiliated-charity.html.

[112] Yaari, "Replacing Hamas."

[113] "Middle East: Iran Back Into Gaza," Amad, October 25, 2015, http://www.amad.ps/ar/?Action=Details&ID=95441

[114] Khaled Abu Toameh, "Analysis: Iran Infiltrates the West Bank," Jerusalem Post, February 9, 2016, http://www.jpost.com/Arab-Israeli-Conflict/Analysis-Iran-Infiltrates-the-West-Bank-444352.

[115] "Palestinian Security Sources: The "Patient" Movement Seeks to Stretch from Gaza to the West," Amad, May 2, 2016, http://www.amad.ps/ar/?Action=Details&ID=109775

[116] Khaled Abu Toameh, "'Corruption Will Let Hamas Take W. Bank,'" Jerusalem Post, January 29, 2010, http://www.jpost.com/Middle-East/Corruption-will-let-Hamas-take-W-Bank.

[117] Palestinian Center for Policy and Survey Research, "Palestinian Public Opinion Poll No (48)," June 2013, http://www.pcpsr.org/survey/polls/2013/p48e.html.

[118] "Muslim Publics Share Concerns about Extremist Groups," Pew Research Center, September 10, 2013, http://www.pewglobal.org/2013/09/10/muslim-publics-share-concerns-about-extremist-groups/.

[119] Hazem Balousha, "Gazans Unimpressed By Hamas Military Parades," Al Monitor, November 20, 2013, http://www.al-monitor.com/pulse/originals/2013/11/hamas-islamic-jihad-military-parade-gaza-crisis.html.

[120] Jonathan Schanzer, Hamas vs. Fatah: The Struggle for Palestine (New York: Palgrave Macmillan, 2008), 110-111.

[121] Ibrahim Barzak and Diaa Hadid, "Gaza Christians Fear for Future of Tiny Community," Associated Press, July 25, 2012, http://bigstory.ap.org/article/gaza-christians-fear-future-tiny-community.

[122] Israel Ministry of Foreign Affairs, "ISA: Data And Trends In Palestinian Terrorism – 2009 Summary," January 15, 2010, http://www.mfa.gov.il/mfa/foreignpolicy/terrorism/palestinian/pages/isa_summary_palestinian_terrorism_2009.aspx.

[123] Ben Hartman, "Shin Bet: West Bank Terror Attacks More Than Doubled in 2013," Jerusalem Post, January 27, 2014, http://www.jpost.com/Defense/Shin-Bet-West-Bank-terror-attacks-more-than-doubled-in-2013-339522.

[124] "Hamas Withdraws 'Anti-Missile' Force From Israel Border," Agence France Presse, February 2, 2014, http://www.naharnet.com/stories/en/116886.

QATAR

> **QUICK FACTS**
>
> Population: 2,258,283 (estimated July 2016)
>
> Area: 11,586 sq km
>
> Ethnic Groups: Arab 40%, Indian 18%, Pakistani 18%, Iranian 10%, other 14%
>
> Religions: Muslim 77.5%, Christian 8.5%, other 14%
>
> Government Type: Emirate
>
> GDP (official exchange rate): $156.6 billion (estimated 2015)
>
> *Quick Facts courtesy of the CIA World Factbook (January 2017)*

OVERVIEW

The tiny Gulf state of Qatar is a study in contradictions. Considerably more liberal than many of its neighbors, Qatar nevertheless is the only country other than Saudi Arabia to espouse Wahhabism as its official state religion. A traditionally conservative country whose authoritarian tribal rulers brook no opposition, Qatar is nevertheless host to the Al-Jazeera satellite television network, whose independent reporting has occasionally led to diplomatic crises with neighboring countries. Moreover, Qatar is host to the Al Udeid air base, regional home of the U.S. Central Command, yet the Qatari government has also provided money and diplomatic support to Islamists in Syria, Libya, and the Sahel, as well as the Muslim Brotherhood in Egypt.

Domestically, Qatar has no active Islamist opposition, for the simple reason that the state has co-opted and involved Islamism in its governance ever since its establishment. Wahhabi thought is especially influential among the Al Thani clan, which has ruled Qatar since the beginning of the nineteenth century. Its embrace of Wahhabism distinguishes Qatar religiously from its other neighbors, while promoting a close relationship—and occasional rivalry—with Saudi Arabia.

ISLAMIST ACTIVITY

Copy Islamism is very much an in-house phenomenon in Qatar. It has been pointed out that a necessary precondition for the rise of an Islamist opposition is a decline in government legitimacy and efficacy.[1] This, in a nutshell, explains the general lack of robust Islamic opposition to the governments of the Gulf States, and Qatar is no exception. A small, exceptionally wealthy country where the government subsidizes everything from petrol to education, Qatar so far has lacked serious challenges to the Islamic legitimacy of its government.

Likewise, there have been very few reported incidents of anti-Western terrorism in Qatar in recent years. In November 2001, two U.S. contractors were shot at the al-Udeid airbase, and attackers attempted to ram the base's gate in 2002.[2] These incidents, however, are believed to have been the work of lone attackers.

In March 2005, Omar Ahmed Abdallah Ali, an expatriate Egyptian, blew himself up outside a theater in Doha. The attack, which killed a British school teacher, was the first suicide bombing in Qatar. Ali was believed to have had ties to al-Qaeda in the Arabian Peninsula, whose leader issued a communiqué two days before the attack calling on local citizens of a number of Gulf states, of which Qatar was at the top of his list,[3] to act against Western interestsIn the aftermath of this attack, allegations were made that Qatar's rulers had been paying protection money to al-Qaeda. A report in London's *Sunday Times* described an agreement between the government of Qatar and al-Qaeda prior to the 2003 Iraq War, under which millions of dollars were paid annually to the terror network to keep Qatar off of its target list, despite the country's role as a U.S. ally.[4] This money was believed to be channeled via religious leaders sympathetic to al-Qaeda, and used to support the organization's activities in Iraq. After the attack in Doha, the agreement was renewed, according to the *Times'* source, "just to be on the safe side."[5]

The *Times* report highlights the fine line that Qatar treads in its relations with the U.S. and its powerful neighbors. Because it hosts the Al Udeid airbase and Camp As Sayliyah, a pre-positioning facility for U.S. military equipment, Qatar is a more attractive target for terrorists than most neighboring countries, whose ties to the U.S. are less tangible. Qatar pays for the upkeep of the bases used by American military forces on its soil; the U.S. pays neither rent nor utilities on them.[6] Neither Qatar nor the U.S. makes any secret of these ties. It is thus surprising that Qatar has not been a more frequent target of al-Qaeda's attacks. The purported payment of protection money to al-Qaeda is one explanation for Qatar's relative safety; another may be that the absence of social and political discontent within the country's borders deprives al-Qaeda of willing local recruits. Homegrown *jihadis* are not as common in Qatar as they are in many neighboring countries.

Moreover, politics in the region are often played out in a very subtle way. While Qatar ostensibly enjoys a close relationship with Washington, these ties are balanced by ties with Islamist groups throughout the region. According to a State Department cable released by Wikileaks, Qatar was deemed "the worst in the region" in its counterterrorism efforts.[7] Qatar's security service was described as "hesitant to act against known terrorists out of concern for appearing to be aligned with the U.S. and provoking reprisals."[8]

Nor is this merely a tactic to defuse Islamist hostility; rather it is consistent with Qatar's long-term strategy. The Qatari government has acquired a reputation as a financial backer of Islamist causes abroad, including terrorist organizations. Several charities based in Qatar have been accused of actively financing al-Qaeda and other terrorist organizations. One of these, the Qatar Charitable Society (QCS), was set up and operated by an employee of the Qatari government.[9]

At the start of the Arab Spring, Qatar threw its weight behind the protest movements in North Africa and the Middle East, playing a major role in almost all the conflicts in the Arab world. Qatar became the first Arab country to grant official recognition to the Libyan rebels, and contributed six Mirage fighter jets to the Western military campaign to depose Muamar Qadhafi. Its financial support of the revolution in Libya may have reached $2 billion, channelled through various opposition figures.[10]

Doha also provided financial aid to Islamist militants fighting in the Sahel region, including al-Qaeda forces that managed to carve out a state in Mali. In 2015, Qatar deployed troops and materiel to Yemen, as part of the Arab coalition's fight against Houthi rebels.[11]

In the Palestinian arena, Qatar has long been the primary financial and ideological sponsor of Hamas. In October 2012, the *emir* became the first head of state to visit the Gaza Strip since Hamas took full control of the territory in 2007. At that time, the *emir* pledged $400 million for infrastructure projects. The timing of the visit, coming just after the upgrade of the Palestinian Authority's status at the United Nations, appears to have been aimed at boosting Hamas's standing against its Fatah rivals.[12] More recently, Doha has coordinated with Israel and the Palestinian Authority to pay Hamas' employees' salaries, and to import construction materials into the Gaza Strip.[13]

In 2013, the Taliban opened an official office in Qatar.[14] The office was briefly closed under pressure from the U.S. and the current Afghan government, but has since reopened to serve as a base for negotiations.[15]

But it is in Syria that Qatar's support for Islamists is most controversial. While Qatari jets have provided symbolic participation in the airpower mission against the Islamic State, Qatar has become a significant financial sponsor of the Islamist elements arrayed against President Bashar al-Assad. In particular, Qatar has provided funding and weapons to *Ahrar al-Sham*— or "Free Men of Syria". Khalid al-Attiyah, then Qatari foreign minister, praised this movement as "purely" Syrian.[16]

Qatar has been openly funding Jabhat al-Nusra since 2013. Much of this funding is provided in the form of "ransom" for Western hostages, kidnapped by the group for exactly this purpose.[17] This is in addition to large sums of money channeled to the group via Qatari charity organizations and individuals, who are allowed to operate freely in the country.[18]

In addition to material support, Doha has provided considerable propaganda support for the Syrian *jihadis* via *Al-Jazeera*. Qatari officials have touted their support of "moderate" jihadi groups as an effective means of fighting the Islamic State.[19] In fact, this support was portrayed in a positive light by the U.S. State Department in its 2014 Country Reports on Terrorism, which cited Qatar's offer "to host a train-and-equip program for moderate Syrian opposition forces."[20]

In fact, with Qatar's help, Jabhat al-Nusra became powerful enough that that U.S. General Petraeus suggested that the U.S. also support the group as the only plausible threat to ISIS in Syria.[21] However, such suggestions ignore the fact that there is no real hierarchy of *jihadi* groups. Alliances and rivalries between the different "camps" are continually shifting, so that support for one group can reach rival groups via mergers and temporary alliances.

In addition, membership in the different *jihadi* groups is fluid; senior leaders of Al Nusra were once members of the Islamic State in Iraq.[22] Al-Nusra has reportedly lost hundreds of fighters to Islamic State over the past few years.[23] These defections lead to the transfer of Qatari-supplied weapons and funds to ISIS, a fact that even Qatar's allies have had to acknowledge. A leaked email published by Wikileaks in October 2016 singled out Qatar and Saudi Arabia as "providing clandestine financial and logistic support to ISIL [ISIS] and other radical Sunni groups in the region."[24]

None of the groups fighting in Syria can be seen as "moderate" in any meaningful sense. Ahrar al-Sham fought alongside Jabhat al-Nusra during the battle for Aleppo and has been accused of at least one sectarian massacre.[25] At the time the organization was being openly supported by Qatar, it was also sharing local authority with the ISIS in Raqqa.[26] Meanwhile Jabhat al-Nusra ostensibly split from al-Qaida in mid 2016, rebranding itself as Jabhat Fateh al-Sham. However, the "split" was in name only; the organization's leader did not in fact renounce ties to its parent group.[27]

Qatar's strategy of simultaneously remaining on good terms with Islamists and with the West has facilitated its role as a mediator in the region, including negotiating for the release of captive U.S. servicemen in Afghanistan in exchange for prisoners held by the U.S. This role, as seen in connection with the al-Nusra hostages, has allowed Qatar to openly bankroll jihadi groups through the payment of ransoms for Western hostages.[28]

At the same time, Qatar's close ties to the Muslim Brotherhood and active support for jihadis have led to strained ties with other countries in the region. In March

2014, Saudi Arabia, the United Arab Emirates, and Bahrain withdrew their ambassadors due to the Qatar's sponsorship of the Muslim Brotherhood and other Islamist groups.[29] After Egyptian president Mohamed Morsi was overthrown in 2013, several members of the Muslim Brotherhood were asked to leave Qatar, as part of a rapprochement agreement signed between Gulf countries.[30] It is not known whether those expelled eventually reentered the country. In December 2016, Egypt accused Qatar of being indirectly responsible for the bombing of a Coptic church which killed 24 people. A statement by the Egyptian government said that the attacker had been instructed by the Muslim Brotherhood in Qatar to plan and carry out the attack in order to promote sectarian strife.[31]

Qatar's continued support of Islamist elements, despite its negative diplomatic impact, reflects the fact that this support goes beyond mere pragmatism, and has a clear ideological basis.[32] At times, this support has been a matter of personal honor. Qatar's ties to the Libyan rebels, for instance, were reportedly mostly on the level of personal connections.[33] Such ties are nothing new; according to American intelligence officials, Abdallah bin Khalid al-Thani, a member of the Qatari royal family, helped wanted al-Qaeda chief Khaled Sheikh Mohammed elude capture in 1996. Abdallah bin Khalid, who was Qatar's Minister of Religious Affairs at the time, reportedly sheltered the wanted man on one of his own farms.[34] Mohammed is believed to have been employed for some years in Qatar's Department of Public Water Works, before slipping out of the country on a Qatari passport just ahead of an American attempt to capture him.[35]

Abdallah bin Khalid was not alone in his sympathies to al-Qaeda. News reports have cited U.S. officials as saying there were others in the Qatari royal family who provided safe haven for al-Qaeda leaders.[36] In late 2013, the U.S. Treasury Department imposed sanctions on several prominent Qataris for providing funds to al-Qaeda and to *jihadis* in Syria.[37] One year later, one of those designated was found to be still employed by the Qatari Interior Ministry, while others were still living at large in the emirate.[38] A U.S.-based think tank has identified over twenty individuals under U.S. or UN sanctions who have benefitted from some form of Qatari negligence or support.[39]

Islamism and Society

Wahhabism—the very strict interpretation of Islam espoused by 18th century preacher Muhammad ibn Abd al Wahhab—has shaped Qatar's history for more than a century. Among the tribes that adopted the *Wahhabi* interpretation in the late 19th century were the Al Thani— in contrast to the ruling Al Khalifas of Bahrain, who rejected *Wahhabism*. When the Al Khalifas attempted to invade the peninsula of Qatar in 1867, the Al Thani and their followers, with the help of the British, repelled the invasion. This victory established the Al Thani family as Qatar's ruling clan. Thereafter, Qatar became the only country other than Saudi Arabia to espouse *Hanbali Wahhabism* as the official state religion.[40] This set the stage for tensions between Qatar and its other neighbors.

Qatar's population is conservative, but overt religious discrimination has been rare. Non-citizens constitute a majority of Qatar's residents, as most are from Southeast Asia or from other Muslim countries, which has minimized the influence of Western culture.[41] Inter-Muslim friction is also minimized by the homogeneity of Qatar's citizenry. Sunni Muslims constitute the overwhelming majority of the population, while Shi'a Muslims account for less than five percent.[42] As a result, the main drivers for Islamist opposition are lacking in Qatar; the government espouses a distinctly Islamist ideology, while social inequities and cultural frictions have been kept to a minimum.

However, in contrast to Saudi Arabia, *Wahhabi* tenets are not officially enforced or strictly adhered to in most public settings in Qatar. Qatari society is generally moderate, and, among Arab countries, its civil liberties are ranked second only to Lebanon.[43] While instances of overt religious discrimination have been rare, anti-Semitic motifs are common in the mainstream media: Israel and world Jewry are frequently demonized in editorials and cartoons.[44]

The need to keep pace with global social and economic development has pushed Qatar to gradually shift its political structure from a traditional society based on consent and consensus to one based on more formal, though not necessarily democratic, institutions. Qatar's constitution institutionalized the hereditary rule of the Al Thani family, but it also established an elected legislative body and made government ministers accountable to the legislature.[45] While formally accountable to no one, the *Emir* is still bound by the checks and balances of traditional Muslim Arab societies; all decisions must be in accordance with *sharia* and must not arouse the opposition of the country's leading families.[46]

In June 2013, Hamad bin Khalifa al-Thani abdicated in favor of his son, British-educated Tamim bin Hamad al-Thani. At 36 years old, Emir Tamim is the youngest head of state in the region and has promised to modernize the country's governmental system and reduce his family's presence in the government. Faced with falling oil prices, the new Emir reduced the number of government ministries, slashed state institutions' budgets and put various social welfare schemes on hold. This was accompanied by hikes in utility rates, gas prices, government fines and service costs.[47] While these reforms are aimed to provide a smooth transition into a post-oil economy, they could negatively impact the popularity of the regime among its citizens.

ISLAMISM AND THE STATE

Qatar's government and ruling family have traditionally been strongly linked to *Wahhabi Hanbali* Islam. Not only is *Wahhabi* Islam the official state religion, but Islamic jurisprudence is the basis of Qatar's legal system. Civil courts have jurisdiction only over commercial law.[48] Qatar's governmental structure, despite a written constitution, conforms closely to traditional Islamic constraints, with tribal and family allegiance remaining an influential factor in the country's politics. There is no provision in Qatar's constitution for political parties, and hence there is no official political opposition.[49] Professional associations and societies, which in other Muslim countries play the role of unofficial political parties, are under severe constraints in Qatar, and are forbidden to engage in political activities.[50] While the official policy has been to support the movements behind the Arab Spring abroad, any such aspirations within the state are dealt with harshly, as in the case of poet Mohammed al-Ajami, who was handed a 15-year prison sentence for a poetry reading in which he called all Arab governments "indiscriminate thieves."[51]

This firm hand when it comes to internal dissent should be contrasted with the considerable leniency shown by authorities toward Qataris accused of funding Islamist activities abroad. What the U.S. government has described as a "permissive" environment for terror finance[52] should be seen as part of a deliberate policy: simply put, the Qatari government has preferred to co-opt rather than oppose Islamism.[53] Religious institutions are carefully monitored by the Ministry of Islamic affairs, which oversees mosque construction and Islamic education. The Ministry appoints religious leaders and previews mosque sermons for inflammatory language that might incite listeners to violence.[54]

Qatar has a longstanding tradition of granting asylum to exiled Islamists and radical preachers from other Muslim countries.[55] Following the 1979 attack on the Grand Mosque in Mecca by an extremist group, Qatar took in a number of radical exiles from Saudi Arabia, including *Wahhabi* scholar Sheikh Abdallah bin Zayd al-Mahmud, who subsequently was appointed Qatar's most senior cleric.[56]

Sympathy for Islamist causes has traditionally been high in Qatari society and among many members of the ruling clan. Sheikh Fahd bin Hamad al-Thani, the second-oldest son of the *Emir*, established a reputation for surrounding himself with *jihadist* veterans of the Afghan War.[57] A number of al-Qaeda leaders are believed to have travelled through Qatar during the 1990s under the protection of members of the ruling clan, including Abu Mus'ab al-Zarqawi and Osama bin Laden.[58] The Chechen leader Zelimkhan Yandarbiyev, who was killed in Doha in 2004, also found refuge for several years in Qatar.

During the 1980s, many Wahhabi exiles were appointed to senior and mid-level positions in Qatar's Interior Ministry, which controls both the civilian security force and the *Mubahathat* (secret police office). After 2003, Emir Hamad bin Khalifa began gradually weeding out the more extreme Islamist elements from government ministries, including the Interior Ministry; the Minister of the Interior, Sheikh Abdallah, a member of the Wahhabi clique, was removed from office in 2004. The Interior

Ministry was then put under the *de facto* control of Sheikh Abdallah bin Nasser bin-Khalifa al-Thani, an *Emir* loyalist. However, a large number of Islamist appointees are believed to remain among mid-level Qatari security officials.[59]

In June 2003, the *Emir* created an independent State Security Agency, answerable directly to him. Additionally, all the most important police, military, and internal security services are headed by powerful members of the ruling family, who in turn answer to the *Emir*.[60] The creation of these parallel security agencies effectively bypassed the Interior Ministry's control of police and public security. These shakeups, however, have had more to do with political alliances than with government opposition to Islamists *per se*. Most Islamists, both domestic and immigrant, have become well integrated into the top echelons of Qatari society.[61]

Among the political exiles who have sought refuge in Qatar are prominent figures of the Muslim Brotherhood, many of whom fled persecution at the hands of Gamal Abdel Nasser's government in Egypt during the 1950s. Some of these exiles reportedly laid the foundations for the Qatari Education Ministry, and taught at various levels there until the early 1980s.[62] More recently, Hamas political head Khaled Mishaal quit his former headquarters under the wing of Syria's Al Assad regime and relocated to Doha.[63]

Given the great success of these elements, the country has no obvious need for an Islamist opposition. In 2007, Kuwaiti Islamist writer Abd Allah al-Nafisi called for the Egyptian Muslim Brotherhood to follow the lead of the Qatari branch and disband altogether. Al-Nafisi noted that from 1960 to 1980, Qatar went through a period of great Islamist intellectual activity and organization. In contrast to the experience of the Muslim Brotherhood in Egypt, the Qatari Muslim Brothers had no real conflict with the state.[64]

One of the most influential—not to mention controversial—voices in Islamist circles today is Egyptian Sheikh Yusuf al-Qaradawi, who has lived in Qatar since 1961. Qaradawi enjoys worldwide exposure via Al Jazeera television, through his weekly program "Sharia and Life" (*al-Shari'a wa-al-Hayat*). Until recently, he also oversaw the Islamist Web portal IslamOnline, established in 1997.[65] Many consider Sheikh al-Qaradawi to be the most influential Islamic scholar alive today; he is viewed as the spiritual leader of the Muslim Brotherhood, and "sets the tone for Arabic language Sunni sermons across the world."[66] Qaradawi has sparked considerable controversy in the West by his support for suicide bombings in Israel and the killing of American citizens in Iraq. Among Muslim audiences, however, his comparatively moderate views on the acceptability of Muslim participation in Western democracies have brought him both praise and condemnation.[67] This mixture of conservatism and reform informs Qaradawi's politics. He is one of the founders of the *wasatiyya* ("Middle Way") movement, which attempts to bridge the gap between the various interpretations of Islam.[68] Yet Qaradawi's political proclivities and involvement have led to some questionable connections: Qaradawi is listed as a founder of the Union of Good (*Itilaf al-Khayr*), a coalition of European Islamic charities now designated by the United States Treasury as a channel for transferring funds to Hamas.[69]

Qaradawi's influence also played a role in the events of the Arab Spring, as his protégés emerged as new leaders, financial backers, religious authorities and politicians.[70] In May 2013, he urged Sunni Muslims to join the *jihad* in Syria against the Assad regime and against Hezbollah.[71] In a region where educational and media influence can determine the lives of dictators, Sheikh Qaradawi is a significant foreign policy asset.

Qatar's policies, though seemingly contradictory, are consistent with two strategic objectives: to buy influence with a number of different forces, while playing off its stronger neighbors, particularly Saudi Arabia and Iran. Uppermost on Qatar's agenda is the need to protect its sovereignty and natural gas wealth, by means of which the country has emerged as a regional player. This strategy may be one of the motivations for Qatar's recent spending spree in Europe. Qatar invests billions of dollars a year in Europe, in real estate, tourist venues, sports and media sectors.[72] These investments are a tool of foreign policy, but also serve an important function in domestic policy. The greater the stake foreign countries have in the stability of the al Thani government, the better. By investing heavily abroad, the al Thanis are buying insurance against an Arab Spring of their own.

This strategy caused a stir when it emerged in 2012 that Qatar had pledged 150 million Euro [$199 million] to investments in French suburbs inhabited by a Muslim majority. While Qatari officials insisted that the move was "just business," critics claimed that the Qataris were using their economic clout to push an Islamist agenda.[73] The issue highlighted the fact that Qatar has become an international superpower when it comes to soft power. The al Thani regime has established itself as second to none in wielding influence through non-military means. Perhaps the greatest weapon in its arsenal is the *Al Jazeera* satellite television station.

Although the Qatari press is free from official censorship, self-censorship is the norm. Defense and national security matters, as well as stories related to the royal family, are considered strictly out of bounds. The country's major radio and television stations, Qatar Radio and Qatar Television, are both state-owned.[74] Although newspapers in Qatar are all privately owned in principle, many board members and owners are either government officials or have close ties to the government. For example, the chairman of the influential daily *Al-Watan*, Hamad bin Sahim al Thani, is a member of the royal family.[75] Meanwhile, Qatar's Foreign Minister, Hamed bin Jasem bin Jaber al Thani, owns half of the newspaper.

Compared to the traditionally conservative and highly censored Arab press, Qatar's *Al Jazeera* satellite network would appear to be a breath of fresh air. Formed in 1996 from the remnants of BBC Arabic TV, which had just been closed down, the station initially offered the kind of free and unfettered discussion of issues not usually broadcast in the Muslim world. *Al Jazeera* quickly established itself as a major international media player, and is increasingly being viewed as a political actor in its own right. *Al Jazeera* is in fact funded by the Qatari government, with its expenses reimbursed by the Ministry of Finance, and Sheikh Hamid bin Thamer, a member of the royal family, heads the station's board of directors.[76]

In recent years, *Al Jazeera* has undergone a process of increasing "Islamization," with many of its more secular staff replaced by Islamists.[77] This process has been accompanied by subtle—and not-so-subtle—changes in the station's reportage of happenings in the field. *Al Jazeera* is alleged to have moved away from its rather ideologically diverse origins to a more populist—and more Islamist—approach.[78] In addition, *Al Jazeera* is increasingly becoming a participant in the sectarian feud between Shi'as and Sunnis. Qatar itself is right in the middle of this battle; on the one hand, it hosts an American military base on its soil, where tanks and vehicles damaged in the fighting are serviced and sent back into battle to protect the Shi'ite-led government of Iraq. On the other, Qatar's Sunni majority sees Shi'ite Iran as the main threat in the region. Qatar supported Saudi Arabia's intervention in neighboring Bahrain to help quell Shi'ite protests, and sent a small contingent of security personnel to protect government sites.[79]

Al Jazeera's Arabic channel has also been heavily involved in promoting the Muslim Brotherhood as a viable player in Egypt, and may well have been the determining factor in the election of Muhammed Morsi to the Egyptian presidency.[80] Many leading figures at *Al Jazeera* news are Egyptians affiliated with the Brotherhood, and Brotherhood guests and loyalists dominate most of the channel's programs on Egyptian political affairs.[81]

Al Jazeera rarely criticizes Qatar's ruling Al Thani family, although other Arab governments come in for severe censure.[82] This has not only infuriated those Arab governments on the receiving end of the station's critical coverage, but also raised the question of Qatari complicity in the destabilization of its neighbors. Libya, for instance, withdrew its ambassador from Qatar between 2000 and 2002 to protest *Al Jazeera's* less-than-complimentary coverage of the Qadhafi regime.[83] In 2002, Saudi Arabia likewise withdrew its ambassador to Doha, partly in response to *Al Jazeera* reportage. (Relations were restored six years later, and *Al Jazeera* has since toned down its Saudi coverage.) Jordan and Lebanon have accused *Al Jazeera* of actively working to undermine their governments, while uncritically supporting their opposition Islamist movements.[84]

Prior to the fall of the Mubarak regime, the Egyptian government repeatedly complained about the open forum given by *Al Jazeera* to representatives of the Egyptian Muslim Brotherhood.[85] It would appear that *Al Jazeera* was in fact a key player in the events that led to the eventual ouster of Mubarak and his replacement by an Islamist regime. In the aftermath of Morsi's ouster, *Al Jazeera* reportedly experienced a wave of desertions by veteran reporters over "biased coverage" and the station's blatant support of the Brotherhood.[86]

It has become increasingly clear that *Al Jazeera's* Islamist shift was a matter of design as much as evolution, reflecting the interests of the Qatari ruling family, as well as the growing popularity of Islamist causes in Arab society. *Al Jazeera* is more than a mirror of public opinion; it is increasingly taking the initiative in influencing events rather than just reporting on them.[87]

For some, there is no doubt that the network is subject to the political dictates of the Qatari government, which has become a significant player in many of the Middle East's disputes despite the country's small size. Government control over the channel's reporting appeared to U.S. diplomats to be so direct that the channel's output is said to have become a subject of bilateral discussions between Washington and Doha. An American diplomatic dispatch from July 2009 noted that *Al Jazeera* could be used as a bargaining tool to repair Qatar's relationships with other countries, and called the station "one of Qatar's most valuable political and diplomatic tools."[88]

Al Jazeera's influence reflects the new reality of an increasingly media-driven Middle East. The station's rivalry with the newer Saudi *Al Arabiya* satellite channel is indicative of a deeper competition for regional influence. Al Jazeera may be seen as an arm of Qatari foreign policy, a sort of electronic *da'wah* (missionary activity). In effect, these governments use their control of the media to create a monopoly on reporting, making the reportage itself a tool in regional rivalries.

Although Al-Jazeera wielded tremendous influence during the events of the "Arab Spring," the fall of the Morsi government in 2013 showed the risks of Qatar's overreaching itself in "making the news" rather than just reporting it. Al Jazeera's reputation in the Arab world suffered from its blatant support of the Brotherhood-affiliated regime. The station's English language staff members in Egypt were arrested and charged with disseminating "false news." Qatar was eventually forced to close its pro-Brotherhood Arabic service to repair relations with Egypt.[89]

However, Al-Jazeera is only one of the means by which Qatar achieves influence. Qatari soft power has increasingly been augmented by investments in arms for Islamist militants in Arab conflicts. Libya was a case in point; by channeling weapons and money to Islamist rebels through personal channels, and largely bypassing the National Transitional Council, Qatar effectively limited the governing body's monopoly on the use of force. This has given Qatar a veto on violence in the country, allowing Qatar to back up its soft power with hard power. In Syria too, Qatar's backing of the insurgency against Assad has gained the country a key role in negotiations—a crucial bargaining chip in the volatile region.

In the Arab world, soft power remains vital. More than in any other region, persuasion and education are tools of dominance. Hence the political logic of *Al-Jazeera*, and hence the huge investment of Saudi Arabia in *da'wah*. What Western countries accomplish via economic dominance, Saudi Arabia has accomplished through financing mosques, and Qatar has accomplished through a studied combination of media influence, economic investment, and military backing.

ENDNOTES

[1] Sheri Berman, "Islamism, Revolution, and Civil Society," Perspectives on Politics 1, no. 2, June 2003, 257-272.

[2] Oxford Analytica, "The Advent of Terrorism in Qatar," Forbes, March 25, 2005, (http://www.forbes.com/2005/03/25/cz_0325oxan_qatarattack.html).

[3] Ibid

[4] Uzi Mahnaimi, "Qatar buys off al-Qaeda attacks with oil millions," Sunday Times (London), May 1, 2005, http://www.timesonline.co.uk/tol/news/world/article387163.ece.

[5] Ibid

[6] Ibidem

[7] Elizabeth Weingarten, "Qatar: 'Worst' on Counterterrorism in the Middle East?" The Atlantic, November 29, 2010, http://www.theatlantic.com/international/archive/2010/11/qatar-worst-on-counterterrorism-in-the-middle-east/67166/

[8] Scott Shane and Andrew W. Lehren, "Leaked Cables Offer Raw Look at U.S. Diplomacy," New York Times, November 28, 2010, http://www.nytimes.com/2010/11/29/world/29cables.html?_r=1

[9] Steven Emerson, Testimony before the House of Representatives Committee on Financial Services, Subcommittee on Oversight and Investigations, February 12, 2002, 8-9.

[10] "Qatar Sends Billions, Hoping for an Islamic Regime in Libya," El-Khabar (Algeria), August 3, 2012, as translated in Al-Monitor, August 3, 2012, http://www.al-monitor.com/pulse/security/01/08/report-warns-about-a-serious-thr.html.

[11] "Qatar deploys 1,000 ground troops to fight in Yemen," Al Jazeera, September 7, 2015, http://www.aljazeera.com/news/2015/09/qatar-deploys-1000-ground-troops-fight-yemen-150907043020594.html.

[12] Acil Tabbara, "Qatar Emir in Gaza: Doha pushes Islamist Agenda to Detriment of Palestinian Unity," Middle East Online, October 23, 2012, http://www.middle-east-online.com/english/?id=55066

[13] Adam Rasgon, "Qatar coordinated payment to Hamas employees with Israel, PA," Jerusalem Post, July 24, 2016, http://www.jpost.com/Middle-East/Qatar-to-pay-salaries-of-Hamas-public-sector-employees-in-Gaza-462209.

[14] Matthew Rosenberg. "Taliban Opening Qatar Office, and Maybe Door to Talks," New York Times, January 3, 2012.

[15] "Taliban reaffirms authority of its Qatar 'political office," Dawn (Karachi), January 25, 2016, http://www.dawn.com/news/1235165.

[16] David Blair and Richard Spencer, "How Qatar is Funding the Rise of Islamist Extremists, "Telegraph (London), September 20, 2014, http://www.telegraph.co.uk/news/worldnews/middleeast/qatar/11110931/How-Qatar-is-funding-the-rise-of-Islamist-extremists.html.

[17] "Funding al-Nusra through Ransom: Qatar and the Myth of the 'Humanitarian Principle,'" CATF Reports, December 10, 2015. http://stopterrorfinance.org/stories/510652383-funding-al-nusra-through-ransom-qatar-and-the-myth-of-humanitarian-principle.

[18] David Weinberg, "Qatar is still negligent on terror finance," The Long War Journal, Aug. 19, 2015. http://mobile.businessinsider.com/qatar-is-letting-2-notorious-terror-financiers-operate-in-the-open-2015-8.

[19] Blair and Spencer, op citml.

[20] U.S. Department of State, Counter-Terrorism Bureau. "Country Reports on Terrorism 2014. "

[21] "Funding al-Nusra through Ransom: Qatar and the Myth of the 'Humanitarian Principle.'"

[22] Ibid

[23] Mariam Karouny "U.S.-led strikes pressure al Qaeda's Syria group to join with Islamic State," Reuters 26 September 2014. http://uk.reuters.com/article/uk-syria-crisis-nusra-insight-idUKKCN0HL11520140926.

[24] Email from John Podesta to Hillary Clinton dated September 27, 2014, https://wikileaks.org/podesta-emails/emailid/3774.

[25] "World Report 2015: Syria: Events of 2014," Human Rights Watch. https://www.hrw.org/world-report/2015/country-chapters/syria

[26] David Blair and Richard Spencer, op. cit.

[27] Thomas Joscelyn, "Analysis: Al Nusrah Front rebrands itself as Jabhat Fath Al Sham," The Long War Journal, July 28, 2016. http://www.longwarjournal.org/archives/2016/07/analysis-al-nusrah-front-rebrands-itself-as-jabhat-fath-al-sham.php|.

[28] Rukmini Callimachi, "Paying Ransoms, Europe Bankrolls Qaeda Terror," New York Times, July 29, 2014, https://www.nytimes.com/2014/07/30/world/africa/ransoming-citizens-europe-becomes-al-qaedas-patron.html; See also Ellen Knickmeyer, "Al Qaeda-Linked Groups Increasingly Funded by Ransom," Wall Street Journal, July 29, 2014, http://online.wsj.com/articles/ransom-fills-terrorist-coffers-1406637010.

[29] Abigail Hauslohner, "Rift Deepens Between Qatar and Its Powerful Arab Neighbors," Washington Post, March 8, 2014.

[30] "Qatar-Gulf deal forces expulsion of Muslim Brotherhood leaders," Guardian (London), September 16, 2014, https://www.theguardian.com/world/2014/sep/16/qatar-orders-expulsion-exiled-egyptian-muslim-brotherhood-leaders.

[31] "Egypt Blames Muslim Brotherhood in Qatar for Involvement in Cairo Cathedral Attack," Ahram Online, 13 December, 2016. http://www.worldaffairsjournal.org/content/egypt-blames-muslim-brotherhood-cairo-church-bombing.

[32] Guido Steinberg, "Qatar and the Arab Spring: Support for Islamists and New Anti-Syrian Policy," SWP Stiftung Wissenschaft und Politik German Institute for International and Security Affairs, February 2012, 4.

[33] "Qatar Sends Billions, Hoping for an Islamic Regime in Libya."

[34] Terry McDermott, Josh Meyer and Patrick J. McDonnell, "The Plots and Designs of Al Qaeda's Engineer," Los Angeles Times, December 22, 2002, http://articles.latimes.com/2002/dec/22/world/fg-ksm22.

[35] Brian Ross and David Scott, "Qatari Royal Family Linked to Al Qaeda," ABC News, February 7, 2003.

[36] Ibid

[37] U.S. Department of the Treasury, "Press Release: Treasury Designates Al-Qa'ida Supporters in Qatar and Yemen," December 18, 2013, https://www.treasury.gov/press-center/press-releases/pages/jl2249.aspx

[38] Robert Mendick, "Al-Qaeda Terror Financier Worked for Qatari Government," Telegraph (London), October 12, 2014, http://www.telegraph.co.uk/news/11156327/Al-Qaeda-terror-financier-worked-for-Qatari-government.html

[39] David Andrew Weinberg, Qatar and Terror Finance – Part I: Negligence (FDD Press, December 2014), http://www.defenddemocracy.org/content/uploads/publications/Qatar_Part_I.pdf.

[40] "Qatar: Wahhabi Islam and the Gulf," country-data.com, n.d., http://www.country-data.com/cgi-bin/query/r-11031.html.

[41] U.S. Department of State, Bureau of Near Eastern Affairs, "Background Note: Qatar," September 22, 2010.

[42] U.S. Department of State, Bureau of Democracy, Human Rights and Labor, International Religious Freedom Report 2010 (Washington, DC: U.S. Department of State, November 17, 2010), http://www.state.gov/g/drl/rls/irf/2010/index.htm.

[43] "Qatar: Political Forces," The Economist, March 11, 2009, http://www.economist.com/node/13216406.

[44] U.S. Department of State, International Religious Freedom Report 2010.

[45] U.S. Department of State, "Background Note: Qatar."

[46] Ibid

[47] Azhar Unwala, "The young emir: Emir Tamim and Qatar's future," September 18, 2016. http://globalriskinsights.com/2016/09/emir-tamim-and-qatars-future.
[48] U.S. Department of State, "Background Note: Qatar."
[49] "Qatar: Political Forces."
[50] U.S. Department of State, International Religious Freedom Report 2010, https://www.state.gov/j/drl/rls/irf/2010/148841.htm .
[51] "Qatar Court Upholds Poet Mohammed al-Ajami's Sentence," BBC, October 21, 2013, http://www.bbc.com/news/world-middle-east-24612650
[52] U.S. Department of the Treasury Press Center, "Remarks of Under Secretary for Terrorism and Financial Intelligence David Cohen before the Center for a New American Security on 'Confronting New Threats in Terrorist Financing'", March 4, 2014, https://www.treasury.gov/press-center/press-releases/Pages/jl2308.aspx . See also Taimur Khan, "US names two Qatari nationals as financiers of terrorism", The National [UAE], August 6, 2015, http://www.thenational.ae/world/americas/us-names-two-qatari-nationals-as-financiers-of-terrorism
[53] David Andrew Weinberg, "Analysis: Qatar still negligent on terror finance", The Long War Journal, August 19, 2015, http://www.longwarjournal.org/archives/2015/08/analysis-qatar-still-negligent-on-terror-finance.php .
[54] U.S. Department of State, International Religious Freedom Report 2010, https://www.state.gov/j/drl/rls/irf/2010/148841.htm
[55] Oxford Analytica, "The Advent of Terrorism in Qatar."
[56] Michael Knights and Anna Solomon-Schwartz, "The Broader Threat from Sunni Islamists in the Gulf," Washington Institute for Near East Policy PolicyWatch no. 883, July 25, 2004, http://www.washingtoninstitute.org/templateC05.php?CID=1761
[57] Ibid
[58] Barry Rubin, ed., Guide to Islamist Movements (London: M.E. Sharpe, 2009), 308-310.
[59] Oxford Analytica, "The Advent of Terrorism in Qatar."
[60] Ibid
[61] "Qatar: Political Forces."
[62] Ehud Rosen, Mapping the Organizational Sources of the Global Delegitimization Campaign Against Israel In the UK (Jerusalem, Israel: Jerusalem Center for Public Affairs, December 24, 2010), http://www.jcpa.org/text/Mapping_Delegitimization.pdf.
[63] Tabbara, "Qatar Emir in Gaza."
[64] Marc Lynch, "Muslim Brotherhood Debates," Abu Aardvark blog, February 28, 2007, http://abuaardvark.typepad.com/abuaardvark/2007/02/muslim_brotherh.html

[65] Reuven Paz, "Qaradhawi and the World Association of Muslim Clerics: The New Platform of the Muslim Brotherhood," PRISM Series on Global Jihad no. 4/2, November 2004, 1-2, http://www.e-prism.org/images/PRISM_no_4_vol_2_-_Qaradhawi.pdf.

[66] Samuel Helfont, "Islam and Islamism Today: the Case of Yusuf al-Qaradawi," Foreign Policy Research Institute E-Notes, January 2010, http://www.fpri.org/article/2010/01/islam-and-islamism-today-the-case-of-yusuf-al-qaradawi/.

[67] Ibid

[68] Ibidem

[69] U.S. Department of the Treasury, "PRESS RELEASE HP-1267: Treasury designates the Union of Good," November 12, 2008, (http://www.treasury.gov/press-center/press-releases/Pages/hp1267.aspx).

[70] Steinberg, "Qatar and the Arab Spring," 4.

[71] Syria conflict: Cleric Qaradawi urges Sunnis to join rebels BBC News, 1 June 2013, (http://www.bbc.com/news/world-middle-east-22741588).

[72] Nadina Shalaq, "Qatar's European Strategy," As-Safir (Lebanon), December 26, 2012, as translated in Al-Monitor, December 27, 2012, http://www.al-monitor.com/pulse/politics/2012/12/qatari-investments-in-greece-highlight-soft-power-strategy.html.

[73] Harvey Morris, "Qatar's Latest Investment Stirs the French," International Herald Tribune, September 25, 2012, http://rendezvous.blogs.nytimes.com/2012/09/25/qatars-latest-investment-stirs-the-french/

[74] Jennifer Lambert, "Qatari Law Will Test Media Freedom," Carnegie Endowment for International Peace Arab Reform Bulletin, December 1, 2010, http://carnegieendowment.org/sada/?fa=42049

[75] Kristen Gillespie, "The New Face of Al Jazeera," The Nation, November 9, 2007.

[76] Ibid

[77] Ibidem; Oren Kessler, "The Two Faces of Al Jazeera", Middle East Forum, Winter 2012, pp. 47-56, http://www.meforum.org/3147/al-jazeera ; Sultan Soood Al Qassemi, "Qatar's Brotherhood Ties Alienate Fellow Gulf States", Al-Monitor, January 23, 2013, http://www.al-monitor.com/pulse/originals/2013/01/qatar-muslim-brotherhood.html ; see also http://foreignpolicy.com/2013/07/12/al-jazeeras-awful-week/

[78] Ibidem

[79] Steinberg, "Qatar and the Arab Spring."

[80] Sultan Soood Al Qassemi, "Morsi's Win Is Al Jazeera's Loss," Al-Monitor, July 1, 2012, http://www.al-monitor.com/pulse/originals/2012/al-monitor/morsys-win-is-al-jazeeras-loss.html#ixzz2I3awUthS

[81] Mohammad Hisham Abeih, "Qatar on Defense over Meddling in Egypt," As-Safir (Lebanon), January 10, 2013, as translated in Al-Monitor, January 10, 2013, http://www.al-monitor.com/pulse/politics/2013/01/qatars-media-and-political-influence-over-egypt.html#ixzz2I36FW8C4.

[82] U.S. Department of State, "Background Note: Qatar."

[83] "Qatar: Political Forces."

[84] Zvi Bar'el, "Is Al Jazeera Trying to Bring Down the Palestinian Authority?" Ha'aretz (Tel Aviv), February 2, 2011, http://www.haaretz.com/print-edition/features/is-al-jazeera-trying-to-bring-down-the-palestinian-authority-1.340716.

[85] Gillespie, "The New Face of Al Jazeera."

[86] Ayman Sharaf. "Al Jazeera staff resign after 'biased' Egypt coverage," Gulf News, July 8, 2013, http://gulfnews.com/news/region/egypt/al-jazeera-staff-resign-after-biased-egypt-coverage-1.1206924

[87] Bar'el, "Is Al Jazeera Trying to Bring Down the Palestinian Authority?"

[88] "Qatar Uses Al-Jazeera as Bargaining Chip: WikiLeaks," The Economic Times (India), December 6, 2010, http://economictimes.indiatimes.com/tech/internet/qatar-uses-al-jazeera-as-bargaining-chip-wikileaks/articleshow/7051690.cms

[89] Hussein Ibish, "Why America Turned Off Al Jazeera," New York Times, February 17, 2016.

SAUDI ARABIA

QUICK FACTS

Population: 28,160,273 (July 2016 est.)

Area: 2,149,690 sq km

Ethnic Groups: Arab 90%, Afro-Asian 10%

Religions: Muslim (official; citizens are 85-90% Sunni and 10-15% Shia), other (includes Eastern Orthodox, Protestant, Roman Catholic, Jewish, Hindu, Buddhist, and Sikh) (2012 est.)

Government Type: Absolute Monarchy

GDP (official exchange rate): $637.8 billion (2015 est.)

Map and Quick Facts courtesy of the CIA World Factbook (January 2017)

OVERVIEW

Since 1744, when the first Saudi emirate was established by a pact between the emir of ad-Diriyyah, Muhammad ibn Saud, and the religious scholar Muhammad ibn Abd al-Wahhab, the puritanical Islamic interpretation now known as Wahhabism has been the official and dominant religious discourse in Saudi Arabia. Although Wahhabism was generally confined to the Arabian Peninsula in its early years, it evolved into a transnational movement in the 1960s when the Saudi government attempted to fight the spread of communism and pan-Arabism that had begun to creep across the Middle East, threatening the region's monarchies.

By the 1970's, as oil prices surged, the Saudi government, headed by Faysal's successor King Fahd, was able to increase its contributions and its influence to Islamic centers and causes in other countries. These efforts enabled the Saudis to spread a puritanical version of Wahabism that became known outside of Saudi Arabia as Salafism. A European Par-

liament report in 2013 estimated that the Saudi government has spent approximately $10 billion to spread Salafism through charitable organizations, some of which have been linked to al-Qaeda's work and networks.[1] From the construction of madrassas (religious schools) in places such as Pakistan and Afghanistan to support of Sunni militants fighting in Iraq, both the Saudi Arabian government and wealthy private individuals in the Kingdom have contributed to the expansion of extremist Sunni Islam.

The Kingdom's ruling family, the al Sauds, have had to strike a precarious balance between the "desert traditions and the demands of the modern world," which has involved the maintenance of political stability, strong relations with the Kingdom's clerics, and the appeasement of the Kingdom's people.[2] Under the moderate and relatively progressive King Abdullah, the Saudi government pushed the country's religious elite to accept reforms to the sharia judiciary, the education system, and women's rights. To maintain stability within the kingdom during the Arab Spring, as protest movements rolled across the Middle East, King Abdullah responded immediately by pouring cash into religious organizations, low-income community housing, and the salaries of government employees. Due to their strong relationship with the monarchy, Saudi clerics across the political spectrum assisted in maintaining stability by standing behind the monarchy and affirming its legitimacy, which enabled the Kingdom avoid a major political crisis.

Since the Arab Spring, Saudi Arabia has been forced to grapple with a shifting balance of power in the Middle East including the threat of the rise of the Islamic State terrorist group, a less-isolated and more assertive Iran, a devastating conflict with its neighbor, Yemen, and the death of King Abdullah which resulted in a complete transformation of its leadership. Islamist religious leaders and scholars—aligned with the government or in opposition to it—continue to play an important but shifting role in the state, the community and in Saudi Arabia's overall image as a global power.

ISLAMIST ACTIVITY

Islamism in Saudi Arabia is characterized by competing intellectual traditions, which—while all conservative and fundamentalist—hold significantly different, and in some ways evolving, ideas about the relationship between Islam and society.

The Rejectionists

The "rejectionists," a pietistic, lower-class Islamic intellectual movement that categorically rejects the legitimacy of the state and its institutions, opposes any role or voice for themselves in the life of the state and in the national political discourse, emerged during the 1950's and 1960's. Rejectionists believe in withdrawing from society and focusing solely on faith and ritual practice, repudiating all schools of Islamic jurisprudence (*fiqh*), and relying solely on the unmediated sayings of the Prophet Muhammad (*hadith*). They confine themselves to isolated, orthodox communities where they educate their children and pursue their distinctive lifestyle. However, they are not monolithic, and some have formed their own socio-political protest movements in spite of the trend's original doctrine.

One of these movements is the *al-Jama'a al-Salafiyya al-Muhtasiba* (JSM), which formed in the 1970s and was inspired by the Syrian religious scholar Nasr al-Din al-Albani.[3] In 1979, JSM, led by Juhayman al-Utaybi, orchestrated an armed takeover of the Grand Mosque in Mecca. Though the Saudis were initially reluctant to use force in one of Islam's holiest sites, they eventually raided the Mosque and ended the siege. After the Grand Mosque incident, the remaining members of JSM fled to Kuwait, Yemen, and the northern Saudi desert, returning to a state of relative isolation. However, Juhayman's ideas have continued to influence others in subsequent years. The JSM's views allegedly influenced three men who were involved in the 1995 bombing in Riyadh, as well as "senior militants" who were part of al-Qaeda's violent campaign in 2003.[4]

The Sahwa

Another intellectual tradition that developed during the 1950s and 1960s is the *Sahwa* ("Awakened") movement, which, unlike the rejectionists, is pragmatic, political and elitist. The *Sahwa* clerics trace their roots back to the rise of the Muslim Brotherhood, whose members were well educated, and who established themselves in the new education and media sectors of Saudi Arabia. As a natural result of their interaction with Muslim Brotherhood members, the *Sahwa* clerics' ideology became a synthesis of *Salafi-Wahhabi* theological teachings and the Brotherhood's political activism.[5] The spread of *Sahwa* teachings in Saudi universities would eventually lead to the group's political reform efforts in the 1990s. However, the *Sahwa* is an extremely diverse faction that includes religious scholars, scientists, doctors, and academics. Its members are commonly divided into at least two main camps: those who follow Hassan al-Banna, the founder of the Brotherhood, and those who follow his more extreme ideological successor, Sayyid Qutb. Their ability to address issues—like politics—that were traditionally outside the purview of the official Saudi religious establishment originally garnered broad public appeal.[6]

The *Sahwa* became widely recognized in 1990 for their virulent opposition to Saudi King Fahd's reliance on a non-Muslim military coalition, led by the United States, to defend the Arabian Peninsula after Saddam Hussein's Iraqi army invaded Kuwait in

1990. Prominent *Sahwa* clerics believed that the legitimacy of the Al Saud leadership and the official Saudi religious establishment had been permanently destroyed by this collaboration with the West.[7] Thereafter, the *Sahwa* called for greater Islamization of Saudi society and demanded a more prominent role in social and foreign affairs.[8]

In 1994, al-Odah, al-Hawali, and nearly 1,300 *Sahwa* affiliates were arrested for their vehement opposition to the Saudi regime.[9] To the leadership's dismay, their five years in prison only cemented the clerics' standing in the eyes of their followers and granted them even greater popular legitimacy than the official *ulema*. When the men were released in 1999, the Saudi government confronted them with the choice of either withdrawing from the public eye or acquiescing to the authority of the state. They chose the latter, and the *Sahwa* splintered as a result. Some of its members have since joined other Saudi Islamist movements, including the jihadist trend, while others abandoned Islamism entirely. For a number of years the *Sahwa* took a more conciliatory tone with the Saudi Arabian regime, and rarely criticized the government.[10] But during the Arab Spring, the split amongst the *Sahwa*, and the challenge they present to the Saudi Arabian regime, became more apparent. In early 2011, several petitions calling for government reform were signed by leading *Sahwa* clerics, but none of them supported calls for the open demonstrations in Riyadh a few months later.[11] For a few years some *Sahwa* and religious scholars remained critical of the regime, but on February 4, 2014, in response to domestic condemnation of the Saudi government's support of the overthrow of Egypt's President Morsi, the Saudi government issued a decree. The decree stated that anyone who provides support (defined loosely and in a variety of ways) to an organization categorized as extremist or defined as a terrorist group could face a prison sentence of 3 to 20 years.[12]

The jihadists

A *jihadist* trend exists in Saudi society, defined by the rise of Osama Bin Laden's al-Qaeda network, but it has faced considerable challenges with the rise of the Islamic State. From 1999 through 2001, conflicts in the Muslim world (Chechnya, Kosovo, and the Palestinian Territories) and a powerful recruiting network in Saudi Arabia enabled Bin Laden to attract a wave of Saudis to al-Qaeda's training camps in Afghanistan. Al-Qaeda's operations have been well-funded by Saudi individuals and organizations. In 2004, the 9/11 Commission reported that Bin Laden created an informal financial network of charities, including the Al Haramain Islamic Foundation and other non-governmental organizations, which allowed Saudi and Gulf financiers to send funds to Arabs fighting in Afghanistan and then later to al-Qaeda.[13]

In early 2002, between 300 and 1,000 Saudi al-Qaeda members returned to Saudi Arabia after the Taliban's fall compromised the network's base of operations in Afghanistan. Two independent cells subsequently formed, and the organization's operatives began preparing for operations by stockpiling weapons, renting safe houses, setting up training camps, and recruiting other "Afghan Arabs."[14] Members were almost entirely men, with the exception of a small number of women who were involved in logistics or the group's media campaign. Al-Qaeda militants were typically older than members of other Islamist groups, with an average age of 27, and most of them had only been educated to the high school level or lower.[15] The cells consisted principally of Saudis, but maintained a small percentage of foreign nationals. The majority of al-Qaeda members were not from regions typically considered to be the most religiously conservative or impoverished rural areas. Instead, the overwhelming majority of the organization was formed by urbanites from Riyadh, most of whom shared previous combat experience in Afghanistan—first against the Soviets and later against the United States.[16]

The Saudi government's aggressive counterterrorism efforts eventually forced al-Qaeda's local branch to relocate across the border in Yemen. In January 2009, the Saudi and Yemeni branches of al-Qaeda merged to become al-Qaeda in the Arabian Peninsula (AQAP), with a number of Saudis assuming leadership positions in the new franchise.[17] AQAP grew more dangerous in just its first year of operations; in August 2009, the organization nearly succeeded in assassinating then Saudi Deputy Interior Minister Prince Muhammad bin Nayef during a gathering at his home in Jeddah.[18] Then, only months later, AQAP coordinated the attempted Christmas Day bombing—carried out by a Nigerian man with explosives in his underwear—of a Northwest Airlines flight traveling from Yemen to Detroit.[19]

In 2014, after AQAP attacked a remote Saudi-Yemeni border checkpoint, the State Department determined the organization has "continued its efforts to inspire sympathizers to support, finance, or engage in conflicts outside of Saudi Arabia and encouraged individual acts of terrorism within the Kingdom."[20] Since then the Saudi government has taken increased action to prevent Saudis from traveling abroad to support extremist groups like al-Qaeda and the Islamic State. However, after the January 2016 execution of a number of al-Qaeda suspects by the Saudi government, al-Qaeda leader Ayman al Zawahiri condemned the government and called for revenge.[21]

The Shi'a

Another Islamic intellectual trend in Saudi Arabia is rooted in the country's Shi'a minority, which is primarily located in the Eastern Province, and constitutes 10-15% of the total population.[22] Having been branded as unbelievers (*kuffar*) since the time of Muhammad ibn Abd al-Wahhab, Saudi Shi'a are still severely marginalized in the modern state.[23] And while Shi'a Islamists have never been as organized as the *Sahwa*, or even the *jihadists* in Saudi Arabia, instances of Shi'a Islamist activity continue to play a significant role in Saudi society and the government's approach to dissent.

An early and frequently cited incident of Shi'a opposition took place in 1980, in the wake of the Islamic Revolution in Iran. Radio Tehran's Arabic channel had been broadcasting propaganda against the Saudi regime to the Shi'a population. The propaganda sparked a riot in Qatif, during which citizens attacked the town's central market.[24] Since that time, the Saudi government has been extremely wary of renewed violence, as well as of Iran's influence in Saudi domestic affairs.

For a brief period, the Arab Spring rekindled opposition from Saudi Arabia's Shi'a population. Shortly after the outbreak of protests in Tunisia in December 2011, Shi'a Islamists in Saudi Arabia began to organize themselves through social media tools like Facebook and Twitter, issuing petitions for political and social reforms such as the transition to a constitutional monarchy and an end to sectarian discrimination. Violent protests erupted in July 2012 in the Eastern Province—which includes not only most of the Shi'a population but also most of the country's oil—after security forces shot and arrested a popular Shi'ite cleric Nimr al-Nimr for instigating "sedition."[25] Shi'a anger continued to bubble in the weeks after Nimr's arrest, with Saudi authorities exacerbating the furor when they fatally shot two men during the demonstrations.[26] The protests in the Eastern Province escalated even further in October 2012, when tens of thousands of angry mourners carried the bodies of three young Shi'a men, slain by Saudi security forces, through the streets of Awwamiya while chanting "Death to al-Saud."[27]

Almost ten months after Saudi authorities arrested al-Nimr, in March 2013, he was put on trial for "sowing discord" and "undermining national unity."[28] Between the trial and the autumn of 2014, Shia protests dissipated. But on October 24, al-Nimr was sentenced to death, along with his nephew, and protests erupted again.[29] A year and four months later, on January 2, 2016, al-Nimr was executed along with 46 other people the Saudi government had labeled "terrorists." In response to the execution, protests erupted in Qatif in the Eastern Province, in Bahrain, and across the Middle East.[30] Angered by al-Nimr's death, Iranian activists attacked and set fire to the Saudi Embassy in Tehran, prompting the severance of diplomatic ties between the two countries.[31]

In response to rising sectarianism in the region and increasing tensions between Iran and Saudi Arabia, Saudi Arabia executed 158 people in 2015, up from 90 in 2014.[32] As of October 19, 2016, Saudi Arabia had executed 134 people.[33]

ISLAMISM AND SOCIETY

With the exception of a brief "*Sahwa* Insurrection" in the early 1990s, Islamist opposition or reformist movements in Saudi Arabia have failed to garner enough societal support to mount a sustained or serious challenge to the ruling House of Saud. This is largely due to the government's use of oil wealth to appease citizens and to co-opt opponents, as well as the Wahhabi mandate of allegiance to the ruler (*wali al-amr*).

Since the rise of the Islamic State, however, there has been a renewed internal debate over the future of Wahhabism. Cole Bunzel, of the Carnegie Endowment for International Peace, has argued that there is a subtly emerging "correctionist" movement regarding Wahhabism within the liberal wing of the religious establishment in Saudi Arabia, and that it has been tolerated much more by society and the government in 2016 than it has in earlier years.[34] Such developments are partially due to the political leadership being preoccupied with consolidating power, but also because of the role that information technologies have played within the Kingdom.

As a social force, the *Sahwa* clerics rose in influence when they challenged the Islamic credentials of the ruling family and religious establishment between 1990 and 1994. Much to the Kingdom's dismay, in some cases their subsequent imprisonment only increased their status and notoriety. Due to Saudi crackdowns and a successful campaign to blame the insurrection entirely on the external forces of the Muslim Brotherhood, the *Sahwa* clerics have since muted their criticism of the regime. Their theology has evolved to reject violence, and argues for civil society and democracy. As they have evolved, they have managed to remain very influential. In recent years, even struggling Arab dictators have sought out stamps of approval from *Sahwa* leaders. The Saudi-owned newspaper al-Arabiya reported on February 27, 2011 that Libyan leader Muammar al-Qadhafi's sons, Seif al-Islam and Al-Saidi, pleaded with al-Odah and Aidh al-Qarnee to issue *fatwas* prohibiting demonstrations in Libya. Both clerics rejected the request, but the incident highlighted the enduring status of *Sahwa* clerics across the Arab and Muslim worlds.

Increasing modernization of information technologies have changed the way that the clerics have engaged with society, and expanded the cleric's influence beyond the traditional Wahhabist/Salafi international network. Between 2011 and 2014, a number of *Sahwa* clerics gained increasing prominence through their use of the Internet. In 2011, *Forbes Middle East* ranked Salman al-Odah fourth on its list of top 100 "Twitterati," who boasted more than 3.4 million Twitter followers, and by 2014 had garnered nearly 1.5 million more followers on Facebook. Today, al-Odah has 11 million followers on Twitter, and almost 7 million on Facebook.[35] Fellow Saudi clerics Muhammad al-Arife and Aidh al-Qarni have been even more successful than al-Odah on social media. Al-Arefe, who is called the "Brad Pitt" of Muslim clerics, has 16 million Twitter followers—more than the total population of the Kingdom of Jordan.[36] Likewise, al-Qarni, a social media star who is known for his self-help book, "Don't be Sad," has 14.5 million Twitter followers.[37] After delivering a lecture in the Philippines in March 2016, al-Qarni was shot and injured in the shoulder, which only increased his notoriety.[38]

The *Sahwa* clerics are not the only brand of Islamists in Saudi Arabia to utilize the Internet to propagate their views—clerics across the spectrum have circumvented traditional modes of religious communication with great success on social media. Their growing popularity could be cause for concern to the Kingdom's leaders, however, as some in the past have used their clout to advocate violence, as when the clerics mobilized Saudis to fight in Iraq against coalition forces in 2004, and when dozens of clerics (not affiliated with the government) signed an online petition calling for Saudi's to engage in jihad against Syria's government.[39]

On the eve of the American siege of Fallujah, twenty-six prominent clerics signed an "Open Sermon to the Militant Iraqi People" that legitimized joining the Iraqi insurgency as part of a "defense *jihad*" against the "aggressor" coalition.[40] Shortly thereafter, the number of Saudis who went to Iraq to fight against Western forces peaked.[41] In June 2012, a number of prominent clerics tried to organize a fundraising campaign for Syrian rebels fighting against President Bashar al-Assad's regime. However, one of the organizations facilitating the transfer of donations was the Revival of Islamic Heritage Society of Kuwait, a charity previously designated as a terrorist entity by the United States and UN for arming and financing al-Qaeda.[42] More recently, despite the government's 2014 decree forbidding Saudi's from fighting against ISIS outside of Saudi Arabia, in the fall of 2015, 53 clerics and academics called for, "all those who are able, and outside of Saudi Arabia, to answer the calls of *jihad*" and fight against Russian forces and the Syrian government in Syria.[43]

In addition to physical and intellectual resistance, Saudi Islamists have long been implicated in terrorist financing across the globe. Since the 1970's, Saudi Arabia has spent more than 4 percent of its GDP per year on overseas aid with "two thirds of that amount going to 'Islamic Activities'" in impoverished countries grappling with extremism, like Yemen, Sudan, Mauritania, Bosnia and Afghanistan.[44] After the events of September 11, 2001, Saudi Arabia and other Gulf countries have been repeatedly criticized for financing terrorism abroad. In 2007, then-Undersecretary of the Treasury for Terrorism and Financial Intelligence Stuart Levey said that, "If I could somehow snap my fingers and cut off funding from one country, it would be Saudi Arabia."[45] Levey's comments were a consequence of the fact that Islamic charities are commonly singled out as the primary source of illicit funds in terror financing cases. Implicating wealthy Saudi's in terrorist financing cases with exact dollar amounts is extremely difficult due primarily to the fact that Saudis prefer cash transactions and donate anonymously. Since giving charitably (zakat) is one of the five pillars of Islam, such organizations receive significant donations anonymously and from all sectors of society.

The final report of the 9/11 Commission determined that there was no evidence that the Saudi government as an institution, or Saudi leadership as individuals, provided support to al-Qaeda, but the Commission noted that al Qaeda raised money directly from individuals in Saudi Arabia, and through "charities with significant government sponsorship."[46] This pattern of funding allegedly stretches back for the past 30 years. In particular, the 9/11 Commission noted the "Golden Chain," a network of Saudi and other Gulf financiers used by Osama Bin Laden to collect and channel funds for the anti-Soviet *jihad* during the 1980s in Afghanistan. The financiers used charities and other NGOs as conduits for their donations to the *jihad*, and this network later became influential in the establishment of al-Qaeda's base in Afghanistan in the late 1990s.[47]

Saudi charities have allegedly financed terrorist groups elsewhere as well. In 2004, families of terror attack victims in Israel filed two civil lawsuits with the U.S. District Court of New York against Arab Bank PLC of Jordan. The families sought $2 billion in damages, accusing the "Saudi Committee for the Support of the Al Quds Intifada," a government-sanctioned charity, of funneling money through Arab Bank branches in the Palestinian Territories to provide "insurance benefits" to the families of suicide bombers and others who were casualties of conflict with Israel.[48] While Arab Bank denied that it had prior knowledge of payments to the families of suicide bombers through its branches, the Saudi Committee's executive manager stated: "We support the families of Palestinian martyrs, without differentiating between whether the Palestinian was a bomber or was killed by Israeli troops."[49]

In another instance of illicit financing, the Pakistani newspaper *Dawn* reported on a leaked 2008 cable from the U.S. Consulate in Lahore to the State Department. The cable alleged that financiers in Saudi Arabia and the UAE were sending nearly $100 million annually to Deobandi and *Ahl-i-Hadith* clerics in southern Punjab. In turn, those clerics were targeting families with multiple children and severe financial difficulties for recruitment, initially under the pretense of charity. Next, a Deobandi or *Ahl-i-Hadith maulana* would offer to educate the children in his school and "find them employment in the service of Islam." During the education phase, the clerics would indoctrinate the children and assess their inclination "to engage in violence and acceptance of *jihadi* culture." Parents then received cash payments of $6,500 for each son chosen for "martyrdom" operations.[50]

Throughout 2016, partially in response to legislation introduced in the U.S. Senate in 2015 as the Justice Against Sponsors of Terrorism Act ("JASTA") which narrowed the scope of the doctrine of sovereign immunity to enable families of the 9/11 victims to make civil claims against a foreign state in response to an act of terrorism, Saudi Arabia aggressively pursued the issue of illicit financing. In the summer of 2016, Daniel Glaser, assistant secretary for terrorist financing at the U.S. Department of Treasury, testified before Congress that Saudi Arabia had emerged as a "regional leader in targeted designations".[51] Saudi Arabia's spokesperson for the Ministry of the Interior claimed that Saudi Arabia had prosecuted more than 240 suspects and froze and investigated more than 117 internal accounts.[52] These activities by the government were also in response to the growing threat of ISIL throughout the region. According to recent polling data, it is estimated that about 5% of Saudi Arabia's population—or over half a million people—support ISIL.[53] And in July, 2016, three suicide bombing attacks bearing the hallmarks of the Islamic State were conducted across the country; an act CIA Director John Brennan described as "unprecedented."[54]

ISLAMISM AND THE STATE

Throughout the 20th century, the Saudi government and its official Wahhabi religious establishment utilized the principles of *hijra, takfir,* and *jihad* to strengthen Saudi political rule. *Hijra* (migration) required individuals to physically migrate to the land of the pious state (Saudi Arabia), which proved useful in settling and indoctrinating the nomads. Later, they used *takfir* (excommunication) to provide the religious blessing for wars against secular Arab leaders like Gamal Abd al-Nasser and Saddam Hussein, and *jihad* (struggle) to embolden young men towards armed conflict against Islam's enemies in Afghanistan and elsewhere.[55] One of the Saudis' central tactics for consolidating their powers is *da'wah* (proselytization). To conduct *da'wah* on a global scale, the Saudi's have developed an extensive network to export and support *Wahhabism*.

Exporting Wahhabism

In 1979 the Monarchy witnessed the Grand Mosque takeover within Saudi Arabia's own borders, the Islamic Revolution in Iran, Shi'a protests in Saudi Arabia's oil-rich Eastern Province, and the Soviet invasion of Afghanistan. Shaken by what it perceived as serious threats to its security and power, the Saudi leadership quickly took drastic measures to assert its leadership in the Islamic world and to appease rising domestic extremism. They accomplished both objectives by increasing its existing exportation of a politicized form of *Wahhabism*, directed as a foreign policy tool against the Soviets and competing strands of Islam alike.[56]

To bolster his legitimacy and to counter the threat of secular governance sweeping the Middle East, in the 1960s King Faysal established a policy of supporting Islamic institutions abroad. In 1962 he created the Muslim World League (MWL) to facilitate the spread of Wahhabi ideology. The MWL supported sects and organizations throughout the world that challenged "heretical" Muslim sects, and eliminated popular religious practices that are forbidden in the Wahhabi interpretation. The MWL supported the Deobandis, *Ahl-i Hadith*, and *Jamaat-e-Islami* in South Asia, while distributing religious literature and funding schools in West African countries like Nigeria, Mali, Ghana, the Ivory Coast, and Guinea.[57]

The Saudis also helped develop other religious organizations, including the World Assembly of Muslim Youth (WAMY), the Al Haramain Foundation, and the International Islamic Relief Organization (IIRO), among others. From 1973-2002, the Saudi government spent more than $80 billion on Islamic institutions and other activities in the non-Muslim world alone, contributing to some 1,500 mosques, 150 Islamic centers, 202 Muslim colleges, and 2,000 Islamic schools.[58] Thanks to Saudi financing in Asia, there are currently more than 10,000 Deobandi-run *madrassas* in

India, Pakistan, and Bangladesh.[59] Saudi Arabia likewise has provided funding to build mosques all over the globe—from Sweden, to Chad, to South Korea, and Los Angeles.[60]

With their unprecedented outreach campaign, the Saudis now sponsor nearly 80 percent of all Islamic institutions in the U.S. and Canada, even though, since 9/11, Islamic institutions in the U.S. have faced increasing scrutiny. Nearly 50 organizations and institutions that have been raided, shut down, or had their assets frozen because of suspected links to terrorism. Among those institutions connected to Saui Arabia were the Muslim World League, World Assembly of Muslim Youth, the Al Haramain Foundation, the SAAR Foundation, the International Institute of Islamic Thought, and the School of Islamic and Social Sciences.[61]

Combating the jihadist threat at home

The Saudi government's approach to combating extremism and domestic terrorism is conducted through its "Security Strategy," which utilizes the security forces and members of the community, and the "Advocacy and Advisory Strategy" which utilizes counseling, advisory, and advocacy campaigns.[62] The advocacy and advisory strategy's "soft" approach to the domestic terrorist threat involves utilizing every form of communication to identify sources of what the government calls "deviant" interpretations of Islam, to correct incorrect understandings of *sharia* law, and to try to convince extremists to follow the right path.[63]

The new approach follows a major initiative pursued by the Kingdom after a series of terror attacks by al-Qaeda in 2003. Between 2003 and 2008, Saudi security forces successfully broke up al-Qaeda cells in the Kingdom by arresting and killing thousands of militants and collaborators suspected of planning terrorist attacks. The approach worked, but only for a time. There were very few attacks in Saudi Arabia until 2014, when the Islamic State staged a series of attacks targeting Shi'ite mosques and the security services.[64] Since then, the Islamic State has carried out over two dozen attacks within the Kingdom, killing several dozen people and injuring hundreds.[65]

To combat the threat, the Saudi government runs two religious rehabilitation programs: a governmental Counseling Program and the independent but government-supported program called *Al-Sakina* (Tranquility).[66] Both rely on clerics, some of them also former radicals, who engage the "deviants" in theological discussions in an attempt to prove their faulty understanding of Islam. Prisoners who have not committed terrorist acts on Saudi soil, and can prove that they have renounced their extreme views, are released and assisted with jobs, government stipends for marriage, education, cars, and housing. Although the Saudis previously claimed a 100 percent success rate for their rehabilitation programs, after the U.S Department of Defense noted the return to militancy of several Guantanamo Bay detainees who had completed the program, the Saudi government now claims a 10 to 20 percent success rate.[67]

The Saudi government also utilizes a "Public Awareness Campaign," which aims to "reinforce the true values of the Islamic faith and to educate Saudi citizens about the dangers of extremism and terrorism."[68] According to the Saudi Embassy in Washington, DC, the campaign primarily promotes public service announcements that are broadcasted on Arabic satellite networks and Saudi television.[69] The Saudi government also leverages interviews with former militants, who have allegedly repented for their wrongdoing and are willing to denounce their former militancy. Among the first former radicals to renounce their views on television were several high profile clerics who were arrested in 2003 following al-Qaeda's attacks in Riyadh.[70]

The Public Awareness Campaign has not fully succeeded in de-radicalizing Saudis or persuading them against joining militant organizations. While Saudi clerics are part of the Kingdom's de-radicalization efforts, at times they offer contradicting messages when they incite sectarian tensions and support fighting *jihad* in foreign countries. During the ongoing civil war in Syria, for example, clerics like Mohamad al-Arefe encouraged Syrian rebels to slaughter Bashar al-Assad's supporters, which include Iran, Hezbollah, and the Syrian Alawite community.[71] Even the Kingdom's Grand Mufti, Abdulaziz Al al-Sheikh, jumped in to denounce Hezbollah, saying, "We urge all politicians and clerics to take substantial measures against this repulsive sectarian group (Hezbollah) and all those [who] back it so as to deter this aggression."[72] A year later, the Grand Mufti declared, "The ideas of extremism, radicalism and terrorism... have nothing to do with Islam and (their proponents) are the enemy number one of Islam."[73] More recently, the opposition clerics and scholars who called for a *jihad* against the Syrian government and its backers, did not contradict the government clerics, but they also did not speak out against traveling abroad for *jihad*.[74]

After the Arab Spring

Since the outbreak of the Arab Spring in late 2010, when massive protests overthrew longtime Saudi allies in Egypt and Tunisia and heralded the rise of Islamists to power, the Saudi government has worked to preempt similar demands for national reforms. As the protest movements rolled through Tunisia, Egypt, and Libya, King Abdullah rushed to avert a crisis of power by issuing subsidy packages worth an estimated $130 billion, creating a Facebook page for the population to tell him their grievances, and increasing the salaries of government workers. The king's measures included 60,000 jobs at the Ministry of the Interior, 500,000 new houses, and a minimum wage for the public sector of 3,000 Saudi Riyals ($800) per month—in contrast, the average private sector wage is only 1,000 SR per month.[75] The government also infused $10.7 billion into its development fund, which offers Saudis interest-free loans to build homes, marry, and start small businesses. An additional $4 billion was designated for the healthcare sector.[76]

To maintain order, the Saudi government also relied on help from the state's clergy, sanctioned and unsanctioned alike, who criticized activists online on Facebook and Twitter, and who issued *fatwas* in support of the regime. On March 6, 2011, the country's highest religious body, the Council of Senior *Ulema*, called on "everybody to exert every effort to increase solidarity, promote unity and warn against all causes giving rise to the opposite," and further warned Saudis about "deviant intellectual and partisan [Shi'a] tendencies" that could threaten Saudi stability.[77] Other clerics threatened potential protesters with violence. Saad al-Buraik, a member of the government's Counseling Program for re-educating extremists, called for "smashing the skulls of those who organize demonstrations or take part in them."[78]

The state's mix of subsidies and clerical advocacy, as well as its robust security deployments, successfully eliminated the threat of a popular uprising, but threats to the Kingdom remain. With the rise of the Islamic State, the increasing strength of Iran, the unruly nature of the Internet and online activism, and a significant power transition, Saudi Arabia continues to wrestle with how to maintain control and legitimacy in a rapidly changing geopolitical and security landscape. Unsanctioned clerics have carved out a substantial platform on social media that may prove difficult for the government to control. Because those clerics have generally played within the state's red lines, they have been largely unhindered in the messaging.[79]

Current and Future Issues

Following the death of King Abdullah on January 25, 2015, his half-brother, King Salman bin Abd al Aziz, came to power and immediately began to assert his authority through various strategic policies. He changed succession plans (like replacing his half-brother Crown Prince Muqrin with his nephew, Prince Mohammed bin Nayef bin Abd al Aziz, the former Interior Minister and head of counterterrorism), released thousands of prisoners except those deemed a threat to security, increased the salaries of public sector employees, curtailed the power of the religious police, dismissed two influential officials who had opposed Wahabi clerics, and, in a nod to ultraconservative clerics, fired the Kingdom's only female Cabinet member.

King Salman's approach to geopolitical changes has been both ideological and practical, similar to his predecessors. As King Salman has leaned more heavily on the traditional cleric establishment to maintain legitimacy, he and his son, the new Deputy Crown Prince, have also moved to restructure the economy in the face of a shifting global energy landscape driven in large part by the United States' new oil independence.[80]

Increasingly concerned with the threat of Iran and its proxies in Yemen, in recent years the Saudi government has also pursued a more aggressive foreign policy defined by its call for the resignation of President Bashar al Assad of Syria, and its military efforts in Yemen beginning in 2015. Three months after coming to power, following the ouster of the Yemeni transitional government in 2015 at the hands of the Houthi rebels and backers of the former Yemeni President Ali Abdullah Saleh, King Salman initiated military strikes in coordination with nine other Middle Eastern countries.[81] Since then, despite a significant number of civilian casualties, Saudi losses, and increased tensions between Iran and Saudi Arabia, the United States has supported the Kingdom in its efforts to reinstate President Hadi in the ongoing conflict.

In April 2016, Deputy Crown Prince Salman announced a long-term oil independence strategy for the country. Included among the radical economic proposals for the country was a commitment to a minor increase in the women's participation rate in the workforce—which will be raised from 22% to 30 % over 15 years. This modest proposal, according to the *Economist*, suggests resistance from the Wahhabi clerical establishment. For a country with a population that has been conditioned to expect oil wealth in exchange for loyalty, and a clerical establishment that is resistant to modernization, a National Transformation Program will be difficult to implement, and may rely entirely on the ability of the young and relatively inexperienced Deputy Crown Prince to move the country in a new direction.[82] His power on social media will play a role, but so will his ability to co-opt the religious establishment and the population under the new terms of a decades-old deal.

Endnotes

[1] Daniel Byman, "The U.S.-Saudi Arabia Counterterrorism Relationship," Brookings Institution, May 24, 2016. https://www.brookings.edu/testimonies/the-u-s-saudi-arabia-counterterrorism-relationship/

[2] "King Abdullah, a Shrewd Force, Who Reshaped Saudi Arabia, dies at 90," New York Times, January 22, 2015, http://www.nytimes.com/2015/01/23/world/middleeast/king-abdullah-who-nudged-saudi-arabia-forward-dies-at-90.html.

[3] "Saudi Arabia Backgrounder: Who Are The Islamists?" International Crisis Group, September 21, 2004, 2, http://www.pbs.org/wgbh/pages/frontline/shows/saud/themes/backgrounder.pdf.

[4] "Rejectionist Islamism in Saudi Arabia: The Story of Juhayman Al-'Utaybi Revisited," 117.

[5] Ondrej Beranek, "Divided We Survive: A Landscape of Fragmentation in Saudi Arabia," Brandeis University Crown Center for Middle East Studies Middle East Brief no. 28, January 2009, 3, http://www.brandeis.edu/crown/publications/meb/MEB33.pdf.

[6] Madawi al-Rasheed, Contesting the Saudi State (Cambridge: Cambridge University Press, 2007).

[7] M. Ehsan Ahrari, "Saudi Arabia: A Simmering Cauldron of Instability?" Brown Journal of World Affairs, Summer/Fall 1999, 220, http://www.watsoninstitute.org/bjwa/archive/6.2/Essay/Ahrari.pdf.

[8] Rachel Bronson, "Rethinking Religion: the Legacy of the U.S.-Saudi Relationship," The Washington Quarterly, Autumn 2005, 127, http://www.twq.com/05autumn/docs/05autumn_bronson.pdf

[9] Shmuel Bachar, Shmuel Bar, Rachel Machtiger and Yair Minzili, Establishment Ulama and Radicalism in Egypt, Saudi Arabia, and Jordan (Washington, DC: Hudson Institute, December 2006), 18, http://www.currenttrends.org/docLib/20061226_UlamaandRadicalismfinal.pdf

[10] When al-Qaeda on the Arabian Peninsula attacked three foreign housing complexes in Riyadh in May 2003, killing 34 and injuring 200, al-Odah and al-Hawali issued a statement with nearly 50 other clerics, condemning the attacks and declaring the perpetrators ignorant, misguided young men. See "Saudi bombing deaths rise," BBC (London), May 13, 2003, http://news.bbc.co.uk/2/hi/middle_east/3022473.stm; Then, in December 2004, al-Odah, Aidh al-Qarni, and 33 other sheikhs signed a statement denouncing London-based Saudi dissident Saad al-Faqih's attempts to organize demonstrations against the regime. See Toby Craig Jones, "The Clerics, the Sahwa and the Saudi State," Center for Contemporary Conflict Strategic Insights, March 2005, 4, http://www.nps.edu/Academics/centers/ccc/publications/OnlineJournal/2005/Mar/jonesMar05.pdf. Subsequently, in January 2005, in response to a failed attack on the Ministry of Interior in Riyadh the previous month, 41 clerics issued a statement on al-Odah's website, Islam Today, warning against actions and discourse targeting the Saudi regime.

[11] Lacroix, Stephanie. "Saudi Arabia's Muslim Brotherhood Dilemma," Washington Post, March 20, 2014.

[12] Ibid.

[13] National Commission on Terrorist Attacks Upon the United States, "The 9/11 Commission Report," July 22, 2004

[14] Thomas Hegghammer, "Islamist Violence and Regime Stability in Saudi Arabia," International Affairs 84, no. 4 (2008), http://hegghammer.com/_files/Hegghammer_-Islamist_violence_and_regime_stability_in_Saudi_Arabia.pdf

[15] Thomas Hegghammer, "Terrorist Recruitment and Radicalization in Saudi Arabia," Middle East Policy, Winter 2006, 42, http://chenry.webhost.utexas.edu/usme/2007/Saudi-Terrorist_Recruitmen_87543a.pdf

[16] Ibid., 45

[17] "Al-Qaeda in the Arabian Peninsula," Al Jazeera (Doha), December 29, 2009, http://english.aljazeera.net/news/middleeast/2009/12/2009122935812371810.html

[18] Margaret Coker, "Assassination Attempt Targets Saudi Prince," Wall Street Journal, August 29, 2009, http://online.wsj.com/article/SB125144774691366169.html

[19] Anahad O'Connor & Eric Schmitt, "Terror Attempt Seen as Man Tries to Ignite Device on Jet," New York Times, December 25, 2009, http://www.nytimes.com/2009/12/26/us/26plane.html

[20] U.S. State Department Bureau of Counterterrorism, Country Reports on Terrorism 2015, April 2016. The report has included similar language since the 2013 report released in April 2014.

[21] "Al Qaeda Chief Tells Jihadist Fighters in Syria: Unite or Die," Reuters, May 8, 2016, http://www.reuters.com/article/us-mideast-crisis-syria-qaeda-idUSKCN0XZ0OA.

[22] Graham, David. "Sheikh Nimr al Nimr and the Forgotten Shiites of Saudi Arabia," The Atlantic, January 5, 2016. https://www.theatlantic.com/international/archive/2016/01/nimr-al-nimr-saudi-arabia-shiites/422670/.

[23] Ahmad Moussalli, "Wahhabism, Salafism, and Islamism: Who is the Enemy?" American University of Beirut, January 2009, 6, http://conflictsforum.org/briefings/Wahhabism-Salafism-and-Islamism.pdf

[24] Rachel Bronson, Thicker than Oil: America's Uneasy Partnership with Saudi Arabia (New York: Oxford University Press, 2006), 147-8.

[25] "Two Die During Saudi Arabia protest at Shia Cleric Arrest," BBC (London), July 9, 2012, http://www.bbc.co.uk/news/world-middle-east-18768703

[26] Toby Matthiesen, "Saudi Arabia's Shiite Escalation," Foreign Policy, July 10, 2012, http://mideast.foreignpolicy.com/posts/2012/07/10/sable_rattling_in_the_gulf

[27] For videos of the protests in Awwamiya, see http://www.youtube.com/watch?v=dPLF5fGvYNA&feature=youtu.be and http://www.youtube.com/watch?v=JQsgTEBoH_E&feature=youtu.be

[28] "Saudi Arabia: Cleric Who Backed Protests on Trial for His Life," Human Rights Watch, May 11, 2013, http://www.hrw.org/news/2013/05/10/saudi-arabia-cleric-who-backed-protests-trial-his-life .

[29] Leila Fadel, "Saudi Cleric's Death Sentence Focuses Shia Anger on Ruling Family," NPR, October 18, 2014, http://www.npr.org/2014/10/18/357108117/saudi-clerics-death-sentence-focuses-shia-anger-on-ruling-family

[30] "Sheikh Nimr al-Nimr: Anger at Execution of Top Saudi Cleric," BBC, January 2, 2016, http://www.bbc.com/news/world-middle-east-35214536

[31] Ben Hubbard, "Iranian Protesters Ransack Saudi Embassy After Execution of Shiite Cleric," New York Times, January 2, 2016, http://www.nytimes.com/2016/01/03/world/middleeast/saudi-arabia-executes-47-sheikh-nimr-shiite-cleric.html

[32] Ibid.

[33] Ben Hubbard, "Saudi Arabia Executes a Prince Convicted in a Fatal Stabbing," New York Times, October 18, 2016, http://www.nytimes.com/2016/10/19/world/middleeast/saudi-arabia-prince-executed-salman.html

[34] Bunzel, Cole. The Kingdom and the Caliphate: Duel of the Islamic States, February 18, 2016.http://carnegieendowment.org/2016/02/18/kingdom-and-caliphate-duel-of-islamic-states-pub-62810.

[35] For Forbes Middle East's List, see www.forbesmiddleeast.com/arabic/الكثر-100-شخصية-عربية-حضوراً-على-توتير/; For Al-Odah's English Twitter Page, see http://twitter.com/Salman_Al_Odah ; For his Arabic page, see www.facebook.com/DrSalmanAlOadah; For his Arabic page, see www.facebook.com/SalmanAlodah

[36] For al-Arefe's Twitter page, see http://twitter.com/MohamadAlarefe; For his Facebook page, see www.facebook.com/3refe

[37] For al-Qarnee's Twitter page, see https://twitter.com/Dr_alqarnee; For his Facebook page, see www.facebook.com/dralqarnee?sk=wall

[38] "Philippine Gunman Attacks and Injures Saudi Preacher," Al Arabiya (Riyadh), March 1, 2016, http://english.alarabiya.net/en/News/2016/03/01/Saudi-preacher-injured-after-gun-attack-in-Philippines.html

[39] McDowell, Angus. "Saudi opposition clerics make sectarian call to Jihad in Saudi Arabia," Reuters, October 5th, 2015. http://www.reuters.com/article/us-mideast-crisis-saudi-clerics-idUSKCN0RZ1IW20151005

[40] "The House of Saud: The Fatwa of the 26 Clerics: Open Sermon to the Militant Iraqi People," PBS Frontline, February 8, 2005, http://www.pbs.org/wgbh/pages/frontline/shows/saud/etc/fatwa.html

[41] Thomas Hegghammer, "Saudis in Iraq: Patterns of Radicalization and Recruitment," Revues.org, June 12, 2008, http://conflits.revues.org/index10042.html

[42] Jonathan Schanzer and Steven Miller, "Saudi Clerics Funnel Cash to Syrian Rebels through Terror Group," Weekly Standard, June 12, 2012, http://www.weeklystandard.com/blogs/saudi-clerics-funnel-cash-syrian-rebels-through-terror-group_647141.html

[43] Al-Saleh, Huda, "52 Saudi clerics, scholars call to battle Russian forces in Syria," Al-Arabiya, October 5th 2015. http://english.alarabiya.net/en/News/middle-east/2015/10/05/Fifty-two-Saudi-clerics-scholars-call-for-fight-against-Russian-forces-in-Syria.html.

[44] Graff, Corinne, Poverty, Development, and Violent Extremism in Weak States, Brookings Institution, 2010, p. 10. Accessed at: https://www.brookings.edu/wp-content/uploads/2016/06/2010_confronting_poverty.pdf

[45] Brian Ross, "U.S.: Saudis Still Filling Al Qaeda's Coffers," ABC News, September 11,2007.

[46] Christopher Blanchard and Alfred Prados, "Saudi Arabia, Terrorist Financing Issues," Congressional Research Service Report, December 8, 2004, http://fas.org/irp/crs/RL32499.pdf

[47] Christopher Blanchard and Alfred Prados, "Saudi Arabia: Terrorist Financing Issues," Congressional Research Service Report, September 14, 2007, 6, http://www.fas.org/sgp/crs/terror/RL32499.pdf

[48] Ibid., 8.

[49] Ra'id Qusti, "Saudi Telethon Funds Go Direct to Palestinian Victims," Arab News (Jedda), May 27, 2002, http://archive.arabnews.com/?page=1&section=0&article=15591&d=27&m=5&y=2002

[50] Qurat ul ain Siddiqui, "Saudi Arabia, UAE Financing Extremism in South Punjab," Dawn, May 22, 2011, http://www.dawn.com/2011/05/22/saudi-arabia-uae-financing-extremism-in-south-punjab.html

[51] Wong, Kristina. "Treasury Official: the Gulf states moving to cut off terrorist financing," The Hill, June 6th, 2016. http://thehill.com/policy/defense/282989-treasury-official-gulf-remains-important-source-of-terrorist-financing

[52] Ibid.

[53] "Is Saudi Arabia to Blame for the Islamic State?" BBC, December 19th, 2015. http://www.bbc.com/news/world-middle-east-35101612.

[54] "Attacks in Saudi Arabia bear hallmarks of Islamic State," Reuters, July 14th, 2016. http://www.reuters.com/article/us-usa-saudi-idUSKCN0ZT-2CL.

[55] Madawi al-Rasheed, Contesting the Saudi State (Cambridge: Cambridge University Press, 2007).

[56] Ibid.

[57] Commins, David. The Wahhabi Mission and Saudi Arabia. New York: I. B. Tauris, 2006.

[58] Alexander Alexiev, "The Wages of Extremism: Radical Islam's Threat to the West and the Muslim World," Hudson Institute, March 2011, 44, http://www.hudson.org/files/publications/AAlexievWagesofExtremism032011.pdf

[59] Alexander Alexiev, "The End of an Alliance," National Review, October 28, 2002, http://old.nationalreview.com/flashback/flashback-alexiev112602.asp

[60] Scott Shane, "Saudis and Extremism, Both the Arsonists and the Firefighters," New York Times, August 25, 2016, http://www.nytimes.com/2016/08/26/world/middleeast/saudi-arabia-islam.html

[61] Alexiev, "The End of an Alliance."

[62] Abdullah F. Ansary, "Combating Extremism: A Brief Overview of Saudi Arabia's Approach," Middle East Policy Journal XV, no. 2, Summer 2008, http://www.mepc.org/journal/middle-east-policy-archives/combating-extremism-brief-overview-saudi-arabias-approach?print.

[63] Ibid.

[64] Ben Hubbard, "Saudi Arabia, Blamed for Spawning Jihadists, is Again their Target," New York Times, July 6, 2016, http://www.nytimes.com/2016/07/07/world/middleeast/saudi-arabia-isis-al-qaeda-jihadists.html

[65] Ibid.

[66] Rabasa et al., Deradicalizing Islamist Extremists; Find the al-Sakina program online at http://www.assakina.com/

[67] Marisa L. Porges, "The Saudi Deradicalization Experiment," Council on Foreign Relations, January 22, 2010, http://www.cfr.org/radicalization-and-extremism/saudi-deradicalization-experiment/p21292

[68] Royal Embassy of Saudi Arabia (Washington, DC), Information Office, "Initiatives and Actions to Combat Terrorism," November 2012, http://www.saudiembassy.net/files/PDF/Reports/Counterterrorism.pdf, page 5

[69] "Initiatives and Actions to Combat Terrorism," 5-6.

[70] Jones, "The Clerics, the Sahwa and the Saudi State," 4.

[71] "الشيخ الحديثي: معركة "القصير" فاصلة في تاريخ الإسلام," Al-Moslim, May 31, 2013, http://www.almoslim.net/node/184327

[72] "Grand Mufti Urges Muslim World to Flay Hezbollah," Saudi Gazette, June 7, 2013, http://www.saudigazette.com.sa/index.cfm?method=home.regcon&contentid=20130607168855

[73] "ISIS Enemy Number One of Islam," Al Arabiya (Riyadh), August 19, 2014, http://english.alarabiya.net/en/News/middle-east/2014/08/19/Saudi-mufti-ISIS-is-enemy-No-1-of-Islam-.html

[74] "Saudi Opposition Clerics Make Sectarian Call to Jihad in Syria," Reuters, October 5, 2015, http://www.reuters.com/article/us-mideast-crisis-saudi-clerics-idUSKCN0RZ1IW20151005

[75] Steffen Hertog, "The Costs of Counter-Revolution in the GCC," Foreign Policy, May 31, 2011, http://mideast.foreignpolicy.com/posts/2011/05/31/the_costs_of_counter_revolution_in_the_gcc

[76] Jonathan Schanzer and Steven Miller, "How Saudi Arabia Survived – So Far," The Journal of International Security Affairs, May 14, 2012, http://www.defenddemocracy.org/media-hit/how-saudi-arabia-has-survivedso-far/.

[77] For the full Arabic text of the fatwa, see http://www.assakina.com/fatwa/6834.html; For an English translation, see www.salafitalk.net/st/viewmessages.cfm?Forum=9&Topic=12255

[78] Madawi al-Rasheed, "Preachers of Hate as Loyal Subjects," New York Times, March 14, 2011, http://www.nytimes.com/roomfordebate/2011/03/14/how-stable-is-saudi-arabia/preachers-of-hate-as-loyal-subjects

[79] Jonathan Schanzer and Steven Miller, Facebook Fatwa: Saudi Clerics, Wahhabi Islam, and Social Media (Washington, DC: FDD Press, 2012) http://www.defenddemocracy.org/media-hit/fdd-releases-cutting-edge-study-of-saudi-social-media1/

[80] Ibid., 5.

[81] "Saudi Arabia Launches Airstrikes in Yemen," BBC, March 26, 2016. http://www.bbc.com/news/world-us-canada-32061632

[82] "Saudi Arabia's Post-Oil Future," The Economist, April 30, 2016, http://www.economist.com/news/middle-east-and-africa/21697673-bold-promises-bold-young-prince-they-will-be-hard-keep-saudi-arabias

SYRIA

> **QUICK FACTS**
>
> Population: 17,185,170 (July 2016 est.)
>
> Area: 185,180 sq km
>
> Ethnic Groups: Arab 90.3%, Kurdish, Armenian, and other 9.7%
>
> Religions: Muslim 87% (official; includes Sunni 74% and Alawi, Ismaili, and Shia 13%), Christian 10% (includes Orthodox, Uniate, and Nestorian), Druze 3%, Jewish (few remaining in Damascus and Aleppo)
>
> Government Type: Presidential republic; highly authoritarian regime
>
> GDP (official exchange rate): $24.6 billion
>
> *Map and Quick Facts courtesy of the CIA World Factbook (January 2017)*

OVERVIEW

Islamism has featured prominently in the politics and policies of modern Syria on a number of different levels. Like other majority Sunni Muslim Arab countries governed by secular autocrats, Syria has a long tradition of Sunni Islamist opposition activity. The fact that the hereditary dictatorship of Syrian President Bashar al-Assad has long been dominated by Alawis, an Islamic offshoot sect viewed as heretical by religious Sunnis, renders it uniquely vulnerable to Islamist challenges. It has managed to survive for nearly a half-century in spite of this Achilles' Heel by brutally suppressing dissent and tightly regulating Sunni religious practices.

Notwithstanding its heavy-handed treatment of Islamists at home, the Assad regime has eagerly armed, financed, and sheltered foreign Islamist organizations committed to fighting its enemies abroad. The sectarian and ideological affiliations of these groups have been varied, ranging from the Shi'a Hezbollah militia in Lebanon to the Sunni Palestinian Hamas movement and al-Qaeda-aligned terrorists battling U.S.-led coalition forces in Iraq after the fall of Saddam Hussein in 2003. In addition to advancing the regime's regional strategic objectives, support for these groups helped defuse Islamist militancy at home by appropriating radical causes that resonated with disaffected youth.

The eruption of a popular uprising against Assad in March 2011 and the country's subsequent collapse into civil war changed everything. Although protests were initially peaceful, multi-sectarian, and explicitly oriented around the pursuit of democratic change, the escalating violence and prolonged breakdown of law and order in many areas of the country were exploited by both indigenous and foreign Islamists (including many who had hitherto supported the regime).

Once the bête noire of secularists, the Syrian Muslim Brotherhood came to dominate the Western-backed Syrian National Coalition. However, more radical Islamist forces on the ground have since eclipsed its influence. Flush with financing from the Arab Gulf (in contrast to cash-starved, poorly-armed, and secular-leaning rebel forces), more radical Salafi-jihadists close to al-Qaeda have gained dominion over key parts of northwestern Syria. Many rallied alongside Iraqi jihadists under the banner of the Islamic State, which seized control of large swathes of Iraq's Sunni heartland in 2013 and 2014.

ISLAMIST ACTIVITY

More than four years of civil war in Syria have enabled an extraordinarily diverse array of Islamist actors to flourish. Broadly speaking, they can be divided into three categories: anti-regime Sunni political Islamists ostensibly committed to advancing their agenda by democratic means; Sunni *Salafi-jihadists* committed to either forcibly establishing an Islamic republic in Syria or using it as a stepping stone to pursue regional and international ambitions; and a small coterie of pro-regime Islamists, mostly Shi'a and non-Syrian.

Political Islamists

The first category of Islamists ranges from the Syrian Muslim Brotherhood (SMB) to various traditionalist, reformist, and moderate Salafi Sunni religious currents that dominate the Syrian opposition in exile.

The Syrian chapter of the Egypt-based pan-Islamic Muslim Brotherhood movement was established in 1946. Despite its status as an offshoot, the SMB differs significantly from the original Muslim Brotherhood in its base of socio-economic support. Whereas the Muslim Brotherhood in Egypt traditionally drew mass support from rural areas, the SMB's base lay in the Sunni urban nobility and middle class.

In 1963, the secular Arab nationalist Ba'ath party seized power and began implementing land reforms and nationalizing industries, which severely threatened middle-class interests.[1] With independent political parties and media outlawed, the mosque became the one semi-protected space where dissidents could voice opposition to regime policies.[2]

As power within the regime became increasingly concentrated among a narrow clique of Alawi officers headed by Gen. Hafez Assad, who assumed the presidency in 1971, Brotherhood agitation intensified. In 1973, violent demonstrations instigated by the Brotherhood led the regime to modify a clause in a proposed new constitution that would not require the president to be Muslim. Instead, Assad persuaded influential Lebanese Shi'ite cleric Musa al-Sadr to issue a ruling certifying that Alawis are Shi'a Muslims and therefore eligible for the presidency.[3]

During the late 1970s, Islamist militants affiliated with the Brotherhood launched an armed insurrection against the Assad regime with the goal of replacing it with an Islamic state. Though the militants had some material support from rival Arab states, they were unable to rally support in rural areas where armed resistance was more tactically feasible. Thus, the rebellion never seriously threatened the regime. Thousands of Islamists were imprisoned, and membership in the Brotherhood was made punishable by death. When militants seized control of large parts of Hama in 1982, regime forces destroyed much of the city, killing tens of thousands.

This episode virtually eradicated the SMB's influence in Syria for the following three decades. Most ranking members of the Brotherhood went into exile,[4] where they splintered into rival factions centered on figures from Aleppo and Hama. Meanwhile, the Assad regime's soaring regional influence in the 1980s dissuaded rival governments from sponsoring armed opposition in Syria. The devastation resulting from the Brotherhood's failed insurrection made dissidents inside Syria wary of any association with Islamism in challenging the regime.

The tenure of Ali Sadreddine al-Bayanouni of the Aleppo wing as head of the SMB from 1996 to 2010 spurred a gradual moderation of the Brotherhood's platform, rhetoric, and tactics.[5] The SMB renounced violence in 2001. In 2004, it adopted a new political platform calling for multiparty democracy and minority rights.[6] Bayanouni also worked to improve the Brotherhood's ties with secular opposition forces. In 2005, the Brotherhood joined secular dissidents inside Syria in signing the Damascus Declaration calling for a "peaceful, gradual" democratic reform process.[7]

After the Damascus Declaration initiative failed to galvanize internal opposition to the regime, the Brotherhood focused its attention on warming up to Western and Arab governments bent on bringing Assad to heel in the wake of his alleged involvement in the 2005 assassination of former Lebanese Prime Minister Rafiq Hariri.[8] In 2006, it formed an alliance with recently exiled former Vice-President Abdul Halim Khaddam, a Sunni ex-Ba'athist with close ties to the Saudi royal family by way of Hariri.[9]

When international and regional pressure on Syria began to wane, however, the Brotherhood tried to reach an accommodation with Assad. In 2009, following Israel's Operation Cast Lead in the Gaza Strip, Bayanouni suspended the Brotherhood's anti-government activities, apparently hoping that Assad would reciprocate by allowing the movement to reestablish a presence inside Syria.[10] When this didn't happen, Bayanouni and his allies were soundly defeated in internal Brotherhood elections in Istanbul the following year. His successor, Mohammad Riad al-Shaqfeh, nevertheless decided to continue the suspension, expressing hope that Turkey would mediate between the Brotherhood and the regime.[11]

The outbreak of mass protests against the Syrian regime in March 2011 took the Brotherhood by surprise. As in other Middle East states experiencing the so-called "Arab Spring," Islamists initially played little discernable role in the unrest.[12] The SMB declined to endorse the uprising for nearly two months,[13] calculating whether its interests would best be served by extracting concessions from a weakened Assad or helping achieve his overthrow. Once it became clear the regime was not going to be able to extinguish the uprising, however, Brotherhood leaders threw their weight fully behind the cause.

The SMB's secretive and elitist structure limited how useful it would be to a popular uprising. This structure served the SMB well when organizing cell-based resistance in the late 1970s and avoiding regime infiltration while in exile, but did not lend itself to mass mobilization. Furthermore, the SMB's predominantly urban social base left it ill-suited to connect with a popular uprising emanating primarily in rural areas and the outskirts of major cities.

Nevertheless, the movement had an advantage over secular exile groups, due to its established organizational hierarchy, large network of members and affiliated Brotherhood chapters around the globe, as well as burgeoning relations with Qatar and Turkey (which turned against the Assad regime several months into the uprising).[14] The SMB played a prominent role in the August 2011 establishment of the Syrian National Council (which brought the exiled Syrian opposition groups under a single umbrella), and its successor organization, the Syrian National Coalition (SNC).[15]

Since then, a number of moderate Islamist currents have vied for influence with the Brotherhood within the SNC. A reformist current, more receptive to liberal democratic norms than the Brotherhood, included the National Action Group, cofounded by Obeida Nahas, who served as political advisor to Bayanouni and was reportedly the architect behind the Brotherhood's short-lived alliance with Khaddam.[16] Much like Turkey's ruling Justice and Development Party (AKP), Nahas and his allies describe themselves as religious conservatives, not Islamists.[17]

The Movement for Justice and Development (MJD), founded in London in 2006 in response to Bayanouni's alliance with Khaddam, actually named itself after the AKP. Its political platform calls for the Syrian constitution to declare Syria a nation of "Islamic civilization and culture," but without making *sharia* a principal source of legislation.[18] The Syrian National Movement (SNM), led by Emad ad-Din al-Rashid, advocates acceptance of the "Islamic reference" (*al-Marja'iyya al-Islamiyya*) as a source of legislation and the basis for the national identity.[19] Former SNC Secretary-General Badr Jamous is affiliated with the SNM.[20]

Another current of devout (though not strictly speaking Islamist) Sunni opposition leaders is composed of *ulema* (traditional Sufi religious scholars) who fled Syria during the revolt, many of whom had acquired substantial followings inside Syria as a result of the Assad's regime's relaxation of controls over religious life in the past decade. Muhammad Kurayyim Rajih's League of the Ulema of Sham (LUS), led mostly by clerics from Damascus and Homs, is the most notable traditionalist group.[21] Moaz al-Khatib of LUS, former *imam* of the Umayyad Mosque in Damascus, served as the first president of the SNC. Current LUS President Sheikh Osama al-Rifai is the spiritual leader of a moderate *Sufi* movement called *Jamaat Zayd* (Zayd's Group), which was allowed by the regime to operate in Syria in the 1990s.[22]

Finally, the Brotherhood and other political Islamist groups have been joined on most issues by a hybrid movement known as the *Sururis*. Based mainly in the Arab Gulf, *Sururism* "blends Salafism with Muslim Brotherhood ideology," notes journalist Hassan Hassan.[23] Named after Muhammad ibn Surur al-Nayef Zayn al-Abidin, a Syrian Islamic scholar initially affiliated with the Brotherhood who emigrated to Saudi Arabia in the 1960s,[24] Sururis adhere closely to the ideological precepts of Salafism (see below), but reject both the political quietism of traditional *Salafis* and (outside of the Syrian context) the *Salafi-jihadist* embrace of violence.

Due in part to lavish financing from donors in the Arab Gulf, Syrian *Sururis* played an influential role in the rebellion. By September 2012, according to scholar Aron Lund, a financing network run by compatriots of the aging Surur and funded primarily by Arab Gulf donors appeared to be "active in supporting both humanitarian and paramilitary Islamist groups."[25]

In April 2014, pro-Brotherhood *ulema* joined together with traditionalists, reformists, and *Sururis* to form the Syrian Islamic Council (SIC), purporting to be an official religious authority for rebel forces. Headed by Osama al-Rifai, it is aligned with the Qatar-Turkey axis and opposed to al-Qaeda-linked extremists.[26] Most Islamists in the SNC have avoided raising divisive social issues, such as veiling women and banning alcohol.

Nevertheless, the perceived dominance of Islamists in the SNC alienated many secular opposition figures. Kamal Lebwany, a dissident physician released from detention in November 2011 after nearly a decade in a Syrian jail, lamented that "the Muslim Brotherhood monopolizes everything" and warning that its pretensions to democracy are "a liberal peel covering a totalitarian, nondemocratic core."[27]

Although the Brotherhood declined to establish a fighting force in Syria bearing its name, it has provided funding to a range of different militias. The Commission for the Protection of Civilians (CPC), established in December 2011, was a primary vehicle for this. The intent of the financing has been less to directly control military units or promote their ideological agenda than to increase the Brotherhood's leverage sufficiently to make gains in an internationally-brokered settlement.[28]

Although the CPC was initially the main source of external financing for the revolt, it was soon supplanted by the fundraising networks of radical *Salafi* preachers based in the Arab Gulf. Many of the CPC's early recipients drifted away as more sources of funding became available, most notably via the Tawhid Brigade, *Ahrar al-Sham*, and *Suqour al-Sham*.[29]

A second umbrella of Brotherhood-backed militias in and around Idlib and Hama was the Shields of the Revolution Commission, nominally loyal to the FSA Supreme Military Command.[30] Over the course of the war, militias affiliated with the Brotherhood have been eclipsed in strength by more radical groups. "Without a negotiated cease-fire," scholar Aron Lund wrote prophetically in mid-2013, "the real outcome of the Syrian conflict is likely to be determined on the battlefield, where the Brotherhood's failure to establish a strong presence could significantly weaken its hand."[31]

The organization that can arguably best be seen as a successor to the Shields of the Revolution Commission is *Faylaq al-Sham*, announced as a merger of 19 brigades in March 2014. The group went on to become a key component of the *Jaysh al-Fath* ('Army of Conquest') coalition set up in 2015 in Idlib province, which will be discussed further below. It has also played a role in fighting in Aleppo, both against the regime and its allies as part of a reconstituted *Jaysh al-Fath* in 2016 and against the Islamic State in the north Aleppo countryside alongside CIA-backed FSA groups with Turkish support.

Regime-backed foreign Islamists

At the beginning of the uprising in March 2011, the Syrian regime retained an impressive array of foreign and domestic Islamist proxies.

In the Palestinian territories, Syria had supported the Sunni Islamist groups Islamic Jihad and Hamas, an offshoot of the Muslim Brotherhood, for two decades. Alongside militant secular Palestinian groups, both were allowed to maintain offices and military bases inside Syria.

In Lebanon, the Assad regime was a principal supporter and conduit to the Shi'a Islamist Hezbollah movement, channeling Iranian arms and funds to the militia as it waged war against Israeli forces occupying southern Lebanon prior their withdrawal in 2000, then intermittently against Israel itself. Syria also co-opted a number of Lebanese Sunni Islamist factions based in and around Tripoli.[32]

Finally, the Syrian regime covertly supported foreign *jihadists* entering Iraq after the fall of Saddam Hussein's regime in 2003.[33] Many Syrian *jihadists* affiliated with Abu Musab al-Zarqawi's al-Qaeda in Iraq (AQI) were allowed to set up safe houses and even recruit volunteers inside Syria.[34] When the Assad regime dialed back its support for Iraqi insurgents in 2007-2008, many of these *jihadis* left Iraq. Hundreds were imprisoned upon their return to Syria, while some were allowed to cross into Lebanon, where they founded the group Fatah al-Islam in the Nahr al-Bared Palestinian refugee camp.[35]

When demonstrations against the Syrian regime first erupted in March 2011, most of the regime's Sunni Islamist allies remained on the sidelines.[36] Once it became clear that Assad was unable to stamp out the uprising by force, however, they abandoned the regime in droves. Hamas leaders departed their longtime home in Damascus for Doha, Qatar, in January 2012,[37] while *Salafi-jihadists* came out squarely in support of the uprising.

Hezbollah, on the other hand, has steadfastly stood by the Syrian regime. The movement has used its considerable political power within Lebanon's quasi-democratic system to ensure that the Lebanese Army and other state security institutions have acted to prevent smuggling and other pro-rebel activities in Lebanon.

In 2012, Hezbollah forces began entering Syria, ostensibly to protect Shi'a shrines but in reality also to bolster pro-regime forces. In mid-2013, Hezbollah forces were instrumental in the regime's recapture of Qusayr, a predominantly Shi'ite Syrian town of 30,000, visible from the Lebanese border and essential to sealing off rebel supply routes into Lebanon.[38]

Besides Hezbollah's overt involvement under its own name with Lebanese fighters, Syria has also seen the deployment of Iraqi, Afghan and Pakistani Shi'a formations in support of the regime, in addition to the development of native Syrian Shi'a militias. The most numerous and effective of these fighters beyond Hezbollah are the thousands of Iraqi Shi'a militiamen.

The first major "international" Shi'a formation was the *Abu al-Fadl al-Abbas* Brigade, which emerged in 2012-2013 and was named after a widely revered military commander in the Battle of Karbala between the progenitors of today's Sunni and Shi'a.[39] Through 2013, a number of more specific formations emerged from the network of the Abu al-Fadl al-Abbas Brigade, mostly composed of and led by Iraqi Shi'a, such as Liwa Assad Allah al-Ghalib, Liwa Dhu al-Fiqar and the Rapid Intervention Regiment. Some of these militias reflect Iranian-backed splinters from the Sadrist trend, feeling let down by Iraqi cleric Muqtada al-Sadr's refusal to endorse fighting in Syria. Aws al-Khafaji, one such splinter cleric who backed the Syria militia mobilization, is the leader of the *Abu al-Fadl al-Abbas* Forces, a militia set up with close links to the Syria-focused groups that emerged out of the Abu al-Fadl al-Abbas Brigade. More recently, Sa'ad Sawar, a Sadrist militia commander who fought in Syria with Liwa Assad Allah al-Ghalib, set up *Jaysh al-Mu'ammal*, recruiting out of Sadr City in Baghdad.

Also through 2013, older Iraqi militias such as the Badr Organization, *Asa'ib Ahl al-Haq* and *Kata'ib Hezbollah* became involved in Syria under their own names, alongside the emergence of new Iraqi militias in Syria like *Saraya al-Khorasani, Harakat Hezbollah al-Nujaba'* and *Kata'ib Sayyid al-Shuhada'*.[40]

Following major advances by the Islamic State through northern and western Iraq in the summer of 2014, many Iraqi fighters returned to Iraq, with Hezbollah supposedly recruiting Lebanese Shi'ites to fill their places.[41] However, with the reversal of a number of Islamic State gains in Iraq and a relative stabilization of the situation, Iraqi fighters redeployed to Syria in considerable numbers through 2015, with a spike likely occurring to coincide with the Russian intervention that began in October 2015. This time around, Iraqi militias that emerged on the home front in 2014, such as Harakat Ansar Allah al-Awfiya' and Harakat al-Abdal, and clearly espousing a pro-Iranian outlook, became involved in Syria alongside the groups that were involved in 2013-2014.

The main units of Afghan and Pakistani Shi'a fighters are Liwa Fatemiyoun and Liwa Zainabiyoun respectively. Both of these groups are affiliated with the Iranian Revolutionary Guard Corps and have mostly recruited Afghan and Pakistani Shi'a who are resident in Iran. The members of these groups generally lack the experience of Lebanese and Iraqi fighters and are used as frontline cannon fodder.

Among Syrian Shi'a, a number of formations have evolved on the basis of the idea of developing a native Syrian Muqawama Islamiya ('Islamic Resistance'). Some of these formations are directly affiliated with Hezbollah, most notably Quwat al-Ridha, which largely recruits from the Homs area; Junud al-Mahdi and the Imam al-Hujja Regiment, which recruit from the villages of Nubl and Zahara' to the north of Aleppo city; and Liwa al-Imam al-Mahdi. A militia that emerged from pro-Assad tribal networks in Aleppo – Liwa al-Baqir – consists primarily of Shi'ified Bekara tribesmen and claims links/affiliation with Hezbollah. Other Syrian 'Islamic Resistance' militias of note are Jaysh al-Imam al-Mahdi (The Imam Mahdi Army, also known as the National Ideological Resistance, which mostly recruits Shi'a and Alawites from Tartous and western Hama, and the Ja'afari Force (Liwa al-Sayyida Ruqayya), which originated from Syrian Shi'a in the Damascus National Defence Forces. The Ja'afari Force was for a time affiliated with Kata'ib Sayyid al-Shuhada', but now claims to be independent.

Salafi jihadists

The Syrian civil war has witnessed a proliferation of militant groups adhering to Salafism, an ultra-orthodox Sunni Islamist current that believes Muslims must return to the ways of *al-salaf al-saleh* (the righteous ancestors) from the time of the Prophet Muhammad and rid themselves of *bidaa* (innovations) that have taken root in the centuries since. The latter include not only such secular conventions as democracy and the nation-state, but also a millennium of Islamic jurisprudence and traditions that have come to define how most Muslims practice their faith. Non-Sunni Muslims and Sufis are viewed as heretics. In sharp contrast to the Muslim Brotherhood and its offshoots, *Salafis* traditionally eschewed participation in politics, focusing instead on daawa (missionary work) to convert Muslim societies to their way of thinking.

During the late 1970s, a younger generation of *Salafis* in the Arab Gulf (many of them expatriates) began to reject the movement's traditional political quietism and either agitate for Islamic rule at home or fight perceived enemies of Islam abroad. Thousands went to South Asia to combat the 1979 Soviet invasion of Afghanistan. After the Soviet withdrawal and the fall of Kabul to the *mujahidin*, many of these so-called "Arab Afghans" returned home to continue fighting for their beliefs or joined Osama bin Laden's expanding al-Qaeda network. Many Arab Afghans later went to Iraq in the wake of the 2003 U.S.-led invasion, where they eventually coalesced into

AQI, rebranded first as the Majlis Shura al-Mujahideen in early 2006 and then the Islamic State of Iraq (ISI) in October 2006 some months after Abu Mus'ab al-Zarqawi's death.

Jabhat al-Nusra and the Rise of the Islamic State

In late 2011, ISI chief Abu Bakr al-Baghdadi began sending undercover operatives into Syria, many of them Syrian nationals. After releasing a January 2012 video statement calling itself *Jabhat al-Nusra* (The Support Front),[42] the new organization claimed responsibility for a multitude of spectacular suicide and Improvised Explosive Device (IED) bombings during the first half of 2012, most notably a February 10 twin bombing in Aleppo that struck a two military facilities, killing 28, and March 17 bombings against the Air Force Intelligence headquarters and Criminal Security department in Damascus, which killed at least 27.[43] *Jabhat al-Nusra* also displayed undeniable prowess on the battlefield, spearheading the capture of numerous regime bases and fortified installations.[44]

Led by a mysterious commander known as Abu Mohammad al-Golani (assumed to be a Syrian with origins from the Golan Heights, though his name may also refer to the Golan neighborhood in Fallujah), *Jabhat al-Nusra* quickly received endorsements from al-Qaeda leader Ayman al-Zawahiri[45] and influential *jihadi* ideologues.[46]

In sharp contrast to ISI's strategy during the Iraq war, which alienated local Sunnis, *Jabhat al-Nusra* developed cooperative relations with non-*jihadist* rebels and limited its mistreatment of civilians. When *Jabhat al-Nusra* was officially designated a terrorist group by the U.S. government in December 2012, the Brotherhood and many FSA commanders publicly defended it.

Fearful that *Jabhat al-Nusra* was growing too independent, in late 2012 Baghdadi began pushing for it to be subsumed under ISI, and in April 2013 unilaterally declared that ISI and *Jabhat al-Nusra* were to merge to form the Islamic State in Iraq and al-Sham (ISIS). However, Golani disputed the merger and appealed to Zawahiri to mediate, declaring a "renewal" of the *bay'a* ('pledge of allegiance') to the al-Qaeda leader. When Zawahiri ruled in favor of Golani, ISIS broke away from al-Qaeda, taking most foreign fighters operating in *Jabhat al-Nusra's* ranks with it.

ISIS aggressively consolidated areas of northern Syria under its control, clashing frequently with other rebels, including *Jabhat al-Nusra*, and even executing several of their military commanders.[47] It soon became clear that ISIS, unlike other rebel groups, was not fighting first and foremost to overthrow Assad—indeed, the regime's endurance had created conditions ideal for its growth. After consolidating contiguous holdings of territory in Syria centered on Raqqa in the wake of infighting with rebels in early 2014, ISIS went on to overrun much of northern Iraq in the spring and summer of 2014. As a result, ISIS officially declared its caliphate on June 29, 2014 and changed its name to "the Islamic State."[48]

In contrast to many other insurgent groups operating in Syria, the Islamic State has derived most of its income from indigenous revenue sources, not outside donations.[49] Besides deriving revenue from taxation and confiscations, the Islamic State gained control of most of the oil-rich province of Deir az-Zor as well as other oil resources in Hasakah, Raqqa and Homs provinces, allowing the organization to make considerable revenue selling off Syrian crude oil (topping up to $1.5 million a day in late 2014, going by the Abu Sayyaf records).[50] As part of the running of the oil industry, the Islamic State has allowed for oil to be purchased from fields under its control and then sold to outside clients, including the Assad regime[51] and rebel-held areas of Syria. When ISIS took over Mosul just before the creation of the caliphate, it was reported to have looted $425 million in cash from the central bank in Mosul after its capture of the Iraqi city in June 2014, making it by some accounts the world's richest terrorist organization.[52] Islamic State finances have since been degraded by coalition airstrikes targeting "cash points" and the oil industry, however. Further, the recapture of territory by local forces acting with coalition support has reduced the Islamic State's taxation base. This has resulted in reductions of salaries and benefits for fighters, who take up a considerable portion of Islamic State expenses.

Jabhat al-Nusra's evolution

Jabhat al-Nusra, which after Zawahiri's ruling in its favor increasingly emphasized openly its al-Qaeda affiliation on the ground (e.g., by inscribing the al-Qaeda name on banners), suffered considerably as a result of the rise of the Islamic State, losing all its holdings in the east by July 2014.[53] Leaked recordings in that month suggested an impending announcement of an Islamic emirate by *Jabhat al-Nusra* to counter the Islamic State's project, though the emirate announcement was then denied in an official *Jabhat al-Nusra* statement. However, the group did not collapse but rather began to show a harsher side, expelling by November 2014 the FSA coalition known as the Syrian Revolutionaries Front, with whom *Jabhat al-Nusra* had previously cooperated in expelling ISIS from Idlib.[54] In addition, *Jabhat al-Nusra* began setting up its own Dar al-Qada (judiciary) branches in various localities in northwest Syria, and forced the Druze community of *Jabal al-Summaq* in northern Idlib province to renounce their faith, most notably destroying the shrines in the process.[55]

In 2015, a number of Islamist, Salafi and *jihadi* groups in the north came to set up the *Jaysh al-Fath* coalition, primarily based in Idlib province and led by *Jabhat al-Nusra* and *Ahrar al-Sham*. Faylaq al-Sham also joined this coalition. Abdullah al-Muheisseni, a Saudi cleric and financier who had moved to Syria, came to serve as a key spiritual and judicial figure in Jaysh al-Fatah. With backing from Turkey, Qatar and Saudi Arabia, the coalition expelled the regime from Idlib city and other key towns in the province, leaving only isolated two Shi'a villages—Fou'a and Kafariya—under siege. The coalition failed to establish a unified governance system in the province, and *Jabhat al-Nusra* experienced its own internal ruptures centered around two dissident figures—Abu Mariya al-Qahtani and Saleh al-Hamawi—who were both involved in the creation of Jabhat al-Nusra but came to believe the group was not being pragmatic enough and insisted on more focus towards unification efforts.

A major impediment to real unity between *Jabhat al-Nusra* and more "mainstream" factions was the issue of *Jabhat al-Nusra's* al-Qaeda ties. Proposals for a merger in January and February 2016 were ultimately rejected because of these connections. Zawahiri around this time recorded a speech entitled "Go forth to al-Sham" (not released until May 2016) that portrayed the Syrian *jihad* as the best hope for establishing an Islamic government that could eventually give rise to the caliphate.[56] Unity of the *mujahideen*, according to Zawahiri, is paramount (an idea he had previously emphasized in a January 2014 speech on Syria in which he placed unity above temporary organizational ties).[57]

By July 2016, the proposal for *Jabhat al-Nusra* to sever public ties with al-Qaeda became a more attractive proposition, partly on account of proposed U.S.-Russian coordination to target the group.[58] The move to "break" ties would put the ball in the court of the factions that objected to the al-Qaeda affiliation in discussions on mergers. In addition, there was hope to score a propaganda move in trying to show that the issue was Western objection to Islam itself, not simply to al-Qaeda links. As a result, with guidance from al-Qaeda, *Jabhat al-Nusra* officially rebranded itself as an independent entity on 28 July 2016, changing its name to *Jabhat Fatah al-Sham* ('Conquest of al-Sham' Front).[59] The move, announced by Golani on video, was notably preceded several hours before by an audio message from Zawahiri's deputy, Abu al-Khayr al-Masri, urging for the necessary steps to be taken to protect the Syrian *jihad*. The fact the message came from *Jabhat al-Nusra's* media wing al-Manara al-Bayda suggests that Masri is as of now residing in Syria, fitting in with a pattern of movement of senior "al-Qaeda central" personnel to Syria. Though some elements within *Jabhat al-Nusra* (e.g., Abu Julaybib) appear to have rejected the rebranding, they do not seem to have influence to divide the ranks.

"Third-way" jihadist groups

In addition to the Islamic State and *Jabhat Fatah al-Sham*, there are a number of smaller *jihadi* factions composed partly or mainly of foreign fighters. These groups have differed in their allegiances and many of them have merged over time with larger formations, including the Islamic State. Some groups that were more closely affiliated with al-Qaeda have merged with *Jabhat Fatah al-Sham*, or remained independent organizations. Some examples of still-independent groups are the Turkestan Islamic Party (composed mostly of Uyghur refugees who have lived in Turkey) and the *Jabhat Ansar al-Din* coalition (featuring a Syrian faction – Harakat Fajr al-Sham al-Islamiya – and a faction founded by Moroccan ex-Guantanamo detainees called Harakat Sham al-Islam). As of December 2016, the *Jabhat Ansar al-Din* coalition components have formally merged into a single entity under that name.

A more "mainstream" current encompasses a broad array of groups funded heavily by *Salafi* activists in the Arab Gulf and Arab Gulf governments themselves, being seen as a means of limiting the growth potential of *Jabhat Fatah al-Sham* and Baghdadi's Islamic State. Most of these groups joined the Syrian Islamic Front, an umbrella coalition established in December 2012, and its successor, the Islamic Front in November 2013. However, the Islamic Front underwent a variety of splits and mergers, with the brand foremost associated at the present time with *Ahrar al-Sham* and groups that have merged into it. Other Islamic Front member groups, such as affiliates of the Aleppo-based *Liwa al-Tawhid* that were ideologically closer to the Muslim Brotherhood, went on to form separate coalitions like the *Shami* Front.

Ideologically, most of the groups that constituted the Islamic Front share much in common with hardline *jihadists*. They have proclaimed rejection of democracy, openly claimed to be fighting for an Islamic state, and have generally not recognized the SNC and the opposition interim government.

Unlike the transnational *jihadists*, however, Islamic Front groups have downplayed or even denied pan-Islamic ambitions (scholar Abdul Rahman Al-Haj calls them "deferred Caliphate" *jihadists*"[60]), avoided anti-Western demagoguery, and adopted slightly less inflammatory rhetoric concerning Syrian minorities.[61] The Islamic Front groups have had few foreign volunteers fighting in their ranks (mostly concentrated in *Ahrar al-Sham*), and none are known to have used suicide attacks significantly.

Most Islamic Front groups have relied heavily on financing from Arab Gulf donors, most of it channeled under the guise of humanitarian aid through Kuwait, which has been the primary hub for private fundraising because of its lax regulatory environment and the political strength of *Salafis*.[62] The tiny oil-rich emirate was dubbed "the Arab world's main clearinghouse" for donations to radical Islamist rebels by the *Wall Street Journal*[63] and "a virtual Western Union outlet for Syria's rebels" by the *New York Times*.[64]

In 2013, the Kuwaiti government prohibited some prominent *Salafis* from preaching to the public[65] and passed new laws bolstering the power of public prosecutors to monitor suspicious transactions and freeze funds.[66] By August 2014, the U.S. government had sanctioned Hajaj al-Ajmi and Shafi al-Ajmi, two prominent Kuwaiti financiers.[67] As a result of these steps, together with UN sanctions and Kuwaiti regulations, their importance has been greatly diminished.

Closer domestic regulation of *Salafi* fundraising may have been intended to pave the way for patronage of Islamic Front factions by the Arab Gulf governments. One of the leading Islamic Front groups, *Jaysh al-Islam*, was formed in October 2013 by the merger of Liwa al-Islam and numerous smaller, Saudi-backed *Salafi* groups operating in the suburbs of Damascus. The Saudi government reportedly offered funding to those who joined, with the apparent intention of halting the expansion of *Jabhat al-Nusra* and ISIS.[68] Liwa al-Islam leader Zahran Alloush, the son of Saudi-based Syrian religious scholar Abdullah Mohammed Alloush, became leader of Jaysh al-Islam. He was subsequently killed in an airstrike in December 2015, succeeded by Issam Bwaydhani. The more "mainstream" outlook of Jaysh al-Islam- that is, operating more within a national framework in comparison with the *jihadist* groups (clearly a result of Saudi influence)- is shown by the fact that the group participated in the opposition body known as High Negotiations Committee that was formed in Saudi Arabia, with the aim of working towards brokering a political solution to the Syrian civil war in 2016. Mohammed Alloush served as the representative on this body. Even so, the group has faced criticism in its main area of influence- the Eastern Ghouta enclave- for running secret prisons and monopolizing power at the expense of other factions, even as it played the leading role in ensuring the Islamic State could not have a foothold in Eastern Ghouta. The group has also had a history of employing harsh sectarian rhetoric and gained further notoriety in late 2015 for an incident of apparently parading Alawite prisoners in cages.[69]

Perhaps more ambiguous in characterization is *Ahrar al-Sham*, which is strongest in Idlib province and the leading faction there alongside *Jabhat Fatah al-Sham*. Founded in late 2011 and led by Hassan Abboud, a former Sednaya detainee, *Ahrar al-Sham* became a leading actor in the Syrian Islamic Front and then the Islamic Front. Though most of the first generation of the leadership was wiped out in a mysterious explosion in late 2014, the group recovered from this predicament. Strongly backed by Turkey and Qatar, the group is open to the idea of engagement on the international stage and has a foreign political relations wing dedicated to this engagement, represented foremost by Labib Nahhas (aka Abu Izz al-Deen), who is seen as embodying the more "moderate" wing of *Ahrar al-Sham*. On the other hand, a lecture by Ali al-Omar, who was then the group's deputy and has since become the overall leader, also situates *Ahrar al-Sham* within the Islamic movements that seek the revival of the Caliphate, framed the conflict in Syria in highly sectarian terms in stressing the need to come together to fight the *'Rafidites'* (a derogatory term for the Shi'a), and spoke highly of the Taliban in Afghanistan as a Sunni movement that could bring together Sunnis of a variety of *madhahib* (schools of thought). Historically, the group had in its ranks Abu Khalid al-Souri, who was appointed by Zawahiri to act as a mediator between *Jabhat al-Nusra* and ISIS, but who was killed in February 2014. In addition, *Ahrar al-Sham* offered condolences on the revelation of the death of Mullah Omar in 2015.

At the present time, the group maintains closer military alliances with *Jabhat Fatah al-Sham* than *Jaysh al-Islam* (Ahrar al-Sham being only a minor group in Eastern Ghouta and the wider south of Syria), but forming unified governing structures within areas taken from the regime has proven more elusive. At the local level in Idlib province, for example, *Ahrar al-Sham* often acts as a local counterbalance to harsher actions by *Jabhat Fatah al-Sham*. The two groups have also supported rival judiciary structures: while *Ahrar al-Sham* is linked with the Islamic Commission, *Jabhat Fatah al-Sham* backs the *Dar al-Qada* (set up in 2014 as *Jabhat al-Nusra's* judiciary branch). In July 2016, a number of *Salafi* and *jihadist* jurists and scholars came together to form the Assembly of al-Sham Scholars, which aims to serve as a single, ostensibly independent judiciary body for the various factions. This development fits in with the notion of grander unification efforts among *Salafi* and *jihadist* factions – an idea that also helped give rise to the formation of *Jabhat Fatah al-Sham*.

However, success in the immediate subsequent unity talks between *Jabhat Fatah al-Sham* and other factions- particularly *Ahrar al-Sham*- proved elusive. A clear reason for this failure is that *Jabhat Fatah al-Sham* does not appear to have fundamentally changed its conduct or ideological end goals, even as those who rejected the rebranding have feared ideological compromise of the jihadist project. This gave rise to suspicion that the rebranding is more of a tactical move rather than a genuine break from al-Qaeda. On a key issue- namely, whether it is acceptable to coordinate operations with Turkish forces to fight the Islamic State in north Aleppo countryside—*Jabhat Fatah al-Sham* reiterated opposition to such action- in keeping with the prior rejectionist stance of *Jabhat al-Nusra*—while *Ahrar al-Sham's* Shari'i council officially endorsed coordination. Though the endorsement does not mean everyone in *Ahrar al-Sham* agreed on the idea, fighters from the group have continued to participate in Turkey's "Euphrates Shield" operations in the north Aleppo countryside against the Islamic State, despite criticism that the "Euphrates Shield" has drawn manpower away from fronts against the regime, allowing the fall of Aleppo city to the regime.

Jabhat Fatah al-Sham's premise for unity talks appears to be based on the notion that other factions should merge under its banner and lose their identities, or at least accept the group as having the main leadership role in a merger body: that is, unity should ultimately be on Jabhat Fatah al-Sham's terms.

The fall of Aleppo to the regime in December 2016—a heavy blow to the wider insurgency—has intensified discussions surrounding a larger merger between factions in the north of the country, the success or failure of which depends heavily on the roles of *Ahrar al-Sham* and *Jabhat Fatah al-Sham*. In effect, two rival unity initiatives appear to have emerged. One of these initiatives is embodied in a statement issued on December 28, 2016 by ten factions, including *Faylaq al-Sham*, the *Shami Front* and *Jaysh al-Islam's* minor northern affiliates.[70] These factions have emphasized their orientation through issuing the statement in the name of the "Free Syrian Army." That is, whatever the Islamist and Salafi tendencies, the project is operating within a clear national framework.

The other unification movement represents a continuation of *Jabhat Fatah al-Sham's* efforts to push for unity, still clearly on its terms and with the intent of orienting the wider insurgency toward its ideological end goals. *Ahrar al-Sham* effectively finds itself caught in the middle between these two unity initiatives. Many in *Ahrar al-Sham's* senior leadership are more sympathetic to the initiative led by *Jabhat Fatah al-Sham*, while others, in particular those associated with the group's wider political outreach efforts such as Labib Nahhas, reject siding with Jabhat Fatah al-Sham as an act of political suicide.[71] There is also a hint of a third-way option in reviving a structure known as the Revolutionary Command Council (RCC), which was set up in late 2014 as the largest alliance attempt at the time between various factions, but came apart over the course of 2015.

ISLAMISM AND SOCIETY

Notwithstanding the steady growth of radical Sunni Islamist forces over the past five years, there was little sign of violent extremism within Syrian society prior to the uprising. However, the spread of radical Islamism has been facilitated by socio-economic conditions in much of Syria on the eve of the uprising, sectarian polarization during the war, and the influx of resources from external sponsors.

Syria is an extraordinarily diverse country. Sunni Arabs are by far the largest ethno-sectarian group, comprising 67 percent of the population. Non-Arab (predominantly Sunni) Kurds number roughly nine percent of the population. The remainder consists of non-Sunni, predominantly Arab religious minorities–Alawis comprise about 12 percent of the population, Christians of various denominations 10 percent, Druze three percent, and various Shi'a denominations around one percent.[72] Communal solidarity (*asabiya*) is very strong among all of these minorities, owing in part to centuries of oppression and discrimination at the hands of Sunni rulers.

Alawis, an offshoot of Shi'a Islam, arguably suffered the most prior to the collapse of the Ottoman Empire at the close of World War I. Branded as heretics by most Sunnis, shunned as deviants by religious Shi'a, and lacking powerful co-religionist regional allies, Syrian Alawis were poor, under-educated, and socially isolated in roughly four dozen remote villages in northwestern Syria.[73]

During the French mandate period (1920-1943), many Alawis and other minorities joined the military as a means of socio-economic advancement, whereas their Sunni counterparts tended to shun cooperation with colonial authorities. Consequently, minorities were overrepresented in the military when Syria gained independence. Many of these officers flocked to the Ba'ath Party, which espoused a secular, non-sectarian, socialist agenda. By 1963, Alawis comprised 65 percent of noncommissioned officers in the Syrian army, which helped pave the way for the Ba'ath coup that year and Hafez al-Assad's subsequent ascent to the presidency in 1971.[74] In the decades that followed, Alawi domination of the security apparatus became even more pronounced.

But Syria was not an "Alawi state." The ruling party's ideology was rigidly non-sectarian – with even references to sect avoided in state-run media. Indeed, in its zeal to erase the appearance of sectarian differences, the Assad regime pushed its own Alawi community to adopt the outer trappings of Sunni Islam (e.g., building mosques, even though Alawis don't customarily use them).[75]

Assad made sure that the façade of civilian government in Syria appropriately reflected Sunni demographic weight. The positions of prime minister, foreign minister, and army commander were nearly always held by Sunnis, for example, as were most parliamentary seats, judicial offices, and other high visibility posts. Many second-generation Alawi power barons later forged business partnerships with Sunnis and some (including Bashar al-Assad) married Sunni women.[76]

For most Syrians, opposition to the regime was not primarily rooted in matters of faith. The Assad regime's statist economic development and social welfare policies gave it sufficiently strong base of rural support cutting across sectarian lines that lasted through the turn of the century.[77] "It is quite plain that the conflict is not about religion," noted historian Hanna Batatu wrote in 1982 as the Brotherhood-led revolt reached its climax. "It is not the beliefs of the Sunnis that have been in danger or under attack since the Ba'thist take-over in 1963, but the social interests of the upper and middle elements of their landed, mercantile, and manufacturing classes."[78] Representing similar constituencies, many traditionalist Sufi preachers in Hama and Aleppo supported the Brotherhood-led revolt against the Assad regime (and in Hama their followers took up arms).[79]

Islamism was an effective tool for mobilizing and channeling mass dissent against an Alawi-dominated regime. Once the leaders using this tool were killed, imprisoned, and exiled, however, Syria enjoyed nearly three decades of relative domestic tranquility, with only sporadic outbreaks of Islamist and sectarian violence. Some observers point to this long stretch of stability as evidence that religious extremism had declined among ordinary Syrians – that bad memories of the Brotherhood's folly had inoculated the country against the appeal of radical Islamism. However, the unrivalled power of the Ba'athist state during this era is sufficient to account for the scarcity of internal Islamist opposition.

Like the rest of the region, Syria began experiencing an Islamic revival during the 1990s, evident in growing mosque attendance, more women wearing the *hijab*, and more men growing beards. Islamic bookshops proliferated and restaurants in many areas of the country stopped serving alcohol.[80]

Hoping to safely channel this religiosity away from political activism, the Assad regime allowed some quietist *Sufi* currents to begin relatively freely, such as the abovementioned Zaydis. For example, a women's charitable organization known as the *Qubaisiaat*—named after the female religious leader, Munira al-Qubaisi, who runs it—saw its influence spread rapidly.[81]

Assad also allowed some traditional *Salafi* charities, funded by donors in the Arab Gulf and Syrian expatriates working there, to operate in rural areas during the mid-2000s, though *Salafism* was a "relatively negligible component of the country's religious scene" at the time of the uprising, notes the International Crisis Group (ICG).[82]

The 2011 Revolt

Militant Islamism certainly was not a cause of the popular uprising that erupted in 2011. There are plenty of socio-economic drivers, most notably a pronounced "youth bulge." Syria's population at the time of 23 million was the youngest in the Middle East outside of the Palestinian territories,[83] with 53 percent below the age of 20.[84]

Bashar Assad's economic reforms solidified support for the regime among the urban elites and middle class, but at the expense of rural areas. UK-based Syrian journalist Malik al-Abdeh characterized the uprising as a "revolution of the rural Sunni working classes against the Alawi-dominated military elite and the urban bourgeoisie (both Muslim and Christian) that has profited from the Assad dictatorship."[85] It was not religion that triggered their decision to rise up to the regime after years of quiet obedience, but the "demonstration effect" of watching Egyptians, Tunisians, and Libyans overthrow their own governments.

Early in the uprising, observers sympathetic to the opposition argued that: "there are few traces of radical Islamism in Syria" and that, should the Assad regime fall, "the chance of Syria turning into an Islamic state is almost nil."[86] But the secular democratic orientation of the uprising steadily eroded as the violence escalated and prospects of a peaceful solution evaporated.[87] This was partly because the regime had little trouble suppressing protests in non-Sunni and mixed towns and neighborhoods, where demonstrations were never large enough to give safety in numbers. In Sunni majority areas, in contrast, demonstrations "were 20 to 30 times larger [and] organized under the semi-inviolable protection of mosques."[88] For ordinary Syrians contemplating whether to protest in the streets, ironically, it was much safer to be a Sunni than to be an Alawi.

Moreover, while it may have been the case that a majority of Christians, Druze, and Kurds – perhaps even Alawis – supported demands for political reform and human rights, they were much less willing than devout Sunnis to take greatest personal risks in challenging Assad. Consequently, regime repression further tilted the demographic composition of uprising by weeding out minorities and those of little religious faith.[89] As the country rapidly slipped into full-blown civil war in early 2012 and it became a question of whether to stand up and fight the regime, the revolutionaries on the ground were almost exclusively Sunni. Sunnification was followed by Islamization as most emerging rebel groups adopted explicitly Islamic names and iconography.

Some attribute this Islamic awakening to the fact that donations from the Arab Gulf states and private Arab donors outpaced assistance from the West. According to such "resource mobilization" explanations,[90] the influx of cash from Salafi donors not only strengthened jihadist forces vis-à-vis the FSA, but also led relatively secular groups within the FSA to adopt Salafi dress and customs.[91] Many rank and file fighters of *Salafi-jihadist* militias are devout Sunnis with no firm extremist convictions. "Size, money, and momentum are the things to look for in Syrian insurgent politics—ideology comes fourth, if even that," notes Lund.[92]

However, much as Pakistan and Afghanistan became the crucible for indoctrinating adventure-seeking youth from across the Arab world into the *Salafi-jihadist* path during the 1980s, conditions in Syria are perfect for giving rise to a new generation of extremists. Already the effects have been felt in attacks in Europe partly caused by returning jihadists, as happened in a shooting incident at the Jewish Museum of Belgium in Brussels in May 2014, as well as the Paris attacks in November 2015. Further, the Islamic State and other *jihadist* groups have made a show of raising and educating children under their wings, giving rise to ideological indoctrination. In addition, the large-scale Shi'a Islamist mobilization to aid the regime has given rise to a much more sectarian-charged atmosphere in the region than prior to 2011.

ISLAMISM AND THE STATE

In the first three decades after the Ba'ath Party seized power in 1963, the Syrian state worked to secularize Syrian society and control Islamic religious expression, especially in the wake of the first Syrian uprising. All formal Islamic institutions were closely managed by the state,[93] while preaching outside of the mosques or outside of appointed prayer times was prohibited. With no independent political parties, media, unions, or other associations allowed to come between citizen and state, neutering the mosques was the final link in the chain.

Only heavily vetted *ulema* (religious scholars) loyal to the regime and willing to actively legitimate it were allowed to preach. The most prominent was Ahmed Kaftaro, head of the Naqshbandi Sufi order and Grand Mufti of Syria from 1964 until his death in 2004. Sermons were typically designed to discourage politicization of religious faith.

The resurgence of Islamic revivalism throughout the Arab world in the 1990s led the Assad regime to take a new direction aimed at endowing Syria with a more authentic Islamic look and feel. The regime released large numbers of Brotherhood members who had been held in Syrian prisons since the early 1980s,[94] while cultivating close ties with Sunni Islamists in the Palestinian territories and elsewhere in the Arab world (its relations with most non-Syrian branches of the Muslim Brotherhood were quite cordial).

Upon ascending to the presidency after his father's death in 2000, Bashar al-Assad continued efforts to promote an Islamic posture. The new president released hundreds of Islamist prisoners, lifted a longstanding ban on wearing female headscarves in Syrian schools,[95] and allowed mosques to remain open between prayer times.[96] He began favorably referencing religion in public speeches,[97] while state universities held Koran reading competitions.[98] The Syrian military even announced that Islamic clergy would be allowed to give lectures to military cadets for the first time in 43 years, a decision that Defense Minister Hassan Tourkmani called a response to "the thirst for God in the barracks."[99]

Rather than seeking to defuse Islamist militancy, state-vetted preachers now sought to harness it in support of the regime. A notable voice was Mohammad Said Ramada al-Bouti, whose televised sermons made him one of the most recognized figures in Syria in the 2000s. Bouti and other state-sanctioned clerics preached that enemies of Islam were conspiring to sow the seeds of *fitna* (civil strife) in Syria and the broader Middle East, using agents ranging from women's rights activists to the Muslim Brotherhood to set brother against brother.[100] In 2003, the aging Kaftaro even issued a *fatwa* calling for resistance to U.S.-led coalition forces in Iraq.

Although falling well short of the kind of unfettered religious freedom that could pose direct political and security threats to the regime, state-modulated Islamization dramatically changed the public landscape of Syria, from styles of dress to architecture.[101]

Whereas the late Hafez al-Assad kept his regime's Palestinian and Lebanese Islamist clients at arms-length and never allowed them to operate unsupervised in Syria, Bashar al-Assad went much further during the Iraq war by allowing militant *jihadists* to preach and recruit inside Syria. The most notable was Abu Qaqaa (aka Mahmoud Qoul Aghassi), a preacher in Aleppo who was allowed to directly recruit local youth to fight in Iraq and even offer weapons training at his mosque. Some have suggested that Abu Qaqaa was, or became, a Syrian intelligence agent, as many of his recruits were tracked and arrested upon their return to Syria. His assassination in 2007 was widely seen as either payback from *jihadists* for betraying them or "disposal" by a regime that no longer needed or trusted him.[102]

In addition to directly sponsoring *jihadist* violence for political and strategic reasons, the regime used its close connections to the Islamist underworld to stage false flag operations designed to cast blame on Islamists. The most infamous is the February 2005 assassination of former Lebanese Prime Minister Rafiq Hariri in Beirut, which was intended to pin responsibility on *Salafi-jihadists* (the Syrian *mukhabarat*, or secret police, even recruited a real, unwitting *jihadist* to make the video-taped claim of responsibility).

During the height of the Assad regime's support for *jihadists* in Iraq, Syria experienced a number of suspicious and ultimately foiled or minimally destructive "terrorist attacks" that were likely orchestrated by the regime to bolster its diplomatic efforts to present itself as a victim of al-Qaeda, notably an April 2004 attack on an abandoned UN building in Damascus.[103]

In the aftermath of the 2005 Syrian withdrawal from Lebanon, the Assad regime allowed numerous Syrian veterans of the Iraq war to infiltrate the country, presumably to create the impression that Lebanon was less secure. There they started a group called *Fatah al-Islam* that fought a bloody 2007 battle with the Lebanese Army that left much of the Palestinian Nahr al-Bared refugee camp in ruins.

As part and parcel of the regime's Islamic "awakening," the *mukhabarat* organized periodic demonstrations designed to give the appearance that Islamists are allowed to assemble and express themselves publicly. In February 2006, as the controversy over a Danish newspaper's publication of cartoons depicting the Prophet Muhammad was sparking Muslim protests worldwide, the regime engineered large riots outside the Danish and Norwegian embassies (both of which were torched).[104]

During the first four months of the uprising, while thousands of pro-democracy protestors were being rounded up, the Assad regime released hundreds of Islamists from its jails, many of them Iraq war veterans who had run afoul of the authorities after returning to Syria in 2008-2009. Many of these parolees later played major roles in the rebellion, including Zahran Aloush, the first leader of *Jaysh al-Islam*; Abdul Rahman Suweis of the *Haqq* Brigade; Hassan Aboud of *Ahrar Al Sham*; Ahmad Aisa Al Sheikh, commander of *Suqour Al Sham*; and possibly *Jabhat al-Nusra* commander Abu Mohammad al-Golani (whose true identity has never been confirmed).[105]

Some interpreted the releases as a horribly botched effort to win the support or at least quiescence of *jihadists*. Others believe that the releases were intended to have precisely the result they had – jumpstarting a violent Islamist insurgency that will lead the international community to think twice about aiding the Syrian opposition, while solidifying support for the regime among minorities and urban, middle-class Sunnis.

Having blamed foreign *jihadists* for the uprising from the very start, the emergence of the Islamic State—a *jihadist* organization full of foreigners that makes no effort to appear civilized—was a blessing for Assad. There is some evidence of the regime having tried to facilitate ISIS' growth versus other rebel factions. For example, regime airstrikes against ISIS bases in some areas of Syria all but stopped when the group began targeting other insurgents in much of 2013 and early 2014.[106] However, fierce battles between the regime and ISIS in the summer of 2014 over control of oil fields, as well as the ISIS conquest of the isolated regime bases in Raqqa province and massacres of personnel in summer 2014, belied claims that ISIS is secretly in league with Assad. In addition, in 2015 the Islamic State launched a military campaign against regime positions in the Homs desert, culminating in the conquest of the ancient city of Palmyra and Qaryatayn. These towns were retaken by the regime with Russian support in the spring of 2016, though the Islamic State then recaptured Palmyra in an offensive in December 2016, while the Syrian regime and Russia were focusing heavily on Aleppo.

Endnotes

[1] Rania Abouzeid, "Who Will the Tribes Back in Syria's Civil War?" Time, October 10, 2012, http://world.time.com/2012/10/10/who-will-the-tribes-back-in-syrias-civil-war/.

[2] Roy Gutman and Paul Raymond, "Syria's Pro-Assad Forces Accused of Targeting Mosques in Civil War," McClatchy Newspapers, June 27, 2013, http://www.mcclatchydc.com/news/nation-world/world/article24750496.html.

[3] Ari Heistein, "Iranian Support for Al-Assad Is Secular: Are Syria's Alawites Really Part of the Shiite Crescent?" Informed Comment, August 19, 2015, http://www.juancole.com/2015/08/secular-alawites-crescent.html.

[4] Thomas Mayer, "The Islamic Opposition in Syria, 1961-1982," Orient 24 (1983); Patrick Seale and Maureen McConville, Assad of Syria: The Struggle for the Middle East, (London: I.B. Tauris, 1988), 320-338.

[5] Mohammad Saied Rassass, "Syria's Muslim Brotherhood: Past and Present," Al-Monitor, January 5, 2014, http://www.al-monitor.com/pulse/politics/2014/01/syria-muslim-brotherhood-past-present.html.

[6] Elin Norman, "A Short Background on the Syrian Muslim Brotherhood and Its Process of Change: 1945-2012," Swedish Defense Research Agency, May 2014.

[7] "Damascus Declaration in English," SyriaComment, November 1, 2005, http://faculty-staff.ou.edu/L/Joshua.M.Landis-1/syriablog/2005/11/damascus-declaration-in-english.htm.

[8] Yvette Talhamy, "The Muslim Brotherhood Reborn: The Syrian Uprising, "Middle East Quarterly 19, no. 2, Spring 2012, http://www.meforum.org/3198/syria-muslim-brotherhood.

[9] Ibid.

[10] Ibidem.

[11] Ibidem.

[12] Nir Rosen, "Islamism and the Syrian Uprising," Foreign Policy, March 8, 2012, http://mideast.foreignpolicy.com/posts/2012/03/08/islamism_and_the_syrian_uprising.

[13] Hassan Hassan, "In Syria, the Brotherhood's influence is on the decline," The National (UAE), April 1, 2014, http://www.thenational.ae/thenationalconversation/comment/in-syria-the-brotherhoods-influence-is-on-the-decline.

[14] Jared A. Favole, "Brotherhood Raises Syria Profile: Islamist Group Tries to Organize Opposition to Assad Regime, as Protests Waiver," Wall Street Journal, May 17, 2011, http://online.wsj.com/article/SB10001424052748703509104576327212414590134.htm; Khaled Yacoub Oweis, "Syria's Muslim Brotherhood rise from the ashes as dominant force in the opposition," Al Arabiya (Dubai), May 6, 2012, http://english.alarabiya.net/articles/2012/05/06/212447.html.

[15] Thomas Pierret, "Syria: Old-Timers and Newcomers," in Robin Wright (ed), The Islamists are Coming: Who They Really Are (Washington, DC: United States Institute of Peace, 2012), 76.

[16] Raphael Lefevre, "Between Pragmatism and Radicalism: The Syrian Muslim Brotherhood and the Ba'ath Regime," in George Joffé, ed., Islamist Radicalisation in Europe and the Middle East: Reassessing the Causes of Terrorism (London: I. B. Tauris, 2012), 173.

[17] Neil MacFarquhar, "Trying to Mold a Post-Assad Syria From Abroad," New York Times, May 5, 2012, http://www.nytimes.com/2012/05/06/world/middleeast/from-abroad-trying-to-mold-a-post-assad-syria.html?_r=1&pagewanted=all.

[18] Pierret, "Syria: Old-Timers and Newcomers."
[19] Ibid.
[20] Thomas Pierret, "The Syrian Islamic Council," Carnegie Endowment for International Peace, May 13, 2014, http://carnegieendowment.org/syriaincrisis/?fa=55580
[21] Ibid.
[22] Ibidem.
[23] Hassan Hassan, "New Syrian Islamic Council repeats the patterns of old," The National (UAE), April 22, 2014, http://www.thenational.ae/thenationalconversation/comment/new-syrian-islamic-council-repeats-the-patterns-of-old.
[24] In Saudi Arabia, Surur developed a large following and influenced the "Islamic Awakening" movement in the Kingdom. Alongside notable Saudi figures such as Salman Al-Ouda (a former student) and Safar Al-Hawali, Surur denounced the Saudi regime after it allowed the entry of U.S. forces into the Kingdom ahead of the 1991 Gulf War. Although the Sururis (al-sururiyyun), as they were derogatively called by the Wahhabi clerical establishment (to highlight the movement's foreign influences), fell into line after the Saudi government began arresting their leaders, they retained a substantial following in the kingdom. Some came out if favor of the Arab Spring uprisings in Egypt and Tunisia, but they have been more reluctant than the Saudi branch of the Brotherhood to press for political change at home. See Jarret M. Brachman, Global Jihadism: Theory and Practice (London: Routledge, 2009), 36-38. See also Abdulaziz Alhies, "Concerns in the Gulf," Al-Ahram (Cairo), December 20, 2012, http://weekly.ahram.org.eg/News/620/21/Concerns-in-the-Gulf-.aspx; William McCants, "Islamist Outlaws: Saudi Arabia Takes on the Muslim Brotherhood," The Brookings Institution, March 17, 2014, http://www.brookings.edu/research/opinions/2014/03/17-saudi-arabia-outlaws-muslim-brotherhood-mccants; Stéphane Lacroix, "Saudi Islamists and the Arab Spring," London School of Economics and Political Science, May 2014, http://eprints.lse.ac.uk/56725/1/Lacroix_Saudi-Islamists-and-theArab-Spring_2014.pdf.
[25] Aron Lund, "Syrian Jihadism," Swedish Institute of International Affairs, September 14, 2012, http://www.ui.se/upl/files/77409.pdf.
[26] Thomas Pierret,"The Struggle for Religious Authority in Syria," Carnegie Endowment for International Peace, May 14, 2014, http://carnegieendowment.org/syriaincrisis/?fa=55593.
[27] Ibid.
[28] Aron Lund, "Struggling to Adapt: The Muslim Brotherhood in a New Syria," Carnegie Endowment for International Peace," May 7, 2013, http://carnegieendowment.org/2013/05/07/struggling-to-adapt-muslim-brotherhood-in-new-syria/g2qm?fa=searchResults&maxrow=20&tabName=pubs&qry=&fltr=&channel=&pageOn=365&reloadFlag=1.

[29] Ibid

[30] Raphaël Lefèvre, "The Brotherhood Starts Anew in Syria," Majalla, August 19, 2013, http://www.majalla.com/eng/2013/08/article55244734.

[31] Lund, "Struggling to Adapt."

[32] Benedetta Berti, "Tensions in Tripoli: The Syrian Crisis and Its Impact on Lebanon," Institute For National Security Studies, May 20, 2012, http://www.inss.org.il/index.aspx?id=4538&articleid=2485.

[33] Raymond Tanter and Stephen Kersting, "Syria's Role in the Iraq Insurgency," inFOCUS Quarterly, Spring 2009, http://www.jewishpolicycenter.org/827/syrias-role-in-the-iraq-insurgency.

[34] U.S. Department of the Treasury, "Treasury Designates Members of Abu Ghadiyah's Network Facilitates flow of terrorists, weapons, and money from Syria to al Qaida in Iraq," February 28, 2008, http://www.treasury.gov/press-center/press-releases/Pages/hp845.aspx.

[35] Peter Neumann, "Suspects into Collaborators," London Review of Books, April 3, 2014 (http://www.lrb.co.uk/v36/n07/peter-neumann/suspects-into-collaborators)

[36] Lee Smith, "Crack-up," Tablet, April 28, 2011, http://www.tabletmag.com/news-and-politics/65981/crack-up/.

[37] Fares Akram, "Hamas Leader Abandons Longtime Base in Damascus." New York Times, January 27, 2012, http://www.nytimes.com/2012/01/28/world/middleeast/khaled-meshal-the-leader-of-hamas-vacates-damascus.html?gwh=58C00E217CFD163EF15817D69C917AF0.

[38] Marissa Sullivan, "Hezbollah In Syria," Institute for the Study of War Middle East Security Report 19, April 2014, http://www.understandingwar.org/sites/default/files/Hezbollah_Sullivan_FINAL.pdf.

[39] Phillip Smyth, "Hizballah Cavalcade: What is the Liwa'a Abu Fadl al-Abbas (LAFA)?: Assessing Syria's Shia "International Brigade" Through Their Social Media Presence," Jihadology.net, May 15, 2013, http://jihadology.net/2013/05/15/hizballah-cavalcade-what-is-the-liwaa-abu-fadl-al-abbas-lafa-assessing-syrias-shia-international-brigade-through-their-social-media-presence/. See also Phillip Smyth, "Hizballah Cavalcade: From Najaf to Damascus and Onto Baghdad: Iraq's Liwa Abu Fadl al-Abbas," Jihadology.net, June 18, 2014, http://jihadology.net/2014/06/18/hizballah-cavalcade-from-najaf-to-damascus-and-onto-baghdad-iraqs-liwa-abu-fadl-al-abbas/.

[40] Sullivan, "Hezbollah In Syria."

[41] "Hezbollah mobilizes to defend Shiite shrines in Syria," Now Lebanon, June 12, 2014, https://now.mmedia.me/lb/en/lebanonnews/551145-hezbollah-announces-general-mobilization-in-syria.

[42] Bill Roggio, "Al Nusrah Front claims suicide attack in Syria," Long War Journal, February 26, 2012, http://www.longwarjournal.org/archives/2012/02/al_nusrah_front_clai.php.

[43] Bill Roggio, "Al Nusrah Front Claims Yet Another Suicide Attack in Syria," Long War Journal, September 2, 2016, http://www.longwarjournal.org/archives/2012/12/al_nusrah_front_clai_9.php.

[44] "Syria Loses Last Idlib Army Base to Nusra Front, Other Groups," Al Jazeera America, September 9, 2015, http://america.aljazeera.com/articles/2015/9/9/syria-loses-last-idlib-army-base-to-nusra-other-groups.html.

[45] "I appeal to every Muslim and every free, honorable one in Turkey, Iraq, Jordan, and Lebanon, to rise to help his brothers in Syria with all what he can, with his life, money, wonders, opinion, and information." As cited in Bill Roggio, "Al Baraa Ibn Malik Martyrdom Brigade forms in Syria," Long War Journal Threat Matrix blog, February 18, 2012, http://www.longwarjournal.org/threat-matrix/archives/2012/02/al_baraa_ibn_malik_martyrdom_b.php.

[46] On March 6, 2012, prominent jihadi cleric Abu Mundhir al-Shinqiti released an online fatwa urging all capable Muslims to join the ranks of Jabhat al-Nusra. See "Fatwa by Senior Salafi-Jihadi Cleric: Muslims Are Obligated to Join the Ranks of the Syrian Jihadi Group 'Jabhat Al-Nusra'," MEMRI Jihad and Terrorism Threat Monitor no. 4565, March 13, 2012, http://www.memri.org/report/en/0/0/0/0/0/0/6168.htm. Other important jihadi ideologues have also given their approval, including the prominent online essayist Sheikh Abu Sa'd al-'Amil, the prominent Jordanian Salafi Sheikh Abu Muhammad al-Tahawi, and the popular Lebanese Sheikh Abu al-Zahra' al-Zubaydi. See Aaron Y. Zelin, "Syria's New Jihadis," Foreign Policy, May 22, 2012, http://www.washingtoninstitute.org/policy-analysis/view/syrias-new-jihadis.

[47] Other Salafi-jihadists were not immune. In May 2014, for example, ISIS militants captured and beheaded Muthana Hussein, a senior commander of Ahrar al-Sham. See "Islamist militias unite under 'code of honor'," Daily Star (Beirut), May 19, 2014, http://www.dailystar.com.lb/News/Middle-East/2014/May-19/256938-islamist-militias-unite-under-code-of-honor.ashx#ixzz35eSDD8nV.

[48] Chelsea J. Carter, "Iraq Developments: ISIS Establishes 'Caliphate,' Changes Name," CNN, June 29, 2014, http://www.cnn.com/2014/06/29/world/meast/iraq-developments-roundup/.

[49] Anne Speckhard, "ISIS's Revenues Include Sales of Oil to the Al-Assad Regime," Huffington Post, April 28, 2016, http://www.huffingtonpost.com/anne-speckhard/isiss-revenues-include-sa_b_9789954.html.

[50] Ibid.

[51] "Rebels in Syria Claim Control of Resources," New York Times, January 28, 2014, http://www.nytimes.com/2014/01/29/world/middleeast/rebels-in-syria-claim-control-of-resources.html?_r=0.

[52] Terrence McCoy, "ISIS just stole $425 million, Iraqi governor says, and became the 'world's richest terrorist group,'" Washington Post, June 12, 2014, http://www.washingtonpost.com/news/morning-mix/wp/2014/06/12/isis-just-stole-425-million-and-became-the-worlds-richest-terrorist-group/.

[53] Daniel Cassman, "Jabhat Fatah Al-Sham (Formerly Jabhat Al-Nusra),"Stanford University, n.d., http://web.stanford.edu/group/mapping-militants/cgi-bin/groups/view/493.

[54] Ibid.

[55] "Syria Conflict: Al-Nusra Fighters Kill Druze Villagers," BBC, June 11, 2015, http://www.bbc.com/news/world-middle-east-33092902.

[56] Thomas Joscelyn, "Ayman Al Zawahiri Discusses Al Qaeda's Goal of Building an Islamic Emirate in Syria," Long War Journal, May 8, 2016, http://www.longwarjournal.org/archives/2016/05/ayman-al-zawahiri-discusses-al-qaedas-goal-of-building-an-islamic-emirate-in-syria.php.

[57] Ibid.

[58] Lisa Barrington and Suleiman Al-Khalidi, "Syria's Nusra Front Says Ending Al Qaeda Ties; U.S. Fears for Aleppo," Reuters, July 29, 2016, http://www.reuters.com/article/us-mideast-crisis-syria-aleppo-idUSKCN108167.

[59] Ibid.

[60] Abdul Rahman Al-Haj, "Salafism and Salafis in Syria: From reform to jihad," The Afro-Middle East Centre (Johannesburg, South Africa), June 22, 2013, http://www.amec.org.za/articles-presentations/syria/361-salafism-and-salafis-in-syria-from-reform-to-jihad.

[61] Aron Lund, "Syria's Salafi Insurgents: The Rise of the Syrian Islamic Front," Swedish Institute of International Affairs, January 2013, 22, http://www.ui.se/eng/upl/files/86861.pdf.

[62] Elizabeth Dickinson, "Playing with Fire: Why Private Gulf Financing for Syria's Extremist Rebels Risks Igniting Sectarian Conflict at Home," The Brookings Institution, December 2013, http://www.brookings.edu/~/media/research/files/papers/2013/12/06%20private%20gulf%20financing%20syria%20extremist%20rebels%20sectarian%20conflict%20dickinson/private%20gulf%20financing%20syria%20extremist%20rebels%20sectarian%20conflict%20dickinson.pdf.

[63] Ellen Knickmeyer, "Kuwaiti Court Upholds Parliamentary Vote, a Setback for Muslim Brotherhood," Wall Street Journal, December 23, 2013, http://online.wsj.com/news/articles/SB10001424052702304244904579276383918948044.

[64] Ben Hubbard, "Private Donors' Funds Add Wild Card to War in Syria," New York Times, November 12, 2013. http://www.nytimes.com/2013/11/13/world/middleeast/private-donors-funds-add-wild-card-to-war-in-syria.html.

[65] Elizabeth Dickinson, "Playing with Fire: Why Private Gulf Financing for Syria's Extremist Rebels Risks Igniting Sectarian Conflict at Home," The Brookings Institution, December 2013, http://www.brookings.edu/~/media/research/files/papers/2013/12/06%20private%20gulf%20financing%20syria%20extremist%20rebels%20sectarian%20conflict%20dickinson/private%20gulf%20financing%20syria%20extremist%20rebels%20sectarian%20conflict%20dickinson.pdf.

"Kuwait scholar Shafi Al Ajami suspended from imamship," Gulf News, August 22, 2013, http://gulfnews.com/news/gulf/kuwait/kuwait-scholar-shafi-al-ajami-suspended-from-imamship-1.1222936. "Kuwait pulls cleric from TV over sectarianism," Al Jazeera (Doha), August 13, 2013,http://www.aljazeera.com/news/middleeast/2013/08/2013813124256264315.html.

[66] Zoltan Pall, "Kuwaiti Salafism and Its Growing Influence in the Levant," Carnegie Endowment for International Peace, May 7, 2014, http://carnegieendowment.org/2014/05/07/kuwaiti-salafism-and-its-growing-influence-in-levant/ha83?reloadFlag=1#.

[67] Asher Berman, "The Syria Twitter Financiers Post-Sanctions," Jihadology, May 18, 2015, http://jihadology.net/2015/05/18/guest-post-the-syria-twitter-financiers-post-sanctions/.

[68] "Saudi Arabia boosts Salafist rivals to al Qaeda in Syria," Reuters, October 1, 2013.

[69] Robert Mackey and Maher Samaan, "Caged Hostages From Syrian President's Sect Paraded Through Rebel-Held Suburb," New York Times, November 1, 2015 http://www.nytimes.com/2015/11/02/world/middleeast/syrian-rebels-say-caged-hostages-will-die-with-them-if-shelling-continues.html?_r=0

[70] Aymenn Jawad al-Tamimi, "Syrian Rebel Mergers: A Harakat Nour Al-Din Al-Zinki Persepctive," Aymenn Jawad Al-Tamimi's Blog, January 7, 2017, http://www.aymennjawad.org/2017/01/syrian-rebel-mergers-a-harakat-nour-al-din-al.

[71] Aqil Hussein, "The Syrian revolutionary command council as a replacement for the merger projects," al-Modon, December 28, 2016 http://www.almodon.com/arabworld/2016/12/28/%D9%85%D8%B4%D8%B1%D9%88%D8%B9%D8%A7-%D8%A7%D9%84%D8%A7%D9%86%D8%AF%D9%85%D8%A7%D8%AC-%D8%A8%D8%A7%D9%86%D8%AA%D8%B8%D8%A7%D8%B1-%D8%A3%D8%AD%D8%B1%D8%A7%D8%B1-%D8%A7%D9%84%D8%B4%D8%A7%D9%85

[72] "Syria," in Central Intelligence Agency World Factbook 2013-14 (Washington, DC: Central Intelligence Agency, 2013), https://www.cia.gov/library/publications/the-world-factbook/geos/sy.html.

[73] Leon Goldsmith, "Alawites for Assad: Why the Syrian Sect Backs the Regime," Foreign Affairs, April 16, 2012, http://www.foreignaffairs.com/articles/137407/leon-goldsmith/alawites-for-assad?page=show; Akil Hashem, "Former Syrian General Akil Hashem on the Uprising in Syria: Without Intervention, No End in Sight," Foreign Affairs, April 16, 2012, http://www.foreignaffairs.com/discussions/interviews/former-syrian-general-akil-hashem-on-the-uprising-in-syria?page=show; Tony Badran, "Divided They Stand: The Syrian Opposition," Mideast Monitor 1, no. 3, September-October 2006, http://www.mideastmonitor.org/issues/0609/0609_3.htm.

[74] Hashem, "Former Syrian General Akil Hashem on the Uprising in Syria: Without Intervention, No End in Sight."

[75] Ayse Baltacioglu-Brammer, "Alawites and the Fate of Syria | Origins: Current Events in Historical Perspective," Ohio State University, January 2014, http://origins.osu.edu/article/alawites-and-fate-syria/page/0/1.

[76] Eline Gordts, "Asma Assad, Wife Of Bashar Assad, Speaks Out," Huffington Post, February 7, 2012, http://www.huffingtonpost.com/2012/02/07/asma-assad-wife-syria_n_1260093.html. Gregory Aftandilian, "Alawite Dilemmas in the Syrian Civil War," Arab Weekly, June 26, 2015, http://www.thearabweekly.com/Special-Focus/891/Alawite-dilemmas-in-the-Syrian-civil-war.

[77] Raymond A. Hinnebusch, "The Islamic Movement in Syria: Sectarian Conflict and Urban Rebellion in an Authoritarian-Populist Regime," in Ali E. Hillal Dessouki, ed., Islamic Resurgence in the Arab World (New York: Praeger, 1982), 150-151.

[78] Hanna Batatu, "Syria's Muslim Brethren," MERIP Reports no. 110 (November-December 1982), 13.

[79] Paulo Pinto, "Dangerous Liaisons: Sufism and the State in Syria," in S. Jakelic and J. Varsoke, eds., Crossing Boundaries: From Syria to Slovakia (Vienna: IWM, 2003), http://www.iwm.at/wp-content/uploads/jc-14-01.pdf.

[80] Eyal Zisser, "Syria, the Ba'th Regime and the Islamic Movement: Stepping on a New Path," The Muslim World 95, no. 1 (January 2005), 60-62.

[81] Ibrahim Hamidi, "The Qubaysi ladies take up Islamic preaching in Syria with government approval," Al-Hayat (London), May 3, 2006, http://faculty-staff.ou.edu/L/Joshua.M.Landis-1/syriablog/2006/05/qubaysi-womens-islamic-movement-by.htm; Andrew Tabler, In the Lion's Den: An Eyewitness Account of Washington's Battle with Syria, (Chicago: Lawrence Hill Books, 2011), 125; Katherine Zoepf, "In Syria, a quiet Islamic revival," New York Times, August 28, 2006, http://www.nytimes.com/2006/08/28/world/africa/28iht-syria3.2620838.html?sq=qubaisiate&st=cse&scp=1&pagewanted=all.

[82] Tentative Jihad: Syria's Fundamentalist Opposition, International Crisis Group, October 12, 2012, 4, http://www.crisisgroup.org/en/regions/middle-east-north-africa/egypt-syria-lebanon/syria/131-tentative-jihad-syrias-fundamentalist-opposition.aspx.

[83] "World Directory of Minorities and Indigenous Peoples," Minority Rights Group International, October 2011, http://www.minorityrights.org/?lid=5266.

[84] David Kenner, "Syria Comes of Age: An extraordinary population boom fuels the revolt against Bashar al-Assad's regime," Foreign Policy, December 8, 2011, http://www.foreignpolicy.com/articles/2011/12/08/syria_population_boom_revolution?page=full.

[85] Malik al-Abdeh, "How I understand the Syrian revolution," syriaintransition.com, March 1, 2012, http://syriatransition.com/2012/03/01/how-i-understand-the-syrian-revolution/.

[86] Hussain Abdul-Hussain, "Syria After Assad," NOW Lebanon, April 13, 2011, http://nowlebanon.com/NewsArchiveDetails.aspx?ID=261197.

[87] This evolution can be tracked in the names of nationwide demonstrations following Friday afternoon prayers, selected each week from among slogans nominated by major activist groups in a poll on the Syrian Revolution 2011 Facebook page. Early rallies had names such as "Friday of Anger," while later on names with religious slogans began to appear, such as "If You Support God He Will Grant You Victory." "The battle to name Syria's Friday protests," Al-Jazeera (Doha), April 14, 2012, http://me.aljazeera.net/?name=aj_standard_en&i=8888&section_name=in_depth_features&guid=201241314026709762&showonly=1.

[88] Gary Gambill, "Assad's Survival Strategy," Foreign Policy, April 6, 2011, http://www.foreignpolicy.com/articles/2011/04/06/assads_survival_strategy?page=full.

[89] "While it is premature to characterize the protests as an Islamist uprising," wrote Gambill three weeks after the start of the uprising, "there is little doubt that those most eager to risk death or severe bodily harm are overwhelmingly Sunni and deeply religious." Gambill, "Assad's Survival Strategy."

[90] Zach Goldberg, Syria's Salafi Awakening: Existential Psychological Primers (Part 1/2), Fair Observer, July 15, 2014, http://www.fairobserver.com/region/middle_east_north_africa/syrias-salafi-awakening-existential-psychological-primers-01474/.

[91] Lund, "Syria's Salafi Insurgents: The Rise of the Syrian Islamic Front," 10.

[92] Lund, "Islamist Groups Declare Opposition to National Coalition and US Strategy."

[93] Zisser, "Syria, the Ba'th Regime and the Islamic Movement," 45.

[94] They were released in several presidential amnesties in December 1991 (2,864 prisoners), March 1992 (600 prisoners), November 1993 (554 prisoners), November 1995 (1,200 prisoners), and 1998 (250 prisoners).

[95] Eyal Zisser, "Syria, the Ba´th Regime and the Islamic Movement," 54.

[96] Sami Moubayed, "The Islamic Revival in Syria," Mideast Monitor 1, no. 3, September-October 2006, http://www.mideastmonitor.org/issues/0609/0609_4.htm.

[97] For example, Assad ended a November 2005 speech at Damascus University with the popular saying "Syria is protected by God" a sentiment completely alien to decades of Ba'athist propaganda. See Bashar al-Assad, "Comprehensive Political Speech Delivered by H.E. President Bashar al-Assad at the Damascus Auditorium," official copy of speech issued by Tishreen newspaper, November 10, 2005, http://www.presidentassad.net/SPEECHES/ASSAD_DAMASCUS_UNIVERSITY_SPEECH.htm;

Tabler, In the Lion's Den, 118.

[98] Tabler, In the Lion's Den, 134.

[99] Ibid., 134.

[100] Wikas, "Battling the Lion of Damascus," 25.

[101] Lina Khatib, Islamic Revivalism in Syria: The Rise and Fall of Ba'thist Secularism (New York: Routledge, 2011), 109-142.

[102] Mohammed Habash, "Radicals are Assad's best friends," The National (UAE), January 1, 2014, http://www.thenational.ae/thenationalconversation/comment/radicals-are-assads-best-friends.

[103] "The Bombing in Damascus: Ten Reasons to Doubt Syria's Claim," Middle East Intelligence Bulletin, May 2004, http://www.meforum.org/meib/articles/0405_s2.htm.

[104] "Syrian protesters set fire to embassies," Associated Press, February 4, 2006, http://www.theguardian.com/world/2006/feb/04/religion.syria.

[105] "Assad regime set free extremists from prison to fire up trouble during peaceful uprising," The National (UAE), January 21, 2014, http://www.thenational.ae/world/syria/assad-regime-set-free-extremists-from-prison-to-fire-up-trouble-during-peaceful-uprising; Raniah Salloum, "From Jail to Jihad: Former Prisoners Fight in Syrian Insurgency," Spiegel (Hamburg), October 10, 2013, http://www.spiegel.de/international/world/former-prisoners-fight-in-syrian-insurgency-a-927158.html.

[106] Ben Hubbard, Clifford Krauss and Eric Schmitt, "Rebels in Syria Claim Control of Resources," New York Times, January 28, 2014, http://www.nytimes.com/2014/01/29/world/middleeast/rebels-in-syria-claim-control-of-resources.html?_r=0.

TUNISIA

QUICK FACTS

Population: Number 11,134,588 (estimated July 2016)

Area: 163,610 sq km

Ethnic Groups: Arab 98%, European 1%, Jewish and other 1%

Religions: Muslim 99.1% (official; Sunni), other (includes Christian, Jewish, Shia Muslim and Baha'i) 1%

Government Type: Republic

GDP (official exchange rate): $43.58 billion (estimated 2015)

Map and Quick Facts courtesy of the CIA World Factbook (December 2016))

OVERVIEW

The self-immolation of twenty-six-year-old fruit vendor Mohamed Bouazizi precipitated mass protests in December 2010. These mass protests led to unprecedented social and political upheaval in Tunisia the following year, and helped launch the larger "Arab Spring" revolutions that swept across the Middle East throughout 2011. The revolution in Tunisia ended the decades-long reign of authoritarian leader Zine el-Abedine Ben Ali, thus ending the restrictive one-party structure that had been the norm in Tunisia since 1956. Into this newly opened field came previously suppressed opposition movements, formerly exiled politicians, and new political groups.

Following the revolution, Tunisia held elections to a National Constituent Assembly on October 23, 2011, following the collapse of Ben Ali's regime. Both domestic and foreign observers judged the elections to be "free and fair."[1] *The National Constituent Assembly was charged with appointing an interim government and writing Tunisia's new constitution.*[2] *In the ensuing vote, the Islamist Ennahda party won the most votes of any single party, gaining control of 90 out of the body's 217 seats.[3] Rather than being a strictly radical movement, Ennahda's members reflect a diversity of opinion on both religious and political issues. Furthermore, the group sought to foster cooperation among Tunisian Islamists in the post-revolutionary political environment.[4]*

Between December 2011 and January 2014, an Ennahda prime minister led the interim government in a coalition with centrist and liberal parties. The resignation of this government in January 2014, the result of a political compromise, seems to validate Ennahda's willingness to operate within established political norms. However, extremist groups have increased their activities, and a country with almost no history of political violence has had to confront Islamist-origin violent demonstrations, political assassinations, and both attempted and actual terrorism. The attack that sparked the most international attention was the assassination of 38 people in Sousse, Tunisia in June 2015. Meanwhile, non-violent salafism has attracted many, especially youth, who are frustrated and disillusioned that the new post-revolution order has been unable to address the issues of jobs, the economy, and social justice.[5]

However, Tunisia's more meaningful role in the wider world of Islamism comes not from its domestic politics, but from its status as a major supplier of foreign fighters. The Tunisian government estimates that approximately 3,000 Tunisians have left home to fight in Syria. Independent analysts and the United Nations estimate that 6,000 – 7,000 have left Tunisia to fight in Iraq, Syria, and Libya in al-Qaeda affiliates and the Islamic State. While exact numbers of foreign fighters are notoriously difficult to estimate, the fact remains that Tunisians make up a significant portion of the estimated 40,000 jihadi fighters that have gone to Syria and Iraq.[6]

Islamist Activity

Ennahda

Founded in 1981, Ennahda was inspired by Egypt's Muslim Brotherhood.[7] During its time in office, the government of Zine el-Abedine Ben Ali suppressed the group as political opposition and exiled its leader, Rachid Ghannouchi, in 1989. After Ben Ali's ouster, Ghannouchi returned to Tunisia, and the party moved quickly to re-establish itself.

Tunisia's modern Islamist movement finds its roots in the Quranic Preservation Society, which was formed in 1970 with the government's approval. The organization was apolitical, dedicated primarily to encouraging piety and faithfulness. It was placed under the Ministry of Religious Affairs and supported by President Bourguiba as a counterweight to the country's political left.[8] Islamists attracted to the Society were not necessarily anti-regime and, in fact, shared some of the regime's views, including its opposition to Communism.[9] They accordingly did not see the need to confront the government and did not see a role for themselves in social and political change, which was the province of the left.

Their approach began to change in the late 1970s, when growing social unrest in other sectors, especially organized labor, politicized the movement. Several Islamists broke from the Quranic Preservation Society—including Rachid al-Ghannouchi, who founded al-Jamaat al-Islamiyya (The Islamic Group) and explicitly called for the end of Bourguiba's one-party rule.[10] In 1978, a year that saw serious economic-based rioting across the country, the "Movement of Islamic Renewal" emerged as a loose-knit coalition of Islamist groups. By the following year, Ghannouchi's group, then called the Mouvement de la Tendence Islamique (MTI), emerged as the backbone of this grouping.[11]

MTI issued a political platform in 1981 that included calls for equitable economic reform, an end to one-party rule, and a return to the "fundamental principles of Islam."[12] These objectives were sufficiently vague and appealing to attract broad support from people across Tunisian society. The group requested recognition as a political party, but was denied such by the government, and most of its leaders were jailed until 1984, when they were released through a general amnesty.[13] Over the course of the 1980s, MTI became younger and more populist in nature, and evolved into a well-organized social and political movement linked with the broader civil rights movement in the country.[14] It was considered pro-democracy and was the first Islamist group in the Arab world to explicitly adopt democratic principles; in his writings, Ghannouchi favored Islamist participation in pluralist politics.[15]

In November 1987, Zine el-Abedine Ben Ali, whom President Bourguiba had recently appointed Prime Minister, ousted the sitting president in a bloodless palace coup. The coup was greeted with relief by the public, as Bourguiba's age and poor health had seriously degraded his judgment and decision-making capabilities. Ben Ali promised reform and democratization, and Ghannouchi, who sought to openly participate in political life, undertook to cooperate with the new President. He signed Ben Ali's "National Pact," which was essentially a social contract between the government and civil and political groups, and then sought to run a list of candidates in the 1989 legislative elections.[16] But Ben Ali soon changed course and, among other measures, prohibited any party's name to contain the words "Islam" or "Islamic" (the prohibition of religiously-identified parties remains in place today.) The MTI duly renamed itself Hizb Ennahda, the Renaissance Party. However, Ben Ali still refused to allow Ennahda to enter the elections as a recognized political party, although he did permit it to field "independent" candidates. Islamists subsequently received 15 percent of the nationwide vote (up to 30 percent in urban areas), but failed to win any seats in the legislature (by contrast, the five recognized secular opposition parties collectively received only 5 percent of the vote).[17] The ruling Constitutional Democratic Rally Party (RCD), the successor to Bourguiba's Neo-Destour (New Constitution) Party, received 80 percent of the vote—a function of both general voter satisfaction and effective regime vote-rigging and polling place intimidation. But the unexpectedly strong performance of the Islamists within the opposition, coupled with Ennahda's increasingly strident political rhetoric, caused the regime to deny Ennahda's second request for recognition. An escalating cycle of protest and repression ensued, and Ghannouchi fled to London in 1989.[18] By 1992, virtually all of Ennahda's leadership had been imprisoned and its organizational capabilities within the country destroyed. Although it was commonly understood that Ennahda was effectively dismantled in the early 1990s, many Tunisians, including Ben Ali, believed it maintained a structure and presence in the country, albeit perhaps a "sleeping" one.[19]

Ennahda's ideology is thoroughly rooted in the ideology of its founder, Rachid Ghannouchi, who views the Koran and the Hadith as "an anchor for political thought and practice."[20] However, he appears to interpret Koranic texts in the context of Western political thinking and modern concepts of political freedoms: the dignity of human beings, human rights, and Koranic prohibitions against Muslim dictators.[21] Ghannouchi himself is a "literalist" and believes that it is the duty of Muslims to establish Islamic government where attainable; in practice, he has endorsed multi-party politics.[22] He does not advocate government by clerics, and has said that "[t]he state is not something from God but from the people... the state has to serve the benefit of the Muslims."[23] His idea of an Islamic political regime appears to be a strong presidential system with an elected president and elected parliament, and considers the parliamentary system a legitimate means of political participation.[24]

Ghannouchi's public statements since his return from exile, and those of other Ennahda figures, have been consistent with this worldview. He has said that his party will accept the outcome of fair and democratic elections, and that he himself will not run for president.[25] In a March 2, 2012 address to a civil society conference, Ghannouchi asserted that, "...We are in need of scholars and intellectuals to debate and study our issues in a climate of freedom, and accept that the legislative institution is the ultimate authority by virtue of being elected."[26] Applying his views to the prevailing political situation in Tunisia at the time, he stated,

> The fact that our revolution has succeeded in toppling a dictator, we ought to accept the principle of citizenship, and that this country does not belong to one party or another but rather to all its citizens regardless of their religion, sex, or any other consideration.[27]

Once in power following the October 2011 elections, however, the Ennahda-led government (Ghannouchi himself assumed no elected or appointed position) appeared to many to be practicing the same sort of majoritarianism and attempting to control all the political levers of national power, in much the same way as the Egyptian Muslim Brotherhood would once it assumed power in Cairo the following year. At the same time, the government was seen as tolerating the disruptive and sometimes violent actions of Salafi elements while simultaneously cracking down on secular demonstrations. In a widely-cited example of this alleged, police allowed the Salafist "occupation" of Manouba University to drag on for several weeks, but quickly used force to break up peaceful anti-Ennahda demonstrations in central Tunis in April 2012.

The issue came to a head with the assassination of two leftist politicians in 2013, killings that were widely seen as the work of Salafists emboldened by Ennahda sympathies. Popular demonstrations against the government grew. Opposition parties, which coalesced into a political umbrella called the "National Salvation Front," called for the dissolution of the National Constituent Assembly and for new elections. Also, the process of writing the country's new, post-Ben Ali constitution had proven to be both protracted and contentious, the economy was still far from robust, and the social environment was one of public frustration and pessimism. Ennahda leaders realized that some sort of national compromise was necessary, lest they go the way of the Muslim Brotherhood and President Morsi in Egypt (albeit not by the hands of the national army). Various compromises were suggested, and Ennahda offered some concessions to its political opponents. Popular demonstrations and civil disobedience waned in the Fall of 2013, and the two sides decided to negotiate a way forward. Finally, a National Dialogue led by Tunisia's labor union federation brokered a compromise in early January 2014, under which the Ennahda-led government would step down in favor of an interim, technocratic administration that would lead the country to new elections, while the Constituent Assembly (about 42% Islamist) would remain and finish the constitution.

All sides agreed to this framework, and by the end of January 2014 the new constitution was drafted and approved by the Constituent Assembly. Serious unrest was avoided, the new constitution was widely accepted, and the country appeared to be moving ahead. At the time, Ennahda appeared to indicate that it would accept the outcome of prospective power-sharing under this structure, with Ghannouchi telling a Washington, DC audience in February 2014 that:

> the Tunisian experience has proven to those doubting the intentions of Islamists that Islam and democracy are compatible, and that victims of decades of repression, marginalization, and exclusion are not carrying hatred or the desire for revenge, but rather an enlightened modernist civil project as embodied in the new Tunisian constitution, which has been adopted with the widest possible consensus.[28]

However, there are indications that younger party members do not see this as a reasonable and necessary compromise, but as the secularist-compelled surrender of political Islam's "main chance" by a weak leadership.[29] Ennahda's philosophies on the relationship between religion and government, meanwhile, have continued to develop over time. In May 2016, during its 10th party congress, 93.5 percent of Ennahda's delegates voted to separate religious and political activities into separate branches. This decision means that elected officials can no longer hold positions both in the party and in broader society, which includes mosques and Islamic organizations.

Ennahda has shown a historical unwillingness to crack down on Salafi-jihadists. This hesitance stems from Ennahda's perception that Salafi-jihadists are young and misguided, as well as from sympathy generated by Ennahda's own history of repression under Ben Ali's regime.[30] Ennahda has counseled Salafi-jihadists to follow a strategy of "bishwaya bishwaya"(slowly, slowly), worried that the aggressive tactics and rapid advance of the latter might alarm opponents. Salafi-jihadists, however, have found that argument unconvincing.[31]

At times, however, Ennahda nonetheless has acted against Islamist elements. In April 2013, it declared Ansar al-Sharia, the largest Salafi group in Tunisia, a terrorist organization.[32] Since then, Ennahda has adopted a more security-oriented approach to Salafi-jihadism, entailing the forced registration of Salafis at police stations and the stationing of plain-clothes police officers in public spaces. While many members of Ennahda are uncomfortable with these measures, as well as with continuing police brutality in Tunisia,[33] the rise of Salafi-jihadism domestically and internationally has made public criticism of these policies challenging.[34]

Other Islamist movements

While Ennahda dominates Tunisian Islamism, other Islamist groups do exist, though they tend to be small in size and loosely organized.

Salafist parties

On May 11, 2012, the Tunisian government granted a license to the Salafist Jebahat el-Islah, (JI), or "Reform Front" to operate as a party under the Political Parties Law (which requires respect for the "civil principles of the state"). It was the first Salafist group to be recognized as such.[35] During this time, Ennahda may have been more inclined to encourage pluralism in Muslim politics in order to better govern a politically diverse country.[36] JI has several leaders who were jailed during the 1980s and claims that it rejects violence, respects democracy, and does not seek to impose duct.[37] A second Salafist party, Al-Rahma ("Mercy") was legalized in July 2012. Its stated goal is the establishment of sharia law. Neither Rahma nor JI are particularly popular.[38] JI remains unswervingly dedicated to bringing sharia law into Tunisia, but younger Salafi-jihadis tend to see the legislative route of enacting sharia as too slow and unwieldy to have much appeal.[39] Furthermore, most of JI's membership consists of older men, and the group has failed to attract younger Tunisians to its cause.[40]

El-Zeituna Party

The non-Salafist El Zeituna Party (named after the historic mosque and school in Tunis) officially announced its establishment in February 2014 and its intention to participate in the next presidential and parliamentary elections. The announcement outlined its position, which is based on the Koran and Sunnah and which "respects the legal legitimacy and the state's constitutional institutions." Its leaders are dissatisfied with the January 2014 constitution, and their goals include reform of the judicial system and establishment of an "Islamic economic system based on the just distribution of wealth."[41]

Ansar al-Sharia Tunisiyya

Ansar al-Sharia Tunisiyya (Supporters of Islamic Law, or AST was established in April 2011. Though there are many groups throughout the world that go by the name of Ansar al-Sharia, these organizations are not part of a united chain of command. Terrorism analyst Aaron Zelin writes: "(Ansar al-Sharia groups) are fighting in different lands using different means, but all for the same end, an approach better suited for the vagaries born of the Arab uprisings."[42] This approach allows the groups to appear to be part of a unified transnational jihadi movement, while in reality addressing the unique environment of each country.

The Tunisian group's founder, Abu Ayyad al-Tunisi, was a jihadist who had fought in Afghanistan and was subsequently arrested and deported to Tunisia as a terrorist in 2003. He was freed with many other prisoners after the revolution.[43] AST has claimed responsibility for the 2012 attack on the U.S. Embassy and the assassinations of liberal politicians Chokri Belaid and Mohamed Brahmi in February and July 2013.[44] Its most recent attack occurred in 2014, when AST militants attacked Tunisian soldiers at checkpoints near the Algerian border. 14 people were killed in that incident.[45]

In July 2014, an AST spokesman declared AST's allegiance to Islamic State emir Abu Bakr Al-Baghdadi.[46] AST has recruited heavily for ISIS in Tunisia, and encourages many young Tunisians to make the journey to Syria. Tunisians travel to Syria to wage jihad alongside a number of groups, but most commonly with ISIS.[47] ISIS also features Tunisians prominently in its own propaganda, often lauding the efforts and martyrdom of Tunisian foreign fighters.[48] However, the extent of the tactical connections between the two groups is unclear. AST, in general, has been less focused on violent attacks and more focused on dawa (proselytization) and community service.[49] As noted in the State Department's 2015 report on terrorist groups, AST's strength and numbers, as well as its foreign aid and financing, remain unknown.[50]

Hizb ut-Tahrir

Another potentially dangerous group is Hizb ut-Tahrir (the Islamic Liberation Party), an international movement founded in 1953 that seeks to re-establish the Islamic Caliphate. This group established a presence in Tunisia in 1973, but historically had only a few dozen members in the country.[51] It emerged publicly after the 2011 revolution and declared its goal of competing in elections and offering its "alternative constitution" to the Constituent Assembly.[52] While the group claims to renounce violence, it does not rule out rebellion and civil disobedience to establish an Islamic state. It believes in the re-establishment of the Muslim Caliphate and in sharia law as the source of the constitution.[53] Its spokesman announced that Hizb ut-Tahrir is preparing for an ideological and political struggle to save the nation.[54] Many Tunisians, including members of Ennahda, believe with good reason that Hizb ut-Tahrir would, if it won an election, ban other parties and implement "one man, one vote, one time."[55] Its request for a license to operate as a political party was initially denied in March 2012 (as was that of the "Tunisian Sunni" party), but that decision was later and Hizb ut-Tahrir became a recognized political party later in 2012.[56] The organization's cooperation with the government proved to be short-lived, however. In September 2016, the Tunisian government requested that a military court ban the group, as it has been accused repeatedly of "undermining public order" since 2012. An anonymous official confirmed that the request had been submitted to a military investigative judge, and that the government was awaiting the judge's reply.[57]

Al-Qaeda in the Islamic Maghreb

Al-Qaeda in the Islamic Maghreb (AQIM), which did not have a significant presence or recruiting base in Tunisia in the past, is now active, especially in the western part of the country. While AQIM has apparently not conducted suicide bomb-type terrorist operations in Tunisia, its "conventional" forces, armed with weapons looted from Libyan arsenals, have engaged Tunisian security forces with deadly results. In 2014, AQIM claimed responsibility for the attack on the home of the interior minister, Lotfi Ben Jeddou.[58]

Some AQIM members have defected to ISIS in recent times,[59] and the group has been weakened in recent years. In 2015, Tunisian counterterrorism operations eliminated much of the group's leadership. Furthermore, ISIS has co-opted some of AQIM's support cells along Tunisia's border with Algeria, taking supplies for themselves.[60]

The Islamic State

The Islamic State does not currently hold any territory in Tunisia, but the country still plays a vital role in the group's operations.[61] As previously discussed, a large percentage of ISIS's foreign fighters come from Tunisia; between 6,000-7,000 Tunisians (of a total of some 40,000 or more foreign fighters) have gone to fight in Iraq, Syria, and Libya to date.[62] ISIS also uses the highly porous border between Tunisia and Libya, where it maintains a sizeable presence, to smuggle guns and fighters into the country.[63] In an effort to further destabilize Tunisia and its economy, ISIS fighters have attacked cities and tourists locales.[64]

ISIS has launched a number of notable attacks in Tunisia to date. In November 2014, ISIS claimed responsibility for the bombing of a presidential guard bus. The blast killed twelve presidential guards.[65] In March 2015, two ISIS-trained gunmen killed 21 tourists and one Tunisian at the Bardo National Museum in Tunis. The Islamic State also took responsibility for the 2015 Sousse shooting that killed 39 and wounded 36. In March 2016, 50 gunmen affiliated with ISIS, many of whom were part of sleeper cells coordinated attacks on "security installations and security personnel in the border town of Ben Guerdane." Security forces killed 49 of the militants, while 17 security officials and seven civilians were killed.[66] In November 2016, the Islamic State claimed the killing of a Tunisian Air Force soldier who was found dead in his home.[67] Two days after the killing, the Tunisian National Security Council announced that it had undertaken a new strategy to fight extremism and terrorism. President Beji Caid Essebsi's office said the strategy was based on "prevention, protection, judicial proceedings and retaliation." No other details about the plan have as yet been revealed.[68]

ISIS has used Libya's virtual collapse to solidify its presence in that nation. There is ample evidence that the group plans to use its base in Libya to begin to infiltrate Tunisia as well. The Ben Guerdane attack (which took place near the border with Libya) illustrates that the Islamic State is quite capable of doing so. The growing chaos and instability in Libya poses a serious security threat for Tunisia. As the Libyan state collapses, ISIS and other jihadi groups will only grow stronger. As ISIS continues to gain ground in Libya, it will step up its attacks in Tunisia, and more incidents as the Ben Guerdane attack may occur. Furthermore, as ISIS gains prestige and power, more young Tunisians may be tempted to cross the border and join the group in Libya.

ISLAMISM AND SOCIETY

Tunisians tend to be moderate in their views and behavior. Habib Bourguiba, the country's first president following its independence from France in the 1950s, was supported by the public and set a moderate political course. Guerrilla warfare and terrorism did not characterize the struggle, and there were no violent purges and settling of accounts among the victors of the sort that led to continued crisis and near-civil war in neighboring Algeria.

Tunisia is an unusually homogenous country for its neighborhood. Ninety-eight percent of its 11 million person population is Sunni Muslim.[69] Shi'ites number perhaps in the thousands, most of them converts to the sect following the 1979 Iranian Revolution.[70] There is a small Jewish community concentrated on the island of Djerba, and there are virtually no indigenous Christians in the country. While there are differences between Arabs and Berbers, ethnicity is not a significant factor, and no "identity politics" exist to fuel conflict and instability. Neither is there a large socio-economic gulf between rich and poor to create tensions. As a result of some very sound economic decisions by the Ben Ali government, Tunisia has developed an expansive urbanized middle class, and a very large percentage of Tunisians have a stake in maintaining the system. There is, however, a geographical "have/have not" gap, and the poorer southern interior has not historically been a focus of development. Most dissident movements, including Islamist forces, have originated in this region, and it was the cradle of the "Jasmine Revolution." Equitable distribution of wealth to all regions remains an important unsolved issue, especially after the revelations of Ben Ali family corruption, and a number of Tunisians have advocated renationalizing and relocating businesses to ensure fairness in the geographical distribution of opportunities.[71]

But relative prosperity was insufficient to prevent upheaval. The 2011 revolution was not about bread and jobs alone. Rather, it was also about dignity and the state's relationship with the people. A stroll along Avenue Habib Bourguiba in downtown Tunis has long provided a useful barometer of the extent of unemployment among young men. Without a job and the means to support a family, these young men cannot marry, start a family, and fully participate in society. Frustration is the result, and a portion of frustrated youth, albeit a very small one, is attracted to the fringes of society, including radical Islamism.

Salafism is growing across the country and, while it does not necessarily manifest in terrorist acts, it is disruptive and often violent. Salafists reportedly control up to 150 mosques in the country, a development being closely watched by the Religious Affairs Ministry.[72] Some of these radical imams are calling young Tunisians to join the jihad against the Syrian regime of Bashar Assad, something of great interest to the Interior Ministry.[73] In recent years, estimates for the number of fighters who have left Tunisia to fight abroad range from 3,000 to 7,000.[74] Furthermore, nearly 700 of these fighters have since returned to Tunisia. Many of these returning fighters are sent to jail or are placed under state surveillance.[75] However, the government has never developed a clear strategy for dealing with these individuals and reintegrating them into society "so they don't turn into time bombs that may explode any moment."[76]

While Islamism has not, and most likely will not, take hold among Tunisians en masse, religious sentiment was growing steadily prior to the revolution. Youth were exposed to this phenomenon primarily at university, especially when secular, modernist, and leftist movements were at best weak and marginalized, and at worst outlawed and suppressed. Beneath the modernism and sophisticated worldview exhibited by the population as a whole, Tunisia is a traditional society that values its religion and cultural heritage. The Ben Ali regime began to recognize this and attempted to "Islamize" society and use religion to support government policies.[77] This "Official" or "Popular" Islam was designed to counter the threat of extremism and terrorism by preaching the values of moderation and tolerance and, at the same time, claiming ownership of Tunisians' Islamic identity, which had been denied by past regimes.[78] This effort was supported by many Tunisians; as an example, Radio Zeytouna, a religious station established in 2009 by the Ben Ali government as a counterweight to Islamist satellite networks, was popular with the public and had a good audience base.

Although Islamists and Ennahda failed over the years to gain the active support of the public, there is sympathy for the vision expressed by the movement—that is, political and economic reform and living by Islamic principles. Most Tunisians do not appear to consider Ghannouchi and other Islamists as saviors of society, but rather simply people who express an appealing vision.[79] Many of those who join the movement do not necessarily support the establishment of an Islamic regime.[80]

Tunisians do not like violent transition, but they do believe in good governance, freedoms, and rule of law. They are very protective of their acquis (patrimony: the shared cultural, political, social, legal experiences), which they believe distinguishes them from their neighbors. Because of this, any political or religious movement that wants to play a role in society will have to preserve and improve these values, and not reject or destroy them.

Islamism and the State

The Tunisian state was hostile to Islamism from independence in 1956 through the end of the Ben Ali regime. Habib Bourguiba, the hero of the liberation and president between 1956 and 1987, dominated the country through force of personality and an efficient political party structure organized down to the lowest grassroots. He made an early decision to devote the country's energies and limited resources to social modernization and economic growth, and not to democracy and political pluralism. Bourguiba steadily consolidated government control over political life in order to avoid the chaos and serial coups d'etat that characterized much of the Arab and African post-colonial experience. The Tunisian people essentially shared this objective and acquiesced to extensive limitations on political participation. Bourguiba's politics were strictly secular, and he insisted that the country would be also. He ignored the country's Arab/Islamic history and connected modern Tunisia directly to a pre-Islamic past—its Carthaginian heritage—while simultaneously secularizing the state and weakening traditional Islamic institutions.[81] At the same time, his regime embarked upon an economic and social development program based on a socialist model. This model failed, and the government changed course; the eventual result was impressive economic performance and very progressive social programs involving public education and literacy, economic mobility, and the position of women in society.

The process of tightening regime control accelerated after the 1987 "palace coup" by Ben Ali, who maintained that no accommodation with Islamists was possible, and who considered Islamism to be a disease against which the public must be "inoculated." The country's 2003 anti-terrorism law allowed the jailing of those threatening national security. It was used almost exclusively against Islamists, primarily Islamist-leaning youths using the Internet "illegally" (i.e., blogging or visiting jihadist websites).[82]

The pre-January 2011 state of affairs in Tunisia was one of comprehensive government domination of the public space and virtually all political activity—not just that of Islamists, but of all potential opposition groups. The state controlled mosque construction, sermon content, religious education, and appointment and remuneration of imams. While these constraints were relaxed by the Ennahda government, imams do not have carte blanche to speak freely. When several imams delivered uncensored Friday sermons attacking politicians, an official from the Ministry of Religious Affairs stated: "in the event of too many excesses, then measures will be taken. Mosques are not meant to be venues for defamation and personal attacks. An imam is not a judge, and the law is above all."[83] The post-January 2014 interim government has again, at least temporarily, limited mosque openings to prayer times only, claiming that many mosques controlled by Salafist imams were preaching jihad and takfirism (accusing another Muslim of apostasy).[84]

Although Ennahda dominated the elected Constituent Assembly and could theoretically have exerted a decisive influence over the new constitution, the Interim Government adopted the same balanced methodology used to draft the 1959 constitution. Six Constituent Assembly subcommittees focused on various parts of the constitution (e.g., the preamble and basic principles, rights and freedoms, the judiciary, legislative and executive powers, etc.). All Constituent Assembly members served in one or another of these subcommittees, in which membership was proportional to the party distribution in the Assembly. Thus, while Ennahda was well represented, it could not pack critical subcommittees with its own members. Perhaps most critically, Ennahda announced its opposition to including sharia in the constitution; the only reference to Islam repeated the 1959 Constitution's Article 1 and states: "Tunisia is a free, independent and sovereign state. Its religion is Islam, its language is Arabic, and its type of government is the Republic. This article cannot be amended."[85] As mentioned previously, Ennahda has taken further steps to separate secularism and religion in its politics, by officially splitting apart those two functions of the party. Tunisia may well continue upon a road of encouraging secular government while recognizing its population's Muslim values.

ENDNOTES

[1] Issandr El Amrani and Ursula Lindsey, "Tunisia Moves to the Next Stage," Middle East Research and Information Project,November 8, 2011, http://merip.org/mero/mero110811.
[2] "Tunisia's Islamist party claims election victory," Telegraph (London), October 25, 2011, http://www.telegraph.co.uk/news/worldnews/africaandindianocean/tunisia/8847315/Tunisias-Islamist-party-claims-election-victory.html.
[3] El Amrani and Lindsey, "Tunisia Moves to the Next Stage."
[4] Haim Malka and Margot Balboni, "Domestic Context: After the Revolution," Center for Strategic and International Studies,June 2016, http://foreignfighters.csis.org/tunisia/domestic-context.html.
[5] Anouar Boukhars, "In the Crossfire: Islamists' travails in Tunisia," Carnegie Endowment for International Peace, January 2014, 13.
[6] Haim Malka and Margot Balboni, "Tunisia: Radicalism Abroad and at Home," Center for Strategic and International Studies, June 2016, http://foreignfighters.csis.org/tunisia/why-tunisia.html.
[7] Aiden Lewis, "Profile: Tunisia's Ennahda Party," BBC, October 25, 2011, http://www.bbc.com/news/world-africa-15442859.
[8] Christopher Alexander, "Opportunities, Organizations, and Ideas: Islamists and Workers in Tunisia and Algeria," International Journal of Middle East Studies 32 (2000), 465-490, 466.
[9] Jennifer Noyon, Islam, Politics, and Pluralism: Theory and Practice in Turkey, Jordan, Tunisia, and Algeria (London: The Royal Institute of International Affairs, 2003), 100.
[10] Alexander, "Opportunities, Organizations, and Ideas."
[11] Susan Walsh, "Islamist Appeal in Tunisia," Middle East Journal 40, no.4 (Autumn 1986), 652.
[12] Ibid., 653.
[13] Ibidem.
[14] Ibidem, 657.
[15] Noyon, Islam, Politics, and Pluralism, 99.
[16] Ibid., 101.
[17] Perkins, A History of Modern Tunisia, 190.
[18] Noyon, Islam, Politics, and Pluralism, 103.
[19] Correspondence of previous chapter author, Larry Velte, with Tunisian academic and lawyer, September 2009.

[20] Noyon, Islam, Politics, and Pluralism, 99.
[21] Mohamed Elhachmi Hamdi, The Politicization of Islam: A Case Study of Tunisia (Boulder, CO: Westview Press, 1998), 107.
[22] Noyon, Islam, Politics, and Pluralism, 101.
[23] As cited in John L. Esposito and Francois Burgat, eds., Modernizing Islam (New Brunswick, NJ: Rutgers University Press, 2003), 78.
[24] Allani, "The Islamists in Tunisia between Confrontation and Participation, 1980-2008," 266.
[25] Al-Munji Al-Suaydani, "Ennahda Movement Leader Talks to Asharq Al-Awsat," ASharq al-Awsat (London) February 7, 2011, http://www.aawsat.com/english/news.asp?section=3&id=24070.
[26] Address by Rached Ghannouchi to the Center for the Study of Islam and Democracy, Tunis, March 2, 2012.
[27] Ibid.
[28] Posted by the Center for the Study of Islam and Democracy, Washington, DC, March 18, 2014.
[29] Discussion by Mokhtar Awad, Brookings Institution, Washington, DC, March 26, 2014.
[30] Monica Marks, "Tunisia's Ennahda: Rethinking Islamism in the context of ISIS and the Egyptian coup," Brookings Institution Project on U.S. Relations with the Islamic World Working Paper, August 2015, 4, , https://www.brookings.edu/wp-content/uploads/2016/07/Tunisia_Marks-FINALE.pdf.
[31] Ibid., 6.
[32] Ibidem, 7.
[33] Ibidem.
[34] Ibidem.
[35] Houda Trabelsi, "Tunisia Approves First Salafist Party," Magharebia, May 17, 2012.
[36] Aaron Zelin, "Who is Jabhat al-Islah?" Carnegie Endowment for International Peace, July 18, 2015. http://carnegieendowment.org/sada/?fa=48885.
[37] Trabelsi, "Tunisia Approves First Salafist Party."
[38] Stefano M. Torelli, Fabio Merone and Francesco Cavatorta, "Salafism in Tunisia: Challenges and Opportunities for Democratization," Middle East Policy XIX, no. 4, Winter 2012.
[39] Anouar Boukhars, "In the Crossfire: Islamists' Travails in Tunisia," Carnegie Endowment for International Peace Paper, January 27, 2014, http://carnegieendowment.org/2014/01/27/in-crossfire-islamists-travails-in-tunisia-pub-54311.
[40] Aaron Zelin, "Meeting Tunisia's Ansar al-Sharia," Foreign Policy, March 8, 2013, http://foreignpolicy.com/2013/03/08/meeting-tunisias-ansar-al-sharia/.
[41] "Tunisia: New Political Party Established" National Tunisian Television ("Alwatania"), February 15, 2014.
[42] Aaron Zelin, "Know Your Ansar al-Sharia," Foreign Policy, September 21, 2012, http://foreignpolicy.com/2012/09/21/know-your-ansar-al-sharia/.

[43] Torelli, Merone and Cavatorta, "Salafism in Tunisia: Challenges and Opportunities for Democratization."
[44] "Ansar al-Sharia in Tunisia (AST)," Counter Extremism Project, 2016, 13, http://www.counterextremism.com/threat/ansar-al-sharia-tunisia-ast.
[45] "Ansar al-Shariah (Tunisia)" Mapping Militant Organizations, Stanford University, August 24, 2016, http://web.stanford.edu/group/mappingmilitants/cgi-bin/groups/view/547#note3.
[46] Jamel Arfaoui, "Tunisia: Ansar Al-Sharia Spokesman Backs Isis," AllAfrica, May 14, 2013, http://allafrica.com/stories/201407090299.html.
[47] "AST," Counter Extremism Project, 20.
[48] Ibid.
[49] Zelin, "Meeting Tunisia's Ansar al-Sharia."
[50] "Chapter Six: Foreign Terrorist Organizations – Ansar al-Shari'a in Tunisia," in U.S. Department of State, Country Reports on Terrorism 2015 (Washington, DC: U.S. Department of State, 2016), https://www.state.gov/j/ct/rls/crt/2015/257523.htm.
[51] Allani, "The Islamists in Tunisia between Confrontation and Participation, 1980-2008," 258.
[52] Interview by previous chapter author, Larry Veldte, with Tahrir spokesman Ridha Belhaj, Assarih (Tunis), March 11, 2011.
[53] Ibid.
[54] Belhaj interview, Al-Jazeera (Doha), March 10, 2011.
[55] Interview with an-Nahda official Abdelfattah Moro, Al-Jazeera (Doha), March 10, 2011.
[56] "Hizb ut-Tahrir Tunisia Spokesman: 'Our Appeal for a License has Been Accepted'," Hizb-ut Tarhri Britain, July 18, 2012, http://www.hizb.org.uk/news-watch/hizb-ut-tahrir-tunisia-spokesman-our-appeal-for-a-license-has-been-accepted.
[57] "Tunisia calls for a ban on radical Islamist party," Al Arabiya, September 7, 2016, http://english.alarabiya.net/en/News/middle-east/2016/09/07/Tunisia-calls-for-ban-on-radical-Islamist-party-.html.
[58] Chapter Six: Foreign Terrorist Organizations – Al-Qa'ida in the Islamic Maghreb," in U.S. Department of State, Country Reports on Terrorism 2015, https://www.state.gov/j/ct/rls/crt/2015/257523.htm.
[59] Jaclyn Stutz, "AQIM and ISIS in Tunisia: Competing Campaigns," AEI Critical Threats Project, June 28, 2016, http://www.criticalthreats.org/al-qaeda/stutz-aqim-isis-tunisia-competing-campaigns-june-28-2016.
[60] Ibid.
[61] Haim Malka and Margot Balboni, Violence in Tunisia: Analyzing Terrorism and Political Violence After the Revolution,Center for Strategic and International Studies, June 2016, http://foreignfighters.csis.org/tunisia/violence-in-tunisia.html.
[62] Haim Malka and Margot Balboni, "Tunisia: Radicalism Abroad and at Home," Center for Strategic and International Studies, June 2016, http://foreignfighters.csis.org/tunisia/why-tunisia.html.

[63] Malka and Balboni, "Violence in Tunisia: Analyzing Terrorism and Political Violence After the Revolution," June 2016, http://foreignfighters.csis.org/tunisia/violence-in-tunisia.html.
[64] Ibid.
[65] Ibidem.
[66] Ibidem.
[67] "Tunisia Takes on Extremism with New 'Terrorism' Strategy," The New Arab, November 8, 2016, https://www.alaraby.co.uk/english/news/2016/11/8/tunisia-takes-on-extremism-with-new-terrorism-strategy.
[68] Ibid.
[69] This and other demographic statistics derived from the U.S. Central Intelligence Agency's World Factbook, https://www.cia.gov/library/publications/the-world-factbook/.
[70] "Tunisia Islamist Trends back to the Forefront," Al-Arabiya (Dubai), February 1, 2011, http://www.alarabiya.net/articles/2011/01/20/134294.html.
[71] Discussions by previous chapter author, Larry Velte, with civil society figures and officials in Tunis, March 10-12, 2011.
[72] Michael Lukac. "Radical Islamists seize control of Tunisia mosques," International Business Times, November 2, 2011, http://www.ibtimes.com/radical-islamists-seize-control-tunisia-mosques-485204.
[73] "Radical Mosques Call Young Tunisians to Jihad in Syria," Agence France Presse, May 18, 2012.
[74] Malka and Balboni, "Tunisia: Radicalism Abroad and at Home."
[75] Sarah Souli, "Tunisia: Why foreign fighters abandon ISIL," Al Jazeera (Doha), March 3, 2016, http://www.aljazeera.com/news/2016/03/tunisia-foreign-fighters-abandon-isil-160301103627220.html.
[76] Maghreb to tighten noose on Syria-bound jihadists," Echourouk (Tunis), February 9, 2014.
[77] Kausch, "Tunisia: The Life of Others."
[78] Correspondence of previous chapter author, Larry Velte, with Tunisian academic and lawyer, September 2009.
[79] Ibid.
[80] Lise Storm, "The Persistence of Authoritarianism as a source of Radicalization in North Africa," International Affairs 85, no. 5, September 2009, 2011.
[81] Noyon, Islam, Politics, and Pluralism, 96.
[82] Hugh Roberts, address before the Center for Strategic and International Studies, Washington, DC, March 21, 2007.
[83] Quoted in Al-Musawwar (Cairo), March 7, 2011.
[84] "The Tunisian Government is waging a campaign to restore the mosques," Ilaf (London) March 24, 2014, http://elaph.com/Web/News/2014/3/885206.html
[85] Duncan Picard, "The Current Status of Constitution Making in Tunisia," Carnegie Endowment for International Peace, April 19, 2012.

UNITED ARAB EMIRATES

QUICK FACTS

Population: 5,927,482

Area: 83,600 sq km

Ethnic Groups: Emirati 19%, other Arab and Iranian 23%, South Asian 50%, other expatriates (includes Westerners and East Asians) 8%

Religions: Muslim (official) 76%, Christian 9%, other (primarily Hindu and Buddhist, less than 5% of the population consists of Parsi, Baha'i, Druze, Sikh, Ahmadi, Ismaili, Dawoodi Bohra Muslim, and Jewish) 15%

Government Type: Federation of Monarchies

GDP (official exchange rate): $375 billion (2015 est)

Quick Facts courtesy of the CIA World Factbook (Last Updated January 2017)

OVERVIEW

In the wake of the September 11, 2001 terrorist attacks on the United States, the United Arab Emirates has been identified as significantly, if indirectly, involved in Islamic terrorism. Two of the nineteen 9/11 hijackers were residents of the UAE, while another had lived there.[1] A decade-and-a-half after those attacks, much of the Arab world remains in a state of upheaval. The government of nearby Bahrain faces the challenge of its Shi'a majority's demands for greater political power, which have engendered a harsh response and occasional violence. In neighboring Yemen, the UAE has committed military, advisory, and economic support to the government of Abed Rabbo Mansour Hadi, in its struggle with Houthi-led forces and al-Qaeda in the Arabian Peninsula (AQAP). Yet the UAE, to all appearances, remains calm. This is due in large part to the cultural setting in which the interpretation and practice of Islam have evolved in the country, as well as to the nature of its leadership since independence in 1971. The founding father of the UAE, and its president until his death in 2004, Zayid bin Sultan Al Nahyan, promoted and personified a conservative but moderate interpretation of Islam, which helped legitimize government efforts to check and contain Islamic extremism. Since 9/11, the UAE has devoted serious efforts to countering Islamic terrorism, the extreme forms of belief that promote it, and the financial support that facilitates it.

Although concerns remain, the country's continued forceful actions to counter Islamic extremism have minimized the possibility of terrorist plots being carried out from or through the UAE, and constrained terrorist financing operations. At various times between December 2011 and November 2016, about 150 Islamists were arrested. They were described in government statements as belonging to an "al-Qaeda cell," and threatening militant attacks. The various charges were alleged violations of Article 180 of the UAE's penal code, which prohibits "establishing, instituting, founding, organizing, administering or joining an association or any branch thereof, with the aim of overthrowing the regime of the State."[2] A 2014 anti-terrorism law further updated national legislation, originally formulated in 2004, allowing expanded use of the death penalty.[3] It seems clear that the arrests and convictions stemmed more from the government's fear of the popular attraction of political Islam in the wake of the Arab Spring than from evidence of an explicit plot to overthrow the government. Since 2011, the government has energetically suppressed manifestations of dissent, criticism, and calls for political reform.[4]

ISLAMIST ACTIVITY

The activity of Islamists in the UAE has historically been constrained by several factors. Islam in the UAE is generally moderate and non-political in nature, and the government closely monitors Muslim organizations, especially those with political agendas. Furthermore, the largest segment of Muslims in the country is South Asian expatriates, who have been drawn there for job opportunities and are subject to expulsion for any behavior deemed threatening to state security. Finally, astute government distribution of the country's vast hydrocarbon wealth has been effective in blunting the kind of discontent that might promote grassroots adherence to Islamism that challenges the writ of the state.

The Muslim Brotherhood

The Muslim Brotherhood (MB) has had an Emirati presence since before the UAE's independence in 1971. In the 1950s and 1960s, educated, professional MB members fleeing Gamal Abdel Nasser's repression in Egypt filled many public and private positions, especially in educational and judicial institutions, gaining significant influence in the UAE in subsequent years.[5] By the 1990s, however, whatever influence the organization exercised had largely dissipated. The Emirati government sought to curb the MB's influence in education by forcing those members employed by the Ministry of Education to renounce the Brotherhood or find employment elsewhere. In 1994, Al Islah, the UAE branch of the MB, was officially proscribed. In 2003, Mohammed bin Zayed Al Nahyan, the crown prince of Abu Dhabi, and senior MB leaders failed to strike a deal to permit the group to operate in the UAE in exchange for renouncing allegiance to its supreme guide and agreeing to halt political activities. Later the same year, UAE authorities initiated transfer of teachers associated with the MB out of the education system and, from 2006, hundreds of expatriate MB members, many in education, were deported.[6] Subsequently, the 2008 defeat of the Brotherhood's candidates in the Kuwaiti parliamentary elections reflected a general setback for the group's attempts to gain a foothold in the Gulf, even as it continued to flounder in the UAE. An Islamist commentator lamenting negative developments for the Brotherhood observed that, in the UAE, "despite some interesting developments among the cadres and the youth of the MB, intense security obstacles prevented them from doing much by way of renewing their thought or engaging in popular actions."[7] Indeed, indications are that the UAE government views the Brotherhood as a political entity whose true aim is to establish a theocracy; thus, the organization is outlawed.[8] In the aftermath of the 2011 Arab Spring, the UAE felt very threatened by the Egyptian MB's perceived attempt to incite Islamist activity in the UAE. While Mohammed Morsi was president of Egypt (June 2012 to July 2013), relations between the two countries remained strained, on account of the Egyptian government's then-prevalent Brotherhood sympathies. As a result, the UAE gave financial aid to President Abdel Fattah al-Sisi, after his overthrow of Morsi.[9]

In November 2014, the UAE released a list of some 83 organizations it had designated as terrorist groups. (The exact number varies slightly in various reports.) A number of allegedly MB-linked organizations were included. Among these were two U.S. groups, the Council on American-Islamic Relations (CAIR) and the Muslim American Society (MAS). The UAE, like its Gulf Arab neighbors, has been concerned that the MB is seen as a legitimate political force in the West. Their action against CAIR and MAS was meant to give support to those in the U.S. government who view negatively those groups, alleged to support the MB, and who wish to officially designate the MB as a terrorist organization. (In 2014 and again in 2015 there were unsuccessful attempts in the U.S Congress to pass legislation calling for President Obama to designate the MB as a foreign terrorist organization. Donald Trump had promised to do so during his presidential campaign and, during his first days in office was being urged to make good on his promise).[10] In June 2016, the UAE Federal Supreme Court convicted a group of four Emiratis and 15 Yemenis (the numbers vary slightly in different reports) of setting up a branch of the MB in the UAE. While one report maintained that the accused intended to overthrow the government, the generally light sentences received by the accused suggest that, though the actual threat was slight, the government continues to feel the need to counter any perceived challenge from the MB.[11]

Al-Islah

Al-Islah, also known as the Reform and Social Guidance Association, is the largest and best-organized opposition group in the UAE. It was originally founded in 1974 as a non-governmental organization (NGO) dedicated to promoting sports and cultural activity as well as charitable work. Throughout the 1980s and 1990s, the group adopted a political reform agenda. In recent years, the government has moved to curb its influence by prohibiting *al-Islah* members from holding public office and other prominent positions. The government now views *al-Islah* as a security threat.[12] As of 2012, the organization was estimated to have as many as 20,000 UAE residents affiliated with it.[13] From December 2011 through 2012, UAE officials, convinced that *al-Islah* was actively working with the MB, especially in Egypt, to challenge the country's political system, arrested a number of the group's members.[14] The crackdown culminated in arrests at the end of 2012 of members of an MB "spy ring" alleged to be collecting secret defense information and contemplating actions calculated to lead to regime change in the UAE. The forceful reaction of the government reflected its fear that Egypt's MB-dominated government was seeking to destabilize the Gulf monarchies by spreading its populist form of political Islam.[15]

The November 2014 list of "terrorist" organizations outlined by the UAE government, and continued arrests of suspected extremists, suggests that, well after the fall of President Morsi and the repression of the MB in Egypt, the UAE continues to perceive *Al-Islah* to be a political threat.[16] However, the UAE appears to lack an internal consensus as to *al-Islah's* true identity; analysts cannot agree on whether it is a chapter of the MB, a group that embraces a similar ideology without organizational links, or is simply deeply influenced by the Brotherhood.[17] These competing views complicate governmental responses to the group. The Emirati government fears that *al-Islah* could become an analog to the MB in Egypt, though it is probably more accurate to characterize the organization as non-revolutionary and focused on the reform and restructuring of government. *Al-Islah's* base has been in Ras al-Khaimah and the other northern emirates, where resentment of the much greater wealth and opportunities in Abu Dhabi and Dubai can fuel Islamist impulses.[18]

Al-Qaeda

The terrorist attacks of September 11, 2001 highlighted links between the UAE and al-Qaeda. Two of the operatives who carried out the attacks were Emiratis, another had resided there during the planning of the attacks, and the planners had frequently transited the UAE. A further connection stems from the UAE being one of only three countries to recognize the Taliban regime in Afghanistan during its time in power (the others were Pakistan and Saudi Arabia).

Since 9/11, there have been no attacks carried out in the UAE or launched from its soil by al-Qaeda, but fairly numerous and credible threats have been reported, although not always with a high level of certainty. However, the presence of al-Qaeda operatives has been established conclusively. In November 2002, the suspected ringleader of the team that had attacked the *USS Cole* in 2000 in Aden, Yemen was captured in Dubai. The same year, credible reports claimed that a considerable number of al-Qaeda fighters captured in Afghanistan were UAE nationals, and that welfare associations in Dubai and Fujairah had been encouraging young men to join terrorist groups. These associations were also accused of sending money to radical groups in Afghanistan and South Asia. Arrests occurring in 2004 suggested that Dubai continued to be a waypoint for al-Qaeda operatives.[19] Then, in July 2005, a new group calling itself "The al-Qaeda Organization in the Emirates and Oman" issued a strong threat against rulers in the UAE, demanding that U.S. military installations in the country be dismantled immediately.[20]

In 2008, the British government issued warnings of the risk of terrorist attacks in the UAE, likely connected to threats from al-Qaeda.[21] Then, in 2009, American officials confirmed a report that UAE authorities had broken up a major terrorist ring in Ras al-Khaimah that spring, which had been plotting to blow up targets in Dubai. In September of the same year, a Saudi tip led to interception in Dubai of explosives, which operatives of al-Qaeda in the Arabian Peninsula (AQAP) claimed to have placed on UPS and FedEx flights.[22] In 2010, there were reports that a network of "semi-legal" mosques dominated by Salafi preachers posed a *jihadi* threat, and there was a purported threat from al-Qaeda. The reports, though coming from backers of Shaikh Khalid bin Saqr Al Qassimi, who is contesting the succession as ruler of Ras al-Khaimah, appeared credible. These occurrences indicate that al-Qaeda still has links to the UAE. Despite some initial press speculation that members of an alleged MB spy ring arrested in December 2013 had links to al-Qaeda, no subsequent reports, official or otherwise, have given any credence to that idea.[23]

Despite these plots and threats, no terrorist group has succeeded in carrying out an operation in the UAE to date, and al-Qaeda is no exception. Some *jihadi* internet forum discussants have suggested that al-Qaeda's failure to strike the UAE reflects lack of popular support for the organization, owing in part to the non-militant nature of Emirati fundamentalists, which in turn constrains al-Qaeda's ability to recruit locals.[24] The government, for its part, has taken measures to counter extremism, including a public awareness campaign conducted by religious authorities about the dangers of violent extremism.[25] On December 15, 2012, in Abu Dhabi, UAE Foreign Minister Sheikh Abdullah bin Zayed Al Nahyan opened the International Center for Excellence in Countering Violent Extremism (ICECVE), also called the Hedayah (Guidance) Center. Deputy Under Secretary of State William Burns represented the U.S. at the center's launch. The center's creation was an outgrowth of the Global Counter Terrorism Forum (GCTF) created by the U.S. Department of State in September 2011, which comprises some 30 countries and seeks to help its members develop research and training in counter-terrorism. The center has, since then, promoted cooperation among members of the GCTF on issues relating to violent extremism, perform research and issue studies on the subject, and offer assistance in capacity building to counter threats. In May 2015, Hedayah initiated implementation of a four year STRIVE Global Program funded by the EU and aimed at increasing the capacity of state and non-state actors to challenge effectively radicalization and recruitment leading to violent extremism. In December 2016, Hedayah and the United Nations Development Program (UNDP) held an international research conference in Jakarta, Indonesia to bring together researchers in the field of countering violent extremism (CVE) to share their recent research findings.[26]

While the threats from militant Islamist groups on Emirati soil appear slight at present, the activities of AQAP in Yemen are of great concern. The UAE, in partnership with U.S. special forces, is combatting AQAP in southern Yemen through military, economic, and humanitarian support. The UAE has focused its efforts in the southern parts of Yemen, while Saudi forces have concentrated their efforts on the anti-Houthi campaign in northern Yemen. The UAE has a unique rapport with the tribes in southern Yemen, as many southern Yemenis fled the civil war in the 1960-70s and settled in the UAE. A significant number of those migrants subsequently joined the UAE's security forces.[27] Beyond these ties, the UAE perceives the Houthis to be a serious national security threat, fearing that they might provide Iran, which is currently giving the Houthi-led forces considerable support, with a greater opportunity to destabilize the Arabian Peninsula.[28]

The Islamic State (Islamic State in Iraq and Syria, Daesh)

The UAE has also manifested its new regional assertiveness in its participation in the struggle against the Islamic State, or ISIS, now the world's leading Islamic terrorist organization. UAE participation in the anti-ISIS coalition was dramatically announced in 2014, when a female Emirati pilot flew her F-16 in the first wave of U.S.-led air attacks against ISIS targets in Syria.[29] In response, ISIS has promised action against Dubai and Abu Dhabi, and a handful of incidents have lent at least some credence to the threat. In January of 2016, the alleged leader of ISIS in the Gulf was put on trial in the UAE Federal Supreme Court, and the following month an ISIS sympathizer was detained for allegedly planning to detonate a grenade in a Dubai restaurant.[30] Also in February 2016, the same court sentenced four Emiratis to death in absentia for joining ISIS and fighting among its ranks in Syria.[31] Furthermore, there is evidence to suggest that money has been smuggled through Dubai to ISIS.[32] In coordination with the U.S., the UAE has taken a significant initiative in the social media front of the struggle with ISIS by establishing the Sawab Center in Abu Dhabi, designed to counter ISIS propaganda efforts online.[33] As with threats from al-Qaeda, the UAE seems reasonably protected from those of ISIS by its vigilance and its generally contented population enjoying the benefits of the country's great wealth.

The Taliban and Haqqani Network

Islamist activity involving South Asian residents in the UAE is significant, and reportedly has included support of terrorist groups operating in Afghanistan, Pakistan, and India. In October 2008, for example, national authorities uncovered a plot involving several individuals, including an Afghan, to provide funds to the Taliban. The U.S. government believes that the Taliban and the affiliated Haqqani Network are funded in part by donors in the UAE, drawing their support from the large Pashtun community there. The Taliban is also known to extort money from Afghan businessmen based in the UAE.[34] However, the size of both voluntary contributions and forced aid is still unknown at this time.

The Haqqani network and the Pakistani Taliban are both on the UAE's list of banned terrorist organizations, which was issued in November 2014.[35] There is evidence to suggest that these classifications do not seriously impede the groups' movements in the UAE. Mullah Akhtar Mohammad Mansour, the former Afghan Taliban leader who was killed in a U.S. drone strike in May 2016, frequently visited the UAE to raise funds for Taliban operations.[36]

Lashkar-e-Taiba

Lashkar-e-Taiba (LeT) developed out of the *Al-e-Hadith* movement, which has roots in both the Middle East and the Indian Subcontinent.[37] The Pakistan-based Islamist LeT reportedly received large amounts of money from Gulf-based networks, including funders in the UAE.[38] There likewise appears to be a link between the UAE and the LeT's terrorist activities carried out against India; an investigation of the 2003 bombings in Mumbai revealed a Dubai connection, through which *Lashkar-e-Taiba* operatives in that emirate colluded with cells in India. Other urban terrorist attacks in India revealed a similar link. An important part of the equation is the set of operational ties between the Student Islamic Movement of India and militant student groups in the UAE, as well as elsewhere in the Gulf. The November 2014 list of terror organizations outlawed by the UAE included *Lashkar-e-Taiba*, and the UAE has worked closely with India to counter terrorist groups, notably the Indian Mujahdeen, which is closely linked with LeT. Intelligence sharing between the two countries led to the UAE turning over key operatives of the Mujahideen who had been hiding in the Emirates to India.[39]

ISLAMISM AND SOCIETY

Estimates of the UAE's population vary greatly. The UN's 2016 estimate is over 9 million while, for the same year, the CIA's estimate is just under 6 million. Native Emiratis are in a decided minority, about 19%, while South Asians (Indians, Pakistanis, Sri Lankans, and Bengalis), account for 50%, Iranians and other Arabs make up 23%, and Westerners and East Asians account for the remaining 8%. Citizens are almost exclusively Muslim, and Islam is the religion of 76% of the entire population.

Christians represent 9% of the population, and Hindus and Buddhists are the largest religious groups among those that comprise the balance.[40] The UAE constitution guarantees freedom of worship and declares all persons equal before the law without discrimination on the basis of religious belief. The State Department has reported that "Christian churches and Hindu and Sikh temples operated on land donated by the ruling families… Other minority religious groups conducted religious ceremonies in private homes without interference." The report added that "Within society there was tolerance for non-Muslims, including for holiday celebrations and traditions, although there was pressure discouraging conversion from Islam.[41] Sunni Emiratis adhere to the Maliki school of Islamic law, which is officially recognized in Abu Dhabi and Dubai, and the Hanbali school that predominates elsewhere (except in Fujairah, where the Shafi'i school holds sway).[42]

Attitudes toward Islamic groups in the UAE are difficult to discern since there is no significant direct popular participation on their part in government. While the constitution mandates freedom of speech, public assembly and association are still subject to government approval. Although the press is among the freest in the Arab world, it exercises self-censorship on sensitive issues, and the broadcast media are government-owned. Thus, attitudes concerning Islamic groups and their activities can be assessed mainly by inference rather than by consideration of explicit expressions of opinion.[43]

Moreover, the identification of Islamist groups is itself somewhat problematic, because there is considerable overlap in the missions of organizations, notably in the areas of philanthropic and religious concern. Curiously, the government identifies fewer than three percent of associations in the UAE as religious.[44] Many of the groups placed under the headings "cultural," "folklore," and "human services" are to one degree or another Islamic in orientation.

The sampling of Islamic groups examined below is broadly representative of those that are active in the UAE. This stratum includes both organizations that are part of native Emirati society and those that belong to various expatriate Muslim communities. To the extent that UAE organizations are identified with the promotion of Islamic objectives, they generally reflect the conservative nature of Islam in the country. However, differences exist; organizations in Dubai tend to reflect the cosmopolitanism of that emirate, with its very large expatriate population, including more than 150,000 from Europe and the United States, while in Abu Dhabi they exhibit a generally more conservative nature in keeping with its character, and in Sharjah they reflect the ruler's commitment to upholding the strong Islamic norms of that emirate.

Emirati Islamic groups

The Mohammed bin Rashid Al Maktoum Foundation was launched in 2007 by the prime minister and ruler of Dubai, who also serves as vice president of the UAE, with a personal donation of a $10 billion endowment (one of the largest charitable donations in history). The Islamic component of the foundation's mission is not explicit, but it is nonetheless significant. A central element of the foundation is the Bayt ul-Hikma, designed to disseminate knowledge in the Arab world and named for the House of Knowledge that represented the apogee of Islamic science and learning in the Abbasid Empire of the Middle Ages.[45]

In Abu Dhabi, the more modestly funded Sheikh Zayed bin Sultan Al Nahyan Charitable and Humanitarian Foundation was established in 1992 with a $100 million endowment. Its mission is more overtly aimed at advancing Islamic goals than that of the Al Maktoum Foundation, and includes the support of mosques, educational and cultural institutions, and the financing of both Emiratis and other Muslims in performing the *Hajj*. The foundation supports humanitarian projects, including a camp and hospital for Syrian refugees in Jordan, and assists low income Emiratis and others in building, refurbishing, and maintaining housing.

The Tabah Foundation is a non-profit institution established in 2005 in Abu Dhabi that seeks to promote a more effective contemporary Islamic discourse to advance Islamic values and counter negative images of Islam. Funded by various institutions and individuals in the UAE, Tabah entered into an agreement with the *Diwan* (Council of State) of the crown prince of Abu Dhabi, Sheikh Mohammed bin Zayed, to develop the Zayed House for Islamic Culture, and it established a media department, comprising both a television and documentary film division.[46]

Islamic groups serving the Indian and Pakistani communities in the UAE

The very large Indian and Pakistani communities in the UAE are served by numerous organizations, each associated with varying degrees of Islamic activity. While Indians clearly constitute the largest single community in the UAE, estimates of their number vary. In 2011, there were some 60 social and voluntary organizations serving the predominantly Muslim Indian community.

By contrast, there are few Islamic organizations in the Pakistani community in the UAE. Most Pakistani organizations in the country are business or financial associations or are devoted to providing aid to earthquake and flood victims in Pakistan. However, there is an Ismaili Centre in Dubai, dedicated in 2003 by the Aga Khan, spiritual leader of the Ismaili community, whose followers in the UAE are Pakistani and Indian expatriates. The site for the center was a gift of Sheikh Mohammed bin Rashid Al Maktoum, ruler of Dubai. The Ismaili Centre, which opened in 2008, is meant to serve, in the tradition of Muslim piety, by promoting enlightenment and mutual understanding among the various elements of the Muslim world community. To that end, it carries out a program of cultural and educational activities.[47]

As the above descriptions suggest, there is little if any political aspect to the missions and activities of the Islamic organizations in the UAE, both those serving the Emirati community and those serving the large expatriate Muslim communities. None could be characterized as extreme in any sense. All would appear to fit well within the mainstream of moderate Islamic activity.

Sporadic signs of extremist activity do exist, however. In April 2010, the Federal Supreme Court sentenced five UAE nationals and an Afghan on charges of funding the Taliban, and government officials indicated that those individuals had also planned to establish an al-Qaeda network in the UAE. At the end of that year, two Pakistanis were put on trial, charged with collecting money and recruiting individuals for al-Qaeda.[48] The scope of terrorist linkage with South Asia would appear to be limited, and, as noted above, anti-terrorist cooperation between India and the UAE has been strengthened. Also, as noted earlier, the UAE has taken the fight to AQAP. While that organization's stated threats against the UAE should not be lightly dismissed, they do not currently constitute a credible danger.

ISLAMISM AND THE STATE

The government of the UAE funds or subsidizes the majority of Sunni mosques in the country, while about five percent are privately endowed. It employs all Sunni *imams*, and provides guidance to both Sunni and Shi'a clergy. Shi'a mosques are considered private, but may receive funds from the government upon request. The Shi'a community is largely concentrated in the emirates of Dubai and Sharjah, with the bulk of its members in the former.[49] A number of new mosques have been built, or are under construction, throughout the country. Notable among them are mosques in Fujairah and Ajman. The Shaikh Zayed Mosque of Fujairah, completed in January 2013, although located in one of the smallest and poorest of the emirates in the UAE, is the second largest in the country, accommodating 28,000 worshippers. Funded by the Zayed bin Sultan Al Nahyan Charitable and Humanitarian Foundation of Abu Dhabi at a cost of $52.1 million, it follows in the mold of its namesake, the Grand Mosque in Abu Dhabi, as an expression of local pride and the ruling family's commitment to Islam. By contrast, the much more modest mosque opened in Ajman in 2011 (designed to hold 1,500 worshippers) is being funded by a donation from Hamad Ghanem Al Shamsi, a member of a distinguished and wealthy Ajman family. In 2015 and 2016, 10 new mosques, all of modest size, were built in Ajman.[50]

In December 2010, plans for four new Shi'a mosques were unveiled by the Khoja Shi'a Ithna-Ashari Jamaat (KSIMC) of Dubai, a private Shi'a religious philanthropy, with the sites for the structures provided by the government of Dubai. Typical of KSIMC activities was a 2013 seminar aimed at developing leadership skills. The members of the Shi'a community, through a Shi'a endowment fund known as the Awqaf Al Jafferiah, raised the funds to construct the mosques.[51] While there is no evidence to suggest that Shi'a (or Sunni) mosques have any connection with political or extremist motives, in 2012 a Khoja Shi'a *madrasa* in Dubai was closed and Shi'a mosque activities were restricted. The UAE government gave no explanation for these actions. These events came in the wake of numerous deportations of Shi'as from the UAE, including long-term Lebanese residents, who were forced to leave the country over fears of possible Hezbollah connections.[52]

From its birth in 1971, the UAE has been supportive of moderate, apolitical Islamic activities, while opposing those that might pose a threat to the government. Shaikh Zayed bin Sultan Al Nahyan, the father of the UAE and its president from inception until his death in 2004, embodied that philosophy both in his rule and in his personal life. He was generous in his support of religious leaders, thus arming himself and the state against attacks from secular or religious quarters. The chief threat to the UAE in the first years of its independence was secular radicalism in the region, especially as given expression by the Marxist government of the People's Democratic Republic of Yemen (PDRY), or South Yemen, and the guerrilla movements supported by the PDRY in their efforts to overthrow the government of the Sultanate of Oman, the UAE's immediate neighbor. Because of Zayed's close and positive relations with the UAE religious leadership, and the lack of extremist Islamic activity in the UAE before the events of September 11, 2001, the UAE's connections with those events was shocking and deeply embarrassing to Zayed and the UAE government.

Post-September 11th, the government reacted promptly (albeit cautiously) to the threat posed by al-Qaeda. While the generally moderate nature of Islamic belief and practice in the UAE precluded broad support for the ideology of al-Qaeda and other extremist groups, popular antipathy for some U.S. government actions in the Middle East has somewhat complicated the government's cooperation with the United States against Islamic terrorism.[53] In 2002, under Zayed's leadership, a contingent of UAE troops was deployed to Afghanistan to help in the struggle to unseat the Taliban, whose government the UAE had recognized before 9/11. Also in 2002, UAE authorities announced that they had arrested Abd al-Rahim al-Nashri, the apparent mastermind behind the October 12, 2000 attack on the *USS Cole* in Aden.[54]

In the past few years, the UAE has taken significant steps to counter Islamic terrorism, generally winning praise from the U.S. government for its efforts. While the general tendency of the UAE's rulers has been to co-opt potential troublemakers, the State Department noted that the UAE's preferred approach was to deny extremists a foothold, rather than permit their participation in the political process.[55] Abu Dhabi Crown Prince Mohammed bin Zayed also cited a threat from Islamic extremism to the country's educational system, and sought to counter this by devoting considerable resources to modernizing curricula. While, in the past, UAE funds given for house construction and humanitarian programs in Gaza may have ended up supporting activities of Hamas, including terrorism, there is evidence that the UAE's position on Hamas has dramatically shifted. The UAE was reportedly aware in advance of Israel's 2014 offensive against Gaza and urged the elimination of Hamas because of its close ties with the MB. Recent UAE support for housing in Gaza has been coordinated with the UN Relief and Works Agency (UNRWA).[56]

There is also concern that the UAE, while acting promptly when provided with evidence of a terrorist threat, does not have a proactive strategy for dealing with it.[57] In the past two years, however, UAE counter-terrorism measures have been robust. State Department reports have summed up UAE anti-terrorist activity by observing that "the UAE has arrested senior al-Qaeda operatives; denounced terror attacks; improved border security; instituted programs to counter violent extremism; investigated suspect financial transactions; criminalized use of the Internet by terrorist groups; and strengthened its bureaucracy and legal framework to combat terrorism."[58] Recently, the UAE demonstrated its cooperation with the U.S. on this front when it accepted 15 detainees from the Guantanamo Bay prison, the largest such transfer during Barack Obama's presidency. In the UAE, the released detainees will be put in a rehabilitation program modeled after a Saudi program designed to de-radicalize the former prisoners.[59]

The UAE has exhibited considerable concern over the threat of Shi'a extremism, prompted largely by fears of infiltration by Iranian agents and Iran-linked sleeper cells that could sabotage critical UAE sectors, including energy and transportation. The existence of both was reportedly revealed in 2007 by a former Iranian consul in Dubai. Actions were taken in 2009, not against Iranians but against Lebanese accused of links to Hezbollah, Lebanon's powerful Iranian-supported militia. The UAE deported 44 Lebanese men, who had worked both in the public and private sectors, for sending small amounts of cash to groups affiliated with Hezbollah. The UAE Foreign Ministry said that the deportations were for violations of a type "that harms the security of the UAE." The UAE remains very concerned about a possible threat from resident Shi'as, especially those from Lebanon. This will continue to be the case as long as Hezbollah and Iran continue actively to support the Assad government in Syria, and as the Sunni-Shi'a divide grows more pronounced and dangerous in the Middle East.[60]

Another area of concern is the flow of money from private donors to support extremist Sunni groups fighting in Syria, like the Islamic State of Iraq, *Jabhat al-Nusra*, and *Ahrar al-Sham*. While some of the funds are specifically targeted at assisting militias, much of the money is raised under the guise of humanitarian assistance. A Gulf-based organization, the Ummah Conference, recruits Muslim (Sunni) volunteers for Syria. Former senior military officers from the UAE head the UAE branch of the organization.[61]

The case of the Bank of Credit and Commerce International (BCCI), which was infiltrated and used for criminal money laundering and terrorist financing before its collapse in 1991, foreshadowed the complex and difficult problems that gained prominence after 9/11, when the UAE, with U.S. support and urging, tackled the problem of the financing of Islamic terrorism. Al-Qaeda was able to use a correspondent banking network to transfer funds from the Dubai Islamic bank to accounts in the United States for use by the 9/11 hijackers.[62] After 9/11, the UAE Central

Bank took steps to counter money laundering. While refusing to ban the traditional *hawala* system of money exchange in wide use between South Asian expatriates in the UAE and their home countries, it imposed strict regulations on it. In 2004, the bank hosted the Second International Hawala Conference to discuss with delegates from around the world more effective monitoring of informal money flows.[63] While the UAE's efforts against money laundering and terrorist financing have been significant, cause for worry remains. Particular attention focuses on Dubai and its large Free Trade Zone, because of its potential facilitation of a variety of criminal and terrorist activities, including the use of front companies, fraud, and smuggling, as well as exploitation of the *hawala* and banking systems. In 2011, the UAE reported that there had been a significant increase in the number of suspicious activity reports submitted by companies to the central bank for 2010 as compared to 2009. While this very likely reflected an improvement in the monitoring of money-laundering practices, the volume itself was cause for concern.[64] In 2013, the U.S. continued to press the UAE on greater coordination of sanctions against illicit financial transactions. American concerns reflect the UAE's large financial services sector and its proximity to Iran. Thus, the U.S. has closely scrutinized the operations of UAE financial institutions and, in 2012, took strong actions against two financial service companies with ties to Iran, pursuing them for alleged sanctions violations.[65] In July 2012, the UAE Central Bank issued regulations that made *hawala* registration mandatory with sanctions for non-compliance. Moreover, the public was cautioned about dealing with unlicensed charities.[66] In October 2014, the U.S. and the UAE established a joint financial counter-terrorism task force. In presenting the initiative, David Cohen, the U.S. Treasury Department undersecretary for terrorism and financial intelligence, stated that: "we have a very good close relationship with the Emiratis in combating terrorist financing…"[67] At the same time, concerns remain about the UAE serving as a haven for funds connected with terrorist activity. This was underscored in a news report concerning a Taliban bombing in Kandahar that killed five UAE diplomats. The report noted that "Dubai has come under scrutiny as a haven for money funneled out of Afghanistan."[68]

The UAE has perceived the Islamist threat in two ways— as the specifically terrorist threat of al-Qaeda and ISIS and as the broad populist threat represented by the MB and Iranian Shi'ism. Cooperation with the U.S. in combatting terrorism and drying up its sources of financing has been increasingly close and effective. There have been no reports of terrorist incidents in the UAE for the past several years. While some concerns remain, especially with respect to laundering and transfer of funds supporting terrorism, the UAE's success in countering terrorism has been impressive. The greater concern in the UAE today is with the impact of the Arab spring and the events it has set in motion. The rise to power of the MB in Egypt was alarming, especially because of the influence that the MB had exercised in the UAE in earlier years and because of the existence of an MB affiliate in the UAE, al-Islah. This accounts for the increased crackdown on dissent and the wide-ranging government identification of "terrorist" organizations, even including two U.S. NGOs. It also explains the expulsion of foreign NGOs working to help build civil society in the UAE, like the NDI and the Gallup Organization. At the same time, fear of Iranian actions and influence, given the UAE's proximity to Iran and its considerable Shi'a minority, has led to harsh treatment of expatriate Shia's, especially those from Lebanon, because of possible links to Hezbollah. These perceived threats have also led to a more assertive role in the Middle East region, including active cooperation with the U.S. against ISIS and against al-Qaeda and the Houthi-led forces in Yemen.

Endnotes

[1] *The 9/11 Commission Report* (New York: W.W. Norton & Company, Inc., 2004), 162, 231, and 168.

[2] Yara Bayoumy, "Seven alleged al Qaeda-linked plotters arrested in United Arab Emirates," Reuters, April 18, 2013, http://worldnews.nbcnews.com/2013/04/18/17806327-seven-alleged-al-qaeda-linked; Brian Murphy, "UAE sentences 69 suspects to prison in mass coup plot trial," Associated Press, July 2, 2013, http://www.foxnews.com/world/2013/07/02/united-arab-emirates-sentences-68-suspects-in-mass-trial-over-alleged-coup-plot.html; Kenneth Katzman, *The United Arab Emirates* (UAE): *Issues for U.S. Policy*) Washington, DC, Congressional Research Service, 2016, 5 and 6; and "UAE jails Emiratis up to 10 years for Islamist links," November 14, 2016, https://www.yahoo.com/news/uae-jails-emiratis-10-years-islamist-links-172617458.html.

[3] Courtney Freer, "The Muslim Brotherhood and the Emirates: Anatomy of a crackdown," *Middle East Eye*, December 17, 2015, http://www.middleeasteye.net/essays/muslim-brotherhood-emirates-anatomy-crackdown-1009823835.

[4] Lori Plotkin Boghardt, "The Muslim Brotherhood on Trial in the UAE," Washington Institute for Near East Policy *Policywatch* no. 2064, April 12, 2013, http://www.washingtoninstitute.org/policy-analysis/view/the-muslim-brotherhood-on-trial-in-the-uae.

[5] Sultan Al Qassemi, "The Brothers and the Gulf," *Foreign Policy*, December 14, 2012, http://www.tvballa.com/2012/12/.../qassemi-al-sultan-and-gulf-brothers.

[6] Sultan Al Qassemi, "Qatar's Brotherhood Ties Alienate Fellow Gulf States," *Al-Monitor*, January 23, 2013, http://www.almonitor.com/pulse/originals/2013/01/qatar-muslim-brotherhood.html; Rachel Ehrenfeld, J. Millard Burr, "The Muslim Brotherhood Deception & Education," American Center for Democracy, April 18, 2013, http://acdemocracy.org/the-muslim-brotherhood-deception-education/; and "Ruling Marks

[7] As cited in Marc Lynch, "MB in the Gulf," *Abu Aardvark blog*, June 10, 2008, http://abuaardvark.typepad.com/abuaardvark/2008/06/mb-in-the-gulf.html.

[8] Samir Salama, "Muslim Brotherhood is Political and not Religious," *Gulf News*, September 22, 2008.

[9] "The UAE and Saudi War on the Muslim Brotherhood Could Be Trouble for the U.S.," *Geopolitical Diary*, November 18, 2014, https://www.stratfor.com/geopolitical-diary/uae-and-saudi-war-muslim-brotherhood-could-be-trouble-us.

[10] Ibid and Adam Taylor, "Why the UAE is calling 2 American groups terrorists," *Washington Post*, November 17, 2014; Freer, "The Muslim Brotherhood and the Emirates" and "The UAE and Saudi War;" Julian Hattem, Cruz bill would designate Muslim Brotherhood as terrorist group," The Hill, November 4, 2015, http://thehill.com/policy/national-security/259099-cruz-bill-would-designate-muslim-brotherhood-as-terrorist-group; and Nahal Toosi, "Activists poke Trump to move faster on Muslim crackdown," Politico, January 24, 2017, http://www.politico.com/story/2017/01/trump-muslim-crackdown-234128.

[11] "Verdict on 'Yemeni Muslim Brotherhood,' Group was accused of setting up a branch of the Muslim Brotherhood," *Emirates 24/7 News*, http://www.emirates247.com/news/emirates/verdict-on-yemeni-muslim-brotherhood-2016-06-13-1.632926.

[12] Pekka Hakala, "Opposition in the United Arab Emirates," European Parliament, Directorate General for External Relations, Policy Department, November 15, 2012, http://www.europarl.europa.eu/committees/en/studies-download.html?...

[13] Jenifer Fenton, "Al-Islah in the UAE," Arabist, August 4, 2012, http://www.arabist.net/blog/2012/.../4/crackdown-on-islamists-in-the-uae.html.

[14] Human Rights Watch, "UAE: Crackdown on Islamist Group Intensifies," July 18, 2012, http://hrw.org/news/2012/07/18/uae-crackdown-islamist; Ali Rashid al-Noaimi, "Setting the Record Straight on al-Islah in the UAE," *Middle East Online*, October 17, 2012, http://www.middle-east-online.com/english/?id=54950.

[15] Al Qassemi, "The Brothers and the Gulf"; *Al Noaimi*, "Setting the Record Straight on al-Islah in the UAE"; Hassan Jouini, "Egypt-UAE Relations Worsen with 'Brotherhood' Arrests," Egypt Daily News, January 4, 2013, http://www.dailystar.com.lb/News/.../2013/Jan.../200804-egypt-uae-relations.

[16] Freer, "The Muslim Brotherhood and the Emirates"; *Amnesty International*, "UAE: Ruthless crackdown on dissent exposes 'ugly reality' beneath facade of glitz and glamour," November 18, 2014, https://www.amnesty.org/en/latest/news/2014/11/uae-ruthless-crackdown-dissent-exposes-ugly-reality-beneath-facade-glitz-and-glamour.

[17] Al Qassemi, "The Brothers and the Gulf"; Yara Bayoumy, "UAE Imprisons Islamist coup plotters," *Daily Star* (Beirut), July 3, 2013; "UAE sentences 69 suspects to prison in mass coup plot trial," Associated Press, July 2, 2013.

[18] Boghardt, "The Muslim Brotherhood on Trial in the UAE."

[19] Christopher M. Davidson, "Dubai and the United Arab Emirates: Security Threats," *British Journal of Middle Eastern Studies*, vol. 36, no. 3, July 1, 2011, pp. 28-29.

[20] Ibid., 446; Reacting to the berthing of U.S. aircraft carriers in Dubai, after their planes had carried out missions to "bombard the Muslims in Iraq and Afghanistan," the organization stated that the UAE's ruling families would "endure the fist of the mujahideen in their faces" if their demand was not met.

[21] Abdul Hamied Bakier, "An al-Qaeda Threat in the United Arab Emirates?" *Jamestown Foundation* Terrorism Focus 5, iss. 25, July 1, 2008, http://www.jamestown.org/single/?no_cache=1&tx_ttnews%5Btt_news%5D=5025.

[22] "Terror Network Dismantled in U.A.E.," Global Jihad, September 17, 2009; "AQAP Unlikely behind UPS Plane Crash - US Officials," *Reuters*, November 11, 2010, http://in.reuters.com/article/2010/11/11/idINIndia-52846520101111

[23] Rania El Gamal, "UAE Says it Arrested a Cell Plotting Attacks," Reuters, December 26, 2012 http://www.reuters.com/article/us-uae-saudi-plot-idUSBRE8BP08Q20121226 and "UAE arrests al-Qaeda cell 'plotters,'" *Al-Jazeera*, April 18, 2013, http://aljazeera.com/news/middleeast/2013/04/20134186290969992.html.

[24] Hamied Bakier, "An al-Qaeda Threat in the United Arab Emirates?" op. cit.

[25] "United Arab Emirates," in U.S. Department of State, International Religious Freedom Report 2011, July 30, 2012, http://www.state.gov/j/drl/rls/irf/2011religiousfreedom/index.htm?dlid=192911#wrapper.

[26] "First International Center for Countering Extremism Opens in Abu Dhabi," *Middle East Online*, December 15, 2012, http://www.middle-east-online.com/english/?id=56089; "Abdullah bin Zayed Opens Hedayah Centre for Countering Violent Extremism," UAE Interact, December 15, 2012; and "Keep Up with Hedayah," *Hedayah/LinkedIn*, nd, https://www.linkedin.com/company/hedayah.

[27] Kyle Monsees, "The UAE's Counterinsurgency Conundrum in Southern Yemen," Arab Gulf States Institute in Washington, August 18, 2016, http://www.agsiw.org/the-uaes-counterinsurgency-conundrum-in-southern-yemen/.

[28] Sigurd Neubauer, "Gulf States See Guantanamo Detainees As Policy Asset," Arab Gulf States Institute in Washington, September 9, 2016, http://agsiw.org/gulf-states-see-guantanamo-detainees-as-policy-asset.

[29] Ian Black, "UAE's leading role against ISIS reveals its wider ambitions," *Guardian* (London), October 30, 2014, https://www.theguardian.com/world/2014/oct/30/uae-united-arab-emirates-leading-player-opposition-isis-middle-east

[30] "UAE court gives four death sentence for supporting ISIS," *Al-Arabiyya* (Riyadh), February 14, 2016, http://english.alarabiya.net/en/News/middle-east/2016/02/14/UAE-Federal-Supreme-Court-sentences-defendants-for-joining-ISIS.html.

[31] Ibid.

[32] Paul Tilsley, "Jihadist couriers? Suspects nabbed at Johannesburg airport with $6M were ISIS-bound, say cops," *Fox News*, September 21, 2015, http://www.foxnews.com/world/2015/09/21/5-suspects-stopped-at-johannesburg-airport-with-6m-cash-headed-for-isis.html.

[33] "U.S., U.A.E. launch anti-ISIS messaging center in Dubai," *CBS News*, July 8, 2015, http://www.cbsnews.com/news/us-uae-launch-anti-isis-messaging-center-dubai/.

[34] "US Embassy Cables: Afghan Taliban and Haqqani Network Using United Arab Emirates as Funding Base," *Guardian* (London), December 5, 2010, http://www.guardian.co.uk/world/us-embassy-cables-documents/242756.

[35] "UAE bans five Pakistan-based outfits among terror groups," *The Economic Times*, November 16, 2014, http://articles.economictimes.indiatimes.com/2014-11-16/news/56137274

[36] Eltaf Najafizada, "Taliban Says Ex-Leader Often Visited United Arab Emirates, Iran," *Bloomberg*, May 26, 2016, http://www.bloomberg.com/news/articles/2016-05-26/taliban-says-ex-leader-often-visited-united-arab-emirates-iran.

[37] Animesh Roul, "Lashkar-e-Taiba's Financial Network Targets India from the Gulf States," *Jamestown Foundation* Terrorism Monitor 7, iss. 19, July 2, 2009, https://jamestown.org/program/lashkar-e-taibas-financial-network-targets-india-from-the-gulf-states/.

[38] Ibid.

[39] Think Chowdury, "India and the UAE: A Partnership Against Terrorism," Swarajya, August 25, 2015, http://swarajyamag.com/world/India-and-uae-a-partnership-against-terrorism

[40] CIA, The World Factbook, United Arab Emirates, updated January 17, 2017, HTTPS://www.cia.gov/library/publications/the-world-factbook/geos/ae.html.

[41] "United Arab Emirates" in United States Department of State, 2014 Report on International Religious Freedom, October 14, 2015, http://www.refworld.org/docid/56210535a.html.

[42] Malcolm C. Peck, The United Arab Emirates: A Venture in Unity (Boulder, CO: Westview Press, 1986), 60.

[43] In the fall of 2010, through an agreement with the Crown Prince Court of Abu Dhabi, the Gallup Organization opened a new research center in Abu Dhabi to conduct inquiries into attitudes of Muslims around the world. While the initial report it issued looked broadly at the state of Muslim-West relations, the Abu Dhabi Gallup Center was set up to perform research specifically on attitudes in the UAE. Most of the UAE polling, focused on non-controversial topics like healthcare access, although a poll on factors hindering women's entrepreneurship in the UAE and other GCC countries was conducted. However, the center was closed down in March 2012, when the UAE government ordered the closure of foreign NGOs, including the U.S.-based National Democratic Institute. Gallup reported that it "made the strategic decision to bring its efforts in Abu Dhabi back to its headquarters in Washington, DC" and that it "will continue to conduct research and publish findings about the region, and will maintain a presence in Dubai."See "Abu Dhabi and Gallup Establish New Research Center," PRNewswire, October 25, 2010, http://www.prnewswire.com/new-releases/abu-dhabi-and-gallup-establish-new-research-center-105668138.html and Vivian Nereim, "Gallup and think tank leave Abu Dhabi," The National, http://www.thenational.ae/news/uae-news/gallup-and-think-tank-leave-abu-dhabi. See also Shibley Telhami, The World Through Arab Eyes (New York: Basic Books, 2013), which presents some interesting results of polling done in the UAE.50.

[44] In 1998, the country's Ministry of Labour and Social Affairs listed 103 associations with only three described as "religious." See Munira A. Fakhro, "Civil Society and Democracy in the Gulf Region," 11th Mediterranean Dialogue Seminar: Security and Development in the Gulf Region, NATO Parliamentary Assembly, Doha, Qatar, November 26-28, 2005.

[45] "Mohammed bin Rashid Al Maktoum Foundation," Revolvy, nd (presumably 2015), https://www.revolvy.com/main/index.php?s=Mohammed%20bin%20Rashid%20AI%20Maktoum%20Foundation&item_type=topic

[46] See Tabah's newsletter, Clarity, its. 1, Fall 2010, for a discussion of its programs, http:/www.tabahfoundation.org/newsletter/pdfs/1/TabahNews-En_201009.pdf.

[47] Aga Khan, "Speech at the Foundation Laying of the Ismaili Center in Dubai," December 13, 2003, http://www.iis.ac.uk/view_article.asp?ContentID=101003.

[48] "UAE Sentences Six Convicted Taliban Agents," *World Tribune*, April 29, 2010, http://www.worldtribune/WTARC/2010/me_gulf0354_04_29.asp; "UAE Tries Two Pakistanis on Qaeda Links: Report," Al Arabiya, (Riyadh), December 28, 2010, http://www.alarabiya.net/articles/2010/12/28/131278.htnl.

[49] "United Arab Emirates," in U.S. Department of State, 2010 Report on International Religious Freedom, November 17, 2010, http://www.state.gov/j/drl/rls/irf/2010/148850.htm.

[50] See "Large Mosque Rising in Fujairah," Fujairah in Focus blog, June 6, 2010, http://fujairahinfocus.blogspot.com/2010/06/large-mosque-rising-in-fujairah-uae.html; see also General Authority of Islamic Affairs & Endowments," A New Mosque for 1500 Worshippers in Ajman," March 15, 2011, hrrp://www.awqaf.gov.ae/Newsitem.aspx?Lang=EN&SectionID=16&Ref ID=1092; and Rezan Oueiti, "New mosques in Ajman make room for everybody," The National, June 16, 2016, http://thenational.ae/uae/new-mosques-in-ajman-make-room-for-everybody.

[51] See KSIMC of Dubai, "Awqaf Al Jafferiah Launches Fund Raising for 4 New Mosque Projects in Dubai," December 14, 2010, http://dubaijamaat.com/latestnewsbloglayout/general-news/591-awqaf-al-jafferiah-lainches-fuind-raising-for-4-new.

[52] Esperance Ghanem, "What is behind UAE deportation of Lebanese nationals?" *Al Monitor*, April 17, 2015, http://www.al-monitor.com/pulse/originals/2015/04/lebanon-nationals-deportation-uae-decision.html#ixzz40DFzmDtB; and "Over 4000 Shiites deported from UAE," Shia World News Facebook, February 13, 2013, https://.facebook.com/newsshia/posts/337686526342852.

[53] See Malcolm C. Peck, Historical Dictionary of the Gulf Arab States, 2nd ed. (Lanham, MD: The Scarecrow Press, Inc. 2008), 144.

[54] Sultan Al Qassemi, "The Sacrifice of Our Troops and a Need for Civil Society," *The National* (Abu Dhabi), February 28, 2010, http://www.thenational.ae/news/the-sacrifice-of-our-troops-and-a-need-for-civil-society; Mohammed Nasser, "Military Expert: Al Qaeda Present in the Gulf... but not Active," Al-Sharq al-Awsat (London), December 29, 2010, http://www.aawsat.com/english/news.asp?section=1&id=23598

[55] "US Embassy Cables: Abu Dhabi Favours Action to Prevent a Nuclear Iran," *Guardian* (London), November 28, 2010, http://www.guardian.co.uk/world/us-embassy-cables-documents/59984

[56] "UAE, Israel have secret meeting, UAE 'offered to fund Israel's Gaza offensive,' *The Peninsula*, July 19, 2014, http://freedmanreport.com/?p=1651; and "600 UAE-funded housing units given to refugees in Gaza, Middle East, News, Palestine, UAE, December 7, 2015, https://www.middleeastmonitor.com/20151207-600-uae-funded-housing-units-given-to-refugees-in-gaza/.

[57] U.S. Embassy Abu Dhabi, "Scenesetter for Counterterrorism Coordinator."

[58] Cited in Kenneth Katzman, The United Arab Emirates (UAE): Issues for U.S. Policy, November 28, 2016, Congressional Research Service.

[59] Jess Bravin and Carole E. Lee, "U.S. Transfers 15 Guantanamo Bay Detainees," *Wall Street Journal*, August 15, 2016, http://www.wsj.com/articles/u-s-transfers-15-guantanamo-bay-detainees-1471303872.

[60] Hair Nayouf, "Iran has "sleeper cells" in the Gulf: Ex-diplomat," *Al Arabiya News*, October 30, 2007, https://english.alarabiya.net/articles/2007/10Abdul H/30/41005.html.; and Abdul Hameed Bakier, "Sleeper Cells and Shi'a Secessionists in Saudi Arabia: A Salafist Perspective," Jamestown Foundation Terrorism Monitor 7, iss. 18, June 25, 2009, http://www.jamestown.org/single/?no_cache=1&tx_ttnews%5Btt_news%5D=35182.; and Esperance Ghanem, op. cit. On fears of Iran and possible "fifth column" activities by UAE residents of Iranian origin, see Katzman, The United Arab Emirates, Congressional Research Service, June 18, 2013, p. 16.

[61] Joby Warrick, "Donors boost Islamists in Syria," *Washington Post*, September 22, 2013.

[62] See Peck, Historical Dictionary of the Gulf Arab States, 297; Steve Barber, "The 'New Economy of Terror:' The Financing of Islamist Terrorism," Global Security Issues 2, iss. 1, winter 2011, 5, 9.

[63] Barber, "The New Economy of Terror"; "Middle East and North Africa Overview," in U.S. Department of State, Office of the Coordinator for Counterterrorism, Country Reports on Terrorism 2005 (Washington, DC: U.S. Department of State, April 28, 2006), http://www.state.gov/s/ct/rls/crt/2005/64344.htm

[64] "Huge Global Problem, Small UAE Improvement," *Money Jihad blog*, February 10, 2011, http://moneyjihad.wordpress.com/2011/02/10/huge-global-problem-small-uae-improvement/

[65] Gregor Stuart Hunter, "U.S. official to focus on illicit finance and sanctions in UAE talks," *The National* (Abu Dhabi), January 27, 2013, http://www.thenational.ae. The two financial service companies were HSBC and Standard Chartered.

[66] Celina B. Realuyo, "Combating Terrorist Financing in the Gulf," The Arab Gulf States Institute in Washington, January 26, 2015.

[67] Taimur Khan, "Joint US-UAE task force to choke off ISIL funding," The National (Abu Dhabi), October 27, 2014, http://www.thenational.ae/world/middle-east/joint-us-uae-task-force-to-choke-off-isil-funding

[68] Said Salahuddin and Erin Cunningham, "Taliban video purports to show American, Australian captives' in tearful pleas to Trump," *The Washington Post*, January 12, 2017, https://www.washingtonpost.com/world/5-uae-diplomats-discussing-aid-projects-killed-in-kandahar-blast/2017/01/11/fa92e870-d7d1-11e6-b8b2-cb5164beba6b_story.html?utm_term=.384df521b00c.

YEMEN

Quick Facts

Population: 27,392,779 (July 2016 est.)

Area: 527,968 sq km

Ethnic Groups: predominantly Arab; but also Afro-Arab, South Asians, Europeans

Religions: Muslim 99.1% (official; virtually all are citizens, an estimated 65% are Sunni and 35% are Shia), other 0.9% (includes Jewish, Baha'i, Hindu, and Christian; many are refugees or temporary foreign residents) (2010 est.)

Government Type: in transition

GDP (official exchange rate): $31.33 billion (2015 est.)

Map and Quick Facts courtesy of the CIA World Factbook (Last Updated January 2017)

Overview

Yemen is a fragile Gulf state home to numerous Salafi-jihadi and Islamist groups, including al-Qaeda in the Arabian Peninsula (AQAP), a leading al-Qaeda affiliate, and an Islamic State branch. Both al-Qaeda and the Islamic State have exploited the conditions created by Yemen's collapse into civil war. The breakdown of the Yemeni state over the course of the civil war will add to historical internal challenges, including political and economic instability, declining oil reserves, severe water shortages, internally-displaced persons (IDPs), and deep-seated ethnic and religious tensions.

Islamist extremist and separatist groups have taken advantage of Yemen's general instability to advance their political agendas and create terrorist safe-havens in the country. The Yemeni government, for its part, has coordinated closely with the United States on counterterrorism operations to target AQAP leaders, including through the use of U.S. drone strikes on Yemeni soil.

The economic, social and security issues that plague the Yemeni state, coupled with civil war, have paralyzed the Yemeni government. It is not able to provide effective governance and security to much of the country. The Zaydi Shi'a Houthi movement is a powerbroker in the Sana'a-based government, having seized control of the state after the collapse of the National Dialogues Conference. AQAP, which governed certain areas for over a year, has expanded its influence and the Islamic State now has a foothold in Yemen. Both groups will continue to operate in the country as long as the civil war continues.

ISLAMIST ACTIVITY

The land of Yemen holds religious significance in Islam. There are two *hadiths* (accounts of the sayings of Muhammad) directly referencing the area. The first prophesies that a Muslim army of 12,000 men will rise from Aden and Abyan in southern Yemen to give victory to Allah. The second states that two religions would not co-exist on the Arabian Peninsula, implying that Islam would overcome the other. Yemen's status in Islam has made it important to international Islamist groups, particularly *Salafi-jihadi* ones.

Yemen has served as a safe haven to opposition and terrorist groups of varying political stripes throughout its history. Prior to the unification of traditionalist North Yemen and Marxist South Yemen in 1990, the latter was used as a sanctuary for a wide array of Palestinian and terrorist organizations with the support of local authorities. Since unification, this tradition of support for subversive groups has continued, but radical Palestinian and leftist organizations have been replaced by extremist Islamist organizations, especially those in opposition to the Saudi monarchy.[1]

Yemen's prolonged civil conflicts, increasing sectarianism and the absence of an effective central government have created the conditions for the development of homegrown Islamist militants like the Houthis, as well as a safe haven for international *Salafi-jihadi* organizations like al-Qaeda. Yemen's education system, which uses textbooks containing some degree of anti-American and anti-Israeli ideology, coupled with an employment rate of around 35 percent, are factors that play into the vulnerability of young men to be exploited by Islamist militant organizations.[2]

Further compounding the problem is the accessibility of weapons through Yemen's vast underground arms market; roughly three guns exist for every one person in Yemen.[3] The Yemeni political and social landscape is replete with tribal leaders and Islamist groups that have the arms and power to deny the Yemeni government a monopoly on the use of violence. Under these conditions, analysts have noted, "piracy, smuggling and violent jihad can flourish, with implications for the security of shipping routes and the transit of oil"[4] through the Red Sea to the Suez Canal.

The ouster of the country's longtime autocratic president, Ali Abdullah Saleh, and the political transition that followed his departure have transformed Yemeni politics. After 33 years in power, Saleh was removed from power following widespread anti-government protests in 2011 during Yemen's Arab Spring. A U.S.-backed, Gulf Cooperation Council (GCC)-brokered transition agreement led to a referendum electing former vice president Abd Rabu Mansour Hadi as Saleh's replacement. Hadi later presided over a National Dialogues Conference to lay the groundwork for a new Yemeni Constitution. The National Dialogue Conference, the forum to address long-standing grievances against the government, included a number of opposition groups and Islamist factions, including Shi'ite Houthi rebels in the north.[5]

Opposition groups decried the transition process after it did not fully shift power from the established elite. The Houthis left the negotiating table and began to militarize, advancing from their northern stronghold to Sana'a, the capital, with Saleh's support.[6] They forced the Hadi government to sign an agreement giving opposition groups, including the Southern Movement (*Hirak*), an umbrella group for southern opposition factions, more power in the government.[7] The Houthi coup culminated in the winter of 2015, when the Hadi government fled the country. An Arab coalition led by Saudi Arabia and including the United Arab Emirates intervened in Yemen in March 2015 in support of the Hadi government.[8] Civil war broke out between two large factions of loose, pragmatic alliances: the Houthi-Saleh faction and those opposed to it, now including the Southern Movement, the Sunni al-Islah party, local tribal militias, and al-Qaeda. The most radical actors on both sides of the civil war are actively promoting sectarianism in Yemen, where it had not been strong before.

Al-Qaeda

Al-Qaeda has a long-standing presence in Yemen. Yemenis ranked second only to Saudis in terms of nationals serving as members of the *mujahideen* who fought the Soviet Union in Afghanistan in the 1980s, a war that constituted a key milestone in the consolidation of radical Islam in Yemen. Yemenis trained under al-Qaeda's high command in Afghanistan throughout the 1990s, up until the U.S. invasion of Afghanistan in 2001.[9]

From its inception until the late 1990s, al-Qaeda maintained training camps in various locations in Yemen.[10] A November 1996 autobiography of bin Laden provided to the Islamist journal *Nida'ul Islam* highlighted the terrorist chief's enduring interest in Yemen and mentioned his support for the *mujahideen* fighting the Communist party in South Yemen in the early 1980s and later in the early 1990s.[11] In 1997, bin Laden reportedly sent an envoy to Yemen to explore the possibility of establishing a base there in the event the Taliban expelled him from Afghanistan.[12] The al-Qaeda leader also listed Yemen as one of six countries "most in need of liberation" in 2003.[13]

In the immediate aftermath of 9/11, the Yemeni government implemented stiff counterterrorism measures and cooperated with the United States to eliminate senior al Qaeda operative Abu Ali al-Harithi in November 2002.[14] By the end of 2003, however, Sana'a began to lag in its counterterrorism efforts and in February 2006 twenty-three al-Qaeda terrorists, including the mastermind of the 2000 *USS Cole* bombing, escaped from a Yemeni prison.[15] An October 2009 report by the American Enterprise Institute (AEI) asserted that:

> "Many Western intelligence analysts viewed elements of the Yemeni security apparatus as complicit in the prison break. The more relaxed security situation in Yemen stemmed both from complacency and the government's perceived need to reallocate security resources to address other domestic threats. Such circumstances made Yemen a favorable alternative location for al-Qaeda to plan, train for, and execute attacks against the regimes of Saudi Arabia and Yemen, both of which it views as hypocritical, apostate puppets of the West."[16]

In the late 2000s, Yemen was a fragile state on the brink of failure focused on putting down the Houthi rebellion in the north. The state's distraction made the country ideal as a base of operations for al-Qaeda in the Arabian Peninsula (AQAP), which represented a merger of Yemeni and Saudi branches of al-Qaeda in January 2009. Yemen was a likely choice for the newly consolidated al-Qaeda movement after the Saudi government imposed a crackdown inside its borders following a series of terrorist attacks in the Kingdom between May 2003 and December 2004 against oil company offices, foreign targets, Saudi government offices, and security targets.[17]

Since its establishment, AQAP has been the most active of al-Qaeda's affiliates in targeting the United States. It has been implicated in a number of terrorist operations, including: a suicide bombing against a group of South Korean tourists in Hadramawt and a South Korean diplomatic convoy to Sana'a; the attempted suicide bombing targeting Saudi Deputy Interior Minister Prince Mohammed bin Nayef; and the ambush and killing of seven Yemeni security officials near the Saudi border.[18]

AQAP repeatedly attempted to attack the United States homeland, or American interests. It claimed responsibility for the attempted Christmas Day 2009 downing of Detroit-bound Flight 253 by Nigerian extremist Umar Farouk Abdulmutallab.[19] AQAP also claimed the cargo plane bomb plot foiled in Dubai and the UK in October 2010, noting it was behind the September 2010 downing of a UPS flight in Dubai, although U.S. officials have found no conclusive connection between the crash and terrorism.[20] The group attempted to attack the United States again in May 2012 (an attack which was thwarted by a Saudi intelligence tip), and was behind the threat stream that closed over twenty U.S. diplomatic missions across the Middle East and North Africa in August 2013.[21]

AQAP is conducting an insurgency within Yemen. The group seeks to mobilize the country's Sunnis behind it against the Yemeni state. AQAP operates within local customs and developed local relations based on pragmatic lines of support.[22] It does not require ideological alignment to support various groups and factions. It uses asymmetrical attacks to degrade Yemeni military capabilities, as well as other forces opposed to it. The group conducts targeted assassinations against military and government leadership, as well as against intelligence officers and local powerbrokers aligned with the government. AQAP has kidnapped individuals for ransom money and could in the future use this tactic to gain political leverage over foreign powers. The kidnapping of Saudi deputy consul Abdallah al-Khalidi at his home in the south Yemeni port city of Aden in March 2012 is one such example.

The number of Yemenis claiming allegiance to AQAP is unknown, although Yemeni Foreign Minister Abu Bakr al-Qirbi claimed in late 2008 that Yemen was playing host to more than 1,000 *jihadist* fighters and al-Qaeda affiliates.[23] This number has increased significantly as AQAP and associated organizations active in Yemen, such as Ansar al-Sharia, have increased their power and influence in southern Yemen. More recently, fighters have traveled from conflicts in Syria and Iraq to Yemen, bringing with them new skills and tactics.[24] Even before the 2011 anti-government protests swept through Yemen, AQAP had been on a path to establishing links with tribes in the Marib, al-Jawf and Shabwah governorates of eastern Yemen.[25]

In the wake of the 2011 uprisings, AQAP sought to capitalize on the political transition, increasing its attacks against government targets. AQAP's insurgent arm, Ansar al-Sharia, seized key cities in the south, including the provincial capital of Abyan province, Zinjibar. Ansar al-Sharia held Zinjibar from May 2011 until the Yemeni military, aided by tribal militias known as Popular Committees, were able to overrun the al-Qaeda "emirates" in late June 2012.[26] AQAP has found a more favorable political climate in the aggrieved Sunni south, though its mass appeal remains limited in a region historically dominated by socialism.

AQAP also conducts an international outreach strategy that is much more pronounced than that of other al-Qaeda affiliates. Anwar al-Awlaki, the late American-born Muslim cleric who became a leading figure within AQAP, ran an online campaign from Yemen to recruit and aid Muslims in foreign countries to carry out attacks that led to over a dozen terrorist investigations.[27] Al-Qaeda's English-language magazine, *Inspire*, has been produced in Yemen since 2010 and provides radicalizing literature and instructions for planning and conducting terrorist attacks.[28] AQAP released a shorter "Guide to Inspire" following the June 2016 Orlando shootings and the July 2016 attack in Nice that analyzed those attacks and provided additional guidance for would-be recruits.[29]

AQAP has strengthened significantly during Yemen's civil war.[30] It controlled al Mukalla, a major port city in southeast Yemen, for a year and also expanded its influence behind the frontlines of Yemen's war.[31] Its influence is growing in Taiz, Yemen's third-largest city, and it continues to have sanctuary in Abyan, al Bayda, Shabwah, Ma'rib and al Jawf. Leadership attrition has not had a significant effect on its operations, and the group continues to show it has developed resilience toward drone strikes. U.S.-backed Emirati counterterrorism operations are only focused on AQAP's presence in key populated areas, allowing the group to continue to develop elsewhere.

The Islamic State

The Islamic State is competing globally with al-Qaeda for leadership of the *Salafi-jihadi* movement. Yemen is key terrain for this contest, not just because of its religious significance but also because of the presence of AQAP.[32] To this end, the late Islamic State military commander Omar al Shishani mentioned Yemen among eight other fields of *jihad* in the Islamic State's celebratory June 2014 video calling for the end of borders that separate Muslims.[33]

Initial support for the Islamic State appeared in Yemen immediately after the group declared a Caliphate in June 2014. A prominent *Salafi-jihadi* cleric, Sheikh Ma'moun Abdulhamid Hatem, was one early supporter of the Islamic State.[34] Sheikh Hatem probably facilitated recruitment in Ibb for the Islamic State even as he remained within AQAP's network.[35] A Saudi Arabian national named Bilal al-Harbi, who was in communication with leadership in Syria by September 2014, was commissioned to gather pledges of allegiance to the Islamic State.[36] Al-Harbi is now one of the group's leaders in Yemen. Islamic State leader Abu Bakr al-Baghdadi recognized the Yemeni branch alongside four other groups in a November 2014 video.[37]

The Islamic State claimed its first attack in Yemen on March 20, 2015, simultaneously bombing two mosques in Sana'a. The attack was the deadliest terrorist incident in Yemen to-date and targeted Zaydi Shi'a.[38] AQAP disavowed responsibility for the attack, noting that it does not target mosques or public spaces. The Sana'a mosque bombings began a series of attacks against targets, many of them civilian, that the Islamic State labeled as being "Houthi." These attacks are part of a global strategy by the Islamic State to increase sectarianism and mobilize the Sunni behind its leadership.[39]

The group shifted its primary focus from targeting the Houthis to targeting an Arab coalition and the Yemeni military and government it backed in October 2015. The Emiratis had led a ground offensive to re-instate the Yemeni government in Aden in July 2015 and were beginning to re-establish the internationally recognized government in the country. Islamic State militants targeted coalition and government sites in Aden on October 6, 2015.[40] The group began regular attacks in Aden through the winter and into spring 2016. It subsequently expanded attacks against the government to the southeastern port city of al Mukalla after an April 2016 Emirati-led offensive regained control of the city from AQAP.[41]

The Islamic State's expansion in Yemen has been limited because of AQAP's strong presence there, and because of how the Islamic State is choosing to operate. The targeting of non-combatants, a practice generally not seen in Yemen, has helped to alienate the population. The Islamic State uses a top-down leadership approach, working with a primarily non-Yemeni leadership body. Its leaders also do not follow Yemeni tribal customs, and in fact reject them entirely. Yemeni members of the Islamic State issued a public denouncement of the Islamic State's leadership in Yemen in two letters in December 2015, rejecting the leadership but reaffirming their allegiance to Baghdadi.[42] The Islamic State core group shut down the rebellion.

The Islamic State's cells in Yemen maintained a low-level of activity in 2016. For most of the year, ISIS only claimed attacks in the Hadramawt and Aden governorates, a significant decrease in activity (as well as the number of active cells)from 2015. ISIS began to claim attacks in central al Bayda governorate in the Fall of 2016, conducting asymmetrical attacks there against Houthi-Saleh forces. As of this writing, ISIS continues attacks against security forces in Aden.

The Houthi Movement

Prior to the 2011 "Arab Spring" uprisings, Yemeni military and security forces were already spread thin. The Saleh regime devoted considerable resources to suppressing a rebellion led by the Houthi family, from where the movement derives its moniker. The Houthis are Zaydi Shi'a and have a stronghold in northern Yemen. They were the most direct threat to the Yemeni state from 2004-2010. The Houthis have been engaged in an on-and-off guerrilla war with the Yemeni government since mid-2004, leading to the death and displacement of thousands. The Saleh regime accused the Houthis of receiving support from Iran and of "trying to reinstate the clerical imamate" (Shi'ite Islamic government) that ruled northern Yemen for roughly 1,000 years prior to 1962,[43] while the Houthis contend they are merely advocating "freedom of worship and social justice."[44]

Currently led by Abdul Malik al-Houthi, the younger brother of the group's founder, Sheikh Hussein Badreddin al-Houthi, the group has accused the Yemeni government of "widespread corruption, of aligning itself too closely with the United States, of allowing too much Wahhabi (fundamentalist Sunni) influence in the country, and of economic and social neglect in predominantly Shi'ite parts of the country."[45]

The origins of the contemporary conflict trace back to 2003, when followers of the group "Believing Youth" shouted anti-American and anti-Israeli slurs inside a Sa'ada mosque where then-president Saleh was attending service at a time when he was trying to maintain strong relations with the West.[46] The Yemeni government responded by killing Hussein al-Houthi in a firefight in September 2004. Houthi's followers took up arms for revenge. The Yemeni military's heavy hand caused collateral damage, drawing additional tribes behind the Houthis and mobilizing a large faction in northern Yemen.

In the years that followed, the Yemeni government and Abdul Malik al-Houthi expressed their readiness for dialogue on a number of occasions. However, several resulting ceasefire agreements proved short-lived. The Yemeni government and Houthis fought six small wars in the decade after 2004. In the fall of 2009, the conflict spilled over the Saudi border as Houthi fighters seized areas within Saudi Arabia and the Saudi military retaliated with air and ground forces to repel the Houthi incursion.[47]

Saudi Arabia has since launched an initiative to fortify its border with Yemen with motion sensors, infrared systems, and GPS trackers.[48] The initiative was launched in tandem with a March 2013 law that mandated the deportation of hundreds of thousands of illegal foreign residents.[49] The International Organization for Migration documents that almost 310,000 Yemenis returned to Yemen from Saudi Arabia between June 1, 2013 and February 28, 2014. A separate estimate found 27 percent of the deportees planned to return to Saudi Arabia when possible. Oman also perceives a security risk and is considering building a barrier along its own border with Yemen.[50]

As the conflict between the Yemeni military and the Shi'ite Houthis escalated, so too did accusations by the Yemeni and Saudi governments of Iranian involvement in arming the Houthis, though the evidence on this score is not conclusive. Overt, unofficial statements by Houthi officials to reporters,[51] recordings of conversations between smugglers and Quds forces,[52] and an intercepted Iranian ship off Yemen's southern coast carrying weapons including 10 Chinese anti-aircraft missiles originating from Iran have been wielded as evidence of Iranian involvement.[53] Tehran has vehemently denied these accusations and condemned Saudi Arabia's involvement in the conflict. Meanwhile, Houthi rebels have accused Saudi Arabia of supporting the Yemeni government and aiding its offensives, a charge which the Saudis have denied.[54]

There is increasing evidence that the Iranian regime is supporting the Houthi-Saleh faction in Yemen. In addition to the interdiction of weapons shipments transported by sea, there have been allegations that Iran is also moving weapons by land, through Oman.[55] The Houthi-Saleh forces, in turn, have used modified ballistic missiles against Saudi Arabia, a capability likely transferred from Lebanese Hezbollah, and an Iranian variant of the Chinese Silkworm missile was identified in the series of attacks against the U.S. naval presence in the Red Sea off Yemen's coast in October 2016.[56]

The Houthis were among many groups that supported the anti-Saleh protests that erupted in January 2011. As the military shifted its resources to restoring security in the capital and combating a growing threat from al-Qaeda in the south, the Houthis were emboldened to expand territorially. This led to clashes with the Sunni al-Islah party, as the two groups jockeyed for power and influence in the northern province of al-Jawf.[57] Adding to the Houthis' list of adversaries, in January 2011 AQAP deputy chief Saeed Ali al-Shihri declared *jihad* against "Iranian-backed Houthi Shiite advocates."[58] From spring 2011 through early 2013, there were reports of sectarian clashes between Houthi militants and Sunni tribes in the northern province of Sa'ada.[59] Another spike in violent activity began in October of 2013 in al-Jawf province after Houthis accused Sunni *Salafis* of recruiting foreign fighters.[60]

Since Saleh was ousted from power in 2011, the reconciliation process under the supervision of President Hadi has granted the Houthis political recognition with 35 of 565 seats at the National Dialogues Conference.[61] The Houthis, however, have continued to exercise military force to expand their influence throughout the process. The decision to divide Yemen into six administrative districts was against Houthi interests because the Houthis' stronghold would be isolated. The Houthis would also be required to compete with another powerful Zaydi family in Sanhan, Sana'a.[62]

The Houthis have had a partnership of convenience with Saleh and his allies since 2014 that has given them control of the capital, Sana'a, and the majority of Yemeni state infrastructure. They have been willing to negotiate a political settlement to the civil war, but have repeatedly rejected the terms put forward by the international community, which favor the Yemeni government. Saleh and the Houthis cut a power-sharing agreement in July 2016, establishing a political council to govern the country split between Saleh's General People's Congress party and the Houthis' Ansar Allah party.[63] The al Houthi-Saleh political council announced a 42-minister "National Salvation Government" on November 28, 2016.[64]

ISLAMISM AND SOCIETY

Historically, Yemeni society has been divided along two main religious identities, the Shi'ite Zaydi sect followed in the country's north and northwest, and the Shafa'i school of Sunni Islam predominant in the south and southeast. Although no accurate and reliable statistics exist, Sunnis are generally acknowledged to represent a majority among Yemen's population of 26 million, while Zaydis claim around 35 percent.[65] There is a strong Sunni *Salafi* trend within certain areas of Yemen. Zaydis are constituents of a Shi'a sect often described as moderate in its jurisprudence.[66]

In his studies of Islamism in Yemen, Laurent Bonnefoy of the Institut Français du Proche-Orient found that "despite episodes of violent stigmatization orchestrated by certain radical groups, the vast majority of the population is at times indirectly (and most of the time passively) involved in the convergence of the once-distinct Sunni and Zaydi religious identities."[67] He cites one such example of this as former president Saleh, who himself is of Zaydi origin but never refers to his primary identity. Bonnefoy goes on to say that: "at the grassroots level, many Sunnis do not mind praying in Zaydi mosques, and vice versa. Consequently, the religious divide only marginally structures political affiliations and adherence to specific Islamist groups."[68]

However, as anti-government protests threatened his presidency, Saleh drew on his Zaydi identity "in an attempt to rally Zaydi tribal solidarity against what he also allegedly framed as a Shafa'i-led protest movement," even going so far as to suggest that he could be the "last Zaydi president."[69] Such actions led to criticism that Saleh was "concentrating on solidifying tribal allegiances even at the cost of exacerbating sectarian divisions."[70] The increase in sectarian tensions in northern Yemen in recent years can be seen, in part, as a result of policies and governing strategies playing competing tribal and sectarian groups off of one another.

Rising sectarianism in the region against the backdrop of the wars in Syria and Iraq is also reflecting in Yemen. The Islamic State is intentionally provoking sectarian actions, as is a small faction of the Houthi movement. Saudi Arabia and Iran both see Yemen as a space for contest, though Yemen is much more important to Saudi Arabia. Iran provides the Houthis with minimal support to drive a Saudi response.[71]

ISLAMISM AND THE STATE

In a March 2009 journal article for *The Middle East Review of International Affairs* (MERIA), Laurent Bonnefoy pointed to the "presence of a strong traditional 'civil society' in the form of tribal and religious groups, most of them armed or capable of opposing the state" as a source in "undermining the regime's capacity to monopolize all the levers of power and fulfilling any totalitarian dreams."[72] For years, the regime maintained such power-sharing arrangements out of self-interest (i.e., weakening its enemies, dividing political and religious groups, etc.). Such arrangements, however, have been unable to withstand a range of endogenous and exogenous shocks.

Over the past decade, divisive policies and shifting political alliances stressed an already fragile system, due in large part to the erosion of the legitimacy and power of the central government. Allegations of widespread corruption, a growing view of the government as an American and Saudi puppet by Islamist groups, and widening economic and resource inequity all contribute to the government's domestic weakness. These trends became more pronounced as the counterterrorism partnership with Washington grew. Since President Hadi's ascension to power, U.S. officials noted "a new determination [and] a new consistency in terms of what the Yemeni government is doing on the counterterrorism front."[73]

The unification of Yemen was initially built upon a partnership between the two former ruling parties of North and South Yemen, within the framework of a power-sharing coalition. However, the Vice President of the coalition government, Ali Salim al-Baidh, who represented the south, fled to the city of Aden in 1993 and accused the government of marginalizing the south and attacking southerners. The conflict that ensued between leaders in the north and south paved the way for increased participation of Islamist groups in the government throughout the 1990s.

Sheik Abdel Majid al-Zindani was a key player during the initial infiltration of radical Islam into Yemen due to his role as a senior Islamic religious leader and prominent Islamist political figure. Zindani was a central activist in recruiting Yemeni *mujahideen* members for the *jihad* in Afghanistan, as well as being himself a combatant against the Soviets during the 1979-89 war. Upon his return to Yemen, Zindani established the Islah Islamic movement, which later became the major political opposition party to former President Saleh's General People's Council. The al-Islah party brought together Yemen's *Salafists*, Muslim Brotherhood members, and also had a significant tribal faction.

After the first multiparty general elections in 1993, al-Zindani became part of the five-man presidential council, while the then-head of al-Islah, Abdallah al-Ahmar, was elected as speaker of parliament.[74] As tensions rose with the socialist leaders in the coalition, President Ali Abdullah Saleh agreed to govern with al-Islah. With the outbreak of war in May 1994 between the Saleh regime in the north and formerly Soviet-aligned separatists in the south, al-Zindani condemned the separatist movements in Yemen as a "foreign conspiracy," and stressed the need both for the unity of Yemen and for allegiance to the regime. Al-Zindani, along with the Islah party, was easily able to rally the returning veterans of the Afghan jihad behind the Saleh regime in the north as a continuation of the jihad that had been waged in Afghanistan against the Marxist regime.

After the victory of Saleh's regime over the southern separatists in July 1994, and with the reunification of north and south Yemen, Saleh rewarded the Afghan veterans for their contribution by incorporating their leaders into the government.[75] One such example of this is Tariq al-Fadli, heir of the sultan of Abyan and former Afghan *mujahideen* leader, who later was appointed by the president to the Majlis al-Shura, the upper house of the parliament. Veteran *jihadists* were thus able to strike what Bonnefoy describes as "a 'covenant of security' deal with the security services on their return home from Afghanistan," under which they would enjoy freedom of movement within Yemen in return for a promise of good behavior inside the country's borders. During this transition, greater participation by the Muslim Brotherhood could be seen in Yemeni politics, with al-Islah members holding several important ministries, including justice, education, trade, and religious affairs.[76]

Throughout the 1990s and into the 2000s, formal and informal integration of numerous Islamist groups into the state apparatus continued. Individuals identifying with various sects of Islam gained important posts in the army and security forces. As a result, repression of Islamist groups was limited, allowing for easy access to political and tribal elites for *Salafists*, *Sufis*, Zaydi revivalists, Muslim Brothers, and some individuals sympathetic to *jihadist* doctrines.[77]

Al-Islah remains entrenched in Yemen's political landscape and in numerous regions of the country. The party seems to have considerable support in the former Marxist South, where a strong anti-socialist movement favors Islamist candidates and platforms over the dominant Yemeni Socialist Party and is currently gaining influence in some areas of the north. Nationally, the Islamist party won an average of 18 percent of the vote during the 1993, 1997, and 2003 parliamentary elections. Although a lack of electoral transparency reduces the significance of these numbers, the influence of al-Islah in Yemen was very sizeable.[78]

Al-Islah gained power in the immediate post-Arab Spring reforms in Yemen. During the transition and the NDC under President Hadi, al-Islah and the Yemeni Socialist Party were the two major parties in the Joint Meeting Parties (JMP), a coalition of former parties opposing the Saleh's GPC party. Al-Islah shared power with the former ruling GPC party and had a significant role, holding 50 seats in the NDC, negotiating and shaping the reforms that were to be instituted by the Hadi government.[79] The addition of the Houthis' party, Ansar Allah, to the NDC negotiations added to the list of Islamist groups represented in the post-Saleh government, which also included the Zaydi al Haqq party. However, it also put President Hadi at odds with many Sunni clerics, including Abd al-Majid al-Zindani, and some within al-Islah.[80]

There was an increase in U.S.-Yemeni counterterrorism cooperation since the ouster of Saleh, and President Hadi made statements openly supporting U.S. drone strikes against al-Qaeda.[81] The U.S. provided military assistance to Yemeni security forces in order to facilitate Yemeni ground operations against AQAP, while conducting direct action operations to eliminate imminent threats from the group.[82] The U.S. administration lauded the partnership in 2014 and described Yemen as a model for future counterterrorism alliances.[83] The model did not survive the outbreak of civil war, however. The Yemeni government now supports U.S.-backed Emirati counterterrorism operations in southern Yemen in addition to sustained U.S. direct action operations against AQAP leadership.

The outbreak of civil war has had a significant effect on Islamism in Yemen, driving Islamists to become more radical and permitting them to expand their reach. The Houthis are empowered in northern Yemen and have expanded governance into the skeleton of the former Yemeni state through the deal with former president Saleh. They have targeted *Salafis* and other Islamists, placing individuals under house arrest. The more hardline faction of the Houthis is dominant, generating sectarian rhetoric. Many *Salafis* and Islah members have fled the country, removing a moderating voice and leaving more radical *Salafis* behind. The tribal faction within Islah lost its national influence. Additionally, Saudi Arabia is empowering Islah and *Salafi* networks in Yemen to counter the Houthis in the civil war. Hadi's vice president is now Lieutenant General Ali Mohsen al-Ahmar, a powerbroker with deep ties into Islah networks.

ENDNOTES

[1] Shaul Shay, The Red Sea Terror Triangle (R. Liberman, trans.) (New Brunswick: Transaction Publishers, 2005), 113-114.

[2] Christopher Harnisch, "Denying Al-Qaeda a Safe Haven in Yemen," American Enterprise Institute Critical Threats Project, October 30, 2009, http://www.criticalthreats.org/yemen/denying-al-qaeda-safe-haven-yemen#_edn2; See also "Yemen Unemployment Rate," Index Mundi, n.d., http://www.indexmundi.com/yemen/unemployment_rate.html.

[3] "Yemen Stems Weapons Trade," Saba Net, September 23, 2008, http://www.sabanews.net/en/news164686.htm; See also "Yemen Moves to Control Arms Trade," Al-Motamar (Sana'a), April 25, 2007, http://www.almotamar.net/en/2463.htm.

[4] Ginny Hill, "Yemen: Fear of Failure," Chatham House Briefing Paper, November 2009, http://www.chathamhouse.org.uk/files/12576_bp1108yemen.pdf.

[5] See Katherine Zimmerman, "Yemen's Pivotal Moment," American Enterprise Institute Critical Threats Project, February 12, 2014, http://www.criticalthreats.org/yemen/zimmerman-yemens-pivotal-moment-february-12-2014.

[6] Alexis Knutsen, "Yemen's Counter-Terrorism Quandary," American Enterprise Institute Critical Threats Project, June 26, 2014, http://www.criticalthreats.org/yemen/knutsen-houthi-counterterrorism-quandary-june-26-2014.

[7] Alexis Knutsen, "Sana'a Under Siege: Yemen's Uncertain Future," American Enterprise Institute Critical Threats Project, September 25, 2014, http://www.criticalthreats.org/yemen/knutsen-sanaa-under-siege-yemens-uncertain-future-september-25-2014.

[8] See Peter Salisbury, "Yemen: Stemming the Rise of a Chaos State," Chatham House, May 25, 2016, https://www.chathamhouse.org/sites/files/chathamhouse/publications/research/2016-05-25-yemen-stemming-rise-of-chaos-state-salisbury.pdf.

[9] Hill, "Yemen: Fear of Failure."

[10] Lawrence E. Cline, "Yemen's Strategic Boxes," Small Wars Journal, January 2, 2010, http://smallwarsjournal.com/blog/journal/docs-temp/339-cline.pdf; Jonathan Schanzer, Testimony before the House of Representatives Committee on Foreign Affairs, February 3, 2010, http://www.pvtr.org/pdf/ICPVTRinNews/HouseForeignAffairsCommitteeHearing-YemenOnTheBrink-ImplicationsForU.S.Policy.pdf.

[11] Bruce Lawrence, ed., Messages to the World: The Statements of Osama bin Laden (London: Verso, 2005), 32.

[12] Jason Burke, Al-Qaeda: The True Story of Radical Islam (London: Penguin Books, 2004), 215.

[13] Harnisch, "Denying Al-Qaeda a Safe Haven in Yemen"; See also Lawrence, Messages to the World, 32.

[14] Gregory Johnsen, "Waning Vigilance: Al-Qaeda's Resurgence in Yemen," Washington Institute for Near East Policy Policywatch 1551, July 14, 2009, http://www.washingtoninstitute.org/templateC05.php?CID=3088.

[15] Ibid.; See also "USS Cole Plotter Escapes Prison," CNN.com, February 5, 2006, http://www.cnn.com/2006/WORLD/meast/02/05/cole.escape/index.html; Harnisch, "Denying Al-Qaeda a Safe Haven in Yemen."

[16] Harnisch, "Denying Al-Qaeda a Safe Haven in Yemen."

[17] "Bombers Attempt Attack On Saudi Oil Facility," New York Times, February 24, 2006, http://www.nytimes.com/2006/02/24/world/africa/24iht-web.0224saudi.html; Christopher Harnisch, "Christmas Day Attack: Manifestation of AQAP Shift Targeting America," American Enterprise Institute Critical Threats Project, December 29, 2009, http://www.criticalthreats.org/yemen/christmas-day-attack-manifestation-aqap-shift-targeting-america#_ednref5; P.K. Abdul Ghafour and Essam Al-Ghalib, "Kingdom Makes Remarkable Headway in Fight Against Terror: Naif," Arab News, November 11, 2004, http://archive.arabnews.com/?page=1&section=0&article=54339&d=11&m=11&y=2004.

[18] Frederick Kagan and Christopher Harnisch, "Yemen: Fighting al Qaeda in a Failed State," American Enterprise Institute Critical Threats Project, January 12, 2010, http://www.criticalthreats.org/sites/default/files/pdf_upload/analysis/CTP_Yemen_Fighting_al_Qaeda_in_a_Failing_State_Jan_12_2010.pdf.

[19] Ibid.

[20] "Al Qaeda Yemen Wing Claims Parcel Plot UPS Crash," Reuters, November 5, 2010, http://www.reuters.com/article/2010/11/05/us-usa-yemen-bomb-idUSTRE6A44PU20101105.

[21] Katherine Zimmerman, "AQAP and the 'Parcel Plot': Assessing this Critical Threats," AEIdeas, November 5, 2010, https://www.aei.org/publication/aqap-and-the-parcel-plot-assessing-this-critical-threat; See also "Al Qaeda Threat to American Interests," American Enterprise Institute Critical Threats Project, August 5, 2013, http://www.criticalthreats.org/al-qaeda/zimmerman/al-qaeda-threat-to-american-interests-august-5-2013.

[22] Katherine Zimmerman, "AQAP: A Resurgent Threat," Combating Terrorism Center at West Point CTC Sentinel, September 11, 2015, https://www.ctc.usma.edu/posts/aqap-a-resurgent-threat.

[23] Hill, "Yemen: Fear of Failure."

[24] Rania El Gamal, "Saudis Hardened by Wars in Syria, Iraq Join Al Qaeda in Yemen," Reuters, March 14, 2014, http://www.reuters.com/article/2014/03/14/us-yemen-security-qaeda-idUSBREA2D0XO20140314.

[25] Gregory D. Johnsen, "The Expansion Strategy of Al-Qa'ida in the Arabian Peninsula," Combating Terrorism Center at West Point CTC Sentinel 2, iss. 9, September 2009, 8-11, http://www.ctc.usma.edu/sentinel/CTCSentinel-Vol2Iss9.pdf.

[26] Jeremy Binnie, "Yemen Overruns Al-Qaeda Enclave," Jane's Defence Weekly, June 28, 2012; See also Katherine Zimmerman, "Al Qaeda's Gains in South Yemen," American Enterprise Institute Critical Threats Project, July 8, 2011, http://www.criticalthreats.org/yemen/al-qaedas-gains-south-yemen-july-8-2011#_edn2; Ahmed Al-Haj, "Yemen Recaptures Center of Al-Qaida-Held City," Associated Press, April 24, 2011; For a chronology of attacks by AQAP in Yemen, visit the "AQAP and Suspected AQAP Attacks in 2010, 2011 and 2012," American Enterprise Institute Critical Threats Project, n.d., http://www.criticalthreats.org/yemen/aqap-and-suspected-aqap-attacks-yemen-tracker-2010.

[27] Eric Schmitt, Mark Mazzetti, and Robert F. Worth, "American-Born Qaeda Leader Is Killed by U.S. Missile in Yemen," New York Times, September 30, 2011, http://www.nytimes.com/2011/10/01/world/middleeast/anwar-al-awlaki-is-killed-in-yemen.html.

[28] Thomas Joscelyn, "Al Qaeda in the Arabian Peninsula Releases 12th Issue of Inspire Magazine," Long War Journal, March 17, 2014, http://www.longwarjournal.org/archives/2014/03/al_qaeda_in_the_arab.php.

[29] Available on www.jihadology.net.

[30] See Katherine Zimmerman, "AQAP: A Resurgent Threat."

[31] Katherine Zimmerman, "2016 Yemen Crisis Situation Report, May 2," American Enterprise Institute Critical Threats Project, May 2, 2016, http://www.criticalthreats.org/yemen/yemen-crisis-situation-reports-may-2-2016; See also "AQAP Expanding behind Yemen's Frontlines," American Enterprise Institute Critical Threats Project, February 17, 2016, http://www.criticalthreats.org/yemen/zimmerman-aqap-expanding-behind-yemens-frontlines-february-17-2016.

[32] See Katherine Zimmerman, "Province Ties to the Islamic State Core: Islamic State in Yemen," in Katherine Bauer, ed, Beyond Syria and Iraq: Examining Islamic State Provinces, Washington Institute, November 2016.

[33] "Islamic State Video Promotes Destruction of Iraq-Syria Border Crossing," SITE Intelligence Group, June 29, 2014, www.siteintelgroup.com.

[34] Katherine Zimmerman, "Exploring ISIS in Yemen," American Enterprise Institute Critical Threats Project, July 24, 2015, http://www.criticalthreats.org/yemen/exploring-isis-yemen-zimmerman-july-24-2015, slide 5.

[35] Sheikh Hatem was killed alongside AQAP militants in al Mukalla, Hadramawt, on May 11, 2015. His co-location with AQAP indicates the continued relationship.

[36] United States Department of the Treasury, "Treasury Sanctions Major Islamic State of Iraq and the Levant Leaders, Financial Figures, Facilitators, and Supporters," press release, September 29, 2015, http://www.treasury.gov/press-center/press-releases/Pages/jl0188.aspx.

[37] "IS Leader Abu Bakr Al-Baghdadi Rallies Fighters, Welcomes New Pledges," SITE Intelligence Group, November 13, 2014, www.siteintelgroup.com.

[38] Alexis Knutsen, "ISIS in Yemen: Fueling the Sectarian Fire," American Enterprise Institute Critical Threats Project, March 20, 2015, http://www.criticalthreats.org/yemen/knutsen-isis-yemen-fueling-sectarian-fire-march-20-2015.

[39] Alexis Knutsen, "Ramadan Bombings in Yemen: Part of ISIS's Global Strategy?" American Enterprise Institute Critical Threats Project, June 17, 2015, http://www.criticalthreats.org/yemen/knutsen-ramadan-bombings-part-isis-global-strategy-june-17-2015.

[40] Joshua Koontz, "2015 Yemen Crisis Situation Report: October 7," American Enterprise Institute Critical Threats Project, October 7, 2015, http://www.criticalthreats.org/yemen/yemen-crisis-situation-reports-october-7-2015.

[41] Jon Diamond and Katherine Zimmerman, "Challenging the Yemeni State: ISIS in Aden and al Mukalla," American Enterprise Institute Critical Threats Project, June 9, 2016, http://www.criticalthreats.org/yemen/zimmerman-diamond-challenging-yemeni-state-isis-in-aden-al-mukalla-june-9-2016.

[42] See Bill Roggio and Thomas Joscelyn, "Divisions Emerge within the Islamic State's Yemen 'Province,'" Long War Journal, December 23, 2015, http://www.longwarjournal.org/archives/2015/12/divisions-emerge-within-the-islamic-states-yemen-province.php.

[43] Hamida Ghafour, "Rebel Without A Clear Cause," The National (Abu Dhabi), August 21, 2009, http://www.thenational.ae/apps/pbcs.dll/article?AID=/20090822/WEEKENDER/708219838/1306; See also Christopher Harnisch, A Critical War in a Fragile Country: Yemen's Battle with the Shiite al Houthi Rebels," American Enterprise Institute Critical Threats Project, August 31, 2009, http://www.criticalthreats.org/yemen/critical-war-fragile-country-yemens-battle-shiite-al-houthi-rebels#_edn3.

[44] Bonnefoy, "Varieties Of Islamism In Yemen."

[45] "Yemeni Government Steps Up Assault On Shiite Rebels," Wall Street Journal, August 12, 2009, http://online.wsj.com/article/SB125007847389825757.html?mod=googlenews_wsj.

[46] Ghafour, "Rebel Without A Clear Cause."

[47] Katherine Zimmerman and Steve Gonzalez, "Tracker: Saudi Arabia's Military Operations Along Yemeni Border | Critical Threats," American Enterprise Institute Critical Threats Project, January 4, 2010, http://www.criticalthreats.org/yemen/tracker-saudi-arabia%E2%80%99s-military-operations-along-yemeni-border.

[48] Glen Carey, "Saudi Arabia Barricades Its Border, U.S.-Style," BusinessWeek, June 27, 2013, http://www.businessweek.com/articles/2013-06-27/saudi-arabia-barricades-its-border-u-dot-s-dot-style.

[49] "Saudi Arabia Deports 427,000 Foreigners in Six Months," Gulf News, April 27, 2014, http://gulfnews.com/news/gulf/saudi-arabia/saudi-arabia-deports-427-000-foreigners-in-six-months-1.1324727.

[50] "Oman Considers Building a Fence on Borders with Yemen," National Yemen, June 1, 2013, http://nationalyemen.com/2013/06/01/oman-considers-building-a-fence-on-borders-with- yemen/.

[51] "Houthi Official Denies Receiving Arms from Iran," The National (Abu Dhabi), March 16, 2012, http://www.thenational.ae/news/world/middleeast/houthi-official-denies-receiving-arms-from-iran.

[52] Eric Schmitt and Robert F. Worth. "Aiding Yemen Rebels, Iran Seeks Wider Mideast Role," New York Times, March 15, 2012, http://www.nytimes.com/2012/03/15/world/middleeast/aiding-yemen-rebels-iran-seeks-wider-mideast-role.html.

[53] "Yemen Says Intercepted Ship Carrying Weapons Was Iranian," Reuters, February 2, 2013, http://www.reuters.com/article/2013/02/02/yemen-iran-arms-idUSL5N0B22GC20130202.

[54] Ibid; Katherine Zimmerman and Steve Gonzalez, "Tracker: Saudi Arabia's Military Operations Along Yemeni Border," American Enterprise Institute Critical Threats Project, January 4, 2010, http://www.criticalthreats.org/yemen/tracker-saudi-arabia's-military-operations-along-yemeni-border; Ariel Farrar-Wellman, "Yemen-Iran Foreign Relations," American Enterprise Institute Critical Threats Project, February 23, 2010, http://www.irantracker.org/foreign-relations/yemen-iran-foreign-relations.

[55] Yara Bayoumy and Phil Stewart, "Exclusive: Iran Steps Up Weapons Supply to Yemen's Houthis via Oman – Officials," Reuters, October 20, 2016, http://www.reuters.com/article/us-yemen-security-iran-idUSKCN12K0CX.

[56] Paul Bucala, Marie Donovan, Emily Estelle, Chris Harmer, and Caitlin Shayda Pendleton, "Iranian Involvement in Missile Attacks on the USS Mason," American Enterprise Institute Critical Threats Project, October 19, 2016, http://www.criticalthreats.org/yemen/iranian-involvement-missile-attacks-uss-mason-october-19-2016.

[57] "Islah Party, Houthi Group Sign Ceasefire Agreement in Jawf," Yemen Post, August 13, 2011, http://yemenpost.net/Detail123456789.aspx?ID=3&SubID=3910.

[58] "Yemen al-Qaida Commander Declares War Against Shiites," Xinhua, January 29, 2011, http://news.xinhuanet.com/english2010/world/2011-01/29/c_13711741.htm.

[59] "Sectarian Violence Continues in North Yemen, 30 Killed," Yemen Post, February 13, 2012, http://yemenpost.net/Detail123456789.aspx?ID=3&SubID=4706; "Death Toll Rises to 20 in Sectarian Violence in Northern Yemen," Xinhua, September 23, 2012, http://news.xinhuanet.com/english/world/2012-09/23/c_131867247.htm.

[60] "At Least 40 Killed in Yemen as Houthi Fighters near Capital," Reuters, March 9, 2014, http://www.reuters.com/article/2014/03/09/us-yemen-clash-idUSBREA2805920140309.

[61] "Representations in the National Dialogue Conference," Yemen Observer, March 18 2013, http://www.yemenobserver.com/national-dialogue/227-representations-in-the-national-dialogue-conference.html.

[62] Katherine Zimmerman, "A New Model for Defeating al Qaeda in Yemen," American Enterprise Institute Critical Threats Project, September 10, 2015, http://www.criticalthreats.org/yemen/zimmerman-new-model-for-defeating-al-qaeda-in-yemen-september-10-2015, 7.

[63] "Signing of the National Political Agreement Between the General People's Congress and its Allies and Ansar Allah and its Allies," SABA.ye, July 28, 2016, http://www.saba.ye/ar/news434879.htm.

[64] "Gulf of Aden Security Review – November 29, 2016," American Enterprise Institute Critical Threats Project, November 29, 2016, http://www.criticalthreats.org/gulf-aden-security-review/gulf-aden-security-review-november-29-2016.

[65] "Yemen," Central Intelligence Agency World Factbook, April 15, 2014, https://www.cia.gov/library/publications/the-world-factbook/geos/ym.html.

[66] Bernard Haykel, Revival and Reform: The Legacy of Muhammad al-Shawkani (Cambridge: Cambridge University Press, 2003), 151.

[67] Laurent Bonnefoy, "Les identités religieuses contemporaines au Yémen: convergence, résistances et instrumentalisations," Revue des mondes musulmans et de la Méditerranée 121-122, April 2008, 201-15; See also Bonnefoy, "Varieties Of Islamism In Yemen."

[68] Ibid.

[69] "Popular Protests in North Africa and the Middle East (II)."

[70] Ibid.

[71] Katherine Zimmerman, "Signaling Saudi Arabia: Iranian Support to Yemen's al Houthis," American Enterprise Institute Critical Threats Project, April 15, 2016, http://www.criticalthreats.org/yemen/zimmerman-signaling-saudi-arabia-iranian-support-to-yemen-al-houthis-april-15-2016.

[72] Bonnefoy, "Varieties Of Islamism In Yemen."

[73] John O. Brennan, interview with Margaret Warner, "U.S. Policy Toward Yemen," Council on Foreign Relations, August 8, 2012, http://www.cfr.org/united-states/us-policy-toward-yemen/p28794.

[74] Bonnefoy, "Varieties Of Islamism In Yemen."

[75] Peter Bergen, Holy War Inc: Inside the Secret World of Osama Bin Laden (London: Weidenfeld & Nicolson, 2001), 190-191.

[76] Bonnefoy, "Varieties Of Islamism In Yemen."

[77] Ibid.

[78] Jillian Schwedler, "The Yemeni Islah Party: Political Opportunities and Coalition Building in a Transitional Polity," in Quintan Wiktorowicz, ed., Islamist Activism: A Social Movement Theory Approach (Bloomington: Indiana University Press, 2003), 205-29; See also Faith in Moderation: Islamist Parties in Jordan and Yemen (Cambridge: Cambridge University Press, 2007), 280.

[79] "Representations in the National Dialogue Conference."

[80] Ashraf Al-Muraqab, "Yemeni Clerics Disapprove of their Exclusion From the National Dialogue," Yemen Times, July 4, 2012, http://www.yementimes.com/en/1587/news/1092/Yemeni-clerics-disapprove-of-their-exclusion-from-the-National-Dialogue.htm; "Yemen President Offers Conditional Dialogue With Al Qaeda," Reuters, September 26, 2012, http://www.reuters.com/article/2012/09/26/yemen-qaeda-idUSL5E8KQ5LF20120926.

[81] Abd Rabu Mansour Hadi, "Yemen's Transition: The Way Forward," Address at the Woodrow Wilson International Center for Scholars, Washington, DC, September 28, 2012, http://www.acus.org/event/yemens-transition-way-forward; See also Greg Miller, "In Interview, Yemeni President Acknowledges Approving U.S. Drone Strikes," Washington Post, September 29, 2012, http://www.washingtonpost.com/world/national-security/yemeni-president-acknowledges-approving-us-drone-strikes/2012/09/29/09bec2ae-0a56-11e2-afff-d6c7f20a83bf_story.html.

[82] See Katherine Zimmerman, "Yemen Model Won't Work in Iraq, Syria," Washington Post, July 17, 2014, https://www.washingtonpost.com/opinions/the-yemen-model-wont-work-in-iraq-syria/2014/07/17/ba0ae414-0d18-11e4-8341-b8072b1e7348_story.html.

[83] White House, Office of the Press Secretary, "Remarks by the President on the Situation in Iraq," June 19, 2014, https://www.whitehouse.gov/the-press-office/2014/06/19/remarks-president-situation-iraq.

Sub-Saharan Africa

COUNTRIES
Ethiopia
Mali
Nigeria
Somalia
South Africa
Tanzania

ETHIOPIA

QUICK FACTS

Population: 102,374,044 (estimated December 2016)

Area: 1,104,300 sq km

Ethnic Groups: Oromo 34.4%, Amhara (Amara) 27%, Somali (Somalie) 6.2%, Tigray (Tigrinya) 6.1%, Sidama 4%, Gurage 2.5%, Welaita 2.3%, Hadiya 1.7%, Afar (Affar) 1.7%, Gamo 1.5%, Gedeo 1.3%, Silte 1.3%, Kefficho 1.2%, other 8.8%

Religions: Ethiopian Orthodox 43.5%, Muslim 33.9%, Protestant 18.5%, traditional 2.7%, Catholic 0.7%, other 0.6%

Government Type: Federal Parliamentary Republic

GDP (official exchange rate): $61.63 billion (and estimated December 2016)

Map and Quick Facts courtesy of the CIA World Factbook (December 2016)

OVERVIEW

The U.S. Department of State has described Ethiopia as "a strategic partner in the Global War on Terrorism"[1] and welcomed "Ethiopia's dedication to maintaining security in the region."[2] The country has received high-level visits from U.S. President Barack Obama and Secretary of State John Kerry, both of whom lauded the partnership between the two countries in addressing governance issues, economic growth, and regional security concerns. The encomia are more than merited, both for the Ethiopian government's actions abroad and for the challenges it faces at home, which the most recent edition of the Department's Country Reports on Terrorism *summarized as follows: "The continuing threat of al-Shabaab emanating from Somalia dominated the Government of Ethiopia's security posture and the Ethiopia National Defense Forces's (ENDF's) counterterrorism efforts in Somalia. Therefore, the Government of Ethiopia's counterterrorism efforts focused on fighting al-Shabaab in Somalia and pursuing potential threats in Ethiopia."[3]*

ISLAMIST ACTIVITY

As of late 2016, Islamist threats to Ethiopia's security are primarily external and emanate from Somalia.

While a certain amount of controversy surrounds the precise details of Islamism's introduction into Ethiopia, a bridgehead seems to have been established in and around the town of Harar fairly early on in the 20th century, perhaps during the Italian occupation (1936-1942), by pilgrims returning from the *hajj*. Later, in the 1960s and 1970s, a number of Oromo students returning from religious studies in Saudi Arabia further propagated political Islam, not only in their native regions but also in Addis Ababa and Wollo. The May 1991 fall of the Derg dictatorship gave new impetus to these trends, as many returning Oromo exiles had been influenced by *Wahhabi* doctrines during their time abroad and the new government's policies facilitated the contact with coreligionists in other countries, who supported the establishment of mosques, schools, and associations.[4] Among the latter were two entities in Addis Ababa: the Ethiopian Muslim Youth Association, founded in the 1990s and linked to the Riyadh-based World Association of Muslim Youth (WAMY), and the Alawiyah School and Mission Center, owned since 1993 by the Saudi-controlled World Muslim League's International Islamic Relief Organization (IIRO).[5] IIRO has also donated food and medical relief to Ethiopia following natural disasters.[6] (In August 2006, the U.S. Treasury Department formally designated the Philippine and Indonesian branches of the IIRO for facilitating terrorism.[7])

Like their *Wahhabi* confrères elsewhere, Ethiopian Islamists have attacked what they regard as syncretism among other Muslims, as exemplified by certain Sufi-inspired practices like pilgrimages to various shrines and the celebration of *Mawlid* (the birthday of the prophet Muhammad). More recently, some zealots have pushed for a stricter observance of what they regard as compulsory practices such as the wearing of pants above the ankles and the use of face coverings by women. The tensions within the Muslim community were further aggravated when a branch of *Takfir wal-Hijrah* ("Excommunication and Exodus"), a radical group which originated in Egypt in the 1970s, was driven from Sudan and decamped first to Gondar and, subsequently, to a northern suburb of Addis Ababa.[8] The group labels most fellow Muslims, including other *Wahhabis*, as *kuffar* ("non-believers"). Although it has caused less of a sensation since the death, in 2004, of its leader in Ethiopia, Sheikh Muhammad Amin, the group continues to exist.[9] Details of the group's activities, capabilities and resources within Ethiopia, however, remain sketchy at best, although one well-respected researcher with extensive fieldwork on the Muslim community in the country has noted that Ethiopian adherents of *Takfir wal-Hijrah* refuse to recognize the national constitution, pay taxes, or carry identification cards.[10]

Al-Qaeda is also active in Ethiopia. The organization has long viewed East Africa as a priority within its overall strategy. According to the Combating Terrorism Center at West Point, the nascent al-Qaeda, then based in Sudan, sought both to establish working relations with Islamist extremists in Somalia and create training camps in ethnic Somali areas of Ethiopia in the early 1990s.[11] When Ethiopia intervened in Somalia in 2006 and again in 2014, for example, al-Qaeda renewed its interest in targeting both the Horn of Africa in general and Ethiopia in particular. However, like with *Takfir wal-Hijrah* (above), accurate information on al-Qaeda's organizational make-up and capabilities in Ethiopia is far from complete, at least at the open-source level. Moreover, there are indications that the foothold al-Qaeda once held in East Africa through links to *al-Shabaab* has eroded, particularly as the Islamic State in Iraq and Syria (ISIS) has gained ground.

Another Islamist group active in Ethiopia is the world's largest *dawa* (proselytizing) movement, *Tablighi Jamaat*. Founded in India in 1929, the group first came to Ethiopia from South Africa in the 1970s. Its activities, however, were very limited until after the fall of the Derg, the Marxist *junta* led by Mengistu Haile Mariam that seized control of Ethiopia after deposing the Emperor Haile Selassie in 1974 and ruled the country until its own overthrow in 1991. Little is known about the group's activities other than that its center of operations seems to be the Kolfe district of Addis Ababa, where it is especially active within the Gurage community that has migrated to the city from their mountainous homeland southwest of there.

The principal Islamist threat to Ethiopia, however, comes from neighboring Somalia. Following the January 1991 collapse of the Muhammad Siyad Barre regime, the last effective central government of Somalia, the rise of *al-Itihaad al-Islamiya* (AIAI, "Islamic Union") posed serious challenges to Ethiopian security—a situation that would persist throughout the 1990s. While the AIAI's primary focus was on the establishment of an Islamist state in Somalia, it also encouraged subversive activities among ethnic Somalis in the Somali region of Ethiopia and carried out a series of terrorist attacks, including the bombing of two hotels in 1996 and the attempted assassination, in 1995 that same year, of cabinet minister Abdul Majeed Hussein, an ethnic Somali Ethiopian whom the AIAI accused of being a traitor. AIAI's hostility to Ethiopia arose from its toxic mix of Islamism with Somali irredentist designs on Ethiopian territory. The exasperated Ethiopian regime finally intervened in Somalia in August 1996, wiping out *al-Itihaad* bases in the Somali towns of Luuq and Buulo Haawa and killing hundreds of Somali extremists, as well as scores of non-Somali Islamists who had flocked to the Horn under the banner of *jihad*.[12]

As it turns out, the defeat was only a temporary setback for Somali Islamists, who regrouped under the banner of the Islamic Courts Union (ICU) with many of the same leaders as AIAI. One such leader was Sheikh Hassan Dahir Aweys, who had served as number two in AIAI and went on to chair the ICU's *shura* and later head the Eritrea-based Alliance for the Re-Liberation of Somalia (ARS), after Ethiopian forces intervened in Somalia in December 2006 in support of the country's internationally-recognized, but weak "Transitional Federal Government." The presence of Ethiopian troops in Somalia, which lasted until early 2009, occasioned an Islamist insurgency spearheaded by the radical *Harakat al-Shabaab al-Mujahideen* ("Movement of Warrior Youth," more commonly known as *al-Shabaab*), a group that was labeled a "specially designated global terrorist" by the U.S. Department of State in 2008.[13] Subsequently, in 2012, the U.S. Department of State added seven *al-Shabaab* leaders to its Rewards for Justice program, offering large rewards for information leading to their locations.[14] In 2014, Ethiopian forces returned to Somalia as official contributors to the African Union Mission in Somalia (AMISOM), prompting renewed calls from *al-Shabaab* to attack Ethiopian forces in Somalia and at home. "We defeated Ethiopia before and we know how to battle them now," *al-Shabaab* spokesman Ali Mohamud Rage said.[15]

Fortunately, much of the pressure from this quarter has been relieved with the military and political setbacks suffered by *al-Shabaab* since it was forced to withdraw from Mogadishu in August 2011.[16] That said, the absence of a major *al-Shabaab* attack in Ethiopia is not due to a lack of effort on the part of the group; in 2013, two suspected *al-Shabaab* operatives were killed when the bomb they were working on exploded in a home in an affluent Addis Ababa neighborhood. No one else was injured, though authorities arrested five people for their involvement and reported that *al-Shabaab* planned to target an upcoming football match.[17] Thus, the resurgence in *al-Shabaab* activities in Somalia in 2016 will, undoubtedly, be closely watched by authorities in Ethiopia.

While the threat from Somalia is external, it cannot be entirely separated from the internal threat to Ethiopian national security posed by dissidents who align themselves with the country's foreign enemies.

Among the latter, Eritrea falls into a category all of its own, given the bitter two-year war which the tiny state precipitated in May 1998 when it occupied a small sliver of territory that had up to then been peaceably administered by Ethiopia. While the regime of Eritrean President Isaias Afewerki is not known for its religiosity, that has not prevented it from supporting Islamist movements that serve its overall strategic objective of undermining the Ethiopian government. To this end, it has at times in the twenty-first century lent support to the Islamist insurgency in Somalia,[18] as well as to the secessionist Ogaden National Liberation Front (ONLF) in Ethiopia, which has frequently partnered with its extremist ethnic kin in Somalia.[19]

ISLAMISM AND SOCIETY

Traditionally, the dominant ethnic group in Ethiopia has been the Amhara, who, together with the Tigray, currently make up about 33 percent of the population, according to the last national census (conducted in 2007).[20] The Oromo, who live largely in the southern part of the country, constitute another 34 percent. Other important ethnic groups include the Somali (6.2 percent), Gurage (2.5 percent), Sidama (4 percent), and Welayta (2.3 percent). Religiously, more than half of the population is Christian, mainly adherents of the Ethiopian Orthodox Tewahedo Church, an Oriental (Monophysite) Orthodox Christian body in communion with the Armenian, Coptic, and Syrian Churches. Evangelical Christianity is the fastest growing denomination in Ethiopia, with some 14 million Protestants counted in the country's last census.[21] Another 34 percent or so is Muslim, drawn primarily from the Oromo and other southern peoples, as well as the ethnic Somali and the Afar. Given that the population of Ethiopia is estimated to number at least 100 million, the country has more Muslims than many Muslim states, including Afghanistan and Saudi Arabia.[22]

Almost all Muslims in Ethiopia are Sunni, with a plurality, if not a majority, adhering to one or another Sufi *tariqa* (order). The most widely followed of these is the Qadiriyya, although the Tijaniyya, Shaziriyya, and Semaniyya orders also have significant followings. Islam is most prevalent in eastern Ethiopia, particularly in the Somali and Afar regions, as well as in many parts of the Oromo region. While institutional Islam in Ethiopia tends to be decentralized, the Ethiopian Supreme Council for Islamic Affairs, formally established (although not accorded *de jure* recognition) in 1976, is treated by the government as "representative of the Ethiopian Muslim community" and accorded the same courtesies as the heads of the Orthodox, Catholic, and Protestant Churches in state ceremonial matters.[23]

Overall, especially in contrast to the rough times experienced under the Derg dictatorship, the Muslim community in Ethiopia has fared better under the Ethiopian Peoples' Revolutionary Democratic Front (EPRDF) government, which lifted its predecessor's restrictions on the *hajj*, ban on the importation of religious literature, and obstacles to the construction of mosques and religious schools.[24] The opening "produced a new consciousness among the Muslim population, generated new religious affiliations and paved the way for Islam in Ethiopia to become more visible."[25]

By and large, Ethiopian Muslims have resisted the attempts of radical co-religionists to promote political Islam. The main reasons for this failure of Islamism to gain traction include not only the deep roots of more traditional forms of Islam, especially those represented by the Sufi orders, and the strength of social ties that cross religious boundaries, but also the fact that the extremists have failed to offer concrete solutions to many of the problems faced by ordinary Ethiopians. By contrast, the government despite its limitations, has managed to deliver impressive rates of economic growth. [26] Nonetheless, the potential does exist for religion to be exploited to mobilize greater support by various separatist or extremist movements.

Beginning in 2011, tensions escalated between some parts of the Muslim community and the Ethiopian government, with the former accusing the latter of interfering in religious matters by allegedly trying to impose the quietist *Al-Ahbash* sect on the country's Supreme Islamic Council. Protests over more than a year drew thousands, and grievances widened to include perceived government interference in Islam and in the selection of the Supreme Islamic Council.[27] In 2015, a court convicted eighteen Muslims who had been arrested during the protests under the country's anti-terrorism law.[28] Activists and some human rights organizations suggested that the trial of these Muslim activists—in addition to other, lower-profile cases—was politicized and not held in accordance with the law.[29]

ISLAMISM AND THE STATE

Following the 1974 overthrow of the Emperor Haile Selassie, the communist Derg regime of Mengistu Hailemariam persecuted religious leaders and discouraged the practice of religion by Christians and Muslims alike. Since the defeat of the dictatorship, and the subsequent assumption of power of the current government led by the Ethiopian Peoples' Revolutionary Democratic Front (EPRDF) in 1991, the policy has shifted to one of religious tolerance, although the formation of political groups on the basis of religion is forbidden. According to the State Department's 2015 annual report on religious freedom, the Ethiopian constitution "requires the separation of state and religion, establishes freedom of religious choice and practice, prohibits religious discrimination, and stipulates the government shall not interfere in the practice of any religion." [30] Also in 2015, "some religious leaders reported interreligious tensions were at a five-year low." [31]

Despite—or perhaps because of—this lack of domestic tension, the Ethiopian government has taken a significant role in regional and international counterterrorism efforts. It served as host for the African Union's Center for Study and Research on Terrorism and in 2008 ratified the Protocol to the OAU Convention on the Prevention and Combating of Terrorism.[32] From 2006 through late 2008, Ethiopia led the efforts in Somalia against extremists connected with the ICU, and provided "critical support" to AMISOM in their efforts against extremist groups.[33] In 2014, Ethiopia intervened again in Somalia in support of AMISOM's effort to fight *al-Shabaab*. The U.S. State Department has generally considered Ethiopia to be an "important regional security partner,"[34] although funds for military assistance "are explicitly limited to nonlethal assistance, training, and peacekeeping support at present."[35]

However, Ethiopia's counterterrorism efforts have drawn mixed reviews. In 2009, Ethiopia passed an anti-terrorism law designed to discourage the formation and activities of radical groups within its borders, carrying penalties ranging up to life imprisonment and even the death penalty. Expressing support for terrorism was likewise criminalized: "Whosoever writes, edits, prints, publishes, publicises, disseminates, shows, makes to be heard any promotional statements encouraging... terrorist acts is punishable with rigorous imprisonment from 10 to 20 years."[36] The legislation, while recognized as an attempt to combat extremism, has drawn criticism from Ethiopia's international partners and from human rights organizations who claim that the law's ambiguous language, as well as its uneven implementation, is an attempt by the EPRDF to cement its power and justify oppression of opposition groups and independent media. [37]

Others have pointed to the country's recent elections as further reason for concern. In May 2010, the EPRDF and its allies won 545 out of 547 seats in the country's parliament. While the lopsided results were partially attributable to divisions within the opposition, they nonetheless raised questions among some analysts about the future of democracy in the Ethiopia.[38] In May 2015, the ruling party's victory in parliament was further cemented when the opposition did not win a single seat.[39]

As of late 2016, widespread demonstrations throughout the country's two largest regions—Amhara and Oromia—were ongoing. Protests began in late 2014 over the government's announcement of a controversial land reallocation scheme; they have continued and expanded in scope to be broadly anti-government. While primarily peaceful, some protesters have engaged in serious property damage—especially affecting foreign-owned businesses. Scores have been arrested, and hundreds have been killed in clashes with security forces.[40] As a result of the ongoing unrest, Ethiopian authorities announced a six-month state of emergency to begin in October 2016, which allows expanded powers to the security services; the government has thus far blamed the unrest on "anti-peace" elements from Eritrea and Egypt.[41] While there is no overt religious element to the current demonstrations, the Ethiopian government's claims of foreign meddling, as well as its restrictions on ordinary citizens as a result of the unrest, bear watching.

Not all experts see cause for concern, however. Rather, they emphasize the progress Ethiopia has made since ousting the Soviet regime in 1991—especially when placed in the context of its neighbors Eritrea, Somalia, and Kenya, all of whom have struggled with instability.[42]

Nevertheless, the potential for conflict remains. After the fall of the communist Derg dictatorship, a constituent assembly convened by the EPRDF government adopted a constitution in 1994 that carried "a radical recognition of diversity and of a new kind of equality."[43] Each ethnic community is accorded the right and duty to manage its own affairs under the aegis of a federal government that serves as the center for state unity. While it is too early to declare the success or failure of this system of ethnic federalism, it does raise the specter of struggles for allegiance between religion and ethnicity. It also creates the distinct possibility that Islam in particular may be used by groups seeking to mobilize their ethnic kin to exercise the secession that the constitution affirms is an inherent part of the "unconditional right of self-determination" accorded to every "group of people who have or share a large measure of common culture or similar customs, mutual intelligibility of language, belief in a common or related identities, a common psychological make-up, and who inhabit an identifiable, predominantly contiguous territory."[44] Against this potential vulnerability—which external foes, both state and non-state will be eager to seize upon—the Ethiopian government will need to maintain constant vigilance, especially as the country enters a new political era and its leaders try to maintain its much-valued stability and economic growth amid rapidly changing societal expectations.

ENDNOTES

[1] U.S. Department of State, Bureau of African Affairs, "Background Note: Ethiopia," June 2009, http://www.state.gov/outofdate/bgn/ethiopia/82233.htm.

[2] U.S. Department of State, Bureau of African Affairs, "Fact Sheet: U.S. Relations with Ethiopia," June 2016, http://www.state.gov/r/pa/ei/bgn/2859.htm.

[3] U.S. Department of State, Office of the Coordinator for Counterterrorism, "Country Reports: Africa Overview," in Country Reports on Terrorism 2015, October 21, 2016, http://www.state.gov/j/ct/rls/crt/2015/257514.htm.

[4] See generally Haggai Erlich, Saudi Arabia and Ethiopia: Islam, Christianity, and Politics Entwined (Boulder, CO: Lynne Rienner, 2007).

[5] Terje Østebø, "The Question of Becoming: Islamic Reform Movements in Contemporary Ethiopia," Journal of Religion in Africa 38, no. 4 (2008), 421.

[6] David H. Shinn, "Ethiopia: Governance and Terrorism," in Robert I. Rotberg, ed., Battling Terrorism in the Horn of Africa (Cambridge, MA and Washington, DC: World Peace Foundation/Brookings Institution, 2005), 98.

[7] Press Release, "Treasury Designates Director, Branches of Charity Bankrolling Al Qaeda Network," U.S. Department of the Treasury, August 2, 2006, http://www.treas.gov/press/releases/hp45.htm.

[8] Timothy Carney, "The Sudan: Political Islam and Terrorism," in ibid., 122.

[9] Østebø, "The Question of Becoming," 422-423.

[10] See Éloi Ficquet, "The Ethiopian Muslims: Historical Processes and Ongoing Controversies," in Gérard Prunier and Éloi Ficquet, eds., Understanding Contemporary Ethiopia (London: Hurst and Company, 2015), 107.

[11] Combating Terrorism Center at West Point, Al –Qa'ida's (mis)Adventures in the Horn of Africa (West Point, NY: U.S. Military Academy, Harmony Project, 2007), 38-40.

[12] Medhane Tadesse, Al-Ittihad: Political Islam and Black Economy in Somalia. Religion, Money, Clan and the Struggle for Supremacy over Somalia (Addis Ababa: Meag printing enterprise, 2002), 156-168.

[13] U.S. Department of State, Office of the Coordinator for Counterterrorism, "Designation of al-Shabaab as a Specially Designated Global Terrorist" (Public Notice 6137), February 26, 2008, http://www.state.gov/s/ct/rls/other/des/102448.htm.

[14] U.S. Department of State, Office of the Spokesperson, "Rewards for Justice – al-Shabaab Leader Rewards Offers" June 7, 2012, http://www.state.gov/r/pa/prs/ps/2012/06/191914.htm.

[15] "Somalia Islamists Vow to Boost Attacks as Ethiopia Joins AU Force," Ahram Online, January 25, 2014, http://english.ahram.org.eg/NewsContent/2/9/92471/World/International/Somali-Islamists-vow-to-boost-attacks-as-Ethiopia-.aspx.

[16] Bronwyn Bruton and J. Peter Pham, "The Splintering of Al Shabaab," Foreign Affairs, February 2, 2012, http://www.foreignaffairs.com/articles/137068/bronwyn-bruton-and-j-peter-pham/the-splintering-of-al-shabaab.

[17] Aaron Maasho, "Ethiopia Says Arrests Five Suspects in Soccer Match Bomb Plot," Reuters, December 19, 2013, http://www.reuters.com/article/us-ethiopia-bombers-idUSBRE9BI14F20131219.

[18] J. Peter Pham, "Eritrea: Regional Spoiler Exacerbates Crisis in the Horn of Africa and Beyond," World Defense Review, October 15, 2009, http://worlddefensereview.com/pham101509.shtml; See also Ahmed Mohamed Egal, "Eritrea's Repayment of its Fraternal Debt to the Somali People," American Chronicle, November 4, 2009, http://www.americanchronicle.com/articles/view/126773.

[19] J. Peter Pham, Testimony before the U.S. House of Representatives Committee on Foreign Affairs, Subcommittee on Africa and Global Health, October 2, 2007, http://foreignaffairs.house.gov/110/pha100207.htm.

[20] "Ethiopia," CIA World Factbook, October 21, 2016, https://www.cia.gov/library/publications/the-world-factbook/geos/et.html.

[21] Emanuele Fantini, "Go Pente! The Charismatic Renewal of the Evagelical Movement in Ethiopia," in Gérard Prunier and Éloi Ficquet, eds., Understanding Contemporary Ethiopia.

[22] "Ethiopia," CIA World Factbook.

[23] Hussein Ahmed, "Coexistence and/or Confrontation?: Towards a Reappraisal of Christian-Muslim Encounter in Contemporary Ethiopia," Journal of Religion in Africa 36, no. 1 (2006), 11-12.

[24] Hussein Ahmed, "Islam and Islamic Discourse in Ethiopia (1973-1993)," in Harold G. Marcus, ed., New Trends in Ethiopian Studies: Social Sciences (Papers of the 12th International Conference of Ethiopian Studies, vol. 1) (Lawrenceville, NJ: Red Sea Press, 1995), 775-801.

[25] Østebø, "The Question of Becoming," 417.
[26] See Alex de Waal, ed., Islamism and its Enemies in the Horn of Africa (Addis Ababa: Shama Books, 2004); See also World Bank, "With Continued Rapid Growth, Ethiopia is Poised to Become a Middle Income Country by 2025," November 23, 2015, http://www.worldbank.org/en/country/ethiopia/publication/ethiopia-great-run-growth-acceleration-how-to-pace-it.
[27] Ficquet, "The Ethiopian Muslims," 117-18.
[28] U.S. Department of State, Bureau of Democracy, Human Rights, and Labor, "Country Report: Ethiopia," in International Religious Freedom Report 2015, 2016, http://www.state.gov/j/drl/rls/irf/religiousfreedom/index.htm?year=2015&dlid=256023.
[29] Morgan Winsor, "Ethiopian Muslims Accused of Terrorism, Jailed for 22 Years After Obama's Visit," International Business Times, August 4, 2015, http://www.ibtimes.com/ethiopian-muslims-accused-terrorism-jailed-22-years-after-obamas-visit-2038177.
[30] U.S. Department of State, "Country Report: Ethiopia."
[31] Ibid.
[32] U.S. Department of State, "Background Note: Ethiopia."
[33] U.S. Department of State, "Country Reports: Africa Overview."
[34] U.S. Department of State, Bureau of African Affairs, "Background Note: Ethiopia," November 5, 2010, http://www.state.gov/outofdate/bgn/ethiopia/158887.htm.
[35] U.S. Department of State, "Fact Sheet: U.S. Relations with Ethiopia."
[36] "Ethiopia Adopts Strict Anti-Terrorism Bill," Agence France Presse, July 7, 2009, http://www.google.com/hostednews/afp/article/ALeqM5hMqgOlskPvo1m_dSE35D1rFeICNw.
[37] Leslie Lefkow, Testimony before the House of Representatives Committee on Foreign Affairs, Subcommittee on Africa and Global Health, June 17, 2010; Human Rights Watch, "Ethiopia: Terrorism Law Decimates Media," May 3, 2013, https://www.hrw.org/news/2013/05/03/ethiopia-terrorism-law-decimates-media.
[38] Barry Malone, "Ethiopia Court Rejects Final Poll Result Challenge," Reuters, July 20, 2010, http://af.reuters.com/article/topNews/idAFJOE66J0RW20100720.
[39] Morgan Winsor, "Ethiopia Election 2015: Ruling Party Declares Historic 100 Percent Victory in Parliamentary Polls," International Business Times, June 23, 2015, http://www.ibtimes.com/ethiopia-elections-2015-ruling-party-declares-historic-100-percent-victory-1979220.
[40] "What is Behind Ethiopia's Wave of Protests?" BBC, August 22, 2016, http://www.bbc.com/news/world-africa-36940906.
[41] "Ethiopia Blames Egypt and Eritrea Over Unrest," BBC, October 10, 2016, http://www.bbc.com/news/world-africa-37607751.

[42] "Ethiopia's Ruling Party Set For Landslide Win," Reuters, May 24, 2010, http://af.reuters.com/article/ethiopiaNews/idAFLDE64N1C220100524.

[43] Jon Abbink, "An Historical-Anthropological Approach to Islam in Ethiopia: Issues of Identity and Politics," Journal of African Cultural Studies 11, no. 2 (1998), 121-123.

[44] J. Peter Pham, "African Constitutionalism: Forging New Models for Multi-ethnic Governance and Self-Determination," in Jeremy I. Levitt, ed., Africa: Mapping New Boundaries in International Law (Oxford: Hart Publishing 2008), 188-190.

MALI

> ## Quick Facts
>
> Population: 17,467,108 (July 2016 est.)
>
> Area: 1,240,192 sq km
>
> Ethnic Groups: Bambara 34.1%, Fulani (Peul) 14.7%, Sarakole 10.8%, Senufo 10.5%, Dogon 8.9%, Malinke 8.7%, Bobo 2.9%, Songhai 1.6%, Tuareg 0.9%, other Malian 6.1%, from member of Economic Community of West African States 0.3%, other 0.4%
>
> Religions: Muslim 94.8%, Christian 2.4%, Animist 2%, none 0.5%, unspecified 0.3%
>
> Government Type: semi-presidential republic
>
> GDP (official exchange rate): $14.1 billion (2015 est.)
>
> *Map and Quick Facts courtesy of the CIA World Factbook (January 2017)*

Overview

Mali continues to experience significant Islamist insurgent violence as Malian and international forces struggle to adequately police a plethora of Islamist and non-Islamist armed groups active in the north of the country. The current instability can be traced back to the 2012 coup d'état and subsequent fracture between the country's north and south (though tensions between the two halves of the country existed long before the coup). In the ensuing political turmoil, Islamist groups were able to take control of the north of the country, prompting an international intervention led by France in January 2013. While French forces, with the assistance of Malian and international troops, successfully regained control of the major Northern towns, large swaths of the north remain unstable and insurgent groups launch frequent attacks against Malian, French, and United Nations forces still present there, as well as civilian targets in the south. As the Malian government struggles to implement the June 2015 peace accord, a durable peace in the country's north remains elusive and it is likely that Islamist activity will continue for the foreseeable future.

ISLAMIST ACTIVITY

Mali declared itself an independent nation in 1960. Since that time, Tuaregs (a Berber ethnic group) that live in the north have repeatedly tried to establish their independence from the Malian government. The National Movement for the Liberation of Azawad (MNLA), a Tuareg separatist group, was formed in October 2011.[1] MNLA is an explicitly religious group, but has allied with Islamist organizations at different points in its history.[2]

Mali's current struggles with Islamism can be traced back to the 2012 *coup d'état* that overthrew the country's democratically elected government. MNLA-led rebellions in the north had restarted early in 2012. Many in the military were frustrated by what they perceived as a lack of support from the government in suppressing these rebellions. The soldiers, called the Green Berets, attacked the presidential palace in Bamako and deposed President Amadou Toumani Touré.

Upon taking power, the Green Berets established the National Council for the Recovery of Democracy and the Restoration of the State (CNRDRE). The group suspended Mali's constitution and dissolved its institutions, promising to restore civilian rule.[3] Within days, the Economic Community of West African States (ECOWAS), the UN, and much of the international community condemned the coup, and in some cases ceased their operations in Mali.[4] ECOWAS suspended Mali from its membership and imposed sanctions against CNRDRE.[5]

Meanwhile, the coup caused enough chaos to benefit the MNLA's cause. On April 2, 2012, the MNLA seized several major cities in the north including Gao, Kidal, and Timbuktu.[6] The MNLA announced a ceasefire on April 6, claiming that they had enough land to form their own state of Azawad.[7] The country was split in two, with Bamako in control in the south and the rebels holding the north.

The MNLA sought the assistance of Islamist groups in its rebellion. These groups included AQIM, *Ansar Dine*, and the Movement for Unity & Jihad in West Africa (commonly referred to as MUJAO, the acronym of its French name, *Mouvement pour l'unicité et le jihad en Afrique de l'Ouest*.). In May 2012, the MNLA and *Ansar Dine* agreed to merge to form an Islamist state.[8] However, the union did not last long. Within less than a week, the two groups clashed over the degree to which *sharia* law would be enforced. Then MUJAO similarly united with the MNLA, and similarly fell out. Thereafter, MUJAO and Ansar Dine worked together to push the MNLA out of Gao in June 2012.[9]

In early December 2012, representatives of *Ansar Dine* and the MNLA agreed to a ceasefire with the government.[10] However by early January 2013, *Ansar Dine* suspended its ceasefire agreement with the government, accusing it of preparing for war.[11] The Islamists then began aggressively moving south towards Bamako. By January 10, Islamist rebels attacked and took control of Konna, a town less than 40 miles from Mopti, where the Malian army maintains a strategic base.[12]

The French government responded by announcing Operation Serval, in which the French government would support Mali in beating back Islamist forces. With French support, the Malian army regained control of Konna on January 11.[13] African troops from the Economic Community of West African States (ECOWAS) also began deployed to the country.[14] French, Malian, and ECOWAS troops quickly retook northern cities and towns in the weeks that followed. However, upon retaking Gao, the French-led forces found themselves conducting counter-insurgency measures, similar to those needed in Afghanistan and Iraq, as the Islamists mounted a counter-attack in February.[15] In August 2014, Operation Serval was replaced by Operation Barkhane. With a mandate focused more on counterterrorism, the 3000-strong force is headquartered in N'Djamena, Chad, and operates across Burkina Faso, Chad, Mali, Mauritania, and Niger. Operation Barkhane was still active as of early 2017.

The Malian government has since signed a number of ceasefires with several armed Tuareg separatist groups, including the MNLA. The most recent, known as the Algiers Accord, was signed in June 2015. Among other things, the peace deal included provisions for former separatist fighters to be integrated into the security force in the north, better representation for the north in central government institutions, and the right for the northern region to form local institutions.[16] The implementation of the peace agreement has been stalled, most notably due the ongoing insecurity in the northern regions, a product of the numerous Islamist militant groups that did not participate in the peace process. After several postponements, local elections were finally held in November 2016 amid reports of violence and inconsistencies.[17]

Militant Islamist groups did not participate in the peace process and are still active in the north and increasingly in the south of the country. While there are a number of distinct Islamist groups, membership between tends to be fluid. As such, multiple groups tend to credibly claim responsibility for terrorist strikes. Analysts have argued that increased counterterrorism pressure from security forces will encourage further collaboration between Mali's Islamist groups.[18]

Al-Qaeda in the Islamic Maghreb (AQIM)

Over time, AQIM has evolved from a local terrorist group seeking to replace Algeria's government with an Islamic one to an al-Qaeda group preaching global *jihad* against the West. Formerly known as the *Group Salafiste Pour la Predication et Combat* (GSPC), AQIM has its roots in the Algerian civil war of the 1990s. In Mali, the group has taken advantage of the country's sparsely populated northern regions where the government has a limited reach. Mali's three northern regions—Timbuktu, Gao and Kidal—contain only 10 percent of the population while accounting for two-thirds of the country's land.[19] As noted by analysts, the group has periodically turned to smuggling and criminality to raise funds, but, at its core, it has remained a highly resilient and pragmatic Islamist insurgency.[20]

In September 2006, GSPC formally merged with al-Qaeda.[21] A few months later, the group rebranded itself as al-Qaeda in the Islamic Maghreb (AQIM). The evolution of GSPC to AQIM changed the group's focus from the "near enemy" (Algeria) to the "far enemy" (the West, particularly the United States and Israel) and the group increasingly targeted foreigners in its North African operations.

GSPC/AQIM, like many Islamist terrorist groups, finances itself through crime. Prior to its merger with al-Qaeda, the group achieved international notoriety when it ransomed 15 European tourists in Algeria in early 2003.[22] It received a reported sum of 5 million Euro.[23] In May 2007, AQIM kidnapped its first foreigner since the 2003 kidnapping. Between 2007 and 2017, there have been a number of additional, high profile kidnappings that illustrate the group's continued ability to operate in northern Mali. The kidnappings serve a dual purpose for AQIM; the activity itself drives foreign investment away from the region, while the ransom payments bring AQIM needed cash for weapons and supplies.[24] In addition to kidnapping, AQIM also engages in profitable smuggling operations in the Sahel with routes going through northern Mali.

In 2016, AQIM and its affiliates launched at least 257 attacks in West Africa.[25] This dramatic increase in attacks—nearly a 150 percent uptick from 2015—underscores the group's ability to successfully recalibrate its strategy and tactics in the face of ongoing counterterrorism efforts and competition from other Islamist groups in the region.[26] At present, there are no credible estimates of force strength for AQIM in Mali available.

While AQIM remains loyal to Al Qaeda's leader Ayman Al-Zawahiri, the group is facing increasing competition from the Islamic State (ISIS).[27]

Ansar Dine ("Defenders of the Faith")

Iyad Ag Ghaly formed *Ansar Dine* ("Defenders of the Faith") in 2011. *Ansar Dine* expanded its reach and power in northern Mali throughout 2012. In January 2013, the group was estimated to have around 1,500 fighters.[28] As previously noted, the group initially worked with the MNLA to take over the north. However, different positions over the adoption of *sharia* law caused the relationship between the two to deteriorate. *Ansar Dine* took control of Timbuktu, Kidal, and Gao in June 2012.[29]

As *Ansar Dine* took control of more and more of northern Mali, the group increasingly pushed a radical interpretation of Islam on Malians. On July 10, 2012, it destroyed two tombs at Timbuktu's ancient Djingareyber mud mosque, a major tourist attraction, angering the city's residents and drawing international condemnation.[30] The Islamist group banned alcohol, smoking, Friday visits to cemeteries, and watching soccer, and required women to wear veils in public.[31] It whipped and beat those who did not adhere to its strict interpretation of sharia law.[32]

As previously discussed, *Ansar Dine* formed and broke a ceasefire with the Malian government in late 2012 and early 2013. As the French intervention gained momentum at the end of January 2013, there were reports that members of *Ansar Dine* crossed into Darfur, Sudan through Niger and Libya.[33]

In June 2016, Ag Ghaly released his first video in almost two years, issuing new threats against the West and commending recent attacks against French forces and UN peacekeepers.[34] On October 31, 2016, Mahmoud Dicko, the president of Mali's High Islamic Council, told reports that he has brokered a truce with Ag Ghaly.[35] However, *Ansar Dine* immediately denied the report, calling the claim "completely baseless."[36]

Movement for Unity and Jihad in West Africa (MUJAO)

MUJAO is a West Africa-based, militant Islamist organization that is allied with *Ansar Dine* and has ties to AQIM.[37] The group made its first public statement on December 12, 2011. Soon after its inception, MUJAO reportedly concluded an agreement with both *Ansar Dine* and AQIM to pursue a common goal of spreading Islamism across the region.[38] The group appears to target West Africa more than its compatriots. The group is largely black African Muslim, rather than of Arab descent, and identifies itself as "an alliance between native Arab, Tuareg and Black African tribes and various *muhajirin* ("Immigrants," i.e. foreign *jihadists*) from North and West Africa."[39] The group appears to fund itself through kidnapping activities.[40]

Like *Ansar Dine*, MUJAO initially had a truce with the MNLA as they jointly fought to take control of Mali's north from Bamako.[41] But in June 2012, MUJAO and its ally *Ansar Dine* pushed the MNLA out of the north-Malian city of Gao.[42] While *Ansar Dine* appears to have taken control of Timbuktu with AQIM, Gao was held by MUJAO.[43] In the advance to Gao, MUJAO reportedly sacked Algeria's consulate and kidnapped seven Algerian diplomats.[44] Once in control, MUJAO imposed a draconian interpretation of *sharia* law on Malians.[45] In August 2013, a significant faction of MUJAO merged with a militant group formerly associated with AQIM to form a new group called *Al-Mourabitoun*.[46]

Al-Mourabitoun ("The Sentinels")

Al-Mourabitoun was formed in August 2013 following a merger between a breakaway segment of AQIM led by Algerian commander Mokhtar Belmokhtar and a faction of MUJAO.[47] Belmokhtar's faction, known as the *al-Mulathamun Battalion* ("the Masked Battalion,"AMB), had previously been part of AQIM, but split into a separate organization in late 2012 after on ongoing dispute with AQIM's *emir*, Abdelmalek Droukdel.[48] Belmokhtar became the commander of *Al-Mourabitoun*, and under his the group claimed responsibility for the January 2013 attack on the Tiguentourine gas facility near Ame.nas, Algeria, which resulted in the deaths of 39 civilians.

The group aims to unite Islamic movements and Muslims across Africa against secular influences, with a particular focus on attacking French interests and French allies across the region.[49] *Al-Mourabitoun* has also been involved in several high-profile attacks against foreigners in central and southern Mali, including the August 2015 attack on the Byblos Hotel in Sévaré, which killed thirteen people, five of whom where UN workers;[50] the March 2015 attack on the La Terrasse restaurant in the capital city of Bamako, which killed five,[51] and the November 2015 attack on the Radisson Blu hotel in Bamako, in which 170 people were taken hostage and nineteen killed.[52] The group has also launched attacks outside of Mali, including collaborating on an attack on the Splendid Hotel in Ouagadougou, the capital of neighboring Burkina Faso, in January 2016 and the March 2016 attack on the Grand Bassam beach resort in Côte d'Ivoire.

In May 2015, *Al-Mourabitoun* co-founder Adnan Abu Walid al Sahrawi alliance to the Islamic State and its founder Abu Bakr al Baghdadi in an audiotape that was released to the Al Akhbar new agency.[53] Several days later, however, Belmokhtar dismissed the pledge of alliance, indicating that al Sahrawi's decision had not been approved by *Al-Mourabitoun's shura* council, a move that seemingly indicated a split in the organization.[54] In the weeks following, local Malian media reported clashes between factions loyal to Belmokhtar and those loyal to al Sahrawi.[55] Al Sahrawi's faction continued to launch attacks in the region, including on a military outpost in Burkina Faso near the border with Mali and on a high-security prison in Niger thought to house militants from Nigeria's *Boko Haram* and AQIM.[56] Following the Radison Blu attack in November 2015, reports indicated that Belmokhtar reunited *Al-Mourabitoun* with AQIM.[57] In October 2016, more than seventeen months after the fact, the Islamic State's Amaq News Agency officially recognized al Sahrawi's oath of allegiance.[58]

Macina Liberation Front (FLM)

The Macina Liberation Front emerged in January 2015 and is led by Amadou Koufa, an ethnically Fulani radical Islamic preacher. In the explosion of post-coup Islamist activity in Mali, Koufa rose to prominence after he led a joint AQIM, *Ansar Dine*, and MUJAO offensive against the town of Konna in early January 2013, the capture of which triggered the beginning of the French intervention in the country.

Notably, the group blends an extremist Islamic ideology with a local ethnic radicalism that is a product of increased insecurity and competition between ethnic groups in central Mali.[59] The term "Macina" refers to the 19th century Fulani-led Islamic Macina Empire that stretched across the central Mali, and Koufa has proved adept at capitalizing on the sense of victimization among ethnic Fulani in the central region of the country. The group is reported to target recruiting to young Fulanis by using local radio stations to broadcast Koufa's Fulani-language sermons, which draw on a narrative of a return to a mythical time when Fulani were the masters of prosperous Islamic faith in West Africa.[60]

Membership in the FLM is estimated to be a few hundred fighters, and the group lacks the numbers to conduct more than small-scale attacks using improvised explosive devices (IEDs).[61] The FLM does, however, often collaborate with other Islamist groups to launch high profile attacks on United Nations peacekeepers and civilian targets. The FLM claimed a role in the November 2015 attack on the Radisson Blu hotel in Bamako[62] and in the July 2016 attack on the Malian military base in Nampala area of the central Segou Region.[63]

Islamism and Society

Mali has a significant Muslim majority, with 94.8 percent of the population adhering to the religion.[64] While the north has experienced a significant uptick in Islamist activity, it is not clear that radical ideology has actually gained a significant foothold across the country. The Islamists, their radical teachings and their imposition of justice have reportedly not been embraced by northerners, many of whom have simply fled into refugee camps in neighboring Mauritania, Burkina Faso, and Niger.[65]

Malian Islam is not typical of other Islamic nations. The country's practice of the religion incorporates animist traditions of the region, including "absorbing mystical elements [and] ancestor veneration."[66] Mali's lengthy history figures prominently in the country's contemporary culture; Malians "regularly invoke Muslim rulers of various pre-colonial states and empires and past Muslim clerics, saints, and miracle-workers from the distant and more recent colonial and post-colonial past."[67] Islam and animism, in other words, have coexisted in Mali for centuries.[68]

Since Islamists took over the north, several French MPs have received reports that Qatar was financing the MNLA, *Ansar Dine*, and MUJAO.[69] Iran has also attempted to peddle influence in Mali.[70] Skeptical of the fundamentalists' ability to influence his country, President Toure commented prior to his ouster that: "Mali is a very old Islamic country where tolerance is part of our tradition."[71]

When the Islamists were in control of the north, they sought to impose their beliefs on the region and to purge Mali of its religious diversity. There have been several instances of Islamist militants destroying shrines and mausoleums in the north, particularly in Timbuktu, claiming the veneration of Sufi saints and scholars was sacrilegious. 16 of the mausoleums destroyed were listed as UNESCO World Heritage Sites.[72] The destruction of these historic shrines was recently ruled a war crime by the International Criminal Court, which sentenced one fighter involved, Ahmad al-Mahdi, to nine years in prison for his participation in the attacks.[73]

While the northern populations initially welcomed the French intervention, frustrations in the north have grown as the French and the United Nations Multidimensional Integrated Stabilization Mission in Mali (MINUSMA) peacekeepers continue to struggle to effectively provide security. There has also been discontent amongst northern populations regarding certain provisions of the 2015 Algiers Accord. In July of 2016, three were killed and dozens wounded when the Malian military open fired on protestors demonstrating against the nomination of former armed militants as local government authorities, as specified by Algiers Accord.[74]

ISLAMISM AND THE STATE

In keeping with the French tradition, religion in Mali "is understood as private and confessional."[75] The Malian constitution, adopted in 1992, maintains the country as a secular state. However, the 1990s saw a dramatic increase in the number of Islamic associations throughout the country, each with varying motivations and religious interpretations.[76] The government formed the High Islamic Council (*Haut Conseil Islamique*) in 2002.[77] While religious political parties are banned under the constitution, Mali's government supports the High Islamic Council as an "official and unique interlocutor of political authorities for all questions relative to the practice of Islam."[78]

The Bush administration began the Pan Sahel Initiative in October 2002 to train African nations in counterterrorism.[79] In June 2005, the program expanded to include more countries from the region, becoming the Trans-Saharan Counter-Terrorism Initiative (TSCTP).[80] The Initiative's Operation Flintlock provides anti-insurgency training to the armies of the seven participating states, including Mali.[81] Operation Flintlock has been reprised on several occasions, most recently in February 2016.[82]

In addition to the American efforts to bolster their military capabilities, Mali and its neighbors have made efforts to coordinate their counterterrorism activities. Algeria held a conference in March 2010 inviting leaders from Burkina Faso, Chad, Libya, Mali, Mauritania and Niger to build a joint security plan to tackle *jihadists*.[83] Subsequently, Algeria, Mauritania, Niger and Mali established a joint military base in Tamanrasset, southern Algeria, in April 2010.[84] Under Operation Barkhane, France has continued its counterterrorism operations and support in the region. In September 2013, in an effort to discourage the growth of radical interpretations of Islam in Mali Malian President Ibrahim Boubacar Keita signed an agreement with the Kingdom of Morocco that would bring 500 Malian *imams* to Morocco for moderate religious training and make available to Malian students religious scholarships at Moroccan universities.[85] Furthermore, Mali's interim government asked the International Criminal Court (ICC) to investigate possible war crimes perpetrated by the Tuareg and Islamist rebels in the north.[86] In September 2016, the ICC convicted former fighter Ahmad al-Mahdi of war crimes.

Overall, the government response to Islamist groups has focused heavily on security solutions and building policing capacity. This has catalyzed two problems. First, heavy-handedness on the part of Malian security forces has tended to exacerbate local grievances and runs the risk of increasing support for Islamist groups. This has already happened to an extent with Mali's Fulani populations, and groups like FLM have found success recruiting among young Fulani populations disaffected after abuses by Malian security services.[87]

Second, a focus on security solutions has been at the detriment of the need to address local social and economic issues in the north of the country. Unfortunately, despite a close relationship between the Malian government and its international partners, President Keita's tenure has been hampered by allegations of corruption and nepotism.[88] Without improving trust in state institutions, service delivery mechanisms, and government accountability, it will be difficult for the government to effectively protect against the allure of Islamist groups to the young and disenchanted, and these groups will continue to capitalize on local crises and insecurity.[89]

Endnotes

[1] Arieff, Alexis. Crisis in Mali. Congressional Research Service, January 13, 2013, https://fas.org/sgp/crs/row/R42664.pdf

[2] Ibid.

[3] Adam Nossiter, "Soldiers Overthrow Mali Government in Setback for Democracy in Africa," New York Times, March 22, 2012, http://www.nytimes.com/2012/03/23/world/africa/mali-coup-france-calls-for-elections.html?pagewanted=all.

[4] ECOWAS, "ECOWAS Statement on the Disturbances in Bamko, Mali," March 21, 2012, http://www.ecowas.int/publications/en/statement/mali21032012.pdf; "UN Condemns Political Instability in Mali After Armed Rebellion," UN News Centre, March 22, 2012, http://www.un.org/apps/news/story.asp?NewsID=41604&Cr=Tuareg&Cr1; Corey Flintoff, "Mali's Coup: Echoes of a Turbulent Past," National Public Radio, March 23, 2012, http://www.npr.org/2012/03/23/149223151/malis-coup-a-setback-for-a-young-african-democracy.

[5] Emergency Mini-Summit of ECOWAS Heads of State and Government on the Situation in Mali (The Economic Community of West African States, March 29, 2012), 19, (http://www.ecowas.int/publications/en/communique_final/mini-sommet/comfinal_mali_2012.pdf.

[6] Neal Conan and Ofeibea Quist-Arcton, "Turmoil in Mali Deepens After Military Coup," National Public Radio, April 5, 2012, http://www.npr.org/2012/04/05/150072681/a-military-coup-creates-political-crisis-in-mali.

[7] "Mali Rebels Announce Ceasefire," ABC News, April 6, 2012, http://www.abc.net.au/news/2012-04-06/mali-rebels-announce-ceasefire/3936824.

[8] "Mali Tuareg and Islamist Rebels Agree on Islamist State," BBC, May 27, 2012, http://www.bbc.co.uk/news/world-africa-18224004?print=true.

[9] "Mali: Islamists Seize Gao from Tuareg Rebels," BBC, June 27, 2012, http://www.bbc.co.uk/news/world-africa-18610618?print=true.

[10] Monica Mark, "Mali Rebel Groups Agree Ceasefire," Guardian (London), December 5, 2012, http://www.guardian.co.uk/world/2012/dec/05/malian-rebel-groups-agree-ceasefire.

[11] "Mali Islamist Group 'Suspends' Ceasefire," VOA News, January 4, 2013, http://www.voanews.com/content/mali-islamist-group-suspends-ceasefire/1577693.html.

[12] Afua Hirsch, "French Troops Arrive in Mali to Stem Rebel Advance," Guardian (London), January 11, 2013, http://www.guardian.co.uk/world/2013/jan/11/france-intervene-mali-conflict.

[13] Ibid.

[14] Christopher Isiguzo and Damilola Oyedele, "Nigeria: Air Force Sends War Planes to Mali Thursday," ThisDay, January 17, 2013, http://allafrica.com/stories/201301170615.html.

[15] David Lewis, "In Mali Town, Counter-Insurgency Task Ties Down French," Reuters, February 14, 2013, http://www.reuters.com/article/2013/02/14/us-mali-rebels-gao-idUSBRE91D1EV20130214.

[16] "Malian rivals sign peace deal," Al Jazeera (Doha), June 21, 2015, http://www.aljazeera.com/news/2015/06/malian-rivals-sign-peace-deal-150620173301883.html.

[17] Adama Diarra and Souleymane Ag Anara, "Mali's Local Elections Marred by Boycotts, Kidnapping," Reuters, November 20, 2016, http://www.reuters.com/article/us-mali-elections-idUSKBN13F0R8?il=0.

[18] Rida Lyammouri, "Attack Highlights Poor Resources of Malian Army and Underscores Collaboration between Islamist Militants," IHS Jane's Terrorism and Insurgency Monitor 16, iss. 8, September 2016.

[19] William B. Farrell and Carla M. Komich, "USAID/DCHA/CMM Assessment: Northern Mali," Management Systems International, June 17, 2004.

[20] J. Peter Pham, "The Dangerous 'Pragmatism' of Al-Qaeda in the Islamic Maghreb," Journal of Middle East and Africa, (2011) 2: 15-29.

[21] Craig Whitlock, "Al-Qaeda's Far-Reaching New Partner," Washington Post, October 5, 2006, http://www.washingtonpost.com/wp-dyn/content/article/2006/10/04/AR2006100402006.html.

[22] Stephen Harmon, "From GSPC to AQIM: The Evolution of an Algerian Islamist Terrorist Group into an Al-Qa'ida Affiliate and its Implications for the Sahara-Sahel Region," Concerned African Scholars Bulletin no. 85, Spring 2010, 17, http://concernedafricascholars.org/docs/bulletin85harmon.pdf.

[23] Raffi Khatchadourian, "Pursuing Terrorists in the Great Desert," The Village Voice, January 12, 2006, http://www.villagevoice.com/2006-01-17/news/pursuing-terrorists-in-the-great-desert/.
[24] Michael Petrou, "Al-Qaeda in North Africa," Maclean's, May 11, 2009.
[25] Caleb Weiss, "Al Qaeda linked to more than 250 West African attacks in 2016," Long War Journal, January 8, 2017, http://www.longwarjournal.org/archives/2017/01/over-250-al-qaeda-linked-attacks-in-west-africa-in-2016.php
[26] Anoar Boukhars, "How West Africa Became Fertile Ground for AQIM and ISIS," World Politics Review, November 29, 2016, http://www.worldpoliticsreview.com/articles/20556/how-west-africa-became-fertile-ground-for-aqim-and-isis.
[27] Sergei Boeke, "Al Qaeda in the Islamic Maghreb: Terrorism, Insurgency, or Organized Crime?" Small Wars & Insurgencies 27, no. 5, 2016, 914-936, http://www.tandfonline.com/doi/full/10.1080/09592318.2016.1208280.
[28] "'Lion of the Desert': Ex-Partner of Germany Leads Malian Islamists," Der Speigel (Hamburg), January 13, 2013, http://www.spiegel.de/international/world/leader-of-malian-islamists-once-helped-german-government-a-878724.html.
[29] Ibid.
[30] "Ansar Dine Destroy More Shrines in Mali," Al Jazeera (Doha), July 10, 2012, http://www.aljazeera.com/news/africa/2012/07/201271012301347496.html.
[31] Michael Lambert and Jason Warner, "Who is Ansar Dine?" CNN, August 14, 2012, http://globalpublicsquare.blogs.cnn.com/2012/08/14/who-are-ansar-dine/.
[32] Adam Nossiter, "Burkina Faso Official Goes to Islamist-Held Northern Mali in Effort to Avert War," New York Times, August 7, 2012, http://www.nytimes.com/2012/08/08/world/africa/burkina-faso-official-visits-mali-in-effort-to-avert-war.html?gwh=.
[33] "Chad Told France That Mali Rebels May Have Entered Sudan – Diplomat," Sudan Tribune, February 26, 2013, http://allafrica.com/stories/201302270345.html.
[34] Conor Gaffey, "Who is Iyad Ag Ghaly, Mali's Veteran Jihadi?" Newsweek, June 29, 2016, http://www.newsweek.com/who-iyad-ag-ghaly-malis-veteran-jihadi-475473.
[35] Idriss Fall, "Mal: Insurgent Group Accepts Cease-fire but With Conditions," Voice of America, October 31, 2016, http://www.voanews.com/a/mali-insurgent-group-ansar-dine-accepts-cease-fire/3573301.html.
[36] "Mali Islamists Still Waging War, Dismiss Ceasefire Report," Voice of America, November 2, 2016, http://www.voanews.com/a/mali-dicko-ansar-dine/3576634.html.

[37] Nossiter, "Burkina Faso Official Goes to Islamist-Held Northern Mali in Effort to Avert War."

[38] "Some Things We May Think About MUJWA," The Moor Next Door, May 30, 2012, http://themoornextdoor.wordpress.com/2012/05/30/some-things-we-think-about-mujwa/.

[39] Andrew McGregor, "Islamist Groups Mount Joint Offensive in Mali," Jamestown Foundation Militant Leadership Monitor XI, iss. 1, January 10, 2013, https://jamestown.org/wp-content/uploads/2013/01/TM_011_Issue01_01.pdf.

[40] Sanders and Moseley, "A Political, Security and Humanitarian Crisis: Northern Mali."

[41] "'Dozens killed' in Northern Mali Fighting," Al Jazeera (Doha), June 28, 2012, http://www.aljazeera.com/news/africa/2012/06/201262891738152474.html.

[42] Ibid.

[43] Nossiter, "Burkina Faso Official Goes to Islamist-Held Northern Mali in Effort to Avert War."

[44] "Some Things We May Think About MUJWA," The Moor Next Door.

[45] Serge Daniel, "North Mali Residents Ready to Resist Islamist Groups," American Free Press, August 14, 2012, http://www.google.com/hostednews/afp/article/ALeqM5jG2uPsDfGOXCBXusjGHvLzlmNvBQ?docId=CNG.5b6400c0bc73c4f95cd82e5991bf5f1a.231.

[46] Bill Roggio, "Al Qaeda Group Led by Belmokhtar, MUJAO Unite to Form Al-Murabitoon," Long War Journal, August 22, 2013, http://www.longwarjournal.org/archives/2013/08/al_qaeda_groups_lead_by_belmok.php.

[47] Ibid.

[48] U.S. Department of State, Office of the Coordinator for Counterterrorism, "Country Reports on Terrorism 2013," April 2014, http://www.state.gov/documents/organization/225886.pdf.

[49] Government of Australia, "Australian National Security: Al-Murabitun," November 5, 2014, https://www.nationalsecurity.gov.au/Listedterroristorganisations/Pages/Al-Murabitun.aspx.

[50] "Mali Hotel Siege: Several Killed in Sevare, Four UN Workers Saved," BBC, August 9, 2015, http://www.bbc.com/news/world-africa-33833363.

[51] "Al-Qaeda-Linked Group Claims Mali Restaurant Attack," Al Jazeera (Doha), March 9, 2015, http://www.aljazeera.com/news/2015/03/al-qaeda-linked-group-claims-mali-restaurant-attack-150309072613760.html.

[52] "Two Arrested in Connection with Bamako Hotel Attack," Guardian (London), November 27, 2015, https://www.theguardian.com/world/2015/nov/27/two-arrested-in-connection-with-bamako-hotel-attack.

[53] Thomas Joscelyn, "Confusion Surrounds West African Jihadists' Loyalty to Islamic State," Long War Journal, May 17, 2015, http://www.longwarjournal.org/archives/2015/05/confusion-surrounds-west-african-jihadists-loyalty-to-islamic-state.php.

[54] "Sahara Islamist Leader Belmokhtar Dismisses Islamic State Pledge: Report," Reuters, May 17, 2015, https://www.yahoo.com/news/sahara-islamist-leader-belmokhtar-dismisses-islamic-state-pledge-170310550.html?ref=gs.

[55] Thomas Joscelyn and Caleb Weiss, "Islamic State Recognizes Oath of Allegiance from Jihadists in Mali," Long War Journal, October 31, 2016, http://www.longwarjournal.org/archives/2016/10/islamic-state-recognizes-oath-of-allegiance-from-jihadists-in-west-africa.php

[56] Conor Gaffey, "Niger Repels Attack on Prison Holding Jihadis from Mali and Nigeria," Newsweek, October 17, 2016, http://www.newsweek.com/niger-repels-attack-prison-holding-jihadis-mali-and-nigeria-510618.

[57] "Mali Extremists Join with Al-Qaeda-linked North Africa Group," Associated Press, December 4, 2015, http://www.cnsnews.com/news/article/mali-extremists-join-al-qaida-linked-north-africa-group.

[58] Joscelyn and Weiss, "Islamic State Recognizes Oath of Allegiance from Jihadists in Mali." Long War Journal. October 31, 2016. http://www.longwarjournal.org/archives/2016/10/islamic-state-recognizes-oath-of-allegiance-from-jihadists-in-west-africa.php

[59] Michael Shurkin, "How to Defeat a New Boko Haram In Mali," Newsweek, September 7, 2015, http://www.newsweek.com/how-defeat-new-boko-haram-mali-369430.

[60] "Mali Islamists Armed Group Push Fighting Beyond Conflict-hit North," Telegraph (London), September 23, 2015, http://www.telegraph.co.uk/news/worldnews/africaandindianocean/mali/11884570/Mali-Islamists-armed-group-push-fighting-beyond-conflict-hit-north.html; Yvan Guichaua and Dougoukolo Alpha Oumar Ba-Konaré, "Central Mali Gripped by a Dangerous Brew of Jihad, Revolt and Self-Defence," The Conversation, November 13, 2016, https://theconversation.com/central-mali-gripped-by-a-dangerous-brew-of-jihad-revolt-and-self-defence-67668.

[61] Rida Lyammouri, "Attack Highlights Poor Resources of Malian Army and Underscores Collaboration between Islamist Militants," IHS Jane's Terrorism and Insurgency Monitor 16, iss. 8, September 2016.

[62] "Mali: Une Seconde Revendication de L'attaque de L'hôtel Radisson," Radio France Internationale Afrique, November 23, 2015, http://www.rfi.fr/afrique/20151123-mali-revendication-attaque-hotel-radisson-front-liberation-macina-bamako?ns_campaign=reseaux_sociaux&ns_source=twitter&ns_mchannel=social&ns_linkname=editorial&aef_campaign_ref=partage_aef&aef_campaign_date=2015-11-23&dlvrit=1448817.

[63] Lyammouri, "Attack Highlights Poor Resources of Malian Army and Underscores Collaboration between Islamist Militants."

[64] "Mali," CIA World Factbook, January 2017, https://www.cia.gov/library/publications/the-world-factbook/geos/ml.html.

[65] Kate Thomas, "In Limbo: Malian Refugees in Burkina Faso," Refugees Deeply, April 20, 2016, https://www.newsdeeply.com/refugees/community/2016/04/20/in-limbo-malian-refugees-in-burkina-faso

[66] Lisa Anderson, "Democracy, Islam share a home in Mali," Chicago Tribune, December 15, 2004, http://articles.chicagotribune.com/2004-12-15/news/0412150328_1_mali-islamic-cinq.

[67] Soares, "Islam in Mali in the Neoliberal Era," 212.

[68] Robert Pringle, "Democratization in Mali: Putting History To Work," United States Institute of Peace Peaceworks no. 58, October 2006, 27, http://www.usip.org/resources/democratization-mali-putting-history-work.

[69] Ségolène Allemandou, "Is Qatar Fuelling the Crisis in North Mali?" France 24, January 23, 2013, http://www.france24.com/en/20130121-qatar-mali-france-ansar-dine-mnla-al-qaeda-sunni-islam-doha.

[70] Willy Stern, "Moderate Islam, African-Style," Weekly Standard, August 4, 2008, http://www.weeklystandard.com/Content/Public/Articles/000/000/015/369mhred.asp.

[71] Anderson, "Democracy, Islam Share a Home in Mali."

[72] Joshua Hammer, "The Race to Save Mali's Priceless Artifacts," Smithsonian Magazine, January 2014, http://www.smithsonianmag.com/history/Race-Save-Mali-Artifacts-180947965/.

[73] "ICC: Mali Fighter Jailed for Destroying Timbuktu Sites," Al Jazeera (Doha), September 27, 2016, http://www.aljazeera.com/news/2016/09/icc-mali-fighter-jailed-destroying-timbuktu-sites-160927093507739.html.

[74] Kamissa Camara, "Violent Protests Have Erupted in Mali. Here's What is Driving Them," Washington Post, August 15, 2016, https://www.washingtonpost.com/news/monkey-cage/wp/2016/08/15/whats-the-role-for-malis-youth-after-the-2015-peace-accord-not-enough-protesters-say/?utm_term=.f9fe8717fb22.

[75] Soares, "Islam in Mali in the Neoliberal Era," 214.

[76] Nicolas Colombant, "Mali's Muslims Steer Back to Spiritual Roots," Christian Science Monitor, February 26, 2002, http://www.csmonitor.com/2002/0226/p08s02-woaf.html.

[77] Ibid.

[78] Soares, "Islam in Mali in the Neoliberal Era," 215.

[79] Harmon, "From GSPC to AQIM," 22.

[80] Ibid., 23.

[81] Ibid.

[82] Emanuelle Landais,"US led Flintlock counter-terrorism exercises end in Senegal, " Deutsche Welle, February 29, 2016, http://www.dw.com/en/us-led-flintlock-counter-terrorism-exercises-end-in-senegal/a-19083235.

[83] "Al-Qaida Digs in to Resist Region's Armies," United Press International, July 6, 2010, http://www.upi.com/Top_News/Special/2010/07/06/Al-Qaida-digs-in-to-resist-regions-armies/UPI-14121278441085/.

[84] "Brief: Saharan Countries' Cooperation Against AQIM," Stratfor, April 21, 2010, http://www.stratfor.com/node/160466/analysis/20100421_brief_saharan_countries_cooperation_against_aqim.

[85] Vish Sakthivel, "Morocco's Move in Mali," Foreign Affairs, January 14, 2014, https://www.foreignaffairs.com/articles/africa/2014-01-14/moroccos-move-mali.

[86] "Mali Asks International Court to Investigate Alleged War Crimes," Los Angeles Times, July 18, 2012, http://latimesblogs.latimes.com/world_now/2012/07/mali-international-court-war-crimes.html.

[87] Boukhars, "How West Africa Became Fertile Ground for AQIM and ISIS."

[88] Grégory Chauzal, "A Snapshot of Mali Three Years After the 2012 Crisis," Netherlands Institute of International Relations, June 8, 2015, https://www.clingendael.nl/publication/snapshot-mali-three-years-after-2012-crisis.

[89] Anoar Boukhars, "How West Africa Became Fertile Ground for AQIM and ISIS," World Politics Review, November 29, 2016, http://www.worldpoliticsreview.com/articles/20556/how-west-africa-became-fertile-ground-for-aqim-and-isis.

NIGERIA

QUICK FACTS

Population: 186,053,386 (estimated December 2016)

Area: 923,768 sq km

Ethnic Groups: Nigeria, Africa's most populous country, is composed of more than 250 ethnic groups; the following are the most populous and politically influential: Hausa and Fulani 29%, Yoruba 21%, Igbo (Ibo) 18%, Ijaw 10%, Kanuri 4%, Ibibio 3.5%, Tiv 2.5%

Religions: Muslim 50%, Christian 40%, indigenous beliefs 10%

Government Type: Federal Republic

GDP (official exchange rate): $490.2 billion (2015 est.)

Map and Quick Facts courtesy of the CIA World Factbook (Last Updated: December 2016)

OVERVIEW

Since its independence in 1960, Nigeria has been plagued by a number of organized militant groups. Among them are Niger Delta militants in southeastern Nigeria, whose grievances are based on extreme environmental degradation, as well as political and economic disenfranchisement. Additionally, there are ethnic-based militants in Nigeria's Middle Belt, where the predominantly Muslim northern region and predominantly Christian southern region meet. There are often conflicts among ethnic groups of different religions over land use. In recent years, Muslim Fulani herders have been increasingly arming themselves and killing Christian villagers in unprecedented numbers, albeit without any centralized coordination. Finally, there are Islamist militants in northern Nigeria, such as Boko Haram and also the potentially violent pro-Iranian Shi'ite Islamic Movement in Nigeria (IMN). These two groups seek to establish an Islamic State in Nigeria (for Boko Haram, a Sunni-Salafi state, and for the IMN a Khomeinist Shi'a state), to institutionalize Islamic law and an Islamic identity for the country, to pry Nigeria out of its alliances with Western countries, and to reorient it towards Islam.

Since September 2010, Boko Haram has become the greatest threat to Nigeria's unity and has been responsible for more violence than any other militant movement in the country (although the Fulani herders may be soon reaching the same level of violence, if not notoriety, as Boko Haram). 20,000 people have been killed in the fighting. Millions more have been displaced, and close to 5 million need food assistance, due to Boko Haram's disruption of the local economy.[1] Boko Haram is the most violent on the spectrum of Islamist movements in Nigeria, but it is divided internally between two factions, one of which is loyal to the Islamic State. This loyalist faction is known as the Islamic State's West Africa Province, or ISWAP, while the other, independent grouping is Jama'atu Ahlis Sunna Lidda'awati wal-Jihad (The Group for Preaching the Prophet's Teachings and Jihad, or JAS). Both are referred to as "Boko Haram" by the media and government, although neither group refers to itself as such.

ISLAMISM ACTIVITY

In addition to JAS and ISWAP, which are northern Nigeria's most violent *Salafist-jihadist* groups, there are thousands of other Islamist groups in Nigeria, including millenarian *mahdists*, *Salafists*, and Shi'a fundamentalists. There are also many religiously moderate, albeit socially conservative, Sufi groups of the Qadiriyya and Tijaniyya orders, as well as Jama'atu Nasril Islam (JNI), a northern Nigerian Muslim umbrella organization led by the Sultan of Sokoto. In contrast to violent Islamist leaders, JNI has called on Muslims to "pray fervently for peaceful co-existence in Nigeria and for Allah to put to shame those who are bent on chaos and unrest."[2]

Nigerian universities have long been hotbeds of Islamist activity. Most leaders who are at the forefront of Islamic extremism in northern Nigeria have their roots in the universities, where they have been able to give theoretical cover to radical ideas and use academic platforms to spread their message. Two noteworthy trends in Nigeria, which are consistent with the rest of the Islamic world, are that youths are the primary demographic group susceptible to radicalization, and that men gravitate towards radicalization more than women.

This section describes four of the most prominent Islamist groups in northern Nigeria: JAS and ISWAP (both commonly referred to as "Boko Haram" in media and government discourse); *Maitatsine/Kala Kato; Jama't Izalat al Bid'a Wa Iqamat as Sunna* (Izala); and the Islamic Movement in Nigeria (IMN).

JAS and ISWAP (Boko Haram)

JAS traces its lineage to Mohammed Yusuf, a Nigerian preacher who maintained his headquarters in northeastern Nigeria's Borno State. He primarily taught that Western education and influence were blasphemous because they contradicted the Quran, and that service in the Nigerian government was unacceptable, as Nigeria was not an Islamic State. Veteran al-Qaeda ideologue Abu Muhammed al-Maqdisi had a significant influence on Yusuf's adoption of a strain of *Salafi-Jihadi* ideology consistent with al-Qaeda's.[3] As Yusuf gained in popularity in the late 2000s, his teachings began to generate opposition from mainstream *Salafists*; one such scholar argued that if Muslims follow Yusuf's advice, then "pagan policemen [who serve in government] will kill and injure Muslims, and when taken to hospitals pagan doctors and nurses [with Western education] will attend to them."[4]

However, although Yusuf began urging his followers, who numbered as many as 280,000 and hailed from Nigeria, Niger, Chad and Cameroon, to prepare for conflict with the Nigerian government, he was not a *jihadist*.[5] During his leadership of the organization (2002 to 2009), his followers did not engage in coordinated violence against the state, although occasional clashes with Nigerian security forces did occur, usually because of the followers' refusal to obey local ordinances. In Yusuf's own words, he believed that sharia law "should be established in Nigeria, and if possible all over the world, but through dialogue."[6]

Yusuf was killed along with approximately 1,000 of his followers in a four-day series of clashes with the Nigerian government in northeastern Nigeria in July 2009. Afterward, Yusuf's deputy, Abubakar Shekau, and other followers announced a jihad against the Nigerian government and security forces, Christians, and moderate Muslim religious and political figures. This was the first time when the group claimed a formal name: JAS. JAS's first attack took place on September 7, 2010, when approximately 50 fighters attacked Bauchi Prison and freed fellow members detained in the July 2009 clashes, making good on the organization's promise that these prisoners would not spend the holiday of *Eid al-Fitr* behind bars. Since then, JAS has carried out more than 1,000 attacks and killed in excess of 10,000 people in an area of operations ranging from its hub of operations in northeastern Borno State to Kogi State in the geographic south of Nigeria, to Sokoto in northwestern Nigeria, to Diffa in Niger, to northern Cameroon, and to N'djamena and other villages around Lake Chad in Chad.[7]

At a minimum, JAS's main objectives are to: 1) remove religious authority from the Sultan of Sokoto and other traditional Muslim leaders and place religious authority in the hands of JAS's religious leaders; 2) create an Islamic state in some or all parts of Nigeria; 3) prosecute the security officers who killed Mohammed Yusuf and other Muslims; and 4) obtain amnesty for all JAS members in prison and compensation for the mosques and the homes of Muslims that have been destroyed in clashes with the government. The latter two goals have, however, progressively become less of a priority for JAS as the militant group has evolved. However, it seems that the group would accept autonomy to live under its own interpretation of Islamic law in a part of Nigeria that restricted entry to the government or security forces, or to any Christian.

However, JAS's killings of innocent Muslims during attacks on the government and security forces—both as collateral damage and as a means to intimidate Muslims in the general population—has been one factor that has bred dissent among the movement's members. In late January 2012, a more internationally oriented faction of the group, which called itself *Jama'atu Ansaril Muslimina Fi Biladis Sudan* (Vanguards for the Protection of Muslims in Black Africa, or "Ansaru"), announced its formation in a video statement and in fliers distributed in Kano.[8] This occurred after Boko Haram's January 20th attacks left more than 170 civilians dead.[9] *Ansaru* has since been proscribed as a terrorist group by the United Kingdom for its alleged involvement in the kidnapping and killing of two British and Italian men in Sokoto State in March 2012, and for being "broadly aligned" with al-Qaeda.[10] *Ansaru* began raising its online media profile in November 2012, around the same time that its fighters carried out a prison break operation in Abuja.[11] Then, in December, *Ansaru* then kidnapped a Frenchman in Katsina, 30 miles from the border with Niger, and warned France that the prisoner's fate would be contingent on France rescinding the law banning the Islamic veil and ceasing its planned attack on the Islamic state in northern Mali (the Frenchman later escaped captivity).[12] In January 2013, *Ansaru* also kidnapped seven foreigners in Bauchi State and killed them the following month, after alleging that the UK and Nigeria were preparing to conduct a rescue attempt (one of the seven captives was British).[13] *Ansaru* also jointly claimed a kidnapping with the larger JAS in December 2013 of a French priest in Cameroon, who was later released for a multi-million dollar sum of money and JAS militants imprisoned in Cameroon.[14]

By 2014, however, *Ansaru* was all but extinct. Despite initially offering itself as a more "humane" alternative to JAS, three factors led to its demise: the French-led intervention in northern Mali in 2012-13, which separated Ansaru from its AQIM patrons, the arrests of key *Ansaru* members by Nigerian special forces, including those who received funding from AQIM, and JAS's assassinations of *Ansaru* commanders who defected from JAS. As the joint claim of the French priest in Cameroon suggested, *Ansaru* members, partly out of desperation, rejoined JAS and brought with them their kidnapping and media specialized skills, especially in the Lake Chad region. Some *Ansaru* members held out in Bauchi State until early 2015, when JAS leader Shekau pledged loyalty to Abu Bakr al-Baghdadi and the Islamic State. Ultimately, however, all of *Ansaru* appears to have been swallowed by the newly announced Islamic State in West Africa Province (ISWAP), or to have withdrawn from militancy.

Several months after JAS reintegrated the bulk of *Ansaru* into its ranks, a second major division occurred when Shekau pledged allegiance to Abu Bakr al-Baghdadi and the Islamic State.[15] In doing so, JAS officially became known as the Islamic State's West Africa Province, or ISWAP. Nigeria, under new president Muhammed Buhari, subsequently launched a large-scale military offensive against ISWAP, which caused the group to lose control of much of the territory in northeastern Nigeria that JAS had controlled prior to the pledge. These battlefield frustrations, as well as lingering ideological disputes between Shekau and the former Ansaru members over his tolerance for killing ordinary Muslims, ultimately led to a fracturing of ISWAP. The former *Ansaru* members became recognized by the Islamic State as ISWAP in August 2016, under the leadership of Muhammed Yusuf's son, Abu Musab al-Barnawi.[16] Shekau, meanwhile, was compelled to leave ISWAP with his loyalist fighters, and subsequently announced in August 2016 that he was reverting to the name JAS.[17]

Today, both ISWAP and JAS remain active, with the former largely operating in the Lake Chad region and the latter focused on Borno State. For the most part, the groups remain at odds with each other.

Other factions more moderate than JAS have also reportedly offered to negotiate with the Nigerian government since 2012, but such groups have little credibility. This is because JAS and ISWAP are behind almost all of the Islamist violence in northern Nigeria, and any truce with the factions other than JAS and ISWAP is likely to be inconsequential.[18]

Maitatsine/Kala Kato

Kala Kato, which means "mere man," in reference to the Prophet, claims to be an offshoot of the Maitatsine sect of the 1980s, which was led by the Cameroonian Mohammed Marwa. Marwa claimed to be a new Prophet of Islam and was known as the "Maitatsine," meaning "the one who damns." Even more extreme than Boko Haram founder Mohammed Yusuf, Marwa condemned anyone who read any book other than the Quran, used watches, cars, bicycles, televisions, cigarettes or any other products that reflected Western life. An antecedent not only to *Kala Kato* but also to Boko Haram, Marwa and his thousands of followers clashed with Nigerian authorities in a battle in Kano in 1980 in which Marwa was killed. Subsequent battles to suppress his followers also took place in Borno State in 1982; Gongola State (present-day Gombe State) in 1984; and Bauchi State in 1985. In December 2009, *Kala Kato* engaged in a series of riots and clashes with the Nigerian security forces in Bauchi State, resulting in the deaths of 70 people, including soldiers, policemen, women and 15 children.[19] The cause of the clashes was Kala Kato's violation of an ordinance against preaching outdoors, which was imposed following the Boko Haram clashes of July 2009.[20] Kala Kato remains one of the most obscure Islamist groups in northern Nigeria, and its leader, Mallam Salisu, has maintained that it "has no link with the Boko Haram followers."[21] Kala Kato remains a small group of approximately 2,000 members, and likely will not have appeal to future generations of Islamists or *jihadists*, who are liable to see Boko Haram as a more "legitimate" group to join because of the credibility it has received from the Islamic State and its greater adherence to general *Salaf-jihadi* ideology.

Jama't Izalat al Bid'a Wa Iqamat as Sunna (Society of Eradication of Innovation and Implementation of the Sunna) (Izala)

The *Izala* movement in Nigeria is an anti-Sufi *Salafist* movement that opposes *bid'a* (innovation) and seeks direct interpretation of the Quran. It was established with funding from Saudi Arabia in the late 1970s, in part as an effort to quell then growing pro-Khomeinist leanings among northern Nigerian Muslims. It opposes the "Westernization" of Nigerian society, albeit while accepting modern technology and sciences and embracing women's education and financial self-sufficiency. With many institutions all over the country and influence at the local, state and even federal levels, Izala has become one of the largest Islamist societies not only in Nigeria, but also in the neighboring countries of Chad, Niger, and Cameroon. The implementation of sharia law in twelve northern states since 2000 has provided legitimacy for the Izala movement, which claims to have been the "vanguard" of the pro-sharia movement.[22]

Today, Izala's most important contribution to the Nigerian Islamist landscape may be simply that it is *not* Boko Haram and presents a credible and non-violent option for Islamists.[23] Nonetheless, the rising anti-Shi'a sentiment in Nigeria, coupled with broader anti-Iranian sentiment in Saudi Arabia and the Middle East, has positioned Izala as the main anti-Shi'a group in Nigeria.[24] In this context, Izala may turn violent not so much as a facet of its Salafi-jihadism, but in an effort to clamp down on Shi'ism in Nigeria.

Islamic Movement in Nigeria (IMN)

The IMN is distinct from other Islamist groups in Nigeria because it is supported by the Islamic Republic of Iran, whereas most other groups (like Izala) are supported by Saudi Arabia and other wealthy Sunni Muslim sponsors. The leader of the IMN, Shaykh Ibrahim el-Zakzaky, alleges that the IMN is only an "Islamic Movement," rather than either "Shi'a" or "fundamentalist," but the common perception of the IMN in Nigeria is that it is in fact a Shi'a movement.[25] Although the IMN's members are mostly Shi'a, the IMN resembles Izala and Boko Haram in that it believes secular authorities should not hold power and that northern Nigeria's traditional religious rulers have allowed government abuses against Muslims by supporting Christian politicians and refusing to stand up for Muslims.[26]

Throughout the 1980s and 1990s, Ibrahim el-Zakzaky and his followers petitioned for the implementation of *sharia* law, and sought to bring about an Islamic revolution similar to that which occurred in Iran in 1979. In the 1990s, followers associated with the IMN carried out a series of attacks in northern Nigeria, the most gruesome of which was the 1994 beheading in Kano of Gideon Alakuka, an Igbo trader who was accused (likely falsely) of desecrating the Quran.[27] When *sharia* law was instituted in twelve states of northern Nigeria in 2000, el-Zakzaky, like Izala, believed there was an over-emphasis on corporal punishments; that the northern governors were illegitimate since they did not come to power through Islamic parties; and that the governors were dishonest people "who amputate the hands of poor people, who steal peanuts, while those who steal millions of tax-payers' money go scot-free."[28] Since 2001, the IMN has committed itself to involvement "in national or international issues that are of concern to Muslims, as well as in solidarity with oppressed sections of the Muslim *Ummah* such as the Palestinians and Iraqis." The movement has also voiced support for Osama bin Laden and al-Qaeda, implying that it would attack U.S. interests in Nigeria if the United States or Israel attacks Iran.[29] El-Zakzaky has also made frequent and well-publicized visits to Iran.[30]

After years of steady growth in followers, particularly around el-Zakzaky's base in Zaria, Kaduna State, in December 2015 the Nigerian army violently cracked down on the IMN, killing around 300 members.[31] El-Zakaky was reported to have been heavily wounded during the crackdown and taken to a military hospital in Lagos. However, rumors persist that he was killed in the incident, because in the year that has followed he has not resurfaced, and many of his close affiliates and family members were likewise killed or missing.[32] The Nigerian government has also restricted public protests that called for more information on el-Zakzaky's whereabouts.[33] This has also led to the initiation of a #Freezakzaky campaign by his followers, and to international criticism of Nigeria for human rights abuses against the IMN.[34] The Nigerian army likely supported the action against the IMN because el-Zakzaky had created a virtual state in Zaria, with its own police, media, and schools. Although unproven, there are also rumors that Saudi Arabia encouraged the elimination of el-Zakzaky in an effort to blunt Iranian influence in Nigeria.[35]

ISLAMISM AND SOCIETY

Nigeria's 170 million citizens are divided almost evenly between Muslims and Christians, with Muslims forming the majority in the northern half of the country and Christians forming the majority in its southern half. With more than 80 million Christians and a roughly equal number of Muslims, Nigeria is both the most populous Christian country in Africa, and the most populous Muslim one. The Hausa and Fulani (often referred to as the "Hausa-Fulani" because of their close cultural interaction for the past several centuries) constitute the largest single Muslim ethnic group in Nigeria, and about one-fourth of its total population. The Muslim Kanuri ethnic group predominates in Yobe and Borno States and is about 5% of Nigeria's population. The Yorubas of southwest Nigeria are about 60% Christian and one of the three largest ethnic groups in Nigeria along with the Hausa-Fulanis and the Igbos of southeast Nigeria. At an estimated 12 million, Yoruba Muslims are second only to the Hausa-Fulanis in terms of total Muslim population in an ethnic group. There are dozens of other predominantly Muslim ethnic groups in Nigeria, including the Shuwa Arabs of Borno State, who trace their lineage to the Arab tribes who migrated into northeastern Nigeria from the Sudan centuries ago.

Almost all Muslims in Nigeria are Sunni Muslims of the Maliki school. However, about 5 to 10% of Nigeria's Muslims are Shi'a, and they can be found throughout northern Nigeria, particularly in Kaduna State but also in large numbers in Sokoto, Kano and Yobe. The number of Shi'a Muslims has increased since the Iranian Revolution of 1979, which brought an Islamic government to power in Iran. Ibrahim el-Zakzaky has been the leader of the Shi'a (IMN) with the financial and ideological support of Iran. The rise of Shi'ism in Nigeria has led to a rivalry between the majority Sunni population and Shi'as, and there have been instances of Sunni mobs or Sunni leaders ordering the destruction of Shi'a mosques and attacking Shi'a communities, with the violence reaching a culmination in December 2015 with the Nigerian army's crackdown on the IMN and general approval of this action from the Nigerian Sunni community.[36]

However, conflict is most frequent between Muslims and Christians as they compete for a greater share of political and economic power in Nigeria. Election season in the country tends to generate the most tension. Muslims tend to believe that, since they constitute more than 70% of Nigeria's population, the 2011 victory of the Christian presidential candidate Goodluck Jonathan over the Muslim candidate Muhammad Buhari (by 58% to 32% of the vote) was likely fraudulent. Anger over this issue has contributed to an increasing sense of marginalization among Nigerian Muslims. Boko Haram has exploited this anti-democracy and anti-Christian tension by staging dozens of attacks on churches and Christians in northern Nigeria. Most recently, Muslim-Christian violence has been seen in the context of Muslim Fulani herdsmen, who are now armed with machine guns (as opposed to the sticks they traditionally carried), raiding Christian farmlands and often killing Christians they find therein. This has, in turn, led to reprisals.[37]

Over-population also contributes to religious tensions as Muslim groups from northern Nigeria migrate into Christian areas in the Middle Belt, prompting competition over land use, as well as competition between the faiths to proselytize new members. The Sultan of Sokoto, who also leads the *Jama'atu Nasril Islam* (JNI), has said that "The rise of secularism and the increasing activities of western evangelical organizations have made it all the more urgent that the message of Islam shall be heard loud and clear and the JNI must play a leading role in this endeavor."

ISLAMISM AND THE STATE

Although the word "secular" is not specifically used in the Nigerian Constitution, Section 101 of that document provides that, "The Government of the Federation or of a State shall not adopt any religion as State Religion." Nonetheless, in practice religion plays such a large role in the state that Nigeria is not truly secular, a status which many religious leaders and citizens acknowledge.[38]

Islam, for example, enters the governmental sphere in several ways: the country observes Islamic holidays such as *Eid el-Fitr*, *Eid al-Adha* and *Milad al-Nabi*; the government is involved in organizing the Hajj pilgrimage; Islamic slogans in the Arabic language are featured on the country's currency and army insignias; Islamic sermons are delivered in public places; and, most significant of all, twelve states in northern Nigeria have implemented sharia law since 2000.

This controversial implementation is inextricably linked to politics, as many northern governors seem to support sharia law less out of religious devotion than out of a desire to portray themselves as "defenders of faith" in order to gain political advantage and to mitigate their lack of support from mainstream Muslims. Through a veneer of dedication to Islam, these politicians attempt to win the support of the masses and stifle criticism or, in many cases, investigations into their corrupt behavior. Some religious scholars have argued that the traditional rulers, including the sultans and emirs, who have no formal authority but serve as political advisers and maintain influence through their social status, are really opposed to sharia law because it does not permit hereditary succession, which is the basis of their positions.[39] Izala, the IMN and Boko Haram all believe that the Sultan and other traditional rulers are apostates for accepting a version of "*half-sharia*" in which secular institutions like elections and democracy exist side by side with Islam.

Although Islam is not formally a state institution in Nigeria, Muslims organizations play an important role in the country. With the advent of sharia law in twelve northern states starting in 1999, these organizations have begun to erode the secular nature of the country. Boko Haram, meanwhile, seeks to completely overthrow both the secular and the traditional Muslim establishment in Nigeria and create an Islamic state akin to the "caliphate" established by ISIS in Iraq and Syria. Although Boko Haram isn't likely to achieve this goal, Islamist groups are nonetheless gaining more and more traction in West Africa, while, in North Africa and the Arab World, pressure to adopt certain tenets of political Islam is becoming increasingly mainstream. A convergence of these forces makes it likely that the secular nature of the Nigerian state will continue to face a challenge from regional Islamist forces, which may in turn erode Nigerian Muslims' support for the secular authorities governing their country.

ENDNOTES

[1] Martin Cuddihy, "Major famine imminent in Nigeria as Boko Haram attacks cripple economy," ABC News, December 1, 2016, http://www.abc.net.au/news/2016-12-02/nigeria-major-famine-imminent-boko-haram/8085946.

[2] "Ramadan: JNI Asks Muslims to Pray for Peaceful Co-Esistence of Nigeria," Sahara Reporters, July 23, 2012, http://saharareporters.com/2012/07/23/ramadan-jni-asks-muslims-pray-peaceful-co-existence-nigeria.

[3] Ibid.

[4] Muhammad S. Umar, "The Popular Discourses of Salafi Radicalism and Salafi Counter-radicalism in Nigeria: A Case Study of Boko Haram." Journal of Religion in Africa 42, no. 2, 2012 , 118-144.

[5] D.N. Danjibo, "Islamic Fundamentalism and Sectarian Violence: The 'Maitatsine' and 'Boko Haram' Crises in Northern Nigeria, University of Ibadan Institute of African Studies Peace and Conflict Studies Programme, 2010.

[6] Emmanuel Goujon and Aminu Abubakar, "Nigeria's 'Taliban' Plot Comeback from Hide-outs," Agence France-Presse, January 11, 2006, http://mg.co.za/article/2006-01-11-nigerias-taliban-plot-comeback-from- hideouts.

[7] Jacob Zenn, "Boko Haram's Dangerous Expansion into Northwest Nigeria," Combating Terrorism Center at West Point CTC Sentinel 5, iss. 10, October 2012, https://www.ctc.usma.edu/posts/boko- harams-dangerous-expansion-into-northwest-nigeria; "Attacks by Boko Haram continue in Niger's Diffa region, forcing more people to flee," United Nations: Africa Renewal Online, June 6, 2016, http:// www.un.org/africarenewal/news/attacks-boko-haram-continue-niger%E2%80%99s-diffa-region-forcing-more-   people-flee-%E2%80%93-un; Vincent Ehiabhi, "Boko Haram Attacks Chad, Kills 10," Naij.com, 2016, https:// www.naij.com/384576-breaking-boko-haram-attacks-chad-for-first-time.html.

[8] "Boko Haram: Splinter Group, Ansaru Emerges," Vanguard, February 1, 2012, http:// www.vanguardngr.com/2012/02/boko-haram-splinter-group-ansaru-emerges/.

[9] Mike Oboh, "Islamist insurgents kill over 178 in Nigeria's Kano," Reuters, January 22, 2012, http:// www.reuters.com/article/us-nigeria-violence-idUS-TRE80L0A020120122.

[10] Government of Great Britain, "Proscribed terror groups or organizations," November 2012, http:// webarchive.nationalarchives.gov.uk/20130128103514/http://www.homeoffice.gov.uk/publications/ counter-terrorism/proscribed-terror-groups/.

[11] "Declared of Jama`atu Ansaril Muslimina Fibiladis Sudan Garki II Abuja," YouTube, November 30, 2012, http://www.youtube.com/watch?v=_1m5-zV3zfU.

[12] Ibrahim Shuaibu, "Islamic Group Claims Responsibility for Kidnapping French Citizen," ThisDay, December 24, 2012.

[13] "Extremist Group in Nigeria Says It Killed 7 Foreign Hostages," Associated Press, March 9, 2013, http://www.nytimes.com/2013/03/10/world/africa/extremist-group-in-nigeria-says-it-killed-7-foreign-hostages.html.

[14] "Vandenbeusch Father Suporers Rally in Discretion," RFI Africa, December 14, 2013. http:// www.rfi.fr/afrique/20131214-france-cameroun-soutiens-pere-vandenbusch-mobilisent-discretion-boko- haram.

[15] Thomas Joscelyn, "Jihadists argue over leadership of Islamic State," Long War Journal, August 4, 2016, http://www.longwarjournal.org/archives/2016/08/jihadists-argue-over-leadership-of-islamic-states- west-africa-province.php.

[16] Aaron Y. Zelin, "New audio message from Abu Bakr al-Shekau: 'Message to the World,'" Jihadology, August 3, 2016, http://jihadology.net/2016/08/03/new-audio-message-from-abu-bakr-al-shekau-message- to-the-world/.

[17] Ibid.

[18] 19

[19] Mohammed Abubakar and Ahmed A. Mohammed, "Kala-Kato crisis: How Latest Bauchi incident erupted," The Daily Trust, January 1, 2010, http://www.dailytrust.com.ng/weekly/index.php/report/3592-kala-kato-crisis-how- latest-bauchi-incident-erupted.

[20] Aminu Abubakar, "Death toll from Nigeria clashes climbs to 70," Agence France Presse, December 30, 2009.

[21] Isa Sa'isu, "Kala-Kato: Meet group with yet another perception of Islam," Weekly Trust, August 15, 2009.

[22] "Controversies about Sharia," Carefronting.org, 2016, http://carefronting.org/controversies-about- sharia/.

[23] Dr. Jonathan N. C. Hill, "Sufism in Northern Nigeria: Force for Counter-Radicalization?" Strategic Studies Institute, May 17, 2010.

[24] "Saudi, Iran stoke Sunni-Shia tensions in Nigeria: experts"Agence France Presse, November 5, 2016, https://au.news.yahoo.com/world/a/33116829/saudi-iran-stoke-sunni-shia-tensions-in-nigeria-experts/ #page1.

[25] "Saudi, Iran stoke Sunni-Shia tensions in Nigeria: experts"Agence France Presse, November 5, 2016, https://au.news.yahoo.com/world/a/33116829/saudi-iran-stoke-sunni-shia-tensions-in-nigeria-experts/ #page1.

[26] Hill, "Sufism in Northern Nigeria: Force for Counter-Radicalization.

[27] Dr. Shedrack Best, "Nigeria: The Islamist Challenge: the Nigerian 'Shiite' Movement," Searching for Peace in Africa, 1999.

[28] Vincent Egunyanga, "El-Zakzaky Blasts Sharia Governors," Daily Champion, April 21, 2002.

[29] Mallam Ibraheem Zakzaky, "Terrorism In The World Today, What Is Terrorism? Who Are The Terrorists?" islamicmovement.org, 2009, www.Islamicmovement.org/sheikh/terrorism2.html.

[30] "Tafiyar Sheikh El-Zakzaky jamhuriyar musulunci ta Iran cikin hotuna," harkarmusulunci.org, May 30, 2009, http://www.harkarmusulunci.org/data.asp?id=101010&lang=1.

[31] Ludovica Laccino, "Nigeria Zaria killings: IMN releases names of 700 missing Shias as Zakzaky returns to Abuja," International Business Times, January 26, 2016, http://www.ibtimes.co.uk/nigeria-zaria-killings-imn-releases-names-700-missing-shias-zakzaky-returns-abuja-1540076.

[32] Garba Muhammad, "Zakzaky, wife suffer life threatening injuries – IMN," Premium Times, July 25, 2016, http://www.premiumtimesng.com/news/top-news/207519-zakzaky-wife-suffer-life-threatening-injuries-imn.html.

[33] Dyepkazah Shibayan, "Zakzakys Followers teargassed in Abuja," The Cable, November 2, 2016, https://www.thecable.ng/zakzakys-followers-teargassed-abuja.

[34] "Nigeria: Gathering In Bauchi after a rally against 'Zaria Carnage' / Photos Part 4th," Ahlul Bayt News Agency, December 14, 2015, http://en.abna24.com/service/africa/archive/2015/12/14/724909/story.html/

[35] Kit O'Connell, "Saudi Arabia Takes Proxy War With Iran To Nigeria As Shias Are Brutalized," Mint Press News, January 15, 2016, http://www.mintpressnews.com/saudi-arabia-takes-proxy-war-with-iran- to-nigeria-as-shias-are-brutalized/212629/.

[36] "Nigerian Shia base knocked down," BBC, August 1, 2007.

[37] Jacbo Zenn, "Leadership Analysis of Boko Haram and Ansaru in Nigeria," Combating Terrorism Center at West Point, February 24, 2014, https://www.ctc.usma.edu/posts/leadership-analysis-of-boko-haram- and-ansaru-in-nigeria.

[38] "Nigeria is Not a Secular State," Sun News Online, August 25, 2011.

[39] Mallam Lawan Danbazau, Politics and Religion in Nigeria (Kano: Tofa Commercial Press, 1991), vii.

SOMALIA

QUICK FACTS

Population: 10,817,354

Area: 637,657 sq km

Ethnic Groups: Somali 85%, Bantu and other non-Somali 15% (including Arabs 30,000)

Religions: Sunni Muslim

Government Type: Federal parliamentary republic

GDP (official exchange rate): $5.8 billion (2014 est.)

Map and Quick Facts courtesy of the CIA World Factbook (Last Updated January 2017) S

OVERVIEW

The U.S. State Department's most recent report on global terrorism trends notes that, despite suffering a series of setbacks in the first half of 2015, al-Shabaab has proven resilient and "adopted increasingly aggressive tactics" aimed at both delegitimizing the Federal Government of Somalia (FGS) and weakening the resolve of the African Union Mission in Somalia (AMISOM) via an increase in attacks on AMISOM military bases in Southern Somalia, as well as attacks in neighboring AMISOM troop-contributing countries.[1] Nevertheless, the group has had to grapple with the death of several key leadership figures as a result of U.S. aerial strikes, the loss of strongholds in parts of south-central Somalia, and, in the view of U.S. authorities, increasing factionalism and defections "as the appeal of the Islamic State of Iraq and the Levant (ISIL) created divisions within al-Shabaab's core leadership."[2] One reason for the group's resilience is the weakness of Somalia's internationally-recognized FGS, whose authority is not widely accepted by Somalis. Hampering the U.S. response to this threat is not only the absence of a capable partner govern-

ment in the Somali capital of Mogadishu but also Washington's failure to creatively engage effective Somali authorities, including those in the unrecognized Republic of Somaliland.[3]

ISLAMIST ACTIVITY

Islamists active in Somalia fall roughly into one of seven principal groups:

Harakat al-Shabaab al-Mujahideen ("Movement of Warrior Youth," al-Shabaab)

Known colloquially as al-Shabaab, this movement arose out of the militant wing of the Islamic Courts Union. Following the defeat of the latter by the Ethiopian intervention in early 2007, al-Shabaab broke with other Islamists who regrouped under the sponsorship of Eritrea to form the Alliance for the Re-Liberation of Somalia (ARS) to oppose the Transitional Federal Government (TFG) then installed in Mogadishu.

Founded in large part due to the efforts of Aden Hashi Ayro, a militant who had trained with al-Qaeda in Afghanistan prior to September 11, 2001, al-Shabaab's schism with other Islamists reflects Ayro's adherence to a more radical *jihadist* ideology that does not countenance cooperation with the non-Muslim Eritrean regime, even against a common enemy. Although divided into several factions even before Ayro was killed by a U.S. aerial strike in May 2008, *al-Shabaab* was an effective fighting force overall. The senior leadership of *al-Shabaab* has included veteran *jihadists* with experience on battlefields abroad, including in Afghanistan, Bosnia, and Kashmir.[4] It managed to seize control of large sections of southern and central Somalia, including parts of Mogadishu, where it has installed a strict Islamist regime that, to the horror of many Somalis, has carried out a number of harsh punishments—among them the stoning of a 13-year-old rape victim for the crime of "adultery" in 2008.[5]

Over time, *al-Shabaab's* leadership split into two principal currents. The first, hard-line faction, consisting primarily of foreign or foreign-funded *jihadists*, follows a transnational *jihadist* agenda, evidenced by the attack on Kenya's Westgate Shopping Mall in 2013 and the subsequent April 2015 attack on Garissa University in Garissa, Kenya—incidents which collectively left over 200 people dead and scores injured. Ahmed Abdi Godane, also known as Mukhtar Abu Zubair, initially spearheaded this faction and proclaimed the group's formal allegiance to al-Qaeda and to Osama bin Laden's successor, Ayman al-Zawahiri, in February 2012.

The other faction, made up of clan-based militia leaders with a more "nationalist" agenda, emphasized expelling foreign forces from Somalia and focusing on local control. At the very end of 2011, the latter group declared its intention to rename itself the "Islamic Emirate of Somalia" and rejected al-Qaeda's branding and objectives, instead focusing primarily on Somalia's domestic challenges.[6]

The internal divisions of *al-Shabaab* helped facilitate its loss of control over Somalia. Since Kenyan and Ethiopian troops joined African Union Mission in Somalia (AMISOM) and Transitional Federal Government forces to expel Al-Shabaab from major cities beginning in late 2011, the group has surrendered its strongholds in numerous regional capitals. Defections of *al-Shabaab* soldiers have increased substantially. In December 2012, Godane admitted to having experienced major defeats, but pledged to continue a guerrilla war against Somali and AMISOM forces.[7]

In 2013, Godane moved against the nationalist faction of the organization, killing or forcing into hiding most of its senior leadership.[8] While Godane himself was killed by a U.S. aerial strike in September 2014, *al-Shabaab* continues to adhere to transnational *jihadism*. Under the leadership of Godane's successor, Ahmed Omar, *al-Shabaab* continues to focus less on holding control of territory and more on launching successful attacks both within Somalia and in neighbouring countries. These attacks include overrunning Ugandan and Kenyan-run AMISOM bases in the southern Somali towns of Janale and El Adde, attacks on hotels and FGS figures in Mogadishu, and attacks on soft targets on neighboring AMISOM troop-contributing countries, including Kenya and Djibouti.

The rise of the Islamic State in the Middle East has created another challenge to the organizational unity of *al-Shabaab*. Several factions of the group in Puntland and Southern Somalia have pledged alliance to the Islamic State, a move that sparked a crackdown on defectors in late 2015 by *al-Shabaab's* senior central leadership.[9] Nevertheless, the Islamic State's media offices continue to encourage al-Shabaab-affiliated fighters in Somalia and members of the Somali diaspora abroad to support the group, and rumors continue to swirl of ongoing clashes between factions loyal to the Islamic State and those loyal to al-Qaeda.[10]

Hizbul Islam ("Islamic Party")

Led by Hassan Dahir 'Aweys, previously the military commander of Somali Muslim Brotherhood offshoot *al-Itihaad al-Islamiyya* (AIAI, the "Islamic Union") and subsequently the chairman of the *shura* of the Islamic Courts Union, *Hizbul Islam* is the product of a merger of several groups. Its primary difference with *al-Shabaab* is that *Hizbul Islam* does not place as much emphasis on global *jihadist* objectives; rather, its two principal demands are the implementation of a strict version of sharia as the law in Somalia, and withdrawal of all foreign troops from the country. Unlike the multi-clan contingency of *al-Shabaab*, *Hizbul Islam* draws its membership and support primarily from 'Aweys' Habar Gedir sub-clan.[11] By and large, *Hizbul Islam* has cooperated with *al-Shabaab,* although the two groups have come into occasional conflict over the division of spoils. *Hizbul Islam* lost control of the strategic town of Beledweyne to al-Shabaab in June 2010, retaining only some territory in the southern and central Somali regions of Bay and Lower Shabelle. Subsequently, during the

Muslim holy month of Ramadan, the two groups cooperated on a joint offensive against TFG and AMISOM forces in Mogadishu. Reports of a merger between the two groups emerged at the end of 2010,[12] but in September 2012 a spokesperson from *Hizbul Islam* announced its split with *al-Shabaab*, citing ideological differences and *al-Shabaab's* weakened position in the region.[13]

Hizbul Islam's stance with respect to the Somali government is unclear, as is the current state of the group. While 'Aweys is reported to have declared war against the regime after Sheikh Hassan Mohamud was elected president in September 2012,[14] the group's spokesman, Mohamed Moalim, was also quoted welcoming the new president and parliament as a "positive development."[15] In fact, 'Aweys came to Mogadishu in June 2013 for talks with government officials, but was arrested and reportedly roughed up.[16] With 'Aweys in custody since then, very little has been heard from his followers.

Mu'askar Ras Kamboni ("Ras Kamboni Brigades")

Founded by Hassan Abdullah Hersi ("al-Turki"), a former military commander for the Islamic Courts, the Ras Kamboni Brigades is based in Middle and Lower Jubba Valley, where it gained control of several strategically located towns which control access to the Kenyan border, including Jilib Afmadoow, and Dhoobley. The group was aligned with *Hizbul Islam* until late 2009, when *al-Shabaab* took control of the port of Kismayo. A faction of Ras Kamboni, led by al-Turki, announced in early 2010 that it was joining forces with *al-Shabaab* and proclaimed its adhesion to "the international *jihad* of al-Qaeda." [17]

The rest of the Ras Kamboni Brigades follows Sheikh Ahmed Mohamed Islam, a.k.a. Sheikh Ahmed Madobe, who served as the former governor of Kismayo from 2006 until the fall of the Islamic Courts Union.[18] Rumored to have strong relations with the Kenyan government, the Madobe-led Ras Kamboni group played a key role in helping the AMISOM, Kenyan, and Somali government forces push al-Shabaab out of the town of Kismayo in October 2012, although some Mogadishu-based Somali government officials denied having cooperated with the "competing militants."[19] In 2013, while continuing to lead the Ras Komboni Brigades against Al-Shabaab forces in the region, Madobe was elected president of the newly established autonomous region of Jubaland.[20]

A spokesperson of the Somali government forces in Juba reported that the group subsequently allied with Ogaden National Liberation Front (ONLF) to fight for control the port city,[21] leading to clashes with government troops in February 2013.[22] However, in August 2013, Madobe signed an Ethiopian-brokered "national reconciliation agreement" with the FGS that allowed him to remain in control of Kismayo at the head of an "interim administration" that would preside over the police forces in Jubaland, while military forces were gradually integrated into the national army.[23]

Ahlu-Sunna wal-Jama'a (roughly, "[Followers of] the Traditions and Consensus [of the Prophet Muhammad]")

The original *Ahlu Sunna wal-Jama'a* was an umbrella group of traditional Somali Muslims organized by General Muhammad Farah 'Aideed as a counterweight to his Wahhabi-inspired opponents in AIAI.[24] In mid-2009, the excesses of *al-Shabaab* led to a revival of the movement to oppose the ideology which *Shabaab* and other Islamist insurgents have appropriated from some of their foreign sponsors. Loosely organized into armed militias on a clan basis and with roots in the Sufi brotherhoods, *Ahlu Sunna wal-Jama'a* fighters in 2010 managed in a number of places to stop what had seemed to be the relentless surge of *al-Shabaab* forces. Trained and assisted by the defense forces of neighboring Ethiopia, which have allowed some of the movement's units the use of its territory, *Ahlu Sunna wal-Jama'a* emerged as a force in southern and central Somalia. However, the group's opposition to *al-Shabaab* should not be confused with support of the TFG. In fact, the group's formal alliance with the TFG in 2010, brought about under tremendous pressure from regional and international actors, has largely fallen apart. In any event, while *Ahlu Sunna wal-Jama'a* has neither the international links nor the global strategic vision of *al-Shabaab*, it has an Islamist agenda of its own—for example, the group has conducted operations against those who it felt were not properly observing the fast of Ramadan—that may set it at odds with the more secular elements of Somali society.[25]

The group took control of several towns and villages in Galgadud and Hiran.[26] After assisting the Somali government fight al-Shabaab for two years, in December 2012, *Ahlu Sunna wal-Jama'a* troops were officially integrated into Somali government forces.[27] In February 2013, the chairman of the executive committee of *Ahlu Sunna wal Jama'a*, Sheikh Mohamed Yusuf Hefow, passed away in a hospital in Mogadishu.[28] Since then, relations between the militia and the FGS have frayed over issues of power in Galgadud, occasioning sporadic clashes between *Ahlu Sunna wal-Jama'a* loyalists and Somali national government forces, notably a February 2015 clash in Guricel that left nine dead.[29]

Al-Islah al-Islamiyya ("Islamic Movement")

In 2004, the U.S. Department of State described *al-Islah* as an "organized Islamic group whose goal is the establishment of an Islamic state," but termed it "a generally nonviolent movement that operates primarily in Mogadishu."[30] Largely displaced during the period when the Islamic Courts Union was ascendant, *al-Islah* underwent something of a revival in Mogadishu with the return of Sharif Ahmed to the head of the TFG in 2009. Its chief role was the administration of schools in the capital which were supported by the group's foreign benefactors. It is not surprising, given how spectacularly state institutions have collapsed in Somalia, that "this naturally promoted fundamentalist trends (such as *al-Islah*) in local Islam, which had previously been largely Sufi in character, and these were encouraged by financial support from Saudi Arabia and other Middle Eastern centers."[31] Hassan Sheikh Mohamed, who was elected head of the Somali government in September 2012, has links with *al-Islah*.[32]

Al-Qaeda

While its earlier foray into Somalia did not prove particularly successful, al-Qaeda remains interested in Somalia both as a theater of operations and as a jumping-off point for terrorist activities in the nearby Arabian Peninsula and elsewhere in Africa.[33] An audio statement released by Osama bin Laden in 2009 in praise of the Islamist insurgency in Somalia and calling upon Muslims to support it underscored this reality.[34] More recently, Ayman al-Zawahiri, bin Laden's successor, endorsed Ahmed Omer, Godane's successor and the current leader of *al-Shabaab*.[35] Even analysts who previously discounted al-Qaeda's involvement in Somalia now acknowledge that since at least early 2008, al-Qaeda advisors have played a critical role in *al-Shabaab* operations,[36] a fact highlighted by the September 2009 strike inside Somalia by U.S. Special Operations Forces which killed Saleh Ali Saleh Nabhan, a Kenyan national wanted in connection with the 1998 bombings of the U.S. embassies in Dar es Salaam, Tanzania and Nairobi, Kenya. At the time of his death, Nabhan was running terrorist training camps and bringing in foreign trainers and fighters to support *al-Shabaab*, presumably at the behest of al-Qaeda. In February 2012, the leadership of *al-Shabaab* formally pledged its allegiance to al-Qaeda leader Ayman al-Zawahiri.[37]

The Islamic State (Islamic State of Iraq and the Levant, Daesh)

Although its success to date has been limited, the Islamic State has made efforts to coopt *al-Shabaab* forces demoralized by their battlefield losses in recent years. In March 2016, the Islamic State claimed its first attack in Somalia, the bombing of an African Union vehicle in Mogadishu, and subsequently released a video showing what it claimed was its first Somali training camp. The group has reportedly attracted several hundred *al-Shabaab* defectors, as well as a number of prominent *imams*, especially in the northeastern part of Somalia.[38]

ISLAMISM AND SOCIETY

Traditionally, the Somali subscribe to Sunni Islam and follow the *Shāfiʿī* school (mahdab) of jurisprudence, which, although conservative, is open to a variety of liberal views regarding practice.[39] Up until the time of Somalia's independence in 1960, there were different movements within the Sunni Islam in Somalia. The most dominant were the Sufi brotherhoods (sing., *tariqa*, pl. *turuq*), especially that of the Qadiriyya order (although the Ahmadiyya order, introduced into Somali lands in the 19th century, was also influential).[40] While traditional Islamic schools and scholars (*ulamā*) played a role as focal points for rudimentary political opposition to colonial rule in Italian Somalia, historically their role in the politics of the Somali clan structure was neither institutionalized nor particularly prominent. In part this is because *sharia* historically was not especially entrenched in Somalia: being largely pastoralists, the Somali relied more on customary law (*xeer*) than on religious prescriptions.[41] Hence, Somali Islamism is largely a post-colonial movement which became active in the late 1980s and which was strengthened by the collapse of the state in 1991 and the ensuing civil war, international intervention, external meddling, and efforts by Somalis themselves at political reconstruction. Absent this chain of events, it is doubtful that militant Islamism would be much more than a marginal force in Somali politics.

Although its adherents often appeal to the early 20th century anti-colonial fight of the "Mad Mullah" Sayyid Muhammad 'Abdille Hassan,[42] Somali Islamism is, at its origins, an import dating back at most to the 1950s. The 1953 establishment in Mogadishu of an Institute of Islamic Studies run by Egyptian scholars from Cairo's al-Azhar University introduced both Arabic language curriculum and contact with the Egyptian Muslim Brotherhood (*al-Ikhwan al-Muslimoon*). As is well-known, unlike the Sufis who emphasize socialization, moral education, and spiritual preparation, the Muslim Brothers stress organization, activism, and the socio-political dimension of change directed toward the creation of a modern Islamic state. After Somalia's independence in 1960, Egyptians opened secondary schools in many of the country's towns. In the 1960s and 1970s, Saudi religious and educational institutions—especially the Islamic University of Medina, the Umm al-Qura University in Mecca, and the Imam Muhammad bin Saud Islamic University in Riyadh—joined al-Azhar in offering scholarships to the graduates of these institutions. This development has parallels with the entrenchment of radical Islam in nearby Sudan via the establishment of the Sudanese Muslim Brotherhood, the precursor to the currently-ruling National Congress Party (formerly the National Islamic Front).

By the 1970s, the nascent Somali Muslim Brotherhood was so visible that the dictatorial regime of Siyad Barre took measures to suppress it, driving its adherents underground. The Somali Muslim Brothers eventually coalesced into two groups: *al-Islah al-Islamiyya* ("Islamic Movement") founded in Saudi Arabia in 1978, and *al-Itihaad al-Islamiyya* (AIAI, the "Islamic Union"), established in the early 1980s. The memberships of the two and their leadership network overlapped considerably. The differences between them were, at least initially, largely a function of the circumstances of their clandestine origins. Both sought the creation of an expansive "Islamic Republic of Greater Somalia" and eventually a political union embracing all Muslims in the Horn of Africa.[43]

The collapse in January 1991 of the Siyad Barre regime led to internecine warfare that laid waste to Somalia. AIAI was forced to withdraw after heavy fighting. This withdrawal, which coincided with the fall of the Derg in neighboring Ethiopia, allowed the Somali Islamists to regroup in the Somali region of Ethiopia where there were also large numbers of refugees from Somalia proper. AIAI tried to seize control of strategic assets like seaports and crossroads. Although it temporarily held the northern port of Bosaso and the eastern ports of Marka and Kismayo, the only area where it exercised long-term control was the economically vital intersection of Luuq, in southern Somalia, near the Ethiopian border, where it imposed harsh *sharia*-based rule from 1991 until 1996. From its base in Luuq, the Islamists of AIAI encouraged subversive activities among ethnic Somalis of Ethiopia and carried out a series of terrorist attacks. The exasperated Ethiopian regime finally intervened in Somalia in August 1996, wiping out AIAI bases in Luuq and Buulo Haawa and killing hundreds of Somali extremists, as well as scores of non-Somalis who had flocked to the Horn of Africa under the banner of *jihad*. From this period emerged the cooperation between Somali Islamists and Ethiopian groups like the Ogaden National Liberation Front (ONLF), which continue to struggle against the newly established government of Ethiopia.

From its inception, AIAI rejected the non-confessional nature of the Somali state and sought to establish an Islamic regime in the country based on a strict *Wahhabi* interpretation of the Muslim faith. When, in the aftermath of the collapse of the Siyad Barre dictatorship, it found the direct road to power blocked by Muhammad Farah 'Aideed, it adopted a more subtle approach based on the establishment of economic and other social programs, together with Islamic courts.[44]

Some Somalis have come to see Islam as an alternative to both the traditional clan-based identities and the emergent criminal syndicates led by so-called "warlords." The increased influence of religion has been largely a phenomenon of small towns and urban centers, although increased adherence to its normative precepts is a wider phenomenon. Islamic religious leaders have helped organize security and other services and businessmen in particular were supportive of the establishment of sharia-based courts throughout the south, which were a precursor of the Islamic Courts Union established in Mogadishu in June 2006. The Islamists attempted to fill certain voids left by state collapse and otherwise unattended to by emergent forces like the warlords. In doing so, they also made a bid to supplant clan and other identities, offering a pan-Islamist identity in lieu of other allegiances.[45]

Given their previous experiences with Somali Islamism, especially in its AIAI incarnation, it was not surprising that, after many of the same extremists emerged in positions of authority in the Islamic Courts Union, the Ethiopians would intervene as they did in 2006 to support Somalia's internationally-recognized but weak "Transitional Federal Government" (TFG), the fourteenth such attempt at a secular national government since 1991.[46] Unfortunately, while the intervention ended the rule of the Islamic Courts Union, it also provoked an insurgency spearheaded by the even more radical *Harakat al-Shabaab al-Mujahideen* ("Movement of Warrior Youth," *al-Shabaab*), a group subsequently designated a "specially designated global terrorist" by the U.S. Department of State in 2008[47] and a "listed terrorist organization" by the Australian government the following year.[48] Even after Ethiopian troops withdrew in early 2009, the Shabaab-led insurgency against the TFG has continued, drawing the African Union Mission in Somalia (AMISOM) deployed to protect the transitional regime deeper into the conflict and causing them to suffer increasing casualties with terrorist attacks like the suicide bombing of September 17, 2009, which killed seventeen peacekeepers and wounded more than forty others,[49] and that of December 3, 2009, which killed three TFG ministers as well as sixteen other people attending a graduation ceremony within the small enclave of Mogadishu thought to still be controlled by the beleaguered regime.[50]

With the end of TFG's mandate in August 2012, the Somali Federal Government was formed—depending on how one counts them, the new entity is either the fifteenth or the sixteenth interim regime since the collapse of the Siad Barre dictatorship in 1991. Hassan Sheikh Mohamud, an educator and civil society activist with ties to *al-Islah* as well as the earlier Union of Islamist Courts, was selected to head the new government, which was formally recognized by the United States in January 2013, the first Somali regime to be accorded that status in more than two decades. While the Federal Government of Somalia, with the help of AMISOM, has managed to roll back al-Shabaab territorial control in southern Somalia, the group continues to regularly strike SFG-affiliated targets in the capital city of Mogadishu, including an attack on the Nasa Hablod hotel in June 2016, which killed a serving government minister, among other victims. As of late 2016, the country is in the midst of a presidential election process, though the vote has been repeatedly delayed due to ongoing insecurity and procedural challenges.[51]

ISLAMISM AND THE STATE

The Somali governmental policy toward Islamism is muddled, compromised by the complicity of the government in Islamist thought and activity. While Somali Islamism was damaged by the military defeat dealt to the Islamic Courts Union following the Ethiopian military intervention in late 2006 and early 2007, the chaos into which the Somali territories (outside Somaliland) subsequently sunk under the aegis of the TFG served to revive their standing, especially given some of the historical linkages between Islamism and pan-Somali yearning.[52] Consequently, Islamists will continue to be a competitive force among the Somalis.

In March 2009, a unity government was established between the TFG and elements of the Alliance for the Re-Liberation of Somalia (ARS). The expansion of the number of seats in the country's parliament to 550, and the election of former ICU leader Sharif Sheikh Ahmed as president, demonstrated the inclusion of a broader spectrum of Islamic ideology in government.[53] The election of Hassan Sheikh Mohamud as president of the Federal Government of Somalia in September 2012 was seen as a further movement towards more moderate, albeit mildly Islamist, leadership.[54] Though Mohamud's tenure has been characterized by a slow improvement in the security situation in the country, extremist elements in Somalia continue to influence and threaten political order. This situation is exacerbated by the withdrawal of AMISOM forces (due to the respective domestic security needs of contributing countries) and a decrease in international support for their deployment in Somalia, which provide a potentially dangerous opening for the militant Islamists.

At the same time, two further topics require elucidation in the context of governmental response:

The Question of Somaliland

Although the sovereignty it reasserted has yet to be formally recognized by any other state, more than a decade and a half have passed since Somaliland (the north-western region of the former Somalia, bordering on Ethiopia and Djibouti) proclaimed the dissolution of its voluntary union with the central government. Perhaps most important, in the context of the rising tide of Islamist militancy in southern and central Somalia, is the fact that Somaliland's reliance on the older system of clan elders and the respect they command "has served as something of a mediating force in managing pragmatic interaction between custom and tradition; Islam and the secular realm of modern nationalism," leading to a unique situation where "Islam may be pre-empting and/or containing Islamism."[55] The consequence of having an organic relationship between Somali culture and tradition and Islam appears to assure a stabilizing, rather than disruptive, role for religion in society in general, and religion and politics in particular. In Somaliland, for example, the population is almost exclusively Sunni Muslim and the *shahada*, the Muslim profession of the oneness of God and the acceptance of Muhammad as God's final prophet, is emblazoned on the flag; yet *sharia* is only one of the three sources of the jurisprudence in the region's courts, alongside secular legislation and Somali traditional law. Unlike the rest of the Somali lands, the region is governed by a democratic constitution which was approved by 97 percent of the voters in a May 2001 referendum and which provides for an executive branch of government, consisting of a directly elected president and vice president and appointed ministers; a bicameral legislature consisting of an elected House of Representatives and an upper chamber of elders, the *guurti*; and an independent judiciary. Somaliland has held presidential elections in 2003 and 2010 and parliamentary elections in 2005, all three of which were judged "free and fair" by international observers. General elections are also scheduled for 2017 and the incumbent president, Ahmed Mohamed Mohamoud, has pledged not to run for a second term.

Not surprisingly, the relative success of Somaliland has drawn the ire of Islamists in southern and central Somalia. In 2008, on the same day that Shirwa Ahmed, a naturalized U.S. citizen from Minneapolis, Minnesota, blew himself up in an attack on the headquarters of the Puntland Intelligence Service in Bosaso, other suicide bombers from al-Shabaab hit the presidential palace, the UN Development Programme office, and the Ethiopian diplomatic mission in the Somaliland capital of Hargeisa.[56]

Since suffering defeats in south and central Somalia, *al-Shabaab* fighters have established footholds in Puntland, posing a major threat to the region's governing institutions and its overall stability.[57] In the past, semi-autonomous Puntland has criticized Somaliland for ignoring the threat posed by the spread of *al-Shabaab* militants in northern Somalia.[58] However, a number of developments—including the effective use of a small coast guard to keep Somaliland largely free of piracy, as well as the 2009 transfer of two Guantanamo Bay detainees to Hargeisa, rather than the less secure Mogadishu—indicate that Somaliland is seen as less vulnerable to militant Islam than south and central Somalia.[59] In February 2013, authorities there responded more forcefully to *al-Shabaab* militants by arresting approximately eighty members, including the son of a Somaliland politician.[60]

Islamism and Piracy

Although incidents of piracy have dramatically decreased since 2012, there was no evidence of anything other than opportunistic instances of cooperation between Somalia's Islamists and pirates. In early 2011, it was reported that *al-Shabaab* had reached a deal with one of the larger piracy syndicates for a 20 percent cut of all future ransoms from piracy and was even opening an office to specifically liaise with the pirates in the port of Xarardheere where the Islamist group would permit the hijackers to anchor seized ships while awaiting ransom payments.[61] A 2011 U.S. Congressional Research Service report cites testimony suggesting that Somali pirates were not directly allied with *al-Shabaab*, but did maintain many of these mutually beneficial financial arrangements.[62]

Thanks to the adoption of best practices in maritime security and increased international patrols, piracy in the Gulf of Aden has declined significantly since 2012. Moreover, al-Shabaab's loss of control of key ports including Xarardheere, Marka, Baraawe, and Kismaayo, to the Somali military and AMISOM further limit opportunities for cooperation between the Islamists and piracy networks.

ENDNOTES

[1] U.S. Department of State, Office of the Coordinator for Counterterrorism, "Country Reports: Africa Overview," in Country Reports on Terrorism 2015, http://www.state.gov/j/ct/rls/crt/2015/257514.htm

[2] Ibid.

[3] J. Peter Pham, "Peripheral Vision: A Model Solution for Somalia," RUSI Journal 154, no. 5 (October 2009), 84-90.

[4] Roland Marchal, "A Tentative Assessment Of The Somali Harakat al-Shabaab," Journal of Eastern African Studies 3, no. 3 (2009), 389.

[5] Chris McNeal, "Rape Victim, 13, Stoned To Death In Somalia," Guardian (London), November 2, 2008, http://www.guardian.co.uk/world/2008/nov/02/somalia-gender.

[6] Brownyn Bruton and J. Peter Pham, "The Splintering of Al Shabaab," Foreign Affairs, February 2, 2012, http://www.foreignaffairs.com/articles/137068/bronwyn-bruton-and-j-peter-pham/the-splintering-of-al-shabaab.

[7] Mojid Ahmed, "Al-Shabaab leader admits defeats," Sabahi, December 17, 2012, http://sabahionline.com/en_GB/articles/hoa/articles/features/2012/12/17/feature-01

[8] Matt Bryden, "The Reinvention of Al-Shabaab: A Strategy of Choice or Necessity?," Center for Strategic & International Studies, February 2014, https://csis-prod.s3.amazonaws.com/s3fs-public/legacy_files/files/publication/140221_Bryden_ReinventionOfAlShabaab_Web.pdf

[9] "Somalia's Al-Qaeda branch warns members against joining IS," Agence France-Presse, November 24, 2015, https://www.yahoo.com/news/somalias-al-qaeda-branch-warns-members-against-joining-075418683.html?ref=gs

[10] Stig Jarle Hansen, "Has Shabaab been weakened for good? The answer is 'yes' and 'no'," The Conversation, October 17, 2016, http://theconversation.com/has-shabaab-been-weakened-for-good-the-answer-is-yes-and-no-67067

[11] "Somalia: Hizbul Islam Group Withdraws Allegiance, Says 'Al Shabaab Is Weakened,'" Garowe Online, September 25, 2012, http://allafrica.com/stories/201209261141.html.

[12] "Somali Islamists al-Shabab and Hizbul Islam 'to merge'," BBC News, December 10, 2010, http://www.bbc.co.uk/news/world-africa-12038556.

[13] "Kenyan Amisom soldier kills six Somali civilians," BBC News, September 24, 2012, http://www.bbc.co.uk/news/world-africa-19698348.

[14] "Somalia: Hizbul Islam Group Withdraws Allegiance, Says 'Al Shabaab Is Weakened.'"

[15] "Kenyan Amisom soldier kills six Somali civilians."

[16] See "Somalia and its Shabab: Are the Islamists Truly on the Ropes," The Economist, July 6, 2013, http://www.economist.com/news/middle-east-and-africa/21580523-new-and-much-lauded-president-finding-it-hard-bury-old-divisions-are.

[17] Abdi Sheikh and Abdi Guled, "Somali Rebels Unite, Profess Loyalty To Al Qaeda," Reuters, February 1, 2010, http://www.reuters.com/article/idUSTRE6102Q720100201.

[18] "The smiling warlord who Controls Ras Kamboni," The Daily Nation, July 11, 2012, http://www.nation.co.ke/Features/DN2/The-smiling-warlord-who-Controls-Ras-Kamboni-/-/957860/1425264/-/12mrtirz/-/index.html

[19] AbdulKadir Khalif, "Somalia in row with militias in captured town," The Daily Nation, October 11, 2012, http://www.nation.co.ke/News/africa/-/1066/1530598/-/14pr6i0/-/index.html.

[20] "Somalia: Kismayo Residents Fear New Clan Fighting," KeydMedia, February 23, 2014, http://www.keydmedia.net/en/news/article/somalia_kismayo_residents_fear_new_clan_fighting/

[21] AbdulKadir Khalif, "Somalia in row with militias in captured town," The Daily Nation, October 11, 2012, http://www.nation.co.ke/News/africa/-/1066/1530598/-/14pr6i0/-/index.html.

[22] "Gulf of Aden Security Review - February 25, 2013,"American Enterprise Institute Critical Threats Project, February 25, 2013, http://www.criticalthreats.org/gulf-aden-security-review/gulf-aden-security-review-february-25-2013.

[23] Andualem Sisay and Abdulkadir Khalif, "Somali Government and Jubaland Strike Peace Deal," Africa Review, August 29, 2013, http://www.africareview.com/News/Somali+government+and+Jubaland+strike+a+deal/-/979180/1972618/-/3a6xv7z/-/index.html.

[24] Menkhaus, ""Somalia And Somaliland," 33.

[25] J. Peter Pham, "Somali Instability Still Poses Threat Even After Successful Strike against Nabhan," World Defense Review, September 17, 2009, http://worlddefensereview.com/pham091709.shtml.

[26] "Somalia's Shabaab seize third town this month after peacekeepers withdraw," Reuters Africa, October 23, 2016, http://af.reuters.com/article/topNews/idAFKCN12N0JZ .

[27] "Somalia: Ahlu Sunna Wal-Jamaa Forces to Join Somali National Army," Sabahi, November 30, 2012, http://allafrica.com/stories/201212040647.html.

[28] "Somalia: A leader of Ahlu Sunna Wal Jama'a Dies," AllAfrica, February 14, 2013, http://allafrica.com/stories/201302141519.html.

[29] "Sufi Militias Repel Somalia Army Counterattack on Town," Hiraan Online, February 12, 2015, http://www.hiiraan.com/news4/2015/Feb/98127/sufi_militias_repel_somalia_army_counter_attack_on_town.aspx.

[30] United States Department of State, "International Religious Freedom Report 2004," 2004, http://www.state.gov/j/drl/rls/irf/2004/35382.htm.

[31] Ioan M. Lewis, A Modern History of the Somali, 4th rev. ed. (Oxford: James Currey, 2002), 299.

[32] "Hassan Sheikh Mohamud: Somalia's new president profiled," BBC News, September 11, 2012, http://www.bbc.co.uk/news/world-africa-19556383.

[33] Kinfe Abraham, The Bin Laden Connection and the Terror Factor in Somalia (Addis Ababa: Ethiopia International Institute for Peace and Development, 2006).

[34] J. Peter Pham, "Bin Laden's Somali Gambit," World Defense Review, March 26, 2009, http://worlddefensereview.com/pham032609.shtml.

[35] Thomas Joscelyn, "Shabaab's Leadership Fights Islamic State's Attempted Expansion in East Africa," Long War Journal, October 26, 2015, http://www.longwarjournal.org/archives/2015/10/shabaab-leadership-fights-islamic-state-expansion.php

[36] Ken Menkhaus, "Somalia: What Went Wrong?" RUSI Journal 154, no. 4 (August 2009), 12.

[37] Katherine Houreld, "Somali Militant Group al-Shabaab Formally Joins al-Qaida," Associated Press, February 9, 2012, https://www.theguardian.com/world/2012/feb/09/somali-al-shabaab-join-al-qaida.

[38] Heidi Vogt, "Islamic State in Africa Tries to Lure Members from al-Shabaab," Wall Street Journal, October 26, 2016, http://www.wsj.com/articles/african-terror-franchise-now-has-competition-from-islamic-state-1477474200.

[39] Ioan M. Lewis, Blood and Bone: The Call of Kinship in Somali Society (Princeton, NJ: Red Sea Press, 1994), 167.

[40] Ioan M. Lewis, Saints and Somalis: Popular Islam in a Clan-Based Society (Lawrenceville, NJ: Red Sea Press, 1998).

[41] Michael van Notten and Spencer Heath MacCallum, eds., The Law of the Somalis: A Stable Foundation for Economic Development in the Horn of Africa (Trenton, NJ: Red Sea Press, 2006).

[42] Robert L. Hess, "The 'Mad Mullah' And Northern Somalia," Journal of African History 5, no. 3 (1964), 415-433; see also Abdi Sheik-Abdi, Divine Madness: Mohammed Abdulle Hassan (1856-1920) (Atlantic Highlands, NJ: Zed, 1993).

[43] Medhane Tadesse, Al-Ittihad: Political Islam and Black Economy in Somalia. Religion, Money, Clan and the Struggle for Supremacy over Somalia (Addis Ababa, 2002), 16-24.

[44] Roland Marchal, "Islamic Political Dynamics In The Somali Civil War," in Alex de Waal, ed., Islamism and its Enemies in the Horn of Africa (Addis Ababa: Shama Books, 2004), 114-146.

[45] Shaul Shay, Somalia between Jihad and Restoration (New Brunswick, NJ: Transaction Publishers, 2007), 93-127; see also Kenneth J. Menkhaus, "Somalia and Somaliland: Terrorism, Political Islam, and State Collapse," in Robert I. Rotberg, ed., Battling Terrorism in the Horn of Africa (Washington, DC: Brookings Institution Press, 2005), 23-47; and Jonathan Stevenson, "Risks and Opportunities in Somalia," Survival 49, no. 2 (Summer 2007), 5-20.

[46] Ken Menkhaus, "The Crisis In Somalia: Tragedy In Five Acts," African Affairs 106, no. 204 (2007), 357-390

[47] U.S. Department of State, Office of the Coordinator for Counterterrorism, "Designation of al-Shabaab as a Specially Designated Global Terrorist" (Public Notice 6137), February 26, 2008, http://www.state.gov/s/ct/rls/other/des/102448.htm.

[48] Commonwealth of Australia, Joint Media Release of Attorney-General Robert McClelland MP and Minister for Foreign Affairs Stephen Smith MP, "Listing of Al-Shabaab as a Terrorist Organisation," August 21, 2009, http://www.foreignminister.gov.au/releases/2009/fa-s090821.html.

[49] "21 Killed In Suicide Attack On African Union Base In Somalia," CNN.com, September 18, 2009, http://edition.cnn.com/2009/WORLD/africa/09/18/somalia.suicide.attack/index.html.

[50] Stephanie McCrummen, "Bombing Kills 19 In Somali Capital," Washington Post, December 4, 2009, A19.

[51] Jason Patinkin, "Somali Elections Postponed Again," Voice of America, September 27, 2016, http://www.voanews.com/a/somali-elections-postponed-again/3526929.html

[52] See J. Peter Pham, "Somalia: Insurgency and Legitimacy in the Context of State Collapse," in David Richards and Greg Mills, eds., Victory Among People: Lessons from Countering Insurgency and Stabilising Fragile States (London: RUSI, 2011), 277-294.

[53] Mohammed Ibrahim, "Moderate Elected President in Somalia," New York Times, January 30, 2009, http://www.nytimes.com/2009/01/31/world/africa/31somalia.html?_r=0

[54] Gabe Joselow, "Somalia Elects New President," Voice of America, September 10, 2012, http://www.voanews.com/content/somalia_parliament_votes_for_new_president/1505008.html

[55] Iqbal Jhazbhay, "Islam And Stability In Somaliland And The Geo-politics Of The War on Terror," Journal of Muslim Minority Affairs 28, no. 2 (2008), 198.

[56] Andrew McGregor, "Somaliland Charges Al-Shabaab Extremists With Suicide Bombings," Terrorism Monitor 6, no. 23 (December 8, 2008), 7-9.

[57] Yara Bayoumy, "Somalia's al Shabaab, squeezed in south, move to Puntland," Reuters, November 9, 2012, http://www.reuters.com/article/2012/11/09/somalia-puntland-shabaab-idUSL5E8M96UZ20121109.

[58] Abdisamad Mooge, "Somaliland: Real terrorism threats in fictional State," Horseed Media, February 25, 2013, http://horseedmedia.net/2013/02/25/somaliland-real-terrorism-threats-in-fictional-state/.

[59] J. Peter Pham, "The Somaliland Exception: Lessons on Postconflict State Building from the Part of the Former Somalia That Works," Marine Corps University Journal 3, no. 1 (2012), 27-28.

[60] Mooge, "Somaliland: Real terrorism threats in fictional State."

[61] Mohamed Ahmed, "Somali Rebels Agree to Ransom Deal with Pirate Leaders," Reuters, February 22, 2011, http://af.reuters.com/article/worldNews/idAFTRE71L1GO20110222.

[62] Lauren Ploch et al., "Piracy off the Horn of Africa," Congressional Research Report, April 27, 2011, 16-17, http://fpc.state.gov/documents/organization/162745.pdf.

SOUTH AFRICA

QUICK FACTS

Population: 54,300,704 (July 2016 est.)

Area: 1,219,090 sq km

Ethnic Groups: Black African 80.2%, white 8.4%, colored 8.8%, Indian/Asian 2.5%

Religions: Protestant 36.6% (Zionist Christian 11.1%, Pentecostal/Charismatic 8.2%, Methodist 6.8%, Dutch Reformed 6.7%, Anglican 3.8%), Catholic 7.1%, Muslim 1.5%, other Christian 36%, other 2.3%, unspecified 1.4%, none 15.1%

Government Type: parliamentary republic

GDP (official exchange rate): $280.4 billion (2015 est.)

Map and Quick Facts courtesy of the CIA World Factbook (Last Updated January 2017)

OVERVIEW

South Africa has a small Muslim population, comprising just 1-2 percent of the country. Despite the relatively small number of Muslims, Islamism has a distinct presence in the nation. South Africa is generally considered peripheral to the global war on terror, given its distance from the traditional hotbeds of Islamism. But in recent years, both transnational and domestic Islamist groups have been active on South African soil. Given the nation's history of political violence, it faces a continued risk of Islamist-inspired violence. In the late 1990s, there were several Islamist attacks in South Africa, and while there have been no recent attacks on South African soil, several recent terror threats illustrate the country's vulnerability to terrorist activity.

The country continues to face significant challenges, including considerable economic and social cleavages left over from the apartheid era, increasing crime rates, and high youth unemployment rates.[1] If not successfully tackled, these factors could contribute to a rise in radicalism and violence. South Africa's liberal democratic government allows religious groups to be active in the country's politics. As a result, Islamist-inspired political parties and organizations that advocate for sharia are present in South African society today, although they do not enjoy mass support.

ISLAMIST ACTIVITY

While South Africa has a history of Islamist-inspired violence dating back to the 1990s, the country has remained on the periphery of current Islamist activity. Nevertheless, global Islamist groups have periodically used South Africa's territory as a staging ground, compounding the danger posed by native Islamist groups that have emerged within South Africa in recent years.

Al-Qaeda

Since the late 1990s, al-Qaeda has used South Africa as both a physical safe haven and a conduit of support. South Africans have also traveled to the Middle East and Central Asia to join al-Qaeda. Similarly, South African *jihadists* have previously fought alongside the Taliban against the Soviet Union, as well as in Kashmir against India and Chechnya.[2]

South Africa has provided safe haven and financial opportunity for al-Qaeda operatives, and has been the subject of credible threats of violence. In January 2007, the U.S. Treasury Department designated two South African cousins, Farhad and Junaid Dockrat, for financing and facilitating al-Qaeda.[3] In addition to acting as an al-Qaeda fundraiser, Junaid also helped send South Africans to Pakistan to train with al-Qaeda, communicating via phone and email with then al-Qaeda operations chief Hamza Rabi'a.[4] In September 2009, the United States government closed its facilities across South Africa after it received credible threats against their safety.[5] The threats reportedly came from an al-Qaeda splinter group.[6] The U.S. State Department reopened its embassies and consulates a few days later. In June 2011, Fazul Abdullah Mohammad, an al-Qaeda operative and mastermind behind the 1998 U.S. Embassy bombings, was killed in Somalia. Reports indicate that he was carrying a South African passport under the name of Daniel Robinson.[7]

Furthermore, evidence has come to light that demonstrates that al-Qaeda's top leadership have an interest in South Africa. In the May 2011 raid conducted by U.S. Navy Seals in Pakistan that targeted Osama bin Laden, the U.S. uncovered revealing information regarding bin Laden's perspective of South Africa. In the documents retrieved during the raid, bin Laden articulated that it may be: "suitable to target Americans in South Africa, because it is located outside the Islamic Maghreb."[8] Bin Laden clearly considered South Africa a potential site of attacks against Americans. However, it is worth noting that bin Laden did not call on his followers to recruit in South Africa or establish a base there, as the group did in Afghanistan.

People against Gangsterism and Drugs (PAGAD)

An organization indigenous to South Africa, People against Gangsterism and Drugs (PAGAD) formed in 1995 in reaction to the extraordinarily high crime rate in the Western Cape.[9] It was also heavily influenced by the *Qibla* Movement, likewise native to South Africa, which developed in the early 1980s "to promote the aims and ideals of the Iranian revolution in South Africa and in due course transform South Africa into an Islamic state."[10] *Qibla* is not directly linked to any violent Islamist activity in South Africa. However, its presence, desire to change South Africa into an Islamic state and influence over other groups indicates that there is potential for the threat to grow. A number of *Qibla* veterans were known to be among PAGAD's ranks.[11]

PAGAD embraced an anti-Western and anti-government ideology. While the group's primary objective was ridding their communities of gang activity and drugs, its ideology and rhetoric was distinctly Islamist. The group held meetings in mosques and its spiritual advisor, Hafiz Abdulrazaq, was given the title *emir* (commander).[12] PAGAD's national coordinator, Abdus-Salaam Ebrahim, legitimized violence in his speeches. He called on Muslims to "prepare themselves with steeds of war against the enemies of Allah (SWT), the enemy of the Muslims and the oppressed people."[13]

In its operations, PAGAD adopted a dual strategy, acting as a community group while simultaneously operating covert military-style cells, known as the G-Force.[14] Through these methods, experts note, "Pagad roused Muslims into action and castigated those who questioned its methods."[15] The group initially targeted drug dealers and gang members and "spawned unprecedented levels of violence" in the Western Cape.[16] Over time, however, the group's *modus operandi* changed. In 1998, it began targeting restaurants and public places as part of its Islamist objectives. During that year, there were a reported 80 pipe bomb explosions in the Western Cape, with the most notorious occurring at a Planet Hollywood restaurant.[17] The group was designated as a Foreign Terrorist Organization by the United States in 2001.[18]

The group has not launched any violent attacks in recent years. In 2000, much of PAGAD's leadership was arrested and prosecuted, bringing the group's activities to a halt. However, as experts point out, "since the underlying reasons for its existence were never addressed, the possible re-emergence of PAGAD or similar organizations cannot be discounted."[19]

Al Shabaab

In 2015, documents leaked to the *Al Jazeera* television network revealed that the South African State Security Agency and foreign intelligence services had prevented terror attacks on South African soil between 2007 and 2010. The thwarted attacks were shown to be linked to Samantha Lewthwaite, known as the "white widow," who resided in South Africa between 2009 and 2011 on a fraudulent South African passport.[20] Lewthwaite was married to Germaine Lindsay, one of the suicide bombers responsible for the death of 26 people in the London underground in July 2005. Lewthwaite has been linked to both the *Al Shabaab* Westgate Mall attack in Nairobi, and the attack on Garissa University in Kenta that killed 148 people.[21]

The Islamic State

In September 2015, the U.S. Embassy issued a security warning regarding a possible terrorist threat to American interests in South Africa.[22] The statement, which came as the Islamic State appealed to its followers to attack Western targets during Ramadan,[23] did not include any specifics regarding the location or timing of the attack but urged U.S. citizens to take the appropriate steps to enhance their personal security. In June 2016, the U.S. Embassy in South Africa again issued a security message to warn U.S. citizens that the U.S. government had "received information that terrorist groups are planning to carry out near-term attacks against places where U.S. citizens congregate in South Africa."[24] The British and Australian Embassies issued similar warnings the same day, encouraging their citizens to be "vigilant" about personal security.[25]

The warnings caused a furor—South African Department for International Relations and Cooperation (DIRCO) and the State Security Agency (SSA) felt that the statements questioned South Africa's ability to protect foreign citizens on its soil. DIRCO questioned the credibility of the threats raising alarm among citizens who doubted the government's capacity to advance counter-terrorism efforts.[26]

In July 2016, the South African authorities arrested twin brothers Tony-Lee and Brandon-Lee Thulsie, along with two accomplices, for plotting to attack the U.S. embassy and a "Jewish Building" in Pretoria. South Africa's State Security Agencies had twice prevented the brothers from leaving to join the Islamic State (IS) in Syria. The brothers were charged with "conspiracy and incitement to commit the crime of terrorism."[27]

It is estimated that approximately 23 South Africans have left the country to join IS in Syria and Iraq to date.[28] South African authorities have kept details of their investigations and monitoring efforts classified. In April 2015, a 15-year old girl was removed from an aircraft leaving South Africa on suspicion that she was travelling to Turkey with the intention of joining the Islamic State.[29] There has been no documented evidence of IS organizing in South Africa.

ISLAMISM AND SOCIETY

Muslims constitute a minority in South Africa, with the majority of South Africans practicing Christianity. In 2010, the Pew Research Center estimated that approximately 1.5 percent of South Africa's 54 million people are Muslim.[30] Since the end of apartheid, the demographics of the Muslim population of South Africa have been changing. The majority of South Africa's Islamic population is comprised of Indians and "coloreds," the accepted term used to describe those of Malay descent.[31] Apartheid and the isolation from the international community that it caused were responsible for a dramatic slowdown of the spread of Islam in South Africa.[32]

As in other countries outside the Muslim world, Islam in South Africa has been influenced by international groups and events. South Africa's position as the economic powerhouse on the continent has made it a destination for immigrants from all over Africa. Reports indicate that immigrants from Central and West Africa have "brought with them a new 'Africanised Islam' more in line with black South Africans' identities than the religion practised by followers with closer links to Asia."[33]

Islamism in South Africa appears to have been more influenced by the Iranian Revolution than by the global *Salafi* movement, with the roots of South Africa's modern radicalism stemming largely from the Ayatollah Ruhollah Khomeini's brand of political Islam.[34] South Africa's Muslims largely identify with more libertarian Sufism, which has been a long established tradition among the Islamic population in the country.[35] *Qibla*'s formation in Cape Town followed on the heels of the Islamic Revolution,[36] and the movement was explicitly created to engender the ideals of the Iranian revolution in South Africa in an effort to one day transform the nation into an Islamic state.[37] As a testament to this fact, the group used the slogan, "One solution, Islamic Revolution."[38]

Qibla also formed the Islamic Unity Convention (IUC) in 1994, which still serves as an umbrella organization to over 250 Muslim organizations in South Africa.[39] It is worth noting that Achmad Cassiem is both a leader in *Qibla* and head of the IUC.[40] The group has boycotted government elections in South Africa "under the pretext that leaders produced by democratic means, such as elections, are illegitimate."[41] It likewise owns a radio station, Radio 786, through which it preaches and promotes its ideology.[42]

While Islamic states like Saudi Arabia and Iran have peddled their influence around the world, their influence in South Africa appears to have been limited. Iqbal Jhazbhay, a senior lecturer at the University of South Africa, notes that nearly all of South Africa's mosques are controlled by the "mainstream" Muslim Judicial Council and "if a Taliban-inclined imam speaks at a mosque and say outrageous things, the worshippers there may ignore him."[43] However, as one report has noted, there are over 600 mosques and over 400 educational centers in South Africa,[44] and it is unclear where the majority of these mosques find their funding. It has been noted, however, that the Muslim Judicial Council is supported by Saudi Arabia.[45]

A number of incidents in recent years have exposed some of the racial and ethnic cleavages in South African society. In August 2012, for example, a Muslim man was beaten to death, reportedly over the fact that he wore a beard.[46] Then, in January 2013, two Muslim students were expelled from their high school in Cape Town for refusing to remove their head coverings.[47] The South African constitution prevents schools from banning wearing certain religious garments including *yamulkes* and headscarves. Within weeks, however, the students were readmitted after a meeting was held between representatives from the school and education department, the parents, a local *imam*, and representatives from the South African Human Rights Commission.[48]

The legacy of apartheid has left deep cleavages within South African society. Within the Muslim community, reports indicate that there is a growing hostility between black Muslims and other Muslims in South Africa. As Israeli scholars Reuven Paz and Moshe Terdman have noted, "[t]he grievances of Black Muslims run the gamut, from racism and exploitation to the unfair distribution of zakat (alms)."[49] The divide presents a factor that could potentially be exploited by Islamists seeking greater influence and followers.

ISLAMISM AND THE STATE

Since the fall of apartheid and the introduction of a true multi-party electoral system, South African politics have been dominated by the African National Congress (ANC). Competing with the ANC are a variety of smaller political parties representing geographical, ethnic and religious groups.

Notably, some advocate for the imposition of *sharia* law as the governing mechanism for the state. One such group is *Al-Jama-ah*, which was created in April 2007 as a political party for South Africa's Muslim youth.[50] Ahead of the 2009 elections, *Al-Jama-ah* aimed its campaign at sixteen and seventeen year olds, noting that, come 2009, they would be eligible to vote. The group advocates for the establishment of *sharia* law in South Africa.[51] Ahead of the elections, the group posted a statement on their website calling on voters to opt for *sharia* law.[52]

Similar to other western states, South Africa's government does not legally recognize Muslim marriages, even those that are monogamous.[53] In 2012, the South African pension fund authority allowed a spouse a portion of their partner's pension after a Muslim divorce had been granted.[54] While the decision does not put in place any binding precedent on the South African courts, some South African Muslims "hope the case could open the way towards acknowledging the dissolution of an Islamic marriage as a divorce in terms of the Divorce Act."[55]

South Africa has porous borders and large immigrant communities that have the ability to harbor *jihadists*.[56] South Africa also suffers from a high crime rate.[57] This propensity towards violence, if coupled with a rise in Islamist activity, may increase the risk of Islamist-inspired attacks against targets within the country. However, the state appears to have been making efforts to reach out to the religious communities in South Africa to "manage the expression of Islam."[58] The ANC's Commission for Religious Affairs, developed in 1995,[59] group meets with the President several times per year to discuss relevant issues.

In terms of its counterterrorist response and readiness, however, South Africa remains lackluster. The South African government has generally hoped that its neutrality in the war on terror and pro-Palestinian stance would spare the nation from being targeted by Islamists.[60]

Furthermore, there has long been concern that South Africa's weak intelligence services and high crime rate would render it vulnerable to large-scale terrorist attacks. In the wake of the U.S. terror warnings in 2016, Minister of State Security David Mahlobo issued his own statement claiming that South Africa remains a "strong and stable democratic country and there is no immediate danger posed by the threat," further urging that there was "no need to panic."[61] The apparently contradictory messages from the South African government and international embassies do not instill confidence that the South African government is taking the threats seriously. An important first step would be the acknowledgement of potential danger from radical Islamic ideology—something currently missing from state discourse.[62]

ENDNOTES

[1] According to the CIA World Factbook, South Africa has an unemployment rate of 24 percent and ranks 173 out of 200 countries in terms of its unemployment rate. "South Africa," CIA World Factbook, August 3, 2010, https://www.cia.gov/library/publications/the-world-factbook/geos/sf.html.

[2] Jane's Islamic Affairs Analyst, December 1, 2006. FULL CITE NEEDED, IF POSSIBLE

[3] U.S. Department of the Treasury, "Treasury Targets Al Qaida Facilitators in South Africa," January 26, 2007, http://www.ustreas.gov/press/releases/hp230.htm.

[4] Ibid.

[5] "South Africa: Security Threat Closes U.S. Diplomatic Offices," AllAfrica.com, September 23, 2009, http://allafrica.com/stories/200909230863.html.

[6] "South Africa: Al-Qaeda Threatened U.S. Offices – Report," AllAfrica.com, September 24, 2009, http://allafrica.com/stories/200909240664.html.

[7] Peter Fabricius, "Al-Qaeda Head had SA Passport – Report," IOL News (South Africa), June 14, 2011. http://www.iol.co.za/news/africa/al-qaeda-head-had-sa-passport-report-1.1083125#.UUnA1leE3u0.

[8] "SOCOM-2012-0000017-HT," in "Letters from Abbottabad," Translated and provided by the Combating Terrorism Center at West Point, n.d., http://www.ctc.usma.edu/posts/letters-from-abbottabad-bin-ladin-sidelined.

[9] Anneli Botha, "PAGAD: A Case Study of Radical Islam in South Africa," Jamestown Foundation Terrorism Monitor 3, iss. 17, September 14, 2005, http://www.jamestown.org/single/?no_cache=1&tx_ttnews%5Btt_news%5D=561.

[10] Ibid.

[11] Goolam Vahed and Shamil Jeppie, "Muslim Communities: Muslims in Post-Apartheid South Africa," in John Daniel, Roger Southall and Jessica Lutchman, eds., State of the Nation: South Africa 2004 – 2005 (Cape Town, South Africa: Human Sciences Research Council Press: 2005), 257.

[12] Heinrich Matthée, Muslim Identities and Political Strategies: a Case Study of Muslims in the Greater Cape Town area of South Africa, 1994-2000 (Kassel, Germany: Kassel University Press GmbH: 2008), 157.

[13] Ibid., 159.

[14] Botha, "PAGAD: A Case Study of Radical Islam in South Africa."

[15] Vahed and Jeppie, "Muslim Communities: Muslims in Post-Apartheid South Africa," 256.

[16] Ibid., 258.

[17] Ibidem.

[18] Holt, "South Africa in the War on Terror."

[19] Botha, "PAGAD: A Case Study of Radical Islam in South Africa."

[20] Agiza Hlongwane and Jeff Wicks, 'White Widow' Paid for South African Passport, IOL Politics, September 29, 2013.

[21] Samantha Payne, "Who is White Widow Samantha Lewthwaite? Shy girl from Aylesbury who became world's most wanted woman," International Business Times, May 22, 2015, http://www.ibtimes.co.uk/who-white-widow-samantha-lewthwaite-shy-girl-aylesbury-who-became-worlds-most-wanted-woman-1502582.

[22] Fred Lambert, "US Embassy in South Africa Issues Terror Attack Warning, UPI, September 9, 2015, http://www.upi.com/Top_News/World-News/2015/09/08/US-embassy-in-South-Africa-issues-terror-attack-warning/5841441748232/.

[23] Reuters, May 22, 2016, Islamic State calls for attacks on west during Ramadan in audio message,

[24] U.S. Embassy Pretoria, "Security Message for US Citizens: Threats to Shopping Areas and Malls," June 4, 2016, https://za.usembassy.gov/security-message-u-s-citizens-threats-shopping-areas-malls/.

[25] Adetula David, "Terrorist Attack Warnings: Here is Why South Africans Should be Worried," Ventures, June 8, 2016, http://ewn.co.za/2016/06/08/International-Relations-responds-to-criticism-on-terror-threat.

[26] Chris Williams (2016) Terror threats and turmoil: a bad time for US-South Africa relations, http://theconversation.com/terror-threats-and-turmoil-a-bad-time-for-us-south-africa-relations-60804

[27] Normitsu Onishi, "South Africa Charges Twins Over Plot to Attack U.S. Embassy and Join ISIS," New York Times, July 11, 2016, http://www.nytimes.com/2016/07/12/world/africa/south-africa-islamic-state.html?_r=0.

[28] Azad Essa, Khadija Patel, "South African families among ISIL's newest recruits", in Al Jazeera, May 29, 2015, http://www.aljazeera.com/news/2015/05/south-african-families-isil-newest-recruits-150529094806722.html

[29] Ministry of State Security of South Africa, "Statement by Minister of State Security, David Mahlobo, MP, on the incident involving a South African and alleged terror links," April 6, 2015, http://www.ssa.gov.za/Portals/0/SSA%20docs/Media%20Releases/2015/Media%20Release%20Statement%20by%20Minister%20of%20State%20Security%20on%20a%20South%20African%20with%20suspected%20terro%20links%206%20April%202015.pdf.

[30] Pew Forum on Religion & Public Life, "Mapping the Global Muslim Population," October 2009, 31, http://pewforum.org/newassets/images/reports/Muslimpopulation/Muslimpopulation.pdf.

[31] Ibid., 253-254.

[32] Nicole Itano, "In South Africa, Many Blacks Convert to Islam," Christian Science Monitor, January 10, 2002, http://www.csmonitor.com/2002/0110/p13s1-woaf.html.

[33] Gordon Bell, "Islam is Spreading among Black South Africans," Reuters, November 14, 2004, http://www.iol.co.za/index.php?set_id=1&click_id=139&art_id=qw1100423885802B264.

[34] Schmidt, "Islamic Terror Is Not a Problem for SA."

[35] Michael Schmidt, Islamic Terror is Not a Problem for SA, November 20, 2004, http://www.iol.co.za/news/politics/islamic-terror-is-not-a-problem-for-sa-227451

[36] Terdman, "Factors Facilitating the Rise of Radical Islamism and Terrorism in Sub-Saharan Africa."

[37] Ibid.

[38] Ibidem.

[39] Botha, "PAGAD: A Case Study of Radical Islam in South Africa."

[40] Ibid.

[41] M. A. Mohamed Salih, "Islamic Political Parties in Secular South Africa," in M. A. Mohammed Salih, ed., Interpreting Islamic Political Parties (New York, New York: Palgrave Macmillan, 2009), 199.

[42] Ibid.

[43] Schmidt, "Islamic Terror Is Not a Problem for SA."

[44] Moulana Ebrahim I Bham, "Muslims in South Africa," Prepared for The Challenges and Opportunities of Islam in the West: The Case of Australia Conference, Griffith University, Brisbane, Australia, March 3-5, 2008, http://www.griffith.edu.au/__data/assets/pdf_file/0006/58308/Bham.pdf.

[45] "Militancy Among South African Muslims," Jane's Islamic Affairs Analyst, October 24, 2006.

[46] Yusuf Abramjee, "Muslim Man Dies after Fight over Beard," News24, August 8, 2012, http://www.news24.com/SouthAfrica/News/Muslim-man-dies-after-fight-over-beard-20120808

[47] "School Hijab Ban Shocks Cape Town Muslims," OnIslam, January 23, 2013, http://www.onislam.net/english/news/africa/461020-school-hijab-ban-shocks-cape-town-muslims.html.

[48] "S. African School Lifts Muslim Headgear Ban," OnIslam, January 25, 2013, http://www.onislam.net/english/news/africa/461038-s-african-school-lifts-muslim-headgear-ban.html.

[49] Reuven Paz and Moshe Terdman, "Islam's Inroads," The Journal of International Security Affairs no. 13, Fall 2007, http://www.securityaffairs.org/issues/2007/13/paz&terdman.php.

[50] Salih, "Islamic Political Parties in Secular South Africa," 195.

[51] "Al Jama-ah Targets Young Voters," The Voice of the Cape (South Africa), October 12, 2007.

[52] "Choose: The Shariah or Unruly Mix," Al-Jama-ah website, November 20, 2008, http://aljama.co.za/2008/11/choose-the-shariah-or-unruly-mix.

[53] Megan Harrington-Johnson, "Muslim marriages and divorce." De Rebus, May 2015:40 [2015], DEREBUS 93, http://www.saflii.org/za/journals/DEREBUS/2015/93.pdf

[54] "S. Africa Pensions Recognize Muslim Divorce," OnIslam, March 17, 2012, http://www.onislam.net/english/news/africa/456258-s-africa-pensions-recognize-muslim-divorce.html.

[55] "S. Africa Pensions Recognize Muslim Divorce," OnIslam, March 17, 2012, http://www.onislam.net/english/news/africa/456258-s-africa-pensions-recognize-muslim-divorce.html.

[56] Ibidem.

[57] Overseas Security Advisory Council (OSAC), "South Africa 2010 Crime & Safety Report," June 9, 2010.

[58] Schmidt, "Islamic Terror Is Not a Problem for SA."

[59] "The ANC and Religion," ANC website, n.d., http://www.anc.org.za/ancdocs/misc/anc_and_religion.html.

[60] Terdman, "Factors Facilitating the Rise of Radical Islamism and Terrorism in Sub-Saharan Africa."

[61] "Government on US Terror Alert: No Need to Panic," Mail and Guardian, June 6, 2016, http://mg.co.za/article/2016-06-06-sa-state-security-department-breaks-silence-on-us-terror-alert.

[62] "Militancy Among South African Muslims."

TANZANIA

QUICK FACTS

Population: 52,482,726 (July 2016 est.)

Area: 947,3000 sq km

Ethnic Groups: mainland - African 99% (of which 95% are Bantu consisting of more than 130 tribes), other 1% (consisting of Asian, European, and Arab); Zanzibar - Arab, African, mixed Arab and African

Religions: Christian 61.4%, Muslim 35.2%, folk religion 1.8%, other 0.2%, unaffiliated 1.4%

Government Type: presidential republic

GDP (official exchange rate):$46.7 billion (2015 est.)

Map and Quick Facts courtesy of the CIA World Factbook (January 2017)

OVERVIEW

Tanzania currently harbors a low level of Islamist activity, especially as compared to regional neighbors such as Egypt, Somalia, Sudan, and Kenya. However, a number of factors—among them secular nationalism, a lame parliamentary democracy, slow and uneven economic growth, and unequal opportunity—have spurred at least some Muslim Africans in Tanzania, as elsewhere, to adhere to Islamism as an ideological alternative.

Like other states in Africa south of the Sahara with large Muslim populations, Tanzania remains vulnerable to the popular unrest that has swept North Africa and the Gulf region since January 2011. The Arab Spring phenomenon presents a "backdoor" opening for radical jihadist Islam, which already maintains a strong presence in North Africa and the Sahel. Tanzania is significant for the number of Muslims in the population (some 18 million people), for its proximity to Somalia, the eastern African cockpit of Islamism, in which both al-Qaeda and ISIS are deter-

mined to vie for influence; and for the character of its internal politics: a one-party-dominant political system, in which the status of the Muslim population is emerging as a divisive political issue.

ISLAMIST ACTIVITY

The bombing of the U.S. embassy in Dar es Salaam in 1998, which killed eleven people and injured eighty-five others, revealed the existence of *jihadi* terrorists in Tanzania. The bombing, however, was not a plot planned inside the country, or even one organized by Tanzanian Muslims, although two Zanzibari residents were implicated. Rather, the attack was actually orchestrated by a handful of Somalis, al-Qaeda operatives and sleepers with regional links to cells in Tanzania and Kenya.[1]

Although no other similarly high-profile attacks occurred for years, Tanzania overall has remained vulnerable to radical Islamists, as a spate of acid and explosive attacks since 2012—as well as the discovery of suspected terror training camps inside Tanzania—confirm.[2] The country has a low-capacity government presiding over a large territorial expanse (one the size of France and Germany combined). Sixty-seven percent of the population lives below the poverty line.[3] *Jihadi* attacks have occurred just across its northern border in neighboring countries of Kenya and Uganda, and small arms and other weapons are readily available on the black market in East Africa. Somali terror group *Al-Shabaab*, which remains a threat to Somalia as well as the broader region, is committed to transnational expansion, including operations in, recruits from, and attacks on Tanzania.[4] With rudimentary border controls, a wide-open coastline and troubled neighbors, Tanzania's large coastal trade and extensive, illegal smuggling industry provide excellent logistical cover for extremists. Meanwhile, the Tanzanian police are unable, and sometimes unwilling, to provide even the most basic public safety services, and major crimes often go unsolved. The Tanzanian National Security Service is more capable than its police force, but is better suited to spying on political opponents than combating criminal networks. These weaknesses make Tanzania a relatively soft target.[5]

The 2012 arrest of Emrah Erdogan, an associate of both al-Qaeda and al-Shabaab, in Dar es Salaam was considered by the Tanzanian National Counterterrorism Center (NCTC) to be a confirmation that extremist organizations "have elements and plans within the country's borders."[6] This looming threat was thrown into the spotlight once again in May 2013 when a church in the predominantly Christian area of Arusha was bombed, wounding over 60. Four Saudi nationals and four Tanzanians were arrested in connection with the attack, but to date no group has claimed responsibility.[7] A series of acid and improvised explosive device (IED) attacks targeting tourists, Christians, and moderate Muslims have occurred since 2012.[8] While no group claimed responsibility, some suggested that a radical Zanzibari separatist group might have inspired—if not carried out—the attacks.[9]

At least three times between 2013 and 2016, authorities raided suspected terror training camps in Tanzania, some of which were recruiting and indoctrinating children.[10] It is unclear which group, is responsible for setting them up, though authorities suggested that al-Shabaab was the prime suspect. While Tanzania is not part of the African Union Mission in Somalia like its neighbors Kenya and Burundi, it is susceptible to the threat of Somali terror group al-Shabaab and its Kenyan affiliate *al-Hijra* (Erdogan, whose case is detailed above, was apprehended in part due to his links to *al-Hijra* members).[11] Both groups have made known their interest in Tanzania—evident especially in the large number of Tanzanian citizens recruited to fight for al-Shabaab in Somalia. More recently, a video message from a cell purported to be aligned with the Islamic State (ISIS) emerged, drawing attention to a third group with its eye on Tanzania, though there is little known about whether the group recruits in person or solely online in Tanzania.[12] The threat of these groups infiltrating Tanzania and carrying out attacks there bears watching, but of equal concern is the transnational power of the radical Islamic ideology that al-Shabaab and ISIS preach, and the potential that Tanzanians could be inspired by the groups to carry out lone wolf attacks.

The potential for volatility and radicalization is higher in Zanzibar, a semi-autonomous archipelago situated off the northeastern Tanzanian coast. The islands are majority Muslim, and thus constitute a prime target for radical figures like Sheikh Ponda Issa Ponda. Ponda has led a smattering of Islamist organizations, including *Simba wa Mungu* (God's Lion) and *Jumuiya ya Taasisi za Kiislam* (Community of Muslim Organizations), which in the past has forcibly taken over mosques in Dar es Salaam and violently targeted tourists.[13] He preaches *jihadi* Islamism and reputedly enjoys ties with al-Qaeda officials.[14] In early 2013, he was convicted of inciting violence "likely to lead to a breach of peace in the country" and given a year-long suspended sentence.[15] Three months later, unidentified men threw acid on two young British tourists in the Zanzibar town of Stone Town in a drive-by attack. Zanzibar authorities immediately arrested Ponda, asserting that his recent meetings with the leaders of the UAMSHO Muslim separatist group may have prompted the attack.[16]

UAMSHO (an acronym for the Association for Islamic Mobilization and Propagation, and also the Swahili word for "Awakening") first began offering public lectures on Islam in the 1990s and later expanded into the sphere of Muslim rights.[17] Its stated goals are to increase the standard of living for Muslims living in Zanzibar and to ultimately achieve Zanzibari independence.[18] UAMSHO's supporters have accused the government of intervening in religious affairs in violation of Article 19 of the Constitution, and they claim that government corruption has led to the moral decline of the country. Finally, they complain that the corrupt government does not properly enforce the laws in Tanzania regulating dress codes and alcohol. The government of Zanzibar, for its part, has accused the group of holding and disseminating fundamentalist views. In addition, various Western groups and think tanks have also accused the group of contemplating terrorist attacks against the tourist industry in Zanzibar, though a 2009 inquiry by the British, American, and Danish embassies in Tanzania found the organization to be non-violent.[19] However, more recently, the group's public image has been tarnished. Tanzanian Prime Minister Mizengo Pinda opined in 2012 that UAMSHO "has of late lost direction and is propagating hatred among the people of Zanzibar."[20]

In 2012, protests against the arrest of some thirty UAMSHO members resulted in the destruction of two churches in Zanzibar; according to Zanzibari police, UAMSHO "was responsible for inciting these riots"—a charge the group has denied.[21] In August 2013, the group was linked to outbreaks of violence, including acid attacks as well as religiously motivated abductions, rioting, and arson.[22] Part of UAMSHO's popularity stems from the formation of the 2010 government of national unity (a coalition between the ruling CCM and opposition CUF in Zanzibar), which to many Zanzibaris closed off the last legitimate, mainstream avenue for expressing their political grievances. In the wake of this agreement, UAMSHO positioned itself as the only group able and willing to bring about positive change for Zanzibari Muslims.

The Ansar Muslim Youth Center (AMYC), based in Tanzania's Tanga region, is another group of potential importance. Thought to be led by Sheikh Salim Abdulrahim Barahiyan, the organization began as an al-Qaeda-linked group before aligning itself with al-Shabaab and *al-Hijra*. Its goal is to "promote moral reform through the propagation of Salafi Islam," and the group exercises considerable influence over a large network of mosques and religious schools in the country.[23] Rather than having a centralized leadership structure, AMYC is "one visible part of a loose network" that includes everyone from hardline Islamic clerics to financiers and recruiters operating across Tanzania.[24] While it is difficult to tell if the group is directly responsible for any recent attacks, the AMYC's danger is its network, through which it has close relations with *al-Hijra* and has reportedly offered safe haven to *jihadists* passing through Tanzania.[25] Using such connections to recruit and fundraise for other radical Islamists may not be far off.

On a broader level, several Islamic groups, associated with a loosely organized movement known as *Ansar al-Sunnah*, seek a purified Islam in Tanzania. Although other revivalists are critical of *Ansar*, saying it is too closely linked to *Salafism, Wahabism, and Hanbalism* (all of which are conservative Muslim religious movements)[26] *Ansar* has recently grown more visible in Tanzania, both in small towns and in larger cities.[27]

So far, however, both movements are largely ripples on the surface of theology and social life across the country. Sufi Islam and Islamic traditions remain mixed with local tribal customs, creating a formidable barrier to radical Islamists.[28] As a further preventative measure, the NCTC intends to work directly with local police to encourage respected figures in Tanzanian communities, including elders and religious authorities, to try to promote conflict resolution through dialogue rather than violence.[29]

Yet it is important to note that these efforts may easily be counterbalanced by foreign influence. In recent years, expatriate *Wahhabis* from Saudi Arabia have been active in Muslim charitable organizations and in schools. According to a 2011 Western intelligence report, the Saudis are spending about $1 million a year in Tanzania to build new mosques and buy influence with the ruling CCM party.[30] "We get our funds from Yemen and Saudi Arabia," says Mohammed Madi, a Zanzibari separatist activist.[31] "Officially the money is used to buy medicine, but in reality the money is given to us to support our work and buy guns."[32] Indeed, *Wahhabi*-style fundamentalists have, on occasion, taken over 30 of the 487 mosques in Dar es Salaam, bombed bars, and beaten women who go out without being fully covered. [33]

ISLAMISM AND SOCIETY

Of Tanzania's population of about 52 million, it is estimated that about one-third are Muslim, nearly two-thirds are Christian, and a small percentage are "animist."[34] The Christian population dominates the southwest and north-central areas of the country. Muslims live largely along the pre-colonial and colonial trade routes: coastal north-south, and east-west. In the past, these routes were active in the transport of slaves, ivory, sisal, coffee and tea. The Zanzibar islands, which once served as the hub of pre-colonial trade, now have a population of roughly 1.3 million, the vast majority of which are Muslim.[35] In the traditional centers of Swahili culture along the coast, Muslims adhere to Sunni Islam, though a sizable minority of Tanzania's Muslims identify as Shi'a.[36]

Tanzania's major, simmering conflict is now the political struggle between the Tanzanian mainland and Zanzibar, which are separate former dependencies of Britain. Despite efforts to tie Zanzibar to the mainland, separatist sentiments never died in the islands.[37] Because many Zanzibaris identify culturally with their alleged Arab ancestry from across the Indian Ocean, rather than the African mainland, the potential for Zanzibari sovereignty remains a political issue linked to religious tensions and thus relevant to the question of the spread of radical Islam.

On the Zanzibar islands, Muslim religious scholars are becoming more influential in setting rules for social behavior—such as enforcing a dress code and attempting to shut down establishments that serve alcohol. High levels of poverty and feelings of marginalization at the hands of the mainland government on the islands continue to contribute to political discontent.[38] Zanzibar, which fared poorly from the economic liberalization of the 1990s, has fallen behind the mainland in economic growth, and its Western-focused tourist industry is small and fragile.[39] Rising crime, as well as high levels of youth unemployment (up to 85% of youth are unemployed in Zanzibar) and drug addiction[40] (estimates suggest that some 7% of Zanzibar's population is addicted to heroin) exacerbate the situation.[41] Thus its dissatisfied population is likely even more vulnerable to radicalization than are the residents of the mainland.

Since the 1980s, wealthy individuals from the Gulf States have funded mosques, *madrassas*, health clinics, and secondary schools in Zanzibar.[42] In addition, young Zanzibari men have received scholarships to study in Medina and Khartoum. Two of Zanzibar's universities are Islamic, funded by Saudi Arabians and Kuwaitis. Zanzibar University is funded by the Darul Iman Charitable Association, while Chukwani College of Education offers classes in Islamic studies and Islamic education. The amount of money provided from abroad is formidable; a 2012 study estimated that Saudi Arabia spends $1 million annually on religious institutions—including schools, radio stations, and mosques—in Zanzibar.[43] As a Zanzibar parliamentarian stated, "it's very difficult for the traditional *madrassas* that are really in poor shape to rival the influence of those that are being funded by foreigners and Wahhabi-based institutions."[44]

Three distinct factors have helped foster an Islamic revival in Tanzania. First, the demise of the single-party state via a 1992 law guaranteeing freedom of political organization allowed for alternative forms of association.[45] Groups that were formerly prohibited have emerged to proselytize for a more purified Islam.[46] Second, new Islamic organizations are opposing formerly state-sanctioned groups.[47] This Muslim revival is part of a "reconnecting" with the Muslim world that is taking place in Tanzania after years of isolation. It parallels, and may be due in part to, the new availability of Islamic satellite television channels and Islamic media in the country.[48] Third, Tanzania remains plagued by poverty. Despite mineral discoveries (including a massive natural gas find in 2016 worth some $8 billion[49]), its economy relies on agriculture, but only a small portion of its land is subject to sustainable cultivation. Comparatively paltry resources, combined with failed economic programs since independence, have translated into a $2,900 per capita GDP, with a large percentage of the population living below the poverty line.[50]

The religious figures leading this revival now portray Muslim traditions as threatened by a secular state, requiring a return to the basics in order to protect the Islamic way of life.[51] The revival includes all age groups and socioeconomic classes. On the Zanzibar islands, the revival is directed toward Muslims who are *munafik* ("Muslims in name only") and the Sufi brotherhoods. On the mainland it is directed toward Christians because of their increasing belief in a version of Islam that is hostile to all other religions.[52] While concerned with the "onslaught and failure" of Western values, the revival in Tanzania also seeks to address the lack of effective governance in the country and tap into widespread dissatisfaction within the Muslim population.[53] The revival groups offer an alternative to the older, state-sanctioned Muslim identity. New sources of information on Islam are now available to Tanzanians, offering alternative avenues from the leading clerics inside the country.

Additionally, the translation of the Quran into Swahili has ensured that the established Arabic-speaking scholars no longer have a monopoly on its interpretation.[54] There is currently an abundance of Islamic literature, tapes, CDs, and DVDs available in Arabic, English, and Swahili. These products are widely available in bookstores, streets, and outside mosques after Friday prayers, further aiding the individualization of Islam and allowing more freedom of interpretation of the religion through expanded access. Thus, the revival is not just directed at the state, but also toward those Muslims perceived as being a part of the state apparatus (consisting largely of an older group of Muslims working within the state's construction of a passive Muslim identity).

For the most part, a long history of cooperation in the name of nationalism has mitigated religious conflict in the country. Indeed, "while there are some ethnic identities and geographic areas that coincide with a certain religious tradition, often other identities, such as class divisions or support for political parties, are cross-cutting and do not reinforce these religious divisions."[55] The legacy of the Tanganyika African National Union's (TANU) emphasis on inter-religious cooperation, has, for the most part, endured.

Yet, in the past decade, circumstances have changed. Prior to the 2015 general elections and a scheduled constitutional referendum (which was later postponed), former President Jakaya Kikwete warned of heightened religious tensions: "You don't need to be a master of astrology to know that the current situation, if left unchecked, could plunge our country into a major conflict between Christians and Muslims."[56] In addition to this general increase in political and sectarian tensions—worsened by political disagreements including the disputed Zanzibar elections, groups like al-Shabaab and ISIS have increasingly appealed to Tanzania's disaffected Muslims. In May 2016, Defense Minister Hussein Mwinyi warned about the radicalization of young Tanzanians and his concern that foreign recruits—previously fighting for al-Shabaab or ISIS—would return to Tanzania, though the government's response to date has primarily been through law enforcement.[57]

ISLAMISM AND THE STATE

The path remains open for simplistic and politicized interpretations of Islam to capitalize on local grievances, such as the integrity of the federation of the mainland and Zanzibar, and to reinterpret those issues as a source of Muslim-Christian tensions. While it is important to note that anti-Christian sentiment thus far has not instigated a wave of Islamist radicalism throughout the rest of the population, the issue of Zanzibari sovereignty is crucial to the problem of this potentially violent reframing.

Tanganyika (the predecessor to Tanzania) came into being after achieving independence from Britain in 1962. Zanzibar achieved independence shortly thereafter, in 1963, and in the election that followed, the Zanzibar Nationalist Party (ZNP) coalition (generally representing the islands' Arab population) narrowly defeated the Afro-Shirazi Party (ASP), which represented the African "labor" class. Subsequently, an uprising of African laborers and ex-soldiers mushroomed into the anti-Arab Zanzibari Revolution of 1964, which overthrew the ZNP government, the Sultan, the Arab elite, and the whole enterprise of constitutional monarchy.[58] Abeid Karume, the leader of the ASP coalition, ruled by decree, warding off any challenges to the new regime. Three months later, Karume and Tanganyikan President Nyerere united Zanzibar and Tanganyika into Tanzania. The rapid pace and questionable constitutionality of these origins remains a background factor to the increasing demands for full autonomy in Zanzibar, a demand which is frequently linked to the differing ethnic and religious composition of the islands' population.

During the early years of one-party socialist rule, President Julius Nyerere was adamant about creating a nation free of racial and religious divisions.[59] The demise of *ujamaa* ("community") socialism in the 1980s, as well as the rise of the multi-party system, permitted region and religion to divide the population, frustrating Nyerere's plans. Today, ethnic differences and overlapping religions have become salient rallying points in the search for the "true" identity of Zanzibar, which have faint echoes on the mainland. All across Tanzania, "people at the grassroots level advance religious identities in pursuit of their interests in regard to spiritual, material, and political interests."[60] The idea of full autonomy was first raised in 1994, but Chama Cha Mapinduzi (CCM), the ruling party since 1963, has constantly rejected the notion.[61]

In Tanzania, religion has taken a subservient position to the unifying nationalist agenda of the CCM. In one notable exception, as a response to transferring control of the nation's education and health administration to the Catholic Church in 1992, the Council for the Propagation of the Quran (commonly known as Balukta) accused the Tanzanian government's National Muslim Organization (Bakwata) of corruption, temporarily seizing its headquarters. Balukta was Tanzania's first militant Islamist group, but its actions were short-lived. President Ali Hassan Mwinyi expelled them from the Bakwata headquarters, and the group was banned in 1993.[62] Since then, most Islamists have tended to be critical of anti-government fundamentalists.

The CCM faces an ongoing challenge from the Zanzibar-based Civic United Front (CUF). A minority party whose various elements have even professed their goal to be to "release Tanzanian society from the dictatorship of Christianity,"[63] the CUF's primary constituents are Zanzibaris of Arab descent. Although its supporters have clashed violently and repeatedly with the police since 1995, the CUF has maintained that it does not use or condone violence as a means of gaining power, preferring to operate through legitimate, democratic means. Yet, it has not totally dismissed the use of violence as a means for establishing itself in Zanzibar, especially if political corruption and marginalization continue to occur there.

Tanzania held general elections in 2015 and, while the contest was considered well-administered, the Zanzibar Electoral Commission annulled results on the island after the opposition looked poised to win (the ruling CCM won handily on the mainland). The subsequent electoral standoff resulted in heightened tensions across Zanzibar; a series of subsequent IED attacks were assumed to be politically motivated. The election annulment effectively ended Zanzibar's government of national unity and simultaneously eliminated what many felt was a last legitimate and mainstream avenue for expressing discontent.[64] There is now a chance that frustrated citizens who feel that they have been ejected from mainstream politics will seek out more radical representation.

To many, political marginalization is a reality in Tanzania. The country faces the common dilemma of post-authoritarian states in Africa: a tropism toward official blandishments or outright control of associations once prohibited under one-party rule. Although the Tanzanian state is officially secular and its constitution guarantees freedom of religion and prohibits religious political parties, smoldering religious tensions in the country belie the effectiveness of this guarantee. The more moderate groups, which offer no structural challenge to the system, are more likely to be candidates for co-optation, while radicals are forced to work outside the system. Thus, the government risks pushing Islamist believers in more radical directions through sheer clumsiness: its entrenched corruption, election rigging, and alleged detentions and torture of opposition members dramatically exacerbate the perception of marginalization among the moderates.

Since the end of socialist rule in the 1990s, people claiming Zanzibari Arab identity have also alleged that the government of Zanzibar (directed by the CCM) deliberately and systematically discriminates against them, denying them access to government jobs, housing, and business licenses. Similar dissatisfaction has spread to the mainland among the coastal Swahili and Arab population.[65] When the Tanzanian government signed "The Prevention of Terrorism Act" into law in December 2002 (largely under pressure from the United States), it further aggravated this demographic and prompted waves of criticism for specifically targeting Muslims. Opponents of the law noted that it borrowed heavily from the *U.S. Patriot Act*, the *British Prevention of Terrorism Act*, and the *Suppression of Terrorism Act* of apartheid South Africa.[66]

Finally, although Muslims have always held key governmental positions (and the presidency has unofficially rotated between a Christian and a Muslim), many Muslims perceive the governing elite as Christian, which contributes to the feeling of marginalization. Such frustrations with the state tend to manifest themselves in attacks upon Christians.[67] Additional dissatisfaction is aimed at the police, since in many Muslim areas, the police are often Christians that tend to disregard local customs and further alienate residents.

Thus, the dynamic in Tanzania bears watching. The rise in tensions has paralleled the rise in political visibility and assertiveness of the Muslim community in the past decade.54 Moreover, al-Shabaab's continued threat to Somalia and its interest in expanding throughout the region—as well as the ideological and increasingly physical presence of ISIS in East Africa—means that Tanzania must remain vigilant against radical external influences, as well as the internal politics and politics that presage violent and dangerous radicalization.

Endnotes

[1] 1 Andre LeSage,"Terrorism Threats and Vulnerabilities in Africa," in Andre LeSage, ed., African Counterterrorism Cooperation: Assessing Regional and Subregional Initiatives. Washington, DC: National Defense University Press, 2007, 87.

[2] Beatrice Materu, "Tanzania: Police Arrest Women, Children at 'Terrorism Training Camp,'" The East African, November 17, 2016, http://allafrica.com/stories/201611170829.html.

[3] "Tanzania" CIA World Fact Book, n.d., https://www.cia.gov/library/publications/the world-factbook/geos/tz.html.

[4] "Al-Shabaab as a Transnational Security Threat," Intergovernmental Authority on Development, March 2016, https://igad.int/attachments/article/1373/1413_ISSP%20Report%20on%20Al%20Shabaab%202016%20FINAL3%20copy.pdf.

[5] Jeffrey Haynes, "Islamic Militancy in East Africa," Third World Quarterly 26, iss. 8 (2005), 1323; William Roseneau, "Al Qaida Recruitment Trends in Kenya and Tanzania," Studies in Conflict and Terrorism 28 (June 2004), 1, 4; Jodi Vittori, Kristen Bremer, and Pasquale Vittori, "Islam in Tanzania and Kenya: Ally or Threat in the War on Terror?" Studies in Conflict and Terrorism 32, no. 12 (2009), 1082; Bruce E. Heilman and Paul J. Kaiser, "Religion, Identity, and Politics in Tanzania," Third World Quarterly, August 2002, 1083; Andre LeSage, "The Rising Terrorist Threat in Tanzania: Domestic Islamist Militancy and Regional Threats," Institute for National Strategic Studies, September 2014, http://ndupress.ndu.edu/Portals/68/Documents/stratforum/SF-288.pdf, 6.

[6] "Tanzania," in U.S. Department of State, Country Reports on Terrorism 2012, 36, http://www.state.gov/documents/organization/210204.pdf.

[7] "Tanzania church attack: Saudis held for 'act of terror,'" BBC, May 6, 2013, http://www.bbc.co.uk/news/world-africa-22425364.

[8] These attacks have occurred both on the mainland and in Zanzibar. LeSage, "The Rising Terrorist Threat in Tanzania," 6.

[9] Mike Pflanz, Gordon Rayner, and Victoria Ward, "Zanzibar Acid Attack: Finger Pointed at Radical Islamic Group as Five Questioned Over Assault on British Teenagers," The Telegraph, August 9, 2013, http://www.telegraph.co.uk/news/worldnews/africaandindianocean/zanzibartanzania/10232580/Zanzibar-acid-attack-finger-pointed-at-radical-Islamic-group-as-five-questioned-over-assault-on-British-teenagers.html.

[10] Deodatus Balile, "Tanzania Dismantles Al-Shabaab Child Indoctrination Camp in Tanga Region," Sabahi, November 15, 2013, http://allafrica.com/stories/201311180387.html.

[11] Canadian Security Intelligence Service, "The Future of Al-Qaeda: Results of a Foresight Project," May 2013, https://cryptome.org/2013/07/csis-alqaeda-future.pdf, 66.

[12] "Al-Shabaab as a Transnational Security Threat," Intergovernmental Authority on Development, 21; "ISIS in Tanzanian Caves: Terror Threat Multiplication," Intelligence Briefs, May 18, 2016, http://intelligencebriefs.com/isis-in-tanzanian-caves-terror-threat-multiplication/. Tanzanians make up the second-largest group of foreign fighters in al-Shabaab; Kenyans are the largest.

[13] Peter Kagwanja, "Counter-terrorism in the Horn of Africa: New Security Frontiers, Old Strategies," African Security Review 15, iss. 3 (2006), 77.

[14] Turner, "'These Young Men Show No Respect for Local Customs'- Globalisation and Islamic Revival in Zanzibar," 239.

[15] Faustine Kapama, "Tanzania: DPP Directs Arrest of Sheikh Ponda for Disobeying Order," allAfrica.com, August 9, 2013, http://allafrica.com/stories/201308090176.html

[16] Mike Pflanz, "Radical preacher wanted over Zanzibar acid attack shot in police raid, Telegraph (London), August 10, 2013, http://www.telegraph.co.uk/news/worldnews/africaandindianocean/zanzibartanzania/10235328/Radical-preacher-wanted-over-Zanzibar-acid-attack-shot-in-police-raid.html

[17] Thembi Mutch, "Zanzibar and the Mainland: The Shaky State of the Union," Think Africa, November 20, 2012, http://thinkafricapress.com/tanzania/zanzibar-tanzania-shaky-state-union-uamsho.

[18] Uamsho, "About Revival," n.d., http://uamshozanzibar.wordpress.com/kuhusu-uamsho/.

[19] Simon Turner, "'These Young Men Show No Respect for Local Customs' –Globalization and Islamic Revival in Zanzibar," Journal of Religion in Africa, 39, 2009, p.242.

[20] "Tanzania: Pinda Concerned With Uamsho Group," AllAfrica.com, June 14, 2012, http://allafrica.com/stories/201206150142.html

[21] Fumbuka Ng'wanakilala, "Zanzibar Islamists Burn Churches, Riot – Police," Reuters, May 27, 2012, http://www.reuters.com/article/zanzibar-protest-idUSL5E8GR1HB20120527.

[22] Nicholas Kulish, "Violent Episodes Grow in Tanzania, an African Haven," New York Times, June 30, 2013, http://www.nytimes.com/2013/07/01/world/africa/violent-episodes-grow-in-tanzania-an-african-haven.html?pagewanted=all&_r=1&.

[23] United Nations, "Report of the Monitoring Group on Somalia and Eritrea pursuant to Security Council resolution 2002 (2011)," July 13, 2012, http://www.marsecreview.com/wp-content/uploads/2012/09/UN_REPORT_2012.pdf.

[24] LeSage, "The Rising Terrorist Threat in Tanzania," 12.

[25] The Future of Al Qaeda: Results of a Foresight Project, Canadian Security Intelligence Service, April 2013, http://www.investigativeproject.org/documents/testimony/394.pdf, 66.

[26] Roman Loimeier, "Perceptions of Marginalization: Muslims in Contemporary Tanzania," in Rene Otayek and Benjamin F. Soares, eds., Islam and Muslim Politics in Africa (New York: Palgrave, 2007), 145.

[27] Turner, "'These Young Men Show No Respect for Local Customs'- Globalisation and Islamic Revival in Zanzibar," 245.

[28] Jeffrey Haynes, "Islamic Militancy in East Africa," Third World Quarterly 26, iss. 8 (2005), 1330.

[29] "Tanzania," Country Reports on Terrorism 2012, 37.

[30] Harvey Glickman, "The Threat of Islamism in Sub-Saharan Africa: The Case of Tanzania," Foreign Policy Research Institute E-Note, April 2011, http://www.fpri.org/enotes/201104.glickman.islamismsubsaharanafrica.html#note8.

[31] Lisa Beyer, "Inside the Kingdom," Time Magazine, September 15, 2003, http://www.time.com/time/magazine/article/0,9171,1005663-8,00.html.

[32] Moshe Terdman, "Factors Facilitating the Rise of Radical Islamism and Terrorism in Sub-Saharan Africa," GLORIA Center Project for the Research of Islamist Movements African Occasional Papers 1 March 2007, 10.

[33] Glickman, "The Threat of Islamism in Sub-Saharan Africa: The Case of Tanzania."

[34] "Tanzania" CIA World Fact Book.

[35] Ibid.; National Bureau of Statistics – Ministry of Finance and Office of Chief Government Statistician – Ministry of State, "Basic Demographic and Socio-Economic Profile, Tanzania Zanzibar," April 2014, http://www.tanzania.go.tz/egov_uploads/documents/TANZANIA_ZANZIBAR_SOCIO_ECONOMIC_PROFILE_sw.pdf, iii.

[36] Pew Forum on Religion & Public Life, "Tolerance and Tension: Islam and Christianity in Sub-Saharan Africa," April 2010, http://www.pewforum.org/files/2010/04/sub-saharan-africa-full-report.pdf, 21.

[37] Haynes, "Islamic Militancy in East Africa," 1330.

[38] Vittori et al., "Islam in Tanzania and Kenya: Ally or Threat in the War on Terror?" 1082; "Tanzania Human Development Report 2014," United Nations Development Programme, 2014, http://hdr.undp.org/sites/default/files/thdr2014-main.pdf, 10.

[39] Turner, "'These Young Men Show No Respect for Local Customs'- Globalisation and Islamic Revival in Zanzibar," 259.

[40] Abigail Higgins, "Fighting Heroin Addiction in Conservative Zanzibar," Al Jazeera (Doha), May 28, 2015, http://www.aljazeera.com/indepth/features/2015/05/fighting-heroin-addiction-conservative-zanzibar-150514102028439.html.

[41] LeSage, "The Rising Terrorist Threat in Tanzania," 8.

[42] Haynes, "Islamic Militancy in East Africa," 1330; LeSage, 81; Vittori et al., "Islam in Tanzania and Kenya: Ally or Threat in the War on Terror?" 1088. As Andre Le Sage points out in "The Rising Terrorist Threat in Tanzania: Domestic Islamist Militancy and Regional Threats," scholars have woefully scarce data on the amount of money that has been donated from the Gulf to East Africa.

[43] Katrina Manson, "Extremism on the Rise in Zanzibar," Financial Times, December 28, 2012, http://www.ft.com/intl/cms/s/0/c85b0054-42c0-11e2-a4e4-00144feabdc0.html#axzz2cXjw2UQ2.

[44] Katrina Manson, "Extremism on the Rise in Zanzibar."

[45] Mohabe Nyirabu, "The Multiparty Reform Process in Tanzania: The Dominance of the Ruling Party," African Journal of Political Science 7, no. 2, 2002, 104.

[46] Loimeier, "Perceptions of Marginalization: Muslims in Contemporary Tanzania," 143.

[47] Turner, "'These Young Men Show No Respect for Local Customs'- Globalisation and Islamic Revival in Zanzibar," 238.

[48] Ibid.; Larson, "Introduction," 20; Heilman and Kaiser, "Religion, Identity, and Politics in Tanzania," 695.

[49] James Burgess, "$8 Billion Natural Gas Find Re-Affirms Tanzania's Status as a Gas Giant," OilPrice.com, March 28, 2016, http://oilprice.com/Energy/Energy-General/8-Billion-Natural-Gas-Find-Re-Affirms-Tanzanias-Status-As-Gas-Giant.html.

[50] The last available statistic for percentage of the population below the poverty line is 67% (2011). With a steady annual GDP growth rate at 7 percent, and as GDP per capita has increased in recent years, it is likely that the number of Tanzanians living below the poverty line has decreased correspondingly, but economic poverty remains a force to be reckoned with. See Bernadeta Killian, "The State and Identity Politics in Zanzibar: Challenges to Democratic Consolidation in Tanzania," African Identities 6, no. 2 (May 2008), 113; see also "Tanzania," CIA World Factbook, November 25, 2016, https://www.cia.gov/library/publications/the-world-factbook/geos/tz.html.

[51] Turner, "'These Young Men Show No Respect for Local Customs'- Globalisation and Islamic Revival in Zanzibar," 240.
[52] Ibid., 238-239.
[53] Larson, "Introduction," 24.
[54] Haynes, "Islamic Militancy in East Africa," 1331.
[55] "Tanzania" CIA World Fact Book.
[56] Fambuka Ng'wanakilala, "Tanzanian President Warns of Rising Religious Tensions Before Referendum," Reuters, March 29, 2015, http://www.reuters.com/article/tanzania-politics-idUSL6N0WV0IM20150329.
[57] "Tanzania Warns of Growing Number of Terrorism Recruits," CCTV Africa, May 12, 2016, https://www.youtube.com/watch?v=M9t7maly0fc; Jaston Binala, "Tanzania: Radicalism Rising in Tanzania but No Panic Yet," The East African, December 19, 2015, http://allafrica.com/stories/201512212852.html.
[58] Greg Cameron, "Narratives of Democracy and Dominance in Zanzibar," in Kjersti Larson, ed., Knowledge, Renewal, and Religion: Repositioning and Changing Ideological and Material Circumstances Among the Swahili on the East African Coast (Uppsala: Nordiska Afrikainstitutet, 2009), 151.
[59] Killian, "The State and Identity Politics in Zanzibar: Challenges to Democratic Consolidation in Tanzania," 115.
[60] Africa Liberal Network, "Civic United Front – Tanzania," 2013, http://www.africaliberalnetwork.org/standard.aspx?i_PageID=138.
[61] Killian, "The State and Identity Politics in Zanzibar: Challenges to Democratic Consolidation in Tanzania," 111.
[62] Barbara G. Brents and Deo S. Mshigeni, "Terrorism in Context: Race, Religion, Party, and Violent Conflict in Zanzibar," The American Sociologist, Summer 2004, 4, 67, http://www.unlv.edu/Faculty/brents/research/terrorZanzibar.pdf.
[63] Douglis G. Anglin, "Zanzibar: Political Impasse and Commonwealth Mediation," Journal of Contemporary African Studies 18, no. 1 (2000), 43-44.
[64] LeSage, "The Rising Terrorist Threat in Tanzania," 8.
[65] Ibid., 705; "Terrorism in Context: Race, Religion, Party, and Violent Conflict in Zanzibar," 67; Haynes, "Islamic Militancy in East Africa," 1330.
[66] Andre Le Sage, "Terrorism Threats and Vulnerabilities in Africa," 87.
[67] Ibid., 705; "Terrorism in Context: Race, Religion, Party, and Violent Conflict in Zanzibar," 67; Haynes, "Islamic Militancy in East Africa," 1330.

Europe

COUNTRIES
Albania
Denmark
France
Germany
Italy
Kosovo
Macedonia
Netherlands
Spain
United Kingdom

ALBANIA

> **QUICK FACTS**
>
> Population: 3,038,594 (July 2016 est.)
>
> Area: 28,748 sq km
>
> Ethnic Groups: Albanian 82.6%, Greek 0.9%, other 1% (including Vlach, Roma (Gypsy), Macedonian, Montenegrin, and Egyptian), unspecified 15.5% (2011 est.)
>
> Religions: Muslim 56.7%, Roman Catholic 10%, Orthodox 6.8%, atheist 2.5%, Bektashi (a Sufi order) 2.1%, other 5.7%, unspecified 16.2%
>
> Government Type: parliamentary republic
>
> GDP (official exchange rate): $11.54 billion (2015 est.)
>
> *Map and Quick Facts courtesy of the CIA World Factbook (December 2016)*

OVERVIEW

While Albanians of all faiths have historically co-existed peacefully, lingering radicalism has since the early 1990s been fueled by external Islamic states and organizations that have established themselves or allied with like-minded local Islamist groups. Since 2011, the conflict in Syria has tapped into an existing extremist underground in the country.

Today's Islamist stirrings in Albania parallel similar developments in other Balkan countries. Such states share several important characteristics: low education and a lack of especially youth employment opportunities, especially for young people; indigenous Muslim populations; a transition from former autocratic socialist or communist governments, and the entrenched presence of foreign Islamist forces attempting to educate local Muslims, build mosques, provide public services, make investments, and otherwise build influence.

While the number of Albanian citizens joining Middle East terrorist groups like ISIS and the Al Nusra Front has significantly declined with these groups' territorial losses since 2015, the question of Islamic radical-

ism remains open in a country that has historically been more nationalist than religious. The more visible role of the Greek-supported Orthodox Church and the Catholic Church has also concerned some Albanian Muslim communities. The failed coup in Turkey in July 2016, which Turkish President Erdogan blamed on U.S,-based cleric Fethullah Gülen, may result in further internal divisions between Sunni Muslims in Albania, with some evincing support for Gülen and his extensive networks of schools and charities, and others opposing them.

While it has not been significantly affected by the European migration crisis, Albania has developed security measures in response to potential radicalization efforts by migrant networks. It uses its status as one of the region's few NATO members to its advantage; the Obama administration committed to supporting counter-terrorism initiatives for the region that would be based in Tirana, including a NATO Center of Excellence for researching the causes of violent extremism.

Nevertheless, the very existence of such ventures indicates that the country does have a problem. Albania has become more known as a producer of jihadists, as several arrests and current trends have indicated. Like other Balkan countries, Albania has passed legislation targeting citizens who have sought to travel to the Middle East to wage jihad, with some effective results. Nevertheless, even though political Islam has thus far failed to make inroads, Islamic extremism will continue to be monitored carefully, due to the larger connections between extremists from Albania and their ethnic kin in nearby Macedonia, Kosovo and Montenegro. Ethnic Albanian extremists also will continue to threaten the authority of the mainstream Muslim community in this wider region.

ISLAMIST ACTIVITY

The population of Albania is 2.8 million.[1] 80 percent of those citizens are Muslims.[2] In this population, there are three distinct groups. The Muslim Community of Albania is the major body representing the country's Sunni Muslims (and Albanian Muslims in general), and is deemed to be the most "legitimate" representative of Albanian Muslims by the state and the international community.[3] Secondly, the World Bektashi Center in Tirana officially represents the Shi'ite Bektashi *Sufi* order (comprising around 20 percent of Albania's Muslim population), which has a longstanding presence in the country and shares some similarities with Turkey's Alevi Muslims.[4] However, the Bektashi order is considered heretical by many Muslims for its more relaxed, liberal practices and differing theology. The Bektashi are particularly despised by the third and most dangerous Islamic group present in Albania—the puritanical minority attracted to *Wahhabism* and other extreme forms of Islam prevalent in the Arab world. The latter population has been involved with recruiting fighters for Middle Eastern conflicts since 2014.

Wahhabis comprise an unknown minority in Albania, as they operate largely outside of official structures. Although they continue to make determined efforts to usurp power from legitimate Islamic representatives, *Wahhabis* have also established parallel institutions, ranging from mosques to schools and charities. In July 2012, a Catholic charity leader voiced alarm over a perceived increase in Islamic fundamentalist attitudes among young Muslims – particularly those returning from schooling in Saudi Arabia and Turkey. This foreign training was associated with increasing fundamentalism.[5]

With the outbreak of the Syria conflict, this fundamentalism has manifested in the form of terrorist recruitment among local youth. This has been noted particularly in the capital, Tirana, and in impoverished villages in southeastern Albania, such as Leshnica, Zagoracan and Rremenj. Since 2011, some 24 young Muslims from these villages alone have disappeared into Syria, where several are presumed to have died in fighting – along with the individual responsible for their recruitment, former Leshnica *imam* Almir Daci.[6] When surveyed in May of 2015, 500 ethnic Albanian fighters were believed to be in Syria and Iraq, with approximately 150 of them Albanian citizens.[7] By August 2016, the number of recruits had dropped considerably, though Albanian experts viewed this decline as reflecting a relative loss of territory – and thus reduced personnel needs – on the part of the Islamic State, rather than a decline in overall radicalism in the country.[8]

Indeed, as elsewhere in Europe, Albania may actually become more at risk of "lone wolf" terrorist attacks with the Islamic State's decline in territorial control in the Middle East and its exhortations to fellow radicals to act alone. As of August 2016, Albania had not yet seen such a terrorist attack. However, a Kosovo Albanian with a prior criminal record did attack and attempt to kidnap several people in the southern town of Vlore that month.[9] This episode caused significant worry among government officials, because Albania has tried in recent years to develop its coastal tourism industry, and any successful attacks would damage this much-needed source of income.

While radicalism remains low, it is significant to note that the Albanian language was one of several chosen by the Islamic State for its propaganda purposes. In fact, the above-mentioned Almir Daci became a well-known propagandist for ISIS, and participated in a brigade specifically composed of Balkan recruits.[10]

A trend in Islamist activities in Albania (and the Balkans in general) is the manipulation of the concept of "civil society." Islamist groups have employed the liberal rhetoric of human rights and religious freedom in pursuit of an Islamic supremacist agenda. This is chiefly done through the public discourse of non-governmental organizations (NGOs) – entities utilized by Western state-builders since the 1990s as tools in the broader democratization movement in post-Communist Eastern Europe. NGOs and charities are also attractive to radical elements for money laundering purposes, as their financial records can easily be manipulated, and they can achieve disproportionate influence in poor, rural areas.[11] And, despite their non-governmental designation, many are in fact informal entities supported by various governments (discussed below).

One of the more conspicuous forerunners of the Albanian Muslim NGO movement (active mostly between 2005-2010) was the Muslim Forum of Albania (MFA). The organization was created in 2005, during a heated feud between moderates and radicals over the official Muslim Community's bylaws. Because of this history, some seasoned foreign and local observers have concluded that the MFA was created to compete with official Islamic bodies.[12] The MFA was accused of creating "parallel structures" from those of the official Muslim Community.[13] Although the MFA claimed merely to be interested in human rights and opposing discrimination against Muslims, its public statements revealed a more dogmatic agenda. Such statements included: attacking Pope Benedict XVI for his comments on violence in Islam; condemning Albanian Christian groups and all church-building initiatives; denouncing the Danish cartoonist who famously drew the depictions of Prophet Mohammed in 2005; petitioning the government to accept Chinese Uighur prisoners being released from Guantanamo Bay; and insinuating that Albania's foreign Islamist residents are oppressed.[14]

The degree of influence that such organizations currently wield over the public discourse remains limited. However, it is clear from their use of the English language and their attempts to petition international organizations to their cause that they are interested not only in the internal, local Albanian audience, but in becoming part of a broader, global Islamic movement. In terms of Albania's national security and social cohesion, the biggest threat that this poses is the potential for Islamists to divide the nation on religious grounds; Albanians have historically taken pride in maintaining ethnic cohesion, despite being cumulatively composed of differing Christian and Muslim groups. If politically-oriented Muslim NGO groups continue to gain influence, it could easily endanger this cooperative legacy.

Most significantly, formal and informal Islamic organizations have been used to challenge the legitimate Muslim leadership in the country in order to implement a more radical policy and to overthrow the leadership. This type of activity has undergone a notable progression in the past decade. While Islamic extremism in Albania once was solely funded and fomented from abroad, in recent years it has found a foothold within the country itself. (The current activities of foreign Islamist charities and groups are discussed in greater detail below.)

As part of this evolution, extremists of Albanian background have been trained abroad, and some have returned to take up active roles in Albania (operating independently or as part of Islamist groups). Significantly, such activities began many years before the Syrian conflict and the rise of ISIS, which have drawn Albanian fighters to the Middle East. For example, following the September 11, 2001 terrorist attacks, the Bush administration asked Albania to shutter several charities suspected to be fronts for radical activity; one, al Haramain, was suspected of organizing the murder of a moderate Muslim Community leader, Salih Tivari, in January 2002.[15] Tivari had pledged to remove foreign Islamist elements from the country. In fact, Albanian authorities believe that local extremists trained in Islamic states actually carried out his murder.[16] In 2006, other Muslim Community leaders received death threats after an extremist group tried, but failed, to change one of the Community's official statutes.[17]

Leadership challenges and internal conflicts within the official Albanian Islamic Community have allowed radical views to proliferate, while the official body remains occupied with its own internal problems. The Islamic Community is Albania's second-largest landowner, and some of the "scandals" surrounding the Community's leadership over the years have concerned alleged profiteering from land sales. This had the effect of dividing the Community's General Council between supporters of then-head *mufti* Selim Muca (in power from 2004 until 2014) and his opponents. On September 21, 2010, following an attempt by Muca's opponents to prosecute him for corruption, a special session of the General Council reconfirmed Muca's authority, and sacked four prominent opponents among the Islamic leadership.[18] This decision came four years after similar infighting, which resulted in the firing of the Mufti of Shkoder, Bashkim Bajraktari. U.S. officials were concerned at the time that Shkoder's Islamic leadership was "stacked with 'extremists'" due to the local influence of the MFA and its international links with the Muslim Brotherhood.[19]

This political jockeying has created internal frictions within Albania's Muslim community, and also distracted its leadership from dealing with attempts by religious extremists to strengthen their foothold. Muca, for example, was criticized for failing to stop the formation of a union of *imams* with reported *Wahhabi* leanings in Kavaja, located between Tirana and the Adriatic coast. In opposition to Muca, the above-mentioned Muslim Forum of Albania held an event in Kavaja in February 2008, attracting Islamists from Kosovo, Macedonia and other parts of the region.[20] A new group, the Union of Islamic Youth, was then registered in Kavaja and believed to be associated with *Wahhabi* elements (though available information about the group is sparse). Local and foreign observers agreed that the Kavaja mosque and its worshippers are increasingly wary of outsiders and seem to have more fundamentalist views.[21]

Ankara has pressured Albania to close Gülen schools, first during President Erdogan's state visit in 2015, and again after the July 2016 coup attempt. While the Albanian government refused to do so, it has come under increasing pressure to tackle the alleged involvement of Gülenist 'parallel institutions' in public administration. Turkey has alleged that Albania is serving as a stronghold for the rival movement. After the coup attempt, Turkey officially requested Albanian police "to investigate and ultimately arrest a number of individuals allegedly supporting Gülen, who media indicated "may include public figures, journalists, analysts and even high-ranking officials."[22] While such requests have put the government in a tough position, Albania's primary allegiance to the US means that it is only likely to crack down on the Gülen movement if Washington does so first.

ISLAMISM AND SOCIETY

A 2009 survey citing Islamic Community officials found that Albania had 568 Sunni mosques, as well as 70 Bektashi *tekkes* (lodges) and mausoleums.[23] By December 2015, however, officials had announced that a grand total of 727 mosques existed in the country – of which at least 200 were not under the control of any official, sanctioned Muslim community organization.[24] Along with criticism from the government made at that time, former Islamic Community deputy director Ermir Gjinishi warned that if the clerical body did not "intervene immediately to change this situation next year, half of the mosques in Albania will pass out of its control."[25]

Albania's cumulative Muslim population accounts for 80 percent of the country's 2.8 million people. Albania also has notable Catholic (10 percent) and Orthodox Christian (20 percent) populations. The latter is located chiefly in the southern part of the country, and includes the country's Greek and Macedonian minorities. The 2009 survey reported over 1,100 Catholic and Orthodox churches in Albania.[26]

Nevertheless, secularism prevails, especially in rapidly-modernizing Tirana, and Albanian Muslims are much less devout in their practice than are ethnic Albanians in neighboring Kosovo and Macedonia. As in these countries and throughout the Balkan region, however, *Wahhabis* have exacerbated divisions within the Muslim community since 2010, with one security official stating in June 2016 that sectarian divisions are now "at the core of the rifts between Muslim communities."[27]

While most Albanians are relatively secular-minded, an important trend for the future will be the relationship between the country's different religious groups. The government was criticized by secularists for its plan to introduce the category of religious affiliation to the 2011 national census, as it could exacerbate the politicking between different faiths.[28] Muslims and Christian proselytizers eye one another warily, and often accuse each other of inappropriate actions. In a 2012 report for the Vatican, Archbishop Angelo Massafra of the Archdiocese of Shkoder-Pult expressed concerns over rising Muslim fundamentalism in Albania, ase well as the perceived involvement of countries like Saudi Arabia and Turkey. He also expressed concerns over the recent opening of a new Islamic university in Tirana.[29] (Known as Bedër University, this center opened in April 2011).[30]

It is likely that the Vatican's concern over the latter is less an expression of fear of radicalism than it is apprehensiveness over any further Islamic "re-awakening" among a relatively secular population. The Vatican has in recent years taken a proactive approach toward expanding its presence in Albania, something that has involved the above-mentioned Papal visit of 2014 and increased involvement of (primarily Italian) Catholic schools and NGOs in Albania.[31] One key event for bolstering Catholicism in Albania and beyond was the September 4, 2016 canonization of Mother Teresa; the revered ethnic Albanian nun was born in Skopje, Macedonia and had ancestry in Kosovo. Tirana's international airport is named for her, and today she is an essential part of the international Albanian "brand." Anecdotal evidence suggests that this has caused an internal debate within Albanian populations of different faiths regarding Mother Teresa's rightful place in Albanian national identity and history.[32]

Albania's internal struggles as a nation questioning its religious values vis-à-vis broader personal and national aspirations have occasionally been heated. For example, in October 2003, the outspoken author Kastriot Myftari was arrested for "inciting religious hatred" after writing that Albanian Muslims should convert to Catholicism. (Myftari was ultimately acquitted).[33] More controversially, in November 2005, Islamists reacted sharply when then-President Alfred Moisiu, speaking before the Oxford Union in England, stated that Albanians followed a "shallow" sort of Islam, as the country's Christian heritage has much deeper roots.[34] The MFA and other Islamist groups accused Moisiu of "insulting Islam."

Inter-religious strife likewise has registered in more tangible ways. When local leaders announced that national hero Mother Teresa would be commemorated with a statue, three Muslim NGOs – the MFA, the Association of Islamic Intellectuals and the Association of Islamic Charities – condemned the initiative as a "provocation" against Islam.[35] (While the MFA was the most visible of the three organizations, the Association of Muslim Intellectuals is older, dating from the early 1990s, paralleling the creation of other, similar Islamist intellectual organizations in Bosnia and elsewhere.[36] In 1991, it was led by Bashkim Gazidede, whose tacit assistance to foreign terrorist-linked entities while serving as director of Albania's national intelligence agency is discussed in detail below.)

Another similar organization, the Albanian Institute of Islamic Thought and Civilization, has kept a fairly low profile, despite having existed since 1996. According to the organization, it is active chiefly in educational areas, such as teaching and translating Islamic texts from Turkish, Arabic and Persian. It also aims to preserve Islamic culture, and maintains links with likeminded organizations both inside the country and abroad.[37] Notably, some of the AIITC's foreign partners are known to have extremist ties. For example, in October 2010 the AIITC announced a plan to cooperate on translation projects with the Libyan World Islamic Call Society (also known as the World Association for the Islamic Call); this Libyan umbrella group of 250 charities, established by the late Libyan strongman Muammar Qaddafi himself, has been linked by American investigators to the dissemination of radical Islam and funding for Hamas.[38]

Foreign Islamic charities still operating in the country have moved beyond the initial phase of relief and infrastructure projects, and are now becoming more involved with social issues. For example, one of Albania's intractable problems – the practice of clan vendettas in the mountainous northeast, which continues to restrict the movement and social life of entire families – has been exploited by foreign Islamists. Dedicated efforts have been made to increase Islamist teaching in these areas, which are historically associated with smuggling, paramilitary activities and isolationism. Hundreds of students are reportedly undertaking Islamic education in rural towns like Koplik, with some going on to study in Turkey or the Middle East.[39] Taking the lead in developing programs to solve vendettas and poverty via Islamic means is the UK-registered (but globally active) charity Islamic Relief,[40] which has operated in Albania since 1991.[41]

The question of foreign influence in the Albanian Muslim community is not limited to the Arab world; as stated, Turkey's presence in Albania is also growing, which may further shape the development of the country's Islamist movements. The Erdogan government's strategic interest in expanding its sphere of influence throughout former Ottoman lands, including Albania, is common knowledge. Turks have justifiable concerns about the state of Ottoman mosques and other historic monuments. The key unknown question regarding Albanian-Turkish cooperation involves the above-mentioned antagonism between Erdogan and Gülen, and the way in which their rivalry will play out in both bilateral relations and within the local Muslim population.

The final aspect of note in Turkey's relationship with Albanian Muslims is the Bektashi order, a more liberal and mystical variety of Islam with strong ties between the two countries, which is denounced by *Wahhabi* elements as heretical. With different factions tolerating and opposing the Bektashi, the degree of Turkish support for them will help determine whether or not they survive in the face of extremist challenges. The Bektashi themselves, who do not engage in proselytizing, are aware that they are vulnerable. However, while Iran has offered funding to help ensure their future, the Bektashi leadership claims that it has not and will not accept funds from Iran.[42]

ISLAMISM AND THE STATE

Historically, the Albanian state's relationship with Islam has been critical in the evolution and practice of Islam in the country. Under Ottoman rule (from the 14th to the early 20th centuries), large numbers of Albanians converted to Islam to capitalize on better opportunities for state employment and career advancement. Sunni Islam became most popular in central and northern Albania, while the Shi'ite Bektashi Dervish order became established, from the 18th century onwards, primarily in southern Albania. The latter, more liberal form of Islam in 1923 dropped Ottoman-enforced practices such as polygamy and the forced wearing of the *hijab* (veil) by women. The same post-WWI Albanian government took in 25,000 members of the Bektashi order expelled from Turkey in 1926 during Mustafa Kemal Ataturk's secularization campaign; the World Bektashi Center remains based in Tirana to this day.

Under the Communist dictatorship of Enver Hoxha, religion was banned from 1967 on, and all religious groups were persecuted by the state. Thus, the most pivotal moment in the modern Albanian state's relationship with Islam came when the first post-Communist government opened its arms to outside Islamist governments and interests in 1990. Then-president (and current prime minister) Sali Berisha himself was not religious, but sought out foreign investment of any kind. His election in 1992 was therefore followed by visits from Kuwaitis who offered an "ambitious" investment plan in exchange for an opportunity to build mosques in Albania.[43] Soon after, the Islamic Development Bank (IDB) began offering substantial investment and opportunities for Albanians to learn Arabic and study in Islamic states.[44] President Berisha also made Albania the first European member of the Organization of the Islamic Conference; one momentous consequence of this decision was the "unilateral abolition" of visa requirements for citizens of Muslim countries, making Albania a desirable option for international fugitive terrorists wanting to disappear into Europe.[45] In this way, several senior al-Qaeda figures were able to establish an operational base on Albanian territory (although that specific network was dismantled in the 1990s).[46]

By 1994, private Saudi investors in the telecom, textile, banking and transport sectors, often through the IDB, were extending multi-million-dollar lines of credit to Albania. In the same year, predating similar investments by the West, the Arab-Albanian Islamic Bank was established in Tirana.[47] Osama bin Laden was reportedly the majority stockholder and founder of this bank.[48] The bank built hundreds of mosques, sent Albanians to Islamic universities abroad, and paid poor Albanians on the condition that their women wear the *chador* (veiled outer garment).[49] Hundreds of young Albanians went to study in Islamic countries, or undertook the *Hajj* – in 1993 alone, more than 1,000 Albanians made the pilgrimage to Mecca.[50] The "true agenda" of the foreign investors was to over time transform Albania into an Islamic state, through economic aid, proselytization, and finally the establishment of Islamic governance.[51]

Most sinister, however, was the Albanian state's relationship with the world's most dangerous Islamist terror networks. While President Berisha was not ideologically motivated, other high-level figures were in fact devoted Islamists, including the late Bashkim Gazidede, then director of the country's national intelligence agency (SHIK). By 1994, the increasing presence of foreign *jihadists* in Islamic charities had made Western security officials "deeply suspicious."[52] Osama bin Laden, at that time based in Sudan, visited Tirana that year, presenting himself as a wealthy Saudi businessman offering humanitarian aid.[53] However, bin Laden was actually sponsoring the charity Al Haramain, later classified as a terrorist entity by the United States government.[54]

The Albanian government likewise welcomed other dangerous charities like the Revival of Islamic Heritage Society, Muwafaq ("Blessed Relief") Foundation, the bin Laden-linked World Assembly of Muslim Youth, Taibah International and Iran's Ayatollah Khomeini Society. Another terror-linked charity, the International Islamic Relief Organization (IIRO), employed Mohammed al-Zawahiri, younger brother of future al-Qaeda second-in-command Ayman al-Zawahiri. He had reportedly been tasked by bin Laden himself with finding "legitimate cover" for Egyptian Islamic Jihad members involved with assassinations or attempted assassinations of Egyptian leaders.[55] The arrival of an Egyptian foreign ministry delegation in Albania in 1995 prompted the CIA to reach out to the by-now highly-compromised SHIK. One detained Islamist became an informant, marking a temporary breakthrough on the intelligence front. The informant in turn revealed the embarrassing truth that Albania had come to be known among *jihadists* as a "safe hotel" where they could hide out with the tacit approval of the state.[56]

Indeed, despite the assistance provided by the SHIK on this occasion, Islamist penetration of Albanian intelligence continued, and assistance provided by the agency to the U.S. suffered a corresponding decline. The SHIK would only be truly reformed once the Berisha government was ousted; in January 1997, the collapse of an investment pyramid scheme left ordinary Albanians penniless, leading to total anarchy and the looting of state arsenals. In April 1997, the SHIK was suspended by the caretaker government. June elections saw the ascent of an Orthodox Christian prime minister, Fatos Nano, who had previously been jailed by Berisha. Ex-SHIK director and *jihad* sympathizer Bashkim Gazidede reportedly escaped to the Middle East, and several arrest warrants were later issued for him by the new government.

The Nano government cooled relations with the Islamic world, irritating Islamist "investors" when it failed to send a delegate to the 1998 OIC conference. A CIA re-training course for the SHIK, and the removal of pro-Islamist SHIK officials and Islamic Community leaders, came at a time when the result of a merger of Ayman al-Zawahiri's Egyptian Islamic Jihad and al-Qaeda was being assessed by the CIA as having produced one of Europe's most dangerous terrorist entities.[57] Local experts in Albania noted that the EIJ's Tirana cell was among its most important, as it was expert in falsifying documents to facilitate the transit of suspected terrorists.[58]

In mid-1998, a renewed round of CIA-ordered SHIK kidnappings of *jihadis* in Tirana led to the rendition of several men to Egypt. Unfortunately, covert American involvement was leaked by "euphoric" SHIK agents, enraging the *jihadist internationale*.[59] A letter released by a London-based al-Qaeda newsletter on August 5, 1998 promised a violent response:[60] just two days later, terrorists bombed the U.S. embassy in Nairobi, Kenya, killing 213 people and injuring more than 4,000. A second embassy attack, in Dar es Salaam, Tanzania, killed 11 and injured 85. These incidents revealed that ongoing counter-terrorist operations in Albania could trigger Islamist attacks globally, which put the Balkan country into the new and nebulous category of "dangerous ally." The U.S. State Department temporarily closed diplomatic facilities in Albania and Americans were warned to avoid the country altogether.

Nevertheless, Albania remained a key ally for the Clinton administration's determined efforts to arm and train Albanian separatists in the neighboring Yugoslav province of Kosovo.[61] (Ironically, at the same time American officials were also stating openly that Albania was hosting Iranian, Chechen, Afghan, Algerian and Egyptian *mujahideen* who were offering their services for a Kosovo *jihad*.[62]) Yet U.S. support for Kosovar Muslims (and Bosnian Muslims in their own previous war against the Serbs) failed to make America beloved throughout the Muslim world. However, during the brief Kosovo refugee crisis in the spring of 1999, the U.S. government allowed massive humanitarian activity to be carried out by some of the very same foreign organizations and individuals that it had identified as dangerous.[63] (The connection between such charities and Albanian extremists active in the Balkans was noted over a decade later, when a radical *imam* was expelled from Kosovo).[64]

It was thus little surprise that adverse security conditions persisted in Albania during the following months. For example, then-Defense Secretary William Cohen had to cancel a celebratory visit to the country in mid-July 1999, as he was being targeted by remaining al-Qaeda operatives in Tirana.[65] Several months earlier, the police had detained a Saudi-trained Albanian national accused of conducting surveillance on U.S. facilities, as well as two well-armed terrorist cell members in Tirana.[66]

Soon after the September 11, 2001 terrorist attacks, U.S. government officials, speaking off the record, disclosed a connection between the al-Qaeda plotters and Albania-based Islamic terrorists.[67] In Tirana, attention turned to Yassin al-Qadi, founder and chief investor in the Muwafaq Foundation. Although he denied all charges, al-Qadi subsequently was designated a terrorist sponsor by the U.S. Treasury Department in October 2001.[68] The multi-millionaire Saudi investor was accused of laundering $10 million for Osama bin Laden through his business interests and charities. In 2002, the Albanian government seized a 15-story business center owned by al-Qadi in Tirana and expelled his business partner, Abdul Latif Saleh; the latter had been associated with the Tirana charities created by al-Qaeda, and was accused by U.S. investigators of cooperating with al-Qaeda while in Albania.[69]

In July 2005 elections, the Nano government was defeated and Sali Berisha reclaimed power. Ex-SHIK chief Gazidede, the charges against him having been dropped since 2003, returned from exile and took up a different position in Berisha's new government (he has since died of natural causes). Although many of the charities and terrorist-linked entities that plagued Albania during Berisha's first stint in power have been uprooted, a new and multifaceted dynamic is visible today in the activities of the Albanian state concerning Islamism.

Albania's membership in the Organization of Islamic Conference – ignored, but not abrogated during the Nanos government – has been restored, in recognition of the OIC's growing influence in the United Nations and as a means of lobbying Muslim countries to recognize Kosovar independence.[70] Through this, the Albanian government is also seeking to show the world that it has some degree of influence in world affairs. At the same time, while it is constitutionally prevented from funding religious facilities, the government approved the Muslim Community's plan to create the Islamic university in Tirana that was opened in 2011. The initiative was presented as a proactive effort to counter extremism by affording students the opportunity to study at home (rather than in the broader Arab world).[71]

Nevertheless, Albania's courtship with foreign Islamic funders, begun in the early 1990s, appears to be continuing, with the Islamic Development Bank (IDB) in October 2010 offering millions of dollars for infrastructure and other projects.[72] The announcement came only three months after Prime Minister Berisha hosted a high-level IDB delegation, and thanked them for their assistance (past and present) in development efforts in Albania.[73] In January 2012, three years after Albania had opened an embassy in the United Arab Emirates, the two countries established a Committee on Economic Co-operation. In addition to its investments in other Balkan states, the UAE in 2012 was funding the construction of the Tirana-Elbasan highway and the airport in Kukes, projects worth roughly $100 million.[74]

The Albanian state's strengthened cooperation with the pro-Islamist government in Turkey, which has its own Balkan aspirations, is yet another sign of current relations with outside Islamist forces. In June 2010, the official headquarters of the Muslim Community of Albania was renovated by the Turkish International Cooperation and Development Agency (TIKA), at a cost of roughly $350,000 REF.[75] At the time, TIKA officials together with Albanian government and Islamic officials disclosed that Turkey plans to reconstruct other Islamic facilities (as it has done since the end of Communism).[76] The Albanian government has also, as stated, green-lighted the Turkish-funded mega-mosque (located, ironically, on George W. Bush Street in central Tirana).

While *Wahhabi* groups remain a distinct minority, the visible presence of Albanian fighters in Syria and Iraq, and their active recruitment efforts in Albania itself, has reoriented the government to take advantage of its strong relations with the U.S. and its own NATO membership. Thus, under the similarly left-leaning administrations of Barack Obama and Albanian premier Edi Rama, plans were laid for a regional center on studying the phenomenon of foreign fighters and countering violent extremism.[77]

Approved in May 2016, this new NATO Center of Excellence will become the first of its kind in the region, and is considered a political victory as much as a security one for the government over regional rivals. However, while the Albanians are thus primed to take a stronger role in the region, lingering competition between Balkan states does not mean that greater trust or intelligence-sharing will result. Rather, it indicates that fighting terrorism and radicalization will remain largely a matter of bilateral or multilateral effort, rather than a truly integrated regional one.

Endnotes

[1] "Population, Total," The World Bank, 2015, http://data.worldbank.org/indicator/SP.POP.TOTL.

[2] See Tracy Miller, ed., Mapping the Global Muslim Population: A Report on the Size and Distribution of the World's Muslim Population (Washington, DC: Pew Research Center, October 2009), http://www.pewforum.org/files/2009/10/Muslimpopulation.pdf.

[3] The community's website is www.kmsh.al.

[4] The official Bektashi order website can be found at www.bektashi.net.

[5] "Turkey, Saudi Arabia Promoting Stricter Islam in Albania," Catholic News Agency, July 20, 2012, http://www.catholicnewsagency.com/news/turkey-saudi-arabia-promoting-stricter-islam-in-albania/.

[6] Aleksandra Bogdani, "Albanian Villages Ponder Local Spike in ISIS Recruits," Balkan Insight, April 25, 2016, http://www.balkaninsight.com/en/article/albanian-villages-ponder-local-spurt-of-isis-recruits-04-22-2016.

[7] Adrian Shtuni, "Ethnic Albanian Foreign Fighters in Iraq and Syria," Combating Terrorism Center at West Point, April 30, 2015, https://www.ctc.usma.edu/posts/ethnic-albanian-foreign-fighters-in-iraq-and-syria.

[8] Fatjona Mejdini, "Drop in ISIS Fighters Reflects 'Low Demand,'" Balkan Insight, August 11, 2016, http://www.balkaninsight.com/en/article/the-decline-of-albanians-fighting-with-isis-related-mostly-with-low-demand-08-11-2016.

[9] Fatjona Mejdini, "Albanian Police Arrest 'Terror Attack' Suspect," Balkan Insight, August 16, 2016, http://www.balkaninsight.com/en/article/albania-police-charge-a-man-from-kosovo-with-terrorism-08-18-2016.

[10] Joby Warrick, "In Albania, Concerns over the Islamic State's Emergence," Washington Post, June 11, 2016, accessible at http://www.stripes.com/news/europe/in-albania-concerns-over-the-islamic-state-s-emergence-1.414273.

[11] Thus, while arguing that Albania's generally tolerant and pro-Western outlook prevents it from becoming radicalized, analyst Arben Kullolli notes that "foreign supporters of Islamic organizations have started to work more intelligently, operating through think-tanks and continuing to convert Albanian Muslims into Wahhabism, especially in poor rural regions." Arben Kullolli, Proselytization in Albania by Middle Eastern Islamic Organizations, (Monterey, CA: Master's Thesis Naval Postgraduate School, March 2009).

[12] See Miranda Vickers, "Islam In Albania," Advanced Research and Assessment Group, Defence Academy of the United Kingdom, March 2008, www.da.mod.uk.

[13] Risto Karajkov, "The Young And The Old: Radical Islam Takes Root In The Balkans," Transitions Online, May 3, 2006, www.tol.cz.

[14] The MFA's official website is www.forumimusliman.org. It has not been updated for some time, however, which seems to indicate that it is no longer very active,

[15] U.S. Treasury Department, "Press Release JS-1703: Additional Al-Haramain Branches, Former Leader Designated By Treasury as Al Qaida Supporters," June 2, 2004, www.ustreas.gov.

[16] Vickers, "Islam In Albania."

[17] Karajkov, "The Young and The Old."

[18] "Selim Muca Reconfirmed As Head Of Albanian Muslim Community," Alsat Television (Skopje), September 20, 2010.

[19] "Impasse Ends After Islamic Council Votes to Dismiss Shkodra Mufti," Wikileaks, Wikileaks Cable 06TIRANA1209. Retrieved January 2013.

[20] Although it was created in the northern city of Shkodra, the MFA has long had a power base in Kavaja.

[21] Vickers, "Islam In Albania."

[22] Ebi Spahiu, "Attack on Gülen Movement Increasingly a Cornerstone of Turkey's Foreign Policy in the Balkans," Eurasia Daily Monitor, Volume 13, Issue 141, https://jamestown.org/program/attack-on-Gülen-movement-increasingly-a-cornerstone-of-turkeys-foreign-policy-in-the-balkans/.

[23] Entela Resuli, "Ne Shqiperi 638 Xhami Me 1.119 Kisha (In Albania There Are 638 Mosques And 1,119 Churches)," Tirana Observer, December 23, 2009.

[24] Fatjona Mejdini, "Uncontrolled Mosques Proliferate in Albania," Balkan Insight, December 17, 2015, http://www.balkaninsight.com/en/article/state-slams-albanian-muslim-over-uncontrolled-mosques-12-17-2015.

[25] Fatjona Mejdini, "Uncontrolled Mosques Proliferate in Albania," Balkan Insight, December 17, 2015, http://www.balkaninsight.com/en/article/state-slams-albanian-muslim-over-uncontrolled-mosques-12-17-2015.

[26] Entela Resuli, "Ne Shqiperi 638 Xhami Me 1.119 Kisha (In Albania There Are 638 Mosques And 1,119 Churches)."

[27] Ebi Spahiu, "Jihadist Threat Persists in Kosovo and Albania Despite Government Efforts."

[28] In any case, the census as completed was inconsistent with perceived reality, for example understating the percentage of Orthodox Christians and increasing the number of non-affiliated persons who would socially and culturally be considered as being from one of the three major faiths.

[29] While the Vatican had not released the detailed report at time of writing, some comments from it were available at the Vatican Insider website: http://vaticaninsider.lastampa.it/fileadmin/user_upload/File_Versione_originale/Sintesi_2012_lingua_italiana_RAPPORTO.pdf.

[30] According to the website of the university, it caters to students from 15 countries with particular focus on Albanians from home and abroad. The university has a capacity of 2000 students at present. See http://www.beder.edu.al.

[31] For a detailed analysis of the role of the Catholic Church in Albania's historic development and current orientation, see Matteo Albertini and Chris Deliso, The Vatican's Challenges in the Balkans: Bolstering the Catholic Church in 2015 and Beyond (Balkananalysis.com, 2015), https://www.amazon.com/Vaticans-Challenges-Balkans-Bolstering-Catholic-ebook/dp/B00S30A7BQ.

[32] This observation is based on numerous interviews by the author with Albanian Muslims and Catholics since 2014.

[33] "Albania," in U.S. Department of State, Bureau of Democracy, Human Rights, and Labor, International Religious Freedom Report 2004 (Washington, DC: U.S. Department of State, 2005), www.state.gov.

[34] The comments that incensed Islamists were perhaps taken out of context; the president was speaking about religious tolerance among the Albanians. Nevertheless he caused a sensation by stating "that part of the Albanians which did not convert into Islam has in its tradition not simply fifteen centuries of Christianity, but two thousand years of Christianity… The Islamism in Albania is an Islam with a European face. As a rule it is a shallow Islamism. If you dig a little in every Albanian you can discover his Christian core." The original text of the speech was published on the official website of the President of Albania, www.president.al.

[35] Llazar Semini, "Mother Teresa Statue Causes Friction," Associated Press, March 20, 2006

[36] Mentioned in Xavier Bougarel, "Islam And Politics In The Post-Communist Balkans," Harvard University Kokkalis Program on Southeastern and East-central Europe, January 28, 2006, 6, http://www.hks.harvard.edu/kokkalis/GSW1/GSW1/13%20Bougarel.pdf.

[37] The group keeps an informative official website, www.aiitc.org.

[38] Matthew Levitt, Hamas: Politics, Charity and Terrorism in the Service of Jihad (New Haven: Yale University Press, 2007), 187. The announcements about book production and translation cooperation between the World Islamic Call Society and the AIITC were posted in October 2010 on the Society's group's official website, www.islamic-call.net, as well as in other Islamic media.

[39] This testimony is recorded in an online summary of a recent trip to Albania by young Islamists from the Turkish IHH (Humanitarian Relief Foundation, or Insani Yardim Vakfi in Turkish), and available at the organization's website, www.ihh.org.tr. The unusually significant proselytizing efforts going on in Koplik in the 1990s were noted long ago, for example in Miranda Vickers and James Pettifer, Albania: From Anarchy to a Balkan Identity (New York: New York University Press, 1997), 100.

[40] On its main website, www.islamic-relief.com, Islamic Relief describes itself as "an international relief and development charity which envisages a caring world where people unite to respond to the suffering of others, empowering them to fulfill their potential."

[41] The charity's efforts to combat clan vendettas and develop rural places like Koplik can be seen on their website, www.islamicreliefalbania.com.

[42] Vickers, "Islam In Albania."

[43] Miranda Vickers and James Pettifer, Albania: from Anarchy to a Balkan Identity, New York University Press, 1997, p 105

[44] Vickers and Pettifer, Albania: From Anarchy to a Balkan Identity, 102-105.

[45] Remzi Lani and Fabian Schmidt, "Albanian Foreign Policy Between Geography And History," The International Spectator XXXIII, no. 2 (April-June 1998).

[46] See Christopher Deliso, The Coming Balkan Caliphate: the Threat of Radical Islam to Europe and the West, Praeger Security International (2007) pp. chapter 2

[47] Grace Halsell, "Special Report: Albania And The Muslim World," Washington Report on Middle East Affairs, June 1994, http://www.washingtonreport.org/backissues/0694/94006020.htm.

[48] J. Milton Burr and Robert O. Collins, Alms for Jihad: Charity and Terrorism in the Islamic World (Cambridge: Cambridge University Press, 2006), 147-149.

[49] Franz Gustincich, "From Lenin To Bin Laden," Gnosis: Online Italian Intelligence Magazine (March 2005), www.sisde.it.

[50] Damian Gjiknuri, "Albania's Counter-Terrorism Policy Options: Finding A Strategy Of Common Sense," U.S. Naval Postgraduate School Thesis, 2004, 12.

[51] Ibid., 15.

[52] Vickers and Pettifer, Albania: From Anarchy to a Balkan Identity, 105.

[53] Chris Stephens, "Bin Laden Opens European Terror Base In Albania," Sunday Times, November 29, 1998.

[54] United States Department of the Treasury, "Press Release JS-1703: Additional Al-Haramain Branches, Former Leader Designated By Treasury As Al Qaida Supporters," June 2, 2004, www.ustreas.gov.

[55] Burr and Collins, Alms for Jihad: Charity and Terrorism in the Islamic World, Ibid, 146.

[56] John Crewdson and Tom Huntley, "Abducted Imam Aided CIA Ally," Chicago Tribune, July 3, 2005.

[57] Andrew Higgins and Christopher Cooper, "CIA-Backed Team Used Brutal Means To Break Up Terrorist Cell In Albania," Wall Street Journal, November 20, 2001.

[58] Kullolli, Proselytization in Albania by Middle Eastern Islamic Organizations, 58.

[59] R. Jeffrey Smith, "US Probes Blasts' Possible Mideast Ties," Washington Post, August 12, 1998.

[60] Deliso, The Coming Balkan Caliphate, 40.

[61] Wayne Madsen, "Mercenaries In Kosovo: The U.S. Connection To The KLA," The Progressive, August 1999.

[62] See "Kosovo Seen As New Islamic Bastion," Jerusalem Post, September 14, 1998, and Barry Schweid, "NATO Braces For Wider Kosovo Fight," Associated Press, June 17, 1998.

[63] For example, see the following, exquisitely detailed summary of Saudi-led refugee efforts, with financial totals, activities carried out, and organizations and individuals involved. Hussein Saud Qusti, "Unsung Heroes," Saudi Aramco World 50, no. 4, April 1999, http://www.saudiaramcoworld.com/issue/199904/unsung.heroes.htm.

[64] Kastriot Duka, an imam originally from Elbasan in Albania, told journalists that he had been assisted in his efforts to build mosques, teach orphans and preach in a Kosovo village during the 1999 relief efforts by a member of an Islamic charity based in Britain. See Paola Casoli, "Terror And Gratitude: Albanian Imam's Kosovo Mission," www.serbianna.com, December 29, 2007. Duka, who continued to rely on funding from UK-based "charities," would be deported from Kosovo back to Albania by Kosovar authorities in March 2010 for allegedly preaching radical Islam. See Linda Karadaku, "Kosovo Deports Self-Proclaimed Imam, Closes Mosque," Southeast Europe Times, March 11, 2010, http://www.setimes.com/cocoon/setimes/xhtml/en_GB/features/setimes/features/2010/03/11/feature-03.

[65] "Pentagon Chief Cancels Albania Visit Over Terror Threat," CNN, July 15, 1999.

[66] The incidents were widely reported, for example see "Albanian Police Arrest More Islamists," RFE/RL Newsline 3, no. 33, February 17, 1999.

[67] Bill Gertz, "Hijackers Connected To Albanian Terrorist Cell," Washington Times, September 18, 2001.

[68] US Treasury Press Release, "JS-2727: Treasury Designates Bin Laden, Qadi Associate," September 19, 2005, www.ustreas.gov.

[69] Ibid.

[70] Author's correspondence with OIC official, October 2010.

[71] Kullolli, Proselytization in Albania by Middle Eastern Islamic Organizations, 62.

[72] As part of this outreach, Albania—along with other IDB member states such as Pakistan, Sudan, Indonesia and Uzbekistan—is slated to receive a portion of a new $772 million tranche for development projects. See "IDB Approves $772m For New Projects," Arab News, October 6, 2010, http://www.gulfbase.com/site/interface/NewsArchiveDetails.aspx?n=153337.

[73] See "Islamic Development Bank Expresses Interest In Albania For Increase Of Bank's Presence Through Private Sector," Balkans.com, July 6, 2010.

[74] Igor Jovanovic, "United Arab Emirates To Invest in Serbian Agriculture," SETimes.com, January 19, 2013.

[75] The event was covered by various local media outlets, as well as foreign Islamist ones. See, for example, "Turkey Rebuilds Albanian Muslim Community's Headquarters," worldbulletin.net, June 30, 2010; See also the official TIKA Web site, www.tika.gov.tr.

[76] Ibid.

[77] Fatjona Mejdini, "Albania to Host NATO Centre on Foreign Fighters," Balkan Insight, June 23, 2016, http://www.balkaninsight.com/en/article/albania-will-host-nato-center-on-foreign-terrorist-fighters-06-23-2016

Denmark

> **Quick Facts**
>
> Population: 5,593,785 (July 2016 est.)
>
> Area: 43,094 sq km
>
> Ethnic Groups: Scandinavian, Inuit, Faroese, German, Turkish, Iranian, Somali
>
> Religions: Evangelical Lutheran (official) 80%, Muslim 4%, other (denominations of less than 1% each, includes Roman Catholic, Jehovah's Witness, Serbian Orthodox Christian, Jewish, Baptist, and Buddhist) 16% (2012 est.)
>
> Government Type: parliamentary constitutional monarchy
>
> GDP (official exchange rate): $302.6 billion (2015 est.)
>
> *Map and Quick Facts courtesy of the CIA World Factbook (Last Updated January 2017)*

Overview

In February 2015, a few weeks after the attack on the Charlie Hebdo magazine in Paris, a young man of Palestinian background attacked a public meeting about freedom of speech and subsequently a synagogue in central Copenhagen. The Islamic State claimed responsibility for the incident, which is believed to be the first Islamist attack to take place in Denmark. In recent years, the Danish government's focus on violent Islamism has centered on the issue of foreign fighters travelling to Syria and the potential threat they could pose when they return. According to the Danish security and intelligence service, PET, approximately 135 people have travelled from Denmark to Syria since 2012.[1]

The history of militant Islamism in Denmark, however, dates back to the 1990s, when veterans of the Afghan jihad against the Soviet Union found safe haven in the country. Today, violent Islamism in Denmark remains far from a well-organized domestic phenomenon, although there have been notable instances of homegrown extremism among Dan-

ish Muslims, with individuals joining foreign militant movements such as al-Qaeda, al-Shabaab and the Islamic State. In the main, however, violent Islamists are very few in number and vastly outnumbered by non-violent Islamist groups.

ISLAMIST ACTIVITY

Militant Islamism in Denmark dates back to the 1990s, when several former *mujahideen* from the Soviet-Afghan war (1980-89) found safe haven there. One of the most prominent personalities in this group was an Egyptian, Talaat Fouad Qassem aka Abu Talal (1957-1995), who was a high ranking member of the militant Egyptian group *al-Gamaat al-Islamiyya*.[2] In 1982, Abu Talal was sentenced to seven years imprisonment in Egypt for his alleged role in the assassination of Egyptian President Anwar Sadat. He escaped during a prison transfer in 1989, and in 1992 an Egyptian court sentenced him to death in *absentia*.[3] In 1989, he went to Afghanistan, where he joined the anti-Soviet *mujahideen* and fought alongside his personal acquaintance, Ayman al-Zawahiri. In 1992, he migrated to Denmark, where he was granted political asylum in three years later.[4]

Abu Talal was extremely well-connected to international *jihadists*. He had close ties to Egyptian cleric Omar Abdel Rahman, the "blind sheikh" who was an unindicted co-conspirator in the 1993 bombing of the World Trade Center, and who visited Denmark twice (in 1990 and 1991 respectively) ahead of that failed plot.[5] Investigations of the World Trade Center attack revealed that three other Egyptians residing in Denmark—and part of the same milieu as Abu Talal—were directly related to the perpetrators of this attack.[6] Abu Talal was also well-connected to Anwar Shabaan,[7] head of Milan's controversial Islamic Cultural Institute, which has been the subject of terrorist investigations since the 1990s. Abu Talal is believed to have been the victim of an early form of extraordinary rendition, the extrajudicial kidnapping and transfer of a person across national borders, when he was intercepted in 1995 in Croatia by U.S. intelligence while on his way to Bosnia. He was apparently sent back to Egypt, where he subsequently disappeared.[8]

Another prominent member of this first generation of *jihadists* was Danish-Moroccan Said Mansour. Mansour hosted Omar Abdel Rahman during one of his visits to Denmark. An ardent supporter of the Algerian terrorist group GIA, Mansour was involved in the distribution of their newsletter, *Al Ansar*, and was affiliated with the notorious London-based Islamist Abu Qatada. Mansour ran a publishing house, Al Nur Islamic Information, through which he disseminated material inciting Muslims to violence. (Materials from Al Nur were subsequently found worldwide at locations related to terrorist investigations in Germany, Italy, Spain, Belgium and the U.S.).[9] In 2007, Mansour was convicted of "incitement to violence" and was released in 2009. Five years later, he was convicted for similar offences and this time stripped of his Danish citizenship.[10]

Following the 2005 London bombings, a new iteration of militant Islamism appeared in Denmark. In contrast to the first generation of the phenomenon, embodied by Abu Talal and Mansour, this second generation is primarily homegrown in nature, and often includes first-generation Danes. The first cases of Islamist terrorism in Denmark after the London bombings were strictly homegrown plots, planned by Danish citizens or residents with few links to Islamist milieus abroad. Since 2007, however, Islamist terrorist plots have also involved "returnees" who have come back to Denmark after joining militant Islamist groups abroad, or—in the aftermath of the so-called "cartoon controversy"—by foreigners with no prior connection to Denmark.

After the outbreak of the cartoon controversy in 2005, and in particular after the republication of the cartoons by several Danish newspapers in 2008, Denmark became a high-end target of militant Islamist organizations, including of al-Qaeda and likeminded groups (*Lashkar-e Taiba*, AQIM, AQAP, and *al-Shabaab*), as well as of autonomous cells operating in Europe. From 2008 through 2010, six plots targeting either the *Jyllands-Posten* daily newspaper or one of the cartoonists have been thwarted. The people behind the first two plots were Danish residents, but in 2009 and 2010, four plots were attempted by foreigners with no prior relation to Denmark.[11]

In December 2010, a Tunisian living in Sweden and two Swedish citizens of Arab descent were arrested on the outskirts of Copenhagen. Yet another Swedish-Tunisian was subsequently arrested in Sweden. All four men were convicted for planning to access *Jyllands-Posten*'s office in Copenhagen and subsequently kill as many employees as possible. The Swedish group was well-connected internationally. One of the convicted previously had spent several years in a training camp in North Waziristan; another had been arrested in Pakistan and Kenya on prior occasions.[12]

Since 2012, a number of Danish citizens and residents has joined the conflict in Syria and Iraq. The Danish intelligence Service, PET, estimates that 135 people at the minimum have traveled to the conflict zone to date.[13] Jakob Sheikh, a journalist from the Danish daily *Politiken*, has collected independent data about 77 Danish citizens or residents who have traveled to Syria, with interesting results. It appears that not all of those who have traveled to this location are *jihadists* or Islamists; while some have joined Islamic State or the Nusrah Front (now Jabhat Fatah al Sham), others have joined secular Kurdish groups or the Free Syrian Army. Irrespective of their affiliation, a large majority of Danish foreign fighters are born and raised in Denmark. A small number of Danish foreign fighters have been convicted upon their return.

Although the Danish security and intelligence service has for years emphasized the threat of Islamist foreign fighters, the first Islamist attack perpetrated in Denmark did not in fact involve a former foreign fighter. In February 2015, a few weeks after the attack on *Charlie Hebdo*, Danish-Palestinian Omar el-Hussein attacked a public meeting about freedom of speech and later the same day a synagogue in central Copenhagen. Two people were killed and several police were wounded, while the perpetrator was subsequently killed in a shootout with police. Hussein was a petty criminal who had just been released from prison, when—apparently inspired by the *Charlie Hebdo* attacks—he decided to carry out violence of his own. The Islamic State subsequently claimed responsibility for the events, and honored Hussein by publishing a glowing obituary in their online magazine *Dabiq*.[14]

The incident is reflective of a larger trend. A majority of the people involved in recent terrorist plots and attacks—in Denmark as well as in other European countries—have a background in criminal environments and not necessarily in radical Islamist groups. Hence, the link between Islamism and terrorism, which is often taken for granted, must and is being examined more closely. The idea of radicalization as a process, where someone increasingly comes under the spell of radical Islamist ideology, no longer has the same analytical traction as it did ten years ago. Pathways eventually leading to terrorism are rarely processes from ideology to violence, but more often lead from one form of violence (gang related crime) to another (terrorism).[15]

However, the number of Muslims in Denmark who actively support violent forms of Islamism is very small. Militant Islamists are by far outnumbered by Muslims involved in non-violent Islamist groups. Among the most controversial is *Hizb ut-Tahrir* (HT). *Hizb ut-Tahrir* put down roots in Denmark in the mid-1980s, although the Danish branch of the organization was not formally established until the mid-1990s.[16] British HT members were instrumental in the establishment of the group's Danish contingent,[17] and the movement's Copenhagen leadership committee was subsequently elevated to head the group's regional affairs, as reflected in its current title "*Hizb ut-Tahrir* Scandinavia."[18] The organization has an estimated 150 active members, but attracts around 1,000-1,200 people to its public meetings.[19]

Ideologically, HT aims to reestablish a Caliphate in the Muslim world. Therefore, unlike the classical Muslim Brotherhood, the group is against the modern notion of the "nation-state." HT considers democracy an un-Islamic invention, and urges Danish Muslims not to engage in politics or take part in elections. It does, however, seek to engage in debates with select intellectuals. The organization as a whole does not engage in violent activities, but supports "defensive *jihad*" in places such as Iraq, Syria, or Afghanistan. The group's public meeting in January 2011 caused considerable controversy, as it endorsed continued resistance in Afghanistan, which was interpreted by many as encouragement to kill Danish soldiers serving there.[20] Former HT spokesperson Fadi Abdullatif was convicted twice for "threats, flagrant insults and incitement to murder" against Jews, as well as against former Danish prime minister (and former NATO Secretary General) Anders Fogh Rasmussen.[21] Various political parties have argued that HT should be banned, and in 2015 after the terrorist attacks in Copenhagen, the Minister of Justice, Mette Frederiksen, made yet another request to ban the group. However, the Danish Attorney General have at several occasions ruled that there were no legal foundations for such a ban.[22]

The extremist group, The Call to Islam (*Kaldet til Islam*) used to be very visible in public and regularly attracted media attention. It had close ties both to the former London-based cleric, Omar Bakri Mohammed, and to his successor in the UK, the notorious Anjem Choudary, who in 2016 was convicted for pledging allegiance to the Islamic State. Back in 2012, The Call to Islam organized demonstrations in front of the French and U.S. embassies, where Bakri and Choudary intervened by delivering speeches from abroad that were screened in front of the embassies. Similarly, they have demonstrated against a parade honoring Danish veterans from the war in Afghanistan; publicly announced the establishment of sharia zones in certain areas of Copenhagen; and during the 2015 elections for parliament, they urged Muslims not to participate in elections and even tore down the election posters of Muslim candidates. After 2012, several people from this group traveled to Syria, where they joined the ranks of the Islamic State; some of them—including the leader-figure Shiraz Tariq—were later reported dead.[23]

Aside from HT and The Call to Islam, The Grimhøj Mosque in the city of Aarhus (*Wakf*) regularly attracts media attention. A large number of the young men and women who travelled to Syria from the city of Aarhus used to attend this mosque, which therefore has come under suspicion of being a hub of radicalization. Political initiatives to close down the mosque have hitherto been fruitless, however, because the imams have a constitutional right to free speech, and therefore are deemed to have committed no infraction of the law.

ISLAMISM AND SOCIETY

Muslim immigration to Denmark began in the 1960s, and proceeded in essentially two waves. During the 1960s and 1970s, immigrants from Turkey, Pakistan, North Africa and the former Yugoslavia came to Denmark to work. After the mid-1970s, a second wave of newcomers to the country was made up primarily of refugees, as well as the families of earlier immigrants who had stayed in Denmark. Conflicts in the Arab and Muslim world (including the Iran-Iraq war, as well as the civil wars in Lebanon, the former Yugoslavia, and Somalia) also prompted Muslim immigration to Denmark, as have the more recent wars in Afghanistan, Iraq and Syria.

While no official census of Muslims in Denmark exists, some preliminary data is available. As of January 2016, the proportion of Muslims in the total population was estimated to 284.000, which is 5 % of the total population. One year before, the number was 4.7% and the increase is a result of the large number of Syrian refugees who came to Denmark in 2015.[24] Denmark's Muslim community is ethnically very diverse. The largest group are Turks (19.9 percent), followed by Iraqis, Lebanese (Palestinians) and Syrians (9.3 percent, 8.7 percent and 8.5 percent, respectively).[25] Today, the main contingents of refugees come from Syria, Afghanistan and Somalia.

A precise estimate of the level of support for violent Islamist groups among Danish Muslims is difficult to obtain since the Danish intelligence service does not make such estimations public. Similarly, it is difficult to identify the reasons some Danish Muslims are attracted to violent Islamism; a general climate of Islamophobia in Denmark is often cited as one such cause, but many other factors also play into such attraction.

It is, however, beyond doubt that, since September 11, 2001, public debates on Islam and Muslims have become increasingly incendiary, culminating with the publication of the infamous 12 cartoons of the Prophet Muhammad in the newspaper *Jyllands-Posten* in 2005 and the surge in the number of refugees seeking asylum in 2015. The year 2001 coincided with the rise to power of a minority right wing government that—for the first time in Danish history—depended on parliamentary support from the country's anti-immigration and Islam-critical nationalist party, the Danish Peoples Party (DPP), to gain the majority. The DPP has been instrumental in articulating a "struggle of values" against Islam, which it considers necessary in order to defend Christianity and "Danishness."[26] In public debates, Islam and Muslim are increasingly framed as a security issue.[27] Successive ministers of foreign affairs have for instance maintained that Islamism constitutes "the most important totalitarian threat today."[28] A spike in the number of refugees in 2015 (primarily from Syria and Afghanistan) has prompted a public discourse that frames refugees as potential terrorists and a threat against Danish values. The current minister for integration, Inger Støjberg, has at several occasions urged Muslims who are not supportive of "Danish values" to "buzz off to their countries of losers."[29]

Recently, several other parties on the far right with ambitions of running for parliament have made their appearance alongside the DPP (in particular the *Nye Borgerlige* and *Danskernes Parti*). These parties argue for an even tougher approach to refugees and immigrants than does the DPP, and repeatedly question the "Danishness" of Muslims, including those who are born in Denmark and hold Danish citizenship. In September 2016, an opinion poll estimated that DPP and Nye borgerlige would get 22.6 % of the votes in case of an election.[30]

Islamism and the State

After the September 11 terrorist attacks and the London bombings in 2005, the Danish parliament passed two Anti-Terrorism Acts (in 2002 and 2006 respectively).[31] The first Act *de facto* amended the Danish penal code by introducing a separate terrorism provision (Chapter 13, §114) that increased the punishment for a variety of previously-proscribed acts if carried out with the *intention* of "frightening a population," or destabilizing "the fundamental political, constitutional, economic or social structures of a country or an international organization."[32] The maximum sentence for committing an offense under the new terrorism provision was raised to life in prison. This Anti-Terrorism Act also penalizes the provision of financial services to terrorist groups and gives authorities new tools to fight terrorism, including secret searches; the logging of telephone and Internet communications; easier access to computer surveillance; expanded ability to refuse or withdraw residence permits, and so forth.

Following the July 7, 2005 subway bombings in London, Danish perceptions of the threat from militant Islamism changed, and the greatest danger became seen as primarily "homegrown" in nature. In order to prevent the domestic processes of "radicalization," a series of preventive measures was set up by the Ministry of Integration in tandem with PET, which established a preventive department in 2007. Over the years, this host of preventive measures has morphed into a "Danish model" that has attracted worldwide attention.[33] The Danish approach to preventing extremism and radicalization is based on extensive multi-agency collaboration between various social-service providers, the educational system, the health-care system, the police, and the intelligence and security services.[34] This approach has abandoned the idea of doing "anti-radicalization"—that is, changing the extremist mindset—in favor of "disengagement," i.e. exit-programs for persons who want to get out of extremist environments in Denmark.[35]

To prevent Danish citizens and residents from going to Syria, a law was passed in 2015, which made it possible for the police to administratively confiscate passports from people who had the intention of travelling to Syria or to similar conflict areas.[36] So far, the police have confiscated only a small number of passports. Moreover, a new law adopted in June 2016 criminalizes the act of entering specific areas in Syria and Iraq without a preceding travel permit issued by the Ministry of Justice.[37]

ENDNOTES

[1] CTA (Center for Terroranalyse), "Terrortruslen mod Denmark" (The Terrorist Threat against Denmark), n.d., https://www.pet.dk/CTA/~/media/VTD%202016/20160428VTDpdf.ashx

[2] Michael Taarnby, "Jihad in Denmark," Danish Institute for International Studies DIIS Working Paper 35, November 2006, 9, http://www.cie.ugent.be/documenten/jihad-dk.pdf.

[3] Ibid.

[4] Tribunale de Milano, "Ruling of Judge Presiding Over Preliminary Investigations," n.d., 44, http://www.washingtonpost.com/wp-srv/world/documents/milan_warrants.pdf.

[5] Taarnby, "Jihad in Denmark," 17; Uwe Max Jensen, "Aros a Terrorist Target?" Nordjyske (Aalborg), September 9, 2010, http://www.nordjyske.dk/dit-nordjyske/forside.aspx?ctrl=10&data=53,3660259,2825,3.

[6] See Manni Crone and Mona Sheikh, "Muslims as Danish Security Issues," in Jørgen S. Nielsen, ed., Islam in Denmark (Plymouth: Lexington Books, 2012).

[7] Taarnby, "Jihad in Denmark," 17.

[8] Human Rights Watch, "Black Hole: The Fate of Islamists Rendered to Egypt," May 9, 2005, http://www.hrw.org/en/node/11757/section/6; Claus Blok Thomsen, "CIA's første bortførte fange kom fra Danmark" [CIA's First Abducted Catch Came from Denmark], Dagbladet Politiken (Copenhagen), October 20, 2007, http://politiken.dk/indland/article399819.ece.

[9] Søren Astrup, "Said Mansour Accepterer Dom" [Said Mansour Accepts Ruling], Dagbladet Politiken (Copenhagen), April 24, 2007, http://politiken.dk/indland/ECE290271/said-mansour-accepterer-dom; Taarnby, "Jihad in Denmark," 22.

[10] Alexander Tange, "Denmark strips man of citizenship after terrorist conviction", Reuters, July 1, 2015 http://www.reuters.com/article/us-denmark-morocco-deportation-idUSKCN0PB4XI20150701

[11] Lene Kühle and Lasse Lindekilde, "Radicalization among Young Muslims in Aarhus," Aarhus University Centre for Studies on Islamism and Radicalization, January 2010, http://ps.au.dk/fileadmin/site_files/filer_statskundskab/subsites/cir/radicalization_aarhus_FINAL.pdf.

[12] Søren Astrup & Frank Hvilsom, "Landsretten giver 12 år for terrorplaner mod JP/Politikens Hus" (High court gives twelve year jail term for plotting terror against JP/Politikens Hus), Politiken, January 31, 2013 http://politiken.dk/indland/art5430383/Landsretten-giver-12-%C3%A5r-for-terrorplaner-mod-JPPolitikens-Hus

[13] CTA (Center for Terroranalyse), "Terrortruslen mod Danmark" (The Terrorist Threat against Denmark), n.d., https://www.pet.dk/CTA/-/media/VTD%202016/20160428VTDpdf.ashx

[14] Dabiq, 8, March 30, 2015, p. 5-6.

[15] Manni Crone, "Radicalization revisited", International Affairs, 92:3, May 2016.

[16] Kirstine Sinclair, "The Caliphate as Homeland: Hizb ut-Tahrir in Denmark and Britain," doctoral dissertation, University of Southern Denmark, 2010, 12.

[17] Ed Husain, The Islamist (London: Penguin, 2008).

[18] Sinclair, "The Caliphate as Homeland," 12.

[19] Ulla Abildtrup, "Forsker: Hizb ut-Tahrir stagnerer" [Researcher: Hizb ut-Tahrir Stagnates], DR, November 16, 2010, http://www.dr.dk/Nyheder/Indland/2010/11/10/113614.htm.

[20] "Hizb ut-Tahrir opfordrer til væbnet kamp" [Hizb ut-Tahrir Calls for Armed Struggle], Information (Copenhagen), December 28, 2010, http://www.information.dk/telegram/254933.

[21] Rigsadvokaten (The Attorney General), Supplerende redegørelse om eventuel opløsning af Hizb ut-Tahrir i henhold til Grundlovens § 78 [Supplementary statement on the potential closure of Hizb ut-Tahrir in accordance with Basic Law § 78], June 2008, http://www.rigsadvokaten.dk/default.aspx?id=58&recordid58=1190, 13, 18

[22] Ibid., 43.

[23] Morten Skjoldager & Jakob Sheikh, "Danske salafisters edderkop er dræbt i Syrien" (The central figure of Danish Salafism killed in Syria), Politiken, September 26, 2013 http://politiken.dk/indland/art5472072/Danske-salafisters-edderkop-er-dr%C3%A6bt-i-Syrien

[24] Brian Arly Jacobsen, "Hvor mange muslimer bor der i Danmark?" (How large is the Muslim population in Denmark), Politiken, April 12, 2016 http://www.religion.dk/religionsanalysen/hvor-mange-indvandrer-lever-i-danmark

[25] Ibid.

[26] Søren Krarup, Systemskiftet. I kulturkampens tegn [Systemic Shift: Characters in the Cultural Battles](Copenhagen: Gyldendal, 2006).

[27] See Crone and Sheikh, "Muslims as Danish Security Issues."

[28] For example, Per Stig Møller, "'Jeg savner de intellektuelle'" ['I Miss the Intellectuals'] Dagbladet Politiken (Copenhagen), December 11, 2010, http://politiken.dk/debat/ECE1139648/jeg-savner-de-intellektuelle/.

[29] Michael Bo Mortensen, "Støjberg til islamister: fis hjem til jeres taberlande" (Støjberg to Islamists: buzz off to your countries of losers), Ekstra Bladet, December 17, 2012 http://ekstrabladet.dk/nyheder/politik/article4000767.ece

[30] Morten Skærbæk, Mathias Gram & Karoline Graulund Nøhr, "Ny måling giver Pernille Vermund og Nye Borgerlige grund til at smile bredt" (New poll gives Nye Borgerlige reason to grin), Politiken, September 23, 2016 http://politiken.dk/indland/politik/article5636967.ece

[31] Jørn Vestergaard, "Dansk lovgivning om bekæmpelse af terrorisme" [Danish Legislation on Terrorism], in Lars Plum and Andreas Laursen, eds., Enhver stats pligt… International strafferet og dansk ret [Duty of Every State… International Criminal Law and Danish Law] (Copenhagen: DJØF Forlag, 2007), 391-424.

[32] Ibid.

[33] Bharati Naik, Atika Shubert and Nick Thompson, "Denmark offers foreign fighters rehab without jail – but will it work?", CNN, October 28, 2014, http://edition.cnn.com/2014/10/28/world/europe/denmark-syria-deradicalization-program

[34] Ann-Sophie Hemmingsen, "The Danish Approach to Countering and Preventing Extremism and Radicalization", DIIS-Report, 2015, 15.

[35] Lasse Lindekilde, "Forebyggelse af radikalisering, miskendelse og muslimsk minoritetsidentitet" [Preventing Radicalization, Misrepresentation and Muslim Minority Identity], Tidsskrift for Islamforskning no. 2, 2010, http://www.islamforskning.dk/Tidsskrift_2_2010/forebyggelse_af_radikalisering.pdf.

[36] Ritzau, "Overblik: Det siger loven om pas og krig" (Overview: The law about passports and war), Berlingske, February 4, 2016 http://www.b.dk/nationalt/overblik-det-siger-loven-om-pas-og-krig

[37] Ministry of Justice, "Regeringen indfører indrejseforbud i kamp mod terror" (Government passes law on travelban to fight terrorism), September 13, 2016.

FRANCE

Quick Facts

Population: 66,836,154 (July 2016 est.)

Area: 643,801 sq km

Ethnic Groups: Celtic and Latin with Teutonic, Slavic, North African, Indochinese, Basque minorities

Religions: Roman Catholic 63-66%, Muslim 7-9%, Buddhist 0.5-0.75%, Jewish 0.5-0.75%, other 0.5-1.0%, none 23-28%

Government Type: Semi-presidential republic

GDP (official exchange rate): $2.422 trillion (2015 est.)

Map and Quick Facts courtesy of the CIA World Factbook (Last Updated December 2016)

Overview

France houses a large Muslim minority, primarily of North African provenance. While many immigrants are non-observant (in line with a general French tendency toward secularism and a de-emphasis of religious affiliation), Islamist organizations actively promote a resurgence of a politicized and ideological Muslim identity. Target groups include youth, especially in the ethnic ghettos of cities where immigrant populations are concentrated. There is considerable tension within the Muslim leadership between advocates of secular French identity and proponents of the Islamist goal of a communitarian cultural separatism. In addition, the trans-Mediterranean immigration patterns and historical French colonial ties to North Africa contribute to a spillover of Islamist terrorist activity from Algeria into France. Jihadist activists with links to al-Qaeda move between Algeria and France, as well as other European countries. French Islamism, in turn, has become part of global jihadist networks.

The Islamic State, also known as ISIS, has recently become a dominant fixture in Islamist terrorist activity in the European Union, particularly France and Belgium, with its ideology often times taking root among young, isolated French or Belgian nationals with secular immigrant parents. Online networking, along with the recruitment of European nationals to train in Syria and subsequently return to the EU, has led to a surge in attacks inspired, or planned, by the Islamic State—including but not limited to the January 2015 attack on the Charlie Hebdo *newspaper and a Jewish supermarket, the November 2015 Paris attack, and the July 2016 attack in Nice.*

The response of the French state has evolved from earlier efforts to portray itself as the bridge between the Arab world and Europe to a more recent insistence on the value of French identity and the importance of secularism, exemplified in regulations such as the 2011 prohibition on concealing one's face in a public space. Furthermore, in contrast to the weak French response to terrorism in the 1980s, France more recently has developed an effective and robust set of counterterrorism and surveillance practices.

Islamist Activity

Union des organizations islamiques de France (UOIF)
Founded in 1983 as a small circle of foreign student activists with Islamist leanings, the Union of Islamic Organizations in France has grown into an umbrella organization claiming to represent between one to two hundred Muslim groups in France.[1] It plays a role in coordinating activities among its member associations, and is the owner of some mosques in the major cities of France. The UOIF is the French member of the London-based Federation of Islamic Organizations in Europe, active in promoting the study of Islam through its European Institute for the Human Sciences, dedicated to Islamic theology and related studies, with two campuses in France.[2] The UOIF has also established several specialized organizations, including the Young Muslims of France (JMF), the Muslim Students of France (EMF), and the French League of the Muslim Woman (LFFM).[3] These organizations contribute to the dissemination of Islamist positions and the construction of separatist communitarian identity politics. While the UOIF presents itself simply as an advocate of Muslim interests, critics point out that it engages in a "double discourse," paying lip service in public to the priority of tolerance for secular French values while at the same time promoting Islamist content (replete with intolerance, misogyny, homophobia and anti-Semitism) to its target populations.[4]

The UOIF has attained considerable public and political resonance through a disproportionate role within the French Council of the Muslim Religion (CFCM), which was established in 2003 by then-Minister of the Interior Nicolas Sarkozy as the official representative body for Muslims in France.[5] The CFCM's responsibilities pertain to interactions between the French state and the Muslim community (e.g., the construction of mosques, oversight of *halal* food, provision of Muslim spiritual services in the military and in prisons, etc). In contrast to the CFCM's administrative and technical functions, the UOIF has wider cultural and political ambitions. "In France, the extremist UOIF has become the predominant organization within the government's Islamic Council where it can eclipse moderate or secular Muslim voices," experts have noted.[6] While the inclusion of the UOIF in the CFCM may have been intended as a strategy of cooptation to move the latter toward the center, it has allowed the relatively small UOIF to emerge as an influential representative of the much more diverse and generally less ideological Muslim population in France.[7]

While the UOIF's explicit goals include the religious, cultural, educational, social and humanitarian needs of the Muslim population of France, with priority given to facilitating religious practice, critics allege that it is close to the Egyptian branch of the Muslim Brotherhood and pursues a goal of communitarian separatism.[8] This agenda involves two aspects: transforming France into a safe haven for radicals engaged in militant Islamist politics in North Africa or elsewhere, especially in the Arab world, while at the same time exercising political identity pressure on the Muslims in France to conform to increasingly repressive interpretations of Islam, a sort of "reactionary and paternalist populism."[9] "The UOIF tries to rein in the Muslims of France. Some associations affiliated with the movement claim the right to say who is a good Muslim and who is, therefore, an apostate," observes Islam expert Fiametta Venner. "This is all the more alarming since these people are not theologians—almost none of the directors of the UOIF pursued studies in this area—and they have a very narrow vision of Islam. They are satisfied with instrumentalizing the religion to pursue a reactionary political project of separatism."[10]

During the 2012 election campaign, Nicolas Sarkozy criticized the UOIF for ties to extremist preachers. Ahmed Jaballah, the President of the UOIF since 2011, insisted on the apolitical character of the organization, while attributing Sarkozy's criticisms to electoral politics. In addition, he articulated a vision of a moderate Islam within the context of French secularism as an alternative to radical tendencies, implicitly carving out a space hospitable to the Muslim Brotherhood but less welcoming of Salafist positions.[11] However, the UOIF has since come under intense pressure, following its designation as a terrorist group by the United Arab Emirates in 2014. National Front politicians, specifically the party's president, Marine Le Pen, has called for the organization's dissolution.[12]

Al-Qaeda in the Islamic Maghreb (AQIM)
Al-Qaeda in the Islamic Maghreb is a terrorist group based primarily in Algeria,

although it operates more widely in North Africa and has links to Europe. Over time, it has transformed from an organization committed to a local Islamist insurgency into a wider network pursuing a program of global *jihad*.

The precise size of AQIM's membership remains elusive. Yet even if its numbers are small, the group has acquired considerable resources thanks to profitable kidnappings and participation in drug trafficking. In 2012, General Carter Hamm, then the head of U.S. Africa Command (USAFRICOM), called AQIM "al-Qaeda's best funded, wealthiest affiliate" and ascribes to it the dominant role in the Malian insurgency.[13] The uprising began in early 2012 and involved AQIM and other Islamist groups building an alliance with Tuareg separatists. That alliance remained unstable and largely collapsed due to the participants' adherence to strict *sharia*.[14] Yet initially, the insurgency appeared poised to penetrate the southern part of the country and threaten the national government in Bamako. In response, French President Francois Hollande authorized a military expedition to prevent an Islamist takeover.

The French presence in Mali, a former colony, has potentially set the stage for new forms of Islamist terrorism in France itself. While France's intervention was met with considerable support from the Malian community in France, the leading French counter-terrorist judge, Marc Trévidic, expressed concern that it could contribute to the recruitment of new terrorists among Islamist sympathizers in France, especially among the young and marginalized members of immigrant communities.[15]

While AQIM is recognized a threat to Europe and the west, because of Al-Qaeda's original focus on attacking western targets an AQIM attack in Europe has not materialized. A 2013 RAND Corporation analysis of AQIM argues that the group lacks the infrastructure and willingness to launch an attack on the West while maintaining their control of the Sahel and its other North African priorities.[16]

The Islamic State
The influence of AQIM, and other Islamist groups in France, has been dwarfed by the emergence of the Islamic State. The Islamic State is a combination of *Salafi jihadists* and Ba'athist military and intelligence personnel who, once ousted from power in Iraq in 2003, took advantage of the civil unrest and disenfranchisement of Sunni Arabs, not only in Iraq, but also in Syria—and whose presence in Syria has only grown as the civil war in that country has dragged on.[17]

In addition to occupying territory in Iraq and Syria, ISIS is a global terror threat known for inspiring attacks throughout the West, particularly in France. France has become a consistent target for ISIS-inspired attacks due to hatred and resentment towards France by *Salafists* caused by its colonial occupation of Algeria, its occupation in Mali, and its participation in U.S.-led coalitions intended to defeat the organization in the Middle East.[18] ISIS recruits followers through online platforms as well as through prisons and existing terror cells, and the open borders in the European Union make it easier for EU nationals to slip into Iraq or Syria for militant training. As of October 2015, approximately 1,800 people were estimated to have left France to join ISIS fighters in Syria. Thereafter, the ability of those same people to return to France to recruit more followers while operating in isolated areas has led to a string of deadly ISIS-inspired attacks.[19]

The January 2015 attack on the satirical newspaper *Charlie Hebdo*, and the attack on a Jewish supermarket that took place in the days that followed, were carried out by three French citizens, two of whom were inspired by al-Qaeda in the Arabian Peninsula (which eventually took credit for planning the attack) and a third, Amedy Coulibaly, who was inspired by ISIS and pledged allegiance to the Islamic State.[20]

In November 2015, ISIS claimed full responsibility for the attacks on the city of Paris where eight gunmen, armed with both explosive belts as well as machine guns, killed 129 people across 6 locations throughout the city, such as the Bataclan theater and a national soccer stadium where President Francois Hollande was attending a match. The Islamic State claimed that the attacks were retaliation for French airstrikes against ISIS fighters in Syria. The attackers were a mix of French and Belgian nationals, many of whom were believed to have visited Syria, committed pervious crimes, had a previous terrorism connection, and were radicalized through existing terror cells or prison encounters.[21]

ISIS inspired attacks also occurred during the summer of 2016, first with the successful attack on Bastille Day in which Mohamed Lahouaiej Bouhlel drove a 19-ton truck through a crowded street in Nice, killing 84 people. ISIS claimed Bouhlel was a "soldier of the Islamic State" and French officials believe he was radicalized through a terror cell in Nice.[22] Also in July 2016, two French nationals raided a church in Northern France and took five people hostage, eventually killing an 84-year-old priest. Both attackers pledged allegiance to ISIS, and one of the attackers was on the radar of police and intelligence agencies for over a year and tried to visit Syria at least once in 2015 before being stopped at the Turkish border.[23]

Islamism and Society

Islam, barely present in France before 1945, arrived along with a wave of immigrant labor, primarily from North Africa. After Catholicism, Islam is now the most common religion in Europe. Muslims make up between five to ten percent of the total population, and Islam is the religion of two-thirds of all immigrants. Since 1872, French law has prohibited any identification of citizens by religion, even for census purposes, so precise numbers are hard to come by, but the *CIA World Factbook* counts

63-66 percent of the French population as Christian (overwhelmingly Catholic), 0.5-0.75 percent as Buddhist, 0.5-0.75 percent as Jewish, 23-28 percent non-affiliated, and 7-9 percent as Muslim.[24] In addition to immigration, many in France's Muslim population are indigenous citizens, having converted from another religion. The Pew Research Center, along with national polls conducted in 2010, found the number of converts at that time at between 70,000 and 110,000.[25] Of the sixteen million Muslims living in the European Union, about a third live in France, concentrated in the Ile-de-France region around Paris, in the south of France and in the country's industrial north.[26] Increased Muslim immigration and recent domestic terror attacks have taken their toll on non-Muslims' attitude towards Islam.[27] For example, an April 2016 poll conducted by IFOP, a French polling center, found that 47 percent of French people felt that Muslims posed a threat to their national identity, up from 43 percent in 2010. The same poll also found that more than 60 percent thought Islam was both too influential and visible in France.[28]

Of the French Muslim population, about a third describes itself as "observant." An extensive secularization of the Muslim population is consistent with the decline of observant practices in other religious traditions in the country. However there are indications that Muslim youth practice their religion at rates higher than the Catholic majority: 65% of practicing Catholics are older than 50, while 73% of practicing Muslims are younger than 54.[29] As of 2016, there were approximately 2,500 mosques in France.[30] In some instances, the construction of new mosques has led to protests, yet Muslim advocates complain that the floor space available for Muslim prayer services remains insufficient.[31]

The rise of a minority Islamism within the Muslim community can be viewed in part as a reaction against the modernization of lifestyles within immigrant communities. The mobilization of Islamist identity frequently involves younger generations rebelling against the aspirations for integration harbored by older generations of immigrants.[32]

Islamist recruitment in France has multiple dimensions. One key venue is the mosque, although of the total number of mosques very few (approximately 120) are considered sources of potential threats.[33] In the months between December 2015 and August 2016, a total of 20 mosques were shut down by French authorities under suspicion of preaching radical Islam. In the same timeframe, France's Prime Minister, Manuel Valls, called for a temporary ban on foreign funding, the most common form of financing, for French mosques to further curb radicalization.[34] In some cases, the mosque *imam* provides the radical ideology, but in others *jihadist* recruiters may be active without the knowledge of the *imam*. Significant recruitment, including proselytization, likewise takes place in prisons; French prison populations are often more than 50 percent Muslim, at times reaching 80 percent in certain areas.[35] Activists reach out both to non-observant Muslim inmates, as well as to non-Muslims who are prospects for conversion. A third avenue of recruitment involves contact with

French *jihadis*—i.e., veterans of the conflicts in Afghanistan, Bosnia, Chechnya and Iraq—who have returned to France and who may form ad hoc groups to support or carry out terrorist attacks.[36] In addition to recruitment in prison and by former jihadis, groups like ISIS target young, often disillusioned French Muslims, both men and women and often-times non-religious, through propaganda videos and social media. Recruiters target those most vulnerable and likely to be radicalized due to lack of societal integration and portray messages of strength, unity, and promise if they become ISIS fighters. Attracting younger recruits online has been incredibly successful in getting men and women to travel to Syria, causing the French government to launch an anti-ISIS communication campaign called Stop Jihadism in early 2015 to try to dissuade French youths from joining the group.[37]

The conflict between modernizing pressure and Muslim identity underlies the controversy surrounding the headscarf, or *hijab*. Islamist pressure to establish separatist communitarian identity focuses on symbols and practices to separate Muslims from secular French society. In 2004, facing a growing Muslim population in public schools with increasing numbers of women wearing the headscarf, the French government promulgated a law banning ostentatious religious symbols in the schools, in the spirit of *laicité*[38], or France's embrace of secularism based on "freedom of conscience and freedom of worship, separation of public institutions and religious organizations, and equality before the law irrespective of their beliefs or beliefs."[39] A 2011 law banning any face covering in public places only added to the controversy around both the *hijab* and the *burqua*, and intensified the conversation around religious freedom. While the laws also pertain to Christian and Jewish symbols, the Muslim headscarf or veil has received the most public scrutiny. These controversial laws underscored the gap between French norms of secular modernity and the neo-traditionalism of Islamist behavior. A primary goal of Islamism involves the assertion of patriarchal norms and the resistance to the spread of equal rights to Muslim women.[40]

Muslim immigrant populations are frequently concentrated in the ethnic ghettos of the *banlieues*, the working-class suburbs surrounding French urban centers, where they remain marginalized, facing discrimination and weathering high unemployment rates. This concentration of social problems has led repeatedly to outbreaks of mass violence. In 2005, in response to the deaths of two teenagers in Clichy-sous-Bois, near Paris, local rioting erupted, spreading rapidly across the country. A state of emergency was declared, resulting in three thousand arrests. Damage to property totaled 200 million Euros.[41] Another series of riots broke out in 2009.[42] Such periodic unrest has contributed to a profound social anxiety about *sécurité*, a term which has implications stretching from crime-in-the-streets to terrorism. Furthermore, the *banlieues* serve as prime recruitment locations for groups such as ISIS, who capitalize on the lack of opportunity and upward mobility that creates discontent amongst some susceptible young Muslims. The situation has only worsened in recent times, as the communities become labeled as guilty or complacent for the recent string of terror attacks in France, creating a dangerous vacuum for radicalization.[43]

ISLAMISM AND THE STATE

A modern liberal democracy with a tradition of secularism dating back to the eighteenth century, France is also a key ally of the United States, despite occasional foreign policy differences. French troops have played an important role in the war in Afghanistan, involvement in Libya, and the coalition to fight ISIS, even as the French state is actively engaged in resisting Islamism, both domestically and internationally.

Building on its history of colonialism, France aspired to become the European gateway to the Arab world through a systematic courting of the post-colonial regimes of North Africa. Public discourse in France, therefore, tended to be more pro-Arab than elsewhere in the West. However, the rise of an emphatically religious Islamism ran counter to French commitments to *laïcité*, generating policy shifts under Sarkozy, an open promotion of French national identity. In October 2009, then-Minister of Immigration Eric Besson called for public debate over "the theme of what it is to be French, what are the values we share, what are the relations that make us French and of which we should be proud." He insisted on a particular valorization of Frenchness: "We must reaffirm the values of French national identity and the pride in being French."[44] This effort by the state to mobilize a focus on nationality was intended as an effort to overcome immigrant (and especially Islamist) separatism, and in the years since, this discussion has shifted increasingly toward secularism. To question the role of religion in the public sphere in France is, above all, a vehicle to inquire about the status of politicized Islam.

Yet the conflict between the republican secularism of the state and the politicization of religion inherent in Islamism continues. In 2009, a debate began over prospective legislation to ban full-length cloaks, the *burqa* and the *niqab* (the latter leaves the eyes uncovered) from public venues. Initially proposed by a Communist mayor of a town with a high Muslim population, its intention was to protect women and to defend French values of secularism. It was adopted with the support of conservative President Nicolas Sarkozy and his party, but the Socialist Party did not oppose it; current Socialist President Hollande has indicated that he does not plan to pursue a retraction of the ban, which has strong popular support.[45] Clothing bans were once again the subject of debate in 2016, when over 30 towns in coastal France imposed a ban on a full-length swimsuit, often referred to as the *Burkini*. While the ban was overturned by some French courts, local officials as well as national figures, such as Prime Minister Valls, were vocal in their opposition to the swimsuit. In the midst of the burkini controversy, the mayor of the Riviera town at the center of the controversy told Muslim women "[i]f you don't want to live the way we do, don't come," while Prime Minster Valls referred to the swimsuit as a "symbol of the enslavement of women."[46]

French counterterrorism practices have faced criticism on civil rights and human rights grounds. The promulgation of laws criminalizing terrorist conspiracies (rather than simply terrorist attacks themselves) has elicited denunciations on the grounds that they represent an ominous expansion of state power. However, this pursuit of conspiracies has been defended as the only way to prevent catastrophic attacks, such as the successful disruption of the plans for terrorist violence at the 2014 World Cup at the *Stade de France*.[47] Still, Amnesty International and other watchdog groups continue to criticize France for its prosecution of conspiracy charges as a "criminal association in relation to a terrorist undertaking."[48]

For civil rights activists, the situation was exacerbated by 2008 legislation that authorized preventive detention in certain cases. After the completion of a sentence, an individual whom a judge deems to be dangerous may face an extended sentence for renewable periods of one year. In addition, the police were granted the authority to develop intelligence files on all individuals over the age of thirteen who are deemed to represent a threat to public order. While criticisms of this counterterrorism regime continue, France was successful in thwarting large-scale domestic attacks for several years leading up to the 2012 Toulouse shootings. Until then, there had been no return to the violence of the 1980s, when terrorists seemed able to act in France with impunity and little fear of sanction. After the Toulouse attack, it was revealed that the perpetrator, Mohammed Merah, had been under surveillance but was nonetheless able to carry out the killings, which lead to public criticism of the counterintelligence community. Marc Trévidic, the former counter-terrorism magistrate, argued that counterintelligence agencies may respond by pulling back their operations precisely in order to avoid this sort of criticism in the future: "After Merah, our policemen are afraid [...] They don't want to monitor people for a long time after they come back [from foreign travel to Islamist territories], because if they monitor someone and this guy commits a bomb attack it will be terrible a second time for [the counterintelligence agency]."[49] The alternative, an early arrest of a potential terrorist, would likely not be upheld due to a lack of sufficient evidence.

However, after it was disclosed that the extremist cell that included the *Charlie Hebdo* attackers had already been known to French intelligence authorities prior to their attacks, French lawmakers responded with a new law designed to intensify intelligence gathering and surveillance. In early 2015, a law was drafted to update the legislative framework to help French security services better define the purposes and types of intelligence-gathering, set up a National Commission for Control of Intelligence Techniques, and authorize new methods to collect metadata from internet providers.[50] While the law passed overwhelmingly in the National Assembly, it is particularly controversial among civil liberties groups because of its provision allowing French authorities access to "digital and mobile phone communications of anyone linked to a 'terrorist' inquiry without prior authorization from a judge." To quell the fears of vocal opponents and concerned citizens, President Hollande has pledged that the law would be reviewed by France's constitutional council to ensure its lawfulness.[51]

In the wake of the Bastille Day attack and the burkini ban controversy of 2016, Hollande saw an opportunity to address the compatibility of Islam and French secularism by setting up the Foundation for Islam in France in August 2016. With the goal of improving relations between France's Muslim population and the French government, Hollande chose Jean-Pierre Chevènement to lead the foundation. In addition to the Foundation, Hollande publicly stated that France must find a way for the state to play a role in financing and building mosques and training clergy to eliminate the possibility of radicalization of imams who are trained abroad.[52]

ENDNOTES

[1] Fiametta Venner, *OPA sur l'Islam de France: Les Ambitions de l'UOIF* [OPA within French Islam: the Ambitions of the UOIF] (Paris: Calman-Lévy, 2005).

[2] The online home of the Institute is http://www.ieshdeparis.fr/.

[3] Venner, *OPA sur l'Islam de France*, 133-153; Michèle Vianès, *Silence, on Manipule: les Islamistes en Manoeuvre* [Exploiting the Silence: Islamists in Action] (Paris: Editions Hors Commerce, 2004), 58.

[4] Venner, *OPA sur l'Islam de France*, 158.

[5] Representation in the CFCM depends on the size of mosque space controlled by an organization. See Vianès, *Silence, on Manipule*, 18-19.

[6] Lorenzo Vidino, "The Muslim Brotherhood's Conquest of Europe," *Middle East Quarterly* 12, no. 1 (Winter 2005), 25-34.

[7] Stéphanie Le Bars, "'Pour la Majorité des Musulmans, la Séperation du Religieux et du Politique est Acquise'" [For the Majority of Muslims, the Seperation of Religion and Politics is Artificial], *Le Monde* (Paris), April 4, 2011, http://www.lemonde.fr/societe/chat/2011/04/04/l-islam-est-il-soluble-dans-la-laicite_1502963_3224.html#ens_id=1460876.

[8] For the objectives of the UOIF, see its official website at http://www.uoif-online.com/v3/spip.php?article20; On the radicalism of UOIF, see the interview with Fiametta Venner, "La Face Cachée de l'UOIF et des Frères Musulmans en France," [The Hidden Side of the UOIF and the Muslim Brothers in France], *Le Post*, March 12, 2009, http://www.lepost.fr/article/2009/12/03/1822346_la-face-cachee-de-l-uoif-et-des-freres-musulmans-en-france.html; On the influence of the Muslim Brothers, see Brigitte Maréchal, *The Muslim Brothers in Europe: Roots and Discourse* (Leiden: Brill, 2008).

[9] Xavier Raufer, ed., *Atlas de l'Islam Radical* [Atlas of Radical Islam] (Paris: CNRS Editions, 2007), 13.

[10] "La Face Cachée de l'UOIF et des Frères Musulmans en France."

[11] "UOIF: 'Il n'y a pas de rupture avec le president de la Republique' [UOIF: 'there is no break with the president of the Republic']," *Le Parisien*, April 6, 2012, http://www.leparisien.fr/societe/religion-ahmed-jaballah-il-n-y-a-pas-de-rupture-avec-le-president-de-la-republique-06-04-2012-1942560.php.

[12] "Islamisme : Il est urgent de dissoudre l'UOIF parrainée par Nicolas Sarkozy," Communiqué de Presse de Marine Le Pen, *Présidente du Front National*, November 18, 2014, http://www.frontnational.com/2014/11/islamisme-il-est-urgent-de-dissoudre-luoif-parrainee-par-nicolas-sarkozy/.

[13] David Lewis, "Al Qaeda's Richest Faction Dominant in North Mali: U.S.," *Reuters*, July 26, 2012, http://www.reuters.com/article/2012/07/26/us-mali-usa-africom-idUSBRE86P1IC20120726.

[14] Jonathan Masters, "Al-Qaeda in the Islamic Maghreb (AQIM)", Council on Foreign Relations, n.d., http://www.cfr.org/north-africa/al-qaeda-islamic-maghreb-aqim/p12717.

[15] Steven Erlanger, "French Intervention in Mali Raises Threat of Domestic Terrorism, Judge Says," *New York Times*, February 23, 2013 http://www.nytimes.com/2013/02/24/world/europe/french-intervention-in-mali-raises-threat-of-domestic-terrorism-judge-says.html?pagewanted=all&_r=0.

[16] Christopher S. Chivvis and Andrew Liepman, "North Africa's Menace AQIM's Evolution and the U.S. Policy Response," *RAND Corporation*, http://www.rand.org/pubs/research_reports/RR415.html.

[17] Jessica Stern, "Why the Islamic State Hates France," *PBSNewshour*, November 18, 2015, http://www.pbs.org/newshour/updates/why-islamic-state-jihadis-are-enraged-by-france/.

[18] Ibid.

[19] The Soufan Group, "Foreign Fighters: An Updated Assessment of the Flow of Foreign Fighters into Syria and Iraq," December 2015, http://soufangroup.com/wp-content/uploads/2015/12/TSG_ForeignFightersUpdate3.pdf.

[20] "ISIS attacks: A Timeline of Terror," *CBS*, n.d., http://www.cbsnews.com/pictures/isis-attacks-a-timeline-of-terror/19/.

[21] Mariano Castillo, Margot Haddad, Michael Martinez and Steve Almasy, "Paris Suicide Bomber Identified; ISIS claims responsibility for 129 dead," *CNN*, November 16, 2015, http://www.cnn.com/2015/11/14/world/paris-attacks/.

[22] Eric Kirschbaum, "Perpatrator of Nice terror attack asked for 'more weapons' before rampage, authorities say," *Los Angeles Times*, July 16, 2016, http://www.latimes.com/world/europe/la-fg-nice-attack-20160717-snap-story.html.

[23] "France church attack: Priest killed by two 'IS militants,'" *BBC*, July 26, 2016, http://www.bbc.com/news/world-europe-36892785.

[24] CIA World Factbook: France, https://www.cia.gov/library/publications/the-world-factbook/geos/fr.html.

[25] Pew Research Center's Forum on Religion & Public Life, "The Future of the Global Muslim Population Projections for 2010-2030," January 2011, 22; "France: comment est évalué le nombre de musulmans," *Le Figaro*, April 5, 2011, http://www.lefigaro.fr/actualite-france/2011/04/05/01016-20110405ARTFIG00599-france-comment-est-evalue-le-nombre-de-musulmans.php.

[26] "L'islam de France aujourd'hui," *Contretemps*, n.d., http://www.contretemps.eu/socio-flashs/islam-france-aujourdhui.

[27] "Unease with Islam on the rise in France and Germany, new poll finds," *France24* (April 29, 2016), http://www.france24.com/en/20160429-france-germany-unease-with-islam-rise-new-poll-finds.

[28] IFOP, Regards croisés sur l'Islam en France en Allemagne, http://www.ifop.com/media/poll/3373-1-study_file.pdf.

[29] "Lislam, première religion en France," *Le Figaro*, October 24, 2012, http://www.lefigaro.fr/actualite-france/2012/10/24/01016-20121024ARTFIG00633-islam-premiere-religion-en-france.php; "En France, des jeunes de plus en plus fidèles à l'islam," *Le Monde*, November 4, 2012, http://www.lemonde.fr/culture/article/2012/11/01/des-jeunes-fideles-a-l-islam_1784520_3246.html.

[30] Yasmeen Serhan, "France's Disappearing Mosques," *The Atlantic*, August 1, 2016, http://www.theatlantic.com/news/archive/2016/08/french-mosques-islam/493919/.

[31] *Portail Religion*, http://www.portail-religion.com/islam/mosquees/mosquees-france.php.

[32] Valérie Amiraux, "From Empire to Republic: the French Muslim Dilemma," in Anna Triandafyllidou, *Muslims in 21st Century Europe: Structural and Cultural Perspectives* (London: Routledge, 2010), 137-159.

[33] Serhan, "France's Disappearing Mosques."

[34] Amiraux, "From Empire to Republic: the French Muslim Dilemma."

[35] Ibidem.

[36] Ibidem.

[37] Margot Haddad, French government fighting online war against jihadist youth recruiting, *CNN*, http://www.cnn.com/2015/02/23/europe/france-anti-jihadist-campaign/.

[38] Alain Houziaux, *Le Voile, que Cache-t-Il?* [The Veil: What Does it Hide?] (Paris: Editions ouvrières, 2004).

[39] "What is Secularism?" http://www.gouvernement.fr/qu-est-ce-que-la-laicite.

[40] Vianès, *Silence, on Manipule*, 51-73.

[41] Centre d'Analyse Stratégique, *Enquêtes sur les Violences Urbaines: Comprendre les Émeutes de November 2005* [Investigations into Urban Violence: Understanding the Riots of November 2005] (Paris: La Documentation Française, 2006).

[42] Angelique Chrisalfis, "Three Nights of Riots in French Town After 21-Year-Old Dies in Police Custody," *Guardian* (London), July 10, 2009, http://www.guardian.co.uk/world/2009/jul/10/french-police-fight-rioting-youths.

[43] Christina Rufini, "Les Banlieues: Searching for the seeds of terror," *CBS News*, January 18, 2016, http://www.cbsnews.com/news/paris-banlieues-seeds-of-terror-isis/.

[44] "Besson Relance le Débat sur l'Identité Nationale" [Besson Relaunches the Debate over National Identity], *Le Monde* (Paris), October 25, 2009.

[45] Steven Erlanger, "Has the 'Burqa Ban' Worked in France?" *International Herald Tribune*, September 2, 2012, http://rendezvous.blogs.nytimes.com/2012/09/02/has-the-burqa-ban-worked-in-france/.

[46] Lauren Said-Moorhouse, "Burkini Ban in Nice overturned by French Court," *CNN*, September 2, 2016, http://www.cnn.com/2016/09/02/europe/france-burkini-ban/.

[47] Ibid., 85-86.

[48] See, for example, Human Rights Watch, "In the Name of Prevention: Insufficient Safeguards in National Security Removals," June 5, 2007, http://www.hrw.org/en/reports/2007/06/05/name-prevention-0; Human Rights Watch, *Preempting Justice: Counterterrorism Laws and Procedures in France* (New York: HRW, 2008), http://www.hrw.org/en/reports/2008/07/01/preempting-justice; "France," in *Amnesty International Report 2009: State of the World's Human Rights* (London: Amnesty International, 2010), http://report2009.amnesty.org/en/regions/europe-central-asia/france.

[49] Erlanger, "French Intervention in Mali Raises Threat of Domestic Terrorism, Judge Says."

[50] Hugh Schofield, "Surveillance law prompts unease in France," *BBC*, May 4, 2015, http://www.bbc.com/news/world-europe-32497034

[51] Angelique Chrisafis, "France passes new surveillance law in wake of Charlie Hebdo attack," *Guardian* (London), May 5, 2015, https://www.theguardian.com/world/2015/may/05/france-passes-new-surveillance-law-in-wake-of-charlie-hebdo-attack.

[52] Tim Hume and Lauren Said-Moorhouse, "Hollande: Republic must create 'Islam of France' to respond to terror threat," *CNN*, http://www.cnn.com/2016/09/08/europe/france-hollande-islam-secularism/.

Germany

> ## Quick Facts
>
> Population: 80,722,792 (estimated July 2016)
>
> Area: 357,022 sq km
>
> Ethnic Groups: German 91.5%, Turkish 2.4%, other 6.1% (made up largely of Greek, Italian, Polish, Russian, Serbo-Croatian, Spanish)
>
> Religions: Protestant 34%, Roman Catholic 34%, Muslim 3.7%, unaffiliated or other 28.3%
>
> Government Type: Federal Republic
>
> GDP (official exchange rate): 3.495 trillion (estimated 2015)
>
> *Quick Facts courtesy of the CIA World Factbook (January 2017)*

Overview

Germany has the highest number of Muslim citizens in Western Europe, as well as in the member states of the European Union as a whole. It is also a hotbed of Islamist activity. Most notably, the attacks of 9/11 were organized in part in Germany by the "Hamburg cell" headed by Mohammed Atta.[1] Today, Islamists from Germany, including homegrown terrorists, pose a real threat to the security of the German state—as well as to that of the United States and other countries, such as Afghanistan, Pakistan, and Iraq.

Islamism in Germany has deep roots, stretching back to a symbiosis between the German state and radical religious elements during the First World War. These ties endured during the Second World War, fueled by the Third Reich's close ties to the Grand-Mufti of Jerusalem, Haj Amin al-Hussaini, and throughout the decades of the Cold War against the Soviet Union, before emerging to challenge the stability of the Federal Republic in the post-Cold War era.

Islamist Activity

Both peaceful political Islam or legal Islamism and violent *jihadism* exist in Germany today. Political Islam of the lawful variant predominates, although instances of *jihadi* activity have been documented as well with the first horrible jihadist attack with a dozen people killed in December 2016. In 2012, Germany's internal security service, the Federal Office for the Protection of the Constitution (*Bundesamt für Verfassungsschutz, BfV*), estimated that some 30 Islamist organizations with a total of 42,550 members were active within the country.[2] This represents an increase of more than 4,000 Islamists from 2011 figures[3], and is mainly the result of Salafist Islamist groups now being included in the tally. In 2013, the BfV estimated that there were 43,190 active members of Islamist organizations within Germany, with *Salafi* Islamist groups growing the fastest.[4] However, by 2015, that number had dropped to 14,120 members of Islamist organizations. One reason for this precipitous drop was the fact that Milli Görüs, a Turkish Islamist group active in Germany, was dropped from the BfV's list in 2014, as the agency no longer considered it a threat to the German constitution.[5] Before, the Federal Agency for the Protection of the Constitution (BfV) estimated Milli Görüs's membership at several 10,000 people, including some 10,000 extremist members (for Milli Görüs see below).[6]

The German security forces mainly focus four jihadist threats in today's Germany: 1) self-radicalized individuals and small groups, 2) those who return from jihad abroad (like fighters for ISIS), 3) those who were hindered to leave the country for jihad and 4) sleepers, well organized by terrorist organizations.[7]

Milli Görüs

Germany has recently changed its views towards the prominent Islamic group *Milli Görüs*. With some 31,000 members as of 2013, the Turkish *Milli Görüs* group is the largest Islamist organization in Germany.[8] As of 2015, the German Security Forces estimated their members of "several 10,000 people," and 10,000 extremists, but with no concrete numbers of membership like in 2013.[9] Founded in the early 1970s by former Turkish Prime Minister Necmettin Erbakan, *Milli Görüs* now runs 323 mosques and associated centers in Germany[10] and receives most of its funding from donations and membership fees.[11] Since January 23, 1995, its umbrella organization has been known as the Islamic Community *Milli Görüs* (IGMG).[12]

For years, the organization has spread anti-Semitic ideology through a range of media. It promotes radical television broadcasts, such as the Iranian TV series *Zehra's Blue Eyes* (which revolves around a fictional Israeli candidate for Prime Minister who kidnaps Palestinian children in order to harvest their organs for Jewish use—and glorifies suicide bombing in response).[13] It also has disseminated written anti-Semitic works, such as Turkish translations of Henry Ford's *The International Jew*.[14] Notably, the dissemination of such literature is contrary to German law, but to our knowledge no legal efforts to prosecute the group has taken place in that respect. At least some portion of the group also has endorsed and promoted *jihadist* activities abroad.[15]

Despite its Islamist character, some state institutions now deal differently with Milli Görüs, including the Office for the Protection of the Constitution in the state of Hamburg, which no longer lists the organization as unconstitutional. Head of that Hamburg office, Manfred Murck, said, Milli Görüs is still not following the democratic system of the Federal System, but he won't count them as enemies of the state anymore.[16] In April 2015, the Vice-Chairman of the Christian Democratic Union (CDU) and head of the opposition in the state of North Rhine-Westphalia, Armin Laschet, visited Milli Görüs in Bremen.[17] Bremen, too, no longer considers Milli Görüs to be against the German constitution. A well known publicist and professor, Werner Schiffauer, a cultural studies scholar, triggered the supposedly changed ideology of Milli Görüs with a controversial book publication about the organization's "change" in 2010. For example, he argued, that parts of Milli Görüs would now allow females to walk alone on the streets, as long as they cover their hair.[18] If we consider former General Secretary of the German Milli Görüs from 2014[19] until 2015, Mustafa Yeneroglu, educated in Germany, who now is a leading AKP politician and head of the "Committee for Human Rights" of the Turkish Parliament in Ankara, doubts arise about the decision to count Milli Görüs not as extremist. During a TV programme in July 2016, he lost control and threatened the moderator to leave her show.[20]

Hezbollah

The Lebanese Shi'ite militia Hezbollah is also active in Germany, where it has had a presence since the 1980s.[21] While it has no official representatives, the organization is known to have grown by the end of 2011 to some 950 members and supporters inside the country.[22] These are still the numbers as of 2015.[23] The terror organization, was established by several Shia militias in 1982 due to the Lebanon War and the Israeli involvement in it. Hezbollah is an Iranian proxy, and close ally of Syrian dictator Assad. Hezbollah' head Nasrallah denies Zionism's existence and denies the existence of a Jewish nation-state as such. The European Union rejected to count the organization as terror organization, like in 2013, when Malta urged the EU not to list them as such.[24] For a long time, Hezbollah was able to work quietly in Germany, which over time became what experts have dubbed its "main fund raising center in Europe."[25] The country has also become a source of arms for the Lebanese militia; Lebanese media outlets reported in 2012 that Hezbollah was buying weaponry in Germany via Iranian-controlled companies.[26]

Hezbollah has managed to maintain a continental presence with virtual impunity until comparatively recently. In 2005, the European Parliament urged member states to ban Hezbollah,[27] but many European countries rejected the plea, including Germany and France. In 2013, the European Union banned the military wing of Hezbollah, a year after the terror organization attacked Israeli tourists in the Bulgarian city of Burgas.[28] April 8, 2014, the German Minister of the Interior, Thomas de Maiziére, declared the organization "Orphans of Lebanon" ("Waisenkinder Libanon e.V.") illegal, due to its rejection of "international understanding," mainly in regard of the Jewish state. The group donated to the Hezballah owned Shahid-Foundation.[29] On November 16, 2015, the German Supreme Administrative Court in Leipzig rejected an objection to the ban and judged that the entire entity of Hezbollah "is an Organization based on the rejection of international understanding, because it rejects the existence of Israel and seeks for her destruction,"[30] "regardless if this pursuit is done in a political, social or terrorist manner."[31] While the German security forces believe Hezbollah to be a dangerous organization, the German government runs short to denounce it as such and does not take action against it.[32]

Hamas

Hamas is estimated to have approximately 300 members in Germany.[33] These activists raise funds for the Palestinian terror group, largely in collaboration with the Palestinian Return Center (PRC) in London.[34] While Hamas does not have any official representatives in the country, it has been known to work through like-minded organizations to raise funds and promote its political objectives there. In July 2010, for example, Germany banned the Humanitarian Relief Foundation, or IHH, because of its close ties to Hamas.[35] The IHH was noteworthy as the organization behind the controversial Gaza Flotilla of May 2010, and is accused of transmitting 6.6 million Euros from Germany to Hamas in the Gaza Strip.[36] The Palestinian Return Center (PRC), the Palestinian Community Germany (Palästinensische Gemeinschaft in Deutschland e.V.) and their allies held a conference with 3,000 participants in Berlin in April 2015.[37]

Muslim Brotherhood

As of 2015, the Muslim Brotherhood (MB) was estimated to have some 1,040 members in Germany.[38] While it has no formal representation in the country, the organization is known to run Islamic centers in Nuremberg, Stuttgart, Frankfurt, Cologne, Marburg, Braunschweig, and Munich.[39]

The Brotherhood has a long history in the Federal Republic, beginning with a 1958 initiative to build a mosque in Munich—an effort which resulted in the creation of the *Islamische Gemeinschaft in Deutschland e.V.* (IGD), the "Islamic Community in Germany." Today, the IGD is headquartered in Cologne and serves as the unofficial representative of the group in national affairs. From 2002 to 2010, it was headed by Ibrahim el-Zayat; since 2010, Samir Fallah has been its head.[40] El-Zayat was general secretary of the World Assembly of Muslim Youth (WAMY), a Saudi organization active in the spread of Wahhabi ideology abroad.[41] The IGD was also a founding member of the London-based Federation of Islamic Organizations in Europe (FIOE).

According to journalist Ian Johnson, FIOE "is headquartered in a small village in northern England" and has established a series of institutions to "push the Muslim Brotherhood worldview."[42]

The IGD ostensibly tries to create a positive political climate for political Islam, and to promote a more pious way of life in Germany. However, it also collects money for Islamist causes abroad, and raised funds for Hamas during the 2009 Gaza war.[43] In 2014, the Government of the United Arab Emirates (UAE) published a list of Islamist terrorist organizations in which the only German group identified was the IGD.[44]

Islamic State (ISIS)

The Islamic State (ISIS) is by far the most dangerous Islamist threat to Germany and Europe today. Due to its recent loss of territory and influence in Syria and Iraq, ISIS has changed its tactics, and has begun prioritizing soft targets in Europe.[45] The attacks in Paris, France in January and November 2015 as well as the 2016 bombing in Brussels, Belgium have shown the significant danger that *jihadists* affiliated with or inspired by ISIS pose in Europe.[46]

Germany has likewise been a target of ISIS-related extremism. On February 26, 2016, a 16 year old Islamist with connections to ISIS attacked a police officer in Hannover and almost killed him. She is now awaiting trial.[47] On July 18, 2016, a young (supposedly 17year old, that is unclear) ISIS follower from Afghanistan attacke five people in a local train near the Bavarian city of Würzburg, almost killing a 31year old Chinese tourist and injuring others as well.[48] Thereafter, on July 24, 2016, an ISIS-affiliated *jihadist* attempted to kill people at the Ansbach Open 2016 in Bavaria. Due to technical problems, his explosives detonated prematurely, killing the *jihadist* and injuring a dozen other people.[49]

Over the past three years, the BfV—working in conjunction with groups such as the Hessian Information- and Competence Centre Against Extremism (HKE)—has sought to track German *jihadists* who travel to Syria and Iraq to join ISIS and other *jihadist* groups. As of June 2015, there were estimated to be 677 such *jihadists* from Germany. In their groundbreaking study (the first of its kind in Europe), they analyze sociological data, including age, gender and religious background or the time-frame who long it took someone to become a *jihadist*.[50] By the end of 2015, the number increased to over 780 people, but since then there has been a significant drop-off in these numbers.[51] This drop is mainly result of the decline of ISIS, but also negative experiences during their time with ISIS, for example, and better controls by the German security forces, who deny *jihadists* to leave the country, as well as the collaboration of a few mosques who try to prevent Muslims from becoming *jihadists*.[52]

Homegrown terrorism

Homegrown terrorism, including domestic groups with connections to international *jihadist* organizations, constitutes a real threat to German security. The country faces potential threats from *jihadists* now resident in Germany, as well as *jihadists* of German origin operating abroad who may eventually return to target the Federal Republic. Both groups can be defined as "third generation" *jihadists*, i.e., those not necessarily under the auspices of al-Qaeda but who share its broad Islamist ideology and terrorist approach.[53] Such elements have been implicated in plots to carry out terror attacks in Germany,[54] as well as being known to have received training from *jihadist* elements abroad.[55] As of 2010, several dozen German *jihadists*—including members of the IJU, the Uzbek Islamic Movement (IBU), the Islamic Movement of Uzbekistan (IMU), and the German Taliban Mujahedin (*Deutsche Taliban-Mudschahidin*, or DTM)—were believed to be active in Pakistan's Waziristan region.[56]

In June 2013, the German government conducted large-scale raids in the states of Saxony, Bavaria and Baden-Württemberg in pursuit of Islamist terrorists believed to be planning attacks via model aeroplanes. All three suspects apprehended as a result are of Tunisian origin, and one allegedly studied aviation at Stuttgart University.[57]

In March 2015, German officials made raids against "Tauhid Germany" in four of its states, a group with some 30 members, they are considered a follow-up organization of the 2012 banned "Millatu Ibrahim." During the raids many computers, cell phones, data carriers and propaganda material, used for recruiting *jihadists* for the "Holy War" were confiscated.[58] After several months of investigation, in November 2016 security forces arrested a number of ISIS supporters, who were accused of having recruited for ISIS in Germany, including one man and his family, who went to Syria. Among the arrested is Ahmad Abdulaziz Abdullah A. aka Abu Walaa, the "preacher without face."[59] For homegrown *jihadists* see also "Isis," above.

Iranian Influence

The influence of the Shi'a variant of Islamism propounded by the Islamic Republic of Iran can be found in Germany as well. The Islamic Center Hamburg (IZH), founded in 1962, is a pro-Iranian institution closely linked to the Islamic Republic. Its head, the Ayatollah Reza Ramezani,[60] was appointed to his post by the Iranian Foreign Ministry in April 2009.[61] The IZH, in turn, tries to spread the ideals of the Iranian Revolution via brochures, events, prayers, rallies, and other activities, and exerts an influence over a number of Islamic organizations within Germany. These include:

- The Islamic Center Salman Farsi Moschee Langenhagen e.V. in Hannover;
- The Academy Baghiatallah e.V. in Bremen;
- The Iranian Islamic Cultural Community Berlin e.V. in Berlin;

- The Islamic Association Bavaria e.V. in Munich; and
- The Ehli-Beyt-Alevit Religious Community Ehli Beyt Alevi Federasyonu e.V. in Frankfurt a.M.[62]

Furthermore, the IZH is actively involved in the following institutions:

- The Council of Islamic Communities in Hamburg;
- The Central Council of Muslims in Germany;
- The Islamic Community of Shi'a Communities in Germany; and
- The Islamic-European Union of Shi'a scholars and Theologians.[63]

Ever since the signing of the Joint Comprehensive Plan of Action (JCPOA) on the Iranian nuclear program in July 2015, Germany's relations with Iran have improved. Despite knowledge of ongoing Iranian attempts to buy military goods,[64] German politics now promotes a normalization of the relationship with Iran.

A Pakistani Islamist, who worked for Iran and spied on Reinhold Robbe, former head of the German-Israel Society ("Deutsche-Israelische Gesellschaft, DIG), was arrested in July 2016. As the suspect had deleted material on his computer, there was no proof and he had to be released. However, no German diplomatic activity was reported in that respect.[65] On the other side, many leading politicians regularly visit Iran. These trips include Vice-Chancellor and member of the Federal Government Sigmar Gabriel, head of the Social Democratic Party, but also politicians and delegations from Saxony, Mecklenburg-West Pomerania and Saxony-Anhalt,[66] for example. Gabriel knows about Iran's extremism,[67] antisemitism and hatred of Israel and mentioned it during his visit, but that will not change the German government's and Germany's economy's[68] stance and collaboration[69] with Iran.[70] There was criticism that a brochure by the Vice-Prime Minister of Saxony, Martin Dulig from the Social Democratic Party, showed several German female politicians with headscarves, as if that Islamist practice is common among non-Muslim German politicians. The German officials said, they did the brochure just for an Iranian audience, which makes things even worse, as the boulevard Bild newspaper pointed out, pointing to anti-headscarf activism in Iran such as by Masih Alinejad.[71]

The Gülen Movement

The Turkish Gülen Movement has become increasingly influential in Germany. Founded by Turkish Islamist Fethullah Gülen (born 1938), it is based on the ideas of Faid Nursi (1876-1960).[72] The Gülen movement runs a number of high schools in Germany[73] and does not publicly advocate violence. To the contrary, it has taken pains to distance itself from bin Laden and al-Qaeda. This stance, however, appears to stem from Gülen's 2004 declaration that non-state actors (such as al-Qaeda) are not permitted to wage war,[74] rather than from an authentic aversion to armed *jihad* writ large. Gülen's Turkish branch of political Islam espouses the idea of the gradual imposition of a *sharia*-based democracy.[75] The Gülen Movement runs at least 20-25 schools in Germany in all, not including some 200 groups for the coaching of pupils after school.[76] There are no official membership numbers available for the Gülen Movement, but the group is believed to be increasingly popular as a result of its educational activities.[77] According to television and media reports in June 2013, Gülen members have tried to influence and coopt democratic parties in Germany.[78] This has clearly been the case in the city of Leipzig, where Gülen members attempted to gain a majority in the city's Social Democratic Party's youth organization, the Young Socialists (Jusos). The Gülen movement also tried to gain influence over the conservative Christian-Social Union (CSU) in Bavaria using the same method.[79] After the attempted coup against Turkish President Recep Tayyip Erdogan and his ruling AKP in Turkey in July 2016, however, German-Turkish followers or alleged followers of the Gülen movement faced attacks and defamation by German-Turkish AKP supporters.[80] Germany has the biggest Turkish community outside of Turkey with over three million Turkish people living in Germany. Turkish immigration started in 1961 with an agreement of the Federal Republic (FRG) and Turkey about so-called "Gastarbeiter," or "guest-workers." (See also below for "Gastarbeiter"). Until 1973 some 900,000 Turkish people came to Germany, most of them stayed in Germany. Other agreements about workers ("guest workers") included Italy (1955), Greece, Spain (1960), Morocco (1963), South Korea (1963), Portugal (1978), Tunisia (1968) and Yugoslavia (1968).[81] These agreements were stopped in 1973 due to the oil crisis.

Salafist elements

German authorities consider *Salafism* to be "the most dynamic Islamist movement," both within Germany and on the global level.[82] *Salafi* groups in Germany are estimated to have increased their number of adherents from 3,800 to some 4,500 between 2011 and early 2013.[83] That growth has continued; as of 2015, some 8,350 Salafists are estimated active in Germany.[84]

This growth has brought with it an increase in militant activity. The first ever "Islamist terror attack" in Germany occurred on March 2, 2011, when Kosovar Serb Arid Uka killed two U.S. soldiers at the Frankfurt International Airport.[85] Uka was discovered to have been in touch with *Salafist* elements via social media outlets, specifically Facebook.[86] He was convicted and sentenced to life in prison in December 2012.[87]

German authorities have begun to respond to the growing threats from these groups. In June 2012, the Islamist network *Millatu Ibrahim* was shut down by German authorities in the first action of its kind against *Salafist* groups.[88] In addition, as of September 2016, according to Hessian MP, Ismail Tipi, there are over 700[89] ongoing investigations against *Salafist* groups such as Dawa FFM (Dawa Frankfurt) and *Die Wahre* Religion (The True Religion). Finally, in March 2013, Germany authorities proscribed *Dawa FFM* and two other groups, *Islamische Audios* and *An-Nussrah*.[90]

According to the head of the Office for the Protection of the Constitution in Hamburg, *Salafists* are the fastest growing elements in Germany's Islamism camp.[91] This may stem from *Salafists'* ability to attract teenagers and young adults by music or social media events, as well as the distribution of the Quran (see below). On April 16, 2016, two 16-year old *Salafists* put a bomb at a Sikh Temple, causing an explosion that injured several people at a wedding. The best known German *Salafist*, a convert named Pierre Vogel, has radicalized many people, and his distance from *jihadist* terror is nothing more than tactical lip-service.[92]

Social media and the Internet have played a crucial role in *Salafist* activity,[93] especially alongside activism in mosques and on the street such as the free distribution of the Quran by the Read ("Lies" in German) campaign. The "Read" Campaign, which started in 2011, was established by Cologne based *Salafist* Ibrahim Abou Nagie, the head of the group *Die Wahre* Religion (The True Religion). Its aim is to distribute no less than 25 million German-language copies of the Quran, in fact they distributed indeed some 3,5 million.[94] May 28, 2016, the state of Hamburg was the first German state to ban the "Read!" Quran distribution, due to its extremist and *jihadist* connections. Other German states might follow suit in the future, including in particular North Rhine-Westphalia.[95]

Finally, November 15, 2016, the organization "The True Religion" was prohibited by the Federal Ministry of the Interior.[96]

Islamism and Society

At 4.5 million, Germany's Muslim population is, alongside France, the highest among the 27 states that make up the European Union (with France having a higher percentage of Muslims).[97] As of December 31, 2015, of 4.5 million, the majority (2.3 million) is from Turkey, while roughly half a million (453,000) from the former Yugoslavia. Iran (84,956), Afghanistan (235,886), Morocco (156,327), Pakistan (110,691), Iraq (135,210), Lebanon (116,634) and Syria (458,482) make up the other significant countries of origin.

For decades, however, the former Federal Republic of Germany did not consider these immigrants to be true citizens, instead terming them *Gastarbeiter*, or guest workers. Over time, however, this fiction has become increasingly hard to sustain; Turkish workers, in particular, stayed in Germany, and their families followed them there. Racism was and remains a widespread phenomenon in Germany, due to the specific German national concept of citizenship, which until recently was defined along blood, rather than territorial, lines. Thus, being born in Germany did not necessarily mean that you were German in the popular conception. This began to change in 1999 with the passage of a new law granting the children of non-German residents citizenship by birth.[98]

Since the attacks of 9/11, and particularly over the past several years, political Islam has become a major topic of public debate in Germany. The wearing of the headscarf, honor killings, forced marriages, and support for terrorism and anti-Zionist activity are among the main topics of discussion surrounding both Islam and Islamism. Yet many newspapers, researchers, and politicians, as well as the general public at large, remain reluctant to deal with these issues.

Those political groups or parties that express their opposition to political Islam do so out of ideological and/or racist grounds, rather than as a result of careful analysis of specific elements of political Islam. Likewise, many groups opposed to Islam are also against other foreigners (as well as those considered to be not "German" enough).

Nevertheless, a tiny but growing number of public intellectuals, scholars, activists, authors, and journalists have emerged publicly as critics of Islamism in recent years. These individuals have faced resistance on the public policy front. Some institutions, like the Berlin Center for Research on Antisemitism (ZfA),[99] have equated any meaningful criticism of Islam with anti-Semitism, often framed as Islamophobia.[100] Many journalists and mainstream scholars even compare or equate Islamist preachers of hate with pro-Western scholars, writers or activists,[101] and reject any military response to Islamism or Islamic *jihad*.[102] Most instead portray Islam as harmless or interesting, and look uncritically upon figures like leading Sunni Islamist Yusuf al-Qaradawi.[103]

Considerable grassroots support for Islamism and even violent *jihad* is visible at the grassroots level in Germany, as evidenced through sporadic rallies in German cities in support of various radical causes. Populist, racist, antisemitic and extremist groups such as the Pegida movement ("Patriots Against the Islamization of the Occident") or the party Alternative for Germany (AfD), are gaining massive support among the German population, with shocking electoral results. Such factions received a major showing in contests for state parliaments in Baden-Württemberg (15,1%), Berlin (14,2%), or the Eastern states of Mecklenburg-Vorpommern (20,8%) and Sachsen-Anhalt (24,3%) in 2016 alone.[104] They agitate against all Muslims and refugees and make no distinction between Islamists, Muslims, or even refugees. The relationship between German society as a whole, and Muslims, can be said to be at a historic low.

ISLAMISM AND THE STATE

Some Islamist groups, such as the Muslim Brotherhood, have been present in Germany for years without engaging any real struggle for power with the government.[105] Others, however, have fared less well in Germany. Hizb ut-Tahrir, for example, was formally banned on January 10, 2003, a decision that was affirmed at the federal level in January 2006.[106] Hezbollah's dedicated television channel, *al-Manar*, was proscribed in hotels and coffee shops in Germany on October 29, 2008.[107] (However, private households in Germany can still watch it via Saudi and Egyptian satellites). More recently, in August 2010, the al-Quds mosque in Hamburg—a *Salafi* religious center known to be a significant source of Islamist indoctrination[108] —was belatedly shuttered.[109]

The German government, for its part, has also attempted to participate in—and to influence—the dialogue over Islam taking place inside the country. In 2006, it established an official "Islam Conference," which continues to convene several times a year. At this venue, leading Muslim congregations, along with independent activists, authors, and scholars, discuss the relationship of Muslims and German society with German politicians, headed by the Federal Minister of the Interior. This approach has garnered disapproval from critics, who say that the conference itself has been co-opted by its inclusion of Islamists and suspicious groups. These include the German Islam Council (*Islamrat für die Bundesrepublik Deutschland e. V.*, or IRD), which was excluded from the Islam Conference in 2010 due to criminal investigations against some of its members over their ties to Islamism.[110] In September 2016, the tenth anniversary of the Islam-Conference was held, but the institution remains highly controversial. "The State is not integrating Islam, but promotes Islamists," critics of the venture have opined.[111]

This schizophrenic approach has led leading critics to contend that Germany, despite its role in international counterterrorism efforts (including Coalition operations in Afghanistan), still lacks a real anti-terror strategy.[112] However, contrary to Spain, England, France or Belgium, Germany has yet to be the victim of a major Islamist attack. National security forces, with cooperation from foreign secret services, have prevented many attacks. Finally, sometimes the *jihadists* have simply had bad luck or have been stopped by Syrian refugees, such as in the case of an ISIS affiliated *jihadist* who, after a protracted chase from Saxony to Leipzig, was apprehended by authorities as a result of a tip from a Syrian refugee. Police found 1.5 kilograms of explosives in the suspect's apartment—leading to the conclusion that they had averted the worst *jihadist* attack in Germany's history.[113] The BfV and the German Government are aware of the possible threat posed by the current refugee crisis in Europe, both to the EU at large and to Germany in particular.[114] However, both organizations emphasize that refugees come to Europe in search of shelter and safety, and prejudice and hatred toward them must be fought.[115] As of April 2016, the head of the Federal Office for the Protection of the Constitution, Hans-Georg Maaßen, said, the Office underestimated IS strategy to bring *jihadists* to Europe and Germany. Maaßen said, "ISIS didn't need to infiltrate *jihadists* among refugees, but they did. We had to learn that lesson."[116] The *jihadist* threat is very acute in Germany as of January 2017. Syrian refugees prevented one of the worst attacks by an ISIS affiliated *jihadist* in October 2016, by delivering a Syrian *jihadist*, who already had heavy explosives for a suicide belt in his apartment, to the police. But then, the German police and the officials at the Leipzig jail completely failed to prevent the *jihadist* from killing himself. They even had an expertise from a psychologist who found out that the aspiring suicide bomber does not want to kill himself. The German public was shocked about the failure of the German security system.[117] On December 19, 2016, the worst *jihadist* attack ever in Germany occurred. 23-year old Tunisian Anis Amri hijacked a truck, killed the Polish driver by a shot in his head and hours later he drove the truck into a Christmas market in the heart of West-Berlin at the Breitscheidplatz, killing eleven people. It turned out that the German security forces were very well informed about the criminal activities of Amri, who was in jail in Italy for four years, for example, and had used many identities as a "refugee" in Germany. The German security forces and the police failed to prevent this horrible massacre, despite they knew about the *jihadist* long before and feared (or at least knew) he might try to kill himself in a suicide attack or another *jihadist* attack. After the attack on December 19, 2016, Amri went to the nearby big train station Zoologischer Garten (Zoo), was filmed by a video camera and showed the Islamic State sign of victory, went to North-Rhine Westphalia, then via the Netherlands, Belgium and France to Italy. In the city of Sesto San Giovanni, near Milano, he was controlled by an ordinary police control at 3.30am. He fired at them, injured a policeman and was killed by his colleague.[118]

ENDNOTES

[1] *The 9/11 Commission Report: Final Report of the National Commission on Terrorist Attacks Upon the United States* (New York: WW Norton & Co., 2004).

[2] Federal Ministry of the Interior, *Verfassungsschutzbericht 2012* [*Annual Report on the Protection of the Constitution 2012*], 2013, https://www.verfassungsschutz.de/download/vsbericht-2012.pdf.

[3] Federal Ministry of the Interior, *Verfassungsschutzbericht 2012* [*Annual Report on the Protection of the Constitution 2012*], 2013, http://www.verfassungsschutz.de/download/vsbericht-2012-vorabfassung.pdf.

[4] Federal Ministry of the Interior, *Verfassungsschutzbericht 2013* [*Annual Report on the Protection of the Constitution 2013*], 2014, https://www.verfassungsschutz.de/de/oeffentlichkeitsarbeit/publikationen/verfassungsschutzberichte/vsbericht-2013.

[5] Federal Ministry of the Interior, *Verfassungsschutzbericht 2014* [*Annual Report on the Protection of the Constitution 2014*], 2015, https://www.verfassungsschutz.de/de/oeffentlichkeitsarbeit/publikationen/verfassungsschutzberichte/vsbericht-2014.

[6] Federal Ministry of the Interior, *Verfassungsschutzbericht 2015* [*Annual Report on the Protection of the Constitution 2015*], 2016, https://www.verfassungsschutz.de/de/oeffentlichkeitsarbeit/publikationen/verfassungsschutzberichte/vsbericht-2015.

[7] Federal Ministry of the Interior, *Verfassungsschutzbericht 2015*, [*Annual Report on the Protection of the Constitution 2015*] https://www.verfassungsschutz.de/de/oeffentlichkeitsarbeit/publikationen/verfassungsschutzberichte/vsbericht-2015, page 152.

[8] Federal Ministry of the Interior, *Verfassungsschutzbericht 2013* [*Annual Report on the Protection of the Constitution 2013*].

[9] Federal Ministry of the Interior, *Verfassungsschutzbericht 2015* https://www.verfassungsschutz.de/de/oeffentlichkeitsarbeit/publikationen/verfassungsschutzberichte/vsbericht-2015.

[10] Federal Ministry of the Interior, *Verfassungsschutzbericht 2009*.

[11] North Rhine-Westphalia Interior Ministry, *Verfassungsschutzbericht 2005* [*Annual Report on the Protection of the Constitution 2005 of North Rhine-Westphalia*], March 20, 2006, http://www.im.nrw.de/imshop/shopdocs/verfassungsschutzbericht_2005.pdf.

[12] Thomas Lemmen, *Islamische Vereine und Verbände in Deutschland* [Islamic Associations and Federations in Germany] (Bonn: Friedrich Ebert Stiftung, 2002), 40. The German name of the group is Islamische Gemeinschaft Milli Görüs e.V.

[13] "Antisemitische Hetzvideos bei der Islamischen Gemeinschaft Milli Görüs [Antisemitic hate videos of the Islamic Community Milli Görüs]," hamburg.de, July 13, 2006, http://www.hamburg.de/archiv/232516/hetzvideos-igmg-artikel.html.

[14] Ibid.

[15] ARD, "Report München," February 8, 2010, http://www.youtube.com/watch?v=-Ka6mV0-99M.

[16] Denis Fengler and Christian Unger: "Milli Görüs ab jetzt unbeobachtet," https://www.welt.de/print/welt_kompakt/hamburg/article126997443/Milli-Goerues-ab-jetzt-unbeobachtet.html.

[17] Kristian Frigelj: "Merkel-Vize zu Besuch bei der Millî-Görüş-Bewegung," https://www.welt.de/politik/deutschland/article139488301/Merkel-Vize-zu-Besuch-bei-der-Milli-Goerues-Bewegung.html

[18] See an enthusiastic review, though, by anthropologist Susanne Schröter, a leading expert in jihad and Islamism, in the Frankfurter Allgemeine Zeitung, August 11, 2010, of Schiffauer's book, http://www.susanne-schroeter.de/files/faz__11.8.2010_kopie.pdf.

[19] Report by the Office for the Protection of the Constitution in the state of Baden-Wurttemberg, June 2014, http://www.verfassungsschutz-bw.de/,Lde/Startseite/Arbeitsfelder/IGMG_+Mustafa+YENEROGLU+ist+neuer+Generalsekretaer.

[20] „Erdogans „Sprachrohr" gerät bei Illner außer Kontrolle," July 22, 2016, https://www.welt.de/vermischtes/article157216544/Erdogans-Sprachrohr-geraet-bei-Illner-ausser-Kontrolle.html

[21] Mark Dubowitz and Alexander Ritzmann, "Hezbollah's German Helpers," Wall Street Journal, April 16, 2007, http://www.defenddemocracy.org/index.php?option=com_content&task=view&id=11779494&Itemid=0.

[22] Nicholas Kulish, "Despite Alarm by U.S., Europe Lets Hezbollah Operate Openly," New York Times, August 15, 2012, http://www.nytimes.com/2012/08/16/world/europe/hezbollah-banned-in-us-operates-in-europes-public-eye.html.

[23] Federal Ministry of the Interior, Verfassungsschutzbericht 2015, https://www.verfassungsschutz.de/de/oeffentlichkeitsarbeit/publikationen/verfassungsschutzberichte/vsbericht-2015, page 192.

[24] https://www.gov.mt/en/Government/Press%20Releases/Pages/2013/July/22/pr1573.aspx.

[25] Anti-Defamation League, "Hezbollah's International Reach," Anti-Defamation League, December 7, 2004, http://www.adl.org/terror/hezbollah_print.asp.

[26] Michal Shmulovich, "Hezbollah Drone Reportedly Manufactured on Germany," Times of Israel, October 17, 2012, http://www.timesofisrael.com/hezbollahs-drone-reportedly-manufactured-in-germany-and-sold-to-iran-lebanese-paper-reports/.

[27] European Parliament, "European Parliament Resolution on the Situation in Lebanon," Strasbourg, France, March 10, 2005, http://www.europarl.europa.eu/sides/getDoc.do?pubRef=-//EP//TEXT+TA+P6-TA-2005-0076+0+DOC+XML+V0//EN.

[28] »Europäische Union setzt Hisbollah auf Terrorliste«, Die Welt, July 22, 2013, https://www.welt.de/politik/ausland/article118262871/Europaeische-Union-setzt-Hisbollah-auf-Terrorliste.html.

[29] https://www.verfassungsschutz.de/de/oeffentlichkeitsarbeit/presse/pi-20140408-wkp-verbot.

[30] Bundesverwaltungsgericht »Vereinsverbot wegen Völkerverständigungswidrigkeit«, November 22, 2015, http://www.bverwg.de/entscheidungen/entscheidung.php?ent=161115U1A4.15.0

[31] Federal Ministry of the Interior, *Verfassungsschutzbericht 2015* [*Annual Report on the Protection of the Constitution 2015*].

[32] http://www.tagesspiegel.de/politik/libanesische-islamisten-miliz-hisbollah-spenden-sammeln-fuer-den-terror-keinen-hats-gestoert/14555884.html

[33] https://www.verfassungsschutz.de/de/oeffentlichkeitsarbeit/publikationen/verfassungsschutzberichte/vsbericht-2015, page194.

[34] Federal Ministry of the Interior, *Verfassungsschutzbericht 2009* [*Annual Report on the Protection of the Constitution 2009*].

[35] Benjamin Weinthal, "Germany Bans IHH for Hamas Links," Jerusalem Post, July 12, 2010, http://www.jpost.com/SpecialSection/Article.aspx?ID=181187.

[36] "Milli Görüs und die Hamas. 'Einfluss auf 60.000 Muslime' [Milli Görüs and Hamas. 'Influence on some 60.000 Muslims']," *Tageszeitung* (Berlin), July 14, 2010, http://www.taz.de/1/politik/deutschland/artikel/1/direkter-einfluss-auf-60-000-muslime/.

[37] Flaggen, Leid und Heimatliebe, taz (tageszeitung), April 26, 2015, http://www.taz.de/!5010871/, Islamisten mit Nahostkarte ohne Israel, Der Tagesspiegel, April 20, 2015, http://www.tagesspiegel.de/politik/palaestinenserkonferenz-in-berlin-islamisten-mit-nahostkarte-ohne-israel/11663508.html.

[38] Federal Ministry of the Interior, *Verfassungsschutzbericht 2015 [Annual Report on the Protection of the Constitution 2015]*.

[39] Federal Ministry of the Interior, *Verfassungsschutzbericht 2009 [Annual Report on the Protection of the Constitution 2015]*.

[40] Ibid.

[41] Ibidem; For possible ties of WAMY to al-Qaeda, see "Al Qaeda linked World Assembly of Muslim Youth (WAMY) Jihad through Da'wa group working with Novib/Oxfam on Somali 'educational' initiatives," *Militant Islam Monitor*, October 16, 2006, http://www.militantislammonitor.org/article/id/2473.

[42] Ian Johnson, Statement before the Human Rights Caucus of the U.S. House of Representatives, February 9, 2006, http://www.aifdemocracy.org/policy-issues.php?id=1727; See also Lorenzo Vidino, "The Muslim Brotherhood's Conquest of Europe," Middle East Quarterly, Winter 2005, 25-34.

[43] Federal Ministry of the Interior, *Verfassungsschutzbericht 2009 [Annual Report on the Protection of the Constitution 2009]*.

[44] UAE Cabinet approves list of designated terrorist organisations, groups, November 15, 2014, http://www.wam.ae/en/news/emirates-international/1395272478814.html.

[45] "Strategy Shift for ISIS: Inflicting Terror in Distant Lands", New York Times, November 15, 2015, http://www.nytimes.com/2015/11/15/world/europe/strategy-shift-for-isis-inflicting-terror-in-distant-lands.html.

[46] Federal Ministry of the Interior, *Verfassungsschutzbericht 2015* [Annual Report on the Protection of the Constitution 2015].

[47] 16-jährige IS-Sympathisantin angeklagt, August 29, 2016, n-tv, http://www.n-tv.de/politik/16-jaehrige-IS-Sympathisantin-angeklagt-article18519826.html.

[48] Report about the Chinese victims, „Der Weg zurück ins Leben nach dem Axt-Attentat von Würzburg," November 16, 2016, http://www.augsburger-allgemeine.de/bayern/Der-Weg-zurueck-ins-Leben-nach-dem-Axt-Attentat-von-Wuerzburg-id39736352.html.

[49] „12 Verletzte bei Bombenanschlag," July 25, 2016, die tageszeitung (taz), https://taz.de/Attentat-in-Ansbach/!5327637/

[50] "Analyse der Radikalisierungshintergründe und -verläufe der Personen, die aus islamistischer Motivation aus Deutschland in Richtung Syrien oder Irak ausgereist sind," December 29, 2015, https://www.bka.de/SharedDocs/Downloads/DE/Publikationen/Publikationsreihen/Forschungsergebnisse/2015AnalyseRadikalisierungsgruendeSyrienIrakAusreisende.html

[51] Private information provided by a representative of the Federal Office for the Protection of the Constitution, September 2016.

[52] „Weniger IS-Sympathisanten reisen nach Syrien und in Irak," November 26, 2016, https://www.merkur.de/politik/weniger-is-sympathisanten-reisen-nach-syrien-und-in-irak-zr-7017740.html

[53] Kai Hirschmann, "Der Jihadismus: Ideologie, Organisation und Bekämpfungsmöglichkeiten [The Jihadists: Ideology, organization and fighting capabilities]," in Kurt Graulich and Dieter Simon, eds., *Terrorismus und Rechtsstaatlichkeit. Analysen, Handlungsoptionen, Perspektiven* [Terrorism and rule of law. Analyses, action options, perspectives] (Berlin: Akademie Verlag, 2007), 99-121, 114.

[54] For a more detailed analysis of the group members, see Rolf Clement and Paul Elmar Jöris, *Die Terroristen von nebenan. Gotteskrieger aus Deutschland* [The terrorists from next door: Holy warriors from Germany] (Munich/Zurich: Piper, 2010); *Radio Deutschlandfunk*, May 12, 2009, http://www.dradio.de/download/104169/.

[55] Yassin Musharbash and Matthias Gebauer, "De Maizière warnt vor Anschlag in Deutschland [De Maizière warns of attack in Germany]," *Der Spiegel* (Hamburg), November 17, 2010, http://www.spiegel.de/politik/deutschland/0,1518,729603,00.html.

[56] ibid.

[57] "Islamist Raids: German Police Shoot Down Model Plane Terror Plot," *Der Spiegel* (Munich), June 25, 2013, http://www.spiegel.de/international/germany/german-police-suspect-remote-controlled-airplane-terror-plot-a-907756.html.

[58] "Vom Rekruten bis zum Rückkehrer", http://jungle-world.com/artikel/2015/15/51764.html.

[59] "Anführer des IS in Deutschland offenbar gefasst", http://www.stern.de/panorama/gesellschaft/razzia--anfuehrer-des-is-in-deutschland-offenbar-gefasst-7138978.html.

[60] On the official homepage of that Islamic Center, http://izhamburg.de/index.aspx?pid=99&ArticleID=47009.

[61] Ibid.

[62] Ibidem.

[63] Ibidem.

[64] Frank Jansen, "Iran will mit allen Mitteln die Atombombe," Tagesspiegel, July 4, 2016, http://www.tagesspiegel.de/politik/verfassungsschutz-iran-will-mit-allen-mitteln-die-atombombe/13829050.html.

[65] „SPD-Politiker im Visier des Iran," Tagesschau.de, January 7, 2017, https://www.tagesschau.de/inland/robbe-105.html

[66] „Wirbel um Broschüre zu Iran-Reise: Auch Frauen aus Sachsen mit Kopftuch," no date available, http://www.lvz.de/Mitteldeutschland/News/Wirbel-um-Broschuere-zu-Iran-Reise-Auch-Frauen-aus-Sachsen-mit-Kopftuch

[67] „Gabriel verteidigt Iran-Reise," n-tv, September 30, 2016, http://www.n-tv.de/politik/Gabriel-verteidigt-Iran-Reise-article18757781.html.

[68] „Umweltcluster Bayern: Besuch iranischer Delegation und Delegationsreise in den Iran," September 19, 2016, http://www.clusterplattform.de/CLUSTER/Redaktion/DE/Kurzmeldungen/Aktuelles/2016/3.%20Quartal/20160919_umweltcluster_iranische_Delegationsreise.html.

[69] „Iran-Handel: Hermesdeckung für Exporte wieder möglich," July 4, 2016, http://www.marktundmittelstand.de/zukunftsmaerkte/iran-handel-hermesdeckung-fuer-exporte-wieder-moeglich-1236511/

[70] „Gabriels Besuch in Teheran endet mit einem Eklat," October 4, 2016, http://www.zeit.de/politik/ausland/2016-10/iran-sigmar-gabriel-treffen-ali-laridschani-absage.

[71] „Protest nach Kopftuchaffäre," June 9, 2016, http://www.bild.de/regional/dresden/kopftuch/protest-sturm-nach-kopftuch-affaere-46201142.bild.html.

[72] Ralph Ghadban, lecture, Aalen, Germany, May 5, 2010.

[73] Author's correspondence with Ralph Ghadban, November 2010.

[74] [74] Ralph Ghadban, lecture.

[75] Ibid.

[76] Author's correspondence with German Islamism expert Claudia Dantschke, Berlin, Germany, April 2011.

[77] Claudia Dantschke, *Muslime – Ihre Einrichtungen und Vereine im Berliner Bezirk Neukölln. Überblick über die Strukturen und ihre religiösen sowie politischen Ausrichtungen. Eine Handreichung für die Jugendarbeit* [Muslims - mechanisms and associations in the Berlin district of Neukölln. Overview of the structures and their religious as well as political adjustments] (Berlin: Zentrum Demokratische Kultur, 2009), 44; For an overview of the Gülen Movement and its ideology, see ibid, 42-45.

[78] TV *Program Exakt*, June 26, 2013, http://web.archive.org/web/20140206031558/http://www.mdr.de/exakt/guelen_bewegung100.html.

[79] Ibid.

[80] "Der Kampf ist in Deutschland angekommen," *Stuttgarter Nachrichten*, July 20, 2016, http://www.stuttgarter-nachrichten.de/inhalt.angriffe-auf-guelen-bewegung-der-kampf-ist-in-deutschland-angekommen.1f291dbf-9e09-43e4-ab28-f135cc1af219.html; "In Deutschland häufen sich Angriffe auf Gülen-Anhänger," *Sueddeutsche Zeitung*, July 22, 2016, http://www.sueddeutsche.de/politik/deutschland-hetzen-drohen-denunzieren-1.3088817.

[81] http://www.bpb.de/politik/hintergrund-aktuell/68921/erstes-gastarbeiter-abkommen-20-12-2010.
[82] Federal Ministry of the Interior, *Verfassungsschutzbericht 2011*, 251.
[83] Ibid; "Islamisten-Szene: Polizei startet Großrazzia gegen Salafisten," Der Spiegel (Munich), March 13, 2013, http://www.spiegel.de/politik/deutschland/islamisten-szene-polizei-startet-grossrazzia-gegen-salafisten-vereine-a-888548.html.
[84] Federal Ministry of the Interior, *Verfassungsschutzbericht 2015*.
[85] Federal Ministry of the Interior, *Verfassungsschutzbericht 2011*, 226.
[86] Ibid, 255.
[87] "Lebenslänglich für Frankfurter Flughafenattentäter," *Focus Online*, February 10, 2012, http://www.focus.de/politik/deutschland/islamistischer-anschlag-lebenslang-fuer-frankfurter-flughafenattentaeter-_aid_712754.html.
[88] "Salafisten: Razzia und Vereinsverbot", http://www.bmi.bund.de/SharedDocs/Pressemitteilungen/DE/2012/06/vereinsverbot.html.
[89] "Ismail Tipi: 710 Ermittlungsverfahren gegen Salafisten und Gefährder in Deutschland", http://www.ismail-tipi.de/inhalte/2/aktuelles/146736/ismail-tipi-710-ermittlungsverfahren-gegen-salafisten-und-gefaehrder-in-deutschland/index.html.
[90] Reiner Burger, "Anschlag auf „Pro-NRW"-Chef verhindert [Attack on „Pro NRW" Chief]," *Franfurter Allemeine Zeitung*, March 13, 2013, http://www.faz.net/aktuell/politik/inland/schlag-gegen-salafisten-anschlag-auf-pro-nrw-chef-verhindert-12112847.html.
[91] "Immer mehr Salafisten in Hamburg erfasst," ndr.de, August 27, 2016, https://www.ndr.de/nachrichten/hamburg/Immer-mehr-Salafisten-in-Hamburg-erfasst,salafismus154.html
[92] "Dschihad im Kinderzimmer," *Die Zeit*, June 2, 2016, http://www.zeit.de/2016/22/islamismus-salafismus-islamischer-staat-jugendliche-schutz/komplettansicht
[93] "Islamismus im Internet. Propaganda – Verstöße – Gegenstrategien," December 2015, http://www.hass-im-netz.info/fileadmin/dateien/pk2015/Islamismus_im_Internet.pdf
[94] "Warum Koran Verschenkaktion ‚Lies!' gefährlich ist," Stuttgarter Nachrichten, March 5, 2015, http://www.stuttgarter-nachrichten.de/inhalt.verfassungsschutz-warum-koran-verschenkaktion-lies-gefaehrlich-ist.69fe7409-cb59-459f-985b-c55c337a6cd3.html; "Das Missionierungsnetzwerk des Ibrahim Abou-Nagie," November 15, 2016, https://www.welt.de/politik/deutschland/article159513618/Das-Missionierungsnetzwerk-des-Ibrahim-Abou-Nagie.html.
[95] "Hamburg geht überfälligen Schritt: Radikale Muslime dürfen Koran nicht mehr öffentlich verteilen," *Huffington Post*, September 12, 2016, http://www.huffingtonpost.de/2016/09/12/hamburg-salafisten-lies-mich_n_11970330.html.

[96] "Vereinigung 'Die wahre Religion (DWR)' alias 'Stiftung LIES' verboten und aufgelöst", https://www.bmi.bund.de/SharedDocs/Kurzmeldungen/DE/2016/11/vereinsverbot-dwr.html.

[97] Anja Stichs, Wie viele Muslime leben in Deutschland? Eine Hochrechnung über die Anzahl der Muslime in Deutschland zum Stand 31. Dezember 2015 Im Auftrag der Deutschen Islam Konferenz (Nuremberg: Federal Office for Migration and Refugees, 2016), http://www.bamf.de/SharedDocs/Anlagen/DE/Publikationen/WorkingPapers/wp71-zahl-muslime-deutschland.pdf?__blob=publicationFile.

[98] "Staatsbürgerschaftsrecht. Reform verabschiedet [New law on citizenship passed]," *Der Spiegel* (Hamburg), May 7, 1999, http://www.spiegel.de/politik/deutschland/a-21229.html.

[99] Conference of the Center for Research on Antisemitism, Technical University Berlin, Berlin, Germany, December 8, 2008, http://zfa.kgw.tu-berlin.de/feindbild_muslim_feindbild_islam.pdf.

[100] The Berlin Center for Research on Antisemitism (ZfA) equated the situation of Jews in the late 19th century with the situation of Muslims today in Germany at a conference dedicated to that topic on December 8, 2008 (see footnote above). See Clemens Heni, "Antisemitism is not the same as Islamophobia," *Jerusalem Post*, December 3, 2008, http://www.jpost.com/Opinion/Op-EdContributors/Article.aspx?id=122938.

[101] A leading voice in equating critics of Islamism with Islamists is historian Wolfgang Benz (head of the above mentioned Berlin Center for Research on Antisemitism (ZfA) from 1990-2011). See his article "Hetzer mit Parallelen. Antisemiten des 19. Jahrhunderts und manche "Islamkritiker" des 21. Jahrhunderts arbeiten mit ähnlichen Mitteln an ihrem Feindbild. [Agitators with Parallels. Anti-Semitism in the 19th Century and some „critics of Islam" in the 21st century use similar tools in portraying their concepts of enemies]," *Süddeutsche Zeitung* (Munich), January 4, 2010, http://www.sueddeutsche.de/politik/antisemiten-und-islamfeinde-hetzer-mit-parallelen-1.59486. For more on Benz and the failure of German (and Western) academia to analyze and confront Islamism, see Clemens Heni, *Antisemitism: A Specific Phenomenon. Holocaust Trivialization – Islamism – Post-colonial and Cosmopolitan anti-Zionism* (Berlin: Edition Critic 2013).

[102] See the German role in the debate about Islam and the West, in David Blankenhorn et al., *The Islam/West Debate: Documents from a Global Debate on Terrorism, U.S. Policy, and the Middle East* (Lanham, MD: Rowman & Littlefield Publishers, 2005).

[103] Qaradawi has been portrayed as "moderate" in the German political discourse, because he rejects suicide bombing i fit is not aimed at Jews and Israel. Heni, *Antisemitism*. For an overview of German Islamic Studies after 9/11 see Clemens Heni, *Schadenfreude. Islamforschung und Antisemitismus in Deutschland nach 9/11* [Schadenfreude. Islamic Studies and antisemitism in Germany after 9/11] (published by The Berlin International Center for the Study of Antisemitism (BICSA), Berlin: Edition Critic 2011).

[104] "Wo die AfD am stärksten ist – und wo am schwächsten," *Stern*, September 5, 2016, http://www.stern.de/politik/deutschland/afd-wahlerfolge--wo-die-rechtspopulisten-am-staerksten-sind---und-wo-am-schwaechsten-7043578.html; Clemens Heni, "Why Jihad and neo-Nazis embrace Brexit and "Bullshit 9.0," *Times of Israel*, June 30, 2016, http://blogs.timesofisrael.com/why-jihad-and-neo-nazis-embrace-brexit-and-bullshit-9-0/, Clemens Heni, "Germany's Hot New Party Thinks America Is 'Run by Zionists,'" *Tablet Magazine*, August 1, 2016, http://www.tabletmag.com/jewish-news-and-politics/209243/germanys-hot-new-party.

[105] ibid; See also Ian Johnson, *A Mosque in Munich: Nazis, the CIA, and the Rise of the Muslim Brotherhood in the West* (Boston and New York: Houghton Mifflin Harcourt, 2010); see also the monograph of Stefan Meining, Eine Moschee in Deutschland. Nazis, Geheimdienste und der Aufstieg des politischen Islam im Westen, Munich: C.H. Beck 2011 [Nazis, Secret Sevices, and the rise of political Islam in the West].

[106] See *Decision by German Federal Administrative Court*, January 25, 2006, http://lexetius.com/2006,604?version=drucken.

[107] John Rosenthal, "Germany Does Not Ban Hezbollah TV," *Pajamas Media*, November 26, 2008, http://pajamasmedia.com/blog/germany-does-not-ban-hezbollah-tv/?singlepage=true.

[108] "Salafistisches Islamseminar in der Taiba – Moschee (ehemals Al-Quds-Moschee), April 9-11,2010 [Salafist Islam seminar in Taliba mosque (former al-Quds-mosque) in Hamburg, April 9-11, 2010]," hamburg.de, April 28, 2010, http://www.hamburg.de/schlagzeilen/2231544/salafismusseminar-fhh-hamburg.html.

[109] "Die 9/11-Moschee ist dicht [9/11 mosque in Hamburg has been shut down]," *Tageszeitung* (Berlin), August 9, 2010, http://www.taz.de/1/leben/alltag/artikel/1/beruehmte-moschee-ist-dicht/.

[110] Statement by the Organizers of the German Islam Conference, May 15, 2010, http://www.deutsche-islam-konferenz.de/cln_117/nn_1319098/SubSites/DIK/DE/DieDIK/NeueTeilnehmer/neue-teilnehmer-node.html?__nnn=true.

[111] vgl.: http://www.deutschlandfunk.de/zehn-jahre-islamkonferenz-die-bundesregierung-hofiert-die.720.de.html?dram:article_id=367026 (eingesehen: 28.09.2016)

[112] Guido Steinberg, *Im Visier von al-Qaida: Deutschland braucht eine Anti-Terror-Strategie* [In the Sights of Al-Qaeda: Germany Needs an Anti-Terror Strategy] (Hamburg: edition Körber Stiftung, n.d.), http://www.koerber-stiftung.de/fileadmin/user_upload/edition/pdf/leseproben/978-3-89684-139-1_001-012_01.pdf.

[113] „Syrer feiern Festnahme des Terrorverdächtigen", SpiegelOnline, October 11, 2016, http://www.spiegel.de/politik/deutschland/chemnitz-wie-syrer-bei-der-festnahme-des-terrorverdaechtigen-halfen-a-1116031.html

[114] Statement by the German Government, May 10, 2016, http://dip21.bundestag.de/dip21/btd/18/083/1808382.pdf.

[115] Ibid.

[116] "Verfassungsschutz: IS falsch eingeschätzt," April 10, 2016, http://www.tagesschau.de/inland/verfassungsschutz-is-101.html

[117] "Syrer bringt die Polizei zum festgesetzten Terrorverdächtigen", https://www.welt.de/politik/deutschland/article158660909/Syrer-bringt-die-Polizei-zum-festgesetzten-Terrorverdaechtigen.html; https://www.welt.de/politik/deutschland/article158724916/Dschaber-al-Bakr-hat-Selbstmord-begangen.html.

[118] „Flucht von Anis Amri 77 Stunden quer durch Europa," January 5, 2017, http://www.spiegel.de/politik/ausland/anis-amri-stationen-seiner-flucht-durch-europa-a-1128683.html; „Fall Anis Amri Verpasste Chancen," January 3, 2017, https://www.tagesschau.de/inland/fall-amri-verpasste-chance

Italy

Quick Facts

Population: 62,007,540 (July 2016 est.)

Area: 301, 340 sq km

Ethnic Groups: Italian (includes small clusters of German-, French-, and Slovene-Italians in the north and Albanian-Italians and Greek-Italians in the south)

Religions: Christian 80% (overwhelming Roman Catholic with very small groups of Jehova Witnesses and Protestants), Muslims (about 700,000 but growing), Atheists and Agnostics 20%

Government Type: Republic

GDP (official exchange rate): $1.816 trillion (2015 est.)

Map and Quick Facts courtesy of the CIA World Factbook (December 16, 2016)

Overview

While Italy has experienced a surge in Muslim immigration over the past two years as a result of the Syrian civil war and a wave of African migration, Islam in both its moderate and radical forms is already a significant presence in the country. The Union of Islamic Communities and Organizations of Italy (UCOII) has been at the forefront of the debate for the representation of the highly fragmented Italian Muslim community. With regard to jihadist *activities, Italy remained simply a logistical base until October 2009, when an attempted bombing by a Libyan radical in Milan shattered popular illusions that the country was safe from extremist attacks. The event sparked significant public debate and the Italian government has slowly begun to strengthen anti-terrorism and surveillance laws in an effort to respond more effectively to Islamism as a political and societal force.*

ISLAMIST ACTIVITY

Italy's Muslim community is extremely diverse and fragmented. Those characteristics, combined with Sunni Islam's intrinsic lack of clerical hierarchy, cause it to suffer from weak internal cohesion and a low level of organization. These characteristics are reflected in the community's chronic inability to produce a unified leadership. Twenty years after the first significant wave of Muslim immigration, Italy's Muslim community is characterized by the presence of many organizations, none of which can legitimately claim to represent more than a fraction of it. Moreover, the relationships among these organizations are often characterized by sharp disagreements and even personal hatreds, leaving the country's Muslims deprived of a unified leadership.

The Italian Islamist panorama, while not as sophisticated as that of many northern European countries, is quite heterogeneous. The one group that has repeatedly made a claim to the leadership of the country's Muslim community is the Union of the Islamic Communities and Organizations of Italy, or UCOII. The union traces its origins to the Union of Muslim Students in Italy (USMI), a small organization of Muslim students that was created in Perugia and other university cities at the end of the 1960s.[1] Comprised mostly of Jordanian, Syrian and Palestinian students, the USMI's ideology was close to the positions of the Muslim Brotherhood.[2] By the second half of the 1980s, when the first notable wave of North African immigrants arrived in Italy, a student organization such as the USMI could no longer satisfy the needs of the new, large Muslim population. In January 1990, representatives of USMI, six mosques from six Italian cities, and 32 individuals formed the UCOII.

Since its founding, the UCOII has been extremely active on the political scene, attempting to become the main, if not the only, Muslim interlocutor of the Italian state. The UCOII has managed to achieve an important position within the Muslim community, thanks to the significant degree of control it exercises over Italian mosques. While its claim to control 85 percent of Italy's mosques is difficult to verify independently, it is undeniable that the UCOII plays a predominant role in the life of Italy's practicing Muslim community and that many mosques are, to varying degrees, linked to it.[3]

While today the organization has no formal ties to the Muslim Brotherhood or any affiliated outfit in the Middle East, its worldview is still inspired by the group's ideology.[4] Like most other Brotherhood-inspired organizations throughout Europe, the UCOII aims at swaying the Muslim population of Italy to its interpretation of Islam through the activities of its capillary network of mosques. Given the lack of other social structures on Italian territory, many Muslim immigrants seeking the comfort of familiar communities congregate in its mosques, which are often seen more as community centers than simply places of worship. The UCOII seeks to use its virtual monopoly over mosques to spread its ideology and exercise what Italian expert on Islam Renzo Guolo has defined as a "diffuse cultural hegemony" over the country's Muslim community.[5] Taking advantage of the community's considerable fragmentation, the UCOII has become the most visible, vocal and organized voice of Italy's Muslims. In terms of representation to the outside world, it can be said that control of the Italian Muslim community has been assumed by an active minority, which has prevailed easily over an unorganized silent majority.[6]

Aside from the UCOII, other Islamist outfits operating in the country, albeit only marginally, are *Hizb ut-Tahrir*, the transnational pan-Islamist Sunni movement, and *Tablighi Jamaat*, the Islamic missionary movement that intelligence agencies worldwide suspect of having been infiltrated by radicals.[7] The Moroccan movement Justice and Charity also has a significant influence on several mosques in northern Italy.[8] Finally, two Shi'a organizations, Naples-based *Ahl al-Bayt* and its Rome-based spin-off, *Imam Mahdi*, have attracted the attention of authorities because of their radical positions and because many of their members are Italian converts with a past association to militant right wing groups.[9] All of these groups and movements operate with various degrees of sophistication and success, competing among themselves and with non-Islamist organizations for influence in the virgin territory that is Islam in Italy.

Due to its activism and association with Italy's mosques, UCOII acts as the main representative for Italy's Muslims. However, the decentralized nature of Italy's Muslim community has led to recent rifts in representation of Islam to the Italian government. For example, in May 2016 the Italian Islamic Confederation, a Rome-based group of most Moroccan immigrants, moved forward in requesting formal recognition from the state as the main Muslim representative despite UCOIIs consistent –although unsuccessful-requests. Another group, the Italian Islamic Religious Community, based in Milan, has also made several unsuccessful requests for recognition but has also failed in both representing the Italian Muslim community as well as gaining state recognition for the religion in general.[10]

The battle that takes place for the control of Islamic places of worship and, more generally, for influence over Italian Muslims, is something that Italian authorities can only watch from afar. Authorities have recently realized this dissonance and in early 2016, Italian interior Minister Angelino Alfano announced he was establishing a council of relations with for Italian Muslims, with the goal of establishing an "Italian Islam." This council will be made up of Islamic religion and culture experts with the state goal of improving integration of Italy's Muslims into the larger Italian cultural community.[11]

In addition, *jihadist* networks have existed in Italy since the late 1980s, though seldom have they targeted the country. Italy historically has been used by various *jihadist* outfits as a logistical base for acquiring false documents, obtaining weapons, and raising funds. This traditional use of Italian territory appeared to change on October 12, 2009, when Mohammad Game, a legal immigrant from Libya, detonated an explosive device hidden on his person at the gates of the Santa Barbara military base in Milan. The attack seriously injured him and lightly injured the *carabiniere* (a member of the Italian paramilitary police) who tried to stop him.

The ensuing investigation revealed that Game had recently become more religious and political. Acquaintances described how he had frequently stated that Italian troops should have left Afghanistan, framing his diatribes in increasingly religious terms. Game reportedly made similar remarks to the ambulance personnel that transported him to the hospital after the attack. Within a few days, authorities arrested two men, an Egyptian and a Libyan, who reportedly had helped Game in his plan. Forty kilograms of the same chemical substances used by Game in the attack were also retrieved in a basement to which the men had access.

Prior to October 12th, Game and his accomplices had begun to attend services at Milan's Islamic Cultural Institute (Viale Jenner mosque), a place that has been at the center of terrorism investigations for almost 20 years. Yet the men did not appear to have acted under the direction of, or even in remote cooperation with, any established group. To the contrary, their characteristics, from their sudden radicalization to the lack of sophistication of their *modus operandi,* resemble that of the homegrown networks that have become common in most European countries but that had not yet then appeared in Italy.

However, the growing number of immigrants and refugees arriving in Italy over the past few years have put some strain on multicultural co-exisistance, or *coestenza*. Muslims in Italy are not isolated and assimilate more seamlessly then in France, for example, which has historically lead to less radicalization and therefore less attacks. Nonetheless, with almost 200,000 migrants from predominantly Muslim countries such as Libya, and Egypt, and the expected influx of Syrian and Iraqi refugees as the EU works with Turkey to discourage arrivals into Greece, Italian citizens and politicians alike are growing concerned about the fiscal and security implications of the migrants. Recent attacks in Paris, Brussels and Germany have only heightened the concerns that radicalized individuals who arrive in Italy may choose to stay.[12]

ISLAMISM AND SOCIETY

Traditionally a country of emigration rather than immigration, Italy only began to attract small numbers of immigrants in the 1970s, with the majority coming from the Philippines and Latin America. The Muslim presence was limited to diplomatic personnel from Muslim countries, a few businessmen and some students. Those numbers increased significantly in the 1980s, when immigrants from North and Sub-Saharan Africa began to choose Italy as their initial or final destination in their migration to Europe. Immigration has peaked since the mid-1990s, and, according to Italy's official census bureau (ISTAT), as of January 2016, there were 5,026,153 foreign citizens residing in Italy.[13] While no exact data on the number of Muslims living in Italy exists, most estimates put the number between one and two million, corresponding to about 2.5 percent of the population.[14]

> [1] Various features characterize Italy's Muslim community, starting with its significant ethnic diversity. The two countries that have consistently contributed the largest number of Muslim immigrants to Italy are Morocco (28.5 percent) and Albania (20.5 percent).[15] Most other Muslims living in Italy come from Tunisia, Senegal, Egypt, Bangladesh, Pakistan, Algeria, Bosnia and Nigeria, contributing to the ethnically diverse community. This ethnic diversity will only grow due to the almost 200,000 migrants who arrived in Italy between January and November 2016, with 21 percent coming from Nigeria, 12 percent from Eritrea, 7 percent from Guinea, Côte d'Ivoire, and The Gambia, 6 percent from Senegal, 5 percent from Mali, Sudan, Bangladesh and 4 percent from Somalia.[16]

Only in the sectarian aspect is Italy's Muslim community quite homogeneous—more than 95 percent of Italy's Muslims are Sunni.[17] Other distinctive characteristics of Italy's Muslim population when compared to other European Muslim communities are its higher number of non-citizens and illegal immigrants, higher percentage of males, and higher level of geographic dispersion.[18]

If there is one certainty about the future of Islam in Italy, it is that its presence will only grow. The influx of immigrants from North and Sub-Saharan African seems to be virtually unstoppable, given migration patterns and socio-economic conditions in Africa. Italy received about 154,000 refugees in 2015 and is projected to receive 170,000 refugees by the end of 2016, 85% of whom come from Africa.[19] Moreover, in the next few years, Italy will start to see second-generation Muslim immigrants, like most other European countries already have. Many of them will hold Italian citizenship and, furthermore, the number of Muslims carrying an Italian passport will also increase through marriages and conversions.

It seems clear that Islam is destined to have a more visible and stable presence in the country and this is already evident in the impressive increase of Islamic cultural centers throughout Italy. According to Maria Bombardieri, the author of *Mosques of Italy*, Italy only has eight official mosques that are "intended as standalone structures… but there are about 800 cultural centers and musalla, which are informal prayer rooms, often housed in garages, basements, and warehouses." These cultural centers serve as proxies for mosques and provide Muslims in Italy with a place to worship as well as serve as a place to hold cultural and educational meetings.[20]

The predominance of the UCOII at the organizational level has strong repercussions on the relationship between the Italian state and the Muslim community and the legal recognition of Islam, a source of major political controversies. The Italian Constitution (Article 19) gives all citizens the right to freely practice and proselytize for any religion (unless its rites are deemed to be against morality). All religions are free to organize themselves and, according to Article 8, their relationship with the state is regulated by law, based on agreements signed by the state with the representatives of each religious community. The Catholic religion enjoys a separate and privileged treatment, which was negotiated by the Vatican and the Italian state in 1929 and then incorporated in the republican Constitution of 1948. In order to be recognized and receive legal and financial benefits similar to those of the Catholic religion, all other religions have to sign an agreement (known in Italian as *intesa*) with the government, which regulates mutual rights and obligations.

Over the last 25 years, various religious communities have done so. Islam, which is *de facto* the country's second largest religion, has not yet been recognized by the Italian state as a religion.[21] While the opposition of some political forces to the recognition of Islam has in some cases interfered with the process, the main reason for this seemingly paradoxical situation is to be found in the lack of a unified leadership in the Italian Muslim community. In order to sign the *intesa* the Italian government needs to find a representative of the Muslim community, something the Italian Muslim community so far has been unable to produce. *Intesa* proposals submitted over the years by various groups that entertain cordial relationships with the Italian state have been turned down, as none of the applicants were deemed able to legitimately claim to represent the majority of Italian Muslims.[22]

Conversely, the Italian state has experienced the opposite problems when dealing with the proposals of *intesa* submitted by the UCOII since 1990. The UCOII seems to be, *prima facie*, the Muslim organization with the largest following and with characteristics that make it the closest of all Italian Muslim organizations to the notion of representation that Italian authorities are looking for. Yet its *intesa* drafts have been turned down because authorities are skeptical of the UCOII's nature and also deemed the draft to be "too ambitious" in asking for state recognition of Islamic festivities, Islamic education in public schools, legal recognition of Muslim weddings celebrated as well as room for Muslims in Italian television.[23] Given these dynamics, Islam is not recognized as an official religion, a situation that creates practical difficulties and generates the perception among many Italian Muslims that authorities discriminate against Islam.

ISLAMISM AND THE STATE

Even though small clusters of *jihadist* groups made plans for attacks against targets in Milan, Cremona, Bologna and Rome in the past, Italian authorities were clear in stating, as of early 2009, that the primary use of Italian soil for radical Islamists has been logistical in nature and that there were no indications of networks planning attacks in Italy or from Italy against other countries.[24] An intelligence report submitted to the Italian Parliament in February 2009 cautioned that the threat in Italy was "multifaceted, volatile, and prone to sudden shifts," but the homegrown threat was then not yet apparent in the country.[25] Italy remains a logistical base for extremist groups, as evidenced by Italian Naval intercepting over 20 ships containing drugs and money intended for territories claimed by ISIS over the period of 2013 to 2015.[26] Furthermore, the suspect of the 2016 Christmas Market attack in Germany, Anis Amri, is rumored to have been radicalized in and Italian prison yet did not carry out his attack there. In a recent interview, terrorist expect Marco Lombardi identified areas around Milan, such as Bergamo and Brescia, where Amri was found and killed, as Islamist hotspots. Lombardi noted that while Italy has relatively few radicalized people because the country has not yet reached a third generation of immigrants, where most radicalization has occurred in countries such as France, and credited Italian intelligence for recognizing early signs of radicalization.[27]

Mohammad Game's homegrown terrorist attack in Milan changed that view. The episode came as a shock to Italian authorities, who for the first time were forced to deal with a case of homegrown Islamist terrorism. In 2009, Former Interior Minister Roberto Maroni publicly stated the Italian government's reassessment of the role of *jihadist* cells operating in the country. He said:

> Until the action in Milan, the cells identified in Italy were involved in fundraising and recruitment. We now believe that there are cells that form, fundraise and train to carry out attacks in Italy. We are not yet at the 'homegrown terrorism' we have seen in the United Kingdom and Spain, but we are very close to it.[28]

Since 2013, authorities have seen a relative growth in homegrown networks in Italy. Growth in online activities by *jihadist* networks caused Italian authorities to crack down on any active members of such groups and punish them under article 270 *quinquies* of the penal code, which criminalizes any facilitation of terrorist training and provides precedent for prosecuting cases where materials are exchanged online.[29] Two notable cases of homegrown radicalization occurred in the province of Brescia. The first case is that of Mohamed Jarmoune, a Moroccan-born man living in Niardo, who spent his time on the internet disseminating *jihadist* materials and networking with *jihadist* sympathizers. Italian authorities monitored Jarmoune for months and finally arrested him in March 2012 after he had narrowed in on Milan's largest synagogue as a potential target. His arrest resulted in a prison sentence of over five years, starting in May 2013, for disseminating terrorist propaganda.[30]

The other Brescia case did not result in a prison sentence. The Jarmoune case led authorities to Anas El Abboubi, another active participant in *jihadist* networks online. Connecting with other *jihadist* sympathizers allowed El Abboubi to learn how to start an Italy-based extremist group, which he eventually tried to do with his blog called Sharia4Italy. El Abboubi was eventually arrested after Italian authorities noticed his militant online presence as well as his searches for apparent targets around the Brescia province. However, the court ruled that he had not violated article 270 *quinquies* and released him.[31] Finally, the previously mentioned 2016 Germany Christmas market attacker, Anis Amri, is said to have been radicalized in Italy. Of Tunisian descent, Amri came to Italy without any identification in 2011 and, after serving 4 years in prison for damaging state property, was kicked out of the Italy in 2015. After Amri was shot and killed in Milan, a video emerged of Amri pledging allegiance to ISIS and its leader Abu Bakr al-Baghdadi.[32]

Unlike the majority of individuals who have been involved in radical activities in Italy before, both Jarmoune and El Abboubi grew up in Italy and were, by all standards, well integrated into Italian society. Both also ran a series of websites and Facebook pages where they shared *jihadist* propaganda and instructions to build explosives and use weapons. The profile of the accused and the dynamics of their networks are quintessentially homegrown, arguably signifying a shift in the *jihadist* threat to Italy.

This evolution worries counterterrorism practitioners, who realize that in tackling the nascent homegrown threat they will not be able to extensively rely on deportations, arguably one of the main legal tools used by Italian authorities in their twenty-year fight against *jihadism*. But most policymakers and the public at large have, for the most part, not yet conceptualized the idea that *jihadism* is not just an external threat but, increasingly, an internal one.

This slowness in grasping the evolution of the phenomenon is not surprising. Unlike most other European countries, which, since 9/11, have engaged in a sustained debate about Islam and Islamism, Italy has followed a different trajectory. As disparate international (terrorist attacks in other countries, global crises) and domestic (the occasional arrest of *jihadist* militants) events appear on the radar, they generate a heated domestic debate that often becomes highly politicized and lacks nuance. In response to these events, the Italian government has begun to strengthen legislation, particularly the Criminal Code, in order to more effectively monitor potential militant or extremist activity. On February 18, 2015 Decree-Law No. 7 entered into effect, calling for stronger legislative and regulatory means for Italian police and armed forces to better anticipate and prevent extremist acts. The law strengthens the surveillance powers of police, and outlines new reforms for criminal punishments for those persons of group of persons identified as terrorists. The law also recognizes the criminality of foreign fighters, those individuals who support a terrorist organization and participate in conflicts abroad. Finally, the law gives the Ministry of the Interior the right to maintain a running list of websites and forums that may be used for recruitment for extremist activities.[33]

To be fair, the violent aspects of Islamism in Italy have, for the most part, been extensively and effectively monitored by Italian authorities since the early 1990s. Over the last 15 years, dozens of complex investigations have brought to light *jihadist* networks throughout the peninsula.[34] The combination of experienced security services and law enforcement agencies, proactive investigative magistrates, and adequate legal framework, such as the 2015 legislation mentioned above, have allowed Italian authorities to be among the most aggressive and successful in Europe in dismantling *jihadist* networks, uncovering extensive links spanning throughout Europe and the Middle East. While these successes have not always been followed by convictions and long sentences once the cases went to trial, it is fair to say that Italian authorities have been quite efficient in keeping in check violent Islamist networks.

Things are quite different, however, when the focus shifts from traditional counter-terrorism measures to a broader frame of analysis. While many European countries have been implementing or at least discussing plans to stem radicalization among their Muslim communities, Italy is severely lagging in even rationally approaching the issue. Moreover, the Italian debate over forms of non-violent Islamism has often shifted, with some notable exceptions, between schizophrenic overreaction, naïve whitewashing, and, most commonly, utter lack of interest. In most other Western European countries, excesses on both sides of the debate, from conflating Islamism with Islam to labeling as racist any question raised over aspects of Islamism, have slowly been replaced by more nuanced and balanced positions. Italy's public debate on the issue, on the other hand, seems to be only occasional and far less mature.

Endnotes

[2] UCOII, "History of UCOII," n.d., http://www.islam-ucoii.it/artcomuni.htm.
[3] Stefano Allievi, "I musulmani in Italia: chi sono e come ci vedono [Muslims In Italy: Who They Are And How They See Us]," Limes, iss 3 (2004), 100.
[4] UCOII, "History of UCOII."
[5] Renzo Guolo, Xenofobi e Xenofili: Gli Italiani e l'Islam [Xenophobes And Xenophiles: Italians and Islam] (Bari: Laterza, 2003), 10.
[6] Ibid., 11.
[7] Ibidem, 5-6.
[8] 59th Report of CESIS (Executive Committee for the Intelligence and Security Services) to Parliament, January-May 2007, 71.
[9] Lorenzo Vidino's interviews with Italian government officials and Muslim community leaders, Rome, Italy, February and July 2007.
[10] "Pulsioni antimondialiste e vecchio antisemitismo [Anti-globalist Trends And Old Anti-Semitism]," SISDEGNOSIS Iss. 4 (2005).
[11] Giacomo Galeazzi and Ilario Lombardo, "Making Space for Islam in Catholic Italy," La Stampa (May 30, 2016), http://www.lastampa.it/2016/05/30/esteri/lastampa-in-english/making-space-for-islam-in-catholic-italy-c9w-ShtisWIyPP8NKbi21jN/pagina.html

[12] "Italy Aims to Integrate Muslims and Shape 'Italian Islam,'" The Local IT (January 19, 2016), http://www.thelocal.it/20160119/italy-strives-to-integrate-muslims-and-shape-italian-islam

[13] Katya Adler, "Migration Crisis: Italy Threatened by National Crisis," BBC News (April 19, 2016), http://www.bbc.com/news/world-europe-36080216

[14] Resident Population on 1st January ,ISTAT, http://stra-dati.istat.it/?lang=en

[15] "Table: Muslim Population by Country," Pew Research Center, January 27, 2011, http://www.pewforum.org/2011/01/27/table-muslim-population-by-country/.

[16] Federico Di Leo, "Il nostro Islam in cifre [Our Islam In Numbers]," Limes, Iss. 3 (2004), 123.

[17] "Italy- Sea Arrivals: UNHCR Update #9" UNHCR (November 2016), http://data.unhcr.org/mediterranean/download.php?id=2327

[18] "Mapping the Global Muslim Population: A Report on the Size and Distribution of the World's Muslim Population", Pew Research Center (October 2009): http://www.pewforum.org/files/2009/10/Muslimpopulation.pdf

[19] "The Situation of Muslims in Italy," European Muslim Union (September 2010), http://emunion.eu/emudoc/EMU%20Country%20Report%20Italy%20-%20September%202010.pdf

[20] Phillip Connor, "Italy on track to surpass Greece in refugee arrivals for 2016," Pew Research Center FactTank (November 2, 2016), http://www.pewresearch.org/fact-tank/2016/11/02/italy-on-track-to-surpass-greece-in-refugee-arrivals-for-2016/

[21] Merelli, Annalisa, "There are over 1.6 million Muslims in Italy— and only eight mosques" Quartz, May 4, 2016, http://qz.com/674377/there-are-over-1-6-million-muslims-in-italy-and-only-eight-mosques/

[22] Non-Catholic groups with an accord [with the Italian Government] include the Confederation of Methodist and Waldensian Churches, Seventh-day Adventists, Assemblies of God, Jews, Baptists, Lutherans, Mormons, Orthodox Church of the Constantinople Patriarchate, and the Apostolic Church, the Buddhist Union and Hindus (2013) https://www.state.gov/documents/organization/222441.pdf

[23] Elena Dusi, "Il fantasma della Consulta," Limes, Iss. 4 (2007), 155.

[24] "The Situation of Muslims in Italy," European Muslim Union

[25] Bi-annual report of the security services to the Italian Senate, February 28, 2009. Pp. 56-7. NEED FULL CITE: Sorry I just don't know where the previous author got this

[26] Ibid, 58.

[27] Rukmini Callimachi and Lorenzo Tondo, "Scaling Up a Drug Trade, Straight Through ISIS Turf," The New York Times (September 13, 2016), http://www.nytimes.com/2016/09/14/world/europe/italy-morocco-isis-drug-trade.html

[28] Kersten Knipp, "Does Italy Play a Special Role for Islamic Terrorists?", DW (December 23, 2016), http://www.dw.com/en/does-italy-play-a-special-role-for-islamic-terrorists/a-36897539

[29] "Maroni: In Italia cellule affiliate ad Al Qaeda [Maroni: In Italy Cells Linked To Al Qaeda]," Apcom, November 6, 2009.

[30] Lorenzo Vidino, "The Evolution of Jihadism in Italy: Rise in Homegrown Radicals," Combatting Counterterrorism Center at West Point (November 26, 2013), https://www.ctc.usma.edu/posts/the-evolution-of-jihadism-in-italy-rise-in-homegrown-radicals.

[31] Ibid.

[32] Ibidem.

[33] Sheena McKenzie, "Berlin attack suspect Anis Amri killed in Milan Shootout," CNN (December 23, 2016), http://www.cnn.com/2016/12/23/europe/berlin-christmas-market-attack-suspect-killed-milan/

[34] "Italy: Updated Legislation on Fight Against Terrorism," Law Library of Congress (March 24, 2016), http://www.loc.gov/law/foreign-news/article/italy-updated-legislation-on-fight-against-terrorism/

[35] For an extensive analysis of jihadist networks in Italy, see Lorenzo Vidino, "Islam, Islamism and Jihadism in Italy," Current Trends in Islamist Ideology 7 (2008).

Kosovo

Quick Facts

Population: 1,883,018 (July 2016 est.)

Area: 10,887 sq km

Ethnic Groups: Albanians 93%, other (Bosniaks, Serbs, Turk, Ashkali, Egyptian, Gorani, and Roma) 7%

Religions: Muslim, Serbian Orthodox, Roman Catholic

Government Type: Parliamentary Republic

GDP (official exchange rate): $6.355 billion (2015 est.)

Map and Quick Facts courtesy of the CIA World Factbook (Last Updated November 2016)

Overview

Islam's footprint in Kosovo dates back seven centuries, to the time of the Ottoman conquest. Although much of the ethnic Albanian-majority population practices a moderate form of Islam, the 1999 NATO intervention and subsequent, prolonged UN mission created the conditions for extremist penetration. Due to the unaccountable governance of a supranational organization, numerous Islamic states and fundamentalist-oriented charities were allowed open access to this economically underdeveloped, war-ravaged corner of Europe. The result today is that, while most Kosovars are still moderate, the country has produced the highest number of foreign fighters per capita among European countries joining ISIS and Al Nusra Front, with 125 fighters for every million people.

As a strong U.S. ally keenly aware that it remains dependent on foreign aid, Kosovo has taken legal and police measures to crack down on extremism. An independent state since 2008, Kosovo (which has a 95% Muslim population) has seen in recent years an increasingly heated domestic discussion regarding the place of religion in society and politics.

While foreign Islamist charities left behind numerous new mosques and religious schools, they failed to re-orient most Muslims toward a strict Wahhabi interpretation of the faith. However, some Kosovar Muslims have sharply criticized their moderate counterparts, not to mention Catholics and Protestant missionaries. Protests over church and mosque construction, as well as the wearing of head scarves in schools, have also become politicized issues within the country.

While it has tended to downplay the role of Islam (and Islamic extremism), the Kosovar government is taking steps to deal with security and social issues associated with radicalization, passing laws against foreign fighters and arresting scores of previous or aspiring homegrown jihadists since 2014. While there are specific connections between Kosovo and the Syrian conflict, in the long term the development of education, health and work opportunities for local youth is probably the greatest challenge Kosovo faces in countering violent extremism. At the same time, the ethnic linkages between Kosovars at home and those in Western European countries has resulted (and will result) in police actions elsewhere on the Continent that in some way involve Kosovo.

ISLAMIST ACTIVITY

Today's Islamist activity in Kosovo was expedited by the 1999 NATO intervention, which replaced Serbian rule with a porous international administration that was preoccupied with matters of inter-ethnic violence, organized crime and institution-building. Relatively little attention was paid to the possibility of Islamic extremism, in part because the narrative of an ethnic nationalist liberation struggle allegedly precluded this possibility. However, estimates made in 2006 that anticipated Kosovar participation in future *jihadist* activities have been proven abundantly correct.[2] The estimates for the number of foreign fighters from Kosovo vary widely, with the Kosovar government claiming an almost complete stoppage of *jihadists* exiting the country.[3] The most recent reliable statistics put the number at some 232 Kosovo-born fighters had joined the ranks of *jihadist* groups, making Kosovo the highest exporter of *jihadists* per capita in Europe.[4]

Several factors account for this trend, not least a poor economy, stalled political and institutional development, a demographic imbalance between males and females and low youth employment rates.[5] Ultimately, though, the participation of Kosovo Muslims in modern *jihad* owes to the support of foreign Islamic donors, who sought to build mosques, schools and NGOs in the country following the 1999 NATO intervention. Although many of these groups have since been closed or voluntarily left, they did provide indoctrination and financial support for impoverished Kosovars at a key post-conflict time. Their influence has lingered and, as we are seeing, has created an extremist fringe that took on a leading role in the Syrian conflict.

Primarily, funding for the wartime resistance, the Kosovo Liberation Army (KLA), came from other means—from the personal donations of patriotic diaspora Albanians, and from Albanian mafia structures involved with heroin distribution in Europe.[6] These smuggling rings were powerful and well-entrenched; over a decade later, in 2011 and 2012, European police in Germany, Switzerland, France and Italy were still combating them.[7]

Cooperation between ethnic Albanian drug cartels and ISIS is today a growing concern. Kosovars have historically been involved in heroin smuggling from Asia and some cocaine smuggling from South America, along with Albanians. But, as with Albania, they are most active through their extensive diaspora networks in Western Europe. After a large-scale police operation to destroy vast cannabis plantations in southern Albania, the business became fragmented, with older clans replaced by more violent adherents to radical Islam. A January 2016 report named Kosovo's most infamous ISIS member, Lavdrim Muhaxheri, as the key link between Albanian drug operations and ISIS recruitment. This is said to mark an increasingly violent and religiously-oriented drug-smuggling outfit in the region, with ties to the Italian and other mafias.[8]

Muhaxheri (born circa 1987) is the best-known Kosovar *jihadist* associated with ISIS (ironically, he previously worked for both the UN administration in Kosovo and NATO in Afghanistan before being radicalized in the small south Kosovo village of Kacanik in 2012).[9] Since 2012, he has appeared in several propaganda videos for ISIS, including one showing him beheading a captive. In an unsettling attempt to justify the crime to Kosovar nationalists, Muhaxheri claimed that he had done "the same thing" as the nationalist KLA had done against the Serbs, in 1999.[10]

Muhaxheri has led ISIS' ethnic-Albanian brigade, and its Albanian-language propaganda campaign. He was also the ideological protégé of the (now jailed) radical Kosovar imam Zekerija Qazimi, as was another field commander, Ridvan Haqifi.[11] In August 2014, Interpol put Muhaxheri on the organization's wanted list. U.S. Secretary of State John Kerry blacklisted the Kosovar *jihadist* as a threat to American national security in the Federal Register on October 2, 2014.[12] Lavdrim Muhaxheri was widely speculated to have died in battle, but new photos indicated that he was alive as of December 2015.[13]

By May 2016, the number of Kosovars (including women and children) who had joined militant groups in Syria and Iraq had reached at least 314 persons, not counting pre-2014 fighters, according to a *New York Times* investigation. This report found that the development and mobilization of a Kosovar *jihadist* force had been accomplished by a "corps of extremist clerics and secretive associations funded by Saudi Arabia and other conservative Arab gulf states using an obscure, labyrinthine network of donations from charities, private individuals and government ministries."[14] While

Kosovo's interior ministry stated in August 2016 that no new recruits were believed to have departed in the past year, some 50 Kosovars had died in battle and another 120 had returned.[15]

Detailed discussion of Islamist activity in Kosovo must begin with an acknowledgement of the complexity and singularity of prevailing local conditions, which cumulatively have created a friendly environment for a certain kind of Islamism to take root. Powerful clan structures and pervasive organized crime have long fueled allegations of criminality and corruption on the part of local and international leaders alike. Frustration among the general public after 1999 was also driven by the perceived lack of political and economic change in the post-Yugoslav "transition" period. The unaccountable and uninvolved nature of an international UN mission that changed staff frequently and had no long-term responsibilities for Kosovo's well-being also hindered prospects of real change.

Kosovo has also been kept in limbo due to a continuing political impasse with Serbia, which refuses to recognize Kosovo's independence. Local and foreign diplomacy since 2000 has thus been almost completely preoccupied with big-picture status issues. With solving this issue seen as a necessary prerequisite to other things, the economy and social services have been neglected. In this situation, Islamists have presented their ideology as a long-term social solution.

The first foreign Islamist actors came to Kosovo in 1999 via in an assortment of Islamic charities. The most important was a Saudi government umbrella organization, the Saudi Joint Commission for the Relief of Kosovo and Chechnya (SJCRKC). It was matched by its official Kuwaiti counterpart, the Kuwaiti Joint Relief Committee (KJRC). Along with then-returning Albanian refugees, representatives of these groups (and the Islamic charities organized within them) entered Kosovo from neighboring Albania, where Albanian and U.S. authorities had been monitoring, and working to control, suspected international terrorist suspects. The Saudis initially allocated over $22.5 million for the rebuilding or new construction of mosques and schools, and also for supporting orphans in Kosovo.[16] However, Kosovo investigators of the now-closed charity found in 2016 that most of the Saudi money could not be accounted for, and that very little has ever actually been given to help orphans.[17]

Aside from charities, a major opportunity for foreign Islamic development, recruitment and intelligence activity came as a result of the broad participation of many nations (including major Muslim states) in the interim UN Mission in Kosovo (UNMIK), and the Kosovo Force (KFOR) peacekeeping units authorized by UN Security Council Resolution 1244. Muslim states like Saudi Arabia, Malaysia, Pakistan, Egypt and Turkey used this rare "official cover" in a previously closed part of Europe to develop their own interests. In October 1999 alone, Saudi sponsors donated 200,000 copies of the Koran in Albanian/Arabic translation as part of efforts to promulgate the Kingdom's official brand of Islamism in the Balkans.[18]

Although the volume of such personnel would gradually diminish over time, and in some cases disappear completely with the progressive downsizing of the UN mission, Kosovo was clearly vulnerable to foreign Islamist penetration in the early years of post-Yugoslav rule. Kosovo's internationally uncertain status also meant a no-visa policy, and with essentially open borders, Kosovo became Europe's primary "safe zone" for foreign radicals. Pressure from the EU – which Kosovo hopes to join someday – led the government to plan to impose visas on over 80 countries in 2013. But, as of August 2016, citizens from over 100 countries (including most of the Gulf states) still did not need visas to enter Kosovo.[19]

From early on, Western experts raised concerns over the arrival of Wahhabism. However, Kosovar Islamic leaders tended to maintain that the appeal of such worldviews was limited and represented no threat to the traditional fabric of Islamic society.[20] Indeed, overly aggressive Wahhabi sponsors angered local Albanian Muslims on a number of occasions, such as when they desecrated tombs and demolished parts of shrines belonging to the traditional Bektashi order of Islam—a more relaxed, Shi'ite-influenced hold-over from Ottoman times that is considered heretical by many Sunnis (including the Wahhabis).[21] This aggressive strategy caused a backlash among local Muslims, leading Wahhabi groups to cease their destruction of "heretical" structures and simply concentrate on building new mosques in the distinctive Arab style.

The dynamic of Islamist activity in Kosovo has changed gradually along with the country's political and social situation. The chronically antagonistic relations between Albanians and Serbs have largely been ethnic in character but, as a 2010 U.S. Department of State report noted, "the close link between ethnicity and religion [have] made it difficult to determine if events were motivated by ethnic or religious animosity."[22]

The motivations behind these animosities and related attacks are indeed difficult to ascertain, though there has undeniably been a religious aspect to violence on both sides. According to Albanian sources, 216 of the 513 mosques that existed in Kosovo in the year 2000 had been damaged in fighting during the 1990s, while over 80 Christian churches and mosques were attacked by Albanians (*after*, not before, the arrival of 40,000 NATO peacekeepers in July 1999).[23] And there is no question that the major post-war conflagration—the country's March 2004 riots, in which 50,000 Albanians targeted Serbs and foreign nationals across Kosovo—had an Islamic aspect as well. For example, after over 30 Serbian Orthodox churches were attacked, DVDs of the destruction were soon being circulated in radical Western European mosques; furthermore, a confidential NATO document subsequently indicated that the alleged masterminds of these pre-planned riots had had ties to Hezbollah and al-Qaeda.[24]

Whereas Kosovo's traditional antagonisms were ethnic in nature (albeit with religious overtones), recent years have seen an emergence of intra-ethnic tensions within the Albanian Muslim community, as well as hostility from Albanian Muslims toward Albanian Catholics and toward local and foreign members of the Catholic and Protestant denominations. This is due to two factors: first, the steady decline of the Serbian minority and Kosovo's 2008 declaration of independence, both of which minimized the Serbs' traditional status as the primary oppressive force restricting the freedom of Albanians; and second, the internal struggles for control between rival Muslim factions, as a young generation trained abroad or exposed to foreign versions of Islam openly contests the worship practices of their elders.

There is potential for this intra-ethnic divide to worsen, as hardline Muslims have expressed anger over the government's perceived preference for promoting a Christian agenda.[25] The enormous Cathedral of the Blessed Mother Teresa occupies a square in downtown Pristina, commemorating the ethnic Albanian nun who is considered an Albanian national hero. She was canonized on September 4, 2016, which will help the Vatican develop its "brand" in Kosovo. The Catholic Church also runs numerous charities and NGOs, as well as a Jesuit boarding school, all of which cause indignation among Muslim extremists.[26]

While Catholicism has an even longer history than Islam does in Kosovo, Islamist activity has also targeted non-native Christian groups. Unsurprisingly, evangelical Christian attempts to convert local Muslims, particularly in more violence-prone provincial areas, have provoked a severe response. Protestants have in the past reported threats and intimidation from local Islamists; in one high-profile case, personal data on members of the Protestant community was reproduced by up to 100 Islamic websites. Subsequently, in May 2010, a missionary reported being physically attacked by Islamists in Prizren, a long-acknowledged center of Islamism in Kosovo.[27] Further, in 2011 Protestants in western Kosovo also complained that dubious legal rulings and local Muslim pressure prevented them opening a church and a cemetery; this restriction "frequently resulted in Protestants being buried in Muslim graveyards and Muslim clerics performing funeral services for Protestants," reported the U.S. State Department in its *International Religious Freedom Report for 2011*. The report also discussed several cases of attacks against Serbian Orthodox shrines and the desecration of a Jewish cemetery in the same year.[28]

More recently, in October 2015, two Serbian churches (including one in the ISIS-linked village of Kacanik) were vandalized. And, in early 2016, police detained four gun-toting men near the Serbian Decani Monastery in western Kosovo. Near that time, explosive material was also found outside a mosque that was known to be critical of *Wahhabi* extremists.[29]

Indeed, tensions within the Muslim community in Kosovo over control of mosques and other religious institutions have long been witnessed, and tend to figure in the longer narrative of alienation and radicalization that finally manifested in the exodus of Kosovar *jihadists* to Syria. For any early example, an elderly *imam* in the Drenica area was attacked in January 2009 by bearded Wahhabis in an act of intimidation, revealing their desire to "take over" the mosque.[30] When mosques have been unavailable, Islamists (especially during the UNMIK period) often appropriate public facilities such as sports halls for fundamentalist preaching. For example, the State Department's 2009 *Country Reports on Terrorism* noted that Kosovo police and the UN Mission in Kosovo "continued to monitor suspected terrorist activity," believing that several NGOs were involved in "suspicious activities." These authorities were also trying "to prevent extremists from using non-governmental organizations to gain a foothold in Kosovo," and "to prevent misuse of facilities for events that had no consent from the relevant religious community."[31]

Even before the Syrian war, Kosovar Albanians were involved in both terrorist cells and organized crime.[32] In the United States, these extremists were implicated in the foiled 2008 attack on Fort Dix in New Jersey,[33] and in a similarly foiled plot against the U.S. Marine Corps base in Quantico, Virginia.[34] In 2012, the shadowy 'Kosovo Hackers Security' group made headlines when it successfully infiltrated the U.S. National Weather Service's computer networks; this was reportedly meant to be "a protest against the U.S. policies that target Muslim countries."[35]

ISLAMISM AND SOCIETY

A 2015 estimate pegged Kosovo's population at almost 1.9 million.[36] Ethnic Albanians comprise 92% of this population, which is on average one of the youngest in any European country. However, the poor economy has led many Kosovars to look for options abroad, and there is a large Kosovar diaspora in Western Europe. Kosovars and Albanians sought to take advantage of the 2015 migrant crisis for economic reasons, comprising one of the largest numbers of asylum-seekers by nationality. Their asylum attempts, however, generally failed, and the individuals in question were returned to their homelands. Germany alone received 102,000 ethnic Albanian migrants in 2015.[37] Despite Kosovo's location in the Balkans, it did not receive a significant influx of migrants during the migrant crisis, because it was off the path that most migrants took to enter Europe, known as the Balkan Route. The Balkan Route runs in from Greece through the Vardar Valley corridor in central Macedonia and northwards through Serbia, reaching Hungary and Austria. Since Kosovo was not on the Balkan Route, it was never really impacted by migrant flows that passed through neighboring Macedonia and Serbia.

Muslims (who include small populations of Roma, Turks, Gorani and Bosniaks) in total are estimated to comprise 95 percent of Kosovo's total population.[38] Approximately three percent of Kosovo's Albanians are Catholic, though this population seems to be increasing, while various foreign Protestant denominations have tried (so far, with less success) to convert Kosovo's Muslims. The beleaguered Serbian Orthodox minority of 120,000 persons is largely concentrated in a few scattered central enclaves, and in more compact northern municipalities around the ethnically divided city of Mitrovica. However, there is also a small Serbian-speaking Slavic Muslim minority, the Gorani, who primarily inhabit the mountainous southwestern area around Dragas, nestled between Macedonia and Albania. The small Roma (Gypsy) minority is mainly Muslim as well, but it is less active, limited by the idiosyncratic Roma lifestyle on the margins of society.

In Kosovo, Islam has played an important role in affecting national identities. The country is often referred to as the "cradle" of the medieval Serbian empire, which left abundant reminders of its presence in the scores of Orthodox Christian churches and monasteries that remain today. However, the area was captured by the Ottoman Turks in the late 14th century, and the Albanian Catholic warlord Skanderbeg (the main national hero) is celebrated today for his resistance to the Turks.

Islam thereafter became the dominant religion, with considerable privileges conferred on those who converted (such as the gradually expanding ethnic Albanian population). During Communist Yugoslav rule, all religions were strictly controlled, while Kosovo's demography underwent two important changes: the Kosovo Albanian population increased even further, and several thousand ethnic Turks and Albanians migrated to Turkey.

The officially recognized Muslim organization in the country is the Islamic Community of Kosovo (in Albanian, *Bashkësia Islame e Kosovës, or BIK*).[39] It is intended to represent the totality of Islam in the country, though there are traditional Bektashi Sufi communities, particularly in western Kosovo, that have certain differences in doctrine and practice. Nevertheless, both the Bektashi and Hanafi Sunni Muslims generally get along and are united by a strong sense of ethnic Albanian nationalism. However, Wahhabi Muslims influenced by foreign ideologies fall outside the structure of the BIK and its control. Their numbers are notoriously difficult to calculate, as there is no strict doctrine or separate institutions governing them; they simply consider themselves "better," more committed Muslims than the rest.

Of Kosovo's approximately 800 mosques, some 240 were built following the 1999 NATO intervention—part of "a deliberate, long-term strategy by Saudi Arabia to reshape Islam in its image, not only in Kosovo but around the world."[40] This mosque-building program and other Islamic activities have been driven not only by the Saudis but by other competing actors like Turkey and Iran. Cumulatively, this rivalry between external powers has damaged social cohesion and led to increasing conservatism. A 2016 study revealed that 57% of Kosovars had greater trust in religious institutions than in state ones, while "Kosovar youth are also becoming increasingly conservative, with their main reference points for spiritual and intellectual guidance being local imams."[41]

As discussed, in the aftermath of the NATO intervention, Muslim charities made extensive efforts in the areas of proselytization, orphan care, Islamic education, banking and loans, and so on. Although their more aggressive efforts met with resistance from Albanians determined to preserve their own traditions and local control, these foreign endeavors have succeeded in some respects. With unemployment remaining high and the social needs of the country's poorest and neediest still often neglected, Islamic groups have sought to style themselves as alternative service providers. Saudi Arabia, Kuwait and other countries thus have built numerous mosques and educational facilities with a clear strategic goal: in the words of one Kosovar commentator, "to create a new generation of loyal Muslims – not (loyal) to Kosovo but to the Islamic international."[42]

Islamists have typically used Islamic NGOs and youth groups to foment protests and shape common policies on these controversial issues. For example, in May and June 2010, Islamist groups organized multiple street protests after a high school student in the town of Ferizaj was expelled for wearing a headscarf. While the Kosovo government has sought to implement strictly secular laws in this regard, a local court gave Islamists room for hope by overturning another similar ban in Vitina. The tension over this issue extends to the workplace, as veiled Muslim women have frequently complained that employers will not hire them.[43]

An indication of the government's concern over religious polarization has been attested to by a new inter-faith body (led by Muslim, Orthodox and Catholic leaders) that meets regularly to discuss better cooperation and references Mother Teresa; though she was born in neighboring Macedonia, the famed nun of Calcutta is considered an ethnic Albanian national hero.[44] The Interfaith Kosovo initiative also holds annual conferences featuring high-profile international speakers, with a common aim of promoting interreligious harmony and confronting extremism; for example, its 2016 event was dedicated to the role of women in countering violent extremism.[45]

Nevertheless, emerging discord between Albanian Muslims and Catholics became apparent in September 2010, when the new Catholic Cathedral of the Blessed Mother Teresa was opened in the capital, Pristina. The building drew the ire of Muslim groups, who chafed at the apparent preferential treatment from the government received by Catholics (who comprise only about 3 percent of the population). They complained with good reason; a 2004 Muslim demand for a grand mosque had been turned down by authorities. Ferid Agani, chairman of the pro-Islamic Justice Party of Kosovo (a small but vocal conservative party which holds three out of Kosovo's 120 parliamentary seats), deemed the refusal "unacceptable," and imams in media testimony derided it as a "political decision."[46] Soon after the Pristina cathedral was opened, threatening graffiti began to appear throughout the city proclaiming that Islamist worship would be conducted in it.[47] Other pro-Islamist figures at the time argued that "fairness" now required a mosque to be built—an argument identical to the one that their co-religionists continue to make throughout the region.

Although the Catholic population of Kosovo is a mere 60,000 persons, it carries disproportionate weight for both historical and contemporary reasons. Before the arrival of the Turks in the late 14th century, Albanians were Catholic. However, as a group, they subsequently converted to Islam for the social benefits granted by the Ottoman conquerors. Therefore, some Albanians tout the idea of "returning" to an "original religion." Furthermore, many believe that becoming Christian will give them a better chance of acceptance in Western Europe[48] — a view again shared by many in the wider Balkan region. In 2005, former Albanian president Alfred Moisiu provoked uproar from Islamist groups following a speech he gave in England in which he stated that Albanians follow a "shallow" sort of Islam, and in fact have deeper Christian roots.[49]

Furthermore, following the erection of the Pristina cathedral, the Vatican upgraded the Catholic Church there to the status of diocese. This action fits a broader trend in recent events indicating the Roman Catholic Church is taking a greater interest in spreading Catholicism in Kosovo. Significantly, on February 10, 2011, the Vatican commissioned its first apostolic delegate to Kosovo, Papal Nuncio in Slovenia Juliusz Janusz. The Church has thus sought to promote Catholicism more strongly against Islamic expansionism.[50] The 2014 visit of Pope Francis to neighboring Albania, and plans for regional celebrations of Mother Teresa's September 2016 canonization, confirm this theory.[51]

Overall, the social and political trends toward increasing Islamic conservatism in Kosovo are not surprising to anyone who has paid close attention to the country since NATO's intervention. Protecting the legacy and righteousness of that intervention has long led U.S. and NATO officials to downplay the presence of Islamism in Kosovo. Western governments in recent years tried to depict Kosovo's brand of Islam as harmless, a sort of "Islam-lite."[52] This narrative has, however, increasingly been challenged by the reality of Kosovar participation in the Syria conflict and related radicalization.

Naturally, the Kosovo government—which aspires to join the EU someday—also wishes to downplay any association with radical Islam. However, as of 2016 contemporary developments and anecdotal evidence point to a new trend toward using Islam as a way to define social identities, ideological beliefs, and cultural choices, and no longer simply as a way of making income, as had been the case with the initial Arab "investment" in Kosovo's people.[53]

ISLAMISM AND THE STATE

In August 2014, Kosovo police arrested 40 people suspected of supporting *jihadists* in Syria and Iraq. In March 2015, the country passed a "foreign fighters" law at the U.S.'s request, as have several other Balkan countries.[55] The law penalizes the act of traveling from one's country to another, typically to the Middle East, with penalties including prison sentences. The law is meant to be a deterrent to prevent people from going to join jihads and keep control of those who have done sone and could pose a threat after returning. In May 2016, police "charged 67 people, arrested 14 imams and shut down 19 Muslim organizations for acting against the Constitution, inciting hatred and recruiting for terrorism," according to the *New York Times*.[56] One of the key radical clerics associated with ISIS, Zekerija Qazimi from Ferezaj, was found guilty of recruiting for the terror group and of inciting hatred, and was jailed for 10 years.[57] Kosovar police further targeted (in a very rare move) a Shi'ite organization in Kosovo run by an Iranian cleric reportedly linked to Iran's *ayatollahs* and accused of funding terrorism.[58]

Elsewhere in Europe, international cooperation with Kosovar authorities has occurred. In November 2015, Italian authorities arrested four Kosovars in the Brescia region, where they had been running an ISIS logistics network linked with Kosovo's most-wanted *jihadist*, Lavdrim Muhaxheri.[59] At home, the Kosovo state is also seeking to counter extremism by other means. One possibility being recommended (in line with similar programs elsewhere in Europe) would offer "*jihad* rehabilitation" opportunities for some of the arrested men involved in the Syrian conflict.[60]

Kosovar-EU relations have been rocky in recent years, with allegations that Kosovo's top leaders profited from wartime organ trafficking and drug smuggling offset by charges of EU corruption in its own Kosovo delegation, in 2014.[61] The relationship between Kosovo's government and its Western partners has also been troubled because of internal political infighting (as when rival Kosovar parliamentarians attacked each with tear gas in 2015 and 2016).[62] The combination of internal political feuding, the unresolved international status of Kosovo and Serbia's non-recognition of the country, as well as endemic economic and social challenges all negatively affect the country's institutional capacity to deal with important but not essential challenges like Islamic extremism.

Amid the turmoil, one country that also saw considerable turmoil in 2016—Turkey—has sought to increase its presence in Kosovo. Unlike Saudi Arabia and other Muslim states, Turkey has a historic and cultural legacy in Kosovo, and thus significant legitimacy there. Since 1999, it has performed considerable development work, investment and political engagement within Kisovo, with significant impact. Among other things, the Erdogan government's Justice and Development Party was the model for Kosovo's Justice Party (Partia e Drejtësisë). Although it was not significantly represented in parliament, its leader was given a cabinet minister post in the previous government. In 2010, the party attempted to pass legislation calling for an introduction of religious education and an end to the state ban on the *hijab* in public schools. While these attempts failed, the closeness of the vote result indicated that individual parliamentarians from a wide range of parties have sympathies with Islam on social grounds.

Kosovo's relationship with Turkey has also been complicated by the failed July 2016 military coup against President Erdogan. As elsewhere in the Balkans, in its aftermath Kosovo was asked by Ankara to close schools linked with the alleged coup mastermind, U.S.-based cleric Fethulah Gulen. The Turkish government also demanded that Kosovo punish a local journalist who had made satirical comments about the coup attempt.[63] The Kosovo government did not do either, and many in the country bristled against perceived intrusiveness. However, the coup has only increased Erdogan's popularity among average Muslims in the Balkans—and Turkey runs Kosovo's airport and electricity supply, while Turkish companies are heavily involved with its road infrastructure development. Kosovo thus faces a delicate balancing act in preserving relations with Turkey, the West and the Islamic world in the years ahead.

ENDNOTES

[1] Joanna Paraszczuk, "Report Finds Alarming Outflow Of Kosovars To Islamic State," Radio Free Europe/Radio Liberty, April 15, 2015, http://www.rferl.org/content/islamic-state-kosovars-fighting-syria-iraq/26957463.html.

[2] For example, see Christopher Deliso, The Coming Balkan Caliphate: the Threat of Radical Islam to Europe and the West (Praeger Security International, 2007). The author is also aware from private discussions with CIA officials that American intelligence had predicted the same scenario as early as 1998, when the Clinton administration was preparing for the NATO bombing campaign.

[3] "Kosovo Hails Sharp Drop in Middle Eastern Fighters," Balkan Insight, October 24, 2016, http://www.balkaninsight.com/en/article/kosovo-plegdes-to-work-closer-to-islamic-comunity-to-fight-radicalism-10-24-2016.

[4] Paraszczuk, "Report Finds Alarming Outflow Of Kosovars To Islamic State."

[5] Adrian Shtuni, "Ethnic Albanian Foreign Fighters in Iraq and Syria," Combating Terrorism Center at West Point, April 30, 2015, https://www.ctc.usma.edu/posts/ethnic-albanian-foreign-fighters-in-iraq-and-syria.

[6] For the first, see Dutch filmmaker Klaartje Quirijns's 2005 documentary The Brooklyn Connection (www.thebrooklynconnection.net), which details how Albanian-American Diaspora leaders were able to raise $30 million for weaponry which they then smuggled to the KLA. There is a vast literature on the second aspect; for example, read the very detailed contemporary testimony of then-Interpol Assistant Director Ralph Mutschke, who gives an impressive assessment of the range of activities, geographical scope, profits and international crime partners of the major Albanian syndicates, as well as comments on links between such organized crime proceeds and terrorism. See Ralf Mutschke, Testimony before the House of Representatives Judiciary Committee, December 13, 2000.

[7] See "International Operation Targeted Large Albanian Drug Trafficking Network," Europol Press Release, July 9, 2012, https://www.europol.europa.eu/content/news/international-operation-targeted-large-albanian-drug-trafficking-network-1683.

[8] Allan Hall and Dan Warburton, "ISIS seizes £4bn drug ring from the Mafia to fund its brutal terror campaign," Daily Mirror (UK), January 17, 2016, http://www.mirror.co.uk/news/uk-news/isis-seizes-4bn-drug-ring-7191800.

[9] "Ekskluzive: Biografia e Lavdrim Muhaxherit" [Exclusive: Biography Lavdrim Muhaxheri]. KosovaPress.com, January 28, 2014.

[10] "Kosovo Albanian Who Beheaded a Man Says He Is Doing the Same Thing KLA Did," Independent.mk, August 2, 2014, http://www.independent.mk/articles/7931/Kosovo+Albanian+Who+Beheaded+a+Man+Says+He+Is+Doing+the+Same+Thing+KLA+Did.

[11] Labinot Leposhtica, "Kosovo Jails Hard-line Imam for 10 Years," Balkan Insight, May 20, 2016, http://www.balkaninsight.com/en/article/kosovo-hard-line-imam-sentenced-to-10-years-in-prison-05-20-2016.

[12] "In the Matter of the Designation of Lavdrim Muhaxheri, also known as Ebu Abdullah el Albani, also known as Abu Abdullah al Kosova, also known as Abu Abdallah al-Kosovi, also known as Abu Abdallah al-Kosovo as a Specially Designated Global Terrorist Pursuant to Section 1(b) of Executive Order 13224, as Amended," FederalRegister.gov. October 2, 2014, https://www.federalregister.gov/articles/2014/10/02/2014-23534/in-the-matter-of-the-designation-of-lavdrim-muhaxheri-also-known-as-ebu-abdullah-el-albani-also.

[13] "Iraq: New photos of Lavdrim Muhaxheri come into sight," RTK Live, December 29, 2015, http://www.rtklive.com/en/?id=2&r=3885.

[14] Carlotta Gall, "How Kosovo Was Turned Into Fertile Ground for ISIS," New York Times, May 21, 2016, http://www.nytimes.com/2016/05/22/world/europe/how-the-saudis-turned-kosovo-into-fertile-ground-for-isis.html?_r=0.

[15] "Kosovo Says No New Cases Of Citizens Joining IS In Iraq, Syria," Radio Free Europe/Radio Liberty, August 24, 2016, http://www.rferl.org/content/kosovo-islamic-state-iraq-syria/27943383.html.

[16] A detailed contemporaneous description of the specific Kosovar refugee relief operations undertaken by Arab groups in Albania, and their subsequent entrance from there into Kosovo, is found in Hussein Saud Qusti, "Unsung Heroes," Saudi Aramco World, July/August 1999. Regarding the role of U.S. and Albanian authorities targeting Islamist groups in Albania during the mid-1990s, see the World Almanac of Islamism chapter on Albania.

[17] Carlotta Gall, "How Kosovo Was Turned Into Fertile Ground for ISIS," op cit.

[18] Frank Brown, "Islam Builds a Future in Kosovo, One Mosque at a Time," BeliefNet, September 12, 2000, http://www.beliefnet.com/News/2000/09/Islam-Builds-A-Future-In-Kosovo-One-Mosque-At-A-Time.aspx.

[19] See the official list, which is updated periodically, here: http://www.mfa-ks.net/?page=2,157.
[20] Ibid.
[21] Examples include United Arab Emirates soldiers forcing Albanian villagers in Vushtrri to destroy two historic graveyards in October 1999, and the Saudi bulldozing of a 16th-century Koranic school and Ottoman library in Djakovica in August 2000. See Jolyon Naegele, "Yugoslavia: Saudi Wahhabi Aid Workers Bulldoze Balkan Monuments," Radio Free Europe/Radio Liberty, August 4, 2000.
[22] See United States Department of State, International Religious Freedom Report 2010.
[23] Brown, "Islam Builds a Future in Kosovo, One Mosque at a Time."
[24] See Deliso, The Coming Balkan Caliphate: The Threat of Radical Islam to Europe and the West, 65-67.
[25] Gjergj Erebara, "Kosovo's New Cathedral Stirs Muslim Resentment," Balkan Insight, October 4, 2010, http://www.balkaninsight.com/en/article/albanians-vie-for-religious-sites.
[26] For a comprehensive overview of the place of the Church in Kosovo and the wider region today, see Matteo Albertini and Chris Deliso, The Vatican's Challenges in the Balkans: Bolstering the Catholic Church in 2015 and Beyond)Balkananalysis.com, 2015), https://www.amazon.com/Vaticans-Challenges-Balkans-Bolstering-Catholic-ebook/dp/B00S30A7BQ.
[27] Cases cited in United States Department of State, International Religious Freedom Report 2010. (Protestant community members have also reported independently to the author that they havebeen physically assaulted by Islamists in Kosovo). This report also notes the official Kosovo Islamic Community's "concerns about radical Islamic groups they alleged were operating from private homes and led by persons from outside of the country."
[28] United States Department of State, International Religious Freedom Report 2011.
[29] Ervin Qafmolla and Kaltrina Rexhepi, "Kosovo Gunmen Arrested Near Serb Monastery," Balkan Insight, February 1, 2016, http://www.balkaninsight.com/en/article/terror-incidents-distress-kosovo-mosques-and-monasteries-02-01-2016.
[30] The story appeared in numerous local media, including on Radio Television Kosova, January 12, 2009.
[31] "Chapter 2 Country Reports: Europe and Eurasia Overview," in United States Department of State, Office of the Coordinator for Counterterrorism, Country Reports on Terrorism 2008 (Washington, DC: U.S. Department of State, April 30, 2009).

[32] The full story of this interaction is reported only partially, and in various sources. See "Kosovo Drug Baron among Terrorists," Blic (Belgrade), September 27, 2006. See also Genc Morina, "Radical Islam: Wahhabism a Danger to Kosovo's Independence!" Express (Pristina), October 15, 2006. For official reactions to the acquittal, see Nina Berglund, "Reaction Mixed to Terror Acquittal," Aftenposten (Oslo), June 4, 2008.

[33] Geoff Mulvihill, "Man pleads guilty in Fort Dix plot case," Associated Press, October 31, 2007.

[34] See Gerry J. Gilmore, "FBI, Navy Foil Alleged Terror Plot on Quantico," American Forces Press Service, September 25, 2009. See also U.S. Department of Justice, "Kosovar National Charged with Terrorism Violations," June 17, 2010.

[35] "Kosovo Group Claims Hack of US Weather Service," Agence France-Presse, October 19, 2012.

[36] See http://www.geoba.se/country.php?cc=XK&year=2015.

[37] Sewell Chan, "How a Record Number of Migrants Made Their Way To Europe," New York Times, December 22, 2015, http://www.nytimes.com/2015/12/23/world/europe/migrant-crisis-europe-million.html.

[38] The 2011 Kosovo census was the first internationally-recognized tally since 1981. Despite the Serb boycott, the EU (which donated 6 million euros to the project) found it generally to have met quality standards. The official Kosovo government statistical office web page for the census is http://esk.rks-gov.net/rekos2011.

[39] The official web site of the BIK is www.bislame.net.

[40] Gall, "How Kosovo Was Turned Into Fertile Ground for ISIS."

[41] Ebi Spahiu, "Jihadist Threat Persists in Kosovo and Albania Despite Government Efforts," Jamestown Foundation Terrorism Monitor 14, iss. 13, June 24, 2016, http://www.jamestown.org/single/?tx_ttnews%5Btt_news%5D=45551&no_cache=1#.V77LZ6KgA3j.

[42] See Genc Morina, "Radical Islam: Wahhabism a Danger to Kosovo's Independence!"

[43] United States Department of State, International Religious Freedom Report 2010.

[44] Linda Karadaku, "Inter-faith Dialogue Expected To Advance Reconciliation," SETimes.com, August, 14, 2013.

[45] The group's official website is www.interfaithkosovo.org.

[46] Gjergj Erebara, "Kosovo's New Cathedral Stirs Muslim Resentment," Balkan Insight, October 4, 2010.

[47] Ibid.

[48] See Christopher Deliso, "Lost in Conversion?" Balkananalysis.com, October 23, 2008, http://www.balkanalysis.com/kosovo/2008/10/23/lost-in-conversion/.

[49] The original text of the speech was published on the official website of the President of Albania, www.president.al.

[50] See Matteo Albertini, "The Vatican's Growing Prominence in Kosovo," Balkananalysis.com, April 14, 2011, http://www.balkanalysis.com/kosovo/2011/04/14/the-vatican%E2%80%99s-growing-prominence-in-kosovo/.

[51] See Albertini and Deliso, The Vatican's Challenges in the Balkans: Bolstering the Catholic Church in 2015 and Beyond.

[52] This could be seen in media pieces printed immediately after the independence declaration, such as "Kosovo Touts 'Islam-lite,'" Associated Press, February 21, 2008.

[53] Several telling examples of this trend are provided in Frud Bezhan, "A Growing Split Between Islamic, Secular Identities In Kosovo," Radio Free Europe/Radio Liberty, August 7, 2016, http://www.rferl.org/content/kosovo-split-islamic-identity-secular-traditions/27906304.html.

[54] Violeta Hyseni Kelmendi, "Kosovo mobilizes to fight religious radicalism and terrorism," Osservatorio Balcani e Caucaso, August 25, 2014, http://www.balcanicaucaso.org/eng/Areas/Kosovo/Kosovo-mobilizes-to-fight-religious-radicalism-and-terrorism-155153.

[55] Una Hajdari, "Kosovo to Jail Fighters in Foreign Conflicts," Balkan Insight, March 13, 2015, http://www.balkaninsight.com/en/article/kosovo-law-to-punish-fighting-in-foreign-conflicts.

[56] Gall, "How Kosovo Was Turned Into Fertile Ground for ISIS."

[57] Leposhtica, "Kosovo Jails Hard-line Imam for 10 Years."

[58] Frud Bezhan, "Charges Against Cleric Put Iran's Balkan Activities Under Spotlight," Radio Free Europe/Radio Liberty, August 1, 2016, http://www.rferl.org/content/kosovo-iran-cleric-arrest/27886917.html.

[59] Matteo Albertini, "Italy and Kosovo Intensify Actions against Another ISIS-linked Group," Balkanalysis.com, December 6, 2015, http://www.balkanalysis.com/kosovo/2015/12/06/italy-and-kosovo-intensify-actions-against-another-isis-linked-group/.

[60] "'Offer Kosovar Fighters 'Jihadi Rehab' to Combat Extremism,'" Balkan Insight, March 24, 2016, http://www.balkaninsight.com/en/article/offer-kosovar-fighters-jihadi-rehab-to-combat-extremism--03-23-2016.

[61] Julian Borger, "EU accused over its Kosovo mission: 'Corruption has grown exponentially,'" Guardian (London), November 6, 2014, https://www.theguardian.com/world/2014/nov/06/eu-accused-over-kosovo-mission-failings

[62] "Opposition MPs let off tear gas in Kosovo parliament," BBC, February 19, 2016, http://www.bbc.com/news/world-europe-35616745

[63] Fatos Bytyci, "Turkey asks Kosovo to punish journalist over coup comments," Reuters, July 26, 2016, http://www.reuters.com/article/us-kosovo-turkey-journalist-idUSKCN1061A1.

Macedonia

> **QUICK FACTS**
>
> Population: 2,100,025 (July 2016 est.)
>
> Area: 25,713 sq km
>
> Ethnic Groups: Macedonian 64.2%, Albanian 25.2%, Turkish 3.9%, Roma (Gypsy) 2.7%, Serb 1.8%, other 2.2% (2002 est.)
>
> Religions: Macedonian Orthodox 64.8%, Muslim 33.3%, other Christian 0.4%, other and unspecified 1.5% (2002 est.)
>
> Government Type: Parliamentary democracy
>
> GDP (official exchange rate): $9.922 billion (2015 est.)
>
> *Map and Quick Facts courtesy of the CIA World Factbook (November 2018)*

Overview

Ethnically- and religiously-divided Macedonia is on the front lines of the European migrant crisis, and was a major transit corridor between Greece and Serbia before that border closed in March 2016. The threat of terrorists posing as migrants has been noted by both local and international authorities. Also, over 100 ethnic Albanian Muslims have fought in jihadist groups like Al Nusra Front and ISIS in Syria and Iraq.[1] This led to the passage of a law on foreign fighters in September 2014, and increasing police activity resulting in the arrests of several alleged terrorist recruiters and fighters.

As in neighboring Kosovo and Albania, Macedonia has been targeted by radical Muslim preachers and Arab-funded charities for many years. By 2014, divisive ethnic politics and the development of an impressionable young generation of Muslims led to the phenomenon of local Albanian youth joining ethnically-based battalions in Syria, or recruiting at home. While approximately 50 fighters have been killed in battle, more have returned home, representing a concern for security planners. There are fewer ethnic Albanians from Macedonia joining the conflict than those from Albania and Kosovo, and those that have joined do not seem to have acquired the same reputations for violence or high levels of leadership.

However, Islamism itself in Macedonia is more pervasive socially and influential politically than in Albania or Kosovo, because of religious and rural-based conservatism, and as a result of specific political tactics employed by radicals in recent years. However, the greatest unknown factor for the future is what impact the aftermath of the failed Turkish coup of July 2016 will have on the behavior and popularity of ethnic Albanian political parties; for, while Macedonia is a strong ally of Turkey, there is internal disagreement within the local Muslim communities and parties regarding support for or opposition to controversial cleric Fethullah Gülen and his Islamic movement. While most Muslims in Macedonia (and the Balkans) do not support Gülen, influential Muslim politicians and commentators are more amenable to him, which raises the possibility of greater religious debate between competing camps in ethnic Albanian political life.

ISLAMIST ACTIVITY

Islamist activity in Macedonia is most widespread in areas where the Muslim population—the vast majority of whom are ethnic Albanians—is concentrated: parts of the capital, Skopje, the towns and villages between Kumanovo and Tetovo (near the border with Kosovo), and numerous towns like Gostivar, Debar, Kicevo and Struga located along the western border with Albania. However, ethnically-mixed areas exist in other regions of the country as well, such as in the central mountain massif south of Skopje. They too provide fertile ground for Islamist activity.

The organization that officially represents Macedonia's Muslim population of 675,000 is the Islamic Community of Macedonia (ICM).[2] As in other regional countries, however, its authority has been challenged by Arab-funded and trained young radicals over an extended period of time. Several violent confrontations have occurred since 2003, sparked by armed extremists seeking to install their candidates in Macedonia's mosques, especially in the capital of Skopje.[3] Later, in July 2010, the ICM's leading cleric, *reis-ul-ulema* Sulejman Rexhepi, admitted that the ICM had lost control over several Skopje mosques, following a fight and near-riot in a mosque under Wahhabi control.[4] And in September 2010 (following a fruitless private appeal to the United States ambassador four months earlier), he publicly called upon U.S. and EU representatives to help the ICM counter the growing influence of radical Islam.[5] Since then, some of the mosques involved have been targeted by police as having provided ideological indoctrination to young Muslims who would travel to Syria to fight.[6]

While international diplomats have for years warned about fundamentalist threats to Macedonia's stability, until the participation of Albanians in the Syrian *jihad* became public in 2014, most considered Islamic infighting to be little more than internal politicking between rival ethnic Albanian parties over property proceeds and other financial interests. Nevertheless, in Macedonia today, fundamentalist Islam (in the form of veiled women, men in traditional garb and long beards, and increased public challenges to secularism) is unmistakably becoming more visible in daily life.[7]

While there is certainly some truth to the skeptics' charge of Islamism as mere "business," the participation of local fighters in Syria and Iraq has provided evidence to the contrary. In late August 2016, while announcing the arrest in Turkey of five Macedonian Albanians en route to Syria, Interior Minister Mitko Chavkov stated that at least 25 other Macedonian citizens had been killed while fighting in the Syrian civil war, and 50 were presumed to still be there.[8]

Rather than destroying existing Islamic institutions, Wahhabi extremists have sought instead to take over authority where they can. To establish control, they have historically used NGOs, charities and publishing entities, domestic and international conferences, political events, "human-rights" activities and various demonstrations.[9] At the same time, these radicals have expedited the goals of Saudi Arabia and other Islamic states by overseeing the construction of hundreds of foreign-funded mosques.[10] The Islamist activity that led to fighters going to the Middle East was concentrated in several mosques in Skopje and Tetovo long associated with radical preachers. However, in many cases authorities have still been unable to arrest these figures because there is no solid evidence that they have done anything illegal.[11]

The complexity of Islamic affairs in Macedonia is growing as multiple internal and external actors vie for power and influence. Aside from the ICM and their Wahhabi opponents funded by the Gulf and other Islamic states, Turkey has a deep footprint in the country, owing to five centuries of Ottoman control. With the long-simmering feud between Turkish president Recep Tayyip Erdogan and controversial cleric Fethullah Gülen finally boiling over with a failed coup against Erdogan's government in July 2016, entrenched interests in Macedonia associated with both sides came under pressure.

This is particularly important when considering that Macedonia's main ethnic Albanian party, the Democratic Union for Integration (DUI), has members privately aligned with the rival Turkish camps (not to mention that Macedonia's small Turkish minority itself has two rival parties). The DUI has been a coalition partner in almost all Macedonian governments since 2002, after it was created by Ali Ahmeti (an ethnic Albanian who led the paramilitary National Liberation Army in the 2001 civil conflict). The Turkish government's demand that regional countries close Gülen-related schools after the 2016 coup put the party in a difficult position. While some party leaders were seen as closer to Gülen, the majority of Muslims in the Balkans supported Erdogan. Diplomatic information alleges that it was actually DUI's Ahmeti who vetoed a governmental proposal to close Gülen entities in Macedonia.[12]

This internal political division could prove especially problematic, since an openly pro-Erdogan ethnic Albanian party, Besa, was created in November 2014. As of 2016, the party had not yet participated in national elections, but is relying on its lack of previous political 'baggage' (like corruption scandals) and its appeal to conservative Muslim voters. While the appeal of the party has not been tested, it has caused concern among both the DUI and its traditional rival, the more nationalist-leaning Democratic Party of Albanians (DPA). The inevitable result in all future elections will be increasing overtures among all three parties for the 'Muslim base' vote in a fairly conservative country.

For its part, the Turkish government and various charities have made the most of their opportunity within the country.[13] Turkey is very active through its international development agency (TIKA) and supported NGOs in reaffirming the tangible signs of its Ottoman legacy in the country.[14] The Erdogan government has long considered Macedonia a key part of its neo-Ottoman foreign policy of "strategic depth."[15] And, not insignificantly in a country that has been actively hunting for foreign investors since 2006, Macedonia has welcomed dozens of major Turkish investors involved in everything from construction to management of the Skopje airport. These business and political ties have strengthened the bilateral relationship tremendously; indeed, when inaugurating the third Bosporus Bridge in August 2016, President Erdogan welcomed Macedonian President Gjorge Ivanov to the ceremony—one of very few leaders to receive that invitation.[16]

President Ivanov has consistently been a strong supporter of Erdogan, for example defending the latter's reaction to 2013 protests in Turkey.[17] Since Turkey is a key ally, this support has (despite Erdogan's pro-Islamist administration) actually benefited Macedonia's fight against terrorism. Indeed, Ivanov's August 25th visit for the bridge opening coincided with the announcement of a joint police and intelligence operation which resulted in the arrest of five Albanians from Macedonia in Istanbul, reportedly planning to join ISIS in Syria (discussed below).

Aside from foreign relations and state-level politics, the bedrock of funding for Islamist networks was established years ago, in often opaque ways, through NGOs and other entities. The official wealth of the ICM itself, in terms of funds, real estate and other assets, is neither publicly known nor discussed. Even less well-known is the total level of funding available to radical groups and the ways in which it is transmitted.

Part of this has to do with established tradition, such as the custom of communal payments seen in the construction of village mosques; locals can simply donate anonymously, drop cash in a box, and so on. Even when police have managed to trace some funds to extremist groups abroad, authoritative figures have never been publicly disclosed. Nor do Islamists, despite their frequent calls for officials to show greater transparency, detail the provenance or amounts of their own funding.[18] As a result, investigators have had to work deductively and, to some extent, rely on anecdotal or comparative information.

In general, officials believe that Islamists in Macedonia (as elsewhere in the region) employ a creative combination of methods to move money. Police sometimes reference the use of Islamic students returning from the Gulf as cash "mules." Other financial sources include proceeds from narcotics trafficking or the sale of items ranging from plastic chairs to silver and gold. To escape the attention of authorities, Islamists sometimes eschew large bank transactions, instead breaking up payments and deposits into smaller amounts.

Finally, funds also come in through donations from ideologically sympathetic businessmen, officials and Diaspora Muslims for religious projects such as mosques, schools and publications.[19] These donations are not always a secret; indeed, the donating country or organization is often prominently displayed on the entrance of the structure in question, or in the beginning of a book.

As discussed above, Islamist activity in Macedonia over the past 20 years has been guided largely by outside interests, such as Saudi and other Gulf state charities and proselytizers. A limited interest has also been evidenced from Pakistani and Malaysian groups.[20] Often, global Islamist NGOs registered locally or via Western Europe (the UK is a major hub) are used as intermediaries. However, since the 1990s, relatively fewer suspicious charities have been allowed to register in the country, in comparison to Albania, Kosovo and Bosnia, due to a measure of resistance from Macedonian security officials.[21]

Specific Islamist activity has taken different forms. One key area is the strategic construction of mosques along major highways, high ridgelines, near pre-existing churches or in close proximity to other mosques. According to a detailed Macedonian newspaper investigation in 2010, over 300 mosques had been built in the previous decade—88 alone between Skopje and Tetovo, the main ethnic Albanian-majority city, in northwestern Macedonia.[22] At a cost estimated by the newspaper to reach $1.5-$2.5 million per mosque, the sum expended is staggering. According to the same report, Saudi Arabia alone committed over $1.2 billion from 2003-2013 for building mosques, providing education, and sending local Muslims on the *Hajj*.[23] More recently, in July 2014, the cornerstone was laid for a Saudi-style, four-minaret mega-mosque in the Skopje district of Topansko Pole. Featuring an educational center, it was expected to be the largest mosque in Macedonia and among the largest in the Balkans.[24]

Aside from mosque construction, Islamists in and with ties to Macedonia have been active around the world. The infamous "Fort Dix Six" plot to attack a U.S. Army base in Ft. Dix, New Jersey involved three ethnic Albanian émigrés from Macedonia, and another from Kosovo.[25] In Switzerland, the popular referendum banning minaret construction began after an Islamist group led by another Albanian originally from Macedonia agitated in favor of such building.[26] During ethnic Albanian paramilitary uprisings in Kosovo and Macedonia in 1999 and 2001, respectively, Albanian Islamists openly sought to raise funds for the cause in Great Britain, Germany and elsewhere in Europe.[27] Although these revolts were generally secular, small numbers of foreign *mujahideen* are now known to have fought in both wars.

At the same time, even before the Syrian crisis and rise of ISIS, Muslims from Macedonia had gone to join al-Qaeda's *jihad* against the United States and the Coalition in Afghanistan (an estimate published in the British media in 2010 put the number at approximately 50).[28] During a joint press conference with Macedonian Prime Minister Nikola Gruevski in January 2010, then-Israeli Foreign Minister Avigdor Lieberman stated that radical Islam in Macedonia and the Balkans was a major concern.[29] This comment came only four months before three Muslims from Macedonia participated in the controversial "humanitarian flotilla" to break the Israeli blockade of Gaza, organized by the Turkey-based Islamic charity Humanitarian Relief Foundation (IHH).[30]

For years, security experts have warned about rising Islamism in Macedonia—albeit without arousing much attention. In late 2004, for example, French counterterrorism expert Claude Moniquet estimated publicly that up to 100 individuals linked to terrorist organizations resided in Macedonia, and that the country was effectively being used as a terrorist safe haven.[31] A year later, Macedonian intelligence officials disclosed that Malaysian proselytizers were regularly arriving to carry out missionary activities in Muslim towns and villages. The influx was a product of necessity; apparently, some of the visiting Islamists had either been expelled or feared being expelled from EU countries, due to political or extremist activities there.[32]

Since the 1990s, hundreds of young Muslims from Macedonia have also gone to study in Islamic states, such as Egypt, Syria, Saudi Arabia and Malaysia, while others have come into contact with radical Islam while working in Europe. An unfortunate long-term result of this trend has been the development of a "next-generation" of local Islamists who have built their own networks. At the same time, Balkan Muslims ensnared by radical Islam while working abroad have developed these networks further upon their return back home. For example, a two-year investigation of radicals in northern Italy by the Divisione Investigazioni Generali e Operazioni Speciali, (The General Investigations and Special Operations Division, or DIGOS) police resulted in the detention of 29 Balkan Muslims, some of whom were from Macedonia and allegedly linked to al-Qaeda.[33]

In 2012, dramatic evidence attesting to these developing radical trends emerged with a series of protests. The first large-scale protest occurred in the Albanian-majority town of Struga, ostensibly in reaction to an annual carnival in the nearby Christian village of Vevchani. The carnival is traditionally light-hearted, poking fun at world leaders, social trends and general society. However, participants at the event mocked Islam, provoking groups of angry protestors to attack churches in Albanian- and Macedonian Muslim-populated villages in western Macedonia, and to even stone a group of Christians on a bus.

In a large and unprecedented protest in Struga, heavily-bearded men waving Albanian and green Islamic flags publicly denounced Christians. Although further investigation and input from intelligence officials revealed that there was a certain amount of local politics and financial interests behind the lurid affair, the demonstration confirmed the presence of extremists and their ability to organize violently on short notice.[34] Most troubling, perhaps, was that the whole incident became a high-level security concern. Top government leaders and foreign diplomats were forced to meet extensively and reaffirm their commitment to work together and overcome ethnic and religious differences.

A second, more serious protest occurred in the capital, Skopje, on May 4, 2012, after a police press conference reported the apprehension of several Albanian "Islamic extremists." The men had been detained after a massive police operation to find the killers of a group of young Macedonian fishermen who had been murdered execution-style, along with an older man who apparently witnessed the scene. The killings sparked the biggest manhunt in state history, dubbed "Operation Monster," in which 600 police officers were deployed. At subsequent protests in Skopje (with smaller ones in Tetovo and Gostivar), several thousand ethnic Albanian youth took to the streets, waving Albanian and Saudi flags and chanting "*Allahu Akbar*" and "death to the Christians." Some were seen wearing provocative shirts with slogans like "Islam will dominate the world" and demanding the establishment of a Greater Albania.[35]

The protest originated at the historic Yahya Pasha Mosque, which had been under Wahhabi control for at least 10 years. Since the young protesters attacked the municipal office of the local (and ethnic Albanian) mayor in the Cair neighborhood of Skopje, security experts also read this as a sign that the extremists are now beyond the control of the ethnic Albanian political mainstream.[36] There were also reports of fights on public buses between Macedonian and Albanian youth and attacks by the latter on elderly Macedonians.

The trial of the suspected gunmen was deferred twice, and witnesses and family members of those killed were only able to face the defendants in court in December 2012 and January 2013.[37] Although police did not charge him with direct involvement, longtime Islamic radical Shukri Aliu was believed to have ignited the protests by calling for an "Arab Spring" uprising targeting the government, and seeking the participation of *imams* throughout the country.[38] Aliu was extradited from Kosovo at the end of 2012 in connection with physical attacks on several *imams* near the village of Kondovo that took place in 2005. In December 2015, a Skopje court overruled an appeal from the five men accused of the murders, upholding life sentences for the crime. This decision sparked complaints from ethnic Albanians, but no protests on a similar level were seen. However, media alleged that the Special Prosecutor's Office (set up in September 2015 to investigate a very opaque 'government wiretapping' affair) would like to revisit the case, so there is room in the future for further ethnic and religious politicization.[39]

ISLAMISM AND SOCIETY

The greatest defining—and most complicating—factor relating to Islamism in Macedonia is its intimate linkage with ethnic identification and ethnic-based politics. Local attitudes toward Islamic groups, and Islam in general, are not rigidly defined and remain in a perpetual state of flux, as does the general sense of ethnic identification among different groups, Christian and Muslim alike. This unique situation arguably makes a true understanding of Islam and society more difficult in Macedonia than in any other country in Europe.

Nearly 70 percent of the national population of 2 million is composed of ethnic Macedonians, a Slavic people who speak a language similar to Bulgarian and Serbian. While most are Orthodox Christian, a small number are Muslim—holdovers from Ottoman times, when those who converted enjoyed special benefits. Ethnic Albanians, who comprise 25 percent of the population, are almost entirely Muslim, predominantly from the Gheg sub-group common to northern Albania and Kosovo.

Other Muslim populations include Turks (four percent of the total population), Roma (around three percent), and about 17,000 Bosniaks.[40] However, a 2011 Pew report on global Muslim population growth trends indicates that, through 2030, Macedonia will experience a higher projected increase in number of Muslims to non-Muslims (5.4%) than any other European country. Pew expects that by 2030 some 40.3% of the total Macedonian population will be Muslim. This demographic trend will have severe political and social implications.[41] However, it should be noted that the unexpected European migration crisis of 2015 will also alter the population balance in Northern European countries, which are far more attractive targets for terrorist attacks than is Macedonia.

The chronic polarization between ethnic Macedonians and Albanians intensified during the 2001 conflict, when Kosovo-led Albanians took up arms, allegedly for more rights and civic employment opportunities, in the so-called National Liberation Army of subsequent DUI president Ali Ahmeti. Under international pressure, a peace treaty—the Ohrid Framework Agreement—was signed shortly thereafter by leaders of the four major political parties existing at that time. The agreement stipulated a quota system for issues like public sector hiring, flag and language use, and so on. Thus followed a territorial decentralization that amounted to political horse-trading between the then-ruling coalition of the Socialist SDSM and the DUI, an ethnic Albanian party formed by the leadership of the former rebel group, the NLA.

The decentralization institutionalized the ascendancy of Islam over large and territorially contiguous swathes of the population, particularly in northern and western Macedonia, where the majority of the country's Albanian Muslims live. The artfully designed new municipalities of 2005 ensured that Albanian mayors would be elected for the first time in ethnically mixed towns like Struga in the southwest, and that historically Turkish municipalities would also fall into Albanian hands. The Turks were rewarded, however, when two ethnically Macedonian Muslim municipalities, Plasnica and Centar Zhupa, were declared "Turkish." However, this new situation also caused resentment within the larger Muslim community as Albanian nationalism was employed to change whole demographics. To win votes, Macedonian Muslim populations were (and are) told that they were "really" Albanian, since they were Muslim; at the same time, savvy Albanians were telling outside observers that they themselves were not particularly religiously observant, in order to avoid being perceived as radicals.

One result of this political tug-of-war was the creation of a new identity: that of the "Torbeshi." Once used in a demeaning fashion, the name derives from the Macedonian word for bag (*torba*); historically, it insinuated that those thus classified would change their religion for whatever riches were given to them (by the previous Ottoman authorities). The ethnically Macedonian Muslims thus classified are typically the odd ones out in society; while they speak the Macedonian language of their Christian kin, they are Muslims like the Albanians. Fitting in with neither side, they are now turning to their religion as a defining factor, or else starting to identify themselves as Muslim Albanians.

Ethnic Albanian parties will continue to pressure the Macedonian Muslims of the western Mavrovo-Rostuse and Struga-area villages to declare themselves Albanians. This process of ethnic "conversion" directly expedites the dreams of Albanian ultranationalists who seek the federalization or territorial division of Macedonia along ethnic and religious lines. A further indication that the Albanian-dominated Islamic Community seeks hegemony over all believers (be they Turkish, Roma, Bosniak or Torbeshi) came with the comments of Reis Sulejmani in 2012 that there should be one national language (i.e., Albanian) in order to "reduce tensions" between Muslims.[42] However, the efforts of ethnic Albanian parties to assimilate more conservative, religiously-minded Torbeshi minorities has also enhanced the parties' religious character.

One victim of the growth of fundamentalist Islam has been the country's more peaceful Bektashi Order—a minority within a minority. Comprised primarily of ethnic Albanians, this more liberal branch of Islam is considered heretical by many Muslims worldwide. In Macedonia, they are particularly despised by Wahhabis, who condemn them as being even worse than Christians and Jews.[43] During and after the brief 2001 war, the country's main Bektashi shrine, the historic Harabati Baba Tekke in Tetovo, was vandalized and partially occupied by Islamic radicals associated with the NLA. Members of the order who have spoken out against the extremists have been threatened and, despite entreaties to successive Macedonian governments, the Bektashis still cannot register themselves as a distinct religious group.

In October 2010, the ICM controversially authorized a rival, so-called "Bektashi" order from the southwestern village of Zajas as the only legitimate such community in Macedonia.[44] However, the "real" Bektashis, whose base is in Tetovo, are recognized by outside Bektashi organizations. They thus criticized DUI-influenced decisions to recognize a parallel Bektashi group that they feared would give the ICM future control over any properties claimed from the state under the denationalization process.[45]

On a broader level, the major social issue within the Muslim community is the gap between the younger and older generations of Muslims. Young Islamists, confident in their own studies in Arab states, tend to depict older leaders of Macedonia's Islamic Community as "communists" who do not understand Islam correctly, due to their different experience growing up in the former Yugoslavia.[46] Yet the perceived discrepancy is rarely put to the test (say, through a televised theological debate). Rather, it is generally carried out through violence and intimidation. Since intimidation is often carried out subtly and occurs within tight-knit communities, it is seldom reported.[47] For the time being, therefore, the primary victims of Islamist activity in Macedonia remain the country's Muslims themselves.

Islamism and the State

In Macedonia, the state's ability to counteract extremism and engage it is conditioned by a unique factor that makes it much more complex than in other regional countries: that is, the increasing tendency of political parties from the ethnic Albanian minority to purposefully blur the boundaries between ethnic and religious identity. This tendency has been seen in social and political life (some examples are noted above), but it also has impeded Macedonian authorities' ability to both pass counter-terrorism legislation and conduct operations. When an Albanian is arrested because of a religiously motivated crime, a backlash often arises that the individual is the victim of ethnic discrimination; and when arrested for nationalist extremism, the counter-argument is made of alleged religious bias. In this situation, police have had to tread carefully, and this more than anything else explains the relatively small number of terrorism-related arrests compared to Kosovo and Albania, where no such ethnic minority problem exists.

Because of the migrant crisis and Syrian civil war, the Macedonian state has had to divert resources and attention from dealing with the domestic Islamist threat. The current crisis began in early 2015, and neatly coincided with the European migration crisis, which saw some one million illegal migrants and refugees transit Macedonia from Greece en route to Western Europe. Keeping control of this flow required considerable police and military assets to be redirected to the country's southern border with Greece and its northern one with Serbia, under the law on crisis situations that was declared by President Gjorge Ivanov in August 2015 and later extended.[48]

In line with a U.S. request and legal assistance, Macedonia passed a foreign fighters law banning the participation of citizens in foreign conflicts on September 3, 2014.[49] While no one voted against it, several prominent members of the ethnic Albanian coalition partner, DUI, abstained. Similar laws have been passed in other Balkan countries since 2014. In Macedonia, it provided a solid base for the state to begin systematically targeting known radical preachers, recruiters and returned foreign fighters from the Middle East.

The results can be seen in several related sweeps by special police, under the title Operation Kelija (Cell). In early August 2015, police targeted mosques, NGO offices and residences associated with recruiters and fighters for ISIS, in Skopje, Tetovo, Gostivar, Kumanovo and Struga.[50] Nine suspects were arrested in the action, including Rexhep Memishi, a well-known radical *imam* opposed to the ICM. Another 27 suspects were at large, believed to be in the Middle East. The US Embassy in Skopje praised the action as a contribution to regional and global efforts against the "evil of terrorism."[51] In March 2016, a court sentenced six persons (including the self-proclaimed *imam*) to seven years in prison.

In July 2016, the operation continued with a further sweep and arrest of four more ISIS-related Islamists.[52] The third part was completed in August 2016, when Turkish police extradited five Macedonian Albanians suspected of having links with ISIS. They had been arrested in the Aksaray neighborhood of Istanbul while preparing to go to Syria.[53] Information from security sources indicates that this was not the first time Macedonian and Turkish police have cooperated on identifying and arresting Macedonian nationals associated with Islamist groups on Turkish soil.

The success of these operations is ironic. While Macedonian police seem finally able to act against Islamic radicals with less danger of causing backlash from local Muslims, the fact that they have to deal with this threat at all indicates the unfortunate outcome of two decades of extremist ideology and infrastructure development in the country. The involvement of young *jihadists* from Macedonia and other Balkan countries in Syria since 2013 is proof of the effectiveness of the ideological, financial and logistical strategies practiced by radical supporters, years before the Syrian crisis provided a trigger for young Muslims to make the transformation from extremists to *jihadists*.

While Macedonia remains frozen out of the EU, owing to the unresolved disagreement with EU member Greece over the country's name (Greece has a province called

Macedonia as well), it has nevertheless enjoyed robust security cooperation with neighbors Serbia, Bulgaria and especially Turkey. Indeed, the level of security cooperation with these countries in the future will greatly influence Macedonia's ability to fight extremism at home. One of the major problems for non-EU members (like Macedonia, Serbia and Turkey) is that they are excluded from the EU's database system that has been used for cataloging asylum seekers (EURODAC). Given the vast number of migrants who have crossed through these countries in recent years, and in light of ongoing concerns that terrorists may be among them, these non-EU countries are being left to create bilateral or otherwise special methods of cooperation and intelligence-sharing. Since the mass migration phenomenon is targeting Northern Europe, not the Balkans, it would be more in the interests of the EU to cooperate with these countries than the other way around. However, for various reasons, the bloc has done an insufficient job in cooperating.[54]

Endnotes

[1] Adrian Shtumi, Ethnic Albanian Foreign Fighters in Iraq and Syria, Combating Terrorism Center at West Point, April 30, 2015. https://www.ctc.usma.edu/posts/ethnic-albanian-foreign-fighters-in-iraq-and-syria/

[2] The ICM's official website is www.bim.org.mk. The BIM acronym comes from the Albanian-language version of the name, Bashkesia Fetare Islame. Note that the institution is oftenreferred to by its Macedonian name and acronym, Islamska Verska Zaednica (IVZ). International sources also refer to it as the Islamic Religious Community (IRC). All of these acronyms refer to the same official body.

[3] The most infamous examples of Salafi violence date from the turbulent reign of former Skopje *mufti* Zenun Berisha, who used a sort of Islamist private guard to take over several mosques, impose preferred candidates for jobs, and generally assert his authority. Accounts of intimidation, beatings and attacks against moderates such as former *Reis* Arif Emini and former Skopje *mufti* Taxhedin Bislimi were widely reported in the local media. A comprehensive account of these events, citing some of the leaders involved, is given in Christopher Deliso, *The Coming Balkan Caliphate: the Threat of Radical Islam to Europe and the West* (Praeger Security International, 2007), 82-86.

[4] Svetlana Jovanovska and Branko Gjorgeski, "Radical Islam In Macedonia Worries Western Observers," *WAZ/EU Observer*, July 8, 2010.

[5] "Macedonia: Moderate Muslims Seek Help Against Sect," Associated Press, September 20, 2010.

[6] "Special forces conduct raid against IS," *The Economist Intelligence Unit*, August 12, 2015, http://country.eiu.com/article.aspx?articleid=833431267&Country=Macedonia&topic=Politics&subtopic_2.

[7] See Deliso, T*he Coming Balkan Caliphate: the Threat of Radical Islam to Europe and the West.*

[8] "MVR so detali: makedonski drzhavjani uapseni vo turtsija planirale zaminuvane na boishtata vo sirija kako del od id," ("MOI details: Macedonian nationals arrested in Turkey planned departure battlefields in Syria as part of ISIS"), *Kurir*, August 27, 2016, http://kurir.mk/makedonija/vesti/mvr-so-detali-makedonski-drzhavjani-uapseni-vo-turtsija-planirale-zaminuvane-na-boishtata-vo-sirija-kako-del-od-id/.

[9] Islamic NGOs in Macedonia include both international franchises and local entities. Some belong to umbrella organizations, allowing them to participate in a variety of events internationally, and thereby network with like-minded ideologues from Islamic states.

[10] Bojan Pancevski, "Saudis Fund Balkan Muslims Spreading Hate Of The West," *Sunday Times* (London), March 28, 2010. Further factual details are cited in "Milijarda Evra Investirani Co Radikalniot Islam (Billion-euro Investment In Radical Islam)," *Nova Makedonija*, July 6, 2010.

[11] According to a senior security official, as of May 2016 some 80 such Islamists were being kept under 24-hour surveillance, as they could not be arrested, but still posed a potential threat. Author interview with Macedonian security official, May 2016.

[12] Author interview with Macedonian official, August 2016.

[13] For example, in the year 2010 alone, some 80 Islamic students from Turkey were known to be studying at the *madrassa* in the eastern town of Stip—with an announced plan for increasing this number in coming years to 500, and eventually to 1,500. "Turski Studenti Go Sardisaa Stip (Turkish Students Occupy Stip)," *Dnevnik* (Skopje), December 28, 2010.

[14] For one example, Turkish State Minister Faruk Celik visited Skopje in December 2010 to mark the TIKA's renovation of the magnificent 15th-century mosque of Mustafa Pasha. He also met with top leaders of the country's Islamic community. See "Turkey Says To Continue Repairing Ottoman Arts In Macedonia," www.worldbulletin.net, December 21, 2010, http://www.worldbulletin.net/servisler/haberYazdir/67671/haber.

[15] For more on the doctrine of "strategic depth" developed by then-Turkish Foreign Minister Ahmed Davutoglu, see Ioannis N. Grigoriadis, "The Davutoglu Doctrine and Turkish Foreign Policy," Hellenic Foundation for European and Foreign Policy (ELIAMEP), April 2010.

[16] "3rd Bosphorus bridge inaugurated," TRT World, August 25, 2016, http://www.trtworld.com/turkey/3rd-bosphorus-bridge-inaugurated-172455.

[17] Sinisa Jakov Marucic, "Macedonians Divided Over President's Support for Erdogan," *Balkan Insight*, July 8, 2013, http://www.balkaninsight.com/en/article/macedonian-president-s-whole-hearted-support-for-endogan-divides-critics/2027/2.

[18] For an example of this prevailing hostile attitude, note the comments of Islamic NGO leader Bekir Halimi to a journalist: "We are fully entitled to receive funding from both governmental and non-governmental sources from Saudi Arabia." See Pancevski, "Saudis Fund Balkan Muslims Spreading Hate Of The West." The article also notes that Halimi "refuses to name the sources of his funding."
[19] Ibid.
[20] Deliso, *The Coming Balkan Caliphate*, 73-78.
[21] For example, a former Macedonian counterintelligence chief, Zoran Mitevski, recounted that in 1996 U.S. diplomats accused him of being "undemocratic" when he blocked several terror-linked Saudi charities from registering in the country. Deliso, The Coming Balkan Caliphate, 81.
[22] "Milijarda Evra Investirani Co Radikalniot Islam (Billion-Euro Investment In Radical Islam)."
[23] Ibid. These figures roughly correspond with those given in Pancevski, "Saudis Fund Balkan Muslims Spreading Hate Of The West," as well as with figures given to the author by Macedonian security officials.
[24] "New Mosque Built in Topansko Pole Will Be the Biggest Mosque in Macedonia," Indepedendent.mk, July 28, 2014.
[25] Three of the men involved in the plot, brothers born in the Albanian-majority town of Debar, were arrested for their role in the failed attacks on U.S. soldiers at Ft. Dix. Garentina Kraja and William J. Kole, "Brothers Behind Fort Dix Plot Were From Pro-U.S. Enclave," Associated Press, May 10, 2007.
[26] Devorah Lauter, "Swiss Voters OK Ban On Minarets," *Los Angeles Times*, November 30, 2009.
[27] Organizations such as the former "Albanian Islamic Society" in London raised money for fighters in 1999 and 2001. British media also reported that mosques frequented by Albanians were also being solicited for war donations. See David Bamber and Chris Hastings, "KLA Raises Money in Britain for Arms," Kosovo.net, April 23, 2000. When ethnic Albanians in Macedonia rebelled in 2001, Jakup Hasipi, a nationalist imam from the remote village of Slupcane in northeastern Macedonia, was dispatched to preach and solicit funds in Albanian Diaspora mosques, in European cities like Leverkusen and Hamburg. As with other leading Islamists, videos of this now-deceased *imam* delivering his sermons in such places are widely available on the Internet.
[28] Pancevski, "Saudis Fund Balkan Muslims Spreading Hate Of The West;" See also "Vahabisti Vrvuvaat Borci Za Dzihad Bo Makedonija" ("Wahhabis Recruit Fighters For Jihad In Macedonia"), *Vecer*, March 29, 2010. These claims correspond with testimony made by different Macedonian security officials and local Muslims to the author since 2004.
[29] A summary of the foreign minister's statements are available on the website of the Israeli Ministry of Foreign Affairs (www.mfa.gov.il).

[30] Goce Mihajloski, "Makedonskite Humanitarsi Se Vratija Od Israel" ("Macedonian Humanitarians Returned From Israel"), *A1 Televizija* (Skopje), June 5, 2010.

[31] Christopher Deliso, "Fissures In Balkan Islam," *Christian Science Monitor*, February 14, 2006.

[32] "Malaysian, EU-Rejected Islamists Penetrate Macedonia," www.balkanalysis.com, September 28, 2005.

[33] "Wahhabis In Labunista Antagonize Locals, As New Details Emerge About Italian Arrests," www.balkanalysis.com, January 5, 2007. Two ethnically Macedonian Muslims were later expelled from Italy; classified DIGOS wiretap transcripts seen by the author indicate that they were in touch with Bosnian radical groups and were aiding the movement of Bosnian and Arab extremists into Macedonia.

[34] See Chris Deliso, "After Macedonia's Islamic Protests, Investigators Search for Significance amidst a Confusing Array of Motives and Clues," www.balkanalysis.com, February 13, 2012, http://www.balkanalysis.com/macedonia/2012/02/13/after-macedonias-islamist-protest-investigators-search-for-significance-amidst-confusing-array-of-motives-and-clues/.

[35] "Macedonia protests signal surge of radical Islam," Euractiv, May 14, 2012, http://www.euractiv.com/enlargement/protests-macedonia-signal-radica-news-512663.

[36] Author interview with Macedonian security official, June 2012.

[37] Sinisa Marusic, "Macedonia Mass Murder Trial Witnesses 'Saw Gunmen,'" *Balkan Insight*, January 18, 2013. Available at http://www.balkaninsight.com/en/article/witnesses-saw-armed-men-at-skopje-s-mass-murder-site.

[38] "Shukri Aliu Povikuval na Arapska Prolet vo Makedonijua," ("Shukri Aliu Called for an Arab Spring in Macedonia"), Sitel TV, December 6, 2012, http://www.sitel.com.mk/shukri-aliu-povikuval-na-arapska-prolet-vo-makedonija.

[39] Sinisa Jakov Marusic, "Macedonia Upholds Albanians' 'Terrorist Murder' Sentences," *Balkan Insight*, December 14, 2015, http://www.balkaninsight.com/en/article/macedonia-court-confirms-terrorist-murders-sentence-12-14-2015.

[40] These numbers derive from the 2002 national census. The data is available in several PDF files on the official website of the State Statistical Office of Republic of Macedonia, www.stat.gov.mk.

[41] *The Future of the Global Muslim Population: Projections for 2010-2030* (Pew Forum on Religion and Public Life 2011). The relevant part of the report is available online at http://www.pewforum.org/future-of-the-global-muslim-population-regional-europe.aspx.

[42] The comments were made after a controversy in which the Roma (Gypsy) minority in the Christian-majority city of Prilep built a mosque, against the wishes of the Albanian-controlled ICM. Aleksandar Pavlevski, "Islamic Leader Calls for Common Language to Reduce Tensions," *SETimes*, November 29, 2012.

[43] Author's interviews with Islamist Muslims, Gostivar, Macedonia, May-June 2010.

[44] "IVZ Prizna Bekteska Verska Grupa Bo Makedonija" ("The IVZ Recognized A Bektashi Religious Group In Macedonia"), *Kanal 5 TV*, October 21, 2010.

[45] "Koj Se Vistinskite Bektasi Vo Makedonija?" ("Who Are The Real Bektashi In Macedonia?"), *Deutsche Welle-Macedonian*, November 14, 2010.

[46] "Opasnost Od Radikalizam I U Macedonikija" ("Danger From Radicalism In Macedonia Too"), *Radio Free Europe/Radio Liberty*, September 11, 2010. In the author's personal experience, the meme of "old Communists" (older, traditionalist Muslims) as being allegedly ignorant is a very pervasive one, and invoked frequently by Islamists in the country.

[47] Some examples include: physical attacks against clerics deemed to be in the way of Islamists and their goals; pressure for females to wear conservative religious dress; orders for moderate Muslims not to associate with Christians; injunctions against shopkeepers against selling alcohol; perpetuation of the archaic custom of arranged marriages for teenage girls; threats against young Muslims seen to be engaging in Western "hedonism;" violence against Muslim journalists seeking to report on any such issues, and so on.

[48] For a detailed account of Macedonia's security response to the migrant crisis, see Chris Deliso, "Macedonian Migration Policy and the Future of Europe," Balkanalysis.com, December 23, 2015, http://www.balkanalysis.com/macedonia/2015/12/23/macedonian-migration-policy-and-the-future-of-europe/.

[49] See Chris Deliso, "Asymmetric Threats Challenge Macedonia before Easter and Elections," Balkanalysis.com, April 25, 2016, http://www.balkanalysis.com/macedonia/2016/04/25/asymmetric-threats-challenge-macedonia-before-easter-and-elections/.

[50] Sinisa Jakov Marusic, "Macedonian Police Targets ISIS Suspects," *Balkan Insight*, August 6, 2015, http://www.balkaninsight.com/en/article/macedonia-launches-anti-terror-busts-08-06-2015.

[51] Sinisa Jakov Marusic, "Macedonia Arrests Nine ISIS Suspects," *Balkan Insight*, August 7, 2015, http://www.balkaninsight.com/en/article/macedonia-arrests-nine-isis-suspects-08-07-2015.

[52] Maja Zuvela, "Macedonian police arrest four suspected of Islamic State links," Reuters, July 9. 2016, http://www.reuters.com/article/us-mideast-crisis-macedonia-idUSKCN0ZP0RV.

[53] "Kelija 3: Five Jihadists from Macedonia, Members of ISIL, Arrested," *Vecer*, August 27, 2016, http://vecer.mk/makedonija/kjelija-3-uapseni-5-dzhihadisti-od-makedonija-chlenovi-na-isis.

[54] Chris Deliso, "Mistrust and Different Priorities Vex EU-Macedonian Security Cooperation," Balkanalysis.com, May 27, 2016, http://www.balkanalysis.com/blog/2016/05/27/mistrust-and-different-priorities-vex-eu-macedonian-security-cooperation/.

NETHERLANDS

QUICK FACTS

Population: 17,016,967 (July 2016 est.)

Area: 41,543 sq km

Ethnic Groups: Dutch 78.6%, EU 5.8%, Turkish 2.4%, Indonesian 2.2%, Moroccan 2.2%, Surinamese 2.1%, Bonairian, Saba Islander, Sint Eustatian 0.8%, other 5.9% (2014 est.)

Religions: Roman Catholic 28%, Protestant 19% (includes Dutch Reformed 9%, Protestant Church of The Netherlands, 7%, Calvinist 3%), other 11% (includes about 5% Muslim and fewer numbers of Hindu, Buddhist, Jehovah's Witness, and Orthodox), none 42% (2009 est.)

Government Type: parliamentary constitutional monarchy

GDP (official exchange rate): $769.9 billion (2015 est.)

Map and Quick Facts courtesy of the CIA World Factbook (January 2017)

OVERVIEW

Historically, the Netherlands has been a country renowned for its religious tolerance. In the Golden Age of the 17th and 18th centuries, the Republic of the United Provinces served as a haven for Jews and Protestants fleeing persecution in other parts of Europe. Muslim immigrants began to join their ranks in the late 19th century. Decades later, as it sought cheap labor during the 1960s, the Dutch government actively encouraged immigration from Indonesia and Suriname, both Muslim-majority countries and former Dutch colonies. Such days, however, have long since passed; ideological conflicts abroad now serve as magnets for aspiring Dutch jihadists, while xenophobia and the looming threat of Islamic terrorism have driven the adoption of increasingly restrictive immigration and asylum policies. In spite of Dutch efforts to proactively counter radicalization and encourage integration, this social transforma-

tion has allowed Islamists to push the political envelope and expose the value gap between the Dutch majority and its immigrant Muslim population.

ISLAMIST ACTIVITY

In December 2012, the Office of the Dutch National Coordinator for Counterterrorism and Security (NCTV) assessed the national threat level as "limited," with little chance of a terrorist attack in the Netherlands or on Dutch interests abroad.[1] Yet only a few months later, in March 2013, NCTV's chief Dick Schoof warned of increasing radicalization among Dutch youth. He declared that nearly 100 so-called "*jihadi* travelers" had departed the Netherlands for Syria, intending to join the civil war there. Their experience in the hostilities was likely to make them "highly radicalized, traumatized and with a strong desire to commit violence, thus posing a significant threat to this country"[2] upon their return. The Dutch General Intelligence and Security Service (AIVD) has also reported that terrorist financing activities and the dissemination of *jihadist* propaganda is currently taking place in the Netherlands in support of al-Shabaab, rendering Somalia yet another (albeit less popular) destination for would-be *jihadists*.[3] As a result of these trends, in March 2013 the government elevated its terror threat level from "limited" to "substantial"—an assessment that would remain in place through the end of 2016, at which point the number of Dutch citizens fighting abroad for extremist causes had doubled to more than 200.[4]

The Dutch government's fear of individual operators traveling abroad to wage *jihad* far predates the Syrian conflict. In fact, multiple Dutch nationals traversing Europe were arrested in the early 2000s, allegedly on their way to fight with other radical Muslims on behalf of the separatists in Chechnya.[5] In January 2002, Indian troops in Kashmir killed two young, "well-integrated" Dutch-Moroccans with ties to Eindhoven's *Salafi* al-Fourkaan mosque. The AIVD, alarmed by this proof that Dutch citizens could indeed be lured into *jihad*, began to investigate domestic recruitment by radical Islamic elements.[6] That December, the AIVD published *Recruitment for the Jihad in the Netherlands: From Incident to Trend*.[7] This memorandum concluded that "the phenomenon of recruitments in the West for the violent Islamic war forms an intrinsic part of a globally spreading radical Islamic movement."[8] Based on its investigation, the AIVD deduced that Islamist recruitment in the Netherlands represents the "first tangible illustrations of a tendency closely related to a stealthy entrance of a violent radical Islamic movement in Dutch society."[9] The AIVD assessed that these recruiters worked with an important principle in mind: that by creating deliberate polarization and antagonism in Dutch society and alienating moderate Muslims from their non-Muslim counterparts, they would increase the appeal of their violent agenda.[10]

It did not take long for the Dutch public to begin sharing these concerns. For many, the brutal murder of filmmaker, politician, and activist Theo Van Gogh in November

2004 finally gave form to the specter of Islamist militancy in the Netherlands. The assailant, Mohammed Bouyeri, was a highly-educated young man who was both raised and radicalized in Dutch society—a true homegrown terrorist. Public anger intensified rapidly in the days that followed van Gogh's murder. At least twelve mosques and two Islamic schools were torched, another was bombarded with Molotov cocktails, and two more schools linked to the al-Fourkaan mosque were victims of explosions. Angry mobs counterattacked, torching at least seven churches and six schools in response.[11] As a result, whereas 12 percent of Dutch voters considered terrorism to be a primary threat to the country in the fall of 2004, that proportion had grown to more than 40 percent less than one year later.[12] The chaos prompted the Dutch government to strengthen its anti-terror legislation and build a preventative strategy to counter domestic radicalization, recommending a commitment to judicial intervention in situations that were likely to lead to violence, criminal activity, or a large-scale rejection of the Dutch democratic legal system.[13] Yet in spite of these measures, the Dutch public continues to believe that terrorism poses a significant threat; for example, the results of a June 2016 Pew Global Attitudes survey reported that 71% of Dutch citizens consider ISIS to be the top threat facing the country.[14]

One of the original targets of the government's strategy was the *Hofstadgrouep*, or the Hofstad Network. Counting Mohammed Bouyeri among its most infamous members, the group was an autonomous radical cell formed in the Netherlands in 2002. The AIVD reported that the group never received significant financial support from outside networks, nor did it appear to possess a "coherent strategy."[15] Bouyeri's arrest and the manhunt that followed swept up eight of the Hofstad Network's other primary personalities. Many, including Dutch convert Jason Waters (also known as Abu Mujahied Amrik), maintained significant ties to the *Salafi* preachers of the al-Fourkaan mosque and other radical institutions. Since the jailing of the group's principal leaders in 2005, the AIVD has regarded the Hofstad Network as in decline, even defunct, but notes that the potential still exists for similar groups to form and foment, further endangering Dutch society.[16]

When tied to specific ethnicities or nationalistic causes, small radical groups may appeal to the multiple Muslim minority communities—particularly Turkish and Moroccan—that reside in the Netherlands. One such example in recent years has been the *Kalifatsstaat* movement, headquartered in Cologne, Germany. Its very name an invocation to reinstate an Ottoman Caliphate across Europe, *Kalifatsstaat* dedicated itself to the restoration of an Islamist state in Turkey.[17] The group's most recent leader was Metin Kaplan, a Turkish militant raised in Germany who had reportedly received funding for his organization from Middle Eastern sources. In November 2000, a German court convicted Kaplan for inciting murder, and he served a four-year sentence. He was later extradited to Turkey, where authorities sentenced him to life in prison for his plans to violently overthrow the country's former, secular government.[18] Historically, the movement has had only a small presence in the Netherlands, and since Kaplan's imprisonment, the organization has had difficulties obtaining financing.

However, given the large Turkish minority residing in the Netherlands, many fear that the activity of such groups threatens the peaceful integration of minorities into their host culture.

Similarly, while some authors dispute the "radical" label attached to the schools and followers of Turkish scholar Fethullah Gülen, the Dutch government's concern with their activities prompted an official investigation into the movement's presence in the Netherlands in 2008. The finding that Gülen-inspired schools promoted "anti-integrative behavior" prompted the government to significantly reduce the level of funding it had previously provided to the movement.[19] Nonetheless, Gülenism continues to arouse suspicions and foster antagonism even among different elements of the Dutch Turkish community: after the failed Turkish military coup of July 2016, which Ankara alleges was masterminded by Gülen, a Turkish state news organization published a controversial list of all Gülen-affiliated organizations and individuals in the Netherlands. Although the Dutch government angrily denounced this foreign interference in their domestic affairs, many concerned parents withdrew their children from the "Gülen-list" schools, resulting in a 20 percent loss to the collective student body.[20]

The radical pan-Islamist organization *Hizb ut-Tahrir* also maintains a small presence in the Netherlands. The group is especially strong in the Rotterdam area, where it has gathered a following among highly educated young Turkish men. Although the number of its followers is assessed to be in the low hundreds, the Dutch National Coordinator for Counter Terrorism's 2016 threat assessments note increased cooperation between *Hizb ut-Tahrir* and various *Salafist* organizations, in spite of their ideological differences, driven in part by the elevated tension in the general public discourse over Islam.[21]

The Moroccan Arrahmane mosque in Amsterdam is the headquarters of the Dutch branch of *Tablighi Jama'at*. Although *Tablighi Jama'at* is in principle an apolitical movement, the Dutch authorities have expressed concern that its ideology may further the "social isolation and radicalization" of vulnerable elements within the Moroccan immigrant community.[22] The mosque's executive committee clashed in 2003 with a group of moderate Muslims who objected to the preaching of *Tabligh* doctrine there. The executive committee defended the organization's weekly use of the mosque by arguing that it had been constructed using funds from donors in Saudi Arabia, Qatar, and the United Arab Emirates, all of which are countries that support *Tablighi Jama'at*.[23] Internationally, in recent years, the movement has increasingly come to be seen as an incubator for aspiring terrorists. Many European recruits are rumored to have used *Tablighi* connections as a pathway into Pakistan, where they then disappeared into the *jihadi* training camps of the Federally Administered Tribal Areas.[24]

Salafists

In its approach to domestic Salafism, the Dutch government applies a framework separating the movement into three "strands:" apolitical Salafism, which encourages *da'wa* (proselytization) and isolation from non-Muslim society; political Salafism, which promotes engagement in society in order to advance the group's specific religious objectives; and *jihadi* Salafism, undoubtedly the most extreme of the three, as it glorifies violence against non-believers.[25] While it is important to recognize that the risks posed by *jihadi* Salafism are much greater and more immediate than those posed by the other two strands, the AIVD's 2015 annual report nevertheless expressed alarm with the overall movement's "polarizing message of intolerance… [which can] constitute a breeding ground for processes of radicalization that eventually lead to violent jihad."[26]

From the mid-1980s until 2001, *Salafism* grew largely unhindered in the Netherlands.[27] *Salafists* are estimated to have access to around 15 percent of all Dutch mosques,[28] with their presence strongest in the el-Tawheed mosque in Amsterdam, the al-Fourkaan mosque in Eindhoven, the as-Sunnah mosque in The Hague, and the Islamic Foundation for Education and Transmission of Knowledge (ISOOK) in Tilburg.[29] Interestingly, Dutch *Salafi* mosques have a multinational membership base, which is a striking contrast to the homogeneous character of the Moroccan or Turkish mosques and organizations in the Netherlands as described above. Muslims from Pakistan, Afghanistan, Turkey, the Middle East, North Africa, and the Horn of Africa, as well as Dutch converts, all visit *Salafi* centers.[30] *Salafi* lectures at these institutions generally draw sizable audiences of at least 100 people,[31] and the centers are considered to be potential sites of radicalization in the Netherlands. As a result, after the 2004 Van Gogh murder, the Dutch government increased its pressure on *Salafi* centers across the country. Public prosecutors could not assemble enough evidence to close the centers outright, but three *imams* of the al-Fourkaan mosque were declared *personae non grata* and deported from the country.[32]

Sources in the U.S. intelligence community reported that "[t]he number of locations, lectures and active preaching at least doubled between 2005 and the first half of 2007."[33] Ideological momentum appeared to slow in 2009 in the face of government and civilian (both Muslim and non-Muslim) opposition. But Dutch *Salafists* now appear to be pursuing different tactics, and as of 2014 the AIVD assesses that the movement is gaining strength once more.[34] The AIVD attributes a large part of this growth to renewed interest in *Salafi* doctrine sparked by the violence and chaos of the Syrian conflict.[35] But there is also evidence that social media and a new generation of traveling *Salafi* preachers are contributing to the movement's renewed appeal; this new generation of independent preachers, typically born and raised in the Netherlands, preaches in Dutch, allowing access to a greater number of potential Dutch converts, and it emphasizes *da'wa* and the expansion of the faith among non-practicing Muslims rather than the espousal of violence and *jihad*.[36] The AIVD notes that even these *da'wa* organizations "have again hardened their tone after a period of relative moderation, becoming more anti-integration, intolerantly isolationist and hostile to any form of dissenting thought."[37]

Eindhoven's al-Fourkaan mosque is the oldest *Salafi* institution in the Netherlands, and the number of prominent orthodox Muslim leaders that have emerged from it is a sign of its influence. Ahmad Salam, considered by many to be the most influential *Salafi* preacher in the Netherlands, was an *imam* and trustee of the al-Fourkaan mosque before he founded the Islamic Foundation for Education and Transfer of Knowledge (ISOOK) in Tilburg in 2000. Mohammed Cheppih, founder of the Poldermosque in Amsterdam and chairman of the Dutch chapter of the Muslim World League, also maintains a connection to the al-Fourkaan mosque, where his father serves as a trustee. Yahia Bouyafa, the leader of the Muslim Brotherhood in the Netherlands, was once a trustee of the Foundation for Islamic Elementary Schools in Eindhoven, an organization linked to the *al-Waqf al-Islami*, a Saudi proselytizing organization.

The network of connections only grows more complex from there. The leaders of mosques in The Hague, Amsterdam, and Tilburg jointly form the board of the Foundation for the Islamic Committee for Ahl-Sunnah in Europe. This foundation is part of a European network of political *Salafis* managed from Saudi Arabia by Syrian *Salafi* leader Adnan al-Arour.[38] In the past, al-Arour has been a primary speaker at Islamic conferences held at the ISOOK mosque in Tilburg and the al-Fourkaan mosque in Eindhoven. In 1999, several members of the radical Hamburg cell (who later carried out the 9/11 attacks) and their associates attended these conferences.[39] That same year, at least three of the 9/11 hijackers—Ramzi Binalshib, Mohammed Atta, and Marwan al-Shehhi—were rumored to have visited the El-Tawheed mosque in Amsterdam.[40] The two young men who were killed in Kashmir in 2002 (one of whom was the son of one of the mosque's board members) had regularly attended services in the al-Fourkaan mosque.[41] One of the board members of *al-Waqf al-Islami* (the body that controls the al-Fourkaan mosque) is Adil Hamad Abderrahman al-Husayni, who was mentioned in the infamous "Golden Chain" document that listed possible funders of al-Qaeda.[42] The AIVD remains wary of this web of al-Fourkaan associations and continues to track them in annual dossiers and reports while advising the mosque to be cautious when issuing invitations to guests. In December 2015, for example, acting on NCTV guidance, Eindhoven mayor Rob van Gijzel barred seven controversial *imams* from speaking at the mosque because of their past glorification of violence committed in the name of Islam.[43]

The Muslim Brotherhood

Although certainly less influential than *Salafi* elements, the Muslim Brotherhood has also gained influence in the Netherlands in recent years, supported by the organization's European umbrella, the Federation of Islamic Organizations in Europe (FIOE). In 2006, Yahia Bouyafa, who serves as the Chairman of the Brotherhood in the Netherlands, convinced authorities in the Slotervaart quarter in Amsterdam to allow him build the first mosque of the FIOE in the Netherlands.[44] The mosque is now believed to be the headquarters of the Dutch Muslim Brotherhood.[45] With the help of the Europe Trust (the European financial vehicle of the Muslim Brotherhood), its Dutch spin-off, the Europe Trust Netherlands, was able to buy its own real estate in The Hague and begin the construction of another mosque in Amsterdam.[46] In both cases, the sources of the two million Euros that funded the construction remained undisclosed.

Some speculated that Bouyafa aspired to gain political influence and take over the representation of the entire Muslim community in the Netherlands, pointing to his campaign to become chairman of one of the two government-approved organizations that represent Dutch Muslims in an official channel of dialogue with the government. Bouyafa is now the chairman of the heterogeneous Contact Group Islam (CGI). This group was created as a counterweight to the Sunni-dominated Contact Body for Muslims and Government (*Contactorgaan Moslims Overheid*, or CMO). The CGI was originally intended to represent Shi'a Muslims, Alawites, Ahmadiyya, and Sufi groups. Yet when Bouyafa took it over, the group fell under Sunni control. The CMO is reportedly highly influenced by the Turkish Milli Görüs movement. The leadership shift meant that both organizations representing Muslims in a dialogue with the Dutch government are Sunni-dominated and highly influenced by the ideology of the Muslim Brotherhood.

Although they cannot compete in size with the Brotherhood, the AIVD deems a number of homegrown radical movements to be threatening as well. Such groups include Behind Bars, Street *Daw'ah*, and Shariah4Holland. Members of these groups have allegedly joined the ranks of those bound for the Syrian civil war.[47] Moreover, they are responsible for hate crimes and public demonstrations, "encourag[ing] anti-democratic and intolerant values… [and] creating a climate in which the use of violence becomes more acceptable."[48] The AIVD's annual report for 2013 assessed that, by virtue of the number of members of these groups who have become foreign fighters traveling to Syria, "they have crossed the line from rhetoric to action. Effectively, the organizations have thus become actual jihadist networks with their core members fighting in Syria and, at home, a wider group of supporters engaged in ever more fervent propaganda."[49]

ISLAMIST ACTIVITY

As of 2014 (the latest such data available), the Dutch Central Bureau of Statistics (CBS), or Statistics Netherlands, reported that legal Muslim residents in the Netherlands accounted for approximately 5% of the country's total population.[50] The illegal Muslim population is much harder to quantify but is also quite substantial.[51] The two largest groups of Muslim immigrants in the Netherlands are Turks (approximately 37 percent of the total Muslim population) and Moroccans (roughly 36 percent).[52] Other large Muslims communities come from Suriname, Afghanistan, Iraq, Somalia,

Pakistan, and Iran.[53] Several thousand native Dutch converts and children of second-generation Muslim immigrants comprise the last piece of the multifaceted Dutch Muslim community.[54]

According to one assessment of Islam in the Netherlands, "whereas today many of the Dutch majority population support the idea of migrants adopting Dutch norms and values, the migrants themselves aspire to a combination of independent cultural development."[55] While it is certainly possible to debate the truth of this statement, there are several other important factors that create a gap between Muslim immigrant communities and the rest of Dutch society. The average age of the Muslim population is much lower than that of the country in general, at 25 years of age for Muslims and 38 for non-Muslims.[56] This age gap, taken in combination with discrepancies in levels of education achieved and language ability, poses a challenge to the seamless integration sought by the Dutch authorities, potentially even increasing the sentiments of disaffection and alienation that can lead to radicalization. The diverse nature of the Muslim community has also prevented any kind of large-scale, viable political movement from forming in support of its varied interests and concerns.[57]

At 2.4% of the country's overall population,[58] Turks make up the largest Muslim community in the Netherlands, and the infrastructure that exists to support them is quite sizable. The main Muslim organizations within the Turkish community belong to mosques under the control of Diyanet (the Turkish religious affairs directorate in Ankara) or to the non-governmental Milli Görüs movement, which is headquartered in Cologne, Germany.[59] This directorate maintains significant power over its diaspora community in the Netherlands, including the right to appoint *imams* for Diyanet-controlled mosques,[60] although all *imams* are required by the Dutch government to take a year-long "integration course" before they are permitted to practice in the country.[61] Diyanet operates through two larger umbrella organizations: the Turkish Islamic Cultural Foundation (TICF, founded in 1979) and the Dutch Islamic Foundation (ISN, founded 1982).[62] Traditionally, the government-controlled official nature of Diyanet has kept it distinct from Milli Görüs. For decades, in fact, the Turkish government was openly hostile to the group, suspicious of the multiple Islamist parties that sprang up in its wake.

In the Netherlands, however, both Diyanet and Milli Görüs cooperate in umbrella organizations such as the Council for Mosques (*Raad voor Moskeeën*) or the aforementioned CMO.[63] Milli Görüs has not been explicitly active in Dutch politics but retains a power base within the insular Turkish community, and its influence continues to grow. Many scholars believe the perception of Milli Görüs in the Netherlands to be more favorable than that of its sister chapter in Germany, asserting that the Dutch government's more tolerant attitude has allowed the organization to establish itself more effectively.[64] While Milli Görüs's image in the Netherlands remains relatively benign, one of its radical offshoots gained international attention in 2008. A cooperative sting spearheaded by France led to the arrest of ten suspects for financing international terrorism. One of the suspects was a Turkish immigrant to the Netherlands, who was accused of collecting funds for Metin Kaplan's *Kalifatsstaat*.[65] In 2013, Deputy Prime Minister Lodewijk Asscher announced that the activities of both Diyanet and Milli Görüs would be monitored closely to ascertain whether or not the way the organizations were operating was inhibiting integration.[66] A vivid example of this trend occurred in 2016 after the failed coup in Ankara, when Gülen-sympathizing Dutch Turks reported that they had been the targets of vandalism and threatened with violence. Allegedly, this hostility came from Dutch Turks who are decidedly anti-Gülenist —a demographic that includes members of Diyanet-controlled mosques.[67] Thus the government has valid reason to fear that poor integration of the Turkish community will cause religious violence and tension to spill over into the broader Dutch society.

Moroccans constitute the second-largest Muslim community in the Netherlands, controlling a full 40 percent of all Dutch mosques.[68] Although the majority of Moroccan immigrants appear to have integrated well into Dutch society, the demographic is disproportionately represented in the government's threat assessments of potential *jihadists*. After 9/11, the Dutch authorities reported that, of the small number of Dutch citizens willing to actively support or carry out violent terrorist activities, most of these potential militants were Moroccan immigrants.[69] More recently, AIVD reports published in 2014 and 2015 affirmed that the majority of Dutch foreign fighters in Syria are also of Moroccan origin.[70][71] There has been a corresponding increase in angry public rhetoric and anti-Moroccan discrimination;[72] in one particularly high-profile example, Geert Wilders, the leader of the nationalist *Partij voor de Vrijheid* (Party for Freedom, or PVV), started a chant at a rally calling for "fewer Moroccans" in the country.

Other outside Islamist organizations also maintain a footprint in Dutch society, including the Saudi-funded Muslim World League. In the Netherlands, the MWL has its home in the Tilburg Islamic Cultural Center.[73] The organization takes responsibility for building mosques, operating cultural centers, and publishing Islamic texts. However, many MWL financers adhere to the fundamentalist *Wahhabi* brand of Islam, which has made many non-Muslims skeptical of its influence.[74]

The Syrian conflict has catalyzed changing attitudes among many Dutch citizens as the wave of refugees seeking asylum in the EU brings the conflict closer to home. The Dutch government has stated that Syrian asylum seekers represented nearly half of all the arrived refugees in the Netherlands in 2015 (approximately 27,700 out of a total 58,880).[75] At the EU Migration Summit in 2015, the Netherlands agreed to accept over the course of two years an additional 7,000 resettled asylum seekers who had originally arrived elsewhere in Europe.[76] As the November 2015 attacks in Paris made clear, foreign fighters en route to Europe from Syria could easily take advantage of the chaos caused by the refugee crisis to return unnoticed. The AIVD reported in 2016 that there were 40 returned fighters back in the Netherlands, and at least 150 still at large in Syria, who would likely "pose a greater threat [upon their return] because they will be better trained and have more combat experience" than those who had returned sooner.[77]

Consequently, the famous Dutch tolerance has decreased somewhat and been replaced by rising xenophobia in the wake of the Syrian conflict and the refugee crisis. In September 2016, the Pew Research Center reported that 61 percent of Dutch citizens think that refugees will increase terrorism in the country; in the same poll, a full third of Dutch respondents said that growing diversity made the Netherlands a worse place to live.[78] As is the case across Western Europe, the presence of large Muslim communities and questions of integration have clearly provoked sentiments of unease and fear among neighbors who blame multiculturalism for increased violence and other social ills.[79] Indeed, the AIVD has noted how radical elements may attempt to exploit these sentiments:

> ...the Islamists involved are indeed aware of the "favorable" polarizing effect of Islamist-inspired violent activities. Such violent activities promote the prejudices of the Dutch population about all Muslims. As a result thereof, Muslims also increasingly get the idea that they are alienated from the Dutch society and the chance that they become susceptible to radical ideas becomes bigger.[80]

ISLAMISM AND THE STATE

As attacks in Paris, Brussels, and Istanbul rocked Europe in 2014 and 2015, the Dutch government proactively took steps to lead anti-extremist efforts on the continent while simultaneously strengthening counterterrorism legislation and border security measures. The Netherlands serves as a member of the Global Coalition to Counter ISIL, conducting airstrikes on behalf of the coalition, and maintaining a liaison in U.S. Central Command. Amsterdam also recognizes the importance of travel intervention in keeping foreign fighters from leaving its territory. As of 2016, the Dutch government is deliberating legislation that allows for harsh administrative sanctions linked to citizenship and freedom of movement. In May 2016, for example, the lower house of the Dutch Parliament approved a controversial bill permitting the revocation of a dual citizen's Dutch nationality if he or she is deemed to have joined a terrorist organization.[81] The government is also now permitted to "impose a notification requirement, an area ban or a restraining order in response to practices that can be placed in connection with terrorist activities or support for them. Examples include contact with other radicalised [sic] people combined with a conspicuous interest in certain properties or events."[82] Notably, both of these penalties can be imposed even without prior criminal convictions for the individual under suspicion.

Another goal of the government's strategy is to isolate radicals, empower the voices of moderate Muslims, and strengthen the bonds between Muslim immigrants and the Dutch democratic political system and society.[83] The Netherlands helps lead the European Commission-sponsored Radicalisation Awareness Network and its Centre of Excellence, and it has championed EU efforts to develop protocols to counter terrorism financing. In August 2014, it began implementation of a Comprehensive Action Programme to Combat Jihadism, intended to "protect the democratic state under the rule of law, to counter and weaken the jihadist movement in the Netherlands and to eliminate the breeding ground for radicalization.[84] Among the important tactics introduced in this program are: an increase in administrative measures to block and disrupt radical *imams* and propagandists; the creation of support networks for those concerned or affected by the perceived radicalization of a loved one; the establishment of a center to monitor social tensions and radicalization; and the formation of an infrastructure to guide the dissemination of narratives and views that counter Islamist doctrine and promote the rule of law.

Another important tenet of the program is its emphasis on combating radicals online. By recognizing the power of social media as a recruiting and dissemination tool, the government is responding with new measures to identify and sanction online producers of propaganda, work with internet companies to proactively dismantle any sites or users violating terms of use agreements, and manage a hotline for citizens to report any online content inciting hatred or promoting violence.

The NCTV is responsible for the implementation of the Programme. The NCTV was born out of the muddled European response to the 2004 Madrid train bombings, at which point the Dutch government realized the dire need to patch the holes in its own counterterror infrastructure. In keeping with its mission "to minimize the risk of terrorist attacks in the Netherlands and to take prior measures to limit the potential impact of terrorist acts,"[85] the NCTV has since focused on the issue of counter-radicalization, launching a joint government and law enforcement operation to "disrupt" the work of the main *Salafi* centers in the Netherlands.[86] The Dutch counter-radicalization approach focuses both on Islamic fundamentalists and right-wing nationalists, since racially-motivated attacks against Muslims (as occurred increasingly after Van Gogh's murder in 2004) can spike hate crimes and deepen feelings of alienation and anger.[87]

This preventative outlook in the current European security environment demonstrate the Dutch government's continued adherence to its so-called "broad approach" to countering radicalization.[88] It is grounded on the idea that "no one is born a terrorist, but first goes through a short or longer process of radicalization before he or she decides to risk the life of other and his or her own for a political objective."[89] Funds allocated for this program support the goal of cooperation with Muslim communities by stimulating partnership and reducing the appeal of Islamist narratives. As explicitly delineated in the Comprehensive Action Programme, law enforcement authorities are encouraged to pursue partnership with moderate mosques and *imams* to negate the polarization pushed by radical elements. At the same time, the government incentivizes integration by Muslim community leaders and individuals. For instance, while the government provides educational subsidies for the training of *imams* at Dutch universities, each participant in the program must first complete a yearlong "integration course" to familiarize themselves with local communities and customs.[90] Law enforcement officials and social workers familiar with local conditions in various towns and villages are designated as official points of contact in such approaches. Skeptics, however, have long derided the utility of the broad approach, given that it oversimplifies the motivations for at-risk individuals, may spark resentment among moderate Muslims, and has little effect on the low-profile, small study groups where such radicalization often occurs.[91][92]

Select elements in the Dutch political discourse, however, threaten the credibility of this approach, thus risking a further increase in social polarization in a way that serves extremist purposes. Particularly in debates over immigration and asylum, the narrative of the looming threat posed by potential radicals gains more ground than that of the government's constructive attempts to head it off. This trend largely began at the turn of this century when the "leader of the Dutch new right" Pim Fortuyn spearheaded a campaign to restrict Dutch immigration and asylum policies.[93] Fortuyn was known not only for his aggressive stance against militant Islam, but also for a hardline belief that Dutch borders must be closed to any further Muslim immigration. He charged that the Netherlands was too small to continue to absorb high numbers of immigrants, and that Islamic values clashed irreconcilably with the permissive Dutch society.[94] After Fortuyn's murder in 2003 by a radical activist (whose motive was reportedly to stop the scapegoating of Dutch Muslims for society's problems),[95] his political mantle was quickly assumed by Geert Wilders, head of the Freedom Party (PVV). Wilders was initially able to leverage his party's crucial position in the ruling Center-right coalition to push the conversation on his priority issues and controversial proposals: stricter regulations on immigration, outlawing the *burqa* and the *niqab*, and a ban on dual nationality (which is held by an estimated 1.5 to 2 million Dutch citizens).[96] The Dutch electorate checked the influence of the PVV in the 2013 parliamentary elections when the party lost 9 seats and, with them, Wilder's ability to advance his agenda legislatively.[97] This perceived backlash was complemented by the 2012 formation of the No Border Network, an alliance of activists and extremists opposed to the restrictive immigration policy of the center-right coalition.

However, Wilders' star appears to be rising once again. The PVV is just one of the hardline Eurosceptic parties that soared in popularity in the lead-up to the United Kingdom's 2016 Brexit vote, and its platform has been gaining ground ever since. In November 2016, for example, 132 of the 150 members of Parliament voted to outlaw wearing the niqab in schools, hospitals, government buildings, and other public places; Wilders vowed to expand this to a total ban in 2017.[98] Wilders makes no secret of his personal views of the threat that Islam poses to Dutch society and to the West, and he has faced legal action for this position. His December 2016 conviction for inciting discrimination against the Netherlands' Moroccan minority did not hurt his party's image;[99] rather, the Dutch Broadcasting Foundation reported increased support for the PVV, due in part to the fact that many Dutch citizens believed it was unfair that Wilders had been tried at all.[100] By the end of 2016, with three months left until the general election, the ruling Liberal party was falling farther behind in the polls, and Wilders and the PVV enjoyed the support of 20-25% of the Dutch electorate[101]—not enough to make Wilders the Prime Minister in the Dutch coalition-based Parliament, but enough to ensure that the contentious agenda outlined Wilders' August 2016 party manifesto will continue to further polarize Parliament and the public debate. The manifesto proposed closure of all Islamic schools and mosques, a ban on the Koran and the wearing of headscarves, and a halt to all immigration from Islamic countries in pursuit of complete "de-Islamization" of the Netherlands.[102] Although the actual passage of any such agenda would require the PVV first to win the election and then to build a strong coalition in Parliament, the propagation of these ideas contributes to social polarization and puts at risk the counter-Islamist agenda that the Dutch government is currently pursuing.

ENDNOTES

[1] United States Department of State, Office of the Coordinator of Counterterrorism, Country Reports on Terrorism 2012 (Washington, DC: U.S. Department of State, May 2013), http://www.state.gov/documents/organization/210204.pdf.

[2] "Netherlands, Germany alarmed over Islamic extremists," Hurriyet Daily News, March 14, 2013, http://www.hurriyetdailynews.com/netherlands-germany-alarmed-over-islamist-extremists-.aspx?pageID=238&nid=42916.

[3] Ministry of Interior of the Netherlands, AIVD (General Intelligence and Security Service), "Annual Report – 2012," 2012, https://www.aivd.nl/english/publications-press/@2999/annual-report-2012/.

[4] National Coordinator for Security and Counterterrorism, "Current threat level for the Netherlands: Substantial," November 14, 2016, https://english.nctv.nl/organisation/counterterrorism/TerroristThreatAssessmentNetherlands/CurrentThreatlevel/index.aspx.

[5] The "Hofstadgroep," Transnational Terrorism, Security, and the Rule of Law, European Commission 6th Framework Program, April 15, 2007, revised April 2008, http://www.transnationalterrorism.eu/tekst/publications/Hofstadgroep.pdf.

[6] E.S.M. Akerboom, "Ten Years of Dutch Counterterrorism Policy," National Coordinator for Security and Counterterrorism, September 9, 2011.

[7] AIVD, Recruitment for the Jihad in the Netherlands: From Incident to Trend, Leidschendam, December 3, 2002.

[8] Ibid.

[9] Ibidem.

[10] E.S.M. Akerboom, "Counter-terrorism in the Netherlands," Tijdschrift voor de Politie (Police Magazine), June 2003, https://fas.org/irp/world/netherlands/ct.pdf.

[11] Ministry of the Interior and Kingdom Relations, National Crisis Centrum, Situation Report NCC2004/81492/nr.1, November 10, 2004; NCC2004/81492/nr.2, November 11, 2004; NCC2004/81759/nr.3; November 12, 2004; November 13, 2004; NCC2004/81759/nr.4, November 15, 2004; NCC2004/81759/nr.6, November 16, 2004; NCC2004/82039/nr.7, November 23, 2004; NCC2004/82663/nr.11, November 26, 2004; NCC2004/83053/nr.12, November 30, 2004; "Golf van aanslagen sinds dood Van Gogh," Brabants Dagblad, November 2004, http://www.brabantsdagblad.nl/algemeen/bdbinnenland/terreur//article28503.ece.

[12] The "Hofstadgroep," Transnational Terrorism, Security, and the Rule of Law.

[13] House of Representatives of the States General, "Letter from the Minister of Internal Affairs & Kingdom Relations and the Minister of Justice," Session 2005-2006, No. 30, September 29, 2005.

[14] Bruce Stokes, Richard Wike, and Jacob Poushter, "Europeans see ISIS, climate change as most serious threats," Pew Research Center, June 13, 2016, http://www.pewglobal.org/2016/06/13/europeans-see-isis-climate-change-as-most-serious-threats/.

[15] The "Hofstadgroep," Transnational Terrorism, Security, and the Rule of Law.

[16] Ibid.

[17] "Profile: The Caliph of Cologne," BBC (London), May 27, 2004, http://news.bbc.co.uk/2/hi/europe/1705886.stm.

[18] Ibid.

[19] Claire Berlinski, "Who is Fethullah Gulen?" City Journal 22, no. 4, Autumn 2012, http://www.city-journal.org/2012/22_4_fethullah-gulen.html.

[20] Janene Pieters, "Dutch politicians outraged over new 'Gulen-list,'" NLTimes.nl, August 31, 2016, http://www.nltimes.nl/2016/08/31/dutch-politicians-outraged-new-gulen-list/.

[21] NCTb, "Terrorist Threat Assessment for the Netherlands 42: Summary," July 2016, 5, https://english.nctv.nl/binaries/dtn42-summary_tcm32-83624.pdf.

[22] Ibid., 25.

[23] Jaco Alberts, "Marokkanen willen 'hun' moskee terug," NRC Handelsblad, September 20, 2003.

[24] See, for example, Omar Nasiri, Inside the Jihad: My life with Al Qaeda (Cambridge: Basic Books, 2006), 109-115.

[25] AIVD and National Coordinator for Security and Counterterrorism, "Salafism in the Netherlands: Diversity and Dynamics," September 2015, 5, https://english.aivd.nl/publications/publications/2015/09/24/salafism-in-the-netherlands-diversity-and-dynamics.

[26] AIVD, "Annual Report 2015: A Range of Threats to the Netherlands," April 2016, https://english.aivd.nl/latest/news/2016/05/27/annual-report-2015-aivd.

[27] National Coordinator for Counterterrorism, Salafism in the Netherlands. A passing phenomenon or a persistent factor of significance? (The Hague, March 2008), 25-26.

[28] Ibid.

[29] Ibidem.

[30] Ibidem.

[31] NCTb, 7e voortgangsrapportage terrorismebestrijding, November 26, 2007, 5516003/07/NCTb, 5.

[32] NCTb, Derde Voortgangsrapportage terrorismebestrijding, December 5, 2005, 5388583/05/NCTb.

[33] NCTb, Derde Voortgangsrapportage terrorismebestrijding, December 5, 2005, 5388583/05/NCTb., 40.

[34] AIVD and National Coordinator for Security and Counterterrorism, "Salafism in the Netherlands: Diversity and dynamics," 8.

[35] Ibid, 8.

[36] Ibidem, 9.

[37] AIVD, "Annual Report 2014: Not only returnees but also 'stay-at-homes' pose a threat," May 13, 2015, 19, https://english.aivd.nl/publications/annual-report/2015/05/13/annual-report-2014-not-only-returnees-but-also-"stay-at-homes"-pose-a-threat.

[38] Chamber of Commerce, dossier number 34153259; NCTb, Salafism in the Netherlands, 31.

[39] Ian Johnson and Crawford, "A Saudi Group Spreads Extremism in 'Law' seminars, Taught in Dutch," Wall Street Journal, April 16, 2003.

[40] "Official: Terrorists Met in Amsterdam," Associated Press, September 13, 2002.

[41] AIVD, "Saudi influences in the Netherlands. Links between the Salafist mission, radicalisation processes and Islamic terrorism," 2004; Chamber of Commerce, Foundation Waqf, dossier number 41091392.

[42] Chamber of Commerce, dossier number 41091392; Tareek Osama, file number 41 (Golden Chain document).

[43] "Eindhoven weert zeven imams die geweld verheerlijken uit moskee [Eindhoven bans seven imams who glorify violence from mosque]," de Volkskrant, December 22, 2015, http://www.volkskrant.nl/binnenland/eindhoven-weert-zeven-imams-die-geweld-verheerlijken-uit-moskee-a4212673/.
[44] Moskee Moslim Broederschap in Slotervaart vormt geen gevaar, April 21, 2009, http://allochtonen.web-log.nl/allochtonen/2009/04/moskee-moslimb.html; "FION announces building of Mosque in Slotervaart (in Arabic)," March 2008, http://www.islamonline.net/arabic/arts/2008/03/01.pdf; "SP wil opheldering ove FION moskee in Slotervaart," February 16, 2009; http://allochtonen.web-log.nl/allochtonen/2009/02/sp-wil-ophelder.html.
[45] Ronald Sandee, The Influence of the Muslim Brotherhood in the Netherlands, NEFA Foundation, December 2007, http://www1.nefafoundation.org/miscellaneous/nefambnetherlands1207.pdf.
[46] Joost de Haas, "MOSLIMBROEDERS RUKKEN OP; Peperduur pand aangekocht voor nieuw 'hoofdkwartier' in Den Haag? 'Achterliggend doel is invoering van sharia' 'Ze zien er niet uit als extremisten,'" De Telegraaf (Amsterdam), May 31, 2008; See also Answers of the mayor of Amsterdam to questions of the Amsterdam city council, February 19, 2009, http://biodata.asp4all.nl/andreas/2009/09012f978057b028/09012f978057b028.pdf.
[47] AIVD, Annual Report 2012, 27.
[48] Ibid.
[49] Soeren Kern, "Dutch Jihadists in Syria Pose a Threat to the Netherlands," Gatestone Institute, May 15, 2014, https://www.gatestoneinstitute.org/4308/dutch-jihadists-syria.
[50] "The Netherlands," in United States Department of State, 2015 Report on International Religious Freedom, August 10, 2016, https://www.state.gov/j/drl/rls/irf/2015/eur/256225.htm.
[51] Sheila Kamerman, "Illegal Aliens like Helen can't hack it in the Netherlands," NRC Handelsblad, February 11, 2010, http://www.nrc.nl/international/Features/article2481118.ece/Illegal_aliens_like_Helen_cant_hack_it_in_the_Netherlands.
[52] "The Position of Muslims in the Netherlands: Facts and Figures," Institute for Multicultural Affairs (Utrecht), 2010, http://www.forum.nl/PortalsInternational/english-pdf/Muslims-in-the-Netherlands-2010.pdf.
[53] Ibid.
[54] "More than 850 thousand Muslims in the Netherlands."
[55] Jan Willem Duyvendak, Trees Pels and Rally Rijkschroeff, "A Multicultural paradise? The cultural factor in Dutch integration policy," Paper presented at the 3rd ECPR Conference, Budapest, Hungary, September 8-10, 2005, 7.
[56] "The Position of Muslims in the Netherlands: Facts and Figures."
[57] Barahim and Ostawar, "The Political Participation of Dutch Muslims."

[58] "Netherlands," CIA World Factbook, January 12, 2017, https://www.cia.gov/library/publications/the-world-factbook/geos/nl.html.

[59] Nico Landman, Van mat tot minaret: De institutionalisering van de islam in Nederland (Amsterdam 1992), 80-82.

[60] "The Netherlands," United States Department of State, 2012 Report on International Religious Freedom.

[61] Freedom House, "Netherlands: Country Report," Freedom in the World 2016, n.d., https://freedomhouse.org/report/freedom-world/2016/netherlands.

[62] Thijl Sunier, et al., "Diyanet: The Turkish Directorate for Religious Affairs in a Changing Environment." VU University Amsterdam, Utrecht University, January 2011, http://www.fsw.vu.nl/nl/Images/Final%20report%20Diyanet%20February%202011_tcm30-200229.pdf.

[63] Heelsum, Fennema and Tillie, Moslim in Nederland, 16.

[64] Ahmet Yukleyen, "State Policies and Islamism in Europe: Milli Görüs in Germany and the Netherlands," Journal of Ethnic and Migration Studies 36, iss. 3, 2010; Gonul Tol, "What Type of Islamism for Europe? Islamism in Germany and the Netherlands." Middle East Institute Insight Turkey 11, no. 1, 2009, 133-149.

[65] John Leicester, "10 arrested in France, Germany, Netherlands in terrorism probe," Associated Press, May 17, 2008, http://www.boston.com/news/world/articles/2008/05/17/10_arrested_in_france_germany_netherlands_in_terror_probe/.

[66] "Pikant: Asscher steunt Nederlandse krant van omstreden Turkse beweging Gulenbeweging start weekblad voor Turkse-Nederlanders en Vlamingen," ["Hot: Asscher Supports a Dutch Newspaper for the controversial Turkish Gulen movement in Dutch and Flemish"] Joop.nl, March 30, 2013, http://www.joop.nl/media/detail/artikel/20297_pikant_asscher_steunt_nederlandse_krant_van_omstreden_turkse_beweging/.

[67] Janene Pieters, "Turkish-Dutch threatened for supporting Gulen," NLTimes.nl, July 19, 2016, http://www.nltimes.nl/2016/07/19/turkish-dutch-threatened-supporting-gulen/.

[68] NCTb, Salafism in the Netherlands, 25-26.

[69] National Security Service (BVD), Annual Report 2001, 17; Landman, Van mat tot minaret, 160-161.

[70] AIVD, "The Transformation of Jihadism in the Netherlands: Swarm Dynamics and New Strength," June 30, 2014, 26, https://www.aivd.nl/publicaties/publicaties/2014/06/30/the-transformation-of-jihadism-in-the-netherlands.

[71] AIVD, Annual Report 2015, 15.

[72] "Netherlands," in United States Department of State, Country Reports on Human Rights Practices for 2015, n.d., https://www.state.gov/j/drl/rls/hrrpt/humanrightsreport/#wrapper.

[73] Islamic Cultural Center in Netherlands," Muslim World League, n.d., http://en.themwl.org/content/islamic-cultural-center-netherlands.

[74] "Muslim World League and World Assembly of Muslim Youth," Pew Research Religion and Public Life Project, September 15, 2010, http://www.pewforum.org/2010/09/15/muslim-networks-and-movements-in-western-europe-muslim-world-league-and-world-assembly-of-muslim-youth/.

[75] "The influx of asylum seekers is changing in terms of composition," Government of the Netherlands, March 14, 2016, https://www.government.nl/topics/asylum-policy/news/2016/03/14/the-influx-of-asylum-seekers-is-changing-in-terms-of-composition.

[76] "Dijkhoff satisfied with outcome EU migration summit," Government of the Netherlands, September 22, 2015, https://www.government.nl/topics/asylum-policy/news/2015/09/22/dijkhoff-satisfied-with-outcome-eu-migration-summit.

[77] AIVD, Annual Report 2015, 15.

[78] Jacob Poushter, "European Attitudes of the Refugee Crisis," Pew Research Center, September 16, 2016, http://www.pewresearch.org/fact-tank/2016/09/16/european-opinions-of-the-refugee-crisis-in-5-charts/.

[79] Steven Erlanger, "Amid Rise of Multiculturalism, Dutch Confront Their Questions of Identity," New York Times, August 13, 2011, http://www.nytimes.com/2011/08/14/world/europe/14dutch.html?pagewanted=all&_r=0.

[80] Ibid.

[81] Wendy Zeldin, "Netherlands: Two New Sets of Administrative Sanctions Proposed to Fight Terrorism," Global Legal Monitor, Library of Congress, June 2, 2016, http://www.loc.gov/law/foreign-news/article/netherlands-two-new-sets-of-administrative-sanctions-proposed-to-fight-terrorism/.

[82] Ibid.

[83] Ibidem; Ministry of Justice, Nota radicalisme en radicalisering, August 19, 2005; 5358374/05/AJS.

[84] Zeldin, "Netherlands: Two New Sets of Administrative Sanctions Proposed to Fight Terrorism."

[85] National Coordinator for Counter Terrorism of the Netherlands, "About the NCTb," n.d., http://english.nctb.nl/organisation/about_the_NCTb/.

[86] NCTb, Derde Voortgangsrapportage terrorismebestrijding, December 5, 2005, 5388583/05/NCTb; Minstry of Justice, Nota radicalisme en radicalisering, August 19, 2005; 5358374/05/AJS.

[87] "Netherlands Sets Plan on Extremism," Associated Press, August 28, 2007, http://www.nytimes.com/2007/08/28/world/europe/28dutch.html?_r=0.

[88] Ministry of Justice and Ministry of Interior, "Operationeel Actieplan Polarisatie en radicalisering 2007-2011," August 27, 2007, http://www.tweedekamer.nl/images/297540141bijlage01_118-182859.pdf.

[89] Akerboom, "Ten Years of Dutch Counterterrorism Policy."

[90] "The Netherlands," United States Department of State, 2012 Report on International Religious Freedom.

[91] Ministry of Justice of The Netherlands, "Court has ruled in case of Hofstad group suspects," March 10, 2006, http://www.rechtspraak.nl/Gerechten/ Rechtbanken/s-Gravenhage/Actualiteiten/Rechtbank+heeft+uitspraak+ged aan+in+zaken+verdachten+Hofstadgroep.htm; Janny Groen and Annieke Kranenberg, Strijdsters van Allah, Radicale moslima's en het Hofstadnetwerk (Amsterdam: J.M. Meulenhoff, 2006) 69-99, 127-137.

[92] Teun Van Dongen, "The Case for Tailored Interventions in the Preventative Approach: Lessons from Countering Jihadism in the Netherlands and the UK," Countering Terrorist Recruitment in the Context of Armed Counter-Terrorism Operations, S. Ekici et al. (Eds), IOS Press, 2016.

[93] Kirsty Lang, "At home with 'Professor Pim,'" BBC, May 4, 2002, http://news.bbc.co.uk/2/hi/programmes/from_our_own_correspondent/1966979.stm.

[94] Ibid.

[95] Ambrose Evans-Pritchard and Joan Clements, "Fortuyn killed 'to protect Muslims,'" Telegraph (London), March 28, 2003, http://www.telegraph.co.uk/news/worldnews/europe/netherlands/1425944/Fortuyn-killed-to-protect-Muslims.html.

[96] "Parliament to press ahead with burqa dual nationality ban laws," DutchNews.nl, May 31, 2013, http://www.dutchnews.nl/news/archives/2012/05/parliament_to_press_ahead_with.php.

[97] "Dutch election: Pro-Europe VVD and Labour Parties win," BBC, September 13, 2012, http://www.bbc.co.uk/news/world-europe-19566165.

[98] Harriet Agerholm, "Dutch government approves partial burqa ban in public places," The Independent, November 29, 2016, http://www.independent.co.uk/news/world/europe/dutch-burqa-veil-ban-holland-votes-for-partial-restrictions-some-public-places-a7445656.html.

[99] Sheena McKenzie, "Geert Wilders guilty of 'insulting a group' after hate speech trial," CNN, December 9, 2016, http://www.cnn.com/2016/12/09/europe/geert-wilders-hate-speech-trial-verdict/.

[100] "Peilingwijzer: opmars PVV zet door," Nederlandse Omroep Stichting [Dutch Broadcasting Foundation], December 21, 2016, http://nos.nl/artikel/2149429-peilingwijzer-opmars-pvv-zet-door.html.

[101] "Geert Wilders' PVV stretches lead in latest poll of polls," DutchNews.nl, December 21, 2016, http://www.dutchnews.nl/news/archives/2016/12/geert-wilders-pvv-stretches-lead-in-latest-poll-of-polls/.

[102] Caroline Mortimer, "The Netherlands' Most Popular Party Wants To Ban All Mosques," Independent (London), August 28, 2016, http://www.independent.co.uk/news/world/europe/netherlands-pvv-leader-geert-wilders-koran-islam-mosque-ban-holland-dutch-pm-favourite-a7214356.html

Spain

> **Quick Facts**
>
> Population: 48,563,476 (July 2016 est.)
>
> Area: 505,370 sq km
>
> Ethnic Groups: Composite of Mediterranean and Nordic types
>
> Religions: Roman Catholic 94%, other 6%
>
> Government Type: Parliamentary constituional monarchy
>
> GDP (official exchange rate): $1.2 trillion (2015 est.)
>
> *Map and Quick Facts courtesy of the CIA World Factbook (Last Updated November 2016)*

Overview

Since the turn of the century, Spain has seen a surge in Muslim immigration. As of 2015, Spain's Muslim population constituted approximately 1.89 million people, nearly four percent of the country's total 48.6 million inhabitants, and a figure that grew by nearly 300,000 in two years.[1] But as Islam in Spain steadily grows, so does the risk of radicalization on its margins. The opposing phenomena of insular religious radicalism and Spanish xenophobia toward Muslim immigrants have obstructed the social integration of this rapidly expanding community. Spain's location as the gateway of the Mediterranean renders it a prime destination for immigrants from North Africa and for foreign radical elements among them. To many such individuals, al-Andalus—the territory of the Iberian Peninsula lost by Islam in the fifteenth century—is no longer simply an abstract cause, but rather a concrete jihadist objective.[2]

Meanwhile, in Spanish political discourse, the issue of Islamic radicalism remains largely taboo, and the government of Prime Minister Mariano Rajoy Brey has been loath to engage in the controversial debates arising from tensions with the country's Muslim minority. However, on the counterterrorism front, the administration's recent efforts indicate a more aggressive, determined approach to the prosecution of suspected terrorists and a dedicated pursuit of effective border security measures.

Islamist Activity

While Spain has not suffered a mass casualty attack since the 2004 Madrid bombings, its geographic location and North African exclaves provide an ideal logistical hub for the transit of supplies and fighters to and from the European mainland. The radical organizations engaging in such activities typically include immigrants from the Maghreb (mainly Algerians and Moroccans who belong to cells originating in their home countries) and from Pakistan, due to the historical presence of a large Pakistani immigrant community in Catalonia. Although such cells and networks have traditionally been small and autonomous, recent investigations by Spanish security forces have detected increasing links with larger groups abroad. At the end of September 2016, the Ministry of the Interior reported that 143 would-be jihadists—of whom 113 were Spanish nationals—had been detained since the government elevated its terror alert level to "4" in 2015.[3]

Organized transnational terrorist groups on Spanish soil date back to the trial and sentencing of the Algerian *Comando Dixan* cell in 2002 and the legal processes against militants from a Catalan *jihadist* network in Santa Coloma de Gramenet in 2006. In 2012, Barcelona's police forces initiated *Operación Kartago* (Operation Carthage) with the stated goal of "neutralizing" the threat of lone-wolf terrorism by preventing potential Spanish terrorists from traveling abroad to seek training.[4] Since then, the export of fighters to eastern conflict zones has remained a key concern, with radicalized individuals continuing attempts to join the Islamic State, al-Qaeda affiliates, and other international terrorist organizations. The U.S. State Department's most recent *Country Reports on Terrorism* assessed that "most" of Spain's 25 returned foreign fighters remain in detention.[5]

From 2015 to 2016 alone, Spanish authorities arrested 83 individuals for links to such organizations.[6] The cases span a wide range of charges, from financing terrorist organizations to public proclamations of intent to murder non-Muslim civilians,[7] and include the dissemination of al-Qaeda propaganda and training,[8] as well as the recruitment of new members for training abroad. Spanish police have compared the lone-wolf style radicalization of these suspects to that of the Tsarnaev brothers, who masterminded the April 2013 Boston Marathon bombings.[9]

In one particularly high profile operation in August 2012, Spanish authorities in cooperation with international security services arrested three al-Qaeda activists for planning a major attack on British Gibraltar during the 2012 Olympic Games. Two of the suspects, Eldar Magomedov and Muhamed Ankari Adamov, were Russian citizens of Chechen extraction, while the group's ringleader, Cengiz Yalzin, was originally from Turkey. Upon investigation of the men's apartments, Spanish authorities found enough explosives to blow up a bus.[10] However, since no specific target had been determined, the judge presiding over the case ruled that intent to commit terrorism could not be definitively proven, and thus the suspects were released.

This incident illustrates the legal difficulties associated with confronting Spanish *jihadist* networks. Several other cases prosecuted on charges of terrorism have resulted in similar acquittals, including:

- The November 2005 arrest of ten Algerians who had allegedly engaged in credit card forgery to raise funds for the GSPC and al Qaeda in Alicante, Granada, and Murcia. Five of these men were tried in the National Court in May 2010. They were acquitted of all terrorism charges, although three of the five were sentenced to prison for forgery.[11]
- The January 2008 arrest in Barcelona of eleven Pakistanis accused of plotting terrorist suicide attacks on the Barcelona metro system on the orders of Taliban leader Baitullah Mehsud. On December 14, 2009, the eleven detainees were found guilty of some of the charges leveled against them, but were found not guilty on the charges of terrorism; it was determined that the plot had not reached the level necessary to be a terrorist conspiracy.[12]
- The May 18, 2010 acquittal by Spain's *Audencia Nacional* (National Court) of two jihadists accused of attempting to make dirty bombs with red mercury.[13]
- The case of five Algerians arrested by Spanish security forces in September 2011 for providing logistical and financial support to al-Qaeda in the Islamic Maghreb (AQIM). All five were released when the judge ruled that there was insufficient evidence to convict.[14]

Alongside this pattern of non-conviction, past U.S. intelligence assessments have confirmed the alarming lack of intelligence on Islamist activity in Spain. In 2012, the Spanish daily *El País* published a Wikileaks cable written by the U.S. Embassy in Madrid in 2005, which reported that Spanish authorities had only minimal intelligence on radical groups in the country and recommended that a counterterrorism center be established at the U.S. consulate in Barcelona.[15] Although it remains unclear whether such a center was ever established, another U.S. cable from 2007 reports that Spanish authorities still deemed Barcelona's large Muslim population "susceptible to jihadist recruitment."[16]

There is an undeniable cause for concern regarding Islamist groups in Spain. Within the nation, five principal Islamist groups either overtly or covertly advocate a rigid adherence to Islamist doctrine and thus provide fertile ground for this kind of radicalization and recruitment. These groups are: the *Salafists, Al Adl wal Ihsane* ("Justice and Charity"), *Hizb ut-Tahrir, Tablighi Jama'at,* and the Muslim Brotherhood. While some of them may display a more moderate public face in order to avoid social marginalization or persecution, some scholars assert that their activities hinder the integration of Muslim communities into the social fabric of Spain.[17] Spanish intelligence sources estimated in 2012 that, of the more than 1,000 mosques throughout the country, 20 percent were involved in the active promotion of radical Islamic doctrine, primarily by calling for the rejection of Spanish society in favor of a strict adherence to a sharia-based lifestyle.[18] To that end, Spain's Interior, Justice and Labor Ministries published a joint 2010 report concluding that, despite the comparatively small percentage of radicals among Spain's Muslims, there are reasons for serious concern regarding both the intensity of their radicalism and their skill in promoting it.[19]

Numerous studies and investigations commissioned by city councils and the *Mossos d'Esquadra* (the autonomous regional civilian police of Catalonia) chronicle the advance of the *Salafist* movement in Spain.[20] *Salafists* are generally concentrated in the regions of Catalonia and Murcia and their surrounding areas. Local newspapers in these areas have reported cases of *Salafi imams* publicly advocating for a radical, violent ideology in their communities. In one such instance, nine men in Reus sentenced a woman accused of adultery to death by stoning. The woman managed to escape, and the men were arrested by the local *Mossos d'Esquadra*.[21] When brought to court, however, such cases have not often led to successful convictions, possibly due to bonds of loyalty between the imams and their congregations that may inhibit objective testimony.[22] However, the May 2013 deportation of Moroccan national, Noureddin Ziani, for disseminating *Salafist* ideology demonstrates that the Spanish government considers such ideas a "threat to society"[23] and is committed to countering them. Spain has also brought criminal charges against a significant number of well-known *jihadist* commanders espousing *Salafism*, including Eddin Barakat Yarkas, alias Abu Dahdah, a Spanish national directly linked to al-Qaeda and the 9/11 attacks. Abu Dadah was sentenced to 27 years in jail for membership in a terrorist organization and conspiracy to commit terrorist acts, although he was released early in 2013 when the Spanish Supreme Court reduced his sentence.[24]

Often, the most radicalized groups on Spanish soil maintain ties with different groups working in North Africa; for instance, the perpetrators of the 2004 Madrid train bombings were *Salafists* who received training abroad from the Moroccan Islamic Group (GICM). These connections open pathways to larger terrorist networks, including AQIM.[25] In other instances, Spain has served as an important hub for foreign *Salafist* organizations, including the Salafist Group for Preaching and Combat (GSPC), whose members frequently interact with the GICM as well as with radicals in Catalonia.[26]

Al Adl wal Ihsan represents another such foreign-based Islamist group, particularly in Spain's southern regions. Founded in 1983 by Moroccan preacher Sheikh Abdesalam Yassine, the group was outlawed by the Moroccan government for its refusal to recognize the religious legitimacy of the Moroccan Crown. Although it does not have as much visibility in Spain, Spanish authorities believe that *Al Adl wal Ihsan* has the potential to "damage the integration of Muslims into Spanish society by defending the prevalence of Islamic law over Western law, and have therefore labeled the group a radical organization."[27] Spanish authorities remain wary of any connection between *Al Adl wal Ihsan* and domestic Muslim organizations; in 2010, for example, the naturalization application of Mounir Benjelloun, vice president of Murcia's Islamic Federation (FIRM), was rejected because of his ties to *Al Adl wal Ihsan*. Benjelloun reportedly forged a close and potentially strategic relationship between FIRM and *Al Adl wal Ihsan*, and since FIRM reportedly controls 45 of the 120 existing mosques and prayer rooms in Murcia, some analysts feared that *Al Adl wal Ihsan* obtained a strong, legitimate platform from which to disseminate its message through this relationship.[28]

Similarly, the municipal government of Ceuta, one of Spain's two North African exclaves, has also expressed concern about the potential for strategic collaboration between *Al Adl wal Ihsan* and *Tablighi Jama'at*, a Sunni proselytization movement whose Spanish off-shoot is led by prominent imam and UCIDE-Ceuta president Laarbi al-Lal Maateis.[29] As with *Al Adl wal Ihsan*, Spanish Intelligence Services have tried to deny citizenship to members of *Tablighi Jama'at* on the premise that they are radicals opposed to social integration. However, the Spanish National Court often overturns such decisions.[30]

Less information is available publicly about *Hizb-ut-Tahrir* (HUT), but in 2007 the *Athena Intelligence Journal* defined the group's three primary activities in Spain as: proselytizing and distributing propaganda, especially to "foment division and confrontation between Muslims and non-Muslims;" increasing its presence in Islamic cultural and social organizations; and advancing an Islamist, anti-Western agenda through online forums and discussions.[31]

The final Islamist group with a major presence in Spain is the Muslim Brotherhood, which became one of the more solidly-established Islamist organizations in Spain through its 1971 affiliation with the Spanish Muslim Association. Radical Muslim Brotherhood elements were especially active in Spain at the turn of this century; Abu Dahdah's network, an al-Qaeda hub based in Madrid, provided funding to the Brotherhood while coordinating logistics for recruits transiting Europe.[32] The Spanish Institute of Strategic Studies (IEEE) notes that the network played a significant part not only in the 9/11 attacks, but also in the attacks in Morocco in 2003 and Madrid in 2004.[33] Although their activity has faded from the media spotlight, the Brotherhood maintains a serious presence in Spain, largely in the regions of Andalusia, Valencia, and Madrid.[34]

ISLAMISM AND SOCIETY

The United Nations' Special Rapporteur on Racism has publicly chastised current trends in Spanish society, asserting that "it is crucial that Spain makes the agenda of combating racism, racial discrimination, xenophobia, and related intolerance a priority... in particular, there is a need for clear and more visible political leadership in combating racism and xenophobia."[35] The nexus of a growing Muslim population and rising distrust or xenophobia among non-Muslim Spaniards may provide a dangerous opportunity for Spanish Islamists to increase their sway among moderate Muslims.

According to the *Unión de Comunidades Islámicas de España* (Union of Islamic Communities in Spain, or UCIDE), Spain's Muslim population in 2015 constituted approximately 1.89 million people, or nearly four percent of the country's total 48.6 million inhabitants.[36] This represents an increase of 300,000 since 2013, when UCIDE reported the same figure to be 1.6 million people, or three percent of the country's 47.4 million inhabitants.[37] Approximately 41 percent of this population consists of natural-born Spanish citizens. Of the remaining 59 percent, 40 percent are Moroccan immigrants, and the remainder comes largely from Algeria, Pakistan, Senegal, Nigeria, the Gambia, and Mali.[38] The percentage is lower than Europe's overall five percent average of Muslim inhabitants, but proportionally similar to Germany (where Muslims make up approximately 3.7% of the population).[39]

These figures result from a striking increase in Muslim immigration to Spain after the turn of the century. Over a ten-year period from 1998 to 2007, Spain nationalized 61,086 Muslim immigrants. Yet in the three subsequent years from 2008 to 2011, 52,095 Muslim immigrants were nationalized – nearly triple the rate of the previous decade.[40] The percentage of Muslims as a subset of the national population has also more than tripled since 2000,[41] and in total, Muslim immigrants account for more than 20 percent of Spain's immigrant population.[42]

The interests of both immigrant and natural-born Muslims in Spain are represented by the Islamic Commission of Spain (CIE), the official Islamic partner of the Spanish government formed in 1992 by the country's two largest Muslim associations: UCIDE and the *Federación Española de Entidades Religiosas Islámicas* (Spanish Federation of Islamic Religious Entities, or FEERI). FEERI's membership leans heavily Moroccan; UCIDE, by contrast, involves Muslim clerics of Syrian and Saudi origin. Another organization, the smaller Junta Islámica de España (Islamic Junta of Spain), is reportedly more overtly political, involving converts to Islam and so-called "progressives" while promoting a distinctive version of Islam that is occasionally at variance with the state.[43] Although none of these three organizations provide figures concerning their membership or structure, it is estimated that FEERI and UCIDE together account for roughly 70 percent of all registered Muslim religious organizations in Spain.[44] But official organizational registration with Spain's Ministry of Justice remains voluntary, and thus such numbers cannot reflect the entire picture. This uncertainty is only likely to intensify as the comparatively explosive growth of the Muslim population in Spain is mirrored by a growth of new Islamic institutions.

While the number of legal, officially approved mosques in the country remains low (no more than two dozen), a large number of cultural associations have sprung up in recent years, filling the need for new venues of worship and prayer. By the end of 2015, the Ministry of Justice's Registry of Religious Entities recorded 44 distinct Islamic religious federations, 1,427 official religious communities, and 20 religious associations.[45] Despite this institutional growth, UCIDE reports that 13% of Spanish Muslim communities lack access to a mosque, while 95% lack an almacabra (Muslim cemetery).[46] Meanwhile, the *Asesoria de Inteligencia y Consultoria de Seguridad*, a private intelligence and risk assessment firm, reported in 2016 that approximately 800 "illegal" (unregistered) mosques currently operate in Spain, while Spanish law enforcement authorities have managed to shut down an additional 100.[47] The invisible nature of such facilities is an understandable frustration to Spanish law enforcement and counterterrorism authorities, which have no way of knowing the nature of the mosques' activities and whether or not they are espousing radical doctrine.

While expanding in size, Spain's Muslim community is also growing increasingly devout. In its April 2010 survey of national religious attitudes, the Spanish government found a marked increase in piousness among the country's Muslims (with religious adherence rising from 41 percent in 2006 to 52 percent in 2009). These statistics stand in stark contrast to the prevailing trend of widespread secularism among the country's native population that has developed over recent decades. For example, less than 20 percent of Spaniards today define themselves as practicing Catholics, compared to 50 percent in 1976. Meanwhile, more than 60 percent of Spanish Muslims regard Islam and democracy as "compatible, but sometimes at personal cost."[48]

Differences between native-born Spanish Muslims or converts and their immigrant counterparts foster divisions in the larger Muslim community, particularly over the issues of interpretation and proper delegation of religious authority. For instance, there is a struggle underway between the competing interpretations of Islam and Islamic law practiced by Morocco and Saudi Arabia. Both versions of Islam are conservative (although the Saudi one is considerably more so), while the Moroccan variant is complicated by Spain's legal possession of North African territory—namely, the exclave cities of Ceuta and Melilla, two smaller territories (Peñón de Vélez de la Gomera and Peñón de Alhucemas), and the Chafarinas archipelago. Morocco's King Mohammed VI has publicly urged the Moroccan Muslim diaspora in Europe to disavow extremist, violent interpretations of their faith.[49] Yet several recent incidents—including the October 2016 arrest of a cell of Moroccan Spanish nationals recruiting children between the ages of 12 and 17 in Ceuta[50]—signify that the exclaves' geographic circumstances render their societies acutely accessible and thus acutely vulnerable to radical elements.

Unlike other immigrant communities in Spain, Muslims are not evenly distributed throughout the country. Due to their location on the African continent, Ceuta and Melilla have a particularly high proportion of Muslim residents. On the mainland,

Spanish Muslims are concentrated in three regions: Catalonia (510,481), Andalusia (300,460), and Madrid (278,976).[51] Andalusia, because of its geographic proximity to North Africa and its need for extensive manpower for agriculture, has attracted comparatively high levels of Muslim immigrants. So has Madrid, which serves as Spain's largest engine of economic growth and thereby provides greater opportunities for employment to immigrants.[52]

But Catalonia accounts for the majority of Muslim immigrants, in part because the region's official antagonism to the Spanish language has led regional authorities to prioritize non-Spanish speaking immigrants in the belief that it would be easier to immerse the newcomers into Catalan separatist culture. Yet this hope may have been ill-founded, as anti-Muslim sentiment has captured Catalan headlines in many well-publicized incidents. Most visibly, a dozen Catalan towns became the first in Spain to ban the *burqa* and the *niqab* in municipal buildings. Lleida, a city in Western Catalonia whose population is a full 25 percent Muslim, is at the epicenter of this movement. Beyond banning the *niqab*, its mayor shut down the city's lone mosque because there were allegedly too many Friday worshippers. In February 2012, angry townspeople began accusing Lleida's Muslims of poisoning dogs in revenge.[53] Such regional unrest has only been magnified by Catalonia's historic secessionist attitudes and Spain's recent economic woes. Against the wishes of Madrid, the regional Catalan government plans to hold a referendum on independence in September 2017. If the referendum succeeds, the would-be state will have to contend with the creation of its own integration, counter-radicalization, and security policies. In that light, the future of the Muslim community in Catalonia is of particular importance.

Intense friction over access to mosques is not limited to Catalonia, however. Rather, it is widespread among rural Spanish communities. Between the mid-1990s and 2012, there were 60 registered disputes between Muslim communities and their Spanish neighbors over the construction of mosques.[54] Riay Tatary, president of UCIDE, has angrily protested what is perceived as a segregationist movement to "exile" mosques by relocating them to areas outside of city and residential neighborhoods.[55] The most publicized incident of this nature occurred in 2012 in Torrejon, a town of 120,000 (of which Muslims comprise nearly 10 percent). The Muslim citizens of the town purchased land to expand the city's mosque, at the time located near the town's center. However, angry protests and petitions from the rest of the town's residents, as well as a demonstration by the anti-immigration Platform for Catalonia, induced the municipal authorities to revoke the building permit and change the site to one near an industrial park outside of town.[56] In other instances, residents have strewn pig's blood and pork meat over potential mosque sites in a deliberate attempt to permanently contaminate the sites in the eyes of Muslims.[57] While revealing a measure of grassroots fear in some areas, these acts have the potential to alienate the moderate Spanish Muslim community, even turning some towards radicalization and retribution.

Although Catalonia has been the focal point of such conflict, it mirrors a xenophobic undertone across Spain that may endanger the peaceful integration of Muslim communities. According to the Pew Global Attitudes Project 2011 Report, 58 percent of non-Muslims in Spain believed that relations between Muslims and Westerners were poor. Sixty-six percent believed that Muslim immigrants do not want to adopt Spanish national customs.[58] Among those asked which religion is the most violent, 87% responded "Islam." Sixty-one percent of those polled expressed concern about Islamic extremism at home. Spain was one of the only Western countries in the project in which the majority of the population (63%) had an unfavorable attitude towards Muslims. Pew also reported that the three top stereotypes about Muslims held by Spanish non-Muslims are "fanatical" (80%), "violent" (61%), and "arrogant" (48%). The report concluded that Spain was the only Western country in which a majority of non-Muslims associate three or more negative characteristics with Muslims.[59] A similar poll conducted by the Economist in 2013 concluded that nearly 65% of Spaniards believe that Islam is not compatible with the West.[60]

Yet simultaneously, Spanish society has shown remarkable openness to the victims of the 2015 refugee crisis, regardless of their religious affiliation. Under the EU's redistribution plan, Spain agreed to accept 15,000 resettled refugees to ease the load on Greece and Italy—a departure from the administration's original figure of just under 3,000, likely due to the pressure of Spanish grassroots organizations urged on by Rajoy's left-wing political rivals.[61] Unlike their counterparts elsewhere in Europe, Spanish groups professing a complete rejection of Islam and Muslim immigrants— including *Plataforma x Catalunya, Spain 2000*, and the newly arrived PEGIDA ("Patriotic Europeans Against the Islamisation of the Occident," a German movement that launched its Spanish branch in 2015)—have been unable to gain significant traction.[62]

It is vital to note that the majority of Spanish Muslims reject the use of violence and consider themselves well integrated into the broader Spanish community.[63] However, for the minority that does not share these feelings, the blend of isolation and xenophobia that they experience is dangerous. Since the Muslim community in Spain is primarily made up of immigrants, it encounters many obstacles to integration: unfamiliarity with the Spanish language, lack of documentation, an unusually high percentage of unmarried men, and frequent unemployment. All of these factors have the potential to increase frustration and estrangement, consequentially increasing the risk of radicalization.[64] The 2010 Religious Attitudes study found that approximately four percent of Muslims in Spain do not condemn the use of violence in pursuit of political objectives, suggesting that this demographic would possibly be more predisposed to radicalization. As the Spanish government struggles with its finances, the resulting social chaos will likely cause increased perceptions of deprivation and insularism among each community—promoting more xenophobia, which will in turn promote more isolationism—which may only make the fractures between the two communities worse.

ISLAMISM AND THE STATE

In spite of the effects of economic crisis, potential Catalan secession, and paralyzing political deadlock, the Spanish government under the leadership of Prime Minister Mariano Rajoy Brey has nevertheless managed to pursue an effective counterterrorism strategy in terms of immigration and border control. Spain helped found the Global Counterterrorism Forum in 2011 and maintains an inter-ministerial Countering Violent Extremism (CVE) working group, described by the U.S. State Department as "tied closely to the fight against illegal immigration and the integration of existing immigrant communities."[65] Spain has also stepped up its cooperation with other Western countries through mechanisms such as the U.S. Immigrant Advisory Program and increased access to Europol information databases on terrorism and organized crime.[66]

While trying to maintain a policy of religious neutrality, the federal government has adopted an assertive stance in pursuit of *jihadist* cells, with varying degrees of success. In July 2015, the country's criminal code was updated to "improve its legal framework to more effectively counter the movement of foreign terrorist fighters to conflict zones, better pursue suspected terrorists without clear affiliation to a known criminal organization, and curtail terrorist preparatory activities online."[67] This legal step—which Amnesty International denounced as so vague that they would be not only ineffective but also an infringement on basic human rights[68]—was likely a response to harsh critiques over the cases described above of multiple terrorist suspects that have been released from Spanish prisons due to excessive punishment or lack of evidence.[69] An inability to convict is an unfortunate consequence of the aggressive policies of quick intervention in cases of suspected terrorism, which was a policy established in 2004 after the attacks in Madrid. In many instances, the police arrest a suspect without having the necessary evidence to guarantee a conviction.

In tandem, Spain has adopted a National Counter Radicalization Strategy, which is promulgated by the national Center for Counter-Terrorism and Organized Crime Intelligence (CITCO). This strategy recognizes that radicalization occurs at the local level and attempts to directly address the causes for grievance posed by, for example, the closure of *almacabras* or lack of access to mosques.[70]

However, outside of traditional security and counter radicalization measures, Spain has been reluctant to articulate a position on political Islamism. In light of the wave of *burqa* bans of the early 2000s, the government under President Luis Rodríguez Zapatero attempted to pass a new, more expansive Religious Freedom Law in order to redefine Spain as secular and neutral to all forms of religious expression.[71] However, the attempt was not successful, and Zapatero acknowledged that the lack of a political and social consensus in Spain prevented the law's passage.[72]

Meanwhile, the controversial issue had gained national prominence with the People's Party's June 2010 proposal of a motion urging the Spanish Senate to extend the *burqa* ban nationwide, both in public buildings and in the street.[73] The Zapatero administration rejected the proposal and blocked the passing of that same motion in Congress days later.[74] Shortly afterward, the ban came under further attack when eleven mosques and prayer rooms run by *Salafist* preachers in Lleida, Barcelona, and Tarragona challenged the ban in court. On its second appeal to the Spanish Supreme Court, the Lleida prohibition was overturned in a landmark March 2013 ruling. However, the ruling was based on the judges' opinion that municipal governments do not have the authority to make a ban that requires the backing of constitutional law. Thus no judicial precedent has yet been set on whether the national government could pass such a measure constitutionally.[75]

Rajoy, who succeeded Zapatero as Prime Minister on December 21, 2011, has appeared to be sensitive to the Spanish Muslim population, and in his public statements since taking office he has been careful to distinguish between "Islam" and "Islamism." However, one particularly controversial legal initiative infuriated Rajoy's opponents and those wary of Islamist doctrine. Sustained Moroccan pressure on the Spanish government led to an agreement passed by both countries in February 2013 (and subsequently incorporated into the Spanish legal code) that gave Moroccan religious authorities the right to "monitor" any Moroccan children adopted by Spanish citizens in order to ensure that the children remain religiously and culturally Muslim during their upbringing. Some critics have called this measure "an unprecedented encroachment of Islamic *Sharia* law within Spanish jurisprudence [and]… a frontal assault on the freedom of religion."[76]

ENDNOTES

[1] Union de Comunidades Islámicas de España (UCIDE), "Estudio demográfico sobre conciudadanos musulmanes," Observatorio Andalusí, February 2016, http://ucide.org/sites/default/files/revistas/estademograf15.pdf; Union de Comunidades Islámicas de España (UCIDE), "Estudio demográfico de la población musulmana [Demographic study of the Muslim population]," Observatorio Andalusi, 2013, http://ucide.org/sites/default/files/revistas/estademograf12.pdf.

[2] In a post-9/11 broadcast, al-Qaeda leader Ayman al-Zawahiri termed the loss of Andalusia a "tragedy." For more, see Rafael L. Bardaji and Ignacio Cosidó, "Spain: from 9/11 to 3/11 and Beyond," in Gary J. Schmitt, ed., Safety, Liberty, and Islamist Terrorism: American and European Approaches to Domestic Counterterrorism (Washington, DC: AEI Press, 2010).

[3] Ministerio del Interior, "La célula yihadista desarticulada hoy en España, Bélgica y Alemania urepresentaba una amenaza grave, concreta y continuada para la seguridad en Europa [Jihadist cell uncovered today in Spain, Belgium, and Germany represents a grave, concrete, and continued threat to European security]," September 28, 2016, http://www.interior.gob.es/es/web/interior/noticias/detalle/-/journal_content/56_INSTANCE_1YSSI3xiWuPH/10180/6424840/?redirect=http%3A%2F%2Fwww.interior.gob.es%2Fes%2Fportada%3Fp_p_id%3D101_INSTANCE_pNZsk8OxKI0x%26p_p_lifecycle%3D0%26p_p_state%3Dnormal%26p_p_mode%3Dview%26p_p_col_id%3Dcolumn-2%26p_p_col_pos%3D2%26p_p_col_count%3D4.

[4] "Interior: la operación de Barcelona persigue 'neutralizar' el terrorismo yihadista [Ministry of the Interior: Barcelona operation attempts to 'neutralize' jihadist terrorism]" Europapress, June 12, 2013, http://www.europapress.es/nacional/noticia-interior-operacion-barcelona-persigue-neutralizar-terrorismo-yihadista-20130612104940.html.

[5] United States Department of State, Office of the Coordinator of Counterterrorism, Country Reports on Terrorism 2015 (Washington, DC: U.S. Department of State, 2016), http://www.state.gov/j/ct/rls/crt/2015/257516.htm.

[6] Vasco Cotovio and Chandrika Naranyan, "Spain arrests 7 suspected of sending guns, bomb materials to ISIS," CNN, February 7, 2016, http://www.cnn.com/2016/02/07/world/spain-terror-arrests/.

[7] Soeren Kern, "Islamic Supremacy Rears its Head in Spain," RealClearWorld, June 22, 2013, http://www.realclearworld.com/articles/2013/06/22/islamic_supremacy_rears_its_head_in_spain.html.

[8] "Spain police arrest 5 Tunisians in Barcelona accused of spreading Internet terror propaganda," FOX News, June 12, 2013, http://www.foxnews.com/world/2013/06/12/spain-police-arrest-5-tunisians-in-barcelona-accused-spreading-internet-terror/.

[9] Goodman, Al, "Spain arrests 2 men suspected of al Qaeda group links," CNN, April 23, 2013, http://www.cnn.com/2013/04/23/world/europe/spain-terror-arrests/.

[10] "Spain had near-miss with terrorism attributed to Chechen group," Public Radio International's The World, April 20, 2013, http://www.pri.org/stories/politics-society/government/spain-had-near-miss-with-terrorism-attributed-to-chechen-group-13569.html.

[11] Al Goodman, "5 Terror Suspects On Trial In Madrid," CNN, May 23, 2010, http://edition.cnn.com/2010/WORLD/europe/03/23/spain.terror.trial/index.html.

[12] See "Recent Highlights in Terrorist Activity," Combating Terrorism Center at West Point CTC Sentinel 3, iss. 1, January 2010, 27.

[13] UCIDE, "Estudio demográfico de la población musulmana."

[14] United States Department of State, Office of the Coordinator of Counterterrorism, Country Reports on Terrorism 2011 (Washington, DC: U.S. Department of State, 2012), http://www.refworld.org/docid/501fbc9f16.html.

[15] "US Embassy feared Barcelona was an Islamist hub," Deutsche Welle, December 12, 2012, http://www.dw.de/us-embassy-feared-barcelona-was-an-islamist-hub/a-6320524.

[16] Ibid.

[17] Rogelio Alonso, "The Spread of Radical Islam in Spain: Challenges Ahead," Studies in Conflict & Terrorism 35, no. 6, 2012, 471-491.

[18] Ibid., 478.

[19] In the study, radical views were found in five percent of the 2,000 adult respondents. See Ministerios de Interior, Justicia y Trabajo, La Comunidad Emigrante En España De Origen Musulmán (Madrid: Demoscopia, April 2010); Comments on this report can be found in Olga R. Sanmartin, "Rubalcaba dice que el gobierno 'observa' las mezquitas radicales [Rubalcaba says the government 'observes' radical mosques']," El Mundo (Madrid), April 8, 2010, 14.

[20] Ferrán Balsells, "El salafismo se hace con el control de cinco mezquitas en Tarragona [Salafism takes control of five mosques in Tarragona]," El País (Madrid), June 21, 2010, 31.

[21] "Un 'juicio' islamista condeno a una mujer a morir por adultera en Reus [An Islamist 'trial' condemns a woman to death in Reus]," ElPeriodico.com, December 5, 2009, http://www.elperiodico.com/es/noticias/sociedad/20091205/juicio-islamista-condeno-una-mujer-morir-por-adultera-reus/print-235772.shtml.

[22] Ferrán Balsells, "La policía: No hay puebas del supuesto juicio islámico de Tarragona [Spanish Police: No Evidence of the Supposed Islamic Trial]," El País (Madrid), June 20, 2010, 27.

[23] "El gobierno del PP acuerda la expulsion definitive de Espana de Ziani por 'difundir ideas Salafistas,'" [The government of the People's Party agrees to Ziani's definitive expulsion from Spain for spreading Salafist ideas), Noticias de Navarra, May 16, 2013, http://www.noticiasdenavarra.com/2013/05/16/politica/estado/el-gobierno-del-pp-acuerda-la-expulsion-definitiva-de-espana-de-ziani-por-difundir-ideas-salafistas.

[24] "Alleged Al Qaeda in Spain chief Abu Dadah released," ANSAmed, May 23, 2013, http://www.ansamed.info/ansamed/en/news/nations/spain/2013/05/23/Alleged-Qaeda-Spain-chief-Abu-Dahdah-released_8754650.html.

[25] See "Marruecos desarticula un grupo terrorista vinculado al 11-M [Morocco arrests terrorist cell connected with the March 11, 2004, attacks]," La Vanguardia (Barcelona), March 3, 2010, 17.

[26] C. Echeverría Jesús, "La conexión paquistaní se consolida también en España [The Pakistani connection also solidifies in Spain]," Grupo de Estudios Estratégicos GEES Analysis, January 23, 2008, www.gees.org.

[27] Jose Maria Blanca Navarro and Oscar Perez Ventura, "Movimientos Islamistas en España [Islamist Movements in Spain]," Insituto Español de Estudios Estratégicos, January 11, 2012, http://www.ieee.es/Galerias/fichero/docs_marco/2012/DIEEEM012012_MovimientosIslamistasenEspana.docx.pdf.

[28] A. Negre, "Justicia vincula a la federación islámica de la región con una organización radical [Justice ties the Islamic Federation of the region to a radical organization]," La Verdad (Murcia), May 6, 2010, 1-3; "UCIDE dice que la federación islámica controla siete mezquitas radicales [UCIDE says that the Islamic Federation controls seven radical mosques]," La Verdad (Murcia), May 7, 2010, 13.

[29] "Movimientos Islamistas en España." See also El Pueblo de Ceuta, July 12, 2009, http://www.elpueblodeceuta.es/200912/20091207/200912073101.html.

[30] Alonso, "The Spread of Radical Islam in Spain: Challenges Ahead," 485.

[31] "Hizb-ut-Tahrir en España," Athena Intelligence Journal 2, no. 2, April 21, 2007, http://www.isn.ethz.ch/Digital-Library/Publications/Detail/?ots591=0c54e3b3-1e9c-be1e-2c24-a6a8c7060233&lng=en&id=47235.

[32] Aaron Mannes, "El Once de Marzo: A Familiar, Maddening Scene," National Review Online, March 12, 2004, http://www.nationalreview.com/node/209873/print.

[33] "Movimientos Islamistas en Espana."

[34] Ibid.

[35] "Spain must make fighting racism and xenophobia a priority – UN Expert," UN News Centre, January 28, 2013, http://www.un.org/apps/news/story.asp?NewsID=44013#.V-1bajc9zww.

[36] UCIDE, "Estudio demográfico sobre conciudadanos musulmanes."

[37] UCIDE, "Estudio demográfico de la población musulmana."

[38] Ibidem; Alonso, "The Spread of Radical Islam in Spain: Challenges Ahead."

[39] "Germany," Central Intelligence Agency World Factbook, May 15, 2013, https://www.cia.gov/library/publications/the-world-factbook/geos/gm.html.

[40] UCIDE, "Estudio demográfico de la población musulmana."

[41] See, for example, Hossein Kettani, "Muslim Population in Europe: 1950-2020," International Journal of Environmental Science and Development 1, no. 2. June 2010, http://www.ijesd.org/papers/29-D438.pdf.

[42] Alonso, "The Spread of Radical Islam in Spain: Challenges Ahead."

[43] The websites of FEERI, UCIDE, and the Junta are, respectively, www.feeri.eu, es.ucide.org, and www.juntaislamica.org. They provide some details as to the organization's ideologies and their program of activities.
[44] Patricia Bezunartea, Jose Manuel Lopez, and Laura Tedesco, "Muslims in Spain and Islamic Religious Radicalism." Microcon, May 2009, http://www.microconflict.eu/publications/PWP8_PB_JML_LT.pdf.
[45] UCIDE, "Estudio demográfico sobre conciudadanos musulmanes."
[46] Ibid., 14.
[47] A. Checa and M. Saiz-Pardo, "Expertos alertan del alto numero de mezquitas encubiertas en la Comunitat Valenciana [Experts warn of a high number of illegal mosques in Valencia]," Las Provincias," May 18, 2016, http://www.lasprovincias.es/comunitat/201605/17/expertos-alertan-alto-numero-20160517003310.html.
[48] Alonso, "The Spread of Radical Islam in Spain: Challenges Ahead."
[49] "Morocco king urges diaspora to reject Islamist extremism," BBC, http://www.bbc.com/news/world-africa-37148105.
[50] "Fernando Lazaro, "La celula de Ceuta reclutaba 'cachorros' de 12 años para el Estado Islámico," El Mundo, October 11, 2016, http://www.elmundo.es/espana/2016/11/10/5823731122601df07f8b4601.html.
[51] UCIDE, "Estudio demográfico sobre conciudadanos musulmanes."
[52] See "Población Musulmana En España [Muslim Population Of Spain]," El País (Madrid), June 10, 2010.
[53] Such reports are still unsubstantiated. See Dale Hurd, "Under Siege? Spain resists Islamic invasion," CBN News, February 12, 2012, http://www.cbn.com/cbnnews/world/2012/february/under-siege-spain-resists-islamic-invasion-/.
[54] Alonso, "The Spread of Radical Islam in Spain: Challenges Ahead," 480.
[55] "Spanish Muslims denounce the 'exile' of their mosques," El País (Madrid), June 3, 2013, http://sociedad.elpais.com/sociedad/2013/06/03/actualidad/1370260356_229615.html.
[56] Guy Hedgecoe, "Local mosque row a Spanish problem," The Irish Times, July 10, 2012, http://www.irishtimes.com/news/local-mosque-row-a-spanish-problem-1.532693.
[57] Alonso, "The Spread of Radical Islam in Spain: Challenges Ahead."
[58] Pew Research Global Attitudes Project, "Muslim-Western tensions persist," July 21, 2011, http://www.pewglobal.org/2011/07/21/chapter-2-how-muslims-and-westerners-view-each-other/
[59] Ibid.
[60] "Islam in Europe," The Economist, January 7, 2015, http://www.economist.com/blogs/graphicdetail/2015/01/daily-chart-2.
[61] "Citizens Pressure the Government of Spain to Welcome in More Refugees," The Local, September 9, 2015, https://www.thelocal.es/20150909/citizens-pressure-spanish-government-to-act-on-refugees.

[62] "Far-right extremist parties find support across Europe," Public Radio International, November 30, 2012, http://www.pri.org/stories/politics-society/far-right-extremist-parties-find-support-across-europe.html.
[63] Alonso, "The Spread of Radical Islam."
[64] Kern, "The Islamic Republic of Catalonia."
[65] United States Department of State, Country Reports on Terrorism 2011.
[66] Ibid; See also United States Department of State, Office of the Coordinator for Counterterrorism, Country Reports on Terrorism 2012 (Washington, DC: U.S. Department of State, May 2013), http://www.state.gov/documents/organization/210204.pdf.
[67] United States Department of State, Country Reports on Terrorism 2015.
[68] "Spain: New Counter-Terrorism Proposals Would Infringe Basic Human Rights," Amnesty International, February 10, 2015, http://www.amnestyusa.org/news/news-item/spain-new-counter-terrorism-proposals-would-infringe-basic-human-rights.
[69] Kern, "Islamic Supremacy Rears its Head in Spain."
[70] Ministerio del Interior, "Plan Estratégico Nacional de Lucha Contra la Radicalización Violenta [National Plan to Combat Violent Radicalization]," 7-8, 2015, http://www.interior.gob.es/documents/10180/3066463/CM_mir_PEN-LCRV.pdf/b57166c1-aaaf-4c0d-84c7-b69bda6246f5%20.
[71] "Ni crucifijos ni funerales católicos [Neither Catholic crucifixes nor funerals]," El Pais (Madrid), June 13, 2006.
[72] Jorge Otero, "Zapatero: 'La ley de libertad religiosa es conveniente, no urgente," Publico.es, November 10, 2010.
[73] "Spanish Senate calls for nationwide burqa ban," Deutsche Press-Agentur, June 23, 2010, http://www.monstersandcritics.com/news/europe/news/article_1565614.php/Spanish-Senate-calls-for-nationwide-burqa-ban.
[74] Alan Clendenning and Harold Heckle, "Spain rejects burqa ban – For Now," Associated Press, July 20, 2010, http://www.huffingtonpost.com/2010/07/20/spain-rejects-burqa-ban_n_653254.html.
[75] Fiona Govan, "Spain overturns Islamic face veil ban," Telegraph (London), March 1, 2013, http://www.telegraph.co.uk/news/worldnews/europe/spain/9902827/Spain-overturns-Islamic-face-veil-ban.html.
[76] Kern, "Islamic Supremacy Rears its Head in Spain."

United Kingdom

Quick Facts

Population: 64,430,428 (July 2016 est.)

Area: 243,610 sq km

Ethnic Groups: white 87.2%, black/African/Caribbean/black British 3%, Asian/Asian British: Indian 2.3%, Asian/Asian British: Pakistani 1.9%, mixed 2%, other 3.7%

Religions: Christian (includes Anglican, Roman Catholic, Presbyterian, Methodist) 59.5%, Muslim 4.4%, Hindu 1.3%, other 2%, unspecified 7.2%, none 25.7%

Government Type: parliamentary constitutional monarchy; a Commonwealth realm

GDP (official exchange rate): $2.65 trillion (2015 est.)

Map and Quick Facts courtesy of the CIA World Factbook (January 2017)

Overview

The United Kingdom is a European hub for numerous forms of Islamist activity, ranging from violent jihadist terrorist cells to "soft power" Islamists.[1] The threat from jihadist terrorists is widely recognized and accepted by both government and civil society in Britain; however, there remains relatively little interest in non-violent Islamists, who hold significant power and influence. While politicians from across the mainstream political spectrum are largely in agreement about the threat faced by terrorism, there is little consensus on how to deal with political Islamism and what role, if any, it should play in countering extremism and terrorism.

Islamist Activity

British Islamists fall into four fluid and often overlapping categories. The groups from these different categories agree on many issues, particularly on the need to withdraw foreign troops from what they describe as Muslim lands, and the central role that *sharia* law should play in the lives of all Muslims. The major differences often surround issues such as participation in the democratic process and the legitimacy and necessity of violent *jihad*.

The Muslim Brotherhood/Jamaat-e-Islami nexus

Although these movements originate from different countries, British manifestations of Egypt's Muslim Brotherhood and South Asia's *Jamaat-e-Islami* are closely aligned in ideological and strategic terms. While they represent only a small minority of British Muslims, groups aligned with these movements are among the best organized and funded of any British Islamic groups.

French Muslim Brotherhood specialist Brigitte Marechal has described how the Muslim Brotherhood in Europe continues to promote Islam as an all-encompassing framework that: "suggests that Islam should be understood as a complete system that concerns state and nation, beliefs and legislation, cult and behavior, and the social, political and historical."[2] This all-encompassing ideology, which Muslim Brotherhood founder Hassan al-Banna referred to as *shumuliyyat al-Islam*, is one of the driving forces for *jihadist* terrorists who are currently trying to enforce their interpretation of *sharia* in Afghanistan, Iraq, Somalia, Yemen and numerous other fronts.

The intention of the Muslim Brotherhood in Britain is to peacefully promote the *shumuliyyat al-Islam* in the hope that it will gradually initiate a reform of society along Islamist lines. Using front groups such as those described below, the organization disseminates its ideology among British Muslims by organizing events and lectures. It has subsequently seen some success in creating culturally and nationally transcendent, "*ummah-centric*" mindsets, whereby young Muslims feel a greater affinity with fellow Muslims around the globe than with their non-Muslim fellow citizens.

Similarly, the British *Jamaat* (established in the UK before the Muslim Brotherhood), are followers of the group's founder, Sayyid Abul A'ala Maududi, and propagate a form of comprehensive Islamic identity through their own set of organizations. Due to their close ideological affinity, the two have effectively formed a partnership: the *Jamaat*, with its roots in Pakistan and Bangladesh, has more appeal to British South Asian Muslims, while the Arab origins of the Muslim Brotherhood give it more traction with British Arabs and North Africans. The main method through which the soft Islamist mission is carried out in Europe is *da'wah* (prosletyzing), whereby Islamist objectives are pursued through missionary and ideological programs.

The main British Muslim Brotherhood institutions and organizations include:•

- *The Muslim Welfare House (MWH)*. Founded as a charity in 1970 with the original aim of assisting foreign Muslim students in Britain, the MWH gradually became one of the central Muslim Brotherhood bodies in the country. It now acts as both a mosque and a community center, and despite its relatively low public profile wields significant influence over the national direction of the movement. The Muslim Brotherhood's connections with the MWH are extensive: until 2007, of the five registered owners and trustees of the MWH, three were also directors of the Muslim Association of Britain (MAB), the Brotherhood's other, more publicly active, representative in the United Kingdom.[3] Among the owners were Mohammed Sawalha, (see below), and Abdel Shaheed el-Ashaal, referred to by the Muslim Brotherhood magazine *Islamism Digest* as a "senior member of the Muslim Brotherhood."[4] Until 2000, el-Ashaal was the company secretary for the Hassan al-Banna Foundation, one of the stated aims of which was "to give a correct image of the thoughts, ideology and life of Imam Shaheed Hassan el-Banna."[5] In 2007, all five trustees were replaced, and at least two of their successors—Wanis al-Mabrouk[6] and Hany Eldeeb[7]—also hold positions within the Federation of Islamic Organizations in Europe (FIOE) or one of its affiliates. The FIOE is the Muslim Brotherhood's European umbrella organization that loosely connects all the group's European front organizations.[8]

- *The Muslim Association of Britain (MAB)*. The MAB is the main British representative of the Muslim Brotherhood global network. It was set up in 1997[9] by Kemal el-Helbawy, then the Muslim Brotherhood's official spokesman in Europe.[10] It has been described by scholars Peter Bergen and Paul Cruickshank as "a Muslim Brotherhood group"[11] and is also the official British representative of the FIOE.[12] The MAB is primarily a political activist organization, which promotes Islamist political thought among British Muslims. Per its website, the MAB "attempts to fill in the gap in terms of Islamic Dawah work in Britain where the call for a comprehensive Islam that encompasses all aspects of life is lacking."[13] This comprehensive Islam is precisely the vision set out in the abovementioned *shumuliyyat al-Islam* as envisioned by Hassan al-Banna.

- *The Cordoba Foundation (TCF)*. TCF was founded as a limited company in 2005 by Anas al-Tikriti, who is also the group's CEO.[14] In 2008, the then-head of the Conservative Party (and former British Prime Minister) David Cameron, identified TCF as a "front for the Muslim Brotherhood" and claimed that "even the most basic research would reveal that the Cordoba Foundation has close connections to people with extremist views, including Azzam Tamimi, the UK representative of Hamas."[15] The role of TCF differs slightly from that of other British Muslim Brotherhood groups in that it describes itself as an "independent research and Public Relations organization."[16] Although it also takes part in political Islamist activism, TCF styles itself as an Islamist think tank that, among other things, publishes a quarterly journal, *Arches Quarterly*, featuring a mix of prominent Islamist thinkers and non-Muslim academics sympathetic to their cause. The foundation remains active as of 2017, despite facing a financial setback in 2014 when HSBC formally closed its longstanding bank accounts.[17]

- *The North London Central Mosque (NLCM)*. Also known as the Finsbury Park Mosque, the NLCM was founded in 1988 as a charity. In the 1990s, it developed a reputation for acting as a center for terrorism recruitment and facilitation under the leadership of the now-convicted extremist *imam* Abu Hamza al-Masri, whose followers included "shoe bomber" Richard Reid and Zacarias Moussaoui, the suspected twentieth 9/11 hijacker. In early 2005, Abu Hamza was removed from the NLCM, and it was taken over by a new management committee made up of senior members of the British Muslim Brotherhood.[18] Its five trustees—Mohamed Kozbar, Mohamed Sawalha, Ahmed Sheikh Mohammed (Treasurer), Abdel Shaheed El-Ashaal (Chairman) and Hafez al-Karmi[19]—were, until 2007, the registered owners of the aforementioned MWH. In addition, all the NLCM trustees, apart from al-Karmi, were also former directors of the MAB. After the takeover, MAB founder Kemal el-Helbawy acted as the mosque's spokesman for a brief period.[20]

The main *Jamaat-e-Islami* organizations and institutes in Britain include:

- *The UK Islamic Mission (UKIM)*. The UKIM was established in 1962 as an official offshoot of the *Jamaat-e-Islami*, with the express goal of establishing the party and its ideology as a major political and social force.[21] With around forty branches, over thirty-five mosques and numerous Islamic schools around the country, it is the single biggest Islamist organization in Britain.[22] Since its inception, the UKIM has used its considerable financial resources to promote Islam in Britain as "a comprehensive way of life which must be translated into action in all spheres of human life" with the eventual aim of "moulding the entire human life in accordance with Allah's will" and creating an "Islamic social order in the United Kingdom in order to seek the pleasure of Allah."[23] The UKIM continues to disseminate the works of Maududi as well as those of senior Muslim Brotherhood figures such as Jamal Badawi.[24]

- *The Islamic Foundation (IF)*. Founded in 1973, the Islamic Foundation (IF) was set up as the official research institute of the burgeoning *Jamaat* network in Britain and is the main publisher and translator of Maududi's works in the country.[25] It is based on a ten-acre campus in Leicester and runs classes and research projects focused on spreading Islamist ideology. In 2000, the IF established the Markfield Institute of Higher Education, which offers postgraduate degrees in Islamic studies and is a crucial center through which the IF develops the *Jamaat's* political ideas.[26] Islam scholar Gilles Kepel has referred to the IF as "one of the most important centres for the propagation of militant Sunni Islamist thinking in the world," also noting that much of its work is in English, which reflects their attempts to "challenge Western cultural hegemony (whether 'secular' or 'Christian') on its own linguistic territory."[27] The IF is also known to be a key facilitator of the close relationship between the British *Jamaat* and Muslim Brotherhood.

- *The East London Mosque (ELM)*. Founded in 1985, the ELM, together with the London Muslim Center, serves the community of Tower Hamlets, one of the largest Muslim populations in the United Kingdom[28] and home to a large British Bangladeshi community.[29] The Mosque is believed to be *Jamaat* affiliated due to its active promotion of the writings and ideological thought of Maududi.[30] The ELM has been the subject of considerable controversy because, in 2003[31] and again in 2009,[32] it provided a platform to American-born cleric Anwar al-Awlaki, one of al-Qaeda's chief ideologues (who was subsequently killed in a U.S. drone strike in September 2011). In the first instance, a third-party group renting the mosque's space hosted al-Awlaki via a videochat, without consulting the mosque. In the second instance, the same third-party group scheduled al-Awlaki for a videotaped lecture;[33] when the mosque discovered it had done so, its officials claim to have discussed the matter with the police, who did not raise objections about the event. While al-Awlaki's visit and activities raised questions about the ELM's Islamist connections, the mosque publicly distanced itself from them. It changed its speaker booking policy after the al-Awlaki controversy in order to thoroughly review and approve both speakers and subject matter before any event is held there.[34]

- *The Islamic Forum of Europe (IFE).* The IFE is a subsidiary organization of the ELM, based within the Mosque's complex. In keeping with the *Jamaat's* mission of promoting an all-encompassing Islamist identity, its mission statement proclaims that "Islam offers a comprehensive system and the challenge to us all is to learn and embody the teachings of Islam and convey them to others in a wise, sensible and beautiful manner," and that the group "helps to enable individuals to learn and apply the basic tools required to achieve this within a collective framework helping to develop the Muslim community and benefit the wider society."[35] The primary mission of the IFE is to train young Muslims in *da'wah*, so that future generations can continue to propagate the movement's message. A six-month investigation by Channel 4 and the *Daily Telegraph* into the IFE and ELM, which culminated in a 2010 documentary, uncovered a detailed Islamist indoctrination program based on the teachings of Maududi. Among the discoveries was the transcript of 2009 IFE recruit training course which told new members that its goal was "to create the True Believer, to then mobilise those believers into an organised force for change who will carry out *dawah, hisbah* [enforcement of Islamic law] and *jihad*. This will lead to social change and *iqamatud-Deen* [Islamic social, economic and political order]."[36]

Muslim political organizations

Campaigning and lobbying is an important tool employed by British Islamists. Presenting themselves as representatives of the rights of persecuted Muslims, Islamist activists have acquired significant support and large media profiles, often appearing as the voice of British Muslims on television and in newspapers.

- *The Muslim Council of Britain (MCB).* In the years following the *Satanic Verses* affair,[37] the British government saw the need for a single umbrella body that could represent the political and social views of British Muslims. This led to the creation of the MCB in 1997, headed by Iqbal Sacranie, one of the most vocal critics of the novelist Salman Rushdie and his controversial book.[38] The MCB expanded rapidly, and eventually claimed to have around 400 Muslim and community groups under its aegis, including the MAB, IFE and ELM. Despite a seemingly wide range of voices within the MCB, the leadership was, and remains, almost exclusively Islamist, taking its ideological cue from Maududi's teachings in particular.[39] After the 7/7 London bombings, the MCB took center stage as the government's main advisors on extremism and radicalization, and used this influential position as an opportunity to attempt to effect real change in the government's foreign policy. Following the attacks, the MCB issued an open letter to then Prime Minister Tony Blair imploring him to change government policy to prevent any future attacks.[40] Its approach to domestic policy is centered on the belief that soft Islamists are the strongest bulwark against al-Qaeda as they can use their supposed credibility among vulnerable British Muslims to prevent them from turning to violence. As part of this approach, the MCB were defenders and supporters of Yusuf al-Qaradawi, the spiritual leader of the Muslim Brotherhood and a global advocate of this bulwark theory. In 2008, when Qaradawi was denied a visa to enter Britain on national security grounds, the MCB, along with the BMI, were openly critical of the government's decision.[41]

- *The Federation of Student Islamic Societies (FOSIS)*. Based in North London, FOSIS was established in 1962 to represent Muslim students in Islamic university societies. A 2009 government report on influential Islamic organizations notes that "the Jamaat-e Islami (JI) along with the Muslim Brotherhood were pioneers in developing student activism through the Federation of Student Islamic Societies (FOSIS)."[42] To this day, FOSIS remains a vehicle for Islamist activism, and coordinates the ideological direction of dozens of British university Islamic societies. It claims to represent over 90,000 students and its events have featured leading British as well as international Muslim Brotherhood and *Jamaat-e-Islami* figures including Anas al-Tikriti,[43] Rashid El Ghannouchi,[44] Azzam Tamimi,[45] Dr. Muhammed Abdul Bari[46] and Jamal Badawi.[47]

- *Muslim Public Affairs Committee UK (MPACUK)*. MPACUK was founded in 2001, in the aftermath of Israel's invasion of the West Bank. As a political lobbyist group with a strongly anti-Zionist outlook, it urges Muslims to become politically active along purely sectarian, Islamist lines, and organizes campaigns against what they perceive as pro-Israel politicians.[48] Referring to themselves as *mujahids* (holy warriors), MPACUK members see their actions as a form of *jihad* against the marginalization and disenfranchisement of Muslims.[49] During the 2010 British General Election, the group organized the "Operation Muslim Vote" campaign, which involved MPACUK activists mobilizing Muslims to vote against "several pro-Zionist war mongering MPs."[50]

Democratic Rejectionists
Unlike the groups profiled above, which have developed a utilitarian approach to democracy, this category of British Islamists rejects any form of participation in the political process. While they acknowledge that other Islamists are gaining influence through their successful manipulation of the system, democracy is still seen as an unacceptable concession. For these organizations, taking part in the current secular democratic system is a form of shirk (polytheism) that recognizes national laws as being above those proscribed by God. Although they differ from Salafi jihadists on issues such as when and where violence is legitimate in order to establish an Islamic state, their stance on secular democracy is almost indistinguishable from that of al-Qaeda and the Islamic State.

- *Hizb ut-Tahrir (HuT)*. HuT is a global revolutionary Islamist political party with a political interpretation of Islam inspired by the Muslim Brotherhood that works toward the re-creation of the Caliphate in the Middle East as an aggressive, expansionist entity with the goal of encompassing the entire globe, thus uniting the global *umma* (community of Muslim faithful).[51] The fundamental differences between the British wings of HuT and the Muslim Brotherhood and *Jamaat* are tactical, not strategic—they share the same goal of creating an Islamic *caliphate*, but disagree on the most effective way to do so. HuT also claims to be non-violent, and the party currently pursues a grassroots strategy which recruits a core of loyal members who work to cultivate Islamist ideology among British Muslims, preparing them for the country's eventual annexation by the Caliphate after they have succeeded in its re-establishment in the Middle East.[52] HuT's recruitment and indoctrination program is often pursued through numerous front organizations based in the heart of major British Muslim communities as well as universities, which organize discussions and other events featuring leading members of the group presenting their ideology as the only true form of Islam. HuT's support for overseas terrorism in the "defensive *jihads*" in Iraq, Israel and Afghanistan and their views on Jews and gays have led them to be banned from appearing on British campuses by the National Union of Students.[53] In addition, senior politicians from both major British political parties, including former Prime Ministers Tony Blair and David Cameron, pledged to ban the group under anti-terrorism legislation. In October 2015, this legislation came about. The British government announced a wide variety of tactics that it hoped would limit radicalization, including bans on online material from radical preachers, the ability to close mosques that support extremism, more limits on extremist radio and television shows, and the ability to pressure internet service providers to remove extremist material.[54]

- *Al-Muhajiroun (ALM)*. ALM was founded in 1996 as a direct offshoot of HuT by the former leader of HuT in Britain, Omar Bakri Mohammed.[55] Mohammed split from HuT due to a dispute with the movement's hierarchy: Bakri wanted it to change tactics and concentrate on establishing an Islamic state in Britain, rather than re-creating the Caliphate in the Middle East. He therefore formed ALM with the aim of creating a cadre of activist Muslims who campaigned for the immediate creation of an Islamic state in Britain. Since its establishment, ALM has also supported "defensive *jihad*" in Israel, Kashmir, Afghanistan and Iraq.[56] The group has campaigned and organized marches on various issues, including a few anti-voting initiatives, and was one of the main driving forces behind the mass protests in London against the Danish Mohammed cartoons in 2004.[57] The group was officially disbanded in 2004 to avoid proscription, though it continued to hold meetings in Islamic centers around the country. After the 7/7 London bombings, Bakri fled the country, handing over the leadership to his deputy, Anjem Choudhary. In 2005, ALM regrouped under the banner of *Ahlus Sunnah wal Jamaah*, and later formed two more offshoots, *al-Ghuraaba* and Saved Sect, both of which were banned in 2006 for glorifying acts of terrorism.[58] Despite the bans, Choudhary and his followers were still able to operate as *Ahlus Sunnah wal Jamaah*, which was never banned, and in 2008 they began working under the name of Islam4UK. A year later, they announced the re-launch of *al-Muhajiroun*.[59] The entire movement was ultimately banned by the government in January 2010.[60] However, this has not stopped the group continuing to organize public meetings under a variety of pseudonyms, leading to a 2014 ban of three additional organizations: Need4Khilafah, the Shariah Project and the Islamic Dawah Association.[61]

"Homegrown" jihadist terrorists

Since the 7/7 attacks, the specter of British "homegrown" terrorism has remained a central concern for the country's security services. Numerous plots, including many in the final stages of planning, have either failed or been prevented from occurring since 9/11. The majority of those convicted on terrorism charges are British citizens, many of Pakistani origin. Between 1999 and 2010, British Pakistanis or Pakistani nationals were responsible for over a quarter of all Islamist-related offences in Britain.[62]

In May 2013, Britain suffered its first domestic fatality to Islamist terrorism since 7/7. Drummer Lee Rigby was murdered in the streets of London by two British extremists, Michael Adebolajo and Michael Adebowale. Adebolajo had unsuccessfully attempted to join up with *al-Shabaab*, the Somali terrorist group, in 2010, and was also known to have spent time within the ALM network in the UK. Subsequently, in December 2015, a man was arrested at a Tube station in Leytonstone after stabbing one person, threatening to stab others, and saying "this is for Syria." The stabbing victim survived. The police and numerous MPs treated the stabbing as a terrorist attack.[63]

ISLAMISM AND SOCIETY

According to the last official estimates, taken from the country's 2011 Census, Britain has a Muslim population of 2.7 million (4.8 percent of the overall population), making them the second largest religious group in the country, after Christians.[64]

It is difficult to gauge the exact level of support for Islamist groups among Muslims in Britain, though a number of polls have tried to assess the sentiments of British Muslims toward both specific British Islamist groups as well as certain aspects of Islamism (such the establishment of *sharia* law and violence in the name of Islam). In 2005, the polling company Populus asked British Muslims about their views on some specific British Islamist organizations. Twenty-five percent of respondents in that survey claimed that the Muslim Brotherhood/*Jamaat e-Islami*-aligned Muslim Council of Britain "absolutely" or "broadly" represented their views, and 19 percent made the same claim about the Muslim Association of Britain, one of the Muslim Brotherhood's main representatives in the country.[65]

Regarding British Muslims' views about certain aspects of Islamism, a 2016 survey administered by ICM found that in most cases, the British Muslim population does not vary greatly from the wider population. The poll suggests that 86 percent of Muslims feel a strong sense of belonging in Britain, and 88 percent said that Britian was a good place for Muslims to live. Four percent of the population said that felt sympathy for suicide bombers, and four percent said they sympathized with people who committed terrorist acts as a form of protest in general.[66]

British Islamist groups are regularly discussed in the mainstream media, often in controversial circumstances. For example, after the deputy secretary of the Muslim Council of Britain, Daud Abdullah, signed a statement in support of violent *jihad* against Israel (see section below for more), it was covered across a range of different newspapers and media outlets.[67] In addition, Member of Parliament Hazel Blears, the government secretary who liaised with the Council, and Daud Abdullah both published articles stating their respective positions.[68]

There is a significant element of Islamist influence in important areas of civic life. The head of the Muslim Council of Britain and Chairman of the East London Mosque, Dr. Muhammed Abdul Bari, sat on a panel for a University College London inquiry into the radicalization of one of its students, Umar Farouk Abdulmutallab,[69] who on Christmas Day 2009 attempted to detonate explosives hidden in his underwear on a plane over Detroit. Considering that Anwar al-Awlaki is widely regarded as a major inspiration for Abdulmutallab's actions, Dr. Bari's involvement in the inquiry was seen by some as inappropriate due to the controversy over the ELM hosting al-Awlaki to speak twice before he became a public figure promoting extremism.[70]

While the Islamic State (ISIS) has emerged as a threat to Europe and the West, its presence has not yet materialized in an attack on the United Kingdom. However, the UK's support of the Unites States' policies and military campaigns against ISIS, along with its own actions to militarily and financially dismantle the group's network, means the UK cannot ignore the threat of potential attacks.[71] Furthermore, according to an October 2016 study conducted by the BBC, more than 850 Britons had travelled to Syria or Iraq in support of ISIS since 2014, and more than 600 others attempting to make the journey had been stopped by authorities. The investigation also uncovered that nearly half of those who went abroad in search of ISIS have returned to the United Kingdom, adding to the threat of a potential domestic attack.[72] Another source of concern for UK politicians and citizens is the surge of immigration, particularly from the Syria and Iraq, that has taken place in recent years. Indeed, mounting concern for the security of the UK's borders and its immigration policies in general were a principal issue in the country's June 2016 referendum, commonly known as Brexit, in which UK citizens voted to leave the European Union.. Many of the arguments in favor of leaving the EU centered on the need to create stronger border controls in order to inhibit the spread of ISIS fighters, and limit their potential entry into the UK.[73]

ISLAMISM AND THE STATE

Since the July 2005 London terror attacks, the relationship between the British state and national Islamist groups has been characterized by inconsistency. The government's counterterrorism strategy, dubbed CONTEST, is split into four parts: Pursue, Protect, Prepare and Prevent. The first three of these priorities are straightforward, hard power methods to be implemented by the security services. The fourth—Prevent, also known as Preventing Violent Extremism (PVE)—was a new and unique approach, which is implemented through the Home Office.[74] Designed with the intention of applying measures which could mitigate the influence and effect of "violent extremists," its primary function was to act as a fund for local community organizations that pledged to tackle radicalization on a grassroots level.

Between 2006 and 2009, the Prevent fund distributed around £12 million to hundreds of organizations around the country, and quickly began to court controversy.[75] Soon after the fund was launched, there were revelations that a number of Islamist organizations were in receipt of Prevent funds despite their involvement in extremist activity. For example, in 2008 it was reported that the aforementioned Cordoba Foundation, while in receipt of Prevent funds, organized an event entitled "Has Political Participation Failed British Muslims?" which included on its panel Abdul Wahid, the Chairman of the British wing of *Hizb ut-Tahrir*.[76]

The issue of the Labour government's dealings with Islamist groups came to a head in early 2009, when the Deputy Secretary General of the Muslim Council of Britain, Daud Abdullah, served as a signatory (along with Mohammed Sawalha of the Muslim Association of Britain) to what became known as the "Istanbul Statement," a conference document calling on the Palestinian authority to "carry on with the jihad and resistance against the occupier until the liberation of all Palestine."[77] At the time, the MCB was a governmental partner on Prevent, and the then-Secretary for the Communities and Local Government, Hazel Blears, warned the MCB that Abdullah must either resign or the government would sever all ties with them. The MCB responded by portraying Blears' request as an attempt to exercise control over an independent Muslim body, refusing to back down. Blears subsequently cut ties with the MCB. Months later, however, Blears was replaced by John Denham, a minister with a more sympathetic view toward the MCB, and they were brought back into the fold shortly thereafter.[78]

Since the Labour party lost power to a Liberal Democrat/Conservative Party coalition in May 2010, the government's stance on the ideology of political Islamist groups such as the MCB shifted and a thorough review into the Prevent strategy led to it being recalibrated the following year. Describing the Prevent program run by the Labour government as "flawed." the Conservative/Liberal coalition government outlined its intent to confront extremist ideology, not just its violent manifestations. Under the new approach, organizations that did not adhere to a belief in equality before the law, democracy and human rights would not be engaged with by the government, and nor would they be funded.[79]

However, implementation of this policy faced challenges from within reluctant elements of the civil service. For example, in June 2010, Home Secretary Teresa May banned Zakir Naik—an Indian cleric who had praised Osama bin Laden and said that "every Muslim should be a terrorist"—from entering the UK because his presence would not be conducive to the public good. However, Charles Farr, the Director of the Office of Security and Counter Terrorism, attempted to undermine this policy and (ultimately unsuccessfully) facilitate Naik's entrance into the country.[80] With Teresa May assuming the role of Prime Minister in 2016, this disparity between government policy and civil service execution may continue to be a problem.

In 2014, then-Prime Minister David Cameron ordered an in-depth investigation into the Muslim Brotherhood and a review and of government policy towards the organization. The review, concluded in December 2015, led Cameron to the following observation of the role of the Muslim Brotherhood in the United Kingdom:

> Parts of the Muslim Brotherhood have a highly ambiguous relationship with violent extremism. Both as an ideology and as a network it has been a rite of passage for some individuals and groups who have gone on to engage in violence and terrorism. The main findings of the review support the conclusion that membership of, association with, or influence by the Muslim Brotherhood should be considered as a possible indicator of extremism.[81]

However, the results of the review were not unanimously agreed upon by all MPs, specifically the House of Commons Foreign Affairs Committee (FCO), which commissioned a second report investigating the Muslim Brotherhood and its political influence on the United Kingdom. The results, released in November 2016, criticized and refuted much of the first report (also known as the Jenkins Report, for former UK Ambassador to Saudi Arabia Sir John Jenkins).

For example, the FCO criticized the Jenkins report for neglecting much of the happenings within the Muslim Brotherhood since its ouster from power in Egypt in 2013, a time the FCO deemed critical for understanding the status and standing of the group in more recent years. It also took aim at the conflict of interest for Jenkins, who was UK ambassador while leading the original review.[82] Opinions about the Muslim Brotherhood, and political Islam in general, in the United Kingdom continue to be a hot button issue for politicians, and the June 2016 referendum to leave the European Union has unknown implications for policy towards Islam in the United Kingdom for years to come.

Endnotes

[1] The term "soft Islamist" will be used throughout this entry to refer to Islamist groups that use "soft power" in pursuit of their goals, in particular the two main revivalist organizations: the Muslim Brotherhood and the Jamaat-e-Islami.

[2] Brigitte Maréchal, "Universal Aspirations: The Muslim Brotherhood In Europe," International Institute for the Study of the Muslim World ISIM Review no.22, Autumn 2008, 36-37.

[3] UK Land Registry, Title Number: NGL700045.

[4] "Six Decades of Repression: An Interview With Adbel Shaheed al-Ashaal," St. Andrews University Centre for the Study of Terrorism and Political Violence Islamism Digest, February 2007.

[5] Hassan al-Banna Foundation Certificate of Incorporation as a Limited Company, Companies House, February 11, 1997.

[6] Federation of Islamic Organizations in Europe, "President Of The Federation And Head Of The Assembly Of Islamic Imams Meet President Of The Commission And European Parliament President," n.d., http://www.euro-muslim.com/En_u_news_Details.aspx?News_ID=214.

[7] "EU Muslim Converts Sharing Experiences," IslamOnline, April 12, 2009, http://www.islamonline.net/servlet/Satellite?c=Article_C&cid=1237706102893&pagename=Zone-English-Euro_Muslims%2FEMELayout.

[8] Maréchal, "Universal Aspirations."

[9] It is unclear if it was originally set up as a limited company. Official company records for the MAB only date back to 1999.

[10] "Kemal El-Helbawy CV," n.d., http://www.khelbawy.com/about.html.

[11] Peter Bergen and Paul Cruickshank, "The Unraveling: The Jihadist Revolt Against Al-Qaeda," The New Republic, June 11, 2008.

[12] Federation of Islamic Organizations in Europe, "FIOE Organisations," n.d., http://www.euromuslim.com/En_u_Foundation_Details.aspx?News_ID=211

[13] Cited on the official website of the MAB, www.mabonline.net.

[14] 2008 Appointments Report for The Cordoba Foundation LTD, Companies House.

[15] David Cameron, speech at the Community Security Trust, London, March 4, 2008.

[16] The Cordoba Foundation, "About us," n.d., http://www.thecordobafoundation.com/about_us.php.

[17] Samuel Westrop, "UK: HSBC Shuts Down Islamist Bank Accounts," Gatestone Institute, August 2, 2014, https://www.gatestoneinstitute.org/4566/islamist-hsbc-banking

[18] "The Battle For The Mosque," BBC News, February 7, 2006.

[19] NLCM press release, "New Era For North London Central Mosque," February 5, 2005.

[20] Bergen and Cruickshank, "The Unraveling."

[21] Michael Whine, "The Penetration of Islamist Ideology in Britain," Hudson Institute Current Trends in Islamist Ideology 1, May 2005.

[22] According to the official website of UKIM, www.ukim.org.

[23] UKIM, "Introduction," n.d., as cited in Giles Kepel, Allah in the West: Islamic Movements in America and Europe (Oxford: Polity Press, 1997).

[24] UKIM, "UK Islamic Mission Dawah: Resource To Online Islamic Books & Articles," n.d., http://www.ukim.org/webpages/Dawah.aspx.

[25] Innes Bowen, Medina in Birmingham, Najaf in Brent: Inside British Islam (Oxford University Press, 2014)

[26] Sayyed Vali Resa Nasr, The Vanguard Of The Islamic Revolution: Jamaat-e-Islami of Pakistan (Berkeley: University of California Press, 1994).

[27] Kepel, Allah in the West.

[28] "East London Mosque: Vision and Mission," n.d., http://www.eastlondonmosque.org.uk/content/vision-mission.

[29] "Ethnicity in Tower Hamlets Analysis of 2011 Census data," 2013, http://www.towerhamlets.gov.uk/Documents/Borough_statistics/Ward_profiles/Census-2011/RB-Census2011-Ethnicity-2013-01.pdf

[30] Samuel Westrop, "Britain Legitimizes, Funds Terrorist Movement," Gatestone Institute, March 3, 2013, https://www.gatestoneinstitute.org/3609/britain-jamaat-islami

[31] Audio of Awlaki's speech at the ELM is available at http://www.youtube.com/watch?v=GyCf25XujkM&feature=youtube_gdata.

[32] Gordon Rayner, "Muslim Groups 'Linked To September 11 Hijackers Spark Fury Over Conference,'" Daily Telegraph (London), December 27, 2008, http://www.telegraph.co.uk/news/uknews/3966501/Muslim-groups-linked-to-September-11-hijackers-spark-fury-over-conference.html; "Councillor Slams Muslim Lecture 'New York In flames' Poster," East London Advertiser, December 31, 2008.

[33] Gordon Rayner, "Muslim groups 'linked to September 11 hijackers spark fury over conference," The Telegraph, December 27, 2008, http://www.telegraph.co.uk/news/uknews/3966501/Muslim-groups-linked-to-September-11-hijackers-spark-fury-over-conference.html.

[34] "East London Mosque and London Muslim Centre Statement on Anwar Awlaki," East London Mosque Trust Management, November 6, 2010, http://archive.eastlondonmosque.org.uk/uploadedImage/pdf/2010_11_07_15_44_46_Awlaki%20Statement%206%20Nov10%20-%20Full%20Statement.pdf

[35] IFE, "Islamic Forum Of Europe: Responding To The Call," n.d., http://www.islamicforumeurope.com/live/ife.php?doc=intro.

[36] Andrew Gilligan, "IFE: Not Harmless Democrats," Guardian (London), March 4, 2010.

[37] After novelist Salman Rushdie published The Satanic Verses in 1988, there were widespread protests and riots by Muslims in Europe, the Middle East and South Asia who considered the content of the book blasphemous and insulting to the Prophet Mohammed. This culminated in the issuing of a fatwa by the Iranian Supreme Leader, Ayatollah Ruhollah Khomeini, in February 1989, which called on Muslims to kill the author in the name of Islam and Mohammed. This saga is widely seen as a watershed moment in the political "awakening" of Western Muslims, and is probably best recounted by Kenan Malik in From Fatwa to Jihad: The Rushdie Affair and Its Legacy (London: Atlantic Books, 2009).

[38] Sacranie famously said of the novelist: "death, perhaps, is a bit too easy for him? His mind must be tormented for the rest of his life unless he asks for forgiveness to Almighty Allah." See "Rushdie In Hiding After Ayatollah's Death Threat," Guardian (London), February 18, 1989.

[39] Martin Bright, When Progressives Treat With Reactionaries: The British State's Flirtation With Radical Islamism (London: Policy Exchange, 2006).

[40] "Full Text: Muslim Groups' Letter," BBC, August 12, 2005, http://news.bbc.co.uk/1/hi/4786159.stm.

[41] "Muslim Outrage As Yusuf al-Qaradawi Refused UK Visa," Times of London, February 7, 2008, http://www.thetimes.co.uk/tto/news/uk/article1917193.ece.

[42] Department for Communities and Local Government, "The Pakistani Muslim Community In England," March 2009.

[43] "FOSIS Annual Conference 2005," http://oldsite.fosis.org.uk/FAC/conference05/poster.jpg.
[44] "FOSIS Annual Conference 2007," http://oldsite.fosis.org.uk/FAC/FAC2007/programme.html.
[45] "FOSIS Annual Conference 2003," http://web.archive.org/web/20030801182249/http:/www.fosis.org.uk/events/articles/annualconf_jun2003.htm.
[46] Ibid.
[47] FOSIS, "Muslim Contribution To Civilisation, Dr. Jamal Badawi, February 2010," n.d., http://fosis.org.uk/sc/calendar/details/94-jamal-badawi-speakers-tour/145%7C139.
[48] MPACUK, "About Us.' http://www.mpacuk.org/us/
[49] MPACUK, "Watford Campaign Starts With A Bang!," April 18, 2010, http://www.mpacuk.org/story/180410/watford-campaign-starts-bang.html.
[50] MPACUK, "Operation Muslim Vote," May 5, 2010, http://www.mpacuk.org/story/020709/operation-muslim-vote.html.
[51] Hizb ut-Tahrir, Hizb ut-Tahrir (London: Al-Khilafah Publications, 2000).
[52] For more on HT in Britain, see Houriya Ahmed and Hannah Stuart, Hizb ut-Tahrir: Ideology and Strategy (London: Centre for Social Cohesion, 2009).
[53] "'Stealth' Islamists Recruit Students," Times of London, October 16, 2005.
[54] Lisa Miller, "David Cameron unveils new anti-terrorism measures allowing parents to block children's passports," ABC News, October 19, 2015, http://www.abc.net.au/news/2015-10-20/david-cameron-proposes-uk-anti-terrorism-laws/6867908.
[55] "Jews Fear Rise Of The Muslim 'Underground,'" Guardian (London), February 18, 1996.
[56] Suha Taji-Farouki, "Islamists And The Threat Of Jihad: Hizb al-Tahrir And al-Muhajiroun On Israel And The Jews," Middle Eastern Studies 36, no. 4, October 2000, 21-46.
[57] "Reaction Around The World To Cartoon Row," BBC, February 4, 2006, http://news.bbc.co.uk/2/hi/europe/4676930.stm.
[58] "Reid Bans Two Radical Muslim Groups," Guardian (London), July 7, 2006.
[59] "Islamist Al-Muhajiroun Relaunch Ends In Chaos Over Segregation Attempt," Guardian (London), June 18, 2009.
[60] "Islam4UK To Be Banned, Says Alan Johnson," Guardian (London), January 12, 2010.
[61] "Ministers ban suspected aliases of banned extremist group," BBC, June 26, 2014, http://www.bbc.com/news/uk-politics-28049374

[62] Robin Simcox, Hannah Stuart & Houriya Ahmed, Islamist Terrorism: The British Connections (The Henry Jackson Society, 2010). These include offenses contrary to anti-terror legislation (namely the Terrorism Act 2000 and the Terrorism Act 2006) and those which include a clear threat designed to intimidate the public, in particular other religious groups.

[63] "Leytonstone Tube station stabbing a "terrorist incident," BBC, DATE NEEDED, http://www.bbc.com/news/uk-35018789

[64] Office for National Statistics, Census 2011, September 2012, http://www.ons.gov.uk/ons/dcp171776_290510.pdf

[65] Poll prepared by Populus on behalf of Times newspaper, December 2005.

[66] Frances Perraudin, "Half of all British Muslims think homosexuality should be illegal, poll finds," The Guardian, April 11, 2016, https://www.theguardian.com/uk-news/2016/apr/11/british-muslims-strong-sense-of-belonging-poll-homosexuality-sharia-law.

[67] "British Muslim Leader Urged To Quit Over Gaza," Guardian (London), March 8, 2009; "Hazel Blears' Standoff With Muslim Council Overshadows New Anti-Terror Launch," Guardian (London), March 25, 2009; "Government Ties With MCB Restored But Not For Deputy," Daily Telegraph (London), January 15, 2010.

[68] Daud Abdullah, "My Reply To Hazel Blears," Guardian (London), March 26, 2009; Hazel Blears, "Our Shunning Of The MCB Is Not Grandstanding," Guardian (London), March 26, 2009.

[69] Umar Farouk Abdulmutallab: Report to UCL Council of independent inquiry panel, University College London, September 2010.

[70] For example, see Paul Goodman, "Why The Conservative Party Should Have Nothing To Do With The East London Mosque," Conservative Home, October 12, 2010. Until May 2010, Mr. Goodman was a Member of Parliament and Shadow Communities Secretary for the Conservative Party.

[71] UK Action to Combat Daesh, https://www.gov.uk/government/topical-events/daesh/about

[72] "Who are Britian's jihadis?" BBC, October 10, 2016, http://www.bbc.com/news/uk-32026985

[73] Clark Mindock, "What The Brexit Means For ISIS: US, EU Terrorism Battle Against Islamic State After UK Vote Could Be Strained," International Business Times, June 24, 2016, http://www.ibtimes.com/what-brexit-means-isis-us-eu-terrorism-battle-against-islamic-state-after-uk-vote-2386430

[74] HM Government, Counter-terrorism strategy (CONTEST), n.d., https://www.gov.uk/government/publications/counter-terrorism-strategy-contest.

[75] For a comprehensive breakdown of all Prevent funded groups, see Tax Payers' Alliance, "Council Spending Uncovered II, No.5: The Prevent Strategy," September 8, 2009.

[76] "Muslim Pressure Group Wins Anti-Democracy Debate," East London Advertiser, February 27, 2008.

[77] "British Muslim Leader Urged To Quit Over Gaza," Guardian (London), March 8, 2009.

[78] "Government Seeks To Recast Relations With British Muslims," Guardian (London), August 10, 2009.

[79] HM Government, Prevent Strategy, June 2011, https://www.gov.uk/government/uploads/system/uploads/attachment_data/file/97976/prevent-strategy-review.pdf

[80] "Theresa May under pressure to sack top adviser in row over ban on Muslim preacher", Telegraph (London), October 19, 2010, http://www.telegraph.co.uk/news/uknews/terrorism-in-the-uk/8071101/Theresa-May-should-sack-top-terrorism-adviser.html

[81] "UK Split over Muslim Brotherhood and Saudi Arabia," Eurasia Review, November 28, 2016, http://www.eurasiareview.com/28112016-uk-split-over-muslim-brotherhood-and-saudi-arabia-oped/

[82] 'Political Islam', and the Muslim Brotherhood Review Sixth Report of Session 2016–17, House of Commons Foreign Affairs Committee, November 2016, http://www.publications.parliament.uk/pa/cm201617/cmselect/cmfaff/118/118.pdf.

EURASIA

COUNTRIES
Azerbaijan
Kazakhstan
Kygrygzstan
Russia
Tajikistan
Turkey
Turkmenistan
Uzbekistan

AZERBAIJAN

> **QUICK FACTS**
>
> Population: 9,872,765 (July 2016 est.)
>
> Area: 86,600 sq km
>
> Ethnic Groups: Azerbaijani 91.6%, Lezghin 2%, Russian 1.3%, Armenian 1.3%, Talysh 1.3%, other 2.4%
>
> Religions: Muslim 96.9% (predominantly Shia), Christian 3%, other <0.1%, unaffiliated <0.1% (2010 est.)
>
> Government Type: presidential republic
>
> GDP (official exchange rate): $35.69 billion (2015 est.)
>
> *Map and Quick Facts courtesy of the CIA World Factbook (Last Updated January 2017)*

OVERVIEW

Bordering both Russia and Iran, and with a close security relationship with both the United States and Israel, Azerbaijan occupies an important geostrategic position. As the former Soviet Union's only Shi'a Muslim majority country, the South Caucasus republic is even more unique. Azerbaijan's geographic location has led to a situation in which various domestic and international forces vie for influence; it has a population of over 9 million people, the majority of whom are closely linguistically and culturally related to the population of nearby Turkey, an extremely antagonistic relationship with neighboring Armenia, and proximity to restive Dagestan, a federal republic of Russia.

Since becoming an independent state in 1991, Azerbaijan has seen an upsurge in Islamist activity emanating from both Sunni and Shi'a organizations. Iranian backed Shi'ite extremists have attempted attacks on targets deemed to be close to the U.S. and Israel, and Sunni jihadists have descended from hotbeds of radicalism in the North Caucasus. In addition, terrorist groups have attempted to exploit organized crime networks and smuggling routes to support their endeavors in the Middle East. The government of Azerbaijan, in its efforts to address the threats emanating from both Sunni and Shi'a radicals, has doubled down on secular governance.

ISLAMIST ACTIVITY

Like many of the post-Soviet states with Muslim populations, Azerbaijan saw a rekindled interest in Islam following its independence in 1991. With an end to state-enforced atheism, the stage was set for domestic and foreign actors to vie for spiritual access to the country's predominantly Muslim community. That community is estimated to be two-thirds Shi'a and one third Sunni.[1] This ratio nevertheless is in flux, given the growing role of various Sunni movements – with *Shafi'i* and *Salafi* missionaries coming from the Arab world, and *Hanafi* activists emanating from Turkey.[2]

Shi'a Radicalism and the role of Iran and Hezbollah

Azerbaijan is situated at the vital geostrategic nexus of Iran, Russia and Turkey. The oil- and gas-rich country shares historical, linguistic and economic ties with all three of these regional powers. Azerbaijan has close ties to both the U.S. and Israel, a relationship Tehran regards with deep suspicion. Furthermore, a quarter of the Iranian population (including Supreme Leader Ayatollah Ali Khamanei) is ethnically Azerbaijani Turkic. Azerbaijan, either by specific actions or simply through its very existence, has great potential to spark anti-Iranian ethnic nationalism, especially in Iran's volatile northeastern provinces.[3] In an effort to counteract the threat emanating from Azerbaijani nationalist movements, Tehran has sought to promote religious movements in Azerbaijan and empower Shi'ite clergy to oppose the Azerbaijani state. The nationalist and autonomist ambitions within Iran's Azerbaijani minority are a sensitive issue, which to date has not received the attention the subject may deserve. The Azerbaijani government has on several occasions alluded to efforts by Tehran to undermine its authority by stirring up religious unrest at home. Officials in Baku alleged in 2002 that Iranian funding and support had contributed to major protests in the Baku suburbs. In mid-2002, then-President Heydar Aliyev alluded to "outside powers" which wished to turn Azerbaijan into an Islamic state, unquestionably a veiled reference to Iran.[4]

In 2006, Azerbaijani authorities foiled a major terror attack involving Iranian operatives and directed at Israeli and Western targets.[5] In the course of the investigation, 15 Azerbaijani citizens were found to have been trained by Iranian security forces. Follow-up investigations led to the prevention of a second attack in 2008 on the Israeli embassy. These plans appear to have been carried out by a secret cell operating on Azerbaijani soil, which had been mobilized by Tehran in collaboration with Hezbollah, in retaliation for the killing of Hezbollah military chief Imad Mughniyeh in Damascus. Prior to the attempted attack, Azerbaijani police apprehended two Hezbollah militants, while suspects of Lebanese, Iranian and Azerbaijani extraction fled across the border to Iran. During trials in October 2009, evidence indicated that both Hezbollah and the Iranian Revolutionary Guard Corps were linked to plot against the Israeli embassy.[6]

Further conspiracies occurred in 2012, in the run-up to the Eurovision song contest, when several attempted attacks against perceived pro-Western and pro-Israeli targets were foiled. First, in January of that year, two men were arrested on charges of plotting to murder two teachers at a Jewish school in Baku. Then, in February 2012, another cell, allegedly trained by the Iranian secret service, came to the attention of Azerbaijani state security.[7] Soon afterward, 22 individuals were arrested on the grounds of planning attacks the embassies of the United States and Israel.

However, a rapprochement between Baku and Tehran since 2012 has led to a decrease of Iranian-linked subversive activity. The Obama administration's hostile attitude toward Azerbaijan and its parallel warming of relations with Iran forced Baku to initiate its own outreach to Iran. Indeed, the Obama Administration strongly pushed for a Turkish-Armenian normalization process that ignored Azerbaijan's concerns over its unresolved conflict with Armenia. As Azerbaijan successfully contributed to halting that normalization process, relations between Washington and Baku soured considerably, with mutual public recriminations that risked undermining the strategic partnership between America and Azerbaijan. As a result, Baku sought to improve relations with other powers, including Iran. While Iranian representatives continue to put pressure on Baku over its close ties to Israel, the improvement of relations appears to have reduced state-sponsored Iranian Islamist activity.

However, the curious case of the town of Nardaran has continued to trouble Azerbaijani authorities. Only a dozen miles outside the capital, the town has been a hotbed of Shi'a radicalism since the mid-1990s, when it gave birth to the defunct Islamic Party of Azerbaijan. Nardaran has long been known for the presence of extremist Shi'a activists and as a hotbed of anti-state Islamism. Following the arrest of over a dozen Islamist activists, including Taleh Bagirov, the leader of the Muslim Unity Movement (MUM) of Azerbaijan, clashes erupted in November 2015 between security forces and local protestors that left seven dead.[8] Among these were two police officers and five alleged Shi'ite militants. The confrontations were followed by series of raids. Security forces surrounded Nadaran and cut off all roads into and out of the district, in order to sweep for weapons and literature, in an effort to head off alleged terrorist activities.

The "Khawarij" and the Forest Brotherhood

Azerbaijan's radical *Salafi* Sunni community has historically revolved around populations in the country's north, bordering Dagestan, and the Abu Bakr Mosque of Baku, which has been seen as a hotbed of terrorist recruitment and violent extremism. While the majority of the congregation is not violent, several prominently connected terrorists, including former Guantanamo Bay inmate Polad Sabir Sirajov, had close ties to the community and served as vectors of radicalization.[9] These community members with extremist sympathies have broken with the leadership of the mosque, earning them the titles of *Khawarij* or "expelled ones."

These *Khawarij* believe they are justified in rebelling against the authority of religious leaders whom they view as having departed from a justified course of violence against civilians. One prominent example of such leadership is Gamat Sulaymanov, the *imam* of the Abu Bakr Mosque, who has made statements against the use of violence against "infidels." Suleymanov was injured in a grenade attack on his congregation in 2008, an incident which killed two and left a further 17 people injured.[10] The attack was likely carried out by the *Khawarij*, who did not take kindly to the *imam*'s conciliatory attitude. Following an investigation of the attack, the Azerbaijani government made a statement in which two Azerbaijani nationals, Ilgar Mollachiyev and his brother-in-law Samir Mehtiyev, both with ties to Sunni radicals in the nearby Dagestan Republic of Russia, were named as suspects.

Both Mollachiyev and Mehtiyev were alleged to have illegally entered Azerbaijan from Dagestan and been involved with setting up the foundations for terrorist cells in Baku and the coastal town of Sumgait. Baku accused the pair of attempting to reestablish the Azerbaijani branch of the "Forest Brothers," a militant group active in the Northern Caucasus that Azerbaijan banned in 2007. Mollachiyev and Mehtiyev were charged with creating an illegal armed group.[11]

Insurgency in Dagestan and the Northern Caucasus

Against the backdrop of the ongoing insurgency in the Northern Caucasus, which to date has claimed hundreds of lives, of both civilian and combatants, Azerbaijan's government has increased law enforcement efforts along the country's northern border.[12] In the wake of the collapse of the Soviet system, the Northern Caucasus became the scene of high levels of violence between Russian security forces and various opposition factions. Over time, resistance to Russian rule took an increasingly Islamic turn, with *jihadi* extremists coming to form the main force of the resistance.[13] While Chechnya has become the focal point of this conflict in the imagination of many observers, the violence has not been confined to that unhappy republic and was quick to spread throughout the region. Dagestan has become the center of the violence, playing host to the majority of clashes in recent years.[14]

Located on the eastern end of the Northern Caucasus, the Republic of Dagestan shares a long border with Azerbaijan. The patchwork of ethnicities that made up the former Soviet Union means that both states share ethnic minority communities, including Avars and Lezgins. Members of both these ethnic minority communities with Azerbaijani citizenship have crossed the Azerbaijani-Russian border to partake in the ongoing Islamist insurgency in the North Caucasus.[15] While the grievances of these groups are primarily directed against Moscow, the rise of Islamic radicalism in the North Caucasus has made *jihadi* groups in the region part of the global *jihadi* movement, and an estimated 1,000 of its members presently fight in Syria and elsewhere.[16]

There is a far more significant and dangerous flow of people and *jihadi* ideology southward into Azerbaijan. *Salafist* ideological streams, funded in part by Islamic organizations in the Gulf States, began entering Azerbaijan from the North Caucasus in the 1990s.[17] Conflict on Russian soil has also repeatedly led to an influx of Chechen and Dagestani fighters, seeking refuge and the opportunity to regroup in Azerbaijan. Most of those crossing into Azerbaijan from the North Caucasus are adherents of *Salafism*, and this fact, combined with the efforts of missionary establishments funded by the oil rich Arab Gulf States, has led to a situation in which there is a significant *Salafist* population in Azerbaijan—estimated to number about 15,000,[18] and in the capital Baku, their focal point has been the Abubakr Mosque.

Though a majority of these *Salafists* are not violent extremists but followers of the purist, nonviolent *Salafi* approach—such as the avowedly apolitical Imam Suleymanov—the potential for violence should not be underestimated. Much of *Salafist* thought is anchored in the belief that the Muslim community can and should be central to the structuring of government. Additionally, it rejects the tenets of multiculturalism and religious plurality. Considering the public priorities of Baku, that rejection sets its adherents on a collision course with state institutions.[19]

The Gülen/Hizmet Movement
Another example of an Islamist group which has ben able to successfully establish itself in post-independence Azerbaijan is the network of the influential, if increasingly controversial, Turkish cleric Fethullah Gülen. Like other missionizing Islamic movements, the Gülen movement saw the end of Soviet state atheism as an opportunity to gain support and followers in the newly independent, and nominally Muslim, states of the Caucasus and Central Asia. Based in Turkey, Gülen's followers were able to leverage linguistic and cultural similarities with the Turkic populations of the former Soviet Union to establish networks of educational institutions in the 1990s to cultivate the new state elites.[20] This, in turn, provided them with a stepping stone to becoming a truly global movement, which is well-represented and headquartered in the United States.

Azerbaijan became the first state outside of Turkey to host Gülen schools. Well-funded, and garnering support from then President Heydar Aliyev, the movement quickly established itself on the Azerbaijani education scene, opening several high schools, a private school, the Qafqaz University and a host of regional centers to promote its activities. Mindful not to antagonize the Azerbaijani government, the movement emphasized shared Turkic identity and cultural values over religious tenets.[21]

Despite this cautious approach, the Gülen movement has suffered significant setbacks in recent years, to put it lightly. The Azerbaijani state has been increasingly focused on training its own population rather than having foreign groups do so. The collapse of the political alliance between Fethullah Gülen and President Erdoğan in 2014 further undermined the position of Gülen supporters abroad, with the Turkish government putting pressure on Baku to curb the activities of the movement in Azerbaijan. Following the July 2016 coup attempt in Turkey, where Ankara was quick to ascribe blame to the Gülenists, Azerbaijani officials rushed to dismiss people in power who were believed to be too close to the movement.[22]

ISLAMISM AND SOCIETY

The majority of Azerbaijan's population of 9.7 million inhabitants self-identify as Muslim, about two thirds of whom are Shi'ites.[23] Sunni Islam is best established in the northern and western regions of the country, especially among the ethnic minorities who live closest to the Northern Caucasus regions of Russia. However, Sunni Islam is gathering strength in the country at the expense of Shi'a traditions, something noted by observers and visible through the influence, not least, of Turkish schools.[24] Azerbaijan's south and east, the areas closest to Iran, have historically been dominated by Shi'a Islam, though decades of Soviet state atheism means that Azerbaijanis in Azerbaijan are generally less observant than their co-ethnics across the border. Under the nationalities policy of the early Soviet period, Azerbaijanis were encouraged to think of Shi'ism as a marker of national identity rather than a guiding principle of spiritual life.[25]

However, following the end of the official state atheism, numerous Azerbaijanis have found new ways to express their religion. A new generation, for whom the Soviet experience is but a vague memory, has taken an interest in public expressions of religiosity. At the same time, both Shi'ite Iran and the Sunni monarchies of the Gulf have sought to encourage the revival of Islamic faith in Azerbaijan, and mold the religious experience of Azerbaijan's youth in a way that favors their own objectives and priorities.

Efforts to promote radicalism have, however, run up on the government's increasingly outspoken secularism, which is firmly entrenched in public discourse despite the quarter century since the demise of the Soviet ideology. The prominence of Islam has prompted debates about the role religion should play in the modern Republic of Azerbaijan, and there remains a deep seated mistrust of Islamism among the Azerbaijani elite.[26] In a situation analogous to that of other post-socialist states with large Muslim populations, radical Islamism in Azerbaijan is fed by the quest for identity in a rapidly changing society, social ills such as corruption, and disappointment over the unfulfilled promises of modernization. Perhaps ironically, Azerbaijan has been subject to criticism from western governments and NGOs for its treatment of Islamist organizations within the country that have developed radical objectives in their criticism of the state.

ISLAMISM AND THE STATE

The major influx of Arab, Iranian and Turkish missionaries into Azerbaijan, tolerated at first in the early 1990s, increasingly became a concern for officials in Baku. Perhaps surprised by the rapidity and scope of these well-funded newcomers on the scene, the government opted for a more decisive course of action. In 1996, the Azerbaijani parliament passed an amendment to the Law on Freedom of Religious Belief which proscribed the participation of "foreigners" in the propagation of 'religious propaganda.'"[27] After deadly riots in the Baku suburb of Nardaran left one person dead and 16 injured in 2002, these measures were expanded to bar anyone who had received religious training abroad.[28]

Further measures to curtail the recruitment efforts of radical Islamists included requiring religious communities to refile their state registration and establishing the State Committee for Work with Religious Associations, which increased state control of religious institutions.[29] The state's efforts to curb the spread of radical Islam are also part of a larger initiative to combat Islamic terrorism. Azerbaijan's counterterrorism policy has included close cooperation with regional as well as international actors, specifically the United States. Baku granted overflight rights and permission for numerous refueling and supply landings to Coalition forces during the military intervention in Afghanistan. Azerbaijani troops themselves took part in operations in Afghanistan, helping in international attempts to stabilize the security situation in Central and South Asia.[30] Azerbaijani officials have also supported international law enforcement through information sharing and joint policing operations.

Following the drawdown of coalition troops from Afghanistan and the rise to prominence of ISIS, Baku has turned its attention to the struggle to contain terrorism emanating from Iraq and Syria. Azerbaijan's leadership has contributed to these international efforts by disrupting the flow of arms and supplies through its territory, by sharing information, apprehending suspected returnee foreign fighters and having state religious authorities, such as the Caucasus Muslim Board, counter the claims of the propaganda savvy organization.

A significant number of legal amendments added every year between 2009 and 2015 have been squarely aimed at tackling the extremist threat and preventing further radicalization. Among these, an amendment to the criminal code ensured that the punishment for "foreign fighters" traveling to Syria became a 15 year-long jail sentence. Similarly the penalty for spreading religious propaganda has been increased to one to two years in prison.[31] Amendments added in 2014-2015 prevented clerics educated abroad (with the exception of those educated in state-approved educational institutions) from working in Azerbaijan, while a 2014 amendment led the State Committee for Work with Religious Organizations to monopolize religious education for the conduct of rites. To fill the need for training clerics, the State Committee expanded its own role and conducted more than 30,000 trainings in 2015-16. However, the amendments were not applied retroactively, which means that any previous training that existing clerics may have received has not been invalidated. Whereas the official state estimate is that 1,800 individuals have already received religious education abroad, the real number is probably higher.[32]

ENDNOTES

[1] United States Department of State, Office of the Coordinator for Counterterrorism, Country Reports on Terrorism 2011 (Washington, DC: U.S. Department of State, July 2012), http://www.state.gov/j/ct/rls/crt/2011/195543.htm

[2] Fuad Aliyev, "The Gülen Movement in Azerbaijan," Current Trends in Islamist Ideology 14 (2013), 90, http://www.currenttrends.org/docLib/20130124_CT14Aliev.pdf.

[3] Ilan Berman, Tehran Rising: Iran's Challenge to the United States (Lanham, MD: Rowman & Littlefield Publishers, 2005), 94-95.

[4] Ibid.

[5] Sebastian Rotella, "Azerbaijan Seen as a New Front in Mideast Conflict," Los Angeles Times, May 30, 2009, http://articles.latimes.com/2009/may/30/world/fg-shadow30.

[6] "Cell Sent By Hezbollah To Attack Israeli Embassy," Yediot Ahronot (Tel Aviv), July 7, 2009, http://www.ynetnews.com/articles/0,7340,L-3743694,00.html.

[7] "Four jailed in Azerbaijan for Eurovision terror plot," Jerusalem Post, December 3, 2012, http://www.jpost.com/International/Article.aspx?id=294463.

[8] Paul Goble, "'A Syrian Echo in Azerbaijan?", Shiites, Police Clash in Nardaran", Eurasia Daily Monitor, vol. 12 no. 14, December 1, 2015. (https://jamestown.org/program/a-syrian-echo-in-azerbaijan-shiites-police-clash-in-nardaran/)

[9] The U.S. Department of Defense's assessment is available online. See Department of Defense, Headquarters, Joint Task Force Guantanamo, "JTF-GTMO Detaine Assessment", January 25, 2008. https://assets.documentcloud.org/documents/82446/isn-89-poolad-t-tsiradzho-jtf-gtmo-detainee.pdf

[10] Elmir Guliev, Central Asia 2008 Analytical Annual (Sweden: Institute for Central Asian, Caucasian Studies & Institute of Strategic Studies of the Caucasus, 2009), 95, http://www.ca-c.org/annual/2008-eng/14.shtml.

[11] "Ilgar Mollachiyev and his brother-in-law Samir Mehdiyev committed explosion in Abu Bakr Mosque", apa.az, September 2, 2008. (http://en.apa.az/print/87964)

[12] Mairbek Vatchagaev, "Azerbaijani Jamaat Cooperates with Caucasus Emirate," Jamestown Foundation Eurasia Daily Monitor 9, iss. 73, April 12, 2012, http://www.jamestown.org/single/?no_cache=1&tx_ttnews%5Btt_news%5D=39262.

[13] Svante E. Cornell, "The 'Afghanization' of the North Caucasus: Causes and Implications of a Changing Conflict," in Stephen Blank, ed., Russia's Homegrown Insurgency (Carlisle, PA: U.S. Army War College, 2012).

[14] John O'Loughlin et.al., " The Changing Geography of Violence in Russia's North Caucasus, 1999–2011: Regional Trends and Local Dynamics in Dagestan, Ingushetia, and Kabardino-Balkaria", Eurasian Geography and Economics, vol. 52 no. 5, 2011, pp. 596-630.

[15] Emil Souleimanov, "Jihadism on the rise in Azerbaijan," Central Asia Caucasus Institute CACI Analyst, May 2, 2012, http://www.cacianalyst.org/?q=node/5766.

[16] Emil A. Souleimanov, "Globalizing Jihad? North Caucasians in the Syrian Civil War", Middle East Policy, vol. 21 no. 3, 2014.

[17] Svante E. Cornell, Azerbaijan since Independence, Armonk: M.E. Sharpe. 2011, 277-279; Sofie Bedford, "Islamic Activism in Azerbaijan: Repression and Mobilization in a Post-Soviet Context," Doctoral thesis before the Stockholm University Department of Political Science, 2009, 104, http://su.diva-portal.org/smash/record.jsf?pid=diva2:200259.

[18] Anar Valiyev, "The Rise of Salafi Islam in Azerbaijan", Terrorism Monitor, vol. 3 no. 13, July 1, 2015. https://jamestown.org/program/the-rise-of-salafi-islam-in-azerbaijan/

[19] Emil Souleimanov, Maya Ehrmann, "The Rise of Militant Salafism in Azerbaijan and its Regional Implications," Middle East Policy 20, no. 3, Fall 2013, http://www.mepc.org/journal/middle-east-policy-archives/rise-militant-salafism-azerbaijan-and-its-regional-implications.

[20] "The Gulen Movement in Azerbaijan & a quid pro quo?" The Perimeter Primate, January 14, 2013, http://perimeterprimate.blogspot.com/2013/01/the-gulen-movement-in-azerbaijan-quid.html.

[21] Eldar Mamedov, "Azerbaijan: Evaluating Baku's Attitude toward the Gulen Movement," Eurasianet.org, February 16, 2012, http://www.eurasianet.org/node/65013.

[22] Altay Göyüşov, "The Gulen movement in Azerbaijan and Erdogan's intervention," MeydanTV, August 02, 2016, https://www.meydan.tv/en/site/society/16428/.

[23] Souleimanov and Ehrmann; Cornell, Azerbaijan Since Independence; International Crisis Group, Azerbaijan: Independent Islam and the State, Europe Report no. 191, March 2008.

[24] Yavuz Kerimoğlu, "Azerbaycan: Toplum ve Siyaset", insamer, April 5, 2016. (http://insamer.com/tr/azerbaycan-toplum-ve-siyaset_275.html)

[25] Bedford, "Islamic Activism in Azerbaijan," 90-91.

[26] Ibid., 98.

[27] State Committee of the Azerbaijani Republic for the work with Religious Organizations, The Law of the Republic of Azerbaijan "On Freedom of Religious Belief," August 20, 1992 (Contains changes and additions of 1996 and 1997), http://www.dqdk.gov.az/eng/zakon_svoboda_e.html.

[28] "В Азербайджане запретят мулл, обучавшихся за границей" Oxu.az, December 2, 2015, http://ru.oxu.az/society/104949.

[29] Bedford, "Islamic Activism in Azerbaijan," 142.

[30] Madeleine Z. Bordallo, "Afghanistan Withdrawal Logistics and Capability of Azerbaijan to Support U.S. Military Requirements," The Sunlight Foundation, August 2012, http://capitolwords.org/date/2012/08/01/E1380-3_afghanistan-withdrawal-logistics-and-capability-of/.

[31] U.S. Department of State, Country Reports on Terrorism 2015 (Washington, DC: United States Department of State, 2016), https://www.state.gov/j/ct/rls/crt/2015/257516.htm.

[32] Svante E. Cornell, Halil Karaveli, Boris Ajeganov, Azerbaijan's Formula: Secular Governance and Civic Nationhood, Silk Road Paper, Central Asia-Caucasus Institute & Silk Road Studies Program, Joint Center, November 2016.

Kazakhstan

> ## Quick Facts
>
> Population: 18,360,353 (estimated July 2016)
>
> Area: 2,724,900 sq km
>
> Ethnic Groups: Kazakh (Qazaq) 63.1%, Russian 23.7%, Uzbek 2.9%, Ukrainian 2.1%, Uighur 1.4%, Tatar 1.3%, German 1.1%, other 4.4% (estimated 2009)
>
> Muslim 70.2%, Christian 26.2% (mainly Russian Orthodox), other 0.2%, atheist 2.8%, unspecified 0.5% (estimated 2009)
>
> Government Type: Presidential republic
>
> GDP (official exchange rate): $128.1 billion (estimated 2015)
>
> *Map and Quick Facts courtesy of the CIA World Factbook (Last Updated January 2017)*

Overview

Unlike its ex-Soviet Central Asian neighbors and Russia, Kazakhstan has rarely seen attacks by religious hardliners. The rhetoric of Islamist danger accompanying the U.S.-led "war on terror" and the experiences of neighboring states with terrorism played a significant role in shaping the Kazakh government's views on the threat of religious extremism and terrorism, and its subsequent counterterrorism responses. A series of terrorist incidents occurred in 2011, shattering Kazakhstan's image of "an oasis of stability" in the ocean of political turmoil. In response, the government intensified its counterterrorism measures and tightened control over religious organizations. Critics of this interference in the business of religious groups maintain that the rise of militant forms of Islam have been exaggerated by the Nazarbayev government, which used the threat of extremism as a pretext for clamping down on religious and political dissent. Some analysts expressed doubts over the official narrative of violent religious extremism, pointing out the criminal backgrounds of Kazakh "terrorists" apprehended to date.

However, concerns over religious extremism persist for a reason. Against the backdrop of deteriorating socio-economic conditions and growing disparities in wealth, there has been some increase in the rank-and-file members of radical Islamic groups in Kazakhstan as well as Kazakh foreign fighters in the Middle East. The most troubling aspect of detained and prosecuted Kazakh jihadists is their relative youth. With more than 40 percent of Kazakhstan's 18.36 million population (July 2016 est.) under the age of 25, the radicalization of youth targeted by Islamist recruiters is becoming an ever higher government priority. Kazakhs who return home from the battlefields of Syria and Iraq will pose another significant, and related, security challenge.

ISLAMIST ACTIVITY

Prior to the wave of terrorist violence in 2011, Kazakhstan had seen little Islamist activity. For both historical and socio-cultural reasons, Kazakh Muslims have been known to be less religious than their Uzbek and Tajik counterparts. The less-developed religious infrastructure, the lack of influential clergy, and the presence of a substantial Christian Russian minority created an unfavorable environment for radicalization of Muslims in Kazakhstan following the break-up of the Soviet Union. The relative socio-economic prosperity in this resource-rich nation has kept Islamic radicalization at bay. Of the 22 terrorist incidents recorded by the National Consortium for the Study of Terrorism and Responses to Terrorism (START) in Kazakhstan since its independence in December 1991, Islamists claimed only three attacks.[1]

The first attack took place in September 2000, when two police officers were shot dead in Almaty. The *Uighur Liberation Organization* (currently known as the East Turkestan Liberation Organization), which advocates an independent "Turkestan" and separatism from China, is suspected of perpetrating that incident.[2] Similar to other terrorist incidents, this attack was minor in terms of lethality, but had a symbolic impact. The incident indicated that Kazakhstan had shifted from being a mere waypoint for Islamist activity to an actual target for extremists.[3]

The following years saw a rise in the activities of *Hizb ut-Tahrir al-Islami* (HT), with the group becoming the primary target of the Kazakh government's counter-extremist efforts. HT is a clandestine radical Islamist organization that operates in 40 countries. In Kazakhstan, HT cells were first detected in 1998 in the country's south. At that time, local authorities intercepted the illegal distribution of leaflets and brochures calling for change in the constitutional system and the establishment of the caliphate. By the year 2000, HT membership in Kazakhstan rose to the low hundreds, and continued expanding in the years that followed, eventually leading to an official ban on the group by the Kazakh government in 2005.[4] Though ostensibly non-violent in nature, there are indications that HT's ultimate goals include a *ji-*

had against America and the replacement of existing political regimes with a caliphate (*Khilafah* in Arabic), a theocratic dictatorship based on *sharia* (Islamic religious law). These key aspects of HT ideology appeal to a small number of Central Asian *Salafists*. What explains the party's success in the region is its ability to adapt its message to local contexts and avoid theological debates.[5]

In 2006, Kazakh and Kyrgyz authorities launched a joint operation that impaired the HT network in both countries[6] and dismantled the routes that were used to deliver propaganda materials with extremist content and financing from abroad.[7] As a result of the operation, Uzbek citizen Otabek Muminov, the leader of the HT "information-analytical center," was detained and extradited to Uzbekistan. Mahamat-Yusuf Mamasadykov, the head of the organization's headquarters for Central Asia, was also apprehended in Jalalabad, Kyrgyzstan.

In 2007-2010, the activities of radical Islamic groups, chief among them HT, but also including *Jamaat Takfir* (which was discovered in Kazakhstan's western region in 2008[8]), focused on the dissemination of Islamist literature and propaganda, as evidenced by the nature of criminal investigations and trials conducted by Kazakhstan's security forces during that time.[9] The members of *Jamaat Takfir* and several other *Salafist* organizations active in the region called for the participation of the faithful in *jihad*, with the objective of establishing a global Islamic state.[10]

Salafism, an ultra-conservative Islamist ideology, came to Kazakhstan by way of the Caucasus and took hold mostly in the Atyrau, Mangistau, and Aktyubinsk regions. There, the ideology has been reinforced by missionaries from Saudi Arabia working in the energy industry in the Caspian region. Kazakh authorities were forced to close the operations of the Almaty Madrasah and the Arab-Kazakh University of Shymkent, but the Culture Center of the Saudi Arabian Kingdom in Almaty still provides education for *Salafis*.[11]

Kazakhstan's National Security Committee (KNB), an internal security service, has also alleged that *al-Jihad al-Islami* (also known as the Islamic Jihad Union, or IJU), an offshoot of the al-Qaeda-affiliated *Islamic Movement of Uzbekistan* (IMU), established its cells in Kazakhstan. The group preaches anti-Western ideology and, like the IMU, opposes secular rule in Uzbekistan.[12] The IJU has been waging *jihad* in the Afghan-Pakistan region, and maintains close ties with al-Qaeda and Taliban leaders. The majority of IJU members come from Central Asia, including a small contingent of Kazakh foreign fighters.[13]

Another battleground in the fight against religious extremism is Kazakhstan's prisons. As efforts to combat the spread of *Salafism* often result in the incarceration of the movement's adherents, many *Salafis* have used the country's penitentiaries as a platform for proselytizing. Their religious message, with its criticism of social injustice, has been successful in attracting new followers from among their fellow inmates. Upon their release, these inmates may go on to join extremist organizations. While the exact number of those radicalized in prisons is unknown, some of the attackers in the terrorist acts in Aktobe and Almaty discussed below had previously spent time in prison for various crimes, according to official sources. In 2011, Kazakhstan's government responded to this situation by closing all mosques, churches and other places of worship in its prisons, and sentencing some prisoners to solitary confinement for praying in their cells.[14] In summer 2016, the Kazakh Ministry of Interior and the Penal Committee government held a roundtable supported by the U.S. Embassy to discuss strategies for preventing radicalization in prisons. These include forensic examination of religious literature entering prisons, organizing meetings between the inmates and theologians, priests, and imams, and working with psychologists to develop approaches to countering violent extremism.[15]

HT and other radical Islamist organizations remain active in Kazakhstan, exploiting the deteriorating economic situation, corruption, and discrimination in parts of the country. The focus of Kazakhstan's counterterrorism measures has recently centered on another group – *Jund al-Kilafah* (Soldiers of the Caliphate, or JaK) – that claimed responsibility for bombings in the western city of Aturau and attacks against police in the southern city of Taraz in 2011. The spate of terrorist violence began with a suicide bombing in May in Kazakhstan's western town of Aktobe, followed by a car explosion in Astana. In July of the same year, security forces carried out an offensive against suspected extremists that left 13 dead in western Kazakhstan. Atyrau became a site of two explosions in October, and the following month two police officers were killed in Taraz.[16]

JaK is a transnational terrorist group based in the North Caucasus and the Afghanistan-Pakistan border region. Its Kazakh wing, known as Zahir Baibars Battalion, was established sometime between 2008 and 2011 by nine Kazakh mercenaries in the Afghan province of North Waziristan. The Battalion became affiliated with JaK in 2011 and continued to lead terrorist operations in the west and south of Kazakhstan. In 2011, JaK released a videotape in which its members threatened the Kazakh government with retaliation if it failed to retract a law banning women from wearing the veil. The following year, JaK published two more videos of attacks against ISAF forces in the Khost province of Afghanistan. It also claimed responsibility for the 2012 Toulouse shooting attributed to Mohamed Merah, a French citizen, who was killed by French police in a shootout.[17]

Kazakhstan's government eventually laid blame for the 2011 terrorist attacks on the Islamists. Initially, however, the government portrayed the 2011 violence as attacks by members of the organized criminal groups sheltering behind the guise of religion. The prosecutors dismissed the May 2011 suicide bombing in Aktobe as the work of Islamists and instead laid the blame on a local kingpin. Another example of the inextricability of Islamism and criminality in Kazakhstan is a series of gunmen attacks in Aktobe on June 6, 2016 that left at least 17 people, including 11 "extremists" dead. Kazakh authorities labeled the incident a terrorist act, but later re-framed it as a foiled *coup d'état*, only to return to the initial interpretation with a twist: the attack was blamed on militants belonging to "non-traditional religious movements" acting on direction from foreign groups. No credible claims of responsibility have ever surfaced for the attack. The government charged Tokhtar Tuleshov, a wealthy Kazakh businessman, and his accomplices, for the attack as well as for the popular protests in response to the land reform announced by President Nazarbayev. Tuleshov was apprehended in January 2016 and charged with drug trafficking, human trafficking, and the financing of a transnational organized criminal group. Several months later, in November 2016, the businessman was charged with plotting the coup against President Nazarbayev, the illegal possession of weapons, and extremism in the closed-door trial by a military court.[18] Another attack by a lone gunman on a police station on July 18, 2016 put Almaty on a high-terrorist alert. The government alleged that the gunman who killed five people, including three policemen, was a radical Islamist.[19] However, the reports of the Ministry of Internal Affairs of Kazakhstan suggest that the perpetrator sought revenge on law enforcement structures for his previous imprisonments.[20] The fact that he dodged his original plan to kill judges due to the large number of civilians present in the courtroom for an attack on the police also does not necessarily conform to traditional terrorist scenarios.

The rise of the Islamic State (ISIS) in the Middle East presents another security threat to authorities in Kazakhstan. ISIS has successfully recruited scores of Central Asian Muslims, who have since moved to Syria and Iraq, in some instances with their families, to fight on the side of ISIS. Several Islamist groups, including the IMU, pledged an oath of allegiance to ISIS.[21] According to Kazakhstan's security services, there are at least 400 Kazakhs now active in the Syria/Iraq theater—an increase of 30 percent from the government's January 2015 estimate.[22] Several propaganda videos (e.g., "Kazakh Fighter Calls His Countrymen to Jihad in Syria or Home," released in July 2014[23] and "How Kazakh Children Execute Enemies of Islam," published in January of 2015) have appealed directly to Kazakh Muslims to join ISIS and to act in support of the caliphate, either at home or in Syria, and have threatened the Nazarbayev government with violent overthrow. No reliable evidence exists to conclude that this new strategy has been working, but the participation of the Kazakh men in insurgency in Syria and Iraq has created a novel problem – the radicalization of Kazakh women who fell under the influence of their extremist husbands or other relatives. A new report released by the International Organization for Migration contends that the tendency for radicalization of women who find themselves in strong social isolation is a new phenomenon emerging in the last five years in the Central Asian states.[24]

ISLAMISM AND SOCIETY

According to Kazakhstan's most recent national census, carried out in 2009, approximately 65 percent of Kazakhstan's citizens identify themselves as Muslim.[25] The majority of Kazakh Muslims adhere to the Hanafi *madhab* (Muslim school of law). Less than one percent of the population professes to be Sunni of the Sha'afi school, or Shi'a, Sufi, or Ahmadi.[26] The highest concentration of practicing Muslims is located in Kazakhstan's southern region, bordering Uzbekistan, where Kazakhstan's Uzbek minority is concentrated. As in neighboring states, the number of mosques in Kazakhstan's has grown significantly since the country's independence. In 1989, there were only 46 mosque congregations in all of Kazakhstan. By 1998, that number had expanded to more than 1,000. By 2003, Kazakhstan had 1652 registered Muslim associations,[27] and in 2009 (the last year for which authoritative figures are available), there were 2,308 registered mosques affiliated with the Spiritual Association of Muslims of Kazakhstan (SAMK), and around 70 independent mosques.[28] The government funded the reconstruction and building of some new mosques, but the majority of new religious infrastructure in Kazakhstan to date has been sponsored from the Arab states.

Modern-day Kazakhs are the descendants of nomadic tribes who converted to the Sunni branch of Islam by the end of nineteenth century. Even after their conversion, these nomads continued to combine their pre-Islamic traditions and practices with the precepts of their new religion.[29] The policies of Tsarist and Soviet Russia only reinforced the blending of indigenous worldviews with Islamic traditions. As a result, Islam has become inseparable from the traditional life course of the Kazakhs and from the community in which these traditions prevail.[30] Today, as in the past, the "Muslimness" of Kazakhs is commonly derived from their ethnic and communal identification, rather than strict observance of Islamic laws and prohibitions.[31]

The SAMK is the organization that leads the Kazakh Muslims adhering to the Hanafi *madhab*, the only official religious school of thought in the republic. Islamic groups practicing their faith outside state-sponsored religious institutions are either regarded as pseudo-Muslim by the SAMK, or as extremist and terrorist by the government. The SAMK official status is that of a religious association, which serves as an independent intermediary between state authorities and its congregation. In practice, SAMK has become an arm of the state, keeping a watchful eye on the Muslim population through the supervision of mosque personnel, licensing construction of mosques, rotation of imams, the coordination of *Hajj* travel, and other forms of control.[32] There are over 1,500 mosques registered with the government.[33] The SAMK, however, does not and cannot control all Islamic organizations and associations in the country. There are many mosques, particularly in the southern part of Kazakhstan, that are not subordinated to the SAMK. Also, local mosques existing in the countryside remain unregistered with the Ministry of Justice. Therefore, they also escape the supervision of the SAMK. According to expert estimates, the number of non-registered mosques, which defy the SAMK's authority, is almost two times greater than that of registered mosques.[34]

ISLAMISM AND THE STATE

Formally, Kazakhstan remains a secular state. The Nazarbayev government has promoted "official" Islam as part of Kazakhstan's cultural identity and in an effort to strengthen economic cooperation with resource-rich states of the Middle East and Asia. It has, however, avoided emphasizing any close relationship between Kazakhstan and Islam. President Nursultan Nazarbayev has promoted the republic as a model of spiritual tolerance, inter-faith dialogue, and a meeting place of various religions. To that end, his government has initiated regular meetings with representatives of religious denominations, and these gatherings evolved into the Congress of World and Traditional National Religions held in Kazakhstan. Nazarbayev also pioneered the idea of the "Palace of Nations," envisioned as a global center for religious and inter-ethnic dialogue. The construction of the palace began in 2004 and a new Temple of Peace and Harmony—housing a mosque, an Orthodox church, a synagogue and a Buddhist temple in a single complex—was inaugurated two years later.[35] The World Forum of Spiritual Culture is another project launched by the government and aimed at fostering spirituality and strengthening dialogue between diverse cultures of the modern world.[36] Human rights groups, however, have lambasted these initiatives for being engineered "in Soviet style top-down fashion" and being intended "for foreigners."[37]

Kazakhstan's constitution adopted in 1995 enshrines the principle of the separation of state and religion. Based on this principle, religious education is prohibited in public schools, and in 2016 Kazakhstan adopted a law banning the hijab in schools across the country.[38] To prevent attempts to politicize Islam, activity by political organizations on a religious basis is legally forbidden in Kazakhstan, and religious political parties are unconstitutional.

Until the early 2000s, Kazakhstan carried out limited measures aimed at countering religious extremism and terrorism. Following 9/11 and intensified regional counterterrorism cooperation, Kazakhstan's government reinvigorated its national counterterrorism policy. To tackle the threat of violent Islamism, in late 2003 the KNB established an Anti-Terrorism Center, which coordinates counterterrorist and counter-extremist activities of various state bodies. The Center also serves as a liaison between Kazakhstan's counterterrorism agencies and similar structures abroad. The Center has administered multiple counterterrorism training exercises, conferences and symposia throughout the republic. In addition, it has engaged in education and public outreach projects, including regular broadcasting about state counterterrorism activities.[39] Kazakhstan's Ministry of Interior (MVD) created its own training center for combating terrorism and extremism in 2005. Kazakhstan's National Guard and State Protection Service also have their own special forces. Today, Kazakhstan's special operation units include *Sunkar* and *Arlan*, both part of the Ministry of Interior; *Kokjal* and *Kalkan*, which are part of the State Protection Service; *Burkit*, which is located within the National Guard; and *Arystan*, which is part of the KNB. Together with special forces of the Defense Ministry, these units are tasked with fighting terrorism, rescuing hostages, apprehending armed criminals, and guarding vital state installations.[40] The personnel of Kazakhstan's special forces receive their training from the elite centers of Russia, the U.S., Germany, Israel, and other states.[41]

In recent years, the Kazakh government has expanded its counterterrorism activities still further. In September 2009, President Nursultan Nazarbaev signed the law "On Counteracting Legalization (Laundering) of Ill-gotten Proceeds and Terrorist Financing."[42] This law enhances Kazakhstan's anti-money laundering/combating terrorism financing (AML/CTF) functions, and brings Kazakhstan into compliance with the "40+9" recommendations of the international Financial Action Task Force on Money Laundering (FATF).[43] The *1999 Law on Countering Terrorism* is still used as the legal basis for combating terrorism in Kazakhstan today.[44] In 2008 the Kazakh parliament considered, but did not pass, a new, stricter counterterrorism law.[45] New amendments seeking to strengthen counterterrorism legislation were brought into the *Oil Majlis* (Kazakhstan's parliament) in September 2016.[46]

Kazakhstan's special operations troops have stepped up their participation in multilateral and bilateral joint exercises, as well as their training with militaries and special units of other states. Particularly notable are the joint counterterrorism and military exercises conducted under the umbrella of the Collective Security Treaty Organization (CSTO) with the participation of the CSTO Rapid Deployment Forces. These include *Grom* (2013-2015), *Interaction* (2009-2015); *Rubezh* (2010-2015); *Tentr-2015*, and *Poisk-2016*, which, for the first time involved reconnaissance units from the participating states. The Shanghai Cooperation Organization (SCO), a six-member security bloc headed by Russia and China, has also been used as a platform for practicing joint counterterrorism responses. The Kazakh government has signed on to a series of agreements dealing with logistical cooperation, and joint efforts to combat the illegal circulation of weapons, ammunition and explosives codified by all members of the SCO member states.[47] Since 2003, the United States and the United Kingdom have supported an annual joint military exercise named *Steppe Eagle*. Furthermore, Kazakhstan has ratified numerous bilateral treaties with foreign nations, which have expanded counterterrorism coordination with foreign capitals.[48]

Parallel with the intensification of counterterrorism measures, Kazakhstan has stepped up its domestic efforts to control religious practices. As a result, the number of the government audits of religious organizations has increased substantially. The seizures of prohibited literature and print equipment additionally likewise have been on the rise. The state has also increased criminal and administrative responsibility for certain types of activities associated with extremism and terrorism, and strengthened religious regulations. In 2002, the government established criminal liability for the advocacy of terrorism and public incitement to commit an act of terrorism, as well as the establishment or leadership of a terrorist group and participation in its activities.[49] In 2005, the country's Criminal Code was amended with another article that criminalized financing of extremism and terrorism. A 2005 extremism law, which applies to religious groups and other organizations, gives the government broad powers in identifying and designating a group as an extremist organization, banning a designated group's activities, and criminalizing membership in a banned organization. HT is prohibited under this law.

In the summer of 2011, citing the need to ensure the freedom of belief and discourage abuses by the country's religious organizations, Kazakhstan's government created an Agency for Religious Affairs. This agency quickly developed a bill on religious activities that Kazakhstan's parliament passed and president signed in October of 2011.[50] The October 2011 law imposed significant new regulations concerning religion, requiring the dissolution and official registration of existing religious groups in the country, and imposing a ban on prayer in the workplace.[51]

In November 2014, Kazakhstan tightened its counter-extremist legislation further by simplifying a procedure for defining a group as terrorist or extremist and confiscating its property. Websites deemed to have extremist or terrorist content have been blocked in the country.[52] Today, the list of banned terrorist and extremist organizations released by the office of the Prosecutor General and approved by the Supreme Court includes, among others: the *Islamic Party of Turkestan*; *Hizb ut-Tahrir*; the *Islamic Movement of Uzbekistan* (IMU); al-Qaeda; the Taliban; the Muslim Brotherhood; *Kongra-Gel*, a Kurdish separatist group; *Boz Kurt* (Gray Wolves), a Turkish right-wing group; Pakistan's *Lashkar-e Taiba*; Kuwait's Social Reforms Society; Lebanon's *Asbat al-Ansar*; and a number of Uighur separatist groups.[53]

The Kazakh government has attempted to balance its restrictions on religious practices and tough anti-extremist measures with several outreach initiatives to its Muslim population. These initiatives have included: a national Program for Ensuring Religious Freedom and Improvement of Relations between the Government and Religions, which is aimed at "increasing the stability of the religious situation" and preventing religious extremism through education and government-sponsored media inserts;[54] conferences; roundtables and seminars on preventing religious extremism for students and youth;[55] and a strengthening of state control over both missionaries and the distribution of religious information.[56]

Kazakhstan's government has used other measures to attempt to discourage youth recruitment into extremist organizations. These measures include initiatives to "re-educate" young people whose religious leanings concern their parents or teachers, public forums dedicated to discussing distinctions between acceptable and unacceptable religious beliefs, and a large-scale program of internet monitoring to censor extremist materials online. The government has also sought to combat extremism by opening a large government-run mosque in Astana, shutting down religious facilities with reported links to extremism, and screening Army recruits for their religious beliefs.[57] In 2013, the government announced plans to launch an educational website called e-ISLAM in hopes of supplanting the websites of other independent Islamic organizations.[58] Recognizing the growing danger of Islamist radicalization of the Kazakh youth and seeking greater participation of the civil society groups in preventing extremist activities in the country, President Nazarbayev created a separate Ministry of Religious Affairs and Civil Society in September of 2016.[59]

ENDNOTES

[1] "Global Terrorism Database – Kazakhstan," National Consortium for the Study of Terrorism and Responses to Terrorism (START), n.d., https://www.start.umd.edu/gtd.

[2] "Kazakh Police Suspect Uighur 'Separatists' Of Murdering Two Policemen," BBC Monitoring, September 2000, http://www.start.umd.edu/gtd/search/IncidentSummary.aspx?gtdid=200009240004.

[3] Dosym Satpayev, "Uzbekistan is Subject to the Worst Risk of Terrorism in the Central Asian Region," Ferghana news, September 13, 2004, http://enews.fergananews.com/article.php?id=599.

[4] Gulnoza Saidazimova, "Kazakhstan: Government Moves to Add Hizb Ut-Tahrir to List of Terror Groups," Radio Free Europe/Radio Liberty, March 18, 2005, http://www.rferl.org/a/1058033.html.

[5] Emmanuel Karagiannis, "Political Islam and Social Movement Theory: The Case of Hizb ut-Tahrir in Kyrgyzstan," Religion, State & Society 33, iss. 2, 2005, 137-150, http://www.tandfonline.com/doi/abs/10.1080/09637490500118638?journalCode=crss20.

[6] "Hizb ut-Tahrir Network Dismantled in Kazakhstan," Interfax-Religion, December 22, 2006, http://www.interfax-religion.com/?act=news&div=2412.

[7] Ibid.

[8] Roger McDermott, "Kazakhstan Cracking Down on Hizb-Ut-Tahrir," Jamestown Foundation Eurasia Daily Monitor 4, iss. 162, September 4, 2007, https://jamestown.org/program/kazakhstan-cracking-down-on-hizb-ut-tahrir/.

[9] Ibid.

[10] Rouben Azizian, "Islamic Radicalism in Kazakhstan and Kyrgyzstan: Implications for the Global War on Terrorism," Defence Academy of the United Kingdom, September 2005, http://webcache.googleusercontent.com/search?q=cache:QDKrVFRHGNUJ:kms2.isn.ethz.ch/serviceengine/Files/RESSpecNet/44044/ichaptersection_singledocument/A46CF13F-6280-4F47-9777-49C0B1400B08/en/10.pdf+&cd=1&hl=en&ct=clnk&gl=us

[11] "Radical Islam in Central Asia: Responding to Hizb ut-Tahrir," International Crisis Group Asia Report no. 58, 2003, 31, https://www.crisisgroup.org/europe-central-asia/central-asia/uzbekistan/radical-islam-central-asia-responding-hizb-ut-tahrir.

[12] "Islamic Jihad Union (IJU)," Counterterrorism Calendar 2009, United States National Counterterrorism Center, n.d., http://www.nctc.gov/site/groups/iju.html.

[13] Bill Roggio and Caleb Weiss, "Islamic Jihad Union Details Its Involvement in Taliban's Azm Offensive," Long War Journal, July 25, 2015, http://www.longwarjournal.org/archives/2015/07/islamic-jihad-union-details-its-involvement-in-talibans-azm-offensive.php.

[14] "Churches and Mosques in Kazakh Prisons Closed; Solitary Confinement for Praying in Cells," AsiaNews.it, November 12, 2011, http://www.asianews.it/news-en/Churches-and-Mosques-in-Kazakh-prisons-closed.-Solitary-confinement-for-praying-in-cells-23158.html.

[15] Penal Reform International, "Preventing Radicalization in Prisons Discussed at Expert Roundtable in Kazakhstan," 12 July 2016, https://www.penalreform.org/news/preventing-radicalisation-in-prisons-discussed-at-expert-roundtable/

[16] Joanna Lillis, "Kazakhstan: Astana Jolted by Terror Incidents," EurasiaNet, November 16, 2011, http://www.eurasianet.org/node/64529.

[17] Terrorism Research & Analysis Consortium (TRAC), "Kazakhstan", https://www.trackingterrorism.org/region/kazakhstan

[18] Catherine Putz, "Kazakh Businessman Given 21 Years for Alleged Coup Plot," The Diplomat, November 8, 2016, http://thediplomat.com/tag/tokhtar-tuleshov/.

[19] Paul Armstrong, "Kazakh City on Red Alert as Gunmen Attack Government Buildings," CNN, July 18, 2016, http://www.cnn.com/2016/07/18/asia/kazakhstan-gun-attacks/.

[20] Kazinform, "Ruslan Kulikbayev Planned to Take Revenge on Law-Enforcement Structures – MIA," 19 July 2016, http://www.inform.kz/en/ruslan-kulikbayev-planned-to-take-revenge-on-law-enforcement-structures-mia_a2926953.

[21] Edward Lemon, "IMU Pledges Allegiance to Islamic State," EurasiaNet, August 1, 2015, http://www.eurasianet.org/node/74471.

[22] Uran Botobekov, "ISIS and Central Asia: A Shifting Recruiting Strategy," The Diplomat, May 17, 2016, http://thediplomat.com/2016/05/isis-and-central-asia-a-shifting-recruiting-strategy/; "Foreign Fighters: An Updated Assessment of the Flow of Foreign Fighters into Syria and Iraq," The Soufan Group, December 2015, http://soufangroup.com/wp-content/uploads/2015/12/TSG_ForeignFightersUpdate3.pdf.

[23] "Kazakh Fighter Calls His Countrymen to Jihad in Syria or Home in IS Video," Site Intelligence Group Western Jihadist Forum Digest, July 16, 2014, https://news.siteintelgroup.com/Western-Jihadist-Forum-Digest/kazakh-fighter-calls-his-countrymen-to-jihad-in-syria-or-home-in-is-video.html.

[24] International Organization for Migration, "Migrant Vulnerabilities and Integration Needs in Central Asia: Root Causes, Social and Economic Impact of Return Migration," Regional Field Assessment in Central Asia, 2016. http://www.iom.kz/images/inform/FinalFullReport18SBNlogocom.pdf

[25] U.S. Department of State, "Kazakhstan," International Religious Freedom Report 2009, http://www.state.gov/j/drl/rls/irf/2009/127366.htm.

[26] Ibid.

[27] Mariya Y. Omelicheva, "Ethnic Dimension of Religious Extremism and Terrorism in Central Asia," International Political Science Review 31, no. 2, 2010, 167-186, https://kuscholarworks.ku.edu/bitstream/handle/1808/10499/omelichevaethnicdimensionofterrorism.pdf?sequence=1.

[28] United States Department of State, "Kazakhstan."

[29] S.G. Klyashtorny and T.I. Sultanov, Kazakhstan: Letopis' Trekh Tysyacheleti (Almaty, Kazakhstan, 1992), 150.

[30] Bruce G. Privratsky, Muslim Turkistan: Kazak Religion and Collective Memory (London, New York: Routledge, 2001), 15.

[31] Mariya Omelicheva, "Islam in Kazakhstan: A Survey of Contemporary Trends and Sources of Securitization," Central Asian Survey 30, no. 2, 2011, 243-256, http://www.tandfonline.com/doi/abs/10.1080/02634937.2011.567069?src=recsys&journalCode=ccas20.

[32] Ibid.

[33] M. Asanbaev, "Religious Situation in Kazakhstan: Potential Conflicts and Risk Factors," Central Asia and the Caucasus, 6 iss. 42, 2006, 76-86, http://cyberleninka.ru/article/n/religious-situation-in-kazakhstan-potential-conflicts-and-risk-factors.

[34] Ibid.

[35] Omelicheva, "Islam in Kazakhstan."

[36] "International Association Peace Through Culture," World Forum of Spiritual Culture, n.d., http://astanaforum.kz/en/.

[37] "Kazakhstan: Religious Freedom Survey," Forum 18, March 20, 2014, http://www.forum18.org/archive.php?article_id=1939.

[38] United States Department of State, "Kazakhstan."

[39] Mariya Omelicheva, Counterterrorism Policies in Central Asia, New York: Routledge, 2011.

[40] Alexander Bogatik, "Kazakh Special Forces Boost Combat Capabilities," Caravanserai, July 18, 2016, http://central.asia-news.com/en_GB/articles/cnmi_ca/features/2016/07/18/feature-01.

[41] U.S. Department of State, Office of the Coordinator for Counterterrorism, Country Reports on Terrorism 2011 (Washington, DC: U.S. Department of State, July 2012), http://www.state.gov/j/ct/rls/crt/2011/195545.htm.

[42] President of the Republic of Kazakhstan, "Law of the Republic of Kazakhstan on Counteracting Legalization (Laundering) of Ill-gotten Proceeds and Terrorist Financing," August 2009, http://www.eurasiangroup.org/legislation-kazakhstan.php.

[43] "Kazakhstan Adopts AML/CFT Legislation," Eurasian Group, September 1, 2009, http://www.eurasiangroup.org/detail/news1/kazakhstan_adopts_aml_cft_legislation/.

[44] "On Counteracting Terrorism," Law #416-1 of the Republic of Kazakhstan, July 13, 1999, as obtained from the SoyuzPravoInform database, http://www.base.spinform.ru/show_doc.fwx?Regnom=1372.

[45] U.S. Department of State, Office of the Coordinator for Counterterrorism, Country Reports on Terrorism 2008 (Washington, DC: U.S. Department of State, April 2009), http://www.state.gov/documents/organization/122599.pdf.

[46] Sputnik, "Kazakh Parliament Considering Proposed Amendments to Counterterrorism Law", 7 September 2016, https://sputniknews.com/asia/201609071045041869-parliament-kazakh-terrorism-amendment/

[47] Shanghai Cooperation Organization, "Chronicle of main events at SCO in 2008," December 31, 2008, http://www.scosummit2012.org/english/documents.htm.

[48] Kazakh National Security Committee, "Press Release: Terrorism and Extremism Counteraction," August 21, 2009.

[49] Omelicheva, Counterterrorism Policies in Central Asia.

[50] Peter Leonard, "Kazakhstan Passes Restrictive Religion Law," Washington Times, October 13, 2011, http://www.washingtontimes.com/news/2011/oct/13/kazakhstan-passes-restrictive-religion-law/#ixzz2JtM6ISfL.

[51] Ibid.

[52] "Kazakhstan Tightens Legislation Against Extremism," Radio Free Europe/Radio Liberty, November 4, 2014, http://www.rferl.org/a/kazakhhstan-nazarbaev-bill-extremism-terrorism-law/26673420.html.

[53] See, for example, "Kazakhstan Updates List of Banned Terrorist Groups," Radio Free Europe/Radio Liberty, October 12, 2006, http://www.rferl.org/a/1071987.html.

[54] U.S. Department of State, "Kazakhstan," International Religious Freedom Report 2009.

[55] Ministry of Internal Affairs of the Republic of Kazakhstan, "Activity of MIA in Counteraction to Extremism in The Territory of the Republic of Kazakhstan,"

[56] U.S. Department of State, "Kazakhstan," International Religious Freedom Report 2009.

[57] "Kazakhstan Struggles to Contain Salafist-Inspired Terrorism," Jamestown Foundation Terrorism Monitor, September 13, 2012, https://jamestown.org/program/kazakhstan-struggles-to-contain-salafist-inspired-terrorism/.

[58] "Kazakhstan to Launch the First Islamic Educational Website," TengriNews, December 12, 2012, http://en.tengrinews.kz/religion/Kazakhstan-to-launch-the-first-Islamic-educational-website-15211/.

[59] Nurlan Yermekbayev, "Why Kazakhstan Created the Ministry for Religious and Civil Society Affairs," The Diplomat, November 10, 2016, http://thediplomat.com/2016/11/why-kazakhstan-created-the-ministry-for-religious-and-civil-society-affairs/.

KYRGYZSTAN

> **QUICK FACTS**
>
> Population: 5,727,553 (estimated July 2016)
>
> Area: 199,951 sq km
>
> Ethnic Groups: Kyrgyz 70.9%, Uzbek 14.3%, Russian 7.7%, Dungan 1.1%, other 5.9% (includes Uyghur, Tajik, Turk, Kazakh, Tatar, Ukrainian, Korean, German)
>
> Religions: Muslim 75%, Russian Orthodox 20%, other 5%
>
> Government Type: Republic
>
> GDP (official exchange rate): $6.65 billion (estimated 2015)
>
> *Map and Quick Facts courtesy of the CIA World Factbook (December 2016)*

OVERVIEW

After 74 years of official atheism, during which the Soviet ideological and political system pushed the Islamic faith out of the social and political life, the past two-and-a-half decades have seen a religious revival in the Kyrgyz Republic. The collapse of the Soviet Union ushered in a return to Islam among the country's population, complete with a renaissance of religio-cultural values and traditions. These religious freedoms are protected by the national Constitution, but have nonetheless come under fire from Kyrgyz political leaders, who fear the political challenge posed by Muslim religious leaders and Islam. This opposition has entailed a reestablishment of governmental control over religious organizations and progressively more restrictive regulations on religious practices.

Official concerns are not without merit. The opening of Kyrgyzstan to the world resulted in an influx of foreign influence in the form of funds (used for the construction and reconstruction of mosques and religious schools), and an upsurge in missionaries from Muslim countries and the publication or importation of religious literature. While this activity has been by and large benign, there are nonetheless troubling signs that

Islamist elements—most prominently the radical grassroots movement Hizb-ut Tahrir—have expanded their influence in the former Soviet republic, capitalizing upon the religious renaissance there that is now underway.

ISLAMIST ACTIVITY

Radical Islam boasts a long and checkered history in post-Soviet Kyrgyzstan. Its roots stretch back to the days after the fall of USSR, when a number of former communist leaders (including Kyrgyzstan's first president, Askar Akayev, and its subsequent leaders) gravitated to Muslim theology and Islamic discourse. Their ideological about-face was by and large tactical; these former Marxists were hardly true believers. Rather, most opted to abandon Soviet dogma and embrace Islamic revivalism as a pragmatic way of staying in power.

To burnish their credentials as champions of Islam, local leaders opened their doors to Saudi-sponsored *Wahhabi* Islam. Riyadh, for its part, took advantage of the invitation, expanding its financial and political foothold in the "post-Soviet space." Thus, in the early 1990s, Saudi influence came to the newly independent states of Central Asia in the form of new mosques and religious education.[1]

The scope of this outreach was staggering. Shamshibek Shakirovich Zakirov, a veteran Kyrgyz expert on religious affairs, estimates that after 1990, ten new mosques were constructed with the help of Saudi Arabia in the Kyrgyz city of Osh alone.[2] The Saudi effort, Zakirov says, also included the provision of *Wahhabi* literature in local languages for these new mosques.[3] This entrenchment of influence was replicated many times over in other corners of the former Soviet Union.

Though initially appreciative of Saudi largesse, Kyrgyz leaders quickly felt its destabilizing potential. Saudi money and educational materials were intended to promote the Kingdom's intolerant, puritan strain of Islam, which encouraged opposition forces to support the creation of an Islamic Caliphate, rather than reinforcing the rule of local post-Soviet governments. By the early 1990s, according to an official Kyrgyz government assessment:

> Numbers of illegal private religious schools [had] increased ... and their contacts with foreign (Saudi) Muslim organizations expanded. As a result of such contacts not only the functioning character of these centers, but also their ideology, changed. Those schools of traditional Islamic education turned into independent radical religious centers, the programs of which, except for training, included the propagation of their own social and political views.[4]

The impact on civil society in Kyrgyzstan was profound. As experts have noted, the question was not one of "a trivial reshuffling of power, but rather a truly radical revolution" in which Wahhabi ideology confronted national secular elites. "National intelligentsia would undoubtedly fall prey to radical Islamization of public life. Secular, atheistic and 'Europeanized' elite would be unable to fit into an Islamic model of development. Iranian and Afghan examples leave no room for illusions."[5]

These fears were made all the more acute by the strategy employed by Kyrgyz Islamic radicals. At home, these people challenged the new "Islamic" ideology of local ruling elites and threatened their positions of power by encouraging Muslim clergy and members of fundamentalist groups to assume state power. Even more ominous, regional experts say that radicals also became active recruiters, encouraging hundreds of young Kyrgyz to venture abroad to study at Islamic educational institutions in nations throughout the Muslim world, often with the active support of radicals in those countries.[6]

Today, the most popular Islamist group in Kyrgyzstan is Hizb-ut-Tahrir (HuT), a broad fundamentalist movement that seeks as a central component of its ideology the "unity of Muslims all over the world." In Kyrgyzstan, HuT has evolved into a political opposition movement, styling itself as the Islamic alternative to regime corruption. Ideologically, however, the movement looks beyond the Kyrgyz state; the declared goal of its programs is "the restoration of Islamic way of life and dissemination of the call (da'vat) to Islam in the world."[7] Officially, HuT renounces the use of violence to achieve this objective. However, there is a broad consensus among experts that the organization serves as an incubator for Islamic radicalism, priming adherents to subsequently take up arms against opponents.

Details about HuT's origins in Central Asia are incomplete. The organization's first cells in Kyrgyzstan, however, are known to have appeared in Jalal-Abad and Osh in 1997–1998. By 1999, the movement had evolved into well-developed structural units, and the number of adherents increased dramatically—driven in part by the repressive measures employed against the group across the border in neighboring Uzbekistan. Since then, HuT's ideas have found fertile ground among the socially disadvantaged Kyrgyz populations of the Kara-Suu, Bazar-Korgon, Suzak, Aravan, Uzgen districts, and within the cities of Osh and Jalal-Abad, especially among ethnic Uzbeks. Membership estimates vary widely, from a few thousand to as many as 40,000.[8]

Since its inception, HuT has boasted a vertical, tightly organized hierarchy. Local branches of the movement depend on the organization's central committee for financial support. Even so, the movement has developed unique strategies for each one of Kyrgyzstan's seven geographic regions, which consist of Batken, Jalal-Abad, Issyk-Kul, Naryn, Osh, Talas, and Chui.[9] It has paid special attention to social projects and outreach, including the provision of assistance to poor families, the distribution of food, and aid to the families of those who have been imprisoned by Kyrgyz authorities. Such charitable activities are aimed at expanding HuT's popularity among the Kyrgyz population. It has also stepped up its proselytization among prison inmates, with some success. Another innovation is the organization's efforts to place its own people in government agencies, including law enforcement units, even though such involvement ostensibly contradicts HuT principles.

With the political and ethnic violence of 2010, HuT's popularity in Kyrgyzstan rose considerably. This was particularly true in ethnic Uzbek communities in the southern regions of the country, as they had been targets of popular and officially-instigated violence in the summer of that year.[10] HuT, on the other hand, offered the Uzbeks a vision of a caliphate that transcended ethnic divisions. Since then, HuT's presence has been steadily increasing, especially among women.[11]

In addition to HuT, the Islamic State of Iraq and Syria (ISIS) has been a constant fixation for Central Asian governments since its inception, and Kyrgyzstan is no exception. Reports indicate that somewhere around six hundred Kyrgyz are fighting with the Islamic State in Syria, and government officials fret over the possibility of their return.[12] However, ISIS has yet to carry out any attacks in Kyrgyzstan. The only organized attack in Kyrgyzstan in recent years, the August 2016 suicide bombing of the Chinese embassy, was carried out by Uighur extremists and not directed against Kyrgyzstan.[13]

Islamism and Society

The establishment of Kyrgyzstan as an independent state in 1991, and the creation of a new constitution enshrining religious freedoms within it, led to a new focus upon Islam in Kyrgyz society. With three quarters of the country's 5.7 million inhabitants identifying as Hanafi Muslim,[14] Islam was indispensable for the development of Kyrgyz nationhood. In the years that followed, the construction of mosques and religious schools (*madrassas*) mushroomed, fueled by aid from Turkey, Egypt, Saudi Arabia and other countries in the Muslim world. With only 39 mosques in 1990, there were 2,362 mosques as recently as 2014, along with 81 official madrassas.[15] The number of Kyrgyz students in Islamic schools likewise surged. National religious traditions and holidays were reinstated after being abolished during the Soviet era.

Kyrgyzstan's religious revival attracted international attention. Missionaries from Muslim countries became involved in local religious activities, and a great deal of religious Islamic literature was published and imported. Muslim missionaries from Turkey and the Arab world found an especially receptive audience in the conservative south of the country. In addition to proselytism, Muslim missionaries built mosques and instituted educational programs and international student exchanges.[16]

This influx of Islamic activity has transformed Kyrgyz society. After the breakup of the Soviet Union, about 55 percent of ethnic Kyrgyz identified as Sunni Muslim; today, that number stands at 97 percent.[17] However, most Islamic practice in Kyrgyzstan is moderate compared to the Arab world, with local traditions playing an outsized role in religious observance. As of 2013, only 54 percent of ethnic Kyrgyz identify religion as being "very important" in their lives. In addition, surveys in the last decade suggest that only 7 percent of Kyrgyz support HuT.[18]

ISIS does not seem to have made significant inroads into Kyrgyz society apart from the 600 or so Kyrgyz nationals fighting abroad; this is evidenced by the lack of terrorist activity in Kyrgyzstan. Kyrgyz are also underrepresented in Syria (in terms of fighters as a percentage of Muslim population) when compared to many Western countries such as France and Australia.[19] While the Kyrgyz authorities occasionally claim to have conducted counter-ISIS operations, it is unclear whether their claims are true, or if they are meant to boost support for the state's lackluster counterterrorism efforts.[20]

ISLAMISM AND THE STATE

Even after the Cold War ended, Central Asia's Soviet-trained political leaders preferred to keep the Soviet model of secularism, fearful of the potential political challenge from Islamic religious leaders. Kyrgyzstan was no different; in the 1990s Kyrgyz authorities re-established state control over religious organizations, and invited former employees of the country's Soviet-era Council for Religious Affairs to serve in its newly-founded State Commission on Religious Affairs. In 1993, the government established the country's highest spiritual governing body—known as the Spiritual Administration of Muslims of Kyrgyzstan (SAMK)—which united the Kyrgyz Muslims, Islamic religious organizations, societies, religious educational institutions, mosques and other groups under its umbrella. Despite these increased controls, religious groups during the 90s and early 2000s enjoyed a relatively high degree of autonomy.

The government sought to curb Islamist influences during this period. Authorities were concerned about the ability of the state to counteract the spread of religious extremism, especially given its limited material, technological, and ideological resources. This was the motivation behind the Kyrgyz Attorney General's Office and the Supreme Court of Kyrgyzstan's 2003 determination to outlaw four organizations: Hizb ut-Tahrir, the Turkistan Liberation Organization, the East Turkistan Islamic Party and the Islamic Party of Turkistan. All were recognized as sponsors or perpetrators of terrorism.

After President Kurmanbek Bakiyev came to power in 2005, official policy towards religion took a decidedly authoritarian turn. The first sign of this change was the killing of Rafiq Qori Kamalov in a joint raid by Kyrgyz and Uzbek police in 2006. Rafiq Qori, a popular preacher from Kara Suu in southern Kyrygzstan, had been a sharp critic of the government's stance towards HuT. A further warning sign came in 2008, when the government arrested scores of Kyrgyz protesting restrictions on an Islamic holiday. The result was extended prison sentences for 32 people, despite a lack of evidence to support the prosecutions.[21] In January 2009, a new religion law went into effect that made religious observance conditional on state permission. In addition, more emphasis was placed on Kyrgyzstan's "traditional" religions—Hanafi Islam and Orthodox Christianity—with many other groups, by extension, being increasingly stigmatized.

The rise of ISIS has led Kyrgyz authorities to further tighten control over Islamic religious practice. A new state concept on religion policy was adopted in 2015 that elevates the role of Hanafi Sunni Islam in Kyrgyz religious life, for example, by only allowing Hanafi Sunni Muslims to be clergy members, religious judges, or muftis. These religious leaders have to submit to screening and accreditation tests which are heavily biased in favor of Hanafi belief. Religious education is also being expanded, naturally, with an emphasis on Hanafism.[22][23]

At the same time, Kyrgyzstan lacks a coherent strategy for countering Islamic radicalism. Many of the measures proposed recently, such as those outlined above, could alienate devout Muslims as a secular state appropriates Islam for strategic ends. It also rests on the false assumption that a strong Hanafi majority will protect against radicalism (the Taliban, for example, is Hanafi, not Wahhabi). Such assertive proposals also preclude the development of an inclusive national identity that can accommodate the growing rift between secular and religious citizens. Furthermore, Kyrgyzstan is not developing any serious programs to counter violent extremism, despite high-level international attention to the issue.[24] Thus, Kyrgyzstan's current trajectory leaves open the possibility for growing Islamic radicalism in the coming decade.

Endnotes

[1] Zeyno Baran. Hizb ut-Tahrir: Islam's Political Insurgency, The Nixon Center, 2004, 71.
[2] Shamshibek Shakirovich Zakirov. Interview by original author Orozbek Moldaliev. Osh, Kyrgyzstan, August 2004.
[3] Ibid
[4] Government of the Kyrgyz Republic, "Islam in Kyrgyzstan: Tendencies of Development," Official Report of the State Commission on Religious Affairs, 2004.
[5] Roald Sagdeev and Susan Eisenhower, Central Asia: Conflict, Resolution, and Change (Eisenhower Institute, 1995), 175.
[6] Shamshibek Shakirovich Zakirov. Interview by original author Orozbek Moldaliev.
[7] "Hizb-ut-Tahrir," n.d., http://www.hizb-ut-tahrir.org (accessed October 6, 2016).
[8] Jacob Zenn and Kathleen Kuehnast, "Preventing Violent Extremism in Kyrgyzstan," U.S. Institute of Peace, October 2014, https://www.usip.org/sites/default/files/SR355_Preventing-Violent-Extremism-in-Kyrgyzstan.pdf

[9] The Embassy of the Kyrgyz Republic in Kuala Lumpur, "Country Profile," n.d., http://www.kyrgyzembassy.my/en/kyrgyz-republic/about-kyrgyzstan/country-profile/.

[10] Zenn and Kuehnast, "Preventing Violent Extremism in Kyrgyzstan."

[11] Ibid.

[12] "Kyrgyz Official: 600 Nationals Fighting in Syria, Iraq," Reuters, August 3, 2016, http://www.rferl.org/a/kyrgyzstan-nationals-fighting-iraq-syria/27897554.html

[13] Joshua Kucera, "Kyrgyz Authorities Describe Multinational, Uighur-Led Plot Against Chinese Embassy," EurasiaNet, September 6, 2016, http://www.eurasianet.org/node/80426.

[14] Central Intelligence Agency, "Kyrgyzstan," in CIA World Factbook (Central Intelligence Agency, 2016), https://www.cia.gov/library/publications/the-world-factbook/geos/kg.html

[15] Franco Galdini, "Islam in Kyrgyzstan: Growing in Diversity." Open Democracy, October 22, 2015, https://www.opendemocracy.net/od-russia/franco-galdini/islam-in-kyrgyzstan-growing-in-diversity

[16] Erica Marat. "Kyrgyzstan: Prospects for Pluralism," Global Centre for Pluralism, May 2015, http://www.pluralism.ca/images/PDF_docs/pluralism_papers/ericamarat_prospectsforpluralism_EN_Global_Centre_for_Pluralism.pdf

[17] Ibid

[18] Ibid

[19] "What Motivates Foreign ISIS Fighters? New Research Has An Answer," Metrocosm, April 26, 2016, http://metrocosm.com/foreign-isis-fighters/

[20] Timur Toktonaliev, "Islamic State Link to Kyrgyzstan Firefight," IWPR, July 27, 2015, https://iwpr.net/global-voices/islamic-state-link-kyrgyzstan-firefight

[21] Nurbek Bekmurzaev, "Kyrgystan vs. The Islamic State: The Capacity of the New Concept of State Policy in the Sphere of Religion to Curb the Threat of Religious Radicalism," The Puls, October 11, 2015, https://pulsofcentralasia.org/2015/10/11/kyrgyzstan-kyrgyzstan-vs-the-islamic-state-the-capacity-of-the-new-concept-of-state-policy-in-the-sphere-of-religion-to-curb-the-threat-of-religious-radicalism-by-nurbek-bekmurzaev/

[22] Ibid

[23] Mushfig Bayram and John Kinahan, "Kyrgyzstan: Religious Freedom Survey, November 2014," Forum18 News Service, November 4, 2014, http://forum18.org/archive.php?article_id=2013.

[24] United States Department of State, Bureau of the Coordinator for Counterterrorism, "Chapter 2: South and Central Asia Overview," in Country Reports on Terrorism 2015 (U.S. Department of State, 2016), http://www.state.gov/j/ct/rls/crt/2015/257518.htm.

RUSSIAN FEDERATION

QUICK FACTS

Population: 142,355,415 (estimated July 2016)

Area: 17,098,242 sq km

Ethnic Groups: Russian 77.7%, Tatar 3.7%, Ukrainian 1.4%, Bashkir 1.1%, Chuvash 1%, Chechen 1%, other 10.2%, unspecified 3.9%

Religions: Russian Orthodox 15-20%, Muslim 10-15%, other Christian 2%

Government Type: semi-presidential federation

GDP (official exchange rate): $1.268 trillion (estimated 2015)

Map and Quick Facts courtesy of the CIA World Factbook (Last Updated January 2017)

OVERVIEW

Muslims today comprise the Russian Federation's second largest confessional group, numbering 20 to 21 million souls, or roughly 14 percent of the country's overall population of approximately 146 million.[1] It is also a group in ideological and societal transition. Although Islamic institutions were largely destroyed and believers forced underground under Soviet rule, Islam has experienced a quick and vibrant, if still ill-defined, revival since the collapse of the USSR, with various ideological tendencies competing for the support of society and state. Among Russia's Muslims, the explosion of ethno-nationalism sparked by the USSR's implosion in the late 1980s and early 1990s has given way to religious identification and the rise of faith-based politics.

Nevertheless, to date, only a small portion of Russia's Muslims has manifested Islamist tendencies, and just a fraction of those have been drawn into violence—either within Russia itself or abroad. However, Russia's ongoing involvement in the Syrian civil war, the rise of exclusionary, ultranationalist identity politics under the government of President Vladimir Putin, and expanding repression and discrimination on the part of the Kremlin have all contributed to disenfranchisement and radicalization among Russia's Muslims. The result is a dangerous distance between the Russian government and the country's Muslim minority— a dynamic that extreme Islamist organizations such as the Islamic State have begun to exploit.

ISLAMIST ACTIVITY
The Caucasus Emirate

The primary Islamist terrorist group in Russia is known as the Caucasus Emirate (CE), or *Imarat Kavkaz*. Encompassing a network of terrorist cells spread across the North Caucasus, the organization is an outgrowth of the radicalization of the Chechen national separatist movement that took place in the 1990s and early 2000s.

The CE evolved from the Chechen separatist movement that emerged amid the Soviet collapse of the early 1990s. Before then, although some radical political Islamic elements existed within Chechen society—and the region's first president, Dzhokar Dudaev, did implement elements of *sharia* law—the Chechen movement was predominantly nationalist in character. This state of affairs persisted through the first Russo-Chechen war (1994-1996), but following the 1996 Khasavyurt peace agreement signed between Russian President Boris Yeltsin and Dudaev's successor, Aslan Maskhadov, the quasi-independent Chechen Republic of Ichkeria (ChRI) devolved into a state of permanent chaos, criminality, and civil strife. The resulting political vacuum was used by a small number of local Islamists, as well foreign extremist elements (including al-Qaeda), to establish a beachhead in the area.

As early as 1996, Ayman al-Zawahiri, then al-Qaeda's second-in-command, attempted to visit incognito and establish a presence in Russia, but he was discovered and deported.[2] In a subsequently published book, he targeted Russia for violent *jihad* and the establishment of an expansive southern Eurasian caliphate.[3] At about the same time, Shamil Basaev, then a Chechen field commander, visited Afghanistan and received training there.[4] Omar Abu Ibn al-Khattab, an al-Qaeda operative, was in Chechnya then as well and, amid the inter-war lawlessness, established camps where perhaps as many as several hundred foreign fighters, as well as local militants, trained in terrorist tactics.[5] These units subsequently spearheaded the August 1999 invasion of neighboring Dagestan, which was organized jointly by Basaev and Khattab and aimed at creating an Islamist enclave there. It was this offensive that set off the second Chechen war.[6]

As during the first Chechen war, Russia deployed a brutal military response, and by 2002 had defeated the militants in conventional war, driving the bulk of the ChRI government and parliament into foreign exile, with many finding refuge in places like Washington, London, Istanbul, Baku, the United Arab Emirates, and Qatar. The more dedicated extremist elements retreated into the mountain forests in southern Chechnya and neighboring Georgia, where they began a classic guerilla insurgency campaign punctuated by occasional large-scale attacks. With national separatist forces isolated abroad, Islamists gradually consolidated power over the movement throughout the next five years.

In the summer of 2002, following the death of Khattab at the hands of Russian security forces, an expanded emergency meeting of the underground remnants of the ChRI government and armed forces convened in the mountains of Chechnya. The meeting served as a *coup d'etat* of sorts; as a result of the gathering, a *sharia*-based order was adopted, with the goal of expanding the insurgency across the North Caucasus.[7] Thereafter, Basaev began to travel across the Caucasus seeking out young radicals and establishing a network of combat cells in Ingushetia, Dagestan, Kabardino-Balkaria, and Karachaevo-Cherkessia.[8] The results produced a series of terrorist incidents in subsequent years, including the October 2002 Dubrovka Theater hostage-taking, a rash of suicide attacks in Moscow in 2003,[9] and the September 2004 seizure of School No. 1 in Beslan in early September—a terrorist incident in which 333 people, including 186 children, were killed. Subsequently, between 2006 and 2010, terrorist activity in Russia saw a significant uptick, rising from just 3 major terrorist attacks in 2006 to 22 in 2010.[10]

This radical activism has continued. The CE has been responsible for scores of high-profile attacks on Russian targets in the North Caucasus and beyond in recent years, including the March 2010 attack on the Moscow subway, the December 2013 bombing of the train station in Volgograd, near the site of the 2014 Olympic Games, and a coordinated December 2014 assault on historic landmarks in Chechnya's capital of Grozny that left at least 20 dead.[11]

More recently, the number of terrorist attacks carried out by the CE and its affiliates in Russia has dipped noticeably—something that Russian officials have been quick to attribute to the Kremlin's robust counterterrorism policies.[12] However, this characterization is deeply misleading, because it discounts the extensive mobilization that has taken place among Russia's Islamist cadres since the Kremlin's military intervention into the Syrian civil war in September 2015. Today, it is estimated that one-quarter of all foreign fighters that have joined the Islamic State in Iraq and Syria are from the territory of the former Soviet Union,[13] and Russian is the third most frequently spoken language among fighters of the Islamic State.[14] Rather than combatting this outflow of militants, Russian authorities appear to be doing the opposite, with government agencies essentially facilitating the departure of terrorists.[15] This, however, appears to be only a temporary solution, and Islamist violence in Russia can be expected to surge anew with the return of these militants from the Middle East in the years ahead.

The CE functions as a decentralized network, consisting of local combat cells loosely tied together and subordinate to sectors, which are in turn subordinated to the CE's "provinces," referred to by the fighters as *veliyats*. Subordination is indicated by the taking of the Islamic loyalty oath (*bayat*). The CE includes five known *veliyats*: *Veliyat Nokchicho* (Chechnya); *Veliyat Gyalgyaiche* (Ingushetia and Ossetia); *Veliyat Dagestan*; the *United Veliyat of Kabardia, Balkaria,* and *Karachai* (the KBR, the KChR, and probably Adygeya); and *Veliyat of the Nogai Steppe* (Krasnodar Krai and Stavropol Krai). An *emir* who has made *bayat* to the CE controls each *veliyat*. The CE's military structure includes: the Caucasus, Dagestan, Volga, and Urals fronts. Combat cells are permitted to design and undertake small-scale operations independently, but larger operations require approval from a higher-ranking *emir*.[16]

The CE is composed of members from each of the Muslim ethnic groups in Russia, as well as members of non-Muslim ethnic groups. Chechens, Ingush and various Dagestani (Avars, Dargins, Kumyks, Nogais, Tabasarans, etc.) predominate, but the Muslim Alans (Karachais and Balkars) and Circassians (Kabards, Cherkess, and Adygs) are also well represented.[17] In short, the CE puts into practice the extremist principle that Islam is universal.

Publicly available information detailing CE's financial sources is limited. It remains likely that Arab and other foreign Islamic governments, businesses, and philanthropists still provide funds, despite the efforts of Russian authorities to prevent it. The local population is known to provide limited financial support in the form of the Islamic *zakat* (charitable contributions), as well as considerable logistical and other material support, such as weapons, safe houses, and food provisions.[18] Support is also generated through criminal activity; during the first Russo-Chechen war and in the period thereafter, the ChRI received funding from elements of the Chechen mafia, narcotics trafficking, illicit oil exports, and the lucrative hostage-taking industry run by Chechen field commander and Moscow mafia chief, Khozh-Akhmed Nukhaev.[19] While these sources were mostly cut off in the years that followed as a result of the displacement of the ChRI leadership and more aggressive international and Russian efforts to combat terrorist financing, there are indications that the organization still generates revenue via illicit means.[20]

The size of the CE's network is extremely difficult to estimate. Extremist sources are silent on the subject, except to refute the accuracy of official Russian estimates, which have tended to downplay the number of active members affiliated with the group.[21] A review of the available literature suggests that it reasonable to assume that there may be more than 1,000 CE fighters, and thousands of additional facilitators.[22] These figures have been affected by the Syrian civil war, which has drawn Russian Islamists to its cause in significant numbers. In the Fall of 2014, Russian security officials estimated that some 800 militants from the North Caucasus had traveled to Syria to take up arms against the Assad regime.[23] By September 2015, that number had swelled to an estimated 2,400—a threefold increase in less than a year.[24] It is unclear what percentage of these mobilized Islamists is made up of CE cadres, but the organization is believed to be heavily represented within the Islamic State.[25]

While the CE has long been a prominent part of the global *jihadist* movement, it has traditionally served as an affiliate of the Bin Laden network, having formally pledged allegiance to al-Qaeda back in April of 2009. However, in 2015, elements of the group broke ranks and formally pledged allegiance to the Islamic State. *Emirs* in Dagestan were the first to formally pledge allegiance to IS,[26] followed by the CE's leading military commander, and Chechnya's *emir*, Aslan Buytukaev, who declared allegiance to IS leader Abu Bakr al-Baghdadi on behalf of all Chechen fighters that summer. Other CE *veliyats* followed soon after. The move created a rift within the organization, with a minority of *veliyat* remaining loyal to the CE (and therefore al-Qaeda). Those that joined the Islamic State, however, were incorporated into an ISIS "governate" encompassing Russia's restive majority-Muslim regions of Dagestan, Chechnya, Ingushetia, Kabardino-Balkaria and Karachayevo-Cherkessia.[27] ISIS *emir* Abu Bakr al-Baghdadi subsequently named Abu Muhammad al-Kadari (Rustam Asilderov) leader of the newly declared Islamic State province, known as the *Velayat Qawqaz*.[28]

The Islamic State has made a point of targeting Russia, if not for its treatment of Muslims internally then certainly for its activities in Syria. October of 2015 saw the downing of a Russian commercial airliner flight from Sharm el-Sheikh to St. Petersburg in an attack orchestrated by the Islamic State.[29] The first IS attack on Russian soil took place in August of 2016, when two men attacked police with a gun and axes. Both were killed as a result, and days later, in the equivalent of a claim of responsibility, IS published a video of their pledges of allegiance to al-Baghdadi.[30] IS has even threatened Russian President Vladimir Putin directly. A video that surfaced in August of 2016 shows masked men in a car calling for IS affiliates to murder Russians and Vladimir Putin himself.[31] In late 2016, the Russian Federal Security Service (FSB) arrested seven IS conspirators in possession of grenades, munitions, and materiel for improvised explosive devices (IEDs). The militants were allegedly planning to attack targets in Moscow and St. Petersburg.[32]

Other Islamists

In the past, suspected al-Qaeda operatives such as Omar Abu Ibn al-Khattab have joined the ChRI/CE, but there is no open source evidence indicating that al-Qaeda or other foreign *jihadist* groups operate in Russia independently from the CE. Russian law enforcement occasionally claims that al-Qaeda operatives number among killed and captured CE fighters, but such claims are never documented. Moreover, al-Qaeda's position in Russia (and elsewhere in the "post-Soviet space") has been largely supplanted over the past couple of years by the Islamic State.[33]

The only other Islamic extremist organization reported to be active in Russia is the *Uighur-Bulgar Jamaat* (UBJ). The group was established between 2006 and 2008 in Bashkortostan by Pavel Dorokhov, an ethnic Russian converted and trained by Taliban camps in Afghanistan.[34] It has sporadically engaged in militancy in Russia's Volga region (encompassing the republics of Tatarstan and Bashkortostan). In 2010, no fewer than 20 members of the UBJ attempted to blow up a gas line in Bashkortostan's Birsk district, and were subsequently killed in a shootout with Bashkir police.[35] In 2012, the group disrupted the long-time peace between religious groups in Tatarstan when they severely injured the region's Grand Mufti, Ilduz Fayzov, and killed his deputy, Valliulla Yakupov.[36] The UBJ also makes up part of the contingent of foreign fighters in Syria, and as of 2013 numbered around 200 in that theater.[37] The UBJ may or may not be one and the same organization as the apparently ethnic Tatar *Bulgar Jamaat*, which fought in Afghanistan around 2009.[38]

Despite being banned in Russia, *Hizb ut-Tahrir* (HuT) maintains a presence in the country as well. Many alleged HuT members are arrested annually, mostly in the republics of Tatarstan and Bashkortostan. By 2012, HuT and other Islamists had penetrated many autonomous mosques and official Islamic institutions in Tatarstan, carried out public demonstrations in tandem with nationalist groups, and organized several automobile caravans flying the HuT flag.[39] According to Memorial, a Russian human rights watchdog, HuT has become a non-violent organization in recent years.[40] Memorial considers 23 of the Muslims arrested in 2016 on charges associated with *Hizb ut-Tahrir* to be "political prisoners," a term it uses to refer to those who have been wrongfully arrested to meet political ends.[41]

Other domestic groups

Several small Tatar groups have Islamist tendencies but are at least equally or predominantly national separatist in nature, confining their activity to the republic of Tatarstan and, to a lesser degree, Bashkortostan. They include: *Azatlyk, Ittifak, Mille Mejlis*, and elements within the *All-Tatar Public Center*.[42] These organizations, have historically confined themselves to occasional declarations, conferences, and small demonstrations, but now increasingly engage in those activities in partnership with Islamist elements such as HuT. Some of their official statements and documents are sent to North Caucasus terrorist websites.[43] None, however, are at present believed to constitute a significant threat to the Russian state.

ISLAMISM AND SOCIETY

Since the collapse of the Soviet Union, Islam has undergone a revival among its traditionally Muslim ethnic groups. According to Russia's leading *mufti*, Chairman of the Council of Muftis of Russia (CMR) Ravil Gainutdin, the number of mosques in Russia grew from 150 in 1991 to some six thousand by October 2005.[44] From 2000 to 2015, mosque construction averaged just over one per day, according to expert estimates.[45]

This explosive growth has been propelled by the size of Russia's Muslim minority itself. While Russia's Muslims remain a distinct minority in Russia, differences in communal behavior—including fewer divorces, less alcoholism and a greater rate of reproduction—have given them a more robust demographic profile than their ethnic Russian counterparts.[46] Thus, according to the United Nations, the fertility of Russia's Muslims, at 2.3, is significantly higher than the overall Russian national fertility rate of 1.7.[47] Other estimates peg the reproductive rate of Russia's Muslims higher still.[48] As a result, a variety of projections have suggested that Russia's Muslims will account for a fifth of the country's total population by the end of this decade, and may make up a majority of Russians by as early as mid-century.[49]

Moreover, migrants (the majority of them Muslim) continue to enter the Russian Federation in search of employment and economic opportunity. In 2013, the total number of migrant workers present on Russian soil was estimated to be 11 million, more than 7 percent of the country's total population.[50] This second cohort helps to augment the size and political reach of Russia's indigenous Muslim community.

Russia's Muslims are divided by geography, history, ethnicity, and divergent confessional movements (Sufis, Sunnis, and Shi'ites) and legal schools (*maskhabs*). The overwhelming majority of Russia's Muslims are Sunni. Shi'a are predominantly located in the southern North Caucasus, particularly among Dagestan's rather small ethnic Lezgin population. Sufism predominates in the North Caucasus, consisting mostly of Naqshbandi and Qadiri *tariqats* (brotherhoods or orders). Each Islamic school of jurisprudence, or *maskhab*, is represented in Russia, but almost all of Russia's Muslims adhere to the Hanafi interpretation. There is, however, a significant Shafi presence in the North Caucasus. Tatarstan's Muslims and the Tatar internal diaspora, meanwhile, are experiencing a revival of the Islamic reformist or *jadidist* school of Islamic thought.

Although Muslim communities can be found all across the length and breadth of the vast federation, the largest concentrations of ethnic Muslims (ethnic groups that traditionally have adhered in overwhelming numbers to the Islamic faith) are found in the North Caucasus's Muslim republics—Chechnya, Ingushetia, Dagestan, Adygeya, Kabardino-Balkaria (KBR), and Karachaevo-Cherkessia (KChR)—and in the Volga and Urals republics of Tatarstan and Bashkortostan. There are also large Muslim populations in Moscow and St. Petersburg, but these are more Russified, urbanized, and secularized than those in other regions, especially the North Caucasus. The Muslims of the North Caucasus remain largely rural, traditionally religious, and indigenously ethnic or clan-oriented.

Russia's other main ethnic Muslim groups, Tatars and Bashkirs, are concentrated to a great extent in the Tatarstan and Bashkortostan Republics. As of the 2010 Russian census, Tatars make up a slim majority in Tatarstan, while ethnic Russians outnumber Bashkirs in Bashkortostan (Bashkiria). Both Tatars and Bashkirs are better integrated into Russian life than are the North Caucasians. Some historically non-Muslim ethnic groups are seeing some of their members convert to Islam, including ethnic Russians.[51]

In terms of political ideology, Russia's Muslims, much like ethnic Slavs, are divided among democrats, conservatives, Eurasianist and Islamist reactionaries. Since, under Russian law, political parties based on any communal identification are forbidden from participating in elections, it is difficult to attain a detailed picture of Muslims' distribution on Russia's political spectrum. Political Islam, however, is in evidence at both the official and unofficial levels. Media controlled by official Islamic structures carry numerous articles on introducing elements of *sharia* law in Russia, including the introduction of Islamic banking and insurance.[52] Also, there are strong anti-American, anti-Western, anti-Israeli, and even anti-Semitic tendencies, not just among Russia's Islamists but among Russia's traditional Muslims as well.[53]

Generally, however, there is only limited support for violent Islamism in both Russia's Muslim and non-Muslim populations. The country's Islamic clergy feels threatened and virulently opposes manifestations of political Islam, and Islamists have found limited support in the Muslim community. That said, many young Muslims are increasingly fascinated by—and sympathetic toward—radical trends, including Islamism as represented by the charismatic fighters of the Caucasus Emirate and, more recently, by the Islamic State.

The Russian government is ill-equipped to deal with this trend. In recent years, the Kremlin has done precious little of substance to address the needs of the country's growing Muslim minority. To the contrary, the ultranationalist identity erected by the government of Vladimir Putin over the past decade has systematically shut Russia's Muslims out of contemporary politics and society, leaving them vulnerable to the lure of alternative ideologies—Islamism chief among them.[54]

ISLAMISM AND THE STATE

Russia's *Freedom of Religion Law of 1997* establishes Islam, along with Orthodox Christianity, Buddhism, and Judaism, as one of the four "traditional" faiths.[55] As of the 2010 Russian census, Muslims make up the second largest group of these (after Orthodox Christianity).

Russia's Muslims are not strongly self-organized. Rather, they are well organized "from above" by the Islamic clergy and the Russian state. Muslim communities must be registered with the government, and each is then incorporated into a regional Muslim Spiritual Administration (MSA), every one of which in turn is included under one of the three main Muslim umbrella organizations: the Council of Muslims of Russia (CMR), the Central Muslim Spiritual Administration (CMSA), and the Coordinating Council of the Muslims of the North Caucasus (CCMNC). The CMR at present is the most influential of the umbrella organizations, with its leader, the ethnic Tatar *mufti* Ravil Gainutdin, on good terms with the Kremlin. Two smaller umbrella organizations—the MSA of the European part of Russia and the MSA of the Asian part of Russia—are subordinated to two of the abovementioned. In all, there are known to be approximately 60 regional MSAs, all of which are included under one or another of the umbrella organizations.[56] These various structures help organize the travel of Muslims to the hajj and to study abroad, support Islamic schools and universities in Russia, and recruit and train Islamic clergy. The various Muslim spiritual councils (*Dukhovnyie Upravlenii Musulman*, or DUM in Russian) receive state funding for muftis' salaries, university and school development, and the building of mosques. Independent Muslim communities and mosques persist but are illegal and are usually discovered by the authorities and incorporated into the official administrations. Typically, these have manifested Islamist tendencies, and some have produced terrorist organizations, leaders, and cadres.[57]

Both the Russian state and official Islamic clergy are strongly opposed to and greatly fear any manifestation of Islamism. As a result, the state has banned political parties based on religion (as well as on ethnicity and gender), and the Islamic clergy cooperates closely with the state apparatus in combating independent Islamic or Islamist groups and supporting reformist, Euro-Islamic, and other more secularized Islamic trends as an antidote to Islamism. Ravil Gainutdin, as well as the leadership of the Republic of Tatarstan, has led in this effort.[58]

Past experience has taught Russian authorities to treat Islamists severely, and they move quickly and often illegally to imprison them for long terms. Arrests of Islamists belonging to non-violent but illegal organizations such as HuT and *Tablighi Jamaat* are often accompanied by official charges of conspiracy to commit terrorist attacks and claims that searches produced not only extremist literature but also weapons and explosives.[59]

The extent to which these policies and practices lead to significant violations of Muslims' civil, political, and human rights, in turn, creates a catalyst for extremist recruitment. Putin-era amendments to Russia's laws "On Extremism" and "On Combating Terrorism" give the Federal Security Service (FSB), the Ministry of Internal Affairs (MVD), Justice Ministry, and General Prosecutor's Office broad leeway in holding suspects and determining what constitutes "extremist literature." Searches are frequently conducted on questionable pretexts, detention can often result in torture, and some convictions are based on exaggerated charges. These practices are more prevalent in the North Caucasus, especially in Chechnya under region president Ramzan Kadyrov, where authorities have even carried out extra-judicial retribution against the families of suspected and actual terrorists, including the abductions of relatives and the burning of homes. Some of this extra-legal law enforcement activity, especially in Chechnya, is carried out by special battalions comprised of former separatist fighters and is driven by local Caucasus customs of blood revenge.

Federal counterterrorism policy has in recent years increasingly focused on "soft power" approaches. Moscow has increased federal contributions to the budgets of republics hardest hit by the CE. As of 2014, the Russian central government was still funding the majority of the budget for the North Caucasus in return for the loyalty of local officials and businessmen.[60] In 2016, some of those youth programs came in the form of media schools that taught students how to promote Russian interests and "standards in journalism."[61]

These efforts have been supplemented by increasingly broad federal authorities to curb perceived terrorist activities. In 2016, Russia passed a series of laws, cumulatively referred to as the "Yarovaya Packet," which expand the definition of "extremism," allowing the criminalization of a highly subjective range of acts and authorizing the prosecution of any person or financier of an act that harms Russians worldwide.[62] The law further tightens the aforementioned organizational structure, requiring official permits for religious activities, including praying, that take place outside of officially recognized religious buildings. It targets outreach and missionary work, confining it to churches and other specific areas, and usually requiring permits. The "Yarovaya Packet" defines "failure to report crime" as a criminal act and sets the accountable age at 14 years for this and other "extremism" charges.[63]

Perhaps most notably, the "Packet" provides the Kremlin with broad oversight over the Internet domain. Under the law's provisions, individuals can now be charged for inciting or justifying terrorism, as well as proselytizing on social media and in emails. "Yarovaya" likewise grants security agencies full access to private communications, as well as requiring telecommunications companies to store all data for at least six months, including conversations and text messages. Meanwhile, "organizers of information distribution" are required to store data for one year and help decrypt information, if necessary.[64]

These "soft power" efforts have been mirrored by a more concrete organizational reconfiguration. In 2016, Russia created a new super-security service known as the National Guard, ostensibly to help the Kremlin better fight terrorism and organized crime.[65] This body encompasses the country's riot police (OMON) and SWAT teams (SOBR), as well as other relevant units, and will work "in close cooperation" with the country's Ministry of Interior Affairs.[66] However, experts note that this new, militarized structure will likely have little actual role fighting terrorism, because its forces are predominantly public security forces, trained to control and deter.[67]

Each of the North Caucasus Muslim republics has carried out its own, and often very different, policies to counter violent Islamism. While Chechnya's Kadyrov has carried out a more brutal policy, Ingushetia's President, Yunus bek Yevkurov, has pioneered a continuous amnesty or "adaptation" policy that seeks to draw fighters out of the forest and back to their families and civilian life by offering reduced or suspended sentences and educational and work opportunities.[68] In 2010, Dagestan established an adaptation commission, which engages in the same work, and in 2011 Kabardino-Balkariya followed suit. In 2012, in an effort to isolate, divide, and rule radical Muslims, Dagestan's authorities helped establish a dialogue between the official Sufi-oriented Muslim Spiritual Administration of Dagestan and the republic's growing Salafi community, the main recruiting pool for the CE. These local policies are aimed at blunting the recruitment efforts of the CE and other radicals.

Nevertheless, recent years have seen a marked uptick in the radicalization and mobilization of elements of Russia's Muslim minority. This is attributable to a number of factors, ranging from a lack of economic integration and opportunity to rising state xenophobia to the growing prevalence of Islamist groups and ideas within the Russian Federation.[69] This mobilization has been exacerbated by the Russian intervention into the Syrian civil war, which has made the country itself the target of various extremist groups. Al-Qaeda's Syrian affiliate, *Jabhat al-Nusra* (now rebranded as *Jabhat Fateh al-Sham*), has called for terrorist attacks within Russia as a retaliatory measure.[70] So, too, has the Islamic State; in November of 2015, the group released a video through its various social media feeds that warned "[w]e will take through battle the lands of yours we wish," and predicted that "[the] Kremlin will be ours."[71] These threats have been followed by concrete incidents of terrorist violence within Russia (detailed above).

These statements highlight the risks inherent in Russia's current foreign policy. By wading into the Syrian civil war on the side of the Assad regime, Russia's government has effectively exacerbated the mobilization—and the radicalization—of its own Muslims. The result could well be a surge of Islamism within, and against, the Russian Federation in the years ahead.

ENDNOTES

[1] The last official census of the Russian population was taken in 2010, and it tallied the national population at 142.9 million. See Vserosiiskii Perepis Naselenie 2010, http://www.perepis-2010.ru/. Since then, various numbers have been floated for the overall size of the Russian population – as well as the proportional size of its Muslim minority. The figures cited above are estimates deemed credible by the authors, but are subject to revision. On Russia's overall population (including the recently-annexed Crimean Peninsula), see Marlene Laruelle, "How Islam Will Change Russia," in Jamestown Foundation, Russia in Decline (forthcoming 2017), https://jamestown.org/program/marlene-laruelle-how-islam-will-change-russia/. The estimated size of Russia's Muslim minority is drawn from the authors' conversations with Russian officials in Washington, DC in the Fall of 2015.

[2] Andrew Higgins and Alan Cullison, "A Terrorist's Odyssey," Wall Street Journal, July 2, 2002; See also Yurii Tyssovskiy, "Terrorist No. 2 Al-Zawahiri spent time in Makhachkalinsky Prison," VEK, July 19, 2002.

[3] Faisal Devji, Landscapes of Jihad: Militancy, Morality, and Modernity (Ithaca, NY: Cornell University Press, 2005), 130-131; Dore Gold, Hatred's Kingdom: How Saudi Arabia Supports the New Global Terrorism (Washington, DC: Regnery, 2003), 137; and Gordon M. Hahn, Russia's Islamic Threat (New Haven and London: Yale University Press, 2007), 36-37.

[4] Michael Reynolds, "False Comfort on Afghanistan," Middle East Strategy at Harvard, August 31, 2009; Mike Bowker, "Western Views Of The Chechen Conflict," in Richard Sakwa, ed., Chechnya: From Past to Future (London: Anthem Press, 2005), 235.

[5] Declassified DIA report NC 3095345, October 16, 1998. http://www.judicialwatch.org/cases/102/dia.pdf; See also Lorenzo Vidino, Al-Qaeda in Europe (Prometheus Books, 2006).

[6] Hahn, Russia's Islamic Threat, 37-39 and 104-110.

[7] "Aslan Maskhadov: 'My sozdadim polnotsennoe Islamskoe Gosudarstvo,'" Kavkaz-Tsentr, March 8, 2010, www.kavkazcenter.com/russ/content/2010/03/08/71101.shtml; See also "Prezident ChRI Sheik Abdul-Khalim. Kto On?" Kavkaz-Tsentr, March 12, 2005, www.kavkazcenter.com/russ/content/2005/03/12/31285.shtml; "Abdallakh Shamil Abu-Idris: 'My oderzhali strategicheskuyu pobedu,'" Kavkaz-Tsentr, January 9, 2006, www.kavkazcenter.net/russ/content/2006/01/09/40869.shtml; Paul Murphy, The Wolves of Islam: Russia and the Faces of Chechen Terrorism (Dulles, VA: Brassey's Inc., 2004), 171-75.

[8] Hahn, Russia's Islamic Threat, 43, 158; Vadim Rechkalov, "'Pochemu spetssluzhby ne mogut poimat' Shamilya Basaeva," Izvestiya (Moscow), December 6-10, 2004; "Shamil Basaev: 'Segodnya voyuet ves chechenskii narod,'" Kavkaz-Tsentr, August 17, 2005, www.kavkazcenter.net/russ/content/2005/08/17/36759.shtml; Aleksandra Larintseva, Timur Samedov, and Olga Allenova, "Koltso kavkazskoi natsionalnosti," Kommersant-Vlast (Moscow), September 29-October 5 2003, 20; Valerii Khatazhukov, "Kabardino-Balkariya Crackdown on Islamists," IWPR'S Caucasus Reporting Service no. 199, August 2003; Mayrbek Vachagaev, "Evolution of the Chechen Jamaat," Jamestown Foundation Chechnya Weekly VI, iss. 14, April 6, 2005; Timur Samedov, "Podozrevaemyie iz 'Yarmuka'," Kommersant Daily (Moscow), December 15, 2004, 4.

[9] A detailed discussion of the 2003 suicide bombing campaign can be found in Yossef Bodansky, Chechen Jihad: Al Qaeda's Training Ground and the Next Wave of Terror (New York: Harper, 2007).

[10] See Robert Johnston, "Terrorist Attacks in Russia." May 22, 2015. http://www.johnstonsarchive.net/terrorism/terr-russia.html

[11] Andrew E. Kramer and Neil McFarquhar, "Fierce Attack by Islamist Militants in Chechen Capital Kills at Least 20," New York Times, December 4, 2014, https://www.nytimes.com/2014/12/05/world/europe/grozny-chechnya-attack.html?_r=0.

[12] Daria Garmonenko, "FSB Sbila v Rossii Terroristichiskoyu Activnost (The FSB has Diminished Terrorist Activity in Russia)," Nezavisimaya Gazeta (Moscow), November 11, 2015, http://www.ng.ru/politics/2015-11-11/100_fsbter.html.

[13] Ibid.

[14] Interview with Evgenia Albats, Ekho Moskvy, November 17, 2015, http://echo.msk.ru/programs/personalno/1659708-echo/.

[15] Michael Weiss, "Russia is Sending Jihadis to Join ISIS," The Daily Beast, August 23, 2015, http://www.thedailybeast.com/articles/2015/08/23/russias-playing-a-double-game-with-islamic-terror0.html.

[16] Hahn, Russia's Islamic Threat, 63-64.

[17] Gordon Hahn, The Caucasus Emirate Mujahedin: Global Jihadism in Russia's North Caucasus and Beyond. (McFarland and Company, Inc., 2014).

[18] "Khazbiev: chinovniki Ingushetii soderzhat boevikov," Kavkaz uzel, July 24, 2009, www.kavkaz-uzel.ru/articles/157053; Alexei Malashenko, "The Kremlin's Violent Underbelly," The Moscow Times, July 29, 2009.

[19] Pavel Khlebnikov, Razgovor s Varvarom: Besedy s chechenskim polevym komandirom Khozh-Akhmedom Nukhaevym o banditizme i islame (Moscow: Detektiv-Press, 2004); Paul Klebnikov, Godfather of the Kremlin: The Decline of Russia in the Age of Gangster Capitalism (Orlando, FL: Harcourt, 2001); A. Khinshtein, Berezovskii i Abramovich: Oligarkhi s bol'shoi dorogi (Moscow: Lora, 2007).

[20] Gordon Hahn, Getting the Caucasus Emirate Right (Washington, DC: Center for Strategic and International Studies. August 2011), https://csis-prod.s3.amazonaws.com/s3fs-public/legacy_files/files/publication/110930_Hahn_GettingCaucasusEmirateRt_Web.pdf.

[21] "MVD RF: na Severnom Kavkaze deistvuyut okolo 500 boevikov," Kavkaz uzel, March 26, 2010,www.kavkaz-uzel.ru/articles/167037/; "Yedelev: v Chechnye deistvuyut do 500 boevikov," Kavkaz uzel, January 21, 2009, www.kavkaz-uzel.ru/articles/148344; "MVD: v Chechnye deistvuyut ne menee 400 boevikov," Kavkaz uzel, February 6, 2008, www.kavkaz-uzel.ru; and "IMARAT KAVKAZ. Moskva pereschitala modzhakhedov. Ikh okazyvaetsya 1500 boitsov," Kavkaz-Tsentr, May 20, 2009, www.kavkazcenter.com/russ/content/2009/05/20/65749.shtml.

[22] Hahn, Russia's Islamic Threat, 67-68.

[23] "Russia Calls for Joint Effort With U.S. to Fight Islamic State," The Moscow Times, September 29, 2014, http://www.themoscowtimes.com/article.php?id=507990.

[24] "Moscow Says About 2,400 Russians Fighting With Islamic State: RIA," Reuters, September 18, 2015, http://news.yahoo.com/moscow-says-2-400-russians-fighting-islamic-state-...

[25] Ivan Petrov, "MVD: Up to 3,500 Russians are fighting for the terrorists in Syria and Iraq," Rossiyskaya Gazeta, March 17, 2016. https://rg.ru/2016/03/17/mvd-na-storone-terroristov-v-sirii-i-irake-voiuiut-do-35-tys-rossiian.html.

[26] Ekaterina Sokirianskaya, "Russia's North Caucasus Insurgency Widens as ISIS Foothold Grows," World Politics Review, April 12, 2016, http://www.worldpoliticsreview.com/articles/18466/russia-s-north-caucasus-insurgency-widens-as-isis-foothold-grows.

[27] "Islamic State Declares Foothold in Russia's North Caucasus," The Moscow Times, June 24, 2015, https://themoscowtimes.com/news/islamic-state-declares-foothold-in-russias-north-caucasus-47666.

[28] "Треугольник Имарат Кавказ, Исламское Государство, аш-Шишани," МКРУ Дагестан, July 27, 2016, http://mkala.mk.ru/articles/2016/07/27/treugolnik-imarat-kavkaz-islamskoe-gosudarstvo-ashshishani.html.

[29] Lizzie Dearden, "ISIS Plane Attack," Independent (London), February 24, 2016, http://www.independent.co.uk/news/world/africa/isis-plane-attack-egypt-terrorists-downed-russian-metrojet-flight-from-sharm-el-sheikh-islamic-state-a6893181.html.

[30] Lizzie Dearden, "Isis claims responsibility for first terror attack in Russia after men try to kill police with gun and axes near Moscow," Independent (London). August 19, 2016, http://www.independent.co.uk/news/world/europe/isis-terror-attacks-news-latest-russia-moscow-balashikha-police-gun-axe-allegiance-video-chechen-a7198731.html.

[31] Dmitri Trenin, "Is Russia Safe From Extremist Attacks Like Those In Europe?" Newsweek, August 12, 2016. http://www.newsweek.com/russia-really-safe-deadly-attacks-isis-france-belgium-germany-488262.

[32] Russian Federal Security Service, "Press Release: Russian FSB and MVD disrupt plans of IS conspirators in Dagestan," December 29, 2016. http://www.fsb.ru/fsb/press/message/single.htm%21id%3D10438055%40fsbMessage.html.

[33] Jonah Goldberg. "Al-Qaeda's out. ISIS is in!" National Review, June 12, 2015, http://www.nationalreview.com/article/419657/al-qaedas-out-isis-jonah-goldberg.

[34] "Member of Extremist Organization, Uyghur-Bulgar Jamaat was Sentenced to 15 Years in a Camp." Kommersant (Moscow), July 20, 2009, http://www.kommersant.ru/doc/1207571.

[35] Vladislav Maltsev, "Bashkirian Jihad," Nezavisimaya Gazeta (Moscow), September 1, 2010, http://www.ng.ru/society/2010-09-01/4_jihad.html.

[36] Leon Aron, "Russia is New Front for Militant Islam," Washington Post, November 13, 2015, https://www.washingtonpost.com/opinions/russias/2015/11/13/3f456156-887c-11e5-9a07-453018f9a0ec_story.html?utm_term=.c9f678c640bf.

[37] "Separatists in Tatarstan announce support of Islamist fighters in Syria," Regnum, June 13, 2013, https://regnum.ru/news/polit/1670767.html.

[38] "Special Agents of the FSB try to fight the UBJ," Komsolmoskaya Pravda, October 26, 2012, http://www.centrasia.ru/newsA.php?st=1351234020. And for the Bulgar Jamaat's Russian-language website, see http://tawba.info orhttp://jamaatbulgar.narod.ru.

[39] See Gordon M. Hahn, Islam, Islamism and Politics in Eurasia Report Nos. 43, 45, 47, 48, 58 and 60, available at https://csis.org/node/33013/publication. On the HuT's penetration of official Islamic structures, demonstrations, and automobile caravans in 2012 see, for example, Rais Suleimanov, "Al'yans vakhkhabizma n national-separtizma v Tatarstane i 'russkii vopros' v regione," RISI, May 2, 2012, http://www.gumilev-center.ru/alyans-vakhkhabizma-i-nacional-separatizma-v-tatarstane-i-russkijj-vopros-v-regione/ and Rais Suleimanov, "Islamskii terrorizm v sovremennom Tatarstane: vakhkhabizm na praktike," Agentsvo politicheskikh novostei, July 25, 2012, www.apn.ru/publications/article26923.htm; See also "V Kazani islamisty proekhali avtokolonnoi s razvernutymi flagami," Regnum.ru, October 26, 2012, www.regnum.ru/news/fd-volga/1586886.html.

[40] Memorial, "Persecution of Hizb ut-Tahrir," October 13, 2015, http://memohrc.org/special-projects/presledovanie-organizacii-hizb-ut-tahrir.

[41] Memorial, "Memorial recognizes 23 Muslims from Bashkotostan as political prisoners," April 26, 2016. http://memohrc.org/news/memorial-priznal-23-h-musulman-iz-bashkortostana-politzaklyuchennymi.

[42] Hahn, Russia's Islamic Threat, 213-214.

[43] For such contacts before 2005, see Hahn, Russia's Islamic Threat, 205-206.

[44] Neil Buckley, "Russia's Islamic Rebirth Adds Tension," Financial Times, October 28, 2005.

[45] Paul Goble, "7500 Mosques Have Been Erected Since Putin Became President," The Interpreter, December 4, 2014, http://www.interpretermag.com/7500-mosques-have-been-erected-in-russia-since-putin-became-president/.

[46] Abdullah Rinat Mukhametov, "Russian Muslims Face Challenges of Demography and Migration," New Eastern Europe, August 14, 2015, http://www.neweasterneurope.eu/articles-and-commentary/1690-russian-muslims-face-challenges-of-demography-and-migration.

[47] Pew Forum on Religion and Public Life, "The Future of the Global Muslim Population: Projections for 2010–2030," January 27, 2011, http://www.pewforum.org/future-of-the-global-muslim-population-russia.aspx.

[48] "Muslim Birthrate Worries Russia," Washington Times, November 20, 2006, http://www.washingtontimes.com/news/2006/nov/20/20061120-115904-9135r/?page=all.

[49] Jonah Hull, "Russia Sees Muslim Population Boom," Al-Jazeera (Doha), January 13, 2007, http://english.aljazeera.net/news/europe/2007/01/2008525144630794963.html; "Cherez polveka Musulmani v Rossii Mogut Stat Bolshenstvom - Posol MID RF [In Half a Century, Muslims in Russia Could Become the Majority - Russia's OIC Ambassador]," Interfax (Moscow), October 10, 2007, http://www.interfax-religion.ru/islam/print.php?act=news&id=20767.

[50] "Russia Has 2nd Biggest Migrant Populace After U.S.," The Moscow Times, September 13, 2013, http://www.themoscowtimes.com/news/article/russia-has-2nd-biggest-migrant-populace-after-us/485966.html.

[51] Although there are no exact figures on the number of converts, it is clear that a Russian/Slavic Islamic community is emerging. According to one report, almost 50 thousand people, mostly ethnic Russians and young women, converted to Islam in the city of Moscow alone from January 2002 to October 2004. This figure comes from a posting on a Qatar-based website IslamOnLine citing an anonymous source from the Council of Muftis of Russia cited in "S 2002 Islam v Moskve prinyali pochti 50 tys. chelovek," Islam.ru, October 7, 2004, www.islam.ru/press/rus/2004/10/07/. An ethnic Russian Muslim community emerged in Omsk in 2004. Aleksei Malashenko, "Shadow of Islam over Europe," International Affairs (Moscow) 50, no. 5 (September-October 2004), 70.

[52] See, for example, Rinat Bekkin, "Esly by ne krizis... R. Bekkin o roste interesa k islamskim finansam v Rossii," Islam.ru, n.d., www.islam.ru/pressclub/gost/esbikaznu/. Islam.ru is affiliated with the MSA of Dagestan and frequently carries articles and interviews on the subject, in particular those of a key lobbyist for the introduction of Islamic financing in Russia, Rinat Bekkin.

[53] Gordon M. Hahn, "Anti-Americanism, Anti-Westernism, and Anti-Semitism Among Russia's Muslims," Demokratizatsiya 16, no. 1 (Winter 2008), 49-60.

[54] David M. Herszenhorn, "Russia Sees a Threat in Its Converts to Islam," New York Times, July 1, 2015, https://www.nytimes.com/2015/07/02/world/russia-sees-a-threat-in-its-converts-to-islam.html.

[55] Russian Federation, Federal Law on Freedom of Religion and Religious Unity. 1997. http://pravo.gov.ru/proxy/ips/?docbody=&nd=102049359.

[56] Shireen Hunter, Islam in Russia: The Politics of Identity and Security (Armonk, NY: M.E. Sharpe, 2002), 54-55.

[57] A. Zhukov, "Kabardino-Balkariya: Na puti k katastrofe," Kavkaz-uzel, n.d., www.kavkaz-uzel.ru/analyticstext/analytics/id/1231255.html.

[58] Ravil Gainutdin, Islam v sovremennoi Rossii (Moscow: Fair Press, 2004), 264-297; Hahn,Russia's Islamic Threat, 183-186.

[59] "Rodnym obvinyaemykh v chlenstve v 'Khizb ut-takhrir' prishlos' proryvat'sya v zal suda," Islam.ru, February 27, 2009, www.islam.ru/rus/2009-02-27/; "V Chelyabinskoi oblasti predstanut pered sudom 5 'khizb ut-takhrirovtsev,'" Islam.ru, August 17, 2009, www.islam.ru/rus/2009-08-17/#27984.

[60] Valery Dzutsati. "Russian Expert Warns North Caucasus Faces Economic Recession." Jamestown Foundation Eurasia Daily Monitor 12, iss. 6, January 12, 2015, https://jamestown.org/program/russian-expert-warns-north-caucasus-faces-economic-recession-2/.

[61] Orysia Lutsevych, "The Long Arm of Russian "Soft" Power," The Atlantic Council, May 4, 2016, http://www.atlanticcouncil.org/blogs/ukrainealert/the-long-arm-of-russian-soft-power.

[62] "The Yarovaya Packet has been accepted into law," Meduza News. June 24, 2016, https://meduza.io/feature/2016/06/24/paket-yarovoy-prinyat-i-eto-ochen-ploho.

[63] Russian Federation, Federal Law #1039101-6 on Changing the Criminal Code of the Russian Federation and Criminal Procedural Code of the Russian Federation and Establishing Extra Counter-Terrorism Measures and Public Safety Guarantees, March 6, 2016.

[64] Russian Federation, Federal Law #1039149-6 on Changing Legislative Acts of the Russian Federation and Establishing Extra Counter-Terrorism Measures and Public Safety Guarantees, March 6, 2016.

[65] Russian Federation, Federal Order on Questions of Federal Service of a National Guard, April 5, 2016.http://kremlin.ru/acts/news/51648

[66] Mark Galiotti, "Putin's New National Guard," In Moscow's Shadows, April 5, 2016, https://inmoscowsshadows.wordpress.com/2016/04/05/putins-new-national-guard-what-does-it-say-when-you-need-your-own-personal-army/.

[67] Ibid.

[68] Robert Coalson, Terrorist Wave Raises Doubts About Moscow's North Caucasus Strategy," Radio Free Europe/Radio Liberty, February 16, 2011, http://www.rferl.org/a/doubts_about_moscow_north_caucasus_strategy/2311376.html.

[69] See generally Ilan Berman, Implosion: The End of Russia and What it Means for America (Regnery Publishing, 2013).

[70] Martin Chulov, "Syrian War's Al-Qaida Affiliate Calls for Terror Attacks in Russia," Guardian (London), October 13, 2015, https://www.theguardian.com/world/2015/oct/13/syria-al-qaida-group-jabhat-al-nusra-terror-attacks-russia.

[71] Malia Zimmerman, "ISIS Coming for the Kremlin, New Video Warns," Fox News, November 12, 2015, http://www.foxnews.com/world/2015/11/12/new-isis-video-says-jihadis-coming-for-kremlin/.

Tajikistan

Quick Facts

Population: 8,330,946 (July 2016 est.)

Area: 144,100 sq km

Ethnic Groups: Tajik 84.3%, Uzbek 13.8% (Includes Lakai, Kongrat, Katagan, Barlos, Yuz), other 2% (Includes Kyrgyz, Russian, Turkmen, Tatar, Arab) (2010 est.)

Religions: Sunni Muslim 85%, Shi'a Muslim 5%, other 10% (2003 est.)

Government Type: Presidential Republic

GDP (official exchange rate): $6.612 (2015 est.)

Map and Quick Facts courtesy of the CIA World Factbook (January 2017)

Overview

The poorest of Central Asia's former Soviet republics, Tajikistan is precariously situated along the lawless northeastern border of Afghanistan and straddles the southern and western ends of the restive Ferghana Valley. The end of Soviet state atheism led to what, to many, appeared to be a sudden reemergence of Islam in the public sphere, much as was the case in other newly independent republics. However, uniquely among the former Soviet bloc, Tajikistan was the site of all out civil war that pitted former communists against opposition forces that included Islamists.

While the civil war came to a close in the late 1990s, sporadic violence has persisted and fears remain that Tajikistan could return to instability. Economic stagnation, a precarious geo-political position and poor political management are all potential factors that could fuel a sudden revival of Islamist militancy. Despite heavy-handed measures aimed at curbing the dangers posed by jihadists and other anti-state movements, sporadic violence has demonstrated the ability of Islamists to survive, and Tajikistan may well prove to be a springboard for further Islamic militancy should the Tajik government make any serious mistakes.

ISLAMIST ACTIVITY

More than any other of the newly independent Central Asian republics, Tajikistan became the scene of intense social conflict and violence after the collapse of the Soviet Union. In the other regional states, the transition was not without challenges—particularly in Uzbekistan, where Islamists briefly took over parts of the Ferghana valley. Yet in Tajikistan, political transition led to outright civil war. Elections in 1991 favored the entrenched communist-era political elite, comprised mainly of *apparatchiks* from the Khujand region. A broad-based coalition of opposition groups which would come to be known as the United Tajik Opposition (UTO) challenged these results, and fighting broke out in early 1992.

The UTO consisted of several different groups with wildly different aims and ambitions: separatists from the ethnically distinct Pamir region, secularists with liberal tendencies, and Islamists. The latter rose to prominence during the course of the fighting, coalescing into the Islamic Renaissance Party of Tajikistan (IRPT). The war raged for five years as the government vied with the opposition for control of the mountainous country, and attracted support from neighboring Uzbekistan and factions in war-torn Afghanistan, as well as from Russia.

In 1997, a peace deal was brokered by the UN and signed by Emomali Rahmonov (today known by Rahmon, having abandoned the Russified version of his name) and Sayid Abdullah Nuri, head of the IRPT, on behalf of the UTO. This agreement ended the civil war and granted the UTO, by this point consisting mainly of the IRPT, a 30 percent share in the government of Tajikistan. The IRPT became the only legal Islamist party in former Soviet Central Asia. Nevertheless, the group's willingness to compromise with secularists and the central government was seen by many as a kind of betrayal of its core principles, and would have to struggle to remain relevant.

In this endeavor, the IRPT had to compete with rival Islamist movements that rose to challenge the credentials it forged during the civil war, while at the same time struggling to maintain power as an official opposition force. In its stead, *Hizb ut-Tahrir* (*HuT*), began to take over the role of the premier Islamist movement in the country. In the late 1990s and early 2000s, HuT was able to mobilize elements of the Tajikistani population to advance its calls for the supposedly non-violent overthrow of the Tajik government.[1]

Contact with the political system, coupled with competition with other more overtly anti-establishment Islamist movements, cost the IRPT popular support in Tajikistan. In parallel, Rahmon's efforts to consolidate power in a manner similar to other regional states led to the gradual undoing of the power-sharing agreement that ended the civil war. Against the backdrop of the rise of the Islamic State and a worsening of the insurgency in Afghanistan following the withdrawal of American troops, the stage was set for Dushanbe's political elite to move against what until then had been Central Asia's only non-proscribed Islamist opposition parties. In the nearly two decades following the cessation of hostilities, Rahmon's People's Democratic Party (PDP) has been able to consolidate its power, while the IRPT, by contrast, lost many of its erstwhile allies in the struggle to maintain a foothold in the political system. At the same time, the geopolitical realities in neighboring Afghanistan have shifted, and the IRPT can no longer draw on reliable allies from across the border.

During a contested election in March 2015, the IRPT proved unable to maintain its foothold in the country's parliamentary system. Alleging intimidation, election fraud, and other irregularities, the IRPT challenged the outcome of the elections. The newly strengthened Tajik government rapidly proceeded to crack down on the party's leadership, charging its members with violating various anti-extremist laws. An armed clash between deputy defense minister Abduhalim Nazarzoda and his supporters and the Tajik police left 26 people dead in September 2015.[2] In the wake of the violence, the government was quick to arrest the leadership of the party, and in February 2016, nine members of the IRPT leadership went on trial for conspiring with Nazarzoda to overthrow the government.[3]

Islamic Movement of Uzbekistan (IMU) and Splinter Groups

Despite its name, the Islamic Movement of Uzbekistan (IMU) was active beyond the borders of Uzbekistan in the late 1990s. Having emerged in the Ferghana Valley in the wake of Soviet collapse, the movement was forced out of Uzbek territory and set itself up in Tajikistan during the civil war, where it took up arms in support of the UTO. In 1999, the group launched a series of raids into Uzbekistan and Kyrgyzstan, engaging police and military units and raising funds through kidnappings. Ultimately the group retreated into Afghanistan, and became embedded in the Taliban's attempts to consolidate its hold over the northern part of the country. During the U.S.-led post-9/11 intervention, the IMU sided with the Taliban, which resulted in the death of its leader, Juma Namangani, and a hasty withdrawal into the tribal areas along Pakistan's border with Afghanistan.[4]

Languishing in Pakistani exile, the IMU shifted its efforts away from directly opposing national governments in Central Asia to becoming specialists firmly entrenched in the world of international terrorism. The highly literate Central Asians, with a history of technical and scientific expertise, are prized throughout the *jihadist* milieu as expert bomb makers. But not until 2010 did the group reemerge in Tajikistan, when it was implicated in the jailbreak of 25 imprisoned Islamists that August and a subsequent attack on Tajik security forces in the Rasht Valley, as well as a car bombing in the northern city of Khujand.[5]

Token attacks notwithstanding, the IMU is a mere shadow of its former self in Central Asia.[6] The group has been confined mainly to Afghanistan and Pakistan in recent years, and was further weakened when the its leader, Usman Ghazi, denounced the Taliban and swore an oath of loyalty to the self-styled *caliph* of the Islamic State of Syria and Iraq (ISIS), Abu Bakr al-Baghdadi. In subsequent clashes with the Taliban, what was left of the IMU was severely weakened, and Usman Ghazi himself likely was killed. However, a surviving faction of the IMU that remains loyal to the Taliban has reconstituted itself, and appears to be taking part in battles against the Afghan government.[7] Other IMU fighters have gathered in Syria under the umbrella of the Imam Bukhari Brigade, which is loyal to al-Qaeda. As the Taliban insurgency shifts into the northern part of Afghanistan, IMU fighters with their avowed hostility toward the secular governments of Central Asia are again coming closer to the border of Tajikistan, and it is not inconceivable that their attention may again be directed at the country in the future.

Hizb ut-Tahrir (HuT)

Hizb ut-Tahrir is unusual because of its agenda of establishing a *caliphate* which unites all Muslims in a single entity by peaceful means, though it remains unclear exactly how this transformation would be brought about without the use of force. Entering Central Asia in the late 1990s, the movement quickly gained in influence as the IRPT and IMU declined in popularity. The IRPT had lost its credibility among Islamists as an Islamic people's movement because of its participation in government, while the IMU fought alongside the Taliban against the U.S.-led intervention in Afghanistan and was all but destroyed in late 2001.

HuT spread its message for Islamic solidarity and an overthrow of the Tajik government through a leaflet campaign which portrayed the country's economic and development woes as a result of secular government. Calls for reform through religion found resonance within both the Tajik and minority Uzbek communities. Despite the group's avowed commitment to non-violence, Central Asian leaderships saw the HuT as an existential threat, and in Tajikistan the movement was declared an "illegal political party" in 1999. This was followed up by a crackdown on alleged members, 500 of whom were arrested between 2000 and 2005.[8]

Since then, HuT has gone underground, and it is difficult to assess how real the presence of the movement is today. In an increasingly anti-Islamist political environment, especially following the 2009 passing of a national "Law on the Freedom of Conscience" that included restrictions on religious communities and religious literature,[9] the movement has likely taken a defensive line and reduced its public profile. While HuT has received the most attention of any organized clandestine group in Central Asia, it is extremely difficult to gauge how many adherents remain within the country and how actively they are proselytizing.[10] It should be noted that while the ascendance of HuT in Central Asia gave birth to a cottage industry of ominous analysis in the West in the 2000s, little has been written on the organization since 2011. Both the Tajik government and HuT itself have an interest in maintaining the appearance of a HuT presence in Tajikistan—but it remains unclear to what extent the movement is still active in Central Asia.

Islamic State of Iraq and Syria

The civil war in Syria and the ongoing turmoil in Iraq have contributed to the rise of the Islamic State of Iraq and Syria (ISIS). With a highly sophisticated propaganda network and strong social media profile, the self-styled *caliphate* quickly became the focus of international media and political rhetoric. With the amount of attention being lavished upon the group, it is perhaps unsurprising that the movement became the focal point of international *jihadist* ambitions. A December 2015 study estimated that between 27,000 and 31,000 people hailing from over 100 countries had opted to become foreign fighters in the ranks of *jihadist* organizations, primarily in Iraq and Syria.[11]

Disturbing as these numbers may be, the number of foreign fighters originating in Central Asia, estimated at ca, 2,000, is comparatively low. According to a report by the Soufan Group, some 386 Tajiks are thought to have traveled to Syria and Iraq to fight for ISIS, compared to about 300 people from Sweden.[12] Furthermore, most Central Asian recruits are known to have been radicalized in Russia, not in their home countries.[13] Nevertheless, Tajik officials have focused on ISIS as a threat to their government, with some justification. In April 2015, Colonel Gulmurod Khalimov, a senior Tajik counterterrorism official trained in the U.S., disappeared, only to reappear in an ISIS propaganda video denouncing the Tajik government and threatening to bring *jihad* to the U.S. and Russia.[14]

Revealingly, Khalimov's propaganda performance included an appeal to Tajik migrants in Russia to rise up against their Russian employers and join the Islamic State. Despite efforts by various Islamist organizations, including ISIS, to win Central Asian recruits for *jihad*, these efforts have so far proven to be relatively ineffective, with far more volunteers coming from Western Europe and the Middle East. The one Central Asian population group which appears to be most vulnerable to *jihadist* propaganda are guest workers in Russia, who are often confronted with difficult living situations, are isolated from the stabilizing influence of their families and local religious leaders, and exposed to overt xenophobia and racism.[15]

ISLAMISM AND SOCIETY

Decades of rule by Moscow left undeniable traces in the languages, cultures and social lives of people in Central Asia. In Part of this legacy is that the Muslim populations in Tajikistan are far less prone to political Islamism than their coreligionists in the other places, like the Arab world. Tajikistan is mostly Sunni, while the small Pamiri communities in the east of the country belong to the Ismaili branch of Shi'a Islam. It is far more common to see alcohol or pork on the menu of restaurants in Dushanbe than it would be in Cairo or Baghdad. Central Asian Muslims have also been heavily influenced by the *Hanafi* School of jurisprudence, which has historically been more amenable to secular government. That being said, the end of communism has led to a reentry of Islam into Central Asian society. Especially in Tajikistan, public religiosity has reappeared in the public sphere, with religious-minded names and clothing styles becoming increasingly prominent.[16]

Tajikistan has seen a more rapid growth of Islamic sensitivities than its northern neighbors. There are several reasons for the heightened level of Islamic solidarity in Tajikistan. Most obviously, the instability of the 1990s gradually made the IRPT the dominant force in the UTO, while liberal or democratic minded opposition forces disappeared over time from leadership roles in a situation analogous to the one we see in Syria today. As a result, Islamist groups gained a foothold during the civil war, the results of which remain to this day.

Independence in Tajikistan was characterized by widespread poverty and the phenomenon of mass labor migration. Some estimates place the number of Tajiks leaving the country for employment in Kazakhstan and Russia at well over a million, which in a country of just under 8 million inhabitants is a staggering number. The biggest exodus took place during the civil war in the 1990s, but the lack of economic opportunity has ensured a steady stream of Tajik migrants down to the present. Indeed, in 2015 the World Bank classified Tajikistan as the country in the world most dependent on remittances, which exceeded 50 percent of GDP.[17] This is in part due to geographic and historical features; Tajikistan's mountainous landscape makes development initiatives difficult, and during Soviet times the country was kept more or less on life support by Moscow, which provided up to a 30 percent of the republic's budget in subsidies. A kleptocratic approach to economic reform has exacerbated existing problems and further undermined faith in state institutions.[18]

In 2008 and 2009, the economic woes of the population came to a head in what has been referred to as Tajikistan "winter crisis." An especially cold year completely overstrained Tajikistan's ageing energy infrastructure, leaving much of the population at the mercy of the elements. Rural areas were especially hard hit, with local people attempting to heat their homes by burning furniture and taking to the thinly wooded (and erosion prone) mountainsides in a desperate search for fuel. Against the backdrop of government assurances that gas and electricity were plentiful, this crisis widened the gap between the state elites and the population at large.

Economic troubles did not end with the spring, however, as in 2009 Tajikistan saw a slowdown in its remittance-based economy. Dependence on the Russian economy has also meant that the Tajik economy has suffered anew in recent years from the after-effects of economic stagnation in Russia, which were first caused by sanctions over Russian aggression toward Georgia in 2008, and since exacerbated by its aggressive foreign policy toward Ukraine. For Tajikistan, this has meant a return-exodus of migrant workers, many of whom have been away for several years.[19]

The Rahmon government has taken only limited measures to combat the issues of poverty and labor migration. Popular resentment has been stoked by the efforts of the government to demonstrate its power through costly public projects, such as the almost quixotic construction of the world's tallest flagpole in 2011 at a cost of $30 million. At the same time that this extravagant prestige project was being developed, the cost of basic commodities within the country spiked, starkly illustrating the disconnect between Dushanbe's priorities and the population at large.[20] More disturbing has been the tendency of the Rahmon regime to narrow rather than broaden its base, relying almost exclusively on the loyalty of a small group of officials hailing from the President's home district of Danghara in Khatlon province.

At the same time, the government has sought to crack down on Islamists, exerting considerable effort to pursue and neutralize suspected terrorists. Following a major prison break in Dushanbe in 2010, during the course of which some 25 convicted militants escaped, Tajik security forces launched what amounted to a military occupation of the Rasht Valley, a hub of Islamist opposition. Between September 2010 and November 2011, some 100 people lost their lives in this operation, and all 25 escapees were either killed or recaptured. Half a decade later, in 2015, similar clashes between security forces and militants in Dushanbe and the town of Vakhdat led to another major crackdown.[21]

Entrenched economic instability and the rise of ISIS's self-styled *caliphate* in Syria and Iraq have conspired to make Islamism more attractive to disenfranchised youth wishing to express political frustrations and counteract a feeling of powerlessness. This is especially acute among the Tajik guest worker population in Russia, which is subject to xenophobic discrimination, difficult living conditions and isolation from family and community ties. At the same time, the operational capacity of Islamists in Northern Afghanistan is increasing due to the most recent incarnation of that nation's interminable civil war. Combined with an uncertain economic future and growing disillusion with the Rahmon government, these developments create conditions in which radical Islamism retains the potential to be a significant threat to Dushanbe's authority.

ISLAMISM AND THE STATE

In recent years, the Tajik government has further intensified existing policies to crack down on suspected Islamists. Citing the dangers of terrorism, the government has sought to limit expressions of religion in the public sphere.[22] The list of proscribed religious movements has steadily grown longer to include the *Hizb ut Tahrir* (banned in 1999), the ostensibly apolitical *Tablighi Jama'at* (banned in 2006) and most recently the IRPT itself. President Rahmon's government even went so far as to ban *Salafism* itself in 2009.[23] Critics argue that what the government claims to be counter-terrorism measures are in actuality merely an attempt to break any form of realistic opposition. The Tajik government has used the accusation of Islamic extremism liberally, including against secular oppositional forces including the "24 Group", whose leader (and former Rahmon business ally) Umarali Quvvatov was assassinated in Istanbul in March 2015. At the same time, the state has also taken steps to monitor non-political religious gatherings and passed legislation to prevent the religious education of children under the age of 18. Such efforts culminated in the 2011 ban on the presence of children at Friday services in mosques, and punitive measures that were taken against the parents of underage violators.[24]

The heavy-handedness of some of these measures exceeds the norm in Central Asia, and has prompted a response from the international community, and Tajikistan's policies in the area of religion have been criticized by bodies such as the European Union, the Organization for Security and Cooperation in Europe and the United States Commission on International Religious Freedom. In part due to this pressure, President Rahmon's government has in the past made concessions, such as repealing some of the stricter prohibitions on religious education.[25] Nevertheless, critics argue that Dushanbe runs the risk of alienating sections of the moderately religious population and galvanizing opposition. Considering the precarious nature of the Tajik economy, which is highly dependent on remittances from guest workers in Russia, a gradual shift northward of the activities of the Taliban and their allies in nearby Afghanistan, and the disappearance of the IRPT as a valve for opposition sentiment, the future of Tajikistan's struggle against radical Islamism will remain fraught with challenges.

Endnotes

[1] Emmanuel Karagiannis, "The Challenge of Radical Islam in Tajikistan: Hizb ut-Tahrir al-Islami," Nationalities Papers 34, no. 1, March 2006.

[2] Edward Lemon, "Violence in Tajikistan Emerges from Within the State", Central Asia-Caucasus Analyst, September 23, 2015, http://cacianalyst.org/publications/analytical-articles/item/13279.

[3] "Islamic Renaissance Party Members Go on Trial in Tajikistan" Eurasianet.org, February 09, 2016, http://www.eurasianet.org/node/77246.

[4] Bill Roggio, "Islamic Movement of Uzbekistan Confirms Leader Tahir Yuldashev Killed," Long War Journal, August 16, 2010, http://www.longwarjournal.org/archives/2010/08/islamic_movement_of_1.php.

[5] Lola Olimova, "Mass Jailbreak Causes Ripples In Tajikistan," Institute for War & Peace Reporting, September 6, 2010, http://iwpr.net/print/report-news/mass-jailbreak-causes-ripples-tajikistan.

[6] "Jacob Zenn, "The IMU is Extinct: What Next for Central Asia's Jihadis", Central Asia-Caucasus Analyst, May 3, 2016, http://cacianalyst.org/publications/analytical-articles/item/13357.

[7] Thomas Joscelyn and Bill Roggio, "Central Asian groups split over leadership of global jihad" Long War Journal, August 24, 2015, http://www.longwarjournal.org/archives/2015/08/central-asian-groups-split-over-leadership-of-global-jihad.php.

[8] Karagiannis, "The Challenge Of Radical Islam In Tajikistan: Hizb ut-Tahrir al-Islami,"

[9] Suhrob Majidov, "Tajikistan: Restriction of Religious Freedoms or Secular State?", Central Asia-Caucasus Analyst, April 8, 2009, https://www.cacianalyst.org/publications/field-reports/item/11819.

[10] "Hizb ut-Tahrir Regional Leader Arrested In Tajikistan," Radio Free Europe/Radio Liberty, June 15, 2011, http://www.rferl.org/content/hizb_ut-tahrir_regional_leader_arrested_n_tajikistan/24235600.html.

[11] "Foreign Fighters: An Updated Assessment of the Flow of Foreign Fighters into Syria and Iraq, the Soufan Group, December 2015, http://soufangroup.com/wp-content/uploads/2015/12/TSG_ForeignFightersUpdate3.pdf.

[12] "Foreign Fighters: An Updated Assessment of he Flow of Foreign Fighters into Iraq and Syria" The Soufan Group, December 2015.

[13] Joanna Paraszczuk, "Most Uzbeks Fighting for IS Came from Russia, Theologian Claims", RFE/RL, March 24, 2015; (http://www.rferl.org/content/most-uzbeks-fighting-for-is-came-from-russia-theologian-claims/26918165.html) Noah Tucker, "Central Asian Involvement in the Conflict in Syria and Iraq: Drivers and Responses", USAID and MDI, 2015. (https://www.usaid.gov/sites/default/files/documents/1866/CVE_CentralAsiansSyriaIraq.pdf); Ryskeldi Satke and Marta Ter, " Are Central Asian migrants in Russia a recruiting ground for Islamic State?" European Council on Foreign Relations, July 27, 2015. (http://www.ecfr.eu/article/commentary_are_central_asian_migrants_in_russia_3080); Daniil Turovsky, "How Isis is recruiting migrant workers in Moscow to join the fighting in Syria", Guardian, May 5, 2015. (https://www.theguardian.com/world/2015/may/05/isis-russia-syria-islamic-extremism).

[14] "Tajikistan police chief defects to ISIS," Guardian (London), May 28, 2015, https://www.theguardian.com/world/2015/may/28/tajikistan-police-chief-defects-to-isis.

[15] Noah Tucker, "Central Asian Involvement in the Conflict in Syria and Iraq: Driver's and Factors" USAID, May 4, 2015, https://www.usaid.gov/sites/default/files/documents/1866/CVE_CentralAsiansSyriaIraq.pdf.

[16] "Tajik Pressure Said to Be Growing over Islamic Dress," Radio Free Europe/Radio Liberty, September 17, 2010, http://www.rferl.org/articleprintview/2160501.html.

[17] "World Bank: Tajikistan is the world's Most Remittance Dependent Country", Asia-Plus News Agency, April 15, 2015, http://www.news.tj/en/news/world-bank-tajikistan-world-s-most-remittance-dependent-country.

[18] Tajikistan: On the Road to Failure (International Crisis Group, February 2009), http://www.crisisgroup.org/~/media/Files/asia/central-asia/tajikistan/162_tajikistan___on_the_road_to_failure.ashx.

[19] James Kimer, "Spurned by Russia, Tajik Labour Migrants Return Home to Build Rogun", Silk Road Reporters, January 13, 2015. http://www.silkroadreporters.com/2015/01/13/spurned-russia-tajik-labour-migrants-return-home-build-rogun/.

[20] "In Tajikistan, The World's Tallest Flagpole… Without A Flag" Radio Free Europe/Radio Liberty, April 24, 2013, http://www.rferl.org/a/tajikistan-flagpole-strong-winds/24967470.html.

[21] "Tajikistan: Digging for Answers About Armed Clashes," Eurasianet.org, September 7, 2015, http://www.eurasianet.org/node/74971.

[22] Farangis Najibullah, "Tajik Officials Keep Sharp Eye on Islamic Teaching," Radio Free Europe/Radio Liberty, August 7, 2010, http://www.eurasianet.org/print/61682

[23] Farangis Najibullah, "Salafi Ban Reflects Tajik Officials' Growing Fear," Radio Free Europe/Radio Liberty, January 9, 2009, http://www.rferl.org/articleprintview/1368347.html.

[24] Alexander Sodiqov, "Bill Banning Children from Mosques Adopted in Tajikistan," Jamestown Foundation Eurasia Daily Monitor 8, iss. 124, June 28, 2011, http://www.jamestown.org/single/?no_cache=1&tx_ttnews%5Btt_news%5D=38104&tx_ttnews%5BbackPid%5D=512.

[25] "Tajik Children, Facing Mosque Ban, To Be Offered Islamic Courses," Radio Free Europe/Radio Liberty, June 27, 2011, http://www.rferl.org/content/tajikistan_children_mosque_ban_islamic_courses/24248140.html.

TURKEY

> **QUICK FACTS**
>
> Population: 80,274,604 (July 2016 est.)
>
> Area: 783,562 sq km
>
> Ethnic Groups: Turkish 70-75%, Kurdish 19%, other minorities 7-12%
>
> Religions: Muslim 99.8% (mostly Sunni), other 0.2% (mostly Christians and Jews)
>
> Government Type: parliamentary republic
>
> GDP (official exchange rate): $735.7 billion (2015 est.)
>
> *Map and Quick Facts courtesy of the CIA World Factbook (Last Updated January 2017)*

OVERVIEW

Turkey has sporadically experienced Islamist terrorism since the Iranian Revolution of 1979, but the level of terrorist activity was relatively low between the 2003 Istanbul bombings, for which both al-Qaeda and the local IBDA-C claimed responsibility, and May 2013, when two car bombs exploded in the town of Reyhanlı, killing 51 and injuring 140, in an attack subsequently claimed by the so-called Islamic State. That bombing marked the beginning of a period of rapidly-escalating terrorism that has made Turkey the European country most victimized by ISIS.

ISIS is believed to be responsible for terrorist attacks in May, 2013, in Reyhanlı, March, 2014, on the Turkish police, June, 2015, in Diyarbakır, and the July, 2015, in Suruç. The bombing in Suruç killed 32 young Kurdish activists are re-ignited the Kurdish-Turkish conflict. On January 12, 2016, an ISIS suicide bomber bombed Istanbul's historic Sultanahmet Square, killing 12 people. On March 19, another suicide bombing in Istanbul's Beyoğlu district killed four and wounded 36.

In September of 2014, Turkey successfully negotiated the release of 49 hostages who had been captured by ISIS and held at the Turkish consulate in Mosul, leading observers to suspect Turkey had forged a tacit non-

aggression pact with the group. But as the 2017 massacre targeting New Year's Eve revelers at an upscale Istanbul nightclub showed, the pact has long since devolved into all-out war.

In September 2014, Turkey joined the US-led coalition against ISIS. Since 2015, Turkey has permitted the US Air Force to use İncirlik and Diyarbakır air bases in southern Turkey for their air campaign against ISIS.

ISIS has declared the Turkish government to be an "apostate regime" allied with the "crusaders."[1]

The return of thousands of radicalized foreign and Turkish fighters from Syria has become a grave concern. As many as 1,200 people linked to ISIS were detained in Turkey in 2015. More than 350 were arrested and imprisoned on suspicion of ties to the group.[2]

The Turkish military's anti-ISIS intervention in Syria, Operation Euphrates Shield, began in August, 2016, in concert with a coalition of Syrian Arab and Turkmen forces, backed by a few hundred Turkish troops. As fighting progressed, Ankara had to send reinforcements. Turkish troops on the ground in northern Syria are now in the thousands. By February 2017, Turkish forces, aided by Russia, had made significant progress against ISIS around the city of Al Bab in northern Syria.[3] *The conflict continues in the region between the Euphrates river to the east and the rebel-held area around Azaz to the west.*[4]

Political Islamism has consistently gained strength since the 1980s, and, with the multiple electoral victories of the Islamist-rooted AKP (Justice and Development Party) since November 2002, has become increasingly visible at the grassroots level, as pious Turks enjoy growing representation in the political process.

The AKP's victory in the 2007 election helped solidify the party's hold on political power, and electoral victories since have given the party a virtual monopoly on the country's judiciary, as well as commanding influence over the executive and legislative branches. It has also adopted an increasingly adventurist and difficult foreign policy. Under then-Prime Minister (now-President) Recep Tayyip Erdogan's increasingly authoritarian rule, Turkey has thrown its weight behind Islamist movements in the region, including Egypt's Muslim Brotherhood and Hamas, and until recently either ignored or facilitated the passage of radical foreign fighters into Syria.

ISLAMIST ACTIVITY

Islamist activity in Turkey generally takes place via one of the three channels: (1) through Islamist terrorist groups; (2) through the activities of charities and business organizations; and (3) through the activities of the Islamist brotherhoods—*tariqa-*

ts, (schools of Sufism) communities and lodges—where political influence leads to cronyism and, ultimately, to corruption. The government has advanced Islamist activities since the 1980s in support of state aims, but it has done so more energetically since the AKP came to power in the last decade.

Terrorist Organizations

IBDA-C

The Islamic Great Eastern Raiders (*İslami Büyükdoğu Akıncılar*, or IBDA) was founded in 1970 as a peripheral youth faction of the National Order Party (*Millî Nizam Partisi*, or MNP), which was at the time headed by Islamic fundamentalist and future Prime Minister Necmettin Erbakan. Under the leadership of Salih Izzet Erdiş (better known as Salih Mirzabeyoğlu), IBDA gained autonomy from the MNP, affixed "Islamic Great East" to its name, and became the first group in the history of modern Turkey to advocate armed struggle in the service of an Islamic revolution. Its ideology, notable and perhaps unique among modern Islamist groups, is a mixture of Sunni Islam, Trotskyism and Platonic idealism, with specifically Turkish sources of inspiration in the Turkish Nakşibendi order and the writings of the Turkish poet, Necip Fazıl Kısakürek (1905-1983). Kısakürek advocated a return to "pure Islamic values" and the restoration of a universal Islamic caliphate in the Muslim world. The secular nature of Turkey, he held, was responsible for the state's inability to ward off what he saw as Western imperialism.[5] IBDA supports the establishment of a "pure Islamic" state to replace the present "corrupt" Turkish regime that is cooperating with the West. It is rigidly anti-Semitic and anti-Christian.

However, the movement is not a populist one. Rather, it endorses an Islamic aristocracy through its project for a Grand Sublime State. No precise estimate of the size of its membership exists. Members organize independently, without any defined hierarchy or central authority, and both its legal and illegal actions are carried out via autonomous local "front" groups, or *cepheler*—IBDA-Cs—that cooperate with other opposition elements in Turkey when necessary.[6] IBDA-C joined al-Qaeda in claiming responsibility for the November 2003 bombings in Istanbul.[7] In April 2004, a *cepheler* assassinated a retired army colonel and his wife in Istanbul.[8] And in the summer of 2008, a front staged an armed attack on the United States General Consulate in Istanbul, killing three police officers who had been defending it. Turkish police claimed to have dismantled several *cephelers* the following year. On October 7, 2014, the group formally pledged its support to the Islamic State.[9]

Turkish Hizbullah

Turkish Hizbullah is a Kurdish Islamic (Sunni) extremist organization founded in the 1980s by Hüseyin Velioğlu, an ethnic Kurd and former student activist, in the southeastern city of Diyarbakır. The organization, which is unrelated to the Lebanese Shi'ite militia of the same name but shares its sympathy for Iran, seeks to establish an Islamic state in three distinct phases: (1) a period of propaganda and indoctrination, known as *tebliğ* (communication); (2) the consolidation of a popular base, known as *cemaat* (community); and (3) a *jihad* to overthrow the secular order and establish an Islamic state.[10] Beginning in the mid-1990s, Turkish Hizbullah expanded its activities from killing Kurdistan Workers' Party (PKK) militants to conducting low-level bombings against liquor stores, bordellos, and other establishments that the organization considered *haram* (forbidden).[11] The Turkish government initially ignored Hizbullah, even hoping that its Islamism might provide an ideological bulwark against the rival PKK's atheistic Marxism. (Many in the Turkish press—supported by compelling individual testimonies—believe that Turkish Hizbullah was in fact formed by the so-called "Deep State," which many in Turkey believe to be comprised of anti-democratic elements in the intelligence services, military, judiciary, and mafia, to counter the growing activity of the PKK). The movement is known for cleaver-assaults, kidnappings, beatings, acid attacks on women not dressed in an Islamic manner, and particularly barbaric means of assassination. Consecutive Turkish governments have accused Iran of using Hizbullah in a similar manner as Hezbollah in Lebanon.[12]

By the late 1990s, Turkish authorities acknowledged that Hizbullah had become a major threat in its own right, and moved against the group.[13] Leader Huseyin Velioğlu was killed in a shootout with Turkish forces at a safe house in Istanbul in January 2000. The incident touched off a series of counterterrorism operations against the group, resulting in some 2,000 detentions and the arrests of several hundred on criminal charges. Turkish Hizbullah has not conducted a major operation since it assassinated the popular Diyarbakır police chief in 2001.[14] In January 2010, five members of the group were freed in accordance with a new national law restricting the amount of time suspects can be held while awaiting the final verdict in their cases.[15]

Hüda-Par, the "Free Cause Party", is a Kurdish Sunni fundamentalist political party that emerged from Turkish Hizbollah. It is reported to be sympathetic to ISIS. Following a decision to end armed struggle in 2002, sympathizers of Turkish Hizbollah founded the Solidarity with the Oppressed Association, *Mustazaflar ile Dayanışma Derneği* or *Mustazaf Der*.[16] In 2010, *Mustazaf Der* held a celebration of the Prophet Muhammad's birthday estimated to have been attended by 120,000 people. A *Diyarbakir* court then ordered the closure of *Mustazaf Der* on the grounds that it was a front for Hizbollah. Societies associated with *Hüda-Par* operate under the umbrella organization Lovers of Prophet (*Peygamber Sevdalıları* in Turkish, *Evindarên Pêyxamber* in Kurdish).[17]

The Caliphate State

The Caliphate State, also known as the Kaplan group and ICB-AFID, is a Turkish fundamentalist terrorist group that operates in Germany and seeks to overthrow the secular Turkish government and establish an Islamic state modeled after Iran. The group was founded by Cemalettin Kaplan, following his parting with the National Vision (*Millî Görüş*) political movement in Turkey. Its immediate purpose is to gather the Muslim masses living in Europe under an Islamic banner to reject democracy and Western culture. Its ultimate goal is to establish a federative Islamic state on Anatolian soil based on *sharia* by overthrowing the constitutional state and the secular order.

Since Cemalettin Kaplan appointed himself "the *Caliph*" in 1994, the organization has been referred to as the Caliphate State. After Kaplan's death in 1995, his son Metin Kaplan was elected the new Caliph, causing divisions within the organization. Following his declaration of *jihad* against Turkey, the new self-styled caliph, Metin, was arrested by German authorities and served a four-year prison sentence in Germany for inciting members of his group to murder a rival Islamic leader. He was then extradited to Turkey, where he was sentenced to life in prison for treason. His followers have reportedly become even more devoted to Kaplan, who is believed to have a fortune worth millions, considering him a martyr for the cause of Allah.[18] The group, organized as *Verband der Islamischen Vereine und Gemeinden e.V.* (Islami Cemaat ve Cemiyetler Birliği/ ICCB) with 1,200 members in Germany and an estimated membership of 5,000 around Europe, was outlawed by the German authorities in 2002.[19] Despite the increasingly Islamist nature of Turkey, the Kaplan group has not changed its attitude toward the Turkish government. Kaplan is still in jail, serving his life sentence, and his followers view that as a grave injustice.[20]

The Army of Jerusalem

The Army of Jerusalem (*Kudüs Ordusu* or *Tevhid-Selam*) is an illegal organization which emerged in 1985. Using the publication of several magazines, including *Tevhid* and *Selam*, as a cover, the group often collaborated with other organizations and received its inspiration from the "Qods (Jerusalem) Force", a paramilitary unit of Iran's Islamic Revolutionary Guard Corps.[21] In the year 2000, twenty-four members were indicted for attempting to overthrow the country's secular regime and establish a state based upon religious law, and for their involvement in the assassinations of several pro-secular journalists and academics during the 1990s. Fifteen of them were subsequently convicted in 2002, with three receiving a death sentence.[22] (The death penalty has since been abolished in Turkey).

Al-Qaeda

Al-Qaeda remains active in Turkey. In 2003, a Turkish chapter of the Bin Laden network surfaced, possibly in collaboration with IBDA-C members, to conduct terrorist attacks against two synagogues, an HSBC bank, and the British consulate.[23] Richard Barrett, the head of the UN's Al Qaeda and Taliban monitoring group, estimated in 2010 that there were over 100 Turkish-speaking al-Qaeda members along the Pakistan-Afghanistan border.[24] Unfortunately, knowledge about al-Qaeda's current size and capabilities within Turkey is undercut by a chronic lack of proper study. Turkish police are generally successful at thwarting al-Qaeda's attacks, and thwarted attacks rarely receive significant media attention. Furthermore, Turkey does not seem a natural target for al-Qaeda, given that it is 99% Muslim with a government heavily influenced by Islamic ideals.[25]

Since the Istanbul bombings, Turkish authorities have cracked down on members running the group's operations in Turkey, sentencing many of them to life in prison.[26] Though no terrorist activity was noted after the 2003 bombings, the recent arrival of thousands of members of the al-Qaeda associate *Jabhat al-Nusra* (designated a terrorist organization by the United States since December 2012)[27] among the estimated 2.7 million Syrian refugees[28] who have fled to Turkey since the start of the Syrian civil war in 2011 have raised concerns about potential for future violence. The Turkish government originally promoted the group as an effective force against Syrian President Bashar al-Assad, criticizing the United States for prematurely designating it as a terrorist organization.[29]

Following bombings near the Syrian border that killed 46 people in May 2013, however, it was widely reported that the Turkish government no longer viewed *al-Nusra* favorably.[30] Despite statements by the Turkish government holding Syria responsible for the explosions,[31] many Turks in the area believe *al-Nusra* was involved. But credible reports of Turkish support for the group have not subsided. On March 21, 2014, *al-Nusra* reportedly crossed into Syria from Turkey and seized the Armenian coastal town of Kassab. The Armenian government called on the UN to protect Kessab, evoked the Armenian genocide, and accused Turkey of allowing *jihadists* to cross their border. Ankara denied the accusations and condemned the charge as "confrontational political propaganda."[32] However, accounts of Turkish involvement have multiple credible sources and are plausible.[33]

Al-Qaeda's presence in Turkey remains under-studied, and its current numbers are difficult to estimate, in part because the Turkish press does not publish the names of people arrested in connection with al-Qaeda (in compliance with Turkish law forbidding the publication of the full names of criminal suspects). Moreover, al-Qaeda operatives use code names. Many of the details of their operations are never reported.[34]

In January 2015, Turkish military documents were leaked; these accused MIT, the national intelligence service, of shipping weapons to al-Qaeda in Syria. Erdogan has insisted these deliveries were destined for Turkmens. The veracity of the account is hard to establish – as is the veracity of much reported about Turkey since the fallout between Erdogan and Gülen. Media outlets have been completely banned from reporting on the incident.[35]

Recently, Al-Qaeda's former affiliate in Syria called on opposition groups not to aid supporting the Turkey-led Euphrates Shield operation in Syria, saying they are a front for a U.S. occupation.[36]

Hizb ut-Tahrir

Hizb ut-Tahrir, founded in 1953, made its way to Turkey in 1978, espousing its aim of establishing an Islamic caliphate and introducing *sharia* law. The Turkish police have frequently detained members of the organization, which was formally outlawed by a Turkish court in 2004.[37] The latest raid came in 2009, with authorities detaining 165 suspected Hizb ut-Tahrir members.[38] Though the exact size and breadth of the group's Turkish branch is not known, documents and maps confiscated during the 2009 raids have exposed the organization's plans to establish a caliphate spanning from Ukraine to Spain in Europe, from Kazakhstan to India in Asia, from Morocco to Gabon and from Egypt to Mozambique in Africa, and from Madagascar to Indonesia in the Indian Ocean.[39] Hizb ut-Tahrir is active in Turkey, despite having been formally banned, and boasts an organizational office in the capital city of Ankara, as well as a dedicated website under the name of *Türkiye Vilayeti*, or Turkish province.[40]

The Islamic State (ISIS)

Until the Turkish government began cracking down on the group, Turkey was an important logistical and financial base for the organization. ISIS's strategy has been to create a division between increasingly fundamentalist Sunnis and others in society by carrying out acts of violence that increase the already-significant tensions along Turkey's sectarian, ethnic, and political fault lines. It moreover seeks to raise the price of Turkey's involvement in the anti-ISIS coalition by staging attacks on foreigners in Turkey as a way of targeting its tourism industry. For example, on January 12, 2016, an ISIS suicide bomber attacked Istanbul's historic Sultanahmet Square, killing 12 people. All of the victims killed were foreign citizens in Istanbul for tourism. In response, the Turkish Army launched tank and artillery strikes on ISIS positions in Syria and Iraq.

ISIS seeks to radicalize the Islamist youth who have become alienated from their communities and encourage them to radical action.[41] The Ankara polling firm Metropoll has found that an overwhelming majority of Turkey's population, 93.6%, do not sympathize with ISIS, but that some 1.3% does.[42] Turkey's population is nearly 79 million, meaning that there are roughly a million potential ISIS recruits in the country.[43] The most fertile recruiting grounds have been the poorest areas in Turkey's Kurdish southeast, where unemployment is roughly six times higher than elsewhere in the country.[44]

The *Dokumacılar* (Weavers) is a branch of ISIS that specifically targets the Kurdish People's Protection Units (YPG) that fought against ISIS during the Syrian Civil War. Estimates of the group's Turkish membership range from 60 to 400.[45] It was linked to both the 2015 Diyarbakır rally bombings that killed 4 people and the 2015 Suruç bombing, which killed 32. The group allegedly participated in the unsuccessful fight against YPG forces during the May-July 2015 offensive by Kurdish People's Protection Units and the Free Syrian Army against the town of Tell Abyad in Syria.[46]

The government's relationship to ISIS militants is the subject of much controversy. Ankara has armed and trained opposition fighters, hosted Syrian dissidents, and backed radical groups like *Ahrar al-Sham*, which works with *Jabhat al-Nusra*, Syria's al-Qaeda franchise.[47] In the past year, Turkey has become far tougher on foreign fighters attempting to travel to Syria via Turkey. But it is unclear how much of the now-extensive radical infrastructure ISIS has implanted in Turkey has been uprooted.[48] Turkey has launched a broad crackdown on militants streaming across its territory. It has deployed undercover surveillance teams at major airports and transit hubs, built new barriers across porous sections of the country's border with Syria, and given its spy service expanded powers to monitor communications between new arrivals in Turkey and suspected Islamic State facilitators waiting to greet them in Syria. It has likewise deepened cooperation with the CIA and other U.S. spy agencies. The CIA and its Turkish counterpart, known as the MIT, operate a supposedly secret coordination center close to the Syrian border.[49]

In March 2016, the *Washington Post* reported that Turkey had deported nearly 3,200 people suspected of foreign-fighter-related activities since the war in Syria began in 2011. 3,000 more people await deportation in "returnee centers". But even these numbers are but a small percentage of the total estimated 35,000 fighters who have traveled to Syria since 2011, with 6,600 of them coming from Western countries. The vast majority of these fighters have entered Syria through Turkey.[50] Cengiz Candar, a Turkish journalist, maintains that Turkey's intelligence service, MIT, helped "midwife" the Islamic State, as well as other *jihadi* groups.[51] Allegations of Turkish collaboration have ranged from military cooperation and weapons transfers to logistical support, financial assistance, and the provision of medical services.[52] It is also alleged that Turkey turned a blind eye to ISIS attacks against Kobani.[53]

CNN Turk has reported that Istanbul neighborhoods such as Duzce and Adapazari have become ISIS gathering spots.[54] Training videos allegedly shot in Turkey have been posted on the Turkish ISIS propaganda website takvahaber.net. CNN Turk further alleges that Turkish security forces could have stopped these developments if they had wanted to.[55]

One reason the Turkish government may have been slow to target ISIS is that most of ISIS's operations in Turkey target political opposition parties and the Kurds. Opposition CHP leader Kemal Kiliçdaroğlu claimed on October 14, 2014 that ISIS offices in Istanbul and Gaziantep were used to recruit fighters.[56] On June 5, 2015, two bombs exploded at an electoral rally in Diyarbakır held by the pro-Kurdish Peoples' Democratic Party (HDP). Four HDP supporters were killed and over 100 were injured as a result. ISIS was suspected, as were the *Dokumacılar*. Subsequently, on October 20, 2015, a massive suicide bombing in Ankara killed 109 people. The government has pointed to ISIS as the responsible party. Evidence has come to light that Ankara's anti-terror department received intelligence of these attacks before the bombings, including the names of the bombers, but did not inform its superiors or the unit responsible for protecting the rally. Furthermore, Ankara police advised its agents to protect themselves against a potential suicide attack during the October 10th rally, but had not organized any measures to protect the rally attendees.[57] The attack had a major impact on Turkish voters, and swung their votes in favor of AKP in the November 1st election.[58]

ISIS has also targeted Turkey's cultural sites. In March 2014, ISIS fighters surrounded the tomb of Suleyman Shah, the grandfather of Osman I, who was the founder of the Ottoman Empire, thus preventing the 38 soldiers guarding it from leaving. The Tomb was located in Syria. In February of 2015, Turkey launched an incursion, complete with hundreds of ground troops, tanks, and drones, to recover Suleyman Shah's remains and rescue the 38 soldiers.[59]

ISIS has attempted to use the threat of terrorism to negotiate with the Turkish government. In September 2013, ISIS threatened Turkey with a series of suicide attacks in Istanbul and Ankara unless Turkey reopened its Syrian border crossings at Bab al-Hawa and Bab al-Salameh. Later, it was revealed that the hostages were exchanged for a ransom and for 180 ISIS militants who had been apprehended or were undergoing medical treatment in Turkey.[60]

Turkey used tanks and artillery to strike ISIS after the January bombing in Istanbul's Sultanahmet Square, and shelled ISIS positions in response to ISIS cross-border shelling.[61] Turkey now permits the United States and other coalition countries to base aircrafts out of the Incirlik and Diyarbakır air bases in southern Turkey for strikes on ISIS.[62]

On August 24, 2016, Turkey launched a military operation in northern Syria, called Operation Euphrates Shield. Ankara claimed that the main objectives of the campaign were to maintain border security, confront ISIS, and deny the Kurdistan Workers' Party (PKK), as well as its Syrian affiliates, a *fait accompli* to create autonomous zones on Turkey's border.

By February 2017, the operation had claimed the lives of 69 Turkish soldiers. The U.S.-led anti-ISIL coalition initially backed the operation, but changed its stance when Ankara decided to push deeper into Al-Bab. Ankara criticized the West for its lack of support, and instead conducted joint air operations with Russia over Al-Bab, with considerable success.[63] Backed by Turkish air, armor and artillery support, Free Syrian Army forces announced the capture of the city, a major stronghold of the Islamic State, on February 24. As of this writing, Turkey played a central role in liberating 770 square miles of territory from the Islamic State.[64]

Charities/Organizations

In their efforts to better organize and expand their reach, Turkish Islamists have expanded their activity from terrorist groups to NGOs. Nearly every *tariqat*, lodge, or brotherhood has formed its own organization, be it charity or business.

The Foundation for Human Rights and Freedoms and Humanitarian Relief (IHH), which organized the May 2010 humanitarian aid flotilla to the Gaza Strip that resulted in a raid by Israeli forces that left nine dead, is not considered a terrorist group by Turkey. The group operates as a humanitarian relief organization and has close ties to Turkey's ruling Justice and Development Party (AKP).[65] Formed to provide aid to Bosnian Muslims in the mid-1990s,[66] it has held "Special Consultative Status" with the United Nations Economic and Social Council since 2004.[67] However, French counterterrorism magistrate Jean-Louis Bruguière has accused the group of helping *mujahedeen* to infiltrate the Balkans in the mid-1990s, and alleges that the IHH is affiliated with al-Qaeda.[68] For its part, the Intelligence and Terrorism Information Center, an Israeli NGO with close ties to the country's military, does not dispute the IHH's legitimate philanthropic activities, but says that the organization is an overt supporter of Hamas and has helped provide weapons and funds for Hamas and other Islamic terrorist groups in the Middle East.[69] IHH continues to undertake broad humanitarian activities in emergency-stricken areas around the globe with an emphasis on those countries with a Muslim population while using these activities as a cover for relations with global jihadist networks.[70] It has been particularly active in Syria.

Another internationally active relief organization is the Kimse Yok Mu association (KYM). Originally founded in 2002, the KYM has since grown into a huge organization operating internationally with the ability to raise large sums of funds, similar to the IHH. Having become heavily involved in the 2004 tsunami in Indonesia, KYM joined Red Crescent (Kızılay), Turkey's state relief organization, and the IHH in aggressively raising funds for Somalia starting in 2010 and 2011.[71] The organization has close ties to the Gülen movement, an Islamist organization that has become a powerful actor within the Turkish state and which is now in an open war with Turkish President Recep Tayyip Erdoğan. KYM seeks to extend influence via charitable activities that complement the activities of the movement's global network of schools and business initiatives undertaken by the Turkish Federation of Businessmen and Industrialists (TUSKON).[72] In the wake of the attempted putsch on July 15, 2016, President Erdogan has been strongly pressing countries around the world to crack down on Gülenist organizations such as Kimse Yok Mu.[73]

Established in 1990, MÜSİAD (the Independent Industrialists and Businessmen's Association) appears to have originally been formed as a more religious counterpoint to the country's predominant business group, the Turkish Industry and Business Association (TUSIAD).[74] The group does not appear to engage in illegal activity, but operates to extend the reach of Islamist capital—what is called *yeşil sermaye* (green money) in Turkey. Green money is basically money from wealthy Islamist businessmen and Middle Eastern countries that, through careful investment, is funneled into legitimate businesses that end up serving as an engine for Islamist parties.[75] MUSIAD and TUSKON differ in the nature of their members, with MUSIAD's members coming from AKP's National Vision arm while those close to Gülen's *cemaat* are organized under TUSKON.[76]

Brotherhoods

One cannot present an accurate picture of Turkey without highlighting the social activities and political influence of Islamist brotherhoods—namely, the *tariqats*, the *cemaats*, the *tekkes*, and their varying extensions. The problem with the brotherhoods does not lie in their political involvement, however corrupt it may be, but rather in the unconditionally submissive tribal nature of the group to a sheik, or a *hoca*, and how the members bow to the wishes of a single gang leader.

While numerous *tariqats* exist, three groups in particular—the *Kadiris*, the *Nakşibendis* and the *Nurcus*—founded the *Milli Nizam Partisi* (National Order Party) in 1970, and then the *Milli Selamet Partisi* (National Salvation Party) a couple of years later. In doing so, they sowed the seeds for the modern political Islamist movement in Turkey. The *Nakşibendis* and the *Nurcus* have increasingly become the dominant forces in Turkey in the last decade, leading to total monopolization of the entire political spectrum after the September 2010 Constitutional Referendum was approved by Turkish voters.[77]

The *Nakşibendis* is the most deeply-rooted tariqat, originating in Central Asia centuries ago, and, in Turkey, is comprised of the *Suleyman, Iskenderpaşa, Erenköy, İsmailağa, Işıkçılar, Menzilci* and *Haznevi* groups (communities and lodges) among others.[78] The *Nakşibendis* have a long track record of supporting conservative parties on the right, including Islamist parties like *Refah* and its modern iteration, the AKP. The *Süleymancıs* have dominated the state-controlled Directorate of Religious Affairs since the 1940s.[79]

The *İsmailağa* lodge has focused on spreading its influence among poor voters,[80] while the *Erenköy* and *Iskenderpaşa* lodges have appealed to middle- to upper-class voters. Numerous Turkish political leaders—including Islamist leader Necmettin Erbakan, prime ministers Turgut Özal and Recep Tayyip Erdoğan—have all been a part of or close to the *Iskenderpaşa* community.[81,82]

The role of the *Süleymancı* was primarily the provision of Quranic education and keeping mosques open after the banning of religious education in 1925. After Quranic courses were again permitted in 1947, students from the movement spread across Turkey. Today, the movement is one of the most broadly organized in Turkey and Europe, especially in Germany where it controls several hundred mosques and Quranic schools. The group is notable in that a large portion of its members never supported the AKP.[83]

While they differ from one another in interpretation, the *Nakşibendi* groups are the foundation upon which Turkish political Islam was built. Their worldview is now the dominant political force in Turkey. The ruling Justice and Development Party (AKP) and the government can accurately be described as a coalition of religious orders.

The *Nur cemaat* emerged sometime in the first quarter of the 20th century (no exact date can be found anywhere, including the movement's own websites) as a Sunni movement based on the teachings of its founder—a Muslim Kurd named Said-i Kurdi (also known as Said-i Nursi), who, in a 1922 letter to Mustafa Kemal Atatürk, demanded that the new republic base itself on Islamic principles.[84] The group was often subjected to pressure by successive Turkish governments until Nursi's death in 1960. Thereafter, the movement has split into different groups, the most active of which is the Fethullah Gülen *cemaat*, which until recently had schools in all regions of Turkey, and still has schools internationally, from Africa to Far East Asia,[85] including the United States. In addition to schools, the movement included the Journalists and Writers Foundation, various businesses including TUSKON, and media outlets such as *Samanyolu TV, Aksiyon Weekly, Zaman,* and its English-language edition, *Today's Zaman* – all of which have now been shut down. According to a detailed 2009 study, the movement seeks to fundamentally transform Turkish society via its extensive network of media, bureaucratic, academic, and economic connections.[86] U.S. government officials have raised concerns over the political agenda of the group as well.[87]

The Gülenists supported the AKP heartily during its first two terms in office, in particular lending critical support to Prime Minister Erdoğan by helping him to imprison their mutual enemies. However, tensions between Erdoğan and the *cemaat* began to surface after the Israeli raid on the Turkish-flagged flotilla in 2010.[88] Those tensions erupted into open hostility on February 7, 2012, when a prosecutor of the "Specially Authorized Judiciary," known to be controlled by the Gülenists, summoned to its office several high-ranking government officials, including the head of national intelligence Hakan Fidan, a trusted Erdoğan advisor, on suspicion of colluding with the Kurdish PKK.[89] Erdoğan perceived the action as an attempt to arrest the Turkish Prime Minister in the same manner the Special Authority Courts had arrested generals of the Turkish Armed Forces.[90] The Special Authority Courts have since been abolished by the Turkish parliament[91] after Erdoğan called them "the state within the state" and said they were going too far.[92] To stop the *cemaat*'s infiltration into the state bureaucracies, the Prime Minister began removing Gülenists from positions in the police, judicial, and education systems.

In May 2013, the allegedly Gülenist governor of Istanbul directed a brutal police response against a small environmental protest in Taksim Park. That incident snowballed into nationwide anti-government protests. Widely known as the Gezi protests, the protests took place in 79 out of 81 provinces in Turkey from May 2013 to late June 2013.[93] Erdoğan's embrace of the exaggerated police brutality can be seen as confirmation of the existence of a chess game between the two forces competing for power, uniting only when confronted by a common adversary, which was the way the protesters were perceived.

Erdoğan next moved to shut down the *dershanes*, schools that serve as the *cemaats*' main recruiting tools. The Gülenists correctly perceived this as an existential threat, and retaliated in a similar manner. On December 17, 2013, prosecutors believed to be associated with the Gülen movement launched a massive corruption probe into government officials, with wiretaps leaked daily that appeared to incriminate the prime minister and everyone around him in malfeasance, skullduggery, and theft. The probe was widely understood to be a form of retaliation by the Gülenists, who are well represented within the police and judiciary.

Erdoğan countered by ferreting out his opponents and stifling journalists, firing or reassigning thousands of police officers, consolidating his control of the judiciary, and shutting down social media sites to plug the leaks. He made it clear that he meant to conduct a full-scale purge of the Gülen movement. This campaign has now kicked into high gear, following the attempted coup attempt of July 2016, which the Turkish government has claimed was carried out in part by a Gülenist faction within the country's military.

Since then, the Turkish government has requested Gülen's extradition from the United States. It has arrested or dismissed thousands of people in the security forces, civil service, and educational institutions suspected of being Gülen followers, as well as banks and other companies said to be associated with Gülen . They have also arrested more than 100 journalists and closed dozens of news media outlets.

Islamism and Society

Turkey's population of nearly 79 million is 99.8 percent Muslim, of whom some 70-85 percent are Sunni, primarily of the *Hanafi* school, although the *Shafi'i* school is also represented. Some 15-25 percent of Turks are Alevis—a heterodox Islamic group with no established doctrine. The remainder include Bektaşi, Câferî, and Alawite Muslims, who comprise about four percent of the population, with the remainder mostly Christians and Jews.[94] During the time of the Ottoman Empire, religious communities were allowed to govern themselves under their own system (*millet*)—*sharia* for Muslims, Canon Law for Christians and *Halakha* for Jews. In the *millet* system, people were defined by their religious affiliations, rather than their ethnic origins. The head of a *millet*—most often a religious hierarch, such as the Greek Orthodox Patriarch of Constantinople—reported directly to the Ottoman Sultan.[95]

After the demise of the Ottoman Empire following the First World War, the Republic of Turkey was founded upon the ideals of modernism and secularism.[96] The founders of the modern republic considered the separation of religion and politics an essential step to adopting Western values and secularism, and as a mandatory condition for its success as a Muslim nation.[97] The new regime therefore abolished the Ottoman sultanate in 1922 and the caliphate in 1924, replacing laws based on *sharia* with European legal codes.[98] Additionally, they switched from the Arabic alphabet to the Latin and from the Islamic calendar to the Gregorian while restricting public attire associated with atavistic Ottoman and religious affiliations (outlawing the fez and discouraging women from wearing the veil).

With the abolition of the caliphate, Islam no longer constituted the basis for the Turkish legal system. However, vestiges remained: despite the abolition of *Şeyhülislam*, the superior authority in the matters of Islam, and the Ministry of Religious Affairs and Pious Foundations,[99] Islam was still preserved as the state religion by the Constitution of 1924.[100] Meanwhile, the Directorate for Religious Affairs, *Diyanet*, was established to oversee the organization and administration of religious affairs. The Unification of Instruction, *Tevhid-i Tedrisat*, brought all educational establishments under the control of the state.[101] Hence, the transformation from a imperial-religious entity to a national entity—from an *ummah* to a modern nation-state—was initiated.

Since the start of multi-party democracy in 1946 and the ensuing victory of the *Demokrat Parti* (the Democratic Party) four years later, the Islamist groups consisting of Sufi brotherhoods—*tariqats*, communities and lodges—and have managed to take advantage of the pandering of political parties in competition for votes. Due to these tactics, brotherhoods have increasingly become powerful players in Turkish politics, often exploiting the deficiencies of the nation's young democratic system. Islamist terrorism has also become a factor since the 1980s, gaining momentum after the 1990s.

The emergence of political Islam in Turkey was connected to the emergence of political Islam elsewhere in the Muslim world, particularly the rise of the Egyptian *Ikhwan al-Muslimeen*, the Muslim Brotherhood. Numerous scholars have noted the influence of key Brotherhood ideologists on former Prime Minister Necmettin Erbakan and the Milli Görüş movement.[102] While the *Ikhwan* is in principle opposed to Sufi orders, this does not appear to apply to the *Naqshbandi-Khalidi* order, which has deep Sunni roots.

In today's Turkey, indigenous Islamist groups imitate the strategies of foreign Islamists. Political sociologists and commentators have long warned of this phenomenon. For example, in a 1999 letter to then-Prime Minister Bulent Ecevit, political scientist Gürbüz Evren warned about the importation of ideas and strategy from the Muslim Brotherhood:

> "The political Islamist segment is currently trying to establish the Egypt-originated "Muslim Brotherhood" model in Turkey. This model aims to create an "alternative society within a society." According to the model, the fundamental needs of the poverty-stricken masses and the low-income segments are designated. Then, hospitals and medi-

cal centers that provide free medical services are established, scholarships are increasingly provided for students, religious educational institutions are disseminated, the number of soup kitchens and charities that hand out clothes and financial aid are increased. On days like wedding days, holidays and child births, people are paid visits to make them feel they are not alone and are given gifts. In short, a society comprised of people who are made to believe that their problems can be solved not by the current order, but via the religion of Islam that embraces them... a society comprised of people who are dressed differently with totally different lifestyles... a society comprised of people who will eventually toil to influence and pressure the rest of the society will be created."[103]

Evren had even warned that a new party based on this model was most likely to be founded out of a cadre of the Islamist *Refah Partisi* (Welfare Party) and *Fazilet Partisi* (Virtue Party). As predicted, the AKP—which contains former members of both *Refah* and *Fazilet*—was founded on August 14, 2001, and went on to win the country's November 2002 parliamentary elections.

Grassroots Islamism in Turkey is also strengthened by the infusion of "green money" from other Middle Eastern states. These vast financial flows, estimated by government officials and Turkish economists at between $6 billion and $12 billion from 2002 to 2005,[104] have given both imported and domestic interpretations of Islamism considerable voice in Turkish society. Moreover, terrorist groups active in Turkey appear to be financed not only through domestic methods (including donations, theft, extortion, and other illicit activity), but also through funds from abroad that contribute to the cost of training and logistics. The amount and origin of such funding is not fully known, but is understood to be substantial. For example, documents recovered in the January 2000 raid against Turkish Hizbullah in Istanbul helped to expose the significant financial and logistical support Iran has provided the group. Since such raids by the security forces often disrupt group activity, foreign support serves as a much-needed lifeline in terms of sanctuary, training, arms, ammunition, food and clothing.[105]

Turkish society in general does not appear as susceptible to radical Islamism as that of other Muslim nations or the Muslim communities in Europe. Traditionally, Turks have tended toward relatively liberal schools of thought in Islam, such as the Hanafi school of jurisprudence, which grants considerable flexibility to the interpretation of religious law. Arab and Kurdish Islam, however, have tended toward the Hanbali and Shafi'i schools of thought, based on the Ashari tradition, which are much stricter.

When surveyed in 2007, 42 percent of Turks reported that they consider themselves unreligious or slightly religious, 37 percent are somewhat religious, and 21 percent identify themselves as very religious or extremely religious (with only 1.6 percent falling into the latter category).[106] Subsequent polls, such as the 2013 Eurobarometer, showed that the number of self-reported atheists had doubled.[107]

However, Islamist groups in the form of "Islamic holdings" have been known to prey on religious communities in Anatolian Turkey and the religious Turkish population in Germany, borrowing directly from lenders without using any financial intermediaries and accumulating large sums of capital.[108] The support for Islamist terror groups by Turkish society, on the other hand, has been negligible and is restricted to the extreme minority.

ISLAMISM AND THE STATE

Since the founding of the Turkish Republic, the Turkish state has made an effort to separate Islam from Islamism. In its attempt to erect a tradition of "state Islam," the government has regulated religious affairs via the *Diyanet* (the Directorate of Religious Affairs established in 1924). The *Diyanet*, directly tied to the office of the Prime Minister, coordinates the building of mosques, trains and appoints *imams*, and determines the topics for weekly Friday sermons by *imams*. Thus, in contrast with other regional states (where governments finance, certify, and supervise mosques but underground radical mosques, Koranic schools, and *imams* successfully compete with government establishments more or less unchecked), state Islam in Turkey has enjoyed a near-monopoly on legitimate expression of the Muslim faith.[109]

Over the years, the formally secular nature of the Turkish state has led to constraints on political participation. Article 2 of the Turkish Constitution, which states, "The Republic of Turkey is a democratic, secular and social state governed by the rule of law,"[110] has served as the basis for the closure of four political parties—the *Millet Partisi* (the Nation Party), *Milli Nizam Partisi*, *Refah Partisi* and *Fazilet Partisi*—each of which was charged with violating the secular nature of the Republic. Twenty-two other parties have been banned for various reasons.[111]

Turkey's transition to a multi-party system and the evolution of Turkish democracy has been marked by friction between the competing pulls of modernization and traditional societal norms. Successful collective political action by tribal leaders, in combination with the appeasement policies of political leaders, has given tribal entities a disproportionate voice in Turkish politics, allowing the more traditional minority to dominate the country's political scene.[112] As a result, even the *Diyanet*, established to control the religious exploitation common in an earlier age, has ended up being dominated by one of the Islamist bodies it was intended to control, namely the Süleymancıs of the Nakşibendi *tariqat*. The outcome has been the further "Sunnization" of Turkey over the years, despite the supposed neutrality of the state toward all religions and their branches.

The U.S. State Department's 2015 Report on International Religious Freedom notes that the Turkish government will not recognize Alevi Muslims' places of worship, despite the High Court of Appeals' ruling that it must, and forces Alevi children to be educated via Sunni Islamic instruction. Furthermore, Turkey persecutes individuals who "openly disrespect" Islamic beliefs. However, many convictions in such cases result in suspended sentences or are overturned.[113] The government funds the construction of Sunni mosques, while restricting other groups' ability to build houses of worship. Furthermore, non-Sunni Muslims face physical violence and threats. Unknown gunmen have fired at Alevi leaders on three separate occasions, and various places of worship have been vandalized.[114]

While the Turkish military has been involved in several interventions (commonly termed as "coups") over the years, only one—the 1997 warning from the country's National Security Council that led to the resignation of Necmettin Erbakan's ruling Islamist coalition—was related to a violation of secularism. Indeed, it was the military coup of 1980 that resulted in the emergence of Islamism as a significant political movement. The left had gained much ground in Turkey; religion was viewed as the natural antidote. Moreover, nationalists had become increasingly radical against the rise of socialist forces. Thus the military espoused a new doctrine of the State, the "Turkish-Islamic Synthesis," the goal of which was to nationalize Islam, Islamize Turkish national identity, and subdue socialist temptations.

The generals who orchestrated the coup sought to use Islam and integrate it into the secular institutions of the Republic. Under the banner of the motto "Mosque, Family, Barracks!" a new era for the Turkish Islamic movements was born. The coup brought with it the expansion of state-run religious services, the introduction of religious education as a compulsory subject in public schools, and the use of the state agency for religious affairs as a tool to promote national solidarity and integration. Sunni Islam became the new source of legitimacy for the Kemalist State.[115]

The behavior of the governing AKP since grabbing 49.9% of the vote in June 2011 has proven political scientist Gürbüz Evren's Muslim Brotherhood model to be valid and exposed new approaches of imposing Islamism on Turkish society. The 2010 Constitutional Referendum weakened the separation of powers that previously existed in the Turkish political system, essentially giving the governing party the power to control all three branches of the government.[116] Nearly all state institutions have been inundated with AKP cadres; any opposition is largely insignificant and has been silenced. In the years since the 2011 elections, not a single resolution out of the 216 attempts by the three opposition parties were accepted, while all 50 of the AKP's resolutions were approved.

The media has long been under threat in Turkey.[117] Turkey leads the world in the number of imprisoned journalists[118] and has dropped from 99th in 2002 to 154th in 2013 (out of 179 nations) in the World Press Freedom Index rankings.[119] With the exception of a few small channels and newspapers, most media outlets support the government. Those who do not abide by the rules may wind up in jail or see their careers ended.[120]

ENDNOTES

[1] Mustafa Akyol, "Islamic State ups rhetoric against Ankara," Al-Monitor, August 11, 2015, http://www.al-monitor.com/pulse/originals/2015/08/turkey-isis-ignores-countrys-islamism.html.

[2] Ceylan Yeginsu, "Turkey Detains 2 ISIS Militants Planning New Year's Even Attack," New York Times, December 30, 2015, https://www.nytimes.com/2015/12/31/world/europe/ankara-turkey-isis-attack.html.

[3] "ISIL fighters 'besieged' in Syria's al-Bab in Aleppo," al Jazeera (Doha), February 6, 2017, http://www.aljazeera.com/news/2017/02/isil-fighters-besieged-syria-al-bab-aleppo-170206172706993.html.

[4] "Al Bab: 'When the tide is turning, ISIL go apocalyptic,'" Al Jazeera (Doha), February 16, 2017, http://www.aljazeera.com/indepth/features/2017/02/al-bab-operation-euphrates-shield-isil-170215103720562.html.

[5] Center for Defense Information, "In the Spotlight: The Great East Islamic Raiders Front (IBDA-C)," October 8, 2004, https://kennisbankterrorisme.nctv.nl/organisatie/islami-bueyuek-dou-akincilar-cephesi-ibda-c.

[6] Yoni Fighel, "Great East Islamic Raiders Front (IBDA-C) – A Profile," International Institute for Counter-Terrorism, January 12, 2003, http://www.ict.org.il/Articles/tabid/66/Articlsid/565/currentpage/19/Default.aspx.

[7] "Turkey Buries Latest Bomb Victims," CNN, November 21, 2003, http://articles.cnn.com/2003-11-21/world/turkey.blast_1_attacks-on-british-interests-bomb-attacks-qaeda?_s=PM:WORLD.

[8] Gareth Jenkins, Political Islam in Turkey: Running West, Heading East? (New York: Palgrave MacMillan, 2008), 203, https://books.google.fr/books?id=kdXGAAAAQBAJ&pg=PA203&lpg=PA203&dq=In+April+2004,++retired+army+colonel++ibda-c&source=bl&ots=ym_w7qSy9x&sig=M2gHGFW0cAvKQ1NFLPm3Bbt_LFk&hl=en&sa=X&redir_esc=y#v=onepage&q=In%20April%202004%2C%20%20retired%20army%20colonel%20%20ibda-c&f=false.

[9] "İstanbul'da IŞİD'cilerden 'iç savaş' toplantısı," Ileri Haber, November 30, 2014, http://ilerihaber.org/istanbulda-isidcilerden-ic-savas-toplantisi/3807/.

[10] Gareth Jenkins, "Back with a Vengeance: Turkish Hezbollah," Jamestown Foundation Terrorism Monitor 6, iss. 2, January 25, 2008, http://www.jamestown.org/programs/gta/single/?tx_ttnews%5Btt_news%5D=4684&tx_ttnews%5BbackPid%5D=167&no_cache=1.

[11] Department of State, "Appendix C: Background Information on Other Terrorist Groups," n.d., http://www.state.gov/documents/organization/31947.pdf.

[12] "Huda-Par's emergence," The Economist, November 23, 2013, http://www.economist.com/news/europe/21590595-islamist-party-turkeys-kurds-huda-pars-emergence.

[13] Jenkins, "Back with a Vengeance."

[14] Department of State, "Appendix C: Background Information on Other Terrorist Groups."

[15] İzgi Güngör, "Release of Turkish Hizbullah members sparks controversy over its future strategy," Hürriyet (Istanbul), January 9, 2010, http://www.hurriyetdailynews.com/n.php?n=release-of-turkish-hizbullah-members-sparks-controversy-over-its-future-strategy-2011-01-09.

[16] Ismail Güney Yılmaz, "Hizbullah: Tebliğ, Cemaat, Cihat," Biamag, April 13, 2013, http://bianet.org/biamag/toplum/145800-hizbullah-teblig-cemaat-cihat.

[17] "Peygamber Sevdalıları Platformu kuruldu," [The Prophet Lovers Platform was Founded] Milli Gazete, April 12, 2009.

[18] "Profile: The Caliph of Cologne," BBC, May 27, 2004, http://news.bbc.co.uk/2/hi/europe/1705886.stm.

[19] "Kaplancılar'ın itirazı kabul edilmedi," [Kaplan Objection was not Accepted] Mynet Haber, November 28, 2002, http://haber.mynet.com/detay/dunya/kaplancilarin-itirazi-kabul-edilmedi/32157.

[20] Hakan Albayrak, "Metin Kaplan Meselesi," Karar, September 16, 2016, http://www.karar.com/yazarlar/hakan-albayrak/metin-kaplan-meselesi-2120#.

[21] "Keleş: Mumcu cinayeti çözüldü," [Keleş: Mumcu's Murder Solved] NTVMSNBC, July 11, 2000, http://arsiv.ntvmsnbc.com/news/16885.asp.

[22] "Ugur Mumcu anılıyor," [Ugur Mumcu Remembered] Hurriyet (Istanbul), January 24, 2002, http://webarsiv.hurriyet.com.tr/2002/01/24/79593.asp.

[23] Emrullah Uslu, "Was Alleged al-Qaeda Attack a Failed Attempt to Occupy the U.S. Consulate in Istanbul?" Jamestown Foundation Terrorism Monitor 5, iss. 27, July 23, 2008, http://www.jamestown.org/programs/gta/single/?tx_ttnews[tt_news]=5073&tx_ttnews[backPid]=246&no_cache=1.

[24] Tolga Tanış, "En az 100 Turk El Kaideci," [More than 100 Turkish al-Qaeda Hands] Hurriyet (Istanbul), October 10, 2010, http://www.hurriyet.com.tr/dunya/16004291.asp.

[25] Karen Hodgson, "The al Qaeda threat in Turkey," Long War Journal, July 8, 2013, http://www.longwarjournal.org/archives/2013/07/the_al_qaeda_threat_1.php.

[26] Ayşegül Usta, "El Kaide'ye 7 muebbet hapis," [7 al-Qaeda get Life in Prison] Hurriyet (Istanbul), February 17, 2007, http://hurarsiv.hurriyet.com.tr/goster/haber.aspx?id=5969387&p=2.

[27] "US blacklists Syrian rebel group al-Nusra," Al Jazeera (Doha), December 11, 2013, http://www.aljazeera.com/news/middleeast/2012/12/2012121117048117723.html.

[28] United Nations High Commission for Refugees, "Regional Overview: Registered Syrian Refugees," September 18, 2016, http://data.unhcr.org/syrianrefugees/regional.php.

[29] Semih İdiz, "Turkey Reconsiders Support For Jabhat Al-Nusra," Al-Monitor, August 13, 2013, http://www.al-monitor.com/pulse/originals/2013/08/turkey-considers-support-for-al-nusra.html.

[30] "Who was behind the Reyhanlı attack?" Deutsche Welle, May 14, 2013, http://www.dw.de/who-was-behind-the-reyhanli-attack/a-16810386.

[31] Matthew Weaver, "Turkey blames Syria over Reyhanli bombings." Guardian (London), May 12, 2013, http://www.theguardian.com/world/2013/may/12/turkey-blames-syria-reyhanli-bombings.

[32] Republic of Turkey, Ministry of Foreign Affairs, "No: 96, 26 March 2014, Press Release Regarding Recent Developments in Latakia / Kesap and Unfounded Allegations in the Press on this Matter," March 26, 2014, http://www.mfa.gov.tr/no_-96_-26-march-2014_-press-release-regarding-recent-developments-in-latakia_kesap-and-unfounded-allegations-in-the-press-on.en.mfa.

[33] Fehim Tastekin. "Fall of Kassab will be costly for Turkey," Al-Monitor, March 31, 2014, http://www.al-monitor.com/pulse/security/2014/03/fall-kassab-syria-costly-turkey.html#ixzz2xwa2cHNs.

[34] Hodgson, "The al Qaeda threat in Turkey."

[35] Fehim Taştekin, "Turkish military says MIT shipped weapons to al-Qaeda," Al Monitor: Turkey Pulse, January 15, 2015, http://www.al-monitor.com/pulse/originals/2015/01/turkey-syria-intelligence-service-shipping-weapons.html#ixzz4NZ2vMCrh.

[36] Alex MacDonald, "Former al-Qaeda affiliate urges Syrian rebels to oppose Turkish invasion," Middle East Eye, September 23, 2016, http://www.middleeasteye.net/news/former-al-qaeda-affiliate-calls-opposition-oppose-turkish-invasion-324667843.

[37] Patrick Wrigley, "Turkey Hems in its Islamist Fringe," Asia Times, August 7, 2009, http://www.atimes.com/atimes/Middle_East/KH07Ak02.html.

[38] "Turkey Detains 165 Suspected Members of Radical Islamist Group Hizb ut-Tahrir," Fox News, July 27, 2009, http://www.foxnews.com/story/0,2933,534927,00.html.

[39] "Hizb-ut Tahrir'in "Hilafet Devletinin toprakları," [Hizb-ut Tahrir's "Caliphate State Lands"] Radikal (Istanbul), July 27, 2009, http://www.radikal.com.tr/Radikal.aspx?aType=RadikalDetayV3&ArticleID=946898&Date=28.07.2009&CategoryID=77.

[40] "Hizb-ut Tahrir Türkiye Vilayeti," n.d., http://turkiyevilayeti.org/html/iltsm/iltsm.html.

[41] Metin Gürcan, "Atatürk Havalimanı saldırısı: IŞİD ne yapmaya çalışıyor?," T24, July 1, 2016, http://t24.com.tr/yazarlar/metin-gurcan/ataturk-havalimani-saldirisi-isid-ne-yapmaya-calisiyor,14930.

[42] Tulin Daloglu "Turks rumored to be joining the Islamic State," Al Monitor: Turkey Pulse, October 1, 2014, http://www.al-monitor.com/pulse/originals/2014/10/turkey-syria-isis-coalition-polls.html#ixzz4NZ5hlEyy

[43] Tülin Daloğlu, "Turks rumored to be joining the Islamic State," Al-Monitor, October 1, 2014, http://www.al-monitor.com/pulse/tr/contents/articles/originals/2014/10/turkey-syria-isis-coalition-polls.html.

[44] Michael Kaplan, "Kurds Joining Islamic State? ISIS Finds Unlikely Supporters Among Turkey's Disgruntled Kurds," International Business Times, July 15, 2015, http://www.ibtimes.com/kurds-joining-islamic-state-isis-finds-unlikely-supporters-among-turkeys-disgruntled-2029924.

[45] Mahmut Bozarslan, "Unraveling Islamic State's Turkish recruitment scheme," Al Monitor: Turkey Pulse, October 23, 2015, http://www.al-monitor.com/pulse/en/originals/2015/10/turkey-syria-isis-adiyaman-suicide-bomber-arsenal.html; "Diyarbakır ve Suruç bombacıları Tel Abyad'da birlikte savaştı'," Radikal, July 22, 2015, http://www.radikal.com.tr/turkiye/diyarbakir-ve-suruc-bombacilari-tel-abyadda-birlikte-savasti-1401886/.

[46] "Diyarbakır ve Suruç bombacıları Tel Abyad'da birlikte savaştı'," Radikal, July 22, 2015, http://www.radikal.com.tr/turkiye/diyarbakir-ve-suruc-bombacilari-tel-abyadda-birlikte-savasti-1401886/.

[47] Michael Weiss, "Syrian Rebels Say Turkey Is Arming And Training Them," Information Clearing House, May 22, 2012, http://www.informationclearinghouse.info/article31399.htm.

[48] Greg Miller and Souad Mekhennet, "Undercover teams, increased surveillance and hardened borders: Turkey cracks down on foreign fighters," Washington Post, March 6, 2016, https://www.washingtonpost.com/world/national-security/undercover-teams-increased-surveillance-and-hardened-borders-turkey-cracks-down-on-foreign-fighters/2016/03/06/baa4ba3a-e219-11e5-8d98-4b3d9215ade1_story.html.

[49] Peter Korzun, "US: Two Military Bases Under Construction in Syria," Strategic Culture Foundation, October 3, 2016, http://www.strategic-culture.org/news/2016/03/10/us-two-military-bases-under-construction-in-syria.html.

[50] Greg Miller and Souad Mekhennet, "Undercover teams, increased surveillance and hardened borders: Turkey cracks down on foreign fighters," Washington Post, March 6, 2016, https://www.washingtonpost.com/world/national-security/undercover-teams-increased-surveillance-and-hardened-borders-turkey-cracks-down-on-foreign-fighters/2016/03/06/baa4ba3a-e219-11e5-8d98-4b3d9215ade1_story.html.

[51] Cengiz Candar, "Will Turkey Midwife Independent Kurdistan?," Al-Monitor, July 14, 2014, http://www.realclearworld.com/2014/07/17/will_turkey_midwife_independent_kurdistan_160143.html.

[52] Anthony Faiola and Souad Mekhennet, "In Turkey, a late crackdown on Islamist fighters," Washington Post, August 12, 2014, https://www.washingtonpost.com/world/how-turkey-became-the-shopping-mall-for-the-islamic-state/2014/08/12/5eff70bf-a38a-4334-9aa9-ae3fc1714c4b_story.html.

[53] David L. Phillips, "ISIS-Turkey Links," Institute for the Study of Human Rights, n.d., http://www.huffingtonpost.com/david-l-phillips/research-paper-isis-turke_b_6128950.html

[54] "İstanbul'da piknik yapıp cihat çağrısında bulundular," CNN Turk, July 29, 2014, http://www.cnnturk.com/video/turkiye/istanbulda-piknik-yapip-cihat-cagrisinda-bulundular.

[55] Ibid.

[56] "Kılıçdaroğlu: 'Davutoğlu belge istiyordun, al sana belge'," Cumhuriyet, October 14, 2014, http://www.cumhuriyet.com.tr/video/video/130347/Kilicdaroglu___Davutoglu_belge_istiyordun__al_sana_belge_.html.

[57] Kadri Gursel, "How Turkish police could have prevented IS massacre in Ankara," Al Monitor: Turkey Pulse, April 18, 2016, http://www.al-monitor.com/pulse/originals/2016/04/turkey-isis-police-can-prevented-ankara-attack.html.

[58] Ibid.

[59] Constanze Letch, "Turkish troops enter Syria to rescue soldiers guarding tomb," Guardian (London), February 22, 2015, https://www.theguardian.com/world/2015/feb/22/turkish-military-completes-operation-to-evacuate-troops-from-tomb-in-syria.

[60] "Turkey swapped 180 IS militants for 49 hostages," Al-Monitor, October 2, 2014, http://www.al-monitor.com/pulse/security/2014/10/turkey-iraq-syria-isis-hostages.html

[61] Tulay Karadeniz and Yesim Dikmen, "Turkish shelling kills 55 Islamic State militants in Syria: military sources," Reuters, May 8, 2016, http://www.reuters.com/article/us-mideast-crisis-syria-turkey-idUSKCN0XZ05R .

[62] Ceylan Yeginsu and Helene Cooper, "U.S. Jets to Use Turkish Bases in War on ISIS," New York Times, July 23, 2015, http://www.nytimes.com/2015/07/24/world/europe/turkey-isis-us-airstrikes-syria.html?_r=1

[63] "Russian and Turkish jets 'bomb ISIL,'" in Syria's Al Bab," Al Jazeera (Doha), January 18, 2017, http://www.aljazeera.com/news/2017/01/russian-turkish-jets-bomb-isil-syria-al-bab-170118130233894.html.

[64] Roy Gutman, "The ISIS Stronghold of Al Bab Falls to Turkish Troops," The Daily Beast, February 23, 2017, http://www.thedailybeast.com/articles/2017/02/23/the-isis-stronghold-of-al-bab-falls-to-turkish-backed-troops.html.

[65] Damien McElroy et al., "Gaza flotilla: Turkey Accused of Behaving like Iran by Israel," Telegraph (London), June 3, 2010, http://www.telegraph.co.uk/news/worldnews/europe/turkey/7801641/Gaza-flotilla-Turkey-accused-of-behaving-like-Iran-by-Israel.html.

[66] "Factbox: Turkish Charity Group Behind Gaza-Bound Convoy," Reuters, May 31, 2010, http://www.reuters.com/article/2010/06/01/us-palestinians-israel-turkey-group-fact-idUSTRE64U4SO20100601.

[67] The list of non-governmental organizations in consultative status with the Economic and Social Council as of September 2009 is available at United Nations Economic and Social Council, E/2009/INF/4, September 1, 2009, http://esango.un.org/paperless/content/E2009INF4.pdf.

[68] "Turkey's Radical Drift," Wall Street Journal, June 3, 2010, http://online.wsj.com/article/SB10001424052748703561604575282423181610814.html.

[69] Alexander Christie-Miller & James Hider, "Turkish Charity that Sent Aid Convoy to Gaza 'has Links to Terrorism,'" Sunday Times (London), June 3, 2010, http://www.timesonline.co.uk/tol/news/world/middle_east/article7142977.ece.

[70] "The Turkish organization IHH provides humanitarian assistance to the famine-stricken regions of Somalia," Meir Amit Intelligence and Terrorism Information Center, May 11, 2011, http://www.terrorism-info.org.il/en/article/17827.

[71] Ismail Einashe, "The Tears of Somalia: Turkey's Moral Foreign Policy," BÜLENT: Journal of Contemporary Turkey, May 7, 2013, http://bulentjournal.com/new-the-tears-of-somalia-turkeys-moral-foreign-policy/

[72] Julia Harte, "Turkey Shocks Africa," World Policy Journal, Winter 2012, http://www.worldpolicy.org/journal/winter2012/turkey-shocks-africa.

[73] Laura Pitel and Jack Farchy, "Turkey's post-coup crackdown moves overseas," Financial Times, August 1, 2016, https://next.ft.com/content/4f8d6d3e-55a3-11e6-befd-2fc0c26b3c60

[74] Eylem Türk, "Ömer Cihad Vardan. Son dönemin yükseleni muhafazakâr dernekler," [The rising conservative associations of the recent era] Milliyet, August 1, 2009, http://www.milliyet.com.tr/Ekonomi/HaberDetay.aspx?aType=HaberDetay&ArticleID=1123854&Date=20.03.2011&Kategori=ekonomi&b=Son%20donemin%20yukseleni%20muhafazak%C3%A2r%20dernekler; TUSIAD US, "Mission Statement," n.d., http://www.tusiad.us/about.cfm?TEMPLATE=1.

[75] Michael Rubin, "Green Money, Islamist Politics in Turkey," Middle East Quarterly, Winter 2005, 13-23, http://www.meforum.org/684/green-money-islamist-politics-in-turkey.

[76] Mustafa Sönmez, "TUSKON'la MUSIAD birbirine girecek (TUSKON and MUSIAD will clash)," Odatv (Istanbul), February 20, 2012, http://www.odatv.com/n.php?n=tuskonla-musiad-birbirine-girecek-2002121200.

[77] "What will the constitutional changes mean for Turkey?" Hurriyet (Istanbul), September 12, 2010, http://www.hurriyetdailynews.com/default.aspx?pageid=438&n=what-the-changes-bring-2010-09-12.

[78] Okan Konuralp, Türkiye'nin tarikat ve cemaat haritası," [Turkey's Religious Order, and Community Map] Hurriyet (Istanbul), September 17, 2006, http://www.hurriyet.com.tr/pazar/5097892.asp?m=1&gid=112&srid=3432&oid=4.

[79] "Süleymancılar: Gizlilik Yemini," [Süleymancılar: A Privacy Oath] Sabah (Istanbul), September 20, 2006, http://arsiv.sabah.com.tr/2006/09/20/cp/gnc113-20060917-102.html.

[80] "Yakın plan tarikat rehberi," [Close-up Sect] Sabah (Istanbul), September 20, 2006, http://arsiv.sabah.com.tr/2006/09/20/cp/gnc111-20060917-102.html.

[81] Timur Soykan, "Naksibendi seyhi oldu," [Naqshibandi Sheikh is Dead] Radikal (Istanbul), February 5, 2001, http://www.radikal.com.tr/2001/02/05/turkiye/01nak.shtml.

[82] Sefa Kaplan, Recep Tayyip Erdoğan: Geleceği Etkileyecek Siyasi Liderler [Recep Tayyip Erdoğan : Anticipating Future Political Leaders] (Istanbul: Doğan Kitap, 2007).

[83] Svante E. Cornell and M. K. Kaya, "The Naqshbandi-Khalidi Order and Political Islam in Turkey," Current Trends in Islamist Ideology, September 3, 2015, http://hudson.org/research/11601-the-naqshbandi-khalidi-order-and-political-islam-in-turkey.

[84] "Said-i Nursi'nin Ataturk'e 88 yillik mektubu," [Said-i Nursi's Ataturk 88-Year Letter] Gazetevatan, January 4, 2011, http://haber.gazetevatan.com/saidi-nursinin-aturke-88-yillik-mektubu/350685/1/Haber.

[85] Okan Konuralp. "Turkiye'nin tarikat ve cemaat haritasi" [Turkey's religious order, and community map] Hurriyet (Istanbul), September 17, 2006, http://www.hurriyet.com.tr/turkiye-nin-tarikat-ve-cemaat-haritasi-5097892.

[86] Rachel Sharon-Krespin, "Fethullah Gülen's Grand Ambition," Middle East Quarterly, Winter 2009, 55-66, http://www.meforum.org/2045/fethullah-gulens-grand-ambition.

[87] "Gülen: Turkey's Invisible Man Casts Long Shadow," Wikileaks, December 4, 2009, http://wikileaks.ch/cable/2009/12/09ANKARA1722.html.

[88] "The Gülenists fight back," The Economist, May 18, 2013, http://www.economist.com/news/europe/21578113-muslim-cleric-america-wields-surprising-political-power-turkey-gulenists-fight-back.

[89] Kadri Gürsel, "Gülenist-AKP clash is now in the open," Al-Monitor, August 16, 2013, http://www.al-monitor.com/pulse/originals/2013/08/turkey-erdogan-akp-gulenism-the-service-power-struggle.html.

[90] Gareth Jenkins, "Ergenekon, Sledgehammer and the Politics of Turkish Justice: Conspiracies and Coincidences," Middle East Review of International Affairs 15, no. 2, June 2011, http://www.gloria-center.org/2011/08/ergenekon-sledgehammer-and-the-politics-of-turkish-justice-conspiracies-and-coincidences/.

[91] "Turkish Parliament abolishes special courts," Hurriyet (Istanbul), June 8, 2012, http://www.hurriyetdailynews.com/turkish-parliament-abolishes-special-courts.aspx?pageID=238&nID=24507&NewsCatID=338.

[92] "Special-authority courts 'going too far,' Turkish PM says," Hurriyet (Istanbul), July 2, 2012, http://www.hurriyetdailynews.com/Default.aspx?pageID=238&nid=22673.

[93] "2.5 million people attended Gezi protests across Turkey: Interior Ministry," Hurriyet (Istanbul), June 23, 2013, http://www.hurriyetdailynews.com/25-million-people-attended-gezi-protests-across-turkey-interior-ministry-.aspx?pageID=238&nid=49292

[94] "Turkey," Central Intelligence Agency World Factbook, May 26, 2011, https://www.cia.gov/library/publications/the-world-factbook/geos/tu.html.

[95] Ilber Ortaylı, "Son İmparatorluk Osmanlı" [The End of the Ottoman Empire] (Istanbul: Timas Yayinlari, 2006), 87–89.

[96] Kemal Karpat, "Modern Turkey," in P.M. Holt et al., eds. The Cambridge History of Islam vol. 1 (Cambridge: Cambridge University Press, 1970), 528; Yael Navaro-Yashin. Faces of the State: Secularism and Public life in Turkey (Princeton: Princeton University Press, 2002).

[97] Stanford J. Shaw and Ezel K. Shaw, History of the Ottoman Empire and Modern Turkey: Reform, Revolution and Republic vol. 2 (Cambridge: Cambridge University Press, 1977), 384.

[98] M. Winter, "The Modernization of Education in Modern Turkey," in Jacob M. Landau, ed., Atatürk and the Modernization of Turkey (Leiden: Brill, 1984), 186.

[99] Karpat, "Modern Turkey," 533-4.

[100] Shaw and Shaw, History of the Ottoman Empire and Modern Turkey, 385.

[101] Republic of Turkey Presidency of Religious Affairs, "The State and Religion in Modern Turkey," n.d., http://www.diyanet.gov.tr/english/weboku.asp?id=795&yid=31&sayfa=10.

[102] Svante E. Cornell, M. K. Kaya, "The Naqshbandi-Khalidi Order and Political Islam in Turkey," The Hudson Institute, September 3, 2015, http://hudson.org/research/11601-the-naqshbandi-khalidi-order-and-political-islam-in-turkey#footNote15.

[103] Author's interview with Gürbüz Evren, Ankara, Turkey, August 2007.

[104] Rubin, "Green Money, Islamist Politics in Turkey," 13-23.

[105] Turkish National Police, " Terör Örgütlerinin Finans Kaynakları," n.d., http://www.egm.gov.tr/temuh/terorizm10_makale5.htm.

[106] "KONDA Research: Religion, Secularism and the Veil in Daily Life Survey September 2007."

[107] Ulaş Dikmen, "Türkiye'deki Ateist Nüfus Hızla Artıyor," Onedio, March 10, 2015, https://onedio.com/haber/turkiye-deki-ateist-nufus-hizla-artiyor-468344.

[108] Gül Berna Özcan & Murat Çokgezen, "Trusted Markets: The Exchanges of Islamic Companies," Comparative Economic Studies (2006), http://pure.rhul.ac.uk/portal/files/778768/Trust%20and%20Islamic%20companies.pdf.

[109] Soner Çağaptay, Düden Yeğenoğlu, and Ekim Alptekin, "Turkey and Europe's Problem with Radical Islam," Washington Institute for Near East Policy PolicyWatch no. 1043, November 2, 2005, http://www.washingtoninstitute.org/templateC05.php?CID=2391.

[110] Constitution of the Republic of Turkey, Article 2, http://www.anayasa.gov.tr/images/loaded/pdf_dosyalari/THE_CONSTITUTION_OF_THE_REPUBLIC_OF_TURKEY.pdf.

[111] "Fazilet, kapatılan 25. Parti," [Virtue, 25th Party Closed] Hurriyet (Istanbul), June 22 2001, http://dosyalar.hurriyet.com.tr/hur/turk/01/06/22/turkiye/85tur.htm.

[112] Mancur Olson, The Logic of Collective Action: Public Goods and the Theory of Groups revised edition (Boston: Harvard University Press, 1971).

[113] United States Department of State, Bureau of Democracy, Human Rights, and Labor, Turkey 2015 International Religious Freedom Report, 2015, http://www.state.gov/j/drl/rls/irf/religiousfreedom/index.htm?year=2015&dlid=256251

[114] Ibid.

[115] See, for example, Banu Eligür, The Mobilization of Political Islam in Turkey (Cambridge: Cambridge University Press, 2014).

[116] Okan Altıparmak, "Is Turkey really a 'vibrant democracy'?" PJ Media, September 30, 2011, http://pjmedia.com/blog/is-turkey-really-a-vibrant-democracy/.

[117] Gareth Jenkins, "A House Divided Against Itself: The Deteriorating State of Media Freedom in Turkey," Central Asia-Caucasus Institute Turkey Analyst 5, no. 3, February 6, 2012, http://www.silkroadstudies.org/new/inside/turkey/2012/120206A.html.

[118] Christophe Deloire and Joel Simon, "Turkey leads the world in jailing journalists," Twin Cities, May 20, 2013, http://www.twincities.com/ci_23268700/deloire-simon-turkey-leads-world-jailing-journalists.

[119] "Turkey falls to 154th in World Press Freedom Index," France24, July 25, 2013, http://www.france24.com/en/20130725-turkey-hurriyet-world-press-freedom-index-media-rsf-reporters-borders.

[120] Oray Egin, "A Turkish press gag: How Erdoğan is suffocating journalists," Vocativ, August 19, 2013, http://www.vocativ.com/08-2013/a-turkish-press-gag-how-Erdoğan -is-suffocating-journalists/

TURKMENISTAN

QUICK FACTS

Population: 5,291,317 (July 2016 est.)

Area: 488,100 sq km

Ethnic Groups: Turkmen 85%, Uzbek 5%, Russian 4%, other 6%

Religions: Muslim 89%, Eastern Orthodox 9%, unknown 2%

Government Type: presidential republic; highly authoritarian

GDP (official exchange rate): $36.57 billion (2015 est.)

Map and Quick Facts courtesy of the CIA World Factbook (January 2017)

OVERVIEW

Over a period of centuries, Islam in Turkmenistan has become an unusual blend of Sufi mysticism, orthodox (Sunni) Islam, and shamanistic Zoroastrian practices. The cult of ancestors is still observed, and reverence for members of the four holy tribes (the owlat) *is still strong. Popular or "folk" Islam is centered around practices and beliefs related to Sufism, the mystical dimension of Islam that originated in Central Asia. The veneration of holy places, which are generally tombs connected with Sufi saints, mythical personages, or tribal ancestors, continues to play an active role in the preservation of religious feeling among the population.*

The pervasive nature of folk Islam, together with the Soviet-era repression of religion and the authoritarian nature of the country's political system, have acted as barriers to the growth of Islamist ideology in Turkmenistan. Thus, the leadership has sought to capitalize on the popularity of Sufism in order to encourage religious beliefs to conform to local popular practices, effectively combating the emergence of Islamism. As in other parts of Central Asia, the distinction between religious and "national" rituals is blurred in Turkmenistan. Since the perestroika period of the late 1980s, the leadership has attempted to co-opt Islam as a fundamental component of its overarching nation-building campaign.

ISLAMIST ACTIVITY

In much of Central Asia, the broad process of re-Islamization that took place in the late 1980s and early 1990s was accompanied by the emergence of political movements that espoused a greater adherence to Islamic tenets. In Turkmenistan, however, there has been no movement to introduce elements of *sharia* or to establish parties based on Islamic principles. The vast majority of the population appears to prefer to disassociate religion from politics altogether, and would be unlikely to lend support to any attempt to replace secular with religious rule, especially if it were to involve a political struggle.

Perhaps more than any other factor, the desire to perpetuate religious beliefs and practices that are widely regarded as "national" traditions in Turkmenistan has disempowered Islamism—an ideology calling for change—as a potent force for social mobilization. Turkmen generally view Islam as a crucial part of national culture, encompassing a set of local customs that sets them apart from outsiders. As such, Islam has a significant secular component that has made it relatively immune to politicization and the penetration of Islamist ideologies. "Folk" Islam (*Islam-i halq*) rather than orthodox Islam *(Islam-i kitab)* is dominant, and is primarily concerned with the celebration of life cycle rituals, the observation of the principle of sacrifice, and the preservation of mystical beliefs. The practice of shrine pilgrimage *(ziyarat)* is at the heart of Islam in Turkmenistan.

To be sure, some of the most widespread practices among Turkmen believers are considered heretical by purist Muslims, such as warding off the evil eye through the use of plants and amulets or performing pilgrimages to the graves of local Sufi saints. As Central Asia expert Ahmed Rashid points out, fundamentalists have criticized Sufi followers to little avail for diverging from the commands of the Koran and tolerating non-Islamic influences.[1] The inherent tension between folk Islam and an Islamist ideology that calls for greater orthodoxy has served to stymie any potential popular support for the latter.

Despite the apparent dearth of Islamist activity, the closed nature of polity and society in Turkmenistan has made it difficult to definitively ascertain the presence or absence of Islamist groups, and has also given rise to speculation that Islamist activity may in fact exist within the former Soviet republic. For example, official reports on an unexpectedly fierce two-day battle that broke out in a northern suburb of Ashgabat in September 2008 provided little information, prompting Russian media and some Western wire services to make unconfirmed assertions that the violence was instigated by Islamist extremists.[2] Similarly, despite reports that the Islamist group *Hizb-*

ut-Tahrir has won converts in Turkmenistan's labor camps and prisons, a significant presence in the country has yet to be established.[3] No other Islamist group is known to have a presence in Turkmenistan, and no terrorist attacks tied to Islamist groups have been reported on Turkmenistani soil since independence.[4] In addition, there has been no noticeable penetration of the Islamic State into the country. This is at least partly due to Turkmenistan's geographic and political isolation, as well as its form of Islam, which is mild even by Central Asian standards.[5]

ISLAMISM AND SOCIETY

In addition to the popular nature of Sufism, the cultural changes that the Soviet Union forced upon the Turkmen population provides a second explanation for the limited appeal of Islamist groups. Some analysts have argued that the Soviet legacy is the key factor hindering the present-day development of Islam and Islamism in Central Asia, given that the region was isolated from the rest of the Muslim world—including its intellectual centers—for more than seventy years.[6] During Soviet rule, Islam in particular was rejected as contrary to modernization, with the consequence that all but a handful of mosques were either closed or turned into museums of atheism. The clergy was persecuted and religious literature was destroyed, all Islamic courts of law, *waqf* holdings (Muslim religious endowments that formed the basis of clerical economic power) and Muslim primary and secondary schools were liquidated. Local shrines acted as the real centers of religious life in the absence of functioning mosques during the Soviet period, thereby ensuring that they have remained an important part of worship in Turkmenistan.

However, while it is undeniable that the aggressive anti-religious campaign launched by the Soviet authorities placed even greater distance between Central Asian Islam and the Islam practiced in "mainstream" Muslim countries in the Middle East, South and Southeast Asia and Africa, Islamic doctrine had never firmly taken root in Turkmenistan as it had in other Muslim areas, including the older, sedentary territories of Central Asia. Well before the Bolshevik Revolution, the Turkmen, like other nomadic peoples, preferred to pray in private rather than visit a mosque.[7] A mobile lifestyle necessarily favored a non-scriptural, popular version of Islam while naturally curtailing the presence of professional clergy. As the expert Adrienne Edgar has noted, any man who could read and recite prayers was given the title of *mullah*, or cleric.[8] Particularly in the nomadic regions, teachers of Sufi orders, or *ishans,* played a more influential role than the *ulema* (Muslim scholars). The independent Turkmen tribes lacked Muslim *kadis* who judged in accordance with Islamic law, with the result that sharia only held sway in the sphere of family law, and was implemented by *mullahs* at birth, circumcision, marriage and funeral ceremonies.[9]

In the twenty-first century, Turkmens continue to be governed less by Islamic law than by tribal customary law, or *adat*, which has been passed down for many centuries. As the majority of Turkmens do not practice their religion in a formal or institutional way, mosques remain conspicuously empty, including one of Central Asia's largest and grandest mosques, the Turkmenbashi Ruhy Mosque in former President Niyazov's hometown of Gypjak, which, despite its capacity to hold 10,000 worshippers, is sparsely attended.[10]

ISLAMISM AND THE STATE

The strict state control of religion is a third, albeit less important, reason why Islamism has thus far failed to attract a significant following in Turkmenistan. Were Islamist groups to appear in Turkmenistan, state security forces would most certainly act swiftly and firmly to repress any and all manifestations of their activities.

In order to prevent the emergence of Islam as a locus of oppositional activity, the Turkmen leadership has acted to thoroughly co-opt the official religious establishment. Beginning in the late 1980s, Saparmurat Niyazov, who was first secretary of the Communist Party of the Turkmen SSR from 1985-1991 and then Turkmenistan's first president from 1991 until his death in 2006, sanctioned the revival of Muslim practices while simultaneously striving to keep religion within official structures. Thus, Niyazov endorsed the construction of mosques, the teaching of basic Islamic principles in state schools, the refurbishment of holy places and the restoration of Islamic holidays. Whereas in 1987 there were only four functioning mosques in the Turkmen SSR, by 1992 that number had risen to eighty-three, with another sixty-four mosques under construction.[11] By 2016, Turkmenistan had more than 400 registered mosques, although it is unclear how many Muslims make use of them.[12] In 1991, Turkmenistan's first *madrassah* (Islamic seminary) was founded in Dashhowuz to help alleviate the country's acute shortage of trained religious clergy. Shrine pilgrimage was acknowledged by Niyazov as a fundamental component of Turkmen identity and even as an expression of patriotism. Seeking to improve their Islamic credentials, both Niyazov and his successor, Gurbanguly Berdimuhammedov, have made pilgrimages to Mecca and Medina.

While the Turkmen government did promote Islam in particular ways, it promoted a very controlled version of Islam. The state banned religious political parties and required that religious communities register with the government. In 1994, the government created the *Gengesh*, (Council for Religious Affairs, and currently replaced with the Committee for Work with Religious Organizations).[13] All senior Muslim clergy belong to the *Gengesh*, of which the chief *mufti*, appointed by the president, is also the deputy chair.[14] The *Gengesh* controls the hiring and firing of all clergy in Turkmenistan,[15] thereby allowing the state to exert control on religious matters down to the village level.[16] In 1997, the government cracked down on Islamic activity and began closing down mosques throughout the nation. This move virtually incapacitated all institutions of Islamic learning in Turkmenistan.[17]

These restrictions endure to this day. Congregations that are not registered are prohibited from gathering publicly and disseminating religious materials, with violators subject to penalties under the country's administrative code. The Dashowuz *madrassah* was closed in 2001, and in 2005 cutbacks were made at the Faculty of Muslim Theology at Magtymguly Turkmen State University, which remained the only official institution for training *imams*. Regular reshuffling of Muslim leaders by the state also keeps clergy in check; from 2003 to 2016, Turkmenistan went through five chief *muftis*, with other Muslim leaders being rotated at a similar rate.[18]

To an even greater degree than other Central Asian Muslims, Turkmens have been unable to travel and receive an education in *madrassahs* abroad. The government has aimed to restrict the population's contact with fellow believers abroad by limiting the number of Turkmen Muslims—including secret police and state officials—performing the *hajj* to Mecca each year to 650 pilgrims, which represents less than a seventh of the quota allocated by the Saudi authorities.[19] As of 2016, the number of Turkmen allowed to perform the Hajj had decreased to 188, due to fears of radicalization.[20]

As in other Central Asian states, Turkmenistan's authorities have sought to limit unwanted Islamist trends by promoting a vision of Islam that is concerned with the preservation of tradition. In similar fashion to neighboring Uzbekistan, the national leadership has attempted to capitalize on the popularity of Sufism in order to encourage religion to conform to local popular practices as well as to combat the emergence of Islamism. So long as orthodox Islamic doctrine rejects and condemns some Sufist practices, such as the veneration of local saints and local shrine pilgrimages[21] as idolatrous, it is held that the promotion of Sufism will serve to dampen any inclination among Turkmen believers to support the more purist—and potentially Islamist—forms of ideology.[22]

Consequently, the leadership of Turkmenistan has taken some steps to foster the Sufi tradition and incorporate it into the regime's larger nation-building project. Thus, the Niyazov leadership provided the mosque and mausoleum complex of the twelfth-century Sufi scholar, Hoja Yusup Hamadani, with a modern-day reconstruction. Located in the Mary *oblast*, this holy site is one of the most important places of shrine pilgrimage in Turkmenistan, even remaining open during the Soviet period, albeit under strict control. Likewise, rather than seeking to prohibit local pilgrimages to sacred places, both the Niyazov and Berdimuhammedov governments have encouraged it, even providing free accommodation for pilgrims in some instances.[23] In 2009, citing fears concerning the spread of swine flu, Turkmen authorities barred aspiring Muslim pilgrims from making the *hajj* to Saudi Arabia altogether, urging them instead to sojourn to 38 sacred sites across the country, although most of the sites had historical or cultural rather than religious significance.[24] As of 2016, the government of Turkmenistan has shown no signs of easing pressure on Muslims, with censorship, educational, and legal restrictions remaining tightly in place.

Under Niyazov, the state-sponsored form of Islam in Turkmenistan underwent an unusual twist when the president made his extensive cult of personality a centerpiece of religious practice by configuring himself as a prophet with his own sacred book, the *Ruhnama* (Book of the Soul). Niyazov regularly urged his country's citizens to study and memorize passages from the *Ruhnama*, making it required reading for university entrance and for work in the public sector, which remained the country's top employer. *Imams* were obliged to display the *Ruhnama* inside mosques and to quote from it in sermons, or face possible removal or even arrest. In direct violation of *sharia*, Niyazov even ordered that passages from the *Ruhnama* be inscribed alongside passages from the Koran on the walls of the cathedral mosque in Gypjak; an inscription above the main arch reads: "*Ruhnama* is a holy book, the Koran is Allah's book."

In 2003, the country's long-serving senior Muslim cleric and deputy chairman of the *Gengesh*, Nasrullah ibn Ibadullah, was replaced for expressing dissent by repeatedly objecting to the *de facto* status of the *Ruhnama* as a sacred book on a par with the Koran, and to its extensive use in mosques. In 2004, he was sentenced to 22 years in prison on treason charges, but was granted amnesty in August 2007.[25] Upon his release, Ibadullah thanked the president and accepted a post as an adviser at the president's State Council for Religious Affairs, thus remaining under the close supervision of administration officials. Since coming to power in 2007, President Gurbanguly Berdimuhammedov has gradually phased out the cult of Niyazov's quasi-spiritual guidebook for the nation.[26]

Under the new president, the state's presence is still pervasive at all levels of religious institutions. *Imams* are still selected by the government via the Commission for Work with Religious Organizations (the successor organ to the *Gengesh*)[27] and the security service. While *imams* are no longer required to recite an oath of allegiance to the president during sermons, they are still required to pray for him.[28] The government provides "recommendations" for sermon content, as well—sermons are expected to convey a state message. This, apparently, has riled some Turkmenistani Muslims, who resent government intrusion into their religious lives.[29]

It is difficult to speculate about the effects of government policy on the religious beliefs of Muslims in Turkmenistan, although much empirical research shows that repression of religious groups generally leads to increased radicalism.[30] Therefore, one would expect to see some mobilization of a religious opposition, and indeed, there is some anecdotal evidence of this. Some unconfirmed reports from Turkmenistani refugees have claimed that there are underground mosques that preach anti-government sermons.[31] In addition, approximately 360 Turkmen Islamists have turned up in Syria, where they have been fighting the Assad government.[32] A former security official from Turkmenistan blames this development on the harsh repression of Turkmenistan's religious groups and the ineptitude of the secret police.[33] Turkmenistan could also prove vulnerable to radical religious teaching due to theological ignorance among its citizens and clergy, ignorance which could facilitate the spread of extremist doctrines. The government has increasingly installed *imams* lacking in religious education; in fact, many viewed Nasrullah ibn Ibadullah as the last official with a proper religious education. Average citizens are rarely exposed to Islamic teaching, and while most households have a copy of the Koran, it is usually in Arabic, which few Turkmen citizens read. Turkmen-language Korans are rare.[34]

As the United States and its allies continue to draw down their forces in Afghanistan, concerns remain that instability from Afghanistan could spread to Central Asia—concerns which are now compounded by the nearly 400 Turkmen fighting in Syria. About a quarter million Turkmen live across the border in Afghanistan, providing a potential pool of recruits for extremist groups. In 2014, reports surfaced that Turkmen border guards had been killed in skirmishes with Taliban fighters.[35] However, there is as yet little evidence that the conflicts in Afghanistan and Syria threaten stability in Turkmenistan.

ENDNOTES

[1] Ahmed Rashid, The Resurgence of Central Asia: Islam or Nationalism? (Karachi: Oxford University Press, 1994), 246-247.

[2] Annette Bohr, "Turkmenistan," in Nations in Transit: Democratization from Central Europe to Eurasia 2009 (New York: Freedom House, 2009), 522, http://www.freedomhouse.org/uploads/nit/2009/Turkmenistan-final.pdf. For an excellent, detailed analysis of both the international and domestic media reports on the September clashes, see Vitaliy Ponomarev, Sobytiia v Ashkhabade 10–13 Sentiabria 2000g [Events in Ashkhabad September 10–13, 2008] (Moscow: Memorial Human Rights Center, November 5, 2008).

[3] Cracks in the Marble: Turkmenistan's Failing Dictatorship, International Crisis Group, January 2003, 25, http://www.crisisgroup.org/~/media/Files/asia/central-asia/turkmenistan/044%20Cracks%20in%20the%20Marble%20Turkmenistan%20Failing%20Dictatorship.ashx.

[4] U.S. Department of State, Bureau of Diplomatic Security, Turkmenistan 2012 OSAC Crime and Safety Report, April 2012, https://www.osac.gov/Pages/ContentReportDetails.aspx?cid=12289.

[5] Jacob Zenn, On the Eve of 2014: Islamism in Central Asia (Washington, DC: The Hudson Institute, June 24, 2013), http://www.currenttrends.org/research/detail/on-the-eve-of-2014-islamism-in-central-asia.

[6] Krzysztof Strachota and Maciej Falkowski, Jihad vs. The Great New Game: Paradoxes of Militant Islamic threats In Central Asia (Warsaw: Centre for Eastern Studies, January 2010), 48-49.

[7] Carole Blackwell, Tradition and Society in Turkmenistan: Gender, Oral Culture and Song (Richmond: Curzon Press, 2001), 35.

[8] Adrienne Lynn Edgar, Tribal Nation: The Making Of Soviet Turkmenistan (Princeton: Princeton University Press, 2004), 26.

[9] W. Konig, Die Achal-Teke. Zur Wirtschaft und Gesellschaft einer Turkmenen-Gruppe im XIX Jahrhundert, 74, as cited in Paul Georg Geiss, Pre-Tsarist and Tsarist Central Asia: Communal Commitment and Political Order in Change (London: RoutledgeCurzon, 2003), 38.

[10] "Turkmenbashi Ruhy Mosque, Gypjak village," Advantour, http://www.advantour.com/turkmenistan/ashgabat/turkmenbashi-ruhy-mosque.htm

[11] Alexander Verkhovsky, ed., Islam i politicheskaya bor'ba v stranakh SNG [Islam and political struggle in the ⊠IS (⊠ommonwealth of Independent States)] (Moscow: Panorama, 1992), 27.

[12] BTI, Turkmenistan Country Report 2016, 7, https://www.bti-project.org/fileadmin/files/BTI/Downloads/Reports/2016/pdf/BTI_2016_Turkmenistan.pdf.

[13] Sally Cummings, Oil, Transition, and Security in Central Asia, Routledge, 2010, pg 14-15.

[14] U.S. Commission on International Religious Freedom, Annual Report 2013 (Washington. DC: USCIRF, April 2013), 176, http://www.uscirf.gov/images/2013%20USCIRF%20Annual%20Report%20%282%29.pdf.

[15] Cummings, Oil, Transition, and Security pg 14-15.

[16] S. Demidov, "Religioznie protsessy v postsovetskom Turkmenistane," [Religious protests in post-Soviet Turkmenistan," Tsentral'naia Aziia i Kavkaz no. 5 (2001).

[17] Cummings, Oil, Transition, and Security pg 14-15.

[18] Felix Corley, "Turkmenistan: Government Changes Islamic Leadership Again," Forum 18 News Service, February 25, 2013, http://www.forum18.org/Archive.php?article_id=1805.

[19] Felix Corley, "Turkmenistan: Eleven-Year Wait on Haj Pilgrimage List?," Forum 18 News Service, August 25, 2014, http://forum18.org/archive.php?article_id=1988.

[20] Dzhumaguly Annayev, "188 Turkmens Go on Hajj," Caravanserai, September 6, 2016, http://central.asia-news.com/en_GB/articles/cnmi_ca/newsbriefs/2016/09/06/newsbrief-01

[21] See Maria Elisabeth Louw, Everyday Islam in Post-Soviet Central Asia (London: Routledge, 2007), 50.

[22] However, as some have noted, the relationship between folk Islam, orthodox Islam and Sufism is complex. While some folk customs might contradict the precepts of sharia, Sufi brotherhoods often successfully used the murid organization to spread orthodox Islam. Geiss, Pre-Tsarist and Tsarist Central Asia, 94n3.

[23] Cracks in the Marble, 25.

[24] Felix Corley, "Turkmenistan: Exit Bans, Haj Ban, Visa Denials Part Of State Religious Isolation Policy," Forum 18 News Service, February 2010, http://www.forum18.org/Archive.php?article_id=1403; Bruce Pannier, "Turkmen Pilgrims Make A Homegrown Hajj," Radio Free Europe/Radio Liberty, November 25, 2009, http://www.rferl.org/content/Turkmen_Pilgrims_Make_A-Homegrown_Hajj/1887880.html.

[25] Gulnoza Saidazimova, "Turkmenistan: President Announces Amnesty, Excluding Political Prisoners," RFE/RL, February 14, 2008, http://www.rferl.org/a/1079475.html

[26] Bohr, "Turkmenistan," in Nations in Transit: Democratization from Central Europe to Eurasia 2010, 544.

[27] Felix Corley, "Turkmenistan: Children's Summer Camp Warning, Fines, New Religion Law, "No Religion" in Army," Forum 18 News Service, April 2016, http://www.forum18.org/archive.php?article_id=2169

[28] USCIRF, Annual Report 2013, 174.

[29] Felix Corley, "Turkmenistan: Religious Freedom Survey, March 2012," Forum 18 News Service, March 2012, http://forum18.org/Archive.php?article_id=1676.

[30] See, for example, Monica Duffy Toft, Daniel Philpott, and Timothy Samuel Shah, God's Century: Resurgent Religion and Global Politics (W. W. Norton & Company, 2011); Brian J. Grim and Roger Finke, The Price of Freedom Denied: Religious Persecution and Conflict in the Twenty-First Century (Cambridge University Press, 2010). For an example specific to Central Asia, see Sebastien Peyrouse, "Islam in Central Asia: National Specificities and Postsoviet Globalisation," Religion, State and Society 35, no. 3 (2007), 149.

[31] Alexey Malashenko, "Turkmenistan: Has There Been a Thaw?" Carnegie Endowment for International Peace, September 2012, 6, http://carnegie.ru/publications/?fa=49681.

[32] Uran Botobekov, "ISIS in Central Asia: A Shifting Recruiting Strategy." The Diplomat, May 17, 2016, http://thediplomat.com/2016/05/isis-and-central-asia-a-shifting-recruiting-strategy/.

[33] Paul Goble, "Turkmenistan's Authoritarianism Leading to Rise of Islamist Radicalism, Former Security Officer Says," Window on Eurasia, June 30, 2013, http://windowoneurasia2.blogspot.com/2013/06/window-on-eurasia-turkmenistans.html.

[34] USCIRF, Annual Report 2013, 176-78.

[35] "Three Turkmen Border Guards Killed on Northern Afghan Border," RFE/RL, May 27, 2014, http://www.rferl.org/a/three-turkmen-border-guards-killed-on-northern-afghan-border/25400305.html

Uzbekistan

> **Quick Facts**
>
> Population: 29,473,614 (July 2016 est.)
>
> Area: 447,400 sq km
>
> Ethnic Groups: Uzbek 80%, Russian 5.5% Tajik 5%, Kazakh 3%, Karakalpak 2.5%, Tatar 1.5%, other 2.5% (1996 est.)
>
> Religions: Muslim 88% (mostly Sunni), Eastern Orthodox 9%, other 3%
>
> Government Type: Presidential Republic; highly authoritarian
>
> GDP (official exchange rate): $66.8 billion (2015 est.)
>
> *Map and Quick Facts courtesy of the CIA World Factbook (January 2017)*

Overview

Uzbekistan's struggles with Islamist groups predate the formation of the country, as several Islamist groups were active in the former Soviet state before the collapse of the USSR. Uzbek militant groups hold sway and significant throughout the wider theater of Central Asia, most notably the Islamic Movement of Uzbekistan (IMU). Prior to his death in 2016,[1] President Islam Karimov attempted to control Islamists in Uzbekistan, with varying degrees of success. Karimov was succeeded by former Prime Minister Shavkat Mirziyoyev,[2] and he may well continue in Karimov's efforts. Central Asia in general, and Uzbekistan in particular, has been a prominent source of foreign fighters traveling to Iraq and Syria to join the Islamic State and other jihadi groups, despite the Uzbek government's attempts to stem the flow.

Islamist Activity

For most of the quarter-century since it declared independence from the USSR, Uzbekistan has been an active arena for a range of Islamist groups. These groups vary in their ideologies, objectives and methods. All, however, share the broad goal of transforming Uzbekistan from its current status as a secular authoritarian regime into a state based upon, and governed by, *sharia* law.

Islamic Movement of Uzbekistan (IMU)

The Islamic Movement of Uzbekistan (IMU) is one of the most important militant groups in Central Asia. The IMU grew out of an amalgam of Islamist groups that were active in the 1990s, most notably the *Adolat* (Justice) group, which was formed by Tahir Yuldashev and Jumabai Hodgiev (aka Juma Namangani). *Adolat* (Justice), formed in 1991, had the aim of building an Islamic state in Uzbekistan.[3] On December 8, 1991, *Adolat* organized an unauthorized rally an captured the office building of the Namangan regional committee of the Communist Party of Uzbekistan, subsequently levying an ultimatum to Uzbek authorities and demanding President Islam Karimov swear on the Koran and proclaim the establishment of an Islamic state.[4] The resulting government clampdown led to thousands of arrests, prompting an exodus of Islamic radicals from Uzbekistan to Tajikistan.[5] In 1992, former Uzbek president Islam Karimov banned Adolat, and Yuldashev and Hodgiev fled to Tajikistan.[6]

About two thousand Uzbeks are estimated to have left the country during the 1990s, with many of them subsequently taking part in Tajikistan's civil war on the side of the United Tajik Opposition (UTO).[7] In Tajikistan the Namangan Battalion (NB) was formed (named after the majority of the group's members, which hailed from the city of Namangan in the Fergana Valley) in 1992. Jumabai Hodgiev became the commander of this militia, which established a network of military bases and training camps for the IMU in northern Tajikistan, mostly in the Jirgatal and Garm regions. The Namangan Battalion was well-armed and developed a special system of training, focusing on guerrilla warfare, sabotage and terrorist activities. Uzbek instructors as well as instructors from Islamic organizations in Afghanistan, Pakistan, Kashmir, and some Middle East countries worked at NB's Tajik bases. Many of them collaborated with foreign intelligence services, most prominently the Pakistani ISI.[8]

During the 1990s, Yuldashev and others traveled to Afghanistan, where they made contact with alumni of the Afghan *jihad* and established training camps for Uzbek militants.[9] These contacts created an avenue for radicalization, and the following years saw a number of Uzbek militants pass through Afghan training camps before returning to Uzbekistan to destabilize the country. Yuldashev and Hodgiev officially formed the IMU by 1998.[10] Following the formation of the IMU, Tahir Yuldashev became its political leader, or *emir*, while Jumabai Hodgiev became the head of its military wing and Zubair ibn Abdurahman (Abdul Rahim) became the head of its press center and an assistant to Yuldashev. The organization's headquarters were established in Peshawar, Pakistan, but later relocated to Kabul, Afghanistan.

NB militants trained in the IMU camps in Tajikistan and abroad, mostly in Afghanistan and Pakistan. These camps formally belonged to Islamist organizations such as al-Qaeda, *Harkat-ul-Ansar, Hezb-e-Islami, Harkat-ul-Mujahideen Tablighi Jamaat*, the Taliban and others. However, in most cases, instructors were Uzbek Islamists affiliated with the Bin Laden network, as well as specialists from Pakistan's ISI.[11] In total, during the 1990s more than a thousand militants of the Islamic Movement of Uzbekistan received military training in training camps in these two countries.[12]

Notably, creating a militia between 500 to several thousand fighters, especially including all the necessary support, clothes, equipment, and arms, poses a significant financial challenge. Accordingly, analysts presume that significant foreign funding aided in the effort.[13] Thereafter, the IMU financed its activities in Central Asia, as well as in other regions, primarily through the support of international Islamist organizations and donations from wealthy members of the Uzbek diaspora in Afghanistan, Turkey and Saudi Arabia. Beginning in the mid-1990s, Uzbek Islamist opposition leaders bolstered this aid with active fundraising activities, with the aim of generating support for a powerful military-political structure.

In 1999, the IMU commenced an organized insurgent campaign against the Uzbek state.[14] Its strategy was not to conduct large-scale violence against Uzbekistan and Kyrgyzstan, but to seize power through terrorism, sabotage, and banditry, all meant to destabilize the country. Its armed incursions in the region continued until U.S. counterterrorist operations in Afghanistan in 2001 weakened the Taliban and al-Qaeda. The IMU also suffered heavy losses in that campaign, including the death of its leader Jumabai Hodgiev near Mazar i-Sharif in November 2001.

The IMU survived by rebranding itself the *Hizb Islami Turkestan*, or the Islamic Party of Turkestan. This organization, which was led by Tahir Yuldashev, maintains the same outlook and ambitions as its precursor. Estimates of its strength vary; according to Pakistani officials, Yuldashev could command as many as 4,800 Uzbek militants, as well as "groups of Chechens, the Libyan Islamic Fighting Group, [and] Uighur militants of the East Turkestan Islamic Movement."[15] The organization is currently believed to be most active in Afghanistan and parts of Pakistan. Yuldashev himself was reportedly killed in August 2009 in South Waziristan as a result of a U.S. Predator drone strike.[16] His death appears to have resulted in a downturn of the group's militant activities, with the last large-scale attack by the IMU being the September 19 2010 ambush on a convoy of government troops in the valley Kamarob of Tajikistan that killed 25 Tajik troops.[17]

Nevertheless, elements of the IMU have remained active, particularly in Afghanistan, where the group remains an ally of both the Taliban and al-Qaeda. In 2012, the International Security Assistance Force and the Afghan armed forces conducted 26 raids against the IMU in eight Afghan provinces—Badakhshan, Baghlan, Faryab, Logar, Helmand. Kunduz, Takhar and Wardak—with eight of them occurring in Kunduz province alone.[18]

However, on July 31, Abu Talut, self-described as a former member of the Taliban, announced that the IMU had broken away from the Taliban and announced that the Islamic Movement Uzbekistan had pledged allegiance to the Islamic State. Within a week, on August 6, 2015, the IMU made their change of affiliation official, releasing a video depicting IMU leader Uthman Ghazi and his fighters pledging allegiance to IS.[19] The IMU statement declared that the Taliban "cannot be trusted," and accused the Afghan militant group of collaboration with Pakistan's spy agency, the Directorate for Inter-Services Intelligence (ISI).[20]

The IMU's August pledge to the Islamic State placed the organization in the center of conflict with Taliban. In December 2015 pro-Taliban Sabiq Jihadmal declared the death of Ghazi in a Twitter message that claimed to show Ghazi's corpse. "On the following day, a pro-IMU fighter gave an account of the group's downfall and elimination. In a message posted on Twitter on December 10, 2015, the jihadist, Tahir Jan claimed that the Taliban and Afghan government entered into an agreement in Zabul to destroy the remainder of the IMU. The Taliban's forces quickly laid siege to the Uzbek's bases, slaughtering hundreds of IMU partisans. Although Ghazi was able to escape, his hiding place was quickly discovered and he was captured.

Jan described the consequences of forsaking the Taliban:

> The former Islamic Movement of Uzbekistan has almost been completely destroyed unfortunately, and maybe less than 10% of those who were in the fronts or on other assignments remain after the events of Zabul.[21]

Not all of these militants are driven by ideology; many of them are known to join foreign *jihads* in order to earn money.[22] According to various estimates, approximately 500 to 3,000 citizens of Uzbekistan are currently fighting in the ranks of the various *jihadist* groups all over the world, with many mobilized through social media.[23]

Akramiyya

The founder of *Akramiyya*, Akram Yuldashev, was born in 1963 in Andijan, Uzbekistan.[24] A teacher by profession, his 1992 treatise "Lymonga Yul" emphasizes that the ultimate goal of his organization is the assumption of power and the creation of an Islamic state.[25] Members of *Akramiyya* called themselves *birodarami*, or brothers, but the people of Central Asia know them as *akramists*. There are now said to be tens of thousands of such "brothers."[26] The organization first appeared in the Ferghana Valley in 1998, where—motivated by the ideology of *Hizb ut-Tahrir*—it espoused a selective reading of the Koran, arguing in favor of *sharia* as the answer to the modern, "unfavorable" period for Muslims in Central Asia. Yuldashev is said to have structured the activities of his group in five phases, beginning with the indoctrination of new members, extending to the accumulation of wealth for charitable Islamic works, and concluding with the gradual, "natural transition" to Islamic rule in Uzbek society.[27]

Ideologically, *Akramiyya* is an outgrowth of the *Ahl al-Quran* movement which existed in the 1940s in Uzbekistan. Members of this movement categorically refused to recognize the teachings of other Sunni schools (*mazh'hab*). They adhered to very austere views, rejected the "Soviet way of life" and did not recognize official clergy. Members of *Akramiyya* believe only in Allah, and do not worship the Prophet Mohammed; they also do not recognize any nation in the world. They ignore state laws, renounce their parents, and subject themselves exclusively to the direction of the group's leaders.[28] Most *Akramiyya* members are of Uzbek nationality. Its members are mostly businessmen with small agricultural enterprises, funds and industrial warehouses. The organization is known to control dozens of commercial firms, which do business under a unified leadership.

Authorities in Tashkent have been targeting *Akramiyya* for some time. Yuldashev was sentenced in the spring of 1998 to two-and-a-half years in prison for violating Article 276 (drug possession) of the Uzbek Criminal Code.[29] In late December of the same year, he received amnesty, only to be arrested again the day after a bombing in Tashkent in February 1999. In May 1999, Yuldashev was sentenced to 17 years in prison under several articles of the Uzbek Criminal Code: 155 (terrorism), 156 (incitement of religious hatred), 159 (encroachment on constitutional system), 161 (sabotage), 216 (unlawful association), 216-1 (luring into an illegal organization), 242 (organization of a criminal association), 244-1 (dissemination of materials against public safety), 276 (drug possession) and 248 (possession of weapons, ammunition and explosives).[30] During the same period (1998-1999), 22 other young members of *Akramiyya* were given various terms in prison.[31] As of this writing, Yuldashev remains jailed in Tashkent.

The organization continued to exist until the Andijan massacre of 2005, when some of its members were shot by state security forces for participating in riots. In its aftermath, many members of fled from Uzbekistan through Kyrgyzstan to the West, leading to the gradual dissolution of the group.

Hizb ut-Tahrir (HuT)

Unlike the IMU, *Hizb ut-Tahrir* (HuT) is a truly transnational movement that enjoys considerable support among young Muslims in Western Europe and has a broad organizational base in London. Hizb ut-Tahrir (HT) was founded in 1952 by Sheikh Taqiuddin al-Nabhani in Jordanian-ruled East Jerusalem. Al-Nabhani died in 1977 and was succeeded by Abu Yusuf Abdul Qadim Zallum, another Palestinian cleric.[32] Zallum left HT's leadership in March 2003, due to his deteriorating health, and died in April 2003. He was succeeded by Ata Ibnu Khaleel Abu Rashta, who previously served as the party's official spokesman in Jordan. Abu Rashta, alias Abu Yasin, is a Palestinian who is believed to have lived most recently in the West Bank. The main goal of the HT movement is to recreate the Caliphate, the Islamic state formally brought to an end in 1924 following the collapse of the Ottoman Empire. Although it claims to be nonviolent, HT acknowledges that violence may eventually be necessary in order to overthrow the regimes standing in the way of the Caliphate. It is anti-

Semitic and anti-American, and disseminates a radical Islamist ideology fundamentally opposed to democratic capitalism and to Western concepts of freedom. While HT as an organization does not engage in terrorist activities, it does operate as an ideological vanguard that supports and encourages terrorist acts.[33] The dissemination of HuT's ideas in Central Asia began in early 1990. In Uzbekistan its membership is estimated to range from 7,000 to 60,000. Reports claim that Kyrgyzstan and Tajikistan have somewhere between 3,000 and 5,000 members each, while Kazakhstan has about 300 members.[34]

There is no evidence that HuT has engaged in violent action.. The group pursues a utopic Islamic state, but rather than using violence, it proposes a three-step plan. First, HuT wishes to educate as many Muslims as possible about its positions and goals. Second, those newly-educated Muslims would share HuT's ideologies with other people in their countries and communities, thus expanding HuT's influence. Third, and finally, this aggregate of the faithful will cause the collapse of secular government. HuT wishes to enact this collapse not through violence, but rather through a shift in loyalty; rather than nations, politics, or ethnicities, people's loyalties will lie with Islam.[35]

The ideology of HuT was imported to Uzbekistan in 1955 by a Jordanian named Atif Salahuddin. That same year, the organization was officially founded in the city of Tashkent, and subsequently in the Andijan, Samarkand, Tashkent and Fergana provinces of Uzbekistan. HuT cells were mostly composed of local youth. Members of HuT were distinguished not so much by their desire for strict adherence to Islamic norms, but by their religious and political activities. Young people enjoyed the opposition position of the party and open discussion of political issues inside the party. HuT acquired adherents first in Uzbekistan, and then migrated to neighboring Kyrgyzstan, Tajikistan and Kazakhstan. In these states, the party first recruited its followers among ethnic Uzbeks, but gradually young ethnic Kyrgyz, Tajiks and Kazakhs became involved in HuT, causing a rapid expansion of the group during the late 1990s.

From 1991 to 1999, HuT was a legal organization in Uzbekistan.[36] Its activities did not attract the attention of Uzbek authorities until May 1998, when party members began to distribute leaflets in public places. The response was rapid; between August and November of 1998, at least 15 members of the Tashkent branch of the party were arrested. Mass arrests of members of HuT throughout Uzbekistan began the following year. "Approximately 6,800 to 7,300 persons were arrested between 1999 and 2001 on suspicion of Islamic extremism or terrorism.[37]

Following the events of September 11, 2001, many members of HuT in Uzbekistan went underground, fearing large-scale retaliation. The group has largely continued to operate covertly to this day, as a result of unprecedented (and often violent) persecution on the part of Uzbek authorities. In recent years, the group has exhibited only nominal activity within Uzbekistan, although experts caution that this lull may be temporary in nature.[38] Elsewhere in the region, however, HuT has expanded its activities. As authorities in Uzbekistan ratcheted up their counterterrorism efforts, party activists were forced to seek refuge among Uzbek communities in neighboring countries, primarily in Kyrgyzstan, to where the headquarters of the party has moved.

ISLAMISM AND SOCIETY

Although the majority (88 percent) of Uzbekistan's population of 28.6 million is Muslim, most of them Sunni, this cohort by and large prefers a secular state system. Muslim leaders in Uzbekistan have demonstrated themselves to be very critical of HuT, and have argued that the movement is essentially a political rather than religious organization, and that Muslims should not be engaged in politics. Former Uzbek President Islam Karimov's intolerance of the group "seemed to catch on with Kazakh, Kyrgyz, and Tajik authorities, who stepped up their repression of the group, arresting, trying, and convicting dozens of members for distributing leaflets and other nonviolent activities."[39] However, some *imams* do not want to alienate members of HuT from their mosques, because the number of parishioners determines the level of donations (*Sadaka-Fitr and zakat*) that flow into their coffers.

While most moderate Muslims in Uzbekistan reject the goals and ideology of the movement, they tend to sympathize with its members because of the repression the latter face at the hands of local authorities, and as a result of the movement's efforts to draw attention to official corruption. HuT leaflets highlighting corruption, inequality and oppression tend to find a receptive ear among the Uzbek population, and especially among its more disadvantaged members. The organization's call for social justice, meanwhile, appears to resonate at a grassroots level among a population that routinely experiences hardship and privation. Nevertheless, neither the IMU nor HuT can claim widespread support anywhere in Central Asia. Both organizations appeal only to a small fraction of the regional population—and then this support is localized, strongest in parts of the Fergana Valley, possibly in south Uzbekistan, and in some areas of Tajikistan. While it is impossible to accurately determine the level of this support, Uzbek observers place the current number of active supporters of these groups at less than 10 percent of the regional population.[40]

Most ordinary Muslims in Uzbekistan do not support political activities in mosques, and do not share radical Islamist ideas. Nevertheless, the scale of support received by radical groups may expand if dissatisfaction with the current political and economic system increases. Support for HuT and other extremists in Uzbekistan is fed more by disappointment with the state of contemporary politics than by a conscious commitment to extremist ideology. After years of government repression, many have been discouraged from trying to use the available ways to protest against the government and the injustices of modern society. Thus, a more radical route holds appeal.

ISLAMISM AND THE STATE

In September 2016, Uzbekistan underwent a political sea change with the death of its longtime president, Islam Karimov. Karimov, the leader of the Uzbek Communist Party during the Soviet era, became president after Uzbekistan's independence from the Soviet Union in 1991.[41]

Virtually from its formation, Karimov's government strived to control the Uzbek population, and temper the political and religious activism of the Uzbek people. In the early 1990s, the government launched a series of measures to eliminate all secular opposition groups, and thereafter directed its attention toward Islamic associations. The government feared that any form of religious expression not controlled by the state could serve as a vehicle for popular discontent. This pattern has continued uninterrupted for the past two decades; state intelligence agencies work to eliminate and marginalize those Islamic leaders who do not share the official vision of religion as an instrument of a state policy. Uzbek security forces, meanwhile, routinely utilize the most repressive methods against Islamic organizations, often failing to differentiate between radical groups like the IMU and more grassroots-oriented ones like *Akramiyya*. Adherents to all of these organizations are subject to arbitrary arrest and torture, based upon suspicions of extremism.[42]

Today, the Uzbek government continues to prosecute anyone engaged in activity regarded as the uncontrolled expression of the Muslim faith. This state repression, however, has been coupled with a subtle and surprisingly sophisticated "soft power" approach to combating Islamist ideology. This approach finds its roots in the nature of Central Asian Islam itself, where the dominant branch of Sunni Islam is the Khanafi school—one of the most tolerant and liberal in that religion. Its pluralistic and largely apolitical disposition is one of the main reasons that Khanafi believers survived and avoided mass repression during the Communist era, when Soviet ideologues sought to eliminate doctrinal competition with Marxism-Leninism.

This approach leverages an asset shared by the Central Asian states: a strong knowledge base with which to fight radical Islamists. Since gaining independence, the countries of the region have managed to educate considerable numbers of knowledgeable experts in Islam. Moreover, in these countries, the *Koran* and *Hadith* have been translated into local languages, and many academics and *imams* are applying their knowledge on a practical level. By necessity, Central Asian governments, especially those in Uzbekistan and Kyrgyzstan, have created and developed an extensive educational system—spanning from kindergarten to university level—that inculcates the moral norms and social principles of tolerant Islam, and which respects the value of human life (be it Muslim, Christian, Jewish, or other). The system provides textbooks for schools, cartoons for children, education for *imams* of local mosques, a network of counselors in Islamic affairs for central and local administrations, and television and radio talk shows that challenge the intolerant *Wahhabi* interpretation of the *Koran* and *Hadith* and provide listeners with a religious alternative.[43]

Mobilization of Foreign Fighters

Central Asian and Russian foreign fighters make up a third of the total *jihadis* that travel to Iraq and Syria.[44] The exact number of Uzbek fighters is difficult to estimate, especially when considering the intricacies of the divide between ethnicity and nationality. Some estimates of Uzbek nationals fighting in Iraq and Syria are as high as 500.[45] But the number of ethnic Uzbek fighters could exceed 1,500.[46] The Uzbek government is trying to stem the tide of Uzbeks traveling abroad to fight in Iraq and Syria.

Radio "Ozodlik" (Uzbek service of Radio "Liberty") reported that at the end of 2015, Uzbek authorities introduced the passport regime in Tashkent. This regime implies that law enforcement agencies were massively checking passports of citizens, registering rented apartments, conducting interviews with citizens who had recently returned from abroad and those who were registered by authorities for their religious beliefs. In some instances, citizens were detained during these "conversations" in the *mahalla* committees (self-government units).

Lieutenant-Colonel Uktam Murodova from the Ministry of Interior stated that the Uzbek law enforcement agencies had reliable information about citizens who traveled abroad for a long time and now were back home. Several arrests of these Uzbeks in late 2015 confirmed this statement. The Independent Human Rights Defenders of Uzbekistan announced that from October 29 to November 18, 2015, more than 200 people were arrested on suspicion of involvement in "ISIS activities". Activists from human rights groups reported about detention of believers who returned to Uzbekistan from abroad that happened in Tashkent and Tashkent region, as well as in Namangan, Kokand and Fergana.

At the end of 2015, there were attempted attacks on the diplomatic offices of foreign states, located in the Uzbek capital. In particular, on the morning of September 28, 2015, attackers threw two Molotov cocktails into the US Embassy in Tashkent, and the Embassy was forced to shut down for several hours.

On September 4, 2015, there was an explosion near the mosque "Tukhtaboy" in Almazar district of Tashkent. In April 2015, pro-ISIS leaflets were distributed at the Transport and Service college in the Tashkent region. Firdaus Salimov, an 18-year-old former student, was arrested and charged with distributing the leaflets. The Uzbek court sentenced him to 9 years in prison.[47]

Uzbek authorities pay great attention to strengthening their police and internal security agencies to counter the internal extremist Islamic terrorist organizations. But at the same time, Tashkent does not focus its efforts on external Islamic threats, especially from the Afghani Taliban. This is manifested in the lack of attention to its own military capabilities. The number of ground troops is only 40 thousand (about 0.01% of the population). Despite the fact that Tashkent inherited a huge storage Soviet base in Termez, it is armed today with only 170 old T-72 and T64 tanks, plus a small number of T-80 tanks. Uzbek Air Force also heavily degraded and now Uzbek strike aircrafts are reduced to two dozen Su-25, supplemented by few combat-ready fighter: 12 Su-27 and 13 MiG-29. Low pay, hazing and corruption are flourishing in the Uzbek arms forces. In general, Uzbekistan will not be able to cope with a serious military challenge alone.[48] According to Uzbek political analyst Farhod Tolipov: "external threats for Uzbekistan are not so great that may make us to expect any offensive of some enemies of the country, only for the reason that in Uzbekistan we have the new president."[49]

According to Vladimir Sotnikov, director of the independent Russia-East-West Center for Strategic Analysis in Moscow, the IMU will move swiftly to exploit any instability in Uzbekistan after the death of President Islam Karimov:

> Though the group's leaders are living in exile in Pakistan, it maintains considerable strength among the ethnic Uzbek population of northern Afghanistan, and could be capable of launching raids inside Uzbekistan as it did in the past... There are also a lot of Uzbek jihadis who've grown disillusioned with the prospects in Uzbekistan and gone off to fight with the Islamic State in Syria and Iraq. For now the domestic situation appears quiet. But there is a possibility that Islamist militants could rise again.[50]

ENDNOTES

[1] "Islam Karimov: Uzbekistan president's death confirmed," BBC, September 2, 2016, http://www.bbc.com/news/world-asia-37260375.

[2] "Uzbekistan's new leader promises major government reshuffle," Reuters, December 14, 2016, http://www.reuters.com/article/us-uzbekistan-president-idUSKBN1431LN?feedType=RSS&feedName=worldNews.

[3] Igor Rotar, "The Islamic Movement of Uzbekistan: A Resurgent IMU?" Jamestown Foundation *Terrorism Monitor* 1, iss. 8, December 17, 2003, http://www.jamestown.org/single/?no_cache=1&tx_ttnews[tt_news]=26187.

[4] Orozbek Moldaliyev, Islam i Politika: Politizatsiya Islama ili Islamizatsiya Politiki? (Islam and Politics: The Politicization of Islam of the Islamization of Politics?) (Bishkek: n.p., 2008), 269; See also A. Starkovsky, "Armia Izgnanikov, Chast I" (Army of Outcasts, Part I) freas.org, January 18, 2004, http://freeas.org/?nid=2367; Vitaly Ponomarev, Ugroza "Islamskovo Ekstremisma" v Uzbekistane: Mifui i Realnosti (The "Islamic Extremist" Threat in Uzbekistan: Myth and Reality) (Moscow: Memorial, 1999).

[5] Ibid; See also Res Publica, September 15-21, 1998.

[6] Thomas M. Sanderson, Daniel Kimmage, and David A. Gordon, From the Ferghana Valley to South Waziristan: The Evolving Threat of Central Asian Jihadists, 2010, CSIS Transnational Threats Project, pg 6, https://csis.org/files/publication/100324_Sanderson_FerghanaValley_WEB_0.pdf.

[7] Michael Falkov, "Islamic Movement of Uzbekistan (IMU): History, financial base and a military structure," Nezavisimaya Gazeta (Moscow), August 24, 2000.

[8] Michael Falkov, "Islamic Movement of Uzbekistan (IMU): History, financial base and a military structure," Nezavisimaya Gazeta (Moscow), August 24, 2000.

[9] Moldaliyev, Islam i Politika, 271

[10] Thomas M. Sanderson, Daniel Kimmage, and David A. Gordon, From the Ferghana Valley to South Waziristan: The Evolving Threat of Central Asian Jihadists, 2010, CSIS Transnational Threats Project, pg 6, https://csis.org/files/publication/100324_Sanderson_FerghanaValley_WEB_0.pdf.

[11] Moldaliyev, Islam i Politika, 271.

[12] Moldaliyev, Islam i Politika, 271.

[13] Author's interview with former IMU member, Osh, Kyrgyzstan, August 11, 2004; See also Alex Alexiev, "Oil Dollars to Jihad: Saudi Arabia Finances Global Islamism," Internationale Politik 1 (2004), 31.

[14] Thomas M. Sanderson, Daniel Kimmage, and David A. Gordon, From the Ferghana Valley to South Waziristan: The Evolving Threat of Central Asian Jihadists, 2010, CSIS Transnational Threats Project, pg 7, https://csis.org/files/publication/100324_Sanderson_FerghanaValley_WEB_0.pdf.

[15] Author's interview with Pakistani researcher, Almaty, Kazakhstan, July 24, 2009.

[16] Bill Roggio, "Tahir Yuldashev Confirmed Killed In U.S. Strike In South Waziristan," Long War Journal, October 4, 2009, http://www.longwarjournal.org/archives/2009/10/tahir_yuldashev_conf.php

[17] "Islamic Movement of Uzbekistan," Country Reports on Terrorism 2010, U.S. State Department, Office of the Coordinator for Counterterrorism, August 18, 2011, www.state.gov/j/ct/rls/crt/2010/170264.htm.

[18] "Afghanistan: IMU leader detained in Kunduz," Fergana News Agency, August 14, 2012, http://www.fergananews.com/news.php?id=19262&print=1, 08.14.2012

[19] INSITE on Terrorism, "2015 Retrospective: How the Fall of the IMU Reveals the Limits of IS' Expansion" by Margaret Foster, https://news.siteintelgroup.com/blog/index.php/submissions/21-jihad/4498-2015-retrospective-how-the-fall-of-the-imu-reveals-the-limits-of-is-expansion

[20] "IMU Declares It Is Now Part Of The Islamic State" by Merhat Sharipzhan, RFE/RL, August 06, 2015, http://www.rferl.org/a/imu-islamic-state/27174567.html

[21] Ibid.

[22] "В Узбекистане показали фильм о молодежи, попавшей в ИГИЛ," Regnum, December 2, 2015, https://regnum.ru/news/2025694.html

[23] "Самосуд общественности в Узбекистане," Radio Free Europe Radio Liberty, February 1, 2016, http://rus.ozodi.org/a/27523134.html.

[24] Bakhtiyar Babadjanov, "Akramia: A Brief Summary," Carnegie Endowment for International Peace, May 2006,http://www.carnegieendowment.org/files/Akramiya.pdf

[25] Ibid.
[26] Author's interview with Uzbek expert on Islam B. Babadzhanov, Tashkent, Uzbekistan, September 14, 2009.
[27] Ibid.
[28] Author's interview with Uzbek expert on Islam I. Mirsaidov, Tashkent, Uzbekistan, September 16, 2009
[29] Moldaliyev, Islam i Politika, 286.
[30] Ibid., 286-287.
[31] Ibidem.
[32] Ahmed Rashid, "Reviving the Caliphate", in Jihad: The Rise of Militant Islam in Central Asia (New Haven: Penguin Books, 2003), p. 119.
[33] Zeyno Baran, "Radical Islamists in Central Asia," in Current Trends in Islamist Ideology, eds. Hillel Fradkin, Husain Haqqani, and Eric Brown, vol. 2 (Washington, D.C.: Hudson Institute, 2005) http://www.hudson.org/content/researchattachments/attachment/1175/20060130_current_trends_v2.pdf
[34] Zeyno Baran, "Radical Islamists in Central Asia," in Current Trends in Islamist Ideology, eds. Hillel Fradkin, Husain Haqqani, and Eric Brown, vol. 2 (Washington, D.C.: Hudson Institute, 2005), 46: http://www.hudson.org/content/researchattachments/attachment/1175/20060130_current_trends_v2.pdf
[35] "Hizb ut-Tahrir al-Islami (Islamic Party of Liberation)," Global Security, n.d., http://www.globalsecurity.org/military/world/para/hizb-ut-tahrir.htm
[36] "From the "Hizb ut-Tahrir" to "Googoosh": the opposition in Uzbekistan is building alliances?" EADaily, September 15, 2016, http://eadaily.com/ru/news/2016/09/15/ot-hizb-ut-tahrir-do-gugushi-oppoziciya-v-uzbekistane-stroit-alyansy
[37] US Department of State, "Country Reports on Human Rights Practices" Bureau of Democracy, Human Rights, and Labor, 2002, March 31, 2003, https://2009-2017.state.gov/j/drl/rls/hrrpt/2002/18400.htm
[38] Author's interview with Uzbek expert on Islam ⊠.P., Tashkent, Uzbekistan, September 11, 2009.
[39] Europe and Central Asia Overview: Human Rights Watch World Report 2003, 2003, https://www.hrw.org/legacy/wr2k3/europe.html.
[40] Timur Kozukulov, Problemy Borby s Religioznim Ekstremismom v Usloviakh Globalizatsiyii v Ferganskoy Doline (Problems of Combating Religious Extremism in the Ferghana Valley under Globalized Conditions) (Osh, Kyrgyzstan: Oshskii Gosudarstviniy Universitet, 2008), 72.
[41] Krishnadev Calamur, "Islam Karimov's Legacy," The Atlantic, September 2, 2016, http://www.theatlantic.com/news/archive/2016/09/islam-karimov-dead/498533/.

[42] See, for example, United Nations Human Rights Committee, "Human Rights Committee Concludes Consideration of Uzbekistan's Third Report," March 12, 2010, http://www.un.org/News/Press/docs/2010/hrct719.doc.htm.

[43] For a detailed analysis of the "soft power" counterterrorism approaches of Central Asian states, see Evgueni K. Novikov, Central Asian Responses to Radical Islam (Washington, DC: American Foreign Policy Council, 2006).

[44] Uran Botokbekov, "ISIS and Central Asia: A Shifting Recruiting Strategy," The Diplomat, May 17, 2016, http://thediplomat.com/2016/05/isis-and-central-asia-a-shifting-recruiting-strategy/.

[45] Uran Botokbekov, "ISIS and Central Asia: A Shifting Recruiting Strategy," The Diplomat, May 17, 2016, http://thediplomat.com/2016/05/isis-and-central-asia-a-shifting-recruiting-strategy/.

[46] Uran Botokbekov, "ISIS and Central Asia: A Shifting Recruiting Strategy," The Diplomat, May 17, 2016, http://thediplomat.com/2016/05/isis-and-central-asia-a-shifting-recruiting-strategy/.

[47] "Uzbek Interior Ministry calls on citizens not to succumb to rumors about 'ISIS,'" Ozodlik, December 21, 2015.

[48] Eugene Pozhidaev, "Risks and prospects of post-Karimov Uzbekistan," EADaily, September 26, 2016, http://eadaily.com/ru/news/2016/09/29/evgeniy-pozhidaev-riski-i-perspektivy-postkarimovskogo-uzbekistana

[49] "There will be no storm in Uzbekistan: EADaily interview with political analyst Farhod Talipova," EADaily, September 12, 2016, http://eadaily.com/ru/news/2016/09/12/uzbekistan-shtormit-ne-budet-intervyu-politologa-farhoda-tolipova-eadaily

[50] Fred Weir, "Uzbek president's failing health raises Islamist worries," Christian Science Monitor, August 29, 2016, http://www.csmonitor.com/World/Europe/2016/0829/Uzbek-president-s-failing-health-raises-Islamist-worries

SOUTH ASIA

COUNTRIES
Afghanistan
Bangladesh
India
Maldives
Pakistan

AFGHANISTAN

Quick Facts

Population: Number 33,332,025 (July 2016 est.)

Area: 652,230 sq km

Ethnic Groups: Pashtun, Tajik, Hazara, Uzbek, other (includes smaller numbers of Baloch, Turkmen, Nuristani, Pamiri, Arab, Gujar, Brahui, Qizilbash, Aimaq, Pashai, and Kyrghyz)

Religions: Muslim 99.7% (Sunni 84.7 - 89.7%, Shia 10 - 15%), other 0.3% (2009 est.)

Government Type: presidential Islamic Republic

GDP (official exchange rate): $18.4 billion (2014 est.)

Map and Quick Facts courtesy of the CIA World Factbook (Last Updated January 12, 2017)

OVERVIEW

Afghanistan is among the countries most affected by Islamic militancy. There are a myriad militant groups varying in size, tactics, and political objectives perpetrating violent Islamist activity. Key groups include the Taliban and their splinter affiliates, the Haqqani Network, Hizb-e-Islami - Hekmatyar, Pakistan-based jihadi *groups such as Lashkar-e-Taiba, Sipah-e-Sahaba, and Tehrik-e-Nafaz-e-Shariat-e-Mohammadi, Jamaat-ul-Ahrar, as well as transnational* jihadi *groups like al-Qaeda and a more recent one, the Afghan offshoot of the Islamic State (IS, ISIS, or* Da'esh*), known as Islamic State in Khorasan Province (ISKP). The largest of these groups active on both sides of the Afghan and Pakistani border remains the Taliban. Under the leadership of their spiritual leader Mullah Mohammad Omar, it seized control of the Afghan state in 1996, effectively ending the Afghan civil war that followed the Soviet invasion of Afghanistan (1979-89). The Taliban regime was subsequently ousted in 2001 by a U.S.-led coalition in response to the September 11,*

2001 terrorist attacks, perpetrated by the Afghan-based al-Qaeda group, led by Osama bin Laden. In the decade-and-a-half since, the U.S.-led coalition and the Afghan government, headed first by former President Hamid Karzai and now by his successor, Ashraf Ghani, have struggled to subdue an insurgency waged by the Taliban and its militant allies, which have enjoyed sanctuaries as well as financial and military support inside neighboring Pakistan.

While the U.S. and international forces ended their combat mission in Afghanistan at the end of December 2014 and withdrew most of foreign troops, the country remains a hotbed of Islamist militancy. Despite fractures in the insurgency, primarily due to the death of Mullah Omar -- (which took place in 2013 but was only publicly announced in mid-2015), the succession and then death of his principal deputy, Mullah Akhtar Mohammad Mansour, and the subsequent appointment of the Taliban's current emir, *Mullah Hibatullah Akhundzada -- the movement persists, threatening a fragile Afghan government.*

ISLAMIST ACTIVITY

The Afghan state continues to fight the Taliban-led insurgency sixteen years after the U.S.-led coalition intervened in Afghanistan. In the first half of 2013 alone, over 1,300 Afghan civilians were killed and an estimated 2,500 injured, a 23 percent increase over 2012.[1] According to UN estimates, in the first half of 2014 alone, civilian casualties sharply rose by 24 percent.[2] In their 2015 mid-year report on Protection of Civilians in Armed Conflict, the UN Assistance Mission in Afghanistan (UNAMA) and the UN Human Rights Office documented almost 5,000 civilian casualties – with close to 1,600 deaths and over 3,300 injured – in the first half of 2015.[3] By the end of December 2015, civilian casualties had risen to over 11,000.[4] In 2016, civilian casualties hit a record high with 3,498 deaths and 7,920 injured, with a tenfold increase in losses caused by the Islamic State.[5] More and more Afghan civilians are killed through ground operations and crossfire than because of improvised explosive devices (IEDs). In total, there has been an estimated 58,736 civilian casualties, with over 21,000 Afghan civilians killed since late 2001, with 2016 as the worst year for Afghan civilians.[6] Meanwhile, 2015 and 2016 were the bloodiest years on record for the Afghan security forces, which have assumed primary responsibility for security from the U.S.-led coalition.[7] In 2015 alone, an estimated 5,000 members of the Afghan National Defense and Security Forces (ANDSF) were killed and another 14,000 were injured while fighting the insurgency.[8] Additionally, in the first eight months of 2016, ANDSF endured 5,523 casualties.[9] The vast majority of these casualties are attributable to the Taliban.

The success of the Taliban is owed, in large part, to its appeal to the broader Afghan population, particularly the south and east of Afghanistan, the country's hotspots from which most Taliban manpower stems. The Taliban's key tactic in eliciting grassroots support, especially among the country's ethnic Pashtun population, is to leverage resentment felt by local Afghan villagers toward the indiscriminate killing of Afghan civilians in U.S. airstrikes and night raids, and perceived disrespect toward local Afghan values and religious norms.

Between 2001 and 2005, the U.S. intervention effectively degraded the Taliban's capabilities and sent their leadership fleeing into Pakistan. During this period, the northern part of Afghanistan was largely free from Taliban activity. Afghanistan's north has traditionally been dominated by ethnic Uzbeks, Tajiks and Hazaras who were previously members of the anti-Taliban Northern Alliance. Taliban tactics in the early years of the war amounted to sporadic raids on U.S. and international forces and attacks on major population centers in the country's south, where the group enjoys the most sympathy. Though Taliban forces were able to control significant swathes of the countryside in the south and east, and along the Afghanistan-Pakistan border, they were unsuccessful in launching major attacks against U.S. and international forces elsewhere. The so-called "swarm attacks" on American and international forces often resulted in heavy losses for the Taliban, which then switched to traditional guerilla and terrorist tactics. When pressure was applied to Taliban strongholds in the south and east of Afghanistan, they simply took refuge across the border in Pakistan's northwestern frontier, or the tribal region, where international troops could not pursue them. Within the tribal region, the Taliban and their allies were concentrated most heavily in the North and South Waziristan Agencies and remain so to the present day. However, the city of Quetta, located in Pakistan's Baluchistan province, served as the headquarters for the exiled Afghan Taliban leadership and was the place where Taliban spiritual leader Mullah Omar supposedly resided.[10] In recent years and months, Baluchistan has become the prime target of the U.S. drone campaign, killing high value Taliban operatives. For instance, in May 2016, a U.S. drone strike killed Mullah Akhtar Mohammad Mansour, the leader of the Afghan Taliban who succeeded Mullah Omar after the Taliban confirmed their spiritual leader had died.[11] Interestingly, according to an official statement issued by Afghan government, Mullah Omar, too, had died in Pakistan in 2013, allegedly in his safe haven of Quetta.[12]

The Taliban's fortunes changed between 2005 and 2008. During this period, a radical Pakistani offshoot of the Afghan Taliban, the *Tehrik-e-Taliban-e-Pakistan* (TTP) or Pakistani Taliban, formed, gaining control over parts of Pakistan's Khyber-Pakhtunkhwa Province (formerly known as the Federally Administered Tribal Areas or FATA). Unlike the Afghan Taliban, with which they share loose links and affiliations, the Pakistani Taliban focused their attacks largely on the Pakistani state, which had largely taken a hands-off approach to the Afghan Taliban residing within its borders.

The Afghan Taliban, which continued to refrain from attacking the Pakistani state, began regrouping in Pakistan and reconstituting their command structure. They expanded operations in Afghanistan, including to the northern province of Kunduz, where a sizeable and sympathetic Pashtun population lives amid Tajiks and Uzbeks. The Taliban also expanded operations in Kunar and Nuristan provinces in the north, and in the west of Afghanistan around Herat province, while consolidating their hold over the Pashtun-strongholds of Kandahar and Helmand in the south.[13] The use of suicide attacks, which were virtually unknown to Afghanistan before 2001, multiplied exponentially between 2005 and 2008, with approximately 100-130 suicide attacks being carried out in the country each year.[14]

During this period, the Afghan Taliban also began to incorporate tactics developed by insurgent and *jihadist* groups in Iraq (namely suicide attacks and IED attacks). At present, IEDs remain the primary cause of casualties in U.S. and international forces in Afghanistan, although a large number of suicide attacks that were directed against international forces, it has proved less successful in recent years than was true in the past.[15] Targeting foreign nationals, especially aid workers, whenever possible, was much more effective as a tactic, and significantly downgraded the efforts of international aid and relief organizations operating in Afghanistan, although the number of such targeted attacks on foreign aid workers remains small. Still, in 2014, the greatest number of attacks on aid workers was in Afghanistan, with more than twice as many attacks than the next most violent setting for aid workers, Syria. There were 54 attacks on aid workers in Afghanistan, and 26 in Syria in 2014.[16]

By 2009, before now-former President Barack Obama came into office, conditions on the ground had deteriorated further, and U.S. and international forces were on the defensive. Throughout the south and east, Taliban "vanguard units" infiltrated towns and began executing pro-Afghan government and especially pro-Karzai political and religious figures, setting up "shadow courts" that administered and delivered swift *sharia* justice, and attacking local Afghan army and police checkpoints and outposts. Most crucially, the Taliban were lent pseudo-legitimacy by the widespread corruption and ineffectiveness of the Karzai government, its local representatives, the police, and the judiciary. Broad swathes of territory were lost, as the United States belatedly began to shift troops from Iraq to Afghanistan with a surge of 30,000 troops and embraced a marked change in counterinsurgency tactics under the leadership of Gen. Stanley McChrystal, then-commander of all U.S. and international forces in Afghanistan.

McChrystal attempted to minimize Afghan civilian casualties and to apply force more judiciously so as not to drive local Afghan villagers who suffered "collateral damage" deaths from coalition operations, particularly airstrikes that caused a sharp increase in civilian casualties, into joining the Taliban. McChrystal made clear that he did not believe the United States and its international partners could "kill our way out of an insurgency."[17] In his major policy speech of December 1, 2009, former

President Obama detailed that the purpose of his surge of U.S. troops in Afghanistan was to strategically defeat the Taliban over the course of eighteen months, before beginning the drawdown of American troops in July 2011.[18] The offensive against Taliban strongholds in the south and east of the country paralleled an increase in the use of remotely-controlled predator drone attacks against Taliban targets in Pakistan's remote tribal agencies, resulting in the killing of dozens of "high-value targets" between 2009 and 2013.

In June 2010, General McChrystal was replaced by Gen. David Petraeus, a war veteran who had previously commanded the surge offensive and counterinsurgency campaign in Iraq (2007-2009). Petraeus launched a more robust effort to rout Taliban insurgents and initiated a policy of using special operations forces to engage in night raids on Taliban hideouts. Although frequent night raids by U.S. special forces proved helpful in dismantling, killing or capturing of high-ranking Taliban operatives across Afghanistan, it also triggered local resentments against American and international forces who oftentimes disrespected local culture and religious beliefs by entering private homes at night, investigating inside mosques, searching Afghan women, and at times holding local villagers in custody without trial. It also stoked tensions between Afghan and U.S. governments after former President Karzai repeatedly complained that any such raids on Afghan homes were in violation of Afghan sovereignty and must be conducted in consultation with Afghan security forces. On July 18, 2011, Gen. Petraeus relinquished command and was replaced by U.S. Marine Corps Gen. Joseph Dunford. Gen. Dunford focused his efforts on a new role for the U.S. military in Afghanistan to "train, advise and assist" the Afghan security forces in advance of the drawdown of U.S. and international troops in December 2014.[19] In the meantime, the United States and Afghanistan negotiated a bilateral security agreement, based principally on the broader Strategic Partnership Agreement (SPA) signed by President Obama and President Karzai in May 2012, with a duration until the end of 2024.[20] In September 2014, the new Afghan National Unity Government led by President Ashraf Ghani and Chief Executive Abdullah Abdullah signed the BSA.[21] The pact serves as a basis for a continued U.S. military presence of an estimated 9,800 U.S. troops and at least 2,000 NATO troops – as part of a new, follow-on NATO-led Resolute Support Mission launched on January 1, 2015 under the command of U.S. Army Gen. John F. Campbell, who was later replaced by the current commander Gen. John W. Nicholson – that will remain in Afghanistan to train, advise, and assist Afghan security forces, and conduct unfettered counterterrorism operations against al Qaeda and its affiliates.[22]

A second major component of Islamist activity in Afghanistan is al-Qaeda, which recently resumed its activities in Afghanistan. Although the core of al-Qaeda is Arab, its ranks also include fighters from Uzbekistan,[23] Turkey,[24] Muslims of European descent,[25] as well as other nationalities.[26] These affiliated radicals cannot be easily distinguished from their counterparts in Pakistan (nor are all of them necessarily members of al-Qaeda Central), and they regularly utilize bases scattered throughout Pakistan's tribal areas, particularly in North Waziristan, to train, plan and plot against Afghan and foreign forces in Afghanistan.

While the Taliban have tried to minimize civilian casualties from suicide and IED attacks, al-Qaeda and its allies have not shown such restraint, and are presumed to be responsible for the many mass-casualty suicide attacks that have occurred in the country since 2005.[27] In addition, al-Qaeda carried out one of the most successful penetration suicide attacks to date against a CIA base in Khost, Afghanistan on December 30, 2009.[28] During the operation, an al-Qaeda double agent, claiming to work for the CIA, detonated a suicide bomb among a group of CIA agents, killing eight of them and makes it a single largest casualty in CIA's history. However, while al-Qaeda and its allies might supply shock troops and suicide bombers to the Taliban, their overall role in the insurgency remains limited. Rather, al-Qaeda's primary aid to the Taliban is in the form of sophisticated Internet and media propaganda.[29] While al-Qaeda once maintained a strong presence in Afghanistan with thousands of militants, it has shrunk significantly in recent years: its total strength is estimated to be between 150-200 operatives that are active in Afghanistan. Meanwhile, al-Qaeda has shifted its battlefield strategy from one of offensive to forging alliances. For example, in June 2016, al-Qaeda leader Ayman al-Zawahiri pledged allegiance to the new leader of the Afghan Taliban, Hibatullah Akhundzada, a largely symbolic move aimed at rebuilding al-Qaeda-Taliban alliance to counter a shared threat: the Afghan offshoot of the Islamic State, the Islamic State in Khorasan (ISK).

The Islamic State in Khorasan, which emerged in Afghanistan in 2015, represents a more recent threat to the Afghan government and people as well as Western presence.[30] Its grand strategic objective is to establish a trans-regional caliphate – by expanding its military presence and menacing activities outside Iraq and Syria (or the Levant) – as part of an "apocalyptic war" against the West.[31] The Islamic State's rationale for its presence in the region is rooted in its interpretation of the Islamic religious texts, which states that an army of true believers will convene in Wilayat Khorasan, (or Khorasan Province, a historic region that encompasses Afghanistan and Pakistan), before the "apocalypse," or the Day of Judgment.[32] Additionally, Islamic State's presence in the region enables the group to challenge and replace its rival, al Qaeda, as the leader of the global *jihadist* movement.[33]

After the group's declaration of a "caliphate" in June 2014,[34] it began to gain support among *jihadist* groups in the "Khorasan" region, particularly in Pakistan. As Pakistan's Tehrik-e-Taliban (TTP) splintered after the death of its leader Hakimullah Mehsud in November 2013, fractures in the group prompted defections, starting with TTP's spokesman Shahidullah Shahid, who publicly announced his allegiance to ISK in October 2014, along with most of the movement's regional commanders, forming Islamic State in Khorasan's most formidable support base in the region.[35] By contrast, the Afghan Taliban do not share ISK's objective of establishing a global caliphate encompassing the entire Muslim community. Instead, the Taliban hold a narrow ethnic and nationalistic agenda of establishing an Islamic Afghan state under their rule, which is the basis for the hostility ISK bears towards the Taliban.[36]

As of March 2016, ISK maintained a sizable presence (between 1,000-3,000 fighters) in eastern Afghanistan, mainly Nangarhar and Kunar provinces.[37] In April 2015, a suicide bomber blew himself up in front of a bank in Jalalabad, the capital of Nangarhar province, killing at least 33 people and injuring more than 100.[38] The Institute for the Study of War reported that on the same day, the Afghan local media had received text messages fromShahidullah Shahib, ISK's spokesperson, claiming responsibility for the attack on behalf of the group.[39] Islamic State in Khorasan also claimed responsibility for the June 2016 assassination of Sher Wali Wardak, a member of the Afghan Parliament.[40] On July 23, 2016, ISK took responsibility for the deadliest attack of the year, and the biggest they have carried out since the onset of their militant operations in Afghanistan, when two suicide bombers detonated their suicide belts among thousands of minority Shi'ite Hazaras (the Islamic sect against whom the Islamic State bears exclusive antagonism) that had gathered near the Afghan Parliament, demanding the reroute of a planned power line through Bamyan province.[41] As a result, over 80 innocent civilians were killed and over 250 wounded.[42] Although Islamic State's presence in Afghanistan is limited so far, the group is starting to gain global attention as a new vanguard of reinvigorated jihadism in Afghanistan.

The third Islamist component present in Afghanistan is the *Hizb-e-Islami* group led by Gulbuddin Hekmatyar. Hekmatyar was an important commander in the anti-Soviet *jihad*, and was allegedly backed by Pakistan's military and intelligence apparatus. During his small stint as the Afghanistan's prime minister during the Afghan civil war in 1990s, he contributed significantly to the destruction of Afghanistan. He later fled to Iran in order to escape the Taliban in 1996. His base of support within Afghanistan collapsed, and although he returned to Afghanistan in 2002, he has not been able to mobilize mass support among Afghans. Most of the fighters that belong to Hizb-e-Islami - Hekmatyar (there do not appear to be any authoritative numbers in this regard) operate in the northeastern parts of the country, close to the border with Pakistan, and many hail from Pashtun ethnic group.[43] The principal division between Hizb-e-Islami - Hekmatyar and the larger Taliban resistance appears to be personal, as Hekmatyar was one of the major *mujahideen* warlords against whom the Taliban fought between 1994 and 1996. Though Hizb-e-Islami - Hekmatyar had previously engaged in talks with the Karzai government (and, most recently, with the National Unity Government), and even though it has been less aggressive in its attacks on U.S. and international forces, the group does appear to be responsible for several attacks targeting Afghan government officials, including assassination attempts against President Karzai in 2007 and 2008.[44] However, in September 2016, the Afghan Government signed a peace deal with Hizb-e-Islami – Hekmatyar, after the group agreed to cease hostilities in return for Afghan Government's recognition of Hizb-e-Islami – Hekmatyar.[45] Subsequently, in February 2017, the United Nations Security Council Sanctions Committee removed Hekmatyar's name from its sanctions list.[46]

Furthermore, 2015-2016 bore witness to some of the deadliest attacks against civilians attributed to the Haqqani network, including an attack that August that killed 43 and wounded more than 300, and an even deadlier attack that left more than 60 dead and some 300 wounded in April 2016.[47]

ISLAMISM AND SOCIETY

Located at the crossroads of the Middle East, Central Asia and South Asia, Afghanistan is divided by geography and ethnicity. The central section of the country is bisected by the Hindu Kush mountains (impassable except through the Salang Pass), while the southern section is divided from Pakistan by the mountainous tribal region and consists of semi-mountainous and arid regions tapering into full desert along the Iranian border.

Ethnically, the estimated 15 million Pashto-speaking Pashtuns of Afghanistan comprise over 40 percent of the population, dominating Afghanistan's south and east along the Pakistani border. Dari-speaking Tajiks make up an additional 25-30 percent of the population and are located in the northeast and along the Iranian border to the west. Significant other minorities include the Uzbeks (approximately 9 percent) located along the border with Uzbekistan to the north, and Hazaras (approximately 9 percent) located in the central mountainous region. A number of other minorities, including Turkmen, Aimaks, Pashais, Kizil Bashis and Baluchis, comprise the rest of the population.[48] Although there is a substantial Shi'ite population in Afghanistan, mainly made up of ethnic Hazaras, it has traditionally not been prone to violent Islamist activity.

In general, Sufism – a less rigid, more mystical variety of Islam - has held a central place in Afghan society. There are three major Sufi orders: the Naqshbandiyya (which tends to be closer to mainstream Sunnism), the Chishtiyya (associated with India) and the Qadiriyya (which is pan-Islamic). The Tajik population has traditionally had a close cultural relationship with the Sufi heritage of Persia, though they are not Shi'ite, while the Pashtuns have been more influenced by the reformist Sunni Deobandi movements originating in India and Pakistan.

Before the Soviet invasion of Afghanistan in 1979, Afghanistan was largely ruled by a semi-secular elite that was either pro-western in its orientation or, later, pro-communist. Afghanistan has traditionally hosted a weak central government more adept at resisting foreign attempts at domination than actually ruling the country. The efforts of reformist rulers such as King Amanullah (1919-29), who sought to establish a strong, liberal regime, were overwhelmingly unsuccessful.[49] Starting in the 1950s, the Union of Soviet Socialist Republics (USSR) established close relations with Afghanistan and gradually built up the local Communist party, an effort that culminated in the overthrow of the Afghan last monarch, King Mohammad Zahir Shah, in 1973 and the establishment of a Communist-dominated regime there five years later. This regime based its power upon the Pashtun Durrani tribe (in opposition to the traditional cultural domination of the Tajiks), but was quickly beset by popular opposition. The USSR came to the aid of the Afghan Communist regime, invading the country in 1979 to bolster it. After the initial invasion, the Soviets remained and became embroiled in a bloody, protracted fight against the U.S.-backed Islamist opposition or *mujahideen* fighters (based out of Peshawar, Pakistan) before ultimately withdrawing in 1989.

Although the conflict ended in defeat for the USSR, Afghanistan's Islamist *mujahideen* were unable to adequately exploit the Soviet Union's withdrawal and instead fell to fighting amongst themselves. The period between 1992 and the rise of the Taliban in 1994-96 was characterized by the Balkanization of Afghanistan. Tribal, *jihadi* and local Islamist leaders were in a frenzy for territory, carved out separate fiefdoms throughout the country and attacked Kabul at will. The ethnic-tribal conglomeration that had been forcefully put together by the Afghan kings in the late 19th century fell apart when central rule collapsed. Separate Uzbek, Tajik and Hazara mini-states were created in the north and west of Afghanistan, while the Pashtun lands in the south and the east fell into chaos. The Uzbek, Tajik and Hazara strongholds were ruled over by strongmen or "warlords" such as Ismail Khan, former governor of Herat province, and Gen. Rashid Dostum, now Afghanistan's First Vice President, who brought a modicum of stability to their regions. During this period, the country's dependence upon the illicit drug trade grew immensely.

The Taliban ("the students" in Farsi) first appeared in Pakistani *madrassas* (schools of Islamic learning) in 1994, portraying themselves as a movement of youth dedicated to eliminating anarchy and chaos.[50] This tribal-religious movement spread into Afghanistan among the Pashtuns living in the country's war-torn south, where *mujahideen*-turned-bandits preyed on the common people. In response, a group of religious students, or Talibs, united under a local *mullah* named Omar and created vigilante groups. These then moved through the Pashtun south, disarming *mujahideen* groups and enforcing strict *sharia* law. By 1995, the Taliban had conquered most of the Pashtun south and had begun to move against Tajiks in the northeast.

Until 1997, the movement appeared invincible, capturing Kabul in 1996, and pushing government supporters led by then-leader of the Northern Alliance, Ahmad Shah Massoud, into the far northeast corner of the country. The Taliban suffered reverses in 1997 and 1998, and responded with massacres. By 2001, they controlled approximately 95 percent of the territory of Afghanistan and ruled the country with their draconian laws, including banning girls from attending schools and introducing capital punishments.

In the absence of international recognition and support except for those offered by Pakistan, Saudi Arabia, and the United Arab Emirates, the Taliban began to rely upon foreign extremist groups like al-Qaeda for financial support. Islamist *jihadi* groups began gravitating toward Afghanistan because of the Taliban's strict imposition of *sharia* law. Their influence was symbolized by the March 2001 destruction of the Buddhas of Bamiyan, Afghanistan's greatest historical site, because they were deemed to be "heathen idols."[51]

When former U.S. President George W. Bush demanded that the Taliban hand over Osama Bin Laden and his affiliates after the attacks of September 11th, the Taliban refused, at first believing al-Qaeda's denials of involvement. Following the U.S.-led invasion, Mullah Omar and other Taliban leadership, owing to a strict Pashtun code of hospitality, doubled down on their relationship with the group.

Yet the Taliban and al-Qaeda do not occupy the same ideological space. The Taliban, whose roots are in the Deobandi reformist school of north India, generally differs from the global *jihadis* of al-Qaeda, who tend to be Arab by ethnicity and Salafi-Wahhabi in ideology. Deobandis, for example, generally do not express the same abhorrence of Sufism and Shi'ism that is characteristic of Salafis. Nevertheless, the Taliban commanders regularly comment favorably on al-Qaeda. Former Taliban leader Mullah Dadullah famously explained: "We like the al-Qaeda organization. We consider it a friendly and brotherly organization, which shares our ideology and concepts. We have close ties and constant contacts with it. Our cooperation is ideal."[52] In August 2015, al-Qaeda leader Ayman al-Zawahiri declared his support for the Taliban as he pledged allegiance to the new (now late) "commander of the faithful," Mullah Mansour, maintaining their relations of reciprocity.[53]

ISLAMISM AND THE STATE

The central government in Afghanistan is fragile and relies upon the support of both local elites (meaning traditional tribal elders and city-based elites) and foreign aid (both governmental and from non-governmental organizations). Traditional tribal support is reflected in the institution of the *loya jirga*, the tribally-appointed consultative body that ratified the Afghan constitution in December 2003. The government's support for political Islam is reflected in Chapter 1, Article 2 of the Afghan Constitution, where it states: "The religion of the state of the Islamic Republic of Afghanistan is the sacred religion of Islam."[54] In general, Islamists sought to portray the Karzai government as one that is subservient to the wishes of the United States and its Western allies, and corrupt and un-Islamic as a whole.[55] Taliban propaganda, for example, routinely referred to former President Karzai as the "new Shah Shuja," a reference to the Afghan king put on the throne by British invaders in the 19th century. Although the Taliban have not been as dogmatic in their opposition to democratic elections as other radical Islamist groups, they have frequently threatened voters with violence.[56]

There are, however, several Islamic parties that are either somewhat allied with the government or participate in the political process. One such example is the comparatively moderate *Jami'at-i Islami*, led by Salahuddin Rabbani, the current foreign minister, which participated in elections and the national political process. Other Islamists maintain an antagonistic relationship with the state, hoping to supplant it in the future, and return the country to *sharia* rule. The Karzai government, during its time in office, often spoke of the possibility of reconciliation with the Taliban,[57] and promulgated at least some aspects of *sharia* law in an effort to co-opt the Islamist opposition into the Afghan government. However, most of its overtures to the Taliban leadership yielded little to no results.

Before the end of the U.S. combat mission in Afghanistan in 2014, the Afghan government and the Obama administration pushed for a negotiated settlement with the Taliban. In July 2013, the Taliban opened diplomatic offices in Doha, Qatar, with the intention of using the facility as a neutral base from which to enter peace negotiations with the United States and Afghanistan. Peace efforts quickly stalled when the Taliban staged a flag-hoisting ceremony thought by the Afghan government and its Western allies to have been a Taliban government in exile, and after they issued unreasonable preconditions for negotiations. While the office was quickly closed, the Doha negotiations with the Taliban have remained moribund ever since.[58] Other signs of a parallel track of engagement are purportedly facilitated by Pakistan. In the summer of 2013, Islamabad released several high-level Taliban prisoners from its custody, including Mullah Abdul Ghani Baradar, who was the long-time second-in-command to Mullah Omar before being imprisoned by Pakistani forces in 2010. Baradar is believed to be one of the few Taliban commanders who could serve as an interlocutor in Afghan-Taliban peace talks, and was rumored to be exploring that option in 2010 shortly before his arrest.[59] However, Baradar's release did not yield any significant results in kick-starting the stalled peace negotiations with the Taliban.

In April 2014, Afghanistan held a presidential election, a protracted process punctuated by allegations of fraud and political uncertainty. In September 2014, the two leading candidates, Ashraf Ghani and Abdullah Abdullah, struck a power-sharing agreement and formed a national unity government. Ashraf Ghani was sworn in as Afghan president and he subsequently created a new position of Chief Executive (the equivalent of a prime minister) for Abdullah Abdullah, the runner-up in the vote. Even though President Ghani had pitched most of his campaign around improvements in government efficiency and addressing corruption, he initially prioritized and used his political capital on negotiating with the Taliban – and, by extension their historic patrons, Pakistan - and like his predecessor, Hamid Karzai, reached out to Pakistan to facilitate the talks, overlooking the ambitious and costly nature of the gambit.[60] In his first foreign trips as the president, President Ghani visited to Pakistan, Saudi Arabia and China to gain support for a reinvigorated campaign in pursuit of a peace settlement with the Taliban.[61] China has even hosted Taliban delegations in Beijing, including in July 2016, in support for the negotiations, but this has not yielded any tangible results as of yet.[62]

As part of the peace and reconciliation campaign, Ghani's government also established a Quadrilateral Coordination Group (QCG), which includes Afghanistan, Pakistan, China and the United States. The QCG planned to meet several times in the spring of 2016, in hopes that Pakistan will end its "undeclared war" against Afghanistan and sincerely bring the Taliban to the negotiating table.[63] However, the Taliban delegation did not attend, causing such frustration among the Afghan delegation that they demanded the Taliban be declared irreconcilable.[64] It was not until April 2016 – after a suicide attack outside Afghanistan's intelligence headquarters, the National Directorate of Security (NDS) claimed 64 lives and wounded almost 350 others[65] -- that President Ghani appeared to fully realize that Pakistan and its Afghan proxies will continue to disregard his pleas for peace, Following the attack, Ghani addressed the nation with the boldest declaration since the 1990s, stating that Afghanistan no longer wants Pakistan to facilitate negotiations with the Taliban, and pledging that those who shed the blood of their own people for the interests of outsiders would be brought to justice. Ghani also declared that amnesty and a lenient approach would no longer define Afghan policy toward militancy, but that Afghanistan's doors would remain open to those who wish to lay down their weapons and reconcile.[66] It remains unclear what the future will bring as relations continue to sour between Afghanistan and Pakistan over Islamabad's duplicitous policy towards Kabul. However, by any measure, Pakistan's subversive role has alienated the country from potential friends in Kabul as well as Washington.

ENDNOTES

[1] Hashmat Baktash and Mark Magnier, "NATO disputes claim of 11 civilian deaths in Afghan strike," Los Angeles Times, September 8, 2013, http://www.latimes.com/world/worldnow/la-fg-wn-afghan-nato-dispute-civilian-deaths-20130908,0,5924476.story.

[2] "Civilian casualties rise by 24 percent in first half of 2014," United Nations Assistance Mission in Afghanistan, July 9, 2014, http://unama.unmissions.org/LinkClick.aspx?fileticket=OhsZ29Dgeyw%3d&tabid=12254&mid=15756&language=en-US.

[3] "Afghanistan: Civilian Casualties Remain at Record High Level in the First Half of 2015 – UN Report," UN Human Rights Office of the High Commissioner, August 2015, http://www.ohchr.org/en/NewsEvents/Pages/DisplayNews.aspx?NewsID=16289&LangID=E.

[4] "Afghanistan: Annual Report 2015 – Protection for Civilians in Armed Conflict," UNAMA & UN OHCHR, February 2016, https://unama.unmissions.org/sites/default/files/poc_annual_report_2015_final_14_feb_2016.pdf.

[5] Grossman, Patricia. "Afghanistan's Civilian Casualties Hit Record High in 2016." Human Rights Watch. February 6, 2017, https://www.hrw.org/news/2017/02/06/afghanistans-civilian-casualties-hit-record-high-2016

[6] Ibid.; "Afghanistan: Annual Report 2015 – Protection for Civilians in Armed Conflict."

[7] "Afghan forces' casualties climbing in 2016, top U.S. commander says." Reuters. July 10, 2016, www.reuters.com/article/us-usa-afghanistan-casualties-idUSKCN0ZQ04H

[8] "2,853 ANA troops killed in Action Since 2003," Afghanistan Times, October 2014, http://old.afghanistantimes.af/news_details.php?id=9352; See also Neta C. Crawford, "War-Related Death, Injury and Displacement in Afghanistan and Pakistan 2001-2014," Costs of War, Watson Institute for International Studies, Brown University, May 2015, http://watson.brown.edu/costsofwar/files/cow/imce/papers/2015/War%20Related%20Casualties%20Afghanistan%20and%20Pakistan%202001-2014%20FIN.pdf.

[9] Gul, Ayaz. "Afghan Forces Suffered 15,000 Casualties in First 8 Months of 2016." Voice of America. October 30, 2016. www.voanews.com/a/afghanistan-us/3571779.html

[10] Gretchen Peters, Seeds of Terror, (New York: Thomas Dunne Books, 2009), 104.

[11] Vanda Felbab-Brown, "Blood and Faith in Afghanistan: A June 2016 Update," The Brookings Institution, June 2016, http://www.brookings.edu/~/media/research/files/papers/2016/05/blood-faith-afghanistan-june-2016-update-felbabbrown/felbab-brown-paper-blood-and-faith-in-afghanistan-may-2016.pdf.

[12] "Mullah Omar: Taliban Leader 'Died in Pakistan in 2013'", BBC News, July 29, 2015, http://www.bbc.com/news/world-asia-33703097.

[13] "Taliban Control Half of Afghanistan, Report Says," Telegraph (London), November 22, 2007, http://www.telegraph.co.uk/news/worldnews/1570232/Taliban-control-half-of-Afghanistan-says-report.html.

[14] Figures are drawn from both the official United Nations report on suicide attacks in Afghanistan (listing 123 for 2006, and 77 for 2007 [until June 30]), and the Afghanistan Conflict Monitor, listing approximately 150 for 2010. See United Nations Assistance Mission in Afghanistan,

[15] "Suicide Attacks in Afghanistan (2001-2007)," September 9, 2007, http://www.reliefweb.int/rw/RWFiles2007.nsf/FilesByRWDocUnidFilename/EKOI-76W52H-Full_Report.pdf/$File/Full_Report.pdf, and "Security Incidents," Human Security Report Project Afghanistan Conflict Monitor, September 2010, http://www.afghanconflictmonitor.org/incidents.html.

[16] "Aid Worker Security Report 2015: Figures at a Glance," Aid Worker Security Database (AWSD), n.d., https://aidworkersecurity.org/sites/default/files/HO_AidWorkerSecPreview_1015_G.PDF.
[17] As cited in Tom Vanden Brook, "Marines Fighting Taliban Strive to Win Afghan Locals' Trust," USA Today, August 3, 2009, http://www.cnas.org/node/3065.
[18] "Full President Obama Speech Text on Afghanistan," Los Angeles Times, December 1, 2009, http://latimesblogs.latimes.com/washington/2009/12/obama-speech-text-afghanistan.html.
[19] Kristina Wong, "Some US Troops to stay in Afghanistan after 2014," Washington Post, September 8, 2013, http://www.washingtontimes.com/news/2013/sep/8/some-us-troops-to-stay-in-afghanistan-after-2014/.
[20] Kenneth Katzman, "Afghanistan: Post-Taliban Governance, Security, and U.S. Policy," Congressional Research Service (CRS), June 2016, https://www.fas.org/sgp/crs/row/RL30588.pdf.
[21] Ibid.
[22] Declan Walsh and Azam Ahmed, "Mending Alliance, U.S. and Afghanistan Sign Long-Term Security Agreement," New York Times, September 30, 2014, http://www.nytimes.com/2014/10/01/world/asia/afghanistan-and-us-sign-bilateral-security-agreement.html?_r=0.
[23] Ahmed Rashid, Jihad: The Rise of Militant Islam in Central Asia (New Haven: Yale University Press, 2002), esp. chapter 7.
[24] Brian Glyn Williams, "On the Trail of the Lions of Islam: A History of Foreign Fighters in Afghanistan and Pakistan, 1980 to 2010," Orbis 55, iss. 2, (2011).
[25] See, for example, Nicola Smith, "Irishman Wants To Kill For Islam," Sunday Times (London), November 15, 2009, http://www.timesonline.co.uk/tol/news/world/ireland/article6917485.ece; Stefan Nicola, "Analysis: German Suspects In Afghanistan," UPI, May 1, 2008, http://www.spacewar.com/reports/Analysis_German_suspects_in_Afghanistan_999.html; "Dozens of Westerners Attending Terror Camps," MSNBC, October 19, 2009, http://www.millennium-ark.net/NEWS/09_Terror/091020.Westerners.terror.camps.html.
[26] Such as Uighur radicals. See B. Raman, "Suspected Death of Yuldashev: Good News for Uzbekistan, China, Germany," South Asia Analysis Group Paper no. 3442, October 3, 2009, http://www.southasiaanalysis.org/%5Cpapers35%5Cpaper3442.html.
[27] "'I Agreed to Become a Suicide Bomber,'" BBC (London), November 12, 2009, http://news.bbc.co.uk/2/hi/south_asia/8357011.stm.
[28] Robert Baer, "A Dagger to the CIA," GQ, April 2010, http://www.gq.com/news-politics/politics/201004/dagger-to-the-cia. For the suicide video, see http://www.youtube.com/watch?v=HB1NJ8zOOso.

[29] See, for example, its online journal, Tala'i' Khurasan, at http://www.e-prism.org/images/kurasan_No.11-_121428_-_28-12-07.pdf.

[30] Salafi derives from the Arabic term "salaf," meaning "the pious predecessors." It refers to members of the Sunni Islamic sect that are strictly and fundamentally orthodox in their beliefs, advocating a return and adherence to the early version of Islam, based on Quran and Sunna.

[31] Harleen Gambhir, "ISIS in Afghanistan," Institute for the Study of War (ISW), December 2015, http://www.understandingwar.org/sites/default/files/ISIS%20in%20Afghanistan_2.pdf.

[32] Ibid.

[33] Ibid.

[34] Matt Bradley, "ISIS Declares New Islamist Caliphate," The Wall Street Journal, June 29, 2014. http://www.wsj.com/articles/isis-declares-new-islamist-caliphate-1404065263.

[35] Ibid.

[36] Akhilesh Pillalamarri, "Revealed: Why ISIS Hates the Taliban," The Diplomat, January 29, 2016, http://thediplomat.com/2016/01/revealed-why-isis-hates-the-taliban/.

[37] Anwal, Mohammad. "Islamic State fighters in Afghanistan flee to Kunar province." Reuters. March 24, 2016, in.reuters.com/article/afghanistan-islamicstate-idINKCN0WQ1KX

[38] Steve Visser and Masoud Popalzai, "ISIS Claims Afghanistan Explosion that Kills Dozens," CNN, July 24, 2016, http://edition.cnn.com/2016/07/23/asia/afghanistan-explosion/.

[39] Ibid.

[40] Ibid.

[41] Ibid.

[42] Ibid.

[43] "Hizb-i-Islami (Islamic Party)," Globalsecurity.org, n.d., http://www.globalsecurity.org/military/world/para/hizbi-islami.htm.

[44] Responsibility for these assassination attempts has been disputed, and the Taliban also claimed the 2008 attempt.

[45] Nordland, Rod. "Afghanistan Signs Draft Peace Deal With Faction Led by Gulbuddin Hekmatyar." The New York Times. September 22, 2016. https://www.nytimes.com/2016/09/23/world/asia/afghanistan-peace-deal-hezb-i-islami.html

[46] "Security Council ISIL (Da'esh) and Al-Qaida Sanctions Committee Removes One Entry from Its Sanctions List." February 3, 2017. https://www.un.org/press/en/2017/sc12705.doc.htm

[47] Felbab-Brown, "Blood and Faith in Afghanistan: A June 2016 Update"; See also Michael Pearson, Masoud Popalzai and Zahra Ullah, "Death Toll Rises After Taliban Attack in Kabul," CNN, April 20, 2016, http://edition.cnn.com/2016/04/19/asia/kabul-explosion/.

[48] "Afghanistan," Central Intelligence Agency World Factbook, June 24, 2010, https://www.cia.gov/library/publications/the-world-factbook/geos/af.html.

[49] Stephen Tanner, Afghanistan: A Military History from Alexander the Great to the war against the Taliban(Cambridge, MA.: Da Capo Press, 2009).

[50] Fahmi Huwaydi, Taliban: jundallah fi al-ma`raka al-ghalat (Beirut: Dar al-Shuruq, 2001), 9-31; For official statements, see http://www.alemarah.info/english/.

[51] Barry Bearak, "Afghan Says Destruction of Buddhas is Complete," New York Times, March 12, 2001, http://www.nytimes.com/2001/03/12/world/afghan-says-destruction-of-buddhas-is-complete.html.

[52] Brian Glyn Williams, "Suicide Bombings in Afghanistan," Jane's Islamic Affairs Analyst, September 2007, 5, http://www.brianglynwilliams.com/IAA%20suicide.pdf.

[53] Noah Browning, Sami Aboudi and Mark Heinrich, "Al Qaeda Leader Zawahiri Pledges Allegiance to New Taliban Chief: Websites," Reuters, August 13, 2015, http://www.reuters.com/article/us-afghanistan-taliban-qaeda-idUSKCN0QI1FO20150813.

[54] The Constitution of Afghanistan, n.d., http://www.afghan-web.com/politics/current_constitution.html.

[55] "Taliban: Winning the War of Words?" International Crisis Group Asia Report no. 158, July 24, 2008, http://www.crisisgroup.org/home/index.cfm?id=5589&l=1.

[56] See "Afghanistan's Election Challenges," International Crisis Group Asia Report no. 171, June 24, 2009, http://www.crisisgroup.org/home/index.cfm?id=6176&l=1.

[57] "Karzai To Lawmakers: 'I Might Join the Taliban,'" Associated Press, April 5, 2010, http://www.msnbc.msn.com/id/36178710/.

[58] "Taliban shuts Doha HQ over 'broken promises," Al Jazeera, July 9, 2013, http://www.aljazeera.com/news/middleeast/2013/07/201379221645539703.html.

[59] Clarence Fernandez, "Pakistan releases former Taliban second-in-command," Reuters, September 21, 2013, http://www.reuters.com/article/2013/09/21/us-pakistan-baradar-idUSBRE98K02S20130921.

[60] Felbab-Brown, "Blood and Faith in Afghanistan: A June 2016 Update."

[61] Ibid.

[62] Ibid.

[63] Ibid.

[64] Ibid.

[65] Samimullah Arif, "Ashraf Ghani's New Plan to Win Afghanistan's Long War Against the Taliban," The Diplomat, April 28, 2016, http://thediplomat.com/2016/04/ashraf-ghanis-new-plan-to-win-afghanistans-long-war-against-the-taliban/

[66] Ibid.

BANGLADESH

QUICK FACTS

Population: 156,186,882 (July 2016 est.)

Area: 148,460 sq km

Ethnic Groups: Bengali at least 98%, ethnic groups 1.1%

Religions: Muslim 89.1%, Hindu 10%, other 0.9% (includes Buddhist, Christian)

Government Type: Parliamentary Republic

GDP (official exchange rate): $226.8 billion (2015 est.)

Map and Quick Facts courtesy of the CIA World Factbook (January 2017)

OVERVIEW

H Islam exerts a profound influence on the society and politics of Bangladesh. Islamist activity in Bangladesh takes three broad forms: the traditional revivalism of grassroots movements such as theHefazate-Islam, Ahl-i-Hadith and Tablighi Jama'at; the incremental political Islam of Islamic political parties (most prominently the Bangladesh Jama'at-i-Islami); and the more radical, subversive activism of jihadist organizations such as the Harkatul Jihad al-Islam (HUJIB) and Jagrato Muslim Janata Bangladesh (JMB), which seek to capture state power through unconstitutional or violent means. Shortly after its independence from Pakistan in December 1971, Bangladesh introduced secularism, before rejecting it in 1975 in favor of a moderate Muslim state. In 1988, Islam became the official state religion. In 2011, Bangladesh again introduced secularism through the 15th amendment to its constitution. Under this new amendment to the constitution despite having the sescular state ideology, Islam as the State religion was retained in the constitution and Bismillahir Rahmanir Raheem (In the name of Allah most gracious and most merciful) was retained on the Preamble to the constitution. Although 'Absolute faith and trust in Allah' was removed from the Constitution, and freedom of religion was revived and the provision for religion-based politics was maintained.[1]

ISLAMIST ACTIVITY

Islamist activity in Bangladesh can be placed in three general categories: the traditional revivalism of grassroots movements, the incremental political Islam of the country's Islamic political parties, and the more radical, subversive activism of *jihadist* organizations.

Islamic revivalism

Hefazat-e-Islam(Hefazat), *Ahl-i-Hadith Bangladesh* (AHAB) and *Tablighi Jama'at* are the three main movements in Islamic revivalism.

Bangladesh *Hefazat-e-Islam* (Hefazat) meaning "Protectorate of Islam in Bangladesh" was born in January 2010, protesting the then Awami league Government's proposed Women Development Policy (Nary Unnayan Nity) which planed to give women the equal rights of inheritance as men[2] contradicting the Quranic law of inheritance.[3] Mawlana Ahmad Shafi, a 93-year-old religious scholar and the chairman of the Bangladesh *Qaumi Madrassa* system[4] is the supreme leader of the Hifazat.[5] The headquarter of Hefazat is located in the port city of Chittagong, The Hefazat enjoys the support of more than 25,000 madrassas, or religious schools, across Bangladesh. Teachers and students at these madrassas belong to these organizations.[6]

The Hefazat-e Islam is a strong alliance of about a dozen Islamic organisations united under one banner very recently.[7] Unlike a political party it acts as a pressure group in order to protect the country from anti-Islamic activities. The organization is claimed to be financed through charity and donations.[8] It does not seek power through elections, but aims to extend its support to those parties who can establish proper Islamic ways of lives. It normally organizes issue oriented program. It acts as the most influencial pressure group in the country. Till today the Hefazat is organized and carrying out religious movement based on 13 point demands including a ban on mixing of men and women in public places, the removal of sculptures and demands for the retention "absolute trust and faith in Almighty Allah" in the preamble of the constitution of Bangladesh.[9] Hefazat-e-Islam has recently come to the centre of national politics by an extraordinary event. It organized a demonstration of about half million people and paralyzed the city of Dhaka on 5 May, 2013 demanding the implementation of their 13 point demands.[10] Among the existing political parties all but Marxist organizations want to build rapport with Hefazat-e-Islam in order to utilize their huge support base in rural Bangladesh to win the future actions. Despite wide ideological differences the main stream political parties like, the Bangladesh Nationalist Party(BNP), Bangladsh Awamileague(BAL), and Bangladesh Jatya Party(BJP) either latent or manifestly try to maintain a liaison with the Hefazat just to exploit their support to win the future elections. The supporters of *Hefazat* say it is campaigning to "save Islam" in Bangladesh, and the detractors fear that it will take the country, "back into the dark ages".[11]

(AHAB) was founded by Siddiq Hasan and Syed Nazir Hossain in British India in the 1830s and found its way to Bengal.

AHAB subscribes to *Wahhabi* ideology, following the exclusionary teachings of Saudi Arabia's Islamic *ulema* (clergy). As part of this worldview, the group does not recognize any single school of law, and relies only on the Quran and *hadith*.[12] AHAB exists in about 40 districts, and claims more than 25 million people as followers.[13] It aims to disseminate the knowledge of the Koran and the *Hadith*, and does not openly involve itself in politics. Instead, it seeks to reorganize the Muslim community and implement the principle of the *Kalemai Tayeba* (faith) in all walks of life.[14] AHAB's funding comes from membership donations and a considerable supply of foreign donations, particularly from Saudi Arabia, Kuwait, and other Arab countries.[15]

Tablighi Jama'at was founded in the 1920s by Mohammad Ilyas Shah with the objective of educating non-practicing Muslims on the subcontinent in how to perform daily prayer (salat) and lead a Muslim life in accordance with the teaching of Prophet Muhammad.[16] *Tablighi* Jama'at aims to bolster Islamic ideals and culture among Muslims.[17] The famous Kakrail mosque in Dhaka serves as the group's headquarters in Bangladesh. The missionary movement is organized by the volunteer work of dedicated religious individuals of all classes, but the middle class is dominant.[18] It organizes meetings, seminars and symposia, as well as an annual *Istema* (assembly) attended by millions of people worldwide—the second largest congregation of Muslims in the world, after the pilgrimage to Mecca. That conference is held annually in the industrial town of Tongi on the banks of the Turag River. Although it does not have links with any political party, *Tablighi Jama'at* receives support from the Bangladeshi government in logistics, maintenance of law and order, traffic, health and sanitation services.[19] Millions of followers are active throughout Bangladesh, and the movement has significant impact on social life within the country. The TJ works for the improvement of the individual's Islamic practices and avoids radicalization/political Islam.

Political Islam

The most important Islamist political party is *Bangladesh Jama'at-I-Islami* (BJI), originally known as simply *Jama'at-i-Islami* (JI). JI was founded in the early 1940s in British India by Islamic ideologue Syed Abul Ala Moududi. After Bangladesh's independence, JI was banned as a communal party in a secular state.[20] Though proscribed, it continued to operate underground. In 1976, renowned JI leader of former East Pakistan Maulana Abdur Rahim resumed JI activities through the formation of a new party called the Islamic Democratic League (IDL).[21] Six JI leaders ran on the IDL ticket and won seats in Bangladesh's parliament in 1979. The JI was then revived and began operating in Bangladesh in 1979 under its acting *emir* (head), Abbas Ali Khan, when the ban on religious-based political parties was withdrawn.[22] Maulana Motiur Rahman Nijami was then elected *emir* in 2002, a post he continued to occupy until he was executed in May 2016 through the verdict of the Highest Court of Bangladesh for his involvement with the War crimes in 1971 during the liberation War of

Bangladesh. After Nijami's death, JI renamed itself BJI and elected Maqbul Ahmed, as its new leader who had been acting as *emir* for six years when real emir Nizami was imprisoned.[23] (See footnote for explanation)

BJI focuses on obtaining power through democratic elections and the constitutional process. BJI believes in both Bangladeshi nationalism and the idea of Islamic democracy. The JI web site shows that "the JIB is striving democratically to enforce God–fearing, honest, and efficient leadership."[24] BJI aims to create national unity and rejuvenate Islamic values in every sphere of national life with the aim to safeguard the country from internal disorder and the attack of outsiders.[25] BJI follows four principles: educating the people with proper Islamic knowledge and organizing them; developing moral values among them; providing social services on the basis of Islamic values; finally, improving the system of governance by replacing the secular and oppressive leadership through God fearing, honest and qualified leadership at all levels through democratic means.[26] BJI is the largest functioning Islamic party in Bangladesh, and is popular among students, the academic intelligentsia, civil servants, the military and other important sectors of Bangladeshi society.[27] However, its overall political impact remains limited; in the country's 1986 parliamentary elections, the JI won 10 seats; in 1991, 18 seats; and in 1996, three seats. In 2001 the JI again secured 17 seats,[28] and finally in the 2008 election, the JI once again received only 2 parliamentary seats with just 4.5 percent of the popular vote.[29] BJI as 18 party alliance partner did not take part in the 2014 parliamentary elections to measure their nationwide current popularity.

The BJI boasts a broad financial network, though its yearly income has never been disclosed publicly. It indirectly operates many financial institutions, including Islamic banks and Islamic insurance companies, as well as private universities, medical colleges and private schools. The Islamic Bank Bangladesh Ltd., a BJI-managed bank, is claimed to have emerged as one of the most successful commercial banks of Bangladesh.[30] These businesses generate huge profits.[31] The ruling Awami league AL government has established its control and monitoring of the financial institutions of JI, most prominently by having four of the five-person board of directors for the bank fired and replaced with pro-government directors, after the bank was accused of financing terrorism in 2014.[32] Unlike other political parties in Bangladesh, the BJI claims that its workers and members contribute money to the party fund according to their capability.[33] The party also has large numbers of supporters and sympathizers in Middle Eastern countries, Europe and North America, who donate regularly.[34] Despite its Islamic ideology, however, BJI has managed to successfully attract western-educated elites,[35] and is now considered to be the premier mainstream Islamic modernist party in the country.

Apart from BJI, many other minor Islamic parties exist in Bangladesh. Although the number of registered Islamic parties stands at just eight, there are more than 100 Islamic parties that exist in one form or another in the country.[36] The most important among them are: the Bangladesh Muslim League, *Nizam-I Islam, Bangladesh Khilafat Andolon, Bangladesh Khilafat Majlis, Islamic Andolon, Jamat-i Ulema Is-*

lam, and the *Islamic Oikko Jote*.[37] All operate legally under the country's constitution, but their organizations are weak and support bases slim. Like BJI, each advocates the imposition of Islamic law in Bangladesh.

Violent Islamist groups

Since the 1990s, al-Qaeda has boasted a considerable presence in Bangladesh, represented by underground organizations such as *Harkatul Jihad al-Islam* (HUJIB), *Jagrato Muslim Janata Bangladesh* (JMB) and *Ansarullah Bangla Team* (ABT). After September 11th and the start of the War on Terror, the al-Qaeda network gravitated even more toward Bangladesh, attracted by the country's fragile economy and weak capacity to combat terrorism.

Harkatul Jihad al-Islam was founded in Bangladesh in 1992, with the goal of establishing Islamic *hukumat* (rule) in Bangladesh via *jihad*.[38] Comprised of veterans of the Afghan *jihad*, HUJIB is reported to have received initial funding from bin Laden's International Islamic Front.[39] In 2005, the Bangladeshi government banned the organization,[40] and in 2008, the U.S. formally listed HUJIB as a terrorist organization.[41] HUJIB's principal areas of activities are limited to the area between Cox's Bazaar, Bangladesh, and the border with Myanmar.[42] The group reportedly maintains six camps in the hilly Chittagong Hill Tract region where its cadres are provided arms training. While there is no authoritative information about the actual size of the group, it is estimated to have around 15,000 members.[43] Since 2005, frequent raids on HUJIB centers by Bangladeshi Rapid Action Battalion (RAB) police and army—and the continuous monitoring of their activities by law enforcement agencies—have significantly weakened the group's capabilities,[44] although it is unknown whether this terrorist outfit is totally eliminated or not. HUJIB reportedly receives financial assistance from Pakistan, Saudi Arabia and Afghanistan via Muslim non-governmental organizations active in Bangladesh.[45] Mufti Hannan, HUJIB's operational commander, launched an attack on British High Commissioner Anwar Chowdhury in 2004. In 2007, he was arrested and sentenced to death for the crime. The appellate Division of the Bangladesh Supreme Court in its final verdict on December upheld the death sentence of Mufti Abdul Hannan and two others in a case filed over the grenade attack on ex-British High commissioner to Bangladesh Anwar Choudhury in 2004.[46]

The *Jammatul Mujahideen Bangladesh* (JMB) came into existence in 1998 with the aim of establishing *sharia* law in Bangladesh through armed revolution. Its supreme leader was Shaikh Abdur Rahman, and second in command was Siddiqur Rahman (a.k.a. Bangla Bhai), who also led its military wing, the *Jagroto Muslim Janata Bangladesh* (JMJB). In 2004, Bangla Bhai unleashed a wave of terror in the northern part of Bangladesh as part of an ostensible war on outlawed Marxist extremists. The targets of the JMB onslaught were judges and lawyers, who were targeted in a bid by the group to establish an Islamic legal system.[47] The group's last large-scale attack was a series of bombings in August 2005. The organization reportedly receives funding from various sources, including individual donors from Kuwait, Saudi Arabia, the UAE, Bahrain, Pakistan, and Libya.[48] Funding for the group also flows through NGOs, which—in spite of their ostensibly humanitarian activism—have aided the activities of the JMB.[49] Several international NGOs—among them the Kuwait-based Revival of Islamic Heritage and Doulatul Kuwait, the UAE-based Al Fuzaira, the Bahrain-based Doulatul Bahrain and the Saudi Arabia-based Al Haramain Islamic Institute—have reportedly provided funding to the group in the past.[50] The JMB reportedly has approximately 10,000 full time and 100,000 part-time members, including teachers, students and ordinary citizens.[51] JMB was banned in 2005 by the government of Prime Minister Khaleda Zia. Its principal leader, Abdur Rahman, its second-in-command, Bangla Bhai, and four other members of the *Majlish-e-sura* (the group's top decision making body) were tried and executed in Bangladesh in 2007.[52] As a result of the execution of their main leaders and strict observation and monitoring of their movements by the law enforcing agencies and government's zero tolerance policy to them, the JMB's activities apparently ceased to exist.

Ansarullah BanglaTeam (ABT) is a militant group that has pledged to uphold al-Qaeda's ideology, and is connected with the organization's Persian Gulf franchise, al-Qaeda in the Arabian Peninsula. It began operating in Bangladesh during 2007 under the name *Jamaat-ul-Muslimin*, but dissolved due to a shortage of funds. The group resurfaced during 2013 as the ABT. The government of Bangladesh banned this terrorist outfit in May 2015 under the country's current anti-terrorism law.[53] This group has been implicated in the attacks and killings of secular bloggers from 2013-2015.[54]

Domestic *jihadism* has also been influenced by the Islamic State, which has begun to exert an influence on Islamist activities in Bangladesh. In 2016, the country experienced a series of terrorist attacks reportedly carried out by homegrown terrorists inspired by the Islamic State (ISIS). The most significant one was the attack on the Holey Artisan Bakery in Dhaka on 1 July 1, 2016, which killed 22 people. The Islamic State claimed the responsibility for the incident, but the Bangladeshi government denied ISIS's involvement and claimed that homegrown militants from JMB were involved.[55] Experts continue to debate whether the gunmen were linked to ISIS, or al Qaeda, or JMB.[56]

Islamism and Society

Bangladesh, widely regarded as a moderate Muslim democracy, is 89.7 percent Muslim and 9.2 percent Hindu, 0.7 percent Buddhists, 0.3 percent Christian. Animist and believers in tribal faith constitute 0.1 percent of the population.[57] More than 98 percent of the population is ethnic Bengali. Non-Bengalis include a minute number of Urdu-speaking Biharis. Among the country's Muslims, more than 99 percent are Sunni and follow the Hanafi school. Several Shi'a and Ahmadiya sects are also represented, albeit only nominally.[58]

Mosques in Bangladesh serve as active centers of religious activity. In the country's 65,000 villages, there are an estimated 133,197 mosques, which act as focal points for daily and weekly prayers and assembly.[59] Local donations, as well as donations from West Asian and African Muslim countries, provide for the construction and maintenance of these religious centers.[60] A parallel structure of some 58,126 *maqtabs* (informal Islamic schools) imparts basic Islamic knowledge to young children (including how to read the Koran, pray, etc.) Mosque *imams* act as influential elders in the country's rural power structure.

Most Bangladeshis follow an orthodox, traditional version of Islam. *Madrassas* (Islamic schools) have long been considered to be the center of traditional Islamic studies and the guardians of the orthodox Islam in Bangladesh. Of these, there are two types: *Qomi madrassas* are private in nature, receive no financial support from the government, and subsist on religious endowments and donations from the faithful. *Alia madrassas*, by contrast, are controlled by the government, which pays 80 percent of the salaries of their teachers and staff, as well as considerable portion of their development budget. One estimate shows that the total number of *madrassas* (both *Qomi* and *Alia*) is 13,406, with 230,732 teachers and 3,340,800 students.[62] These schools constitute the main current of traditional Islam in Bangladeshi society.

ISLAMISM AND THE STATE

The forty-five-year political history of Bangladesh is typified by an official embrace of and accommodation with Islam by a succession of ruling governments. The current government in Bangladesh struggles with the role of Islamism in public life.

At the time of the country's independence in December 1971, the government of Sheikh Mujibur Rahman introduced a secular democracy and later, one-party authoritarianism. But enforced secularism eventually provoked backlash from the Muslim majority,[63] leading to greater inclusion of Islam in public life. Prime Minister Rahman (commonly known as "Mujib") established public foundations in Bangladesh for the research and analysis of Islamic culture and society. Under his direction, Bangladesh also joined the Organization of the Islamic Conference (OIC, today known as the Organization of Islamic Cooperation). Beyond that, however, the practice of Islam in political form was severely circumscribed.

This balance was shattered in 1975 by a *coup d'etat* that unseated Mujib and installed a military regime in his government's place. Bangladesh's new rulers wasted no time dropping secularism from the constitution and inserting a proviso emphasizing "absolute trust and faith in Almighty *Allah*."[64] Simultaneously, the new government allowed Islamic political parties, through a constitutional amendment, to return to politics, and included a constitutional addendum compelling Bangladesh to maintain fraternal relations among the Islamic countries based on Islamic solidarity.[65] After the assassination of President Ziaur Rahman in May 1981, power was assumed by General Hossein Mohammad Ershad, who established Islam as the state religion, ushering a period of relative religio-political stability.

In 1990, however, the Ershad regime was ousted as a result of a massive political revolt and purge. Khaleda Zia, Rahman's widow, assumed power and became the first female prime minister in the new parliamentary democracy. Like her late husband, Zia pursued a pro-Islamic policy both domestically and abroad. In 1996, Sheikh Hasina, one of Mujib's surviving daughters, rose to power as part of the opposition Awami League (AL) political party, only to be subsequently ousted by a coalition government with Khaleda Zia at its helm.

Hasina has demonstrated a willingness to make common cause with religious radicals for political gain, signing an agreement with *Khilafat Majlis*—a group considered by some to be a pro-Taliban Islamist group—as a strategy to win the country's January 2007 election. The ploy worked, and in 2008 Sheikh Hasina returned to power, further buoyed by her pledge "not to harm Islam."[67]

Despite her earlier partnership with *Khilafat Majlis*, Hasina has reinforced secularism and generally sought to combat Islamist forces. In February 2009, her government passed two key pieces of legislation: the Money Laundering Prevention Act (MLPA) and the Anti-terrorism Act (ATA).[68] The former empowered the Bangladesh Bank to freeze the accounts of suspected terrorist financiers, and directed it to take preventive measures against monetary transactions that might be used for financing terror acts. Together with the ATA, it also instituted the death penalty for terror financing and politically motivated acts of violence.[69] Furthermore, Hasina's government has aggressively prosecuted "war criminals" – Bangladeshis who sided with Pakistan during the war for independence – many of whom later became members of JI. This strategy effectively weakened Islamic forces, especially the JI.[70]

In 2011, the government imprisoned the top leaders of the JI and their allies on the grounds of their alleged involvement in crimes against humanity during the Bangladesh's war for independence in 1971. A tribunal, dubbed the International War Crimes Tribunal (ICT), was founded to try the accused. However, the validity of the ICT soon came into serious question. *The Economist* magazine published an investigative report showing that the chief of the tribunal, Judge Nizamul Haq, had worked improperly by taking written advice and suggestion through e-mail and Skype conversations from an unauthorized Brussels-based lawyer regarding the trial.[71] At that point, the ICT had already sentenced five BJI leaders to death by hanging. Apart from those sentences, the ICT sentenced two other leaders to death, but the appellate division reduce one man's sentence to life in prison, while the other escaped. National and international media as well as human rights organizations, have questioned the ICT's track record.[72] The death sentences also provoked violent protests that resulted in the deaths of 100 people.[73]

Another key blow in the fight against JI came in 2011 as well, the Bangladesh Parliament passed the 15th amendment of the constitution. The amendment re-introduced secularism as the official framework of the state, but retained Islam as the state religion. In August 2013, the High Court of Bangladesh declared JI illegal, on the grounds that its character violated the newly secular constitution of the country.[74] Unless it wins an appeal, it will be a banned organization and unable to enter the January 2014 national election.[75] Indeed, the appeal court did not give its verdict yet and the ruling coalition led by Awamileague captured all 300 seats, whereas 153 cadidates declared uncontested winners in the parliament in the aftermath of the elections boycott by the 18 party election alliance led by the BNP, one of the largest political parties in Bangladesh.[76] In a 2016 decision Bangladesh's High Court upheld Islam as the official religion of the Muslim-majority Bangladesh and legalized the co-existence of secularism and state religion Islam.[77]

Endnotes

[1] Constitutional Amendments in Bangladesh,online: http://studiesbangladesh.blogspot.ca/2011/06/constitutional-amendments-constitution.html

[2] Julien Bouissou, "Bangladesh's radical Muslims uniting behind Hefazat-e- Islam ", The Guardian 30Jul2013. online: https://www.theguardian.com/world/2013/jul/30/bangladesh-hefazat-e-islam-shah-ahmad-shafi

[3] According to Quranic law, a daughter's share is half of a son's. In the proposed Women Development Policy, daughters were suggested to inherit equal property rights. For details on Muslim Family Law, see, Farah Deeba Chowdhury, Islam and Women's Income :Dowry and Law in Bangladesh, (London: Routledge,2017),35-48.

[4] The Qaumi madrassa is one of the two madra systems in Bangladesh. These madrassas are run by the community or the people (Qaum), as opposed to the state. Like charitable organizations, these institutions are financed through donations of the community. The Qaumi madrassas in Bangladesh are founded in light of the Darul Ulum Deoband in Uttar Pradesh, India founded in 1867. Hathazari Qaumi Madrassa is the first one established in Bangladesh following the Deobond model. These madrassas are also known as Khwarijee madrassas, which means that they are outside Government control.See, "Modernization of Madrassa Education in Bangladesh: A Strategy Paper", Bangladesh Enterprise Institute (BEI) Dhaka, Bangladesh June 2011 online: ttp://ndc.gov.bd/lib_mgmt/webroot/earticle/2379/modernization_of_madrasa_education_in_Bangladesh.pdf.

[5] Born in Rangunia in Chittagong district, Maolana Shafi earned higher education in Islamic Studies in Deoband in India. He returned to teaching at the Hat-hazari madrassa, where he had once studied, and later became its Principal. See, Toufique Imrose Khalidi, "Behind the rise of Bangladesh'sHifazat",online:http://www.aljazeera.com/indepth/featur es/2013/05/201356134629980318.html

[6] Sabir Mustafa "Hefazat-e Islam: Islamist coalition" BBC Bengali Service 6 May 2013 http://www.bbc.com/news/world-asia-22424708

[7] Ibid.

[8] Julien Bouissou,op.cit.

[9] The 13 point demands raised by the Hefazat-e-Islam are the following: 1.Reinstate the phrase "Absolute trust and faith in the Almighty Allah" in the Constitution as one of the fundamental principles of state policy;2.Pass a law providing for capital punishment for maligning Allah, Islam and the Prophet Muhammad and for starting smear campaigns against Muslims; 3.Stop all propaganda and "derogatory comments" about the Prophet Muhammad by "atheist leaders" of the Shahbagh movement, atheist bloggers and other anti-Islamists; arrest them and ensure stern punishment to them; 4.Stop attacking, shooting, killing and persecuting the Prophet-loving Islamic scholars, madrassa students and people united by belief in Allah; 5.Release all the arrested Islamic scholars and madrassa students;6.Lift restrictions on mosques and remove obstacles for the holding of religious programmes; 7. Declare Qadianis (Ahmadiyyas) non-Muslim and stop their publicity and conspiracies; 8.Stop foreign cultural intrusions, including free-mixing of men and women and candle-light vigils, and put an end to adultery, injustice and shamelessness, among other things, committed in the name of freedom of expression and the individual; 9. Stop turning Dhaka, the city of mosques, into a city of idols, and stop installing sculptures at road intersections, colleges and universities.10.Scrap anti-Islam women policy and education policy and make Islamic education mandatory from primary to higher secondary levels; 11.. Stop threatening and intimidating teachers and students of the Qawmi madrassas, Islamic scholars, imams and khatibs;12. Stop creating hatred among the younger generation against Muslims by misrepresentation of Islamic culture in the media; 13. Stop anti-Islam activities by non-governmental organisations, evil attempts by Qadianis and conversion by Christian missionaries in Chittagong Hill Tracts and elsewhere in the country. See, Frontline, May 17,2013. Online: http://www.frontline.in/world-affairs/the-13-demands/article4650805.ece.

[10] Julien Bouissou opcit.

[11] Ibid.

[12] Sufia M. Uddin, Constructing Bangladesh,: Religion, Ethnicityand Language in an Islamic Nation (Chapel Hill: The University of North Carolina Press, 2006), 56.

[13] "Ahle Hadith: New moves in religion-based politics". PROBE News Magazine. 23 September ,2010, http://web.archive.org/web/20120324204417/http://www.probenewsmagazine.com/index.php?index=2&contentId=596.

[14] K.M. Mohsin, "The Ahl-I Hadis movement in Bangladesh,"in Rafiuddin Ahmed,ed. Religion,Nationalism and Politics in Bangladesh(New Delhi: South Asian publishers,1990), 179-182.

[15] The Kuwait based NGO Saudi Revival of Islamic Heritage (RIHS) is the main source of funding to the Ahle Hadith Bangladesh. See PROBE News Magazine Dhaka, 9, iss. 14, September, 2010, 24-30, online: http://www.probenewsmagazine.com. On this issue also see, Militancy Mumtaz Ahmad Ahl-e-Hadith Movement in Bangladesh: History, Religion, Politics and Militancy " online: http://www.iiu.edu.pk/wp-content/uploads/downloads/ird/downloads/Ahl-e-Hadith-Movement-in-Bangladesh-Complete.pdf

[16] Uddin, Constructing Bangladesh, 161-62.

[17] Ahmed Shafiqul Huque and Muhammad Yehia Akhter, "The Ubiquity of Islam: Religion and Society in Bangladesh" Pacific Affairs 60, no.2 (1987), 217.

[18] M. Rashiduzzaman, "Islam, Muslim Identity and Nationalism in Bangladesh," Journal of South Asian and Middle Eastern studies 18, no. 1 (1994), 54.

[19] Ibid.

[20] Banglapedia: Jamaat-e-Islami Bangladesh, n.d., http://en.banglapedia.org/index.php?title=Jamaat-e-Islami_Bangladesh.

[21] Ibid.

[22] Ibidem.

[23] Moqbul Ahamed was the acting Ameer and Motiur Rahman Nizami was the actual ameer duing 2010-2016, when Nizami was imprisoned. See Rafiqul Islam Azad " Maqbul Ahmed 'elected' Jamaat ameer,"The Independent, 21 September 2016. Online: http://www.theindependentbd.com/home/printnews/60962.

[24] Bangladesh Jamat-e-Islami, online: http://www.jamaat-e-islami.org/en/aboutus.php

[25] See the official website of Bangladesh Jamaat-e-Islami at http://www.jamaat-e-islami.org/en/details.php?artid=MTQ4.

[26] Porichity, Jamaati-Islami Bangladesh (Dhaka: 1981) p,5,p.10.

[27] IshtiaqHossain and Noore Alam Siddiquee, "Islam in Bangladesh: the role of the Ghulam of Jamaat-I Islami ," 384.

[28] Banglapedia, "Jamaat-e-Islami Bangladesh."

[29] Zaglul Haider, "The Ninth General Election in Bangladesh: The Fall of the Bangladesh Nationalist Party and the Rise of the Bangladesh Awami league" The Journal of South Asian and Middle Eastern Studies 34, no.3 (2011), 79.

[30] Ferdous Ahmad, "Islamic Banking Blooms in Bangladesh" online: http://islamicbanking.info/islamic-banking-in-bangladesh/

[31] See, Jamaat-e-Islami and its financial resources, online: http://www.bangladeshlivenews.com/home/article-details/4560/column/Jamaat-e-Islami+and+its+financial+resources/.

[32] Golam Mowla, "How govt is taking control of Islami Bank," Dhaka Tribune, April 26, 2016, http://archive.dhakatribune.com/bangladesh/2016/apr/26/how-govt-taking-control-islami-bank#sthash.sR2DhIFn.dpuf.

[33] Supporters and workers of other parties do not make contribution to the party fund on a monthly basis, they collect money from the party leaders, and big businessmen, while, the BJI workers and supporters contribute a fixed amount of money to the party fund regularly/monthly basis.

[34] The party's supporters, workers and well-wishers working abroad regularly contribute to the party fund, whether monthly, annually or occasionally as part of their political and moral responsibilities. Author's interviews with JI leaders and activists, Bangladesh, August 2006.

[35] Talukder Maniruzzaman, "Bangladesh Politics: Secular and Islamic Trends," in Rafiuddin Ahmed, ed., Religion, Nationalism and Politics in Bangladesh (New Delhi: South Asian Publishers, 1990), 84.

[36] The Islamic parties registered with the Election commission are: JI, Bangladesh Tarikat Federation, Bangladesh Khilafat Andolon, Bangladesh Muslim League, Jamiate Ulamaye Islam Bangladesh, Islamic Front Bangladesh, and Islami Oikko Jote (IOJ). See Mubashar Hasan, "The Geopolitics of Political islam in Bangladesh," Harvard Asia Quarterly 14, nos. 1-2, 2012, 65.

[37] Emajuddin Ahmad and D.R.J.A. Nazneen, "Islam in Bangladesh: Revivalism or Power politics?" Asian Survey 30, no.8, 1990, 802.

[38] Summit Ganguly, "The Rise of Islamist Militancy in Bangladesh" United States Institute of Peace Special Report, August 2006, http://www.usip.org/files/resources/SRaug06_2.pdf.

[39] Bruce Vaughn, Islamist Extremism in Bangladesh (Washington, DC: Congressional Research Service, January 31, 2007), http://www.fas.org/sgp/crs/row/RS22591.pdf.

[40] See "Harkatul Jihad banned at last," Daily Star, October 18, 2005, http://www.thedailystar.net/2005/10/18/d5101801033.htm.

[41] Ibid.

[42] "Harkat-ul-Jihad-al Islami Bangladesh (HuJI-B)," South Asia Terrorism Portal, n.d., http://www.satp.org/satporgtp/countries/bangladesh/terroristoutfits/Huj.htm.

[43] Ibid.

[44] Ibidem.

[45] Ibidem.

[46] "SC uphpholds death penalty for Mufti Hannan,2 others " The Daily Star,December 8,2016

[47] "Jama'atul Mujahideen Bangladesh," South Asia Terrorism Portal, n.d., http://www.satp.org/satporgtp/countries/bangladesh/terroristoutfits/JMB.htm.

[48] Ibid.

[49] Joyeeta Bhattacharjee, "Understanding 12 extremist groups of Bangladesh," Observer India, June 7, 2009, http://www.observerindia.com/cms/export/orfonline/modules/analysis/attachments/Bangladesh-Militant-Groups_1246945884723.pdf.

[50] "Jama'atul Mujahideen Bangladesh," South Asia Terrorism Portal.

[51] Ibid.

[52] Abdul Kalam Azady 26,2015., "Six Militant Linchpins Hanged," New Age (Dhaka), March 31, 2007, http://www.newagebd.com/2007/mar/31/front.html.

[53] Rohit Inani, "Bangladesh Bans a Hard-Line Islamist Group Suspected of Killing Atheist Bloggers" Time, May 16,2015,online: http://time.com/3895853/bangladesh-atheist-blogger-ansarullah-bangla-team-banned/; "Ansarullah Bangla Team Banned," Dhaka Tribune, May 26, 2015.

[54] Ibid.

[55] "Bangladesh police blames JMB for Dhaka cafe attack," The Indian Express, July 9, 2016, http://indianexpress.com/article/world/world-news/bangladesh-police-blames-jamaatul-mujahideen-bangladesh-jmb-for-dhaka-cafe-attack-2903911.

[56] Alexander Stark, "Dhaka attack part of a larger pattern of terrorism in Bangladesh," The Diplomat, July 22, 2016.

[57] BANBEIS, Bangladesh Bureau of Educational, Information, And Statistics, online:http://www.banbeis.gov.bd/bd_pro.htm

[58] For example, the international Sunni organization Khatma Nabuat continuously puts pressure on the government to declare the Ahamadya sect as non-Muslim.

[59] Rashidduzzaman, "Islam, Muslim Identity and Nationalism in Bangladesh," 36-60.

[60] Ahamed and Nazneen, "Islam In Bangladesh: Revivalism or Power politics?" 798.

[61] Mumtaz Ahmad, " Madrasa Education in Pakistan and Bangladesh," in Satu P. Limaye, Mohan Malik and Robert G. Wirsing, eds., Religious Radicalism and Security in South Asia (Honolulu, Hawaii: Asia Pacific Centre for Security Studies, 2004), 101.

[62] Ibid., 105.

[63] Rashed Uz Zaman, "Bangladesh-Between Terrorism, Identity and Illiberal Democracy: The Unfolding of a Tragic Saga," Perception 17, no. 3, 2012, 159.

[64] Rounaq Jahan, Bangladesh Politics: Problems and Issues,(Dhaka: The University Press Limited,1980),210.

[65] Zaglul Haider, The Changing Pattern of Bangladesh Foreign policy: A Comparative study of the Mujib and Zia regimes (Dhaka: The University Press Limited, 2006), 204.

[66] Bruce Vaughn, Bangladesh: Background and U.S. Relations (Washington, DC: Congressional Research Service, August 2, 2007), 4, http://www.fas.org/sgp/crs/row/RL33646.pdf.

[67] "Hasina promises no laws against Quran, Sunnah", BDNews24.com, online: http://bdnews24.com/bangladesh/election-2008/2008/12/15/hasina-promises-no-laws-against-quran-sunnah.

[68] "10 Bills Sail Through Opposition Protest," New Age (Dhaka), February 25, 2009, http://www.newagebd.com/2009/feb/25/front.html#1.

[69] "Bangladesh Enacts Tough Anti-Terrorism Law," Hindustan Times, June 13, 2008, http://www.hindustantimes.com/Bangladesh-enacts-tough-anti-terrorism-law/Article1-317131.aspx.

[70] United States Commission on International Religious Freedom, USCIRF Annual Report 2010 - Additional Countries Closely Monitored: Bangladesh, 29 April 2010, Online, http://www.unhcr.org/refworld/docid/4be28407d.html.

[71] "The trial of the birth of a nation," The Economist, (London), December 15, 2012, http://www.economist.com/news/briefing/21568349-week-chairman-bangladeshs-international-crimes-tribunal-resigned-we-explain.

[72] Human Rights Watch, "Bangladesh: Azam Conviction Based on Flawed Proceedings",online: https://www.hrw.org/news/2013/08/16/bangladesh-azam-conviction-based-flawed-proceedings.

[73] The conviction of Sayeedi, a Jamaat-e-Islami party leader, sparked protests last year leaving more than 100 dead..See, "Bangladesh Islamist Delwar Sayeedi death sentence commuted"BBC News, 17 September 2014, http://www.bbc.com/news/world-asia-29233639

[74] "Bangladesh Court declares Jamaat illegal," Al-Jazeera (Doha), August 1, 2013, www.aljazeera.com/news/asia2013/08.

[75] Ibid.

[76] Freedom House reports on 2014 Bangladesh elections: "In national elections held on January 5, 2014, the BNP and 17 allied parties boycotted the vote to protest what they said were unfair elections, leaving the majority of elected seats (153) uncontested and ensuring an AL victory. The AL won 234 parliamentary seats, and independents and minority parties captured the remainder." See, Freedom in the World, Online : https://freedomhouse.org/report/freedom-world/2015/bangladesh

[77] Davi Berggmen, "Bangladesh court upholds Islam as religion of the state," Al-Jazeera, March 28, 2016, http://www.aljazeera.com/news/2016/03/bangladesh-court-upholds-islam-religion-state-160328112919301.html.

INDIA

QUICK FACTS

Population: 1,266,883,598 (July 2016)

Area: 3,287,263 sq km

Ethnic Groups: Indo-Aryan 72%, Dravidian 25%, Mongoloid and other 3%

Religions: Hindu 79.8%, Muslim 14.2%, Christian 2.3%, Sikh 1.7%, other and unspecified 2%

Government Type: federal parliamentary republic

GDP (official exchange rate): $2.251 trillion (2015 est.)

Map and Quick Facts courtesy of the CIA World Factbook (January 12, 2017)

OVERVIEW

Few countries have felt the deadly consequences of Islamist extremism more than India. Situated next to Pakistan, a key sponsor and instigator of international Islamist terrorism, the South Asian region is host to a multiplicity of centers of Islamist militancy that have affected India, including Iran, the principal driver of Shia militancy; Afghanistan and Bangladesh where Sunni militancy has flourished, and the Arab world, where radical interpretations of Sunni Islam have affected the large community of expatriate Indian workers and their families.

However, the Indian Muslim community has in large part refused to yield to the call of militancy. A community of well over 172 million Muslims[1]—the second largest in the world after that of Indonesia[2]—lives in relative harmony within India's multicultural, multi-religious, secular democracy. Such coexistence is not without its frictions: strife between the various religious communities has been a significant feature in India since (and, indeed, long before) the carnage of the partition of India in 1947. That conflict, in which the British Indian Empire was cleaved in two, saw nearly half a million people killed. However, the Indian Muslim community has largely rejected broader attempts at radicalization and indoctrination, and remains integrated into the fabric of Indian society.

Arguably the greatest impact of Islamist terrorism in India has been felt in the state of Jammu and Kashmir, where a separatist movement, inspired by Sunni extremism and sustained by Pakistani support, has plagued the region for over two-and-a-half decades.[3] Islamist terrorist attacks on a smaller scale by both foreign and indigenous groups, meanwhile, have occurred in many other parts of the country.

ISLAMIST ACTIVITY

Islamist terrorism in India, overwhelmingly generated and supported by Pakistan, has long found its principal concentration in the north Indian state of Jammu and Kashmir (J&K). Though J&K has often been the site of Islamist violence, the situation has improved in recent years, as the changes on the world stage since 9/11 and Pakistan's growing instability have led to a diminution in violence. At its peak, Islamist violence in J&K killed over 4,500 people through 2001. In 2015, J&K saw 174 fatalities caused by Islamist terrorism, though there was a spike in 2016, with annual fatalities rising to 267.[4]

India has been confronted with Pakistani-backed Islamist subversion virtually since the birth of both nations,[5] but experienced an asymmetric escalation after 1988, when then-Pakistani dictator General Zia-ul-Haq, flush from the successful *jihad* against the Soviets in Afghanistan (1980-1989), decided to extend his strategy to J&K. Successive governments in Islamabad have actively sustained this policy, leading to unrelenting terrorism in J&K for over two and a half decades and inflicting—as of 2016—a total of 44,145 fatalities.[6]

Gradually, as international pressure to curtail *jihad* in J&K mounted and as domestic circumstances in Pakistan worsened, terrorist groups largely controlled by Pakistan's notorious spy agency, the Inter-Services Intelligence Directorate (ISI),[7] have increasingly found it necessary to base their cadres in areas outside of J&K. They have also had to rethink their approach within a wider pan-Islamist ideological framework that dovetails more seamlessly into the psyche of extremist groups and the logic of the "global *jihad*." Ever growing levels of Islamist subversion and terrorism were sustained across India since the start of the new century,[8] culminating in the Mumbai attacks of November 26, 2008,[9] though there has been a dramatic fall in incidence and fatalities since.

The networks and support structures of the multiplicity of Islamist terrorist organizations operating in India have been painstakingly constructed by the ISI and backed by enormous flows of financial support from West Asia, as well as from affluent expatriate Muslim communities in the West, as part of a sustained strategy of "erosion, encirclement and penetration" that has been exhaustively documented elsewhere.[10]

Lashkar e-Taiba (LeT)

Under the command of Hafiz Mohammad Saeed, the ISI created *Lashkar e-Taiba (LeT)*, in the Kunar province of Afghanistan. LeT is part of the "al-Qaeda compact"[11] and is a member of the "International Islamic Front for the struggle against the Jews and the Crusaders" *(Al-Jabhah al-Islamiyyah al-'Alamiyyah li-Qital al-Yahudwal-Salibiyyin)* established by Osama bin Laden in February 1998. In 1993, LeT's forces were diverted to the Pakistan-backed *jihad* in J&K, where it has operated continuously since. At the same time, LeT has extended its networks and strikes across the rest of India, crystallizing the strategy that Saeed first articulated publicly on February 18, 1996, in an address at the Lahore Press Club: "The *jihad* in Kashmir would soon spread to entire India. Our *mujahideen* would create three Pakistans in India."[12]

The organization is headquartered at Muridke on a large plot of land widely acknowledged to have been gifted to it by the Pakistan government,[13] and is known to have run terrorist camps in Muzaffarabad and Gilgit (in Pakistan-occupied Kashmir), Lahore, Peshawar, Islamabad, Rawalpindi, Karachi, Multan, Quetta, Gujranwala and Sialkot. The group operates at least 16 Islamic centers, 135 secondary schools, 2,200 offices and a vast network of *madrassas* (religious seminaries), orphanages, medical centers and charities across Pakistan.[14] The U.S. State Department's 2008 *Report on International Religious Freedom* noted that: "schools run by Jamat-ud-Dawa [LeT's sister organization] continued... teaching and recruitment for Lashkar-e-Tayyiba, a designated foreign terrorist organization."[15]

Until its designation as a terrorist group by the UN Security Council in December 2008, the LeT published a number of journals, papers and websites.[16] Crucially, it remains loyal to Pakistan and, unlike many other organizations created by the ISI which have since turned against Islamabad or whose loyalties are now suspect, continues to coordinate its activities with Pakistani state agencies. Finances for the group—as for all Pakistan-backed Islamist terrorist groupings—are provided via tacit state support, including the transfer of large quantities of fake Indian currency that Indian Intelligence sources contend, on the basis of interrogations of arrested terrorists and couriers, is printed at Pakistani Security Presses at the Malir Cantonment in Karachi, and at Lahore, Quetta and Peshawar.

Significant in this regard is the Indian government's August 2009 announcement that it intends to take up the issue of the importation of currency standard ink and paper by Pakistan from the UK, Sweden and Switzerland, with various international agencies, including Interpol.[17] In addition to very substantial seizures of fake Indian currency notes (FICN) from Pakistan-linked couriers, there have been instances of such currency also being recovered from Pakistan Embassy staff.[18] India's Ministry of Home Affairs has reportedly found that "the ISI has managed to get access to the configuration, specifications and other secret codes of the genuine Indian currency notes from six European companies that supply Indian currency papers fitted with security features, and another company in Switzerland that supplies the security ink used in printing these currency notes in India."[19] Neutralizing FICN in circulation was also one of the objectives of the demonitisation of INR 1000 and 500 notes in November 2016, and there were claims that this had led to the closure of printing presses in Pakistan where FICNs were printed.[20]

LeT's financial sources also include "charitable" contributions that support both its vast social network across Pakistan and its terrorist activities. These sources can range from external contributions from diaspora communities to international Islamist charities, including several prominent ones from Saudi Arabia. The Pakistani state channeled a large proportion of international aid received in the wake of the earthquake in Kashmir in 2005 through the LeT, withholding state relief operations in order to facilitate the LeT's further consolidation in the affected areas.[21]

There is now no doubt that the massive terrorist attack on Mumbai November 26-29, 2008—in which Pakistan-backed militants went on a four-day shooting and bombing rampage in India's commercial capital, killing 164 and wounding over 300—was engineered by the LeT, which is now permitted to operate openly in Pakistan under a different name, *Jamaat-ud-Dawa* (JuD), after its supposed official ban (imposed as a result of U.S. pressure) in 2002. American involvement and pressure on Pakistan in the aftermath of that attack forced some apparent action against visible leaders of the LeT/JuD, though a long process of denial and obfuscation by Pakistan's top leadership and authorities suggests that the group will be allowed simply to reinvent itself under a new identity, as it has done previously.

As a result of tremendous international focus and pressure, the LeT has not been able to execute many significant incidents of terrorist violence in India outside J&K since the Mumbai attacks of 2008. Yet the group nevertheless was reportedly involved in at least four prominent incidents since outside J&K, namely: the Pune German Bakery blast (February 13, 2010); the Mumbai serial blasts (July 13, 2011); the Delhi High Court Blast (September 7, 2011); and the Dinanagar Police Station attack in Gurdaspur, Punjab (July 27, 2015). Moreover, the group's involvement was confirmed in at least 91 incidents (36 of them violent) in J&K during 2011, 66 incidents (26 of them violent) in 2012, 51 incidents (12 of them violent) in 2013, 61 incidents (27 of them violent) in 2014, 66 incidents (33 of them violent) in 2015, and another 67 incidents (39 of them violent) in 2016.[22]

The Harkat Triad

In addition to the LeT, the three most significant terrorist groups that operate in India comprise the "Harkat Triad". These groups are the *Harkat-ul-Jihad-Islami* (HuJI), the *Harkat-ul-Mujahideen* (HuM) and the *Jaish-e-Mohammad* (JeM), each of which is also linked to the Taliban and al-Qaeda.

HuJI came into existence in 1980 and fought the Soviets in Afghanistan. After the Afghan war, HuJI focused much of its resources on the fighting in Kashmir while also dispatching cadres to fight in other Islamist campaigns in a number of other countries, including Bosnia, Myanmar and Tajikistan. HuJI was one of the organizations that sent hundreds of its *mujahideen* into Afghanistan after 2001 during the campaigns against the Northern Alliance and the U.S.-led coalition's Operation Enduring Freedom, and is also a member organization of bin Laden's "International Islamic Front." However, the emergence and consolidation of more effective terrorist organizations has marginalized HuJI in Pakistan. Consequently, the group is now strongest in Bangladesh, where HuJI Bangladesh (BD) was established as a distinct organization with direct aid from Osama bin Laden in 1992, and now seeks to establish Islamic *hukumat* (rule) there.[23] Since 2005, HuJI-BD has been involved in a number of major Islamist terrorist operations in India, executing joint operations with Pakistani terrorist groups including the LeT, the JeM and HuM, and coordinates closely with the ISI.

HuM is one of the original member organizations of bin Laden's International Islamic Front. It was established in 1985 at Raiwind in Pakistani Punjab by Maulana Samiul Haq and Maulana Fazlur Rehman, leaders of factions of the *Jamiat-ul-Ulema-e-Islam* (JUI), to participate in the *jihad* against Soviet forces in Afghanistan. Samiul Haq's *madrassa*, the Dar-ul-Uloom Haqqania at Akora Khattak near Peshawar, later emerged as a primary training ground for the Taliban, and also came to dominate the HuM's terrorist mobilization and training projects. Within months of its creation, the HuM was exporting recruits to Afghanistan, initially from Pakistan and Pakistan-occupied Kashmir, but subsequently from other countries, including Algeria, Egypt, Tunisia, Jordan, Saudi Arabia, Bangladesh, Myanmar and the Philippines.[24] The primary area of HuM's activities, after the Afghan campaigns, was J&K, though it has suffered a continuous erosion of its stature as a leading player, as the *Lashkar-e-Taiba* and HuM's breakaway, *Jaish-e-Mohammed*, consolidated their role through a succession of dramatic attacks, both within and outside Pakistan.

JeM is one of the most virulent Pakistani groups operating in India. It was established in early 2000, following known terrorist Azhar Masood's triumphant return to Pakistan upon his release from India as part of a hostage exchange. Masood, originally part of HuM, split with that organization as a result of differences over matters of "finance and influence."[25] Bin Laden is believed to have extended generous funding to the JeM.[26] The JeM has also been extraordinarily successful in motivating second-generation South Asian Muslims in the West to join the *jihad*. These include Ahmed Sayeed Omar Sheikh, one of the conspirators in the 9/11 attacks in the U.S. and journalist Daniel Pearl's killer, as well as "Abdullahbhai," a Birmingham (UK) resident who served as the first suicide bomber in Jammu & Kashmir in the Badami Bagh incident of December 2000. JeM has been very active in recent times, and was involved in two of the deadliest attacks in India in 2016. On January 2, 2016, JeM terrorists attacked an India Air Force base at Pathankot in Punjab, killing seven soldiers. All six attackers were also killed.[27] In September 2016, after infiltrating from across the Line of Control (the *de facto* border between Pakistan and India), JeM terrorists attacked the administrative base of a Brigade of the Indian Army in Uri, Baramulla District. The militants killed 18 soldiers and injured 19. Two of the injured soldiers died subsequently, raising the death toll to 20.[28]

HM is the second-largest terrorist formation operating in J&K after LeT in terms of strength and capacity to carry out terror strikes.[29] India, the United States, and the European Union have declared HM a terrorist group. Overseas, HM is allegedly backed by Ghulam Nabi Fai's Kashmir American Council and Ayub Thakur's World Kashmir Freedom Movement in the U.S. Early in its history, the Hizb established contacts with Afghan *mujahideen* groups such as Hizb-e-Islami, as part of which some of its cadres allegedly received arms training. In January 2013, it was reported that HM had joined hands with HuJI to engage in operations to strike fear among Kashmiris.[30] The proscribed Students Islamic Movement of India is also believed to have links with the *Hizb-ul-Mujahideen*.[31]

At one time, HM was the most important militant group of the Harkat Triad in terms of its effectiveness in perpetrating terrorist violence, but has been progressively marginalized by LeT and JeM, as those groups have become more central to Pakistan's strategic objectives in India. More recently, with the LeT and JeM bases and networks in Pakistan coming under increasing international scrutiny, there has been some effort to restore HM's operational ascendancy in J&K. It has, however, met with limited success in this endeavor, as the group's operational leadership was systematically decimated in the 2008-2010 timeframe.[32] Nevertheless, the group continues to operate openly from its headquarters at Muzzafarabad in Pakistan-occupied Kashmir, under the leadership of Yusuf Shah (a.k.a. Syed Salahuddin), who also serves as the chairman of the United Jihad Council—a conglomerate of India-directed *jihadi* organizations supported by the Pakistani state and also headquartered at Muzzafarabad.

Other factions

There are a number of other Pakistan-based groups operating in India, playing roles of varying significance in the machinery of Islamist terror that has been assembled over the years, including some that boast substantial Indian membership.[33] The most important among them in recent years has been the Student's Islamic Movement of India (SIMI). SIMI has been involved in terrorist activities, principally as a facilitator to various Pakistan-based groups, since the 1990s, providing a range of services, such as couriers, safe havens and communications posts, for specific terrorist operations or terrorist cells. Since 9/11, however, SIMI's significance in Pakistan's strategic perspective has grown, as Islamabad came under increasing international pressure to dismantle the terrorist networks it had constructed and deployed. Pakistan has sought, consequently, to project an increasing proportion of its operations in India as "indigenous terrorism" purportedly sparked by "discontented Muslims," and the role of "indigenous terrorists" has seen an abrupt spike. SIMI's role in these operations has gradually increased. Initially, its cadres joined with the various Pakistani groups to participate in collaborative operations, and eventually, in the Ahmedabad and Delhi bombings of July and September 2008, respectively, operating "independently" under the identity of the "Indian Mujahideen." Crucially, however, the top leadership and cadres of SIMI receive safe haven, training and resources from, Pakistan, and it is there that their operational command centers are located.[34]

The Indian Mujahideen (IM) is believed by intelligence agencies to be a shadow amalgam of the SIMI. As the pressure of arrests built up on the top SIMI leadership, the most radical elements within the organization went on to form IM, with SIMI continuing as the "feeder agency" for IM recruits, engaging in continuing political mobilization and ideological subversion. IM leaders like Mohammad SadiqueIssar Sheikh, Riyaz Bhatkal, Iqbal Bhatkal, Amir Reza Khan and Tariq Ismail, have all graduated from SIMI. On February 23, 2012, IM's ideologue and principal recruiter, Mohammad Kafeel Ahmed, confirmed that SIMI's vast networks were now being used by the IM. Intelligence sources indicate that money raised through arms smuggling, circulation of fake currency, *hawala* transactions, extortion and the diversion of political funds had, by late 2012, made the IM worth an estimated INR 450 million (about USD 8.5 million),[35] with a large chunk of this money coming from Saudi Arabia. IM is the first India-based terrorist group to be designated as a foreign terrorist organization (FTO) by the U.S., according to a September 19, 2011 notification.[36] The group has reportedly been found to be involved in ISI-LeT-led attacks, prominently including the Pune German Bakery blast (February 13, 2010), Mumbai serial blasts (July 13, 2011), the Delhi High Court Blast (September 7, 2011), and the twin blasts in Hyderabad, Andhra Pradesh (February 21, 2013).

Global *jihad's* apparent appearance in India, evidenced by the formation of Al Qaeda in the Indian Subcontinent (*Jamā'at Qā'idat al-Jihād fī Shibh al-Qārrah al-Hindīyah or Organization of the Base of Jihad in the Indian Subcontinent, AQIS*), and the Islamic State announcements regarding Khorasan Province (which includes the Indian Subcontinent), has attracted enormous interest. In reality, the impact of AQIS has been non-existent, and the impact of the Islamic State, negligible.

After the fall of Mosul, Iraq in June 2014 and the Islamic State's declaration of a Caliphate soon thereafter, there was a flurry of interest in the Islamic State in India. Some 23 Indians were confirmed to have joined the Islamic State in 2014[37] and, after a protracted lull, 21 Indians from the southern state of Kerala are reported to have subsequently travelled to Syria.[38] The latter group included six women and three children.[39] Six of the first group were confirmed to have been killed, and two have returned to India. Another 30-odd individuals, interdicted in their attempts to travel to Syria to join Daesh, have also been detained, counseled and returned to their families. In addition, there have been 66 arrests of individuals plotting terrorist activities in the name of the Islamic State in India, particularly in a network mobilized by Muhammad Shafi Armar, the surviving leader of the *Ansar ul Tawhid fi bilad al Hind* (AuT), a group that pledged allegiance to the Islamic State in August 2014.[40]

There have also been a few incidents of flag waving, provocative posters and occasional symbolism (such as wearing Islamic State T-shirts in one incident in Tamil Nadu in August 2014). However, to date, the Islamic State has not been linked in any way to any attack on Indian soil.

Likewise, though AQIS exists in India, its impact has been minimal. On September 3, 2014, Ayman al Zawahiri announced the formation of AQIS with Maulana Asim Umar, a leader of a breakaway faction of the Indian Mujahiddeen based in Pakistan, as its chief. Significantly, India has been unsuccessfully targeted by al-Qaeda at least since 1996, when Osama bin Laden referred to India as being among the lands where the Muslims were living under "oppression," and thus a legitimate theater of *jihad*.[41] There has, as of this writing, been no incident of terrorist violence related to AQIS, and no significant recruitment on Indian soil.

ISLAMISM AND SOCIETY

Islamism in Indian society occupies a continuous ideological spectrum. Indeed, many of the root ideologies that have fed terrorism in South Asia find their sources on Indian soil—though, as already stated, at least some of these sources have sought to distance themselves from the interpretations and activities of terrorists.

Four broad sources can be identified on the landscape of revivalist, fundamentalist and extremist Islamism in South Asia: the Deobandi school; the Barelvi school; the modernist-revivalist streams, such as the influential *Jamaat-e-Islami*; and the *Ahl-e Hadith*, which finds its inspiration in *Wahhabi* doctrines and support and funding from Saudi Arabia.

The Deobandi, the oldest of these four groups, dates back to 1867 and the establishment of the Dar-ul-Uloom seminary at Deoband, a small town in western Uttar Pradesh in India. Founded by Maulana Muhammad Qasim Nanautawi and Maulana Rashid Ahmed Gangohi, the seminary developed a structured curriculum with an overwhelming emphasis on religious education based on original Arabic texts, rather than on later and "corrupted" interpretations. The impetus for these developments was the marginalization of the Muslim community in British India, and concerns about the growth of Western and other non-Islamic influences. The Deobandis formally subscribe to the Hanafi School of Islamic jurisprudence, and emphasize a puritanical interpretation of the faith.

In 1919, Deobandi leaders created a political front, the *Jamiat Ulema-e-Hind* (JUH). Later, the demand for a separate state of Pakistan for Muslims of the subcontinent split the JUH, and the *Jamiat Ulema-e-Islam* (JUI) came into being in 1945, uniting the votaries of Partition. This group lent its support to the dominant political formation favoring the communal division of British India, the Muslim League (ML). The JUI and a variety of Deobandi formations have been immensely influential, both socially and politically, in Pakistan, shaping the course of sectarianism, extremism and militancy. The Taliban in Afghanistan and the Harkat Triad in India also claim Deobandi affiliation. Significantly, however, the *ulema* of the Dar-ul-Uloom Deoband have repeatedly and explicitly condemned all aspects of terrorism, stating that "there is no place for terrorism in Islam" and declaring it to be an "unpardonable sin."[42] In February 2008, for instance, the Deoband Ulema organized an anti-terrorism conference at the Dar-ul-Uloom, which was attended by "tens of thousands of clerics and students from around India."[43]

The Barelvi order, established by Ahmed Raza Khan toward the end of the 19th century in Uttar Pradesh state, also adheres to an interpretation of the Hanafi School, but one that is at wide variance with the Deobandi reading. The Barelvi School, in fact, seeks to emphasize the very syncretic elements of South Asian Islam that were explicitly rejected by the Deobandis. Deeply influenced by mystical Sufi practices and beliefs, it attributes many extraordinary perhaps even divine qualities to the Prophet, conceiving of him more as a holy presence than a mortal man. They likewise believe strongly in the power of intercession by holy personages and saints, and give greater import to the personal (rather than social and political) aspects of religion. Unsurprisingly, the Barelvi philosophy is anathema to the puritan reformist movements and schools of Islam, which condemn the Barelvis as shrine- and grave-worshipping deviationists. The Barelvis have not been significantly associated with terrorism in India, and have been systematically targeted by Deobandi terrorist groups in Pakistan.[44]

Another movement is *Ahl-e Hadith*, a relatively small movement that has benefited enormously from Saudi support in recent times. It represents one of the most radicalized elements within the Sunni fundamentalist factions of South Asia. Inspired by Sayyed Ahmed 'Shaheed' (The Martyr) of Rae Bareilly (in the present Indian State of Uttar Pradesh), who fought the Sikh Maharaja Ranjit Singh in 1826-31 in the Peshawar region, the *Ahl-e Hadith* has sought to restore Islam to the purity of the original faith, as articulated in the Koran and the *Hadith*. It formally claims to be distinct from the Wahhabis, but the movement's beliefs and practices have much in common with the dominant creed of Saudi Arabia. While the *Ahl-e Hadith* insists that it does not follow any one of the four schools of Islamic jurisprudence, its practitioners have moved progressively closer to the Hanbali interpretation that is also the basis of

Wahhabi practices. Their interpretation of Islam is puritanical and legalistic, and they reject all manner of perceived deviations and "idolatrous" practices that they claim have crept into the other major traditions. While its numbers are believed to be small and the movement no longer has more than a trace presence in India, it has remained vibrant in Pakistan, from where it has exercised disproportionate influence and demonstrated a great capacity for violence in recent years. *Lashkar-e-Taiba* proclaims adherence to the *Ahl-e Hadith* ideology.

The *Jamaat-e-Islami* is one of the most influential revivalist movements in South Asia, and has had tremendous political influence, both in pre-Partition India and, subsequent to its creation, in Pakistan. It is the most explicitly political of the various movements and categorically denies the very possibility of a distinction between the religious and the political or, indeed, even between the religious and the personal, within a genuinely Islamic order. Abu AlaMaududi, the ideologue and founder of the *Jamaat-e-Islami*, declared that in an Islamic state—the ideal and objective of the organization—"no one can regard his affairs as personal and private... An Islamic state is a totalitarian state."[45] Maududi sought to "enunciate an all-inclusive school of Islamic thought," one that was "not bound by any school of law."[46] To a large extent, *Jamaat* practice follows upon interpretations of Maududi's vision.

Hizb-ul-Mujahideen and the Students' Islamic Movement of India trace their roots to *Jamaat* ideology. Nevertheless, the *Jamaat-e-Islami* Hind rejects all linkages with these groups, including SIMI—which it created as its student wing in 1977, but which was "expelled" in 1981 due to its increasing radicalization. The Hizb remains intimately connected with the *Jamaat-e-Islami* Jammu & Kashmir.

Tablighi Jamaat (TJ) is a radical Muslim revivalist movement, founded by Muhammad Ilyas in 1926 in Mewat (in the present Indian State of Haryana), which reaches out to Muslims of all social and economic classes and seeks to purify the Islamic faith of all "idolatrous deviations." One of the most rapidly growing Islamist organizations, TJ primarily operates in India, Pakistan and Bangladesh, but has extended its network in other parts of the world as well. It is "a loosely controlled mass movement, not a rigidly controlled organization" and "has no fixed membership and the leaders of the movement do not exercise a total control on its activists."[47] TJ's founder, Mohammad Illyas, emphasized the *jihad-bin-nafs*, or the internal *jihad* of the spirit, over the *jihad-bin-saif*, jihad by the sword, and the organization has long been criticized by other Islamists for its apolitical orientation. In recent years, however, linkages between TJ followers and Islamist terrorism have surfaced with increasing frequency.[48]

Today, some of the Indian Muslim community's disadvantages are structural, and relate to accidents of history and of geography. The partition divested the community of its leadership and its elites across North India, and Muslims have remained largely directionless and socially, politically and economically underdeveloped over the intervening decades. On virtually all social indicators, Muslims are worse off than compared to the other major religious communities in India. Higher poverty and illiteracy levels in the community limit capacities for productive employment, especially at higher levels. 26.5 percent of Muslim Other Backward Castes (OBCs) and 19.3 percent of other Muslims were below the poverty line in urban areas and 30.8 percent of Muslim OBCs and 25 percent of other Muslims were below the poverty line in rural areas in 2011-2012, as compared to an Indian average of 13.7 and 25.7 percent, respectively.[49] Literacy among Muslims stands at 57.3 percent as against a national average of 63.1 percent.[50] The distribution of Muslim populations has a crucial impact on these factors: The community is disproportionately located in some of the poorest, most backward and ill-governed States of India. In 2011, for instance, just four of India's 28 States and seven Union Territories—Uttar Pradesh (38.4 million), Bihar (17.5 million), West Bengal (24.6 million), and Assam (10.6 million)—with some of the poorest human-development profiles in the country, accounted for 53.04 percent of India's Muslim population.[51] Relatively higher Muslim population growth, disproportionately concentrated in the most backward regions and among the most disadvantaged population segments, only serves to exacerbate existing ills. Higher poverty and illiteracy levels are directly related to higher reproduction rates among the Muslims, though rates have declined proportionately among segments of the Muslim population that have escaped these blights.[52] Significantly, in many of the better-administered and more prosperous States, the gap between the general population profile and the Muslim population profile tends to diminish on a number of variables. In Kerala, for instance, Muslim literacy in 2011 stood at 93.29 percent[53] compared to a State average of 94 percent.[54] Nevertheless, Muslim poverty remains higher than the average in most States in the country.

In terms of Muslim education, it is crucial to understand that the Indian *madrassa* has little in common with the *"jihad* factories" that have been established in a large proportion of Islamic educational institutions in Pakistan and, to some extent, in Bangladesh as well. There are no authoritative estimates of the number of *madrassas* in India, but recent approximations put the figure at between 30,000 and 45,000.[55] Divergent estimates put the proportion of Muslim children going to *madrassas* variously at 2.3 and 4 percent of the 7-19 years age group. The proportion is higher in rural areas and among males.[56] The government runs programs supporting modern curricula in *madrassas*, and a significant number of such institutions have accepted such curricula.[57] Crucially, *madrassas* are often found to be providing the only option for schooling in areas where the state's education system has failed. However, the Union Ministry of Home Affairs has developed a "multipronged" policy focusing on counter-radicalization, involving several ministries and state governments, and including a program for skill development for *madrassa* students.[58]

Nevertheless, a fraction of *madrassas* have been found to have at least some linkages with the Islamist extremist enterprise, and there has been a pronounced growth of such institutions—funded from outside the country—along the most porous stretches of India's borders. In February and March 2006, for instance, officers of a border security agency disclosed that 2,365 mosques and *madrassas* had sprung up on the Indian side of the Indo-Nepal border, and some 700 had done so on the Nepal side, over the preceding decade—of which some 50 or 60 were considered "sensitive."[59] A significant rise in the number of *madrassas* along the Indo-Bangladesh border also has been reported.[60] At least some terrorist incidents have been linked backward to networks established among elements within the mosque-*madrassa* complex in the country.[61]

There has also been a proliferation of Wahabi *madrassas* and mosques in troubled Jammu & Kashmir, with the *Ahl-e-Hadith* leading the pack. These have reportedly been funded overwhelmingly through *hawala* channels and through physical transfer of currencies across the Line of Control with Pakistan. While intelligence and enforcement agencies are well aware of the problem, they remain mute bystanders in the absence of a political mandate to act, and because of the 'sensitive' nature of the issue.[62] Similar patterns are visible in several other states across the country.[63]

ISLAMISM AND THE STATE

"India's secular democratic constitution," scholar and diplomat Husain Haqqani observes, "empowers the country's Muslims more than their co-religionists in Muslim majority states."[64] India's constitutional and legal order is rigorously secular[65] and goes out of its way to protect minorities or to accommodate them through "reverse discrimination" provisions.

Nevertheless, Muslims—along with other disadvantaged groups—do endure significant discrimination in a deeply inequitable social, economic and political order. Weak governance and a crumbling justice system across vast areas of the country have meant that injustice, neglect and injury are often disregarded, and their victims have little practical recourse, despite the elaborate framework of statutory provisions. While the broad trajectory of trends in "communal violence" is not discouraging,[66] periodic bloodbaths—the worst of these in the new millennium in Gujarat in 2002, where some 2,000 persons were killed, primarily Muslims—continue to poison relationships between communities, and undermine the confidence of the country's minorities in the institutions of the state. 62 persons were killed, 98 injured and over 55,000 displaced in the most recent of major cycles of communal rioting, in Uttar Pradesh in 2013.[67] Crucially, such violence often "bears the imprimatur of the state,"[68] as parties in power abandon constitutional values and subvert the agencies of the state.

Among the most visible indicators of systemic discrimination against Muslims in India is their share in government employment, which relatively recently stood nationwide at 4.9 percent of the total number of such employees, when Muslims constituted 13.4 percent of the country's population.[69] When tallied in 2016, Muslims made up just 3.3 percent of the Indian Administrative Service and 3.2 percent of the

Indian Police Service.[70] Much of this is, however, a consequence of poor education and the relative paucity of qualified aspirants to these posts. Thus, "the success rate of Muslims is about the same as other candidates," though "the small number of Muslim candidates appearing in the written examination of the Civil Services is a cause of concern."[71]

Despite the popular narrative, however, the successes of Islamist radicalism demonstrate no coherent correlation to specific grievances, atrocities or deprivations among the Muslim community.[72] Islamist extremism is, in fact, rooted in a powerful, sustained process of ideological mobilization that has its roots in Pakistan. Indian Muslims have overwhelmingly resisted these efforts at subversion and radicalization. Nevertheless, fringe elements within the community remain vulnerable to radicalization and recruitment by terrorist and anti-state forces. Clearly, areas with heavy Muslim concentrations would be more susceptible to such extremist mobilization, and these vulnerabilities are compounded where these areas lie along borders with hostile neighbors—particularly Pakistan and, at least until recently, Bangladesh. The growth of *madrassas*, particularly where these are substantially foreign-funded, along and on both sides of India's borders, is, in this context, a matter of deep concern, though only a small minority of all *madrassas* in the country have proven to be susceptible to radicalization.

The critical element of India's abiding success against radical Islamist mobilization is the constitutional and civilizational underpinnings of secularism within the country. Of course, Indian society and politics have yet to become "socially and emotionally secular,"[73] despite Constitutional secularism and a long history of confessional coexistence. The periodic recurrence of communal conflagrations and manifestations of religious extremism are evidence of this. Nevertheless, structural and cultural factors constrain even radical players from their greatest excesses. For instance, electoral considerations have repeatedly forced the Hindu right to accommodate Muslim concerns. Similarly, even where some state agencies have colluded with extremist elements—as, for instance, in the Gujarat riots of 2002—constitutional checks and balances have, eventually, reasserted themselves to bring offenders to some measure of justice.

While the threat of Islamist radicalization and terrorism has endured for decades, and Pakistan gives every sign of being intent upon an asymmetric war of attrition, Indian responses have remained largely fitful, event-led and *ad hoc*. Indeed, India has no clearly articulated counterterrorism policy.[74] This deficiency is compounded by endemic deficits of capacity in the security, intelligence and justice systems,[75] which make any planned and comprehensive response impossible. As noted elsewhere,

> The absence of strategy and the incoherence of tactics have long afflicted India, as the country finds itself responding continuously and insufficiently to provocations by its neighbors, and to a rising tide of subversion and ter-

rorism. Worse, the pattern of responses has, with rare exception, reflected a quality of desperation and directionless-ness that, after decades of contending with these problems, is impossible to fathom. With over 25 years of Pakistan-sponsored Islamist terrorist activity on Indian soil, the country is still to correctly define the problem that confronts it, or to craft an appropriate 'strategic architecture' and to derive policies and practices that are in conformity with such an overarching design.[76]

If Islamist terrorism, nevertheless, gains little traction, and if the state is still able to achieve significant successes against both terrorists and against extremist ideologies, the credit must go to small handfuls of exceptionally dedicated individuals in the intelligence and security community, on the one hand, and an enveloping culture that rejects terrorism on the other. India's democracy, which has gone great lengths to accommodate minority sentiments, is a part of this culture, and it is through the instruments and dynamics of democracy that extremism is constrained.

ENDNOTES

[1] The 2011 population of Muslims was estimated at 172.2 million according to the Census of India, 2011, http://www.census2011.co.in/religion.php.
[2] Pew Research Center, "Ten Countries with the Largest Muslim Populations, 2010 and 2050," April 2, 2015, http://www.pewforum.org/2015/04/02/muslims/pf_15-04-02_projectionstables74/
[3] Indeed, low-grade jihadi subversion and Pakistani incursions commenced almost from the moment of Partition. See Praveen Swami, India, Pakistan and the Secret Jihad: The Covert War in Kashmir 1947-2004 (New Delhi: Routledge, 2007).
[4] Violence in J&K peaked in 2001, with 4,507 fatalities in that year, and remained continuously at the high intensity conflict level between 1990 and 2006. For the first time since insurgency started, it came down to three figures in 2007. All data from the Institute for Conflict Management, South Asia Terrorism Portal, "Fatalities in Terrorist Violence 1988 – 2016," n.d.,
http://www.satp.org/satporgtp/countries/india/states/jandk/data_sheets/annual_casualties.htm]
[5] Swami, India, Pakistan and the Secret Jihad.
[6] "Fatalities in Terrorist Violence 1988 – 2016."
[7] See, for instance, Ashley Tellis, Testimony before the House of Representatives, Committee on Foreign Affairs, Subcommittee on the Middle East and South Asia, March 11, 2010, http://www.carnegieendowment.org/files/0311_testimony_tellis.pdf.
[8] See Institut e for Conflict Management, South Asia Terrorism Portal, "Islamist Terrorist Attacks Outside J&K, Punjab And Northeast 2000-2016,"

n.d., http://www.satp.org/satporgtp/countries/india/database/Islamist_Terrorist_Attacks_Outside_J&K_Punjab_Northeast.htm; and Institute for Conflict Management, South Asia Terrorism Portal, "ISI related modules Neutralised outside J&K and Northeast, 2004-09," n.d., http://satp.org/satporgtp/countries/india/database/ISImodules.htm.

[9] On November 26, 2008, a group of ten terrorists from Pakistan, affiliated with Lashkar-e-Taiba, with demonstrated connections to the ISI-Army-State structure in Pakistan, attacked multiple targets in the coastal city and India's financial capital, Mumbai. 166 persons were killed in this terrorist outrage. The attack was covered live virtually throughout the 62 hours of its execution by India's many television channels. Conversations between the terrorists and their handlers in Pakistan were fully recorded by Indian and American intelligence agencies, and subsequent investigations have established linkages not only to the LeT in Pakistan, but to a number of serving and retired Army officers there. See Government of India, Ministry of Home Affairs, Annual Report 2008-09, 2010, 20; Mumbai Terrorist Attack: Dossier of Evidence, by Government of India July 6, 2009, http://www.investigativeproject.org/document/277-mumbai-terror-attacks-dossier-of-evidence; Rajeev Deshpande, "26/11 Probe: US may ask for Pak major's extradition," Times of India, December 9, 2009; "Five army officers held for link with Chicago suspects," Daily Times, November 25, 2009; "Headley Link: 5 Pak Army officers held," Hindustan Times, December 23, 2009.

[10] Ajai Sahni, "South Asia: Extremist Islamist Terror and Subversion," in K.P.S. Gill and AjaiSahni, eds., The Global Threat of Terror: Ideological, Material and Political Linkages (New Delhi: ICM-Bulwark Books, 2002), esp. 212-229; Tellis, Testimony before the House of Representatives, Committee on Foreign Affairs, Subcommittee on the Middle East and South Asia; Swami, India, Pakistan and the Secret Jihad.

[11] The expression was used by the then-Indian National Security Advisor, M.K. Narayanan, to describe the global network of al-Qaeda-linked organizations. See Bruce Tefft, "LeT is part of al Qaeda Compact," The Hindu, August 14, 2006.

[12] See, Ajai Sahni, "Offensive from Pakistan," Wars within Borders, n.d., http://www.satp.org/satporgtp/ajaisahni/09fablime04.htm.

[13] See, for instance, Aarish Ullah Khan, "The Terrorist Threat and the Policy Response in Pakistan," Stockholm International Peace Research Institute Policy Paper no. 11, September 2005, 22. Khan notes, "The land for building the complex was given by the government of President Zia ul-Haq, with a huge investment from Abdul Rehman Sherahi, as a gift to Markaz al Dawawal Irshad during the jihad years…"; See also Mariam AbouZahab and Olivier Roy, Islamist Networks: The Afghan–Pakistan Connection (Hurst: London, 2004), 32, and Amir Rana, "Jamaat ud Dawa splits," Daily Times (Lahore), 18 July 2004.

[14] John Wilson, "Lashkar-e-Taiba: New Threats Posed by an Old Organization," Jamestown Foundation Terrorism Monitor 3, iss. 4, May 5, 2005, http://www.jamestown.org/single/?no_cache=1&tx_ttnews%5Btt_news%5D=314.

[15] "Pakistan," in U.S. Department of State, Bureau of Democracy, Human Rights and Labor, International Religious Freedom Report 2008 (Washington, DC: U.S. Department of State, 2009), http://www.state.gov/g/drl/rls/irf/2008/108505.htm.

[16] These include www.jamatuddawa.org; an Urdu weekly called Gazwa; an English-language monthly, Voice of Islam; an Urdu monthly, Al Dawa; an Arabic monthly, Al Rabat; an Urdu youth magazine, Mujala-e-Tulba; and an Urdu weekly, Jihad Times.

[17] Vishwa Mohan, "India to take up fake currency note issue at global fora," Times of India, August 4, 2009.

[18] Ajit Kumar Singh, "Subversion sans Borders," Outlook India, November 20, 2006, http://www.outlookindia.com/article.aspx?233169; Tara Shankar Sahay, "Hijackers with Pak military intelligence, says ISI ex-chief," rediff.com, January 3, 2000.

[19] Aman Sharma, "Economic Terror no Fake Threat," India Today, August 5, 2009, http://indiatoday.intoday.in/site/Story/55177/LATEST%20HEADLINES/Economic+terror+no+fake+threat.html. See also, for further details, Ajai Sahni, "Blood Money," Defence & Security of India, April 2009, http://www.satp.org/satporgtp/ajaisahni/09ASdsivw.htm.

[20] "Fake currency printing press in Pakistan have to shut now: Kiren Rijiju", The Economic Times, November 9, 2016, http://economictimes.indiatimes.com/news/politics-and-nation/fake-currency-printing-press-in-pakistan-have-to-shut-now-kiren-rijiju/articleshow/55335954.cms]. A January 7, 2017, report, quoted an unnamed senior official as saying, "Pakistan had been printing fake Indian currency notes in its government printing press in Quetta and its security press in Karachi. Post demonetisation, Pakistani state and non-state actors had no option but to shut shops of fake Indian currency notes" Vasudha Venugopal, "Note ban takes toll on terror; Pak counterfeit presses close, Kashmir violence dips 60%", Economic Times, January 7, 2017, http://economictimes.indiatimes.com/news/politics-and-nation/note-ban-takes-toll-on-terror-pak-counterfeit-presses-close-kashmir-violence-dips-60/articleshow/56383135.cms

[21] See, for instance, Jan McGirk, "Kashmir: The Politics Of An Earthquake," OpenIndia, October 18, 2005, http://www.opendemocracy.net/conflict-india_pakistan/jihadi_2941.jsp.

[22] Numbers compiled from the South Asia Terrorism Portal's "Timelines," n.d., www.satp.org.

[23] Harkat-ul-Jihad-al Islami Bangladesh (HuJI-B), Terrorist Group, Bangladesh, South Asia Terrorism Portal, http://www.satp.org/satporgtp/countries/bangladesh/terroristoutfits/Huj.htm. See also, "Harkat ul Jihad Islami – Bangladesh", Tracking Terrorism, https://www.trackingterrorism.org/group/harakat-ul-jihad-i-islami-bangladesh-huji-b.

[24] B. Raman, A Terrorist State as a Frontline Ally, 2002, Lancer Publishers, India, page 23.

[25] Praveen Swami, "The Tanzeems and their leaders", Frontline, Volume 17 - Issue 17, Aug. 19 - Sep. 01, 2000, http://www.frontline.in/static/html/fl1717/17170200.htm

[26] See, for instance, Jamal Afridi, "Kashmir Militant Extremists," Council on Foreign Relations Backgrounder, July 9, 2009, http://www.cfr.org/publication/9135/.

[27] "Manohar Parrikar says all six terrorists killed, Pathankot airbase combing still underway,", The Indian Express, January 6, 2016, http://indianexpress.com/article/india/india-news-india/manohar-parrikar-says-all-six-terrorists-killed-pathankot-airbase-combing-still-underway/

[28] "Uri attack: Another soldier succumbs to injuries, death toll rises to 20", The Indian Express, September 30, 2016, http://indianexpress.com/article/india/india-news-india/uri-attack-another-soldier-naik-rajkishor-singh-succumbs-to-injuries-3057140/

[29] "Lashkar reviving women cadre in J&K: Govt," Times of India, March 22, 2012, http://timesofindia.indiatimes.com/india/Lashkar-reviving-women-cadre-in-JK-Govt/articleshow/12361679.cms.

[30] Harkat and Hizb join hands, Pak Observer, January 2, 2013, http://www3.pakobserver.net/201301/02/detailnews.asp?id=189815, Harkat and Hizb join hands in Kashmir, http://www.timesnow.tv/INDIA/Hazrat--Hizb-join-hands-in-Kashmir/videoshow/4417910.cms.

[31] South Asia Terrorism Portal, "Hizb-ul-Mujahideen," n.d., http://www.satp.org/satporgtp/countries/india/states/jandk/terrorist_outfits/hizbul_mujahideen.htm.

[32] See Kanchan Lakshman, "J&K: Dying Embers of Terror," South Asia Terrorism Review 7, no. 29, January 7, 2009; Praveen Swami, "A homecoming for yesterday's jihadists?" The Hindu (Chennai), August 21, 2009.

[33] A detailed listing and profile of principal groups can be found at South Asia Terrorism Portal, "India: Terrorist, insurgent and extremist groups,"n.d., http://www.satp.org/satporgtp/countries/india/terroristoutfits/index.html.

[34] See, for instance, Praveen Swami, "Islamism, modernity and Indian Mujahiddeen," The Hindu (Chennai), March 23, 2010; "The Lashkar-e-Taiba's Army in India," The Hindu (Chennai), January 17, 2009; "Lashkar trained Indian terrorists pose growing threat," The Hindu (Chennai), December 19, 2008.

[35] "Vicky Nanjappa, "How the Indian Mujahideen raised Rs 45 crore in two years", Rediff.com, October 11, 2012, http://www.rediff.com/news/report/how-the-indian-mujahideen-raised-rs-45-crore-in-two-years/20121011.htm, [The earlier given source "Indian Mujahideen raked in Rs. 40 crore in last two years: IB" India TV, September 12, 2012, http://www.indiatvnews.com/news/india/indian-mujahideen-raked-in-rs-crore-in-last-two-years-ib-17661.html has been updated and says only 40 crore, not 45 crore],

[36] Designated Foreign Terrorist Organizations, Bureau Of Counterterrorism, Foreign Terrorist Organizations, Diplomacy in Action, US Department of State, http://www.state.gov/j/ct/rls/other/des/123085.htm

[37] Ajai Sahni, "Breaking News: ISIS is not coming! ISIS is not coming!", Scroll.in, February 11, 2016, http://scroll.in/article/803373/breaking-news-isis-is-not-coming-isis-is-not-coming.

[38] Praveen Swami, "From fish curry to war: 'Indian in Syria' calls out to his homeland", The Indian Express, July 14, 2016, http://indianexpress.com/article/india/india-news-india/from-fish-curry-to-war-indian-in-syria-calls-out-to-his-homeland-2912568/.

[39] Munish Pandey, "22 from Kerala have already joined Daesh", Mumbai Mirror, September 13, 2016, http://timesofindia.indiatimes.com/city/mumbai/22-from-Kerala-have-already-joined-Daesh/articleshow/54305744.cms.

[40] Union Ministry of Home Affairs, reply to Unstarred Question No. 1404 in the Lok Sabha (Lower House of Parliament), July 26, 2016.

[41] Ajai Sahni, "Vulnerabilities and Resistance to Islamist Radicalization in India," Middle East Institute, January 12, 2015, http://www.mei.edu/content/map/vulnerabilities-and-resistance-islamist-radicalization-india.

[42] "Darool-Uloom Deoband says terrorism is anti-Islam," Reuters, February 26, 2008.

[43] Ibid.

[44] Jawad Syed, Edwina Pio, Tahir Kamran, Abbas Zaidi, Faith-Based Violence and Deobandi Militancy in Pakistan, November 2016, Palgrave Macmillan, UK.

[45] Abu A'laMaududi, "Political Theory of Islam," as cited in K.K. Aziz, Pakistan's Political Culture (Lahore: Vanguard, 2001), 265.

[46] Seyyed Vali Reza Nasr, Mawdudi & the Making of Islamic Revivalism (New York: Oxford University Press, 1996), 114.

[47] Yoginder Sikand, "Plane 'Plot': Media Targets TablighiJama'at," The Milli Gazette, August 19, 2006, http://tablighijamaat.wordpress.com/2008/06/16/plane-plot-media-targets-tablighi-jamaat/#more-19; See also Yoginder Sikand, The Origins and Development of the Tablighi Jama'at (1920-2000): A Cross-Country Comparative Study (Hyderabad: Orient Longman, 2001).

[48] Praveen Swami, "Shattered certitudes and new realities emerge in terror link investigation," The Hindu (Chennai), July 8, 2007.

[49] Report of the Post Sachar Evaluation Committee, September 29, 2014, http://iosworld.org/download/Post_Sachar_Evaluation_Committee.pdf. .
[50] Amitabh Sinha, Sagrik Chowdhury "42.7 per cent Muslims illiterate, says Census," The Indian Express, September 1, 2016, http://indianexpress.com/article/india/india-news-india/muslim-illiteracy-rate-india-census-report-education-3006798/
[51] Muslim Religion Census 2011, All India Religion Census Data 2011, Religion Census 2011, Population Census 2011, Census of India 2011, http://www.census2011.co.in/data/religion/2-muslims.html.
[52] Absolute population of Hindus was 1,210,854,977 in 2011 and Muslims, 172,245,158, Census of India, 2011, http://www.census2011.co.in/religion.php. The Total Fertility Rate (TFR) is falling faster in Muslims than in Hindus. In the National Family Health Survey (NFHS) 1 (1992-93), fertility numbers for Muslims and Hindus were 4.4 and 3.3, a gap of 1.1. In NFHS 2 (1998-99), the numbers for Muslims and Hindus fell to 3.59 and 2.78, and the gap, therefore, to 0.8. And in NFHS 3 (2005-06), the numbers were 3.1 and 2.7; the gap 0.4. Poonam Muttreja, "Population growth slowing for all; on sex ratio, Muslims better than Hindus", The Indian Express, August 27, 2015, http://indianexpress.com/article/explained/population-growth-slowing-for-all-on-sex-ratio-muslims-better-than-hindus/
[53] Dr. J. K. Bajaj, "The Continuing Decline Of Hindus In Kerala", Swarajya, April 25, 2016, http://swarajyamag.com/politics/the-continuing-decline-of-hindus-in-kerala.
[54] Kerala Population Census data 2011: Kerala Literacy Rate 2011, http://www.census2011.co.in/census/state/kerala.htm.
[55] Manzoor Ahmed, in his study of Indian Muslim education, estimated the number of madrassas at around 30,000. Manzoor Ahmed, Islamic Education: Redefinitions of Aims and Methodology (New Delhi: Genuine Publications, 2002), 32. Yoginder Sikand puts the number at about 30,000. Yoginder Sikand, Bastion of the Believers: Madrassas and Islamic Education in India (New Delhi, Penguin India, 2005), 95. Shabeeb Rizvi's estimate goes as high as 45,000. Shabeeb Rizvi, "The rise and rise of Wahabism," Telegraph (New Delhi), May 10, 2009, www.telegraphindia.com/1090510/jsp/7days/story_10942907.jsp#.
[56] Sachar Committee Report, 77.
[57] See Yoginder Sikand, "Voices for Reform in the Indian Madrasas," in Farish A. Noor and Yoginder Sikand, eds., The Madrasa in Asia (Amsterdam: Amsterdam University Press, 2008), 31-65, esp. 59-64.

[58] Abhishek Bhalla, "Skills boost for India's Muslim children: Government plans training programmes for madrasas to combat ISIS radicalisation threat," Mailonline India, December 8, 2015, http://www.dailymail.co.uk/indiahome/indianews/article-3351596/Skills-boost-India-s-Muslim-children-Government-plans-training-programmes-madrasas-combat-ISIS-radicalisation-threat.htm

[59] Vishwa Mohan, "A New Terror Trail Leads to Nepal," Times of India, February 12, 2006; "1900 madrassas mushrooming along Indo-Nepal border," rediff.com, March 24, 2006, http://www.rediff.com/news/2006/mar/24border.htm.

[60] Union Minister of Home in the Ministry of Home Affairs Vidyasagar Rao, Rajya Sabha (Upper House of Indian Parliament), Unstarred Question no. 700, March 6, 2002. In December 2014, India raised the issue of proliferation of madrassas on their side of the India-Nepal border with Kathmandu, and sought cooperation in checking anti-India activities by such religious schools that were being funded and supported by Pakistan's ISI and the Dawood Ibrahim terror syndicate. See Rakesh Kumar Singh, "India seeks Nepal help to stem ISI-Funded Madrasas," Daily Pioneer, December 18, 2014, http://www.dailypioneer.com/todays-newspaper/india-seeks-nepal-help-to-stem-isi-funded-madrasas.html. The largest number of madrasas and mosques has come up in the border areas of Lower Assam, Bihar and Bengal that share a boundary with Nepal and Bangladesh. "Along with the madrasas, a large number of Muslim-focused NGOs have also sprung up in the area bordering Nepal. Most of these madrasas and NGOs promote anti-India activities. The NGOs receive substantial and completely unregulated funding from Saudi Arabia, Kuwait and other Islamic countries, and work to radicalise the local youth," an unnamed intelligence official said. Abhinandan Mishra, "Madrasas on India-Bangla border under watch," Sunday Guardian, October 25, 2014, http://www.sunday-guardian.com/news/madrasas-on-india-bangla-border-under-watch.

[61] See, for instance, Praveen Swami, "Fortresses of Faith," Frontline 23, iss. 20, October 7-20, 2006; K.P.S. Gill, "Gujarat: New Theatre of Islamist Terror," South Asia Intelligence Review 1, no. 11, September 30, 2002, http://www.satp.org/satporgtp/sair/Archives/1_11.htm.

[62] Asit Jolly, "The Wahabi Invasion," India Today, December 23, 2011, http://indiatoday.intoday.in/story/saudi-charities-pump-in-funds-through-hawala-channels-to-radicalise-kashmir-valley/1/165660.html.

[63] Vicky Nanjappa, "How Saudi funder Rs. 1,700 crore for Wahabi influence in India," OneIndia, June 25, 2015, http://www.oneindia.com/india/wikileaks-how-saudi-funded-rs-1-700-crore-wahabi-influence-india-1787820.html.

[64] Husain Haqqani, "India's Islamist Groups," Hudson Institute Current Trends in Islamist Ideology 3, 2006, 22.

[65] Justiciable "fundamental rights" under the Constitution, for instance, guarantee equality before law and equal protection by the law; prohibit discrimination on the grounds of religion, race, caste, sex and place of birth; freedom of conscience and right to freely profess, practice and propagate religion; right to manage religious institutions and affairs; protection of minorities right to conserve language, script or culture; right to establish and administer educational institutions of their (minorities') choice, etc.

[66] "Muzaffarnagar riots: Sahai report absolves UP government, blames others", Rediff.com, October 2, 2015, http://www.rediff.com/news/special/exclusive-up-riots-report-absolves-govt-blames-others/20151002.htm.

[67] NeeraChandoke, "The new tribalism," The Hindu (Chennai), April 4, 2002.

[68] High Level Committee Report on Social, Economic and Educational Status of the Muslim Community of India (New Delhi: Akalank Publications, January 2007), p. 165.

[69] Zeeshan Shaikh, "Ten years since Sachar report, Muslims still 3 per cent in IAS, IPS," The Indian Express, August 18, 2016, http://indianexpress.com/article/india/india-news-india/ten-years-since-sachar-report-muslims-still-3-in-ias-ips-2982199/

[70] "Muslims on par with others in UPSC exams", Rediff.com, December 14, 2006, http://www.rediff.com/news/report/muslim/20061214.htm.

[71] See, for example, Praveen Swami, India, Pakistan and the Secret Jihad: The Covert War in Kashmir, 1947-2004 (London: Routeledge, 2007), 2.

[72] Partha S. Ghosh, "Demographic Trends of Muslim Population in India: Implications for National Security," Demographic Dynamics in South Asia And their Implications on Indian Security (New Delhi: Institute for Conflict Management, unpublished 2006), 29.

[73] For a detailed assessment, see Ajai Sahni, "Counter-terrorism and the 'Flailing State,'" Eternal India 1, no. 5, February 2009, http://www.satp.org/satporgtp/ajaisahni/09AS-7EtInd.htm.

[74] For details, see Ajai Sahni, "Strategic Vastu Shastra," South Asia Intelligence Review 7, no. 24, December 22, 2009; AjaiSahni, "The Peacock and the Ostrich," South Asia Intelligence Review 8, no. 7, August 24, 2009.

[75] Ajai Sahni, "Counter-terrorism and the 'Flailing State.'"

Maldives

> **Quick Facts**
>
> Population: Number 392,960 (July 2016 est.)
>
> Area: 298 sq km
>
> Ethnic Groups: South Indians, Sinhalese, Arabs
>
> Religions: Sunni Muslim (official)
>
> Government Type: Presidential Republic
>
> GDP (official exchange rate): $3.27 billion (2015 est.)
>
> *Map and Quick Facts courtesy of the CIA World Factbook (January 2017)*

Overview

The Maldives, an Indian Ocean archipelago nation, has faced a number of internal challenges in recent years, from economic and environmental concerns to radical Islam and political infighting. However, what has attracted global attention is the country's status as a safe haven for the growth of a radical strain of Islam. This Sunni-majority Islamic nation has been confronting a grassroots Islamist surge that has been overlooked for over a decade, and the country has proven fertile ground for transnational jihadist recruitment. The nation has been struggling to cope with Salafi jihadist ideology, which has gained ground among large swaths of the population and among the nation's youth in particular, with reports emerging of young Maldivians participating in the ongoing Syrian civil war.

ISLAMIST ACTIVITY

The Islamic Foundation of the Maldives (IFM)

The Islamic Foundation of the Maldives (IFM) is non-profit religious organization. IFM was founded in April 2009 by Ibrahim Fauzee, an Islamist previously arrested in Karachi, Pakistan, and detained at Guantanamo Bay for his links to al-Qaeda. According to its previous website (now defunct), the IFM aims to "promote and protect Islamic tenets and ethics, create religious awareness, and to uphold social events within the boundary of Islamic principles and [the] Religious Unity Act in the Maldives." The IFM's Islamic activism was highlighted when Mohamed Nazim, a Maldivian, was assaulted after he raised some doubts about Islam and his own religious beliefs during a meeting addressed by Islamic preacher Zakir Naik. In 2010 The IFM immediately urged the government and court to strip Nazim of his citizenship and sentence him to death (based on Islamic *sharia* and the Constitution of Maldives), if he did not repent.[1] Nazim relented, reportedly under duress, and publicly apologized for questioning Islam.

Jamiyyatul Salaf

One of the most prominent Islamist groups is the Jamiyyatul Salaf (JS), a non-governmental religious group that propagates an ultra-conservative strain of Islam. JS has *Wahhabi/Salafi* lineage and a strong anti-secular ideology. It supports Islamizing education and promotes intolerance toward other religions, especially Christianity. Many of its members are known to have been educated in Saudi Arabia and Pakistan. As part of its campaign to raise Islamic awareness and promote the values of Islam, the group regularly invites Islamic preachers and scholars to the Maldives in conjunction with the country's Ministry of Islamic Affairs. The JS is also actively engaged in moral policing: in 2008, it declared music to be *haram* (forbidden) and forced a school library in Male to close because it contained Christian books. In 2012, vehement pressure from radical and other conservative religious groups like JS prompted the Islamic Affairs ministry to issue guidelines on permissible public behaviour, including any prohibiting mixed-gender dance events.

In November 2011, Jamiyyatul Salaf activists demonstrated against the UN Human Rights chief Navi Pillay's comments on flogging and the country's "discriminatory" constitutional provisions. The JS has received some political support in its anti-UN campaign, especially from political parties, including the Dhivehi Rayyithunge Party (DRP) and the PPM. JS has recommended the use of Saudi-style beheadings and firing squads over lethal injections for a convicted murderer in accordance with the Islamic principle of *Qiasas* (equal retaliation).[2]

JS remains at the forefront of pro-Islamic activities in Maldives and issues religious edicts and guidelines intermittently to enforce various Islamic grievances. For example, in June 2016, JS's member Sheikh Sameer issued an edict through social media discouraging Maldivians from participating in the International Yoga Day, which according to him "is not permissible for Muslims because it is part of Hinduism."[3]

Adhaalath Party

One of the most significant Islamist political party in the Maldives is the *Adhaalath* (Justice) Party (AP). More radical political parties like AP control the nation's Ministry of Islamic Affairs, and they have long advocated for the strict implementation of *sharia* in all parts of the Maldives. The party holds conservative views on gender issues—opposing, for instance, the eligibility of women in presidential elections. Under its influence, the Ministry of Islamic Affairs has regularly invited foreign scholars and preachers with extreme religious views to the Maldives to address large and small groups on religious matters. Foreign Islamic scholars and preachers like Zakir Naik (India),[4] Bilal Phillips (Jamaica), and Sheikh Abdur Raheem Green (UK) with extreme religious views and misogynist outlooks are among those to have been invited to the Maldives by the Ministry.[5] Zakir Naik, a "televangelist" who runs the satellite television channel "Peace TV," is known for his preaching sessions and his inflammatory comment that "every Muslim should be a terrorist."[6]

AP has also banned visits to Sufi tombs and shrines because its leadership deemed praying there to be un-Islamic. The party supports reinstating a ban on public visits to the Medhu Ziyaaraiy, the tomb of Abu Barakat Berberi, who is credited with introducing Islam to the Maldives.[7] The country's Islamic Ministry, however, has ordered the shrine to remain open on the condition that no flags would be hoisted in or around it.

AP has also urged the government to ban music and songs that have been harming Maldivian youths. According to the pro-Islamist political party, "Cigarettes, music and Internet are gateways to higher addictions like alcohol, pornography and hard drugs. Attack root cause and save our kids."[8] However, despite pressure from pro-Islamist groups, Male administration refrained from imposing any legal proscription on music or dance.[9]

Members of JS and AP vehemently criticized former President Mohamed Waheed Hassan Manik when he asked for a review of the conviction of a minor who was sentenced to flogging by a juvenile court on Feydhoo Island.[10] According to AP, flogging is the penalty for fornication under *sharia* and maintains that the "purpose of penalties like these (flogging) in Islamic Sharia is to maintain order in society and to save it from sinful acts [...] and no one has the right to criticise any penalties specified in Islam."[11]

Malé Attack

The first and to date only Islamist terrorist attack in the country took place in the national capital, Malé, in September 2007, when a crude bomb blast injured nearly 12 foreigners, including tourists from the UK, Japan, and China. The attack targeted the tourism industry for its alleged un-Islamic practices and sinful influence on local culture. Subsequently, a massive crackdown prompted extremists to flee the country, mostly to neighbouring Pakistan and Sri Lanka. Three terrorists—Mohamed Sobah, Moosa Inaz and Ahmed Naseer—confessed to the crime and were sentenced to 15 years in jail in connection with the attack.[12] The search and sweep operation that ensued after the bombing uncovered an illegal *Dar-ul-Khair* mosque located on an isolated island in October 2007, where many extremists were hiding. The situation erupted into a violent confrontation between radical members of the mosque and security forces. The standoff at *Dar-ul-Khair* was featured in an al-Qaeda propaganda video in November 2007, which raised concerns within the country's security circles that the transnational terrorist group was gaining a foothold in the country. The propaganda video, titled: "Your brothers in the Maldives are calling you," was made by a hitherto unknown group known as *Ansar Al Mujahideen* and posted on the al-Qaeda-linked *Al-Ekhlaas* web forum, in order to attract recruits and raise capital for militant activities in the Maldives.[13] Maldivian authorities eventually unearthed similar Islamist outposts, such as an island located in North Ari atoll that provided safe heaven to extremists.

A subsequent al-Qaeda video circulated in November 2009 and featured Ali Jaleel, a Maldivian national who fought alongside pro-Taliban forces in Pakistan. Soon thereafter, another recruitment video featured a previously unknown al-Qaeda cell operating covertly in unregulated *madrasas* in the Maldives, and exhorted *jihadists* to travel to the country.[14]

The Pakistan Connection

There have been many instances of Maldives citizens traveling to Pakistan to engage in terrorist activities. In 2009, nine Maldivians were arrested in Pakistan's Waziristan tribal region during security raids at the militant training camps there.[15] Later that year, Maldivian al-Qaeda member Abu Jaleel and two of his associates carried out a suicide attack on Pakistan's Inter-Service Intelligence Agency headquarters in Lahore.[16] In the early weeks of February 2010, nine alleged Maldivian terrorists who had been arrested in Pakistan's troubled South Waziristan tribal region in March 2009 were repatriated to the Maldives.[17] According to national police, the nine suspects had ties to the bombing that took place in Malé's Sultan Park in September 2007, and they may have left the country for Pakistan via Sri Lanka for further training and indoctrination.[18] They were repatriated by the government to the Maldives in two phases, for de-radicalization. The suspects included Yusuf Izaadhy (who, according to a leaked U.S. cable, was planning to establish a terror group in the Maldives with the assistance of a Pakistan-based group) and two other individuals identified as Easa Ali, and Hasnain Abdullah Hameedh.[19]

In 2016, Mohamed Abdul Rahman was charged with terrorism and participating in a foreign war. Abdul Rahman travelled to Pakistan in 2007 under the pretext of continuing his studies, and engaged in militant activity there for almost ten years.[20]

In February 2010, the government estimated that there were 200-300 unregistered Maldivian students in Pakistan.[21] The offer of free education in Pakistani madrassas is widely acknowledged as a core means of radicalizing Maldivians locally, with well-meaning parents sending their children off on scholarships to "study Islam."[22] Though there is no recent statistics regarding the number of Maldivians students are presently undergoing various educational courses, bilateral ties in the sphere of education was boosted with an Memorandum of Understanding (MoU) during the Maldivian President Abdullah Yamin Abdul Gayoom's visit to Pakistan in May 2015.[23] In the past, the Maldivian government, including former President Mohamed Nasheed, has admitted that Pakistan-based terrorist groups have successfully recruited hundreds of Maldivian Muslims to fight against government forces in Pakistan.[24]

The Islamic State

The transnational jihadi movement has affected the Maldives in the same way that it has affected many other parts of the world. Maldivian youths are reportedly joining the al-Qaeda-affiliated *Jabhat Fateh al-Sham*, formerly known as the *Al-Nusra Front*, which is active in Iraq and Syria, as well as the Islamic State. While government sources insist that fewer than 50 youths have joined *jihadi* groups, various reports suggest that nearly 250 Maldivians have travelled to Syria and Iraq so far to participate in the ongoing civil strife in the Middle East alongside foreign militants affiliated with al-Qaeda or the Islamic State.[25] In March 2016, three Maldivians were arrested in Turkey while attempting to illegally cross over into Syria. These individuals, identified as Munnawar Abdulla, Ahmed Latheef and Ahmed Suhail, were extradited to the Maldives the same month.[26]

One explanation for Maldivian youths' interest in becoming foreign fighters is stargeted media. The Bilad Al Sham Media (BASM) is an online media forum, presumably run by Maldivians in Syria, that propagates and publicizes Maldivian jihadists and their heroics in the battlefields.[27] It has detailed the experiences of Maldivian *jihadis*, mostly young university students, as they travelled to Syria through a transit country with the hope of establishing an Islamic state that would ultimately "liberate the Islamic world" and achieve the global of an "Islamic caliphate."[28]

The Islamic State of Maldives

Reports of the establishment of the Islamic State of Maldives (ISM), purportedly a local branch affiliated with the Islamic State, emerged in July 2014, coinciding with the country's Independence Day celebrations. An Islamic State flag was hoisted for the first time in the capital Male's Raalhugandu area. ISIS flags were also seen during the early August 2014 protest march against Israel's military operations in the Gaza Strip, with protestors burning both American and Israeli flags. There were banners and flags clearly displaying the Maldivian flag crossed out with a message in the local Divehi language stating: 'This flag is directly under the slavery of America. If there was any independence, it would have been possible to implement Allah's Shari'a. Don't mock yourself, talking about independence."[29] The other banner with ISIS's flag depicted the message: "If you want real independence, try and get under the shelter of this flag. That will be the day when we break free from the shackles of the Kuffar and celebrate. Insha Allah."[30]

ISM has been active in popular social networking sites for *jihadist* propaganda, such as Facebook, Twitter, and YouTube. Its primary purpose is to promote the Islamic State in the Maldives, to create awareness about the Islamic State and to convey its messages to the Maldivian people. It urged Maldivian youth to: "strive for the Caliphate and to stand up against the existing democratic system of governance," which, according to the ISM, has "ruined Maldives."[31]

Conflicting allegiances notwithstanding, a whole new generation of young men appears to be gravitating to radical Islamist ideals, using social media, such as Twitter and Facebook, to propagate violence and intolerance, and to display the flags and insignia of jihadist groups. These youth have two things in common: the desire to have strict sharia implemented in the Maldives, and a hatred for democracy (which is viewed as un-Islamic). There have also been repeated incidents of Islamist vigilantes abducting and interrogating young men in Malé and elsewhere and forcing them to identify online activists advocating secularism or professing atheism through social media sites. Soon after the abduction of journalist Ahmed Rilwan in August 2014, the Islamic State of Maldives released a video on YouTube that depicted the execution of U.S. journalist James Wright Foley. It also contained a message threatening to kill Maldivian atheists, stating, "We shall borrow your heads."[32]

ISLAMISM AND SOCIETY

The Maldivian population is almost 100% Muslim, with citizenship strictly confined to practitioners of the Islamic faith. Most Maldivian Muslims belong to the *Shafi* school of Sunni Islam. The official language of the Maldives is Dhivehi.

The culture of the Maldives has undergone changes in recent years, and many believe it is progressively being *Wahhabized* and more and more adherents (particularly among the youth) are following a *Salafi-jihadi* ideology. In January 2011, an investigative report citing Maldivian intelligence officials concluded that Maldivian youths are increasingly attracted to the idea of transnational jihad, as discussed above.[33]

The influence of external and more extreme Islamic ideologies can be seen in changing dress codes for women, the increasing frequency with which men wear long beards, and in the name changes adopted by foreign-funded mosques around the country. Although the full veil is illegal in the Maldives (and even headscarves are banned for female television anchors), many women on Himandhoo Island have begun to cover themselves completely.[34] Ahmed Naseem, who served as foreign minister until the bloodless coup of February 2012 that toppled the democratically elected government of Mohamed Nasheed (Maldives Democratic Party), has stated that religious orthodoxy has become the norm in the Maldives, with an increasing number of Maldivians receiving sponsored madrassa education in Pakistan and Saudi Arabia.[35]

Maldivian women in particular are targeted in this environment. They face public floggings for adultery and rape. A 2009 investigation found that Muslim courts in the country had sentenced almost 150 women to public flogging for adultery.[36] Reports citing data from the Criminal Court show that there were 67 women who were flogged for adultery in 2010. Out of the 129 fornication cases that were filed in 2011, 104 people were sentenced. 93 of those sentenced were women. A young woman from the island of Feydhoo was raped by her stepfather, and then convicted of premarital sex in a juvenile court. She was sentenced to 100 lashes and eight months of house arrested in February 2013.[37]

In 2014, the Islamic jurisprudence body known as the Fiqh Academy publicly rejected a woman's right to consent to sex in a spousal relationship. The vice president of the academy, Dr. Mohamed Iyaz Abdul Latheef, said, "With the exception of forbidden forms of sexual intercourse, such as during menstrual periods and anal intercourse, it is not permissible under any circumstance for a woman to refrain from it when the husband is in need… [and should show] complete obedience to her husband."[38] The Academy has also endorsed other degrading and harmful practices, such as female genital mutilation.[39]

In 2015, woman, a mother of five, was convicted by a local judge on a remote island for adultery and giving birth out of wedlock, and sentenced to death by stoning. This sentencing, the first of its kind in Maldivian history,[40] was reportedly issued under section 1205 of the penal code, which states that Islamic *sharia* punishments must be meted out to persons found guilty beyond a reasonable doubt of committing a crime for which punishment is prescribed in the sharia.[41] However, the Maldivian Supreme Court overturned the ruling.

The attempt to implement strict *sharia* in the Maldives has on occasion triggered confrontation and violence. Many liberal intellectuals, writers and activists who have challenged the idea of the strict implementation of Islamic practices have been targeted. Dr. Afrasheem Ali, a renowned liberal religious scholar and lawmaker, was assassinated in early October 2012,[42] and there were attempted assassinations against two writers and social activists: Aishath Velezinee in January 2011[43] and Khilath Rasheed in June 2012.[44]

The Ministry of Islamic Affairs claims to have developed de-radicalization methods and has been taking measures to curb the activities of the various transnational Islamic organizations that have arrived in the Maldives in recent years.[45] However, radical interpretations of Islam and calls for *jihad* against non-believers are finding an increasing number of supporters in the Maldives. Islamist hardliners have called for adopting "Arabesque" alternatives in all aspects of life, including determining the age at which women reach puberty and proscribing how convicts should be executed in an "Islamic way."[46]

Other instances of rising extremism in the Maldives include the "Defend Islam" campaign of December 23, 2011.[47] Demonstrators with placards and banners stating "We stand united for Islam and the nation," "No idols in this holy land," "No to the Zionist Murderers," and "We stand for peace" descended on the streets of Malé, accusing then-president Mohammed Nasheed's administration of defiling Islam, promoting Western ideals and culture, and restricting the spread of more austere Islamic practices. The campaign and demonstrations in support of Islam were spearheaded by Islamic non-governmental organizations and some mainstream pro-Islamic political parties, including the Adhaalath Party and the party of former President of Maumoon Abdul Gayoom, the Progressive Party of the Maldives (PPM).

Hundreds of Maldivians took to the streets in September 2012, protesting against a film made by an independent filmmaker based in the U.S. entitled *Innocence of Muslims*, which was widely perceived as offensive to the Prophet Muhammad and sparked protests worldwide. The rally, which was called "In Protection of the Prophet Muhammad," resulted in the burning of an American flag and the display of placards with anti-American and anti-Jewish slogans such as "May Allah Curse America" and "Maldives: Future Graveyard of Americans and Jews."[48]

ISLAMISM AND THE STATE

With the adoption of the country's 1997 constitution, Islam became the state religion, and the chain of nearly 1,200 coral islands that make up the Maldives was declared officially Islamic.[49] Non-Muslims are forbidden from proselytizing and conducting public worship in the Maldives. Any Muslim who converts to another faith is breaking *sharia* law and can lose his or her citizenship. Migrant workers of other religions are denied the ability to practice their faith. The government also prevents the import of non-Muslim books and other religious items. However, people from other religions are given permanent residence permits to work, mostly in the country's hospitality industry, which serves as the economic lifeline of the Maldives. Despite its economic benefits, many radical Islamic groups active in the Maldives have denounced what they view as tourism's negative influence on local Islamic culture.

In July 2000, then-President Maumoon Abdul Gayoom, reportedly under pressure from radicals, declared in a public address that there is no room in the Maldives for any religion but Islam. He reiterated his stance on numerous occasions, and went on to accuse foreigners of destroying religious unity by introducing other faiths.[50] Gayoom claimed that the Maldives achieved and sustained its sovereignty by adhering only to Islamic principles. During the reign of Gayoom, who was himself an alumnus of Cairo's famed Al Azhar University, where he studied Islamic jurisprudence, the country experienced a new Islamic revival. In the 1980s and early 1990s, intense Islamic indoctrination was undertaken under the government's direct patronage, and mosques (miski) were built en masse. During that time, Quranic schools also emerged as major educational institutions. Gayoom has been accused of having brought Islamic fundamentalism into the country, and of using "Islam as a tool of governance."[51] Under the Gayoom regime, Islamic preachers and madrassas received unconditional political and financial support.[52]

After almost three decades of authoritarian rule, the Maldives became a multi-party democracy in 2008 with the election of the liberal Mohamed Nasheed as President. Although Nasheed's party, the Maldivian Democratic Party (MDP), has progressive views on religion, its main ally, the *Adhaalath* Party, holds conservative views on religious and cultural matters. According to one official, there were at least seven Islamist radicals running in the 2008 elections, though all of them lost.[53] However, Nasheed did not remain popular for long. Due to his economic strategy and alleged anti-Islamic policies, discontent reached a crescendo when Nasheed's government arrested Judge Abdulla Mohamed on January 16, 2012. A politico-religious coalition (the December 23 Alliance for Defending Islam) then accused Nasheed of violating the Maldivian constitution.

In February 2012, Nasheed was ousted in what was believed to be a bloodless coup[54] and replaced by then-Vice President Mohammed Waheed Hassan Manik. Though the alleged coup was never proven,[55] Nasheed claimed that he was forced out of office by security personnel at the behest of opposition political parties. The President of the Adhaalath Party, Sheikh Imran Abdulla, and PPM Vice President Umar Naseer were reportedly responsible for orchestrating the ouster of Nasheed.[56]

Nasheed's MDP government had resisted calls from extremists to shut down the country's luxury tourist resorts that serve alcohol, pork, and facilitate "pleasure tourism." Since Nasheed's ouster from power, the Islamic Ministry, which is responsible for religious affairs in the Maldives, has proposed the adoption of "Islamic tourism" without these basic elements, arguing that it works in Saudi Arabia where alcohol is not available, even at posh hotels frequented by Westerners. Political parties like the Gayoom-led PPM call for an alternative economy based on oil, rather than depending on the "anti-Islamic" tourism industry that facilitates public dancing, singing and massage parlors. Gayoom and others who propagate this Islamic tourism may find more takers among the conservative populace, but this development will certainly impact the future of the Maldives' famed tourism industry.

In the post-Nasheed era, there was a renewed call for the implementation of sharia in all walks of life in the Maldives. His immediate successor, President Mohammed Waheed Hassan, was seen as more favorable to radical Islamist ideas, or at least passive in the face of their overtures, ignoring extremists and allowing them to freely advocate their beliefs.[57] The Islamic Ministry has admonished young jihadis in only the mildest terms, stating that "No Muslim scholar in the Maldives has called on Maldivians to participate in foreign wars, but there are youth, who get emotional from what they see, of the suffering of Muslims, there are Maldivian youths who want to avenge that." The October 2015 Anti-Terrorism Act criminalized the act of leaving the Maldives to fight in a foreign war or joining a banned terror group. The offence is punishable by a jail term of between 10 to 20 years.

Under Waheed Hasan's administration, Islamic Affairs minister Sheikh Mohamed Shaheem Ali Saeed, who is a member of the *Adhaalath* Party, waged a virulent campaign against Christians and what he termed "Freemasons" for conspiring to erase Islam from the Maldives.[58] This tactic was not unexpected, as a common political smear in the Maldives is more liberal politicians being accused of promoting Christianity or conducting business with Jews. Shaheem Ali, who remains among the chief advocates of puritanical Islamic beliefs in the Maldives, reportedly published a book where he proposed the idea that the Maldives should become an emirate of a Middle Eastern country, such as Saudi Arabia. According to sources, Sheikh Shaheem indeed appears to be working towards this goal, as he has made significant effort as a Minister to steer Maldivian foreign policy towards Arabic countries while distancing it from the West.[59]

Under the new Progressive Party of Maldives government led by President Abdulla Yameen since mid November 2013, there are now efforts being undertaken to replace the ultra conservative Fiqh Academy, in spite of vehement criticism from various Islamic organizations as well as opposition political parties. In April 2016, the country's parliament amended the 1994 Religious Unity Act to set up a new Supreme Council for Islamic affairs, or *Fatwa Majlis*, with the authority to issue *fatwas* or legal opinions on religious disputes.[60] It is to be noted, however, that the same Fiqh Academy of Maldives that is currently under fire issued a *fatwa* in August 2015 prohibiting participation in foreign civil wars.[61]

In the Maldives, there is an ever-growing risk of religious extremism now as underground Islamic vigilante and criminal groups have been increasing, and intimidating progressive voices to remain silent. Now that a string of youths have already joined global *jihadi* organizations and are spreading their wings travelling to remote war zones and undergoing trainings and indoctrination, their return to Maldives will be far more dangerous to the Maldivian society and for the region at large, as their heroics back home would draw more takers and followers for future *jihad*, making Maldives a potential safe haven for transnational *jihadi* foot soldiers.

ENDNOTES

[1] IFM's previous webportal had published this release titled, "Islamic Foundation's views about the apostate," May 29, 2010, https://web.archive.org/web/20131006040534/http://islamicfoundationofthemaldives.org/sites/default/files/Press%20release%202.pdf; Also "See, Islamic Foundation calls for death sentence if apostate fails to repent", Minivan News Archive, June 1, 2010 http://minivannewsarchive.com/politics/islamic-foundation-calls-for-death-sentence-if-apostate-fails-to-repent-7606

[2] "Religious NGO Jamiyyathul Salaf recommends beheading, firing squad over lethal injection," Minivan News Archive, February 26, 2013, http://minivannewsarchive.com/society/religious-ngo-jamiyyathul-salaf-recommends-beheading-firing-squad-over-lethal-injection-53689

[3] "Despite cloud of Islamist criticism, Yoga Day events in the Maldives go off without a twist", Scroll India News, June 22, 2016, https://scroll.in/article/810439/despite-cloud-of-islamist-criticism-yoga-day-events-in-the-maldives-go-off-without-a-twist.

[4] Zakir Naik's visit (May 25-31, 2010) was organized by the Islamic Foundation (IFM) and Islamic Affairs ministry. See the transcript of Zakir Naik's response to Mohamed Nazim at the Male's Maafaanu stadium, 28 May 2010, Minivan News Archive, http://minivannewsarchive.com/files/2010/05/Dr_Zakir_Naik_and_Nazim-1.pdf

[5] Bilal Philips created a major controversy when he preached that it was Islamic to marry off young girls as soon as they reached puberty, irrespective of their age, an idea that was endorsed by the Salaaf (JS). Phillips visited the Maldives along with Abdur Raheem Green on the invitation of JS in the first week of June 2010. The JS's misogynistic ideals and preaching have drawn criticism in the past and triggered the creation of a feminist movement in Maldives, known as Rehendhi. JJ Robinson, "Feminist group launches letter writing campaign against sponsors of Dr Bilal Philips event", Minivan News Archive, May 27, 2010.

[6] Naik was banned from entering the UK for his speeches in June 2010 and most recently, in November 2016, his organization Islamic Research Foundation (IRF) was banned by Indian government. See, "Modi govt bans Zakir Naik's NGO Islamic Research Foundation for 5 years", Firstpost, November 15, 2016, http://www.firstpost.com/india/modi-govt-bans-zakir-naiks-ngo-islamic-research-foundation-for-5-years-3107076.html. For his most outrageous comment, see, for example, "Every Muslim Should be a Terrorist," https://www.youtube.com/watch?v=Bxk5AAA5FbI

[7] "Sacred Shrine Opened to Public," Dhivehi Observer, March 29, 2009, (Archived in) http://doreview.blogspot.in/2009/03/sacred-shrine-opened-to-public.html

[8] "Maldives cracks down on men and women dancing together", Agence France Presse /NDTV.com, September 14, 2012, http://www.ndtv.com/world-news/maldives-cracks-down-on-men-and-women-dancing-together-499304

[9] "Maldives: President rejects ministry's ban on mixed-gender dance events", Arts Freedom, September 18, 2012, https://artsfreedom.org/maldives-president-rejects-ministrys-ban-on-mixed-gender-dance/

[10] "Maldives girl, 15, sentenced to 100 lashes for 'fornication", The Guardian, March 01, 2013, https://www.theguardian.com/world/2013/mar/01/maldives-girl-100-lashes-fornication

[11] "15 year-old rape victim deserves flogging for separate crime of fornication: Adhaalath Party", Minivan News Archive, February 28, 2013, http://minivannewsarchive.com/politics/15-year-old-rape-victim-deserves-flogging-for-crime-of-fornication-adhaalath-party-53861

[12] "Three people involved in Sultan Park bombing sentenced to 15 years", December 2007, http://www.policelife.mv/page/19695

[13] "Ansar Al Mujahideen Targets the Maldives", Threat Watch, November 2007, http://threatswatch.org/rapidrecon/2007/11/ansar-almujahideen-targets-the/

[14] "First Video of al-Qaeda in Maldives Released," Adnkronos International, November 20, 2009, http://www.adnkronos.com/AKI/English/Security/?id=1.0.1575824650.

[15] "Nine Maldives jihadists held in Pakistan", The Hindu, April 04, 2009, http://www.thehindu.com/todays-paper/Nine-Maldives-jihadists-held-in-Pakistan/article16608723.ece.

[16] "The Maldives and US link in ISI office attack, The News (Karachi), March 08, 2013.

[17] "9 Armed Maldivians Arrested in Waziristan," Miadhu News, April 2, 2009; "Maldivian Detainees Repatriated from Pakistan," Minivan News Archive, February 8, 2010. http://minivannewsarchive.com/politics/maldivian-detainees-repatriated-from-pakistan-3296

[18] "Aim was to Perform Jihad by Targeting Non Muslims – Police," Miadhu News, November 8, 2007.

[19] Al-Qaeda associates active in Maldives: State Department cable, Haveeru Daily, December 6, 2010.

[20] Hassan Mohamed, "Trial begins for Maldivian man 'who fought in Pakistan for nine years", Maldives Independent, January 15, 2017, http://maldivesindependent.com/politics/maldivian-man-who-fought-in-pakistan-for-nine-years-brought-to-trial-128388.

[21] United States Department of State, Office of the Coordinator of Counterterrorism, Country Reports on Terrorism 2010 (Washington, DC: U.S. Department of State, August 2011), http://www.refworld.org/docid/4e5248203c.html.

[22]   Author's (Animesh Roul) Interview with J J Robinson, Former editor, Minivan News. (March 2013).
[23]   "Pakistan, Maldives sign four MoUs", Dawn, May 07, 2015, https://www.dawn.com/news/1180523
[24]   "Radicals in Pak Recruiting our Youth: Maldives," CNN-IBN (New Delhi), October 25, 2009. http://www.news18.com/videos/india/maldives-pres-intw-327314.html
[25]   "Maldives again downplays jihadist threat, places number at 49", Mihaaru, June 16, 2016, http://en.mihaaru.com/maldives-again-downplays-jihadist-threat-places-number-at-49/
[26]   "Three Maldivians en route to Syria extradited", Maldives Independent, March 24, 2016, http://maldivesindependent.com/society/three-maldivians-en-route-to-syria-extradited-122998
[27]   "Bilad al Sham Media" http://biladalsham.wordpress.com/; Also See, Bilad al Sham Media's Facebook page (presently defunct), https://www.facebook.com/pages/Bilad-Al-Sham-Media/253167868224266
[28]   Ahmed Rilwan, "Maldivian militant killed in Syrian suicide attack, claims online jihadist group", Minivan News Archive, May 25, 2014, http://minivannewsarchive.com/politics/maldivian-militant-killed-in-syria-suicide-attack-claims-online-jihadist-group-85600
[29]   Author's translations of the Graffitis under the Flags.
[30]   Author's translations of the Graffitis under the Flags.
[31]   ISM social media site has since been blocked, Screen shot available, with Author
[32]   ISM social media site has since been blocked. Screen shot available, with Author
[33]   Anupam Dasgupta, "A Male-Volent Link," The Week, January 16, 2011.
[34]   "Maldives Moves against Veiled Women, Jihadis," Daily Times (Lahore), November 15, 2007.
[35]   Tom Wright, "Islamism Set Stage for Maldives Coup," Wall Street Journal, February 11, 2012, http://www.wsj.com/articles/SB10001424052970203824904577215050907606404.
[36]   Andrew Buncombe, "150 Women Face Adultery Flogging on Maldives," Independent (London), July 22, 2009, http://www.independent.co.uk/news/world/asia/150-women-face-adultery-flogging-on-maldives-1757150.html
[37]   Neil Merritt, "Fifteen year-old's appeal of flogging sentence for fornication stalled in High Court," Minivan News Archive, August 3, 2013, http://minivannewsarchive.com/politics/fifteen-year-olds-appeal-of-flogging-sentence-for-fornication-stalled-in-high-court-61850

[38] Even though the president of the Maldives called it "un-Islamic," the Fiqh Academy's fatwa on the subject may have adherents within the Maldivian society. See, Fiqh Academy Vice President Dr.Mohamed Iyaz Abdul Latheef's views, as cited in "President Yameen vetoes sexual offences bill," Minivan News Archives, January 15, 2014, http://minivannewsarchive.com/politics/president-yameen-vetoes-sexual-offences-bill-75176.

[39] Zaheena Rasheed , "Fiqh Academy VP endorses female genital mutilation", Minivan News Archives, February 6, 2014, http://minivannewsarchive.com/politics/figh-academy-vp-endorses-female-genital-mutilation-77037

[40] "Maldives court sentences woman to death by stoning," Maldives Independent, October 18, 2015. http://maldivesindependent.com/crime-2/maldives-court-sentences-woman-to-death-by-stoning-118541.

[41] Shahindha Ismail and Mushfique Mohamed, "Why the sentence on death by stoning is unconstitutional," Maldives Independent, October 20, 2015, http://maldivesindependent.com/feature-comment/sentence-on-death-by-stoning-is-unconstitutional-118640.

[42] "MP Afrasheem stabbed to death," Haveeru Online, October 2, 2012.

[43] "ICJ says Velezinee attack politically motivated," Haveeru Daily, January 6, 2011.

[44] "Slashed journalist claims attack was targeted assassination by Islamic radicals," Minivan News, July 2, 2012.

[45] "Islamic Ministry Proposes Extremist Rehabilitation Centre," Minivan News Archive, March 18, 2010, http://minivannewsarchive.com /society/islamic-ministry-proposes-extremist-rehabilitation-centre-4640

[46] Author's (Animesh Roul) Interview with J J Robinson, Former editor, Minivan News. (March 2013).

[47] See "Protests proceed peacefully as a majority defends Islam", Minivan News Archive, December 23, 2011, http://minivannewsarchive.com/politics/protests-proceed-peacefully-as-a-majority-defends-islam-29826

[48] "Protests over anti-Islamic movie spread to the Maldives," Minivan News Archives, September 15, 2012, http://minivannewsarchive.com/society/protests-over-anti-islamic-movie-spread-to-the-maldives-43852.

[49] Article 10 of the Maldivian Constitution states the religion of the Maldives is Islam and Islam shall be the basis for all laws in the land. The constitution granted right to freedom of expression in Article 27; however, it stipulates that the right only exists as long as it is "not contrary to any tenet of Islam."

[50] Gayoom said while addressing a 4,000 strong crowd that "We want to bring reform to the Maldives, reform that leaves no room for other religions." See "Asia's Longest-Serving Leader in Maldives Run-Off," Associated Press, October 27, 2008.

[51] Maldivian Democratic Party leader Mohamed Latheef once said that Gayoom is the person who brought Islamic fundamentalism to the Maldives. See "Radical Islam Shows up in Maldives," CNN-IBN (New Delhi), June 21, 2007, http://ibnlive.in.com/news/maldives-turns-to-islamic-extremism/27821-2.html.

[52] "Maumoon Abdul Gayoom - the Father of Maldivian Extremism," Dhivehi Observer, October 10, 2007; Aishath Valenzinee, "Gayoom's abuse of faith," Himal South Asian, October 2007, http://www.dhivehiobserver.com/editorial/Islamic_Extremism_Maldives__101007.html; See also http://himalmag.com/component/content/article/1325-.html

[53] Anupam Dasgupta, "A Male-Volent Link," The Week, January 16, 2011, (Archived in) http://www.maldivestoday.com/2011/01/18/a-male-volent-link/.

[54] The anti-Nasheed wave existed before due to his economic policy and alleged anti-Islamic policies, it came into open with the arrest of Judge Abdulla Mohamed on January 16, 2012 when a politico-religious coalition (December 23 Alliance for Defending Islam) accused him of violating the Maldivian constitution. The pro-Islamic alliance led by the President of Party Sheikh Imran Abdulla and Vice President of Progressive Party of Maldives (PPM) Umar Naseer reportedly orchestrated the ouster of Nasheed.

[55] An independent Commission of National Inquiry (CoNI) ruled out any coup and the findings largely supported by the U.S. and the Commonwealth of Nations. See "Nasheed ouster not a coup: probe panel," August 30, 2012, http://www.thehindu.com/news/international/nasheed-ouster-not-a-coup-probe-panel/article3839500.ece.

[56] Azra Naseem, "Operation Haram to Halal – the Islamist role in replacing Nasheed with Waheed", Minivan News, February 18, 2012, http://minivannews.com/politics/comment-operation-haram-to-halal-the-islamist-role-in-replacing-nasheed-with-waheed-32294. Also see Tom Wright, "Islamism Set Stage for Maldives Coup," Wall Street Journal, February 11, 2012, http://online.wsj.com/article/SB10001424052970203824904577215050907606404.html.

[57] "No other presidency granted more freedom to religious scholars than the current regime- Shaheem," Miadhu Daily, February 1, 2013.

[58] "Islamic Ministry claims Christians, Freemasons secretly working to 'eradicate' Islam in the Maldives," Minivan News Archive, February 12, 2013, http://minivannewsarchive.com /politics/islamic-ministry-claims-christians-freemasons-secretly-working-to-eradicate-islam-in-the-maldives-52751.

[59] Author's Interview with Azra Naseem.

[60] "President authorized to constitute religious advisory body", Maldives Independent, November 22, 2016, http://maldivesindependent.com/politics/president-authorised-to-constitute-religious-advisory-body-127839

[61] The fatwa reads, "Travelling to Islamic countries where groups belonging to Islamic countries create havoc and instability in the name of jihad will open avenues for enemies of Muslims to interfere in the affairs of Muslim countries." , See, "Fiqh Academy issues fatwa on Jihad", Maldives Independent, August 25, 2016, http://maldivesindependent.com/society/fiqh-academy-issues-fatwa-on-jihad-116727

Pakistan

> **Quick Facts**
>
> Population: 201,995,540 (estimated 2016)
>
> Area: 796,095 sq km
>
> Ethnic Groups: Punjabi 44.68%, Pashtun (Pathan) 15.42%, Sindhi 14.1%, Sariaki 8.38%, Muhajirs 7.57%, Balochi 3.57%, other 6.28%
>
> Religions: Muslim (official) 96.4% (Sunni 85-90%, Shia 10-15%), other (includes Christian and Hindu) 3.6%
>
> Government Type: Federal republic
>
> GDP (official exchange rate): $271.1 billion (estimated 2015)
>
> *Map and Quick Facts courtesy of the CIA World Factbook (January 2017)*

Overview

Pakistan was established in 1947 as a homeland for South Asia's Muslims following the end of British colonial rule on the Indian Subcontinent. The majority of Pakistanis practice a moderate form of Sufi Islam, but Islamist political parties exercise significant influence within society and through the courts, as well as help shape political debates, foreign policy, and the development of legislation. Moreover, throughout Pakistan's history, its military and intelligence services have created and cultivated ties with violent Islamist groups to achieve regional strategic objectives. The U.S. war in Afghanistan following the September 11, 2001 terrorist attacks, and Pakistan's role in fighting terrorism in recent years, has severely complicated the Islamist militant landscape in Pakistan. The emergence of the Pakistani Taliban – an amalgam of anti-state militants that formed in 2007 in reaction to the Pakistan military's storming of the notorious Red Mosque in the heart of Islamabad – has threatened to destabilize the nation. The Pakistani Taliban has conducted countless terrorist attacks throughout the country over the last nine years, killing nearly 30,000 civilians and security forces, and prompting a major Pakistan Army operation against the militants during the last two years.

Pakistan will continue to grapple with its status as a Muslim constitutional democracy, and with developing ways to channel Islamist ideologies that have played a significant role in its identity since 1947. While Islamist political parties are unlikely to take power in the near future, they will continue to influence the country's legal framework and political discourse in ways that restrict personal freedoms, subordinate women and minorities, and enhance the role of clergy within the country's democratic institutions. While societal attitudes will also shape Islamist trends in Pakistan, it can be argued that the military's posture and attitude toward violent Islamists will be the single most important factor in determining the future direction of the country, i.e., whether it remains positively engaged with Western countries or takes a decisively Islamist turn that severs its traditionally strong relations with the United States.

ISLAMIST ACTIVITY

Pakistan's Federally Administered Tribal Areas (FATA), which consist of seven semi-autonomous tribal agencies along the border with Afghanistan, constitute one of the most dangerous terrorist safe havens in the world today. In 2002, al-Qaeda's leadership moved from Afghanistan into Pakistan's North and South Waziristan sections of the tribal border areas, where they established networks with like-minded Pakistani groups such as the *Jaish-e-Muhammed* (JeM) and the *Lashkar-e-Taiba* (LeT).[1] The Obama administration's aggressive campaign of drone strikes in the region from 2010–2012 has helped degrade al-Qaeda's leadership ranks and disrupted the group's ability to plan and carry out international terrorist attacks. Pakistani denunciations of the drones for infringing on the country's sovereignty and complaints from international human rights organizations about civilian casualties resulting from drone strikes, however, have led the U.S. administration to curb their use in recent years. All told, there have been over 400 U.S. drone strikes in Pakistan since January 2008, including the strike that killed Taliban leader Mullah Akhtar Mansour in Pakistan's Baluchistan province in May 2016.[2]

Pakistan has long relied on violent Islamist groups to accomplish its strategic objectives in both Afghanistan and India. Pakistan's support for groups that fight in Afghanistan—namely the Afghan Taliban and the Haqqani network—and those that primarily attack India (like the JeM and LeT) remains undiminished, even as it has stepped up its military operations in the tribal border areas against the *Tehrik-i-Taliban Pakistan* (TTP, or the Pakistani Taliban).[3]

There are around 150,000 Pakistani troops deployed along the Pakistan-Afghanistan border. Since 2002, the U.S. has provided nearly $14 billion to Pakistan in the form of Coalition Support Fund (CSF) reimbursements for Pakistan's military deployments and operations along the Afghan border.

The Afghan Taliban

Pakistan's military and intelligence services (particularly the Inter-Services Intelligence Directorate, or ISI) historically have had close ties with the Afghan Taliban, which ruled Afghanistan from 1996–2001. Before the terrorist attacks of September 11, 2001, the Pakistani government openly supported and recognized Taliban rule in Afghanistan. Although Pakistani officials largely disagreed with the Taliban's harsh interpretation of Islam, they viewed the movement as their best chance to achieve their own strategic objectives in the region. Pakistan continued to support the Taliban into the late 1990s, long after Osama bin Laden took refuge there in 1996 and despite the growing problems that it created in Islamabad's relations with Washington. Pakistan's high-stakes policy vis-à-vis the Taliban derived from its aims of denying India, as well as Iran and the Central Asian countries, a strong foothold in Afghanistan and ensuring a friendly regime in Kabul that would refrain from making territorial claims on Pakistan's Pashtun areas along the Pakistan-Afghanistan border.

Despite pledging to break ties with the Taliban after the U.S. invasion of Afghanistan in 2001, Islamabad failed to crack down forcefully on its leaders or to actively disrupt their activities in Pakistan. Indeed, U.S. officials have acknowledged that officials within Pakistan's Inter-Services Intelligence (ISI) directorate maintain relationships with Afghan Taliban leaders and see benefits in keeping good ties with the Taliban in the expectation that the Taliban will again play a role in Afghan politics.[4]

Hopes for a negotiated Afghan settlement were raised in July of 2015, when Pakistan played host to face-to-face talks between the Afghan government and Taliban leaders. However, weeks later, just before a second round of talks was scheduled to be held, reports surfaced that Taliban supreme leader Mullah Omar had died two years prior, causing disarray within the Taliban movement. Pakistan helped install Omar's successor, Mullah Akhtar Mansour, who was subsequently killed in a U.S. drone strike on May 21, 2016. The leadership crisis within the Taliban and escalating Taliban violence in Afghanistan, including a major truck bombing in Kabul on April 19th that killed nearly 65, have closed the door on negotiations for the foreseeable future.

Al-Qaeda

The unilateral U.S. raid in Abbottabad, Pakistan on May 2, 2011, that eliminated Osama bin Laden exposed deep fissures in U.S.-Pakistan relations. Pakistanis were incensed that the U.S. did not take its leadership into confidence before the raid. U.S. officials, on the other hand, were incredulous that the world's most wanted terrorist could live in a Pakistani garrison town for six years without the knowledge of officials within the military establishment. U.S. Senator Susan Collins (R-Maine) said the bin Laden killing revealed the "double-game" Pakistan is playing and called for stricter conditions on U.S. aid to the country.[5] U.S. Secretary of State Hillary Clinton told Members of Congress in June 2011 that a review of intelligence turned up no information indicating that top Pakistani leaders knew about bin Laden's presence in Abbottabad. She added, however, that it was possible that lower-level Pakistani officials were involved in protecting the international terrorist.

Pakistan's subsequent arrest of a Pakistani doctor, Shakil Afridi, who helped the U.S. track bin Laden's whereabouts through a fake vaccination campaign, was a further blow to bilateral relations. Afridi was initially sentenced to 33 years in prison by a Pakistani tribal court on trumped-up charges of supporting a militant group. In August 2013, however, the sentence was overturned, and a retrial was ordered.[6] Pakistani authorities privately acknowledge he is being punished for helping the CIA. In mid-December 2016, a senior Pakistani official said that Pakistan would be willing to discuss the release of Dr. Afridi, possibly through a presidential pardon, with the Trump administration.[7]

The Obama administration's intensive drone campaign in Pakistan's tribal border areas has helped degrade al-Qaeda and hindered its ability to plot and train for terrorist attacks across the globe. Pakistani officials and media outlets regularly criticize the drone missile strikes as a violation of Pakistani sovereignty, but the program appears to be at least tacitly accepted at the highest levels of the Pakistan government. Of more than 400 drone strikes in Pakistan since 2004, only the strike on Mansour in May and one other have taken place outside the tribal areas. The U.S. attack on Mansour angered Pakistani officials, who called it a "violation of sovereignty."

Due to Pakistani public anger over the drone campaign and complaints from human rights organizations about the number of civilian casualties, the U.S. administration has reduced considerably its reliance on drones. There were only 10 drone strikes in Pakistan in 2015, down from a peak of 128 strikes in 2010.

Tehreek-e-Taliban Pakistan (TTP)

The Tehreek-e-Taliban Pakistan (TTP), an amalgamation of Pakistani militant groups loosely affiliated with al-Qaeda and the Afghan Taliban, was formed in 2007 and has conducted numerous suicide attacks that since 2012 have killed over 9,000 Pakistani civilians and 2,400 Pakistani security forces.[8]

In the six weeks before Pakistani elections in May 2013, the TTP took responsibility for attacks that killed scores of election workers and candidates, mainly from the secular-leaning political parties. Nawaz Sharif's Pakistan Muslim League/Nawaz (PML/N) party ran on a campaign of supporting negotiations with the TTP and failed to denounce the attacks on the electoral process. Six months after winning the elections, the Nawaz Sharif government offered to engage in talks with the TTP. The

TTP-government talks officially started in January 2014 but did not last long. The TTP claims of instituting a cease-fire were undermined by continued attacks against civilians and security forces.

Talks broke down altogether following a major TTP attack on the Karachi airport that killed 36 in June 2014. One week later, the Pakistani military announced the launch of a new military offensive against TTP bases in North Waziristan called *Zarb-e-Azb* ("Strike of the Prophet's Sword"). The Pakistani Army intensified their counterterrorism operations following an attack on a military school in Peshawar in December 2014 that killed 130, mostly children. Military operations in the FATA reportedly contributed to a nearly fifty percent decline in the number of terrorist attacks in the country in 2015, as compared to 2014.[9]

The National Action Plan (NAP) to combat terrorism passed by the Pakistani parliament in January 2015 has further contributed to the decrease in terrorist attacks, as well as laid initial groundwork for delegitimizing extremist ideologies. The plan includes steps like lifting the moratorium on the death penalty for terrorists, establishing special military courts to try terrorists, curbing the spread of extremist literature and propaganda on social media, freezing the assets of terrorist organizations, and forming special committees, comprised of army and political leaders, in the provinces to implement the NAP.

Still, Pakistan has a long way to go in reversing the tide of extremism and terrorism in the country, as evidenced by several major terrorist attacks that occurred earlier this year. On January 20, militants stormed a university in the Pakistani city of Charsadda, killing at least 20 students and teachers. Afghanistan-based TTP leader Omar Mansour claimed credit for the attack (Mansour's faction of the TTP was also behind the 2014 attack on the school in Peshawar).[10] A U.S. drone strike in eastern Afghanistan subsequently killed Mansour in July of 2016.

Another splinter group of the TTP, Jamaat-ul-Ahrar, was responsible for a suicide bombing at a park in Lahore this past Easter. The group said it directly targeted Christians and that the bombing was a message to the Pakistani government that "we will carry out such attacks until Sharia is imposed in the country."[11] While the attack was directed at Christians, most victims were Muslim, and about half of the 72 killed were children.

There were two major attacks in Baluchistan in 2016, one on August 8th in Quetta, which targeted a hospital and in which 70—mostly lawyers—were killed.[12] ISIS claimed credit for another attack, which took place on October 25th, on a police academy in Quetta, killing 61 Pakistani cadets—although Pakistani authorities blamed a local anti-Shi'a group, the *Lashkar-e-Jhangvi*.[13]

The Haqqani Network

Jalaluddin Haqqani—a powerful independent Afghan militant leader whose followers operate in the border areas between Khost in Afghanistan and North Waziristan in FATA—reportedly died in 2014. Haqqani had been allied with the Afghan Taliban for nearly 20 years, having served as tribal affairs minister in the Taliban regime in the late 1990s, and was known to be close to Pakistan's intelligence service. Jalaluddin's son, Sirajuddin, has taken over operational control of the militant network and currently serves as the number two leader of the Afghan Taliban.

The Haqqani network has been a major facilitator of the Taliban insurgency in Afghanistan, and responsible for some of the fiercest attacks against U.S. and coalition forces. Haqqani forces were responsible for a suicide attack against the Indian embassy in Kabul in July 2008 that killed two senior Indian officials and over 50 others; a suicide attack on a CIA base in Khost Province in December 2009 that marked the most deadly attack on the CIA in 25 years; a multi-hour siege of the U.S. embassy in Kabul in September 2011; and—most recently—a major truck bombing in Kabul on April 19, 2016 that killed 65.

The source of the Haqqanis' power lies primarily in their ability to forge relations with a variety of different terrorist groups (al-Qaeda, the Afghan Taliban, the Pakistani Taliban, and India-focused groups like the Jaish-e-Muhammed), while also maintaining links to Pakistani intelligence. Pakistani military strategists view the Haqqani network as their most effective tool for blunting Indian influence in Afghanistan. Credible U.S. media reports indicate that the Haqqani network, in cooperation with Pakistani intelligence, was responsible for the bombing of the Indian embassy in Kabul in July 2008, killing more than 50 people, including two senior Indian officials.[14] U.S. officials have appealed to Pakistani leaders to crack down on the Haqqani network, but have been rebuffed with declarations that the Pakistani military is overstretched and incapable of taking on too many militant groups at once.

On September 7, 2012, under pressure from the U.S. Congress, the U.S. State Department listed the Haqqani Network as a Foreign Terrorist Organization (FTO). An organization designated an FTO is subject to financial and immigration sanctions. The designation also publicly stigmatizes the organization, which can help garner cooperation from foreign governments. The U.S. has killed several Haqqani network leaders in Afghanistan and in Pakistan's tribal border areas since the FTO designation.

The U.S. has also begun to block military aid to Pakistan due to its failure to crack down on the Haqqanis. The U.S. withheld $300 million in CSF payments to Pakistan in FY 2015 because the administration could not certify to Congress that Pakistan's military offensive in the tribal border areas included operations against Haqqani bases.[15] Furthermore, Congress blocked U.S. funding for the transfer of eight F-16 aircraft to Pakistan in the first half of 2016 because of Islamabad's lack of action against the Haqqani sanctuary within its borders.[16]

Lashkar-e-Taiba and Jaish-e-Mohammed

Groups like the Lashkar-e-Taiba (LeT) and Jaish-e-Mohammed (JeM, formerly the Harakat-ul-Ansar) focused their attacks throughout the 1990s on Indian security forces in Jammu and Kashmir, but now conduct attacks throughout India and target both Indian and Western civilians. The Pakistani government's failure to shut down groups like JeM and LeT, who were responsible for the November 2008 attacks in Mumbai, is creating instability in the region and increasing the likelihood of additional international attacks, particularly against India, but also involving citizens of other nations. In March 2010, Pakistani-American David Headley, who was arrested in Chicago in early October 2009, pleaded guilty in a U.S. court to involvement in both the Mumbai attacks and a plot to attack the offices of a Danish newspaper for publishing caricatures of the Prophet Mohammed. In four days of testimony and cross-examination, Headley detailed meetings he had with a Pakistani intelligence officer, a former Army major, and a Navy frogman, all of whom were among the key players orchestrating the assaults. Headley's revelations have raised questions about whether there was official Pakistani involvement in the Mumbai attacks.[17]

Following the Mumbai attacks, Islamabad responded to U.S. and Indian pressure by arresting seven LeT operatives, including those that India had fingered as the ringleaders of the attacks: Zaki ur Rehman Lakhvi and Zarar Shah. The Pakistani government also reportedly shut down some LeT offices throughout the country. Despite these actions, there are indications that the LeT continues to operate relatively freely in the country. Pakistan released from detention LeT founder Hafez Muhammed Sayeed in June 2009, when the Lahore High Court determined there was insufficient evidence to continue his detainment. Sayeed has taken an increasingly public role in Pakistan and frequently speaks at political rallies, where he calls for jihad against India. In 2012, the U.S. issued a $10 million reward for information leading to his arrest and conviction.[18] As further evidence of its unwillingness to act against the LeT, Pakistan released Zaki ur Rehman Lakhvi from jail in April 2015, just days after the U.S. approved the sale of nearly $1 billion in military equipment to Pakistan.

The LeT has put down roots in Pakistani society, especially in central and southern Punjab, through its social welfare wing, the Jamaat-ud-Dawa (JuD), which runs schools and medical clinics. The headquarters of the LeT/JuD is a 200-acre site outside Lahore in the town of Muridke. The JuD increased its popularity through its rapid response in helping victims of the October 2005 earthquake in Pakistani Kashmir. The U.S. government views the JuD as a surrogate or front organization of the LeT. The U.S. State Department designated the LeT as a Foreign Terrorist Organization in December 2001, and later included the JuD on the Specially Designated Global

Terrorist Designation list as an alias of the LeT.[19] On December 11, 2008, the United Nations Security Council imposed sanctions on JuD, declaring it a global terrorist group.[20]

There are well-known links between both the LeT and JeM to international terrorism. Shoe bomber Richard Reid apparently trained at a LeT camp in Pakistan; one of the London subway bombers spent time at the LeT complex in Muridke; and al-Qaeda leader Abu Zubaydah was captured from an LeT safe house in Faisalabad, Pakistan. The LeT signed Osama bin Laden's 1998 *fatwa* calling for Muslims to kill Americans and Israelis.

Reports indicate that one of the prime suspects in the 2006 London airliner bomb plot had family ties to Maulana Masood Azhar, the leader of JeM. The JeM has also been linked to the kidnapping and brutal murder of *Wall Street Journal* reporter Daniel Pearl in January 2002. Pakistan officially banned the JeM in 2002, but Azhar has never been formally charged with a crime. Indeed, reports indicate Masood Azhar addressed a large public rally in Pakistan via phone in early 2014 and called on his supporters to resume *jihad* against India. Furthermore, the JeM conducted a major attack on the Indian air base at Pathankot in early January of 2016, just six days after Indian Prime Minister Narendra Modi had made a surprise goodwill visit to Lahore, where he met with Pakistani Prime Minister Nawaz Sharif.

Indo-Pakistani tensions escalated further following a September 18th, 2016 attack by Pakistan-based terrorists on an Indian military base in Kashmir that killed at least 18 Indian soldiers. Ten days later, India launched surgical strikes across the Line of Control (LoC) to neutralize terrorist bases inside Pakistani territory. Shelling and firing across the LoC, which had become an almost-daily occurrence, has decreased subsequently, but rhetoric from both Pakistani and Indian officials remains heated, and there is a continued risk for military escalation.[21]

The Islamic State (ISIS)

ISIS has sought to gain the allegiance of various terrorist groups in the region and in January 2015 officially announced the formation of its Khorasan "province." Khorasan is an Islamic historical term used to describe the area encompassed by Afghanistan, parts of Pakistan, and parts of other countries bordering Afghanistan. According to the relevant *Hadith* (sayings attributed to the Prophet Muhammad), South-Central Asia plays a key role in establishing a global caliphate. The *Hadith* contains references to the Ghazwa-e-Hind (Battle of India), where the final battle between Muslims and non-Muslims before the end times will supposedly take place. One *Hadith* further says that an army with black flags will emerge from Khorasan to help the "Mahdi" (the prophesied redeemer of Islam) establish his caliphate at Mecca.[22]

So far, only a handful of TTP leaders and a few disgruntled Afghan Taliban leaders have pledged their allegiance to ISIS leader Abu Bakr al-Baghdadi. The Pakistan-based anti-Shi'a sectarian outfit Jundullah reportedly pledged support to ISIS in late 2014.[23] The number of fighters that have traveled from South Asia to fight with ISIS in Iraq and Syria also is relatively low. The International Centre for the Study of Radicalization estimates that around 500 fighters have travelled from Pakistan to join the ranks of the group.[24] In July 2015, a U.S. drone strike in the eastern Afghan province of Nangahar killed more than two dozen ISIS fighters, including Shahidullah Shahid, former spokesman for the Pakistani Taliban, who had defected to ISIS ranks the year before.[25]

ISIS' inability so far to make significant inroads into Pakistan is largely due to the well-established roots of al-Qaeda in the region. There is some concern that ISIS may eventually gain influence among the educated urban middle class in Pakistan since it has had success in recruiting among this cohort globally. However, most analysts are largely skeptical about the future prospects of ISIS in Pakistan.[26]

Al-Qaeda leader Ayman al-Zawahiri has sought to strengthen relations with Pakistan-based terrorist groups and make inroads with the Muslim populations in other parts of South Asia to help fend off ISIS encroachment. In September 2014, Zawahiri made a video announcement launching an al-Qaeda wing in the Indian Subcontinent (AQIS). In the video, Zawahiri assures Muslims in India, Bangladesh, and Burma that the organization "did not forget you and that they are doing what they can to rescue you from injustice, oppression, persecution, and suffering."[27] Just two days after the launch of AQIS, the group attempted to attack a Pakistani navy frigate in order to use it to target American naval assets in the Indian Ocean.

ISLAMISM AND SOCIETY

The strategic environment in South Asia over the last 30 years, and the Pakistani response to regional challenges, has influenced Islamist trends in society and heightened religious-inspired violence. The war against the Soviets in Afghanistan in the 1980s and the Islamization policies of Pakistani president General Zia ul-Haq during the same period strengthened Islamist political forces and puritanical sects like the Deobandis over the more moderate Barelvis.[28] The influence of Sufism, dating back to the eighth and ninth century in South Asia, also has had a moderating influence on how most Pakistanis practice and interpret the Islamic faith.

Muslim revivalist movements developed late in the nineteenth century in South Asia in response to the decline in Muslim power in the region and as a reaction to British colonial rule. The first attempt to mobilize pan-Islamic sentiment on the Subcontinent was in 1919 through the launching of the Khilafat movement, which agitated against the abolition of the Ottoman caliphate.[29] Although the movement dissolved after the Turkish government abrogated the Muslim caliphate in 1924, it roused Muslim political consciousness and catalyzed a sense of communal identity.[30]

The Jamaat-e-Islami was founded by Islamic scholar Maulana Abul Ala Maududi in 1941. Maududi came of age as British colonial rule was ending on the Subcontinent and an Indian national identity was developing. Witness to Hindu-Muslim communal tensions, Maududi believed the only way Muslims could safeguard their political interests was to return to a pure and unadulterated Islam that would not accommodate Hindus. He denounced nationalism and secular politics and held that the Islamic state was a panacea for all the problems facing Muslims. He further held that for Muslims to mobilize their resources against the Hindus, they had to break free of any Western influences.[31] Reflecting Maududi's early linking of the Muslim struggle with both Indian Hindus and western forces, modern Islamist extremist literature in Pakistan draws parallels between British colonial rule in the nineteenth century and U.S. ascendancy since the middle of the twentieth.[32]

In contrast with Maududi, Pakistan's founding father and leader of the Muslim League, Muhammed Ali Jinnah, supported the idea of Islam serving as a unifying force, but envisioned the country functioning largely as a secular and multiethnic democratic state. Thus, although the argument to establish a separate Pakistani state was based on religious exclusivity, Jinnah's ultimate goal was not to establish Pakistan as a theocratic state.[33] However, soon after the creation of Pakistan, debate about the role of religion in the country's constitutional and legal systems was increasingly influenced by the idea that Islamic principles should inform the conduct of the state.[34]

Maududi's contrasting vision for Pakistan created problems for him and the JI during the early years after partition. Pakistani authorities questioned the allegiance of JI members to the state and even incarcerated Maududi for his controversial positions on the Indo-Pakistani dispute over Kashmir.[35] After spending time in jail, Maududi eventually stopped questioning the legitimacy of the Pakistani state and focused on encouraging Islamization of the government and the adoption of an Islamic constitution.

Today's Jamaat-I-Islami (JI) political party in Pakistan, led by Siraj-ul-Haq, draws most of its support from middle class urban Pakistanis. It has generally performed only marginally at the polls, capturing about five percent of the vote in most elections held during the last two decades. The party's influence on Pakistani politics and society outweighs its electoral performance, though, primarily because of its effectiveness in mobilizing street power, its ability to influence court cases, and its adeptness at using Pakistan's Islamic identity to bring pressure on military and democratic governments alike to adopt aspects of its Islamist agenda.[36] In the 2002 elections, the JI formed an alliance with five other religious political parties, and the coalition garnered over 11 percent of the national vote. The resulting coalition of Islamist parties grabbed enough votes in Khyber Pakhtunkhwa (KPK) to form the government, marking the first time the Islamists were charged with running a provincial government (see below).

The other major Islamist movement in South Asia is the Deobandi movement. This movement originated in 1866 in the city of Deoband in the Indian state of Uttar Pradesh with the establishment of the Dur ul-Ulum *madrassa*, (a Muslim religious school), which is still the largest operating Deobandi *madrassa*. Deobandism was a reformist movement that developed in reaction to British colonialism and from the belief among Muslim theologians that British influence on the Indian subcontinent was corrupting the religion of Islam. The Deobandis solidified a puritanical perspective toward Islam for South Asian Muslims, much as the Wahhabis have done in present-day Saudi Arabia.[37]

Although Deobandi clerics were initially concerned with strengthening the Islamic character of individuals and society, several of them later became politically focused and joined the Jamiat Ulema-e-Hind (JUH), a political party established in pre-partition India in 1919.[38] In the lead-up to partition, the Deobandis split between those who supported Gandhi's Indian National Congress and those who supported the creation of a separate state of Pakistan as proposed by Muslim League leader Muhammed Ali Jinnah. The pro-Muslim League faction became the Jamiat Ulema-e-Islam (JUI), while the JUH maintained links with the Indian National Congress, arguing that the creation of Pakistan would divide and weaken the Muslims of the Subcontinent.[39]

The Deobandis gained considerable strength during the war against the Soviets in Afghanistan in the 1980s when *madaris* (plural of *madrasa*) mushroomed in Pakistan, partially to accommodate the three million Afghan refugees that fled there. The Taliban leaders who made their debut in Kandahar, Afghanistan in 1994 came mostly from these Deobandi *madrassas*.[40] As a political party, JUI draws support from rural voters, mostly among Pashtuns in the northwest.

Three wars and several military crises with India have also bolstered the influence of religious extremists, with the backing of the Pakistani state. During the 1990s, the JI focused its agenda on supporting Kashmiri militants, while the JUI turned most of its attention to supporting the Taliban in Afghanistan. More recently, both the JUI and JI have rallied their political supporters against U.S. policies in the region, taking advantage of high levels of anti-American sentiment fueled by the post 9/11 American and NATO military presence in Afghanistan and U.S. pressure on Pakistan to tackle terrorists on its own soil. Most Pakistanis blame their country's counterterrorism cooperation with the U.S.—not past support for religious extremists—for the incessant suicide bombings and attacks across the nation that have claimed more than 9,000 civilian lives since 2012.

The erosion of respect for religious pluralism in Pakistan has also been facilitated by exclusionary laws and the proliferation of minority-hate material in public and private school curriculums. Several studies have also documented a broad-based connection between *madrassa* education and the propensity toward gender, religious, and sectarian intolerance and militant violence in Pakistan.[41] *Madaris* are spread throughout Pakistan, but most analysts believe that only about 5–10 percent of Pakistani school children attend these Islamic seminaries. A number of these schools are financed and operated by Pakistani Islamist parties, such as the Jamaat-e-Ulema Islam (JUI), and by Pakistani expatriates and other foreign entities, including many in Saudi Arabia. In a seminal study entitled "Islamic Education in Pakistan," South Asia scholar Christine Fair notes that while there is little evidence that *madaris* contribute substantially to direct recruitment of terrorists, they do help create conditions that are conducive to supporting militancy.[42] While mainstreaming and expanding the curriculums of *madaris* is part of reversing extremist trends, it is equally important for Pakistan to improve and modernize its public education sector and to revise textbooks that encourage an intolerant and militant culture.

Discrimination against religious minorities—including Christians, Hindus, Sikhs, Ahmadis, and Shi'a—has led to a threefold increase in religious and sectarian violence in the country over the last 30 years. The rising violence against the Shi'ite community (which makes up about 25 percent of Pakistan's total population) has been part of the upward trend in sectarian attacks. In May 2015, gunmen attacked a bus in Karachi, killing 45 Ismaili Shi'a. In January 2015, at least 61 people were killed after a bombing at a Shi'a mosque in Shikarpur, while two years prior in January and February 2013, sectarian attacks including bombings in Quetta killed nearly 200 Shi'a.

In recent years, most of the attacks against Pakistani Shi'a have been carried out by the Lashkar-e-Jhangvi (LJ), a Sunni militant organization that receives inspiration and support from al-Qaeda. The Pakistan government has begun to crack down on LJ and target its leadership over the past year. In July 2015, one week after his arrest, LJ founder and supreme leader Malik Ishaq and over a dozen of his followers were killed in a police encounter.[43]

The minority Ahmadi community also is suffering severely from the growing culture of religious intolerance in Pakistan. The Ahmadiyya Jamaat has approximately 10 million followers in the world, including approximately 3 to 4 million in Pakistan. Toward the end of the 19th century, Mirza Ghulam Ahmad (1835-1908), founder of the Ahmadiyya Jamaat, broke with centuries-old Islamic dogma by claiming to be an Islamic prophet. (Mainstream Muslims believe that the Prophet Mohammad was the last prophet.) Six years after Pakistan's independence, Islamists led by Anjuman-i-ahrar-i-Islam (Society of Free Muslims) started a mass movement to declare the Ahmadi sect as non-Muslim, arguing that Ahmadiyya was an entirely new religion that should not be associated with Islam. In late May of 2010, militants armed with hand grenades, suicide vests, and assault rifles attacked two Ahmadi mosques, killing nearly 100 worshippers.[44] Human rights groups in Pakistan criticized local authorities for their weak response to the attacks and for their failure to condemn the growing number of kidnappings and murders of members of the Ahmadi community. In December 2014, a member of the Ahmadi community in Gujranwalla was shot and killed five days after an extremist cleric called Ahmadis "the enemy" in a rant on a popular Pakistani television show.

Christians also are increasingly bearing the brunt of rising Islamist extremism in Pakistan. There have been numerous incidents of violence against Christians and their worship areas in the last few years. In the largest attack to date targeting the Christian community, on September 22, 2013, 85 people were killed during Sunday services when dual suicide bombers attacked a church in Peshawar, Pakistan. The group responsible for the attack, a faction of the *Tehrik-e-Taliban Pakistan* (TTP), said they were retaliating against U.S. drone strikes in Pakistan's tribal border areas. More recently, a splinter group of the TTP carried out a suicide attack against Christians celebrating the Easter holiday at a park in Lahore in March 2016.

The public reaction to the early 2011 murders of two senior Pakistani officials for advocating changes to the country's blasphemy laws demonstrates growing religious intolerance within Pakistani society. When Pakistani Punjab Governor Salman Taseer was assassinated on Jan 4, 2011, after pushing for scrapping the blasphemy laws (which are often misused against religious minorities), several hundred Pakistani clerics signed a statement condoning the murder and warning Pakistanis against grieving his death. Two months later, Pakistani Minority Affairs Minister Shahbaz Bhatti was also gunned down. Bhatti's murderers left pamphlets at the scene of the crime, explaining that they killed him because of his opposition to the blasphemy laws.

The London-based think tank Quilliam warned in its August 2009 report that Pakistani youth are a prime target for Islamist recruitment.[45] With the segment of Pakistan's population between ages 15-24 estimated to be around 36 million, and those below the age of 15 an additional 58 million,[46] the need for specific policies to counter the Islamist agenda is apparent. The Quilliam report argues that without the development of a compelling Pakistani identity, pan-Islamism is starting to fill the void.[47]

There have been some recent signs that the Nawaz Sharif government is slowly seeking to reverse extremist trends in society. The most notable was the government's follow-through with the execution of Mumtaz Qadri, the murderer of Salman Taseer. Despite street protests in all of Pakistan's major cities against the execution of Qadri, the government resisted intervention against the Supreme Court's decision, and the death sentence was carried out on February 29, 2016.

The Nawaz Sharif government took another step forward in support of religious minorities in mid-December 2016 by renaming the National Center for Physics after Nobel Prize-winning physicist Abdus Salam, a member of the Ahmadi community. Even though Salam received the Nobel Peace Prize in 1979, his achievement was largely ignored in Pakistan because of the stigma attached to the Ahmadi faith.[48] One week after the government's gesture, however, there were two major incidents of religious persecution against the Ahmadi community. In the first, Pakistani police raided an Ahmadiyya central office in Rabwah, where they beat up staffers, looted the office, and made arrests without a warrant.[49] In a second incident, a mob comprised of more than 1,000 people descended on an Ahmadi place of worship in Chakwal, Punjab.[50]

The Supreme Court also agreed in 2015 to review the case of Asia Bibi. Bibi, a mother of five and a farmworker, was arrested in 2009 after her Muslim co-workers alleged that she had committed blasphemy during an argument about sharing a water bowl. In November 2010, she was sentenced to death by a Pakistani trial court—a decision that was upheld by the Lahore High Court in October 2014. The outcome of the review is still pending.

The 2007 Red Mosque siege and the events that followed have played a significant role in Pakistani society's current perception of Islamist movements. Early in 2007, students of the notorious Red Mosque in the heart of Islamabad, and an adjacent *madrassa* for women, launched a vigilante-like campaign to force their view of Islam on the Pakistani people. They burned CD and video shops, took over a local children's library, and kidnapped women whom they accused of running a brothel, as well as several Pakistani policemen.

On July 5, 2007, Pakistani troops started a clearing operation to force the students to vacate the mosque and *madrassa*. While 1,200 students surrendered and the government sought to negotiate a peaceful resolution, over one hundred armed militants hunkered down in the mosque and *madrassa* and vowed to fight until death. Five days later, military troops stormed the buildings. After two days of fierce fighting, the military gained control of the premises, but only after 19 soldiers and 62 militants were killed.

The Pakistani public reacted negatively to the military operation, with Islamist circles questioning the use of force against the country's own citizens and mosques, and more liberal commentators faulting the government for allowing the situation to get out of hand in the first place, noting the past strong ties of Pakistani intelligence to the mosque. The Islamist political parties faced a dilemma in that they largely agreed with the policies the Red Mosque leaders were pursuing but did not support the idea of engaging in violent confrontation with the government to achieve these goals.[51] Following the military operation that ended the siege, then-JI leader Qazi Hussain held the state "wholly responsible" for the confrontation. In addition, the two Islamist parties hailed the Red Mosque militants as "*mujahideen* who fought for enforcing Islam in its true spirit."[52]

However, ever since April 2009, when pro-Taliban militants moved from the Swat Valley into neighboring districts following a peace deal with the government, most observers have believed that the militants overplayed their hand and revealed their long-term intentions of expanding influence throughout Khyber Pakhtunkhwa (KPK). Pakistanis living outside of the northwest province had previously believed the Taliban's activities could be contained within the tribal areas and Swat Valley. A video that circulated in the Pakistani national media in early April 2009 showing Taliban leaders whipping a young girl also helped turn Pakistani public opinion against the militants.

In early 2009, the Pakistan military, with backing from the central government, pursued a peace deal with the pro-Taliban militant group, the *Tehreek-e-Nafaz-e-Shariat-e-Mohammadi* (TNSM, or "Movement for the Enforcement of Islamic Law"), whose objective is to enforce sharia throughout the country. In 2007, the movement succeeded in taking over much of the Swat Valley in the settled areas of KPK. The Pakistan military deployed some 12,000 troops to the area for 18 months in 2007-2008 before ceding the territory to the militants. The surrender of the valley occurred despite the overwhelming vote in favor of the secular Pashtun Awami National Party in the February 2008 elections, demonstrating that the people of the region did not support the extremists' agenda but were merely acquiescing in the absence of support from the government to counter the militants.

Tensions came to a head in mid-April 2009, when the pro-Taliban forces moved from the Swat Valley into the neighboring district of Buner. On April 24, 2009, under both Pakistani public and U.S. pressure, the Pakistan Army deployed paramilitary troops to the region and then-Chief of Army Staff (COAS) General Ashfaq Kayani sent a warning to the militants that the Army would not allow them to "impose their way of life on the civil society of Pakistan."[53] The statement was a positive first step in clarifying Pakistani policy toward the militants and was followed by aggressive military operations.[54] By mid-summer, the Pakistan military cleared the militants from the Swat Valley, and normalcy began to return to the region.

The Pakistani public was outraged when Malala Yousafzai—a fifteen year-old girl who openly advocated for the education of girls in the Swat Valley—was shot by militants in early October 2012 as she boarded a bus from school. Yousafzai miraculously survived the assassination attempt and continues to advocate for female empowerment and education. She is the youngest person ever to have won the Nobel Peace Prize.

The Army's resolve in fighting militants in the Swat Valley, and more recently in North Waziristan, signals greater clarity within the military establishment about the threat to the state from the Pakistani Taliban. However, there are few signs the Pakistani Army leadership is ready to accommodate U.S. requests to crack down on other groups that target U.S. and coalition forces in Afghanistan, like the Jalaluddin Haqqani network that operates out of North Waziristan and Afghan Taliban leaders that operate mainly from Quetta, Baluchistan.

ISLAMISM AND THE STATE

Following the 9/11 attacks, former Pakistani President Pervez Musharraf broke off official ties with the Taliban, supported the U.S. invasion of Afghanistan, granted overflight and landing rights for U.S. military and intelligence units, facilitated logistical supply to military forces in Afghanistan, and contributed substantially to breaking up the al-Qaeda network in the region. Pakistan helped captured scores of senior al-Qaeda leaders, most notably 9/11 mastermind Khalid Sheikh Mohammed.

However, the government's various relationships with Islamist groups were not entirely severed, and progress in this regard has been mixed. In addition to sporadic military operations, the Pakistani government in the past pursued several peace deals with the militants, which contributed to destabilizing the Pakistani state and facilitating insurgent attacks against coalition forces in Afghanistan.

The first peace deal in March 2004, referred to as the Shakai Agreement, was interpreted by locals as a military surrender.[55] A February 2005 peace agreement with now-deceased TTP leader Baitullah Mehsud also backfired, emboldening Mehsud to form the *Tehrik-e-Taliban Pakistan*. Baitullah Mehsud directed a string of suicide attacks against both Pakistani security forces and civilians in 2008-2009. Mehsud was killed by a U.S. drone strike in August 2009 and was replaced by Hakimullah Mehsud, who was also killed by a drone strike in November 2013.

The Pakistan military remains powerful, despite the first successful peaceful transfer of power from one democratically-elected government to another in May 2013. Thus the country's success in countering violent Islamist movements will largely be determined by both the military's capabilities in beating back Islamist insurgencies in the northwest part of the country, as well as its policies toward violent extremist groups it continues to nurture.

Throughout Pakistan's troubled political history, both military leaders and democratic politicians have contributed to the Islamization of society and political discourse. Pakistan has endured military rule for about half its existence (during the periods 1958–1971, 1979–1988, and 1999–2008). Even when democratic governments have been in power, the Pakistani Army continued to wield tremendous influence, particularly on matters related to foreign policy and the country's nuclear program. The Army leadership has proved itself adept at using religion and Islamist political parties to stifle political opposition. During the 2002 elections, then-President Musharraf pursued steps, such as campaign restrictions and candidate selection policies, which favored the Islamist parties over the democratic opposition, thus helping religious parties garner their greatest percentage of votes ever and catapulting the Islamist coalition to power in KPK.

In contrast to their showing in the 2002 elections, Pakistan's Islamist political parties performed poorly in the country's February 2008 and May 2013 elections. In 2008, the JI boycotted the election, and the other Islamist parties garnered only two percent of the national vote. In 2013, the JUI/F won 10 seats, and the JI only three seats in the National Assembly.

The democratic parties, during their tenures, have also sought to co-opt the religious parties in various ways and use religion to consolidate their power base. Pakistan's first elected Prime Minister, Zulfiqar Ali Butto, passed a resolution in 1974 declaring Ahmadis to be non-Muslims. The legislation barred Ahmadis from calling themselves Muslims, calling their places of worship mosques, performing the Muslim call to prayer, and using the traditional Islamic greeting in public. In 1998, when he was serving his second stint as Prime Minister, Nawaz Sharif proposed a law to introduce sharia as the law of the land. If passed, it would have nullified the existing civil code and made Sharif the *Amir-ul-Momineen* (Commander of the Faithful) with absolute power. Fortunately, the motion failed.

What has been most damaging to the democratic character of Pakistan—and contributed significantly to the country's current instability—has been the Pakistan military's reliance on religious militants to achieve strategic objectives vis-à-vis Afghanistan and India.[56] The Pakistani Army's support for militancy as an instrument of foreign policy has eroded religious tolerance and created strong links between the Islamist political parties and militant groups.[57]

The Obama administration has challenged the Pakistanis on their lack of consistency in countering terrorist groups in the region and their failure to crack down on the Afghan Taliban and related groups that threaten the U.S. and coalition mission in Afghanistan. The Kerry-Lugar bill passed by the Senate in September 2009 (the *Enhanced Partnership with Pakistan Act of 2009*) authorized $7.5 billion in civilian aid to Pakistan over a five-year period but also conditioned military assistance on Pakistani measures to address terrorist threats. Former U.S. Director of National Intelligence Admiral Dennis Blair testified before Congress on February 2, 2010, "Pakistan's conviction that militant groups are strategically useful to counter India are hampering the fight against terrorism and helping al-Qaeda sustain its safe haven."[58]

In September 2012, the Obama administration did not certify Pakistan for military aid because it failed to meet the counterterrorism benchmarks stipulated by the law. Instead the Administration took advantage of a national security waiver contained in the law to waive the conditions and thus allow U.S. military aid to continue to flow to Pakistan. In February 2013, the Administration again issued a waiver to allow the transfer of major defense equipment.

More recently, the U.S. Congress has used its authority to block U.S. military aid for Pakistan. The *National Defense Authorization Act* (NDAA) for FY2015 stipulated that $300 million of the $1 billion in CSF funding appropriated for Pakistan could no longer be subject to Presidential waiver authority. Thus, when the Administration failed to certify that the Pakistan military's operations in the tribal areas included attacking Haqqani Network bases, Congress blocked the transfer of $300 million in CSF payments to Pakistan. The NDAA for FY2016 authorized another $900 million in CSF funding for Pakistan, with $350 million being ineligible for waiver.

The military confrontation following the siege of the Red Mosque in 2007, the aggressive military operations in the Swat Valley in 2009, and the on-going *Zarb-e-Azb* operations in North Waziristan against the TTP, all demonstrate that in certain situations the Pakistan military is prepared to confront extremists, even those with whom it previously had an intelligence relationship. The army links to religious militants revolve more around regional strategic calculations than deep sympathies with the Islamists' ideology. Thus, while it may take time to fully sever ties between elements of the military/ISI establishment and Islamist militant groups, this outcome is certainly possible. Indications that the Red Mosque confrontation caused some dissent within the Army ranks demonstrate the challenges of convincing the Pakistan military to confront its former proxies without causing major discord within the only Pakistani institution capable of taking on the militants. Any such process will take time and circumspection in order to anticipate and minimize the chances of revolt inside the military ranks.

The strength and professionalism of the Pakistani Army, combined with the democratic impulse of middle class Pakistanis who are familiar with a tradition of practicing moderate Islam, should act as bulwarks against a potential Islamist revolution similar to the one in Iran in 1979. However, until Pakistan takes a more comprehensive approach to defeating Islamist extremism within its borders by cracking down on all Islamist extremists (not just on those groups that attack the Pakistani state), Pakistan's future will be at risk.

The hardening stance toward Pakistan among Members of the U.S. Congress signals that America's patience with Pakistan's dual policies toward terrorism is wearing thin. While completely isolating Pakistan and disengaging with its leadership is not a realistic policy option, it is likely that U.S.-Pakistan relations will continue on a downward trend, unless there is a substantial change in Pakistan's policies toward terrorist groups that threaten both regional stability as well as fundamental U.S. national security interests.

ENDNOTES

[1] Haider A.H. Mullick, "Pakistan's Security Paradox: Countering and Fomenting Insurgencies," Joint Special Operations University Report 09-9 (Hurlburt Field: JSOU Press, 2009), 50.

[2] Bill Roggio, "Charting the Data for U.S. Airstrikes in Pakistan 2004–2015," Long War Journal, n.d., http://www.longwarjournal.org/pakistan-strikes.

[3] K. Alan Kronstadt, "Direct Overt U.S. Aid Appropriations for and Military Reimbursements to Pakistan, FY2002-FY2017, Congressional Research Services Memo for Congress, February 24, 2016, https://www.fas.org/sgp/crs/row/pakaid.pdf.

[4] "Senate Armed Services Committee Holds Hearing on the Situation in Afghanistan," Congressional Testimony, General John R. Allen, Senate Armed Services Committee, March 22, 2012, http://www.rs.nato.int/images/20120322_sasc_hearing_allen_transcript.pdf.

[5] Stephanie Condon. "After Osama Bin Laden's Death, Congress Puts Pakistan on the Hot Seat." CBSNews, 3 May 2011. http://www.cbsnews.com/news/after-osama-bin-ladens-death-congress-puts-pakistan-on-the-hot-seat/.

[6] "Bin Laden Doctor Shakil Afridi to Be Retried." BBC News, 29 Aug. 2013. http://www.bbc.com/news/world-asia-23882900.

[7] Ayaz Gul, "Pakistan 'Willing' to Discuss Freedom for Doctor Who Helped Find Bin Laden," voanews.com, December 16, 2016, at http://www.voanews.com/a/pakistan-doctor-who-helped-find-bin-laden/3638778.html.

[8] "Fatalities in Terrorist Violence in Pakistan 2003-2016," South Asia Terrorism Portal, n.d., http://www.satp.org/satporgtp/countries/pakistan/database/casualties.htm.

[9] Pakistan Security Report 2015, Pak Institute of Peace Studies, n.d., http://pakpips.com/downloads/293.pdf.

[10] "Taliban faction releases video of four BKU attack militants," Dawn.com, January 23, 2016, http://www.dawn.com/news/1234887/taliban-faction-releases-video-of-four-bku-attack-militants?utm_source=feedburner&utm_medium=feed&utm_campaign=Feed%3A+dawn-news+(Dawn+News).

[11] Shaiq Hussain and Erin Cunningham, "Taliban Splinter Group Claims Attack on Christians at Pakistan Park; 60 dead," Washington Post, March 27, 2016, at https://www.washingtonpost.com/world/explosion-kills-at-least-15-at-park-in-pakistans-lahore-reports-say/2016/03/27/00e49d32-f42e-11e5-958d-d038dac6e718_story.html.

[12] Syed Ali Shah, "70 dead as blast hits Quetta Civil Hospital after lawyer's killing," Dawn, August 9, 2016, https://www.dawn.com/news/1276183.

[13] "Quetta attack: Militants kill dozens at Balochistan Police College," BBC, October 25, 2016, http://www.bbc.com/news/world-asia-37757914.

[14] Mark Manzetti and Eric Schmitt, "Pakistanis Aided Attack in Kabul, U.S. Officials Say," New York Times, August 1, 2008, http://www.nytimes.com/2008/08/01/world/asia/01pstan.html.

[15] Jamie Crawford. "US Holds up $300 Million for Pakistan over Terrorism." CNN, 4 Aug. 2016.

[16] Franz-Stefan Grady. "US Won't Subsidize Pakistan's Purchase of F-16 Fighter Jets." The Diplomat, 4 May 2016. http://thediplomat.com/2016/05/us-wont-subsidize-pakistans-purchase-of-f-16-fighter-jets/.

[17] Katherine Wojtecki, "Chicago Man Pleads Guilty to Terror Plots," CNN.com, March 18, 2010, http://www.cnn.com/2010/CRIME/03/18/headley.plea/index.html.

[18] "Rewards for Justice - Lashkar-e-Tayyiba Leaders Reward Offers." U.S. Department of State. 03 Apr. 2012.

[19] U.S. Department of State, Office of the Coordinator for Counterterrorism, Country Reports on Terrorism 2008 (Washington, DC: U.S. Department of State, April 30, 2009), http://www.state.gov/s/ct/rls/crt/2008/122434.htm.

[20] Zahid Hussain and Eric Bellman, "Pakistan Says It May Outlaw Islamic Group," Wall Street Journal, December 11, 2008, http://online.wsj.com/article/SB122889700300394357.html.

[21] Lisa Curtis, "Indian Strikes against Pakistani Terror Bases: U.S. Must Ensure No Further Escalation," The Daily Signal, September 20, 2016, http://dailysignal.com/2016/09/30/india-strikes-across-line-of-control-to-neutralize-terrorist-bases-in-pakistan/.

[22] Husain Haqqani, "Prophecy and the Jihad in the Indian Subcontinent," Current Trends in Islamist Ideology 18 (2015), 6.

[23] Farhan Zahid and Muhammad Ismail Khan, "Prospects for the Islamic State in Pakistan," Current Trends in Islamist Ideology 20 (2016), 69.

[24] Peter R. Neumann, "Foreign fighter total in Syria/Iraq now exceeds 20,000; surpasses Afghanistan conflict in the 1980s," International Centre for the Study of Radicalization, January 26, 2015, http://icsr.info/2015/01/foreign-fighter-total-syriairaq-now-exceeds-20000-surpasses-afghanistan-conflict-1980s/.

[25] Sudarsan Raghavan and Tim Craig, "Suspected U.S. drone strikes kill key Islamic State figures in Afghanistan," Washington Post, July 9, 2015, https://www.washingtonpost.com/world/us-drone-strike-kills-key-islamic-state-figure-in-afghanistan/2015/07/09/f4114ab2-2636-11e5-b621-b55e495e9b78_story.html.

[26] Zahid and Khan, "Prospects for the Islamic State in Pakistan."

[27] Lisa Curtis, "Al-Qaeda Announces New Affiliate in South Asia," The Daily Signal, September 4, 2015, http://dailysignal.com/2014/09/04/al-qaeda-announces-new-affiliate-south-asia/.

[28] For a discussion of the Barelvi school of Islamic thought, see Haider A.H. Mullick and Lisa Curtis, "Reviving Pakistan's Pluralist Traditions to Fight Extremism," Heritage Foundation Backgrounder no. 2268, May 4, 2009, http://www.heritage.org/Research/AsiaandthePacific/bg2268.cfm.

[29] Joshua T. White, Pakistan's Islamist Frontier: Islamic Politics and U.S. Policy in Pakistan's North-West Frontier Province (Arlington, VA: Center on Faith and International Affairs, 2008), 25.

[30] Seyyed Vali Reza Nasr, The Vanguard of the Islamic Revolution: The Jamaat-I-Islami of Pakistan (Berkeley, CA: University of California Press, 1994), 11.

[31] Ibid, 4-8.

[32] Husain Haqqani, "The Ideologies of South Asian Jihadi Groups," Current Trends in Islamist Ideology 1 (2005), 12.

[33] Stephen Philip Cohen, The Idea of Pakistan, (Washington, DC: The Brookings Institution, 2004), 161.

[34] Fatima Mullick and Mehrunnisa Yusuf, Pakistan: Identity, Ideology, and Beyond (London: Quilliam, August 2009), 11.

[35] Nasr, The Vanguard of the Islamic Revolution, 121.

[36] White, Pakistan's Islamist Frontier, 38.

[37] Mullick and Curtis, "Reviving Pakistan's Pluralist Traditions to Fight Extremism."

[38] White, Pakistan's Islamist Frontier, 25.

[39] Ibid., 26.

[40] Haqqani, "The Ideologies of South Asian Jihadi Groups," 21.

[41] Mullick and Curtis, "Reviving Pakistan's Pluralist Traditions to Fight Extremism."

[42] C. Christine Fair, "Islamic Education In Pakistan," United States Institute of Peace, March 26, 2006, http://home.comcast.net/~christine_fair/index.html.

[43] "Malik Ishaq: Pakistan Sunni Militant Chief Killed by Police," BBC, July 29, 2015, http://www.bbc.com/news/world-asia-33699133.

[44] Rizwan Mohammed and Karin Brulliard, "Militants Attack Two Ahmadi Mosques In Pakistan; 80 Killed," Washington Post, May 29, 2010, http://www.washingtonpost.com/wp-dyn/content/article/2010/05/28/AR2010052800686.html.

[45] Mullick and Yusuf, Pakistan: Identity, Ideology, and Beyond, 9.

[46] Ibid., 2.

[47] Ibidem, 9.

[48] Pamela Constable, "Pakistan honors Nobel winner in physics 37 years late. But his religion still stirs anger," Washington Post, December 6, 2016, https://www.washingtonpost.com/world/pakistan-honors-nobel-winner-in-physics-37-years-late-but-his-religion-still-stirs-anger/2016/12/06/87702e82-bba4-11e6-94ac-3d324840106c_story.html?utm_term=.f2c6aeb4a5a0.

[49] Haroon Balogun, "Gunmen raid Ahmadiyya central office," Vanguard, December 9, 2016, http://www.vanguardngr.com/2016/12/gunmen-raid-ahmadiyya-central-office/.

[50] Imran Gabol, "Mob 'besieging' Ahmadi place of worship in Chakwal dispersed by police," Dawn, December 13, 2016, https://www.dawn.com/news/1302057.

[51] Joshua T. White, "Vigilante Islamism in Pakistan," Current Trends in Islamist Ideology 7 (2008), 56.

[52] Ibid, 59.

[53] "Pakistani Taliban Withdraw from Key Northwestern District," Voice of America, April 24, 2009.
[54] Lisa Curtis, Testimony before the U.S. Senate Committee on Homeland Security and Governmental Affairs, Subcommittee on Federal Financial Management, Government Information, Federal Services, and International Security, July 7, 2009.
[55] C. Christine Fair and Seth G. Jones, "Pakistan's War Within," Survival 51, no. 6 (December 2009–January 2010), 171.
[56] Yusuf, "Prospects of Youth Radicalization in Pakistan: Implications for U.S. Policy," 10; Frederic Grare, Reforming the Intelligence Agencies in Pakistan's Transitional Democracy (Washington, DC: Carnegie Endowment for International Peace, 2009), 23.
[57] Yusuf, "Prospects of Youth Radicalization in Pakistan: Implications for U.S. Policy," 19-20.
[58] Dennis C. Blair, "Annual Threat Assessment of the US Intelligence Community for the Senate Select Committee on Intelligence," February 2, 2010, http://intelligence.senate.gov/100202/blair.pdf.

EAST ASIA

COUNTRIES
Australia
China
Indonesia
Malaysia
Thailand

AUSTRALIA

Quick Facts

Population: 22,992,654 (July 2016 est.)

Area: 7,741,220 sq km

Ethnic Groups: English 25.9%, Australian 25.4%, Irish 7.5%, Scottish 6.4%, Italian 3.3%, German 3.2%, Chinese 3.1%, Indian 1.4%, Greek 1.4%, Dutch 1.2%, other 15.8% (includes Australian aboriginal .5%), unspecified 5.4%

Religions: Protestant 30.1% (Anglican 17.1%, Uniting Church 5.0%, Presbyterian and Reformed 2.8%, Baptist, 1.6%, Lutheran 1.2%, Pentecostal 1.1%, other Protestant 1.3%), Catholic 25.3% (Roman Catholic 25.1%, other Catholic 0.2%), other Christian 2.9%, Orthodox 2.8%, Buddhist 2.5%, Muslim 2.2%, Hindu 1.3%, other 1.3%, none 22.3%, unspecified 9.3%

Government Type: parliamentary democracy (Federal Parliament) under a constitutional monarchy; a Commonwealth realm

GDP (official exchange rate): $1.257 trillion (2015 est.)

Map and Quick Facts courtesy of the CIA World Factbook (January 2017)

Overview

The shallow presence and short history of Islamism in Australia is a function of the country's comparatively small Muslim population (just 1.7 percent of its total of 21.5 million, or approximately 366,000 people).[1] By global standards, the threat of Islamist violence in Australia is relatively low. While recent years have seen several Islamists convicted of terrorism-related offenses, none of these trials have provided evidence of any specific, well-developed terror plots that were nearing execution. Generally, Australia has not proven fertile ground for global terrorist organizations, despite some attempts by such groups to recruit and fundraise there. The overwhelming majority of those convicted under the country's anti-terrorism laws seem to have belonged to small, independent, self-starting groups with no clear connection to any well-established global terrorist organi-

zation. *Similarly, the very few individuals to have been in contact with such organizations have long since left them, and have shown little, if any, intention of undertaking terrorist acts in Australia. Notably, however, the threat of terrorism associated with the Islamic State (ISIS) has spiked within the country in recent months.*

ISLAMIST ACTIVITY

The Benbrika group

In November 2005, Australian federal and state intelligence and law enforcement agencies carried out the largest counterterrorism raids in the country's history as part of a long-running investigation known as Operation Pendennis. Seventeen people were arrested and charged across Sydney and Melbourne at that time, with another charged a week later and an additional three charged in late March 2006.[2] The senior figure in the affair was Abdul Nacer Benbrika, also known as Abu Bakr, an immigrant from Algeria who, at the time of his arrest, was variously reported as being 45 or 46. The rest of those charged were considerably younger, mostly between 18 and 28. All except one came from immigrant families, with the dominant ethnicity among them Lebanese. A majority of the Melbourne group was Australian-born, and one of the accused was an Anglo-Australian convert to Islam. Neither the Melbourne nor Sydney groups seem to have been highly educated or wealthy. Most were tradesmen or laborers, and only one participant had a graduate degree. Moreover, several had minor criminal records for fraud, theft and firearms charges.[3]

Members of the Melbourne cluster were all charged with being members of a terrorist organization involved in the fostering or preparation of a terrorist act (a legal designation under Australian law). Some were also charged with providing resources or making funds available to a terrorist organization, as well as possessing materiel connected to terrorism. Benbrika himself was also charged with intentionally directing the activities of a terrorist organization.[4] The Sydney cluster faced more serious charges of conspiring to plan a terrorist attack.

The Melbourne trial commenced first, resulting in seven convictions, four acquittals, and one retrial. In February 2009, Benbrika was sentenced to 15 years in prison with a non-parole period of 12 years—considerably less than the maximum 25-year sentence available under the relevant legislation.[5] It is possible this was due to the relatively embryonic nature of the group. The court found that the group had not reached the stage of plotting to blow up specific targets. By contrast, the Sydney cluster was more advanced, with considerable stockpiles of weapons and chemicals.[6] In October 2009, following the longest-running criminal trial in Australian legal history, five of its members were convicted (in addition to four others who had pled guilty) and subsequently sentenced to prison terms ranging from 21 to 28 years.[7]

Links between the Benbrika group and global terrorist organizations seem to have been sparse. Of the Melbourne cluster, Ango-Australian Shane Kent was the only one to have attended a training camp overseas in Afghanistan where he reportedly pledged allegiance, and may have been introduced, to Osama bin Laden.[8] Nevertheless, prosecutors dropped charges alleging Kent provided support to al-Qaeda.[9] The Sydney cluster seems to have had some deeper international experience, with up to three of them having visited *Lashkar-e-Taiba* (LeT) training camps in Pakistan.[10] Benbrika himself, however, appears to have had no sustained contact with global terrorist organizations. The only encounter on the public record was in 1994, when the British-based al-Qaeda sheikh Abu Qatadah visited Australia as a guest of the Melbourne-based *Salafi imam* Mohamed Omran. News reports suggest Benbrika's radicalization can be traced to his exposure to Abu Qatadah's speeches during that tour.[11]

Abu Qatadah's host, Mohamed Omran, is one of Australia's highest-profile *Wahhabi-Salafi imams*, the head of the Ahlus Sunnah Wa-l-Jamaah Association, and a central figure in any consideration of radical Islamism in Australia. In addition to his connections with Abu Qatadah, he has been named in Spanish court documents as an associate of al-Qaeda's Abu Dada (a charge which he has denied).[12] At the time of Abu Qatadah's speaking tour of Australia, and for several years thereafter, Benbrika was one of Omran's followers. Their relationship seems to have ended some years before Benbrika's arrest, when he left Omran's organization because he found it insufficiently radical.[13] Benbrika's own followers in the Melbourne cluster appear to have continued attending Omran's center, but there is no doubt that Benbrika was their most important influence at this time.[14]

Ideologically, the Benbrika group clearly held to a *Wahhabi-Salafi* ideology. First, the group viewed the world as divided between "true" Muslims and everyone else. Second, it believed that Islam was under attack from the Western world, particularly the United States, but also Australia.[15] Third, the group held that the perceived campaigns against Islam waged by the West in Afghanistan and Iraq compelled the group's members an obligation as devout Muslims to act in defense of Islam. That obligation took the form of an individual religious obligation to embark upon violence in Australia. Thus, the group's views of their militancy were larger defensive, rather than imperial; they saw themselves as acting in the defense of Islam, rather than proceeding from an explicit desire to Islamize Australia or the world.

Consistent with its independent, self-starting nature, the Benbrika group was informally and independently funded. Some members would contribute to a sanduq, or central fund, mainly through minor crimes such as car theft and credit card fraud.[16] By all accounts, it received no external funding from well-established terrorist organizations.

Operation Neath

August 2009 saw the culmination of Australia's second-largest counter-terrorism operation, in which five men were ultimately arrested and charged with conspiring to plan a terrorist attack on Holsworthy Barracks, an Australian Army training base.[17] The apparent plan was for members of the group to kill as many Australian soldiers as they could with automatic weapons before they themselves were killed.[18] The matter is currently before the courts.

The five men, all Australian citizens from Melbourne, were ethnically Lebanese and Somali. Authorities believe they were part of a broader group of 18 men, also ethnically Lebanese and Somali.[19] The group seems to have similar professional and educational backgrounds to the Benbrika group discussed above. None were believed to have graduate-level education, and most were either laborers or taxi drivers.[20] Likewise, there appears to have been an absence of a well-formulated overarching ideology; although the group was definitively *Wahhabi/Salafi* in orientation, its political narrative appears to have been reactive and defensive. Members regularly expressed anger at the presence of Australian troops in Muslim countries, possibly Iraq and Afghanistan, although they did not mention these places by name.[21]

Unlike the Benbrika group, however, there appears to be no clear religious authority figure in this case. All of those charged were young, and while the contours of the group will emerge more fully as evidence is presented in court, publicly available information suggests the group to be horizontal in structure.

The other key development in this case is the group's Somali connection—the first alleged involvement of Somali Australians in radical Islamist activity. Indeed, a 2007 investigation by the Australian Federal Police of extremism within the Australian Muslim Somali community found no evidence of any illegal activity.[22] However, authorities believe that the group apprehended in Operation Neath possessed links with Somalia's *al-Shabaab*, an al-Qaeda affiliate banned in the United States, and which American authorities allege has been actively recruiting Somali-American Muslims.[23] News reports suggest several members of the group had attempted to travel to Somalia to train with al-Shabaab.[24] A spokesman for *al-Shabaab*, however, has denied the allegations, claiming it has "no involvement at all" with the group and no people based in Australia.[25]

Operation Appleby

Operation Appleby appears to be the longest running anti-terror operation in Australia. Beginning in September 2014, the most prolific raid conducted involved 800 law enforcement agents in Brisbane and Sydney.[26] The raid was response to intelligence that suggested that Muhammad Ali Baryalei, a senior Australian member of the Islamic State, had ordered Australian Islamists to "kidnap and murder a randomly chosen non-Muslim member of the Public."[27] The pre-emptive raids conducted resulted in 16 arrests, though only one, Omarjan Azari, was charged. As of late 2016, 15 people have been charged from the intelligence gathered within Operation Appleby, with the latest arrest occurring on May 26, 2016.[28]

In April 2015, law enforcement authorities in Melbourne used the Preventative Detention Order (PDO) to hold a terror suspect without charge.[29] Although the PDO bill was introduced into legislation in 2005, this was the second time in Australian history it had been used. The first invocation of PDOs was in a September 2014.[30] Finally, the law was slated to expire in December 2015 but was extended in 2018.

Individuals connected to terrorism

While the above events are certainly the most important in the history of Islamist militancy in Australia, several other individual Islamists have been convicted of terrorism-related offenses. Some of these have been Australian citizens who have made connections with Islamist terrorist groups overseas. Others are foreign nationals who attempted unsuccessfully to infiltrate Australia. None are presently active members of radical Islamist organizations. They are:

- David Hicks, an Anglo-Australian convert to Islam who travelled to Albania and joined the Kosovo Liberation Army (KLA).[31] Hicks undertook four weeks of training with the KLA and enlisted with NATO, but the conflict ended before he could do any fighting, and he was sent home under NATO orders.[32] Upon returning to Australia he attempted to join the Australian Army, but was rejected.[33] In November 1999, he flew to Pakistan, where he spent three months in a *Lashkar e-Taiba* training camp. From there, he traveled on to Afghanistan where he spent eight months in 2001 in an al-Qaeda training camp.[34]

  Following the U.S.-led invasion of Afghanistan, Hicks was sent to the front line to fight with the Taliban. He insists he saw no action, and never fired his weapon. Indeed, the front to which he was sent collapsed only hours after he arrived. Hicks was captured detained in the Guantànamo Bay detention facility for just under five-and-a-half years. In March 2007, Hicks was formally charged with providing material support for terrorism and tried before a Special Military Commission. He pleaded guilty and became the first person convicted by the Guantànamo Military Tribunal. He was sentenced to seven years' imprisonment, all but nine months of which was suspended.[35]

  Hicks has since served his sentence and been released into the Australian community. Initially, he was placed under a control order that required him to report to a police station three times weekly. The control order expired in December 2008, however, and the Australian Federal Police did not seek to renew it—indicating Hicks was no longer considered a threat.[36] Moazzam Begg, a former Guantànamo Bay detainee who met Hicks in detention, has said that Hicks is no longer a Muslim, and ceased being one some time early in his detention.[37]

- Joseph Thomas, who in early 2001 travelled to Afghanistan to join the Taliban's fight against the Northern Alliance. Thomas spent a week on the front line in Afghanistan after his training, but did not participate in any combat. Over the four months that followed, he was in contact with senior al-Qaeda figures such as Ayman al-Zawahiri, Mohammed Atef, and Saif el Adel, seeking help with income and accommodation. He claims he did not know who these people were at the time.[38] With the commencement of the U.S.-led invasion of Afghanistan, Thomas remained to fight American forces. At that time, he shared a guesthouse with 9/11 planner Ramzi bin al-Shibh, and was asked by al-Qaeda's

Abu Zubaida to "do some work."[39] Thomas' time with Abu Zubaida took him to Pakistan, where he met the alleged mastermind of the *USS Cole* bombing, Khalid bin Attash. Bin Attash asked Thomas to undertake an attack in Australia.[40] Thomas was given $3,500 and a plane ticket to Australia for this purpose. However, he has maintained at all times that he had no intention of executing such an attack, and that the money he received was merely compensation for his time and maintenance, rather than for terrorism.[41] Yet, before he could board his flight, Thomas was arrested by Pakistan's ISI, and subsequently was tortured.

Around this time, the Australian Federal Police and the Australian Security and Intelligence Organization questioned Thomas, who provided a detailed statement. In June 2003, Pakistani authorities released Thomas and flew him to Australia, where he remained free for around 17 months until being arrested. Thomas was charged with receiving funds and resources from a terrorist organization that would assist in a terrorist attack, as well as with travelling on a falsified passport.[42] Following a high-profile trial, Thomas was acquitted of the most serious offenses—largely because most of the evidence on which they were based was tainted by his torture at the hands of the ISI. At the end of the appeal process, Thomas was finally convicted on the falsified passport charge, as well as for receiving funds from a terrorist organization. He was sentenced to nine months' in prison, and upon his release, was made subject to a control order that, among other restrictions, prohibits him from contacting certain figures involved in terrorism and imposes a curfew.[43]

- Faheem Lodhi, an Australian citizen, immigrated to Australia from Pakistan in 1996. In June 2006, he was convicted of acting in preparation for a terrorist attack and sentenced to 20 years' imprisonment. Key elements of the prosecution's case included that Lodhi had sought information about chemicals capable of making explosives, possessed a terrorism manual, and had maps of the electricity grid.[44] It is suspected that he was targeting the national electricity supply, as well as various Army barracks and training areas. During the trial, it emerged that Lodhi had trained with LeT in Pakistan, where he met al-Qaeda operative Willie Brigitte. Lodhi was also Brigitte's main contact when Brigitte visited Australia.[45] Brigitte himself was deported from Australia for visa violations, before finally being convicted in a French court and sentenced to nine years in prison for planning a terrorist attack in Australia.[46]

- Jack Roche, a British immigrant to Australia who converted to Islam in his late 30s. Soon after his conversion, Roche had contact with twin brothers Abdulrahman and Abdulrahim Ayub, who are suspected of being Australia's representatives of the Indonesian terrorist group *Jemaah Islamiah* (JI). The Ayub twins sent Roche to Malaysia and JI leader Hambali. From there, Roche was sent to Pakistan, where he trained in explosives in an al-Qaeda camp and met Osama bin Laden.[47] Al-Qaeda subsequently asked Roche to return to Australia to gather information about the Israeli embassy in Canberra, as well as on Joseph Gutnick, a wealthy Jewish-Australian businessman. In June 2000, Roche set to work, filming the outside of the embassy. However, he could not go through with the attack and went to the Australian Intelligence and Security Organization to tell them of these events. Yet, in Roche's words, "no one seemed to be particularly interested in what was going on." [48]

It was only after the Bali bombings in October 2002 that Australian law enforcement and security agencies took a fresh look at domestic militancy, which resulted ultimately in Roche's arrest and conviction for the embassy plot.[49] He was sentenced to nine years in prison with a parole period of half that time, and was released in May 2007.[50]

- Musa Cerantonio is an Australian preacher who used social media to both express his support for ISIL and propagate ISIL-related propaganda (Lambert, 2016, 12 January).[51] He was first arrested in 2014 in the Philippines while allegedly attempting to travel to Syria (Wood, 2015, March).[52] Upon his arrest, he was deported to Australia. Cerantonio is regarded as an influential advocate for ISIL (Oakes & Clark, 2016, 11 May).[53] While precise levels of his influence are unclear, Cerantonio is alleged to have associated with Singaporean ISIL sympathizer Zulfikar Shariff (Lim, 2016, 29 July).[54] In May 2016, he, along with five others, was arrested for attempting to sail to Indonesia, before travelling to ISIL controlled territory (Safi & Robertson, 2016, 11 May).[55]

- Numan Haider was the perpetrator of the September 2014 Endeavour Hills attack, in which he stabbed two anti-terrorism officers from the Joint Counter-Terrorism Team (Oakes, 2014, 25 September).[56] He was killed during the attack. Haider was also alleged to have associated with Al-Furqan. Subsequent inquiries into the incident have revealed evidence suggesting Haider viewed ISIL propaganda on his mobile phone two days prior to the attack (Longbottom, 2016, 22 March).[57] He was also said to have attempted to find out Tony Abbott's schedule. Haider, who came from a "moderate" Muslim family, was said to have been radicalized "within months."[58]

- Man Haron Monis was the perpetrator of the December 2014 hostage crisis at the Lindt Chocolate Café in Sydney. The 50-year-old Iranian held 17 people hostage for 16 hours in the café.[59] Monis was deemed to have been mentally and emotionally unstable prior to the attack. After police negotiations failed, he was killed when police stormed the building.[60]

- Omar Succarieh was accused of both funding terrorists abroad and attempting to aid Agim Kruezi's (failed) migration to Syria.[61] Arrested in 2014, he allegedly financed *Jabhat Al-Nusra*.[62] Police believe he sent at least $27,000 to them.

- Sevdet Besim was arrested for plotting the foiled 2015 Anzac Day attack.[63] Besim intended to "run over a police officer, cut off his head and go on a violent rampage that would end in his own death."[64] He claimed to have been inspired by his friend, Numan Haider. Besim plotted the attack online with a teenager living in the UK.

Non-violent Islamist groups

Given Australia's status as a liberal democracy, Islamist groups can form freely and remain in existence provided they remain within the law. Accordingly, a number of Islamist organizations remain active in Australian society.

The most worrisome, from a security perspective, is Mohamed Omran's Ahlus Sunnah wa-l-Jamaah Association. Nothing on the public record links the Association to violence directly, and its representatives have consistently denied their support for terrorism.[65] However, public concerns surround Omran because of his connections with the al-Qaeda figures discussed above, and as a result of his own statements in support of Osama bin Laden, whom he insists was not involved with the 9/11 attacks.[66] While the organization is said to be fundamentally apolitical, it has voiced support for violent jihadist resistance against both the occupation of Palestine, and the "Western" forces in the Afghan and Iraq wars.[67] In this context, the ASWJ is viewed as an organization that has occasionally strayed "from its civic-social mainstay into the realm of radical politics."[68]

The other prominent *Wahhabi-Salafi* organization of note is the Islamic Information and Services Network of Australasia, headed by Samir Mohtadi. This organization is more politically moderate than other *Wahhabi-Salafi* groups, and broke from Omran's group many years before domestic terrorism became a public issue. Mohtadi testified during the trial of the Benbrika group, saying that he warned Benbrika he would notify the authorities if he intended to do "anything stupid," and that Australia was a "peaceful country."[69]

A range of other *Wahhabi-Salafi* organizations with similar attitudes exist, most notably Sydney's Global Islamic Youth Centre, led by Sheikh Feiz Mohamed, though it appears unconnected to Omran's group. None of these groups publicly advocate the forceful Islamization of Australia. To the extent they are radical, they tend to articulate their activism in defensive terms, rather than offensive ones. Mohtadi's group is focused on *dawah* (proselytization) rather than the forceful transformation of society.

The Al-Furqan Islamic Information Centre was a bookstore that "doubled" as a *musallah*, primarily for young Muslims, in South Melbourne.[71] It was led by Harun Mehicevic after he decided to part ways with the Ahlus Sunnah Wal Jamaah (ASWJ) centre in 2011.[72] Like ASWJ, Al-Furqan's theological position is built upon Salafism. While it is unclear if Mehicevic advocated a politicized brand of *Salafism*, the organization was linked with at least six alleged and known Australian terrorists: Neil Prakash, Numan Haider, Adnan Karabegovic, Sevdet Besim, Harun Causevic, and Mohomod Unais Mohomed Ameen.[73]

Prakash and Ameen have appeared in ISIL propaganda videos from ISIL controlled territories.[74] After being subject to multiple police raids since 2012, Mehicevic made the decision to cease Al-Furqan's operations in 2015.[75] However, it has been alleged that Al-Furqan continues to operate covertly from a suburban leisure centre in Dandenong, Melbourne (Minear & Dowling, 2015, May 2).[76] Notably, Mahicevic himself has not been accused or charged for terrorist offences. Rather, it has been alleged that he was asked to assist the Australian Security Intelligence Organization (ASIO) by leveraging on position to "spy" on ISIL.[77]

The most overtly Islamist organization in Australia is undoubtedly *Hizb ut-Tahrir*. The group attracted a slew of media attention following the 2005 London bombings, when banning the group became a topic of public discussion in Australia, mirroring Britain's public calls for a ban on the group.[78] HuT treats the establishment of "the Khalifah system as explicit ideological aspiration."[79] Its methodology is based on non-violent resistance against secular democracy, and specifically relies on demonstrating the (in their view) intellectual, moral, and functional superiority the *Khalifah* system of governance vis-à-vis any other.[80] As such, HT appears to rely heavily on its online publishing arm, wherein critiques of Australian policies, particularly those on counter-terrorism, are commonplace (Hizb ut-Tahrir Australia, n.d.-c).[81] However, while HuT is a major presence in many countries, its members in Australia are very small in number and confined mostly to Sydney.[82]

ISLAMISM AND SOCIETY

As a nation with a British political inheritance, a very small Muslim population and a strong enduring alliance with the United States, Australia is not a welcoming environment for Islamist movements, particularly violent ones. Islamism has no discernible public or governmental support as an ideology. Anyone who calls publicly for the incorporation of some part of Islamic law (typically family law) into the Australian legal system faces swift denunciation, to say nothing of those who openly support more radical Islamist ideas.[83]

Accordingly, none of the aforementioned Islamist organizations receive government patronage, and there is little if any evidence that their popularity and level of support in the Australian community extends significantly beyond their own memberships. Debate continues in Australia as to whether or not HuT, for instance, should be banned.[84]

As the Muslim population of Australia continues to grow, both through population expansion and immigration, Muslim organizations can be expected to expand in size and number. Within a span of 20 years (between 1991 and 2011), the Muslim population increased from 125, 000 to 500,000 However, while an increase in the number of mosques is inevitable as a result, there is no evidence of a surge in mosque construction, and there is nothing in the public domain to suggest an impending rise in terrorist activity beyond what has been seen since 2005. It is probably true that HuT's voice is gradually becoming louder (facilitated by media attention) but it remains closely monitored and of marginal influence.[85]

Funding arrangements for Islamic organizations are more difficult to discern. The record to date suggests that would-be terrorist groups in Australia are not reliant on overseas funding for their plots, and indeed, as discussed above in relation to the Benbrika group, have attempted their own fundraising, often through fraudulent means.

More mainstream Islamic organizations have long been recipients of funding from both Australian and overseas governments. Among the most active has been the Saudi government, which is thought to have spent around AU$120 million (roughly 91 million in U.S. dollars) in Australia since the 1970s.[86] It is reasonable to assume that this financial support played an important role in the emergence of *Wahhabi* Salafism in Australia over the decades that followed. In this regard, there have been periods of consternation in the Australian press over funding from the Saudi government, particularly of esteemed institutions such as Australian universities.[87] There is little to suggest, however, that funding flows from abroad have increased in the past decade, while the associated media coverage indicates that such funding arrangements would be heavily scrutinized once publicly known. The Australian government, too, has actively funded Islamic studies in Australian universities—most directly through the establishment of a National Centre of Excellence in Islamic Studies across three universities in three states at a cost of AU$8 million ($6 million U.S.).[88] The center was conceived as part of the government's social cohesion, harmony and security strategy, and aims at teaching Islam in an Australian context.[89]

ISLAMISM AND THE STATE

The Australian government responded to the 9/11 terrorist attacks and the subsequent 2002 Bali bombings with a flurry of legislative activity. The suite of anti-terrorism laws introduced since that time have created new terrorism-related offenses and greatly expanded the powers of police and intelligence agencies.[90] These laws have certainly been controversial for their impact on civil liberties, and there has been much criticism of the legislative process that produced them,[91] as well as the occasionally improper use of these powers and instances of improper conduct by police and intelligence agencies.[92]

Australian authorities have also taken some steps towards a social approach to counterterrorism. In September 2005, the Howard government established a Muslim Community Reference Group to look into areas of social need in Muslim communities, including those elements thought to contribute to radicalization, such as education, employment and social cohesion.[93] Similarly, some police forces around the country, including the Australian Federal Police, have expanded their community engagement programs.[94] Led by the Australian Federal Police (AFP), the National

Disruption Group (NDG) was established in 2014 to execute the deradicalization of returning Australian foreign fighters.[95] Within the NDG, federal police collaborate with academics, religious leaders, and psychologists to conduct to facilitate the deradicalization process.[96]

Not all of these measures have been well received among Australian Muslims. The introduction of anti-terrorism laws caused significant Muslim protest, and these measures have been regularly criticized by Muslim groups for contributing to further alienation and facilitating coercive and intimidating behavior from authorities.[97] While there is some evidence suggesting that the impact of harsh legislation and the negative tone of public discourse are having a radicalizing effect in Australia, [98]this is impossible to quantify. Similarly, the Muslim Community Reference Group has faced criticism for being a forum for lecturing to the Muslim community and encouraging Muslims to identify radicals for the government under the guise of community engagement, as well as for perpetuating the connection between Muslims and terrorism.[99] In February 2015, the state established a website to enable individuals to report any extremist propaganda they might chance upon online).[100] This initiative was also widely criticized within the Muslim community as a transgression of their rights.

In September 2014, the threat level of terrorism in Australia was raised from "medium" to "high," indicating the imminent likelihood of a terrorist attack in Australia).[101] This was the first time the threat level had been increased since 2002. The threat level assessment was based on a four-tier system, with "extreme" being the highest possible level. The threat level was maintained at "high" at least until September of 2015.[102] In November 2015, the threat level assessment system changed from a four-tier to a five-tier one in response to the "changing domestic and international security landscape."[103]

Upon its introduction, the threat level assessment was indicated as "Probable," indicating that Australian intelligence believes that terrorists have both the capability and intention to conduct an attack.[104] Australia's National Security website indicates the threat level to still be "Probable."[105] Both "high" (the 3rd highest in the four-tier system) and "Probable" (the 3rd highest in the five-tier system) indicate the same quantitative and qualitative threat levels (Keenan, 2015, 26 November).[106] Then Prime Minister Tony Abbott said this five-tier system ("Not Expected," "Possible," "Probable," "Expected," and "Certain") would be easier for laypeople to comprehend.[107]

Finally, as of April 1, 2016, the state intends to introduce a post-sentence preventative detention order bill to enable the state to prolong and maintain the detention of "high risk offenders" who are deemed to be beyond the help of rehabilitation.[108] It does not appear that this law has been introduced yet.

The threat from Islamism in Australia, especially the radical variant, while real and continuing, has grown significantly since 2013. To date, in spite of the occasional overuse of force, attempts at law enforcement have been successful in monitoring and prosecuting the main threats stemming from Islamic radicalism. However, the large number of Australian citizens (close to 62 since 2015) that have joined ISIS indicates that the organization has established links in Australia. Most of these recruitments have taken place through social media which has resulted in Australia deploying various strategies to counter the ISIS threat in the cyber space.[109]

Endnotes

[1] Figures derived from "Australia," CIA World Factbook, November 9, 2010, https://www.cia.gov/library/publications/the-world-factbook/geos/as.html.

[2] "Tip Off Led To Intense 16-Month Investigation," The Age (Melbourne), September 17, 2008, http://www.theage.com.au/national/tipoff-led-to-intense-16month-investigation-20080916-4hxp.html?page=-1.

[3] Mitchell D. Silber and Arvin Bhatt, Radicalization In The West: The Homegrown Threat (New York: New York City Police Department, 2007), 27-28

[4] "Benbrika Guilty Of Terrorism Charges," ABC Radio The World Today, September 15, 2008, http://www.abc.net.au/worldtoday/content/2008/s2364860.htm.

[5] "Benbrika Jailed For 15 years," The Age (Melbourne), February 3, 2009, http://www.theage.com.au/national/benbrika-jailed-for-15-years-20090203-7w7y.html.

[6] "Five Guilty Of 'Mass' Terror Plot In Sydney," Daily Telegraph (Surry Hills), October 16, 2006, http://www.news.com.au/national/five-guilty-of-mass-terror-plot-in-sydney/story-e6frfkvr-1225787524969.

[7] "Long Sentences For Sydney Terror Plotters," ABC Radio PM, February 15, 2010, http://www.abc.net.au/pm/content/2010/s2820249.htm.

[8] "Terror Suspect 'Met Osama,'" Australian Associated Press, December 20, 2005, http://www.smh.com.au/articles/2005/12/20/1135032012529.html.

[9] "Shane Kent Pleads Guilty On Eve Of Terror Trial, But Al-Qa`ida Charge Dropped," The Australian, July 28. 2009.

[10] Silber and Bhatt, Radicalization In The West: The Homegrown Threat, 51.

[11] "Suspect Linked To radical UK Cleric," Times of London, November 13, 2005, http://www.timesonline.co.uk/tol/news/world/article589625.ece.

[12] Sally Neighbour, "How They Spotted Terror Suspects," The Australian, November 4, 2005, 2.

[13] "Terror Links To Radical Sheikhs," The Australian, November 10, 2005, 1.

[14] Ibid.

[15] "Long Sentences For Sydney Terror Plotters."

[16] 'Tip-Off Led To Intense 16-month Investigation," The Age (Melbourne), September 17, 2008, http://www.theage.com.au/national/tipoff-led-to-intense-16month-investigation-20080916-4hxp.html; Silber and Bhatt, Radicalization In The West: The Homegrown Threat, 52.

[17] "Army Base Terror Plot Foiled," The Australian, August 4, 2009, 1; Milanda Rout, "Terror Suspect Saney Aweys Says He's 'Victimised' In Prison," The Australian, November 7, 2009, http://www.theaustralian.com.au/news/nation/terror-suspect-saney-aweys-says-hes-victimised-in-prison/story-e6frg6nf-1225795202644.

[18] Cameron Stewart, "Phone Call Sparked Operation Neath," The Australian, August 4, 2009, 1, 4.

[19] Ibid.

[20] Ibid.

[21] "Army Base Terror Plot Foiled."

[22] Ibid.

[23] Spencer S. Hsu, "U.S. Says Men Ran Terror Network," Washington Post, November 24, 2009, http://www.washingtonpost.com/wp-dyn/content/article/2009/11/23/AR2009112303999.html.

[24] "Phone Call Sparked Operation Neath."

[25] "Militant Somali Group Denies Australia Link," ABC News, August 7, 2009, http://www.abc.net.au/news/stories/2009/08/07/2648501.htm.

[26] Andrew Zammit, "Islamic State Spurs Increased Jihadist Activity in Australia," The Jamestown Foundation: Terrorism Monitor, February 20, 2015, https://jamestown.org/program/islamic-state-spurs-increased-jihadist-activity-in-australia/.

[27] Andrew Zammit, "Islamic State Spurs Increased Jihadist Activity in Australia," The Jamestown Foundation: Terrorism Monitor, February 20, 2015, https://jamestown.org/program/islamic-state-spurs-increased-jihadist-activity-in-australia/.

[28] Australia Federal Police and Victoria Police, "Media Release: Additional man charged as a result of Operation Middleham", Australian Federal Police, May 27, 2016, https://www.afp.gov.au/news-media/media-releases/media-release-additional-man-charged-result-operation-middleham.

[29] Loretta Florance, "Preventative Detention Orders explained: What rights does a person have?" ABC News, April 21, 2015, http://www.abc.net.au/news/2015-04-20/preventative-detention-orders-explained/6405154.

[30] Svetlana Tyulkina & George Williams, "Preventative detention orders in Australia", University of New South Wales Law Journal 738 Vol.38, no.2: 2015.

[31] Raymond Bonner, "Australian Terrorism Detainee Leaves Prison," New York Times, December 29, 2007, http://www.nytimes.com/2007/12/29/world/asia/29hicks.html?_r=1.

[32] "The Case Of David Hicks," ABC Television 4 Corners, October 31, 2005, http://www.abc.net.au/4corners/content/2005/s1494795.htm.
[33] Ibid; "Australian Terrorism Detainee Leaves Prison."
[34] "The Case of David Hicks."
[35] Michael Melia, "Australian Gitmo Detainee Gets 9 Months," Washington Post, March 31, 2007, http://www.washingtonpost.com/wp-dyn/content/article/2007/03/31/AR2007033100279.html.
[36] Australian Federal Police National Media Release, "David Hicks' Control Order Not To Be Renewed," November 20, 2008, http://www.afp.gov.au/media_releases/national/2008/david_hicks_control_order_not_to_be_renewed.
[37] Penelope Debelle, "Hicks No Longer A Muslim: Ex-Detainee," The Age (Melbourne), June 24, 2006, http://www.theage.com.au/news/national/hicks-no-longer-a-muslim-exdetainee/2006/06/23/1150845378125.html.
[38] Penelope Debelle, "Hicks No Longer A Muslim: Ex-Detainee," The Age (Melbourne), June 24, 2006, http://www.theage.com.au/news/national/hicks-no-longer-a-muslim-exdetainee/2006/06/23/1150845378125.html.
[39] Penelope Debelle, "Hicks No Longer A Muslim: Ex-Detainee," The Age (Melbourne), June 24, 2006, http://www.theage.com.au/news/national/hicks-no-longer-a-muslim-exdetainee/2006/06/23/1150845378125.html.
[40] Penelope Debelle, "Hicks No Longer A Muslim: Ex-Detainee," The Age (Melbourne), June 24, 2006, http://www.theage.com.au/news/national/hicks-no-longer-a-muslim-exdetainee/2006/06/23/1150845378125.html.
[41] Penelope Debelle, "Hicks No Longer A Muslim: Ex-Detainee," The Age (Melbourne), June 24, 2006, http://www.theage.com.au/news/national/hicks-no-longer-a-muslim-exdetainee/2006/06/23/1150845378125.html.
[42] Penelope Debelle, "Hicks No Longer A Muslim: Ex-Detainee," The Age (Melbourne), June 24, 2006, http://www.theage.com.au/news/national/hicks-no-longer-a-muslim-exdetainee/2006/06/23/1150845378125.html.
[43] "Government Places Curfew On Jack Thomas," ABC Television Lateline, August 28, 2006, http://www.abc.net.au/lateline/content/2006/s1726436.htm.
[44] Leonie Lamont, "Lodhi 'Deserves' 20 Years," The Age (Melbourne), August 23, 2006, http://www.theage.com.au/news/national/lodhi-gets-20-years/2006/08/23/1156012586528.html.
[45] "Bomb Plotter 'Guilty By Association' With Brigitte," The Australian, November 6, 2007, 9.
[46] "Brigitte Jailed For Planning Aust Terrorist Attacks," ABC News Online, March 16, 2007, http://www.abc.net.au/news/newsitems/200703/s1873090.htm.
[47] Sally Neighbour, "My Life As A Terrorist," The Australian, December 4, 2007, http://www.theaustralian.com.au/national-affairs/defence/my-life-as-a-terrorist/story-e6frg8yx-1111115023061.
[48] Ibid.

[49] "Jack Roche: The Naive Militant," BBC, June 1, 2004, http://news.bbc.co.uk/2/hi/asia-pacific/3757017.stm.

[50] "Terrorist Roche Released From Jail," ABC News Online, May 17, 2007, http://www.abc.net.au/news/newsitems/200705/s1925403.htm.

[51] Olivia Lambert, "Radical Islamic State preacher Musa Cerantonio breaks silence," news.com.au, January 12 2016, http://www.news.com.au/national/victoria/news/radical-islamic-state-preacher-musa-cerantonio-breaks-silence/news-story/f8730bddd0267a230394f2d00e08fc39.

[52] Graeme Wood, "What ISIS Really Wants", The Atlantic, 1 March 2015, https://www.theatlantic.com/magazine/archive/2015/03/what-isis-really-wants/384980/.

[53] Dan Oakes and Sam Clark, "Islamic preacher Musa Cerantonio among five arrested over alleged plan to join Islamic State," ABC News, May 11 2016, http://www.abc.net.au/news/2016-05-11/preacher-among-five-arrested-over-alleged-plan-to-join-is/7403344.

[54] Lim Yan Liang, "Singaporean Zulfikar Mohamad Shariff, 44, detained under ISA for promoting violence and ISIS, radicalising others," Strait Times, July 29, 2016, http://www.straitstimes.com/singapore/44-year-old-singaporean-detained-under-isa-for-promoting-violence-and-isis-radicalising.

[55] Michael Safi & Josh Robertson, "Musa Cerantonio among men arrested after allegedly trying to sail to Indonesia", The Guardian, last modified 11 May 2016, https://www.theguardian.com/australia-news/2016/may/11/musa-cerantonio-among-men-arrested-after-allegedly-trying-to-sail-to-indonesia.

[56] Dan Oakes, "Melbourne shooting: What we know about Abdul Numan Haider, shot dead after stabbing anti-terrorism officers at Endeavour Hills," ABC News, September 25, 2014, http://www.abc.net.au/news/2014-09-24/what-we-know-about-abdul-numan-haider/5767044.

[57] Jessica Longbottom, "Numan Haider's phone used to access 'disgusting' IS videos, Tony Abbott's schedule, inquest told," ABC News, March 22, 2016, http://www.abc.net.au/news/2016-03-21/numan-haider-thought-it-was-ok-to-behead-people-inquest-told/7263210.

[58] Melissa Davey, "Rapid radicalisation: the case of Numan Haider shocks family and experts alike," The Guardian, March 24, 2016, https://www.theguardian.com/australia-news/2016/mar/25/rapid-radicalisation-the-case-of-numan-haider-shocks-family-and-experts-alike.

[59] "Man Haron Monis: 'Damaged' and 'unstable,'" BBC, December 16, 2014, http://www.bbc.com/news/world-australia-30484419.

[60] Patrick Begley, "Lindt cafe siege: Officer who shot Man Haron Monis describes final moments", The Sydney Morning Herald, last modified 25 July 2016, http://www.smh.com.au/nsw/lindt-cafe-siege-officer-who-shot-man-haron-monis-describes-final-moments-20160725-gqcwix.html.

[61] Louisa Rebgetz, "Alleged terror financier Omar Succarieh denied bail for third time", ABC News, last modified 15 February 2016, http://www.abc.net.au/news/2016-02-15/omar-succarieh-denied-bail-for-third-time/7169700.

[62] Kristian Silva, "Brisbane suicide bomber's brother also fighting in Syria: police," Brisbane Times, September 20, 2014, http://www.brisbanetimes.com.au/queensland/brisbane-suicide-bombers-brother-also-fighting-in-syria-police-20140919-10jjog.html.

[63] Australian Associated Press, "Anzac Day terrorism plot: Sevdet Besim 'wanted to emulate Numan Haider'", The Guardian, last modified 1 August 2016, https://www.theguardian.com/australia-news/2016/aug/01/anzac-day-terrorism-plot-sevdet-besim-wanted-to-emulate-numan-haider.

[64] Australian Associated Press, "Anzac Day terrorism plot: Sevdet Besim 'wanted to emulate Numan Haider'", The Guardian, last modified 1 August 2016, https://www.theguardian.com/australia-news/2016/aug/01/anzac-day-terrorism-plot-sevdet-besim-wanted-to-emulate-numan-haider.

[65] "Militant Networks," The Australian, November 18, 2006, http://www.theaustralian.com.au/news/features/militant-networks/story-e6frg6z6-1111112542554.

[66] "Sheikh Moves To Clarify Bin Laden Comments," ABC Television Lateline, July 25, 2005, http://www.abc.net.au/lateline/content/2005/s1422054.htm.

[67] Dr S A Hamed Hamed Hosseini & Wafa Chafic, "Mapping the Socio-Cultural Contexts of Political Identity Formation Among Young Muslim Australians: A Primary Profile", School of Humanities and Social Sciences, the University of Newcastle, Research Paper, No.2 (2016).

[68] Dr S A Hamed Hamed Hosseini & Wafa Chafic, "Mapping the Socio-Cultural Contexts of Political Identity Formation Among Young Muslim Australians: A Primary Profile", School of Humanities and Social Sciences, the University of Newcastle, Research Paper, No.2 (2016).

[69] "Moderate Cleric Claims Benbrika Described Australia As A Land Of War," ABC Radio PM, August 2, 2006, http://www.abc.net.au/pm/content/2006/s1704344.htm.

[70] Richard Kerbaj, "Radical Phones Home For Sermons," The Australian, July 26, 2007, 1.

[71] Michael Safi, "Closure of al-Furqan puts spotlight on role of Islamic bookshops in extremism," The Guardian, April 23, 2015, https://www.theguardian.com/australia-news/2015/apr/23/closure-of-al-furqan-puts-spotlight-on-role-of-islamic-bookshops-in-extremism.

[72] James Dowling, "Revealed: The split that created Al-Furqan", Herald Sun, last modified 16 May 2015, http://www.heraldsun.com.au/news/victoria/revealed-the-split-that-created-alfurqan/news-story/516eb4edada14b35d5beeb6949775299.

[73] "Al-Furqan: The names linked to a shuttered Islamic Centre in Melbourne," ABC News, March 7, 2016, http://www.abc.net.au/news/2016-03-02/al-furqan-islamic-centre-melbourne-names-linked/7214472.

[74] Ibid.

[75] "Melbourne's Al-Furqan Islamic Centre, attended by several terrorism accused, closes its doors," ABC News, April 23, 2015, http://www.abc.net.au/news/2015-04-23/melbournes-al-furqan-islamic-centre-closes-effective-immediately/6414316.

[76] Tom Minear & James Dowling, "Islamic State-linked group Al-Furqan still meeting at suburban sports centre after shutting book shop," Herald Sun, May 2, 2015, http://www.heraldsun.com.au/news/law-order/islamic-statelinked-group-alfurqan-still-meeting-at-suburban-sports-centre-after-shutting-book-shop/news-story/edfee9bd3d3eb2ee6314a135d4f19424.

[77] Charles Miranda, "Controversial Melbourne preacher Harun Mehicevic was 'asked to spy on ISIS', say parents," news.com.au, May 13, 2016, http://www.news.com.au/national/controversial-melbourne-preacher-harun-mehicevic-was-asked-to-spy-on-isis-say-parents/news-story/4f93963291fdbf739ca5363fc3a4924f.

[78] See, for example, Janet Albrechtsen, "It Is Time We Banned Hizb ut-Tahrir," The Australian, July 8, 2007, http://blogs.theaustralian.news.com.au/janetalbrechtsen/index.php/theaustralian/comments/it_is_time_we_banned_hizb_ut_tahrir/P50/.

[79] Hosseini & Chafic, "Mapping the Socio-Cultural Contexts," p.39.

[80] "FAQs about Hizb ut-Tahrir", Hizb ut-Tahrir Australia, last modified 13 February 2016, http://www.hizb-australia.org/2016/02/faqs-hizb-ut-tahrir/.

[81] "Press Release", Hizb ut-Tahrir Australia, accessed http://www.hizb-australia.org/media/press-releases/.

[82] Barney Zwartz, "Working On The Margins," The Age (Melbourne), January 13, 2007, http://www.theage.com.au/news/in-depth/working-on-the-margins/2007/01/12/1168105181403.html.

[83] See, for example, the reflections of Age journalist Barney Zwartz after he reported on a call for an Islamic family law tribunal. Barney Zwartz, "Sharia In Australia: Sanity Or Shocking," Sydney Morning Herald, October 18, 2009, http://www.smh.com.au/opinion/blogs/the-religious-write/sharia-in-australia-sanity-or-shocking/20091018-h32b.html.

[84] See for example, Sally Neighbour, "Hardliners Teach How To Get Islamic State In Sydney," The Australian, July 8, 2010, http://www.theaustralian.com.au/news/nation/hardliners-teach-how-to-get-islamic-state-in-sydney/story-e6frg6nf-1225889152531; Carl Ungerer and Anthony Bergin, "Cry Halt When Islamists Take Liberties," The Australian, July 9, 2010, http://www.theaustralian.com.au/news/opinion/cry-halt-when-islamists-take-liberties/story-e6frg6zo-1225889557751.

[85] Sally Neighbour, "Extremists With Caliphate On Their Minds, Not Bombs In Their Belts," The Australian, July 2, 2010, http://www.theaustralian.com.au/news/world/extremists-with-caliphate-on-their-minds-not-bombs-in-their-belts/story-e6frg6ux-1225887074605.

[86] Richard Kerbaj and Stuart Rintoul, "Saudis' Secret Agenda," The Australian, May 3, 2008, http://www.theaustralian.com.au/news/features/saudis-secret-agenda/story-e6frg6z6-1111116230270.

[87] "Saudi Money; Australian Universities and Islam – where is the line in the sand?" ABC Radio National The Religion Report, April 30, 2008, http://www.abc.net.au/rn/religionreport/stories/2008/2231183.htm.

[88] Minister for Education Science and Training, "$8m For Centre Of Excellence For Islamic Education National Action Plan," July 16, 2006, http://www.dest.gov.au/Ministers/Media/Bishop/2006/07/B002160706.asp.

[89] Ibid.

[90] See, for example, the Security Legislation Amendment (Terrorism) Act 2002 (Cth), the Australian Security and Intelligence Organisation Legislation Amendment (Terrorism) Act 2003 (Cth) and the National Security Legislation Amendment Bill (No. 1) 2014

[91] See, for example, Andrew Lynch, "Legislating With Urgency—The Enactment Of The Anti-Terrorism Act [No 1] 2005," MULR 30, iss. 3 (2007), 747-781.

[92] See, for example, the legal judgments in R v Ul-Haque, NSWSC 1251 (2007); R v Mallah, NSWSC 358 (2005); R v Thomas, VSCA 165 (2006).

[93] Janet Phillips, "Muslim Australians: E-Brief," Parliamentary Library of Australia, March 6, 2007, http://www.aph.gov.au/library/INTGUIDE/SP/Muslim_Australians.htm.

[94] See, for example, "Building A Relationship With Melbourne's Islamic community," Platypus Magazine 97, December 2007, 28-29, http://www.afp.gov.au/__data/assets/pdf_file/64549/28_29_Building_a_relationship.pdf.

[95] Andrew Colvin, "Australian Strategic Policy Institute - Building Capabilities for Tomorrow", Australian Federal Police, last modified 25 February 2016, https://www.afp.gov.au/news-media/national-speeches/australian-strategic-policy-institute-building-capabilities-tomorrow.

[96] Debra Killalea, "Anzac Day terror plot: Do deradicalisation programs really work?" news.com.au, April 26, 2016, http://www.news.com.au/national/courts-law/anzac-day-terror-plot-do-deradicalisation-programs-really-work/news-story/62dfccc34da6796a1c10476eec8e7096.

[97] See, for example, Australian Muslim Civil Rights Advocacy Network, submission no 88, Parliamentary Joint Committee on ASIO, ASIS and DSD Review of Division 3 Part III of the ASIO Act 1979: ASIO's Questioning and Detention Powers, https://www.aph.gov.au/HOUSE/committee/pjcaad/asio_ques_detention/subs/sub88.pdf.

[98] Sharon Pickering, David Wright-Neville, Jude McCulloch and Peter Lentini, Counter-Terrorism Policing and Culturally Diverse Communities: Final Report 2007 (Clayton: Monash University, 2007)

[99] See, for instance, Basia Spalek and Alia Imtoual, "Muslim Communities And Counter-Terror Responses: 'Hard' Approaches To Community Engagement In The UK And Australia," Journal of Muslim Minority Affairs 27, iss. 2, August 2007, 185-202, 193-196.

[100] George Brandis, "Reporting Violent Extremism Online," Attorney-General for Australia, February 9, 2015, https://www.attorneygeneral.gov.au/Mediareleases/Pages/2015/FirstQuarter/9February2015-ReportingViolentExtremismOnline.aspx.

[101] Emma Griffiths, "Terrorism threat: Australian alert level raised to high; terrorist attack likely but not imminent," ABC News, September 13, 2014, http://www.abc.net.au/news/2014-09-12/australia-increases-terrorism-threat-level/5739466.

[102] John Coyne, "The New Norm In Australia Is A High Terror Threat Level," The Huffington Post, September 17, 2015, http://www.huffingtonpost.com.au/john-coyne/the-new-norm-in-australia-is-a-high-terror-threat-level/.

[103] George Brandis, "Overview of the National Terrorism Threat Advisory System," Attorney-General's Department AU, November 25, 2015, https://www.youtube.com/watch?v=StfXo6B_VgY.

[104] Michael Keenan, "New National Terrorism Threat Advisory System," Ministry of Justice, November 26, 2015, https://www.ministerjustice.gov.au/Mediareleases/Pages/2015/FourthQuarter/26-November-2015-New-National-Terrorism-Threat-Advisory-System.aspx.

[105] "National Terrorism Threat Advisory System," Australian National Security, https://www.nationalsecurity.gov.au/Securityandyourcommunity/Pages/National-Terrorism-Threat-Advisory-System.aspx.

[106] Keenan, "New Terrorism Threat."

[107] Australian Associated Press, "Terrorism alert system moves from four levels to five – to be simpler, says PM", The Guardian, last modified 23 July 2015, https://www.theguardian.com/australia-news/2015/jul/23/terrorism-alert-system-moves-from-four-levels-to-five-to-be-simpler-says-pm.

[108] George Brandis, "COAG to strengthen national security legislation," Attorney-General for Australia, April 1, 2016, https://www.attorneygeneral.gov.au/Mediareleases/Pages/2016/SecondQuarter/1-April-2016-COAG-to-strengthen-national-security-legislation.aspx.

[109] Katharine Murphyu , "Australia taking cyber fight to Isis, Malcolm Turnbull to confirm" Guardian, 22 November 2016

CHINA

Quick Facts

Population: 1,373,541,278 (July 2016 est.)

Area: 9,596,960 sq km

Ethnic Groups: Han Chinese 91.6%, Zhuang 1.3%, other (includes Hui, Manchu, Uighur, Miao, Yi, Tujia, Tibetan, Mongol, Dong, Buyei, Yao, Bai, Korean, Hani, Li, Kazakh, Dai and other nationalities) 7.1%

Religions: Buddhist 18.2%, Christian 5.1%, Muslim 1.8%, folk religion 21.9%, Hindu < 0.1%, Jewish < 0.1%, other 0.7% (includes Daoist (Taoist)), unaffiliated 52.2%

Government Type: communist state

GDP (official exchange rate): $11.39 trillion (2015 est.)

Map and Quick Facts courtesy of the CIA World Factbook (Last Updated January 2017)

Overview

Prior to 1949, China's Nationalist government recognized Muslims as one of the "five peoples" constituting the Chinese nation—along with Manchus, Mongols, Tibetans and Han. The Communist Party of China (CPC) has maintained this recognition and continued to push Muslims toward integration. China, in the words of one official, "allows the practice of religion, but not at the expense of the state."[1] In all, Beijing recognizes ten separate Muslim nationalities, the largest being Uighurs, Hui and Kazakhs.

The spread of Islam in China, particularly in the Xinjiang Uighur Autonomous Region—a sprawling western expanse of inhospitable deserts and mountains—has long been a source of official concern, resulting in numerous laws restricting assembly, as well as religious practices and teaching. These repressive measures have also led to the incarceration and persecution of political activists and vocal nationalists. More subtly, the Chinese state has made efforts to dilute Uighur dominance demographi-

cally through the transplantation of Han Chinese to the province. This policy has resulted in a material shift in the demographics of the region; according to official estimates, Han Chinese, who made up just 6 percent of the overall population of Xinjiang in 1949, comprised 38 percent of the provincial total as of 2014.[2]

Put succinctly, "to be a practicing Muslim in Xinjiang is to live under an intricate series of laws and regulations intended to control the spread and practice of Islam."[3] Nevertheless, signs suggest that Islam's popularity within China continues to grow, along with Uighur dissatisfaction with official policies, particularly in Xinjiang. Chinese officials ascribe rising social and political tensions in the province to the growing influence of radical Islam – rather than to repressive state policies. As such, they see radical Islam as an external threat to what would otherwise be a peaceful and happy Chinese religious minority.[4]

ISLAMIST ACTIVITY

Chinese authorities collectively classify separatism, extremism, and terrorism as the "three forces" that represent a threat to the nation. Chinese authorities divide their struggle against these evils into five phases between 1990 and 2007.[5] During this period, religious radicalism underwent a significant metamorphosis, culminating in the rise of groups such as East Turkestan Islamic Movement (ETIM), also known as the Turkistan Islamic Party [TIP], or *al-Hizb al-Islami al-Turkistani*, the East Turkestan Islamic Reform Party, the East Turkestan Democratic Reform Party, and the East Turkestan Justice Party.

The Xinjiang Autonomous Region is the epicenter of concerns about Islamic extremism, and the focal point of China's long-running anti-terror campaign. Xinjiang is China's largest province, spanning more than 1.6 million square kilometers in the country's extreme west. Its territory abuts eight foreign nations, five of which—Kazakhstan, Kyrgyzstan, Tajikistan, Afghanistan and Pakistan—are majority Muslim. According to official Chinese statistics, Muslims make up the barest of majorities (just over 11 million) of Xinjiang's population of 22 million. Of these, the largest ethnic bloc is the Uighur, who number over 11 million.[6]

Relations between Xinjiang and the Chinese central government have long been fraught, and recent years have seen escalating efforts by Beijing to repress and control residents there. This campaign is complex, since radical Islamism and Uighur separatism are inextricably linked in the minds of many Chinese officials and citizens. Han Chinese—even those with progressive attitudes toward democracy—often cannot see the difference between a politically active Uighur and a separatist.[7]

Uighurs have long lived as *de facto* second class citizens within China, with many denied economic opportunity and political representation over the past five decades—and with little attention paid, at least until recently, to the living standards and economic conditions affecting them. Over time, a comparatively tiny fraction of Uighurs, what experts have defined as "a very small minority within the minority,"[8] has become politically active through illegal and/or militant groups. The goal of these organizations is, invariably, the promotion of Uighur rights and separatist tendencies in Xinjiang.

In December of 2003, China's Ministry of Public Security released a list of organizations deemed to pose a threat to the state. The document listed four distinct groups—the East Turkestan Islamic Movement (ETIM, also known as the Turkestan Islamic Party, or TIP), the East Turkestan Liberation Organization (ETLO), the *World Uighur Congress*, and the East Turkestan Information Center—as well as eleven individuals.[9] Of these, only ETIM/TIP remains active today.

While there is broad consensus regarding some of these organizations (ETIM, for example, was designated as a Foreign Terrorist Organization by the U.S. Department of State in September 2002), the status of others remains hotly contested, due largely to suspicions that their blacklisting was driven by political considerations on the part of the Chinese government.[10] Indeed, although U.S. officials concurred with Beijing in the case of ETIM/TIP, they have historically resisted Chinese pressure to designate other Uighur groups as terrorists.[11]

Until quite recently, China did not have a terrorism problem, at least not as commonly understood in the West. Prior to 2008, low-grade insurgent activity did occur sporadically. Nevertheless, regional law enforcement agencies appeared to have effectively neutralized Islamist radicals. However, over time, the state's increasingly tight controls on speech, movement, and the practice of Islam engendered widespread frustration and anger among Chinese Muslims. A growing resentment of heavy-handed state intervention in religious life—not the insidious intervention of foreign influences, as Beijing claims—solidified the separatist movement and strengthened its grassroots support. This, in turn, catalyzed large-scale and violent Uighur anti-government riots in 2008-2009, and has perpetuated sporadic instances of violence since. These have included, among other incidents, a March 2014 Uighur attack on a train station in Yunnan province,[12] a January 2015 small-scale riot in Xinjiang,[13] a July 2015 police raid that resulted in the deaths of three purported Uighur terrorists in Shenyang,[14] and the death of four people at the hands of Uighur assailants in Xinjiang in February 2017.[15]

Over time, this unrest has prompted a change in Islamist groups active in Xinjiang—most directly, ETIM/TIP. Thus, while previously only nominally connected to external Islamist networks (such as al-Qaeda), following the 2008-2009 timeframe groups such as *Hizb ut-Tahrir* and the al-Qaeda linked *Islamic Movement of Uzbeki-*

stan (IMU) began to exert greater influence over ETIM/TIP's ideology and tactics,[16] with the latter reportedly involved in the training of the group's militants.[17] ETIM/TIP ideology promotes Uighur independence and resistance against the suppression of Islam in Xinjiang. For example, one Uighur separatist publication, *Turkistan al-Muslimah* (Muslim Turkistan), regularly links Islam and separatism by claiming that ETIM/TIP is "seeking freedom and independence and to be ruled by God's Shari'a."[18]

Information regarding ETIM/TIP is tightly controlled by the Chinese government, and as a result little is known about the group's current size, strength and sources of funding. Nevertheless, the organization's increasingly strident Islamist rhetoric in recent years, as well as its surge of attacks against Chinese targets, which have been carried out in spite of deepening state repression, suggest that the organization continues to constitute a real—albeit limited—threat to Chinese security.

Over the past several years, both the Islamic State and al-Qaeda have begun targeting China with both threats and online propaganda.[19] Al-Qaeda leader Ayman al-Zawahiri has labeled China an enemy of the Muslim world, as has the leader of the al-Qaeda-affiliated TIP, Abdul Haq.[20] The Islamic State, meanwhile, released a propaganda video in early 2017 highlighting Chinese Uighurs living and training to fight in the Islamic State, as well as depictions of the torture Uighurs suffer at the hands of the Chinese government.[21]

Nevertheless, the Islamic State has yet to gain a significant foothold within China, although its ideology has begun to resonate among the country's disaffected Muslims. Official state media has estimated that approximately 300 Chinese Muslims have joined the group's ranks in Iraq and Syria to date.[22] Other calculations, however, have put the number significantly lower, at 118.[23] Nevertheless, Chinese Muslims do have a notable presence within the Islamic State's rump *caliphate*. A 2016 study by the New America Foundation, a Washington, DC-based think tank, noted that ISIS fighters from China were overwhelmingly Uighur in ethnicity, and hailed from Xinjiang. Moreover, these fighters tended to be older than the average foreign fighter, and in many cases brought their families with them, suggesting that they intended to stay with the Islamic State for the foreseeable future.[24]

ISLAMISM AND SOCIETY

As of 2015, the Muslim population of China was estimated to be 1.7 percent of the total, or 23,142,104 people out of a population of 1,332,810,869.[25] The largest segments of this population are Uighurs, Hui and Kazakhs, which have been formally recognized by the Chinese state since 1949.

The Uighurs, a Turkic Muslim minority, populate the rugged, oil- and mineral-rich territory of Xinjiang that constitutes one-sixth of China's total land mass. Uighurs are the largest ethnic group in Xinjiang, accounting for approximately half of the region's total population of roughly 21 million.[26] Uighurs have practiced Sunni Islam since the 10th century, and the faith has experienced a revival among the community in recent years. As of 2008, Xinjiang was estimated to be home to approximately 24,000 mosques and 29,000 religious leaders.[27]

Uighurs have had an historically tense relationship with the Han Chinese majority, and thus many support the idea of independence, or at least greater autonomy, for Xinjiang. In fact, Uighur activists often refer to Xinjiang as East Turkistan, as it was called during its former days as an independent republic.

The Uighur community has numerous grievances against the Chinese government: restrictions on their religion, language and culture; official policies that encourage Han emigration to Xinjiang to dilute the strength of the Uighur ethnic identity; and common Han discrimination towards Uighurs. China's authorities reject the validity of these complaints, saying Uighurs should instead be grateful for Xinjiang's rapid economic development and targeted investment from the government over the last decade. Beginning in 2008, these racial and religious tensions fueled Uighur protests against state restrictions on Islam. A simultaneous series of radical Uighur attacks against the authorities and their Han neighbors only precipitated increasingly restrictive countermeasures. Ultimately, this cycle culminated in the mob violence of July 2009.

With no real voice in politics at the national level, the political interests of the Uighur community are largely represented by the World Uyghur Congress (WUC). The WUC is the most well known international Uighur political organization. It is an umbrella group of smaller Uighur nationalist organizations formed after the East Turkestan National Congress and the World Uyghur Youth Congress merged in April 2004.[28] The WUC claims to "peacefully promote the human rights, religious freedom, and democracy for the Uyghur people in East Turkistan."[29] Beijing, on the other hand, asserts that the WUC is a front through which Western nations can clandestinely channel funds and weapons into Xinjiang and undermine the integrity of the Chinese state.[30]

With a population of over 10 million scattered throughout China, the Hui make up just under half of the country's Muslims.[31] They are most numerous in the Ningxia Hui Autonomous Region, Gansu, Qinghai, Henan, Hebei, Shandong, and Xinjiang. Although anthropologists and historians debate their origin, Hui ancestors include Central Asians, Persians, Han Chinese, and Mongols. During the Tang and Yuan Dynasties, people from Central Asia and Persia migrated to China along the Silk Road. Over the centuries, their descendants intermarried with Mongols and Han Chinese, giving rise to the Hui people. Over time, the Hui have lost their proficiency in Arabic and Central Asian languages and adopted Chinese as their native tongue. Today's Hui are best understood as Sinicised Muslims that (unlike other official Muslim groups) look Han and speak Mandarin or other local dialects. Unlike the Uighurs—whose claim to Xinjiang predates that of the Han—the Hui settled in areas already dominated by ethnic Hans.[32] The Hui today enjoy far more religious freedom than they did in the first decades of Communist rule, when all religion was repressed. However, greater religious freedom has also increased mosque attendance among Hui—a tendency that many Han interpret as clannish.

Finally, approximately 1.5 million Kazakh Muslims reside in the north of Xinjiang, on the border with the Central Asian republic of Kazakhstan.[33] Unlike the Hui, Kazakhs speak their native language and feel a close connection to clans in neighboring Kazakhstan. In Kazakh society, rituals are generally performed in accordance with Islamic tradition, and include prayers, fasting, observance of the *Hajj* (pilgrimage to Mecca), and adherence to Islamic burial rites. Similarly, Kazakhs supplement their official legal marriages with traditional ceremonies. Generally speaking, Kazakh Muslims have maintained a better relationship with the Han than have the Uighurs.[34]

The tight controls on information in China (particularly in Xinjiang), coupled with the severe penalties for either financial or rhetorical support for unrecognized Islamic organizations, make it impossible to determine who donates to Islamist groups, and how much. However, it appears that the Uighur community (rather than the Hui or Kazakhs) is the primary domestic constituency and support base for Islamist movements that call for Xinjiang's independence. *Turkistan al-Muslimah*, for instance, publishes articles on government persecution of Uighurs, but does not mention the plight of Hui or Kazakh Muslims in Xinjiang.[35] The magazine publishes only the names of "martyred" Uighurs, and in its first issue, the journal stated its aim as exposing "the real situation of our Muslim nation in East Turkistan, which is living under the occupation of the Communist Chinese."[36] Publications of this ilk do not appear to exist within either the Hui or Kazakh communities.

Xinjiang's economic situation has only exacerbated the potential for extremism among its populace. In 2012, the *People's Daily* reported that the poverty rate was 13.8 percent higher in regions populated by ethnic minorities in comparison with the national average.[37] Furthermore, Xinjiang's economy depends on subsidies from Beijing, and in 2014 made up 60 percent of the region's budget.[38] Uighurs, meanwhile, feel the economic strain and stresses of the situation in Xinjiang acutely. Farming remains the primary source of income for approximately 80 percent of Uighurs in the poor southern portion of the province.[39] Many face discrimination in the job market, both over their ethnic and religious heritage. This discrimination is exacerbated by the linguistic barrier between the Uighurs and the rest of China.[40] One government program, known as Xinjiang Class, sends thousands of Uighur and Han students from Xinjiang to other parts of China to continue their education and seek job opportunities. Approximately 50 percent of those students, however, are ultimately forced to return to Xinjiang.[41]

Islamism and the State

The Chinese state maintains an intricate system of control over its Muslim minorities. The regional Commission on Religious and Ethnic Affairs (CREA) closely monitors China's Islamic educational institutions, which span grades one through 12. Its teachers and clergy are thoroughly vetted by the parallel Islamic Association to ensure they do not harbor extremist ideas or tendencies. In practice, this has created a series of state-sponsored and tightly-controlled religious schools for Chinese Muslims.[42] This has included the underwriting of academic efforts to "reinterpret" Islamic scriptures so that they are more in keeping with Chinese society and values, as well as the promotion of communist ideas and integration among different ethnic groups (namely, the Uighur and the Han, with intermarriage actively encouraged by authorities). It has also advocated bilingual education (both Uighur and Mandarin) for the region's residents.[43]

The Chinese government has invested heavily in Islamic education. China currently has 10 Islamic institutes nationwide, but the most prominent is the Islamic Institute of Xinjiang in Urumqi. Now some three decades old, the Institute has a capacity of 450 students and turns out between 40 and 80 graduates per year. As of September 2016, it had graduated roughly 750 alumni, all of whom go on to become *imams* themselves, mostly within China.[44]

Funding for the Institute comes from the country's Islamic Association. However, the Institute was originally built thanks to a grant from the World Islamic Union, suggesting at least some economic (and perhaps ideological) involvement from the broader Muslim World. Currently, curriculum at the facility is 30 percent academic and 70 percent religious (including Quranic recitation, the study of the *hadith*, and other subjects). The average course of study lasts five years, and students are nominated to attend the institution by their local communities, with candidacies considered by regional authorities to ensure they are in keeping with the larger ideological bent of religious policy.[45]

This investment is part of a strategy to reduce the exposure of local Muslims to radical ideas and teachings now proliferating throughout the greater Middle East. However, China's Muslims are not hermetically walled off from divergent ideological strains of the religion. Notably, a small minority receives additional religious education abroad at institutions in Libya or Pakistan, or at Egypt's famed Al-Azhar University—a potential "weak link" that could lead to their exposure to the radical ideas now proliferating throughout the greater Middle East.[46] That said, according to local Chinese officials and administrators in Xinjiang, China has developed long-term relationships with these intuitions and they have yet to experience adverse consequences from sending students to these schools.[47]

Limits on religious activity likewise abound. Prior to the 2008-2009 timeframe, propaganda and education controls, coupled with an ample security presence, appeared to suppress Islamist activity within China's Muslim communities. However, as previously discussed, in July of 2009, Xinjiang's capital of Urumqi became the site of several days of violent clashes between the local Uighur and Han communities—a culmination of months of simmering ethnic and communal tensions throughout the region. The initial demonstrations, and armed counter-protests, left more than 150 dead, marking the largest instance of public violence in China since the 1989 Tiananmen Square massacre.[48]

The government response to the Urumqi riots was sharp and swift. Among its numerous policies, it suspended all text-messaging and Internet services in Xinjiang between July 2009 and January 2010.[49] Authorities in Yining "smashed two violence gangs, and arrested more than 70 suspects," according to Jiao Baohua, secretary of the Yining city CPC committee.[50] Since then, the Chinese state has implemented a series of new measures designed to prevent further violence. Thousands of armed police, special police, and public security personnel began to patrol the Uighur sections of Urumqui and carry out raids.[51] The government issued new ordinances calling on local businesses and residents to register guests with the authorities[52] and temporarily restricting travel after dark.[53]

The state has expanded it propaganda efforts, and increased its control over legal and information services. Propaganda efforts included the implementation of a "political education" campaign to promote "new model citizens with a modern attitude."[54] Legal controls included new restrictions on—and warnings to—lawyers,[55] as well as death sentences for some rioters and harsh prison sentences for others.[56]

Since then, authorities have sought to more rigidly enforce laws and provisions that severely restrict the practice and teaching of Islam. These regulations, which had been on the books for years, are now publicly posted online and on banners throughout Xinjiang.[57] Examples of policies that limit Islamic activity included half-hour limits on sermons, prohibitions on prayer in public areas and prohibitions on the teaching of the Quran in private. They also include restrictions on worship, with Muslims only permitted to attend mosques in their hometowns, and restrictions on government workers and CPC members from attending mosques.[58]

Two of Islam's five pillars—the sacred fasting month of Ramadan and the *Hajj*—are also restricted. Authorities use propaganda and control of passports to compel Muslims to join government-run *Hajj* tours that deliberately reduce exposure to Islamist teachings.[59] Local governments in Xinjiang have even expanded their policies to encompass bans against traditional clothing. In 2015, legislators in Urumqi banned women from wearing *burqas* in public. In other cases, men in religious garb with full bears have been banned from riding public buses. The city of Karamay also banned veils, large beards, and several forms of Islamic dress.[60] The Chinese government has also applied a variety of other invasive measures to weaken Uighur communities, including explicitly ordering Muslim restaurant and store owners to sell alcohol and cigarettes, and promote them in "eye-catching displays."[61] The government has also banned fasting during Ramadan,[62] and indicated that parents or guardians who "encourage or force" their children to be religious should be reported to the police. Though China claims to allow religious freedom, minors are not allowed to participate in religious expression, and there have been crackdowns on covert *madrassas* in the past several years.[63]

In 2014, a massive contingent of 200,000 Communist Party officials visited 8,000 villages in Xinjiang. Formally, the officials were there to listen to local grievances and improve the relations of local communities with the state. In actuality, however, they worked to establish a vast network of informers designed to keep tabs on villages throughout Xinjiang.[64] Following the uptick in inter-ethnic violence and terror later in 2014, 3,000 former members of the People's Liberation Army were deployed to Xinjiang communities. The former soldiers were under thirty years old and were meant to fortify security in the region.[65]

Nevertheless, instances of violence continue to occur. In December 2016, attackers drove a car into a government building and set off explosives, killing one.[66] In February 2017, three attackers, allegedly Uighurs, killed five people before being shot by police. In response, tens of thousands of police in full riot gear and military vehicles participated in at least four military "parades" as a show of force the same month.[67] Official Chinese policy continues to endorse combatting these and other instances of unrest with increased shows of force and military personnel, despite claims that tightened government control over religion are to blame over extremism causes.

Today, Xinjiang remains an inhospitable place for Muslims. A vicious cycle of repression and rebellion exists, in which the state's suppression of Islam broadens the appeal of extremist Islamist ideologies among Uighurs. Furthermore, the implications of radicalization are increasingly international, as the issue affects China's level of cooperation with its neighbors and South Asian partners. In one instance Beijing was able to pressure Cambodia into deporting a group of asylum-seeking Uighurs back to China. After they returned to China, the Uighurs were placed in a residence outside of Beijing, where they were compelled to disclose the names of all of those that had helped them escape China. Within a week of their deportation, China rewarded Cambodia with a package of new trade deals worth over $1 billion.[68]

Chinese officials believe that Xinjiang, despite its past history of independence, represents "an integral part of China."[69] As such the PRC will not brook any activism that they view as separatist in nature. Indeed, authorities have cracked down harshly on instances of real or perceived dissent, resulting in a massive—and ongoing—security operation in the region. To date, according to Chinese scholars, some 2,000 extremist groups and cells have been dismantled by Chinese security forces.[70]

Against this backdrop, many officials in Xinjiang—and at least some in Beijing—have come to view their country's official policy of "reform and opening up" as potentially dangerous, insofar as it permits greater expression and political activism. This perception, moreover, is amplified by the growing stature of Xinjiang as an integral part of China's westward expansion strategy, commonly known as the "One Belt, One Road."

Since it was first proposed in 2013 by Chinese President Xi Jinping, the "One Belt, One Road" initiative (OBOR) has become a centerpiece of Chinese foreign policy. A sprawling framework for the development of trade and commercial ties with the countries of Eurasia, it is comprised of two distinct parts: a land-based economic "belt" along the historic Silk Road trading route of antiquity, and a maritime "silk road" connecting China with oceangoing economies of Middle East and South Asia. Official Chinese tallies of the projected economic scope of OBOR are not readily available, but China's policy banks, primarily the China Export-Import Bank and Silk Road Fund, have indicated they will make up to $4 trillion in concessionary loans to OBOR countries to support about 900 projects built by Chinese state-run companies.[71]

While OBOR will undoubtedly spur vast growth and new international connections for the PRC, it nonetheless represents a double-edged sword for Beijing. While the initiative is designed to expand prosperity, and to make China a key power center in Eurasia, the facilitation of the transit of goods and people along the "road" will bring with it heightened potential for the intrusion of radicalism, and the infiltration of militants into the PRC.

Chinese officials are keenly aware of these risks. Greater interaction with the majority-Muslim states of Central Asia carries with it a potential for increased extremism within China's own borders—a reality that is likely to spur greater rigidity and repression, particularly toward the Uighur minority, which Beijing sees as particularly susceptible to radicalization. This same rationale drives China's ongoing efforts to "harmonize" Xinjiang, transforming cities like Urumqi—which, until recently, retained a distinct Central Asian and Islamic character—into facsimiles of other Chinese urban centers.

Endnotes

[1] Interviews by American Foreign Policy Council scholars, Xinjiang, China, June 2008.
[2] Statistics Bureau of Xinjiang Uygur Autonomous Region, "3-8 Number of sub-nationalities in major years," January 25, 2016, http://www.xjtj.gov.cn/sjcx/tjnj_3415/2015xjtjnj/rkyjy_2015/201603/t20160315_492327.html.

[3] Edward Wong, "Wary Of Islam, China Tightens A Vise Of Rules," New York Times, October 18, 2008, http://www.nytimes.com/2008/10/19/world/asia/19xinjiang.html?_r=3&hp&oref=slogin.

[4] Interviews by American Foreign Policy Council scholars, Xinjiang, China, September 2016.

[5] Interviews by American Foreign Policy Council scholars, Xinjiang, China, June 2008.

[6] Statistics Bureau of Xinjiang Uygur Autonomous Region, "3-8 Number of sub-nationalities in major years."

[7] Louisa Greve, Testimony before the Congressional-Executive Commission on China, February 13, 2009, http://frwebgate.access.gpo.gov/cgi-bin/getdoc.cgi?dbname=111_house_hearings&docid=f:48222.wais.

[8] Randal G. Schriver, Testimony before the U.S. House of Representatives Committee on Foreign Affairs, Subcommittee on International Organizations, Human Rights and Oversight, June 16, 2009, http://www.internationalrelations.house.gov/hearing_notice.asp?id=1083.

[9] "China identifies Eastern Turkestan Terrorist Organizations," PLA Daily, December 16, 2003, http://www.globalsecurity.org/wmd/library/news/china/2003/china-031216-pla-daily01.htm.

[10] Schriver, Testimony before the U.S. House of Representatives Committee on Foreign Affairs, Subcommittee on International Organizations, Human Rights and Oversight.

[11] Ibid.

[12] Beina Xu, Holly Fletcher, and Jayshree Bajoria, "The East Turkestan Islamic Movement (ETIM)," Council on Foreign Relations CFR Backgrounder, September 4, 2014, http://www.cfr.org/china/east-turkestan-islamic-movement-etim/p9179.

[13] "Don't make yourself at home," The Economist, January 15, 2015, http://www.economist.com/news/china/21639555-uighurs-and-tibetans-feel-left-out-chinas-economic-boom-ethnic-discrimination-not.

[14] "Three 'Xinjiang terrorists' shot dead by police in China," BBC, July 14, 2015, http://www.bbc.com/news/world-asia-china-33517512.

[15] "Eight dead after knife attack in China's western Xinjiang region," Telegraph (London), February 15, 2017, http://www.telegraph.co.uk/news/2017/02/15/eight-dead-knife-attack-chinas-western-xinjiang-region/.

[16] Rodger Baker, "China and the Enduring Uighurs," Stratfor Terrorism Intelligence Report, August 6, 2008, https://www.stratfor.com/weekly/china_and_enduring_uighurs.

[17] Murad Batal Al-Shishani, "Journal of the Turkistan Islamic Party Urges Jihad in China." Jamestown Foundation Terrorism Monitor 7, iss. 9, April 10, 2009, https://jamestown.org/program/journal-of-the-turkistan-islamic-party-urges-jihad-in-china/.

[18] Ibid.

[19] Uran Botobekov, "Al-Qaeda and Islamic State Take Aim at China," The Diplomat, March 8, 2017, http://thediplomat.com/2017/03/al-qaeda-and-islamic-state-take-aim-at-china/.
[20] Ibid.
[21] Ibidem.
[22] Adam Taylor, "ISIS recruits from China don't fit a typical profile – and Beijing may be partially to blame," New York Times, July 20, 2016, https://www.washingtonpost.com/news/worldviews/wp/2016/07/20/how-isis-fighters-from-china-differ-from-other-foreign-fighters/?utm_term=.866747ec269b.
[23] Nate Rosenblatt, All Jihad is Local: What ISIS' Files Tell Us About Its Fighters, The New America Foundation, July 2016, 23, https://na-production.s3.amazonaws.com/documents/ISIS-Files.pdf.
[24] Ibid.
[25] Raymond Lee, "Muslims in China and their Relations with the State," Al Jazeera Centre for Studies, August 26, 2015, http://studies.aljazeera.net/en/reports/2015/08/2015826102831723836.html.
[26] Statistics Bureau of Xinjiang Uygur Autonomous Region, "3-8 Number of sub-nationalities in major years."
[27] Wong, "Wary Of Islam, China Tightens A Vise Of Rules."
[28] "Introducing the World Uyghur Congress," Official Website of the World Uyghur Congress, n.d., http://www.uyghurcongress.org/en/?cat=149.
[29] Ibid.
[30] "Jiangdu, gai kongxi cilue," (Uighur separatists changed terrorism strategy) Ta Kung Pao (Hong Kong), August 11, 2008, http://www.takungpao.com/news/08/08/11/BJ-945008.htm.
[31] Statistics Bureau of Xinjiang Uygur Autonomous Region, "3-8 Number of sub-nationalities in major years."
[32] Richard Baum, China Watcher: Confessions of a Peking Tom (Seattle: University of Washington Press, 2010), 204.
[33] Statistics Bureau of Xinjiang Uygur Autonomous Region, "3-8 Number of sub-nationalities in major years."
[34] Iraj Bashiri, The Kazakhs of China (n.p., 2002), https://www.academia.edu/10187200/The_Kazakhs_of_China.
[35] Al-Shishani, "Journal of the Turkistan Islamic Party Urges Jihad in China."
[36] Ibid.
[37] "Poverty rate higher in ethnic minority areas," People's Daily, November 29, 2012, http://english.peopledaily.com.cn/90882/8039388.html.
[38] Dexter Roberts, "China Tries to Bring Growth to Its Restless Xinjiang Region," Bloomberg Businessweek, December 11, 2014, https://www.bloomberg.com/news/articles/2014-12-11/chinas-development-of-xinjiang-spurs-resentment-from-uighurs.
[39] Ibid.

[40] "Don't make yourself at home."
[41] Ibid.
[42] Interviews by American Foreign Policy Council scholars, Xinjiang, China, June 2008.
[43] Interviews by American Foreign Policy Council scholars, September 2016.
[44] Ibid.
[45] Ibidem.
[46] Interviews by American Foreign Policy Council scholars, Xinjiang, China, June 2008.
[47] Ibid.
[48] "The Riots In Xinjiang: Is China Fraying"" The Economist, July 9, 2009, http://www.economist.com/node/13988479.
[49] Andrew Jacobs, "China Restores Text Messaging in Xinjiang," New York Times, January 17, 2010, http://www.nytimes.com/2010/01/18/world/asia/18china.html.
[50] Zhu Jingzhao, "Xinjiang yining dadiao liangbaoli fanzui tuanhuo, zhuabu shean qishiyuren," (Yining, Xinjiang wiped out two groups of violent crime suspects, arrested more than 70 people) Zhongguo Xinwen She (Beijing), July 13, 2009, http://news.qq.com/a/20090713/001079.htm.
[51] "Jiehou Wulumuqi jianwen: wending yadao yiqie," (Life in Urumqi after the festival: Stability is everything), Ta Kung Pao (Hong Kong), July 18, 2009, http://www.takungpao.com/news/09/07/18/xjsl_xgbd-1113938.htm.
[52] Government of the People's Republic of China, "Riot-Hit Urumqi To Tighten Migrant Population Administration," August 9, 2009, http://www.gov.cn/english/2009-08/09/content_1387239.htm.
[53] "China Imposes Curfew In Capital Of Xinjiang," Kyodo News Agency (Japan), September 7, 2009, http://home.kyodo.co.jp/modules/fstStory/index.php?storyid=458736.
[54] Xi Wang, "Ideological Campaign Launched in Xinjiang" Radio Free Asia, February 17, 2012, http://www.rfa.org/english/news/uyghur/campaign-02172012144813.html.
[55] Human Rights Watch, "China: Xinjiang Trials Deny Justice, Proceedings Failed Minimum Fair Trial Standards," October 15, 2009, http://www.hrw.org/en/news/2009/10/15/china-xinjiang-trials-deny-justice.
[56] Cui Jia, "Murderers in Urumqi riots will not appeal," China Daily (Beijing), October 27, 2009.http://www.chinadaily.com.cn/cndy/2009-10/27/content_8852664.htm.
[57] Wong, "Wary Of Islam, China Tightens A Vise Of Rules."
[58] Ibid.
[59] Ibidem.

[60] Steven Jiang, "China bans wearing burqa in biggest Muslim city," CNN, January 14, 2015, http://www.cnn.com/2015/01/13/world/asia/china-burqa-ban/.

[61] Simon Denyer, "China orders muslim shopkeepers to sell alcohol, cigarettes, to 'weaken' Islam," Washington Post, May 5, 2015, https://www.washingtonpost.com/news/worldviews/wp/2015/05/05/china-orders-muslim-shopkeepers-to-sell-alcohol-cigarettes-to-weaken-islam/?utm_term=.86b80fa76626.

[62] "China bans Muslims from fasting Ramadan in Xinjiang," Al Jazeera (Doha), June 18, 2015, http://www.aljazeera.com/news/2015/06/china-bans-ramadan-fasting-muslim-region-150618070016245.html.

[63] "China's new rules for Xinjiang ban parents from encouraging or forcing children into religion," South China Morning Post, October 12, 2016, http://www.scmp.com/news/china/policies-politics/article/2027342/chinas-new-rules-xinjiang-ban-parents-encouraging-or.

[64] Tom Phillips, "China launches massive rural 'surveillance' project to watch over Uighurs," Telegraph (London), October 20, 2014, http://www.telegraph.co.uk/news/worldnews/asia/china/11150577/China-launches-massive-rural-surveillance-project-to-watch-over-Uighurs.html

[65] Tom Phillips, "China sends thousands of troops to combat violence," Telegraph (London), November 28, 2014, http://www.telegraph.co.uk/news/worldnews/asia/china/11259959/China-sends-thousands-of-troops-to-combat-Xinjiang-violence.html.

[66] "Xinjiang attack: four 'terrorists' and one bystander killed, says China," Guardian (London), December 28, 2016, https://www.theguardian.com/world/2016/dec/29/xinjiang-attack-four-terrorists-and-one-bystander-killed-says-china.

[67] Josh Ye, "Massive show of force staged in China's Xinjiang region after terrorist attack," South China Morning Post, February 17, 2017, http://www.scmp.com/news/china/policies-politics/article/2071788/massive-show-force-staged-chinas-xinjiang-region-after.

[68] Seth Mydans, "After Expelling Uighurs, Cambodia Approves Chinese Investments," New York Times, December 21, 2009, http://www.nytimes.com/2009/12/22/world/asia/22cambodia.html.

[69] Interviews by American Foreign Policy Council scholars, September 2016.

[70] Ibid.

[71] "Our bulldozers, our rules," The Economist, July 2, 2016, http://www.economist.com/news/china/21701505-chinas-foreign-policy-could-reshape-good-part-world-economy-our-bulldozers-our-rules.

INDONESIA

QUICK FACTS

Population: 258,316,051 (estimated July 2016)

Area: 1,904,569 sq km

Ethnic Groups: Javanese 40.1%, Sundanese 15.5%, Malay 3.7%, Batak 3.6%, Madurese 3%, Betawi 2.9%, Minangkabau 2.7%, Buginese 2.7%, Bantenese 2%, Banjarese 1.7%, Balinese 1.2%, Acehnese 1.4%, Dayak 1.4%, Sasak 1.3%, Chinese 1.2%, other 15%

Religions: Muslim 87.2%, Christian 7%, Roman Catholic 2.9%, Hindu 1.7%, other 0.9% (includes Buddhist and Confucian), unspecified 0.4%

Government Type: Republic

GDP (official exchange rate): $941 billion (estimated 2015)

Quick Facts courtesy of the CIA World Factbook (January 2017)

OVERVIEW

The world's largest Muslim population lives not in the Middle East, but in Southeast Asia. Out of Indonesia's population of 255.9 million people, some 223.1 million—or just over 87 percent—is Muslim.[1] Indonesia is the largest Muslim-majority democracy in the world. Furthermore, Indonesia is also one of the most pluralistic societies in the world in terms of the ethnic, linguistic, cultural, and religious affiliations of its population. Much of this diversity is attributable to the country's geography, with the Indonesian archipelago consisting of more than 17,800 islands and islets.

The Indonesian government officially recognizes only five religions—Islam, Protestantism, Catholicism, Buddhism, and Confucianism. The pluralism of the archipelago has meant that Indonesia has been given to conflict and pogroms for much of history, but from 1966 on much of this was contained by the repressive authoritarian regime of former Indone-

sian President Suharto. *The end of Suharto's thirty-two year rule in 1998 resulted in intense jockeying for newfound political space in Indonesia on the part of various social and political groups and organizations, including Muslims.*

In Indonesia, Islamism is not a monolithic phenomenon.[2] While the virulent brand of Islamist activism epitomized by the ideology and agenda of both jihadi and paramilitary groups is undoubtedly a feature of the broader social-political terrain in post-Suharto Indonesia, they form but a small faction of the wider Muslim community. And while trends of religious conservatism are clearly evident in the social and cultural sphere in recent years, this has not translated to significant support for the Islamist agenda of the implementation of Islamic state and Islamic law

ISLAMIST ACTIVITY

Indonesia won its independence from the Dutch in 1945. Since then, the nation been divided over the legal status of Islam in the multi-ethnic and multi-religious state. Issues such as adopting *sharia* into the Indonesian Constitution and the establishment of an Islamic state are still hotly contested, but Islamic political parties have begun to adopt a more inclusive political agenda. These groups promote a pluralistic ideology and focus on the implementation of universal Islamic values.

Political Parties

Partai Keadilan Sejahtera – PKS ("Prosperous Justice Party")

PKS is the most organized of all Indonesian Islamist parties, with some 400,000 carefully selected and well-trained cadres. It has also cultivated an image of collective decision-making in which no individual leader stands out. Additionally, PKS has successfully contained its internal differences and prevented public schisms. The party is popular with the modernist Islamic constituency, especially among students and educated middle-class Muslims. Apart from representing its members' aspirations in parliament and engaging in *tarbiyah* (educational) activities, PKS provides public services. For example, PKS set up a *Pos Keadilan* ("Justice Post") from which its members could provide assistance to affected communities in ethnic/religious conflicts or natural disasters. In December 1999, a year after PKS's official founding, its social services were institutionalized into the *Pos Keadilan Peduli Umat* (Justice Post Concerning Muslim Society), and expanded to include assistance to farmers in selling their underpriced crops.[3]

(PKS) was originally founded in July 1998. The party emerged from the 1980s organization *Lembaga Da'wah Kampus* (LDK), or "University Students' Body for Islamic

Predication."[4] LDK formed partially in response to the suppression of student movements in the late 1970s. The Muslim Brotherhood in Egypt and its *dawah* (proselytization) activities in mosques also inspired radical Muslim students in the LDK. The LDK is also linked to the Brotherhood's educational system. By the early 1980s, LDK had expanded into a large organization and its alumni subsequently entered the political arena.[5] Eventually, those alumni established the PKS.

In Indonesia's 2004 elections, PKS secured 7.3 percent of votes, and 45 out of 550 seats, in the country's parliament, making it the only Islamic party to improve its position since the previous election. The party then retained a similar level of popular support in the 2009 elections. PKS's success over time has in part been due to a political agenda that emphasized not the implementation of *sharia* or the creation of an Islamic state, but the broadly popular theme of "clean and caring government" in opposition to incumbent parties—both Islamist and secularist—that were widely perceived by voters to be corrupt and elitist.[6] Nonetheless, PKS is still considered a religious party, with its primary focus the promotion of Islamic values.

The powerful *tarbiyah* movement found in secular state universities is essential for the group's success.[7] Campus activism is one of the main conduits of Islamic political communication in Indonesia. That activism is also in line with the party's advocacy for a transformation of society. The *tarbiyah* movement engages its members through hundreds of regular gatherings, sometimes on a weekly basis. These meetings are not only attended by the upper echelons of the party, but also by ordinary people. Often, these meetings do not even focus on significant political issues, but rather on religion and religious understanding. Furthermore, these meetings become catalysts for member interaction, establishing party discipline and helping new recruitment. This level of regular contact gives PKS easy, meaningful access to thousands of its followers. Given this extensive political machinery, PKS is well placed to mobilize members quickly during election times.

The image of PKS as a clean party, free of corruption, has in recent years been undermined by several controversies. This includes the imprisonment of PKS lawmaker Muhammad Misbakhun for fraud and the resignation of another PKS lawmaker, Arifinto, for watching pornography during a parliamentary session. In addition to these internal crises, PKS lost influence in the ruling coalition in 2011 when President Susilo Bambang Yudhoyono replaced the party's research and technology minister, Suharno Surapranata, with environment minister Gusti Muhammad Hatta in a cabinet reshuffle. The move was purportedly a response to the Islamist party's departure from coalition positions on policy issues. Subsequently, in February 2013, party president Luthfi Hasan Ishaaq was detained on corruption charges in a move that shocked the party membership. He was jailed for sixteen years.

Despite these controversies, however, the party suffered only a 1 percent dip in support in the subsequent April 2014 parliamentary elections. Analysts have argued that strong campaigning, particularly by secretary-general Anis Matta, as well as efficient party machinery, helped to contain the fallout from these corruption cases.

Partai Kebangkitan Bangsa – PKB ("National Awakening Party")

The PKB, whose stronghold lies in East Java, was established specifically to contest parliamentary elections in June 1999 in the wake of the political downfall of former president Suharto the preceding May. It was established as the political arm of the *Nahdlatul Ulama* (NU), a rural-based Islamic organization of thirty million adherents with a liberal pluralist agenda that withdrew from active politics in 1984. Chaired by Matori Abdul Djalil, its effective leader was Abdurrahman Wahid, who headed the NU. In the election of June 1999, it secured third place with 17.4 percent of the vote and fifty-one out of 462 electoral seats, behind *Partai Demokrasi Indonesia-Perjuangan* and *Partai Golongan Karya* (Golkar). Following the election, Abdurrahman Wahid was elected party president by the People's Consultative Assembly. The PKB has, however, been unable to sustain its momentum, managing to secure only 10.5 percent of the votes in 2004 and just five percent in 2009, and fifty-two seats and twenty-eight seats, respectively. These poor performances can be attributed to internal conflicts and intra-family disputes arising from Abdurrahman Wahid's decision to sack a string of party chairmen, including his own nephew.

The party experienced a change in fortunes when Rusdi Kirana, a successful non-Muslim businessman and owner of Indonesia's largest airline, Lion Air, joined the party and became deputy chairman. Later, the chairman of the NU, Said Agil Siraj, openly endorsed the party during its 2014 campaign. In the 2014 election, the PKB proved to be the most successful of the Islamic parties, securing about nine percent of the vote due to its strengthened relations with the NU and strong campaign funding.

Partai Bulan Bintang – PBB ("Crescent Star Party")

The PBB claims to be the descendant of Masyumi, the largest Islamic party of the 1950s, and was founded in July 1998. Masyumi was banned in the 1960s by President Sukarno, and its leaders were jailed. After they were released, former Masyumi leaders decided to establish the DDII (*Dewan Da'wah Islamiyah Indonesia*) to maintain its members and leadership networks, as well as to insulate themselves from further political gridlock and turbulence. The DDII is a modernist Islamic organization and has close relations with other similar bodies such as the Muhammadiyah and Persis.[8] The PBB was eventually formed from this collective.

As heir to the Masyumi legacy, PBB espouses a classic Islamist political agenda including the introduction of elements of *sharia* into the Constitution. Both the PBB and PPP (elaborated below) advocated the formal introduction of *sharia* into the constitution in the 2002 annual session of the People's Consultative Assembly. In the 2004 elections, the party garnered 2.6 percent of votes, a slight increase from its previous performance in the 1999 elections.[9] However, in 2009, the party won only 1.8 percent, failing to meet the mandated 2.5 percent legislative threshold and losing its seats in the People's Representative Council. The marginal support for the party was again evident during the 2014 elections, when it garnered a mere 1.5 percent of the vote.

Partai Persatuan Pembangunan – PPP ("United Development Party")

The PPP emerged from a merger of four Islamic parties during Suharto's reign in 1973, and was one of the three legal parties during the New Order. From 1973-1998, the PPP was politically neutered, but remained the medium for the expression of Islamic concerns within the regime. While the PPP never posed a serious threat to the then-incumbent Golkar party, it defeated Golkar in strongly Islamic provinces such as Aceh and occasionally posed a serious challenge to Golkar's electoral dominance in West Sumatra, South Sumatra, East Java and South Kalimantan. The PPP's status as the main opposition party ended when Abdurrahman Wahid withdrew the NU from the party in 1984, which meant the loss of 30 million votes. Most NU leaders resigned after this turn of events.

The party's share of votes has declined drastically over the years, with its popularity dropping by more than two percent (to 8.2 percent of votes) in 2004 as compared to its performance in the 1999 elections. In 2009, the party's share dropped further, to 5.3 percent of votes, earning it 37 seats in the People's Representative Council. Its popularity improved marginally in 2014, when it secured 6.5 percent of the votes due to strong patronage ties with Religious Affairs Minister Suryadharma Ali and Public Housing Minister Djan Faridz. Worthy of note is the fact that the PPP has managed to endure the transition from a regime-sponsored party to a democratic party after 1998 because it retained some standing as a voice of Islamic interests and because of the continued involvement of a range of both modernist and traditionalist Islamic leaders who had participated in the party during the Suharto era.[10]

Like the PKS and PBB, the PPP officially states that its ideological basis is Islam. The PBB, PPP, and PKS all share similar perspectives on sharia, but differ on the means by which to pursue their aims. The PKS does not focus on the formal adoption of sharia, but the PBB and PPP advocate amending the Indonesian Constitution to incorporate the principles of Islamic jurisprudence.

Radical Salafi Islamist Groups

Front Pembela Islam – FPI ("Front of the Defenders of Islam")

The FPI was founded by Muhammad Rizieq Syihab, a young man of Hadrami descent born into a family of sayyids (reputed descendants of the Prophet Muhammad).[11] Before establishing FPI, Syihab was a prominent religious preacher in addition to being a religious teacher in an Islamic school in Central Jakarta.[12] *Laskar Pembela Islam* (LPI), the paramilitary division of FPI, was a loosely organized entity with an open membership.[13] The majority of its members were from mosque youth associations and a number of Islamic schools (*madrassas*) in Jakarta. Other members, particularly among the rank and file, were simply unemployed youths, including those from the notorious *preman* (thug) groups, whose motivation in joining was economic reward for carrying out militant actions. Members were indoctrinated by Syihab, who taught that they should "live nobly, or better, die in holy war as a martyr."[14] LPI eventually succeeded in expanding its network to cities outside Jakarta. It claims to have established eighteen provincial and more than fifty district branches with tens of thousands of sympathizers throughout the country.[15]

LPI first made its presence felt on the national stage in a mass demonstration on August 17, 1998, where it denounced Megawati Soekarnoputri's presidential candidacy. In line with its puritanical ideological beliefs, it became "the most active group in conducting what it called *razia maksiat* (raids on vice)" to assert its political demands more visibly.[16] Moreover, the group demanded that the government abrogate the policy of *asas tunggal* ("sole foundation") which required all political and social organizations to accept the longstanding ideology of the state, *Pancasila*.[17] In addition, the group rallied support for the adoption of the Jakarta Charter, which would have given Islamic law constitutional status. On one occasion, the group also reportedly ransacked the offices of the National Human Rights Commission, which it felt "had not been objective in its investigation of the Tanjung Priok massacre (where the army had shot hundreds of Muslim demonstrators)."[18] In addition, the FPI also threatened Americans in Indonesia, apparently in retaliation for the United States' attack on the Taliban in Afghanistan.[19]

In 2016, FPI was at the forefront of protests against Jakarta gubernatorial candidate Basuki "Ahok" Tjahaja Purnama for the alleged crime of blasphemy. These protests culminated in two rallies in Jakarta which took place on November 4th and December 2nd. The first rally was attended by between 150,000 to 250,000 people, while the second was much larger, with attendance estimated at 500,000 to 750,000.[20]

Laskar Jihad – LJ ("Holy War Force")

LJ first captured the attention of the public in early 2000. It mobilized in response to purported Christian violence against Muslims in the Moluccas, an archipelago within Indonesia, and the apparent inability of the Indonesian central government to protect local Muslims. The LJ was a paramilitary group established by Ja'far Umar Thalib and leading Salafi personalities such as Muhammad Umar As-Sewed, Ayip Syafruddin and Ma'ruf Bahrun.

Before its militant turn in 2000, LJ had mostly been an apolitical and quietist movement, though it was influenced by puritanical Wahhabi Salafism.[21] Many of its members were educated and were at some point part of campus Islamic student movements, or had been in surreptitious contact with Darul Islam, an Islamist militant group (discussed in further detail below). They had come under the charismatic influence of Thalib, who had spent years studying in conservative and radical circles in Saudi Arabia and Yemen, after which he had been dispatched to Afghanistan to take part in *jihad*.[22] It is widely known that from 1994 to 1999, the cadres of LJ contented themselves with teaching and preaching Wahhabi Islam. However, it was the conflict in the Moluccas, alluded to earlier, that propelled them into radical activism and violence. Shortly after the conflict started, the group established a training camp in West Java and was dispatching thousands of its members to the Moluccas, both as relief workers as well as fighters.[23]

Modelled after a military organization, LJ consisted of "one brigade divided into battalions, companies, platoons, teams and one intelligence section."[24] As its symbol, the group adopted the image of two crossed sabres under the words of their creed: "La ilaha illa Allah, Muhammad Rasul Allah" (there is no God but Allah and Muhammad is His messenger).[25]

In terms of its doctrinal positions, LJ dismisses man-made laws in favor of its own interpretation of *sharia*. It rejects notions of democracy and popular sovereignty, maintaining that they fundamentally contradict the teachings of Islam. The group was also outspoken in its condemnation of Megawati Sukarnoputri's presidency on the grounds that she was a woman. Although the organization claims that it is not interested in politics – and specifically, in replacing the current regime with an Islamic state – during the height of its activism, LJ repeatedly instigated violent street riots, often claiming to do so in the pursuit of *sharia*. Other acts of violence included attacks on cafes, brothels, gambling dens and other places, which they considered representations of vice.

In the aftermath of the Bali bombings of October 2002, public opinion swung decidedly away from these local paramilitary groups as Indonesian Muslims expressed outrage at the targeting of co-religionists. At the same time, their patrons from the security services withdrew support and endorsement because of international attention. Both FPI and LJ were quickly disbanded.

Radical Non-Salafi Islamist Groups

Majelis Mujahidin Indonesia – MMI ("Jihad Fighter Group of Indonesia")

The MMI "places a different emphasis on sharia discourse than does LJ and FPI, associating it with the Jakarta Charter and the historical struggle of the Darul Islam movement" (described below).[26] It appears to be a front for various groups that have some relation to the Darul Islam. The group's key organizer is Irfan S. Awwas and its chief religious authority is Abu Bakar Ba'asyir.

Of the militant organizations that have become active during the post-New Order era in Indonesia, the MMI is arguably one of the oldest. According to observers, "it is a loose alliance of a dozen minor Muslim paramilitary organizations that had been scattered among cities such as Solo, Yogyakarta, Kebumen, Purwokerto, Tasikmalaya and Makassar. Notable member groups are *Laskar Santri* (Muslim Student Paramilitary Force), *Laskar Jundullah* (God's Army Paramilitary Force), *Kompi Badar* (Badr Company), *Brigade Taliban* (Taliban Brigade), *Corps Hizbullah Divisi Sunan Bonang* (God's Party Corps of the Sunan Bonang Division), *Front Pembela Islam Surakarta* (Front of the Defenders of Islam of Surakarta/FPIS) and *Pasukan Komando Mujahidin* (Holy Warrior Command Force)."[27]

MMI members continue to lobby for the incorporation of *sharia* into the country's constitution, particularly at the local and regional level in former Darul Islam strongholds. One of the MMI's main objectives is to establish an Islamic *khilafah* (caliphate). MMI has also been active in making calls for *jihad*, particularly in the Moluccas and other troubled spots. In contrast to the large-scale mobilization of *LJ*, however, MMI has preferred to operate in small units that are well trained and armed.

Hizb-ut-Tahrir – *("Party of Liberation")*

HuT is a political organization founded in 1952 in Lebanon by Taqi al-Din al-Nabhani.[28] It is unclear when HuT came to Indonesia, but some scholars trace the organization's presence as far back as the 1970s. In Indonesia, the party is commonly known as HTI, or Hizb-ut-Tahrir Indonesia.

Before the fall of Suharto's regime, HTI remained underground, moving from one mosque to another. It avoided any documentation or public coverage that might reveal its existence and activities. Therefore, HTI's presence was largely unknown until President Suharto stepped down. During the subsequent era of *Reformasi* (political reform), however, the group made its appearance through several public rallies. But, for fear of prosecution, HTI has never revealed the identity of the leader of its Indonesian branch. Its public representative, Ismail Yusanto, claims that he is just the group's spokesperson.

HTI advocates the implementation of *sharia* in Indonesian culture, viewing Islam as not just a religion but also a political system and way of life.[29] Like the MMI, its most important objective is to establish an Islamic *khilafah*.[30] The group also espouses the promulgation of one global government for all Muslims. It is not surprising, therefore, that this group rejects the idea of nationalism or the nation-state.

Darul Islam and Jemaah Islamiyah

The Darul Islam movement, led by S. M. Kartosoewirjo, first emerged in the mid-1940s in West Java as part of the broader armed anti-colonial movement against Dutch reoccupation after the Second World War. Kartosoewirjo declared the formation of an Indonesian Islamic State *Negara Islam Indonesia* (NII) based on *sharia* in 1949. At the same time, armed elements from the Darul Islam movement launched insurgency operations against the newly formed Indonesian Republic, which Kartosoewirjo viewed as a betrayal of the anti-colonial enterprise. By 1954, the movement had spread to Central Java, Aceh, South Sulawesi, and South Kalimantan, posing a serious internal security threat. A combination of military campaigns and offers of amnesty to Darul Islam members, however, gradually eroded the influence of the movement.[31]

The collapse of the Darul Islam Movement did not signal the end of Islamist extremism. Rather, it forced those extremist forces to evolve and take on a different, more clandestine form. In 1993, a new and more lethal extremist movement known as al-Jama'ah al-Islamiyyah – commonly referred to as *Jemaah Islamiyah*, or JI – was founded by two former Darul Islam leaders, Abdullah Sungkar and Abu Bakar Ba'asyir. JI saw itself as the heir of Darul Islam, although it sought to achieve the goal of an Islamic state through more militant means, including the deliberate targeting of civilians. Many prominent members of JI were veterans of the *jihad* against the Soviet Union in Afghanistan during the 1980s, and had been recruited through Darul Islam channels.[32] The Bali bombings of October 2002, however, proved to be a watershed for JI, sparking an internal debate over the issue of the killing of Muslims and whether the organization should focus its immediate attention on proselytization rather than bombings in order to advance its goals.

Together with a crackdown by Indonesian security forces, this schism eventually forced a split in JI, with a hardline faction led by two key Malaysian leaders – Noordin Top and Azahari Husin – breaking away from the main organization and continuing a reign of terror with the Australian Embassy bombing (September 2004), the JW Marriott Hotel in Jakarta (August 2003), and the Marriott and Ritz-Carlton hotels in Jakarta (July 2009). While security operations have since led to the deaths of both men, the spring 2010 emergence of a heretofore unknown group in Aceh, called Al-Qaeda in Indonesia, underscores the fact that while on the run from increasingly effective security operations, jihadi groups and individuals may be active and evolving.

Furthermore, Islamic *jihadi* extremism found new expression in Indonesia through the growing appeal of the Islamic State of Iraq and As-sham, otherwise known as ISIS, in the country. Since 2014, videos have surfaced of Indonesians who have arrived in Iraq and Syria and who are engaging in armed conflict in support of ISIS and other *jihadi* groups such as Jabaat al-Nusra. At the time of writing, it is estimated that 500-700 Indonesians have made their way to these conflict zones in the Middle East, but it is difficult to determine conclusively what the exact number is.[33] Notably, a significant number of these are women and children.[34]

Indonesia was the victim of the first ISIS-inspired attack in Southeast Asia. This occurred on January 14, 2016, when self-proclaimed followers of ISIS set off bombs at a Starbucks outside the Sarinah mall and at a nearby police outpost, and gunfire broke out on the streets at Jalan Tamrin in the heart of Jakarta.[35] While the casualty toll was limited, it could have been higher had the militants succeeded in conducting the attack on a much larger and more popular shopping mall, as was their original intent. They were discouraged by the tight security at that mall.

The emerging influence of ISIS has caused a split in the Indonesian *jihadi* community. Pro-ISIS elements include followers of the late Poso-based *jihadi* leader, Santoso, as well as Aman Abdurrahman, who is currently incarcerated but who has actively translated ISIS material into Indonesian for mass consumption in Indonesia. In Syria, the Indonesian Bahrum Naim claims to be the leader of "ISIS Indonesia," although at this writing there is no clear evidence that such a group exists. It is important to note that *Jemaah Islamiyah* is at odds with ISIS as a result of both theological and personality differences. Ironically, because of its anti-ISIS position, *Jemaah Islamiyah* has been granted a public platform in the country of late, from which it has readily denounced ISIS. An example is how Abu Tholut (Imron), a convicted terrorist serving a prison sentence in Indonesia, has been given airtime to criticize ISIS. Notwithstanding the higher visibility of ISIS today, in Indonesia *Jemaah Islamiyah* maintains a much larger following. Moreover, *Jemaah Islamiyah* has, over the years, managed to regroup and consolidate, as well as recruit new members.[36]

ISLAMISM AND SOCIETY

Like most of the Muslim world, Indonesia was not immune from the global Islamic resurgence that began in the late 1960s and early 1970s as a consequence of the failure of Arab nationalism. During this period, numerous students made their way to the great Islamic learning centers of the Arab world. Many were also sent to secular schools and universities in Europe on government scholarships, where Islamic civil society movements were active among Muslim communities. Locally, an Islamic *dawah* (proselytization) movement began in Bandung around the campus-based Salman mosque and soon spread across the country to other tertiary education institutions. This movement was organized around study groups modelled after the Egyptian Muslim Brotherhood, as previously discussed. The related *tarbiyah* (education) movement began in the early 1980s at various university campuses.[37] The legacy of this process remains evident today in the increased social activism of the country's various Muslim communities.

A driving force for the development of the *dawah* movement was the socio-political suppression of Islamist intellectuals. The Suharto administration had placed substantial restrictions on the expression of religiously-referenced political aspirations on the part of the Muslim majority, to the extent that socially active Muslim groups like the

NU and Muhammadiyah were effectively de-politicized. More conservative Muslims were also concerned about the increasing assertiveness of what was thought to be "liberal" Islamic ideas in Indonesian society. In the words of one scholar:

> the general mass media, as another manifestation of the public sphere, tended to serve as the state ideological apparatus in championing modernization. The media was thus preconditioned to be sympathetic to the renewal movement. Realizing that the public sphere was hostile to their ideo-political aspirations, the Islamist intellectuals created a subtle and fluid social movement, which was relatively impervious to state control, as a new foundation for constructing collective solidarity and identity."[38]

Salafi influences within the country can largely be traced to the late 1950s, when a small number of modernist Muslim intellectuals were attracted to the ideas of the Muslim Brotherhood.[39] However, it was not until the late 1970s and early 1980s that these ideas and organizational techniques began to win a sizeable following. The main group influenced by these ideas was known as the *Tarbiyah* group. Unlike in Malaysia, where Islamists leaders had direct relationships with fundamentalist *Ikhwan* and *Jamaat* leaders, Indonesian Islamist leaders learned these ideas mainly through Indonesian translations of books written by *Ikhwan* activists.

During this period, Indonesia was still ruled by the authoritarian New Order regime, which was extremely suspicious of Islamic parties and groups. It was Indonesia's fifth Prime Minister, Mohammad Natsir, and his organization, the DDII, that was chiefly responsible for encouraging Islamic student activism in Indonesian universities.[40] While it is difficult to establish the extent of Natsir's relationship with *Ikhwan* and *Jamaat* leaders, it is clear that he played a major role in facilitating the travel of Indonesian students to *Ikhwan* and *Jamaat*-dominated universities in the Middle East and Pakistan. He was also responsible for introducing the *Ikhwan's* religio-political ideas and methods of organization to Muslim students on various campuses. It was these students who established the *Lembaga Dakwah Kampus*, LDK (Campus Proselytising Network). *Ikhwan*-inspired students subsequently formed a separate organization, the *Kesatuan Aksi Mahasiswa Muslim Indonesia*, (KAMMI) ("Indonesian Muslim Undergraduate Action Association"). With the collapse of the New Order regime, activists of KAMMI formed what would become PKS, which was discussed at the beginning of this chapter. PKS maintains strong links with the broader transnational Salafi network, often attending international Islamist gatherings organized by the *Ikhwan* and *Jamaat*.

While conservative forces aligned themselves behind the Salafi movement and the various social and, eventually, political organizations, alternative patterns of thinking were also emerging elsewhere within the Indonesian Muslim community. During the late 1970s and early 1980, people – particularly younger intellectuals – sought to recalibrate Islam's role in Indonesian society. This phenomenon, initially called the "reform movement" (*gerakan pembaruan*) and more recently "cultural Islam" (*Islam kultural*), consciously rejected the political agenda and aspirations of Islamist parties since independence and sought to redefine Islam's relations with—and role in—the state from a purely apolitical, cultural perspective. Among the chief proponents of this movement were former president Abdurrahman Wahid and the well-known intellectual, the late Nurcholish Madjid.[41]

Cultural Islam was particularly critical of political Islam (or Islamist activism) on several counts. Islamist parties had experienced very limited success in achieving their goals. Moreover, they had not been able to unite Muslims politically, nor managed to garner a majority of votes at general elections. Neither had they succeeded in getting Islamic laws implemented in local or national government. What was required instead, proponents of cultural Islam believed, were alternative ways of achieving the aspirations of Indonesian Muslims to live pious lives—aspirations that had in fact been hampered by the preoccupation of Islamist leaders with politics.

The position of supporters of Cultural Islam on the formal role of the *sharia* in the state was highly controversial. Many younger intellectuals repudiated the concept of an Islamic state, arguing that the Quran contains no prescription for the structure of the state. Instead, they supported the religiously neutral *Pancasila* as the basis of the Indonesian state, asserting that the pluralism and religious equality inherent in the concept were consistent with Islamic principles. In addition, this sentiment disputed the notion that Muslims should only support Islamic parties. Pluralist, "deconfessionalized" parties were not less virtuous for Muslims to belong to than exclusively Islamic ones, they argued.[42]

The democratization of Indonesia was a critical factor in expanding the space for Islamic discourse and activism. Along with the proliferation of faith-based political parties, Indonesia also witnessed the emergence of many Islamic civil society groups, including the radical organizations introduced above. This included Muslim groups whose interpretation of Islamic scripture was deemed by the mainstream as unorthodox. One such movement was the Liberal Islam Network, or Jaringan Islam Liberal, a movement that shunned received wisdom and encouraged critical thinking among Muslims. Formed in early 2001, it has come under heavy criticism from fundamentalist quarters in the Indonesian Muslim intellectual community, including the Majelis Mujahidin Indonesia. At the same time, the movement has also had an uneasy relationship with more moderate organizations such as the NU.[43]

An increasing concern in this climate of openness has been the instances of hostility and even violence perpetrated by more extremist Muslim groups against fringe organizations. Such is the case against the Ahmadiyah, an Islamic sect of South Asian origin deemed deviant by the two largest Muslim organizations in Indonesia, Nahdlatul

Ulama and Muhammadiyah. While *fatwas* against the Ahmadiyah have not resulted in violence against them by NU and Muhammadiyah members, the Ahmadiyah have nevertheless been victimized by the FPI. On January 28, 2011, members of FPI attacked an Ahmadiyah mosque in Makassar and forced the congregation to evacuate the premises before destroying their property.[44] Since then, attacks on Ahmadiyah places of worship and members by Muslim vigilante groups such as FPI have become all too frequent. The Indonesian government of Susilo Bambang Yudhoyono appears either unable or unwilling to stem this vigilantism.

At its annual convention in August 2015, NU introduced the concept of "Islam Nusantara" or "Islam of the archipelago" into the discourse of Islamic thought and practice in Indonesia. Conceptualized as a counter-narrative to the virulent ideology of groups such as ISIS, Islam Nusantara is predicated on what is essentially Indonesia's rich Islamic tradition, which promotes peace, moderation, and tolerance. Despite the ambiguity surrounding the concept, ambitious NU and Indonesian leaders such as Said Aqil Siradj have suggested that Islam Nusantara could potentially take on a transnational character and be embraced and practiced by Muslims throughout the world. Yet the concept is not without controversy. Not only are the expansionist aspirations of its progenitors far too ambitious – it is difficult to envisage Arab Muslims in the heartland embrace a movement that emerged from the peripheries of the "Muslim World" - the legitimacy of the concept itself remains debated within Indonesian circles, including among NU leaders themselves. Conservative critics of Islam Nusantara have dismissed it as *Bida'a* (innovation), which is forbidden in Islam. Others have criticized it as the contamination of "pure" Islam by Javanese culture, the dominant culture in Indonesia.

Indonesia's reputation for religious tolerance suffered a notable blow in 2016. Radicals mobilized by the National Movement to Guard the MUI Fatwa, a collection of Islamist groups, staged two massive rallies calling for the conviction of Jakarta's incumbent governor, Basuki "Ahok" Tjahaja Purnama, for blasphemy against the Quran. Purnama is a blunt, ethnically Chinese, Christian politician. As the nomenclature of the Islamist movement that organized the rallies denotes, the rallies were inspired by an MUI *fatwa* that declared Basuki a blasphemer for making reference to the Quran in a campaign rally speech. Under pressure from this Muslim social movement, the Indonesian government of President Joko "Jokowi" Widodo took the decision to distance itself from Basuki, who had hitherto been an ally of President Jokowi himself, and limited its intervention to calls for restraint.[45]

ISLAMISM AND THE STATE

While Indonesia is often considered a secular state, it is officially a state based on religion as premised in the first principle of the *Pancasila*, which enshrines "belief in Almighty God" (*KeTuhanan yang Maha Esa*). This was, in effect, a compromise between those wanting a secular state and those favoring an Islamic state. While there is no official state religion or formal acknowledgment of the authority of religious law in the constitution, the use of the term "Almighty God" implies monotheism, a concession to Muslim sentiment.

Indonesia's political and constitutional history reveals that among the most divisive debates surrounds the formal role of Islam in the state and the question of the position of *sharia* in the constitution. Much of this debate focused on the Jakarta Charter, an agreement struck between Muslim and nationalist leaders on June 22, 1945 as part of the preparations for Indonesia's independence. The most controversial part of the charter was a seven-word clause: "with the obligation for adherents of Islam to practice Islamic law" (*dengan kewajipan menjalankan syari'at Islam bagi pemeluk-pemeluknya*). Although often portrayed as an attempt to make Indonesia an Islamic state, the inclusion of these seven words in the constitution would not, by itself, have had this effect. Rather, it was left to Islamic parties to demonstrate whether they could garner sufficient support in parliament to advance *sharia*-based legislation.[46] Islamic leaders did, however, succeeded in having a stipulation inserted into the draft constitution that mandated the president be a Muslim.

On August 18, 1945, the day after the proclamation of independence, pro-charter Muslim leaders came under strong pressure from "secular" Muslims, nationalists, and religious minorities to drop the seven words regarding the practice of Islamic law, despite the initial agreement of the committee responsible for finalizing the constitution. Those opposing the clause were concerned that the embryonic Indonesian nation would collapse as pressure from Islamists caused the non-Muslim dominated outer islands to secede. Eventually, Muslim leaders were persuaded, in the interest of national unity, to exclude the charter. In addition to that, the clause requiring the president of the country to be Muslim was also dropped.

It was not until the 1970s that Islam experienced a resurgence in Indonesia. That period witnessed a surge in mosque attendance, enrollment in religious classes, adoption of Islamic dress (including the veil, worn by women), and expansion of Muslim education and social organizations. Although there were a small number of extremists at its fringe, the Islamic resurgence was never politically radical. Its primary social impulse was pietistic and ethical, aimed at heightening the role of Islam in social life.[47]

The resurgence put greater pressure on the government to make concessions in favor of Indonesia's Muslims. In response, Suharto began to extend greater aid to the country's Muslim community in the late 1980s, increasing state subsidies for mosque building, Islamic education, Muslim television programming, the celebration of religious holidays, and preferential treatment for Muslim entrepreneurs in state contracts. He lifted an earlier ban on the veil in state schools, and imposed tighter restrictions on the activities of Christian missionaries. The president even went as far as to sponsor an Islamic faction in the armed forces, previously a bastion of conservative secular nationalism, with the assistance of his son-in-law, Prabowo Subianto.[48]

The slew of legislative and institutional concessions to the Muslim community was a strong indicator of the New Order's stance towards Islam. Prominent among them were "the expansion of the authority of religious courts in 1989, the establishment of the Indonesian Muslim Intellectuals association (ICMI) in 1990, lifting of the ban on female state school students wearing *hijabs* in 1991, the upgrading of government involvement in alms collection and distribution, the founding of an Islamic bank (BMI) in 1992, and the abolition of the state lottery (SDSB) in 1993."[49]

While major Muslim organizations agreed to cooperate with the New Order regime in facilitating and implementing its social and educational initiatives, they also subtly pressed for democratic reforms. This challenge from moderate Muslims led Suharto to change his political strategy in the mid-1990s, and to reach out to hard-line groups like *Dewan Dakwah Islamiyah Indonesia* (DDII - Indonesian Council for Islamic Predication) and *Komite Indonesia Untuk Solidaritas dengan Dunia Islam* (KISDI – the Indonesian Committee for Solidarity of the Islamic World), which had developed reputations for being strongly anti-Western and anti-Christian. Suharto's efforts had a backlash effect, however. "With the onset of the Asian economic crisis in late 1997, support for the Suharto regime waned, and the President was forced from power in May 1998."[50]

Nevertheless, the end of Suharto's rule did not spell the end of efforts to exploit religious tensions for political advantage in Indonesian politics. After May 1998, and in the wake of the upheaval of post-Suharto democratisation in Indonesia, more than a few politicians and leaders appealed to ethno-religious sentiments in order to enhance their credentials. The tactic had an especially bloody consequence in Maluku, Central Kalimantan, and Sulawesi, upsetting a delicate demographic balance between Christians and Muslims with the rise of sectarian paramilitaries and bloody campaigns of ethnic cleansing.

Despite the lack of official support for the implementation of *sharia*, the issue appears to be gaining some traction at the regional level. One such case would be the north Sumatran province of Aceh, where sharia was promulgated under special autonomy laws in early 2002, though there is intense debate within the local Islamic community over the scope of the laws and the details of their implementation. The *sharia* issue has also attracted strong support from Muslim groups in South Sulawesi, West Sumatra and Banten, but is still far short of receiving majority support. In a number of districts in West Java, sharia has been implemented in a *de facto* fashion by local Muslim groups, often in concert with district government officials and *ulama*.[51]

The prevalence of cases of *sharia*-inspired laws and by-laws being adopted in Aceh and several other local districts, especially conservative variants associated with hudud law, is rooted in the agreement between the Indonesian government and the Free Aceh Movement, where the introduction of *sharia* law was one of the concessions made to end a decades-old separatist insurgency (even though it was not clear that this was demanded by the Free Aceh Movement).[52] After implementation, there has been very little evidence that the Indonesian government harbors any intention to slow down, let alone overturn, this gradual process of *shariaization*, despite the fact that, as critics have pointed out, it runs contrary to Indonesia's secular constitution.

ENDNOTES

[1] "Indonesia," CIA World Factbook, n.d., https://www.cia.gov/library/publications/resources/the-world-factbook/geos/id.html.

[2] Greg Fealy, "Divided Majority: Limits of Indonesian Political Islam," in Shahram Akbarzadeh and Abdullah Saeed, eds., Islam and Political Legitimacy (London: Routledge/Curzon, 2003), 151.

[3] Anies Rasyid Baswedan, "Political Islam in Indonesia: Present and Future Trajectory," Asian Survey 44, no. 5 (October 2004), 677.

[4] Ibid., 675.

[5] Bambang Sulistiyo and Alfian, "Voices of Democracy from Within the Tarbiyah," in Asrori S. Karni, ed., A Celebration of Democracy (Jakarta: PT. Era Media Informasi, 2006), 200.

[6] R. William Liddle and Saiful Mujani, "Indonesia in 2004: The Rise of Susilo Bambang Yudhoyono," Asian Survey 45, no. 1 (January 2005), 123.

[7] Ibid., 121.

[8] The NU was a non-political Islamic organization that was founded in 1926, became a political party in 1952, and participated in the 1955 and 1971 elections. In 1973, the NU was merged into the PPP. In 1984, the NU declared itself kembali ke khittah (return to origin) as a non-political religious movement, and officially retreated from partisan politics. The NU remained neutral until it made a return to partisan politics by establishing the PKB (National Awakening Party) in July 1998.

[9] Stephen Sherlock, The 2004 Indonesian Elections: How the System Works and What the Parties Stand For (Canberra: Centre for Democratic Institutions, Research School of Social Sciences, Australian National University, 2004), 17.

[10] Ibid., 32.

[11] See Noorhaidi, "Islam, Militancy and the Quest for Identity in Post New Order Indonesia," Letters Proefschriften, 2005, http://igitur-archive.library.uu.nl/dissertations/2006-0705-200332/c1.pdf, 3.

[12] Ibid.

[13] Sherlock, The 2004 Indonesian Elections, 17.

[14] Noorhaidi, "Islam, Militancy and the Quest for Identity in Post New Order Indonesia," 6.

[15] For more details, see Edward Aspinall, "Indonesia," in Bogdan Szajkowski, ed., Revolutionary and Dissident Movements of the World (London: John Harper Publishing, 2004).

[16] Noorhaidi, "Islam, Militancy and the Quest for Identity in Post New Order Indonesia," 4.

[17] M. Rizieq Syihab, Kyai Kampung: Ujung Tombak Perjuangan Umat Islam (Ciputat: Sekretariat FPI, 1999).

[18] "Police Question Rights Body Over FPI Attack," Jakarta Post, May 26, 2010.

[19] "Indonesia's Muslim militants," BBC (London), August 8, 2003, http://news.bbc.co.uk/2/hi/asia-pacific/2333085.stm.

[20] Greg Fealy, "Bigger than Ahok: Explaining the 2 December Rally," December 7, 2016, http://indonesiaatmelbourne.unimelb.edu.au/bigger-than-ahok-explaining-jakartas-2-december-mass-rally/.

[21] Salafis are those who attempt to reform Islam by taking it away from its traditional association with syncretism and re-orienting it towards scripturalism.

[22] Syihab, Kyai Kampung: Ujung Tombak Perjuangan Umat Islam.

[23] See Kirsten E. Schulze, "Laskar Jihad and the Conflict in Ambon," Brown Journal of World Affairs 9, iss.1 (Spring 2002).

[24] Noorhaidi. Laskar Jihad: Islam, militancy and the quest for identity in post-New Order Indonesia (Utrecht: Utrecht University, 2005), http://igitur-archive.library.uu.nl/dissertations/2006-0705-200332/c1.pdf, 6.

[25] Ibid

[26] See Martin van Bruinessen, "Genealogies of Islamic Radicalism in Post-Suharto Indonesia," in Joseph Chinyong Liow and Nadirsyah Hosen (eds.), Islam in Southeast Asia vol. IV (London: Routledge, 2009), 52-53. In the 1950s, the Darul Islam (DI, the Islamic State) movement, spread to South Sulawesi and Aceh under the leadership of Kahar Muzakkar and Daud Beureu'eh respectively. At its core, DI is a political movement which was dissatisfied with the policies of the central government under President Sukarno. However, they used Islam to legitimize their existence and at the same time to denounce the nation-state of Indonesia.

[27] Noorhaidi, "Islam, Militancy and the Quest for Identity in Post New Order Indonesia," 7.

[28] Saiful Umam, "Radical Muslims in Indonesia: The Case of Ja'Far Umar Thalib and The Laskar Jihad," Explorations in Southeast Asian Studies 6, no. 1 (Spring 2006), 11.

[29] Ibid.

[30] Ibidem.

[31] Greg Fealy, Virginia Hooker and Sally White, "Indonesia," in Greg Fealy and Virginia Hooker, eds., Voices of Islam in Southeast Asia: A Contemporary Sourcebook (Singapore: Institute of Southeast Asian Studies, 2006), 49.

[32] Ibid.

[33] Foreign Fighters: An Updated Assessment of the Flow of Foreign Fighters into Syria and Iraq, The Soufan Group, December 2015, pg. 8. http://soufangroup.com/wp-content/uploads/2015/12/TSG_ForeignFightersUpdate4.pdf.

[34] The respected observer of extremism in Indonesia, Sidney Jones, estimates that up to 40 percent of Indonesians in Syria and Iraq are women and children under the age of 15. See Sidney Jones, "Understanding the ISIS Threat in Southeast Asia," ISEAS Yusof Ishak Institute, Discussion Paper, January 12, 2016, p.2. http://www.iseas-rof.sg/sites/live.rof2016.site.gsi.sg/files/ROF%20Session%204a.pdf.

[35] Sidney Jones, "Battling ISIS in Indonesia," New York Times, January 18, 2016, http://www.nytimes.com/2016/01/19/opinion/battling-isis-in-indonesia.html?_r=0.

[36] "Extremist Group Jemaah Islamiyah Active Again, Recruiting and Collecting Funds," Straits Times, February 15, 2016, http://news.asiaone.com/news/asia/extremist-group-jemaah-islamiyah-active-again-recruiting-and-collecting-funds.

[37] Andreas Ufen, "Mobilising Political Islam: Indonesia and Malaysia Compared," Commonwealth & Comparative Politics 47, no. 3 (2009), 316. For further reading on the dakwah movements and tarbiyah movements, see Yudi Latif, "The Rupture of Young Muslim Intelligentsia in the Modernization of Indonesia," Studia Islamika 12, no. 3 (2005), 373-420, and Salman, "The Tarbiyah Movement: Why People Join This Indonesian Contemporary Islamic Movement," Studia Islamika 13, no. 2 (2006), 171-240.

[38] Latif, "The Rupture of Young Muslim Intelligentsia in the Modernization of Indonesia," 391. Some scholars refer to the renewal movement (gerakan pembaharuan) as reform movement (gerakan pembaruan).

[39] Muhammad Natsir was the former Prime Minister and Information Minister of Indonesia. He was leader of the Masyumi party, which was banned under the New Order regime in 1965. For more on Natsir, see Luth Thohir, M. Natsir: Dakwah dan Pemikirannya, (Jakarta: Gema Insani, 1999).

[40] Any Muhammad Furkon, Partai Keadilan Sejahtera: Ideologi dan Praksis Kaum Muda Muslim Indonesia Kontemporer (Jakarta: Penerbit Terajau, 2004), 124.

[41] Greg Fealy, "Divided Majority: Limits of Indonesian Political Islam," in Shahram Akbarzadeh and Abdullah Saeed, eds., Islam and Political Legitimacy (London: RoutledgeCurzon, 2003), 161.

[42] Ibid., 162.

[43] Anita Rachman, "Fundamental differences to the fore at NU meeting," Jakarta Globe, March 25, 2010.

[44] Hadianto Wirajuda, "Ahmadiyah attack a threat to Indonesia's democracy," Jakarta Post, February 10, 2011.

[45] Greg Fealy, "Bigger than Ahok: Explaining the 2 December Rally," December 7, 2016, http://indonesiaatmelbourne.unimelb.edu.au/bigger-than-ahok-explaining-jakartas-2-december-mass-rally/.

[46] Fealy, "Divided Majority: Limits of Indonesian Political Islam," 155.

[47] Robert W. Hefner, "State, Society, and Secularity in Contemporary Indonesia," in Theodore Friend, ed., Religion and Religiosity in the Philippines and Indonesia (Washington: Southeast Asia Studies Program, 2006), 42.

[48] Ibid.

[49] Fealy, "Divided Majority: Limits of Indonesian Political Islam," 163.

[50] Ibid.

[51] Ibidem, 164-165.

[52] Dewi Kurniati, "Shariah in Aceh: Eroding Indonesia's secular freedoms," Jakarta Globe, August 18, 2010.

Malaysia

Quick Facts

Population: 30,949,962 (July 2016 est.)

Area: 329,847 sq km

Ethnic Groups: Malay 50.4%, Chinese 23.7%, Indigenous 11%, Indian 7.1%, other 7.8%

Religions: Muslim 60.4%, Buddhist 19.2%, Christian 9.1%, Hindu 6.3%, Confucianism , Taoism, other traditional Chinese religions 2.6%, other or unknown 1.5%, none 0.8%

Government Type: Constitutional monarchy

GDP (official exchange rate): S$302.7 billion (2015 est.)

Map and Quick Facts courtesy of the CIA World Factbook (January 2017)

Overview

Malaysia has long been viewed as a developed, pro-Western and moderate Muslim-majority country. In recent decades, however, the country as a whole has been experiencing a swing toward Islamic conservatism. This shift appears to be gaining momentum, as evidenced by the increasing popularity of sharia law in public discourse, the state-sanctioned suppression of civil rights and liberties in the name of Islam, the inability of civil courts to stand up against controversial sharia court decisions, increasing cases of moral policing by Islamic religious authorities (including the policing of non-Muslims, in some instances), and more frequent references to the "Islamic state."[1] This increasing visibility of Islam in Malaysian society and politics is driven not only by the Islamist opposition party Parti Islam Se-Malaysia (Islamic Party of Malaysia, or PAS), but also by the United Malays National Organization (UMNO), whose members were apparently the architects of Malaysia's brand of progressive, moderate Islam.[2] Alternative actors such as non-governmental orga-

nizations (NGOs) and civil society groups likewise are increasingly participating in the politicization of Islam in Malaysia today, at times even eclipsing mainstream political parties in terms of intensity.

Islam in Malaysia is arguably fragmented and variegated in both substance and expression, with religious vocabulary and idioms being mobilized by the state, opposition forces, and a wide array of civil society groups. While Malaysian Islamists nominally operate within the boundaries of the country's mainstream political processes, they also work to define those boundaries. Moreover, even as the Muslim opposition attempts to shed its doctrinaire image in pursuit of an agenda of reform, the "moderate" UMNO-led government has pursued an agenda that has resulted in the constriction of the country's cultural and religious space.

ISLAMIST ACTIVITY

PAS - Parti Se-Islam Malaysia (Pan Malaysian Islamic Party)

PAS was established as the Pan Malaysian Islamic Party in 1951 by dissidents from UMNO's Bureau of Religious Affairs, and has participated in every Malaysian parliamentary election since 1955.[3] Since its inception, PAS has advocated for the promotion of Malay interests and the protection of Muslim rights. In its early days, PAS maintained a more rural constituency, particularly among ethnic Arabs and religiously-educated Malays.[4] By 1982, however, PAS's political stance was infused with Islamist aspirations. During this time, old-guard ethno-nationalists were voted out via party elections and replaced by *ulama* (religious scholars) leadership. This transformation coincided with burgeoning sentiments among Malay-Muslims that Islam is *addin* (a way of life), and had to be accorded greater prominence not only in their personal lives, but in the public sphere as well.[5]

The global resurgence of Islamic consciousness during the 1970s and early 1980s, coupled with the religious leadership epitomized by the likes of Fadzil Noor, Abdul Hadi Awang and Nakhaie Ahmad, contributed to the party's pronounced Islamic agenda.[6] The result has been a public battle between PAS and UMNO that hinges on the discourse of morality, with PAS admonishing UMNO for marginalizing the position of Islamic laws and the political leadership's failure to observe Islamic ethics and morals. From the outset, the party's goal was a *sharia*-based state in which economic, political and social systems conformed to Islamic values.

While PAS's commitment to its religious agenda had in the past prevented the party from fruitful cooperation with secular opposition allies,[7] a steady expansion of PAS's support base in states such as Terengganu, Kedah and Perlis and in the universities throughout the country in the 1990s indicated the party's rising popularity and the appeal of *sharia*-centered politics. The party's outlook is buttressed by its unyielding belief that the creation of an Islamic state is both a viable and necessary alternative to the UMNO-dominated secular state. Since 1990, when it was returned to power in the state of Kelantan, PAS has presented draft proposals to the parliament for the introduction of *hudud* criminal law in Kelantan.[8] Similar efforts were made after the PAS electoral triumph in Terengganu in 1999. However, as criminal law falls under the jurisdiction of the federal and not the *sharia* courts, the motions were withdrawn on both occasions.

A turning point in the party's Islamic-state agenda came in the run-up to the March 2008 elections. Given the party's dismal showing in the 2004 elections, PAS leaders promised to soften the party's stance on the Islamic-state issue.[9] Ex-deputy prime minister of Malaysia and current PKR adviser Anwar Ibrahim echoed this shift, claiming: "PAS's intention to establish an Islamic state is no longer an issue."[10] In the 2008 election, PAS distanced itself from the Islamic-state objective and attempted to leverage the disenfranchisement of Malaysia's ethnic minorities in the wake of UMNO's rallying call of Malay primacy.[11]

In an obvious effort to woo non-Muslim votes, PAS leaders made clear that their campaign at the national level would focus on a manifesto that holds out the promise of a welfare state system, known as *"negara kebajikan,"* accessible to all Malaysians.[12] Components of this agenda included populist initiatives such as free education, free water utilities throughout the country, cheaper fuel and health subsidies.[13] Furthermore, wealth and income distribution would be pursued through a taxation policy that targeted revenue from large businesses in order to offset subsidies earmarked for the poor.[14] Not only was the welfare-state concept intended to dull the edges of its Islamist agenda, the PAS hoped it would enhance the appeal of the party across the electorate, particularly since specific reference had also been made to issues of meritocracy and the importance of the presence of non-Malay ministers.[15] Indeed, these were all important developments in ensuring non-Muslim support for PAS in the 2008 elections, in which the party made considerable gains and raised its total number of seats in the National Parliament from 7 to 23. In a continuation of this trajectory, the party also created a non-Muslim wing in 2010, and planned to field non-Muslim candidates in mixed seats during the next election.

PAS fulfilled its promise and fielded non-Muslim candidates during the 2013 general elections.[16] When the election took place on May 5, 2013, the incumbent coalition *Barisan Nasional* (BN), led by incumbent Prime Minister Najib Razak, maintained a majority in Parliament despite a resurgence of the opposition. In protest, *Pakatan Rakyat* (PR), the minority coalition of which PAS is a part, demonstrated against the election results. Although the PR coalition's other constituent parties—the secular Democratic Action Party (DAP) and the moderate PKR—agitated on the basis of electoral malfeasance, the PAS took the opportunity to advocate for an Islamic state, and rumors of a possible "Malaysian Arab Spring" have since circulated among opposition leaders.[17]

Within PAS, rumblings of dissatisfaction over the party's less than stellar electoral performance began to grow. It had not gone unnoticed by some PAS leaders that the party was defeated in areas with a Malay-majority populace. The party has since lost two seats of the 23 it won in 2008. Some PAS leaders later attributed the decline in the party's popularity among its core Malay base to its support for the dismantling of longstanding race-based affirmative action policies.[18]

At the PAS *muktamar* (annual congress) held at the end of 2013, the gulf between those who wished to return to a more conservative religious stance and the progressives who wished to continue building on inclusive political engagement widened considerably. Although several conservatives were voted into PAS's central committee at the 2013 *muktamar*, the overall make-up of the party did not change. As such, despite resentments held by a sizeable segment within PAS, the party nevertheless remained with the PR coalition.[19]

However, by 2015, PAS conservatives had actively renewed its *hudud* implementation agenda, with the PAS-dominated Kelantan state assembly unanimously passing amendments to the Syariah Criminal Code that would approve *hudud*.[20] Inevitably, this move met with strong condemnation from its coalition allies, DAP and PKR. After PAS leadership was firmly secured by the conservatives at the 2015 *muktamar*, PAS severed its ties with PR. Several months later, the progressive faction, which was sidelined within PAS, split to form a new political party, the *Parti Amanah Negara*.

PAS's strategy of cooperation with the secular-oriented opposition coalition did not result in further electoral gains in 2013, and this likely provided the impetus for conservatives within the party to re-establish their dominance. Since then, PAS has redoubled its efforts to pursue the implementation of its *hudud* agenda. In 2016, PAS president Abdul Hadi Awang succeeded in having his Private Member's Bill, on amendments that would increase the penalties meted out under the Syariah Courts (Criminal Jurisdiction) Act, tabled in Parliament.

Radical Salafi groups

Malaysia is home to a pair of notable radical Islamist groups who adhere broadly to the exclusionary Salafi strain of political Islam:

The KMM (*Kumpulan Mujahidin Malaysia/Kumpulan Militan Malaysia*, or Malaysian Mujahidin Group/Malaysian Militant Group), an alleged underground militant group, was uncovered as a result of its attempted bombing of a shopping mall in Jakarta in August 2001. The group is reported to favor the overthrow of the Malaysian government and the creation of a regional Islamic state.[21]

KMM differs from other militant organizations in Malaysia in terms of its reach. Though established in Malaysia, several sources have indicated that KMM enjoys close links with *Jemaah Islamiyah* in Indonesia.[22] Nevertheless, the exact nature of this relationship remains murky. Despite inconclusive evidence, Malaysian intelligence sources also revealed that KMM allegedly participated in religiously inspired riots in Maluku and Ambon in 2000, and supplied arms to radical Muslims involved in those incidents.[23] Subsequent arrests found leaders having in their possession "documents on guerrilla warfare and map reading, along with studies of militant groups in the Philippines, Chechnya, Afghanistan and Indonesia."[24] In response, Malaysian security forces launched a nationwide operation to detain remaining KMM members. Eventually, up to seventy KMM members were detained without trial under the ISA (Internal Security Act) for allegedly trying to overthrow the government through violent means in the name of *jihad*.[25] Most of the detained members have since been released and the organization has been outlawed.

Al-Maunah (Brotherhood of Inner Power) was a non-governmental organization involved in the teaching of martial arts, particularly the development of one's inner powers and the practice of Islamic traditional medicine. At its most prolific, it was said to have more than 1,000 members in Malaysia and overseas, particularly in Tripoli, Libya.[26]

In June 2000, the *Al-Maunah* movement managed to successfully carry out an arms heist from two Malaysian Armed Forces military camps in Perak. The heist served as a major source of embarrassment for the government, given that the members of the group managed to penetrate the camp's security infrastructure by dressing up in military fatigues and driving jeeps painted in camouflage green, indicating the likelihood that the heist was an inside job.[27] According to police reports, the group had at least several hundred members led by a former army corporal, Mohammad Amin Razali. Several other sources revealed that civil servants, security services personnel, and even some UMNO members numbered among its ranks.[28] Upon ascertaining *Al-Maunah's* responsibility for the arms heist, Malaysian security forces embarked on a high-profile operation against the organization's camp in Sauk, Perak in July 2000 where nineteen members were eventually captured. Apprehended members of *Al-Maunah* were subsequently charged with treason and plotting to overthrow the government, with the intention of establishing an Islamic state. *Al-Maunah* no longer exists.

It is important to note that both KMM and *Al-Maunah* cite local issues as the primary causes of their grievances, pursuing a predominantly domestic political agenda. For example, the *Al-Maunah* perpetrators demanded the resignation of Prime Minister Mahathir and his cabinet, while in the case of the KMM, its three key objectives—"to seek religious purity among Malay-Muslims", "to ensure that PAS' political struggle was maintained and encouraged", and "to implement *shari'a* within Malaysia"—all pertained to domestic political concerns, despite efforts on the part of the government to link them to a transnational terrorist agenda.[29]

Additionally, evidence linking these militant movements with external organizations remains nebulous and inconclusive. Although these domestic movements share some degree of ideological affinity as well as rudimentary contacts with external organizations, they are purportedly not controlled by any outside group.[30] Therefore, despite attempts to associate KMM with external groups and regional objectives such as the grandiose vision of a *Darul Islam Nusantara* in the region, no mention was made about links with either *Jemaah Islamiyah* or Al-Qaeda in the formal charges leveled against the organization. KMM was charged under the Internal Security Act (ISA) solely for its attempt to overthrow the government.[31]

In recent years, a growing concern for the influence of the Islamic State's (ISIS) ideology has enveloped Malaysia. Unlike in Indonesia and the Philippines, however, where pro-ISIS sentiments have coalesced around existing extremist groups, in Malaysia the phenomenon has mostly taken the form of self-radicalized individuals, most of whom have had little to no prior affiliation with any extremist groups. On June 28, 2016, a grenade was tossed into the Movida Restaurant and Bar in Puchong, Selangor state, in Malaysia. The perpetrators of the attack were arrested several days later and upon investigations, it was revealed that they had received instructions from Muhammad Wanndy Muhammad Jedi, a Malaysian *jihadi* believed to be based in Syria fighting with ISIS.[32]

ISLAMISM AND SOCIETY

Muslims constitute some 60 percent of the Malaysian population, with Buddhists accounting for nearly 20 percent, Christians nearly 10 percent, and Hindus just over 6 percent. Malaysian society on the whole has been experiencing a swing toward Islamic conservatism. This swing seems to be gaining momentum, as demonstrated by the increasing popularity of *sharia* in public discourse, state-sanctioned curtailment of civil rights and liberties in the name of Islam, the incapacity of civil courts to challenge controversial *sharia* court decisions, increasing incidences of moral policing by Islamic religious authorities (including policing of non-Muslims in some instances), and the alarming regularity of references to an "Islamic state."

With the changing complexion of PAS, and the UMNO-led government's systematic Islamization of the bureaucracy, social consciousness and political discourse in Malaysia has assumed a much more religious dimension. This has resulted in an intensification of the UMNO–PAS competition where the focus is on linking credibility and legitimacy to Islam. However there is also a concurrent Islamic discourse rooted in an increasingly vibrant civil society that encompasses NGOs as well as alternative expressions of Islamic consciousness (namely, alternative media sources beyond the mainstream government-controlled channels). Even as the heavily contested politics of UMNO and PAS began to converge, a parallel form of civic activism was emerging, which has brought together not just political parties but also professional, civil society, educational, and religious institutions.

NGO activism in Malaysia generally peaks during periods of major social upheaval in this otherwise comparatively peaceful sociocultural environment. Recently, the issues of apostasy, religious freedom, and the sanctity of the *sharia* have spurred a round of NGO political activism that has challenged the hegemony of the state along with the policies of the opposition PAS. Muslim and non-Muslim groups that extend across the political spectrum have, in their own way, spoken for and against the positions and policies of UMNO and PAS, at times compelling these mainstream political parties to negotiate their politics and recalibrate their narratives.

Islamic NGOs and civil society organizations are not the sole challengers of the religio-political agenda of both UMNO and PAS. Considering the demographic realities of Malaysia, any debate on Islamism elicits responses from the non-Muslim community as well. In recent times, non-Muslims have voiced concerns over their place in Malaysian society, and their ability to hedge against the intensification of Islamist discourse and its increasingly hegemonic nature.

The Malaysian Consultative Council for Buddhism, Christianity, Hinduism, and Sikhism (MCCBCHS) is an example of a non-Muslim interfaith organization that seeks to enhance dialogue and cooperation, not only among Buddhists, Christians, Hindus, and Sikhs, but also between these communities and Muslims in Malaysia. Since 2001, the MCCBCHS has been leading an effort driven by the non-Muslim community to establish an Inter-Religious Council (IRC) that would encourage dialogue across religious boundaries. In particular, the MCCBCHS felt that the "proper procedures" regarding marriage, divorce, and child custody issues relating to converts to Islam required clarification from Islamic clerics.[33] The group believed that there were "several gray areas in this matter, which has caused much emotional suffering and confusion for family members of converts," aside from the tension it placed on intercommunal relations.[34]

In Malaysia, civil society groups represent popular discourse in its most organized and mobilized form. Conversely, cyberspace and various alternative media sources are the new outlets and pathways of political expression that take Islamist debates deeper into Malaysian society.[35] Controversies related to various judicial rulings on the matter of apostasy, declarations by Malay-Muslim political leaders that Malaysia is an Islamic state, and the government's apparent intolerance for open discussions on the "sensitive" issue of Malay-Muslim rights and primacy, have highlighted the increasingly vital role these new forms of expression play on the Malaysian political scene. They can both provide a forum for contrarian views, or for support of the government's policies couched as a defense of the faith. Weblogs (henceforth referred to as blogs), chat rooms, and listservs have been shown to contribute to the shaping and constraining of larger political debate.

It is important to note that some of the most intense national debates spanning a range of issues at the heart of the rise of Islamism in Malaysia—namely apostasy,

Islamic governance and government, the sanctity of the constitution and of *sharia* law—are taking place not in the sphere of mainstream partisan politics but in cyberspace among ordinary citizens. This situation points to how Malaysian society is polarized over the question of Islam's salience as an ordering principle for law and politics.

There is a noticeable schism between the opinions and perspectives found on Malay-language blogs and English-language blogs regarding Islamic state declarations and high-profile *murtad* (apostasy) cases. While individuals from a variety of ethnic and religious backgrounds comfortably indulge in English-language blogs, Malay-language blogs seem largely monopolized by Malay-Muslims.[36] Another discernible trend is that, regardless of ethnicity and religion, there is a general consensus on English-language blogs in relation to the status of Malaysia as an Islamic state. A comparison with Malay blogs would show a clear disjuncture of perspectives on the issue. In the same vein, reactions to the high-profile apostasy cases that have emerged in recent years show that sentiments are divided along religious lines, regardless of language. In general, Malay and English blogs show an acute contrast in opinions, with the former expressing decidedly more conservative and exclusionary views and the latter conveying more openness to the idea of conversion out of Islam and to the principle of religious freedom writ large.

ISLAMISM AND THE STATE

Islamization in Malaysia is essentially a social-change phenomenon with significant political implications. It has been accelerated by the UMNO and PAS's search for an Islamic ideal that would translate into legitimacy, popularity, and electoral support. By placing greater significance on Islamic laws, values, and practices, the early 1980s saw UMNO and PAS enter a "race" to determine which of the two parties' visions of Islam would be most successful in Malaysia.

When Mahathir Mohammad assumed office in July 1981, the global Islamic resurgence was at its peak. In an effort to build on this trend, Mahathir set out to Islamize the Malaysian government, enacting a number of policies to achieve these ends. This Islamization campaign was made public during the UMNO general assembly in 1982, when Mahathir announced that the party would embark on a new strategy that aimed "to change the attitude of the Malays in line with the requirements of Islam in this modern age."[37]

The UMNO government not only ordered the restructuring of a range of Islamic institutions (both in scale and in scope), it also expanded the state bureaucracy to accommodate the return of a growing number of Malaysian students sent abroad on government scholarships during the Mahathir administration for degrees in Islamic studies, as well as the graduates of local Islamic institutions. The government also transformed the operations of *sharia* courts and mosques, and reorganized banking structures, foundation and charity work, *zakat* collection, as well as educational institutions. Making religious knowledge a 'regular' subject (in other words, one that could be tested like history or math) in the mainstream school curriculum was one of the Mahathir administration's most significant and controversial endeavors. The Islamic Teachers Training College was established in 1982 to accommodate this change in syllabi. Another notable high point of Mahathir's enterprise of creating and restructuring Islamic institutions was the introduction of Islamic banking.[38] With the creation of an Islamic bank, the larger objective of the Islamizing the economy was achieved; it was also an important expression of Mahathir's interpretation of Islamic values (*Nilai-nilai Islam*), whereby Malays can "seek wealth in a moral and legal way" and "obtain prosperity in this world and hereafter."[39]

At the same time, Mahathir worked actively to suppress other interpretations of political Islam at odds with his own. Events like 1987's Operation Lallang,[40] the banning of *Al Arqam* (a Muslim minority religious sect) in 1994, and the arrests of several prominent political figures, particularly from PAS, demonstrated the Mahathir administration's willingness to use the Internal Security Act to remove all obstacles perceived to be standing in the way of the government's Islamization policies and broader political agenda, even when the actual threat posed by some of these actors was questionable.

In the ongoing debate over the appropriate role of *sharia* law, unresolved structural tensions exist related to the question of jurisdiction and enforcement powers over alleged wrongdoings that have a religious aspect. These tensions are apparent at two stages. In the first level, confusion is caused by the legal governance system, at times hybridized in terms of a combination of *sharia* and constitutional law, and at times parallel, revolving around the Malaysian constitution and reinforced by the system of federalism that brings about a dispersal of power on the issue of the formulation of Islamic law. Essentially, states may have the power to formulate religious laws, but these formulations require ratification by the federal Parliament in order to be codified as legally binding and enforced.

The second is the dynamic that defines the relationship between civil and Islamic law. In a 1988 constitutional amendment, Article 121 1(A) stipulated that federal high courts "shall have no jurisdiction in respect of any matter within the jurisdiction of the *shari'a* courts." Criminal law falls under federal jurisdiction, but the constitution is ambiguous in such a way that it assigns power to create and punish offenses against the laws of Islam, which has allowed many state religious authorities to interpret their jurisdiction expansively.

The boundaries of Muslim politics in Malaysia may seem straightforward, with PAS serving as the Islamist opposition on one end, which demands that Malaysia's public spaces be governed by *sharia*, and by UMNO, the "secularist" Muslim government that is apparently set on restricting Islamism and keeping religion within the private sphere, at the other. However, this is an illusion. As recent controversies over apostasy and the right of non-Muslims to use the word "Allah" show, differences between UMNO and PAS are not set in stone. While PAS has begun taking inclusive positions on issues relating to Islam, the UMNO has become discernibly strident and "fundamentalist" in its defense of the primacy and exclusive rights of Muslims.

In other words, the track record of PAS is considerably more inconsistent than its strident rhetoric about exclusivist Islamism suggests, while the ostensibly "secularist" UMNO party harbors many Islamist tendencies. This latter trend has been especially noticeable since the Mahathir administration, with many elements of a conservative and orthodox Islamic government being put in. Even more telling was an UMO state assemblyman's suggestion, in July 2012, that the state government in Johor seriously consider implementing "true *hudud* law" that would govern non-Muslims as well. This represents a striking departure from PAS's position on the implementation of *hudud* in Malaysia, which it has always claimed would be applicable only to Muslims.[41]

Nevertheless, since the 2013 general elections, there has been a notable convergence of interests, at least on the surface, between the two long-standing political rivals. For instance, all 12 UMNO state assemblymen in Kelantan chose to support the amendment by PAS that approved *hudud*, which was unanimously passed in the state assembly in 2015.[42] This was followed by the UMNO-led government's decision in 2016 to fast-track hearings in Parliament on PAS president's private member bill, which would increase penalties for crimes under the Syariah Court (a court of Islamic law).[43] Given the negative impact on its public image stemming from corruption allegations involving Prime Minister Najib Razak, UMNO could very well be motivated by a desire to signal to the largely conservative Malay electorate that it too is serious about *hudud*, and willing to cooperate with PAS for the greater good of Islam in Malaysia.[44]

ENDNOTES

[1] Consider, for example, how former UMNO president and Malaysian prime minister Abdullah Badawi regularly made references to Islam in his public speeches, or how Mingguan Malaysia [Malaysia Weekly], a best-selling government-linked daily, has weekend columns offering advice on various matters pertaining to religion in everyday life. Malaysia has also regularly hit the country-level limit set by the Saudi government for Haj pilgrims, and there is now a three-year waiting list for Malaysians wanting to make the pilgrimage.

[2] Angel M. Rabasa, Political Islam in Southeast Asia: Moderates, Radicals and Terrorist (New York: Oxford University Press Inc., 2003), 39.

[3] Saliha Hassan, "Islamic non-governmental organizations." in Meridith L. Weiss and Saliha Hassan, eds., Social Movements in Malaysia (New York: Routledge, 2003), 98.

[4] Joseph Chinyong Liow, "Political Islam in Malaysia: Problematising Discourse and Practice in the Umno-PAS 'Islamisation Race,'" Commonwealth and Comparative Politics 42, no. 2 (July, 2004), 186.

[5] Ibid

[6] Ibidem

[7] See Joseph Chinyong Liow, Piety and Politics: The Shifting Contours of Islamism in Contemporary Malaysia (New York: Oxford University Press, 2008), 58-64.

[8] Beh Lih Yi, "PAS to 'soften' stance on Islamic state", Malaysiakini, January 20, 2005, http://www.malaysiakini.com/news/33013.

[9] Ibid.

[10] Azamin Amin, "Hindraf: PAS kesal hak asasi rakyat dicabuli" ("HINDRAF: PAS regrets human rights abuses"), Harakah Daily, November 25, 2007, http://www.harakahdaily.net/bm/index.php/utama/hindraf-pas-kesal-hak-asasi-rakyat-dicabuli.html. PAS was careful to warn, however, that it did not agree with all of Hindraf's demands either. See Dato' Seri Tuan Guru Abdul Hadi Awang, "Hak berhimpun diakui, tetapi sebahagian tuntutan Hindraf melampau" ("HINDRAF's right to assemble must be respected but some of its demands are unacceptable"), Harakah Daily, December 3, 2007, http://www.harakahdaily.net/bm/index.php/arkib-utama/hak-berhimpun-diakui-tetapi-sebahagian-tuntutan-hindraf-melampau.html.

[11] Basiron Abdul Wahab, "Pilihan raya umum: Negara kebajikan, tabung biasiswa antara tawaran PAS" ("General elections: PAS offers a welfare state and bursary fund"), Harakah Daily, August 28, 2007, http://www.harakahdaily.net/bm/index.php/arkib-pahang-darul-makmur/pilihan-raya-umum-negara-kebajikan-tabung-biasiswa-antara-tawaran-pas.html.

[12] "PAS mampu lahirkan negara kebajikan bila diberi peluang tadbir pusat" ("PAS can establish welfare state if allowed to administer at the federal level"), Harakah Daily, January 22, 2008, www.harakahdaily.net/bm/index.php/arkib-kelantan-darul-naim/pas-mampu-lahirkan-negara-kebajikan-bila-diberi-peluang-tadbir-pusat.html; See also Basiron Abdul Wahab, "Pilihan raya umum: Negara kebajikan, tabung biasiswa antara tawaran PAS" ("General elections: General elections: PAS offers a welfare state and bursary fund"), Harakah Daily, August 28, 2007, http://www.harakahdaily.net/bm/index.php/arkib-pahang-darul-makmur/pilihan-raya-umum-negara-kebajikan-tabung-biasiswa-antara-tawaran-pas.html.

[13] Muda Mohd Noor, "PAS akan lantik orang Cina jadi menteri" ("PAS will appoint Chinese minister"), Malaysiakini, February 6, 2008, http://www.malaysiakini.com/news/77875

[14] Ibid.

[15] James Hookway, "Malaysia's Islamic Party Unveils New Election Weapon: Christian Candidates," Wall Street Journal, April 15, 2013.

[16] Nile Bowie, "Is Malaysia Teetering on the Edge of an Islamist Knife?" Global Research 16, May 2013.

[17] Mohamed Nawab Mohamed Osman, "Islam, ethnicity and political power: Malay voting pattern in the 13th Malaysian elections," in Mohamed Nawab Mohamed Osman, ed., The 13th Malaysia Elections: Issues, Trends and Future Trajectories (Singapore: S. Rajaratnam School of International Studies, Nanyang Technological University, 2014), 63.

[18] James Chin, "Malaysia in 2013: Najib's Pyrrhic Victory and the Demise of 1Malaysia," Southeast Asian Affairs (2014), 181.

[19] Asrul Hadi Abdullah Sani, "PAS wants hudud laws for Kelantan: What you need to know about the laws," Straits Times, March 20, 2015.

[20] Terrorism Research Center, "Terrorist Group Profiles. Kumpulan Mujahidin Malaysia (KMM)," n.d., http://www.terrorism.com.

[21] See Kamarulnizam Abdullah, "Islamic Militancy Problems in Malaysia," SEACSN Bulletin, January-March 2003.

[22] Ibid

[23] "Asian Militants With Alleged Al Qaeda Ties Are Accused Of Plotting Against Embassies," Asian Wall Street Journal, January 2, 2002.

[24] Ibid.

[25] "Religious Cults And Sects, Doctrines And Practices: Al-Ma'unah," apologeticsindex.org, n.d..

[26] Liow, Piety and Politics, 7.

[27] "Two Policemen And Nine More Soldiers Identified As Belonging To The Movement," New Straits Times, July 13, 2000.

[28] Kamarulnizam Abdullah, "Islamic Militancy Problems in Malaysia," SEACSN Bulletin, January-March 2003, 7.

[29] Liow, Piety and Politics, 16.

[30] Ibid

[31] 'KL police see ISIS hand in grenade attack', Straits Times, July 5, 2016.

[32] "Suhakam to Consider Proposal to Set Up Interreligious Council," New Straits Times, August 27, 2002.

[33] Ibid

[34] See, for example, Marc Lynch, Voices of a New Arab Republic: Iraq, Al Jazeera, and Middle East Politics Today (New York: Columbia University Press, 2006).

[35] Needless to say, this general remark is made based on the comments of bloggers who actually sign their names to their posts.

[36] See Mahathir's speech at the 33rd Annual UMNO General Assembly, Kuala Lumpur, Malaysia, September 10, 1982.

[37] See Norhashimah Mohd. Yasin, Islamisation/Malaynisation: A Study on the Role of Islamic Law in the Economic Development of Malaysia: 1969–1993 (Kuala Lumpur, Malaysia: A. S. Noordeen, 1996), 261–64. The bank did not offer any interest on deposits it received. Instead, it would share the profits earned from investing the deposits with the bank's customers. The bank was also not charging interest on credit that it extended.

[38] Hajrudin Somun, Mahathir: The Secret of the Malaysian Success (Kuala Lumpur, Malaysia: Pelanduk Publications, 2004), 164.

[39] Operation Lallang was carried out on October 27, 1987 by the Malaysian police to prevent the occurrence of racial riots due to the provocation by the ruling government towards DAP. The operation saw the arrest of 106 persons under the Internal Security Act (ISA) and the revoking of the publishing licenses of two dailies, The Star and the Sin Chew Jit Pohand two weeklies, The Sunday Star and Watan.

[40] Shazwan Mustafa Kamal, "Soi Lek flays Johor UMNO rep over hudud proposal," Malaysiainsider, July 2, 2012, http://www.themalaysianinsider.com/malaysia/article/soi-lek-flays-johor-umno-rep-over-hudud-proposal.

[41] Joceline Tan, "Big day for Kelantan hudud move," The Star, March 19, 2015.

[42] Rachel Middleton, "Uproar in Malaysia as PM Najib Razak's ruling party fast tracks tabling of opposition's hudud laws," International Business Times, May 31, 2016.

[43] Saleena Saleem, "Malaysia's Right Wing Push: Chinese Swing Benefitting BN?" RSIS Commentaries CO16162, June 29, 2016.

PHILIPPINES

QUICK FACTS

Population: 102,624,209 (estimated July 2016)

Area: 300,000 sq km

Ethnic Groups: Tagalog 28.1%, Cebuano 13.1%, Ilocano 9%, Bisaya/Binisaya 7.6%, Hiligaynon Ilonggo 7.5%, Bikol 6%, Waray 3.4%, other 25.3%

Religions: Catholic 82.9% (Roman Catholic 80.9%, Aglipayan 2%), Muslim 5%, Evangelical 2.8%, Iglesia ni Kristo 2.3%, other Christian 4.5%, other 1.8%, unspecified 0.6%, none 0.1%

Government Type: presidential republic

GDP (official exchange rate): $311.7 billion (estimated 2015)

Map and Quick Facts courtesy of the CIA World Factbook (January 2017)

OVERVIEW

Since 1972, the overwhelmingly Catholic Philippines has confronted long-running Muslim secessionist insurgencies in the Southern islands of Mindanao and in the Sulu archipelago. Government corruption, crippling poverty and low levels of human development have fueled Muslim demands for an independent homeland. Yet the three primary groups engaged in insurgent activity in support of separation were themselves divided along tribal and ideological lines.

In the years since 2002, the United States has increased military assistance to the Philippine government and the Armed Forces of the Philippines (AFP). Furthermore, since 2004 the United States has deployed some 500 Special Forces personnel to the southern Philippines to provide intelligence support and training. Nonetheless, the AFP are hobbled by corruption, limited by outdated equipment, and often stretched too thin. The AFP found itself on better footing following the peace process with the Moro Islamic Liberation Front (MILF) in 2014 but still faces ongoing threats from other insurgent and radical groups. There are now questions regarding the continuation of U.S. security assistance and the Filipino state's approach to insurgencies following the 2016 election of Rodrigo Duterte as president. Nevertheless, positive political and social trends continue as they relate to the insurgencies in Mindanao and Sulu, and in turn have lessened incidents of violence..

ISLAMIST ACTIVITY

The Philippines lacks any truly broad-based Islamic movements. The Muslim Brotherhood is not strongly represented in the country, nor do the Philippines have any large Muslim civil society organizations, such as Indonesia's *Nadhalatul Ulama* or *Mohammidiyah*. There are three main organizations capable—to various degrees—of engaging in religious-inspired violence in the Philippines: The Moro National Liberation Front (MNLF), the Moro Islamic Liberation Front (MILF), and the Abu Sayyaf Group (ASG). Each of these insurgent groups is riddled with factionalism, leadership contests, and disputes over tactics. Moreover, there is no Muslim or Islamist political party at the national level. Although the MNLF ostensibly acts like a political party, and will contest elections in the Autonomous Region of Muslim Mindanao (ARMM), it is weak and factionalized. Since 2006, it has not governed the ARMM.

Moro National Liberation Front

Nur Misuari, a Manila-based Muslim academic, founded the MNLF in the early 1970s, and for the next decade it served as the sole revolutionary organization for the indigenous Muslim population, known as the Moros. The MNLF was an ethnonationalist movement, and predominantly secular, although it included Islamist elements. The group received considerable material and financial support from Libyan leader Col. Muammar Qadhafi, whose *Green Book* espoused leftist Muslim anti-colonialism.[1] The MNLF was closely allied with the communist New People's Army, which launched its own insurgency at the same time, prompting a declaration of martial law and the country's subsequent deterioration.

In 1976, Qadhafi attempted to broker a peace agreement, but the government showed little interest in implementing the proposed autonomy deal. After the failed talks, the MNLF became internally divided and suffered significant battlefield losses to the AFP. They never posed a serious military threat to the Republic of the Philippines again. In 1996, the MNLF and the government signed the Tripoli Accords, which established the Autonomous Region of Muslim Mindanao (ARMM).[2] Nur Misuari became the governor of the region, which included only five provinces; the other eligible provinces having failed to pass plebiscites. Some two thousand MNLF combatants were integrated into the AFP and the national police.[3] The ARMM agreement was never fully implemented and the region never achieved the promised political and economic autonomy. Rampant corruption and inept leadership also hobbled the ARMM, and these problems remain prevalent to this day.

In 2001, the MNLF executive committee voted to replace Misuari, who in turn staged a short-lived rebellion against the government. The rebellion was quickly put down and Misuari was captured, thereafter living under house arrest until 2007 (though he was never formally charged). He secured release from formal government monitoring in 2008. The MNLF lost control of the ARMM government in the 2006 elections, and the organization largely fell into disarray afterward. Though Muslimin Semma formally heads the Executive Council, Misuari and his loyalists do not recognize his authority. In 2007, certain MNLF units took up arms again, joining forces with the Abu Sayyaf.[4] The organization has shed its secular image, now espousing a 'light' version of Islamism.[5] Misuari continues to court controversy with public statements regarding relations between Manilla and the Moro majority south, but by and large he has removed himself from most active efforts of the group he founded.

The MNLF remains deeply factionalized and largely ignores the fact that the political aspirations of the Moro have diversified considerably. The causes that inspired MNLF's formation remain the rallying call of the group, but greater political engagement among the Moros and a greater willingness to discuss Moro grievances by the government has slowly eroded MNLF's relevance. Among Moro extremist groups, it can be said that the Moro Islamic Liberation Front (MILF) holds greater influence than MNLF today. Elements of the MNLF occupied parts of Zamboanga City in 2013, in an effort to derail a peace process between the Philippines government and MILF. Approximately 200 MNLF members fought AFP units, forcing the city to cease commerce, government services, transportation systems, and schools until the attack stopped. Since that time, MNLF has waded into and out of the peace process.

MNLF's supporters primarily come from the Tausig population in the Sulu area. MNLF's more concentrated support in the Sulu area brought the group into greater direct dispute with members of Abu Sayyaf (ASG). Specifically, ASG's kidnapping and banditry throughout the area drew greater attention from AFP forces that in turn further strained the local population and undercut MNLF's political operations. Following the election of Rodrigo Duterte in 2016, the administration has signaled its willingness to sit down with MNLF to discuss sources of the ongoing dispute. Concerns have been expressed throughout Mindanao that President Duterte's willingness to hold separate talks with the MNLF may lead to an intensification of the conflict.[6]

Moro Islamic Liberation Front

The Moro Islamic Liberation Front (MILF) is the largest armed Islamist organization in the country. Salamat Hashim, a Muslim scholar educated at Egypt's Al Azhar university, broke away from the MNLF in 1978 and formally founded the MILF in

1984, basing its headquarters in the *Jamaat-I Islamiya's* compound in Lahore, Pakistan. The MILF saw itself as part of the global *jihad*, inspired by the influence of the *mujahideen* in Afghanistan.[7] From the start, the MILF was far more Islamist than the secular, ethno-nationalist MNLF, and its avowed goal was to establish an Islamic homeland for the Moros.[8] The MILF began as a small group, whose growth and popularity caught Philippine forces by surprise. The MILF rejected the 1996 MNLF-Government peace pact that established the ARMM and benefited from mass defections from MNLF ranks as a result of that agreement.[9] By 1999, the MILF had over 11,000 men under arms and controlled vast swaths of central Mindanao. Yet it was never able to broaden that base of support throughout the Sulu archipelago, where the ethnic Tausig-dominated MNLF remained strong.

Starting in 1996, members of the nascent terrorist organization and regional al-Qaeda affiliate, *Jemaah Islamiyah* (JI), began to conduct training for their members and MILF combatants in MILF camps.[10] Al-Qaeda-affiliated individuals have long been rumored to assist JI with financing and operational assistance, but JI never became fully affiliated with al-Qaeda.[11] However, in 1997 the MILF and Philippine government under President Fidel Ramos, who had just concluded an autonomy agreement with the MNLF the previous year, began formal peace talks. The 2000 election of President Joseph Estrada, however, led the government to revert to a hardline stance. Estrada ordered the country's military to resume operations against the group, culminating in the capture of the MILF's main base camp. Peace talks resumed in 2001, following Estrada's ouster via a popular uprising. His successor, President Gloria Macapagal Arroyo, resumed peace talks with the MILF in 2002. Nonetheless, in 2003 peace talks broke down and wide-scale fighting erupted, with Philippine military personnel seizing several large MILF camps.

Since the mid-2003 death of Salamat Hashim, the MILF has been led by Chairman Ebrahim Murad and Vice Chairman Aleem Abdulaziz Mimbintas. Murad has *de facto* accepted a broader autonomy agreement, cognizant that the MILF could not win an independent homeland on the battlefield. Formal talks over autonomy began in 2003, and in November 2007 a draft autonomy agreement over the MILF's "ancestral domain" was finally concluded.[12] Nonetheless, Christian lawmakers in Mindanao, the Armed Forces of the Philippines (AFP) and hardline members of the cabinet rejected the agreement in December 2007. The country's Supreme Court found it to be unconstitutional in August 2008.[13] As a result, widespread fighting resumed. Although President Arroyo pledged to restart talks, formal talks did not resume before her term ended in May 2010. The breakdown of talks led to renewed fighting by the MILF and attacks on Christian villages in 2008-09, which left 400 dead and thousands displaced. The stalled peace process also saw the withdrawal of the small Malaysian-led contingent of peace monitors at the end of 2009. Formal talks faltered in 2010, as President Arroyo completed her lame-duck term in office.

The MILF remains the country's largest Muslim group, strongly represented among the Maguindanao and Maranao ethnic groups, though it has little following among Tausigs. The past decade has seen a weakening of the MILF relative to its peak strength in 1999-2000.

In February 2011, as the administration of President Benignoy Aquino, Jr. prepared to resume formal negotiations with the MILF, a hard line commander left the MILF and vowed to resume offensive military operations.[14] The MILF previously was known to receive funding from Saudi Arabia and other Gulf sources, although the scope of this aid is not publicly known. Much of money received from outside sources is thought to have dried up, with the group forced to look towards alternative sources of income from within the Philippine economy. The MILF engaged in criminality, such as extortion and a limited amount of kidnapping, as well as the production of marijuana for profit, throughout its existence.

In part because of its shrinking array of strategic options and limited financial resources, MILF's leadership proved to be open to negotiations with the Philippine government under President Benigno S. Aquino III. He used the MILF's weaknesses and growing public demand for a cessation of hostilities to successfully build consensus on both sides for a political settlement in 2012. The negotiated pact called for the creation of a semi-autonomous region called Bangsamoro that would have greater political and economic separation from Manila, thus alleviating Moro fears about domination by the Christian north, but remain a part of the Republic of the Philippines.[15] Bangsamoro would replace the Autonomous Region in Muslim Mindanao as the political unit covering the southern island, and the plan upon the agreement being reached in 2014 was to allow international aid organizations and development groups to begin economic development.[16]

Yet, like prior "breakthroughs" in negotiations between the disputing parties, discussions broke down in the summer of 2013. MILF representatives feared delay by government negotiators was in preparation of amendments to the initial pact, while the Philippine government became apprehensive that the Moro population would push for greater autonomy than initially agreed upon without necessary protections being worked in. The peace has held for the past several years, though tensions on both sides remain high. The election of Duterte has thus far been seen by many of the leaders in MILF as a positive development, because the new president is seen as being far more flexible in the pursuit of peace than his predecessor. The establishment of a tentative peace has allowed MILF segments to focus on internal issues that in turn have increased factionalism throughout the group's ranks and even led to incidents of violence.[17]

The MILF works very closely with the Islamic clergy across Mindanao, and has deputized many clergy to serve as Islamic judges in the shadow government that the MILF runs in the territory under its control. The MILF is the leading voice for the Maranao and Maguindanao tribes, as well as a handful of smaller tribes such as the Yaccans on Basilan Island. The MILF has very little support amongst the Tausigs in Sulu or Tawi Tawi. It controls significant territory in Lanaao del Sur, Cotabato, Maguindanao, Sultan Kudarat, Sharif Kabungsan and Sarangani provinces, as well as territory in provinces in other parts of the southern Philippines.

Despite all this, the MILF should be in a much stronger position than it is currently. In the areas it controls, the group provides little in the way of social services. It has some *madrassas* and a small medical corps, but is not able to match—or compete with—the resources marshaled by the Philippine state. In some ways, the MILF actually alienates the very community it seeks to represent. The MILF is a largely horizontal organization, and individual base commanders often compete over turf; i.e., what villages they can tax. There is also growing concern about the peace process; while most Muslims in the region rejoiced over the agreed pact in late 2012, the government has dragged its feet in finalizing all the points and MILF commanders have become increasingly anxious to resume combat operations.

There are hard-core elements of the MILF who have never accepted the peace process and took action to discredit the moderate leadership of MILF chairman Ebrahim el Haj Murad. In July 2010, one of the most conservative religious commanders, Ustadz Ameril Umbra Kato, quit the organization, and has subsequently attracted the organization's more radical youth, unhappy with the stalled peace process, away from the fold.[18] The longer the peace process drags on, the more likely the hardliners will feel vindicated. The MILF claims to be 12,000 to 15,000 members in size,[19] although circumstantial evidence suggests the organization is significantly smaller and weaker today. The protracted peace process similarly has weakened the MILF's battlefield preparedness.

Abu Sayyaf

The third Islamist organization active in the Philippines is the Abu Sayyaf Group (ASG), an organization that vacillates between terrorism and criminality. The ASG was founded in 1991 by a veteran of the Afghan *mujahideen*, Abdurrajak Janjalani, apparently with seed money from al-Qaeda.[20] Concomitantly, Osama bin Laden's brother-in-law, Muhmmed Jamal Khalifah, moved from Quetta, Pakistan—where he ran a branch of the Rabitat (Muslim World League—to the Philippines.[21] From 1991 to late 1994, he ran branches of two Saudi charities, the Muslim World League and the Islamic International Relief Organization, in Mindanao and Sulu—organizations that Philippine security forces saw as conduits of aid for the various Moro secessionist organizations.

From 1991-1995, the Abu Sayyaf, which was mainly comprised of ethnic Tausig defectors from the larger and more secular Moro National Liberation Front (MNLF), carried out a spate of bombings, assassinations and kidnappings against non-secular targets, including churches and Christian missionaries in Sulu province. Following a loss of support from al-Qaeda in 1995, the group degenerated and became synonymous with bold kidnapping attacks, such as the April 2000 raid on the Malaysian island of Sipidan and the May 2001 assault on the Philippine resort island of Palawan. Together, these attacks netted the group some 50 foreigners, which it proceeded to hold for ransom.

Between 2000 and 2001, the ASG took some 140 hostages including schoolchildren, teachers, priests and western tourists, and was responsible for the death of 16 of these captives. Starting in 2003, the ASG all but ceased kidnapping and—in conjunction with members of the Indonesian-based JI —resumed a campaign of terrorist attacks, including the bombing of a ferry in February 2004 that killed 116 people. Between 2004 and 2007, the few kidnappings that the group did perpetrate resulted in executions, not ransoms. The shift had much to do with the consolidation of power carried out in 2003 by Khadaffy Janjalani, the younger brother of the organization's founder, who sought to return the group to its secessionist roots, as well as with the neutralization of several other leaders following the onset of U.S. training and assistance to the Philippine military in early 2002.

By early 2005, several top JI leaders were known to be in Jolo, protected by the ASG. An August 2006 campaign by the Armed Forces of the Philippines, supported by a contingent of U.S. Special Forces troops who provided training and intelligence, led to a sustained offensive against the ASG through mid-2007. In September 2006 and March 2007, respectively, Khadaffy Janjalani and Abu Solaiman were killed. Both were key leaders in the organization. The ASG was weakened as a result and from 2007 through 2010 returned to kidnapping schemes.[22]

The current leadership of the ASG is more fragmented than in previous eras. Isnilon Totoni Hapilon, the group's hardline commander on Basilan, remains a prominent leader. The size of the ASG is estimated to be between 300-400 fighters at any given time. However, it is often supported and bolstered by disaffected MNLF combatants and gains members who have been radicalized elsewhere.[23] The ASG has increased kidnapping since 2007, and has frequently beheaded individuals for whom ransom is not paid.[24] Maritime attacks on private vessels near Sulu province have also become a common form of violence. Nonetheless, the ASG targets U.S. forces when possible, such as with the October 2009 IED attack in Jolo that killed two U.S. Special Forces soldiers. Abu Sayyaf's forces and leadership remain primary targets of AFP and U.S. forces, but remain at large by successfully avoiding raids. Hapilon made global headlines when he publicly issued a statement in August of 2014 swearing affiliation with ISIS and in turn, was recognized as ISIS' designated leader in the Philippines in early 2016 with the new name of Sheik Mujahid Abu Abdullah al-Filipini. The areas where ASG operates have become one of several hotspots in Southeast Asia for targeted ISIS recruitment.[25] There is ample speculation regarding how closely tied ASG and ISIS are, but the existence of ties at all is a troublesome development for the AFP.[26]

ASG has social support within the Philippines, but it is not particularly strong. In the Sulu archipelago, and in particular Jolo Island, there is support for the group—albeit for no other reason than that it is a closely-knit society based on clan and kinship. The group itself is not wildly popular, nor does it have a positive message or social agenda. The ASG simply has a vehemently anti-Christian, anti-state, and anti-American identity. It relies on kidnappings for much of its funding. Almost all kidnapping victims occur against individuals who appear to be Christian. On the few occasions that the ASG has kidnapped Muslims, it has tended to execute them, because they were working on U.S.-funded projects. When the ASG receives foreign funds, kidnapping ceases and bombings resume. This cyclical pattern limits the group's appeal, attractive to only a small segment of ethnic Tausig society. By and large, the ASG is rejected by both Muslims and Christians because of its conduct, but clan-based loyalties and kinship ties sustain them. To date no authoritative polling has been done to quantify the level of support the ASG enjoys, either in the Sulu archipelago or in the Philippines at large.

ISLAMISM AND SOCIETY

Islam came to the Philippines via Yemeni traders who spread the religion throughout the Malay and Indonesian archipelagos beginning in the 14th Century. Spanish colonization led to brutal clashes, and the Muslims—known as Moros, a derivation of the Spanish word Moors—took great pride in their resistance to colonial domination. When the Philippines became an American colony, the Moros continued their fight for independence, and only after U.S. military intervention was the southern Philippines pacified.

At the end of World War II, when the U.S. was preparing Philippine independence, Moro leaders requested that the United States give them their own independent homeland. The U.S., however, never acknowledged this request, and the Muslim region was incorporated into the Republic of the Philippines. Decades of Christian migration fundamentally altered the ethnic balance, and in vast swaths of the region, Muslims became the minority. By almost every measure of human development, however, the Muslim region lags behind the rest of the country. Today, the Philippines are 82.9 percent Catholic, 5 percent Muslim, and 2.1 percent Evangelical Christian.[27]

One of the most interesting trends in the Philippines is the spread of "Balik Islam"— literally, "return to Islam." Balik Islam is a movement of Christian converts to Islam, which remains the fastest growing religion in the Philippines. Conversion takes place through two general processes. One is the conversion of workers while overseas in the Middle East,[28] often for financial reasons (since being a Muslim can lead to better job opportunities). The other, which takes place in the Philippines, is via the network of Balik Islam centers scattered throughout the archipelago, primarily in slum areas of cities. For instance, of the 1,890 *madrassas* in the Philippines, only 1,000 or so are in Mindanao; the remainders are spread across the rest of the country. The center of Balik Islam is in the northern city of Baguio, on Luzon Island. Much of the funding for Balik Islam's *da'wa* work comes from the Gulf.[29] Balik Islam preaches a *Salafi* interpretation of Islam, and encourages its members to live in exclusive parallel communities.[30] A radical fringe of Balik Islam, the Rajah Solaiman Movement, has worked closely with the ASG and been implicated in a number of terrorist acts.

There are two major organizations that lead the Balik Islam movement: the Islamic Studies Call and Guidance (ISCAG) and Islamic Wisdom Worldwide Mission (IWWM). Both have been substantially funded from Middle East and Gulf sources. The IWWM is the successor organization of a front foundation used by Osama bin Laden's brother-in-law, Mohammed Jamal Khalifa, who was forced out of the Philippines in late 2004.[31] The organization was thought to have been used in the planned terrorist operations of Ramzi Yousef and his uncle Khalid Sheikh Mohammed. ISCAG was established in the mid-1990s in Saudi Arabia by a group of primarily Balik Islam converts. ISCAG is a rapidly growing NGO and has been featured in the press, due to its rapid expansion of operations and sponsorship of mosque and *madrassa* construction. The organization has come under more scrutiny by state authorities after its original head, Humoud Mohammad Abdulaziz al-Lahim, was forced out of the Philippines in April 2002 on allegations of sponsoring terrorism. ISCAG remains a focus of the state's investigative agents to explore ties to violent extremism.

ISLAMISM AND THE STATE

The Philippine government has a mixed history with its Muslim citizens. There is ample suspicion of the Muslim minority by the Catholic majority, which has translated into structural discrimination within the national economy. Yet the emergence of a powerful Moro identity that in turn inspired more intense legitimate political advocacy and violent extremism has encouraged the state to pay closer attention to Moro concerns. The details of the 2014 agreement signed between the government and the MILF included guarantees of greater political access and stronger political autonomy. Islamic courts for family law are active in the country's south. Mosque and *madrassa* construction generally proceed unhindered. Overall, Islam is the fastest growing religion in the country, and as mentioned above, the Balik Islam movement is robust.

This has led to extensive contacts between the Philippines and the broader Muslim world. The country has observer status in the Organization of Islamic Cooperation, or OIC (formerly the Organization of the Islamic Conference); has increased the number of pilgrims it sends on the *hajj* to Saudi Arabia; and has allowed foreign aid organizations, *da'wa* organizations and Islamist charities to have access to the country.[32] The presidential administration in Manila likewise has an office of Muslim affairs, and Muslims are increasingly making political inroads as candidates beyond the southern provinces.

Muslims in Mindanao and Sulu have been angered at the loss of ancestral domain to Christian migration, heavy-handed government responses to Muslim secessionist movements, and the slow implementation of promises by the government as part of various peace pacts. There is also concern that the government's extensive counter-terrorism cooperation with the United States since 9/11 has hardened government elements against any type of compromise with Moro groups. This is again where the election of Rodrigo Duterte may prove significant. Duterte hails from Mindanao and his primary base of support is concentrated there. Despite his reputation as a political wildcard, the Philippine population as a whole has found the start of Duterte's administration to be a success. His populist persona and a desire for quick government action has created concerns over the status of rule of law in Philippines. The administration's anti-drug campaign remains popular with the broader public but legal groups, opposition parties, and human rights organizations are growing concerned. Duterte's populism also is also popular among the Moro population. The hope in the south is that, as a local and as a politician less interested in appearances, he will push forward the peace process to greater stability.

The peace agreement between MILF and the government remains extremely popular throughout the country, especially among moderate Muslims in the south. The agreement has continued to largely dissuade MILF elements from engaging in conflict, while joint operations with the United States and improved operational capability have isolated Abu Sayyaf. This, of course, could change if the geopolitical orientation of the Philippine state shifts away from cooperation with the U.S. In that eventuality, joint operations with the United States may curtail or even cease, and new strategic partners for the Philippine state may arise. The government's footing has gradually improved over the past decade as they have used security assets in a more efficient manner, diversified the socio-economic tools used to assist development in the south, and used political dialogue to ease tensions with groups willing to negotiate. As such, insecurity will continue to define portions of the Philippines and terrorism, especially by ASG, will be a focus of AFP, but the state's positive steps over the past decade or so can be expected to deliver continued benefits to the entire country.

Endnotes

[1] On October 7, 1971, Libyan leader Muammar Qadhafi stated that if "the genocide still went on against the Muslims in the Philippines," he would assume responsibility" for protecting them. That year he established the Islamic Call Society (ICS) to support Islamic revolutions around the world. The ICS became a major force in Libyan foreign policy-making and had offices not just in Africa, but also in Thailand, Malaysia, the Philippines, and Indonesia. Khadhafi, through the ICS, became the major patron of the MNLF. See Saleh Jubair, Bangsamoro: A Nation Under Endless Tyranny, 3rd ed. (Kuala Lumpur: IQ Marin SON BHD, 1999), 150.

[2] The ARMM was established on November 6, 1990 by Republic Act 6734. It was legally possible to do so because of the promulgation of a new constitution in 1987 that allowed for the establishment of autonomous regions.

[3] Deidre Sheehan, "Swords into Ploughshares," Far Eastern Economic Review, September 20, 2001, 30-31. This USAID program is known as the Livelihood Enhancement and Peace Project. For more on this project, see Dan Murphy, "Filipinos Swap Guns for Rakes," Christian Science Monitor, March 5, 2002.

[4] Veronica Uy, "Duereza to MNLF: Deal with Malik," Philippine Daily Inquirer, April 16, 2007.

[5] Zachary Abuza interviews with MNLF leaders, Sulu, Zamboanga and Cotabatao, June 2007.

[6] Alexis Romero, "Duterte eyes separate talks with Nur Misuari," Philippine Star, November 9, 2016, http://www.philstar.com/headlines/2016/11/09/1642085/duterte-eyes-separate-talks-nur-misuari.

[7] Salamat Hashim, The Bangsamoro Mujahid: His Objectives and Responsibilities (Mindanao, Bangsamoro: Bangsamoro Publications, 1985), 18-19.

[8] Derived from the MILF's old webpage, http://morojihad.stcom.net/milf.html.

[9] Rasmia Alonto, "Interview: We Assert our Legitimate Rights to Self-Determination, That Is, Independence," in Salamat Hashim, Referendum: Peaceful Civilized, Diplomatic and Democratic Means of Solving the Mindanao Conflict (Camp Abu Bakre As-Siddique: MILF Agency for Youth Affairs, 2002), 45; Rigoberto Tiglao, "Hidden Strength: Muslim Insurgents Shun Publicity and Grow in Power," Far Eastern Economic Review, February 23, 1995.

[10] Indonesian National Police (INP), "Interrogation of Mohammad Nasir bin Abbas," Jakarta, Indonesia, April 18, 2003.

[11] Preeti Bhattacharji, "CFR Backgrounder: Philippines," Council on Foreign Relations, June 1, 2009.

[12] In addition to the five provinces of the ARMM, the MILF demanded an addition 1,478 villages, while the government contended that only 618 villages were majority-Muslim. Ultimately the two sides agreed on 712 villages. See "Philippines in 'Separatist Deal,'" BBC, November 15, 2007, http://news.bbc.co.uk/2/hi/asia-pacific/7096069.stm.

[13] Manny Mogato, "MILF: Peace Talks now in 'Purgatory,'" Reuters, August 31, 2008.

[14] MILF Admits Major Split Ahead of Talks," Agence France Presse, February 5, 2011.

[15] For an overall account of the pact see Whaley's "Philippine Government Signs Pact with Muslim Rebels," from the New York Times, October 15, 2012.

[16] See the World Bank's plans for FASTRAC (Facility for Advisory Support for Transition Capacities) in the Philippines at www.worldbank.org/en/news/press-release/2013/04/29/moro-islamic-liberation-front.

[17] Noel Tarrazona, "How Philippine militants internal conflict affects peace," Asia Times, November 16, 2016.

[18] MILF Admits Major Split Ahead of Talks," Agence France Presse, February 5, 2011.

[19] Rigoberto Tiglao, "MILF Boasts Bigger, Better Army," Philippine Daily Inquirer, June 9, 2000.

[20] For the history of the Abu Sayyaf, see Zachary Abuza, Balik Terrorism: The Return of the Abu Sayyaf (Carlisle, PA: Strategic Studies Institute, Army War College, September 2005).

[21] National Intelligence Coordinating Agency, "Mohammad Khalifa's Network in the Philippines," n.d., 2.

[22] Zachary Abuza, "The Demise of the Abu Sayyaf Group in the Southern Philippines," CTC Sentinel, June 15, 2008.

[23] Veronica Uy, "Duereza to MNLF: Deal with Malik," Philippine Daily Inquirer, April 16, 2007.

[24] "Philippine Abu Sayyaf jihadists behead German hostage in video," BBC, February 27, 2017, http://www.bbc.com/news/world-asia-39102762.

[25] Per Liljas, "ISIS Is Making Inroads in the Southern Philippines and the Implications for Asia Are Alarming," Time, April 14, 2016, http://time.com/4293395/isis-zamboanga-mindanao-moro-islamist-terrorist-asia-philippines-abu-sayyaf/

[26] IBID.

[27] "Philippines," The CIA World Factbook, December 2016, https://www.cia.gov/library/publications/the-world-factbook/geos/rp.html.

[28] Overseas foreign workers are the backbone of the Philippine economy. Although, they only comprise six percent of the population, their share of the country's GDP is 11 percent. There are over one million OFWs from the Philippines in the Middle East.

[29] Though dated, the best study of the Balik Islam phenomenon is Luis Q. Lacar, "Balik Islam: Christian Converts to Islam in the Philippines, c. 1970-98," Islam and Christian-Muslim Relations 12, no. 1 (January 2001), 39-60, esp. n4, 57.

[30] Simon Montlake, "In Philippines, A Watchful Eye on Converts," Christian Science Monitor, November 28, 2005.

[31] Abuza, Zachary, "Balik-Terrorism: The Return of the Abu Sayyaf", Strategic Studies Institute, September 2005.

[32] Hilman Latief, "Gulf Charitable Organizations in Southeast Asia," Middle East Institute, December 24, 2014, http://www.mei.edu/content/map/gulf-charitable-organizations-southeast-asia

THAILAND

> **QUICK FACTS**
>
> Population: 68,200,824
>
> Area: 513,120 sq km
>
> Ethnic Groups: Thai 95.9%, Burmese 2%, other 1.3%, unspecified 0.9% (2010 est.)
>
> Religions: Buddhist (official) 93.6%, Muslim 4.9%, Christian 1.2%, other 0.2%, none 0.1% (2010 est.)
>
> Government Type: Constitutional Monarchy; note - interim military-affiliated government since May 2014
>
> GDP (official exchange rate): $390.6 billion (2015 est.)
>
> *Map and Quick Facts courtesy of the CIA World Factbook (Last Updated January 2017)*

OVERVIEW

Since January 2004, the three southernmost provinces of Thailand have been affected by an ethno-nationalist insurgency. This Malay-Muslim rebellion is not new to the predominantly Buddhist kingdom of Thailand; rather, it has erupted sporadically ever since the 1902 Sino-British border demarcation carved out a Malay majority in the southern provinces of Yala, Pattani, Narathiwat, Satun and parts of Songkhla. Official Thai government policy has focused on the assimilation of the 1.3 million Muslims in the country's southernmost provinces (of the total 1.8 million people living there), which has only further alienated the local population. The Malays of this region see the Thai government as outsiders occupying their homeland, and meet any attempts at assimilation with resistance. Thai Muslims are more amenable to the assimilation movement.

An all-out insurgency raged from the mid-1960s to the early 1990s. However, the insurgents themselves were plagued by factional and ideological strife. The insurgency was comprised of a loose amalgamation of secular-leaning ethno-nationalists and groups affiliated with the Malayan Communist Party. In the first wave of armed insurgencies, all groups were committed to complete independence. As time wore on, positions changed: some favored independence, while others simply wanted greater autonomy within Thailand. Today, all insurgent groups, except for the Barisan Revolusi Nasional (BRN), would settle for less than full independence. The insurgency eventually collapsed for various reasons, including a widening gap between combatants on the ground and their leaders living in exile. The Thai government, though fairly brutal in its counterinsurgency operations at first, was able to capitalize on the disorganization of these groups. The government began offering general amnesties and showering the region with development funds. In the mid-1990s, the last major insurgent group, the Pattani United Liberation Organization (PULO), accepted the government's amnesty, and by 2002 the government declared victory. Yet local grievances remained deep-seated, and after a decade-long incubation, the insurgency re-ignited in 2004.

Though it began on a small scale, missteps by Thai government, political opportunism, and accusations of widespread human rights violations have led to an increase in the scope of the violence and level of support for the current insurgency. Now in its thirteenth year, and sixth government, no end is in sight, with more than 7,000 people dead and nearly 10,000 wounded. While violence declined dramatically in 2008, it increased anew from 2009-2013, and continued even after the start of peace talks in February 2013 between Thailand's National Security Council and the BRN (Barisan Revolusi Nasional), with Malaysia acting as facilitator.

ISLAMIST ACTIVITY

The southern Thailand conflict is ostensibly an ethno-religious one, being waged by ethnic Malay Muslims in Thailand's south against the Thai security forces.[1] However, a more detailed analysis suggests that the conflict is driven more by local political concerns than a quest for global *jihad*.[2] In the view of Patani Malays, Thailand's policy of assimilation comes at the expense of their ethno-religious identity. The Thai state prefers to frame the conflict primarily as a religious one, rather than as a question of national policy or governance.

The vast majority of the current generation of Patani Malay combatants fall under the command of the *Barisan Revolusi Nasional* (BRN), one of the longstanding separatist movements that, like many others, surfaced in the mid-1960s in response to Thailand's policy of assimilation. That policy included the move to ban all *madrassas* in the region and demand that only Thai language, customs and traditions be taught. The insurgents are locally referred to as *juwae* in local Malay dialect or *perjuang* in standard Malay, both of which mean "fighter." The *juwae/perjuang* are organized in small cells and scattered through out the Malay-speaking region. The insurgents are provided with only a vague idea of the rules of engagement and guidelines from BRN leaders. These directives center on the limitation of their violent activities in terms of geographical scope or the theater of violence. Combatants are not permitted to carry out violence outside the region unless they are specifically instructed to do so. As control over the movement is extremely fluid, cell members turn to criminal gangs and crime syndicates to make extra cash, though this occurs only very rarely.[3]

BRN cadres, along with those of other separatist organizations, disarmed in the late 1980s. But unlike other organizations, BRN managed to maintain its network and infrastructure, and thus was able to revive quickly and take up arms anew in 2004. BRN's main support is found in the hundreds of *madrassas* that dot the entire Malay-speaking region in the south of Thailand. By contrast, other long-standing separatist groups were unable to revive their respective networks of fighters when unrest flared in 2003, and thereafter decided to enter into a political dialogue with the Thai government. In August 2015, these groups merged into one umbrella organization, known as MARA Patani, pursuant to their talks with the government. However, it has since become clear that MARA Patani does not have any true control over insurgents on the ground.

At present, militant Malay youth in the South embrace *Shafi'i* Islam rather than the *Salafism* or *Wahhabism* of many other global *jihadi* outfits. Their agenda is driven as much by ethnic and political concerns as religious ones. While the local Malay Muslim villagers in the Thailand's far south support the movement, the insurgents do not have the support of the Thai Muslims. Militants acquire weapons either by stealing them or by keeping them after battles with government forces or local village defense volunteers. They buy or steal materials for bombs.

ISLAMISM AND SOCIETY

There are about seven million Thai Muslims, 44 percent of whom are ethnically Malay and reside in the three deep southern provinces of Pattani, Yala and Narathiwat and the four Malay-speaking districts of Songkhla province. The remaining 56 percent of Thai Muslims are multi-ethnic and are scattered throughout the rest of the country.[4] The majority of southern Muslims speak Patani-Malay as their primary language. They are not fluent in the official Thai language. Patani Malay is identical to Kelantanese Malay spoken across the border in Myanmar and remains an important identity marker for local communities.

The Malay Muslims of Thailand's south strongly emphasize the ethnic aspect of their adherence to the religion of Islam. Their ethnicity and religion are both key and deeply interconnected parts of their experiences and identity. Ethnicity and religion are intermingled, resulting in the formation of an ethnicized view of Islam. From the Malay perspective, mere religious conversion to Islam is not enough; rather, according to them, one has to *masuk Melayu*—"become a Malay"—in order to be accepted as a Muslim. The strong convictions of the Malay *ulema*, their role as custodians of religion and ethnic tradition, and their sturdy network thus render them important players in the ongoing insurgency so far as they keep the Patani Malay narrative and identity alive and encourage the Muslim population to question the Thai state-constructive narrative.

In fact, the first person who tried to negotiate the terms for coexistence between the Thai state and Patani was an Islamic cleric, Haji Sulong Toemeena, who was a reformist and political activist educated in Mecca, Saudi Arabia. Upon returning to Pattani in 1930, he engaged in the reform of the Malay Muslim community and represented Malay Muslim interests before the government. Principally, Sulong sought political autonomy for the south within a federal system as proposed by the then Thai Prime Minister Pridi Phanomyong. In 1947, Haji Sulong made several demands of the central government. These demands centered on the issue of political freedom for the Malays and the preservation of Malay language and cultural identity. The only religious demand concerned the recognition and enforcement of *sharia* (Islamic law). Since his mysterious death in 1954, Haji Sulong has become a symbol of resistance to the Thai state. He was believed to have been abducted and killed by a Thai death squad.

Today, the Malay Muslims of southern Thailand view national integration as equivalent to cultural disintegration for, according to them, Thai Buddhism and Malay Islam are "closed systems" belonging to two fundamentally different orientations. The conflict in the Patani region has also become an excuse for continuing Thai nationalism and Islamophobia.

ISLAMISM AND THE STATE

In the face of the reemergence of the southern insurgency—marked by bombings and executions—the ruling government of Prime Minister Thaksin Shinawatra responded with excessive force and imposed martial law on the deep south. Two particular episodes, the first in April 2004 and the second that October, stand out, having left a lasting imprint on the insurgency.

The Krue Se Jihad

After the imposition of martial law in the south on April 28, 2004, insurgents attacked 11 security posts in Yala, Songkla and Pattani. The resulting battles led to the death of 105 Muslim militants and five security personnel, 17 of the militants have been arrested. Thirty-seven of the militants were killed in the blockade of the Krue Se mosque, where militants are reported to have engaged in mystical religious prayer services comprised of the recitation of sacred verses and the drinking of holy water after the evening prayer. The militants were led to believe that these rituals would make them invincible to the police and invulnerable to bullets. They were suspected of belonging to a radical religious group called *Hikmat Allah Abadan* or *Abadae* (Brotherhood of the Eternal Judgment of God), led by a religious teacher by the name of Ismail Yaralong, also known as Ustaz Soh. The cell was secretive, and members were indoctrinated with mystical-leaning beliefs that they could become invisible and invincible.[5]

A 34-page Jawi/Malay language booklet, *Berjihad di Patani*, was found on the body of one of the dead militants. Published in Kelantan, Malaysia, it called for a separate Patani state and for the extermination of people of different religious faiths should they stand in the way. It concludes by suggesting the formation of a constitutional state of Patani based on the Sunni-*Shafi'i* school of law. Local clerics who studied the booklet described it as more of an organizational manual aimed at motivating the combatants, rather than a theological work. It also reflects the local *Shafi'i* school of thought and how it incorporates animism, popular beliefs, and pre-Islam practices that continue even today in this historically contested region.

The Krue Se mosque incident led to a large public media debate about the methods being used to quell the insurgency. The Thaksin government was also criticized for dismantling the Southern Border Provincial Administration Center (SBPAC) and the Combined 43rd Civilian-Police-Military Command (CPM 43). Established in 1981 during the period of democratization, these two bodies played an important role in educating the local Malay Muslims about integrating and assimilating in the Thai society. The SBPAC served as a sounding board for feedback on how to implement national accommodation policies—an important procedure, because government officials sent to work in the south come largely from majority-Buddhist areas of the country. They have frequently been accused of being culturally insensitive to Malay-Muslim values, thus perpetuating the conflict and resentment.

The Takbai Incident

Violence spiraled out of control in another episode in the Takbai district of Narathiwat in October of 2004, when police accused a group of village defense volunteers of handing their government-issued weapons to insurgents, and arrested them. In response, a large group of Muslims held a rally outside the Takbai district police station. Seven were killed when soldiers and police moved against the mob, and a further 78 died of suffocation after they were piled into trucks to be transported to a military camp. The government was sharply criticized for excessive use of force, neglect, and human rights violations, as well as Prime Minister Thaksin's refusal to apologize for the tragedy. The incident became part of the insurgent narrative to reinforce the notion that the state has never treated Patani Malays fairly.

The government set up an independent fact-finding commission into the incident, which yielded criticism of the method of transport and its supervision by inexperienced, low-ranking personnel. Ultimately, however, the commission did not find that the deaths had been caused intentionally, but did find some senior security officials to be at fault, and suggested that compensation be paid to the families of those who died, were injured or went missing.

In 2006, General Sonthi Boonyaratkalin launched a bloodless coup and removed Thaksin Shinawatra. Former army chief General Surayud Chulanont became prime minister. Surayud officially apologized for the Takbai massacre and other atrocities committed by the Thai state against the Patani people. He also invited the international community to help Thailand develop and reconcile the conflict in the far south.

Surayud sought to reconnect with older generations of separatists of PULO and BRN, hoping that they would take on a mediating role between the government and the new generation of younger insurgents, who are now even more devoted to their cause and radically more violent in their approach. However, *Barisan Revolusi Nasional-Coordinate* (BRN-C), the most active insurgent group, rejected negotiations. While other groups did not respond, General Surayud's government remained open to talks and to the possibility of granting autonomy (albeit not separation).

The interim government also revived the Southern Border Provinces Administrative Center (SBPAC), the civilian-military-police task force that had played a crucial role in offering a forum for dialogue between the locals and the authorities until its dissolution by Thaksin. The body's main task is development of the south, through the creation of pilot projects that, if successful, are turned over to the respective local ministries for further management.

By all indications, Prime Minister Surayud was sincere in his attempted solution for the southern conflict, but his preoccupation with national politics took up much of his time and energy. His government's apology and dialogue-centered approach was not supplemented with other measures, such as delivery of justice, recognition of local language and culture, and allowing the locals to manage their own affairs. Nevertheless, Surayud's apology marked the beginning of a more peaceful governmental approach to the conflict, supplanting Prime Minister Thaksin's approach of meeting violence with violence. However, this shift did not curb the number of assassinations, abductions and bomb attacks.

The Samak government proposed initiating joint military and private business ventures in the south with the intention of boosting the local economy and offsetting the insurgency. By this time, the central government was bogged down in political bickering with an opposition group outside parliament called the People's Alliance for Democracy (PAD), which was bent on driving the PPP government from office. Out of necessity, the government was forced to fully transfer to the army all responsibility for dealing with the southern insurgency. The army promptly initiated a full-scale operation to suppress the violence. Though this approach has reduced the number of violent attacks, violent episodes continue, including assassinations, disappearances, human rights abuses, and the shooting of Muslim religious teachers. To date, authorities have by and large ignored these problems, which has only resulted in the further alienation of the Malay Muslims from Thai society.

During July 2008, an obscure group claiming to be the "real" separatists came forward to announce a ceasefire. It was soon revealed, however, that they were former separatist leaders who retained little influence among the insurgency and the new, young, and faceless group of insurgents who controlled it.

In late 2008, the Bangkok government sent a retired general to Bogor, Indonesia, to meet with leaders from various separatist organizations. Indonesian Vice President Jusuf Kalla organized the event. It was meant to be both secret and unofficial, despite the fact that it was Prime Minister Samak himself who had reached out to the Indonesian government for help. When the event became public, the Thai government immediately backed away from the meeting.[6]

The 2011 Thai elections led to the victory of the Pheu Thai Party, also supported by former Prime Minister Thaksin Shinwatra. Yingluck Shinwatra, Thaksin's sister and the leader of the Pheu Thai party, became the first female Prime Minister of Thailand. In March 2012, Thaksin met with separatist leaders in Kuala Lumpur, Malaysia in an attempt at reconciliation, but fell short of apologizing for his heavy-handed approach to the southern conflict when he was prime minister.[7] Peace talks were attempted once again on February 28, 2013 between Thailand's National Security Council and the BRN, with Malaysia acting as a mediator. But in the months since the talks were announced, violent attacks have increased, and several insurgent groups remain absent from the negotiating table.[8]

ENDNOTES

[1] Michael K. Jerryson, Buddhist Fury : Religion and Violence in Southern Thailand (Oxford/New York: Oxford University Press, 2011); Imtiyaz Yusuf and Lars Peter Schmidt, eds., Understanding Conflict and Approaching Peace in Southern Thailand, Second Edition (Konrad Adenauer Stiftung, 2006); Duncan McCargo, Tearing Apart the Land: Islam and Legitimacy in Southern Thailand (Cornell University Press, 2008); Wan KadirChe Man, Muslim Separatism : the Moros of Southern Philippines and the Malays of Southern Thailand (Singapore: Oxford University press, 1990); Surin Pitsuwan, Islam and Malay Nationalism: A Case Study of Malay-Muslims of Southern Thailand (Thai Khadi Research Institute: Thammasat University, 1985).

[2] "Southern Thailand: Insurgency, Not Jihad," International Crisis Group Asia Report no. 98, May 18, 2005, https://www.crisisgroup.org/asia/southeast-asia/thailand/southern-thailand-insurgency-not-jihad.

[3] Author Don Pathan's interviews with Thai military officials.

[4] Imtiyaz Yusuf, "Ethnoreligious and Political Dimensions of the Southern Thailand Conflict" in Amit Pandya and Ellen Laipson, eds.. Islam and Politics: Renewal and Resistance in the Muslim World (Washington DC: The Henry L. Stimson Center, 2009), 44.

[5] Author Don Pathan's interviews with members of cells led by Ustaz Soh.

[6] Adianto P. Simamora, "Kalla insists Thai peace talks received 'valid authorization," The Jakarta Post, October 9, 2008, http://www.thejakartapost.com/news/2008/09/27/kalla-insists-thai-peace-talks-received-039valid-authorization039.html-0.

[7] Don Pathan, "Deep South peace talks lead back to square one," The Nation, May 13, 2013, http://www.nationmultimedia.com/opinion/Deep-South-peace-talks-lead-back-to-square-one-30205515.html

[8] "BRN YouTube clip threatens talks," Bangkok Post, April 29, 2013, http://www.bangkokpost.com/news/local/347469/brn-demands-hard-to-believe.

GLOBAL MOVEMENTS

MOVEMENTS
Canada
Al-Qaeda
Boko Haram
Fetullah Gülen
Hezbollah
Hizb ut-Tahrir
Lashkar e-Taiba
Muslim Brotherhood
Tablighi Jamaa'at
Taliban

AL-QAEDA

> **QUICK FACTS**
>
> Geographical Areas of Operation: East Asia, Eurasia, Europe, Latin America, Middle East and North Africa, North America, South Asia, Sub-Saharan Africa
>
> Numerical Strength (Members): Exact numbers unknown
>
> Leadership: Ayman al-Zawahiri
>
> Religious Identification: Sunni Islam
>
> *Quick Facts courtesy of the State Department Country Report on Terrorism 2015*

OVERVIEW

Al-Qaeda remains the most notorious Islamist terrorist group in existence today, and by 2017 the extent of its rise in global strength has become clear to keen observers. The 2007-09 defeat of major affiliate al-Qaeda in Iraq (AQI, which would later become the Islamic State of Iraq and al-Sham, or ISIS) had spurred a shift in al-Qaeda's strategic thinking. AQI had come to be seen by Iraqi Sunnis as a foreign imperialist force, thus prompting local opposition in the form of the Sahwa (Awakening) movement, while at the same time attracting a massive U.S. counterinsurgency response. Intent on avoiding being put in that position again, al-Qaeda began emphasizing localization (making its affiliates appear to be an organic part of local aspirations) and the use of front groups, which would make the question of whether a militant group was part of its orbit more ambiguous.

This strategy's success has been facilitated by a confluence of factors. The "Arab Spring" revolutions gave the group more operating room than ever before, due to both the policies of emerging governments and the diminishing capacity of regional states to control their own territory. Growing regional competition between Sunni states and Iran further expanded al-Qaeda's space to maneuver. Al-Qaeda positioned itself as anti-Iran, as well as a bulwark against ISIS's rise. Further, al-Qaeda was able to "rebrand" by contrasting itself with ISIS, portraying itself within the Middle East and North Africa region as the more "moderate," rational, and perhaps even controllable jihadist alternative. Al-Qaeda happily let the majority of Western and Middle Eastern states' counterterrorism and counterinsurgency resources target ISIS.

On July 28, 2016, Abu Muhammad al-Julani, the emir of one of al-Qaeda's most powerful branches—Jabhat al-Nusra, based in Syria—held a press conference where he announced that his group, moving forward, would "have no links whatsoever with foreign parties."[1] Nusra took on the new organizational name Jabhat Fateh al-Sham (JFS). However, this "dissociation" was likely deceptive rather than genuine. Far from the diminution of al-Qaeda's global brand, the emergence of JFS may signal that al-Qaeda no longer views ISIS as a serious challenge to its network, and is returning to the strategy of localization and front groups that characterized its primary response to the opportunities presented by the Arab Spring revolutions. This conclusion is further underscored by ISIS's growing struggles, including coalition military pressure being brought to bear simultaneously on its major holdings of Mosul and Raqqa. ISIS's decline as a territorial entity means that al-Qaeda is well on its way to again being seen as the most powerful jihadist organization in the world.

HISTORY & IDEOLOGY

Though the attacks of September 11, 2001 are the most profound symbol of al-Qaeda's notoriety, the group finds its roots in another, more conventional, war. Al-Qaeda was formally created in the latter years of the Afghan-Soviet war (1979-1989).[2] Various theories have been offered about the etymology of "al-Qaeda"—which in Arabic literally means "the base"—including that it refers to a "database" of names of Arab-Afghan *mujahideen* compiled by al-Qaeda's first *emir*, Osama bin Laden, and Palestinian jihadist theoretician Abdullah Yusuf Azzam.[3] However, there is no reason to doubt bin Laden's own explanation: that "al-Qaeda" was originally used as a generic phrase to denote the *mujahideen's* base of combat or operations.[4] This is borne out by the fact that al-Qaeda sometimes refers to itself as *qaedat al-jihad*, or "base of *jihad*."[5]

Coming on the heels of the Islamic Revolution in Iran, when Islamist fervor had reached a fever pitch internationally, the Afghan-Soviet conflict attracted *jihadists*, and other fighters and supporters from across the Arab world. Among them was Saudi multi-millionaire Osama bin Laden, who, in conjunction with Azzam, opened a "services bureau" (*maktab al-khidamat*) in Peshawar, Pakistan, supporting the Afghan *jihad*.[6] Ayman al-Zawahiri, an Egyptian physician who rose to become al-Qaeda's *emir* following bin Laden's death in May 2011, also made periodic stops in Peshawar, lending his medical skills to the care of wounded *mujahideen*.[7] Bin Laden eventually entered Afghanistan to fight the Soviets, and often recounted his spiritual, near-death experiences and feelings of tranquility in the midst of furious shelling.[8]

The victory of the *mujahideen* over the Soviets, and the subsequent collapse of the USSR, instilled a sense of destiny and invincibility in the *mujahideen*. It was viewed as a harbinger of even greater Muslim glory to come.[9] Ascribing their win to divine intervention, Islamists and *jihadists* became more confident of their destiny to defeat better-equipped and more technologically advanced foes.

After returning to his homeland of Saudi Arabia, where he was hailed as a hero, Osama bin Laden found another opportunity to test the mettle of his cadre of seasoned *mujahideen*, popularly known as the "Afghan Arabs" or "Afghan alumni." That test was Iraqi president Saddam Hussein's 1990 invasion of Kuwait. This, along with neighboring Saudi Arabia's fear that it was next on Saddam's list of targets, furnished bin Laden with an opportunity to rally his now-unemployed fighters, this time to defend not just a peripheral Muslim nation but the very sanctity of Arabia, home of the *haramain* (the Two Holy Mosques in Mecca and Medina). He petitioned the Saudi monarch, King Fahd, to allow the Afghan Arabs to defend the country, only to be rebuffed. Fahd opted instead to accept the U.S.'s offer to deploy its "infidel" troops on Arabian soil. Bin Laden later referred to the U.S. troop presence in Saudi Arabia in his 1996 declaration of war against America as the West's greatest aggression against the *Ummah*.[10]

Saudi Arabia's acceptance of American soldiers on its soil turned bin Laden against the Saudi monarchy. Because of his outspoken criticisms, the former war hero was ostracized and exiled from the Kingdom, and forced to flee to Sudan. Khartoum had just experienced its own Islamist *coup d'état*, after which it welcomed fundamentalists from across the globe. During this time (1992-1996), Ayman al-Zawahiri and his organization, the Egyptian Islamic Jihad, also used Sudan as a base to launch attacks against the Egyptian government. Zawahiri eventually merged the Egyptian Islamic Jihad with al-Qaeda, and expanded the scope of its *jihad* well beyond Egypt's borders.[11]

Bin Laden's early sponsorship of terrorist attacks against U.S. interests, along with Zawahiri's botched terrorist missions against the Mubarak regime (including failed assassination attempts on the Egyptian Prime Minister and President Mubarak himself),[12] brought international pressure down on the Sudanese government to evict al-Qaeda. They eventually did so, and in 1996 al-Qaeda's leadership returned to Afghanistan and found refuge with another Islamist regime, the Taliban. That militant group, whose leadership was composed of former students indoctrinated in Pakistan's madrassas, had risen out of the chaos that followed the Soviet withdrawal from Afghanistan. The Pakistan-backed Taliban government welcomed bin Laden and his Afghan Arabs, and allowed them to set up militant bases and training camps.

Al-Qaeda is a *Salafist* organization. *Salafism* denotes the emulation of the Prophet Muhammad and the first three generations of Muslims, *al-salaf al-salih* (righteous predecessors). Al-Qaeda's ultimate goal is to resurrect a global Caliphate that enforces *sharia* law. But the *Salafist* worldview is not unique to al-Qaeda. Rather, it is a form of Islamism increasingly subscribed to by other Islamist activists, both militant and non-violent.[13] Under the "originalism" inherent in the *Salafist* approach, centuries of jurisprudence about *sharia* according to Islam's *madhahib* (four mainstream schools of thought) can no longer dictate to the believer what the Islamic faith truly means.

Al-Qaeda justifies the attacks of September 11, 2001, in which nearly 3,000 civilians were killed, with the *sunna* (examples or acts from the Prophet Muhammad's life), which tells of Muhammad employing catapults during the siege of the town of Ta'if.[14] Similarly, al-Qaeda excuses the act of killing women and children by referring to reported permission to do so granted by Prophet Muhammad.[15] Al-Qaeda also supports "martyrdom operations" by reference, for example, to a Qur'anic verse that calls on believers to "kill and be killed" (Surah 9:111). Other verses simply call for violence, such as the famous "sword verse": "fight and slay the Pagans wherever ye find them, and seize them, beleaguer them, and lie in wait for them in every stratagem (of war)."[16]

Another practice regularly used by al-Qaeda and other Islamist groups is *taqiyya*,[17] a doctrine that espouses deceiving the enemy when the latter is in a dominant position or during war, two conditions that al-Qaeda believes apply today. In his lengthy treatise, "Loyalty and Enmity," Zawahiri dedicates an entire section to *taqiyya*, quoting classical *ulema* (clerics) who believed that Muslims under the authority of non-Muslims should behave loyally while harboring feelings of hatred toward them.[18] In another treatise, Zawahiri quotes Muhammad's famous assertion that "war is deceit."[19] While al-Qaeda has readily justified violence and terror, it has also taken on a softer, more methodical image in recent years to give itself more operating space. This underappreciated strategic shift is discussed at length below.

GLOBAL REACH

From 2010 onward, the Obama administration heavily pushed the idea that al-Qaeda's "core" leadership had been significantly eroded. In the summer of 2010, then-CIA Director Leon Panetta estimated there were only 50-100 al-Qaeda members in Afghanistan.[20] The idea that al-Qaeda's core leadership was in steep decline gained more adherents after bin Laden's death in May 2011. In July 2011, Panetta said that the U.S. was "within reach of strategically defeating al-Qaeda."[21]

Similarly—and related—both the administration and many independent observers believed in early 2011 that the revolutionary events of the "Arab Spring" would marginalize al-Qaeda. Former CIA deputy director Michael Morell, describing the prevailing analytic outlook at the time, wrote that the CIA "thought and told policymakers that this outburst of popular revolt would damage al Qaʻida by undermining the group's narrative. Our analysts figured that the protests would send a signal throughout the region that political change was possible without al Qaʻida's leading the way and without the violence that al Qaʻida said was necessary."[22]

Assessments concerning the decline of al-Qaeda's core leadership were always questionable, but even when most analysts thought that the group's core was badly damaged, nobody doubted that its affiliates remained robust. As one U.S. counterterrorism official put it in 2010—mirroring the conventional wisdom of the time—"while (core) Al Qaeda is now struggling in some areas the threat it poses is becoming more widely distributed, more geographically diverse. The rise of affiliated groups such as Al Qaeda the Arabian Peninsula and Al Qaeda in the Islamic Maghreb is a troubling development."[23]

Al-Qaeda in the Arabian Peninsula (AQAP) may be al-Qaeda's most capable affiliate organization. The group resulted from a merger of al-Qaeda's Saudi and Yemeni franchises in January 2009. While it attempted several attacks against foreign targets at its inception, AQAP has also exhibited a persistent local focus, and has exploited the recent chaos of Yemen's civil war.

In 2010, Yemen's government estimated the group's strength to be just 200 to 300 members,[24] though unofficial estimates at that time put the number somewhat higher, at between 500 and 600 militants.[25] AQAP has grown in size and scope since then. In 2011-2012, AQAP succeeded in gaining control of large swathes of territory in southern Yemen. This prompted a major response from the Yemeni government, forcing the organization into a "strategic retreat" from Abyan Province.[26]

But thereafter, a civil conflict erupted between Iran-backed Houthis, Sunni tribes, and the forces of nominal president Abd Rabbuh Mansur Hadi. AQAP benefited from this chaos, and even succeeded in positioning itself as somewhat useful to the GCC states of Saudi Arabia and U.A.E., which intervened to counter Iranian gains. At one point, AQAP gained control over Yemen's fifth-largest city, al-Mukalla.[27] Though AQAP later retreated from the urban areas of Mukalla, it continues to control surrounding territory, and has a powerful foothold in Yemen.

Also prominent among al-Qaeda's regional franchises is *al-Qaeda in the Islamic Maghreb*, or AQIM. AQIM was formed in September 2006, when Algeria's radical Salafist Group for Call and Combat (GSPC) joined forces with al-Qaeda. With the merger, the organization's focus became broader, as compared to the GSPC's narrower goal of ousting Algeria's Bouteflika regime. The organization now "has aspirations of overthrowing apostate African regimes and creating an Islamic Caliphate," according to the U.S. Department of State.[28] AQIM is currently headed by Abdelmalek Droukdel, its founder and a veteran of the *jihad* against the Soviet Union in Afghanistan.

By late 2012, AQIM was the dominant force in Northern Mali, and instituted a harsh brand of *sharia* in the territory under its control.[29] France intervened in January 2013, after which AQIM's Northern Mali safe haven became less tenable. AQIM adapted by moving parts of its organization to southwest Libya.[30] Thereafter, AQIM played a central role in an insurgency in Mali that has significantly heated up from 2015-17.[31] AQIM's capabilities were further bolstered when it reunited with the master terrorist Mokhtar Belmokhtar and his splinter group *al-Murabitun* in December 2015. This rapprochement was announced following a notorious attack on Bamako's Radisson Blu Hotel.[32] Thereafter, Belmokhtar's arm of AQIM continued to carry out deadly attacks on hotels and resorts in West Africa that are popular with Westerners. AQIM has also continued high-profile kidnappings of European hostages.

Nor are AQAP and AQIM the only al-Qaeda affiliates that are growing in power and prominence. The Somali militant group *al-Shabaab* was the dominant military force in southern Somalia until an offensive against it led by the African Union Mission in Somalia (AMISOM) pushed it from its urban strongholds in 2011-12. Despite those setbacks, Shabaab has in recent years become a noticeably more potent insurgent force.[33] Today AMISOM's grip on the urban areas of Somalia is weakening, and al-Shabaab appears to be the strongest force in the country's rural areas.

RECENT ACTIVITY

Though the Arab Spring revolutions did not diminish al-Qaeda in the way that many experts had predicted, when ISIS emerged as an independent challenger from within the *jihadist* ranks, many observers thought this was the development that would finally push al-Qaeda to the margins. Though it did not do so, ISIS's emergence has in fact had a tremendous impact on al-Qaeda.

ISIS had once been a part of al-Qaeda, where it was known as al-Qaeda in Iraq (AQI). The organization suffered significant setbacks during the course of the Iraq War. (Throughout its history, the group has taken several names, including AQI, the Islamic State of Iraq, the Islamic State of Iraq and al-Sham, or ISIS, and, most recently, the Islamic State.)

During the Iraq war, AQI grew in influence, ultimately becoming, in the words of Col. Peter Devlin, the "dominant organization of influence" in Iraq's majority-Sunni Anbar province by August 2006.[34] But the group suffered a catastrophic collapse in popular support as a result of the brutal policies of its leader, Abu Musab al-Zarqawi. Against the instructions of al-Qaeda's leadership,[35] Zarqawi adopted a policy of indiscriminately targeting and butchering local Sunnis and Shi'ites in Iraq deemed to be at variance with his exclusionary interpretation of Islam. The backlash to these excesses helped form and sustain the so-called Sunni "Awakening," which served as a critical complement to the Bush administration's "surge" of forces into Iraq in 2007.

Following the onset of instability in neighboring Syria as well as the drawdown of U.S. troops from Iraq, ISIS staged a bloody comeback. ISIS first attained a significant foothold in Syria, where the regime of Bashar al-Assad was struggling against an array of opposition forces. ISIS soon captured land in northeast Syria. It did so initially in conjunction with al-Qaeda's local Syrian affiliate, *Jabhat al-Nusra*, but internal infighting between the two prompted al-Qaeda head Ayman al-Zawahiri to intervene.[36] Zawahiri ordered ISIS to leave Syria and return to Iraq, a command with which it refused to comply.

Thereafter, a strategic and ideological schism developed between al-Qaeda and ISIS. In February 2014, Zawahiri formally disavowed ISIS.[37] In June 2014, ISIS launched a dramatic offensive from Syria into Iraq, capturing a broad swath of territory, and by the end of the month declared that it had reestablished the caliphate. In doing so, the late ISIS spokesman Abu Muhammad al-Adnani stated that the *caliph*, Abu Bakr al-Baghdadi, had become the "leader for Muslims everywhere."[38] Adnani's statement also declared that the caliphate's establishment made all competitor organizations—a category that included al-Qaeda—legally void.

The competition between al-Qaeda and ISIS for primacy in the *jihadist* movement soon reached a fever pitch. ISIS began loudly trying to lure al-Qaeda's affiliates into its own orbit, and succeeded in winning over a couple of less significant pro-al-Qaeda groups, Sinai's *Ansar Bayt al-Maqdis* and Nigeria's *Boko Haram* (which had been an undeclared al-Qaeda affiliate). The U.S. intelligence community estimated at that time that ISIS could field as many as 31,000 men under arms.[39] This number was likely an underestimate.[40] ISIS was also, at the time, perhaps the richest militant group in the world, with assets valued at around $2 billion.[41] ISIS controlled segments of northern Iraq and eastern Syria equivalent to the size of the United Kingdom.[42]

But despite the massive advantages it enjoyed in both territory and resources, ISIS's strategy was fraught with problems from the start. The group purposefully surrounded itself with enemies, including by betraying allies and attacking forces that were not at war with it.[43] Due to the group's aggressiveness, including launching a genocidal campaign against the Yazidi minority group that posed no military threat to it, ISIS provoked an international response. In September 2014, the Obama administration authorized air strikes against ISIS in Iraq and Syria, and worked to create a coalition, including both European nations and Gulf Arab states, to coordinate the fight against the Islamic State. The anti-ISIS fight was slow going at first, with extremely conservative targeting rules limiting the air campaign.[44] Nevertheless, ISIS has lost significant ground over time, with its losses spiraling in the latter half of 2016. Further, despite the noise ISIS has made about expanding internationally, the group did not succeed in making a significant dent in al-Qaeda's global network, and in fact has been outmaneuvered by al-Qaeda and its allies in most theaters outside the Iraq-Syria caliphate.[45]

Meanwhile, al-Qaeda has been able to pivot off of ISIS's raw brutality to undertake a strategic shift that it had sought since AQI's defeat in Iraq. Bin Laden had written about the need to change public perceptions of the organization prior to his death. In a May 2010 letter to Atiyah Abd al-Rahman, he proposed that al-Qaeda should "correct [the mistakes] we made," and "reclaim ... the trust of a large segment of those who lost their trust in the jihadis."[46] In other words, bin Laden viewed AQI's conduct as a black mark on how al-Qaeda was perceived globally, and he thought correcting al-Qaeda's image was vital. He cautioned that if al-Qaeda alienated the public, it could win "several battles while losing the war at the end."[47] Some of the early efforts at changing al-Qaeda's public image were reflected in Zawahiri's "General Guidelines for Jihad," released in September 2013.[48] The document aims to reduce the amount of unnecessary violence associated with al-Qaeda, including advising affiliate organizations not to kill women and children, and also to stop attacking markets and mosques where Muslims could be killed.

As the Arab Spring revolutions struck, al-Qaeda undertook further adaptations and exploited developments in the region. One of al-Qaeda's adaptations was making use of front groups to conduct *dawa* (evangelism) and other forms of public outreach, in the form of organizations like *Ansar al-Sharia* in Tunisia and Libya. *Jabhat al-Nusra* in Syria initially functioned as a front group until ISIS's loud entry into Syria, and its subsequent claim that *Nusra* was subservient to it, forced *Nusra emir* Abu Muhammad al-Julani to make his relationship with al-Qaeda public. This use of front groups allowed al-Qaeda to gain adherents locally without attracting outside counterterrorism resources against it.

Al-Qaeda also sought to mirror what the United States had done when it defeated AQI in 2007-09, and became more population-centric. Al-Qaeda built relationships with other armed groups, including those that were not *jihadist*. For example, after a coalition of Islamist armed groups, including Nusra, captured the Syrian city Idlib in April 2015, *Nusra's* Julani said that his group did not "strive to rule the city or to monopolize it without others."[49] This approach contrasted with that of ISIS, which wanted to dominate all other groups, including Sunni militias.

Thus, while ISIS's emergence was a real challenge for al-Qaeda, ISIS's rise also presented an opportunity. In contrast to al-Qaeda's efforts to tone down its brutality, and appear more rational or even "moderate," ISIS broadcast its brutality to the world, and reveled in its increasingly ingenious and repulsive methods of torturing and murdering its victims.

Al-Qaeda used ISIS as its rhetorical foil. Not only did it contrast itself with ISIS's brutality, but al-Qaeda also downplayed its own successes. The world was worried about ISIS's growth, and for good reason, and al-Qaeda was content to allow the bulk of counterterrorist and counterinsurgent resources focus on ISIS. Typifying this strategy is a June 2015 interview in *The Guardian* with senior al-Qaeda religious figures

Abu Muhammad al-Maqdisi and Abu Qatada. Maqdisi said that al-Qaeda's organization had "collapsed," and Abu Qatada described Zawahiri to be "isolated."[50] This portrayal was almost certainly disinformation.

On July 28, 2016, *Nusra's emir*, Abu Muhammad al-Julani, held a press conference in which he announced that his group would, from then on, "have no links whatsoever with foreign parties." Nusra adopted the new name *Jabhat Fateh al-Sham* (JFS). This move was widely interpreted as JFS dissociating itself from al-Qaeda, but the heavy presence of al-Qaeda senior leaders in Syria makes it likely that Julani considers al-Qaeda to be a non-foreign party.[51] It seems that the rebranding of *Nusra* as JFS signals a return to al-Qaeda's pre-ISIS strategy for Syria, in which the local affiliate has taken on a different name and a different brand, and is allegedly independent.

Al-Qaeda has survived and thrived despite recent challenges. The Arab Spring did not marginalize it, but presented it an opportunity to grow. ISIS did not eclipse it, but presented it the opportunity to undertake a rebranding that it had sought ever since AQI's defeat. The signs of al-Qaeda's growing strength are evident in multiple theaters, including in its return to Afghanistan and the intensifying al-Qaeda-linked insurgencies in Mali and Somalia. AQAP and AQIM remain potent and destabilizing forces.

Endnotes

[1] "Syrian Nusra Front announces split from al-Qaeda," BBC News, July 29, 2016, http://www.bbc.com/news/world-middle-east-36916606.

[2] John Rollins, Al Qaeda: Profile and Threat Assessment (Washington, DC: Congressional Research Service, July 25, 2011), http://www.fas.org/sgp/crs/terror/R41070.pdf.

[3] Ibid

[4] "Transcript of Bin Laden's October Interview," CNN, February 5, 2002, http://archives.cnn.com/2002/WORLD/asiapcf/south/02/05/binladen.transcri....

[5] "Al-Qaeda Deputy Ayman al-Zawahiri Claims Responsibility for the London Bombings, Discusses Elections in Afghanistan, and Declares: 'Reform Can Only Take Place through Jihad,'" Middle East Media Research Institute Special Dispatch No. 989, September 20, 2005, http://www.memri.org/report/en/0/0/0/0/0/0/1480.htm.

[6] Lawrence Wright, The Looming Tower: Al-Qaeda and the Road to 9/11 (New York: Random House, 2007), 119.

[7] Ibid., 52-54.

[8] Mark Long, "Ribat, al-Qa'ida, and the Challenge for U.S. Foreign Policy," Middle East Journal 63, no. 1, Winter 2009, http://muse.jhu.edu/journals/the_middle_east_journal/v063/63.1.long.pdf

[9] Rohan Gunaratna, "Al Qaeda's Ideology," Current Trends in Islamist Ideology, May 19, 2005, http://www.currenttrends.org/research/detail/al-qaedas-ideology.

[10] Douglas Jehl, "Holy War Lured Saudis as Leaders Looked Away," New York Times, December 27, 2001, http://www.nytimes.com/2001/12/27/world/a-nation-challenged-saudi-arabia....

[11] "Mapping Militant Organizations: Egyptian Islamic Jihad," Stanford University, July 31, 2012, http://www.stanford.edu/group/mappingmilitants/cgi-bin/groups/view/401

[12] "Egyptian Islamic Jihad," Encyclopedia of the Middle East, n.d., http://www.mideastweb.org/Middle-East-Encyclopedia/egyptian_islamic_jiha....

[13] Christian Caryl, "The Salafi Moment," Foreign Policy, September 12, 2012, http://www.foreignpolicy.com/articles/2012/09/12/the_salafi_moment; see also the description of divisions within Salafism in Monica Marks, "Youth Politics and Tunisian Salafism: Understanding the Jihadi Current," Mediterranean Politics 18, no. 1 (2013), 109.

[14] Quintan Wiktorowicz and John Kaltner, "Killing in the Name of Islam: Al-Qaeda's Justification for September 11," Middle East Policy 10, no. 2, Summer 2003, http://publikationen.stub.uni-frankfurt.de/files/12030/killing_in_the_na....

[15] Raymond Ibrahim, The Al Qaeda Reader (New York: Doubleday Publishers, 2007), 165.

[16] At Taubah, Surah 9: Repentance, http://www.muslimaccess.com/quraan/arabic/009.asp#5.

[17] For a detailed discussion, see Raymond Ibrahim, "How Taqiyya Alters Islam's Rules of War," Middle East Quarterly 17, no. 1, Winter 2010, http://www.meforum.org/2538/taqiyya-islam-rules-of-war.

[18] Ibrahim, The Al Qaeda Reader, 73-74.

[19] Ibid., 142.

[20] Jack Date, "CIA Director Leon Panetta: Serious Problems with Afghanistan War but Progress Being Made," ABC News, June 27, 2010, http://abcnews.go.com/ThisWeek/cia-director-panetta-exclusive-intelligen....

[21] Elisabeth Bumiller, "Panetta Says Defeat of al Qaeda is 'Within Reach,'" New York Times, July 9, 2011, http://www.nytimes.com/2011/07/10/world/asia/10military.html?mtrref=www.nytimes.com&_r=0.

[22] Michael Morell, The Great War of Our Time: The CIA's Fight Against Terrorism from al Qa'ida to ISIS (New York: Twelve, 2015).

[23] Quoted in Assaf Moghadam and Brian Fishman, "Debates and Divisions Within and Around Al Qa'ida," in Assaf Moghadam and Brian Fishman, eds., Self-Inflicted Wounds: Debates and Divisions al-Qa'ida and its Periphery (West Point, NY: Combating Terrorism Center, December 2010), 11-12, http://www.dtic.mil/cgi-bin/GetTRDoc?AD=ADA536531.

[24] "Western Counter-Terrorism Help 'Not Enough for Yemen,'" BBC, December 29, 2009, http://news.bbc.co.uk/2/hi/8433844.stm.

[25] Pascal Boniface, "Al-Qaida: De L'Afghanistan Au Yemen?" Le Nouvel Observateur, September 16, 2010, http://pascalbonifaceaffairesstrategiques.blogs.nouvelobs.com/archive/20....

[26] Andrew Michaels and Sakhr Ayyash, "AQAP's Resilience in Yemen," CTC Sentinel, September 24, 2013, http://www.ctc.usma.edu/posts/aqaps-resilience-in-yemen.

[27] Daveed Gartenstein-Ross & Bridget Moreng, "Al Qaeda is Beating the Islamic State," Politico, April 14, 2015, http://www.politico.com/magazine/story/2015/04/al-qaeda-is-beating-the-islamic-state-116954.

[28] U.S. Department of State, Country Reports on Terrorism 2013.

[29] Zachary Laub, "CFR Backgrounder: Al-Qaeda in the Islamic Maghreb (AQIM)," Council on Foreign Relations, March 27, 2015, http://www.cfr.org/terrorist-organizations-and-networks/al-qaeda-islamic-maghreb-aqim/p12717.

[30] U.S. Department of State, Country Reports on Terrorism 2013.

[31] Mark Leon Goldberg, "In Mali, Peacekeepers Have Become the Target of an Insurgency. This is Unprecedented," UN Dispatch, June 1, 2016, http://www.undispatch.com/deadliest-peacekeeping-mission/.

[32] Daveed Gartenstein-Ross & Nathaniel Barr, "Neither Remaining Nor Expanding: The Islamic State's Global Expansion Struggles," War on the Rocks, February 23, 2016, http://warontherocks.com/2016/02/neither-remaining-nor-expanding-the-islamic-states-global-expansion-struggles/.

[33] See, for example, Bill Roggio and Caleb Weiss, "Shabaab Strikes Police Department Headquarters in Mogadishu," Long War Journal, July 31, 2016, http://www.longwarjournal.org/archives/2016/07/shabaab-strikes-police-department-headquarters-in-mogadishu.php.

[34] Peter Devlin, "State of the Insurgency in al-Anbar," U.S. Marine Corps intelligence assessment, August 17, 2006, available at http://www.washingtonpost.com/wp-dyn/content/article/2007/02/02/AR2007020201197.html.

[35] See Ayman al-Zawahiri, letter to Abu Musab al-Zarqawi, n.d., available at https://www.ctc.usma.edu/posts/zawahiris-letter-to-zarqawi-english-translation-2.

[36] Bassem Mroue, "Syria and Iraq al Qaeda Merger Annulment Announced by Ayman al Zawahiri," Associated Press, June 10, 2013, http://www.huffingtonpost.com/2013/06/10/syria-iraq-al-qaeda-merger-annu....

[37] "Expert: ISIS' Declaration Of Islamic State 'Poses A Huge Threat To Al Qaeda,'" CBS, June 30, 2014, http://washington.cbslocal.com/2014/06/30/expert-isis-declaration-of-islamic-state-poses-a-huge-threat-to-al-qaeda/.

[38] See "Sunni Rebels Declare New 'Islamic Caliphate,'" Al-Jazeera (Doha), June 30, 2014, http://www.aljazeera.com/news/middleeast/2014/06/isil-declares-new-islamic-caliphate-201462917326669749.html.

[39] Jim Sciutto, Jamie Crawford and Chelsea J. Carter, "ISIS Can 'Muster' Between 20,000 and 31,500 Fighters, CIA Says," CNN, September 12, 2014, http://www.cnn.com/2014/09/11/world/meast/isis-syria-iraq/.

[40] Daveed Gartenstein-Ross, "How Many Fighters Does the Islamic State Really Have?," War on the Rocks, February 9, 2015, http://warontherocks.com/2015/02/how-many-fighters-does-the-islamic-state-really-have/.

[41] Martin Chulov, "How an Arrest in Iraq Revealed Isis's $2bn Jihadist Network," The Guardian, June 15, 2014, http://www.theguardian.com/world/2014/jun/15/iraq-isis-arrest-jihadists-wealth-power.

[42] Ian Johnston, "The Rise of Isis: Terror Group now Controls an Area the Size of Britain, Expert Says," Independent (London), September 3, 2014, http://www.independent.co.uk/news/world/middle-east/the-rise-of-isis-terror-group-now-controls-an-area-the-size-of-britain-expert-claims-9710198.html.

[43] Daveed Gartenstein-Ross, "The Islamic State's Vulnerability," War on the Rocks, September 17, 2014, http://warontherocks.com/2014/09/the-islamic-states-vulnerability/.

[44] See, for example, Eric Schmitt, "U.S. Caution in Strikes Gives ISIS an Edge, Many Iraqis Say," New York Times, May 26, 2015, http://www.nytimes.com/2015/05/27/world/middleeast/with-isis-in-crosshairs-us-holds-back-to-protect-civilians.html.

[45] Gartenstein-Ross & Barr, "Neither Remaining Nor Expanding: The Islamic State's Global Expansion Struggles."

[46] Letter from Osama bin Laden to Atiyah Abd al-Rahman, May 2010, SOCOM-2012-00000019, http://www.jihadica.com/wp-content/uploads/2012/05/SOCOM-2012-0000019-Trans.pdf.

[47] Ibid

[48] Ayman al-Zawahiri, "General Guidelines for Jihad," As-Sahab Media, September 2013, https://azelin.files.wordpress.com/2013/09/dr-ayman-al-e1ba93awc481hirc4ab-22general-guidelines-for-the-work-of-a-jihc481d-c4ab22-en.pdf.

[49] Abu Muhammad al-Julani, "Victory from God and Conquest is Close," Al-Manarah al-Bayda Foundation for Media Production, April 1, 2015, http://jihadology.net/2015/04/01/al-manarah-al-bay%E1%B8%8Da-foundation-for-media-production-presents-a-new-audio-message-from-jabhat-al-nu%E1%B9%A3rahs-abu-mu%E1%B8%A5ammad-al-jawlani-victory-from-god-and-conque/.

[50] Shiv Malik, Mustafa Khalili, Spencer Ackerman and Ali Younis, "How Isis Crippled Al-Qaida," The Guardian (London), June 10, 2015, http://www.theguardian.com/world/2015/jun/10/how-isis-crippled-al-qaida.

[51] Thomas Joscelyn, "Al Nusra Front Rebrands Itself as Jabhat Fath al-Sham," Long War Journal, July 28, 2016, http://www.longwarjournal.org/archives/2016/07/analysis-al-nusrah-front-rebrands-itself-as-jabhat-fath-al-sham.php.

BOKO HARAM

> **QUICK FACTS**
>
> Geographical Areas of Operation: Northern Nigeria, northern Camaroon, Lake Chad Basin, and southeast Niger.
>
> Numerical Strength (Members): Membership is estimated to be several thousand.
>
> Leadership: Abu Musab al-Barnawi
>
> Religious Identification: Sunni Islam
>
> *Quick Facts Courtesy of the 2015 edition of the U.S. State Department's Country Reports on Terrorism*

OVERVIEW

Boko Haram is an Islamist militant group in northern Nigeria and the Lake Chad region. However, after Boko Haram leader Abubakar Shekau pledged allegiance to the Islamic State leader Abu Bakr al-Baghdadi in March 2015, Boko Haram began to be called "Islamic State's West Africa Province", or ISWAP. When the Islamic State dropped Shekau from its leadership position in ISWAP in August 2016 in favor of another leader, Shekau revived Boko Haram anew. Thus, ISWAP now operates alongside Boko Haram, although there are major ideological barriers to collaboration between the two factions.

Boko Haram traces its ideological origins to the Nigerian Salafi imam Mohammed Yusuf. Yusuf was killed during the 2009 Boko Haram uprising. Abubakar Shekau was Yusuf's deputy during his lifetime, and his successor after his death. When the Islamic State demoted Shekau in August 2016 as a result of a long-standing feud within ISWAP's ranks, the Islamic State named Abu Musab al-Barnawi, Yusuf's son, as Shekau's successor. Al-Barnawi still leads ISWAP today.

Under Yusuf, Boko Haram sought to create an Islamic State in northern Nigeria based on the model of the Taliban in Afghanistan. However, it was not until Shekau took power in 2010 that Boko Haram began to build international connections and gain international legitimacy in the jihadist community. In 2014, the group announced an "Islamic State" in areas under Boko Haram control in northeastern Nigeria. This announcement was a harbinger of growing ties with and Shekau's signaling to the Islamic State and would culminate with Shekau's declaration of allegiance to al-Baghdadi in 2015 and al-Baghdadi's acceptance of the declaration with great fanfare from various Islamic State provinces in the week after Shekau's pledge. But soon after the pledge, a combined Nigerian and regional military offensive forced Boko Haram to abandon territories it conquered in northeastern Nigeria, causing Shekau's declared state to collapse. At the same time, the Islamic State also faced pressure from national armies, rival rebels, and international forces in Iraq, Syria, and Libya. That pressure limited the extent to which the Islamic State could support new provinces, such as ISWAP. However, even if direct operational coordination was minimal as a result of these pressures, the Islamic State fully integrated its media operation with that of ISWAP and has maintained ISWAP as an "official" province ever since Shekau's pledge.

In joining Islamic State, Shekau lived up to Yusuf's belief that an Islamic State "should be established in Nigeria, and if possible all over the world," but there were differences between the two men's ideologies.[1] Shekau's emphasis was strictly on militancy and jihadism, while Yusuf combined preaching with preparing for jihad more concretely, such as by sending young men to Afghanistan to learn how to build bombs.[2] While Yusuf commonly appeared on television and radio as a preacher, he also surreptitiously sent followers to the Sahel, Sudan, Pakistan and Afghanistan to receive funds to build madrasas and mosques, and so they could acquire militant training and advice from al-Qaeda in preparation for an inevitable confrontation with the Nigerian government. That confrontation finally occurred in July 2009 and led to Yusuf's death.[3]

In recalling this history, Abu Musab al-Barnawi said in the interview with Islamic State that announced his usurpation of Shekau's position and ascension to wali (governor), on August 3, 2016 that: "The group went through stages and many developments in its jihadi march, and among these developments was its thorough striving to rescue its captives who were captured in the first assault on the group, its sending its soldiers to the Greater Sahara to be trained there, and also its transitioning from the stage of guerrilla warfare to the stage of empowerment and spreading control. Also among most prominent developments was that historic development that astonished the entire world, when our pledge of allegiance was announced to the Caliph of Muslims, al-Qurashi [Abubakar al-Baghdadi], may Allah preserve him."[4]

ISWAP under al-Barnawi has already evolved from being a local threat to a sub-regional threat, with attacks in Nigeria, Niger, Chad and Cameroon. There are signs that ISWAP not only has networks throughout Africa and beyond, as evidenced by the Islamic State relationship, but that it has operational cells in Senegal and other West Africa countries.[5] *It may only be a matter of time before Islamic State uses sub-Saharan African foreign fighters who trained in Libya to carry out attacks through West Africa on behalf of ISWAP in a similar way to how European foreign fighters trained in Syria have done the same in France, Belgium and Germany. Meanwhile Shekau's Boko Haram may not have the strong Islamic State regional and global connections that al-Barnawi's ISWAP now has, but it nonetheless still operates throughout the Lake Chad sub-region and is a significant sub-regional threat*

History and Ideology

Yusuf led Boko Haram from 2002 to 2009. He preached that "Western education is sinful," which in Hausa language translates to *Boko Haram* (*Boko* can mean "Book" or, more broadly, "Western education," and *Haram* means "sinful" or "forbidden"). Yusuf also taught that employment in the Nigerian government and participation in democracy was *haram* for Muslims because Nigeria was not an Islamic State. He also preached that activities, such as sports or listening to music, were haram because they could lead to idol worship.[6]

Yusuf's estimated 280,000 followers, who came from Nigeria, Niger, Chad and Cameroon, either listened to his sermons in-person or on audiocassettes. They became known in northern Nigeria and abroad as the "Nigerian Taliban" because of their adherence to the theology of the Taliban in Afghanistan, which Nigerian Taliban members cited as their source of inspiration along with Osama bin Laden.[7] Yusuf's anti-Western and anti-education ideology appealed to many northern Nigerian Muslims that believed Nigeria was losing its Muslim identity to Western influence and Christianity. They also felt that the secular government was failing to provide adequate services to the people of northern Nigeria.

Before the British colonial period (1850 – 1960), a large swath of northern Nigeria, southern Niger and Cameroon were under the rule of the Sokoto Caliphate (1804 – 1903), while Nigeria's Borno and Yobe States and parts of northern Cameroon, southeastern Niger and western Chad were under the rule of the Borno Empire (1380 – 1893). The British disbanded both of these Muslim empires and established the Northern Nigeria Protectorate in 1900, which later became part of colonial Nigeria in 1914, and then part of independent Nigeria in 1960. Colonization brought with it British education, including Western schools and Christian missionaries. By the time of Nigerian independence in 1960, southern Nigeria, where British influence was strongest, especially in cities like Lagos and the oil hub Port Harcourt, was economically more powerful and had higher levels of education than northern Nigeria. Moreover, its population, which was largely animist before the arrival of the British, was by 1960 predominantly Christian. Northern Nigeria, on the other hand, was and remains predominantly Muslim, although since independence the influence of Islamic practices from Saudi Arabia and the Middle East, such as *Salafism* and Shiism, have become among the most prominent strands in northern Nigerian Islam and heavily influenced the doctrines of Muhammed Yusuf and his followers.

When democracy was institutionalized in Nigeria in 1999 after several failed attempts at political liberalization, some northern Nigerian Muslims saw democracy as a byproduct of American influence and a ploy that would lead to the marginalization of northern Nigerian Muslims or dilute the Islamic identity of the region.[8] As a result twelve states in northern Nigeria adopted *sharia* laws since 2000. But *Salafists* like Boko Haram founder Mohammed Yusuf considered this only "half-*sharia*" because it was not imposed throughout the entire country and the traditional Islamic leaders still mixed *sharia* with secular institutions like electoral democracy and co-ed schooling.[9]

As a result of the perceived weakened Islamic identity and diluted form of Islam practiced in northern Nigeria, Yusuf's rallying cry when he founded Boko Haram in 2002 was the creation of a true Islamic state and the elimination of all forms of Western influence and education.[10] According to Yusuf, for a short-lived period in 2003, several thousand members of the Nigerian Taliban: "left the city, which is impure, and headed for the bush, believing that Muslims who do not share their ideology are infidels."[11] They called their encampment, which was located two miles from Nigeria's border with Niger, "Afghanistan."

The local government ordered the Nigerian Taliban to leave "Afghanistan" when the community failed to respect local ordinances. The friction between the Nigerian Taliban and the local government led to frequent clashes. During one battle in early 2004, several hundred members of the Nigerian Taliban attacked the residences of local government leaders, regional officials, and the divisional police. They killed several policemen and stole police weapons and vehicles.[12] The Nigerian security forces responded to the attacks by killing several Nigerian Taliban members, arresting a number of others, and destroying "Afghanistan."

In 2004, Yusuf's followers attempted four attacks on Nigerian security forces, three of which failed. For the next five years, Yusuf's followers generally avoided conflict with the Nigerian government and security forces. Yusuf fled to Saudi Arabia in 2005 but returned shortly thereafter when northern Nigerian politicians assured him that he would not be harmed. He was arrested several times between 2005 and 2009, but for the most part he maintained an uneasy truce with the government and security forces.

The apparent truce came to an end in July 2009 when Yusuf's followers and the security forces engaged in battles in Borno State and several other states in northeastern Nigeria for four days. Police captured Yusuf and killed him in an extrajudicial execution. During the uprising, more than 700 people were killed, many of them innocent bystanders.[13]

While the government and Yusuf's followers blamed each other for instigating the clashes, conflict may have been inevitable given Yusuf's rising popularity in northeastern Nigeria. His popularity, combined with his rejection of the legitimacy of the Nigerian State; his sermons encouraging his followers to hoard weapons in preparation for battle; and his establishment of training and financial contacts with al-Qaeda during the mid-2000s; all gave Yusuf credibility as a serious threat. Yusuf's followers were said to have received "coded messages from Pakistan… on how to carry out terrorist activities against American interests in Nigeria."[14] The rapid acceleration in militant capabilities of Yusuf's followers starting in 2010 also attested to the training they received from al-Qaeda. That training could not have happened if Yusuf did not forge alliances with al-Qaeda, especially AQIM, throughout the mid-2000s.

During the year after Yusuf's death, Yusuf's followers went underground in Nigeria or took refuge in Niger, Chad and Cameroon, all of which border Borno State. Shekau, who was Yusuf's deputy, reportedly went into hiding in the "desert between Chad and Sudan," although other reports suggest he was simply in hiding in northern Nigeria all along[15] In July 2010, Shekau, who Nigerian security forces believed was killed in the July 2009 clashes, emerged in a video statement as Boko Haram's new leader. His video message was issued "on behalf of my *mujahideen* brothers in some African territory called Nigeria… to the soldiers of Allah in the Islamic State of Iraq in particular." It warned that: "*Jihad* has just begun… O America, die with your fury."[16] On October 2, 2010, AQIM's media wing, al-Andalus, also published a statement by Shekau to the Shumukh al-Islam *jihadist* web forum, which marked the first time that AQIM disseminated an official message from another militant leader or group. In the message, Shekau offered "glad tidings" and mourned the deaths of two al-Qaeda in Iraq leaders and offered: "condolences on behalf of the Mujahideen in Nigeria to the Mujahideen in general, in particular to those in the "Islamic State of Iraq, Osama bin Laden, Ayman Al-Zawahiri, Abu Yahya Al-Libi, Abu Abdullah Al-Muhajir, the Emir of the Islamic State in Somalia, the Emir of Al-Qaeda in the Islamic Maghreb, the Emir of the Mujahideen in Pakistan, in Chechnya, Kashmir, Yemen, the Arabian Peninsula, and our religious clerics whom I did not mention."[17]

Shekau would remain leader from 2010 through his pledge of allegiance of al-Baghdadi in March 2015 and until August 2016, when rival factions endorsed by Islamic State deposed him. The transition of power culminated in the Islamic State's announcement on August 3, 2016 that the new *wali* (governor) of "West Africa Province" was Abu Musab al-Barnawi. Shekau, in turn, reverted back to his pre-West Africa Province title of "*imam*" of Boko Haram (*Jamaatu ahlis Sunna li'Dawati wal Jihad*), while still maintaining his loyalty to Abu Bakr al-Baghdadi as Caliph, possibly in the hopes of one day reuniting with al-Barnawi in ISWAP or to fight with and defeat al-Barnawi and reclaim the leadership of ISWAP.

Global Reach

Boko Haram has only claimed to have carried out one attack in the predominantly Christian oil-producing zones of southern Nigeria. That attack occurred in June 2014, when Shekau claimed responsibility for a female suicide bombing at Apapa Port in Lagos in June 2014 (Shekau did not, however, refer to the identity of the attacker).[18] This was the second female suicide bombing that Boko Haram carried out and represented the start of what by the end of 2016 would amount to more than 120 such female suicide bombing operations involving more than 200 women and girls (often in tandem or trios) in attacks Nigeria, Niger, Chad and Cameroon.[19]

Boko Haram's attacks have instead been concentrated in northern Nigeria, especially Borno State, with occasional large bombings in the Middle Belt region, as well as in northern Cameroon, Niger and Chad. In April 2012, Boko Haram militants, including Shekau, were reportedly in northern Mali with the Movement for Unity and Jihad in West Africa (MUJWA), al-Qaeda in the Islamic Maghreb (AQIM), and Ansar al-Din when the Islamist militias established the "Islamic State of Azawad" in northern Mali.[20] A French-led military intervention eventually expelled them from the region in early 2013.[21] During that time, Boko Haram reportedly took part in attacks on the forces of the secular Tuareg-led militia, the National Movement for the Liberation of Azawad (MNLA) and the Malian army, as well as the kidnapping of Algerian diplomats at their consulate in Gao, Mali.[22]

After the French-led military intervention, some of these Boko Haram members returned to northern Nigeria and used similar tactics of desert warfare to overrun Nigerian military barracks throughout Borno State.[23] This allowed Boko Haram to become the de-facto military power in large swaths of Borno State in 2014 and provided grounding for Shekau's announcements in 2014 that Boko Haram established an "Islamic State." The videos carried the same visual signatures of Islamic State's own releases and hinted that a pledge from Shekau to al-Baghdadi was in the making.[24] This control over territory in northeastern Nigeria, combined with Shekau's charismatic persona and imitations of Abu Musab al-Zarqawi and Boko Haram's tactics, such as kidnapping and proudly enslaving the more than 250 schoolgirls from Chibok, impressed the Islamic State and facilitated its eventual recognition of Boko Haram as ISWAP.

Coinciding with Boko Haram's merger with the Islamic State in March 2015, Nigeria and regional militaries from Niger, Chad and Cameroon launched incursions into northeastern Nigeria to oust Boko Haram from the territories it controlled. This, in turn, led Boko Haram to retaliate against all of these countries. In February 2015, Boko Haram sent a tandem of a male and female suicide bomber to attack Diffa, Niger. In June 2015, Boko Haram sent two suicide bombers to N'djamena, Chad to attack the government buildings. The Islamic State later claimed those operations.[25] Later, two other suicide attackers targeted markets in N'djamena, while other suicide bombers, often female, began to target islands in Lake Chad with regularity. Cameroon had been a target of Boko Haram's as early as 2014, even before the regional military offensive against the group. By 2015, Boko Haram was targeting Cameroon's northern region as frequently as northern Nigeria, again also primarily using women as suicide bombers.[26]

Cameroon's large-scale counterinsurgency effort, however, rolled back Boko Haram attacks in the country by 2016. Chad, too, managed to mitigate further Boko Haram attacks in the country by 2016, possibly based on the way it dealt with factions of Seleka in Central African Republic or rebels in Darfur, by coming to a tacit truce or understanding with Boko Haram, which was by then known as ISWAP. According to Chadian analysts, the country's President Idriss Deby needs both foreign aid to keep coming and Chad's trade route through northern Cameroon to remain open. Chad may have made a deal to not interfere in ISWAP operations so long as ISWAP would not close the northern Cameroon transportation routes or attack Chad. At the same time, Chad may leverage its ability to "control" ISWAP to demand concessions in terms of foreign aid from France and other Western countries with a subtle threat that if aid is not forthcoming Chad will allow Boko Haram to reign free around the Lake Chad region. Whatever the cause, after Boko Haram attacks, around Lake Chad in Chad in early 2016 and suicide bombings in N'djamena in June 2016 the country has managed stay relatively free of any further ISWAP or Boko Haram attacks since then.

Niger, however, has suffered the brunt of ISWAP attacks in 2016, with several large-scale ISWAP operations in Diffa and Bosso in the country's southeast. A June 2016 raid by more than 100 ISWAP militants destroyed a military barracks in Bosso.[27] ISWAP filmed a video entitled: "Invading Niger: Scenes from Liberating the Nigerien Apostate Army Camp in the Area of Bosso."[28] ISWAP released the video via the Islamic State's media channels in July 2016 and may have done so in anticipation of and as a promotion for Abu Musab al-Barnawi's imending ascension to ISWAP's leadership position.

ISWAP has established cells in Senegal in 2015 and 2016. They, however, are not yet focused on carrying out attacks but rather recruitment, financing and training.[29] There are approximately 100 Nigerians and several dozen Senegalese with the Islamic State in Libya. With the Islamic State struggling to hold territory in Libya and Abu Musab al-Barnawi's more internationally connected ISWAP faction now in charge of these regional realationships, ISWAP could activate cells of Nigerian and Senegalese ex-foreign fighters in Libya. Activating those cells would launch ISWAP's first attack outside of the Lake Chad region.

There are, however, no signs at this time ISWAP is planting cells in Europe for attacks. Rather, the Islamic State is using its Syria network to carry out attacks in Europe. It is the Libya network that is likely to be responsible for attacks throughout Africa, including those under the banner of ISWAP.

Recent Activity

From the time of Shekau's pledge to al-Baghdadi until August 3, 2016, the formerly-bombastic Shekau was not seen publicly in any video or propaganda material, although the Islamic State still recognized him as its *wali* (governor). During this time, Shekau and his former rival for Boko Haram leadership, Mamman Nur, were locked in a factional feud, with the two of them sending audios behind-the-scenes condemning one another.[30]

Mamman Nur is wanted by Interpol and the FBI for masterminding the UN Headquarters attack in Abuja in August 2011 in coordination with al-Qaeda in the Islamic Maghreb (AQIM), which killed more than 20 people.[31] He accuses Shekau of being dictatorial, religiously uncompromising, and killing or maiming (via *sharia* punishment) innocent Muslim civilians and burning down mosques over small "violations," including being disloyal to Shekau, selling a goat against Shekau's orders, or holding a government ID card.[32] Nur's criticisms of Shekau resemble those of other breakaway groups, such as the Yusufiya Islamic Movement in 2011 and AQIM-aligned Ansaru in 2012-2013.

Shekau was forced to back down after Nur's condemnations and the Islamic State's announcement on August 3, 2016 that Abu Musab al-Barnawi, who was aligned with Nur, was the new *wali* of ISWAP.[33] In an audio clip released on Youtube, also on August 3, Shekau reverted to his former position and declared himself *imam* of *Jamaatu ahlis Sunna li'Dawati wal Jihad* (the original name of Boko Haram before the formation of ISWAP), thus showing that Shekau had left ISWAP.[34] On August 7, Boko Haram also released a video on Youtube for the first time since Shekau returned to his role as *imam* of Boko Haram. The video marked Shekau's his first public appearance since before he pledged allegiance to al-Baghdadi in March 2015.[35] In the beginning of the video, Shekau's military *emir*, who was also a *sharia* judge for Boko Haram and then ISWAP, leads a march of about 100 fighters. He then reads a scripted message to the "caliph of Muslims, Abubakar al-Baghdadi" in response to the "sudden" news about a new *wali*—al-Barnawi. The military *emir* says Boko Haram will refuse to follow al-Barnawi and will only follow Shekau because al-Barnawi does not adhere to "*authentic Salafism.*" In the last few minutes of the video, Shekau appears. Like his bombastic pre-ISWAP persona, he fires a gun in the air in the style of Abu Musab al-Zarqawi and screams: "Praise be to Allah, who made *jihad* the greatest form of worship" and "die in your frustration" to the "tyrants of America, France, Germany and the United Nonsense [Nations]." In subsequent videos in September 2016, and an audio message in November 2016, Shekau reiterated that Boko Haram was still loyal to al-Baghdadi and opposed to al-Barnawi's leadership. He also claimed that his militants would continue *jihad* regardless of their affiliation.[36] Furthermore, Shekau condemned the electoral victory of the "pagan" and "homosexual" November 2016 Donald Trump over the "prostitute" Hillary Clinton in the U.S. presidential election, thus making clear that the U.S. remains the main target of his enmity.[37]

The leadership change makes ISWAP's future likely to be more regional, especially in regards to potential expansion in West Africa. Both Nur and al-Barnawi are far more internationally connected than Shekau and they are now the top figures in ISWAP, which could prompt them to launch an attack outside the Lake Chad region. If the organization manages to successfully orchestrate attacks outside its home base, its power in the jihadi world and already-intense notoriety will only grow. Meanwhile, if ISWAP begins to take on a more regional dimension, it could open up opportunities for Shekau to reclaim the mantle of *jihad* in Nigeria. In essence, ISWAP could evolve into a more regional militant group while Boko Haram limits its focus to Nigeria alone.

ENDNOTES

[1] Emmanuel Goujon & Aminu Abubakar, "Nigeria's 'Taliban' Plot Comeback from Hide-outs," Agence France-Presse , (Maiduguri), January 11, 2006;
[2] "Nigerian 'Trained in Afghanistan,'" BBC, September 2, 2009. http://news.bbc.co.uk/2/hi/africa/8233980.stm
[3] . Ikechukwu Nnochiri, "Danger Alert: Al-Qaeda Boss in West Africa Lives in Kano," Odili.net, April 8, 2012.
[4] Islamic State, al-Naba Weekly Newsletter #41, August 23, 2016 available at: http://jihadology.net/2016/08/02/new-issue-of-the-islamic-states-newsletter-al-naba-41/; http://www.vanguardngr.com/2016/08/know-boko-harams-new-leader-abu-musab-al-barnawi/.

[5] Tamba Jean-Matthew, "3 imams charged with terrorism in Senegal," Africa Review, November 9th, 2015, http://www.africareview.com/news/Senegalese-imams-charged-with-terrorism-/979180-2949060-dv12q3z/index.html; "Coup de Filet Anti Boko Haram Au Sénégal: La cellule de Abu Youssouf," Dakaractu, déciméehttphttp://www.dakaractu.com/COUP-DE-FILET-AN-TI-BOKO-HARAM-AU-SENEGAL-La-cellule-de-Abu-Youssouf-decimee_a115021.html; http://www.buzz.sn/news/boko-haram-attirerait-il-autant-de-senegalais-que-la-branche-libyenne-de-lei/34207; "Peer Raises Fears Over UK Charity's Alleged Links to Boko Haram," Guardian, September 9, 2012, https://www.theguardian.com/world/2012/sep/09/uk-charity-boko-haram.

[6] Umar, Muhammad, S. "The Popular Discourses of Salafi Radicalism and Salafi Counter-radicalism in Nigeria: A Case Study of Boko Haram," Journal of Religion in Africa, 2012.

[7] Aminu Abubakar, "Nigerian Islamist sect threaten to widen attacks," March 29, 2010.

[8] Simeon H.O. Alozieuwa, "Contending Theories on Nigeria's Security Challenge in the Era of Boko Haram Insurgency," The Peace and Conflict Review, 2012.

[9] Karen Brulliard, "For Many, Nigeria's Moderate Form of Sharia Fails to Deliver on Promises," Washington Post, August 12, 2009.

[10] Farouk Chothia, "Who are Nigeria's Boko Haram Islamists?" BBC, January 11, 2012.

[11] Emmanuel Goujon and Aminu Abubakar, "Nigeria's 'Taliban' Plot Comeback from Hide-outs," Agence France-Presse (AFP) (Maiduguri), January 11, 2006.

[12] Benjamin Maiangwa and Ufo Okeke Uzodike, "The Changing Dynamics of Boko Haram Terrorism," al-Jazeera, July 31, 2012.

[13] Spiraling Violence: Boko Haram Attacks and Security Force Abuses in Nigeria, Human Rights Watch, October 11th, 2012. https://www.hrw.org/report/2012/10/11/spiraling-violence/boko-haram-attacks-and-security-force-abuses-nigeria.

[14] "Chapter 2 -- Country Reports: Africa Overview," U.S. Department of State, April 30, 2008, http://www.state.gov/j/ct/rls/crt/2007/103705.htm; Ahmad Salkida, "Nigeria: Sect Leader Vows Revenge," Daily Trust, July 27, 2009, http://allafrica.com/stories/200907270879.html.

[15] "Nigerian Taliban Reportedly Reforming to Strike Again a Year After Uprising," Agence France-Presse, July 16, 2010.

[16] "Nigerian Islamist leader threatens US: monitors," AFP, July 14, 2010.

[17] "Periodical Review July 2010 – No. 2," International Institute for Counterterrorism, August 2010.

[18] Robyn Dixon, "Nigeria depot blast was a suicide bombing, security analysts say," The Los Angeles Times, July 10th, 2014, http://www.latimes.com/world/africa/la-fg-nigeria-lagos-terror-20140710-story.html; Tim Cocks, Isacc Abrak, "Boko Haram leader claims blast in Nigeria's Lagos," Reuters, July 13, 2014, http://uk.reuters.com/article/uk-nigeria-violence-idUKKBN-0FI0IG20140713.

[19] "Boko Haram Widely Deploying Female Suicide Bombers," The Clarion Project, December 15, 2014, http://www.clarionproject.org/news/boko-haram-widely-deploying-female-suicide-bombers; "Boko Haram Turns Female Captives into Terrorists," The New York Times, April 7, 2016 http://www.nytimes.com/2016/04/08/world/africa/boko-haram-suicide-bombers.html.

[20] "Boko Haram Leader Shekau Reportedly Found in Mali," Daily Post Nigeria, January 19, 2013, http://dailypost.ng/2013/01/19/boko-haram-leader-shekau-reportedly-found-in-mali/.

[21] Jacob Zenn, "Nigerians in Gao: Was Boko Haram Really Active in Northern Mali?" African Arguments, January 20, 2014

[22] "Dozens of Boko Haram in Mali's rebel-seized Gao: sources," Al-Arabiya News, April 9, 2012, https://www.alarabiya.net/articles/2012/04/09/206611.html

[23] "Boko Haram Militants Shows Off Weapons 'Captured' From An Army Barack Raid," Sahara TV, April 29, 2013, https://www.youtube.com/watch?v=El-O37TNIm4; Jacob Zenn, Boko Haram's Evolving Tactics and Alliance in Nigeria, Combatting Terrorism Center, June 25, 2013, https://www.ctc.usma.edu/posts/boko-harams-evolving-tactics-and-alliances-in-nigeria; Kareem Ogori, "Boko Haram Raids Army Barracks, Kills 22," Blueprint, March 4, 2013.

[24] "Boko Haram Militants Display Control Of Captured Towns In Northeastern Nigeria," Sahara TV, November 10, 2014, https://www.youtube.com/watch?v=77YwVoM7_JA

[25] "Bloody Weekend as Boko Haram Strikes Chad, Nigeria," Africa News, February 5, 2016, http://www.africanews.com/2016/01/31/bloody-weekend-as-boko-haram-strikes-chad-nigeria/; "Chad Executes 10 Boko Haram Fighters over Deadly Attacks." BBC News, August 29, 2015, http://www.bbc.com/news/world-africa-34100484.

[26] "A female suicide bomber killed by a poisoned arrow in Cameroon," Reuters France, May 4, 2016, https://francais.rt.com/international/20091-femme-kamikaze-tuee-par-fleche.

[27] "Boko Haram retakes Niger town of Bosso, says mayor," Reuters, June 6, 2016. http://www.reuters.com/article/us-nigeria-security-niger-idUSKC-N0YS1TY.

[28] S.J. Prince, "WATCH: New ISIS Video Aims to 'Liberate Niger' With Boko Haram," Heavy, http://heavy.com/news/2016/07/new-isis-islamic-state-daesh-amaq-news-pictures-videos-wilayat-west-africa-wilayat-gharb-afriqiya-boko-haram-bosso-army-camp-attack-full-uncensored-youtube-video/. /

[29] "Terrorism: over 23 Senegalese joined Boko Haram," Press Afrik, February 25, 2016, http://www.pressafrik.com/Terrorisme-plus-de-23-Senegalais-ont-rejoint-Boko-Haram_a146725.html

[30] Jacob Zenn, Leadership Analysis of Boko Haram and Ansaru in Nigeria, Combatting Terrorism Center, February 24, 2014, https://www.ctc.usma.edu/posts/leadership-analysis-of-boko-haram-and-ansaru-in-nigeria; "Nigeria Sets $175,000 Bounty For Mamman Nur, The Alleged UN Office Bomber," Sahara Reporter, September 18, 2011, http://saharareporters.com/2011/09/18/nigeria-sets-175000-bounty-mamman-nur-alleged-un-office-bomber; "New Boko Haram Leader, al-Barnawi, Accuses Abubakar Shekau Of Killing Fellow Muslims, Living In Luxury" Sahara Reporters, August 5, 2016, http://saharareporters.com/2016/08/05/new-boko-haram-leader-al-barnawi-accuses-abubakar-shekau-killing-fellow-muslims-living.

[31] "Abuja attack: Car bomb hits Nigeria UN building," BBC, August 27, 2011, http://www.bbc.com/news/world-africa-14677957. http://www.bbc.com/news/world-africa-14677957

[32] "New Boko Haram Leader, al-Barnawi, Accuses Abubakar Shekau of Killing Fellow Muslims, Living in Luxury," Sahara Reporters, August 5, 2016, http://saharareporters.com/2016/08/05/new-boko-haram-leader-al-barnawi-accuses-abubakar-shekau-killing-fellow-muslims-living.

[33] Islamic State, al-Naba Weekly Newsletter #41, August 2, 2016 available at: http://jihadology.net/2016/08/02/new-issue-of-the-islamic-states-newsletter-al-naba-41/; "Al-Urwah al-Wuthqa Foundation Presents a New Video Message from Boko Haram", Jihadology, January 27, 2015, http://jihadology.net/2015/01/27/al-urwah-al-wuthqa-foundation-presents-a-new-video-message-from-from-boko-ḥarams-jamaat-ahl-al-sunnah-li-dawah-wa-l-jihad-interview-with-the-official-spokesma/.

[34] (Video has been removed for violating YouTube's Terms of Service,) https://www.youtube.com/watch?v=AhYR37fvB-k&feature=youtu.be.

[35] "New video message from Jamāʿat Ahl al-Sunnah li-l-Daʿwah wa-l-Jihād's Abū Bakr Shekau: 'Message From the Soldiers,'" Jihadology, August 7, 2016, http://jihadology.net/2016/08/07/new-video-message-from-jamaat-ahl-al-sunnah-li-l-dawah-wa-l-jihads-abu-bakr-shekau-message-from-the-soldiers/.

[36] "New video message from Jamāʿat Ahl al-Sunnah li-l-Daʿwah wa-l-Jihād's Abū Bakr Shekau: 'Message to the World,'" Jihadology, September 24, 2016, http://jihadology.net/2016/09/24/new-video-message-from-jamaat-ahl-al-sunnah-li-l-dawah-wa-l-jihads-abu-bakr-shekau-message-to-the-world/.

[37] Abdurasheed Adamu, "boko haram leader Abubakar shekau warns Donald trump, claim," November 14, 2016, https://www.youtube.com/watch?v=2Z2rAR-lSBU.

Fetullah Gülen Movement

Quick Facts

Geographical Areas of Operation: East Asia, Eurasia, Europe, Latin America, Middle East and North Africa, North America, South Asia, Sub-Saharan Africa, Australia

Numerical strength (members): There are somewhere between three and six million Gülen followers although exact numbers are impossible to offer because, as Ihsan Yilmaz stated, the boundaries of this "collectivity" are "extremely loose and difficult to specify."

Leadership: Fetullah Gülen

Religious identification: Mainstream Sufism

Quick Facts courtesy of Ihsan Yilmaz's, "Inter-Madhhab Surfing, Neo-Ijtihad, and Faith Based Movement Leaders" and Claire Berlinski's, "Who is Fethullah Gulen?" (Autumn 2012)

Overview

Fetullah Gülen, a charismatic Turkish preacher, inspired and leads the Gülen movement. Unlike many other organizations in this compilation, the Gülen movement claims to be pacifist and focused on providing quality educations to the communities all over the world of which it is a part, ostensibly working toward the modernization and democratization of Turkey. However, there is compelling evidence to suggest that the Gülen movement is focused more on cultivating its own social power than anything else. Furthermore, the movement operates internally in an undemocratic fashion. Critics accuse its vast network of charter schools of illegally funneling millions of American taxpayer dollars to Turkish businesses. Critics inside Turkey accuse it of infiltrating the Turkish government and military and staging a bloody failed coup on July 15, 2016. On December 11, 2015, the Gülen movement was classified as a terrorist organization in Turkey under the name Gülenist Terror Organization (Fetullahçı Terör Örgütü, FETÖ) or Parallel State Organization (Paralel

Devlet Yapılanması, *PDY)*. *Gülen continues to give weekly talks (*Bamteli *and* Herkul Nağme*), which are uploaded to Herkul.org and regularly downloaded by some 20,000–50,000 listeners.*

HISTORY AND IDEOLOGY

According to Fetullah Gülen's website (http://www.Gülenmovement.com), he is:

> ...an authoritative mainstream Turkish Muslim scholar, thinker, author, poet, opinion leader and educational activist who supports interfaith and intercultural dialogue, science, democracy and spirituality and opposes violence and turning religion into a political ideology.

The site notes that he was "the first Muslim scholar to publicly condemn the attacks of 9/11 (in an advertisement in the *Washington Post*)." It also celebrates his infinite modesty. Yet there is more to the story. Gülen at the height of his power was an immensely powerful figure in Turkey, and—to put it mildly—a controversial one. He is also a powerful figure globally.

To understand Gülen, it is critical to understand the history of the Nurcu movement. Said Nursî, a Sunni Muslim in the Sufi tradition, was one of the great charismatic religious personalities of the late Ottoman Caliphate and early Turkish Republic; his Qur'anic commentary, the *Risale-i Nur*, became the basis for the formation of reading circles known as *dershanes*. These evolved into so-called "textual communities" devoted to reading and internalizing Nursî's commentaries.

The *dershanes* gradually spread throughout Anatolia. Hakan Yavuz, a Turkish political scientist at the University of Utah who was formerly quite sympathetic to Gülen, notes that the Nurcu movement:

> ...differs from other Islamic movements in terms of its understanding of Islam ... As a resistance movement to the ongoing Kemalist modernization process, the Nurcu movement is forward-looking and pro-active. Said Nursî offers a conceptual framework for a people undergoing the transformation from a confessional community (Gemeinschaft) to a secular national society (Gesellschaft)... Folk Islamic concepts and practices are redefined and revived to establish new solidarity networks and everyday-life strategies for coping with new conditions.[1]

Gülen's movement, or *cemaat*, arose from roughly a dozen neo-Nur textual communities, and Gülen is best described as being in Nur's mold, but more devoted to the Turkish state. Born in 1941, Gülen hails from a village near Erzurum, the eastern frontier of what is now the Turkish Republic. This territory was bitterly contested by the Russian, Persian and Ottoman empires and the zone of some of the bloodiest communal conflicts in modern memory. The region gave rise to a strongly nationalist version of Islam. Gülenists do not—contrary to one frequent misconception—view the Russians or the Persians as their friends.

While Gülen presents a tolerant Sufi image today, his early career was notable for statements, sermons, and publications notable for their intolerance toward those whom he considered enemies of Islam. In one sermon, allegedly dating from 1979, Gülen energetically chastises his flock for failing to prevent infidels (*gâvur*) from controlling of all of the holy places of Islam: "Muslims should become bombs and explode, tear to pieces the heads of the infidels! Even if it's America opposing them." He further curses those who are indifferent to this cause.[2] In another, he says: "Until this day missionaries and the Vatican have been behind all atrocities. The Vatican is the hole of the snake, the hole of the cobra. The Vatican is behind the bloodshed in Bosnia. The Vatican is behind the bloodshed in Kashmir. They have lobby groups in America and Germany."[3]

In unrevised editions of books from his early career, such as *Fasildan Fasila* and *Asrin Getirdigi Tereddutler*, Gülen called the Western world the "continuous enemy of Islam." Of Christians, he wrote: "After a while they perverted and obscured their own future." Jews have a "genetic animosity towards any religion;" and have used "their guile and skills to breed bad blood" to threaten Islam from the beginning of time, "uniting themselves with Sassanids, Romans and crusaders." He averred that: "the Church, the Synagogue and Paganism form the troika that has attacked Islam persistently." "In any case," he wrote, "the Prophet considers Islam as one nation and the *Kuffar* as the other nation."[4]

At the end of the 1990s, Gülen changed either his mind or his tactics, forging warm ties with the Vatican and other tablemates of the Interfaith Dialogue platform. In 1999, he fled to the United States, ostensibly for medical treatment, ensconcing himself at the heart of what he once considered the Devil's headquarters. Since then, he has presented himself as the great cultural reconciler. Many Turks, however, still view him as an archconservative *imam* with extremist views about women, atheists, and apostates. He has neither acknowledged nor apologized for his former views. The earlier books have been revised without comment.

Two notable points about Gülen's theology: First, he differentiates between *tebliğ* and *temsil*. The former means open proselytism, and he strongly dissuades his followers from this. He urges them instead to practice *temsil*—living an Islamic way of life at all times without uttering the word "Islam" or other "dangerous words." *Temsil* missionaries are to set a good example, embodying their ideals in their way of life. It is very visible that in Turkey, at least, the embodiment of these ideals involves a highly segregated role for women.

Second, Gülen holds publicly that Muslims and non-Muslims once lived in peace because the Ottoman Turks established a tolerant environment. To implement this peaceful cohabitation again, Turks should become leaders in the promotion of tolerance among religions. Latif Erdoğan and Davut Aydüz, both authors sympathetic to Gülen and perhaps even "inspired" by him, argue that the *cemaat's* key goal is to give Turkey a pivotal role in the international political environment. "Turkey will be the representative of justice in the world... Turkey should show the meaning of civilization to the world once more."[5]

Once in power, Gülen's organization forged an uneasy alliance with the Justice and Development Party of Turkish President Recep Tayyip Erdogan, although tensions between the two political partners persisted. These broke into the open beginning in June 2007, when police discovered a crate of grenades in an Istanbul slum.[6] Investigators claimed that they belonged to a shadowy group of conspirators called *Ergenekon*. The organization is accused of being an outgrowth of the so-called "Deep State"—a secret coalition of high-level figures in the military, the intelligence services, the judiciary, and organized crime. Allegedly, it planned to stage a series of terrorist attacks throughout Turkey and use the ensuing chaos as the pretext for a military coup. In the years since, thousands of Turks have been arrested in mostly pre-dawn raids, including hundreds of military officers and academics, NGO spokesmen, theologians, and journalists.

According to Turkish journalist Asli Aydintasbas, in 2009 then-prime minister Recep Tayyip Erdogan began replacing key figures in police intelligence, narcotics, anti-terrorism, and surveillance units headed by known Gülenists. This led to the so-called the Ergenekon investigation. She reports that the eavesdropping capabilities of the military and police were combined under a newly created body, also staffed by Gülenists:

> For the purposes of the Ergenekon trials, the investigators, the prosecutor, and later the judges were a clique who have mostly graduated from Gülen schools, participated in Gülen network's gatherings, were allies of the movement, acted in unison, or were openly known as Gülenists within the police force. Major stories about the case were first published in Gülen-related news outlets, such as Samanyolu, Zaman, Bugün or Taraf. A noticeable number of those arrested in the case and in subsequent probes were nationalists or hardline Kemalists who had criticised or attacked the Gülen network over the years.[7]

In 2009, a new round of mass arrests began, targeting the so-called KCK—the urban wing of the extremist Kurdish Workers Party, or PKK. In 2010, the so-called *Balyoz*, or Sledgehammer, case began when the self-styled liberal *Taraf* newspaper published allegedly leaked reports of the military's plans to stage a coup, first creating a pretext, and chaos, by bombing two mosques and accusing Greece of shooting down a Turkish plane. These plans, passed to prosecutors, formed the basis for their case. In total, thousands were imprisoned as a result.[8]

Turkish, U.S., and German forensic experts subsequently concluded that the digital evidence on a number of CDs in the Balyoz case was forged.[9] As the scholar Dani Rodrik writes,

> Today it is widely recognized that the coup plans were in fact forgeries. Forensic experts have determined that the plans published by Taraf and forming the backbone of the prosecution were produced on backdated computers and made to look as if they were prepared in 2003. A quasi-judicial United Nations body has slammed the Turkish government for severe violations of due process during the trial. Erdoğan and his close associates, once fully behind the charges, now talk about fabricated evidence and concede that there was a plot against the military. The 230 defendants held in jail (including Çetin Doğan) were eventually released on June 19th, 2014, following a unanimous ruling by the constitutional court finding the defendants' right to a fair trial had been violated.[10]

These waves of arrests were united by obvious evidence of judicial manipulation; despite this, all were supported by media outlets associated with Gülen, which refused to report on claims that the evidence was fraudulent.[11]

It is plausible to suspect that the movement functions like a mafia, and did indeed infiltrate the organs of the state in a way that further corrupted its already corrupt justice system, used this power to intimidate or imprison those who objected to this, and exploited Islamic sensibilities to do this. This line of argument has been supported by numerous informed assessments. The late University of Ankara history professor Necip Hablemitoğlu, a highly vocal critic of the Gülen movement, in his book *Köstebek* ("The Mole"), alleged that the Gülen movement had infiltrated the Turkish police. He was assassinated in 2002, shortly after its publication. The case has never been solved.12 Similarly, Adil Serdar Saçan, former director of the organized crimes unit in the Istanbul Directorate of Security, gave an interview to Kanaltürk TV in 2006 in which he said that Gülen sympathizers had thoroughly penetrated the state's security apparatus:

> *During my time at the [police] academy, those in the directorate who did not have ties to the [Gülen] organization were all pensioned off or fired in 2002 when the AKP came to power... Belonging to a certain cemaat has become a prerequisite for advancement in the force. At present, over 80 percent of the officers at supervisory level in the general security organization are members of the cemaat.*[13]

In 2008, Saçan himself was arrested on suspicion of involvement in Ergenekon. Similarly, the journalist Ahmet Şık was arrested just as he was about to publish *The Imam's Army*, a book detailing the Gülen movement's pervasive influence within the Turkish bureaucracy, police force, and judiciary. From prison, he sent a handwritten note to the American journalist Justin Vela, who published part of it in the magazine *Foreign Policy*:

> *The Ergenekon investigations are the most important part of allowing the cemaat to take power in the country. I must say that the deep state is still intact. Just the owner has changed. What I mean by this ownership ... is composed of the coalition of AKP and the* cemaat. .... *'Something' has come to power in Turkey, but not sharia. I can't name that 'thing' properly.*[14]

Asli Aydintasbas claims that, in 2010, Erdoğan and President Abdullah Gül removed the Gülen movement from the National Security Political Document. This list of security threats, popularly known in Turkey as the Red Book, is approved by the National Security Council and details Turkey's national security doctrine. Its contents are never published. Journalist Metin Gurcan confirms that in 2010, "religious reactionary trends," often a euphemism for the movement, were removed. (They were reportedly reinstated in 2014, according to Gurcan.[15])

Erdoğan strongly backed the Gülenists' efforts against the so-called deep state. "I am the prosecutor of this case," he said, and his team ridiculed critics who charged the *cemaat* was taking over the country's deep state.[16]

There is strong circumstantial evidence to suggest that Gülen's supporters manufactured evidence during the sham trials of senior military figures; Gülenist press organs were keen to promote easily dismissed and contradictory evidence as fact, and did so even as that evidence became more contradictory and absurd. No one knows how or why Gülenists were involved in those trials, so no one yet understands the extent and the nature of Gülen's involvement in Turkish politics and the military.

There are reasons to believe that the Gülen movement need not be seen as a threat to America. For example, the movement has become, for pragmatic reasons, friendlier to Israel than is the ruling AKP. Moreover, followers of the movement tend to loathe Iran, and its publications—such as the English-language *Today's Zaman*—regularly ran scathing denunciations of the Islamic Republic.[17] Toward America, the movement is on the surface relatively warm—as would be expected, since Gülen is in exile in the U.S. and has considerable business interests there.

However, President Tayyip Erdoğan, Prime Minister Binali Yıldırım, and many politicians from different parties believe Gülen planned and executed the July 15,

2016 coup attempt. The Turkish government calls Gülenists within the Turkish state a "parallel structure organization."[18] Sources within the military, according to the well-connected Turkish journalist Murat Yetkin, likewise claim that the plotters were known or suspected Gülen sympathizers.

Gülen has strongly denied any involvement. He has denounced the coup attempt, and accused Erdoğan, in turn, of staging the coup himself as a pretext for the brutal crackdown now underway on those suspected of involvement. Turkey has requested Gülen's extradition from the U.S. to face trial. The United States' failure to do so expeditiously has placed great strain on the bilateral relationship, with Turkish officials accusing the United States of staging the coup or, at least, of harboring the coup-plotter.

GLOBAL REACH

There are somewhere between three and six million Gülen followers—or, in the term they prefer, people who are "inspired" by him. An exact figure is impossible to offer, for, as one of the inspired, Ihsan Yilmaz, explains, the boundaries of this "collectivity" are "extremely loose and difficult to specify."[19] Skeptical observers note that Gülen's followers tend to deny their association with him. In 2006, for example, in a cable released by Wikileaks, U.S. consulate officers in Istanbul remarked that "[w]hile on the surface a benign humanitarian movement, the ubiquitous evasiveness of Gülenist applicants—coupled with what appears to be a deliberate management of applicant profiles over the past several years—leaves Consular officers uneasy, an uneasiness echoed within Turkey by those familiar with the Gülenists..."[20]

The value of the institutions inspired by Gülen—which existed on every populated continent—has been estimated, variously, as ranging from $20 to $50 billion. The movement, according to researchers such as Hakan Yavuz, had three coordinated tiers: businessmen, journalists, and teachers and students.[21] Financial support for its activities came largely from the so-called "Anatolian bourgeoisie." This newly-wealthy class funded the building of hundreds of private high schools, universities, colleges, dormitories, summer camps, and foundations around the world. Followers, moreover, controlled banks and major financial institutions, and built a vast media empire that owned one of the leading Turkish dailies, *Zaman*, and its English-language counterpart—which was not its precise translation—*Today's Zaman*, as well as the Turkish television station STV, and many magazines and academic journals. As of this writing, however, virtually all of these organs abroad have been closed down in response to the Turkish government's lobbying of foreign governments following the July 2016 coup attempt.

One researcher, Ahmet Insel, described the *cemaat's* regional organizations in developing nations thus:

There is a strong leader, a manager cadre (which knows about the economy and about a people that work much and earn little), and a central inspection mechanism, which centers itself around the person of the leader (Gülen) and manifests the internal coherence of the group.[22]

Wherever the movement establishes itself, similar patterns emerge. Thus, in Central Asia, French researcher Bayram Balcı notes that "Nurcu group members—whom we can consider as missionaries—are sent by the movement with the aim of making contact with important companies, bureaucrats and personalities in order to appraise local needs. They then invite some of these important personalities to Turkey... Nurcu organizations receive them and show them the private schools and foundations of the cemaat, without ever mentioning this word. Thanks to these contacts it then becomes easy to prepare the work in Central Asia."[23]

Almost every top commander and general since Kanan Evren has spoken out against Gülen and warned of Gülenist infiltration, even if they did not identify him by name, referring instead to *cemaatler* and *irtica*—reactionaries. The military has always been obsessively careful about its recruits' loyalty, in part for fear of them. But this does not necessarily mean they succeeded in keeping them out, as the recent coup attempt suggests.

Quite a number of Turkish military sources believe that there are or were large numbers of Gülenists in the nation's armed forces; top commanders and generals have long spoken against Gülen and warned of attempts at infiltration. That Gülen says he has always been against military interventions doesn't make it true—he himself is known to have lavishly praised the army following the 1980 coup. The army has long purged Gülenists amid their ranks, however, to the extent they could detect them. But Erdoğan put an end to those the purges during the period after he took power, when he and Gülen closely collaborated.

Gülen himself lives in the Poconos, where he fled to avoid prosecution in Turkey on charges of trying to infiltrate the state. He inspires his followers from a rural tourist hub in northeast Pennsylvania, and has become, among other things, one of the most powerful figure in the world of American charter schools. Before his overt split with then-prime minister Recep Tayyip Erdogan, his supporters, Turkish politicians, and leading businessmen often visited him at his American compound.

The Gülenist Schools

There now are Gülen schools in every continent but Antarctica. To date, 95 countries with Gülen schools have been identified, while estimates—and the pronouncements of Gülenists themselves—suggest that at its height that network was broader still, stretching to perhaps as many as 140 countries with an active educational and proselytizing presence.[24]

In 2001, Gülen was granted an immigrant visa as a "religious worker," and soon after received his green card.[25] In the decade-and-a-half since, he has been able to amass sufficient manpower and influence to effectively lobby several Commanders-in-Chief, woo countless members of Congress, and become the largest operator of charter schools in America, funded with millions of taxpayer dollars, many of these issued in the form of public bonds. These schools have come under scrutiny by the FBI and the Departments of Labor and Education, which have been investigating their hiring practices, particularly the replacement of certified American teachers with uncertified Turkish ones who are paid higher salaries than the Americans, exploiting loopholes in H1-B visa laws.[26] They have also been hired as PE teachers, accountants, janitors, caterers, painters, construction workers, human resources managers, public relations specialists, and lawyers.

The schools, moreover, have been credibly and frequently charged with channeling school funds to other Gülen-inspired organizations, bribery, using the schools to generate political connections, unfair hiring and termination practices, and academic cheating—the latter charges ranging from grade-changing schemes to the accusation that some science fair projects have been completed by the teachers. In 2011, the *New York Times* reported that Gülen charter schools in Texas were funneling some $50 million in public funds to a network of Turkish construction companies, among them Atlas, which was identified with Gülen in a 2006 cable from the American Consul General in Istanbul that was subsequently released by WikiLeaks.[27]

Dozens of Texans, ranging from state lawmakers to congressional staff members to university professors, have taken trips to Turkey financed by Gülen's foundations. The Raindrop Foundation paid for State Senator Leticia Van de Putte's recent travel to Istanbul, according to a recent campaign report.[28] Thereafter, in January 2011, she co-sponsored a Senate resolution commending Gülen for "his ongoing and inspirational contributions to promoting global peace and understanding."[29]

Federal authorities are investigating several of the movement's schools for violating immigration laws and forcing employees to send part of their paychecks back to Turkey.[30] Nationwide, the charter schools have expanded aggressively with financing through public bond issues. The Texas schools borrowed more than $200 million through these offerings. The State Legislature and the Texas Education Agency are investigating, as is the federal Department of Education. Quite a number of people who have questioned these practices have been threatened with lawsuits for "defamation."

Importantly, there is no evidence that Islamic proselytizing takes place at these schools, and there is considerable evidence that the schools are viewed positively by students and parents alike. Graduates perform reasonably well, and some perform outstandingly.

Among other things, the schools are moneymakers for members of the *cemaat*. They are loaded with private, state and federal funding. The Ohio charters received more than $27 million in public funds, including stimulus money. They've likewise proved an amazingly effective forum for soliciting donations to Gülen's organizations. The FBI and the Departments of Labor and Education have investigated whether employees are forced to kick back part of their salaries to the *cemaat*.[31] The federal investigation was closed without any criminal charges.[32] The charter school experiment has resulted in the United States being the only country in the world where the Gülen Movement has been able to establish schools fully funded by the host country's taxpayers.

Despite continuing questions and concerns and the uncertainty in the Gülen movement's future given the recent political tension with Turkey, charter schools still exist all over the world. The *Wall Street Journal* reported in 2016 that around 150 U.S. charter schools were tied to the Gülen movement.[33]

RECENT ACTIVITY

As Turkish journalist Asli Aydıntaşbaş details,

> Hundreds of think-tankers, congressional staffers, and several members of the US Congress [have] visited Turkey on tours organized by such Gülen outfits as Rumi Forum. The group's pro-Western views and moderate form of Islam were particularly attractive in the post-9/11 atmosphere. A congressman who came to Istanbul in 2012 on such a tour did not know much about the movement (or the Gülenist-led trials where dozens of journalists were behind bars) but described the group to me in glowing terms as "the anti-mullahs".
>
> Gülen-related entities and individuals were also able to do fundraising at the local level, since many had become naturalized residents of the US, and could make contributions to election campaigns in Texas, New Jersey and, New York at a national level.[34]

But while the Gülen movement developed its contacts in the United States, its connections to Turkey's political elite grew shakier. As previously discussed, the AKP had relied upon the Gülen movement to eliminate secularist establishment in the state and the military, once the military was sidelined, the inevitable happened: The AKP and the Gülen movement descended into a struggle for the control over the state.

Long-rumored tensions between Gülen and Erdoğan broke into the open in the immediate aftermath of the Gezi uprising of May 2013, when the Gülen movement issued an 11-article communiqué to dispute "accusations and charges" that it claimed came from AKP quarters.[35]

Shortly afterward, Turkish police carried out dawn raids against leading businessmen and allies of the prime minister.[36] They alleged that the targets of the raids had helped Iran bypass international financial sanctions by sending gold to the regime in Tehran in exchange for oil and natural gas. Gülenists were assumed to be behind the raids. On December 17, 2013, corruption several bureaucrats, ministers, mayors, and family members of the ruling Justice and Development Party, leading to widespread protests and calls for the resignation of the government.[37] Erdoğan immediately attributed the raids to a Gülenist set-up.[38] The whistleblowers who had tipped off the police leaked rumors that Erdogan's sons were next to be arrested. They released, on social media, recordings that purported to be Erdogan telling his son, Bilal, to rid their home of a billion dollars.[39]

This sparked an outright civil war among Turkey's Islamists. On December 14, 2014, Turkish police arrested more than two dozen senior journalists and media executives connected with the Gülen movement on various charges. The government raided and closed all Gülen-linked media, and began seizing companies that belonged, or were widely believed to belong, to Gülen supporters. It began purging the bureaucracy, particularly the police and judiciary. The preparation of a list of military officers, to be purged in August 2016, is widely speculated to have precipitated the July 15th coup.

The failed military coup in Turkey that began on the evening of July 15th left more than 150 dead and over 1,100 injured.[40] It was the fifth coup attempt in Turkey since 1960, but the first in which the military turned its fire against its own citizens. The AKP was very nearly decapitated; Erdoğan escaped assassination by minutes. Unthinkably, and inexplicably, the aspiring *junta* also bombed the Turkish parliament, the symbol of the democracy it claimed to be acting to rescue. It was the most serious coup plot in Turkey since the military takeover in 1980. Hundreds of officers and up to 10,000 soldiers from the army, air force, navy, and gendarmerie were mobilized.

Immediately after the failed coup, General Hulusi Akar's aide, Infantry Lt. Col. Levent Türkkan, confessed his allegiance to Gülen. His testimony reinforced longstanding rumors that Gülenists are sufficiently well represented in the military to furnish their protégés with the answers to the military academy's examination questions. "Yes, I am a member of the parallel establishment," he said. "I am from the Fethullah Gülen community.... After I was brought to the aide-de-camp position at the General Staff, I started to execute the orders given on behalf of the community."[41] Sources within the military, according to the well-connected Turkish journalist Murat Yetkin, likewise claim that the plotters were known or suspected Gülen sympathizers.

While in all likelihood there was Gülenist involvement in the coup plot, it is not known whether they were its only authors. The putschists' manifesto appealed to classically Kemalist tropes and dramaturgy. They called themselves "Yurtta Sulh Komitesi," or the "Peace at Home Committee," in an appeal to Atatürk's famous slogan, "Peace at home. Peace in the world." This doesn't necessarily indicate Kemalist involvement, and may have been a dog whistle calculated to lure Kemalists into the streets in support of the coup.[42] Gülen himself has strongly denied any involvement. He has denounced the coup attempt, and accused Erdoğan, in turn, of staging the coup as a pretext for the brutal crackdown now underway on those suspected of involvement.[43]

It will be many years, if ever, before we fully understand the coup plot. But some of the conclusions drawn in the immediate aftermath in the Western media make no sense. Many commentators were quick, for example, to accept Gülen's intimation that the scale of the purge indicated that the coup attempt was staged by Erdoğan himself, in some kind of Turkish "Reichstag Fire." It is true that the lists of people to purge were prepared in advance, but that doesn't mean that Erdoğan staged the coup. Beginning in 2012, the AKP had visibly, explosively, and publicly fallen out with Gülen's flock, so of course these lists were ready. The president took advantage of the coup plot to accelerate a purge, but it does not necessarily mean that he staged it. Nor is the longstanding tension between Erdoğan and Gülen proof that Gülen led the plot, though it would be credulous to dismiss the idea of his involvement out of hand.

According to Ahmet Şık,[44] a journalist who was arrested after writing a book that charged the Gülenists with extensive infiltration of the Turkish state, the coup was headed by Gülenist officers who had been planning to stage it before a promotions meeting in August, when they were due to be dismissed. Their plans were discovered, he writes, and they knew they were to be arrested at 4am on Saturday morning.[45] He believes the officers, aware they had been betrayed, decided to attempt the coup early on Friday night. This would explain why the coup was so poorly planned. Consistent with this, Erdoğan has acknowledged he knew of "military activity" at least seven to ten hours before the coup.

The number of arrested and purged since the coup attempt has been breathtaking. At least 40,000 have been detained,[46] including at least 10,000 soldiers and, for reasons that remain unclear, 2,745 judges.[47] Thousands of teachers have been suspended and their licenses revoked on allegations of loyalty to Gülen. More than 100,000 people have been "arrested and fired from their jobs."[48]

It is widely believed both by the Turkish public and the government that the United States sponsored the coup attempt—a belief fueled, particularly, by Gülen's residency in the United States. In response, on July 16, 2016, then- U.S. Secretary of State John Kerry encouraged the Turkish government "to present us with any legitimate evidence that withstands scrutiny" for an extradition request.[49] On August 2, 2016, due to escalating tensions over Gülen, Erdoğan questioned Turkey's relationship with the United States and criticized the West for supporting terrorism and backing the coup-plotters.[50] Washington has insisted it needs more evidence of Gülen's guilt before extradition, to which Erdoğan said: "When you asked for the return of a terrorist, we did not ask for documentation... Let us put him on trial."[51] Although he didn't specify the threat, the *Wall Street Journal* concluded from his tone that he had "raised the prospect of a prolonged closure of the Incirlik air base in southern Turkey if he didn't get his way." Suleyman Soylu, Turkey's labor minister, has overtly stated the U.S. was behind the coup.[52]

Gülen is prepared to fight an extradition request in U.S. courts, so this is apt to be a contentious issue between the U.S. and Turkey for a long time to come. Both Gülen and the Turkish government have well-paid lawyers and PR firms to ensure their side of the feud is ably represented. For its part, the Trump administration has not made its priorities and thoughts regarding Gülen's extradition clear, although Lt. General Michael Flynn, now the U.S. National Security Advisor, has stated that he believes the U.S. should extradite Gülen back to Turkey.[53]

ENDNOTES

[1] MH Yavuz, "Towards An Islamic Liberalism?: The Nurcu Movement and Fethullah Gülen," Middle East Journal 53, no. 4, Autumn 1999.

[2] "Fethullah Gülen's exemplary preaching," Haber 5, June 13, 2010, http://haber5.com/video/fethullah-Gülenden-ibretlik-vaaz .

[3] "Fetullah Gülen'in İç Yüzü/ 3. Bölüm" YouTube video, April 2, 2007, http://www.youtube.com/watch?v=SRAyGkE1q50#t=4m51s.

[4] Gulen's early writings are out of print and hard to find, but digital copies are archived on various social media sites. See, for example, http://www.flickr.com/photos/eksib612/sets/72157631747801352/.

[5] Unal Bilir, "'Turkey-Islam': Recipe for Success or Hindrance to the Integration of the Turkish Diaspora Community in Germany?" Journal of Muslim Minority Affairs 24, no. 2, October 2004.

[6] Dan Bilefsky, "In Turkey, Trial Casts a Wide Net of Mistrust," New York Times, November 21, 2009, http://www.nytimes.com/2009/11/22/world/europe/22turkey.html.

[7] Asli Aydintasbas, "The Good, The Bad, and the Gülenists: The Role of the Gülen Movement in Turkey's Coup Attempt," European Council on Foreign Relations, September 2016, 5.

[8] As of 2010, Gareth Jenkins reported that 600 had been detained in the Ergenekon trials: "The Devil in the Detail: Turkey's Ergenekon Investigation Enters a Fourth Year," vol. 3, no. 13 of the Turkey Analyst, https://www.turkeyanalyst.org/publications/turkey-analyst-articles/item/219-the-devil-in-the-detail-turkeys-ergenekon-investigation-enters-a-fourth-year.html; the numbers vary according to whose reporting it, but in 2011, Bianet put the number of people detained in the KCK trial at 7748. BIA News Center, October 6, 2011, http://bianet.org/bianet/siyaset/133216-30-ayda-kckden-7748-gozalti-3895-tutuklama. In 2011, CNN Türk reported that 66 Balyoz suspects were in custody: "3. Balyoz iddianamesi" mahkemede

[9] Evidence altered in Balyoz case, says expert," Hürriyet Daily News, November 29, 2011, http://www.hurriyetdailynews.com/default.aspx?pageid=438&n=evidence-altered-in-balyoz-case-says-expert-2011-11-29; "Balyoz lawyers complain about court to top board," Hürriyet Daily News, April 17, 2012, http://www.hurriyetdailynews.com/balyoz-lawyers-complain-about-court-to-top-board.aspx?pageID=238&nID=18577&NewsCatID=338.

[10] Dani Rodrik, "The Plot Against The Generals," June 2014, 1, http://drodrik.scholar.harvard.edu/files/dani-rodrik/files/plot-against-the-generals.pdf.

[11] As of 2010, Gareth Jenkins reported that 600 had been detained in the Ergenekon trials. See Gareth Jenkins, "The Devil in the Detail: Turkey's Ergenekon Investigation Enters a Fourth Year," Turkey Analyst 3, no. 13, July 5, 2010, https://www.turkeyanalyst.org/publications/turkey-analyst-articles/item/219-the-devil-in-the-detail-turkeys-ergenekon-investigation-enters-a-fourth-year.html; the numbers vary according to the reporting, but in 2011, BIANET put the number of people detained in the KCK trial at 7748. See BIA News Center, October 6, 2011, http://bianet.org/bianet/siyaset/133216-30-ayda-kckden-7748-gozalti-3895-tutuklama. In 2011, CNN Türk reported that 66 Balyoz suspects were in custody. See "'3. Balyoz iddianamesi' mahkemede," CNN Turk, November 11, 2011, http://www.cnnturk.com/2011/turkiye/11/11/3.balyoz.iddianamesi.mahkemede/636423.0/index.html.

[12] "Necip Hablemitoğlu kimdir, kim öldürdü nasıl öldü?" A24, September 30, 2016, http://www.a24.com.tr/mehmet-ali-yalcindag-istifa-etti-haberi-40075640h.html?h=11

[13] Rachel Sharon-Krespin, "Fethullah Gülen's Grand Ambition, Turkey's Islamist Danger," Middle East Quarterly, Winter 2009, 55-66.

[14] Justin Vela, "Behind Bars in the Deep State," Foreign Policy, January 11, 2012, http://foreignpolicy.com/2012/01/11/behind-bars-in-the-deep-state/

[15] Metin Gurcan, "Erdogan angles to tag Gulenists as a national security threat," Al-Monitor, October 20, 2014, http://www.al-monitor.com/pulse/originals/2014/10/turkey-national-security-threat-gulen-movement.html.

[16] "Cemaat devlete sızmış, buna kargalar güler,'" NTV, February 20, 2012, http://www.ntv.com.tr/turkiye/cemaat-devlete-sizmis-buna-kargalar-guler,FMxmUxVJhUqKz-8NGPbZnQ.

[17] See, for example, Lale Kemal, "Erdogan to Obama: You Left Iraq in Iran's Hands," Today's Zaman, March 21, 2012, http://www.todayszaman.com/columnists/lale-kemal-274942-erdogan-to-obama-you-left-iraq-in-irans-hands.html

[18] "Structure of Turkey's 'parallel state' revealed," Anadulo Agency, December 12, 2015,http://aa.com.tr/en/turkey/structure-of-turkeys-parallel-state-revealed/491482.

[19] Ihsan Yilmaz, "Inter-Madhhab Surfing, Neo-Ijtihad, and Faith-Based Movement Leaders," in Peri Bearman, Rudolph Peters and Frank E. Vogel, eds., The Islamic School of Law: Evolution, Devolution, and Progress (Cambridge: Harvard University Press, 2005), 191, http://www.academia.edu/333445/Inter-Madhhab_Surfing_Neo-Ijtihad_and_Faith-Based_Movement_Leaders

[20] U.S. Department of State internal cable, "Fethullah Gülen: Why Are His Followers Traveling," May 23, 2006, released by WikiLeaks on August 30, 2011, http://dazzlepod.com/cable/06ISTANBUL832/.

[21] M. Hakan Yavuz, Islamic Political Identity in Turkey (New York: Oxford University Press, 2003), 184.

[22] Bilir, "'Turkey-Islam.'"

[23] Bayram Balci, "Fethullah Gülen's Missionary Schools in Central Asia and their Role in the Spreading of Turkism and Islam," Religion, State and Society 31, iss. 2, 2003, http://www.tandfonline.com/doi/abs/10.1080/09637490308283.

[24] A comprehensive list of estimates, drawing from various foreign sources, can be found at http://turkishinvitations.weebly.com/every-continent-but-antarctica-the-numbers.html

[25] Abigail Hauslohner, Karen DeYoung, and Valerie Strauss, "He's 77, frail and lives in Pennsylvania. Turkey says he's a coup mastermind," Washington Post, August 3, 2016, https://www.washingtonpost.com/national/hes-frail-77-and-lives-in-pennsylvania-turkey-says-hes-a-coup-mastermind/2016/08/03/6b1b2226-526f-11e6-bbf5-957ad17b4385_story.html?utm_term=.03a199345070.

[26] See, for example, Joseph M. Humire, "Charter Schools Vulnerable to Controversial Turkish Movement," The Hill, March 10, 2016, http://thehill.com/blogs/congress-blog/education/272424-charter-schools-vulnerable-to-controversial-turkish-movement.

[27] Stephanie Saul, "Charter Schools Tied To Turkey Grow In Vegas," New York Times, June 6, 2011, http://www.nytimes.com/2011/06/07/education/07charter.html.

[28] Ibid.

[29] Ibidem.
[30] Martha Woodall and Claudio Gatti, "U.S. Charter-School Network with Turkish Link Draws Federal Attention," Philadelphia Inquirer, March 20, 2011, http://articles.philly.com/2011-03-20/news/29148147_1_Gülen-schools-Gülen-followers-charter-schools; "FBI Investigation of Gülen Schools (a.k.a., Harmony Science Academies in Texas)," Education News, March 24, 2011, http://www.educationnews.org/commentaries/insights_on_education/152233.html; Yigal Schleifer, "More Scrutiny for Gülen Schools in the US," Eurasianet, June 6, 2012, http://www.eurasianet.org/node/65507.
[31] Ibid.
[32] Jeremey Roebuck and Martha Woodall, The Inquirer, July 16, 2016, http://www.philly.com/philly/news/20160716_Turkey_s_president_blames_Muslim_cleric_in_the_Poconos_for_military_coup.html.
[33] Beckie Strum, "Gulen Movement's Charter Schools May Be Caught Up in Turkey-U.S. Standoff," Wall Street Journal, July 19, 2016, http://www.wsj.com/articles/gulen-movements-charter-schools-may-be-caught-up-in-turkey-u-s-standoff-1468967536.
[34] "The good, the bad and the Gülenists," European Council on Foreign Relations, Sep. 23 2016 http://www.ecfr.eu/publications/summary/the_good_the_bad_and_the_gulenists7131
[35] Kadri Gursel, "Gulenist-AKP Clash Is Now in the Open," Al-Monitor, August 16, 2013, http://www.al-monitor.com/pulse/fr/contents/articles/opinion/2013/08/turkey-erdogan-akp-gulenism-the-service-power-struggle.html.
[36] Lonna Lisa Williams, "Turkey: Erdogan faces new protests over corruption scandal," Digital Journal, December 28, 2013,http://www.digitaljournal.com/news/world/erdogan-faces-new-protests-over-corruption-scandal/article/364759.
[37] Çetin Aydin, "İstanbul'da yolsuzluk ve rüşvet operasyonu," Hurriyet, December 17, 2013, http://www.hurriyet.com.tr/istanbulda-yolsuzluk-ve-rusvet-operasyonu-25378685.
[38] Alexander Cristie-Miller, "The Gulen movement: a self-exiled iman challenges Turkey's Erdogan," Christian Science Monitor, December 29, 2013, http://www.csmonitor.com/World/Middle-East/2013/1229/The-Gulen-movement-a-self-exiled-imam-challenges-Turkey-s-Erdogan.
[39] Cengiz Çandar, "The Erdogan tapes," Al-Monitor, February 27, 2014, http://www.al-monitor.com/pulse/originals/2014/02/supporters-deny-taped-conversation-erdogan-son.html.
[40] See, for example, Gul Tuysuz and Eliott C. McLaughlan, "Failed Coup in Turkey: What You Need to Know," CNN, July 18, 2016, http://edition.cnn.com/2016/07/18/middleeast/turkey-failed-coup-explainer/.

[41] Mesut Hasan Benli, "Top Turkish commander's aid admits allegiance to Gülenists," Hurriyet Daily News, July 20, 2016, http://www.hurriyetdailynews.com/top-turkish-commanders-aide-admits-allegiance-to-gulenists-.aspx?PageID=238&NID=101851&NewsCatID=341.

[42] Asli Aydıntaşbaş, "The good, the bad and the Gülenists," European Council on Foreign Relations, September 23, 2016, http://www.ecfr.eu/publications/summary/the_good_the_bad_and_the_gulenists7131.

[43] Tim Arango and Ceylan Yeginsu, "Turks Can Agree on One Thing: U.S. Was Behind Failed Coup," The New York Times, August 2, 2016, https://www.nytimes.com/2016/08/03/world/europe/turkey-coup-erdogan-fethullah-gulen-united-states.html?mtrref=undefined.

[44] Claire Berlinski, "A Prisoner of Conspiracy," City Journal, April 15, 2011, https://www.city-journal.org/html/prisoner-conspiracy-10831.html.

[45] Cihan Tugal, Turkey coup aftermath: between neo-fascism and Bonapartism, 18 July 2016. Open Democracy http://leftunity.org/wp-content/uploads/2016/08/After_the_coup_final.pdf.

[46] See, for example, "Turkey Orders 400 Arrests in Continuing Post-Coup Crackdown," Reuters, January 21, 2017, http://europe.newsweek.com/turkey-orders-400-arrests-post-coup-crackdown-545947?rm=eu.

[47] "Turkey: Mass arrests after coup bid quashed, says PM," BBC News, July 16, 2016, http://www.bbc.co.uk/news/world-europe-36813924; Sheena McKenzie and Ray Sanchez, "Turkey coup attempt: Erdogan rounds up suspected plotters," CNN, July 18, 2016, http://edition.cnn.com/2016/07/17/asia/turkey-attempted-coup/index.html.

[48] Tim Arango, Ceylan Yeginsu, and Safak Timur, "Turks See Purge as Witch Hunt of 'Medieval' Darkness," New York Times, September 16, 2016, https://www.nytimes.com/2016/09/17/world/europe/turkey-erdogan-gulen-purge.html.

[49] Bradley Klapper, "US-Turkish tensions rise after failed coup attempt," Associated Press, July 16, 2016, http://bigstory.ap.org/fd1bd31fed-39440cbf95ffd76a7550bf.

[50] "Erdogan accuses West of 'writing script' for Turkey coup," Telegraph (London), August 2, 2016,http://www.telegraph.co.uk/news/2016/08/02/erdogan-accuses-west-of-writing-the-script-for-turkey-coup/.

[51] "The Latest: Erdogan calls on us not to delay cleric's return," Associated Press, August 18, 2016, http://bigstory.ap.org/article/62bc096608264827878202279f9cb76b/latest-car-bombings-turkey-kill-6-wound-over-120.

[52] "After the coup, Turkey turns against America,"The Economist, Jul 18th 2016 http://www.economist.com/news/europe/21702337-turkish-media-and-even-government-officials-accuse-america-being-plot-after.

[53] Jack Moore, "Donald Trump adviser: U.S. should extradite coup suspect Fetullah Gulen to Turkey," Newsweek, November 10, 2016, http://www.newsweek.com/us-should-extradite-coup-suspect-fethullah-gulen-turkey-says-trump-adviser-519534.

HEZBOLLAH

QUICK FACTS

Geographical Areas of Operation: Europe, Latin America, Middle East and North Africa, North America, and Sub-Saharan Africa

Numerical Strength (Members): Thousands of supporters, several thousand members, and a few hundred terrorist operatives

Leadership: Hassan Nasrallah

Religious Identification: Shia Islam

Quick Facts Courtesy of the U.S. State Department's Country Reports on Terrorism (Last Updated 2015)

OVERVIEW

Hezbollah ("the Party of God") is not only a major political party and provider of social services in Lebanon, it is also a militant organization that fields both a well-armed and well-trained militia in Lebanon and a terrorist wing integrated with elements of Iranian intelligence services operating abroad. Even as the movement has undergone a process of "Lebanonization," through which it has successfully insinuated itself into the Lebanese parliamentary political system, it remains committed not only to its Lebanese identity but to its revolutionary pan-Shi'a and pro-Iran ones as well.

HISTORY AND IDEOLOGY

Founded in the wake of the Israeli invasion of Lebanon in 1982, Hezbollah was the product of a Shi'a awakening in Lebanon. On the one hand, Hezbollah was the outgrowth of a complex and bloody civil war, during which the country's historically marginalized Shi'a Muslims attempted to assert economic and political power for the first time. Hezbollah was also a by-product of Israel's effort to dismantly the Palestine

Liberation Organization (PLO) by invading Southern Lebanon in 1982. That awakening followed the disappearance of Sayyid Musa al-Sadr in 1978 and the Islamic Revolution in Shi'ite Iran the following year. Long neglected by the Lebanese government and underrepresented in the country's social and political institutions, Lebanese Shi'a leaders organized to empower their disenfranchised community. Already eager to follow in the footsteps of the Iranian revolution, young Lebanese Shi'a were driven to break with established parties and gravitated to Hezbollah as a result of the Israeli invasion and subsequent occupation of southern Lebanon. Iran was more than willing to help, eager as it was to export its Islamic revolution to other Shi'a communities throughout the Middle East. Iranian assistance included financial backing and training at the hands of the Islamic Revolutionary Guard Corps (IRGC) and was facilitated by a Syrian regime pleased with the prospect of developing a proxy in Lebanon capable of preventing Israel and its allies in Lebanon from controlling the country. It was the IRGC, however, that shaped Hezbollah's ideological foundations and informed its operational policies.

Hezbollah is simultaneously a Lebanese party, a pan-Shi'a movement and an Iranian proxy group. These multiple identities form the foundation and context for the group's ideology of Shi'a radicalism. The establishment of an Islamic republic in Lebanon was a central component of Hezbollah's original political platform, released in 1985, though the organization shifted away from that goal in subsequent years.[1] The fight against "Western Imperialism" and the continued conflict with Israel also feature prominently in that document, and those tenets continue to be critical rallying points. Hezbollah is ideologically committed to the Ayatollah Ruhollah Khomeini's revolutionary doctrine of *Velayat-e faqih* (Guardianship of the Jurist), creating tension between its commitment to the decrees of Iranian clerics, its commitment to the Lebanese state, and its commitment to the sectarian Shi'a community in Lebanon and its fellow Shi'ites abroad. As a result, its objectives include the sometimes competing goals of establishing an Islamic republic in Lebanon; promoting the standing of Shi'a communities worldwide; undermining Arab states with Shi'a minorities in an effort to export the Iranian Shi'a revolution; eliminating the State of Israel; challenging "Western imperialism;" and coordinating with the paramilitary wing of Iran's IRGC, known as the Quds Force. Unable to harmonize all of these wide-ranging ideological drivers, Hezbollah was at times driven to ineffective steps in an effort to fulfill its goals. Hezbollah brought massive damage to Lebanese infrastructure, but rose in pan-Shi'a popularity, after it dragged both Israel and Lebanon into a war neither wanted by crossing the UN-demarcated Israel-Lebanon border and killing three Israeli soldiers while kidnapping two others in July 2006.

By 2008, Hezbollah appeared to have overcome the political setbacks incurred by the massive damage cause to Lebanon's infrastructure in the July 2006 war. Local criticism arose again in May 2008. With the position of the country's president vacant since the previous November, an ongoing political crisis presented the backdrop for what would prove to be the most violent intrastate fighting in Lebanon since the country's fifteen-year civil war ended in 1991. In early May of 2008, the Lebanese government reported that it had discovered a Hezbollah surveillance camera situated at the Beirut airport. The ensuing criticism by Hezbollah's political opponents, and pro-Hezbollah protests throughout Beirut left nearly 100 dead and 250 wounded.[2] While the Lebanese Armed Forces (LAF) ultimately deployed and stopped the fighting, Hezbollah successfully leveraged its military strength for political advantage over the already-weakened Lebanese government. The result, after five days of Qatari mediation, was the Doha Agreement, under which Hezbollah secured a "blocking third's" worth of representation in a new national unity government, giving it the potential to obstruct any future government initiative.

The Doha Agreement left the issue of Hezbollah's weapons—maintained in blatant violation of UN Security Council resolutions 1559 and 1701—unresolved, allowing it to remain the only militia in Lebanon with a private arsenal of weapons. Preventing serious discussion of this issue at the talks in Doha was a public relations coup for Hezbollah, which was left politically exposed after turning its guns on fellow Lebanese. Despite the insertion of a more robust United Nations presence in southern Lebanon in the wake of the July 2006 war, Hezbollah had successfully restocked its arsenal of missiles. Indeed, Hezbollah was then believed to have more rockets, with longer ranges and larger payloads, than it did prior to the 2006 war.[3]

These political gains, however, were followed by a significant reversal. In May 2009, the German weekly *Der Spiegel* revealed that the UN special tribunal investigating former Lebanese Prime Minister Rafiq Hariri's assassination had implicated Hezbollah.[4] In early January 2011, it became evident that the Tribunal's chief prosecutor, Daniel Bellamere, would submit a draft indictment to the pre-trial judge for review. Hezbollah pre-empted the indictment's release and withdrew its support for Saad Hariri's government, forcing its collapse.[5] Subsequently, aided by sympathetic leaders of Lebanon's Christian and Druze communities, Hezbollah was able to raise billionaire Najib Mitaki to the premiership, cementing its control over the Lebanese state.[6]

However, Hezbollah now finds its position in Lebanon under growing threat, in large part thanks to the role the organization and its chief sponsor, Iran, have played in propping up the regime of Bashar al-Assad in Syria since the outbreak of the civil war there in March 2011.

GLOBAL REACH

Before its recent foray into the Syrian war, Hezbollah was already well known for several international terrorist attacks, most notably the 1992 and 1994 bombings of the Israeli embassy and Jewish community center (AMIA), respectively, in Argentina, the 1995 Khobar Towers attack in Saudi Arabia. More recently, Hezbollah claimed responsibility for the 2012 bombing of an Israeli tourist bus in Burgas, Bulgaria.[7]

Hezbollah's global footprint, however, is broader still, with support networks in regions as far afield as Africa, Southeast Asia, North and South America and Europe. Hezbollah receives significant financial backing from the contributions of supporters living abroad, particularly from Lebanese nationals living in Africa, South America and other places with large Lebanese Shi'a expatriate communities. Over time, these communities developed into a global support network available not only to raise funds, but also to provide logistical and operational support for Hezbollah operations. Such support networks, sometimes comprising a few individuals and in other cases larger, more organized cells, have developed in Latin America, North America, Europe, Africa and in Middle Eastern countries with minority Shi'a populations such as Saudi Arabia.

Hezbollah has leveraged its support networks in Europe to help operatives use the Continent as a launching pad for entering Israel to conduct attacks or collect intelligence there since the 1990s. Hezbollah's most successful European operation to date came on July 18, 2012. In Burgas, Bulgaria, Hezbollah bombed a tour bus carrying Israelis, killing the Bulgarian bus driver and five Israelis, and wounding some thirty more.[8]

After months of often acrimonious deliberations, senior European officials gathered in Brussels in July 2013 to announce that all 28 EU member states agreed to add Hezbollah's military wing – not the organization itself – to the EU's list of banned terrorist groups. At the time, European officials pointed to the blacklisting as a shot across the bow. "This is a signal to terrorist organizations," German Foreign Minister Guido Westerwelle warned. "If you attack one of our European countries, you get an answer from all of them." Regardless, evidence reveals that Hezbollah's military wing is still plotting attacks across Europe, and that the EU's words have not dissuaded the organization whatsoever.

Throughout the 1990s, Hezbollah maintained an active support network in Southeast Asia as well. Hezbollah infiltrated at least one Malaysian operative, Zinal Bin-Talib, into Israel to collect intelligence.[9] Hezbollah has conducted significant fundraising in Southeast Asia, nearly succeeded in bombing the Israeli embassy in Bangkok in 1994,[10] and collected intelligence on synagogues in Manila and Singapore.[11] Hezbollah members are known to have procured and cached weapons in Thailand and the Philippines.[12] They collected intelligence on El-Al's Bangkok office and on U.S. Navy and Israeli commercial ships in the Singapore Straits.[13] The network additionally recruited local Sunni Muslims and sent several to Lebanon for training.[14] In January 2012, Thai police arrested Hussein Atris, a Lebanese national carrying a Swedish passport, at Bangkok's Suvarnabhumi Airport.[15] After questioning Atris led authorities to a three-story building on the outskirts of Bangkok containing a stockpile of 8,800 pounds of already distilled chemicals used to make explosives.[16] Some of the explosives, disguised as cat litter, were intended to be shipped abroad. Bangkok had already been described as "a center for a [Hezbollah] cocaine and money-laundering network," but it was now clear that the city also served as a hub for explosives in addition to logistics and transportation.[17]

In Africa, Hezbollah operatives have long helped finance the group's activities by dealing in conflict diamonds in places like Sierra Leone and Liberia. According to David Crane, the prosecutor for the Special Court in Sierra Leone, "Diamonds fuel the war on terrorism. Charles Taylor is harboring terrorists from the Middle East, including al-Qaeda and Hezbollah, and has been for years."[18] Hezbollah also raises funds in Africa from the local Shi'a expatriate community. In some cases, Shi'a donors are unwittingly conned into funding Hezbollah, while in others they are knowing and willing participants in Hezbollah's financing efforts.[19] In 2002, Ugandan officials disrupted a cell of Shi'a students who were recruited by Iranian intelligence agents and sent on scholarships to study at the Rizavi University in Mashhad, Iran. Upon their return, one student recruit, Shafri Ibrahim, was caught, while another, Sharif Wadulu, is believed to have escaped to one of the Gulf States. The two were trained by Iran's Ministry of Intelligence, together with new Lebanese Hezbollah recruits, and sent home with fictitious covers to establish an operational infrastructure in Uganda.[20]

Hezbollah activity in South America has been well documented, including its frenetic activity in the Tri-Border region. The group's activities received special attention in the wake of the 1992 bombing of the Israeli embassy in Buenos Aires, Argentina and the 1994 bombing of the AMIA Jewish community center there. What is less well known, however, is that Hezbollah is also active in Chile, Venezuela, Cuba, Panama and Ecuador. Of particular concern to law enforcement officials throughout South America is Hezbollah's increased activity in free trade zones, especially under the cover of import-export companies.[21]

Finally, Hezbollah maintains a sizeable presence of supporters and operatives in North America. The U.S. Treasury Department has designated Hezbollah charities in the Detroit area, while individuals and cells have been prosecuted across the U.S. and Canada for raising funds and procuring weapons and dual use technologies like night vision goggles. The most prominent case to date occurred in Charlotte, North Carolina, where Hezbollah operatives engaged in a cigarette smuggling enterprise raised significant sums for Hezbollah while maintaining direct contact with Sheikh Abbas Haraki, a senior Hezbollah military commander in South Beirut.[22] Members of the Charlotte cell received receipts back from Hezbollah for their donations, including receipts from the office of then-Hezbollah spiritual leader Sheikh Mohammad Fadlallah. The Charlotte cell was closely tied to a sister network in Canada that was primarily engaged in procuring dual-use technologies such as night vision goggles and laser range finders for Hezbollah operational squads. The Canadian network was under the direct command of Hajj Hassan Hilu Lakis, Hezbollah's chief military procurement officer, who is also known to procure material for Iran.[23]

Recent Activity

Today's Hezbollah faces existential challenges over its active participation in the war in Syria. By siding with the Assad regime, the regime's Alawite supporters, and Iran, and taking up arms against Sunni rebels, Hezbollah has placed itself at the epicenter of a sectarian conflict that has nothing to do with the group's purported raison d'être: "resistance" to Israeli occupation.

Speaking in late May 2014, Hezbollah Secretary General Nasrallah declared that the battle in Syria was Hezbollah's fight: "We will continue along the road, bear the responsibilities and the sacrifices. This battle is ours, and I promise you victory." To that end, Hezbollah went "all-in" fighting alongside Assad regime loyalists and Iranian Revolutionary Guardsmen against Syrian rebels. The impact of Hezbollah's involvement cannot be overstated, as was seen most clearly in the battle for Qusayr, where Hezbollah gunmen reportedly fought house to house, took significant losses, and played the decisive role in turning the tide against the rebels who ultimately lost the battle. That battle also laid bare the myth that Hezbollah was not fighting in Syria. Although Hezbollah had already admitted it was fighting in Syria, it insisted that it was only either fighting along the border to protect ethnic Lebanese living on the Syrian side of the border, or protecting Shi'a shrines, specifically the Sayyeda Zeinab shrine in Damascus. These narratives used by Hezbollah and its allies in Iran and Iraq have pervaded their propaganda in the past two years.

Hezbollah's destabilizing activities in Syria date almost to the beginning of the country's uprising in 2011. Within weeks of the uprising, Nasrallah himself called on all Syrians to stand by the regime. As reports emerged in May 2011 that Iran's Qods Force was helping the Syrian regime crack down on anti-government demonstrators, Hezbollah denied playing "any military role in Arab countries." But by the following month, Syrian protesters were heard chanting not only for Assad's downfall, but also against Iran and Hezbollah. Video footage showed protesters burning posters of Nasrallah. According to a senior Syrian defense official who defected from the regime, Syrian security services were unable to handle the uprising on their own. "They didn't have decent snipers or equipment," he explained. "They needed qualified snipers from Hezbollah and Iran." Over time, Hezbollah increasingly struggled to conceal its on-the-ground support of the Assad regime. In August 2012, the U.S. Treasury Department blacklisted Hezbollah, already on the Department's terrorism list, this time for providing support to the Assad regime. Since the beginning of the rebellion, Treasury explained, Hezbollah had been providing "training, advice, and extensive logistical support to the Government of Syria's increasingly ruthless efforts" against the opposition. Hezbollah's "resistance" rhetoric notwithstanding, U.S. officials informed the UN Security Council in October 2012, "the truth is plain to see: Nasrallah's fighters are now part of Assad's killing machine." Two months later, a UN report confirmed Hezbollah members were in Syria fighting on behalf of the Assad government.

In the Spring of 2013, Hezbollah took on a more public presence in the fight against the Syrian rebels when martyrdom notices for fallen Hezbollah fighters began to appear on the group's official and unofficial websites, forums, and Facebook pages. Based on Hezbollah's organization structure and disciplined messaging, it is likely these notices were sanctioned by the leadership in the organization despite the fact that they did not publicly admit to being involved in Syria until late May. Determining the number of fighters Hezbollah has sent to Syria is difficult to ascertain, but according to French intelligence sources its believed that 3,000-4,000 individuals have made the trip to assist the Assad regime. The numbers may be slightly higher according to other sources, in the range of 4,000-5,000 fighters on the ground in Syria at a time and rotating in and out of the country on thirty day deployments. Hezbollah has proven to be an invaluable fighting force for Iran and the Assad regime. Yet the losses have been heavy – Hezbollah has lost at least one thousand fighters in Syria, along with senior Hezbollah leader Mustafa Badreddine, reportedly killed in an explosion in Damascus in May 2016. Given Badreddine's role as head of the group's External Security Organization and its forces in Syria, his death represents Hezbollah's biggest loss since the 2008 assassination of former "chief of staff" Imad Mughniyah.

The impact of the Syrian war on Hezbollah has been nothing short of dramatic, shifting the group's focus from battling Israel and contesting the political space within Lebanon to engaging in regional conflicts beyond the country's borders. Hezbollah deployed a unit to Iraq to train Shi`a militants during the Iraq war, where it worked in close cooperation with Iran, but its deep commitment on the ground in the war in Syria underscores the group's new, regional, pan-Shi`a focus. With the notable exception of Syria, Hezbollah's regional reorientation is most obvious in its increased operational tempo in the Gulf.

In Yemen, a small number of Hezbollah operatives have been training Houthi rebels for some time, but in early 2016 the Gulf-backed Yemeni government claimed to have physical evidence of "Hezbollah training the Houthi rebels and fighting alongside them in attacks on Saudi Arabia's border."[24] Three years earlier, the U.S. government revealed that Khalil Harb, a former special operations commander and a close adviser to Secretary General Hassan Nasrallah, was overseeing Hezbollah's activities in Yemen. He has also traveled to Tehran to coordinate Hezbollah's operations in Yemen with Iran.[25] Former Hezbollah specials operations commander in southern Lebanon Abu Ali Tabtabai, who also spent time fighting in Syria, is likewise reported to have been sent to Yemen.[26] Hezbollah has never been open about these deployments, but Hezbollah Deputy Secretary-General Naim Qassem did warn in April 2015 that Saudi Arabia would "incur very serious losses" and "pay a heavy price" as a result of its Yemen campaign.[27]

Beyond Yemen, Hezbollah's support for terrorist groups in the Gulf region also continues unabated. In January, authorities in Bahrain arrested six members of a terrorist cell tied to Hezbollah and blamed for a July 2015 explosion outside of a girls' school in Sitra.[28] In August 2015, Kuwaiti authorities raided a terrorist cell of 26 Shi'a Kuwaitis. The cell was accused of amassing "a large amount of weapons, ammunition, and explosives."[29] After media outlets reported alleged links between the cell, Iran, and Hezbollah, the public prosecutor issued a media gag order on the investigation.[30] In January 2016, a Kuwaiti court sentenced a Kuwaiti and an Iranian national to death for spying on behalf of Iran and Hezbollah.[31] In June, a court in Abu Dhabi found the wife of a "prominent Emirati" guilty of spying for Hezbollah.[32] The following month, a Kuwait court sentenced a Shi`a member of parliament in absentia for issuing statements deemed insulting to Saudi Arabia and Bahrain and for calling on people to join Hezbollah.[33]

In 2013, a Hezbollah sleeper cell was discovered in the United Arab Emirates. According to court proceedings in April 2016, "the terrorist cell used sex and alcohol" to recruit a group of agents that provided "information about government, security, military and economic institutions as well as UAE's arms deals with various countries to the Hezbollah agents." The prosecution claimed that "two Emiratis, four Lebanese, and a Canadian-Egyptian woman" were blackmailed into participating in the spying scheme. The court case came shortly after the UAE convicted three Lebanese men with setting up a Hezbollah cell.[34]

Set against this aggressive activity in the Gulf, it was little surprise that in March 2016 the Gulf Cooperation Council (GCC) labeled Hezbollah a terrorist group. Since then, the Gulf States have cracked down on Hezbollah supporters and financiers within their borders.[35] The GCC designated Hezbollah as a terrorist organization over the "hostile actions of the militia who recruit the young people (of the Gulf) for terrorist acts."[36] The Arab League and the OIC followed suit within weeks.[37] This seemingly rapid series of condemnations was three years in the making, however. In June 2013, GCC countries came to the unanimous conclusion that Hezbollah was a terrorist group, and several member states began taking discrete actions against the group's supporters in their countries.[38] In May 2014, Saudi authorities withdrew the business license of a Lebanese national linked to Hezbollah,[39] and a GCC offer to engage Iran in dialogue if Tehran changed its policy on Syria fell on deaf ears.[40] In January 2016, the Saudi government released a report on Iranian-sponsored terrorism that focused heavily on Hezbollah, spanning the group's militant activities from the 1980s to the present.[41]

Hezbollah's intensified involvement in the Gulf is a function of the sustained geopolitical and sectarian tensions between Saudi Arabia and Iran. These tensions spiked in January when Saudi Arabia executed Shi'ite Sheikh Nimr al-Nimr on charges of sedition and taking up arms against Saudi security forces. The sheikh's death sparked outrage across the Shi'a world, and, in Iran, two Saudi diplomatic compounds were stormed in protest. Saudi Arabia sought condemnation of the attacks from the Arab

League and the OIC, and both organizations responded accordingly. Lebanon, however, offered only "solidarity." This perceived slight spurred Saudi Arabia to cut off monetary support to Lebanon and pull funds from Lebanese banks.[42] Bahrain and the UAE fell in line with the Saudis, issuing travel warnings and travel bans, respectively, for Lebanon.[43] A month after the execution and protests, Saudi Arabia blacklisted four companies and three Lebanese businessmen, citing their relationships to Hezbollah.[44] The United States had designated these companies and individuals a year earlier, but the Saudi actions indicated a heightened focus on Hezbollah by the kingdom.[45]

Nasrallah has tried to justify Hezbollah's overreach into proxy wars around the region by presenting the issue as one of Lebanese national security. In July 2016, Sheikh Nabil Qaouq, the deputy head of Hezbollah's Executive Council, derided Saudi Arabia for supporting terrorism in Lebanon and throughout the region. The terrorists "who staged bombings in Beirut, Hermel and the Bekaa, and who abducted and slaughtered the (Lebanese) servicemen are al-Qaida's branch in Lebanon and Syria (Abdullah Azzam Brigades) and al-Nusra Front, and al-Nusra Front is today fighting with Saudi weapons," Qaouq charged. Qaouq accused the Saudis of continuing to arm Jabhat al-Nusra "although it has murdered us, executed our servicemen and continued to occupy our land in the Bekaa," noting that Saudi sponsorship of terrorism "poses a real threat to Lebanese national security."[46]

In August 2015, Ahmed al-Mughassil, the military chief of Saudi Hezbollah, was apprehended in Beirut and deported to Saudi Arabia. Mughassil had allegedly lived in Lebanon for years under the protection of Hezbollah.[47] The Farsi-speaking Mughassil may provide insight into the clandestine operations of Iran and its proxies around the region. In the current sectarian environment in the region, the circumstances of the arrest are themselves a source of intrigue. Just as Hezbollah-Saudi tensions are mounting, a Hezbollah operative who evaded capture for years was suddenly caught and deported to Saudi Arabia.

Even more significant is what happened next door in Syria eight months later. Hezbollah was dealt a heavy blow in May with the loss of its most prominent military figure, Mustafa Badreddine. The assassination of Badreddine shocked Hezbollah; the group lost an especially qualified commander with a unique pedigree as the brother-in-law of Mughniyah and a confidante of Nasrallah. Yet most confounding to Hezbollah was that Israel, Hezbollah's arch enemy, was not the assassin. Though Hezbollah outlets quickly pinned blame for the attack on Israel, Nasrallah soon took to the airwaves to personally announce that there was "no sign or proof leading us to the Israelis." Nasrallah quickly added that Hezbollah is "not afraid to blame Israel when necessary," but in this case, "our investigations led us to the [Sunni] terrorist groups."[48]

For some within Hezbollah, the Saudis will come up as likely players behind the scenes, possibly supporting the Sunni rebels Nasrallah says were behind the attack. Indeed, there would be historical precedent for this. The Saudis reportedly supported the Lebanese militants who targeted Sheikh Mohammad Hussein Fadlallah in a failed assassination attempt in 1985.[49] In fact, the United States has been fairly open about that fact that it has partnered with GCC countries and others to counter Hezbollah's activities.[50]

Hezbollah's pivot toward the Gulf should not be seen as a pivot away from Israel, however. To the contrary, Hezbollah sees a pernicious, budding alliance between the United States, Saudi Arabia, and Israel that is directly benefiting the Sunni *takfiri* militants it is fighting in Syria and, to a lesser extent, elsewhere in the region. And while Hezbollah is taking active measures to prepare for the next, eventual war with Israel, it is eager to avoid such a conflict at the present time given its significant investment of personnel and resources in the Syrian war next door and its desire not to give Israel a pretext to either enter that war on the side of the Sunni rebels or take advantage of Hezbollah's deployment there to target the group's military presence and rocket arsenal in south Lebanon. Moreover, Hezbollah has been trying to extend its reach into the Palestinian Territories. In August 2016, Israeli authorities detained several Hezbollah cells in the West Bank. The members, some of whom had been ordered to commit an imminent attack against IDF forces in the area, had been recruited online by Hezbollah operatives in Lebanon and the Gaza Strip.[51]

Yet Hezbollah's international operations are not limited to its home region. In June 2015, the latest Hezbollah plot in Europe was thwarted in Cyprus, where Hussein Bassam Abdallah, a dual Lebanese-Canadian citizen, was found to have stockpiled 8.2 tons of ammonium nitrate, a popular chemical explosive. Abdallah was convicted by a Cyprus court for his participation in a terrorist group (Hezbollah), possessing explosives, and conspiracy to commit a crime. It was the second time in three years that a Cypriot court has sentenced a Hezbollah operative to prison for plotting an attack within the country.[52]

According to Israeli investigators, Hezbollah was using Cyprus as a "point of export" from which to funnel explosives elsewhere for a series of attacks in Europe.[53] Indeed, the plot was already in motion: investigators believe the explosives used in the 2012 Burgas bus bombing may have come from the batch of chemicals stored in Cyprus.

Not only did Hezbollah actively maintain an explosives stockpile in Cyprus, the group retained the operatives, infrastructure and reach to engage in operations across Europe. Over the course of time Abdallah maintained this explosives stockpile, Hezbollah remained active across Europe, from a 2012 bombing thwarted in Greece to the arrest and deportation of a Hezbollah operative in Denmark in 2013 who arrived on a commercial ship for purposes still unknown. Four months after the EU ban, in late 2013, two Lebanese passengers were caught at a Brussels airport with nearly 770,000 euros in their possession. At least some of this cash was suspected to be intended for Hezbollah's coffers, Europol reported. A few months later, Germany raided the offices of the Orphan Children Project Lebanon in Essen, accusing the group of serving as a Hezbollah fundraising front organization. Germany's domestic intelligence agency recently reported that Hezbollah maintains some 950 active operatives in the country.

Hezbollah weapons and technology procurement operations continue in Europe as well. In July 2014, the U.S. Treasury Department blacklisted a Lebanese consumer electronics business, Stars Group Holding, along with its owners, subsidiaries, and "certain managers and individuals who support their illicit activities." Together, they functioned as a "key Hezbollah procurement network" that purchased technology around the world -- including in Europe -- to develop the drones Hezbollah deploys over Israel and Syria.[54]

After months of often acrimonious deliberations, senior European officials gathered in Brussels in July 2013 to announce that all 28 EU member states agreed to add Hezbollah's military wing – not the organization itself – to the EU's list of banned terrorist groups. At the time, European officials pointed to the blacklisting as a shot across the bow. "This is a signal to terrorist organizations," German Foreign Minister Guido Westerwelle warned. "If you attack one of our European countries, you get an answer from all of them." Regardless, evidence reveals that Hezbollah's military wing is still plotting attacks across Europe, and that the EU's words have not dissuaded the organization whatsoever.

The Treasury Department is moving more frequently to designate terrorists and targeting key individuals and companies facilitating Hezbollah's international misdeeds, with a focus on those with ties to the Islamic Jihad Organization, Hezbollah's terrorist arm.[55] President Barack Obama signed legislation in December 2015 that aims to "thwart" the group's "network at every turn" by imposing sanctions on financial institutions that deal with Hezbollah or its al Manar television station.

The Treasury designations – which freeze assets and impose sanctions – kicked into high gear in June 2016, when the U.S. targeted a high-level operative, Adham Tabaja and his company, al-Inmaa Group. Treasury had already targeted Hezbollah's military procurement front organizations and some of the businesses that run them, such as Stars Group Holdings in Lebanon and foreign subsidiaries that supplied components for the unmanned aerial vehicles Hezbollah deploys over Syria and Israel. Treasury also targeted associates of Mr. Tabaja—one of whom, Husayn Ali Faour, is a member of Hezbollah's Islamic Jihad, whose company supplied vehicles—and other Hezbollah procurement agents and financiers.

October 2016 brought arrests of a lawyer in Paris and a businesswoman in Atlanta who, according to the criminal complaint, conspired to launder narcotics proceeds and engage in international arms trafficking. The businesswoman told an undercover agent that she had associates in Hezbollah who were seeking to purchase cocaine, weapons, and ammunition, the U.S. government has charged.[56] The lawyer suggested that he could use his connections with Hezbollah to provide security to narcotics shipments.

Hezbollah's dependence on money laundering and drug trafficking has continued and even expanded as its monetary situation has deteriorated, strained by tightened U.S. sanctions and the costly Syrian war effort. In February 2016, the U.S. Drug Enforcement Administration (DEA) implicated Hezbollah in a multi-million-dollar drug trafficking and money laundering network that spanned four continents.[57] According to the DEA report, Hezbollah had relationships with South American drug cartels in a cocaine-smuggling network to Europe and the U.S. The proceeds funded a money-laundering scheme known as the Black Market Peso Exchange and provided Hezbollah with "a revenue and weapons stream."[58]

Tensions over the AMIA bombing and the indictment of senior Iranian officials for their roles in the attack resulted in poor diplomatic relations between Argentina and Iran for many years. Then, in 2007, Argentine representatives suddenly ceased their years-long policy of walking out of UN meetings whenever an Iranian official spoke. Despite the standing Argentinean indictments of Iranian officials, Argentina and Iran agreed in 2011 to form a "truth commission" to jointly investigate the 1994 bombing. The merits of this "partnership" were questionable from the outset, but doubts were exacerbated with the mysterious death of Argentine prosecutor Alberto Nisman in 2015. Nisman, who presided over the ongoing AMIA investigation, had filed charges that the Argentine government, specifically then-President Cristina Fernández de Kirchner and Foreign Minister Héctor Timerman, planned a cover-up of Iran and Hezbollah's role in the AMIA bombing in exchange for a political deal between the government of Iran and Argentina.[59] The day before he was due to present his case to the Argentine parliament, Nisman was found dead in his apartment. Despite his tragic and untimely demise, the work Nisman and his team had already conducted exposed not only the circumstances behind the AMIA attack, but Iran's ongoing intelligence operations in South America.

In May 2015, the man described by Argentinean authorities as the driving force behind the AMIA bombing, Mohsen Rabbani, told Argentinean TV that Nisman's investigation was based on nothing more than "the inventions of newspapers without any proof against Iran."[60] In fact, however, the most powerful proof against Iran was evidence of Rabbani's own role in the plot, from running a network of intelligence agents in Buenos Aires to purchasing the van used as the car bomb in the attack. Rabbani, moreover, remains active: according to Nisman's more recent investigations, Iranian agents in Argentina acting at Rabbani's behest and reporting directly back to him were conspiring to concoct fake 'new evidence' to supplant the real evidence collected in the case.[61] A small victory came in December 2016, when an Argentine court reopened the case on former President Fernandez and her role in concealing Iranian responsibility in 1994.[62]

One of the group's most recently foiled plots was in Peru and involved a Hezbollah operative married to a U.S. citizen. Peruvian counterterrorism police arrested the Hezbollah operative in Lima in November 2014, the result of a surveillance operation that began several months earlier. In that case, Mohammed Hamdar, a Lebanese citizen, arrived in Peru in November 2013 and married a dual Peruvian-American citizen two weeks later. When he was arrested in October, police raided his home and found traces of TNT, detonators, and other inflammable substances. A search of the garbage outside his home found chemicals used to manufacture explosives.[63]

In the run-up to the 2016 Rio Olympics, Brazilian authorities arrested former Hezbollah member Fadi Hassan Nabha. According to police, Nabha served in Hezbollah's special services and had weapons and explosives training.[64] September 2016 saw two more arrests of key Hezbollah operatives in the region: Khalil Mohamed El Sayed and Mohammed Jalil. El Sayed, a Lebanese naturalized Paraguayan, was arrested while trying to enter Argentina using counterfeit documents. The U.S. has investigated El Sayed for six years for his involvement in Hezbollah, and Brazil has accused El Sayed for involvement in drug and arm trafficking for over eight years. Jalil, also a Lebanese-Paraguayan attempting to enter Argentina on false papers, was arrested on similar charges, including affiliation with Hezbollah, drug and arms trafficking, along with credit card fraud. Jalil is wanted in the U.S., Brazil, and Paraguay.

In August 2016, Nasrallah expressed Hezbollah's international ambitions in no uncertain terms. "If Hezbollah emerged from the 2006 war a regional force," Nasrallah declared, "it will emerge from Syria crisis an international force."[65] In light of both the scope and pace of its contemporary international operations, this confidence is not entirely unfounded.

ENDNOTES

[1] Rafid Fadhil Ali, "New Hezbollah Manifesto Emphasizes Political Role in a United Lebanon," Jamestown Foundation Terrorism Monitor 7, iss. 38, December 15, 2009, http://www.jamestown.org/single/?no_cache=1&tx_ttnews[tt_news]=35830&tx_ttnews[backPid]=13&cHash=42a34967d2

[2] Nadim Ladki, "Lebanese Forces Pledge Crackdown; Force To Be Used to Quell Fighting That Has Killed 81," Montreal Gazette, May 13, 2008.

[3] Israel Defense Forces, Strategic Division, Military-Strategic Information Section, "The Second Lebanon War: Three Years Later," July 12, 2009, http://www.mfa.gov.il/MFA/About+the+Ministry/Behind+the+Headlines/The-Second-Lebanon-War-Three-years-later-12-Jul-2009

[4] "Report: Mughniyeh's brother-in-law suspect in Hariri killing," Yediot Ahronot (Tel Aviv), July 7, 2010, http://www.ynetnews.com/articles/0,7340,L-3927186,00.html

[5] Laila Bassam, "Hezbollah and Allies Resign, Toppling Lebanon Government," Reuters, January 12, 2011, http://www.reuters.com/article/2011/01/12/us-lebanon-hariri-resignation-idUSTRE70B26A20110112

[6] "Hezbollah-Backed Najib Mikati Appointed Lebanese PM," BBC, January 25, 2011, http://www.bbc.co.uk/news/world-middle-east-12273178

[7] "Israelis Killed in Bulgaria Bus Terror Attack, Minister Says," CNN, July 18, 2012, http://www.cnn.com/2012/07/18/world/europe/bulgaria-israel-blast/index.html.

[8] "Israelis Killed in Bulgaria Bus Terror Attack, Minister Says," CNN, July 18, 2012, http://www.cnn.com/2012/07/18/world/europe/bulgaria-israel-blast/index.html.

[9] Zachary Abuza, "Bad Neighbours: Hezbollah in Southeast Asia," Australia/Israel Review, November 2006, http://www.aijac.org.au/review/2006/31-11/abuza31-11.htm

[10] Ely Karmon, "Fight on All Fronts: Hizballah, the War on Terror, and the War in Iraq," Washington Institute for Near East Policy Research Memorandum no. 45, December 2003, http://www.washingtoninstitute.org/templateC04.php?CID=18

[11] Abuza, "Bad Neighbours."

[12] John T. Hanley, Kongdan Oh Hassig, and Caroline F. Ziemke, "Proceedings of the International Symposium on the Dynamics and Structures of Terrorist Threats in Southeast Asia, Held at Kuala Lumpur, Malaysia," Institute for Defense Analyses, September 2005.

[13] Ibid.; "Hizbollah Recruited Singaporeans: The Muslims Were Recruited Through religious Classes in Singapore to Aid a Plot to Blow Up US and Israeli Ships," Straits Times (Singapore), June 9, 2002; "Indonesian Government Expect Escalation in Terrorist Bombings; Hizballah Ops Out of Singapore Also Noted," Defense & Foreign Affairs Daily 20, no. 104 (2002).

[14] Maria A. Ressa, Seeds of Terror: An Eyewitness Account of Al-Qaeda's Newest Center of Operations in Southeast Asia (New York: Free Press, 2003); Hanley, Hassig and Ziemke, "Proceedings of the International Symposium on the Dynamics and Structures of Terrorist Threats in Southeast Asia, Held at Kuala Lumpur, Malaysia."

[15] Dudi Cohen, "Bangkok Threat: Terrorist's Swedish Connection," Yediot Ahronot (Tel Aviv), January 15, 2012, http://www.ynetnews.com/articles/0,7340,L-4175513,00.html; "Second Terror Suspect Sought, Court Issues Warrant for Atris's Housemate," Bangkok Post, January 20, 2012, http://www.bangkokpost.com/news/local/275914/second-terror-suspect-sought.

[16] James Hookway, "Thai Police Seize Materials, Charge Terror-Plot Suspect," Wall Street Journal, January 17, 2012, http://online.wsj.com/article/SB10001424052970204555904577164632227644906.html; Sebastian Rotella, "Before Deadly Bulgaria Bombing, Tracks of a Resurgent Iran-Hezbollah Threat," Foreign Policy, July 30, 2012, http://www.foreignpolicy.com/articles/2012/07/30/before_deadly_bulgaria_bombing_tracks_of_a_resurgent_iran_hezbollah_threat?wp_login_redirect=0

[17] Thomas Fuller, "In Twisting Terror Case, Thai Police Seize Chemicals," New York Times, January 16, 2012, http://www.nytimes.com/2012/01/17/world/asia/thai-police-in-bangkok-seize-bomb-making-material.html

[18] "U.N. Prosecutor Accuses Taylor of Al Qaeda Links; More," United Nations Foundation UN Wire, May 15, 2003,http://www.unwire.org/unwire/20030515/33747_story.asp

[19] Douglas Farah, "Hezbollah's External Support Network in West Africa and Latin America," International Assessment and Strategy Center, April 15, 2009, http://www.strategycenter.net/research/pubID.118/pub_detail.asp

[20] Matthew Levitt, "Hizbullah's African Activities Remain Undisrupted," RUSI/Jane's Homeland Security and Resilience Monitor, March 1, 2004.

[21] Matthew Levitt, "Hezbollah Finances: Funding the Party of God," in Jeanne K. Giraldo and Harold A. Trinkunas, eds.,Terrorism Financing and State Responses: a Comparative Perspective (Palo Alto: Stanford University Press, 2007).

[22] United States v. Mohamad Youssef Hammoud, et al., United States Court of Appeals for the Fourth District; U.S. Department of the Treasury, "Twin Treasury Actions Take Aim at Hizballah's Support Network," July 24, 2007, http://www.treasury.gov/press-center/press-releases/Pages/200772410294613432.aspx

[23] Ibid.

[24] Angus McDowall, "Yemen government says Hezbollah fighting alongside Houthis," Reuters, February 24, 2016, http://www.reuters.com/article/us-yemen-security-idUSKCN0VX21N

[25] U.S. Department of the Treasury, "Press Release: Treasury Sanctions Hizballah Leadership."

[26] Itamar Sharon, "'Six Iranians, including a general, killed in Israeli strike,'" Times of Israel, January 19, 2015, http://www.timesofisrael.com/six-iranians-also-said-killed-in-alleged-israeli-strike/?wptouch_preview_theme=enabled.

[27] Zeina Karam, "Hezbollah accuses Saudi Arabia of 'genocide' in Yemen," Times of Israel, April 13, 2015, http://www.timesofisrael.com/hezbollah-accuses-saudi-arabia-of-genocide-in-yemen.

[28] "Bahrain says it dismantled Iran-linked terror cell," Agence France-Presse, January 6, 2016, http://www.timesofisrael.com/bahrain-says-it-dismantled-iran-linked-terror-cell.

[29] U.S. Department of State, "Country Reports on Terrorism 2015," June 2016, https://www.state.gov/j/ct/rls/crt/2015/.
[30] Ibid.
[31] Yara Bayoumy, "Kuwait court sentences two to death for spying for Iran, Hezbollah," Reuters, January 12, 2016, http://www.reuters.com/article/us-kuwait-security-idUSKCN0UQ0RS20160112.
[32] "UAE Jails Emirati Woman on Charges of Spying for Hezbollah," Agence France-Presse, June 28, 2016, http://www.timesofisrael.com/uae-jails-emirati-woman-on-charges-of-spying-for-hezbollah/.
[33] "Kuwait jails Shiite MP for insulting Saudi, Bahrain," Agence France-Presse, July 27, 2016, http://www.al-monitor.com/pulse/afp/2016/07/kuwait-politics-trial-saudi-bahrain.html.
[34] Abdulla Rasheed, "Iran set up Hezbollah cell in UAE, court hears," Gulf News, April 18, 2016, http://gulfnews.com/news/uae/government/iran-set-up-hezbollah-cell-in-uae-court-hears-1.1715716.
[35] "GCC declares Lebanon's Hezbollah a 'terrorist' group," Al Jazeera (Doha), March 2, 2016, http://www.aljazeera.com/news/2016/03/gcc-declares-lebanon-hezbollah-terrorist-group-160302090712744.html.
[36] Ibid.
[37] "Arab League labels Hezbollah a 'terrorist' group," Al Jazeera (Doha), March 16, 2016, http://www.aljazeera.com/news/2016/03/arab-league-labels-hezbollah-terrorist-group-160311173735737.html.; "Islamic summit slams Hezbollah for 'terrorism.'"
[38] Sultan Al-Tamimi, "GCC: Hezbollah terror group," Arab News, June 3, 2016, http://www.arabnews.com/news/453834.
[39] Fahd Al-Zayabi, "Saudi Arabia launches financial sanctions on Hezbollah," Al Sharq Al-Awsaat (London), May 29, 2014, http://english.aawsat.com/2014/05/article55332700.
[40] Al-Tamimi, "GCC: Hezbollah terror group."
[41] Royal Embassy of Saudi Arabia, "Fact Sheet: Iran's Record in Supporting Terrorism and Extremism," January 20, 2016, https://www.saudiembassy.net/fact-sheet-irans-record-supporting-terrorism-and-extremism-0.
[42] Anne Barnard, "Saudi Arabia Cuts Billions in Aid to Lebanon, Opening Door for Iran," New York Times, March 2, 2016, https://www.nytimes.com/2016/03/03/world/middleeast/saudi-arabia-cuts-billions-in-aid-to-lebanon-opening-door-for-iran.html.
[43] "Saudi and UAE ban citizens from travelling to Lebanon," Al Jazeera (Doha), February 23, 2016, http://www.aljazeera.com/news/2016/02/saudi-uae-ban-citizens-travelling-lebanon-160223154000581.html.
[44] Rania El Gamal and Sam Wilkins, "Saudi Arabia blacklists four firms, three Lebanese men over Hezbollah ties," Reuters, February 26, 2016, http://www.reuters.com/article/us-mideast-crisis-saudi-lebanon-idUSKCN0VZ1C2.
[45] Ibid.

[46] "Concerned over its terror labeling Hezbollah urges Saudis to review decision," YaLibnan, July 9, 2016, http://yalibnan.com/2016/07/09/concerned-over-its-terror-labeling-hezbollah-urges-saudis-to-review-decision/.

[47] Matthew Levitt, "Anatomy of a Bombing," Foreign Affairs, September 1, 2015, https://www.foreignaffairs.com/articles/lebanon/2015-09-01/anatomy-bombing.

[48] Matthew Levitt and Nadav Pollak, "Hizbullah Under Fire in Syria," Tony Blair Faith Foundation, June 9, 2016, http://www.washingtoninstitute.org/policy-analysis/view/hizbullah-under-fire-in-syria.

[49] Matthew Levitt, Hezbollah: The Global Footprint of Lebanon's Party of God (Washington: Georgetown University Press, 2013), 27.

[50] At the release of the State Department's annual terrorist report in June, a senior U.S. official highlighted these efforts. "Confronting Iran's destabilizing activities and its support for terrorism was a key element of our expanded dialogue with the countries of the Gulf Cooperation Council, following the leaders' summit at Camp David in May of [2015]. We've also expanded our cooperation with partners in Europe, South America, and West Africa to develop and implement strategies to counter the activities of Iranian-allied and sponsored groups, such as Hezbollah." U.S. Department of State, "Country Reports on Terrorism 2015 Special Briefing with Justin Siberell, Acting Coordinator for Counterterrorism," June 2, 2016.

[51] "Hezbollah cells in West Bank busted by Israeli security forces," Jerusalem Post, August 18, 2016.

[52] Detailed in Matthew Levitt, "Inside Hezbollah's European Plots"; The Daily Beast, July 20, 2015, http://www.thedailybeast.com/articles/2015/07/20/inside-hezbollah-s-european-plots.html

[53] Gili Cohen and Reuters, "Cyprus Police Foil Planned Hezbollah Attacks Against Israeli Targets in Europe," Haaretz, May 29, 2015, http://www.haaretz.com/israel-news/1.658716.

[54] U.S. Department of the Treasury, "Treasury Sanctions Procurement Agents Of Hizballah Front Company Based In Lebanon With Subsidiaries In The UAE And China," July 10, 2014, https://www.treasury.gov/press-center/press-releases/Pages/jl2562.aspx.

[55] Detailed in Matthew Levitt, "The Crackdown on Hezbollah's Financing Network," Wall Street Journal, January 27, 2016, http://www.washingtoninstitute.org/policy-analysis/view/the-crackdown-on-hezbollahs-financing-network

[56] United States Department of Justice, United States Attorney's Office Eastern District of New York, Two Hezbollah Associates Arrested On Charges Of Conspiring To Launder Narcotics Proceeds And International Arms Trafficking," October 9, 2015, https://www.justice.gov/usao-edny/pr/two-hezbollah-associates-arrested-charges-conspiring-launder-narcotics-proceeds-and.

[57] Detailed in Matthew Levitt, "Don't Forget, or Deny, Hezbollah's Brutal Crimes," National Post, July 20, 2016, http://www.washingtoninstitute.org/policy-analysis/view/dont-forget-or-deny-hezbollahs-brutal-crimes

[58] United States Drug Enforcement Administration, DEA and European Authorities Uncover Massive Hizballah Drug and Money Laundering Scheme," February 1, 2016, https://www.dea.gov/divisions/hq/2016/hq020116.shtml.

[59] Hugh Bronstein and Luc Cohen, "Argentine court revives bombing cover-up case against Fernandez," Reuters, December 29, 2016, http://www.reuters.com/article/us-argentina-fernandez-idUSKBN14I1LT.

[60] Uki Goni, "Iran denies involvement in 1994 Argentinian Jewish centre bombing," Guardian, May 19, 2015, https://www.theguardian.com/world/2015/may/19/iran-argentina-jewish-centre-amia-bombing.

[61] Alberto Nisman, "Nisman report (dictamina) on sleeper cells – Extended Summary," March 4, 2015, http://albertonisman.org/nisman-report-dictamina-on-sleeper-cells-extended-summary/.

[62] Hugh Bronstein and Luc Cohen, "Argentine court revives bombing cover-up case against Fernandez," Reuters, December 29, 2016, http://www.reuters.com/article/us-argentina-fernandez-idUSKBN14I1LT.

[63] Mitra Taj, "Lebanese Detainee in Peru Denies Hezbollah Link, Says Police Coerced Confession," November 14, 2014, http://www.haaretz.com/middle-east-news/1.626415.

[64] "Brazil nabs former Hezbollah member wanted for drug trafficking," Reuters, July 29, 2016, http://www.reuters.com/article/us-olympics-rio-security-idUSKCN1091V5.

[65] "S. Nasrallah: Hezbollah Will Emerge from Syria War as an International Force," al-Manar, August 19, 2016, http://archive.almanar.com.lb/english/article.php?id=282798

Hizb ut-Tahrir

> **Quick Facts**
>
> Geographical Areas of Operation: East Asia, Eurasia, Europe, and the Middle East and North Africa
>
> Numerical Stregnth (Members): Unknown
>
> Leadership: Ata Abu Rashta
>
> Religious Identification: Sunni Islam
>
> *Quick Facts Courtesy of the Counter Extremism Project,*

Overview

Banned throughout the Middle East, South Asia, and Central Asia as well as in a few European states,[1] yet ostensibly nonviolent in its methods, Hizb ut-Tahrir al-Islami (The Party of Islamic Liberation, or HT) is a global Islamist organization that defies easy categorization. It is not engaged in traditional religious missionary work, and although it is heavily influenced by the Leninist model, it is neither a conventional political party (it eschews political participation) nor a violent revolutionary organization or terrorist group.[2] In many ways, Hizb ut-Tahrir *(HT) operates in the gray zone between politics, activism and extremism.*

History and Ideology

Taqiuddin an-Nabhani al-Filastyni, an Islamic scholar of Palestinian origin, founded HT in Jordanian-occupied East Jerusalem around 1953. An-Nabhani had been a student at Egypt's prestigious al-Azhar University, and had interacted with members of the Muslim Brotherhood during his time there (although it is not clear if he ever became a member).[3]

The group's platform and ideology are well defined. HT views itself not as a religious organization, but rather as a political movement whose ideology is based on Islam.

Therefore, it disavows nationalism, capitalism, and socialism as western ideologies alien to Islam. Instead, the organization seeks to re-establish the Caliphate that ruled Muslims following the death of the Prophet Muhammad under the four "righteous Caliphs."[4] Furthermore, the group rejects contemporary efforts to establish Islamic states, claiming that Sudan, Iran and Saudi Arabia, among others, do not meet the necessary criteria.

The modern Caliph envisioned by an-Nabhani and HT controls the religion, army, economy, foreign policy and political system of the Caliphate. In fact, HT explicitly rejects democracy and favors *sharia*—Islamic law—as the law of the land. It is left up to the Caliph and his deputies to interpret and apply it and thereby solve all social, economic, and ethnic problems that the *ummah* (the Islamic community) may face. Arabic will be the state language, which non-Arabic speakers would have to learn. One element that makes Hizb ut-Tahrir different from many other Islamist groups is that the group has welcomed female members. However, women are barred from key positions in the proposed Caliphate such as that of Caliph, Chief Judge, and provincial governors. An *amir* (defense minister) will be appointed by the Caliph to prepare the people for and to wage war against non-believers, including the United States, the European countries and Israel. Military conscription will be mandatory for all Muslim men over 15.[5]

HT has criticized attempts by other Islamist parties (such as the Islamic Revival Party of Tajikistan, the Muslim Brotherhood, and Hamas) to utilize democratic structures by holding ministerial posts in existing governments, or to participate in the electoral and legislative processes in order to achieve some influence in high-level decision-making.[6] Instead, HT has favored peaceful, but radical, political change through the demolition of the existing state apparatus and the construction of a new Islamic state. Nevertheless, HT does not favor the idea of forcibly seizing the state and mandating that society accept its ideology; rather, it prefers to persuade society to gradually accept its ideas, which would lead inevitably to a change in regime. As one expert has explained: "Rather than slogging through a political process that risks debasing the Quran and perpetuating the *ummah's* subjugation to the West, Hizb ut-Tahrir aims at global, grassroots revolution, culminating in a sudden, millenarian victory… when Muslims have achieved a critical mass of Koranic rectitude."[7]

HT's strategy to achieve this goal consists of three stages.[8] The first is to recruit members and built a strong organization. This stage is followed by HT's "interaction" with the *ummah* in an effort to impose its principles as the only legitimate version of Islam, one "stripped of all cultural accretions and purged of alien influences."[9] Finally, the ensuing grassroots revolution will re-establish the Caliphate.

The scenario for broadening the Caliphate which plays out in HT literature involves one or more Muslim countries coming under the organization's control, creating a base from which it will be able to convince others to join the fold, generating what is in essence a domino effect. Leaders of HT—citing the lack of political space for opposition parties throughout the Muslim world, increasing despair and a lack of economic opportunity—believe that much of the Muslim World is approaching a "boiling point," making it ready for an Islamist takeover. The group seeks to take advantage of dispossessed populations to seize power in particular states, such as those in Central Asia, Pakistan, or Indonesia, as a prelude to the establishment of a broader Caliphate, removing wayward Muslim regimes and eventually overthrowing non-Muslim ones as well. The organization welcomed the overthrow of Arab dictators during the Arab Spring revolutions.

It is widely reported that HT shuns violence in the pursuit of these goals. That is certainly true at the early stages in the organization's strategy, and while there is no evidence that the organization is responsible for terrorist or guerilla attacks, HT's understanding of political violence is more nuanced than current analysis of the group suggests. Emmanuel Karagiannis and Clark McCauley provide two ways of summarizing the ideological complexities of HT's position on violent action: "The first is to say that they have been committed to non-violence for fifty years. The second is to say that they have been waiting fifty years for the right moment to begin violent struggle."[10]

These two perspectives may not be as different as they appear at first glance. Historically, few groups are unconditionally committed to nonviolence, and "Hizb ut-Tahrir is not exceptional but typical in this regard. Its commitment to nonviolent struggle is conditional and the condition sought is the declaration of *jihad* by legitimate authority,"[11] the Caliph. HT also endorses defensive *jihads*, where Muslims are required to fight against an invader if attacked—a position that clearly has the potential to be interpreted very broadly and has been applied by the group to Coalition forces in Iraq and Afghanistan.[12] Moreover, the group was proscribed in Denmark after distributing pamphlets urging Muslims to "kill [Jews] wherever you find them, and turn them out from where they have turned you out."[13]

But even within Muslim majority countries, where the organization attempts to win over mass support in the hope that one day its adherents will rise up in peaceful demonstrations to overthrow the regimes they live under, HT has developed the concept of *nusrah* (seeking outside assistance) from other groups such as the militaries of target states.[14] It might be argued that HT's preferred method of political change to establish the Caliphate is in fact a *coup d'état* by the military that would have first embraced Islam as its guiding politico-religious principle. It is relevant here to note that HT encouraged elements within the Jordanian armed forces to attempt just this in 1968 and 1969, and the group was later linked to a failed 1974 coup attempt in Egypt.[15]

From HT's point of view, the justification for non-violence lies in the example of the Prophet, who criticized the pagan leaders of Mecca, gathered followers around him, and initially resisted the use of force to establish the Islamic state.[16] Indeed, according to one expert:

> The Party still thinks that it must follow the strategy of the Prophet: like Muhammad in Mecca, they must preach without violence. In practical terms, it means that when HT achieves a large following for its ideology, they could overthrow… regimes through peaceful demonstrations. Also like Muhammad in his war against the Arab tribes in Mecca, they could get outside assistance or nusrah from the military to organize a coup.[17]

Although HT as an organization does not adopt violence as a means to achieve its goals, another source of concern is that the group may radicalize members who then go on in their individual capacities to conduct violent acts. According to Zeyno Baran, "Hizb ut-Tahrir is part of an elegant division of labor. The group itself is active in the ideological preparation of the Muslims, while other organizations handle the planning and execution of terrorist attacks… Hizb ut-Tahrir today serves as a *de facto* conveyor belt for terrorists."[18] Indeed, several notable militants associated with more radical Islamist groups are known to be previous members of HT, as was the case with Omar Sharif. British intelligence officials discovered a cache of HT literature in the home of Sharif, a British citizen who attempted to blow himself up in a Tel Aviv bar in 2003.[19]

Similarly, there is concern in many quarters about what is perceived to be HT's disingenuous dual track strategy of grassroots activism amongst Western Muslims on one hand and engagement with wider Western society on the other. Houriya Ahmed and Hannah Stuart from the London-based Centre for Social Cohesion discuss HT activism in Britain as consisting of two messages and two complementary aims, one for the UK's Muslim communities and one for the wider public and specifically intellectuals and opinion-makers such as journalists and politicians. Presenting itself as the vanguard of Islam, HT works within the British Muslim communities to promote political identification with Muslims globally and discourage any other sense of political loyalty. Within wider society, HT works to present Islamism, the Caliphate, and their interpretation of *sharia* law as a non-threatening and viable alternative to current political thinking.[20]

They add that, "[i]n order to mainstream HT ideology amongst Western Muslim communities and avoid rejection by wider society, the party has downplayed its more intolerant beliefs and presents itself as defending 'true' Islam in the face of a perceived Western 'War on Islam.'"[21] The group has denounced the declaration of a caliphate by ISIS in Syria and Iraq because it did not follow the Prophet's methodology and the security situation there is too precarious.[22]

GLOBAL REACH

Whatever the concerns and criticisms regarding HT's goals and methods, it is increasingly clear that it is a movement with a significant following in many parts of the world. Some even claim that, "of all the banned Islamist groups in the former Soviet Union, Hizb ut-Tahrir is the only one that can be called a mass organization."[23] It is also a popular organization among young Muslims in Western Europe[24] and national conferences in the U.S. and Canada in July 2009 indicate a resurgence of HT activism there.[25] The group's major organizational center is said to be in London, where most of its literature is published and a good deal of its fundraising and training occurs,[26] although some claim that Ata Abu Rashta, HT's current global leader, is based in Lebanon.[27]

Relatively little is known about HT's organizational structure, chain of command, or leadership. What is clear is that the organization is cell-based, and heavily influenced by the Marxist-Leninist revolutionary model that controls HT's worldwide activities and drastically reduces the possibility of the penetration of outsiders into its leadership echelons. The global leader of HT meets with regional leaders who distribute literature and funding to district leaders, who in turn redistribute these items as well as provide strategic direction during their monthly meetings to individual cells. For operational security, most cell members only know other people in their cell and are kept in the dark about other cells operating locally, nationally, and regionally.[28] Indeed, Ahmed and Stuart claim that:

> HT's ideology and strategy are centralized. HT global leadership issues strategy communiqués to the executive committees of national branches, which then interpret them into a localized strategic action plan... Whilst HT core ideology stressed the indivisibility of the Muslim 'ummah' and rejects national identity, national strategies often reflect the ethnic origins of the various Muslim communities... National executives are encouraged to interpret strategy to best suit their localized needs.[29]

Because the group operates clandestinely in most parts of the world, its global membership numbers are unknown. Rough estimates of its strength in Central Asia alone range from 20,000 to 100,000.[30] Emmanuel Karagiannis estimates that there are around 25,000 members and many more sympathizers in the region,[31] with the majority in the Ferghana Valley in Uzbekistan and thousands of members in Tajikistan and Kyrgyzstan alongside "hundreds (perhaps thousands) in Kazakhstan and Russia, as well as Azerbaijan and the Ukraine."[32] The group's support base consists of college students, the unemployed, factory workers and teachers,[33] but it also seems to be making particularly strong headway behind prison walls,[34] where between 7,000 and 8,000 of its members are thought to reside in Uzbekistan alone.[35]

HT's growth in Central Asia has been significantly, though unintentionally, fueled by the repressive tactics adopted by the regimes there. With few exceptions, the states that emerged out of the Soviet Union smother, rather than engage, their political opposition. The anti-democratic policies adopted by these regimes unwittingly expand the influence of extremist groups like HT and the Islamic Movement of Uzbekistan from the margins of national political discourse to its center. When there is no room for moderate and reasonable opposition, the only channel for change comes through radical elements. Thus, in May 2015, British members of HT gathered outside the Uzbek embassy in London to commemorate the tenth anniversary of the Andijan massacre, despite the fact that the group was not directly involved.[36]

South and Southeast Asia are also strongholds of HT activism. The organization claims that it has recruited "tens of thousands" of members in Indonesia.[37] While these numbers are difficult to verify, a 2007 HT conference there drew somewhere between 80,000 and 100,000 attendees from around the world.[38] HT also holds regular public protests and demonstrations in Pakistan and Bangladesh. The organization's presence at universities "points to a deliberate strategy of targeting students."[39] Yet, the group has been banned in both countries. HT also has a presence of unknown strength in, among other places, Syria, Iraq, Turkey, Palestine, Lebanon, Egypt, Tunisia, Afghanistan, Malaysia, China, Canada, Australia, South Africa, Russia, and Ukraine.

Much like its opaque membership, HT's secrecy makes it difficult to investigate its sources of funding. However, it appears that most of its money is raised in Europe, the Middle East, and South Asia.[40] Members are expected to contribute to the operational costs of the organization, including such mundane outlays as printing leaflets.[41] Organizational costs for HT remain relatively low because most members live in and operate out of their own homes and very few, if any, volunteers are paid.[42] However, a great deal of the organization's technology in Central Asia has been funded and imported from abroad, signifying both the international scope of the movement and potentially the complicity of at least some officials responsible for customs and border controls among local governments.[43]

Recent Activity

During the past five years, HT activities in Western countries have included the organization of protests, sit-ins and petitions. The group asked Muslims to abstain from the 2015 parliamentary elections in Great Britain.[44] HT staged a protest against the killing of civilians in Aleppo outside the Syrian embassy in London in December 2016.[45] In the United States, the local branch organized two events about the siege of Aleppo by Syrian regime forces and pro-Iranian militias.[46] In November 2015, the group organized a conference in Australia against "forced assimilation".[47] The branch of HT in Australia has become increasingly active in recent years due to the presnce of a sizeable Arab community.

South Asia has remained an important area of HT activities. The Pakistani branch suffered a major blow in March 2012 when 19 members, including some university professors, were arrested by police in Lahore.[48] The newly-established branch of HT in Afghanistan organized a conference, with limited participation, on corruption in April 2012.[49] Despite being banned by the Bangladeshi government in October 2009, HT organized a rally in Dhaka in December 2012. The local branches have maintained strong links to the Pakistani and Bangladeshi communities in the UK.

Members of Hizb ut-Tahrir were arrested in Muslim-populated areas of Russia in August 2012.[50] Three months later, 18 HT members were arrested in Moscow, although the group claimed that the actual number of its arrested members was much higher.[51] As a result, the Palestinian branch of HT organized a protest at the Russian Representative Office in Ramallah, as did the Indonesian branch outside the Russian embassy in Jakarta.[52] The Russian security agencies have also arrested members in the Crimea following the annexation of the peninsula by Moscow in March 2014.[53]

Although state repression has led to a decrease of HT activities in Central Asian republics, Hizb ut-Tahrir has made inroads in southern Kyrgyzstan, which has suffered from ethnic tensions in recent years.[54] Moreover, the group held a demonstration outside the Uzbek embassy in Brussels during Islam Karimov's visit to the European Union and NATO in January 2011, which was apparently the first open manifestation of HT in Belgium.[55] Nevertheless, it seems that the group has scaled down its activities in Central Asia following the Arab Spring.

There are indications that the group's leadership has shifted its focus to Arab countries. Following the Arab Spring revolutions of 2010-2012, there is a renewed quest for religious identity, which partly manifests itself in a renewed interest in political Islam. HT organized a much-publicized female conference in Tunisia in March 2012.[56] Additionally, HT has paid increased attention to the crisis in Syria by organizing public events and protests, including one in Chicago on December 24, 2011. The group even organized a protest in the Syrian city of Aleppo on November 9, 2012.[57] In April 2013, female members of HT staged a press conference in Amman, Jordan to discuss the situation in Syria, especially as it relates to women and children.[58] The group has also faced a few setbacks in the region. In September 2016, the Tunisian government considered the banning of ban Hizb ut-Tahrir because it is "undermining public order".[59] During the same month, the Jordanian government arrested 15 senior members of Hizb ut-Tahrir for campaigning against changes to the school curriculum.[60]

The group is likely to maintain its level of engagement in Arab countries. It has paid increased attention to human right abuses committed by authoritarian regimes in North Africa and the Levant. The ongoing Syrian crisis has also allowed Hizb ut-Tahrir to mobilize Muslims living in western countries. The group has also launched a campaign for the support of the Rohingya Muslims in Burma. In this way, it has portrayed itself as a defender of Muslim populations in war zones. Finally, the group will probably attempt to increase its activities in Muslim-majority countries in South and South-East Asia.

ENDNOTES

[1] Hizb ut-Tahrir is banned in countries such as Bangladesh, Denmark, Germany, Jordan, Kazakhstan, Kyrgyzstan, Pakistan, Russia, Syria, Tajikistan, Turkmenistan, and Uzbekistan, among others.

[2] "Understanding Islamism," International Crisis Group, Middle East/North Africa Report no. 37, March 2, 2005, 4fn11.

[3] Taqiuddin an-Nabkhani, The Islamic State (Lahore: Hizb ut-Tahrir, 1962).

[4] Tyler Rauert, "The Next Threat from Central Asia," The Journal of International Security Affairs 9, Fall 2005, 28.

[5] Members of Hizb ut-Tahrir in Britain, The Method to Re-establish the Khilafah and Resume the Islamic Way of Life (London, Al-Khilafah Publications, 2000), 67.

[6] Matthew Herbert, "The Plasticity of the Islamist Activist: Notes from the Counterterrorism Literature," Studies in Conflict and Terrorism 32 (2009), 399

[7] Olivier Roy, Globalized Islam: The Search for a New Ummah (New York: Columbia University Press, 2004), 248.

[8] Herbert, "The Plasticity of the Islamist Activist," 399

[9] Emmanuel Karagiannis and Clark McCauley, "Hizb ut-Tahrir al-Islami: Evaluating the Threat Posed by a Radical Islamic Group That Remains Nonviolent," Terrorism and Political Violence 18 (2006), 328.

[10] Ibid.

[11] Rauert, "The Next Threat From Central Asia," 28; See also A. Elizabeth Jones, Testimony before the U.S. House of Representatives Committee on International Relations, Subcommittee on the Middle East and Central Asia, Washington, DC, October 29, 2003.

[12] Christian Caryl, "Reality Check: The Party's Not Over," Foreign Policy, December 22, 2009.

[13] "Radical Islam in Central Asia: Responding to Hizb ut-Tahrir," International Crisis Group Asia Report no. 58, June 30, 2003, 8.

[14] Suha Taji-Farouki, A Fundamental Quest: Hizb ut-Tahrir and the Search for the Islamic Caliphate (London: Grey Seal, 1996), 27, 168

[15] Karagiannis and McCauley, "Hizb ut-Tahrir al-Islami," 325

[16] Zeyno Baran, Hizb ut-Tahrir: Islam's Political Insurgency (Washington, DC: The Nixon Center, 2004), 11.

[17] Ariel Cohen, "Hizb ut-Tahrir: An Emerging Threat to U.S. Interests in Central Asia," Heritage Foundation Backgrounder no. 1656, May 30, 2003

[18] Didier Chaudet, "Hizb ut-Tahrir: An Islamist Threat to Central Asia?" Journal of Muslim Minority Affairs 26, no. 1, April 2006, 117

[19] Caryl, "Reality Check: The Party's Not Over."

[20] Houriya Ahmed and Hannah Stuart, Hizb ut-Tahrir: Ideology and Strategy (London: Centre for Social Cohesion, November 2009), 69.

[21] Ibid., 7.

[22] Mamdooh Abu Sawa Qataishaat, "Media Statement Regarding ISIS's Declaration in Iraq", Media Office of Hizb ut-Tahrir, Wilayah of Jordan, July 1, 2014, http://www.hizb.org.uk/current-affairs/media-statement-regarding-isiss-declaration-in-iraq

[23] "Central Asia: Islamists in Prison," International Crisis Group Asia Briefing no. 97, March 15, 2009, 3. See also Emmanuel Karagiannis, Political Islam in Central Asia: The Challenge of Hizb ut-Tahrir (New York: Routledge, 2010), 2.

[24] Jane's Terrorism and Insurgency Center, Hizb ut-Tahrir, October 26, 2009, URL?

[25] See Daniela Feldman, "Islamic extremists hold open conference in Chicago," Jerusalem Post, July 22, 2009, 7; See also "Open House with Hizb ut-Tahrir," invitation from Hizb ut-Tahrir Canada, www.torontomuslims.com/events_display.asp?ID=9232

[26] Ariel Cohen, "Radical Islam and the U.S. Interests in Central Asia", Testimony before the U.S. House of Representatives Committee on International Relations, Subcommittee on the Middle East and Central Asia, October 29, 2003.

[27] Ahmed and Stuart, Hizb ut-Tahrir: Ideology and Strategy, 52.

[28] Jane's, Hizb ut-Tahrir.

[29] Hizb ut-Tahrir: Ideology and Strategy, 68.

[30] "Radical Islam in Central Asia: Responding to Hizb ut-Tahrir," 17.

[31] Karagiannis, Political Islam in Central Asia: The Challenge of Hizb ut-Tahrir, 58.

[32] "Central Asia: Islamists in Prison," 3.

[33] Ahmed Rashid, Jihad: The Rise of Militant Islam in Central Asia (New York, NY: Penguin Books, 2002), 124.

[34] See "Central Asia: Islamists in Prison."

[35] Shiv Malik, "For Allah and the Caliphate," New Statesman 17, no. 824 (2004).

[36] "Andijan Massacre: Uzbek Embassy Picket, 11am 9th May 2015," Hizb ut-Tahrir: The Liberation Party, Britain, May 5, 2015, http://www.hizb.org.uk/current-affairs/andijan-massacre-uzbek-embassy-picket-11am-9th-may-2015.

[37] Ahmed and Stuart, Hizb ut-Tahrir: Ideology and Strategy, 55.

[38] "Stadium Crowd Pushes for Islamist Dream," BBC, August 12, 2009, http://news.bbc.co.uk/2/hi/south_asia/6943070.stm; see also "At massive rally, Hizb ut-Tahrir calls for a global Muslim state," Christian Science Monitor, August 14, 2007.
[39] Ahmed and Stuart, Hizb ut-Tahrir: Ideology and Strategy, 57.
[40] Jane's, Hizb ut-Tahrir.
[41] Ibid.
[42] Ibidem.
[43] Rauert, "The Next Threat From Central Asia," 31.
[44] Hizb ut-Tahrir Britain, "The Futility of British Elections", April 22, 2015, http://www.hizb.org.uk/election-2015/the-futility-of-british-elections
[45] Hizb ut-Tahrir Britain, "Raise your voice, Break the silence, Support you ummah in Aleppo", December 16, 2016, http://www.hizb.org.uk/wp-content/uploads/2016/12/demo-aleppo.jpg
[46] Hizb ut-Tahrir America, "Aleppo, Syrian Crisis and Solution", December 17, 2016, https://hizb-america.org/aleppo-syria-crisis-solution/ and Hizb ut-Tahrir America, "Stand up for Aleppo", December 23, 2016, https://hizb-america.org/stand-up-for-aleppo/
[47] Rosie Lewis, "Hizb ut-Tahrir: National Anthem is Forced Assimilation", The Australian, November 2, 2015, http://www.theaustralian.com.au/indepth/community-under-siege/hizb-uttahrir-national-anthem-is-forced-assimilation/news-story/5aac76c3ec65454d63f7f323f326e597
[48] "19 Hizb ut-Tahrir Men Booked Under Sedition Law, Jailed," The Nation, April 14, 2012, http://www.nation.com.pk/pakistan-news-newspaper-daily-english-online/national/14-Apr-2012/19-hizb-ut-tahrir-men-booked-under-sedition-law-jailed
[49] Hizb ut-Tahrir, "Press Release – Hizb ut-Tahrir Wilayah Afghanistan Organizes Conference in the Capital on Corruption, Causes and Solution," April 5, 2012, http://www.hizb-ut-tahrir.info/info/english.php/contents_en/entry_17159.
[50] "Five Alleged Members of Banned Hizb ut-Tahrir Arrested in Chelyabinsk," Radio Free Europe/Radio Liberty, August 1, 2012, http://www.rferl.org/content/members-hizb-ut-tahrir-arrested/24663122.html
[51] Mairbek Vatchagaev, "Moscow Recognizes Hizb ut-Tahrir Operates Inside Russia," Jamestown Foundation Eurasia Daily Monitor 9, no. 213, November 20, 2012, http://www.jamestown.org/programs/edm/single/?tx_ttnews%5Btt_news%5D=40139&cHash=10b65985b87adb678a9638d6f77a7c58; See also the HT statement on its Russian-language website, located at http://hizb-russia.info/index.php/khizb-ut-takhrir/proklomatsii/strany-zapada/rossiya/777-massovye-obyski-i-zaderzhaniya-musulman.html.

[52] "Hizb ut-Tahrir Palestine: Protest at the Russian Representative Office in Ramallah," khilafah.com, December 6, 2012, http://www.khilafah.com/index.php/activism/middle-east/15116-hizb-ut-tahrir-palestine-protest-at-the-russian-representative-office-in-ramallah; "Hizb ut-Tahrir Demands Russia Release Members," Radio Free Europe/Radio Liberty, November 29, 2012, http://www.rferl.org/content/hizb-ut-tahrir-russia-indonesia/24784504.html.

[53] Hizb ut-Tahrir Australia, "Russia Arrests More HT Members in Crimea on Fabricated Terror Charges", October 13, 2016, http://www.hizb-australia.org/2016/10/russia-arrests-more-ht-members-in-crimea-on-fabricated-terror-charges/

[54] Jacob Zenn, "Hizb ut-Tahrir Takes Advantage of Ethnic Fault Lines in Tatarstan, Kyrgyzstan," Jamestown Foundation Eurasia Daily Monitor 9, no. 218, November 29, 2012, http://www.jamestown.org/single/?no_cache=1&tx_ttnews%5Btt_news%5D=40174.

[55] Bruno De Cordier, "Why Was Hizb ut-Tahrir Protest in Brussels the Biggest?" neweurasia.net, January 28, 2011, http://www.neweurasia.net/photoblog/why-was-hizb-ut-tahrir-protest-in-brussels-the-biggest/

[56] HuT England, "HT Press Statement for the International Women's Conference on Women and the Khilafah," March 15, 2012, http://www.hizb.org.uk/current-affairs/press-statement-international-womens-conference-on-women-and-the-khilafah

[57] "Protest in Aleppo, Syria by Hizb ut-Tahrir," khilafah.com, November 9, 2012, http://www.khilafah.com/index.php/activism/middle-east/14986-video-protest-in-aleppo-syria-by-hizb-ut-tahrir

[58] Hizb ut-Tahrir, "Hundreds of Women to Gather at a Critical Press Conference in Jordan Organised by Hizb ut-Tahrir," April 24, 2013, http://www.hizb-ut-tahrir.info/info/english.php/contents_en/entry_24835

[59] "Tunisia pushes for court ban on political party that calls for caliphate", Middle East Eye, September 7, 2016, http://www.middleeasteye.net/news/tunisia-pushes-court-ban-political-party-calls-caliphate-1380588769

[60] Hizb ut-Tahrir Australia, "Jordan Arrests 15 Senior HT Members Including Respected Scholars", September 30, 2016, http://www.hizb-australia.org/2016/09/jordan-arrests-15-senior-ht-members-including-respected-scholars/

ISLAMIC STATE

QUICK FACTS

Geographic Areas of Occupation: East Asia, Eurasia, Europe, Latin America, Middle East and North Africa, North America, South Asia, Sub-Saharan Africa

Strength: Estimates at year's end suggested between 19,000 and 25,000*

Leadership: Abu Bakr al-Baghdadi

Religious Identification: Sunni Islam

(Quick Facts courtesy of the U.S. State Department's Annual Country Reports on Terrorism, Last Updated 2015)

*These estimates only reflect membership in Syria and Iraq

OVERVIEW

The "Islamic State," or ISIS (the Islamic State of Iraq and Syria), refers to a Salafi Islamist militant faction that traces its origins back to a jihadist group led in the late 1990s by the Jordanian Abu Musab al-Zarqawi. Moving to Iraq in 2002, the group began as one of several militias challenging the U.S.-led military presence in the country, eventually contesting for leadership among the various mujahideen groups. Initially independent of al-Qaeda, Zarqawi swore allegiance to Osama bin Laden in 2004, and his group became The Al-Qaeda Organization in the Land of the Two Rivers (better known as al-Qaeda in Iraq, or AQI). Despite al-Zarqawi's death in June 2006, the MSC became the Islamic State in Iraq (ISI) in October 2006 in expectation of establishing an Islamic state in conquered territory modeled on a Salafi conception of the "pure" Islamic state that existed during the formative years of Islam's ascendance. This vaultingly ambitious "Islamic State" project would be temporarily undermined by an increasingly successful American-led counterinsurgency campaign in Iraq from 2007 to 2010.

In May 2010, ISI announced the selection of Abu Bakr al-Baghdadi as its leader. Al-Baghdadi announced in a 2012 speech that the group was prioritizing the freeing of imprisoned group members and targeting police personnel. As U.S. troops departed Iraq in December 2011 the Iraqi Government of Prime Minister Nouri al-Maliki assumed an increasingly sectarian character, deeply alienating the Sunni Arab population. ISI then launched a series of successful raids to liberate captured members from Iraqi prisons and sent fighters to establish a presence in 2011 in Syria amid an uprising against President Bashar al-Assad.

By April 2013, Abu Bakr al-Baghdadi attempted to assert his control over the ISI-al-Qaeda joint project in Syria by announcing the creation of ISIS, making the al-Qaeda-affiliated Nusrah Front part of his organization. Fissures in the jihadist ranks deepened as ISIS' leadership bid was rejected by both al-Qaeda leader Ayman al-Zawahiri and Nusrah Front amir Abu Muhamad al-Julani. Yet, as jihadists increasingly joined the ranks of ISIS, the organization succeeded in taking the major Syrian city of Raqqa in August 2013 from rival groups. Continued unrest in Iraq opened the doors for ISIS to take the major city of Fallujah in January 2014. A disavowal of ISIS by al-Qaeda in February 2014 barely seemed to slow the momentum of the group in Iraq's Anbar province.

The shockingly swift and easy June 2014 takeover of Mosul and much of Iraq's Sunni Arab north propelled ISIS to the front and center of global media attention. Buoyed by an image of invincibility and authenticity, the ISIS propaganda juggernaut issued a call for Muslims worldwide to emigrate and build the nascent state. ISIS's brutal treatment of religious minorities in northern Iraq led to the creation of a U.S.-led military coalition against it. ISIS began suffering losses, most notably when it lost control of the Mosul Dam in August 2014 and the besieged city of Amerli in September 2014. While more than 10,000 Coalition airstrikes slowed ISIS momentum in Iraq and parts of Syria, the organization demonstrated its potency by scoring major victories in Ramadi, Iraq and Tadmur, Syria in spring 2015. Meanwhile, its potent propaganda and revolutionary image of an idealized Islamic state reborn at the "End of Days" continues to attract a steady stream of new recruits and oaths of allegiance from substantial Salafi jihadist groups in Libya, West Africa, and Egypt, as well as pockets of fighters scattered throughout turbulent regions of the Muslim world. By 2016, ISIS was confronting an ongoing series of important military reversals and defeats on the ground in its Syria-Iraq heartland. By October 2016, the long expected offensive against Mosul, the largest city held by ISIS, had begun and quick initial progress was replaced by a slow and deadly grind in urban areas. As of early 2017, the fighting is still ongoing. With Turkish-backed Syrian rebels and their bitter Syrian Kurdish rivals succeeding in making some progress against ISIS in Syria. Facing enemies on every side and still implacable in its methods and ambitions, the Islamic State, both on the ground and in cyberspace, is ceding ground slowly and bitterly and has revolutionized the world of Islamism.

HISTORY & IDEOLOGY

A few months after the death of Abu Musab al-Zarqawi in 2006, the al-Qaeda in Iraq-led Mujahideen Shura Council (MSC) became the Islamic State of Iraq (ISI). An October 15, 2006 statement announcing the new entity compared it in size to the 7th century state of Medina under the Prophet Muhammad, and called for Muslims everywhere to support the state, which would be the precursor to a resurrected Caliphate to be based in Baghdad.[1] A month later, a 20-minute audio file by Abu Hamza al-Muhajir, a veteran Egyptian *jihadist* who had replaced al-Zarqawi as *emir* of al-Qaeda in Iraq, contained his pledge of allegiance to Abu Omar al-Baghdadi, the "Qurayshi and Hashemi, descendant of Hussein, Commander of the Faithful." Al-Muhajir pledged his "12,000 fighter strong Army of al-Qa'ida" to the new leader and called on other Iraqi *jihadist* groups to unite under Al-Baghdadi's standard.[2] He declared that this was the beginning of a new phase "where we put down the foundations for the project of an Islamic caliphate." While ostensibly still part of al-Qaeda, the new organization revealed a revolutionary agenda that would dramatically impact 21st century *Salafi jihadism*.

The announcement of the Islamic State did not emerge out of a vacuum. It was designed to mimic the most "authentic" Islamic state that existed during the time of the Prophet Mohammed and the idealized period of the Righteously Guided Caliphs (622-661 A.D.). Al-Qaeda, by contrast, focused on prioritizing the conflict against the West and especially the United States, and saw the creation of the Caliphate as an eventual goal, to be pursued when conditions improved and there was consensus among the Muslim *umma* (community of believers).

Al-Zarqawi himself spoke in 2004 about a near-future apocalyptic state arising out of Mesopotamia. "The spark had been lit in Iraq," he said, "and its flames will blaze, Allah willing, until they consume the armies of the Cross at Dabiq."[3] In 2005, an AQI spokesman specifically listed the "re-establishment of the Righteously-Guided Caliphate" as one of the group's principal goals, along with *jihad* and "renewing pure monotheism which was sullied by the filth of polytheistic elements."[4] In 2006, with increased insurgent momentum and success in Iraq, the leaders of ISI sought to make this ambitious agenda a reality.

By December 2006, the Islamic State's new proto-*caliph* dismissed Osama bin Laden as the "sheikh of the Mujahideen" in his inaugural speech and offered the American military safe conduct out of Iraq provided they leave their heavy weapons behind and depart within a month. Abu Omar al-Baghdadi claimed that 70 percent of Sunni tribal sheikhs supported the new organization and that more than 13 *jihadist* groups had joined. He even boasted that the new state sought to establish an empire stretching from Spain to China.[5] Criticism from dissident *jihadists* toward Baghdadi's astonishing declaration were not long in coming, with some complaining that the new entity was fighting other *jihadist* factions rather than infidels in order to compel their submission.[6]

The Islamic State pursued a dual strategy of fighting the Iraqi government and American forces on one hand, and rival insurgent factions on the other. In March and April 2007, ISI clashed with the 1920 Revolution Brigade and with Ansar al-Sunna. At the same time, suicide car bombs (VBIEDs) killed hundreds in Tel Afar, Al-Hillah and at a Baghdad market.

Abu Omar al-Baghdadi's third speech, in March 2007, announced that Jews and Christians living among Muslims were now considered fair game and that Sunni Muslims who participate in the Iraqi political process were considered apostates who could be lawfully killed. Much of the rest of his remarks focused on rival Islamist groups who participated in a "fierce multi-faceted media attack on the nascent State of Islam."

A fourth speech by the ISI "Commander of the Faithful" later in 2007 extolled the great accomplishment of the Islamic State:

> "The people of Iraq today are one of the greatest nations on earth in maintaining *tawheed* (strict monotheism), for there is no polytheistic Sufism being propagated or shrines being visited or innovated festivals being celebrated, or candles being lit of a pilgrimage being made to a pagan totem, because the people of Iraq have destroyed all these shrines with their bare hands so Allah alone would be worshipped."[7]

The image of what ISIS would become was visible in August 2007, when the group orchestrated its bloodiest attack to-date in Iraq: a series of truck bombs in the Yazidi towns of Kahtaniya and Jazeera which killed between 500 and 900 people and injured 1,500 more.[8] While the group remained active in killing and bombing, U.S. and Iraqi counter-insurgency operations, aided by the increasingly effective, U.S.-backed Sons of Iraq or "*Sahwa*" (Sunni tribes armed to fight al-Qaeda) was taking its toll.

Abu Omar's fifth speech threatened Iran with a two-month deadline to stop aiding Shi'a in Iraq or face war. The threat extended to any Sunni Arab country doing business with Shi'a. His sixth speech, in September 2007, castigated Sunnis, both politicians and tribesmen, working against the Islamic State and threatened terrorism against Sweden for the publication of cartoon depicting the Prophet Muhammad as a dog:

> "Every sniveling coward dares to insult us, from the worshippers of the Cross, to the worshippers of the Devil (Yazidis), even the worshippers of the cow. Our honor and blood have become the cheapest thing in all the world and when we try to arise from our slumber to regain our glory and the dignity of our past, we are stabbed in the back."[9]

Abu Omar's next speeches seemingly referenced a group with a powerful idea that was flailing to maintain relevance. His eighth, in December 2007, decried Arab nationalism as an invention of Arab Christians aimed at weakening Islam: "to Hell with the proponents of darkness who want the return of the Ba'athist Army." In the hopes of fanning the dying embers of *jihad*, his ninth speech was dedicated to the Israeli-Palestinian conflict. Meanwhile, the death toll in Iraq in January 2008 had fallen to its lowest mark in almost three years.[10] Perhaps as a sign of desperation, the group seemed to have used two women suffering from mental illness as suicide bombers in another Baghdad market attack in February 2008.[11]

The Islamic State's "Minister of War," Abu Hamza al-Muhajir, resurfaced in October 2008 with a revealing 44-minute interview. Al-Muhajir explained that establishing the Islamic State had always been a dream of Iraqi *jihadists*, but that conditions had been ripe for the establishment of an entity that would embody and protect Iraq's (and the region's) Sunni Arab Muslims. He seemed to make clear that the decision to try and establish a "state" was only made after the death of Abu Musab al-Zarqawi. He also revealed that the military commander of the Islamic State had been a former Colonel in Saddam's army, and that the point of *jihad* was to secure a State in order to enforce God's law following the precedent of Muhammad in Medina.[12]

Abu Omar al-Baghdadi marked the second anniversary of the Islamic State in October 2008 in a defiant speech, given the increasing success of the Iraqi Security Forces (ISF) at the time. He boasted that it was better to kill one *rafidah* (Shi'a) than a hundred Crusaders.[13] The election of a new American president in November 2008 engendered still another speech directed at the President-elect and at the Christians more broadly, calling on them to purge their religion of the "corruptions" instituted by Emperor Constantine at Nicaea.

Despite increasing success by the ISF, the Islamic State continued to strike out with its deadliest operation of the year on April 23, 2009, a dual suicide bomb attack that killed around 130 in Baghdad and Diyala. A June 2009 communique followed, expressing frustration at the nationalist orientation of some Sunni *jihadist* groups, which had still refused to join ISI.

A month later, Abu Omar condemned Iraqi authorities and those who cooperate with them, especially the Sunni Arab Islamist Iraqi Islamist Party (IIP). He urged Sunnis to repent, join *Salafi* Islam "for the age of nationalism, pan-Arabism and Ba'thism is gone for good." He warned about the threat posed by Shi'a seeking to extend a belt from Tehran to Beirut by spreading influence in Sunni-majority areas.[14] An August 2009 coordinated attack in Baghdad featured several car bombs and mortar shells hitting government ministries, killing over a hundred and wounding over 500 in what was described as the worst attack since the Yazidi bombings two years before.

Leveraging intelligence provided by a high-ranking ISI prisoner, U.S. and Iraqi forces succeeded in killing both ISI War Minister Abu Hamza al-Muhajir and Abu Omar al-Baghdadi on April 18, 2010. U.S. Vice-President Joe Biden called it a "potentially devastating blow" to the group. A subdued statement on May 16 announced the naming of Abu Bakr al-Baghdadi as the new leader of the Islamic State of Iraq.

While the Islamic State of Iraq was announced in 2006 at a period that seemed to be especially propitious for success, Abu Bakr al-Baghdadi (Ibrahim Awad al-Badri al-Samarrai) took over an organization in disarray, with its top leaders killed, disunity in the ranks of Sunni Arabs, and the seeming growing success of both the Iraqi Security Forces and the Sunni Awakening Movement in Anbar Province.

Abu Bakr al-Baghdadi was a long-time radical *Salafi* cleric whose extended family had both ties to the Ba'ath Party and military of Saddam Hussein and to the larger constellation of *Salafi* networks in the region. A *Salafi jihadist* before the U.S. invasion of Iraq in 2003, he eventually rose to become the head of the Islamic State's important Sharia Committee and member of its most senior councils.[15] He now set a course to revive the organization's fortunes, doubling down on terrorist attacks, focusing on peeling away dissident Sunnis and expanding its territory.[16]

On August 25, 2010 a string of suicide bomb attacks hit Iraqi cities from Mosul to Basra during the month of Ramadan. The coordinated attacks were described by ISI as an "earth-shaking wave" carried out by "battalions of monotheists" for the sake of the "blessed prisoners." These actions were led by the "Commander of the Faithful, Abu Bakr al-Baghdadi." The ISI statement also included a mention of support to *jihadist Al-Shabaab* fighters in Somalia.[17] An even higher-profile attack occurred October 2010, with the massacre of Christian worshippers attending a Mass at the Syrian Catholic Cathedral in Baghdad.[18] The Islamic State press release that followed sought to tie the killing, which may have been a failed hostage taking, to events in Egypt involving the supposed conversion of some Coptic women to Islam.[19]

Al-Baghdadi's profile remained low while ISI continued to carry out terrorist attacks in 2011. One particularly notorious attack, however, targeted Iraq's best-known Sunni mosque in Baghdad during Ramadan.[20] With the American military departure complete in December 2011, the government of Prime Minister Nuri al-Maliki began to unravel some of the hard-won gains in forging a multi-sectarian consensus,[21] and terrorist actions claimed by the Islamic State began to grow. In January 2012, large scale attacks against Shi'a civilians struck during the Arbaeen rituals in three Shi'a holy sites.[22]

Al-Baghdadi re-appeared in an audio message on July 21, 2012 announcing an extended campaign to free all *jihadist* prisoners and capture territory. This effort, dubbed "Destroying the Walls," presaged a series of coordinated attacks whose lethality and sequencing showed that the group was bouncing back after the departure of U.S. forces.[23] The use of VBIED "waves," often aimed at Iraqi Shi'a neighborhoods, was now a standard tool in the arsenal of the Islamic State.[24]

The growing popular revolt against the regime of Syrian President Bashar al-Assad in 2011 led to the outbreak of increasingly savage and sectarian fighting there. The first al-Qaeda fighters, sent from the Islamic State in Iraq, arrived in Syria that year and began organizing. The new Syria-focused organization, the Nusrah Front, was announced in January 2012 and was led by a veteran Syrian *jihadist* named Abu Muhammad al-Julani who had spent years fighting in Iraq. According to one source, al-Julani came from a middle class family in Damascus and the "Al-Julani" *kunya* referred not to the Golan Heights of Syria but to the Al-Julani neighborhood of Fallujah where he had distinguished himself.[25]

Blessed by al-Qaeda Central's leadership and ISI, al-Julani grew his organization, often working in concert with other Islamist rebel factions. By April 2013, the Islamic State sought to reassert its control over the Nusrah Front, which it claimed to have funded and created, an assertion of control rejected by al-Julani and by al-Qaeda's leader Ayman al-Zawahiri. Battle-tested and ruthless, the now newly-renamed ISIS took the major Syrian city of Raqqa, not from the Assad regime but from other rebel groups, including the Nusrah Front.[26] With Raqqa swollen with internally displaced persons (IDPs) from other parts of Syria, for the first time the Islamic State had full, uncontested control over a major population area. *Jihadists*, both Arab and foreign, flocked to the group, among them the famed Chechen *jihadist* Abu Omar al-Shishani and his hardened fighters.[27]

ISIS launched eight separate attacks on Iraqi prisons from July 2012 to July 2013, two of which resulted in the release of at least 600 prisoners.[28] The successful attack on the Abu Ghraib facility in July 2013 released, among others, the ISIS Minister of War, Abdul Rahman al-Bilawi.[29] The group's new military campaign, announced in July 2013 and titled "Soldiers Harvest," aimed at intimidating and wearing down Iraqi Security Forces, especially in Sunni majority areas of Iraq that ISIS sought to control. ISIS spokesman al-Adnani claimed that the operation actually began in Syria but also seemed to focus on Iraq's Ninewa and Northern Diyala areas.[30] Overall, the situation in Iraq steadily deteriorated, with the level of violence in 2013 reaching levels not seen in five years.

In December 2013, ISIS succeeded in entrapping and killing the leadership of the Iraqi Security Force's 7th Division in a synchronized attack involving multiple suicide bombers near Rutbah.[31] That same month, seemingly oblivious to the storm brewing, Iraqi Prime Minister Nouri al-Maliki cracked down on Sunni critics in Anbar province.[32] In January 2014, a resurgent ISIS rapidly took over the Iraqi city of Fallujah.[33] This major ISIS achievement, coming after its overall resurgence and success in Syria, was dismissed by President Barack Obama as "various local power struggles and disputes" by rival *jihadists*.[34] By this time, however, the number of foreign fighters in Syria, most of them part of ISIS, exceeded the number that had gone to fight in Afghanistan against the Soviets.[35]

While ISIS videos featured all sorts of telegenic European and exotic recruits from Chile or Cambodia, the group's leadership remained overwhelmingly Iraqi and Syrian, except for notable field commander Al-Shishani.[36] A core of that leadership came from the officer corps of Saddam Hussein's former army.[37] One other prominent exception was the firebrand ISIS cleric from Bahrain, Turki al-Bin'ali, who aggressively confronted the enemies of the Islamic State among the regional *ulema* (group of Muslim scholars).[38]

ISIS' encounter with Syria and its friction with al-Qaeda's sclerotic leadership led to a revolution in the way it produced propaganda. Previously, much of its video production was focused internally on events inside Iraq.[39] While the elements of soaring ambition, extreme sectarianism, and vivid violence had always been hallmarks of ISIS propaganda, this was now coupled with polished technical means and an expanding social media network. Many of the themes encapsulated in ISIS propaganda were not new, but their impact grew substantially the deeper the organization embedded itself in the Syrian conflict.[40] The Islamic State's media campaign first dealt at length with Syria in January 2013.[41] Its long running series "Windows Upon the Land of Epic Battles" ran from 2013 to 2014, documenting the organization's growth and success and its melding of the battlefields of Iraq and Syria into one.

The February 2014 disavowal of ISIS by al-Qaeda leader Ayman Zawahiri seemed to slow the organization down. A loose coalition of Islamist rebels succeeded in driving ISIS away from the Idlib and Aleppo areas shortly thereafter.[42] Al-Qaeda now fully realized that ISIS was nakedly challenging it for supremacy of the worldwide *jihadist* movement, and doing so on the highest profile of all battlefields.[43] ISIS' propaganda and military objectives dovetailed in "Clanging of the Swords, Part IV," a lengthy video exercise in psychological warfare preparing the ground for a military offensive in Northern Iraq by terrifying ISF recruits.[44]

On June 4, 2014 an ISIS operation to take Mosul was launched under the command of former Abu Ghraib detainee Abu Abdurahman al-Bilawi, who ended up being killed early in the fighting. Within a week, the city had fallen and several ISF divisions had disintegrated. Tremendous stores of U.S.-supplied weapons and materiel were captured. Determined and ruthless ISIS fighters, outnumbered 15 to one, had gained an astonishing victory.[45] Subsequently, the northern town of Tal Afar fell, as did much of Anbar Province, including several key border crossings. Mosul's ancient Christian community was extinguished in one fell swoop as all Christians were expelled *en masse*.[46] As many as 500,000 Iraqi citizens from a variety of religious and ethnic communities were displaced by ISIS victories. Tikrit and the oil refinery town of Baiji also fell as ISIS forces moved south toward Baghdad but intervention by Iranian-supported militias prevented the fall of the strategically significant city of Samarra.

Abu Bakr al-Baghdadi then took the fateful step the Islamic State had repeatedly hinted at since 2006, restoring the institution of the Caliphate and declaring himself Caliph over all the Muslims. In a unique appearance for the cameras at Mosul's Nuri Mosque on June 29, 2014, "Caliph Ibrahim" called for Muslims to join the new Caliphate.

An official ISIS document, released in Arabic and English, announced that "it is incumbent upon all Muslims to pledge allegiance to the Khalīfah Ibrāhīm and support him (may Allah preserve him). The legality of all emirates, groups, states, and organizations, becomes null by the expansion of the Khilāfah's authority and arrival of its troops to their areas."[47]

A key element of both its actions on the ground and its propaganda continued to be ISIS' bitter hatred and violence towards Shi'a Muslims. This took the form of concrete action as well. In its single worst massacre up to that point, the group killed as many as 1,100 unarmed Shi'a Iraq Air Force cadets at Camp Speicher in Tikrit in June 2014.[48]

The ISIS media package was now complete. A call to emigrate to, defend, and build an Islamist utopian state, strongly associated with apocalyptic discourse, was coupled with an emotional appeal to righteous violence and an austere, rigid and fierce identity attractive to modern youth looking for purpose in life.[49] ISIS' use of social media even included professionally-produced *anasheed*, or a capella songs by male voices permitted by the traditionally-intolerant *Salafi* Islam.[50]

As resistance to the ISIS offensive in central Iraq stiffened in August 2014, ISIS succeeded in massacring hundreds of Sunni tribal fighters who fell into its hands in Anbar province,[51] and then turned its attention to northern Iraq, largely populated by Iraq's Kurdish minority. ISIS advances against Kurdish *Peshmerga* (militia) and evidence of genocide practiced against the Yazidi religious minority in the Sinjar region eventually drew the United States into the conflict with a campaign of air strikes carried out as part of a new strategy to "degrade and ultimately destroy" the Islamic State.[52]

As ISIS military advances in Iraq slowed and were even reversed in some cases (the strategic Mosul Dam was re-taken from ISIS, the threat to the Iraqi Kurdish capital of Irbil was eliminated, and the besieged Shia town of Amerli was relieved), the group turned its attention, and its new military equipment, toward Syria. An August 2014 uprising by the Sunni Arab Shaitat tribe in Deir ez Zour was brutally suppressed, with ISIS killing nearly one thousand men in a graphic warning to Arab tribes in the region.[53]

In September 2014, an ISIS offensive to take the Syrian town of Kobani, controlled by the Kurdish People's Protection Units (YPG), on the Turkish border dragged on for months and eventually led to an ISIS defeat in January 2015. The fighting and multiple airstrikes aimed at helping Kurdish fighters, however, reduced most of the city to rubble. While checked in its advance on Baghdad, ISIS succeeded in massacring hundreds of captured Sunni Tribal fighters in Anbar province in late 2014.[54]

Meanwhile, ISIS responded to new U.S. and Coalition operations by orchestrating a series of high-profile beheadings of Western and Japanese hostages, including journalists and aid workers, over the next few months. Beginning with the beheading of American journalist James Foley in August 2014 and ending with the killing of two Japanese hostages in January 2015, seven individuals were killed in polished video productions aimed at projecting an impression of power and vengeance.

The group's encounter with Christian populations led it to revive the practice of the *jizya* tax on non-Muslims as part of a plan intended to humiliate "protected" religious groups.[55] As it slavishly sought to imitate aspects of the period of formative Islam, it also boasted about the revival of sex slavery, principally of Yazidi girls and women, adding that "we will conquer your Rome, break your crosses, and enslave your women."[56]

The image of ISIS as a *jihadist* colossus "here to stay and spreading" was powerful in continuing to attract foreign fighters and the allegiance of *jihadist* groups scattered throughout the Muslim world. A 2014 UN report claimed that more than 15,000 foreigners from more than 80 countries had joined ISIS "on an unprecedented scale."[57] On September 24, 2014, an Algerian *jihadist* group that had pledged loyalty to ISIS beheaded a French hostage.[58] ISIS-affiliated groups claimed actions in its name in Lebanon, Gaza and Libya.

While oil production and smuggling into Turkey and Syria have proved to be major sources of financing for the group, other, less well-known, streams of revenue exist as well. These include kidnapping and looting, including the sale of pilfered antiquities and personal property, combined with new tax revenue schemes in the burgeoning ISIS empire.[59]

The principal message of ISIS to Muslims elsewhere continued to be that they should immigrate as soon as possible to the Islamic State, as long as borders remained open.

Failing that, foreigners should pledge allegiance (give *bayat*) to the ISIS Caliph and carry out lone wolf attacks.[60] A spate of such attacks was carried out in Western Europe, Canada, the United State and Australia throughout 2014, receiving high-level publicity.[61]

By early 2015, the physical borders of the Islamic State seemed to have stabilized, stretching from the outskirts of Aleppo in Syria down to central Iraq. The group controlled two large cities, Raqqa and Mosul, and many smaller towns. Several million people, mostly Sunni Arab Muslims, lived under their black banner and the nascent State worked aggressively to promote an image of success. It also sought to prove its capacity to build a functioning state that could implement Islamic law literally, whether through public punishments or acts of charity and governance.

Thousands of Coalition airstrikes had exacted a toll on ISIS in Iraq and Syria, making defeat possible where there were counterforce units on the ground, such as Kurdish *Peshmerga* or Iraqi Security Forces and militias. Yet foreign fighters continued to flock to ISIS-controlled Syria in a steady if not overwhelming stream.

While much of its propaganda focused on building rather than destroying, ISIS sought to continue to manipulate the news cycle by producing unusual or visually arresting "morality plays" that would attract attention, even if negative, by documenting acts such as the killing of homosexuals by throwing them off of buildings or the burning alive of a Jordanian Air Force pilot.[62]

The continuing potency of ISIS in its heartland of Syria and Iraq was graphically underscored in May 2015, when the group succeeded in seizing the historic Syrian town of Palmyra, where it wantonly vandalized much of Palmyra's famed antiquities.[63] Shockingly, given Coalition airpower and ISF attention, ISIS also managed to seize the capital of Anbar province in Ramadi.[64] The military victories disrupted a budding narrative that the group was at least contained if not in decline.

Despite those victories, ISIS was unable to prevent advances by Kurdish forces in Northern Syria, which succeeded in taking the key gateway city of Tel Abyad in June 2015, thereby making it somewhat more difficult for recruits to reach ISIS in Syria.[65] Kurdish fighters backed by coalition aircraft also tightened their hold on the region of Kobani and the city of Al-Hasakah. In response, ISIS sought to expand south and west towards Syria's largest cities and rampaged through Eastern Homs province.[66]

The online appeal of ISIS continued despite the enhanced efforts of Western governments and social media companies to blunt it. One prominent U.S. media account related in detail how ISIS supporters in Europe and the Middle East were able to "turn" a young American woman living in isolated, rural Washington State through the use of social media.[67] And a detailed study of the organization's media activities in April 2015 found ISIS releasing 123 different media items in Arabic in a given week, portraying the group as "winners, competent and pious."[68] An aggressive media campaign in June 2015 pushed the creation of the new ISIS gold *dinar* as a blow to Western capitalism and the U.S. economy.[69]

ISIS efforts in 2015 to expand its scope in the Arabian Peninsula and Gulf were underscored by suicide bomb attacks on Shi'a mosques in Saudi Arabia and Kuwait. The organization called for Shi'a to be killed anywhere possible in Saudi Arabia.[70] Saudi authorities arrested hundreds of ISIS supporters inside the Kingdom, supposedly disrupting other terrorist plots.[71]

The high-profile crisis created by a flood of refugees desperately seeking to enter Europe, most of them Muslims and many of them from Syria, provoked a flurry of ISIS messaging against the phenomenon in September 2015. Portraying it as a betrayal of Islam, ISIS spokesmen and fighters vehemently called on Muslims to turn immediately to the "Land of the Caliphate" rather than to the "House of Unbelief," where they run the risk of being humiliated or converted to Christianity.[72] Similar campaigns from ISIS tried to take advantage of events in areas outside its rule with varying degrees of success. A series of videos supporting Palestinian knife attacks against Israelis seemed to have had no discernable impact but a similar string of polished video material from various ISIS states encouraging the Somali *Al-Shabaab* to switch allegiance from Al-Zawahiri to Al-Baghdadi did presage a change in loyalty of at least one *Al-Shabaab* faction in October 2015.[73]

GLOBAL REACH

ISIS' own ranks were augmented by an informal network of online *Salafis*, operating in Western languages and in Arabic, which had already been growing. ISIS' embrace of social media platform Twitter in 2013, to a degree al-Qaeda had never entertained, enabled the organization to reach larger populations faster.[74] The number of pro-ISIS Twitter accounts almost doubled from 2012 to 2013, and then more than doubled again in 2014.[75] As ISIS expanded into Syria, it presented more material in various languages, including English, German, French, Russian, Azeri, Kurdish, and Chechen. The group's Al-Hayat Media Center (HMC), dedicated to producing propaganda in languages other than Arabic, eventually even produced material in the Uighur dialect of China.[76]

ISIS' battlefield successes turbocharged its media appeal, leveraging a wave of enthusiasm among *Salafi-jihadists* worldwide despite the condemnation from most mainstream Sunni Muslim clerics, as well as by supporters of al-Qaeda.[77] Influential Islamist cleric Abu Muhammad al-Maqdisi, conservative Sunni leader Yusuf al-Qaradawi, and even the pro-Caliphate movement *Hizb ut-Tahrir* all criticized the establishment of the ISIS Caliphate.[78] The organization, however, was undaunted. A new online English-language magazine, *Dabiq*, recalling the apocalyptic battlefield of

Islam's past, now appeared.[79] Its first issue trumpeted the return of the Caliphate. The publication promised to focus on the key ISIS themes of *tawhid* (monotheism), *manhaj* (truth-seeking), *hijrah* (migration), *jihad* (holy war) and *jama'ah* (community)."[80]

The seeming success of the ISIS caliphate has reverberated worldwide throughout the ranks of *jihadist* movements, with many pledging allegiance to the organization. The network's supposed 33 provinces stretched at its height in 2015 from Africa to Pakistan, although more than half are within the confines of historic Iraq and Syria and some existed only on paper. In December 2014, *Ansar Beit al-Maqdis*, operating out of Egypt's Sinai Peninsula and increasingly challenging the Egyptian military, pledged its loyalty.[81] In March 2015, *Boko Haram*, in the midst of a major insurgency against Nigeria and neighboring countries stretching back more than a decade, formally announced that it was now the caliphate's West Africa Province.[82]

ISIS supporters in chaotic Libya had real success on the ground in 2015. After eventually being driven by rival *jihadists* from Derna, the group was able to take over the region of Sirte including Muammar al-Qaddafi's home town of the same name, where it sought to both govern and expand by building on the framework established by previous groups like Ansar al-Shariah.[83] ISIS in Libya supported two major terrorist attacks in neighboring Tunisia, at the Bardo Museum in March 2015 and at seaside resorts in Sousse in June 2015. Both attacks sought to kill foreigners and deliver major blows against Tunisia's economy.

The ISIS Libya branch was involved in two more media massacres, a February 2015 video showing the killing of 21 Coptic Christian workers, ostensibly in retaliation for alleged Coptic mistreatment of Coptic women who had supposedly converted to Islam (the same excuse used in the October 2010 attack on the Syrian Catholic Church in Baghdad) and the April 2015 killing of 30 Ethiopian Christians.[84]

ISIS also scored an important advance in the Russian Caucasus with the announcement of the *Kavkaz Wilaya* (Caucasus province) of the Islamic State in June 2015. A non-Chechen, Rustam Aselderov, an ethnic Dargin from Daghestan, assumed leadership of an entity aimed at fighting the Russian government and its local allies and also in rivalry against a rump pro-Al-Qaeda Caucasus Emirate.[85] This reality mirrors the situation in Syria, with rival factions of Caucasus fighters, mostly Chechens, pledging loyalty to bitterly opposed rivals in both ISIS and the Nusrah Front and serving as one more pretext for Russian military intervention in Syria as of September 2015.[86]

As pressure increased in its Syria-Iraq heartland in 2015-2016, the Islamic State sought to respond by highlighting the work of potential franchises and outlets in South Asia. ISIS focused on the work of local *Jihadists* in Bangladesh moving towards its orbit who launched a wide-ranging campaign against religious minorities, secularists, and Muslims seen as insufficiently pious or Sunni.[87] Considerable efforts were also extended to prepare for a newly branded ISIS *Wilaya* in the Southern Philippines, again by absorbing and reorganizing existing *jihadist* fighters under the ISIS banner.[88] ISIS global organizing was accompanied by an ongoing high profile, high volume media campaign across multiple platforms, geographic areas and languages.[89]

Recent Activity

By late 2015, several obvious trends began to emerge that would reshape the development of ISIS as a movement. Military pressure on the ground from various actors began to shrink ISIS rule in its heartland in Syria and Iraq. The Syrian Arab Army, reinforced by massive Russian support and that of Iranian-supported units (including Hezbollah), succeeded in relieving the long-besieged airbase at Kweiris, east of Aleppo, in November.[90] This was followed by an offensive in early 2016 that recaptured most territory lost by Assad forces in eastern Homs to ISIS in the summer of 2015, including Palmyra and Al-Qarytayn.[91]

Meanwhile mostly Kurdish forces under the U.S.-supported Syrian Democratic Forces (SDF), which also included some Arab, Turkmen and Syriac Christian militia fighters, continued to press their advantage against ISIS in northern Syria. After advances in Al-Hasakah, U.S. airdrops of weapons helped in the taking of Al-Hawl (November 2015), the strategic Tishrin Dam on the Euphrates (December 2015), and Al-Shahhadah (February 2016). By June 2016, an SDF offensive had quickly encircled the key town of Manbij (which once had so many foreign fighters that it was dubbed "Little London"[92]) taking it in August 2016 and threatening the last remaining open supply corridor for ISIS to the Turkish border. Continued military pressure and economic losses also led ISIS to halve its soldiers' salaries and take other emergency financial actions in 2016.[93]

In Iraq, the Iraqi Security Forces, including a large and controversial Popular Mobilization Unit (PMU) militia element, slowly expanded operations to retake Anbar Province from ISIS.[94] By December 2015, the heavily damaged provincial capital of Ramadi was back in government hands. The ISF took the towns of Hit (April 2016), Al-Rutbah on the Amman-Baghdad highway (May 2016) and, finally, the highly symbolic city of Al-Fallujah (June 2016), which had been held by ISIS for more than two years. The ISF then shifted to areas south of Mosul, eventually taking the Qayyarah airbase in July 2016 after a months-long offensive. Also lost in July was the Islamic State's most famous foreign commander, Abu Omar al-Shishani, who was killed in an airstrike while ISIS spokesman and the key head of external operations Abu Muhammad al-Adnani was killed the next month.

Sirte, Libya has long been bruited as a potential backup caliphate site, should ISIS lose control of Raqqa and Mosul. Anti-ISIS forces launched an offensive against Sirte in April 2016. The campaign was a slow and bloody one, but anti-ISIS forces retook Sirte in December 2016. As of early 2017, the country still remains a theater of *jihadist* activity.[95]

But if military progress has been slow but steady on the ground against the "physical" caliphate, ISIS as an idea and a way of violence still seemed powerful and resilient. An ongoing, in depth study of ISIS supporters in the United States launched by George Washington University in December 2015 documented relatively small but still unprecedented levels of ISIS mobilization among Americans.[96] This research was underscored in the popular mind by high profile ISIS inspired terrorist attacks in San Bernardino (December 2015) and Orlando (June 2016). In both cases, following an ISIS template, the perpetrators pledged loyalty to ISIS "Caliph" Al-Baghdadi during the actual attack. The Orlando shooting was the deadliest terrorist attack on U.S. soil since September 11, 2001.[97]

While the online "virtual" caliphate is more contested than ever before (by social media companies, civil society, and government), and the scope of some ISIS amplifiers has been scaled back as a result, the group's propagandists still have the ability to surge in the media space at will and get their message out. Thus, as pressure has increased on platforms such as Facebook, YouTube and Twitter, the Islamic State and its defenders have found effective alternative online safe havens such as Telegram, Justepaste.it and Internet Archive. And despite progress in this field by anti-ISIS forces, the virtual ISIS footprint is still massive.[98]

Moreover, if ISIS military victories have become increasingly scarce, a spate of spectacular terrorist operations have to date maintained the perception that the Islamic State is still both viable and lethal. In the Middle East, the toll has been stunning. From the downing of a Russian Metrojet flight over Sinai in October 2015 to repeated attacks in Istanbul and Ankara in 2016 to constant, multiple suicide bombings in Syria and Iraq against government forces, other rebel groups, and religious and ethnic minorities, the Islamic State has ably used these operations as the caliphate's own version of heavy artillery, airstrikes, and high profile media events.[99]

Attacks beyond the Middle East have garnered the group even more attention, mostly distracting from bad news of military reverses in Syria and Iraq. It is now clear that the Islamic State did use the massive refugee flows from Syria to smuggle in operatives into Western Europe.[100] But while the planning and structure of attacks in Paris (November 2015) and Brussels (March 2016) may differ greatly from seemingly more individual, inspired efforts in Orlando or Nice, France (July 2016), the extensive media attention and the spike in fear and anger are the same.[101]

Particularly noteworthy was the month of carnage that was Ramadan (roughly early June to early July) 2016. Al-Adnani's call for Ramadan attacks in a May 22nd audiofile was resoundingly answered.[102] By the end of the month, after successful high profile attacks in Orlando; Magnanville, France (where an ISIS killer livestreamed his murders); Istanbul; Dhaka, India; Baghdad, and Medina and a score of thwarted attacks elsewhere, ISIS officially claimed to have killed or injured more than 5,200 people during Ramadan (almost 2,000 of them Shi'a Muslims).[103]

The long-awaited offensive against Mosul, the largest city held by the Islamic State, was launched on October 17, 2016 and was able to regain the Nineveh Plain area and enter the Eastern suburbs of the city.[104] By the end of 2016, the two-month offensive by Iraqi Security Forces had brought them deep into Eastern Mosul but they encountered fierce resistance, including repeated ambushes and waves of suicide bombers.[105] Both in Mosul and in Northern Syria where Turkish-backed Syrian rebel forces made slow progress, and ISIS was clearly losing. However, it was losing slowly and continued to fight savagely and with tremendous persistence.

Today, the Islamic State "core state" is indeed under growing, seemingly irreversible military pressure. But a wounded ISIS remains a deadly, high profile reality—one capable of counterattacking ferociously and repeatedly lashing out at its many enemies, near and far, and of boasting about it.

Citations

[1] "Islamic State Announcement Subtitles Eng 15/10/2006," youtube.com, October 15, 2006, https://www.youtube.com/watch?v=s1DsXuDHIk0.

[2] Nadia Abou el-Magd, "al-Qaida in Iraq Claims 12,000 Fighters," Washington Post, November 10, 2006, http://www.washingtonpost.com/wp-dyn/content/article/2006/11/10/AR2006111001624_pf.html.

[3] "Al-Zarqawi's Message to the Fighters of Jihad in Iraq on September 11, 2004," Middle East Media Research Institute Jihad and Terrorism Studies Project, September 15, 2004, http://www.memri.org/report/en/0/0/0/0/0/0/1219.htm.

[4] Nimrod Raphaeli, "'The Sheikh of the Slaughterers': Abu Mus'ab Al-Zarqawi and the Al-Qaeda Connection," Middle East Media Research Institute, July 1, 2005, http://www.memri.org/report/en/0/0/0/0/0/0/1406.htm.

[5] Nibras Kazimi, "Just a Thought… (upated)," Talisman Gate, December 30, 2006, http://www.talismangate.blogspot.com/2006_12_01_archive.html.

[6] Ibid.

[7] Nibras Kazimi, "Abu Omar al-Baghdadi's Fourth Speech: the 'State of the Union' is iffy," Talisman Gate, April 17, 2007, http://www.talismangate.blogspot.com/2007/04/abu-omar-al-baghdadis-fourth-speech.html.

[8] Michael Howard, "'They won't stop until we are all wiped out.' Among the Yezidi, a people in mourning," Guardian (London), August 17, 2007, http://www.theguardian.com/world/2007/aug/18/iraq.topstories3.

[9] Nibras Kazimi, "Asia Cup Replaces Koran in Resolving Tribal Disputes," Talisman Gate, September 28, 2007, http://talismangate.blogspot.com/2007_09_01_archive.html.

[10] "Rocket blast kills 3 U.S. soldiers in Iraq," Associated Press, March 12, 2008, http://www.nbcnews.com/id/23591348/ns/world_news-mideast_n_africa/t/rocket-blasts-kills-us-soldiers-iraq/#.Vf8a2_lVhBc.

[11] Richard A. Oppel Jr., "Files for Suicide Bombers Show No Down Syndrome," New York Times, February 21, 2008, http://www.nytimes.com/2008/02/21/world/middleeast/21iraq.html?_r=0.

[12] Nibras Kazimi, "Abu Hamza al-Mujahir's Interview: Very Revealing," Talisman Gate, October 27, 2008, http://talismangate.blogspot.com/2008/10/abu-hamza-al-muhajirs-interview-very.html.

[13] Pascal Combelles Siegel, "Islamic State of Iraq Commemorates its Two-Year Anniversary," Combating Terrorism Center, October 15, 2008, https://www.ctc.usma.edu/posts/islamic-state-of-iraq-commemorates-its-two-year-anniversary.

[14] Speech of Abu Omar al-Baghdadi (in Arabic), July 8, 2009, https://archive.org/details/293aoao

[15] William McCants, The Believer: How an Introvert with a Passion for Religion and Soccer Became Abu Bakr al-Baghdadi, Leader of the Islamic State (The Brookings Institution, September 1, 2015), http://www.brookings.edu/research/essays/2015/thebeliever.

[16] Ibid.

[17] Aaron Y. Zelin, "The Islamic Emirate of Afghanistan Spokesman's Remarks about Petraeus' New Propaganda Machine," Jihadology, August 29, 2010, http://jihadology.net/2010/08/page/2/.

[18] ALWUHELI, "كشف الدالة جريمة كنيسة سيدة النجاة بصحب بغداد والي," Youtube, January 1, 2011, https://www.youtube.com/watch?v=pfKVQwSKh0E.

[19] Bill Roggio, "Al Qaeda in Iraq claims massacre at Christian church in Baghdad," Long War Journal, November 1, 2010, http://www.longwarjournal.org/archives/2010/11/al_qaeda_in_iraq_cla.php.

[20] "Baghdad suicide bomber kills 29 in attack on Sunni mosque," Associated Press, August 28, 2011, http://www.theguardian.com/world/2011/aug/29/baghdad-suicide-bomber-kills-29.

[21] Dahr Jamail, "Rivals say Maliki leading Iraq into 'civil war'," Al Jazeera (Doha), December 28, 2011, http://www.aljazeera.com/indepth/features/2011/12/2011122881820637664.html.

[22] Martin Chulov, "Iraq's Shias targeted in deadly bomb blasts," Guardian (London), January 5, 2012, http://www.theguardian.com/world/2012/jan/05/iraq-shias-targeted-bomb-blasts.

[23] Sam Wyer, "The Islamic State of Iraq and the 'Destroying the Walls' Campaign," Institute for the Study of War Security Update, September 21, 2012, http://www.understandingwar.org/sites/default/files/ISWSecurityUpdate_Islamic-State-Iraq.pdf.

[24] Joel Wing, "The Rebirth of Al Qaeda in Iraq, An Interview with Jessica Lewis of the Institute for the Study of War," Musings on Iraq, November 25, 2013, http://musingsoniraq.blogspot.com/2013/11/the-rebirth-of-al-qaeda-in-iraq.html.

[25] Comments to the author from a journalist at a pan-Arab media outlet, June 2015.

[26] Sarah Birke, "How al-Qaeda Changed the Syrian War," New York Review of Books, December 27, 2013, http://www.nybooks.com/blogs/nyrblog/2013/dec/27/how-al-qaeda-changed-syrian-war/.

[27] "Omar al-Shishani," Counter Extremism Project, n.d., http://www.counterextremism.com/extremists/omar-al-shishani.

[28] Wing, "The Rebirth of Al Qaeda."

[29] Mushreq Abbas, "Al-Qaeda Militants Raid Iraq's Abu Ghraib, Taji Prisons," Al-Monitor, July 26, 2013, http://www.al-monitor.com/pulse/originals/2013/07/iraq-al-qaeda-prison-raid-abu-ghraib.html#.

[30] Jessica D. Lewis, "AQI's 'Soldiers' Harvest' Campaign," Institute for the Study of War Backgrounder, October 9, 2013, http://www.understandingwar.org/sites/default/files/Backgrounder_SoldiersHarvest.pdf.

[31] Bill Roggio, "Al Qaeda suicide team kills Iraqi general, 17 officers," Long War Journal, December 21, 2013, http://www.longwarjournal.org/archives/2013/12/al_qaeda_suicide_tea.php.

[32] Joel Wing, "Inside the Surge: An Interview With Prof. Peter Mansour, former Executive Officer to Gen. Petraeus," Musings on Iraq, December 31, 2013, http://musingsoniraq.blogspot.com/search?updated-min=2013-01-01T00:00:00-08:00&updated-max=2014-01-01T00:00:00-08:00&max-results=50.

[33] Liz Sly, "Al-Qaeda force captures Fallujah amid rise of violence in Iraq," Washington Post, January 3, 2014, https://www.washingtonpost.com/world/al-qaeda-force-captures-fallujah-amid-rise-in-violence-in-iraq/2014/01/03/8abaeb2a-74aa-11e3-8def-a33011492df2_story.html.

[34] [34] David Remnick, "Going the Distance," New Yorker, January 27, 2014, http://www.newyorker.com/magazine/2014/01/27/going-the-distance-david-remnick.

[35] Peter R. Neumann, "Foreign fighter total in Syria/Iraq now exceeds 20,000; surpasses Afghanistan conflict in the 1980s," International Center for the Study of Radicalisation, January 26, 2015, http://icsr.info/2015/01/foreign-fighter-total-syriairaq-now-exceeds-20000-surpasses-afghanistan-conflict-1980s/.

[36] Alberto M. Fernandez, "Abu Talha Al-Almani – ISIS's Celebrity Cheerleader," Middle East Media Research Institute, August 13, 2015, http://www.memri.org/report/en/0/0/0/0/0/0/8704.htm.

[37] Hamza Hendawi and Qassim Abdul-Zahra, "ISIS Top Brass is Iraqi Army's Former Best and Brightest," Ha'aretz (Tel Aviv), August 8, 2015, http://www.haaretz.com/news/features/1.670177.

[38] Cole Bunzel, "The Caliphate's Scholar-in-Arms," Jihadica, July 9, 2014, http://www.jihadica.com/the-caliphate%E2%80%99s-scholar-in-arms/.

[39] Aaron Y. Zelin, "al-Furqān Media presents a new video message from the Islamic State of Iraq: 'Clanging of the Swords, Part 1'," Jihadology, June 30, 2012, http://jihadology.net/2012/06/30/al-furqan-media-presents-a-new-video-message-from-the-islamic-state-of-iraq-clanging-of-the-swords-part-1/.

[40] Emerson Brooking, "The ISIS Propaganda Machine is Horrifying and Effective. How Does It Work?" Council on Foreign Relations, August 21, 2014, http://blogs.cfr.org/davidson/2014/08/21/the-isis-propaganda-machine-is-horrifying-and-effective-how-does-it-work/.

[41] Abu Mohammed Al-Adnani, "Seven Facts," Fursan Al-Balagh Media, January 2013, https://azelin.files.wordpress.com/2013/01/shaykh-abc5ab-mue1b8a5ammad-al-adnc481nc4ab-22the-seven-facts22-en1.pdf.

[42] Liz Sly, "Renegade al-Qaida faction withdraws from Syrian border town of Azaz," Guardian (London), March 4, 2014, http://www.theguardian.com/world/2014/mar/04/isis-al-qaida-rebels-syria-azaz.

[43] "Al-Qaeda-ISIS Split: Tactics Over Strategy," The Soufan Group TSG IntelBrief, February 6, 2014, http://soufangroup.com/tsg-intelbrief-al-qaeda-isis-split-tactics-over-strategy/.

[44] Patrick Kingsley, "Who is behind ISIS's terrifying online propaganda operation?" Guardian (London), June 23, 2014, http://www.theguardian.com/world/2014/jun/23/who-behind-isis-propaganda-operation-iraq.

[45] "Terror's new headquarters," The Economist, June 14, 2014, http://www.economist.com/news/leaders/21604160-iraqs-second-city-has-fallen-group-wants-create-state-which-wage-jihad.

[46] Jonathan Krohn, "Has Last Christian Left Iraqi City of Mosul After 2,000 Years?" NBC News, July 27, 2014, http://www.nbcnews.com/storyline/iraq-turmoil/has-last-christian-left-iraqi-city-mosul-after-2-000-n164856.

[47] "This is the Promise of Allah," Al Jazeera (Doha), n.d., https://ia902505.us.archive.org/28/items/poa_25984/EN.pdf.

[48] "Iraq: 1095 Soldiers are still Missing Since the 'Speicher Massacre" at the Hands of DAESH," CNN.com, September 18, 2014, http://arabic.cnn.com/middleeast/2014/09/18/iraq-isis-camp-speicher.

[49] Charlie Winter, "The Virtual 'Caliphate': Understanding Islamic State's Propaganda Strategy," Quilliam Foundation, July 2015, http://www.quilliamfoundation.org/wp/wp-content/uploads/publications/free/the-virtual-caliphate-understanding-islamic-states-propaganda-strategy.pdf.

[50] Alex Marshall, "How ISIS got its anthem," Guardian (London), November 9, 2014, http://www.theguardian.com/music/2014/nov/09/nasheed-how-isis-got-its-anthem.

[51] Martin Chulov, "ISIS kills hundreds of Iraqi Sunnis from Albu Nimr tribe in Anbar province," The Guardian, October 30, 2014, http://www.theguardian.com/world/2014/oct/30/mass-graves-hundreds-iraqi-sunnis-killed-isis-albu-nimr.

[52] Mark Landler, "Obama, in Speech on ISIS, Promises Sustained Effort to Route Militants," New York Times, September 10, 2014, http://www.nytimes.com/2014/09/11/world/middleeast/obama-speech-isis.html?_r=0.

[53] Alberto M. Fernandez, "Massacre and Media: ISIS and the Case of the Sunni Arab Shaitat Tribe," Middle East Media Research Institute, June 23, 2015, http://www.memri.org/report/en/0/0/0/0/0/0/8622.htm.

[54] Orla Guerin, "Iraq: Sunni tribe 'left for slaughter' by Islamic State," BBC, November 10, 2014, http://www.bbc.com/news/world-middle-east-29984668.

[55] Alberto M. Fernandez, "ISIS's View of Christians Echoes that of Official Saudi Fatwas," Middle East Media Research Institute, June 1, 2015, http://www.memri.org/report/en/0/0/0/0/0/0/8592.htm.

[56] Allen McDuffee, "ISIS is Now Bragging About Enslaving Women and Children," The Atlantic, October 13, 2014, http://www.theatlantic.com/international/archive/2014/10/isis-confirms-and-justifies-enslaving-yazidis-in-new-magazine-article/381394/.

[57] Spencer Ackerman, "Foreign jihadists flocking to Iraq and Syria on 'unprecedented scale' – UN," Guardian (London), October 30, 2014, http://www.theguardian.com/world/2014/oct/30/foreign-jihadist-iraq-syria-unprecedented-un-isis.

[58] "Islamic State Algerian Group Beheads French Hostage Hervé Gourdel," LeakSource, September 24, 2014, http://leaksource.info/2014/09/24/graphic-video-islamic-state-algerian-group-beheads-french-hostage-herve-gourdel/.

[59] Janine di Giovanni et al., "How Does ISIS Fund its Reign of Terror?" Newsweek, November 6, 2014, http://www.newsweek.com/2014/11/14/how-does-isis-fund-its-reign-terror-282607.html.

[60] Jessica Lewis McFate and Harleen Gambhir, "ISIS's Global Messaging: Strategy Fact Sheet," Institute for the Study of War, December 2014, http://www.understandingwar.org/sites/default/files/GLOBAL%20ROLLUP%20Update.pdf.

[61] Ibid.

[62] Rod Nordland and Anne Barnard, "Militants' Killing of Jordanian Pilot Unites the Arab World in Anger," New York Times, February 4, 2015, http://www.nytimes.com/2015/02/05/world/middleeast/arab-world-unites-in-anger-after-burning-of-jordanian-pilot.html.

[63] Stuart Manning, " Why ISIS wants to erase Palmyra's history," CNN, September 1, 2015, http://www.cnn.com/2015/08/26/opinions/manning-palmyra-isis/.

[64] Anne Barnard and Hwaida Saad, "Frantic Message as Palmyra, Syria, Fell: 'We're Finished,'" New York Times, May 21, 2015, http://www.nytimes.com/2015/05/22/world/middleeast/syria-palmyra-ruins-isis.html?_r=0.

[65] Elliot Ackerman, "The Story of the Story at Tal Abyad," New Yorker, June 20, 2015, http://www.newyorker.com/news/news-desk/the-story-of-the-story-at-tal-abyad.

[66] "ISIS seize key Syrian town in Homs," Al Arabiya (Riyadh), August 6, 2015, http://english.alarabiya.net/en/News/middle-east/2015/08/06/ISIS-seizes-key-Syrian-town-in-Homs-.html.

[67] Rukmini Callimachi, "ISIS and the Lonely Young American," New York Times, June 27, 2015, http://www.nytimes.com/2015/06/28/world/americas/isis-online-recruiting-american.html.

[68] Aaron Y. Zelin, "Picture or it Didn't Happen: A Snapshot of the Islamic State's Offical Media Output," Perspectives on Terrorism 9, no. 4, August 2015, http://www.terrorismanalysts.com/pt/index.php/pot/article/view/445/876.

[69] Colin Freeman, "Islamic State mints its own 'Islamic Dinar' coins," Telegraph (London), June 23, 2015, http://www.telegraph.co.uk/news/worldnews/islamic-state/11694838/Islamic-State-mints-its-own-Islamic-Dinar-coins.html.

[70] AlAlam, "ISIS in Saudi Calls for Killing Shiites," LiveLeak, May 30, 2015, http://www.liveleak.com/view?i=5d6_1433006966.

[71] "Saudi arrests 431 ISIS-linked suspects," Al Arabiya (Riyadh), July 18, 2015, http://english.alarabiya.net/en/News/middle-east/2015/07/18/Saudi-arrests-431-ISIS-linked-suspects-.html.

[72] "ISIS Fighters to Refugees: Do Not Migrate to France or Germany, 'Migrate Immediately to the Islamic State'," Middle East Media Research Institute Jihad and Terrorism Threat Monitor, September 17, 2015, http://www.memrijttm.org/isis-fighters-to-refugees-do-not-migrate-to-france-or-germany-migrate-immediately-to-the-islamic-state.html.

[73] Robyn Kriel and Briana Duggan, "Al-Shabaab Faction Pledges Allegiance to ISIS," CNN, October 23, 2015, http://www.cnn.com/2015/10/22/africa/al-shabaab-faction-isis/.

[74] J.M. Berger and Jonathon Morgan, "The ISIS Twitter census: Defining and describing the population of ISIS supporters on Twitter," The Brookings Institution, March 2015, http://www.brookings.edu/research/papers/2015/03/isis-twitter-census-berger-morgan.

[75] Ibid.

[76] Aymenn Jawad Al-Tamimi, "New Islamic State Nasheed in Uyghur Language," Jihad Intel, July 7, 2015, http://jihadintel.meforum.org/167/new-islamic-state-nasheed-in-uyghur-language.

[77] "Al-Qaeda Leader Rejects ISIS Caliphate, Predicts Imminent 'Islamic Spring,'" Middle East Media Research Institute Jihad and Terrorism Threat Monitor, September 10, 2015, http://www.memrijttm.org/al-qaeda-leader-al-zawahiri-rejects-isis-caliphate-predicts-imminent-islamic-spring.html.

[78] "Islamic State's 'caliph' lauds Iraq rebellion," Al Jazeera (Doha), July 6, 2014, http://www.aljazeera.com/news/middleeast/2014/07/islamic-state-caliph-lauds-iraq-rebellion-201475125745177772.html.

[79] "The Islamic State's (ISIS, ISIL) Magazine," The Clarion Project, September 10, 2014, http://www.clarionproject.org/news/islamic-state-isis-isil-propaganda-magazine-dabiq.

[80] Ibid.

[81] Khalil al-Anani, "ISIS Enters Egypt: How Washington Must Respond," Foreign Affairs, December 4, 2014, https://www.foreignaffairs.com/articles/middle-east/2014-12-04/isis-enters-egypt.

[82] "Islamic State 'accepts' Boko Haram's allegiance pledge," BBC, March 13, 2015, http://www.bbc.com/news/world-africa-31862992.

[83] Jon Lee Anderson, "ISIS Rises in Libya," New Yorker, August 4, 2015, http://www.newyorker.com/news/news-desk/isis-rises-in-libya.

[84] Alberto M. Fernandez, "ISIS's View of Christians Echoes that of Official Saudi Fatwas," Middle East Media Research Institute, June 1, 2015, http://www.memri.org/report/en/0/0/0/0/0/0/8592.htm.

[85] Derek Flood, "The Islamic State Raises Its Black Flag Over The Caucasus," Combating Terrorism Center at West Point, June 29, 2015, https://www.ctc.usma.edu/posts/the-islamic-state-raises-its-black-flag-over-the-caucasus.

[86] Joanna Paraszczuk, "Why Russian Propaganda Links Chechen Militants, IS, And Assad's Coastal Stronghold," Radio Free Europe/Radio Liberty, September 14, 2015, http://www.rferl.org/content/why-russia-propaganda-links-chechens-is-latakia/27248094.html.

[87] Michael Kugelman and Atif Jalal Ahmad, "Will ISIS Infect Bangladesh?" The National Interest, December 8, 2015, http://nationalinterest.org/feature/will-isis-infect-south-asia-14538.

[88] Charlie Winter, "Signs of a Nascent Islamic State Province in the Philippines," War on the Rocks, May 25, 2016, http://warontherocks.com/2016/05/signs-of-a-nascent-islamic-state-province-in-the-philippines/.

[89] Mary-Ann Russon and Jason Murdock, "Welcome to the bizarre and frightening world of Islamic State channels on Telegram," International Business Times, May 23, 2016, http://www.ibtimes.co.uk/welcome-bizarre-frightening-world-islamic-state-channels-telegram-1561186.

[90] Aron Lund, "Strategic Implications of Assad's Victory at Kweiris," Carnegie Endowment for International Peace, November 10, 2015, http://carnegieendowment.org/syriaincrisis/?fa=61941.

[91] "Syrian army 'retakes' al-Qaraytain near Palmyra from IS," Deutsche Welle, March 4, 2016, http://www.dw.com/en/syrian-army-retakes-al-qaraytain-near-palmyra-from-is/a-19161553.

[92] Josie Ensor and Magdy Samaan, "The town nicknamed 'Little London' at the heart of Islamic State's war," Telegraph (London), January 11, 2016, http://www.telegraph.co.uk/news/worldnews/islamic-state/12091228/The-town-nicknamed-Little-London-at-the-heart-of-Islamic-States-war.html.

[93] Lizzie Dearden, "ISIS cuts salaries, brings in fines and releases prisoners to make up cash shortage caused by airstrikes – report," Independent (London), February 16, 2016, http://www.independent.co.uk/news/world/middle-east/isis-budget-cuts-iraq-syria-pay-bonuses-air-strikes-oil-militants-food-snickers-a6877226.html.

[94] Ahmed Rasheed and Stephen Kalin, "Slow gains in Anbar set pace for Iraq's anti-IS offensive," Reuters, August 6, 2015, http://www.reuters.com/article/us-mideast-crisis-iraq-anbar-idUSKCN0QB1HR20150806.

[95] Abdur Rahman Alfa Shaban, "Over 240 Libyan soldiers killed in anti-ISIS combat in Sirte," Africanews, July 12, 2016, http://www.africanews.com/2016/07/12/over-240-libyan-soldiers-killed-in-anti-isis-combat-in-sirte/.

[96] "ISIS in America," George Washington University Center for Cyber and Homeland Security, June 2016, https://cchs.gwu.edu/isis-in-america.

[97] Ashby Jones, "Orlando Shooting Ranks Among Deadliest Attacks in U.S.," Wall Street Journal, June 12, 2016, http://www.wsj.com/articles/orlando-shooting-ranks-among-deadliest-attacks-in-u-s-1465746043.

[98] Alberto Fernandez, Testimony before the Senate Committee On Homeland Security And Governmental Affairs, July 6, 2016, http://www.memri.org/report/en/0/0/0/0/0/0/9304.htm.

[99] Karen Yourish, Derek Watkins and Tom Giratikan, "Where ISIS has Directed and Inspired Attacks Around the World," New York Times, March 22, 2016, http://www.nytimes.com/interactive/2015/06/17/world/middleeast/map-isis-attacks-around-the-world.html.

[100] Mark Thiessen, "How ISIS Smuggles Terrorists Among Syrian Refugees," Newsweek, April 27, 2016, http://www.newsweek.com/how-isis-smuggles-terrorists-among-syrian-refugees-453039.

[101] Brian Jenkins, "Is the surge in terrorist attacks coincidence or coordinated campaign?" The Hill, July 11, 2016, http://thehill.com/blogs/pundits-blog/homeland-security/287182-is-the-surge-in-terrorist-attacks-coincidence-or.

[102] Maher Chmaytelli, Stephen Kalin and Ali Abdelaty, "Islamic State calls for attacks on the West during Ramadan in audio message," Reuters, May 22, 2016, http://www.reuters.com/article/us-mideast-crisis-islamicstate-idUSKCN0YC0OG.

[103] Lisa Daftari, "ISIS claims 5,200 victims in Ramadan campaign of terror," Fox News, July 13, 2016, http://www.foxnews.com/world/2016/07/13/isis-claims-5200-victims-in-ramadan-campaign-terror.html.

[104] 'The Battle for Mosul, the Story So Far," BBC, December 9, 2016, http://www.bbc.com/news/world-middle-east-37702442.

[105] Dominic Evans and Stephanie Nebehay, "Iraq Says Army Makes Gains in Grueling Mosul Battle," Reuters, December 10, 216, http://www.reuters.com/article/us-mideast-crisis-iraq-idUSKBN13Z0G9?feedName=topNews&feedType=RSS

LASHKAR-E TAIBA

QUICK FACTS

Geographical Areas of Operation: South Asia

Numerical Strength (Members): Exact numbers unknown; estimated several thousand members in Pakistan and India

Leadership: Hafiz Muhammad Saeed

Religious Identification: Sunni Islam (Wahhabi)

Quick Facts courtesy of the U.S. State Department's Country Reports on Terrorism (Last updated 2015)

OVERVIEW

Of the many terrorist groups operating in South Asia, Lashkar-e Taiba (LeT) is one of the most potent. Founded in Pakistan in the mid-1980s, LeT was generously supported by Pakistan's Inter-Services Intelligence (ISI) as a proxy in its conflict with India. Since then, LeT has built a substantial infrastructure running schools and social services throughout Pakistan, while simultaneously carrying out deadly, sophisticated attacks throughout India and Afghanistan. From its founding, LeT's ambitions were global in nature, and the group now boasts a presence in some twenty-one countries. After the November 2008 massacre in Mumbai, India—a terrorist attack which claimed the lives of over 180 people and specifically targeted foreigners—the international community recognized that LeT represents a global threat.

HISTORY AND IDEOLOGY

Lashkar-e Taiba (LeT), variously translated from Urdu as Army of the Pure, Army of the Righteous, or Army of the Good, is technically the name of the armed wing of the radical Pakistani Islamist charitable group *Jamaat-ud-Dawa* (JuD), i.e., the Society for Preaching. Prior to the 2008 Mumbai attack, LeT was viewed primarily as an actor in the ongoing conflict in Jammu and Kashmir. However, from its founding, LeT voiced global ambitions and viewed undermining Indian rule in Jammu and Kashmir as a stepping-stone to the dissolution of India and ultimately the reinstatement of Muslim rule over the Indian sub-continent and beyond.[1] (Throughout this chapter, for clarity, use of the term LeT will refer to the group's entire network of linked charitable and terrorist organizations.)

LeT itself was formally founded in 1990, but its origins go back to 1985, when a pair of professors at the University of Engineering and Technology in Lahore, Hafiz Mohammed Saeed and Zafar Iqbal, founded JuD, a small missionary group dedicated to spreading the *Ahl-e-Hadith* (AeH) interpretation of Islam. (The *Ahl-e-Hadith* interpretation of Islam is closely related to the Wahhabis of the Arabian Peninsula and is a minority sect within Pakistan.[2]) LeT's embrace of *Ahl-e-Hadith* is relatively unusual for Pakistan-based militant groups, most of which adhere to the Deobandi interpretation of Islam.

In 1986, JuD merged with an organization founded to facilitate the participation of Pakistani followers of the *Ahl-e-Hadith* sect in the *jihad* against the Soviets in Afghanistan. This new organization was called *Markaz al-Dawa-wal-Irshad* (MDI), the Center for Preaching and Guidance.[3] Among MDI's cofounders was Osama bin Laden's religious mentor, Abdullah Azzam.[4] Hafiz Saeed became the *emir* of both MDI and subsequently of LeT, when the latter was established in 1990 as MDI's armed wing.[5]

LeT is unique among the Ahl-e-Hadith groups in Pakistani because it holds *da'wa* (preaching) and *jihad* (fighting) as equal and essential components of Islam. LeT's charitable wings carry out extensive outreach in an effort to convert Pakistanis to their interpretation of Islam. Many LeT recruits undergo military training, and some are sent to fight for LeT in Jammu and Kashmir, or more recently, Afghanistan. At the same time, LeT's armed operations help its recruitment and outreach efforts by inspiring disaffected Pakistanis.[6]

LeT's first front was Afghanistan, but by the time LeT was founded, the war against the Soviets was waning. According to one report, only five LeT operatives were killed fighting in Afghanistan before LeT withdrew from the conflict as different factions of the Afghan *mujahideen* turned on each other.[7]

When the people of the disputed Indian province of Jammu and Kashmir rebelled against India in the late 1980s and early 1990s, Pakistan's Inter Service Intelligence agency (ISI) sought to take advantage of this turmoil and destabilize its neighbor. One of the lessons Pakistan's generals had drawn from the Afghan war was how to use proxy forces against a more powerful enemy and how to hurt the enemy without provoking a full-scale war.[8]

Initially, Pakistani strategists supported the Jammu and Kashmir Liberation Front, but found that organization supported an independent Kashmir, rather than Kashmiri accession to Pakistan. In turn, Pakistan shifted its support to Islamist groups that the ISI believed would be more effective and easier to control.[9] In this regard, LeT was an ideal proxy because it was ideologically committed to *jihad*, had an ethnic composition similar to that of the Pakistani military, swore its loyalty to the state, and represented a minority sect within Pakistan.[10]

For its part, LeT readily shifted its focus to Jammu and Kashmir, which it saw as the closest of many open fronts in the global *jihad*. Despite its focus on Jammu and Kashmir, LeT's ultimate goal was the "liberation" (meaning establishment of Muslim rule) of the Indian subcontinent. To facilitate plausible deniability for Pakistan's role in fomenting violence in Jammu and Kashmir, the ISI urged MDI to split its operations, formally establishing LeT as the militant wing of the organization.[11]

The earliest known LeT operation in India took place in 1990, when LeT operatives ambushed a jeep carrying Indian Air Force personnel.[12] In 1993, LeT attacked the army base in Poonch, a major coup in terms of their ability to carry out attacks against hard targets.[13] However, the group's presence was not publicly recognized until early 1996, when a group of LeT terrorists carried out the first of many massacres targeting minority groups within Kashmir, killing 16 Hindus in Kashmir's Doda district.[14] These massacres, which generally targeted ethnic and religious minority communities within Jammu and Kashmir such as Sikhs and Hindus, were intended to provoke ethnic strife and to polarize communal relations within Jammu and Kashmir.[15] Perhaps the most notable of these massacres occurred on March 20, 2000, on the eve of President Bill Clinton's official visit to India, when LeT terrorists (along with members of *Hizbul Mujahideen*, another Pakistan-backed terrorist organization) massacred 35 Sikhs at Chattisinghpora in Anantnag.[16]

Besides its deadly massacres, LeT has carried out innumerable attacks in Jammu and Kashmir, targeting Indian government and military installations and disrupting elections by intimidating voters and targeting political leaders. LeT developed bomb-making skills, building and planting IEDs to target Indian army vehicles and adeptly mixed high and low technology to communicate and carry out operations.[17]

This shift does not indicate that LeT lost all interest in Afghanistan in the 1990s. However, its main operational focus was Kashmir. According to LeT expert Stephen Tankel, several possible factors—from LeT's *Ahl-e-Hadith* background to a desire on the part of Pakistani intelligence to keep the group separate from other terrorist actors—could explain why LeT's activities and freedom of movement were constrained in Afghanistan during the 1990s.[18]

One of LeT's signature tactics has been *fidayeen* attacks, in which small, heavily armed and highly motivated two- to four-man squads strike significant or symbolic targets in an effort to cause mass casualties and humiliate the enemy. One early *fidayeen* operation occurred in November 1999, when a team of LeT terrorists infiltrated the supposedly secure headquarters of India's 15 Corps at the Badami Bagh cantonment in Srinagar (the capital of Jammu and Kashmir) killing the Public Relations Officer and seven of his staffers. The attackers then fought off Indian soldiers for almost 10 hours before being killed.[19] A month later, LeT terrorists attacked the Police Special Operations Group Headquarters and killed a dozen Indian security personnel. These attacks were not limited to security forces. In January 2001, six LeT operatives attempted to enter Srinagar Airport, and in August 2001, three LeT *fidayeen* killed 11 inside the Jammu Railway station.[20] LeT has carried out dozens of such *fidayeen* attacks over the years.

Fidayeen attacks are distinct from suicide bombings, a tactic that LeT has refrained from using. Unlike suicide bomb attacks, the *fidayeen* (translated as "those who sacrifice themselves in order to redeem themselves") can, at least theoretically, survive the attack. *Fidayeen* attacks are an important LeT recruiting tool. LeT publishes their exploits, and substantial numbers of *fidayeen* do survive and return to Pakistan, where they help recruit new members.

Although violence in Kashmir peaked in the mid-2000s and has decreased substantially since, LeT has remained active in the region. In January 2010, for example, LeT operatives held off security forces for 22 hours after storming a hotel in Srinagar and killing a civilian and a policeman.[21]

Although the bulk of LeT operations have taken place in Jammu and Kashmir, the group was never confined to that arena. From its beginnings, LeT sought to target India. As early as 1992, Hafez Saeed sent Azam Cheema, a top LeT commander, to India to recruit Indian Muslims. Taking advantage of Hindu-Muslim communal tensions, Cheema had some success, and his network carried out a number of low-level bombings across India.[22] Karim Abdul Tunda, who was arrested on the Indian-Nepal border in August 2013, was one these early LeT recruits. He is suspected of involvement in over 40 terror cases in India, both directly and coordinating operations from Pakistan.[23] Indian police arrested LeT operatives in the 1990s, but LeT was not well known at the time and Indian authorities did not realize the extent of the LeT operation in their country.[24]

Just as the ISI supports LeT as a proxy in order to maintain plausible deniability, LeT fosters proxies in India among radical Islamist militias in India. LeT's most important ally within India is the Indian Mujahideen (IM). Established by Indian Muslims radicalized by community violence, IM's members are primarily drawn from the ranks of the Students Islamic Movement of India (SIMI).[25] LeT, along with several other Pakistani terror groups, provided support to IM, including training, cash, weapons, explosives, and false travel documents. One of IM's founders, Mohammed Sadiq Israr Sheikh, is believed to have traveled to Pakistan in part on a legitimate Pakistani passport supplied by ISI through LeT; he met with LeT leaders in Pakistan, attended an LeT training camp, and recruited other Indian Muslims to attend LeT training camps.[26]

Some analysts argue that IM is little more than an outgrowth of LeT and the ISI, which was established when Pakistan, under U.S. pressure, reduced its support for armed operations in Jammu and Kashmir.[27] According to these analysts, IM was an outgrowth of "The Karachi Project" which brought together a number of Pakistani militant groups including LeT to attack India.[28] Other analysts view IM as an independent organization, but allied with LeT:

> "…most Indian militants did not perceive themselves as proxies for either Lashkar or Pakistan.... In other words, the group [LeT] was a force multiplier for Indian militancy, rather than a key driver of it. Further, while Lashkar was the chief external outfit providing support for Indian jihadism, it was not the only one."[29]

The Gulf is often a critical region of LeT-IM communications and recruitment because many Indians travel to the Gulf for work and can then relatively easily travel on to Pakistan.

IM has been held responsible for numerous deadly attacks throughout India, most of them before 2012. While LeT's preferred tactic is the *fidayeen* assault, IM's specialty has been IEDs made with pressure cookers packed with ammonium nitrate and fuel oil. It is often difficult to determine if an attack was a LeT operation in which IM provided support, an IM-LeT joint operation, or an IM operation that received LeT support. There may also have been attacks by IM in which they did not receive direct LeT support, but LeT training and support helped IM build the necessary organizational capabilities to carry out the attack. Indian officials have cracked down hard on IM in recent years, and in March 2014 they claimed to have arrested the group's entire top leadership.[30] Since then, IM has not been particularly active.

Jihad is central to LeT's worldview, but so is *da'wa* (preaching). LeT runs a vast network of offices, schools, medical centers, and media outlets within Pakistan to proselytize LeT's Ahl-e-Hadith theology. LeT's headquarters are at a 200-acre compound in Muridke, outside of Lahore, designed to be a "pure" Islamic city with a madrassa, a hospital, a market, residences, and farmland. To demonstrate the purity of the city, televisions and pictures are banned, with entertainment limited to cassettes of warrior songs.[31]

LeT runs a network of primary and upper-level schools that serve over 18,000 students. They are not, technically, *madrassas*; while LeT pushes its view of Islam, the schools also teach other subjects. However, LeT's worldview is infused into every component of education. The former head of LeT's education department explained that in the basic reader the alphabet is used to emphasize *jihad*, "'Alif' for Allah, 'Be' for Bandooq (gun), 'Te' for toop (cannon) and so on." Because of the poor state of Pakistan's public education, LeT schools are an attractive alternative. LeT also subsidizes the fees for those who cannot pay.[32]

LeT is also a major healthcare provider, running hospitals, mobile medical centers, and an ambulance service. Over 2,000 doctors volunteer their services part-time and are trained to use their contact with patients as an opportunity to proselytize. LeT believes these activities are necessary to counter-act the influence of NGOs and Christian missionaries. As in LeT's education system, the organization is providing a service desperately needed by many impoverished Pakistanis.[33] LeT has also been on the forefront of disaster relief, which also raises the organization's profile and reputation in Pakistan. LeT was one of the first organizations to respond to the 2005 Kashmir earthquake[34] and has delivered aid to refugees who were displaced by the fighting in the Swat Valley in 2008 and the 2010 floods.[35]

The effectiveness with which LeT and JuD have managed to serve the role of a shadow state cannot be stated enough. Consider that as early as 2005, LeT's assets included a 190-acre campus in Muridke, outside Lahore, which featured 500 offices, 2200 training camps, 150 schools, 2 science colleges, 3 hospitals, 11 ambulances, a publishing empire, a garment factory, an iron foundry, and woodworks factories. Salaries were in some cases 12 to 15 times greater than those offered for similar jobs in the civilian state sector.[36]

LeT has an extensive media arm, publishing several magazines in Urdu, English and Arabic with publications targeted to specific communities such as women and students. The flagship publication, *Majalah al-Dawa*, is an Urdu-language monthly with a circulation of about 60,000.[37] *Jihad* is a regular theme in these publications, and they regularly feature testaments from "martyrs," LeT operatives killed in the service of *jihad*.[38] LeT has used the internet to propagate its message, broadcasting an internet radio show and maintaining websites and Facebook pages. However, international scrutiny has led the Pakistani government to shut down these sites. LeT also holds conferences and rallies throughout the country.[39] These have continued despite the supposed ban on LeT and often feature speeches by Hafez Mohammed Saeed, notwithstanding the $10 million bounty on him under the U.S. Rewards for Justice program.[40]

LeT's large social service and paramilitary operations are expensive to operate. However, the organization has been both creative and systematic in its fundraising efforts. According to one report donation boxes for the *jihadi* groups are present in every third or fourth shop in Pakistani markets throughout the country. LeT publications include calls for donations. LeT also raises money from wealthy supporters in the Arabian Peninsula and from the large Pakistani expatriate community around the world. Often these donations are channeled through a variety of international Islamist charities, such as the International Islamic Relief Organization and the al-Rashid Foundation.[41]

One notable LeT fundraising operation is collecting the skins of sacrificial animals after holidays and selling them to tanneries. In 2010, JuD reportedly collected 100,000 skins, netting a profit of $1.2 million.[42] LeT uses a range of low and high-tech means to involve people in this campaign. For example, within Pakistan, LeT announces this campaign via loudspeaker, but internationally, it allows individuals to contribute to the purchase of a sacrificial animal online and then donate the skin to LeT.[43]

Besides the ISI stipend, the Pakistani civilian government has also contributed to LeT. In June 2010, the Punjab provincial government allocated 80 million rupees (about $1 million) to LeT-affiliated schools and hospitals.[44]

Another possible source of support to LeT's operations in India is D-company, the organized crime group led by Dawood Ibrahim. While his present location is unknown (most Indians believe he may be based in Pakistan), his criminal network extends well beyond India and the Subcontinent and into the Middle East. Ibrahim, who is heavily involved in the heroin trade and various forms of smuggling, is believed to be a major donor to LeT, with his smuggling networks purportedly used to help LeT move operatives in and out of India.[45]

GLOBAL REACH

Although the vast majority of LeT's operations have been in India, it is a terrorist group of global reach and ambition. LeT's global network has multiple components. LeT has allied with other Islamist groups around the world, including al-Qaeda, and has developed its own network of supporters internationally for fundraising and logistical support. LeT has also become a magnet for Islamists worldwide seeking training. Finally, and most worrisome, LeT is increasingly operating against NATO forces and India in Afghanistan and has on several occasions directed plots outside of the Indian sub-continent.

While LeT's rhetoric focuses on India, it has never discussed India exclusively. LeT statements have long vilified a coalition of Hindus, Jews, and Christians, colorfully termed the "Brahmanic-Talmudic-Crusader" alliance that seeks to destroy the *ummah*, the international Muslim community.[46] In a 1998 speech, Hafez Saeed stated:

> Lashkar-e-Taiba will ultimately plant the flag of Islam on Delhi, Tel Aviv, and Washington. All evil in the world emanated from the WhiteHouse which would be blown up and if the US Army took action against the Muslims it would be opposed by Lashkar-e-Taiba.[47]

LeT communications call for *jihad* to overthrow the oppressors of Muslims everywhere. LeT rhetoric frequently targets Israel and at one point called for Pakistan to deploy a hydrogen bomb to "make the USA yield before Pakistan."[48]

LeT's affiliation with the international Islamist terror movement is deep and extensive. As discussed above, LeT's links to al-Qaeda, the leading organization of the *jihadist* movement, go back to the very founding of the organizations and the joint legacy of Abdullah Azzam, who was instrumental in the creation of both al-Qaeda and LeT's predecessor, MDI.

The connection between LeT and al-Qaeda was more than rhetorical. LeT has sheltered and trained many notable al-Qaeda figures. Ramzi Yusuf, the mastermind of the 1993 World Trade Center bombing and nephew of 9/11 organizer Khalid Sheikh Mohammed, is known to have been sheltered in LeT safehouses.[49] After 9/11 and the U.S. invasion of Afghanistan, LeT assisted with the exfiltration of al-Qaeda personnel from Afghanistan into Pakistan and beyond, providing safe houses, safe passage, travel documents, and logistical support.[50]

Even after 9/11, several al-Qaeda operatives trained with LeT. Richard Reid, the infamous terrorist who attempted to detonate his shoes as part of an al-Qaeda plot on a U.S.-bound flight, had trained with LeT prior to joining al-Qaeda. Two of the 2005 London subway bombers, Mohammad Siddique Khan and Shehzad Tanweer, may also have received training from LeT.[51]

While LeT was focused on its anti-India objectives, many group members were embedded in an international network of Islamist organizations. It has long offered support to other extremist groups battling those it perceives as enemies of Islam. LeT has offered rhetorical and occasionally financial support to Islamists in Chechnya, Gaza, the Philippines, ad the Balkans.[52] The Islamic Movement of Uzbekistan (IMU), a group with the goal of overthrowing the Uzbek regime and replacing it with a *sharia*-based government, has long-standing ties with LeT and receives support from the organization.[53] IMU's militant network in fact extends well beyond LeT; it also cooperates with the Pakistani Taliban and Lashkar-e-Jhangvi. In 2015, the IMU pledged its allegiance to the Islamic State, though a faction retaining the name IMU and its loyalties to al-Qaeda still exists today.[54] Over the last two years, it has flirted with the Islamic State faction based in Afghanistan and Pakistan. LeT is also plugged into the international networks of Islamist fundraisers such as the Al Akhtar Trust or the Al Rashid Trust, which were founded to fund militant groups, including LeT.[55]

When al-Qaeda's training infrastructure in Afghanistan was destroyed, LeT's camps were largely untouched due to Pakistan's protection; thus, the camps took up the mantle of training militants from across the international Islamist movement.[56] This training support is provided to militants from numerous organizations in South Asia, such as *Hizbul Mujahideen* (HuM), *Jaish-e-Mohammed* (JeM), *Harkat-ul-Jihad-ul-Islami* (HuJI), and the Taliban, among others.[57] Furthermore, radical Muslims worldwide have travelled to Pakistan to train with the LeT.

Besides being a magnet for Islamists worldwide, LeT has established its own global footprint to support its terror activities. Within the Indian sub-continent, LeT has safehouses and supporters in Bangladesh, Nepal,[58] and the Maldives[59] that facilitate the infiltration of operatives into India. LeT also has supporters in the Gulf region who raise funds, but also recruit Indians working in the Gulf and coordinate travel to Pakistan for training. But LeT's network extends far beyond Asia, into Europe and even the United States. There is evidence that LeT opened an office in Lodi, California, and counterterrorism officials "cite evidence in recent years of fundraising or recruiting efforts in Canada, Britain, Australia and the United States."[60] There has also been evidence of LeT activity in Germany, as stated by the German Interior Minister,[61] a cell that raised money and was armed with explosives was arrested in Spain,[62] and (as will be discussed below) LeT had an active presence in France.[63]

Despite its international network, vast resources, and unmitigated rage against the West for most of its existence, LeT has almost exclusively targeted India. However, this has begun to change over the past decade. The attacks in Mumbai in which foreigners, and particularly Israelis and Americans, were targeted was one example. But LeT is becoming increasingly involved in the fight against NATO and the United States in Afghanistan. More ominously, LeT operatives have, on several occasions, hatched plots beyond the Indian sub-continent that directly target Western interests.

The vast majority of attacks LeT has executed other than in India have occurred in Afghanistan. In part, these attacks have been consistent with LeT's willingness to serve as a proxy for Pakistani intelligence. Pakistan's military leadership is deeply concerned that increased Indian influence in Afghanistan will leave Pakistan surrounded. Several LeT attacks have reflected this Pakistani concern. At first, LeT's support for the Afghan Taliban in their fight against NATO forces was informal, granting LeT fighters leave to travel to Afghanistan and join the Taliban on their own initiative. This was a useful safety valve for LeT. Many LeT members were frustrated that the Pakistani government had allied with the Americans and was cracking down on LeT activities against India in Jammu and Kashmir. In 2004 and 2005, LeT began to formally support its members traveling to Afghanistan to fight alongside the Taliban.[64] LeT fighters played a significant role in an attack on a U.S. base in Wanat, Nuristan in which insurgents nearly overran the base.[65] LeT also carried out a number of high-profile strikes against Indian targets in Afghanistan, including a July 2008 car-bombing of the Indian Embassy[66] and a February 2010 *fidayeen* attack on Kabul guesthouses hosting Indians.

LeT has also begun to act operationally within the West. A notable case of an attempted LeT attack in the West is that of Willie Brigitte, a French convert to Islam.

Initially Brigitte sought to enter Afghanistan to join the Taliban. When he could not do so, Brigitte spent several months training at a LeT camp in Pakistan in late 2001. He then was dispatched to Australia, where he linked up with other LeT operatives to carry out a series of attacks, with potential targets including a nuclear reactor and Australian military bases. Ultimately, after France alerted Australia's domestic intelligence agency, ASIO, of the threat posed by Brigitte, he was deported to France where he was convicted of providing support to terrorists and sentenced to nine years in prison.[67]

In spring 2004, LeT dispatched several operatives to Iraq to fight the Americans and British. Led by a high-level LeT operative named Danish Ahmed, the team was arrested by British forces in April 2004. LeT was exploring the possibility of sending fighters to Iraq but ultimately did not have the right links to the clandestine networks. Nonetheless, this incident highlights that LeT was taking a more expansive view of its conflict with the West.[68]

David Headley, a Pakistani-American, is perhaps the most notorious Western LeT operative. He is both an example of a Western recruit to LeT and of attempts by the organization to directly attack the West. Headley's involvement with LeT lasted for seven years, during which time he trained at least five times at LeT camps in Pakistan, shuttled back and forth between the United States, Pakistan, and India on the organization's behalf, and, perhaps most integrally, selected and scoped out attack locations for the Mumbai attack.[69] He was ultimately arrested in Chicago a year after the 26/11 attacks and was convicted in January 2013 to 35 years in federal prison for his role in the attacks.[70]

Recent Activity

Lashkar-e-Taiba currently finds itself in a difficult position. Unlike many of the other Islamist groups in Pakistan, it has remained loyal to the Pakistani state, and even serves Pakistan's government as an intermediary to other radical groups.[71] At the same time, LeT's primary arena for *jihad*, Jammu and Kashmir, has been increasingly closed off to it. Violence in the region has decreased from hundreds of civilians killed annually by terrorists only a decade ago to less than a score killed annually.[72] Jammu and Kashmir remain restive, and LeT and other Pakistani extremists continue to attempt to wage their battle there. But they are receiving far less support from the government of Pakistan, which is under international pressure and is seeking to improve relations with India.[73] The 26/11 assault on Mumbai may have been one outgrowth of this internal tension (as well as an effort to derail warming Indian-Pakistani relations.)

Additionally, LeT has been unable to capitalize on new developments in the global jihadist sphere. The emergence of ISIS over the last few years has not threatened LeT, but neither has it helped strengthen LeT. When ISIS announced the establishment of a chapter in the Afghanistan/Pakistan region in early 2015, some observers noted that LeT could be a logical partner for ISIS in the South Asia region, given that both groups adhere to the Salafist sect of Sunni Islam. By contrast, most South Asian terror groups—from the Taliban to the sectarian Lashkar-e-Jhangvi (LeJ)—belong to the Deobandi sect, which ISIS rejects. Observers contended at the time that some renegade LeT members, frustrated about their group's less active role in Kashmir and across India, could jump ship to ISIS.[74]

Instead, ISIS has chosen to partner with other local militant groups, and particularly LeJ. For ISIS, its preference appears to be to link up with groups in South Asia that share its targeting preferences—LeJ, like ISIS, is deeply sectarian and frequently targets Shia Muslims—even if they don't share ISIS's Salafist sect. Another reason that helps explain why ISIS has not taken an interest in partnering with LeT is the latter's ties to the Pakistani state, which ISIS wants to destroy.

Not surprisingly, LeT does not appear to have much respect for ISIS. In late 2015, the two organizations engaged in a nasty war of words through each other's respective propaganda magazines.[75]

All this said, despite their differences, LeJ and ISIS, like all Islamist terrorist groups, are cut from the same general ideological cloth. For this reason, one cannot rule out the possibility of a temporary marriage of convenience motivated by a need to target a common enemy—such as U.S. soldiers or Indian civilians in Afghanistan. Still, even these occasional tactical collaborations, were they to be established, would likely have a very limited impact on LeT's overall capacities.

That being said, several attacks did target Jammu and Kashmir and broader India in 2015 and 2016. Terrorists hit Indian military facilities in Pathankot in the state of Punjab in January 2016, and in Uri in Jammu and Kashmir in September 2016. They also hit a police station in the town of Gurdaspur in Punjab in July 2015. India blamed another Pakistan-based anti-India terror group, *Jaish-e-Mohammed*, for the first two attacks. Yet posters were reportedly spotted in the Pakistani town of Gujranwala in October 2016 that announced that LeT would hold last rites *in absentia* for one of the four attackers in the Uri attack—suggesting a level of LeT involvement.[76] However, this may have been more a case of LeT trying to assert its continued relevance and potency than a genuine claim of responsibility. Meanwhile, the Gurdaspur attack was initially blamed by Indian officials on terrorists linked to LeT.[77] However, there was little else said by New Delhi about LeT's role in the months since the Gurdaspur attack took place.

After the Uri attack, one of the deadliest on the Indian military in decades, India retaliated with what it described as a "surgical strike"—a limited attack on Pakistani militant facilities along the Line of Control. According to Indian media reports drawing on military assessment reports, LeT suffered significant damage, including the loss of 20 fighters.[78] However, given that some of the Indian media's reporting on the incident was later contradicted by government officials and subsequent reports, such findings should be regarded with some degree of skepticism.

Over the course of 2015 and 2016, Indian officials often warned of terror threats to India posed by LeT.[79] They also alleged that the group was behind the protests that convulsed Jammu and Kashmir in the summer of 2016 after Indian security forces killed Burhan Wani, a popular young militant affiliated with the Kashmiri separatist group *Hizb-ul-Mujahideen*.[80] However, there is insufficient open source information on which to judge the veracity of these claims.

LeT's expanded international profile since the 26/11 attacks has also hurt the organization's ability to carry out terror attacks. The 2012 arrest of Abu Jundal highlighted increased Saudi-Indian counter-terror cooperation.[81] India's arrests of Karim Abdul Tunda and Yassin Bhatkal will reduce, although not eliminate, LeT's ability to carry out attacks within India. Finally, expanded international scrutiny in general will make it more difficult for LeT to move operatives and plan major attacks.

Furthermore, LeT's compromised future prospects should be viewed through the prism of a deepening U.S.-India security relationship. Washington's messaging, and particularly since 2014, has suggested emphatically that the United States—which lost six citizens in the 2008 Mumbai attack—is fully behind New Delhi in its efforts to combat the LeT threat. Tellingly, a White House statement issued in September 2016, following a conversation between U.S. National Security Advisor Susan Rice and her Indian counterpart Ajit Doval, stated that: "Ambassador Rice reiterated our expectation that Pakistan take effective action to combat and delegitimize United Nations-designated terrorists individuals and entities, including Lashkar-e-Tayyiba..."[82] With Washington and New Delhi poised to increase arms sales and intelligence sharing as their defense relationship grows, India's capacity to attack LeT (and other anti-India militants) on Pakistani soil—particularly through the use of lightning cross-border strikes and other limited covert measures—could well be enhanced in the coming years.

Furthermore, LeT has reportedly suffered setbacks in its operations outside of India. According to the Afghan government, for example, 19 members of LeT were killed in airstrikes in eastern Afghanistan in October 2016.[83]

Despite these setbacks and threats, however, LeT continues to operate openly in Pakistan. In recent years LeT rallies have protested NATO transports traveling through Pakistan, U.S. drone strikes, Indian water policies, and improved trade relations with India. LeT has spearheaded a coalition of Islamist groups opposed to these efforts, which is known as the *Difa-e-Pakistan Council* (Defense of Pakistan.)[84]

Despite a $10 million bounty under the U.S. Rewards for Justice program, LeT chief Hafez Muhammed Saeed continues to travel throughout Pakistan and speak at rallies, including anti-India protests in the heart of Islamabad. Saeed also regularly gives academic lectures at colleges in the Pakistani province of Punjab. Several top LeT leaders are being tried in Pakistan for their role in the 26/11 attacks. But the extremely slow pace of the judicial process suggests that the Pakistani government is not committed to seeing justice served.[85] Indeed, Zakiur Rehman Lakhvi, a top LeT leader implicated by India in the 26/11 attacks, has been in and out of jail for several years and has been out on bail since 2015. In January 2017, Pakistan announced that it had placed Saeed under house arrest. This wasn't the first time Saeed experienced this fate; he had also been detained in this way in 2008 and 2009, only to be released soon thereafter. Given Pakistan's poor track record on seeking justice for top LeT leaders, independent analysts expected that this latest detention would not last long either.

Prime Minister Narendra Modi's administration has shown little interest in improving India's relationship with Pakistan. Modi is a Hindu nationalist, whose party has expressed virulently anti-Pakistan views. Due to this point of conflict, LeT's anti-India extremism may well continue to resonate with large segments of society across Pakistan, and particularly in the province of Punjab where the group is based. In 2016, Modi threatened to revisit, or even revoke, the Indus Waters Treaty—a water-sharing accord that ensures the Indus, a critical water source for Pakistan, flows downstream unencumbered into Pakistan from India.[86] Modi's threat will provide more ammunition for LeT propaganda, which has long used India's alleged "water theft" as a chief talking point.

Ultimately, LeT holds the values of *jihad* as a central tenet of its ideology. Its current period of relative restraint will be difficult to maintain. Either the organization will again seek to launch terrorist spectaculars, possibly farther afield from its previous areas of operation. Alternately, frustrated LeT cadres may begin to plot attacks on their own initiative. This may have been the case when David Coleman Headley, the key plotter of the Mumbai attacks, began scouting targets in Denmark.[87] LeT likewise remains ideologically committed to violence and is a formidable organization with the resources and skills needed to launch major, deadly terror attacks. Revelations that it is embracing technological innovations—including a new mobile application that enables its communications in Jammu and Kashmir to be more secure[88]—highlight the group's willingness to adjust to the times as it prepares to continue its fight into the future.

Endnotes

[1] Stephen Tankel, "Lashkar-e-Taiba: Past Operations and Future Prospects," New America Foundation, April 27, 2011, https://www.newamerica.org/international-security/policy-papers/lashkar-e-taiba/.

[2] Yoginder Sikand, "Islamist Militancy in Kashmir: The Case of Lashkar-e-Taiba," in Aparna Rao, Michael Bollig and Monika Bock, eds., The Practice of War: Production, Reproduction and Communication of Armed Violence (London: Berghahn Books 2007).
[3] Ibid.
[4] Wilson John, "Lashkar-e-Toiba: New Threats Posed By An Old Organization," Jamestown Foundation Terrorism Monitor 3, no. 4, May 5, 2005, http://www.jamestown.org/single/?no_cache=1&tx_ttnews[tt_news]=314.
[5] Tankel, "Lashkar-e-Taiba."
[6] Muhammad Amir Rana, A to Z of Jihadi Organizations in Pakistan, Saba Ansan, trans., (Pakistan: Mashal Books, 2006), 298-300.
[7] Ibid., 317-18.
[8] Praveen Swami, India, Pakistan and the Secret Jihad: The Covert War in Kashmir, 1947-2004 (London: Routledge, 2007), 145.
[9] Ibid., 170-80.
[10] Joshua Adlakha, The Evolution of Lashkar-e-Tayyiba and the Road to Mumbai, Unpublished dissertation for Georgetown University, 2010.
[11] Ibid.
[12] A. Abbas, "In God We Trust," The Herald, January 2002.
[13] Sikand, "Islamist Militancy in Kashmir: The Case of Lashkar-e-Taiba," 206.
[14] South Asian Terrorism Portal, "Incidents and Statements involving Lashkar-e-Toiba: 1996-2007," n.d., accessed September 16, 2013, http://www.satp.org/satporgtp/countries/india/states/jandk/terrorist_outfits/lashkar_e_toiba_lt2007.htm.
[15] Praveen Swami, "Turning the Snow Red," Frontline 17, no. 17 (August 19–September 1, 2000), http://www.frontline.in/static/html/fl1717/17170160.htm.
[16] Barry Bearak, "A Kashmiri Mystery," New York Times Magazine, December 31, 2000, http://www.nytimes.com/2000/12/31/magazine/a-kashmiri-mystery.html?pagewanted=all&src=pm.
[17] Peter Chalk & C. Christine Fair, "Lashkar-e-Tayyiba leads the Kashmiri insurgency," Jane's Intelligence Review 14, no. 10, October 17, 2002, 1-5.
[18] Stephen Tankel, "Lashkar-eTaiba in Perspective: An Evolving Threat," Counterterrorism Strategy Initiative Policy Paper, New America Foundation, February 2010, http://carnegieendowment.org/files/Lashkar-e-Taiba_in_Perspective.pdf.
[19] Praveen Swami, "A growing toll," Frontline, 16, no. 24, November 13-26, 1999, http://www.frontline.in/static/html/fl1624/16240390.htm.
[20] For an in-depth chronology of LeT operations, see South Asia Terrorism Portal, "Incidents involving Lashkar-e-Toiba: 1996-2007," http://www.satp.org/satporgtp/countries/india/states/jandk/terrorist_outfits/lashkar_e_toiba_lt2007.htm.

[21] "Siege ends at Lal Chowk; 2 militants gunned down," ExpressIndia.com, January 7, 2010, http://expressindia.indianexpress.com/karnatakapoll08/story_page.php?id=564467

[22] Praveen Swami, "Pakistan and the Lashkar's Jihad in India," The Hindu, December 9, 2008.

[23] Dwaipayan Ghosh, "Tunda fed IM sleeper cells via border operations," Times of India, September 4, 2013, http://articles.timesofindia.indiatimes.com/2013-09-04/kolkata/41764390_1_indian-mujahideen-terror-attacks-delhi-police.

[24] Tankel, "Lashkar-e-Taiba."

[25] C. Christine Fair, Students Islamic Movement of India and the Indian Mujahideen: An Assessment, (Seattle, WA: The National Bureau of Asian Research, January 2010).

[26] "13/7 Accused Haroon Naik met Osama, Lakhvi in Pak: ATS," The Hindu, February 7 2012, http://www.thehindu.com/news/national/137-accused-haroon-naik-met-osama-lakhvi-in-pak-ats/article2869467.ece.

[27] Vicky Nanjappa "How the Indian Mujahideen was formed." Rediff.com, July 29, 2008, http://www.rediff.com/news/2008/jul/29ahd9.htm.

[28] Animesh Roul, "After Pune, Details Emerge on the Karachi Project and its Threat to India," CTC Sentinel 3, no. 4, April 2010, http://www.ctc.usma.edu/posts/after-pune-details-emerge-on-the-karachi-project-and-its-threat-to-india.

[29] Tankel, Storming the World Stage, 144.

[30] Rahul Tripathi, "Entire Top Indian Mujahideen Leadership Nabbed in 8 Months," Indian Express, March 30, 2014, http://indianexpress.com/article/india/india-others/im-impounded/.

[31] Jessica Stern, Terror in the Name of God: Why Religious Militants Kill (New York: HarperCollins, 2003), 114.

[32] Arif Jamal, "From Madrasa to School," News, December 15, 2002.

[33] Shushant Sareen, The Jihad Factory: Pakistan's Islamic Revolution in the Making (India: Observer Research Foundation, 2005), 243-46.

[34] Praveen Swami, "Quake came as a boon for Lashkar leadership," The Hindu, November 17, 2005.

[35] Saeed Shah, "Pakistan floods: Jamaat-ud-Dawa, Islamists linked to India's Mumbai attack, offer aid," Christian Science Monitor, August 4, 2010.

[36] Neil Padukone, "The Next Al-Qaeda? Lashkar-e-Taiba and the Future of Terrorism in South Asia," World Affairs Journal, November/December 2011, http://www.worldaffairsjournal.org/article/next-al-qaeda-lashkar-e-taiba-and-future-terrorism-south-asia.

[37] Everything You Want to Know About LeT," Hindustan Times, February 20, 2010, http://www.hindustantimes.com/Everything-you-want-to-know-about-the-LeT/H1-Article1-511059.aspx.

[38] Mariam Abou Zahab, "'I shall be waiting for you at the door of paradise:' The Pakistani Martyrs of the Lashkar-e Taiba," in Rao, Bollig and Bock, eds., The Practice of War: Production, Reproduction and Communication of Armed Violence, 167.

[39] Amir Mir, "The Gates are Open," Outlook India, January 19, 2009, http://www.outlookindia.com/article.aspx?239500.

[40] Annie Gowen, "Pakistan, India spar in Kashmir in worst border violence in years," Washington Post, September 12, 2013, http://articles.washingtonpost.com/2013-09-12/world/41982669_1_indian-controlled-kashmir-india-and-pakistan-muslim-majority-pakistan.

[41] Sareen, The Jihad Factory, 290-93.

[42] "Banned Outfits Raise Cash from Sacrifice Day," Dawn (Karachi), November 24, 2010, http://www.dawn.com/2010/11/24/banned-outfits-raise-cash-from-sacrifice-day.html.

[43] Sareen, The Jihad Factory, 298.

[44] "Pakistan 'Gave Funds' to Group on UN Terror Blacklist," BBC, June 16, 2010, http://www.bbc.co.uk/news/10334914.

[45] VS Subrahmanian et al., Computational Analysis of Terrorist Groups: Lashkar-e-Taiba (New York: Springer Verlag, 2013), 216.

[46] C. Christine Fair, testimony presented before the House Homeland Security Committee, Subcommittee on Transportation Security and Infrastructure Protection, March 11, 2009, http://www.rand.org/pubs/testimonies/CT320/.

[47] Friday Times, November 21-27, 1998, cited in Sareen, The Jihad Factory, 310.

[48] Evan Kohlmann, "Expert Witness: Synopsis of Testimony, Regina v. Mohammed Ajmal Khan, Palvinder Singh, and Frzana Khan, Exhibit EK/1" (UK: Snaresbrook Crown Court, 2006), http://nefafoundation.org//file/ekletwitnessreport.pdf.

[49] Mariam Abou Zahab and Olivier Roy, Islamist Networks: The Afghan-Pakistan Connection (New York: Columbia University Press, 2004), 42.

[50] Tankel, "Lashkar-e-Taiba."

[51] Ibid., 162-66.

[52] Peter Bergen, Holy War Inc.: Inside the secret world of Osama Bin-Laden (New York: Free Press, 2001).

[53] Bill Roggio, "Al Qaeda video highlights fighting in Ghazni." Long War Journal, July 13, 2013.

[54] Bill Roggio and Caleb Weiss, "Islamic Movement of Uzbekistan faction emerges after group's collapse," The Long War Journal, June 14, 2016, http://www.longwarjournal.org/archives/2016/06/islamic-movement-of-uzbekistan-faction-emerges-after-groups-collapse.php.

[55] South Asian Terrorism Portal, "Al-Rashid Trust," n.d., www.satp.org/satporgtp/countries/pakistan/terroristoutfits/Al-Rashid_Trust.htm.

[56] Tankel, "Lashkar-e-Taiba."

[57] Neil Padukone, "The Next Al Qaeda? Lashkar-e-Taiba and the Future of Terrorism in South Asia," World Affairs, November/December 2011, 67-72.

[58] Tankel, Storming the World Stage, 144.

[59] Animesh Roul, "Jihad and Islamism in the Maldive Islands," Jamestown Foundation Terrorism Monitor, February 12, 2010, https://jamestown.org/program/jihad-and-islamism-in-the-maldive-islands/.

[60] Josh Meyer, "Extremist group works in the open in Pakistan," Los Angeles Times, December 18, 2007.

[61] Mohit Joshi, "Lashkar-e-Taiba members in Germany, interior minister says." TopNews, December 12, 2008.

[62] Jesus Duva, Monica Ceberio Balaza, and Jorge A. Rodriguez, "Three Al Qaeda members detained in Spain," El Pais, August 2, 2012.

[63] Tankel, Storming the World Stage, 165.

[64] Ibid., 194.

[65] "Surge of the Insurgents," Jane's Terrorism and Security Monitor, September 5, 2008.

[66] Praveen Swami, "Kabul Attack: U.S. Warning was accurate," The Hindu, August 3, 2008, http://www.thehindu.com/todays-paper/Kabul-attack-U.S.-warning-was-accurate/article15271791.ece

[67] Tankel, "Lashkar-e-Taiba."

[68] Praveen Swami, "Lashkar renews anti-American polemic," The Hindu, May 9, 2004, http://www.hindu.com/2004/05/09/stories/2004050902141000.htm.

[69] Adlakha, The Evolution of Lashkar-e-Tayyiba and the Road to Mumbai.

[70] Steven Yaccino, "Planner of Mumbai Attacks is Given 35-Year Sentence," New York Times, January 24, 2013.

[71] Abou Zahab, "'I shall be waiting for you at the door of paradise:' The Pakistani Martyrs of the Lashkar-e Taiba,", 114.

[72] South Asia Terrorism Portal, "Fatalities in Terrorist Violence 1988-2013," n.d., http://www.satp.org/satporgtp/countries/india/states/jandk/data_sheets/annual_casualties.htm.

[73] Tankel, Storming the World Stage, 174-177.

[74] Arif Rafiq, "Islamic State Goes Official in South Asia," February 4, 2015, http://thediplomat.com/2015/02/islamic-state-goes-official-in-south-asia/.

[75] Rohan Joshi, "Is a Clash Between Lashkar-e-Taiba and ISIS Imminent?" Business Standard, December 15, 2015, http://www.business-standard.com/article/punditry/is-a-clash-between-lashkar-e-taiba-and-isis-imminent-115121500156_1.html.

[76] Praveen Swami, "Pakistan: Lashkar-e-Taiba Claims Uri Attack in Posters in Gujranwala," Indian Express, October 26, 2016, http://indianexpress.com/article/india/india-news-india/uri-attack-lashkar-e-taiba-pakistan-terrorism-gujranwala-3103034/.

[77] "Lashkar-e-Taiba Behind Gurdaspur Terror Attack, Confirms MHA," Business Standard, July 27, 2015, http://www.business-standard.com/article/news-ani/lashkar-e-taiba-behind-gurdaspur-terror-attack-confirms-mha-115072701297_1.html.

[78] PTI, "Pakistan-Based Lashkar-e-Taiba Suffered Maximum Damage in Surgical Strikes," Indian Express, October 12, 2016, http://indianexpress.com/article/india/india-news-india/lashker-e-taiba-suffered-maximum-damage-in-surgical-strikes-3073562/.

[79] See, for example, Vicky Nanjappa, "Kill All Hindu Leaders Ahead of Polls: IB Intercept States," One India, November 21, 2016, http://www.oneindia.com/new-delhi/kill-all-hindus-leaders-ahead-of-polls-ib-intercept-states-2268072.html.

[80] "Lashkar-e-Taiba Fueling Large-Scale Protests in Kashmir: India," Times of India, August 10, 2016, http://timesofindia.indiatimes.com/india/Lashkar-fuelling-large-scale-protests-in-Kashmir-India/articleshow/53633232.cms.

[81] Sebastian Rotella, "Militant Reaffirms Role of Pakistan in Mumbai Attacks," Foreign Policy, August 9, 2012.

[82] White House, Office of the Press Secretary, "Statement by NSC Spokesperson Ned Price on National Security Advisor Susan E. Rice's Call with National Security Advisor Ajit Doval of India," September 28, 2016, https://www.whitehouse.gov/the-press-office/2016/09/28/statement-nsc-spokesperson-ned-price-national-security-advisor-susan-e.

[83] "Egyptian Militant Among 19 Killed in Kunar Province," Khaama Press, November 1, 2016, http://www.khaama.com/egyptian-militant-among-19-killed-in-kunar-province-of-afghanistan-02193.

[84] Arif Rafiq, "The Emergence of the Difa-e-Pakistan Islamist Coalition," CTC Sentinel, March 22, 2012.

[85] Richard Leiby, "Pakistani militant Hafiz Mohammad Saeed seeks protection from bounty hunters," Washington Post, April 22, 2012.

[86] Shubajit Roy and Amitabh Sinha, "Blood and Water Can't Flow Together, Says PM Modi at Indus Water Treaty Meeting, Govt Plans Cross-Border River Strategy," Indian Express, September 27, 2016, http://indianexpress.com/article/india/india-news-india/indus-water-sharing-treaty-india-pakistan-modi-border-security-underwater-sensor-uri-3051968/.

[87] Stephen Tankel, "Lashkar-e-Taiba, Mumbai, and the ISI," Foreign Policy, May 20, 2011.

[88] "Terror Goes Hi-Tech: Lashkar-e-Toiba Develops App for its Operations," Zee News, October 14, 2015, http://zeenews.india.com/news/india/terror-goes-hi-tech-lashkar-e-toiba-develops-app-for-its-operations_1809936.html

MUSLIM BROTHERHOOD

> **QUICK FACTS**
>
> Geographic Areas of Operation: Europe, Middle East and North Africa, North America, and Sub-Saharan Africa
>
> Numerical Strength (Members): Exact numbers unknown; estimated in the millions
>
> Leadership: Mohammad Morsi (Egypt), Mohammed Badie (Egypt), Mahmoud Ezzat (Egypt), Khairat al-Shater (Egypt), Mahmoud Ghozlan (Egypt), Ali Saddredine Bayanouni (Syria), Boudjerra Soltani (Algeria), Sheikh Sadeq Abdallah bin Al-Majed (Sudan), among others
>
> Religious Identification: Sunni Islam
>
> *Quick Facts Courtesy of The Clarion Project Special Report on The Muslim Brotherhood (2015)*

OVERVIEW

Founded in Egypt in 1928, the Muslim Brotherhood is one of the world's oldest, largest and most influential Sunni Islamist groups. In the first decades of its existence, the movement was actively involved in the efforts to drive the British out of Egypt, and it later participated in the 1948 war against the State of Israel's emergence. Its primary purpose, however, was creating an Islamic state in Egypt, which it hoped to use as a foothold to create a new caliphate. Following Gamal Abdel Nasser's assumption of power in Egypt in 1954, the Brotherhood was formally outlawed. President Anwar Sadat gradually permitted its reemergence during the 1970s, and in the decades that followed it was sometimes repressed and otherwise tolerated but always illegal. Throughout this period, the movement developed a wide network of social and religious charities and programs, expanding its influence across the entire Muslim world and beyond.

Simultaneously, it underwent key ideological evolutions, such as formally distancing itself from internal elements that were advocating the violent overthrow of non-Islamic regimes in the 1970s. This move, how-

ever, put the Brotherhood at odds with other Islamist movements, which continued to advocate violence. While the movement did not join the 2011 Arab Spring uprising until its fourth day, its involvement was ultimately pivotal. It was also a key beneficiary of President Hosni Mubarak's overthrow, after which it translated its traditional social influence into tangible political power. However, a year after a Muslim Brotherhood-dominated government led by Mohammad Morsi assumed power, the Egyptian military responded to massive protests by removing Morsi from office. The resulting (and ongoing) crackdown on the Brotherhood has severely degraded the group's leadership and capabilities inside Egypt.

History and Ideology

The *Jama'at al-Ikhwan al-Muslimin* (Society of the Muslim Brothers) was founded in 1928 by Hassan al-Banna, a young primary school teacher from the city of Isma'iliyya in southern Egypt.[1] In its original form, the Brotherhood was a religious, youth and educational group. It advocated moral reform and a revival of Islam in Egypt and the Middle East to combat what al-Banna viewed as Western-inspired secularization. Inspired by the thinking of Muslim scholars Muhammad Abdu (1849-1905), Rashid Rida (1865-1935) and Jamal al-Din al-Afghani (1839-1897), al-Banna was convinced that the process of "Westernization" had corrupted his fellow Muslims, and that secular sentiments were among the principal reasons for the decline of Islamic societies. He felt that the weaknesses of the Muslim world could only be cured by implementing Islam as an "all-embracing concept," meaning that Islamic principles as defined by the Brotherhood (or those educated according to the Brotherhood's theories) should govern every aspect of life.

Al-Banna envisioned the Brotherhood as a mechanism for promoting this vision throughout Egypt from the grassroots up. To this end, during the Brotherhood's early years, he focused on establishing Brotherhood offices and local organizational structures across Egypt, to promote the Brotherhood's vision. Al-Banna introduced a multi-stage process through which the Brotherhood would achieve its political goals: it would recruit individuals, whom it would indoctrinate throughout a process known as *tarbiya*; those individuals would then raise families that would lead Islamic lifestyles; these families would help promote the Brotherhood's vision in the society; once the society broadly embraced the Brotherhood's vision, it would implement its particular interpretation at the state level, until Egypt was an Islamic state; and once this process took place in multiple countries, they would all unify under the banner of a new caliphate.

Beyond outlining this process, Al-Banna focused on promoting unity within the group. The recruitment and indoctrination was therefore designed to weed out dissenters, and ensure that all members were committed to the Brotherhood's vision and was willing to follow its leaders' orders. He further rallied Egyptian Muslims around vague Islamist slogans, promising a "return to Islam" and assuring supporters that "the Qur'an is our constitution" and marshaled his supporters to populist causes such as resisting British rule in Egypt and opposing Zionism. While the process of becoming a Muslim Brother was quite rigid and the organization was, for much of its history, exclusivist, these slogans helped the Brotherhood develop a broader following even among non-members.

Al Banna outlined his vision through a series of epistles, including one titled "On Jihad." In this piece, Al Banna argued that too many Muslims were passively watching as their values were overcome by the brand of modernity that Westernization brought. He called supporters to invest themselves in pressing back against the tide of Westernization. However, al-Banna believed that *jihad* was not restricted to the struggle against *kuffar* (apostates), but was in fact a more comprehensive awakening of Muslim hearts and minds. In the 1930s, Al-Banna's opposition to British rule and influence found expression as his organization began to recruit followers who saw the appeal in its ideology on issues ranging from poverty and education to nationalism and the nascent Israeli-Palestinian conflict.

As the movement grew, it faced domestic repression. During this period, the group constructed an armed "secret apparatus," which sought to protect the organization but also used offensive violence. Al-Banna's relationship with this apparatus is disputed, but it was blamed for numerous violent incidents during the 1940s, including the 1948 assassination of the country's prime minister. Al-Banna himself was assassinated in February 1949, likely in retaliation.

After Al Banna's death, the government accelerated its repression of the group. Nearly 4,000 members were arrested in 1949, and most were not released from prison until after the Free Officers Revolution in 1952. Hassan Al Hudaiby, a judge, succeeded Al-Banna as the Brotherhood's leader, but struggled to control the organization because he lacked Al-Banna's charisma.

The Brotherhood collaborated with the military officers who ousted King Farouk during the 1952 Free Officers Revolution, and thus anticipated having influence in the new government. But after a brief period of cooperation, the Brotherhood was outlawed along with all other political parties. Following a failed assassination attempt in 1954, President Gamal Abdel Nasser escalated the crackdown on the organization, imprisoning most of its leadership, sending many Brothers into exile, and effectively eliminating it on the ground for much of the next two decades.

During this period, the most radical tendencies within the Brotherhood emerged, led by its chief ideologue, Sayyid Qutb, a literary critic whose brief stay in the United States repelled him from Western values. While in prison, Qutb wrote his manifesto *Milestones*, which has since inspired generations of violent *jihadis*. In *Milestones*, published in 1964, Qutb argued that the Muslim world had regressed to the pre-Islamic state of ignorance known as *jahiliyya*, and advocated *jihad* against *jahili* political and societal influences as a remedy. Qutb thereby cast contemporary Arab governments, including Egypt's, as non-Islamic, and urged his followers to take up arms against it. The Egyptian government responded by banning *Milestones* and executing Qutb in prison in 1966.

While the Brotherhood regards Qutb as a martyr and continues to teach his writings, it distanced itself from his most radical arguments. In this vein, during the late 1960s, Muslim Brothers in prison refuted Qutb's view that contemporary Arab governments were non-Islamic by promoting *Preachers Not Judges*, a pamphlet which was later attributed to the second leader of the Muslim Brotherhood, Hassan Hudaiby. In *Preachers Not Judges*, Hudaiby rejects violent *jihad* and envisions a greater role for the individual in ascertaining an Islamic path. Both Qutb and Hudaiby believed that governments not working in obedience with God's will interfered with an individual's ability to choose the right path in their pursuit of righteousness. Hudaiby, however, feared that violence would only further cloud the individual's ability to choose correctly. He thus advocated more gradual change that centered on education as the antidote for *jahiliyyah*.

In the decades that followed, Qutb and Hudaiby would represent competing trends both within the organization, as well as within the world of Islamism more broadly. Brotherhood "Qutbists" typically favored insularity and ideological purity, whereas those from the "Preachers Not Judges" stream favored outreach and even working with non-Islamists in pursuit of common short-term objectives. More importantly, though, those Islamists who favored Qutb's call for violent *jihad* gravitated towards *jihadi* movements, and represented the Brotherhood's main competitor within Islamism. These groups included al-Gamaa al-Islamiya and the Egyptian Islamic Jihad.

When President Anwar Sadat succeeded Nasser in 1970, he gradually gave greater freedom to Islamists, viewing them as useful for countering the socialist nationalist adherents to Nasserism who threatened his authority. This, combined with the upsurge in Islamist activity that followed the 1967 Arab-Israeli War, catalyzed an explosion of Islamist activity on university campuses. When Muslim Brothers were ultimately released from prison during the mid-1970s, they recruited from this new generation of Islamists in reestablishing the Brotherhood. For the most part, those who joined the Brotherhood during this period rejected violent *jihad* within Egypt, and this deepened the rift between the Brotherhood and *jihadist* organizations, the latter of which were implicated in Sadat's assassination in 1981.

Under President Hosni Mubarak, who succeeded Sadat, the Brotherhood remained an illegal organization but was permitted to participate in parliamentary elections as independents. It also used moments of relative freedom to expland its societal influence through its nationwide recruitment of Islamists and massive social services network. It first participated in elections in 1984, when it formed a coalition with the nationalist New Wafd Party, which won 58 parliamentary seats. Three years later, the Brotherhood aligned with the Socialist Labor Party and the resulting coalition won 60 seats.

The Brotherhood's success at the polls, however, often came at a price, as the Mubarak regime viewed its Islamist ideology and committed following as a significant threat, and thus repressed it to prevent it from gaining greater influence. In this vein, dozens of Muslim Brotherhood leaders were arrested and sentenced to five years in prison immediately prior to the 1995 elections, in which the Brotherhood only won one seat. Ten years later, after the Brotherhood won an impressive 88 of 444 contested seats in parliament, the regime began another major crackdown: two chief financiers – businessman Hassan Malek and deputy supreme guide Khairat al-Shater – were arrested and given seven-year sentences, and the 2007 constitutional amendments were designed to restrict religious parties from future elections.[2] Then, during the 2010 parliamentary elections, which were widely considered to be the most rigged in Egypt's history,[3] the regime's repression prevented the Brotherhood from winning any seats.

Fearing even greater repression, the Brotherhood initially stayed on the sidelines during the January 25, 2011 protests that began Egypt's version of the "Arab Spring". But when it appeared that the demonstrations would succeed, the organization mobilized its followers to participate in the pivotal January 28, 2011 "Friday of Rage" protests, during which Egypt's police force effectively collapsed.

GLOBAL REACH

Although banned and clandestine for most of its history, the Muslim Brotherhood has expanded throughout the Muslim world, especially in Egypt's neighboring countries—Lebanon, Syria, Iraq, Sudan, Jordan, and the Palestinian territories—as well as in the Arabian Peninsula (Saudi Arabia, Kuwait, Yemen, Oman, and Bahrain). The movement has also achieved global status by expanding well beyond its traditional Middle Eastern borders and into the West. For decades, these different offshoots have remained largely autonomous from their Egyptian base and independent from one another, making it inaccurate to characterize the Brotherhood as a coherent and homogenous organization.

The Brotherhood first began to spread its ideology throughout the Middle East in the 1930s, essentially as a response to Western colonial presence. In Palestine, the movement was established in 1935 by the brother of al-Banna himself, Abd al-Rahman, along with other figures such as Izz al-Din al-Qassam, who was one of the leaders of the armed resistance against the British.[4] At the time, the Brotherhood's activities were primarily of a social and religious nature, and included the creation of associations, schools and the establishment of mosques intended to "bring an Islamic generation up."[5] It was in 1987, in the context of the first *Intifada* (Palestinian uprising), that the Brotherhood politicized itself by founding the Islamic Resistance Movement – more commonly known as Hamas[6] – which in turn took on a greater military bent. In contrast, such politicization occurred earlier in countries like Syria and Jordan, where the Brotherhood became an opposition force to the regime in the first years after national independence.[7] The Islamic Action Front (IAF),[8] the Jordanian Brotherhood's political wing, is, for instance, the country's only established opposition party.

In Syria, after the 1963 Ba'athist coup, the Brotherhood became the main (Sunni) opposition force to the ruling (Shi'ite Alawite) Assad clan. The conflict quickly developed into an open armed struggle, culminating in the Hama uprising of 1982 that the regime brutally crushed, effectively eliminating the movement when it killed thousands of its members.[9] After that, the movement ceased to be active politically inside the country, and maintained only a skeletal support network there, as most of its leadership regrouped in exile.[10]

Since the beginning of the Syrian uprising in 2011, the Brotherhood has joined the anti-regime movement.[11] Led by former leader in exile Riyad al-Shaqfeh,[2] its members initially held the most seats within the Syrian National Council (SNC). Non-Islamists, however, objected to the Brotherhood's strength and the SNC has since been replaced by other opposition coalitions in which the Brotherhood has less influence. Syrian Muslim Brothers also chaired relief committees that distribute aid and money to the rebels. However, other Islamist groups have played a much greater role in the fighting, and at the time of this writing the Syrian Muslim Brotherhood is a bit player in the overall conflict.

In Jordan, the Brotherhood similarly positioned itself as a leading player in the 2011 anti-government protests and denouncing public corruption and poverty.[13] As in most other countries where the Brotherhood operates, however, the movement there seeks to change the system from within.[14] In Iraq, the Brotherhood-affiliated Iraqi Islamic Party was banned during the 1960s and forced underground by Saddam Hussein. It reemerged after the 2003 U.S.-led invasion, and has since displayed an ambiguous posture, voicing harsh criticism of the U.S. and Iraq's new political elites while still participating in the transitional process.[15]

In the Gulf, the Brotherhood has branches in several countries, most of which were established by Brothers who were driven out of Egypt in the 1950s. Many found shelter in Saudi Arabia, but their doctrine was seen as a challenge to that country's official Wahhabi creed. The movement was never allowed to deal with religious issues, and therefore invested its energies in the educational field as an alternate way of disseminating its ideology. This led to the emergence of movements like the "Awakening" (*Sahwa*), known for its support of rebellion against the Saudi leadership.[16]

Elsewhere, such as in the United Arab Emirates and Qatar, the Brotherhood relied on a strong intellectual and media presence to influence local populations.[17] With the exception of Oman, where the Brotherhood has faced severe crackdowns, the movement also managed to gain seats in parliaments across the region: in Kuwait via the *Hadas* movement;[18] in Yemen through Islah or the "Congregation for Reform;"[19] and in Bahrain through *Al-Minbar*, although this group has lost its prominence since the rise of Shi'ite opposition.[20]

In North Africa, the Brotherhood's expansion was also fueled by resentment of colonial rule. In Algeria, its members joined the uprising against the French during that country's war for independence before being marginalized by the secular FLN party. In the 1990s, the Algerian Brotherhood did not join *jihadist* factions in their fight against the state; instead, the group favored a peaceful resolution of the conflict and a return to democracy, even taking part in the coalition backing current president Abdelaziz Bouteflika in the early 2000s.[21] In Tunisia, the Brotherhood influenced Islamists, in particular *Ennahda* (the Renaissance Party) founded in 1989, whose leaders advocate democracy and pluralism "within an Islamist framework."[22] Formerly outlawed by the Ben Ali regime, *Ennahda* made a historic return in the wake of the 2011 "Jasmine Revolution"[23] and became a legal party, benefiting from considerable popular support in the parliamentary elections and winning 40 % of the votes. It later responded to resistance by ceding power and joining a transition process with Tunisia's other political forces, culminating with the election of a non-Islamist government. Domestic opposition to Islamism has forced *Ennahda* to downplay its Islamism, and in 2016 *Ennahda* leader Rachid Ghannouchi formally distanced the movement from political Islam, hinting that the movement would instead focus on outreach work (*dawa*).

In Morocco, the Justice and Development party also won the largest number of seats in the 2011 parliamentary election, gaining 27% of the votes and becoming the country's major opposition party. In Libya, the Brotherhood has maintained a presence since the 1940s when King Idris I offered Egyptian Brothers refuge from persecution. However, after seizing power in a coup, Muammar al-Qadhafi considered the Muslim Brothers a menace and actively worked to eliminate them. Despite this repression, the Brotherhood maintained a vast network of sympathizers in Libya.[24] The Party of Justice and Construction (the political arm of the Muslim brotherhood in Libya) has gained seats in the legislative body since Qadhafi's death.[25] Finally, in Sudan the Brotherhood enjoys a significant, though informal, presence, and has launched mass Islamization campaigns that have allowed its representatives to infiltrate virtually all state institutions.[26]

In addition to its traditional geographic reach, the Brotherhood has gained significant ground in Europe through regional forums like the Federation of Islamic Organizations in Europe, the Forum of European Muslim Youth and Student Organizations, and the European Council for Fatwa and Research.[27] Starting in the 1960s, members and sympathizers of the group moved to Europe and established a vast and sophisticated network of mosques and Islamic charities and schools, such as those in England (Muslim Association of Britain), France (Union des Organisations Islamiques de France), Germany (Islamische Gemeinschaft Deutschland), and Italy (Unione delle Comunita' ed Organizzazioni Islamiche in Italia).[28] With considerable foreign funding and the relative tolerance of European governments seeking to engage in a dialogue with Muslim minorities,[29] Brotherhood-related organizations have gained prominent positions on the Continent's sociopolitical scene, presenting themselves as the legitimate representatives of Muslim communities in Europe and "moderate" interlocutors for governments and the media.

In addition to its presence in Europe, the Brotherhood has also reached out to Muslims in the United States, where its members have been present since the 1960s. The movement launched its first long-term strategy there in 1975, focusing on proselytizing efforts and the creation of specific structures for youth and newly arrived Muslim immigrants. Seeking to exert political influence at the state and federal levels, Muslim Brothers have been represented in multiple religious organizations such as the Muslim Students' Association (MSA), the Islamic Society of North America (ISNA), the Islamic Circle of North America (ICNA), the Muslim American Society (MAS) and a variety of other activist groups. On May 22, 1991, the Brotherhood issued a programmatic memorandum titled "The General Strategic Objective for the [Brotherhood] in North America,"[30] which highlighted its goal to penetrate the heart of American society. The memorandum stated that all Muslims had to "understand that their work in America [was] a grand *jihad* in eliminating and destroying Western civilization from within and sabotaging its miserable house by their hands so that God's religion [Islam] is victorious over all religions."[31]

RECENT ACTIVITY

When Mubarak was ousted from power on February 11, 2011, the Brotherhood believed that the moment for it to transition from promoting its Islamism within the society to implementing it within the state had come, and it therefore formed a political party – the Freedom and Justice Party (FJP) – as its political vehicle. When a small segment of Brotherhood's youth opposed this sharp turn towards politics, the Brotherhood quickly banished them, thereby preventing fissures from forming within the organization. These Brotherhood youths later formed the Egyptian Current Party, which won zero seats in the 2011-2012 parliamentary elections. The Brotherhood's FJP, by contrast, anchored an alliance of eleven parties, which won more than 47 percent of the seats. The second largest bloc belonged to *Salafist* parties, which won approximately 24 percent of the seats.[32]

In the FJP-dominated parliament, Muslim Brothers held either the chairmanship or deputy chairmanship of 18 of 19 committees, Salafists MPs were granted the chairmanships of three committees, and Brotherhood leader Saad al-Katatny was appointed parliamentary speaker.[33] The core issue before this parliament was the selection of the Constituent Assembly, which was tasked with drafting Egypt's next constitution. Despite their differences, the Brotherhood and Salafists collaborated to select a Constituent Assembly that was approximately 65 percent Islamist. Non-Islamist Assembly members, as well as representatives from Al-Azhar, the judiciary, and the Coptic Church, responded by boycotting the Assembly, and a court ultimately disbanded it in April 2012, a mere two weeks after it was formed. The Brotherhood also used their dominance of the parliament to chip away at the SCAF's political legitimacy, and escalate what had been a dormant power struggle between the junta and the Islamists.[34] In March 2012, in response to the FJP's attempt to use the parliament to declare no confidence in the SCAF-backed government, the SCAF issued a statement that effectively threatened the Brotherhood with a crackdown akin to the Nasser days.[35]

This was one reason that the Brotherhood reneged on its prior pledge, made in February 2011, before Mubarak was overthrown, that it would not run a presidential candidate.[36] The second reason why it reneged was the emergence of former Muslim Brotherhood leader Abdel Moneim Abouel Fotouh as a leading presidential candidate as the May/June 2012 presidential elections approached. Abouel Fotouh had declared his intention to run in early 2011, and the Brotherhood banished him for doing so against its orders. The Brotherhood, however, feared that if it did not run a candidate, many of its members would ultimately vote for Abouel Fotouh, thereby rewarding someone who failed to follow the Brotherhood leaders' orders and threatening chaos in the Brotherhood's ranks.[37]

So in late March 2012, the Brotherhood announced that Khairat al-Shater, a wealthy businessman and senior member of the organization, would be the FJP's presidential candidate. Two weeks later, Shater was disqualified from running by the national electoral commission due to his prior imprisonment under Mubarak,[38] as were other leading contenders.[39] The Brotherhood, however, was prepared for this possibility and had already nominated FJP chairman Mohammed Morsi as a backup. The final list featured thirteen candidates, including Mubarak's former Prime Minister Ahmed Shafiq, Nasserist former parliamentarian Hamdeen Sabbahi, and former Foreign Minister Amr Moussa. The elections took place on May 23-24, 2012, with Morsi ultimately securing victory with 24 percent of the vote.[40] A month later, Morsi was named the winner of a run-off election against Shafik, in which he garnered 51.7 percent of the vote.[41]

Prior to winning the election, however, relations between the Brotherhood and the state institutions deteriorated further. On June 14, a court disbanded the FJP-controlled parliament, arguing that it had been elected unconstitutionally because the electoral format did not give an equal opportunity to political independents.[42] A few days later, in anticipation of a possible Morsi victory, the Supreme Court of Armed Forces, Egypt's highest military body, issued a constitutional declaration that protected the military from any future president's oversight and granted itself legislative authority. As a result, the Brotherhood and its allies occupied Tahrir Square before the presidential elections results were announced, threatening chaos if Morsi was not named Egypt's next president.

The SCAF's constitutional declaration meant that when Morsi was sworn in on June 30, 2012, there was no parliament, no new constitution, and his precise powers were undefined. On August 12, however, Morsi used a major attack in the Sinai the previous week as a pretext for firing the SCAF's leaders, promoting director of military intelligence[43] Abdel Fatah al-Sisi to defense minister, and issuing a new constitutional declaration granting himself legislative power until a new parliament was sworn in.[44]

This action made Morsi Egypt's undisputed power holder, at least legally. But in November 2012, it appeared as though a second Constituent Assembly, which parliament had appointed before it was disbanded in June, was going to be nullified by the courts just as the first one had been. Morsi responded by issuing another constitutional declaration that protected the Constituent Assembly from the courts, but also placed his own edicts above any judicial oversight. It was effectively a total power grab, and when mass protests broke out, Morsi used the ensuing political crisis to ram a theocratic constitution through to ratification.

While the new constitution passed by 64 percent through referendum, the political crisis persisted for months, with increasingly violent protests against Morsi erupting with greater regularity. Meanwhile, the economy plummeted, lines for gas extended around city blocks, and power shortages created outages lasting many hours on end.[45] As a result, on June 30, 2013, millions of Egyptians took to the streets to demand Morsi's removal. When Morsi refused to compromise, the military responded by ousting him on July 3, 2013.

In the wake of the coup, the Brotherhood gathered is members and allies in northern Cairo's Rabaa al-Adawiya Square and Giza's al-Nahda Square. Protesters denounced the interim government installed to replace Morsi as illegitimate. After negotiations between the new government and the Brotherhood broke down, security forces violently cleared these protests on August 14, 2013, killing at least 800 civilians, according to Human Rights Watch.[46]

After the Rabaa massacre, the government arrested tens of thousands of Brotherhood leaders and supporters. Then, following a massive terrorist incident in al-Mansoura in December 2013, the government labeled the Muslim Brotherhood as a terrorist group.[47] Ultimately the government's crackdown on the Brotherhood appears to have been successful: with its leaders in prison, exile, or hiding, the organization has been decapitated, rendering it incapable of executing a nationwide strategy within Egypt. Meanwhile, the Brotherhood faces a significant internal crisis pitting younger members, who want to fight the current government with violence, against older leaders, who fear that Brotherhood violence will legitimate the regime's crackdown.[48] The Brotherhood youth's wing appears to have won internal elections that were held in 2014, which explains the Brotherhood's January 2015 statement calling for jihad and martyrdom in fighting the regime. But the "old guard" has rejected these elections, creating a rift that has not been resolved as of this writing. While deputy supreme guide Mahmoud Ezzat, who heads the "old guard" faction, called for reunifying the organization (presumably under his leadership), its youth-oriented "revolutionary" faction appeared to consolidate its power with new elections in late 2015, after which some of its older members resigned from their leadership posts.[49]

Due to these internal disagreements as well as the Egyptian government's repression of it, the Brotherhood no longer represents a significant threat to the current regime. While some Brotherhood sympathizers formed militant groups that have targeted security forces and state infrastructure, such as Revolutionary Punishment and Hasm, these groups have failed in their goals of destabilizing the Egyptian regime. The regime has sought to prevent the Brotherhood's possible reemergence by shutting down its social services activities and implementing strict restrictions on mosque preaching. In this vein, in mid-2016, the Egyptian government mandated that imams read government-approved sermons in Friday prayers. This edict was also intended to constrain Salafist , despite the fact that the leading Salafist party – the Light Party – supported Morsi's overthrow and is the only Islamist group still participating in Egyptian politics.

ENDNOTES

[1] For an overview of the Muslim Brotherhood's core ideology, see Hassan al-Banna's writings and memoirs, particularly the Letter To A Muslim Student, which develops the main principles of the movement. For the English translation, see http://www.jannah.org/articles/letter.html; see also Brynjar Lia, The Society of the Muslim Brothers in Egypt: The Rise of an Islamic Mass Movement, 1928-1942 (New York; Ithaca Press, 1998) and Richard Paul Mitchell, The Society of the Muslim Brothers (London & New York: Oxford University Press, 1969).

[2] Nathan J. Brown and others, "Egypt's Controversial Constitutional Amendments," The Carnegie Endowment for International Peace (23 Mar. 2007): <http://carnegieendowment.org/files/egypt_constitution_webcommentary01.pdf>.

[3] Josh Stacher, Adaptable Autocrats: Regime Power in Egypt and Syria (Stanford: Stanford University Press, 2012) 7.

[4] Amnon Cohen, Political Parties in the West Bank under the Jordanian Regime, 1949–1967 (Ithaca, NY: Cornell University Press, 1982).

[5] Ziad Abu-Amr, "Hamas: A Historical and Political Background," Journal of Palestine Studies 22, no. 4, Summer 1993, 5-19.

[6] See the Palestinian Territories chapter of the American Foreign Policy Council's World Almanac of Islamism.

[7] Robin Wright, Dreams and Shadows: the Future of the Middle East (New York: Penguin Press, 2008); Olivier Carré and Gérard Michaud, Les Frères musulmans: Egypte et Syrie (1928–1982) [The Muslim Brothers: Egypt and Syria (1928-1982)] (Paris: Gallimard, 1983).

[8] Jillian Schwedler, Faith in Moderation: Islamist Parties in Jordan and Yemen (Cambridge: Cambridge University Press, 2006).

[9] See the Syria chapter of the American Foreign Policy Council's World Almanac of Islamism.

[10] Radwan Ziadeh, "The Muslim Brotherhood in Syria and the Concept of Democracy," Paper presented at CSID's 9th Annual Conference, May 14, 2008, https://www.csidonline.org/9th_annual_conf/Radwan_Ziadeh_CSID_paper.pdf.

[11] Khaled Yacoub Oweis, "Syria's Muslim Brotherhood rise from the ashes," Reuters, May 6, 2012, http://www.reuters.com/article/2012/05/06/us-syria-brotherhood-idUSBRE84504R20120506.

[12] Youssef Sheikho, "The Syrian Opposition's Muslim Brotherhood Problem," Al-Akhbar (Cairo), April 10, 2013, http://english.al-akhbar.com/node/15492.

[13] Heather Murdock, "Muslim Brotherhood Sees Opportunity in Jordan," Washington Times, March 1, 2011, http://www.washingtontimes.com/news/2011/mar/1/muslim-brotherhood-sees-opportunity-in-jordan/.

[14] Curtis R. Ryan, "Islamist Political Activism in Jordan: Moderation, Militancy and Democracy," Middle East Review of International Affairs 12, no. 2, June 2008, 1-13, http://www.gloria-center.org/2008/06/ryan-2008-06-01/.

[15] See the Iraq chapter of the American Foreign Policy Council's World Almanac of Islamism; for further details, see "Iraqi Islamic Party," globalsecurity.org, n.d., http://www.globalsecurity.org/military/world/iraq/iip.htm.

[16] Toby Craig Jones, "The Clerics, the Sahwa and the Saudi State," Center for Contemporary Conflict Strategic Insights 4, no. 3, March 2005, http://kms1.isn.ethz.ch/serviceengine/Files/ISN/34006/ichaptersection_singledocument/90678113-7f09-49dc-8c77-e546acacb75a/en/jonesmar05.pdf.

[17] See the United Arab Emirates and Qatar chapters of the American Foreign Policy Council's World Almanac of Islamism.

[18] See the Kuwait chapter of the American Foreign Policy Council's World Almanac of Islamism.

[19] See the Yemen chapter of the American Foreign Policy Council's World Almanac of Islamism; Amr Hamzawy, "Between Government and Opposition: The Case of the Yemeni Congregation for Reform," Carnegie Endowment for International Peace Carnegie Papers no. 18, November 2009, http://www.carnegieendowment.org/files/yemeni_congragation_reform.pdf.

[20] Kenneth Katzman, Bahrain: Reform, Security, and U.S. Policy (Congressional Research Service, September 2013), http://www.fas.org/sgp/crs/mideast/95-1013.pdf.

[21] "Islamism, Violence and Reform in Algeria: Turning the Page," International Crisis Group Middle East Report no. 29, July 30, 2004, http://www.crisisgroup.org/en/regions/middle-east-north-africa/north-africa/algeria/029-islamism-violence-and-reform-in-algeria-turning-the-page.aspx.

[22] See the Tunisia chapter of the American Foreign Policy Council's World Almanac of Islamism; Rajaa Basly, "The Future of al-Nahda in Tunisia," Carnegie Endowment for International Peace Arab Reform Bulletin, April 20, 2011, http://www.carnegieendowment.org/arb/?fa=show&article=43675.

[23] "As Tunisians Cheer Egypt, Islamist Leader Returns," NPR, January 30, 2011, http://www.gpb.org/news/2011/01/30/as-tunisians-cheer-egypt-islamist-leader-returns?utm_source=feedburner&utm_medium=feed&utm_campaign=Feed%3A+GPBNewsFeed+%28GPB+News%29.

[24] Paul Cruickshank and Tim Lister, "Energized Muslim Brotherhood in Libya Eyes a Prize," CNN, March 25, 2011, http://articles.cnn.com/2011-03-25/world/libya.islamists_1_moammar-gadhafi-libyan-regime-benghazi?_s=PM:WORLD.

[25] "Libya Muslim Brotherhood mulls Cabinet Withdrawal," Agence France-Presse, September 12, 2013, http://english.alarabiya.net/en/News/middle-east/2013/09/12/Libya-Muslim-Brotherhood-mulls-Cabinet-withdrawal-.html.

[26] Gabriel R. Warburg, "The Muslim Brotherhood in Sudan: From Reforms to Radicalism," Project for the Research of Islamist Movements (PRISM), August 2006, http://www.e-prism.org/images/Muslim_BROTHERS.PRISM.pdf.

[27] Lorenzo Vidino, "The Muslim Brotherhood's Conquest of Europe," Middle East Quarterly XII, no. 1 (Winter 2005), 25-34, http://www.meforum.org/687/the-muslim-brotherhoods-conquest-of-europe.

[28] Ibid.

[29] Ibidem.

[30] Douglas Farah, Ron Sandee and Josh Lefkowitz, "The Muslim Brotherhood in the United States: A Brief History," NEFA Foundation, October 26, 2007, http://counterterrorismblog.org/upload/2007/12/nefaikhwan1007%5B1%5D.pdf.

[31] Ibid.

[32] Eric Trager, Arab Fall: How the Muslim Brotherhood Won and Lost Egypt in 891 Days (Washington: Georgetown University Press, 2016) 107.

[33] Sherif Tarek, "El-Katatni: From prisoner to speaker of parliament," Ahram Online (Cairo), January 24, 2012, http://english.ahram.org.eg/NewsContent/1/0/32600/Egypt//ElKatatni-from-prisoner-to-speaker-of-parliament.aspx.

[34] Trager (2016) 122-124.
[35] Trager (2016) 126.
[36] Trager (2016) 127-130.
[37] Trager (2016) 127-130.
[38] According to a rule banning candidates with prior criminal convictions from running in the elections. See Jeffrey Fleishman, "Egypt disqualifies 3 leading presidential candidates," Los Angeles Times, April 14, 2012, http://articles.latimes.com/2012/apr/14/world/la-fg-egypt-candidates-20120415.
[39] "Muslim Brotherhood and Salafists excluded from presidential poll," Asia News, April 16, 2012, http://www.asianews.it/news-en/Muslim-Brotherhood-and-Salafists-excluded-from-presidential-poll-24512.html.
[40] Although some contest the electoral results. see Borzou Daragahi, "Egypt nervously awaits election results," Financial Times, June 22, 2012, http://www.ft.com/cms/s/0/a17de564-bc5b-11e1-a470-00144feabdc0.html#axzz21WobfdCf.
[41] Trager (2016) 136-137.
[42] Trager (2016) 140-141.
[43] Trager (2016) 158-159.
[44] Trager (2016) 159-161.
[45] Trager (2016) 212.
[46] Ali Omar, "Muslim Brotherhood responds to NCHR Rabaa report," Daily News Egypt, March 8, 2014, http://www.dailynewsegypt.com/2014/03/08/muslim-brotherhood-responds-nchr-rabaa-report/.
[47] Salma Abdelaziz and Steve Almasy, "Egypt's interim Cabinet officially labels Muslim Brotherhood a terrorist group," CNN, December 25, 2013, http://www.cnn.com/2013/12/25/world/africa/egypt-muslim-brotherhood-terrorism/.
[48] Eric Trager and Marina Shalabi, "The Brotherhood Breaks Down: Will the Group Survive the Latest Blow?" Foreign Affairs (17 Jan. 2016): <https://www.foreignaffairs.com/articles/egypt/2016-01-17/brotherhood-breaks-down>.
[49] Amr Darrag, "Statement of My Retirement from Political Work," Facebook, December 22, 2016, https://www.facebook.com/amr.darrag.9/posts/1188793107837161.

TABLIGHI JAMAA'T

QUICK FACTS

Geographical Areas of Operation: East Asia, Eurasia, Europe, the Middle East and North Africa, South Asia, and Sub-Saharan Africa

Numerical Strength (Members): Estimated from 70 to 80 million

Religious Identification: Sunni Islam

OVERVIEW

Tablighi Jama`at, or "[Islamic] transmission group," is a vast, transnational Islamic propagation and re-pietization organization. It is estimated to be active in at least 165 nations throughout the world. Its annual assembly in Tongi, Bangladesh, is larger than any other in the Islamic world except for the Hajj itself,[1] and estimates of TJ's membership range from 12 to 80 million.[2] Officially apolitical and preferring word-of-mouth instruction to public written or online communiqués, TJ has heretofore flown largely under the analytical radar, unlike other pan-Islamic groups such as Hizb ut-Tahrir and the Muslim Brotherhood, which are much more political, higher-profile and overt. But TJ's global presence and growing influence in both Muslim and non-Muslim majority countries make it arguably the modern world's most dynamic Islamist group.

HISTORY AND IDEOLOGY

Tablighi Jama'at, or TJ, began in British-ruled India, emerging from the Islamic Deoband movement active in South Asia.[3] From its inception in 1867, the Deoband movement fused some aspects of Sufism with the study of the *hadith* and strict adherence to *sharia*, as well as advocating non-state-sponsored Islamic *da`wah* (missionary activity).[4] In the late 19th and early 20th centuries, the Muslim minority in British India felt itself caught between the resurgent Hindu majority and the small but British-supported Christian missionary agenda.

TJ's founder, Mawlana Muhammad Ilyas (1885-1944), graduated from the central Deoband *madrassa* in 1910 and, while working among the Muslim masses of Mewat, India (just south of Delhi) came to question whether education alone could renew Islam.[5] He eventually decided that "only through physical movement away from one's place could one leave behind one's esteem for life and its comforts for the cause of God."[6] Indeed, some have even described his movement, TJ, as the missionary arm of the Deobandis.[7] Other Muslim groups in the subcontinent, notably the Barelvis,[8] had previously developed the idea of itinerant missionary work—*tabligh*[9]—in order to counter Hindu (and Christian) conversions of Muslims, but it was Ilyas' genius to teach that *tabligh* should be the responsibility of each and every individual (male) Muslim.[10] He aimed to recapitulate the alleged piety and practice of Muhammad and his companions in the 7th century A.D., and as such was concerned not just with Hindu or Christian inroads into the Muslim community but with stemming the rising tide of Westernization and secularization. Unlike other contemporary Islamic renewers, Ilyas did not believe that Islam could be reconciled with Western science, technology and political ideologies.[11]

In the mid-1920s, Ilyas enjoined upon his followers the practice of *gasht*, "rounds" in Persian: going to those Muslims who lived near a mosque and summoning them to Quran study and prayer. By the mid-1930s, Ilywas was promulgating a more detailed program of belief and praxis. This new doctrine went beyond the five pillars of Islam[12] and belief in the usual Islamic doctrinal staples,[13] to include:

- Islamic education (especially of children, at home),
- Modest Islamic dress and appearance (shaving the moustache and allowing the beard to grow long),
- Rejection of other religions,
- High regard for other Muslims and protecting their honor,
- Propagating Islam,
- Self-financing of tabligh trips,
- Lawful means of earning a living, and
- Strict avoidance of divisive and sectarian issues.[14]

The missionary procedure of TJ incursion into new territories follows a regular pattern. An initial "probing mission" is followed by TJ entrenchment into several local mosques which are increasingly controlled by the organization and eventually either taken over by TJ or, barring that, supplanted by TJ-built or -controlled mosques.[15] From these mosques, the TJ teams teach their beliefs and practices to local Muslims, initially approaching local religious leaders, then intellectuals and professionals, followed by businessmen and, finally, conducting outreach to the general Muslim community.[16]

There is a typology of Islamic renewal/reform movements as either 1) emulative (adopters of Western ideas); 2) assimilationist (attempting to reconcile Islamic and

Western concepts and practices); or 3) rejectionist (allowing only strictly Islamic answers to the challenges of personal and collective life).[17] *Tablighi Jama`at* is clearly in the last category, based on its promulgation of strict adherence to the Quran and *sharia*, as well as its emphasis on emulating the lifestyle of Islam's founder, Muhammad. However, while undeniably conservative, even puritanical, whether TJ serves as an incubator for *jihad* remains the subject of some debate.

The movement teaches *jihad* primarily as personal purification rather than as holy warfare.[18] This may be because, following Deobandi doctrine, TJ takes the utilitarian approach that martial *jihad* is not wise when the *umma* is weak, rather than because it disavows violent *jihad* altogether.[19] In any event, because TJ eschews *jihad* of the sword currently, it has met with the disapproval of Saudi clerics, with TJ missionaries banned from preaching in the Kingdom of Saudi Arabia and a number of online Wahhabi *fatwas* listing TJ as a "deviant" group, alongside Shi`ites.[20] However, practical connections between TJ practitioners and acts of terror (such as the 1998 attacks in Dar es Salaam, Tanzania and Nairobi, Kenya), as well as anecdotal evidence that Ilyas himself believed he was "preparing soldiers" for *jihad*,[21] paint a more complex—and possibly threatening—picture of the organization.

The available data today indicates that TJ, at least in the preponderance of locations around the world where it is found, can be considered *ipso facto* a passive supporter of *jihadist* groups via its reinforcement of strict Islamic norms, intolerance of other religious traditions and unwavering commitment to Islamizing the entire planet. TJ is thus both like and unlike its major transnational Islamic rivals: *Hizb al-Tahrir* (HuT) (dedicated to re-establishing the Caliphate); the Muslim Brotherhood (focused on expanding *sharia*'s scope in both the Muslim and non-Muslim world); and the Gülen Movement (devoted to re-establishing Turkish power in the Islamic, and greater, world in order to advance Islam). TJ is much less political than any of these organizations, and much more focused on personal Muslim piety. However, its eschewal of politics (at least publicly) has enabled TJ, in most places, to escape suppression by wary government organs. Whether TJ ever decides to risk this situation of state tolerance by transforming into an active supporter of *jihadist* movements remains to be seen.

Global Reach

Under Mawlana Yusuf, Ilyas' son, TJ expanded out of India and Pakistan to much of the rest of the world, and expanded its mission from simply re-pietizing Muslims to undertaking efforts to convert non-Muslims to Islam.[22] Most of the Muslim-majority nations of the world saw the infusion of some TJ presence between the end of World War II and the 1960s, with the exception of Soviet Central Asia.[23] It would not be until the end of the Cold War, post-1991, that the "Stans" opened up to TJ teams. TJ has been perhaps most successful in Africa, where it is at work in at least 35 of the continent's 52 countries.[24]

Africa

Gambia, in West Africa (whose 1.5 million people are 90 percent Muslim), may be the hub of TJ activity in that part of the continent.[25] First established in Gambia in the 1960s, TJ's popularity there was limited until the 1990s, when its missionaries' knowledge of English (spoken prevalently in Gambia as well as in India and Pakistan) and the global Islamic resurgence made many Gambian Muslims, especially Gambian youth, more receptive to the organization's agenda. Currently, some 13,000 Gambians are estimated to be involved with TJ. Some Gambian Muslim leaders, steeped in West Africa's heavily Sufi tradition, have expressed fears of TJ coming to dominate the country.[26]

In 99-percent-Muslim Morocco, TJ was introduced in 1960 under the name *Jama`at al-Tabligh wa-al-Da`wah* (JTD), although it was not recognized by the government until 1975.[27] While proselytizing to Moroccan Muslims to re-Islamize their lives, JTD also makes hospital calls upon sick Muslims. But TJ's main focus is on increasing ritualized conduct—persuading Moroccans to eat, drink, prepare for bed and sleep, go to the market, and bathe in the proper ways, emulating the Prophet Muhammad.

TJ has also committed a number of teams to Mali, Mauritania and Niger,[28] a three-country region of some 26 million people, the vast majority of them Muslim. The local version of Islam was more aligned with Sufism, but by the late 1990s, TJ had a substantial presence.[29] Shortly after 9/11, the government of Mali extradited 25 TJ members.[30] This crackdown did little to slow the group's growth in the region, particularly among the Touareg tribal leaders, who in turn have hastened to point out that the group's activities are totally unconnected to global *jihad*.[31] As the Toaureg's long-running rebellion exploded into a civil war in 2012, the impact of TJ's Salafist inroads became evident. Alongside the traditional Touareg separatist group Mouvement National Pour la Liberation de l'Azawad (MNLA) the Islamist Ansar ud-Dine (Defenders of the Faith) emerged. Ansar ud-Dine began establishing harsh Sharia law in areas it controlled including the historic city of Timbuktu, it also allied with al-Qaeda of the Islamic Maghreb.[32] Mali's Islamists were pushed back when the French intervened, but they have continud their violent campaign with high-profile attacks throughout the country. In March 2017, the leader of Ansar ud-Dine, Iyad Ag Ghaly, appeared in a video where he appeared to be the leader of a new coalition of Islamist terrorist groups that pledged their allegiance to al-Qaeda.[33] Iyad Ag Ghaly had been a Toaureg tribal leader and diplomat, known for his drinking and corousing. In the early 1990s he encountered TJ missionaries and then travelled to Pakistan where he became devout began his path to radicalism.[34]

South Africa has also become a focal point for TJ's work, despite the fact that 85 percent of its population of 55 million is Christian.[35] South Africa shares a legacy of British rule with India and Pakistan, and some two million of its people are of South Asian origin, of whom perhaps half are Muslim. TJ's "Sufi-lite" orientation and its Deoband origins give it legitimacy with many South African Muslims—although the more *Salafi/Wahhabi* groups dislike any hint of Sufism and denigrate TJ for "un-Islamic" practices such as asking for Muhammad's intercession and promoting the reading of other books in tandem with the Quran. Many Muslims in South Africa, encouraged by TJ, also became disenchanted with majority Christian rule after rules were relaxed on abortion, prostitution and other "immoral" activities. TJ appears to have contributed to, and possibly sparked, the polarization of the Muslim community in Africa's southernmost country.[36]

TJ also has a significant presence in Eastern Africa. This is partly because of geographical proximity to the subcontinent but also because, like South Africa, there are substantial expatriate Indian and Pakistani communities there, particularly in Tanzania, Kenya and Uganda. Perhaps one-third of Tanzania's population of 52 million is Muslim (but over 90 percent of the population on the islands of Zanzibar[37] and Pemba is Muslim). Kenya is home to about five million Muslims (out of a population of over 46 million, mostly Christian) and the majority of Uganda's 38-million-people is Christian, with almost 14 percent of the population Muslim.[38] The founder of Uganda's Allied Democratic Force, a Muslim separatist group that straddles the border between Uganda and the Demorcatic Republic of Congo (DRC), Jamil Mukulu converted to Islam under the auspices of TJ. Founded in 1989, in recent years the groups presence in the Eastern DRC has grown and they have been responsible for large-scale massacres. They are also linked to al-Shabaab in Somalia.[39]

But TJ has been most visible in Tanzania, particularly on Zanzibar, where its message of "return to Islam" has been received as complementary to *Wahhabi/Salafi* ideology. These two strains of Islamic renewal have come together in the preaching of militant TJ members such as Zahor Issa Omar, who, from his base on Pemba, travels to mainland Tanzania, Kenya and Uganda to advocate *jihad*, reportedly supported by Saudi *Wahhabi* money and even *khutbah* ("sermon") outlines.[40] More traditionalist Tanzanian Muslim leaders consider TJ to be an intruder bringing a foreign brand of Islam, mainly because of the group's opposition to full-blown Sufism.[41] There are anecdotal claims that TJ serves as a conveyor belt, at least indirectly, to Islamic terrorism.[42] Two of the al-Qaeda terrorists indicted in the 1998 bombings of the U.S. embassies in Dar es Salaam and Nairobi—Khalfan Khamis Mohammad and Ahmed Khalfan Ghailani—were Zanzibaris previously involved with TJ.[43]

There is conflicting data on the relationship between the neo-*Wahhabi* al-Shabaab militia which controls much of southern and central Somalia and TJ. In 2009, a story surfaced that al-Shabaab had attacked a TJ mosque, killing at least five of its members.[44] However, in mid-2010 Indian media cited at least one terrorism analyst who claimed that TJ "has been very active in Somalia, including sending terror fighters to Al Shabaab."[45] TJ members have continued to be attacked by al-Shabaab, although TJ may continue to act as an inadverdent feeder to the more violent group. Regardless, there are numerous reports indicating an extensive TJ presence in Somalia through at least 2015.[46]

Southeast Asia

Aside from Africa, one of TJ's major theaters of operations has been Southeast Asia—so much so, in fact, that the organization's members active in the region no longer use Urdu or Hindi to communicate, but rather rely on the Malay or Indonesian languages.[47] TJ has been active in Indonesia since 1952, and in its far-eastern province of Irian Jaya (West Papua, the western half of the island of New Guinea) since 1988.[48] Originally a phenomenon of the large urban areas' working classes there, it has increasingly penetrated the smaller cities, towns and villages.[49]

TJ has tried, with limited success, to exploit the Jakarta-supported transmigration of thousands of Muslims from the rest of Indonesia to heavily-Christian West Papua; as of 2009, only perhaps 1,000 Muslims had joined TJ there.[50] TJ teams are stymied by indigenous Papu customs (especially the affinity for pork) and the large Christian missionary presence.[51] More recent reports show little headway. The efforts in West Papua are an experiment, as TJ proselytizing focuses primarily on Muslims and in areas with large Muslim communities. TJ's risk averse apolitical approach appears to hamper its efforts in West Papua because more aggressive efforts to win converts might trigger backlash in the delicate ethnic and religious environment.[52]

TJ has, counterintuitively, been more successful in majority-Buddhist Thailand.[53] In 2003, some 100,000 Muslims from Southeast and South Asia came to a mass TJ gathering at Tha Sala in Nakhon Si Thammarat province.[54] In two decades, TJ has made inroads not only among the five percent of the country's 66 million citizens who are Muslim, but even among Buddhists—one effective strategy has been to play up the Sufi, mystical side of TJ while also practicing asceticism similar to that of Buddhist monks. However, TJ activities have also polarized the Thai Muslim communities; many traditionalist Muslims dislike the long absence of husbands and fathers on TJ mission treks, while more modernist Muslims denigrate TJ members as "fanatic *mullahs*" who neglect their families and have given up on the world. However, TJ in Thailand gives every indication of being well on its way to creating an independent mosque network that can serve as an alternative to the existing national Muslim association created by the Thai government. While TJ has continued to proselytize, when Islamist violence flared up in southern Thailand after 2004, leading to communal conflict, the number of Arab and South Asian TJ missionaries visiting Thailand declined dramatically.[55]

The Indian Subcontinent

The heart of TJ activities is in the Indian subcontinent, where it was founded. In Pakistan the group has obtained significant prominence. In the 1980s, as part of his

Islamization campaign, Pakistan's President, General Zia al-Haq, attended TJ annual conclave in Raiwind (Pakistan's largest Sunni gathering, attended by by hundreds of thousands.)[56] General Javed Nasir, director of Pakistan's all-powerful Inter-Services Intelligence for a year in the early 1990s, was an open member of TJ who expanded ISI engagement with religious extremists, including supporting TJ proselyitizing in Chechnya, Dagestan, and Xinjiang.[57] Nasir was forced into retirement as a result of U.S. pressure.[58]

Pakistan is one of the world's centers of radical Islam and home to numerous terrorist organizations. There is significant cross-fertilization between TJ and these groups. While TJ's leadership insists that it eschews violence and rejects efforts by terrorist groups to infiltrate their ranks, there is significant evidence of groups like *Lashkar-e-Taiba* and *Lashkar-e-Jhangvi* attempting to recruit from TJ's ranks.[59] There are also reports that *Harkat-al-Mujahedin*, a Pakistani terrorist group active in the Kashmir battle was founded by TJ members and that thousands of TJ members have trained in its camps.[60] Recent stories suggest that the Pakistani Taliban are using death threats and kidnappings to force singers and actors to renounce their former professions and join TJ —indicating, if true, a troublesome intersection between South Asian Islamic militancy and ostensibly peaceful Islamic missionaries.[61]

The United States and Europe

In the West, there may be as many as 150,000 TJ members in Europe, mainly in the UK (where they tend to be of South Asian descent) and France and Spain (where TJ members from North Africa predominate).[62] TJ's European headquarters is at the Markazi Mosque in Dewsbury, in the British Midlands.[63] In February 2016 Hafiz Patel, who had been the leader of TJ in Europe for decades died. In 1978 he established the mosque in Dewsbury. Under Patel's influence TJ has been a dominant influence in shaping Islam in the UK.[64]

In 2007 TJ in the UK announced plans to build a "megamosque" with room for over 10,000 worshippers and 190 foot high minarets. The site was adjacent to the site of the London 2012 games and engendered substantial community opposition. The plan was rejected by the local government and then TJ appleaed. Finally in 2015 the government made a final decision to block the proposed project.[65]

In the United States, some analysts claim that there may be as many as 50,000 Muslims affiliated with TJ,[66] and that the influential Islamic Circle of North America (ICNA) cooperates with, and hosts, TJ teams and activities.[67] TJ's North American headquarters is alleged to be either at the al-Falah Mosque in Queens, New York,[68] or at the Masjid al-Noor in Chicago.[69]

There have been numerous cases of Western recruits to al-Qaeda who had links to TJ. In the early 2000s, French intelligence asserted that about 80% of French radical Islamists were from the ranks TJ. Two of the London subway bombers and Richard Reid (the shoe bomber) both had been involved in TJ. A number of prominent American Muslims have been linked to TJ (including "American Taliban" John Walker Lindh, the "Lackawanna Six" and al-Qaeda operative José Padilla).[70] Simlarly in the United Kingdon, Mohammed Siddique Khan and Shehzad Tanweer, two of the London Subway bombers, began their path to Islamic extremism at the TJ mosque in Dewsbury. But they left that mosque because they found it apolitical and were exposed to calls for violent *jihad* elsewhere.[71]

The extent of TJ's role in the radicalization process is not clear. Lindh initially converted to Islam under the auspices of TJ, but in Pakistan left them to join the Taliban. The Lackawanna Six, Yemeni-Americans who travelled to Afghanistan and fight with the Taliban (and who were disillusioned with bin Laden and returned to the U.S.) claimed to be members of TJ going to study in Pakistan. However, they were not affiliated with the organization.[72]

Recent Activity

Upon Mawlana Yusuf's death in 1965, Ilyas' grand-nephew Mawlana In`am al-Hasan assumed leadership of TJ, and subsequently directed the group's activities for the following three decades. Then, beginning in 1995, and for the next decade or so, the organization was supervised by a collective leadership based at Nizamuddin, New Delhi and consisting of Mawlana Sa`d al-Hasan (grandson of Yusuf), Zubayr al-Hasan (son of In`am) and Izhar al-Hasan (another relative of Ilyas').[73] In recent years, Mawlana Sa`d has moved to the fore, once again giving TJ a single spiritual leader.[74] Yet it is also noteworthy that the world's most famous TJ personality, officially, is not Sa`d but the group's *emir* in Pakistan, Hajji Muhammad Abd al-Wahhab—who, according to Oman's Royal Islamic Strategic Studies Centre, is the 16th most influential Muslim in the world.[75]

Despite the fact that "the Tablighis have apparently moved from a fringe phenomenon to the mainstream of Muslim society in South Asia,"[76] they engender no small measure of opposition from other Muslims on their home ground. From one side, TJ is attacked by Barelvis, whose mystical Sufi leadership deems the group "a thinly disguised front for the Wahhabis"[77] and has orchestrated armed attacks on TJ members. Some Barelvi propagandists even accuse TJ of being a tool of the British, Americans and Indians, employed to drain Muslims of *jihadist* zeal.[78] From the other side, the Ahl-i Hadith groups charge TJ with abandoning the concrete concerns of the world for a vacuous mysticism.[79] And Jama`at-i Islami, the Islamic political organization established by Sayyid Abu ala `Ali Mawdudi, considers TJ a threat to its own powerful position in Pakistani society, and disparages TJ's alleged lukewarm attitude toward establishing a caliphate.[80] At least some Islamic groups outside of South Asia appear even more ill-disposed toward TJ, evidenced by the fact that in October 2010 Pakistani intelligence was reporting that "four foreign militants have been assigned by their commanders to assassinate two prominent leaders of Tablighi Jamaat."[81]

TJ does not always succeed in its attempts at winning foreign hearts and minds for strict Sunni Islam. In early 2010, almost a hundred members of the organization were arrested in Tajikistan and given lengthy jail sentences for running afoul of that country's laws against miscreant versions of Islam.[82] While in nearby Kazakhstan there have been numerous instances of TJ members being arrested for advocating extremism, although human rights groups accuse that government of repressing the exercise of religious activity in order to marginalize any potential opposition.[83]

Perhaps the most significant question about TJ is the extent of its role in leading followers to violent extremism. As described above, there have been several incidences of violent Islamists who started their path with TJ.

TJ's complex relationship to terrorism is illustrated in the case of Mubin Shaikh (the undercover agent that helped Canadian authorities disrupt the "Toronto 18" terrorist cell.) Shaikh had grown up studying with TJ in Canada. When he chose to become more religious he travelled to Pakistan with TJ but in the course of his missionary work came into contact with the Taliban. Shaikh states that TJ is separationist and non-political. Since he was seeking a more political and martial life, he found the Taliban's message of *jihad* appealing (he later rejected violence and has since advised the Canadian and American governments on countering violent extemism). Shaikh argues that TJ is not a "conveyor belt to violent extremism" for the vast majority of its members, but, as was his case, it can galvanize identity crises making individuals more susceptible to extremism and bring them into contact with more radical actors.[84]

As the Islamic State (IS) has displaced al-Qaeda as the world's most prominent Islamist terrorist group, TJ has again emerged as a possible feeder to this newer terrorism threat. A survey of the more than 50 Indians who have gone to fight for IS in Iraq and Syria found that nearly a third had been linked to TJ.[85] A group of French Muslims had also attended a TJ mosque before traveling to Syria to fight for IS.[86] Syed Rizwan Farook, who along with his wife Tashfeen Malik, committed the San Bernadino massacre in December 2015 and pledged loyalty to IS, had worshipped at a TJ mosque in San Bernadino.[87]

Ultimately, TJ is perhaps the modern world's most effective Islamic group at fostering pan-Islamic identity—one only has to be a Muslim to join and enter a "virtual transnational space" where every Muslim is immediately part of the Dar al-Islam.[88] As such, TJ is both a help and a hindrance to more political and "extremist" Islamic groups—the former because it promotes and reinforces the entire non-Muslim world as "other;" the latter because TJ can provide a feeling of Muslim solidarity sans sharia or the sword.[89]

ENDNOTES

[1] Yoginder Sikand, The Origins and Development of the Tablighi Jama'at, 1920-2000: A Cross-Country Comparative Survey (Hyderabad: Orient Longman, 2002), 2-12.

[2] Pew Forum on Religion and Public Life, "Muslim Networks and Movements in Western Europe: Tablighi Jama'at," September 15, 2010, http://pewforum.org/Muslim/Muslim-Networks-and-Movements-in-Western-Europe-Tablighi-Jamaat.aspx.

[3] Sikand, The Origins and Development of the Tablighi Jama'at, 1920-2000, 2-77; See also Muhammad Khalid Masud, ed., Travelers in Faith: Studies of the Tablighi Jama'at Movement as a Transnational Movement for Faith Renewal (Leiden: Brill, 2000), esp. "Introduction" and Chapter One, "The Growth and Development of the Tablighi Jama'at in India."

[4] Ira Lapidus, A History of Islamic Societies (Cambridge: Cambridge University Press, 1988), 725-26.

[5] Masud, Travelers in Faith, 6.

[6] Ibid., 7.

[7] Shireen Burki, "The Tablighi Jama'at: Proselytizing Missionaries or Trojan Horse?" Journal of Applied Security Research 8, no. 1, January-March 2013, 101.

[8] Founded by Ahmad Riza Khan Bareilly (1856-1921), the Ahl al-Sunnat ("Family of the Sunnah") movement—popularly known as Barelvis or Barelwis—advocated Islamic renewal much as did the Deobandis, although Barelvis were (and are) "more inclined toward the emotional or magical," according to Usha Sanyal, Ahmad Riza Khan Barelwi: In the Path of the Prophet (Oxford: Oneworld, 2005), 129.

[9] In Arabic-speaking Islam, the word usually employed for such work is da'wah; but in Urdu, in India and, later, Pakistan, tabligh ("transmission, communication, propaganda") came to be substituted.

[10] Sikand, The Origins and Development of the Tablighi Jama'at, 1920-2000, 48.

[11] Ibid., 66ff.

[12] Profession of faith ("there is no god but Allah and Muhammad is his messenger"), fasting during the daytime during Ramadan, praying at the appointed five daily times, zakat (tithing 2.5 percent) and going on the Hajj once in a lifetime.

[13] Such as the infallibility of the Koran, the existence of angels and djinn, the standard eschatological doctrines about the Mahdi, the Dajjal, and the apocalyptic struggles at the end of time.

[14] Masud, Travelers in Faith, 10-11.

[15] Farish A. Noor, "The Arrival and Spread of the Tablighi Jama'at in West Papua (Irian Jaya), Indonesia," S. Rajaratnam School of International Studies RSIS Working Paper, February 10, 2010, http://www.rsis.edu.sg/publications/WorkingPapers/WP191.pdf.

[16] Masud, Travelers in Faith, 134-35.

[17] This paradigm is adapted from Albert M. Craig et al., eds., The Heritage of World Civilizations. Volume II: Since 1500. Seventh Edition (Upper Saddle River, NJ: Pearson Prentice-Hall, 2006), 812-816.

[18] Barbara Metcalf, "'Traditionalist' Islamic Activism: Deoband, Tablighis, and Talibs," Social Science Research Council/After September 11, November 1, 2004, http://essays.ssrc.org/sept11/essays/metcalf.htm.

[19] Burki, "The Tablighi Jama`at: Proselytizing Missionaries or Trojan Horse?" 102-03.

[20] Yoginder Sikand, "A Critique of the 'Tablighi-as-Terrorist Thesis," n.d., http://www.uvm.edu/~envprog/madrassah/TablighiCritique.htm

[21] Masud, Travelers in Faith, 106.

[22] Ibid., 121.

[23] Ibidem, 125-130.

[24] As extracted from http://tablighijamaat.wordpress.com/2008/05/13/worldwide-tablighi-markaz-address/.

[25] Marloes Janson, "The Prophet's Path: Tablighi Jama`at in The Gambia," Institute for the Study of Islam in the Modern World Review 17 (Spring 2006), 44-45.

[26] Ibid., 45.

[27] Masud, Travelers in Faith, 161-173.

[28] Baz Lecocq and Paul Schrijver, "The War on Terror in a Haze of Dust: Potholes and Pitfalls on the Saharan Front," Journal of Contemporary African Studies 25, no. 1 (2007), 141-166.

[29] Stephen Harmon, Terror and Insurgenecy in the Sahara-Sahel Region: Corruption, Contraband, Jihad and the Mali War of 2012-2013 (New York: Routledge, 2014), pg. 159.

[30] Lecocq and Schrijver,151.

[31] Ibid, 155.

[32] David Graham, "Mali's Tangled Mix of Jihad and Civil War," The Atlantic, Nov. 20, 2015, https://www.theatlantic.com/international/archive/2015/11/mali-hotel-hostage-crisis/417021/

[33] Conor Gaffey, "African Jihadi Groups Unite and Pledge Allegiance to al-Qaeda," Newsweek, March 3, 2017, http://www.newsweek.com/al-qaeda-groups-unite-sahel-563351

[34] William Lloyd-George, "The Man Who Brought the Black Flag to Timbuktu," Foreign Policy, October 22, 2012, http://foreignpolicy.com/2012/10/22/the-man-who-brought-the-black-flag-to-timbuktu/

[35] "General Household Survey 2013," Statistics South Africa, June 18, 2014, http://www.statssa.gov.za/publications/P0318/P03182013.pdf

[36] Goolam Vahed, "Contesting Orthodoxy: the Tablighi-Sunni Conflict among South African Muslims in the 1970s and 1980s," Journal of Muslim Minority Affairs 23, no. 2, October 2003, 313-334; See also Masud, Travelers in Faith, 206-221.

[37] Zanzibar was the power base of the Omani Sultans who had taken control of the coastal areas of East Africa and the lucrative Muslim slave trade in the late 17th century and in 1856 was made the capital of the Omani Sultanate there; as such Zanzibar has been, under German, British and then independent Tanzanian rule, a hotbed of Islamic political thought and aspirations.

[38] Population figures from The CIA World Fact Book, 2016 (Washington, DC: Central Intelligence Agency, 2016), https://www.cia.gov/library/publications/the-world-factbook/docs/contributor_copyright.html.

[39] Sunguta West, "The Rise of ADF-NALU in Central Africa and Its Connections with al-Shabaab," Jamestown Foundation Terrorism Monitor, Volume 13, Issue 1, January 9, 2015, https://jamestown.org/program/the-rise-of-adf-nalu-in-central-africa-and-its-connections-with-al-shabaab/#.Vlx70nbhCUl.

[40] Gregory Pirio, African Jihad: Bin Laden's Quest for the Horn of Africa (Trenton, NJ: The Red Sea Press, 2007), 167ff.

[41] For example, Maalim Mohammad Idriss has stated that TJ and Wahhabism both pervert Islam and wrongly undermine Sufi traditions and practices. Ibidem, 168.

[42] Fred Burton and Scott Stewart, "Tablighi Jamaat: An Indirect Line to Terrorism," STRATFOR, January 23, 2010, http://www.stratfor.com/weekly/tablighi_jamaat_indirect_line_terrorism.

[43] Pirio, Radical Islam in the Greater Horn of Africa, IAQ, Inc., February 2, 2005, http://www.dankalia.com/africa/0101205023.htm.

[44] "Somalia: 5 Pakistani Preachers Killed Outside Tawfiq Mosque," Huffington Post, August 12, 2009, http://www.huffingtonpost.com/2009/08/12/somalia-5-pakistani-preac_n_257257.html.

[45] "Indian Jihadis in Qaida's Somalia Arm?" Times of India, August 23, 2010, http://timesofindia.indiatimes.com/india/Indian-jihadis-in-Qaidas-Somalia-arm-/articleshow/6399366.cms.

[46] "Somalia: Al-Shabaab Beheads Teenage Boy in Beledweyne," Sabahi, January 6, 2015, http://allafrica.com/stories/201501071116.html and "Somali Government Official Survives Car Bomb Explosion," Somali Update, February 27, 2015, http://somaliupdate.com/articles/5845/Somali-Government-Official-Survives-Car-Bomb-Explosion

[47] Farish Noor, "On the Permanent Hajj: the Tablighia Jama'at in South East Asia," South East Asia Research 18. no. 4, December 2010, 729-30.

[48] Noor, "The Arrival and Spread of the Tablighi Jama'at in West Papua (Irian Jaya), Indonesia," 1-10.

[49] Noor, 1-10.

[50] Noor, 18.

[51] Noor, 14, 16, 22.

[52] Farish Noor, "Locating the Tablighi Jama'at of West Palua in the Grander Structure of the Tablighi Jama'at in Indonesia and Southeast Asia," in eds. Juliana Finucane and R. Michael Feener, Proselytizing and the Limits of Religious Pluralism in Contemporary Asia, (Singapore: Springer, 2014)

[53] Alexander Horstmann, "Inculturation of a Transnational Islamic Missionary Movement: Tablighi Jamaat al-Dawa and Muslim Society in Southern Thailand," SOJOURN: Journal of Social Issues in Southeast Asia 22, iss. 1, April 2007, 107-131, http://findarticles.com/p/articles/mi_hb3413/is_1_22/ai_n29344399/.

[54] Ibid.

[55] Farish Noor, Islam on the Move: The Tablighi Jama'at in Southeast Asia (Amsterdam: Amsterdam University Press, 2012), pg. 182.

[56] Hussain Haqqani, Pakistan: Between Mosque and Military (Washington, DC: Carnegie Endowment for International Peace, 2005), 151.

[57] B. Raman, "Dagestan: Focus on Pakistan's Tablighi Jamaat," South Asia Analysis Group, September 15, 1999, http://www.southasiaanalysis.org/%5Cpapers%5Cpaper80.html.

[58] Haqqani, 292.

[59] Jane Perlez, "Pakistani Group, Suspected by West of Jihadist Ties, Holds Conclave Despite Ban," New York Times, November 19, 2007, http://www.nytimes.com/2007/11/19/world/asia/19jamaat.html

[60] Alex Alexiev, "Tablighi Jamaat: Jihad's Stealthy Legions," Middle East Quarterly 12, no. 1, Winter 2005, 3-11, http://www.meforum.org/686/tablighi-jamaat-jihads-stealthy-legions.

[61] "Taliban Threatens Pakistani Singers and Actors with Death," Telegraph (London), March 15, 2009, http://www.telegraph.co.uk/news/worldnews/asia/pakistan/4992107/Taliban-threatens-Pakistani-singers-and-actors-with-death.html.

[62] Pew Forum, "Muslim Networks and Movements in Western Europe: Tablighi Jama`at."

[63] William Langley, Roya Nikkahah, James Orr, David Bamber, and Massoud Ansari, "Army of Darkness," Telegraph London), August 20, 2006, http://www.telegraph.co.uk/news/1526793/Army-of-darkness.html.

[64] "Hafiz Patel, influential British Muslim leader, dies at 92," February 19, 2016, BBC News, http://www.bbc.com/news/uk-35615205.

[65] Andrew Gilligan, "Islamic group blocked from building 'Britain's biggest mosque' in London," The Telegraph, October 25, 2015, http://www.telegraph.co.uk/news/uknews/11953462/Islamic-group-blocked-from-building-Britains-biggest-mosque-in-London.html

[66] Burton and Stewart, "An Indirect Line."

[67] Alexiev, "Tablighi Jamaat: Jihad's Stealthy Legions," 3-11.

[68] Salah Uddin Shoaib Choudhury, "What Is Tablighi Jamaat," Family Security Matters, June 4, 2010, http://familysecuritymatters.org/publications/id.6384/pub_detail.asp.

[69] Thomas Gugler, "Parrots of Paradise—Symbols of the Super Muslim: Sunnah, Sunnaization, and Self-Fashioning in the Islamic Missionary Movements Tablighi Jama`at, Da`wat-e Islami, and Sunni Da`wat-e Islami," July 2007, 1, http://www.zmo.de/mitarbeiter/gugler/parrots%20of%20paradise.pdf; See also "Fact Sheet on U.S. Treasury Endorsement of Sharia Compliant Finance," n.d., http://usastopshariah.wordpress.com/background/.

[70] Alexiev, "Tablighi Jamaat: Jihad's Stealthy Legions."

[71] Burki, "The Tablighi Jama`at: Proselytizing Missionaries or Trojan Horse?" 106.

[72] Susan Sachs, "A Muslim Missionary Group Draws New Scrutiny in U.S." New York Times, July 14, 2003, http://www.nytimes.com/2003/07/14/us/a-muslim-missionary-group-draws-new-scrutiny-in-us.html.

[73] Gugler, "Parrots of Paradise—Symbols of the Super Muslim," 1; Dietrich Reetz, "The 'Faith Bureaucracy' of the Tablighi Jama`at: An Insight into their System of Self-organization (Intizam)," in Gwilym Beckerlegge, ed., Colonialism, Modernity and Religious Ideologies: Religious Reform Movements in South Asia (New Delhi: Oxford University Press, 2008), 98-124.

[74] Reetz, "The 'Faith Bureaucracy' of the Tablighi Jama`at," 109.

[75] Joseph Lumbard and Aref Ali Nayed, eds., The 500 Most Influential Muslims 2010 (Amman, Jordan: Royal Islamic Strategic Studies Centre, 2010), 58-59.

[76] Ibid., 121.

[77] Yoginder Sikand, "The Tablighi Jamaat's Contested Claims to Islamicity," n.d., http://www.indianmuslimobserver.com/2010/06/issues-tablighi-jamaats-contested.html.

[78] Ibid.

[79] Ibidem.

[80] Ibidem.

[81] "Intelligence Report: Foreign Militants Tasked to Assassinate Tablighi Jamaat Leaders," Middle East Media Research Institute, October 29, 2010, http://www.thememriblog.org/urdupashtu/blog_personal/en/31633.htm.

[82] "Tajikistan: Jail Terms and Massive Fines—But for What Crimes?," FORUM 18 News Service, May 19, 2010, http://www.forum18.org/Archive.php?article_id=1446.

[83] Felix Corley, "Kazakhstan: Is Sharing Faith a State Security Issue?" George Fox University Occasional Papers on Religion in Eastern Europe 37, iss. 1, Article 7 (2017), http://digitalcommons.georgefox.edu/cgi/viewcontent.cgi?article=2006&context=ree

[84] Stefano Bonino, "In Conversation with Mubin Shaikh: From Salafi Jihadist to Undercover Agent Inside the "Toronto 18" Terrorist Group," Perspectives on Terrorism 10, no. 2 (2016), http://www.terrorismanalysts.com/pt/index.php/pot/article/view/502/html.

[85] Azaan Javaid, "NIA's study of arrested Indian ISIS fans busts common myths," Daily News & Analysis, January 20, 2017, http://www.dnaindia.com/india/report-nia-s-study-of-arrested-indian-isis-fans-busts-common-myths-2294253

[86] Andrew Higgins, "A French Town Linked to Jihad Asks Itself Why," The New York Times, January 16, 2015, https://www.nytimes.com/2015/01/17/world/europe/french-town-struggles-over-departures-for-jihad.html?_r=0

[87] William Finnegan, "Last Days: Preparing for the Apocalypse in San Bernadino," The New Yorker, February 22, 2016, http://www.newyorker.com/magazine/2016/02/22/preparing-for-apocalypse-in-san-bernardino

[88] "Rejected: the Mosque Plan That Grew So Big It Attracted the Wrong Sort of Crowd," Independent (London), December 5, 2012.

[89] Noor, "On the Permanent Hajj: the Tablighia Jama'at in South East Asia," 722, 732.

TALIBAN

> **QUICK FACTS**
>
> Geographical Areas of Operation: Number (estimated WHEN)
>
> Numerical Stength (Members): Approximately 25,000
>
> Leadership: Moulavi Haibatullah Akhunzada
>
> Religious Identification: Sunni Islam
>
> *Quick Facts courtesy of Stanford Univeristy's Mapping Militant Organizations (July 2016)*

OVERVIEW

The Taliban is a Sunni fundamentalist militant group, founded by Mullah Mohammad Omar, that emerged in 1994 during the Afghan Civil War (1992-1996). The Taliban, or "religious students" in Pashto, was just one of many factions in the civil war. The group led a brief but well-received campaign to rid southern Afghanistan's Kandahar region of its predatory commanders and bandits in the spring of 1994. The group continued to grow in size and power, and in 1996 it seized Kabul and took control of the Afghan government. In 2001, the Taliban refused to hand over al-Qaeda leader Osama bin Laden to the United States government. In response, the U.S. and NATO forces invaded Afghanistan and toppled the regime.

Many of the Taliban's top leadership, including Mullah Omar, slipped over the border into Pakistan and reestablished an ad hoc command-and-control center in the Pashtunabad neighborhood of Quetta, earning the moniker "the Quetta Shura" from U.S. and Afghan intelligence agencies. The Taliban slowly metamorphosed into a more organized, centralized, and capable organization, and by 2006 launched a protracted campaign of violence and intimidation throughout Afghanistan's southern and eastern provinces. Similarly, a Pakistani offshoot of the Taliban emerged as several tribal shuras supportive of the Afghan Taliban pledged bayat (allegiance) to Mullah Omar and began cross-border attacks providing manpower, weapons and logistical support to insurgent fronts in eastern Afghanistan and beyond.

After the drawdown of American and coalition forces from Afghanistan at the end of 2014, which ended the NATO-led ISAF mission, the coalition began a new, follow-on mission, called the Resolute Support (RS) on January 1, 2015. As part of the Resolute Support Mission, the United States and coalition forces are now engaged in a train, advise, and assist mission to support the Afghan security forces to maintain increased security across the country. In September 2014, the United States and Afghanistan's newly-elected National Unity Government signed the Bilateral Security Agreement, which provided the basis for the United States and NATO coalition to leave behind an estimated 9,800 U.S. troops and 5,500 coalition troops in Afghanistan.

The Resolute Support mission serves two main purposes: to train and assist the Afghan national security forces, and conduct unfettered counterterrorism operations against al Qaeda, its affiliates, and the Afghan offshoot of the Islamic State, or ISIS Khorasan.[1] According to the original Agreement, the number of U.S. troops was to be reduced to 5,500 before the end of 2016. But, given Afghanistan's deteriorating security situation and the ANSF's lack of requisite capacities as a counterinsurgent force,[2] the U.S. instead delayed the impending troop drawdown and committed to maintaining a residual force of 8,400 troops in Afghanistan through the end of the Obama administration.[3]

HISTORY AND IDEOLOGY

The Taliban rose to power after Afghanistan's devastating civil war (1992-1996). It renamed the country the Islamic Emirate of Afghanistan and quickly implemented a strict interpretation of sharia (Islamic law). The core of the original Taliban movement originated from a clerical *andiwal* (war comrades) network of Islamic conservatives, made up of *madrassa*-educated ethnic Pashtun men from poor or lower class backgrounds.

The Taliban has been highly resilient due to three attributes: it is centralized and therefore efficient; flexible and diverse, therefore adaptable to local contexts, and; highly pragmatic in its use of narco-resources to finance itself.[4] But the question of just who the Taliban is remains largely unknown. Some experts interpret the movement to be a loose network of militants based along tribal lineage, others describe the Taliban as a Pakistani-created and funded proxy army, while still others suggest the Taliban are an umbrella organization of various militant networks, marginalized tribes and clans, as well as criminal gangs, some of whom pledge allegiance to the core element of the former Taliban government, Mullah Mohammad Omar. The organizational construct of the Taliban movement in Afghanistan, its offshoots, and its Pakistani extension, the *Tehrik-i-Taliban* Pakistan, are presented below.

Quetta Shura Taliban (QST)

The remnants of the former Taliban government manifested itself as the *Quetta Shura* in 2002. Initially, the movement consisted of a ten man Rahbari Shura (Leadership Council) consisting of eight old-guard Taliban military commanders from southern Afghanistan and two others.[5] In October 2006, it announced the creation of the *majlis al-shura* (Consultative Council) consisting of 13 members and some additional "advisers."[6] Since that time, the *Quetta Shura* has become far more complex. As the Taliban began to spread its influence and gain de facto control of some rural areas in southern Afghanistan, the *Quetta Shura* began assigning shadow government positions to various areas and regions with heavy Taliban footprint and support. The *Quetta Shura* ballooned in size, likely because of its effort to manage and bring some organizational efficiency to what was and essentially is a franchise of tribal and communal networks with loose ideological relations.

In April 2013, Taliban *emir* (leader) Mullah Mohammad Omar died after falling ill. The news of his death was kept secret among a handful of Taliban leaders for more than two years, on tactical grounds. After his death, the Taliban continued to release official statements under his name. Furthermore, the group published his biography in April 2015 to mark his 19th year as their supreme leader, stating that the *emir* "remains in touch" with daily Afghan and world events. In July 2015, the Taliban released a statement, wherein Mullah Omar backed peace talks with the Afghan government as a "legitimate" route to ending the conflict and the occupation of foreign forces in Afghanistan. This farce continued until July 2015, when Afghan intelligence announced the Taliban leader had died years earlier in a hospital in Pakistan.[7] Later that month, the Taliban itself confirmed Mullah Omar's death. Subsequently, Mullah Omar was succeeded by his deputy, Mullah Akhtar Mansour – who served as the Minister of Civil Aviation during Taliban regime – in a hasty selection process that was disputed by high-ranking leaders of the movement.[8] Soon after Mullah Mansour's accession, fractures began to appear in the movement, as some of its political and military leadership members, including the prominent Mullah Abdul Zakir, Mullah Mansour Dadullah (brother of former senior commander Daddulah), and Mullah Mohammad Rasool (the governor of Nimroz during Taliban regime), protested that the late *emir's* son, Mullah Mohammad Yaqub—who asserted that Pakistan engineered Mullah Mansour's succession—should become the leader.[9] They accused Mansour of "hijacking the movement because of personal greed," which led to the creation of a splinter group, the High Council of Afghanistan Islamic Emirate, led by Mullah Rasool.[10] The split soon erupted into infighting between the two sides, with Mansour's side gaining the upper hand, as the clashes led to Mullah Dadullah's death due in November 2015.[11] Intense clashes under the leadership of Mullah Rasool continued into the spring of 2016.

In January 2015, news emerged that Mullah Abdul Rauf Alizai had sworn allegiance to the Islamic State's Afghan offshoot, known as Wilayat Khorasan, and had been appointed its deputy commander, after falling out with Taliban. (The U.S. State Department would formally declare the Wilayat Khorasan a Foreign Terrorist Organization (FTO) in early 2016.[12]) The following month, however, Alizai was killed by a U.S. drone strike in Helmand province while travelling in a vehicle full of explosives and ammunitions with his brother-in-law and four Pakistani militants.[13]

In August 2015, al Qaeda leader Ayman al-Zawahiri pledged allegiance to the Taliban, declaring his support for Mansour. In September 2015, the Taliban captured the northern city of Kunduz province, which helped rally some of the heavyweight dissidents, including Mullah Abdul Zakir, Umar's brother Mullah Abdul Manan Akhund, and son Mullah Yaqub, to acquiesce to Mansour accession as "commander of the faithful."[14] Subsequently, Manan was named the head of *Dawat Wal Irshad*, the Preaching and Guidance Commission, and Yaqub was given a seat on the executive council of *Quetta Shura*, as well as in the Military Commission by making him the military chief of 15 provinces.[15] On August 8, 2016, the Taliban announced that Mullah Rasool's deputy, Mullah Baz Mohammad, and Mullah Akhtar Mohammad Akhund, another recalcitrant commander in Uruzgan, together with their followers, had reunited with the Taliban.[16] At this time, it has not been established whether the breakaway faction of Mohammad Rasool will reintegrate with the main group as well.

In May 2016, a U.S. drone strike killed Mullah Mansour in a remote village of Pakistan's Balochistan province, which shares a border with Iran.[17] On May 25, the Taliban confirmed Mansour's death and selected one of his deputies, Mawlawi Haibatullah Akhunzada, as its new leader. As his honorific title *Mawlawi* (used for a high-level of religious scholarship) suggests, Akhunzada was previously committed to the religious affairs of the movement, and was not directly involved in the command structure, which is why he lacks "any familiarity with the bigger issues," according to the former head of Afghanistan's intelligence agency, Rahmatullah Nabil.[18] Akhunzada has left the operational command of the movement in the hands of his deputies: the incumbent and *de facto* leader of the Haqqani Network, Sirajuddin Haqqani, and the young Mullah Mohammad Yaqub.[19] According to one Taliban commander, who spoke to reporters about the Taliban leadership on condition of anonymity, the two deputies have already "divided Afghanistan into two parts," each wanting to control his own front.[20]

Since the onset of his administration, current Afghan President Ashraf Ghani has prioritized reconciling with the Taliban by reaching out to Pakistan to facilitate negotiations, as well as by establishing a Quadrilateral Coordination Group (QCG), which includes Afghanistan, Pakistan, China, and the United States, in pursuit of a peace settlement. However, the Taliban has continued its offensives and refused to attend the peace talks. As a result, in the first quarter of 2016, Ghani effectively eschewed amnesty and passivity as a policy option toward the insurgency, yet continued to welcome those who wish to reconcile.[21]

In May 2016, the new Taliban leadership announced it would not resume peace talks with the Afghan government and would remain committed to battlefield operations. The decision was driven by the conviction of many of the movement's commanders that political settlement to the conflict is not a desired option, given the attainable prospect of victory over the Afghan government. This view has been strengthened by the movement's recent offensives in nearly half of the country's 34 provinces, particularly the capture of a city in Kunduz in September 2015 (in which the Taliban freed 600 prisoners, including nearly 150 insurgent fighters), and again in August 2016, when Taliban fighters seized Khanabad district in Kunduz, a province that holds symbolic and strategic significance to the Taliban as it was once its key northern stronghold.[22] Afghan security forces subsequently retook both territories, however. Since a political settlement does not seem to be in the offing, the two sides will likely remain in what experts have termed a "mutually hurting stalemate."[23]

Tehrik-i-Taliban Pakistan

Tehrik-i-Taliban Pakistan is an umbrella front bringing together rogue resistance organizations like *Lashkar-e Jhangvi, Jaish-e Muhammad, Sipah-e Sahaba Pakistan*, and possibly some of the banned Kashmiri groups like *Harakat ul-Mujahedin*.[24] Though the group was officially formed in 2007, its seeds were sown as early as 2001 as a result of Afghan-Pakistani militant communication and collaboration.

Following the U.S.-led invasion of Afghanistan in October 2001, Taliban supporters and sympathizers in Pakistan's western tribal areas quickly pledged support and provided additional manpower and resources to help the Afghan Taliban resistance. The Pashtun tribes who dominate the western tribal agencies of Pakistan share ancestral lineages with many of Afghanistan's Pashtun tribesmen and both have long resisted colonial attempts at occupation. Even in a modern context, the core of the Afghan resistance movement against the Soviet occupation of Afghanistan was based in these same areas, using Peshawar as a *de facto* capital and the tribal agencies of North and South Waziristan as training areas and key junctions for transiting personnel and weapons into Afghanistan.

The initial flow of Taliban fighters into Pakistan's Federally Administered Tribal Areas (FATA) became a tidal wave following the collapse of the Taliban regime in Kandahar and after the monumental battle of Tora Bora in December 2001 and the subsequent spring 2002 battle of the Shah-i-kot Valley (known in the West as "Operation Anaconda"). Along with the Taliban came hundreds of fleeing Arab and foreign fighters linked to al-Qaeda, many of whom settled among their Pashtun supporters and sympathizers in North and South Waziristan. Home of the legendary *mujahedeen* commander Jalaluddin Haqqani, North Waziristan is also the operational space of many al-Qaeda leaders and the network of Hafiz Gul Bahadur.

Baitullah Mehsud soon emerged as a charismatic Pakistani version of Mullah Omar. Young, radical but oddly not schooled in Islamic *madrassas*, Baitullah hailed from the Mehsud tribe and gained prominence in February 2005 when he signed a "peace accord" with the Pakistani government.[25] As part of that deal, Baitullah pledged not to support al-Qaeda and restrained his forces from attacking Pakistani state targets and military targets in exchange for the end of Pakistani military operations in South Waziristan. The deal disintegrated in 2006, leaving South Waziristan a largely independent militarized zone where Taliban officials and al-Qaeda leaders found sanctuary. Baitullah Mehsud commanded a core of 5,000 hardened loyalists, mostly tribally affiliated Mehsud kinsmen, launching spectacular raids and ambushes against the superior Pakistani military forces.[26]

On December 14, 2007, a militant spokesman announced the formation of the *Tehrik-i-Taliban Pakistan* (TTP). Baitullah Mehsud was appointed the *emir* of TTP's forty-man shura; Hafiz Gul Bahadur was appointed as the *naib emir* (deputy); and Maulana Faqir Mohammad of the Bajaur Agency was appointed third in command.[27] The TTP consolidated its objectives to enforcing *sharia* throughout the FATA, uniting against NATO forces in Afghanistan by supporting Mullah Omar's Afghan Taliban, seeking to remove Pakistani military checkpoints from the FATA, and vowing to protect the Swat district and Waziristan from future Pakistani military operations. Following the Pakistani government's siege of the Red Mosque in Islamabad in July 2007,[28] Baitullah Mehsud and the TTP turned its guns on the Pakistani government. The following month, forces loyal to Mehsud humiliated the Pakistani military when they ambushed and captured 200 government soldiers.[29] Subsequently, the December 2007 assassination of Pakistan's former two-time Prime Minister Benazir Bhutto reverberated around the world and drew considerable attention to the deteriorating security situation in the country.

The Pakistani government quickly blamed Baitullah Mehsud and the TTP for orchestrating the assassination of Bhutto, offering transcripts of alleged phone conversations with Mehsud and his operatives discussing the attack, a claim Mehsud and the TTP strongly denied.[30] Rifts between rival commanders under the TTP banner impacted the organization's unity throughout 2008, eventually leading to major disputes between Hafiz Gul Bahadur, Baitullah Mehsud and Maulvi Nazir. An increase in U.S. drone strikes targeting militants in North and South Waziristan strained the TTP as top and mid-level leaders died throughout 2008 and 2009 and scores more were arrested in 2010. The Pakistani military moved on the TTP and the TSNM in Bajur and Swat, prompting a closer cooperation among militants who renewed their vows of union in February 2009 when they formed the *Shura-Ittehad-al-Mujahedeen* (United Mujahedeen Council) which again brought Hafiz Gul Bahadur, Baitullah Mehsud, Maulavi Nazir and Siraj Haqqani together.

Major Pakistani military ground operations (under the rubric of *Operation Rah-e Nijat*) targeted the TTP in South Waziristan in October 2009, concluding by April 2010. Beginning in October 2009, the Pakistani military launched a major offensive against Taliban strongholds in South Waziristan. The symbolic village of Makeen, the hometown of Baitullah Mehsud, as well as Ladha, Kotkai, Kaniguram, and Sararogha were the primary targets of the operation.[31] Pakistani Prime Minister Yousaf Raza Gilani, in announcing the completion of the ground offensive on December 19, 2009, claimed that 589 Taliban fighters and their supporters had been killed in the offensive and that 79 Pakistani soldiers also died in combat.[32]

Just prior to the South Waziristan operation, on August 5, 2009, an American UAV strike killed Baitullah Mehsud, his second wife, and several of his bodyguards. A chaotic rebuttal from TTP spokesmen denied his death, but within two weeks, and following an alleged power struggle within the TTP for the top leadership position, the TTP acknowledged Mehsud's death and announced Hakimullah Mehsud as his replacement.

In October 2013, Pakistan's Prime Minister, Nawaz Sharif, paid an official visit to Washington in an effort to strengthen U.S.- Pakistan relations as well as to solidify America's commitment to ensuring security and stability in Pakistan and the region.. Eight days later, on November 1, a U.S. drone strike killed Hakimullah Mehsud along with his uncle after a meeting with several senior Taliban leaders in a small mosque.[33]

Following Mehsud's death, Maulana Fazlullah, the founder of TTP's Swat chapter, presided over a tumultuous period for the organization, marked by ideological differences and internal rivalries.[34] In May 2014, a powerful faction of TTP, the Mehsud tribe, parted ways with the central leadership of the organization after failed attempts at peace talks and convincing Fazlullah to give up "un-Islamic" practices, such as "the killing of innocent people, kidnapping for ransom and extortion."[35] The new breakaway faction calls itself *Tehrik-e-Taliban Pakistan-South Waziristan* (TTP-SW), and is led by Khalid Mehsud (aka Khan Said Sajna), the former Chief of TTP's South Waziristan chapter, who was listed by the U.S. State Department as a SDGT on October 21, 2014.[36] Khalid Mehsud was reportedly killed in U.S. drone strike in Afghanistan's Khost province on November 25, 2015.[37] However, Azam Tariq, the faction's spokesman, denied reports of Mehsud's death, and the faction has since continued to fight against the Pakistani state and foreign forces in Afghanistan under the leadership of the Afghan Taliban.[38]

Fractures in TTP led to speculation about a weakening of the group, however, the organization's activities have intensified. In June 2014, TTP militants stormed into a cargo area of Pakistan's Jinnah International Airport in Karachi, leaving more than 20 people dead.[39] In response, Pakistan's Army and Air Force launched a counterterrorism operation in North Waziristan called *Zarb-e-Azb* the same month, aimed at TTP and terrorists of "all hues and colors," which had killed over 1,800 militants by the end of the year.[40] TTP's responses included the November 2014 attack on a paramilitary checkpoint at Wagah border with India that killed around 60 people, and the attack on a military-run public school in Peshawar the following month, in which TTP militants entered classrooms, shooting and killing 145, including 132 children.[41] The attack prompted a global response. Even the Afghan Taliban, with which the TTP is closely affiliated, condemned the attack as a "deliberate killing of innocent people, women and children [which is] against Islamic principles," and offered their condolences to the victims.[42] Pakistan's government responded by lifting the six-year moratorium on the death penalty for militants convicted on terrorism-related charges, and intensified the North Waziristan military operation, *Zarb-e-Azb*, which has killed some 3,500 "terrorists" as of September 2016, according to the Pakistani military's top spokesman, Lieutenant General Asim Bajwa.[43]

In August 2014, a second splinter group, called *Jamaat-ul-Ahrar*, formed in Mohmand tribal agency near Peshawar under the leadership of Omar Khalid Khorasani, who had served as a spokesman to Fazlullah until he was sacked after accusing the leader of deviating from the movement's ideology by opening negotiations with the Pakistani government.[44] The attacks attributed to Khorasani's breakaway faction included the November 2014 twin bombings in Mohmand Agency, which targeted peace committee volunteers, killing six;[45] twin bombings at two churches in Lahore on March 15, 2015, which killed 15 people;[46] the March 27, 2016 suicide attack on members of a Pakistani Christian community at a park in Lahore that killed over 70 and injured more than 340;[47] and the suicide attack on a local mosque in Mohmand agency on September 16, 2016 that killed 28 people.[48]

Khorasani's *Jumaat-ul-Arhar* rejoined the TTP in March 2015 following temporary peace talks between Taliban and the Afghan government, which they feared would leave them baseless and caught between the Pakistani military and a potentially inhospitable Afghanistan.[49] Khorasani was subsequently killed by a U.S. drone strike in July 2016.[50]

In September 2016, General Asim Bajwa claimed Operation *Zarb-e-Azb* had succeeded in defeating terrorists and all but declared the operation over.[51] The TTP's new leader for North Waziristan, Akhtar Mohammad Khalil, who was appointed in spring 2016 by the main *emir*, Mullah Fazlullah (believed to be hiding in Afghanistan), appeared in a video released in mid-September on the TTP's official propaganda outlet, Umar Media, countering Pakistani military's claims.[52] The video features three Pakistani security personnel captured and put on display, as well as TTP fighters firing rifles, rockets, mortars and machine guns at Pakistani troops in remote mountainous areas.[53]

Most of the regional commanders of TPP have pledged allegiance to the Islamic State, and have close relations with ISIS's regional offshoot, *Welayat Khorasan*. However, despite their affiliation with and support for IS Khorasan, TTP appears committed to its core anti-state philosophy and campaign against the Pakistani government and military establishment. Looking ahead, some TTP's disgruntled members may be coopted into IS Khorasan, but the possibility of the entire group merging with IS Khorasan appears very unlikely. Still, all signs point to an inescapable reality that TTP's end is not yet in sight.[54]

The Haqqani Network

The Haqqani Network is based out of a Taliban bastion in neighboring Pakistan. The village of Dande Darpa Khel near Miramshah (North Waziristan) is its main headquarters, while Zambar village in the northern Sabari district in Khost province serves as the group's major operations hub.[55] The group also maintains a major presence in the Zadran dominated districts between Paktia and Paktika provinces, which also serve as a major transit point for insurgents infiltrating into Logar province and southern Kabul.

Jalaluddin Haqqani, who was never part of the original Taliban movement of Mullah Omar, was coopted into the Taliban in 1996 after the religious militia neared his stronghold of Paktia. Haqqani was allowed by Mullah Omar to operate his network as an offshoot under auspices of the Taliban regime. He (and later his oldest son Siraj Haqqani) has pledged *bayat* (allegiance) to Mullah Omar, becoming the Minister of Tribal and Border Affairs, the Governor of Paktia and eventually the Taliban's overall military commander under its ruling regime. In 2003, Jalaluddin led the Taliban's strategy for the eastern zone. Suspected of suffering from lupus for some time, the elderly Haqqani handed the reins of his terror network over to his son Siraj in 2007 after developing health issues.

The Haqqanis hold clout on both sides of the border and, through Siraj's leadership, the group provides a critical bridge to Pakistani Taliban groups and al-Qaeda-linked foreign fighters. Electronic signal intercepts by U.S. and Indian intelligence agencies reportedly confirm a link between ISI officers and Haqqani operatives who are said to have jointly planned and executed the deadly suicide car bomb attack against Indian embassy in Kabul on July 7, 2008.[56] In September 2012, the U.S. formally designated the *Haqqani Network* as a foreign terrorist organization.

A series of complex assaults against Afghan government and economic institutions in Kabul, Jalalabad, and Khost cities have been attributed to the *Haqqani Network* and its "Kabul Strike Group"- a shadowy guerrilla front that plans and conducts sophisticated attacks that often include a commando style raid with suicide-bombers against urban targets. On February 19, 2011, a brazen day-light attack against Jalalabad's main bank, which involved gunmen and suicide bombers dressed as border police, killed at least 42 people and wounded more than 70 in one of the deadliest attacks ever carried out by the *Haqqani Network*.[57]

Past attacks attributed to the *Haqqani Network* include the multi-pronged assault on two Afghan ministries and a prison headquarters in Kabul that left 19 people dead and more than 50 wounded; an 11-man commando-style suicide bombing raid against several government facilities in Khost City; and the July 4, 2009 assault against a remote U.S. outpost in Paktika's Zerok district that killed two U.S. soldiers and injured four others. On July 21, 2009, suicide bombers armed with rocket-propelled grenades and assault rifles attacked government installations and a U.S. base in the cities of Gardez and Jalalabad. However, one of the most brazen attacks attributed to the *Haqqani Network* occurred in Kabul on October 4, 2009 when terrorists dressed in police uniforms assassinated the security guard protecting the UN's guest house and stormed the facility, eventually detonating several suicide vests and killing at least twelve people, including six UN personnel. The deadly suicide bombing of an CIA forward operating base in Khost on December 30, 2009 that killed seven senior CIA operatives and a Jordanian intelligence offer has been speculatively attributed to the *Haqqani Network*, the TTP and al-Qaeda in Afghanistan. In June 2013, *Haqqani Network* fighters staged a large-scale coordinated attack with 13 suicide bombers on two high-profile Afghan government targets, including the Kabul International Airport.

The *Haqqani Network* was at its zenith in the period between 2004 and 2010, during which time it boasted more than 3,000 fighters and supporters. However, following the deaths and arrests of several Haqqani sons and hardline commanders, the network's influence has faded somewhat. By mid-2015, rumors emerged that Jalaluddin Haqqani had died the previous year following a protracted illness.[58] Pakistani intelligence and the leader's relatives reportedly confirmed his death; however, Taliban spokesman Zabiullah Mujahid rejected reports of Haqqani's demise.[59]

Despite all the turbulence, the network has demonstrated persistent capability to carry out operations, particularly those focused on Kabul. In 2011, three high-profile attacks were attributed to the *Haqqani Network*: the attack on Intercontinental Hotel in Kabul on June 28, 2011; the truck bombing in Wardak province on September 10, 2011 that injured 77 U.S. soldiers; and the September 13, 2011 coordinated attacks on U.S. Embassy and NATO headquarters in Kabul, killing 16 and leaving more than 160 injured.[60] In June 2012, the network's militants carried out a 12-hour siege of a popular hotel on the outskirts of Kabul, leaving at least 20 dead.[61] After a relative lull in their terror campaign in 2013 through mid-2014, the network resumed its offensives with by back-to-back attacks in the summer of 2014: on July 15, the network carried out a truck bomb attack in a market located in a remote eastern district in Afghanistan, killing 72 people, and then, two days later, suicide attacks targeted Kabul airport with volleys of grenades, killing 5 people.[62] On June 22, 2015, militants staged a coordinated attack on the Afghan parliament, with a suicide car bomb and gunfire, which killed five people and seven attackers.[63] The Taliban claimed responsibility, but Afghan intelligence alleged that the *Haqqani Network* was responsible, backed by Pakistan's ISI.[64]

The network has engendered a global response. In 2011, the then-Chairman of the U.S. Joint Chiefs of Staff, Adm. Mike Mullen, the Haqqani Network "as a veritable arm" of ISI in testimony before the Senate Armed Services Committee.[65] In early 2015, the Pakistani government officially outlawed the *Haqqani Network*, mainly in response to the military public school attack and pressures from the U.S. to stop differentiating between "good" and "bad" militants.[66] However, the country's promises and policies never translated into effective practical counterterrorism as they merely focused on displacing rather than destroying the network. In May 2016, the U.S. Congress proposed a $300 million cutoff in military aid to Pakistan if the network's "safe havens and freedom of movement" were not "significantly disrupted."[67] Two months later, reimbursements allocated for Pakistan's counterterrorism and counterinsurgency operations were suspended, following former U.S. Defense Secretary Ash Carter's refusal to certify that Pakistan had made any noteworthy efforts in dismantling the Haqqani and other terrorist networks.[68]

Hezb-i-Islami Gulbuddin (Party of Islam)

A young Islamist named Gulbuddin Hekmatyar, a Kharoti Pashtun from the northern Afghan province of Kunduz, formed the *Hezb-i-Islami - Gulbuddin* political faction in Pakistan in 1976 in response to the growing influence of leftist movements in the Afghan government and university campuses. During the 1980s, Hekmatyar, along with guidance from Pakistan's intelligence services and financial assistance from U.S. and Saudi intelligence services, propelled *Hezb-i-Islami* into the biggest *mujahedeen* organization fighting the Soviet occupation. Hekmatyar is infamous for his brutal battlefield tactics and backstabbing political deals, including the assassination of many of his political rivals.[69]

The U.S. military has estimated Hekmatyar's forces to number around 400-600, although experts suggest the number is more likely to total around 1,500 full-time fighters.[70] *Hezb-i-Islami* cadres have fallen out of favor with many Taliban fronts at the local level, with violent clashes and killings attributed to both sides occurring throughout 2010.[71] Unlike the Taliban, *Hezb-i-Islami* leaders have participated in clandestine and overt talks with the Afghan government since 2009, both abroad and in Afghanistan-an indicator the group is militarily weakened and biding its time for a political rebirth and to bolster its rank-and-file. In February 2003, the U.S. Department of State designated Gulbuddin Hekmatyar a SDGT for having participated and supported terrorist acts committed by al-Qaeda and the Taliban.[72] At the same time, the United Nations also included Hekmatyar on its sanctions list against known terrorists, which would obligate all UN members states to impose sanctions on the group, including asset freezes.[73] Hekmatyar loyalists were politically active in the former Afghan government led by Hamid Karzai, with several occupying important cabinet level positions, including Abdul Hadi Arghandiwal as the Minister of Economy, and Karim Khurram as President Karzai's Chief of Staff.

HIG has never had a prominent battlefield presence like the Taliban. Their onslaughts have primarily been high-profile attacks, such as a suicide bombing of September 2012 in Kabul – carried out in retaliation for a film mocking Prophet Mohammad – killing 12 people, including eight South African nationals working for a USAID-chartered air service, and another attack in May 2013 when a Toyota Corolla, packed with explosives, rammed into a pair of American military vehicles in Kabul, killing 16 people, including 6 Americans (two soldiers and four contractors).[74] The attack was carried out as a reaction to the talks about a long-term security deal between Kabul and Washington.

HIG is the most reconcilable of all the insurgent groups involved in the current peace process. In January 2010, Hekmatyar and the Karzai administration initiated talks on reconciliation in Kabul, followed by HIG delegation's attendance of the Afghan government's consultative peace *Loya Jirga* a few months later in June – the two sides subsequently met in June 2012 academic conference in Paris, and again in Chantilly, France, in December 2012 – to discuss issues and terms of reconciliation.[75] Talks were cast into limbo as Afghanistan and the United States negotiated a bilateral security agreement, which ensured a long-term U.S. and NATO presence in Afghanistan.

In the 2014 Afghan elections, Hekmatyar reportedly told his partisans to vote for his deputy, Qutbuddin Helal, who ran for president as an "independent," gathering a meager 2.75 percent of the vote.[76]

In May 2016, the Afghan National Unity Government and Hekmatyar came close to finalizing a 25-point peace agreement, which is widely regarded as a model for future peace deals between the Afghan government and other insurgent groups, like the Taliban, with much more significant presence, to follow suit.[77] On September 22, 2016, the Afghan government signed a draft of the long-awaited peace deal with HIG.[78] The terms of the agreement call for the faction to cease hostilities in exchange for recognition by the government, its support for the delisting of Hekmatyar as a SDGT and the removal of U.S. and UN sanctions against him.[79] However, the HIG representative, Mohammad Amin Karim, simultaneously said that the group will "keep struggling until the last foreign soldier leaves," as "the restoration of independence is our main demand."[80] The U.S. Embassy in Afghanistan issued a statement, lauding the accord and welcoming it as "an Afghan-led, Afghan-owned peace process."[81] Additionally, the deal entails the arrangement of Hekmatyar's re-establishment in Afghanistan and its political apparatus by granting him an "honorary post" in the government, which does not entail power sharing.[82] Even though the agreement is a breakthrough, as it represents the first qualified success in the Afghan government's protracted peace campaign, it is still fragile and easily reversible, particularly given Hekmatyar's history of breaking agreements and changing sides in a political conflict.

GLOBAL REACH

The Afghan Taliban movement has restricted its area of operations to attacks within the borders of Afghanistan, although violent clashes in the frontier areas with Iran and Tajikistan have occasionally been reported. These clashes are likely smuggling operations gone awry, as Afghanistan's frontier regions with Iran and Tajikistan are well-established narcotics and weapons smuggling routes. Occasionally, Afghan Taliban leaders have threatened attacks against NATO countries whose soldiers are operating in Afghanistan (namely Germany, Spain and the UK) although none of the terrorist attacks in any of these countries have ever been attributed to the Taliban.[83] In the fall of 2009, the Taliban made an effort to promote a new "foreign policy" by releasing several statements on their website declaring the movement poses no regional or international security threat. Mullah Omar repeated this rhetoric in one of his two annual *Eid* statements to the Afghan people, which appeared in mid-November 2010.[84] In June 2015, Mullah Mansour sent a letter to ISIS leader Abu Bakr al-Baghdadi, warning him to stop making separate *jihadist* inroads in Afghanistan or the group would face the consequences of Taliban retaliation.[85]

The Pakistani Taliban or TTP, especially following the Baitullah Mehsud's reign of terror between 2007 and 2009, have shown interest in not only attacking the Afghan government and security targets but also Pakistani state institutions and security targets. On several occasions in 2008 and 2009, Baitullah Mehusd threatened to launch attacks against international targets, including the White House.[86] On January 19, 2009, Spanish authorities seized 14 suspected associates of the TTP in Barcelona on suspicion of plotting a series of suicide-bomb attacks, which were to coincide with the run-up to the March 9 parliamentary elections and the March 11 anniversary of the Madrid commuter train bombings.[87] Similarly, the TTP claimed credit for the April 4, 2009 shooting attack at an immigration center in Binghamton, New York where 13 people lost their lives to a lone gunman. However, investigators quickly identified the gunman as a deranged Vietnamese immigrant with no ties to international terrorist groups or radical Islamist movements.

On May 1, 2010, Faisal Shahzad, a Pakistani-American, made a failed attempt to detonate a car bomb in Times Square in New York City. Shortly thereafter, in an interview with NBC's "Meet the Press," U.S. Attorney General Eric Holder said that based on the initial evidence collected, Shahzad was working with the Pakistani Taliban and that the movement directed the plot. In fact, TTP's top commander, Qari Hussain, who trained suicide bombers (calling them "the atomic weapons of Muslims") and plotted operations against the West, orchestrated the attack.[88] He was reported to have been killed in 2012 by a U.S. drone strike in North Waziristan.[89]

Mehsud's close association with Arab al-Qaeda leaders and Uzbek militants in South Waziristan partially explained his global-*jihadist* rhetoric. Following his death in August 2009, the TTP's shura struggled to nominate a new leader that pleased both the Pashtun tribal constituency and the more global minded *jihadists* of al-Qaeda. Al-Qaeda's influence won out, and Hakimullah Mehsud, the radical TTP commander of the Orakzai Agency, became the new *amir* for the TTP. Hakimullah ordered a number of deadly attacks against Pakistani and U.S. military targets in the region with some reports indicating he helped facilitate the suicide bombing attack against a U.S. intelligence base in eastern Khost province of Afghanistan. The deadly attack killed eight CIA officers and left six others severely injured on December 28, 2009.

RECENT ACTIVITY

Since the attack on the Army Public School in Peshawar in December 2014, the TTP and its affiliates have continued their offensives in Pakistan. The group has targeted civilians, government and military personnel, (as mentioned above), with the most recent high-profile attacks carried out on August 8, 2016, when suicide bombers targeted a government hospital in Quetta, Balochistan. In that attack, 77 people were killed and more than a hundred were injured. There was also a suicide attack on a mosque in Mohmand Agency the next month, all of which demonstrates the group's resiliency and persistence.[90]

The United Nations Assistance Mission in Afghanistan (UNAMA) estimates that, in the first half of 2013 alone, over 1,300 Afghan civilians were killed.[91] In 2014, the estimated civilian casualties were 10,548, including 3,699 civilian deaths, and 6,849 injuries—a staggering 22 percent rise.[92]

For the first half of 2015, UNAMA and the UN Human Rights Office documented almost 5,000 civilian casualties in Afghanistan – with close to 1600 deaths and over 3,300 injuries.[93] By the end of December 2015, civilian casualties had risen to over 11,000, most of which were attributed to the Haqqani network, including the attack in August that killed 43 and wounded more than 300, and an even deadlier attack on the Afghan intelligence directorate in April 2016 that left more than 60 dead and some 300 wounded.[94] The vicious trend continued into 2016, with 11,418 civilians recorded killed or maimed in that year.[95] Ground engagements, mostly by anti-government elements (60 percent), continue to be the main cause of civilian casualties, followed by complex and suicide attacks and improved explosive devices (IEDs).[96]

Meanwhile, in 2013 and 2014, the Afghan security forces – which have assumed primary responsibility for security from American and coalition forces – endured a staggering number of casualties.[97] The Afghan Ministry of Defense estimated that almost 1,400 soldiers lost their lives in 2013 alone fighting the insurgency.[98] Additionally, the year 2014 bore witness to an even higher death toll for Afghan security forces, with 1,868 soldiers and 3,720 police killed in the line of duty.[99] Furthermore, 2015, a year of survival for Afghanistan, wasthe bloodiest year on record for the Afghan security forces, marked by casualties reported at over 20,000 deaths and injuries, according to Gen. John Nicholson, commander of U.S. and coalition forces in Afghanistan.[100] The grim uptick continued into 2016 marked by the attack on April 19 that targeted a security compound responsible for protecting government VIPs and contractors in Kabul – killing 64 and injuring more than 300.[101] Two months later, in June, Taliban suicide bombers attacked a police convoy in the western outskirts of Kabul, carrying 215 recently graduated cadets in five buses, two of which were destroyed by explosions, killing nearly 40 cadets.[102]

The Taliban remains resilient and reportedly gained and lost control of at least 35 of Afghanistan's 398 districts. The group continues to contest for territory in at least another 35 districts and is more any time since their ouster in 2001.[103]

Endnotes

[1] Declan Walsh and Azam Ahmed, "Mending Alliance, U.S. and Afghanistan Sign Long-Term Security Agreement," New York Times, September 30, 2014, https://www.nytimes.com/2014/10/01/world/asia/afghanistan-and-us-sign-bilateral-security-agreement.html?_r=0.

[2] Lauren McNally & Paul Bucala, The Taliban Resurgent: Threats to Afghanistan's Security, Institute for the Study of War (ISW), March 2015, http://www.understandingwar.org/sites/default/files/AFGH Report.pdf

[3] Melanie Garunay, "An Update on Our Mission in Afghanistan," The White House, July 6, 2016, https://www.whitehouse.gov/blog/2016/07/06/update-our-mission-afghanistan

[4] Willis Dorronsoro, "The Taliban's Winning Strategy in Afghanistan," Carnegie Endowment for International Peace, 2009, http://carnegieendowment.org/files/taliban_winning_strategy.pdf

[5] Amin Tarzi and Robert D. Crews. "The Taliban and the Crisis of Afghanistan." May 2009, p. 295. http://www.hup.harvard.edu/catalog.php?isbn=9780674032248

[6] Antonio Giustozzi, Koran, Kalashnikov, and Laptop: the Neo-Taliban Insurgency in Afghanistan (New York: Columbia University Press, 2008), 46-47, 83, 90.

[7] "Taliban Admit Covering up Death of Mullah Omar," BBC News, August 31, 2015, http://www.bbc.com/news/world-asia-34105565

[8] Kenneth Katzman, Afghanistan: Post-Taliban Governance, Security, and U.S. Policy, Congressional Research Service, June 2016, http://www.fas.org/sgp/crs/row/RL30588.pdf This source has been updated as of January 2017 Note: Much of this information is taken from a series of U.S. Department of Defense (DoD) reports entitled, "Progress Toward Security and Stability in Afghanistan." The latest one was issued in December 2015, covering June 1 to November 30, 2015. http://www.defense.gov/Portals/1/Documents/pubs/1225_Report_Dec_2015_-_Final_20151210.pdf

[9] Ibid, Katzman, Afghanistan: Post-Taliban Governance, Security, and U.S. Policy.

[10] Dawood Azami, "Why are the Taliban Resurgent in Afghanistan?" BBC, January 2016, http://www.bbc.com/news/world-asia-35169478

[11] Ibid.

[12] "Afghanistan Drone Strike 'Kills IS Commander Abdul Rauf,'" BBC, February 2015, http://www.bbc.com/news/world-asia-31290147; See also U.S. Department of State, "Foreign Terrorist Organizations," n.d.,http://www.state.gov/j/ct/rls/other/des/123085.htm

[13] "Afghanistan Drone Strike 'Kills IS Commander Abdul Rauf'," BBC News, February 2015, http://www.bbc.com/news/world-asia-3129014 And, "Foreign Terrorist Organizations," U.S. Department of State,http://www.state.gov/j/ct/rls/other/des/123085.htm

[14] Katzman, Afghanistan: Post-Taliban Governance, Security, and U.S. Policy.

[15] Bill Roggio, "Taliban Appoints Mullah Omar's Brother, Son to Key Leadership Positions," Long War Journal, April 5, 2016, http://www.longwarjournal.org/archives/2016/04/taliban-appoint-mullah-omars-brother-son-to-key-leadership-positions.php.

[16] Bill Roggio, "Former Senior Taliban Leader with Jihadist Group," Long War Journal, August 10, 2016, http://www.longwarjournal.org/archives/2016/08/senior-former-taliban-leader-reconciles-with-jihadist-group.php

[17] Kenneth Katzman, Taliban Leadership Succession, Congressional Research Service, May 26, 2016, https://www.fas.org/sgp/crs/row/IN10495.pdf

[18] "New Taliban Leader Mullah Haibatullah Gets Ultimatum from Afghanistan Government," Associated Press, May 29, 2016, http://www.news.com.au/world/asia/new-taliban-leader-mullah-haibatullah-akhundzada-gets-ultimatum-from-afghanistan-government/news-story/5dc98f1ce3dbcc8c7e3cc1f0c62cd529.

[19] Katzman, "Taliban Leadership Succession.

[20] "New Taliban Leader Mullah Haibatullah Gets Ultimatum from Afghanistan Government."

[21] Samimullah Arif, "Ashraf Ghani's New Plan to Win Afghanistan's Long War Against the Taliban," The Diplomat, April 28, 2016, http://thediplomat.com/2016/04/ashraf-ghanis-new-plan-to-win-afghanistans-long-war-against-the-taliban/.
[22] Katzman, Taliban Leadership Succession.
[23] Azami, "Why are the Taliban Resurgent in Afghanistan?"
[24] Thomas Ruttig, "The Other Side: Dimensions of the Afghan Insurgency: Causes, Actors and Approaches to 'Talks,'" Afghanistan Analysts Network, July 2009, 24.
[25] Amir Mir, "War and Peace in Waziristan," Asia Times, May 4, 2005.
[26] Amir Mir, "The Most Wanted Pakistani Talib," Pakistan Post, December 10, 2007.
[27] Ibid.
[28] Carlotta Gall and Salman Masood, "At Least 40 Militants Dead as Pakistani Military Storms Mosque After Talks Fail," New York Times, July 10, 2007, http://www.nytimes.com/2007/07/10/world/asia/10pakistan.html
[29] Christina Lamb, "High-Profile Victories in the Battle Against Terror," Times of London, August 9, 2009.
[30] "Fighters Deny Bhutto Killing Link," Al Jazeera (Doha), December 30, 2007.
[31] Kotkai is the home village of TTP leader Hakeemullah Mehsud, and Kaniguram is a village where Uzbek militants established a headquarters and training area.
[32] "South Waziristan Offensive Over: Pakistani PM," CBC News, December 12, 2009, http://www.cbc.ca/world/story/2009/12/12/south-waziristan-offensive-ends.html.
[33] Tim Craig, "Drone Kills Taliban Chief Hakimullah Mehsud; Pakistan Accuses U.S. of Derailing Peace Talks," Washington Post, November 2, 2013, https://www.washingtonpost.com/world/asia_pacific/pakistani-official-accuses-us-of-sabotage-as-drone-targets-taliban-leaders-in-northwest/2013/11/01/1463d0c2-431d-11e3-b028-de922d7a3f47_story.html
[34] Juliet Perry, "Who Are the Pakistan Taliban?" CNN, January 20, 2016, http://edition.cnn.com/2016/01/20/asia/pakistan-taliban-profile-2016/
[35] Mushtaq Yusufzai, "Pakistan Taliban Fractures Over 'Un-Islamic' Kidnapping and Killing," NBC News, May 28, 2014, http://www.nbcnews.com/news/world/pakistan-taliban-fractures-over-un-islamic-kidnapping-killing-n116476
[36] Ibid; United States Department of State, Bureau of Counterterrorism, "Individuals and Entities Designated By the State Department under E.O 13224," n.d., http://www.state.gov/j/ct/rls/other/des/143210.htm

[37] Hameedullah Khan, "Paksitan Taliban Commander Allegedly Killed by Drones," Al Jazeera (Doha), November 26, 2015, http://www.aljazeera.com/news/2015/11/pakistan-taliban-commander-allegedly-killed-drones-151126094717789.html
[38] Ibid.
[39] Sophia Saifi, Sanjay Gupta & Salma Mohsin, "Militants Attack Karachi Airport; 21 Killed In Clashes," CNN, June 9, 2014, http://edition.cnn.com/2014/06/08/world/asia/pakistan-karachi-airport-attack/
[40] Julia Thompson, "A Small Measure of Progress," Foreign Policy, December 22, 2014, http://foreignpolicy.com/2014/12/22/a-small-measure-of-progress/
[41] Jon Boone, Dozen Killed in Suicide Attack at Pakistan-India Border Post," Guardian (London), November 2, 2014, https://www.theguardian.com/world/2014/nov/02/suicide-attack-wagah-border-bomb-blast-pakistan-india-flag-lowering; See also Mina Sohail, "Pakistan Responds to the Peshawar School Massacre," The Diplomat, December 26, 2014, http://thediplomat.com/2014/12/pakistan-responds-to-the-peshawar-school-massacre/
[42] Perry, "Who Are the Pakistan Taliban?"
[43] Ibid; Sohail, "Pakistan Responds to the Peshawar School Massacre."
[44] Ihsanullah Tipu Mehsud & Declan Walsh, "Hard-Line Splinter Group, Galvanized by ISIS, Emerges From Pakistani Taliban," New York Times, August 26, 2014, http://www.nytimes.com/2014/08/27/world/asia/hard-line-splinter-group-galvanized-by-isis-emerges-from-pakistani-taliban.html?_r=0.
[45] Zahir Shah Shirazi, "Twin Blasts Kill at Least Six in Mohmand," Dawn (Karachi), November 7, 2014, http://www.dawn.com/news/1142941/twin-blasts-kill-at-least-six-people-in-mohmand
[46] "Deadly Blasts Hit Pakistan Churches in Lahore," BBC, March 15, 2015, http://www.bbc.com/news/world-asia-31894708
[47] Sophia Saifi, "In Pakistan, Taliban's Easter Bombing Targets, Kills Scores of Christians," CNN, March 28, 2016, http://edition.cnn.com/2016/03/27/asia/pakistan-lahore-deadly-blast/
[48] Iftikhar Firdous, "At Least 28 Killed in Suicide Blast at Mohmand Agency Mosque," Express Tribune, September 16, 2016, http://tribune.com.pk/story/1182675/huge-explosion-mosque-mohmand-agency/
[49] Catherine Houreld & Saud Mehsud, "Pakistani Splinter Group Rejoins Taliban Among Amid Fears of Isolation," Reuters, March 12, 2015, http://www.reuters.com/article/us-pakistan-militants-alliance-idUSKBN0M81WF20150312
[50] Jibran Ahmad, "Pakistan Says Leader of School Attack Killed in U.S. Drone Strike," Reuters, July 14, 2016, http://www.reuters.com/article/us-pakistan-taliban-idUSKCN0ZT21O

[51] Bill Roggio, "TTP Commander of North Waziristan Touts Operations in Pakistan," The Long War Journal, September 14, 2016, http://www.longwarjournal.org/archives/2016/09/ttp-commander-for-north-waziristan-touts-operations-in-pakistan.php

[52] Ibid, The Long War Journal, September 14, 2016

[53] Ibid, The Long War Journal, September 14, 2016

[54] Harleen Gambhir, "ISIS in Afghanistan," Institute for the Study of War (ISW), December 2015,http://www.understandingwar.org/sites/default/files/ISIS in Afghanistan_2.pdf

[55] Matthew DuPee, "The Haqqani Networks: Reign of Terror," Long War Journal, August 2, 2008.

[56] Mark Mazzetti and Erich Schmitt, "Pakistanis Aided Attack in Kabul, US officials Say," New York Times, August 1, 2008, http://www.nytimes.com/2008/08/01/world/asia/01pstan.html.

[57] Rafiq Sherzad, "Afghan Attack Toll Rises, Making it Worst in 8 Months," Reuters, February 20, 2011; Bill Roggio, "Afghan Intel Links Jalalabad Bank Attack, Other Suicide Attacks to Pakistan," Long War Journal, February 27, 2011, http://www.longwarjournal.org/archives/2011/02/afghan_intel_links_j.php#ixzz1FOQFf0x2.

[58] Zahir Shah, "Haqqani Terror Network Founder May have Died a Year Ago," CNN, August 1, 2015, http://edition.cnn.com/2015/08/01/asia/pakistan-haqqani-network-leader-death/

[59] Ibid.

[60] Ibid, Kenneth Katzman, Afghanistan: Post-Taliban Governance, Security, and U.S. Policy, Congressional Research Service, June 2016, http://www.fas.org/sgp/crs/row/RL30588.pdf

[61] "NATO Commander links Haqqani network to Kabul attack," Reuters, June 22, 2012, http://uk.reuters.com/article/uk-afghanistan-hotel-haqqani-idUKBRE85L0ND20120622

[62] Carlotta Gall, "Terror Group Back on the Offensive in Afghanistan," New York Times, July 17, 2014, http://www.nytimes.com/2014/07/18/world/asia/kabul-airport-comes-under-attack-from-militants.html?ref=topics

[63] "Taliban Stages Deadly Attack on Afghan Parliament," Al Jazeera (Doha), June 22, 2015, http://www.aljazeera.com/news/2015/06/explosions-gunfire-rock-afghan-parliament-kabul-150622060232229.html

[64] Ayesha Tanzeem, "Pakistan Rejects Afghan Allegations on Parliament Attack," Voice of America, June 25, 2015, http://www.voanews.com/a/kabul-blames-haqqani-network-pakistan-for-parliament-attack/2836385.html

[65] Katzman, Taliban Leadership Succession.

[66] Mehreen Zahra-Malik, "Pakistan Bans Haqqani Network After Security Talks with Perry," Reuters, January 16, 2015, http://www.reuters.com/article/us-pakistan-militants-haqqani-idUSKBN0KP1DA20150116

[67] Marvin G. Weinbaum & Meher Babbar, "The Tenacious, Toxic Haqqani Network," Middle East Institute, September 7, 2016, http://www.mei.edu/content/tenacious-toxic-haqqani-network.
[68] Ibid.
[69] The most notorious attack against political rivals in known as the "Farkhar massacre" when a Hekmatyar sub-commander named Sayed Jamal killed 30 of Ahmed Shah Massoud's Shura-e Nezar commanders after a joint-meeting on July 9, 1989. Ishtiaq Ahmad, Gulbuddin Hekmatyar: An Afghan Trail from Jihad to Terrorism (Islamabad: Pan Graphics, 2004), 24.
[70] Giustozzi, Koran Kalashnikov and Laptop, 132.
[71] Matthew DuPee and Anand Gopal, "Tensions Rise Between Hizb-i-Islami and the Taliban in Afghanistan," Combating Terrorism Center at West Point CTC Sentinel, August 2010.
[72] U.S. Department of State, "Designation of Gulbuddin Hekmatyar as a Terrorist," February 19, 2003, https://2001-2009.state.gov/r/pa/prs/ps/2003/17799.htm
[73] Ibid, U.S. Department of State, February 19, 2003
[74] Ibid, Kenneth Katzman, Afghanistan: Post-Taliban Governance, Security, and U.S. Policy, Congressional Research Service, June 2016, http://www.fas.org/sgp/crs/row/RL30588.pdf- For specifics on the Kabul attack that killed 12 including 8 South African nationals, see Anita Powell, "8 South Africans Killed in Afghanistan," VOA News, September 18, 2012, http://www.voanews.com/a/suicide-bomber-attacks-foreigners-near-kabul/1510019.html
[75] Ibid, Kenneth Katzman, Afghanistan: Post-Taliban Governance, Security, and U.S. Policy, Congressional Research Service, June 2016, http://www.fas.org/sgp/crs/row/RL30588.pdf
[76] Thomas Ruttig, "Almost Signed? The Peace Agreement with Hezb-e-Islami," Afghanistan Analysts Network, May 21, 2016, http://www.afghanistan-analysts.org/wp-content/uploads/wp-post-to-pdf-cache/1/almost-signed-the-peace-agreement-with-hezb-e-islami.pdf
[77] Katzman, Taliban Leadership Succession.
[78] Rod Nordland, "Afghanistan Signs Draft Peace Deal with Faction Led by Gulbuddin Hekmatyar," New York Times, September 22, 2016, https://www.nytimes.com/2016/09/23/world/asia/afghanistan-peace-deal-hezb-i-islami.html.
[79] Ibid.
[80] Ibidem.
[81] Ibidem.
[82] Ibidem.

[83] David Montero, "Taliban to Germany: Leave Afghanistan or lose Oktoberfest," Christian Science Monitor, September 28, 2009; "Taliban Threatens Attacks on West: Spanish Radio," Agence France-Presse, November 26, 2008; "Dead Taliban Leader was Training U.S. Recruits," ABC News The Blotter, May 14, 2007.

[84] "Taliban Leader Mullah Omar Issues Statement on Eid Al-Adha, Rejects Media Reports of Peace Talks as 'Baseless Propaganda' Aimed at 'Wrongfully Raising Hollow Hopes in the Hearts of… People,'" Middle East Media Research Institute Special Dispatch no. 3380, November 15, 2010, http://www.memri.org/report/en/0/0/0/0/0/0/4769.htm.

[85] Eilish O'Gara, "Taliban Letter Warns ISIS to Stay Out of Afghanistan," Newsweek Europe, June 16, 2015, http://europe.newsweek.com/taliban-letter-warns-isis-stay-out-afghanistan-328820.

[86] Sara A. Carter and Eli Lake, "Taliban Threatens Attack in D.C.," Washington Times, April 1, 2009, http://www.washingtontimes.com/news/2009/apr/01/fbi-issues-alert-on-tali....

[87] Kathryn Haahr, "Spanish Police Arrest Jamaat al-Tabligh Members in Bomb Threat," Jamestown Foundation Terrorism Focus 5, iss. 6, February 13, 2008, http://www.jamestown.org/single/?no_cache=1&tx_ttnews%5Btt_news%5D=4722.

[88] Bill Roggio, "Taliban Eulogize Qari Hussain, Chief of Suicide and International Operations," Long War Journal, December 20, 2013, http://www.longwarjournal.org/archives/2013/12/taliban_eulogize_qar.php.

[89] Ibid.

[90] "Timeline of Deadliest Insurgent Attacks in Pakistan," Express Tribune, March 28, 2016, http://tribune.com.pk/story/1074142/timeline-of-deadliest-insurgent-attacks-in-pakistan/; See also "Lahore Attack: Anguish Families Bury Their Dead," Express Tribune, March 29, 2016,http://tribune.com.pk/story/1074654/lahore-attack-anguished-families-bury-their-dead/; See also "At Least 28 Killed in Suicide Blast at Mohmand Agency Mosque," Express Tribune, September 16, 2016,https://tribune.com.pk/story/1182675/huge-explosion-mosque-mohmand-agency/.

[91] "Afghanistan: Civilian Casualties Remain at Record High Level in the First Half of 2015 – UN Report," UN Human Rights Office of the High Commissioner, August 2015, http://www.ohchr.org/en/NewsEvents/Pages/DisplayNews.aspx?NewsID=16289&LangID=E

[92] "Civilian Casualties in Afghanistan Rise by 22 Percent in 2014," UNAMA, February 18, 2015, http://unama.unmissions.org/civilian-casualties-afghanistan-rise-22-cent-2014

[93] Ibid.

[94] "Afghanistan: Annual Report 2015 – Protection for Civilians in Armed Conflict," UNAMA & UN OHCHR, February 2016, https://unama.unmissions.org/sites/default/files/poc_annual_report_2015_final_14_feb_2016.pdf; See also Vanda Felbab-Brown, The Brookings Institution, May 2016, https://www.brookings.edu/wp-content/uploads/2016/06/Felbab-Brown-Paper-BLOOD-AND-FAITH-IN-AFGHANISTAN-May-2016.pdf

[95] "UN Calls on Parties to Take Urgent Measures to Halt Civilian Casualties, as Numbers for 2016 Reach Record High," UNAMA, February 6, 2017, https://unama.unmissions.org/un-calls-parties-take-urgent-measures-halt-civilian-casualties-numbers-2016-reach-record-high.

[96] Ibid, "UN Calls on Parties."

[97] Rod Nordland, "Afghanistan Signs Draft Peace Deal with Faction Led by Gulbuddin Hekmatyar," New York Times, September 22, 2016, http://www.nytimes.com/2016/09/23/world/asia/afghanistan-peace-deal-hezb-i-islami.html?ref=world&_r=0

[98] "2,853 ANA troops killed in Action Since 2003," Afghanistan Times, October 2014, http://old.afghanistantimes.af/news_details.php?id=9352; See also Neta C. Crawford, "War-Related Death, Injury and Displacement in Afghanistan and Pakistan 2001-2014," Costs of War, Watson Institute for International Studies, Brown University, May 2015, http://watson.brown.edu/costsofwar/files/cow/imce/papers/2015/War%20Related%20Casualties%20Afghanistan%20and%20Pakistan%202001-2014%20FIN.pdf

[99] Ibid.; See also Azam Ahmed, "The Hardest (and Most Important Job in Afghanistan," New York Times, March 8, 2015, http://www.nytimes.com/2015/03/08/magazine/the-hardest-job-in-afghanistan.html.

[100] Courtney Cube & Erik Ortiz, "Afghanistan Sees 20 Percent Rise in Casualties of Security Forces, Police: Official," NBC News, July 28 2016, http://www.nbcnews.com/news/world/afghanistan-sees-20-rise-casualties-security-forces-police-u-s-n618921

[101] Michael Pearson, Masoud Popalzai & Zahra Ullah, "Death Toll Rises After Taliban Attack in Kabul," CNN, April 20, 2016, http://edition.cnn.com/2016/04/19/asia/kabul-explosion/

[102] Kareem Fahim & Mohammad Fahim Abid, "Taliban Attack on Afghan Police Cadets Kills at Least 33," New York Times, June 30, 2016, http://www.nytimes.com/2016/07/01/world/asia/taliban-afghanistan-police-convoy-bombings.html?_r=0

[103] "Taliban Controls or Contests 70 Districts in Afghanistan," Long War Journal, October 16, 2015, http://www.longwarjournal.org/archives/2015/10/taliban-controls-or-contests-70-districts-in-afghanistan.php

CONTRIBUTORS

Afghanistan

Javid Ahmad (2017 Edition)
Javid Ahmad is a nonresident fellow with the Atlantic Council's South Asia Center and a senior intelligence manager at iJET International, a risk management firm, where he manages a fifteen-member team of intelligence analysts and provides analytical content and assessments to business and government clients. He is also a senior policy adviser to Afghanistan's minister of finance, focusing on devising policies and strategies on anti-money-laundering and counterterrorism financing issues. Additionally, he is a nonresident fellow at the Modern War Institute at West Point, where he researches and publishes on pressing security and counterterrorism issues in South Asia.

Previously, Javid worked on South Asia supporting the Pentagon's Afghanistan-Pakistan Hands program and the US Naval Postgraduate School. He also worked as a program coordinator for Asia for the German Marshall Fund of the United States, a Washington-based think tank. In addition, he has worked for the NATO HQ in Brussels, *The Voice of America*, and the Afghan embassy in Washington. He has also worked on governance issues for organizations in Kabul. Javid's writing has appeared, *inter alia*, in *The New York Times, The Washington Post, The Financial Times, The Wall Street Journal, Foreign Policy, CNN.com, Foreign Affairs, The National Interest,* and *The Daily Beast*. He has a BA in international relations from Beloit College and an MA in security studies from Yale University.

William Goodyear (2014 Edition)
Will Goodyear is the Gulf Research Associate and Special Researcher for the Director at the Near East-South Asia Center at the National Defense University. His research interests include Environmental and Natural Resource Security, International Aid and Development, Islamist Politics, and the Modern History of the Arab World.

David Cook (2011 Edition)
David Cook is associate professor of religious studies at Rice University

specializing in Islam. He did his undergraduate degrees at the Hebrew University in Jerusalem, and received his Ph.D. from the University of Chicago in 2001. His areas of specialization include early Islamic history and development, Muslim apocalyptic literature and movements (classical and contemporary), radical Islam, historical astronomy and Judeo-Arabic literature. His first book, *Studies in Muslim Apocalyptic*, was published by Darwin Press in the series Studies in Late Antiquity and Early Islam. Two further books, *Understanding Jihad* (Berkeley: University of California Press) and *Contemporary Muslim Apocalyptic Literature* (Syracuse: Syracuse University Press) were published during 2005, and *Martyrdom in Islam* (Cambridge: Cambridge University Press 2007) as well as *Understanding and Addressing Suicide Attacks* (with Olivia Allison, Westport, Conn.: Praeger Security Press, 2007) have been completed recently. Cook is continuing to work on contemporary Muslim apocalyptic literature, with a focus upon Shi'ite materials, as well as preparing manuscripts on *jihadi* groups and Western African Muslim history.

Brian Williams (2011 Edition)
Dr. Williams is an Associate Professor in the Department of History at the University of Massachusetts, Dartmouth. His fields of teaching and research include conflict in contemporary Islamic Eurasia, and nationalism and Identity in the Caucasus/Central Asia.

Al-Qaeda
Daveed Gartenstein-Ross (2017 Edition)
Daveed Gartenstein-Ross is a Senior Fellow at the Foundation for Defense of Democracies. His professional focus is on understanding how violent non-state actors (VNSAs) are transforming the world, and how states are in turn trying to adapt to this challenge. Gartenstein-Ross has specialized in jihadist movements, including undertaking detailed research into al-Qaeda, the Islamic State (ISIS), Ansar al-Sharia in Tunisia, Boko Haram, and ISIS's Wilayat Sinai. He is also the Chief Executive Officer of Valens Global, a consulting firm focused on the challenges posed by VNSAs, as well as a Fellow with Google's Jigsaw, an Associate Fellow at the International Centre for Counter-Terrorism – The Hague, and an Adjunct Assistant Professor in Georgetown University's Security Studies Program

Ilan Berman (2014 Edition)
Ilan Berman is Vice President of the American Foreign Policy Council in Washington, DC. An expert on regional security in the Middle East, Central Asia, and the Russian Federation, he has consulted for both the

U.S. Central Intelligence Agency and the U.S. Department of Defense, and provided assistance on foreign policy and national security issues to a range of governmental agencies and congressional offices. Berman is the author or editor of six books: *Tehran Rising: Iran's Challenge to the United States* (Rowman & Littlefield, 2005), *Dismantling Tyranny: Transitioning Beyond Totalitarian Regimes* (Rowman & Littlefield, 2005), *Taking on Tehran: Strategies for Confronting the Islamic Republic* (Rowman & Littlefield, 2007), *Winning the Long War: Retaking the Offensive Against Radical Islam* (Rowman & Littlefield, 2009), *Implosion: The End of Russia and What it Means for America* (Regnery Publishing, 2013), and *Iran's Deadly Ambition: The Islamic Republic's Quest for Global Power* (Encounter Books, 2015).

Jared Swanson (2014 Edition)
Jared Swanson is a former Research Associate at the American Foreign Policy Council. He provides research support for AFPC initiatives and develops quantitative tools and methods to assist with analysis. His research interests include U.S. strategic priorities and development programs in Africa and the Middle East. He has published writings on the Middle East and South Asian Maritime Security issues. Swanson is a graduate of the University of Oregon.

Raymond Ibrahim (2011 Edition)
Raymond Ibrahim is associate director of the Middle East Forum, author of *The Al Qaeda Reader* (Doubleday, 2007), and deputy publisher of The Middle East Quarterly. A widely published author on Islam, he regularly discusses that topic with the media, including *Fox News, C-SPAN, Reuters, Al-Jazeera, NPR, CBN,* and *PBS*. Mr. Ibrahim guest-lectures at the National Defense Intelligence College (Washington, D.C.), briefs governmental agencies (such as U.S. Strategic Command), provides expert testimony for Islam related lawsuits, and has testified before Congress regarding the conceptual failures that dominate American discourse concerning Islam. He began his career as a reference assistant at the Library of Congress' Near East Section.

Albania

Christopher Deliso (2011, 2014, and 2017 Editions)
Christopher Deliso is an American journalist and author concentrating on the Balkans. Over the past decade, Chris has established a dedicated presence in the Balkans, and published analytical articles on related topics in numerous relevant media outlets, such as *UPI, The Economist Intelligence Unit,* and *Jane's Islamic Affairs Analyst* and *Jane's Intelligence Digest*. Chris is also the founder and director of the Balkan-interest news and current affairs website, www.balkanalysis.com, and the author of *The Coming Balkan Caliphate: The Threat*

of Radical Islam to Europe and the West (Praeger Security International, 2007).

Algeria
Yahia Zoubir (2011, 2014, and 2017 Editions)
Yahia H. Zoubir is Professor of International Studies and International Management, and Director of Research in Geopolitics at EUROMED MANAGEMENT, Marseille School of Management, France. His recent works include, *Global Security Watch: The Maghreb* (Praeger, 2013); *North Africa: Politics, Region, and the Limits of Transformation* (Routledge, 2008); "The Sahara-Sahel Quagmire: Regional and International Implications," *Mediterranean Politics* (Nov.2012); "Tilting the Balance toward Intra-Maghreb Unity in Light of the Arab Spring," *International Spectator* (Sept. 2012); "The Libya Spawn, What the Dictator's Demise Unleashed in the Middle East," Snapshot, *Foreign Affairs* (July 2012); "The End of the Libyan Dictatorship: The Uncertain Transition," *Third World Quarterly* (July 2012); "Algeria's Path to Political Reforms: Authentic Reforms?" Middle East Policy (July 2012); "Algeria and Russia: Reconciling Contrasting Interests," *The Maghreb Review* (Sept. 2011); "The United States and Libya: The Limits of Coercive Diplomacy," *Journal of North African Studies* (2011); and, "The United States and the Maghreb: Strategic Interests" (chapter in *America's Challenges in the Greater Middle East*, 2011). He serves on the board of numerous international academic journals. Zoubir is also an international consultant for governments and businesses.

Australia
Mohamed Nawab Mohamed Osman (2014 and 2017 Editions)
Mohamed Nawab Mohamed Osman is the Coordinator of the Malaysia Program and a Research Associate with Contemporary Islam Programme at the S. Rajaratnam School of International Studies (RSIS), Nanyang Technological University, Singapore. His research interests include the domestic and international politics of Southeast and South Asian countries, transnational Islamic political movements and counter-radicalization. Nawab has written various papers, books and journal articles relating to his research interests. Some of these articles have been featured in prominent journals such as *Southeast Asia Research, South Asia, Pacific Review, Studies and Conflict in Terrorism, Terrorism and Political Violence*, and *Indonesia and the Malay World*. Several of his articles have been featured in leading dailies such as *The Straits Times, India Express, The Nation* (Thailand), *Jakarta Post, Manila Times* and *Today's Zaman* (Turkey). Nawab is also a social activist and serves as the Vice-President of the Professional Expatriate Network of Singapore. He also

sits in the boards of Association of Muslim Professionals, Jamiyah Singapore and Forum for Islamic and Democracy in Southeast Asia. As a former student activist, he served as President of National University of Singapore.

Waleed Aly (2011 Edition)
Waleed Aly is a lecturer in the Global Terrorism Research Centre at Monash University in Melbourne, Australia. His research interests include homegrown radicalization and the relationship between identity politics and political violence.

Azerbaijan
Svante E. Cornell and Julian Tucker (2017 Edition)
Svante E. Cornell joined the American Foreign Policy Council as Senior Fellow for Eurasia in January 2017. He also servs as the Director of the Central Asia-Caucasus Institute & Silk Road Studies Program, and a co-founder of the Institue for Security and Development Policy, Stockholm. His main areas of expertise are security issues, state-building, and transnational crime in Southwest and Central Asia, with a specific focus on the Caucasus and Turkey. He is the Editor of *The Central Asia-Caucasus Analyst*, the Joint Center's bi-weekly publication, and of the Joint Center's *Silk Road Papers* series of occasional papers.

Cornell is the author of four books, including *Small Nations and Great Powers*, the first comprehensive study of the post-Soviet conflicts in the Caucasus, and *Azerbaijan Since Independence*. Cornell is an Associate Research Professor at Johns Hopkins University's Paul H. Nitze School of Advanced International Studies. He was educated at the Middle East Technical University, received his Ph.D. in Peace and Conflict Studies from Uppsala University, and holds an honorary degree from the National Academy of Sciences of Azerbaijan. He is a member of the Swedish Royal Academy of Military Science, and a Research Associate with the W. Martens Center for European Studies in Brussels. Formerly, Cornell served as Associate Professor of Government at Uppsala University.

Mr. Julian Tucker is a Research Coordinator at the Stockholm China Center of the Institute for Security and Development Policy. He recently completed his Master of Arts in Central Asian Studies at the Humboldt University in Berlin, Germany. He also pursued Uzbek language and history courses at the Samarkand State Institute of Foreign Languages in Uzbekistan. He holds a BA in Anthropology and Middle Eastern Languages from McGill University in Montreal, Canada. Mr. Tucker's research interests include the implications of regional authority and security structures in Central Asia for international development efforts. At the China Centre his work will focus primarily on the One Belt One Road Initiative and Maritime Security in The South China Sea.

Ariel Cohen (2011 Edition)
Ariel Cohen is a Senior Research Fellow at The Kathryn and Shelby Cullom Davis Institute for International Studies at the Heritage Foundation. He received his Ph.D. from the Fletcher School of Law and Diplomacy at Tufts University in Massachusetts. Dr. Cohen is also a member of the Council of Foreign Relations, International Institute of Strategic Studies in London, and Association for the Study of Nationalities. His research interests include the economic development and political reform in the former Soviet Republics, and continuing conflicts in the Middle East. He has on multiple occasions testified on Russian and Eurasian politics, economics, and law before the U.S. Congress. Dr. Cohen has also published numerous pieces of writing.

Bahrain
Don Radlauer (2011 and 2017 Editions)
Donald Radlauer is the foremost expert on the demographics of the victims from the phase of the Israeli-Palestinian Conflict that began in September of 2000. He is an Associate of the International Policy Institute for Counter-Terrorism (ICT) where he has published and lectured extensively on topics relating to terror finance, counter-terrorism, casualty statistics, asymmetric conflict, and radicalization via "virtual communities." Mr. Radlauer is the Lead Researcher for the ICT's "Al-Aqsa Intifada" Database Project where he developed the project's technological infrastructure and wrote the projects findings in the study *An Engineered Tragedy*. Mr. Radlauer studied History and Sociology of Science at the University of Pennsylvania. He is also a director and co-founder of the Institute for the Study of Asymmetric Conflict.

Bangladesh
Zaglul Haider (2011, 2014, and 2017 Editions)
Zaglul Haider is a professor of Political Science at the University of Rajshahi. He received his PhD in Political Science from Clark Atlanta University in Atlanta, Georgia, U.S.A and did an LLM from Osgoode Hall Law School, Canada. Dr. Haider has published a good number of articles in European, North American and South Asian academic journals. His articles appeared in *The Security Dialogue, Asian Survey, The Round Table, African and Asian Studies, Asian and African Studies, South Asian and Middle Eastern Studies,* and *Asian Profile and Regional Studies*. Dr. Haider's book, *The Changing*

Pattern of Bangladesh Foreign Policy: A Comparative Study of the Mujib and Zia Regimes, was published by the University Press Limited in 2006.

Boko Haram
Jacob Zenn (2011, 2014, and 2017 Editions)
Jacob Zenn is an analyst of African and Eurasian Affairs for The Jamestown Foundation and author of the Occasional Report entitled *Northern Nigeria's Boko Haram: The Prize in al-Qaeda's Africa Strategy*, published by The Jamestown Foundation in November 2012. In 2012, he conducted field research in Nigeria, Niger, Chad and Cameroon on the socio-economic factors behind the Boko Haram insurgency. Mr. Zenn earned a J.D. from Georgetown Law, where he was a Global Law Scholar, and a graduate degree in International Affairs from the Johns Hopkins SAIS Center for Chinese-American Studies in Nanjing, China. He has spoken at international conferences on Boko Haram and is frequently interviewed and cited in international media.

Bolivia
Joseph Humire (2014 and 2017 Editions)
Joseph M. Humire is a global security expert, focusing on the nexus between security, defense and economic freedom. Humire's research and investigations on the crime-terror nexus, radical Islam and Iran's influence in Latin America has been sought after by various entities within the U.S. government as well as think tanks and private sector clients throughout the hemisphere. Currently the Executive Director of the Center for a Secure Free Society (SFS), Humire is developing a global network of security and defense specialists that are focused on the intersection of security, intelligence, defense and economic development. Prior to this, Humire spent seven years with the United States Marine Corps, deployed to many hot spots around the world, including Iraq and Liberia, and partook in the first multinational military exercise in Latin America—Unitas 45-04. He is also a graduate from George Mason University with a degree in Economics and Global Affairs. Humire co-edited *Iran's Strategic Penetration of Latin America* (Lexington Books, 2014).

Douglas Farah (2011 Edition)
Douglas Farah is president of IBI Consultants LLC and a senior fellow at the International Assessment and Strategy Center. For twenty years, he was a foreign correspondent and investigative reporter at *The Washington Post*, where he won numerous awards for his work. In addition to his national security consulting work he is a regular lecturer at universities, government agencies

and foreign policy groups. He has testified before Congress on numerous occasions, has written two books and numerous articles and monographs.

Brazil
Joseph Humire (2014 and 2017 Editions)
Joseph M. Humire is a global security expert, focusing on the nexus between security, defense and economic freedom. Humire's research and investigations on the crime-terror nexus, radical Islam and Iran's influence in Latin America has been sought after by various entities within the U.S. government as well as think tanks and private sector clients throughout the hemisphere. Currently the Executive Director of the Center for a Secure Free Society (SFS), Humire is developing a global network of security and defense specialists that are focused on the intersection of security, intelligence, defense and economic development. Prior to this, Humire spent seven years with the United States Marine Corps, deployed to many hot spots around the world, including Iraq and Liberia, and partook in the first multinational military exercise in Latin America—Unitas 45-04. He is also a graduate from George Mason University with a degree in Economics and Global Affairs. Humire co-edited *Iran's Strategic Penetration of Latin America* (Lexington Books, 2014).

Canada
Candice Malcolm (2017 Edition)
Candice Malcolm is a best-selling author, a nationally syndicated columnist with the Toronto Sun and Postmedia papers, and an international fellow with the Centre for a Secure Free Society in Washington, D.C. She is the founder of the True North Initiative, an independent, non-profit research and educational organization in Canada that seeks to champion sound immigration and security policies for the 21st century. Candice is the author of two best-selling books, *Generation Screwed* and *Losing True North*. She is a former advisor to the Minister of Citizenship and Immigration Canada, the former director of research at Sun News Network, and the former Director of the Canadian Taxpayer's Federation in Ontario.
Born and raised in Vancouver, British Columbia, Candice is a ninth generation Canadian and loves to travel; she has visited over 80 countries. Candice has master's degrees in international relations and international law, and splits her time between Toronto and San Francisco, with her husband Kasra.

Micah Levinson (2011 Edition)
Micah Levinson is a former Junior Fellow at the American Foreign Policy Council. Trained in government and political economy, he earned a B.A.

from Harvard University and an M.A. from Washington University in St. Louis, Missouri. He also holds a certificate in counterterrorism from the Interdisciplinary Center in Herzliya, Israel. Micah's research focuses on revolutionary groups and the stability of authoritarian regimes, and he has published on these topics in Politics, Philosophy & Economics and has contributed to *The Political Economy of Democracy and Tyranny*, edited by Norman Schofield.

China
Ilan Berman (2017 Edition)
Ilan Berman is Vice President of the American Foreign Policy Council in Washington, DC. An expert on regional security in the Middle East, Central Asia, and the Russian Federation, he has consulted for both the U.S. Central Intelligence Agency and the U.S. Department of Defense, and provided assistance on foreign policy and national security issues to a range of governmental agencies and congressional offices. Berman is the author or editor of six books: *Tehran Rising: Iran's Challenge to the United States* (Rowman & Littlefield, 2005), *Dismantling Tyranny: Transitioning Beyond Totalitarian Regimes* (Rowman & Littlefield, 2005), *Taking on Tehran: Strategies for Confronting the Islamic Republic* (Rowman & Littlefield, 2007), *Winning the Long War: Retaking the Offensive Against Radical Islam* (Rowman & Littlefield, 2009), *Implosion: The End of Russia and What it Means for America* (Regnery Publishing, 2013), and *Iran's Deadly Ambition: The Islamic Republic's Quest for Global Power* (Encounter Books, 2015).

Joshua Eisenman (2011 Edition)
Joshua Eisenman is Senior Fellow in China Studies at the American Foreign Policy Council. A former professional policy analyst on the staff of the Congressionally-mandated U.S.-China Economic and Security Review Commission, he is currently a Ph.D. Candidate in the political science department at the University of California, Los Angeles. Mr. Eisenman received his MA in International Relations with specializations in China studies and international economics at Johns Hopkins University's Paul H. Nitze School of Advanced International Studies (SAIS) and a BA in East Asian Studies and Chinese language from The George Washington University. He speaks and reads Mandarin Chinese.

Denmark
Manni Crone (2011, 2014, and 2017 Editions)
Manni Crone is a Danish translator and holds a Ph.D. in Political Science

from the Institut d'études politiques de Paris and the DEA from l'École des Hautes Études en Sciences Sociales. She has translated, among other works, *Boris Vian* and *Francis Picabia* from French to Danish together with Asger Schnack. She is an assistant professor at the Department of Political Science at the University of Copenhagen, where she conducts research in Islam, secularism, and religious influence on policy formation.

Egypt
Eric Trager (2017 Edition)
Eric Trager, the Esther K. Wagner Fellow at The Washington Institute, is an expert on Egyptian politics and the Muslim Brotherhood in Egypt. He was in Egypt during the 2011 anti-Mubarak revolts and returns frequently to conduct firsthand interviews with leaders in Egypt's government, military, political parties, media, and civil society. His writings have appeared in numerous publications, including *The New York Times, The Wall Street Journal, Foreign Affairs, The Atlantic,* and *The New Republic*.
Trager is the author of *Arab Fall: How the Muslim Brotherhood Won and Lost Egypt in 891 Days* (Georgetown University Press, 2016) which chronicles the precipitous rise to power of Egypt's Muslim Brotherhood, culminating in the election of President Mohamed Morsi in 2012, and its sudden demise just a year later. The book also assesses the current state of Egyptian politics and the prospects for a reemergence of the Brotherhood.
Dr. Trager has served as an adjunct professor at the University of Pennsylvania, where his doctoral research focused on Egyptian opposition parties. From 2006-2007, he lived in Egypt as an Islamic Civilizations Fulbright fellow, where he studied at the American University in Cairo and received his M.A. in Arabic studies with a concentration in Islamic studies. He served as a research assistant at The Washington Institute from 2005 to 2006 upon graduation from Harvard University with a degree in government and language citations in Arabic and Hebrew.

Alexander Brock (2014 Edition)
Alexander Brock is a JD candidate at the University of California, Berkeley, school of law, and is also the translation reviewer for *National Geographic Magazine's* Arabic edition. He previously worked as a research associate for Middle Eastern studies at the Council on Foreign Relations in Washington, DC. He is a former Fulbright Scholar to Cairo, Egypt, where he conducted research on Islamic philosophy at Cairo University. He received his BA in Philosophy with a minor in Arabic from Dickinson College in Carlisle, PA.

Myriam Benraad (2011 Edition)

Myriam Benraad is a research fellow in the Middle East and Mediterranean doctoral program of the Paris Institute of Political Studies (Sciences Po), and at the Center for International Studies and Research (CERI). She is also an Associate Fellow at the Washington Institute for Near East Policy in Washington, DC.

Ethiopia
J. Peter Pham (2011, 2014, and 2017 Editions)
J. Peter Pham is Vice President for Research and Regional Initiatives at the Atlantic Council as well as Director of the Council's Africa Center. He also serves as Vice President of the Association for the Study of the Middle East and Africa (ASMEA) and Editor-in-Chief of its refereed *Journal of the Middle East and Africa*.

Fetullah Gülen Movement
Claire Berlinski (2014 and 2017 Editions)
Claire Berlinski is a former Senior Fellow for Turkey at AFPC. Ms. Berlinski is a City Journal contributing editor, a freelance investigative journalist, traveler writer, biographer, and novelist who lives in Istanbul. She is the author of *Menace in Europe: Why the Continent's Crisis is America's, Too*, and *There is No Alternative: Why Margaret Thatcher Matters*.
Her journalism has been published in *The New York Times, The Washington Post, The Los Angeles Times, First Post, The Oxford International Review,* The *American, Asia Times, The Globe and Mail, The New York Sun, The Weekly Standard, National Review, Policy Review, Radio Free Europe*, and *World Affairs Journal*, among others. She is also author of two spy novels and frequent guest on local and international radio talk shows.

France
Anonymous (2017 Edition)
AFPC thanks our anonymous authors for their generous contributions to the *World Almanac of Islamism*.

Russell Berman (2011 and 2014 Editions)
Russell A. Berman is the Walter A. Haas Professor in the Humanities at Stanford University and a Senior Fellow at the Hoover Institution. His areas of specialization include modern European culture, trans-Atlantic relations, anti-Americanism and terrorism. Recent publications include *Fiction Sets You Free: Literature, Liberty and Western Culture* (Lincoln: University of Iowa Press, 2007), *Anti-Americanism in Europe: A Cultural Problem* (Stanford:

Hoover Press, 2008) and *Freedom or Terror: Europe Faces Jihad* (Stanford: Hoover Press, 2010).

Germany
Clemens Heni (2011, 2014, and 2017 Editions)
Dr. Clemens Heni is the Director of the Berlin International Center for the Study of Antisemitism (BICSA), www.bicsa.org. He is the author of four books, including his new book in 2013, a 648 page study on Antisemitism: *A Specific Phenomenon – Holocaust Trivialization – Islamism – Post-colonial and Cosmopolitan anti-Zionism* (www.editioncritic.de). He publishes both in English and German and is a regular speaker at international conferences, dealing with topics like anti-Semitism, Islamism, Israel, the Middle East, contemporary Germany, the Holocaust and related topics.

Hezbollah
Matthew Levitt: Hezbolah (2011, 2014, and 2017 Editions)
Matthew Levitt is a senior fellow and director of The Washington Institute's Stein Program on Counterterrorism and Intelligence, and an adjunct professor at Johns Hopkins University's Paul H. Nitze School of Advanced International Studies (SAIS). Previously, he served as deputy assistant secretary for intelligence and analysis at the U.S. Department of the Treasury and earlier still as an FBI counterterrorism analyst. He is the author of several books, including *Hamas: Politics, Charity and Terrorism in the Service of Jihad* (Yale University Press, 2006) and *Hezbollah's Global Reach: The Worldwide Presence of Lebanon's Party of God* (Georgetown University Press, 2013).

Hizb ut-Tahrir
Emmanuel Karagiannis (2014 and 2017 Editions)
Emmanuel Karagiannis is Assistant Professor of International Relations at the University of Macedonia's Department of Balkan, Slavic and Oriental Studies in Thessaloniki, Greece and a Research Associate of Bryn Mawr College's Solomon Asch Center for the Study of Ethno-political Conflict in the United States. He is the author of *Political Islam in Central Asia: The Challenge of Hizb ut-Tahrir* (New York: Routledge, 2010).

Tyler Rauert (2011 Edition)
Tyler Rauert is a Professor of International Law and Political Violence at the Near East South Asia Center for Strategic Studies of the National Defense University. He focuses on the study of just war theory, the law of armed conflict, human rights, transnational organized crime, and security in the

Middle East and South Asia. The views expressed herein do not represent those of the National Defense University, the Department of Defense, or any other branch of the U.S. government.

India
Ajai Sahni (2011, 2014, and 2017 Editions)
Ajai Sahni is the founding member and Executive Director of the Institute for Conflict Management. His focus of study is on security issues in South Asia, and as the Executive Director of the Institute, he has acted as a consultant for various national and state governments in regards to internal security issues. Dr. Sahni is also the Editor of the South Asian Intelligence Review and the Executive Editor of the quarterly journal, *Faultlines: Writings on Conflict and Resolution*. He is a member of the Council for Security Cooperation in the Asia Pacific – India. He has written extensively on issues pertaining to conflict and development in South Asia. Dr. Sahni received his Ph.D. from Delhi University.

Indonesia
Joseph Chinyong Liow (2011, 2014, and 2017 Editions)
Joseph Chinyong Liow is Associate Dean and Professor of Comparative and International Politics at the S. Rajaratnam School of International Studies, Nanyang Technological University, Singapore. He is the author of *Piety and Politics: Islamism in Contemporary Malaysia* (New York: Oxford University Press, 2009) and *Islam, Education and Reform in Southern Thailand* (Singapore: ISEAS, 2009).

Islamic Republic of Iran
Ilan Berman (2011, 2014, and 2017 Editions)
Ilan Berman is Vice President of the American Foreign Policy Council in Washington, DC. An expert on regional security in the Middle East, Central Asia, and the Russian Federation, he has consulted for both the U.S. Central Intelligence Agency and the U.S. Department of Defense, and provided assistance on foreign policy and national security issues to a range of governmental agencies and congressional offices. Berman is the author or editor of six books: *Tehran Rising: Iran's Challenge to the United States* (Rowman & Littlefield, 2005), *Dismantling Tyranny: Transitioning Beyond Totalitarian Regimes* (Rowman & Littlefield, 2005), *Taking on Tehran: Strategies for Confronting the Islamic Republic* (Rowman & Littlefield, 2007), *Winning the Long War: Retaking the Offensive Against Radical Islam* (Rowman & Littlefield, 2009), *Implosion: The End of Russia and What it Means for*

America (Regnery Publishing, 2013), and *Iran's Deadly Ambition: The Islamic Republic's Quest for Global Power* (Encounter Books, 2015).

Iraq

Renad Mansour (2017 Edition)
Since 2008, Renad has held research and teaching positions focusing on issues of comparative politics and international relations in the Middle East. His research at Chatham House explores the situation of Iraq in transition and the dilemmas posed by state-building.
Prior to joining Chatham House, Renad was an El-Erian fellow at the Carnegie Middle East Centre, where he examined Iraq, Iran and Kurdish affairs. Renad is also a research fellow at the Cambridge Security Initiative based at Cambridge University and from 2013, he held positions as lecturer of International Studies and supervisor at the faculty of politics, also at Cambridge University. Renad has been a senior research fellow at the Iraq Institute for Strategic Studies in Beirut since 2011 and was adviser to the Kurdistan Regional Government Civil Society Ministry between 2008 and 2010. He received his PhD from Pembroke College, Cambridge.

Marisa Sullivan (2014 Edition)
As Deputy Director at the Institute for the Study of War (ISW), Marisa Cochrane Sullivan supervises the Iraq and Afghanistan Projects. Ms. Cochrane Sullivan also conducts research on Iraqi political dynamics, Shi'a militia groups, and the security environment in central and southern Iraq. Ms. Cochrane Sullivan has also authored numerous publications on these issues, including Balancing Maliki and The Fragmentation of the Sadrist Trend. Ms. Cochrane Sullivan holds a Bachelor's Degree in International Studies from Boston College, where she held a Presidential Scholarship and won the prestigious McCarthy Award for her scholarship in the Social Sciences. She has also studied at the London School of Economics and Political Science.

Hussain Abdul-Hussain (2011 Edition)
Hussain Abdul-Hussain is an expert on the Middle East and the Washington correspondent of Kuwaiti daily *Al Rai*. Abdul-Hussain previously worked for the Congressionally-funded Arabic television channel *Alhurra*, and for Beirut's *Daily Star*. He has contributed articles to *The New York Times, The Washington Post, The Christian Science Monitor, The International Herald Tribune* and *USA Today*, and has appeared on both *CNN* and *MSNBC*. He appears regularly on Arabic satellite television channels. Abdul-Hussain is a graduate of the American University of Beirut.

Islamic State
Alberto Fernandez (2017 Edition)
Alberto M. Fernandez is Vice-President of the Middle East Media Research Institute (MEMRI) and a board member of the Center for Cyber and Homeland Security at George Washington University. Ambassador Fernandez served as a U.S. Foreign Service Officer from 1983 to 2015, and as the State Department's Coordinator for the Center for Strategic Counterterrorism Communications from March 2012 to February 2015. From 2009-2012, he served as U.S. Ambassador to the Republic of Equatorial Guinea; prior to that, he was U.S. Charge d'Affaires to the Republic of Sudan (June 2007-May 2009), Director for Near East Public Diplomacy (2005-2007), Director for Iraq Public Diplomacy (2004-2005) and in senior public diplomacy positions at the U.S. Embassies in Afghanistan, Jordan, Syria, and Guatemala.

Israel
Lorena Atiyas Lvovsky (2017 Edition)
Lorena Atiyas Lvovsky is Researcher at the International Institute for Counter-Terrorism (ICT), and serves as the ICT External Relations Manager, facilitating ICT cooperation with academic, security and governmental bodies.
Atiyas Lvovsky holds a BA in Government, graduating with distinction, from the Lauder School of Government, Diplomacy, and Strategy at the Interdisciplinary Center (IDC) Herzliya, Israel. Ms. Atiyas Lvovsky is currently pursuing a MA with a Thesis from the Lauder School of Government, Diplomacy, and Strategy at the IDC Herzliya, Israel.

Micah Levinson (2014 Edition)
Micah Levinson is a former Junior Fellow at the American Foreign Policy Council. Trained in government and political economy, he earned a B.A. from Harvard University and an M.A. from Washington University in St. Louis, Missouri. He also holds a certificate in counterterrorism from the Interdisciplinary Center in Herzliya, Israel. Micah's research focuses on revolutionary groups and the stability of authoritarian regimes, and he has published on these topics in *Politics, Philosophy & Economics and has contributed to The Political Economy of Democracy and Tyranny*, edited by Norman Schofield.

Barak Seener (2011 Edition)
Barak Seener is a Research Fellow in Middle Eastern Studies at the Royal

United Services Institute (RUSI). Prior to his time at RUSI, Seener was one of the founding members of the Henry Jackson Society in Westminster, and was the Society's Director for the Greater Middle East Section. As an expert on the Middle East and the Israel-Palestine controversy, he has appeared on multiple TV networks such as *Al-Jazeera, BBC, CNN, Bloomberg*, and has published extensively for the Hudson Institute, *Middle East Quarterly, Muslim World*, and *The Jerusalem Post*. Mr. Seener holds a Master's degree in International Security and Global Governance from Birbeck College, University of London and a BA in History and Politics from Queen Mary, University of London.

Italy

Anonymous (2017 Edition)
AFPC thanks our anonymous authors for their generous contributions to the *World Almanac of Islamism*.

Lorenzo Vidino (2011 and 2014 Editions)
Lorenzo Vidino, Ph.D., is an academic and security expert who specializes in Islamism and political violence in Europe and North America. Currently a senior fellow at the Center for Security Studies, ETH Zurich, he previously held positions at the RAND Corporation, the Belfer Center for Science and International Affairs, Kennedy School of Government, Harvard University, the U.S. Institute of Peace, and the Fletcher School of Law and Diplomacy. He has taught at Tufts University, the University of Maryland (START), the National Defense University and the University of Zurich. He is the author of three books and frequent articles in several prominent newspapers and academic journals. He has testified before the U.S. Congress and consults with governments, law firms, think tanks and media in several countries. A native of Milan, Italy, he holds a law degree from the University of Milan Law School and a doctorate in international relations from the Fletcher School of Law and Diplomacy.

Jordan

Ehud Rosen (2014 and 2017 Editions)
Ehud Rosen is an expert on modern political Islam, focusing on the ideology and history of the Muslim Brotherhood in the Middle East and Europe. He is a senior researcher at the Jerusalem Center for Public Affairs and teaches at Bar-Ilan University. Among his relevant publications are "The Muslim Brotherhood's concept of education," *Current Trends of Islamist Ideology* (vol. 7, November 2008), and *Reading the runes? The United States and the Muslim*

Brotherhood as seen through the Wikileaks cables, co-authored with Dr. Martyn Frampton), (The Historical Journal, 2013).

Shmuel Bar (2011 Edition)
Dr. Bar is Director of Studies at the Institute of Policy and Strategy, Interdisciplinary Center Herzliya, Israel. He retired from the Israeli civil service in 2003 after 30 years as an intelligence analyst, during which he specialized in Jordanian, Palestinian, Iranian and Syrian affairs, and ideological and operational aspects of the *jihadi-Salafi* movement and served in various senior positions in Israel and abroad. Dr. Bar holds a Ph.D. in History of the Middle East from Tel-Aviv University (1989), M.A. (*Magna cum Laude*) in History of the Middle East from Tel-Aviv University (1984) and a B.A from The Hebrew University of Jerusalem, 1974, in Jewish and Middle Eastern History. He has published numerous books and papers on Middle Eastern affairs, terrorism and radical Islam.

Yair Minzili (2011 Edition)
Yair Minzili is a senior research fellow at the Institute for Policy and Strategy. He is a veteran expert on Islamic radicalism and has specialized and published on the Islamic movement in Jordan and the strategies of the Jihadi-salafi movements.

Kazakhstan
Mariya Y. Omelicheva (2017 Edition)
Mariya Y. Omelicheva is an Associate Professor in the Department of Political Science at the University of Kansas. She holds PhD (2007) in Political Science from Purdue University and JD in International Law (2000) from Moscow National Law Academy. Dr. Omelicheva's research and teaching interests include international and Eurasian security, counterterrorism and human rights, democracy promotion in the post-Soviet territory, Russia's foreign and security policy, and terrorism/crime nexus in Eurasia. She has published on these subjects in *Terrorism and Political Violence, Europe-Asia Studies, International Journal of Human Rights, Central Asia Survey, Cambridge Review of International Relations*, and other journals. She is the author of *Counterterrorism Policies in Central Asia* (Routledge 2011), which received an Outstanding Academic Title award by Choice, and *Democracy in Central Asia: Competing Perspectives and Alternate Strategies* (University Press of Kentucky 2015), and editor of *Nationalism and Identity Construction in Central Asia: Dimensions, Dynamics, and Directions* (Lexington 2015).

Ariel Cohen (2011 and 2014 Editions)
Ariel Cohen is a Senior Research Fellow at The Kathryn and Shelby Cullom Davis Institute for International Studies at the Heritage Foundation. He received his Ph.D. from the Fletcher School of Law and Diplomacy at Tufts University in Massachusetts. Dr. Cohen is also a member of the Council of Foreign Relations, International Institute of Strategic Studies in London, and Association for the Study of Nationalities. His research interests include the economic development and political reform in the former Soviet Republics, and continuing conflicts in the Middle East. He has on multiple occasions testified on Russian and Eurasian politics, economics, and law before the U.S. Congress. Dr. Cohen has also published numerous pieces of writing.

Kosovo
Christopher Deliso (2011, 2014, and 2017 Editions)
Christopher Deliso is an American journalist and author concentrating on the Balkans. Over the past decade, Chris has established a dedicated presence in the Balkans, and published analytical articles on related topics in numerous relevant media outlets, such as UPI, The Economist Intelligence Unit, Jane's Islamic Affairs Analyst and Jane's Intelligence Digest. Chris is also the founder and director of the Balkan-interest news and current affairs website, www.balkanalysis.com, and the author of The Coming Balkan Caliphate: The Threat of Radical Islam to Europe and the West (Praeger Security International, 2007).

Kuwait
Kristian Coates Ulrichsen (2014 and 2017 Editions)
Kristian Coates Ulrichsen, Ph.D., is the Baker Institute fellow for Kuwait. Working across the disciplines of political science, international relations and international political economy, his research examines the changing position of Persian Gulf states in the global order, as well as the emergence of longer-term, non-military challenges to regional security. He is a visiting fellow at the LSE Middle East Centre and an associate fellow at Chatham House in the United Kingdom.

Coates Ulrichsen has published extensively on the Gulf. His books include *Insecure Gulf: the End of Certainty and the Transition to the Post-Oil Era* (Columbia University Press, 2011) and *The Political Economy of Arab Gulf States* (Edward Elgar Publishing, 2012). He is currently completing a book on Qatar and the Arab Spring and has been commissioned to write a textbook on the Gulf and international political economy. Coates Ulrichsen's articles have appeared several academic journals, and he consults regularly on Gulf issues for Oxford Analytica and the Norwegian Peacebuilding Resource Centre. He also authors a monthly column for Gulf Business News and Analysis.

Aviv Oreg (2011 Edition)
Aviv Oreg is a veteran officer of the Israeli intelligence community, mostly covering issues related to the global *jihad* phenomenon and its most dominant entity factor – the al-Qaeda organization. His last position was as head of the "Al Qaeda and Global Jihad" desk in the IDF's military intelligence. Since the summer of 2007, Mr. Oreg has served as the founding president of Ceifi T, an investigative consulting firm composed of veterans of the Israeli intelligence community that offers comprehensive research, analysis and counseling services of the global *jihad* phenomenon.

Kyrgyzstan

Cory Bender (2017 Edition)
Cory Bender is the Program Officer for Central Asia at the Institute for Global Engagement. He received a bachelor's degree in Russian Studies and Political Science from the University of Massachusetts Amherst. Before coming to IGE, Bender worked at the American Foreign Policy Council, and conducted research on Central Asia at the Hudson Institute's Center for Political-Military Analysis. He also interned at the U.S. Embassy in Moscow, where he coordinated public affairs and consular programs. In 2011, Bender studied abroad at the American University of Central Asia in Bishkek, Kyrgyzstan, where he also worked as an Editorial Assistant at the Institute for Public Policy, a Bishkek-based think tank. He studied Russian in Kazan, Russia as a Critical Language Scholar and at Middlebury College, where he was a Kathryn Davis Fellow. He is originally from Chelmsford, Massachusetts and currently resides in Alexandria, Virginia.

Evgeuni Novikov (2014 Edition)
Evgueni Novikov is an expert with extensive on-the-ground experience in Islam and considerable practical experience in the Central Asia and Persian Gulf regions. Dr. Novikov was one of top experts on Islamic affairs for the Soviet government. He is the author of a number of articles and of several books, including *Gorbachev and the Collapse of the Soviet Communist Party: The Historical and Theoretical Background* (Peter Lang, 1994) and *Central Asian Responses to Radical Islam* (AFPC, 2006).

Orozbek Moldaliev (2011 Edition)
Orozbek Moldaliev is one of the best-informed Central Asian experts on terrorism and radical Islam. Dr. Moldaliev is professor and head of the Department of World Politics and International Relations at the Diplomatic Academy of the Kyrgyz Republic. Both a faithful Muslim and an established

intellectual, he has published 36 books and articles on Islam, Islamic terrorism and problems of Central Asian national security.

Lashkar-e Taiba

Michael Kugelman (2017 Edition)
Michael Kugelman is the Asia Program Deputy Director and Senior Associate for South Asia at the Woodrow Wilson Center, where he is responsible for research, programming, and publications on the region. His main specialty is Pakistan, India, and Afghanistan and U.S. relations with each of them. Mr. Kugelman writes monthly columns for Foreign Policy's South Asia Channel and monthly commentaries for *War on the Rocks*. He also contributes regular pieces to *The Wall Street Journal's* Think Tank blog. He has published op-eds and commentaries in *The New York Times, The Los Angeles Times, Politico, CNN.com, Bloomberg View, The Diplomat, Al Jazeera,* and *The National Interest,* among others. He has been interviewed by numerous major media outlets including T*he New York Times, The Washington Post, Financial Times, Guardian, Christian Science Monitor, National Geographic, BBC, CNN, NPR,* and *Voice of America*. He has also produced a number of longer publications on South Asia, including the edited volumes *Pakistan's Interminable Energy Crisis: Is There Any Way Out?* (Wilson Center, 2015), *Pakistan's Runaway Urbanization: What Can Be Done?* (Wilson Center, 2014), and *India's Contemporary Security Challenges* (Wilson Center, 2013). He has published policy briefs, journal articles, and book chapters on issues ranging from Pakistani youth and social media to India's energy security strategy and transboundary water management in South Asia.

Aaron Mannes (2014 Edition)
Aaron Mannes is a researcher at the University of Maryland's Laboratory for Computational Cultural Dynamics, a PhD candidate at the University of Maryland's School of Public Policy, and a co-author of *Computational Analysis of Terror Groups: Lashkar-e-Taiba* (Springer 2013) as well as numerous popular and scholarly articles on terrorism and international affairs. He can be reached through his website—www.aaronmannes.com.

Michael Garber (2014 Edition)
Michael Garber is a research assistant at the University of Maryland's Laboratory for Computational Cultural Dynamics and earned a Masters with a concentration in international security affairs from the University of Maryland's School of Public Policy.

Ashley Tellis (2011 Edition)

Ashley Tellis is a foremost expert in the fields of non-proliferation, South Asian strategic issues and U.S. Foreign Policy. Dr. Tellis is currently a senior associate at the Carnegie Endowment for International Peace, and has served as the senior advisor to the Undersecretary of State for Political Affairs in negotiating the civil nuclear agreement with India. Prior to his position at the Carnegie Endowment, he was commissioned into the U.S. Foreign Service, where he served as senior advisor to the ambassador at the U.S. embassy in New Delhi. Dr. Tellis is the author and co-author of several books, and has contributed greatly to many annual volumes and journals. Dr. Tellis holds a BA and MA from the University of Bombay ad received a second MA and his PhD from the University of Chicago.

Lebanon

Aaron Mannes (2017 Edition)
Aaron Mannes is a researcher at the University of Maryland's Laboratory for Computational Cultural Dynamics, a PhD candidate at the University of Maryland's School of Public Policy, and a co-author of *Computational Analysis of Terror Groups: Lashkar-e-Taiba* (Springer 2013) as well as numerous popular and scholarly articles on terrorism and international affairs. He can be reached through his website—www.aaronmannes.com.

Ian Garner (2014 Edition)
Ian Garner is the Mediterranean Research Associate at the NESA Center, National Defense University. His research interests include insurgency and state building, democratization, energy, and Islamic social movements.

Robert Rabil (2011 Edition)
Robert Rabil is the director of graduate studies and an associate professor of Middle Eastern Studies at the Florida Atlantic University's Department of Political Science. Dr. Rabil is an expert on Middle Eastern affairs, having written several books and multiple articles dealing with the Arab-Israeli Conflict, Radical Islam, Hezbollah, Lebanon, Israel, Iraq, and Syria. He served as chief of emergency of the Red Cross in Lebanon's Baabda ditsrict during the country's civil war. He also was project manager of Iraq Research and Documentation Project, a project affiliated with Harvard University and funded by the US State Department. Dr. Rabil holds a Master's degree in Government from the Harvard University Extension School and a Ph.D. in Near Eastern and Judaic Studies from Brandeis University.

Libya

Chloe Thompson and Brian J. Carpowich (2017 Edition)
Chloe Thompson is a Research Fellow and Program Officer at the American Foreign Policy Council. She serves as the Managing Editor of the *World Almanac of Islamism*. Her previous work with AFPC involved research on the military use and strategic implications of unmanned aerial vehicles, as well as militant groups in the Middle East and Latin America. Ms. Thompson joined AFPC in June 2016 after graduating with High Honors from Carnegie Mellon University.

Brian J. Carpowich is a Research Intern at the American Foreign Policy Council who focuses on Radical Islamism, Terrorism and Middle Eastern security concerns. He is also pursuing a Master of Arts in International Affairs at George Washington University, where he studies both International and Transnational Security issues. He graduated from Saint Vincent College in 2016 with a BA in Political Science and a minor in International Studies. Mr. Carpowich has also received a Certificate in Middle Eastern Studies from the American University in Dubai.

Aaron Y. Zelin (2014 Edition)
Aaron Y. Zelin is the Richard Borow Fellow at the Washington Institute for Near East Policy where his research focuses on how jihadi groups are adjusting to the new political environment in the era of Arab uprisings and Salafi politics in countries transitioning to democracy. He also serves as a consultant and lecturer at the U.S. Military Academy at West Point's Combating Terrorism Center's Practitioner Education Program. Zelin is a frequent contributor to *Foreign Policy*, *Foreign Affairs*, and *The Atlantic*, and is the author of the New America Foundation's 2013 study *The State of the Global Jihad Online*. He independently maintains the widely cited website Jihadology.net and co-edits the blog al-Wasat.

Aviv Oreg (2011 Edition)
Aviv Oreg is a veteran officer of the Israeli intelligence community, mostly covering issues related to the global *jihad* phenomenon and its most dominant entity factor – the al-Qaeda organization. His last position was as head of the "Al Qaeda and Global Jihad" desk in the IDF's military intelligence. Since the summer of 2007, Mr. Oreg has served as the founding president of CeifiT, an investigative consulting firm composed of veterans of the Israeli intelligence community that offers comprehensive research, analysis, and counseling services of the global jihad phenomenon.

Malaysia
Joseph Chinyong Liow (2011, 2014, and 2017 Editions)
Joseph Chinyong Liow is Associate Dean and Professor of Comparative and International Politics at the S. Rajaratnam School of International Studies, Nanyang Technological University, Singapore. He is the author of *Piety and Politics: Islamism in Contemporary Malaysia* (New York: Oxford University Press, 2009) and *Islam, Education and Reform in Southern Thailand* (Singapore: ISEAS, 2009).

Maldives
Animesh Roul (2011, 2014, and 2017 Editions)
Animesh Roul is the Executive Director at Society for the Study of Peace and Conflict, (www.sspconline.org) a Delhi-based policy research think-tank. In his earlier stint he worked as a Research Associate at New Delhi-based Institute for Conflict Management, which hosts a leading terrorism database on South Asia (www.SATP.org). He holds a Master of Philosophy degree from the School of International Studies, Jawaharlal Nehru University, New Delhi and has a master's degree in Modern Indian History. Mr. Roul specializes in counterterrorism, radical Islam, terror financing, armed conflict and issues relating to arms control and proliferation in South Asia. He has written for *Terrorism Monitor, The CTC Sentinel, Jane's Intelligence Review, Militant Leadership Monitor,* and *CBW Magazine,* among others. He is also serving as executive editor of *South Asia Conflict Monitor* (SACM), a monthly E-bulletin on armed conflicts and terrorist violence in South Asia.

Mali
Julian Wyss (2017 Edition)
Julian Wyss is the assistant director of the Atlantic Council's Africa Center. Prior to the Atlantic Council, Julian worked in the humanitarian aid sector, including supporting Syrian refugee populations as an intern for the Danish Refugee Council (DRC) in Jordan, and assisting with the resettlement of newly arrived Iraqi and Afghani refugees at the International Rescue Committee (IRC) in Northern California. Julian later employed his expertise in refugee support as the program director for the *Salam Neighbor* project, a documentary film about life in a Syrian refugee camp. He has also worked as a consultant in the humanitarian sector, most notably for the Disasters Emergency Committee (DEC) in London, UK.
Julian holds an MSc in International Development and Humanitarian Emergencies from the London School of Economics and Political Science (LSE) and a BA in International Relations/Political Science from Carleton

College, where his senior thesis involved field research on the influence of religious civic organizations in Mali. His professional interests include conflict, humanitarianism, migration, and security in the Sahel.

Laura Grossman (2011 and 2014 Editions)
Laura Grossman is a Research Analyst for the Foundation for Defense of Democracies' Iran Energy Project. She co-authored *Homegrown Terrorists in the U.S. and the U.K.* and *Terrorism in the West 2008* with Daveed Gartenstein-Ross, in addition to *Iran's Energy Partners* and *Iran's Chinese Energy* Partners with Mark Dubowitz. She holds a BA in History from the University of Michigan and an MS in Global Affairs from New York University.

Mauritania

Martin A. Ewi (2014 and 2017 Editions)
Martin A. Ewi joined the Institute for Security Studies in July 2010, as a Senior Researcher, International Crime in Africa Programme (ICAP), Pretoria Office. He previously served as a Political Affairs Officer at the headquarters of the Organisation for the Prohibition of Chemical Weapons (OPCW) based in The Hague, the Netherlands from 2005 to 2010. Before joining the OPCW, Mr Ewi was in charge of the African Union Commission's counter-terrorism programme in Addis Ababa, Ethiopia, where he was concurrently in charge of security strategic issues from 2002 to 2005.

Mr. Ewi holds a MA degree in International Peace Studies from the University of Notre Dame, at Southbend, Indiana, United States of America. He also holds a BA (with Distinction) in Peace Studies and International Politics from Juniata College in Huntingdon, Pennsylvania, United States of America. His research focus is in the area of counterterrorism and the competences of regional organizations in Africa on strategic security issues.

Daniel Zisenwine (2011 Edition)
Daniel Zisenwine is the author of two books, *The Maghrib in the New Century* (University Press of Florida, 2007) and *The Emergence of Nationalist Politics in Morocco* (Tauris Academic Studies, 2010). Dr. Zisenwine is a Research Fellow at the Moshe Dayan Center for Middle Eastern and African Studies. He holds a Ph.D. from the Tel Aviv University.

Morocco

J. Peter Pham (2014 and 2017 Editions)
J. Peter Pham is Vice President for Research and Regional Initiatives at the Atlantic Council as well as Director of the Council's Africa Center. He also

serves as Vice President of the Association for the Study of the Middle East and Africa (ASMEA) and Editor-in-Chief of its refereed *Journal of the Middle East and Africa*.

Marc Ginsberg (2011 Edition)
Marc Ginsberg served as U.S. Ambassador to Morocco under President Clinton, and before that as Deputy Senior Advisor to the President for Middle East Policy from 1979-1981. He is Senior Vice-President of APCO Worldwide and President of Layalina Productions, a producer of television series and documentaries for Middle East television networks.

Muslim Brotherhood

Eric Trager (2017 Edition)
Eric Trager, the Esther K. Wagner Fellow at The Washington Institute, is an expert on Egyptian politics and the Muslim Brotherhood in Egypt. He was in Egypt during the 2011 anti-Mubarak revolts and returns frequently to conduct firsthand interviews with leaders in Egypt's government, military, political parties, media, and civil society. His writings have appeared in numerous publications, including *The New York Times, The Wall Street Journal, Foreign Affairs, The Atlantic,* and *The New Republic.*

Trager is the author of *Arab Fall: How the Muslim Brotherhood Won and Lost Egypt in 891 Days* (Georgetown University Press, 2016), which chronicles the precipitous rise to power of Egypt's Muslim Brotherhood, culminating in the election of President Mohamed Morsi in 2012, and its sudden demise just a year later. The book also assesses the current state of Egyptian politics and the prospects for a reemergence of the Brotherhood.

Dr. Trager has served as an adjunct professor at the University of Pennsylvania, where his doctoral research focused on Egyptian opposition parties. From 2006-2007, he lived in Egypt as an Islamic Civilizations Fulbright fellow, where he studied at the American University in Cairo and received his M.A. in Arabic studies with a concentration in Islamic studies. He served as a research assistant at The Washington Institute from 2005 to 2006 upon graduation from Harvard University with a degree in government and language citations in Arabic and Hebrew.

Myriam Benraad (2011 and 2014 Editions)
Myriam Benraad is a research fellow in the Middle East and Mediterranean doctoral program of the Paris Institute of Political Studies (Sciences Po), and at the Center for International Studies and Research (CERI). She is also an Associate Fellow at the Washington Institute for Near East Policy in Washington, DC.

Netherlands

Margot van Loon (2014 and 2017 Editions)
Margot van Loon is a former Junior Fellow at the American Foreign Policy Council. She conducts research, editing, and analysis in support of multiple AFPC publications. She formerly served as the Project Coordinator for AFPC's *World Almanac of Islamism*. A graduate of American University, her research focuses on U.S. foreign policy and public diplomacy. Her commentary has appeared in *U.S. News and World Report*.

Ronald Sandee (2011 Edition)
Ronald Sandee has served as the director of analysis & research at the NEFA Foundation since June 2006. Previously, he worked as a senior analyst at the transnational affairs desk at the Dutch Ministry of Defense. He focuses his research on core al-Qaeda in the Afghanistan-Pakistan area, terrorism in Africa and radicalization in Europe and the U.S.

Nicaragua

Jon Perdue (2014 and 2017 Editions)
Jon B. Perdue is the author of *The War of All the People: The Nexus of Latin American Radicalism and Middle Eastern Terrorism* (Potomac Books, 2012). Perdue is a noted scholar and researcher on issues of international terrorism, human rights, strategic communication, and peripheral asymmetric warfare. Mr. Perdue serves as the Senior Fellow for Strategic Research at the Center for a Secure Free Society, a Washington, DC think tank focused on economics and security, and as the Director of Latin America Programs at The Fund for American Studies. He co-edited the book *Rethinking the Reset Button: Understanding Contemporary Russian Foreign Policy*, and also wrote the foreword.
Mr. Perdue's articles have been published in numerous magazines and newspapers, including *The Washington Times, Investors Business Daily*, and *The Miami Herald*, as well as a variety of newspapers in Latin America. In 2010, Mr. Perdue served as an expert witness in a precedent-setting human rights trial in the Miami Circuit Court, and in 2009 he traveled to Honduras as part of a senior U.S. delegation to take part in the historic Honduran presidential elections as an international observer.

Douglas Farah (2011 Edition)
Douglas Farah is president of IBI Consultants LLC and a senior fellow at the International Assessment and Strategy Center. For twenty years, he was a foreign correspondent and investigative reporter at *The Washington Post*, where

he won numerous awards for his work. In addition to his national security consulting work he is a regular lecturer at universities, government agencies and foreign policy groups. He has testified before Congress on numerous occasions, has written two books and numerous articles and monographs.

Nigeria
Jacob Zenn (2014 and 2017 Editions)
Jacob Zenn is an analyst of African and Eurasian Affairs for The Jamestown Foundation and author of the Occasional Report entitled *Northern Nigeria's Boko Haram: The Prize in al-Qaeda's Africa Strategy*, published by The Jamestown Foundation in November 2012. In 2012, he conducted field research in Nigeria, Niger, Chad and Cameroon on the socio-economic factors behind the Boko Haram insurgency. Mr. Zenn earned a J.D. from Georgetown Law, where he was a Global Law Scholar, and a graduate degree in International Affairs from the Johns Hopkins SAIS Center for Chinese-American Studies in Nanjing, China. He has spoken at international conferences on Boko Haram and is frequently interviewed and cited in international media.

Pakistan
Lisa Curtis (2011, 2014, and 2017 Editions)
Lisa Curtis is a senior research fellow at the Heritage Foundation. She specializes in America's economic, security and political relationships with India, Pakistan, Afghanistan, and other South Asian countries. Curtis has testified before Congress on more than a dozen occasions on topics relating to India, Pakistan, radical Islamists, and America's image abroad. Prior to her work at the Heritage Foundation, Curtis was a member of the professional staff of the Senate Foreign Relations Committee, in charge of South Asian affairs for then chairman Sen. Richard Luger (R-Ind). Curtis also served abroad in the U.S. Foreign Service, where she was assigned to the U.S. embassies in Pakistan and India. She received her BA in Economics from Indiana University.

Palestinian Territories
Grant Rumley (2017 Edition)
Grant Rumley is a research fellow at the Foundation for Defense of Democracies, where he focuses on Palestinian politics. Grant has published in leading media outlets including Foreign Affairs and Foreign Policy, and contributed commentary to The New York Times, Reuters, and Newsweek. He is the author of the 2015 FDD report *The Race to Replace Mahmoud*

Abbas: Understanding and Shaping Palestinian Succession.
Prior to joining FDD, Grant was a visiting fellow at Mitvim, The Israeli Institute for Regional Foreign Policies, where he authored, *Back to Basics: The Evolution of the Palestinian UN Campaign.* While in Jerusalem, Grant also founded and edited The Jerusalem Review of Near East Affairs. Previously, Grant served as a consultant in Washington on issues related to counter-terrorism, the Middle East, and war-gaming strategies.

Grant has an MA in Middle East Studies from the Hebrew University of Jerusalem and a BA in International Relations from Michigan State University. In 2010, he studied Arabic at the University of Alexandria, Egypt, and from 2012-2013 was a Rotary Ambassadorial Scholar.

Jonathan Schanzer (2014 Edition)
Jonathan Schanzer is vice president for research at the Foundation for Defense of Democracies. Jonathan worked as a terrorism finance analyst at the U.S. Department of the Treasury, where he played an integral role in the designation of numerous terrorist financiers. A former research fellow at the Washington Institute for Near East Policy, Dr Schanzer is author of two books and two monographs. His 2008 book, *Hamas vs. Fatah: The Struggle for Palestine* (Palgrave Macmillan), is still the only book on the market that analyzes the internecine conflict between the two most powerful Palestinian factions. His 2004 book, *Al-Qaeda's Armies: Middle East Affiliate Groups and the Next Generation of Terror* (Washington Institute for Near East Policy), was the first to explore the al-Qaeda franchises of the Middle East. More recently, Dr. Schanzer co-authored a monograph in 2010 with FDD's executive director Mark Dubowitz titled, *Palestinian Pulse: What Policymakers Can Learn From Palestinian Social Media* (FDD Press). Using proprietary technology, this study collected data from thousands of Arabic language websites to reveal the trends, thoughts, and perceptions of Palestinians online, with a focus on those that could impact current U.S. policies. In 2012, he co-authored another cutting edge study, using the same technology, with FDD researcher Steven Miller titled, *Facebook Fatwa: Saudi Clerics, Wahhabi Islam and Social Media* (FDD Press). This cutting edge study explores the way in which Saudi religious figures disseminate their messages to the wider Muslim world.

David Barnett (2014 Edition)
David Barnett is a former research associate at the Foundation for Defense of Democracies (FDD). His research focused on Palestinian politics as well as Salafi jihadist groups in the Palestinian Territories and Sinai Peninsula. He has been cited in numerous publications including *The Washington Post, The New York Times,* and *Foreign Policy.*

Raymond Ibrahim (2011 Edition)
Raymond Ibrahim is associate director of the Middle East Forum, author of *The Al Qaeda Reader* (Doubleday, 2007), and deputy publisher of *The Middle East Quarterly*. A widely published author on Islam, he regularly discusses that topic with the media, including *Fox News, C-SPAN, Reuters, Al-Jazeera, NPR, CBN,* and *PBS*. Mr. Ibrahim guest-lectures at the National Defense Intelligence College (Washington, D.C.), briefs governmental agencies (such as U.S. Strategic Command), provides expert testimony for Islam related lawsuits, and has testified before Congress regarding the conceptual failures that dominate American discourse concerning Islam. He began his career as a reference assistant at the Library of Congress' Near East Section.

Philippines
Jeffrey S. Payne (2014 and 2017 Editions)
Jeffrey S. Payne is a Research Fellow and Academic Affairs Manager at the Near East-South Asia (NESA) Center at the National Defense University, which he joined in 2012 after serving for five years as an Instructor of Political Science at Butler University. As a Research Fellow at the NESA Center, Payne conducts analysis on Chinese foreign policy, South Asian security affairs, maritime security, and transnational movements. While at Butler, he taught classes on Asian politics, social movements, international relations, and political economy. Payne has also served as a consultant for the World Bank and as a faculty member for DePauw University. Payne received his Master's Degree from Indiana University. Originally hailing from the Midwest, he has lived in China and traveled extensively throughout Asia.

Zachary Abuza (2011)
Zachary Abuza is Professor of National Security Studies at the National War College and Professor of Political Science and International Relations at Simmons College. He is the author of four books on politics and security issues in Southeast Asia.

Qatar
Yael Shahar (2011, 2014, and 2017 Editions)
Yael Shahar is the Director for the Database Project Institute for Counter-Terrorism at the IDC Herzliya. Ms. Shahar also heads the International Institute for Counter-Terrorism's (ICT) OSINT project. She specializes in the study of technological trends as applied to terrorism and intelligence sharing. She is a dynamic speaker, and has lectured worldwide on topics

related to trends in terrorism, non-conventional and techno-terrorism, threat assessment and asymmetric conflict. Ms. Shahar studied Physics and Philosophy of Science at the University of Texas and at the Hebrew University in Jerusalem. She has also served as a reservist in the IDF hostage rescue unit, and is a director and co-founder of the Institute for the Study of Asymmetric Conflict.

Russia
Ilan Berman and Heather Stetten (2017 Edition)
Ilan Berman is Vice President of the American Foreign Policy Council in Washington, DC. An expert on regional security in the Middle East, Central Asia, and the Russian Federation, he has consulted for both the U.S. Central Intelligence Agency and the U.S. Department of Defense, and provided assistance on foreign policy and national security issues to a range of governmental agencies and congressional offices. Berman is the author or editor of six books: *Tehran Rising: Iran's Challenge to the United States* (Rowman & Littlefield, 2005), *Dismantling Tyranny: Transitioning Beyond Totalitarian Regimes* (Rowman & Littlefield, 2005), *Taking on Tehran: Strategies for Confronting the Islamic Republic* (Rowman & Littlefield, 2007), *Winning the Long War: Retaking the Offensive Against Radical Islam* (Rowman & Littlefield, 2009), *Implosion: The End of Russia and What it Means for America* (Regnery Publishing, 2013), and *Iran's Deadly Ambition: The Islamic Republic's Quest for Global Power* (Encounter Books, 2015).

Heather Stetten joined AFPC as a Junior Fellow in December 2016. A specialist in Russia studies, Heather holds a Master's Degrees from the Kathryn Davis School of Russian at Middlebury College in collaboration with the Russian State University for Humanities in Moscow. A former AFPC researcher, she previously worked with Transparency International and the Higher School of Economics in Moscow to write reports in English and in Russian on corruption in state-run corporations and best practices for setting up provisional governments in newly formed nations.

Gordon Hahn (2011 and 2014 Editions)
Gordon Hahn is a Senior Researcher for the Center for Terrorism and Intelligence Studies (CETIS) and an academic fellow at Smolny College in St. Petersburg, Russia. He has taught extensively on the topics of Russian domestic and foreign policy at Stanford, St. Petersburg State (Russia), Boston, American, and San Jose State Universities. Dr. Hahn is the author of two books and is published in many Russian and English language scholarly

journals. He specializes in Muslim politics and terrorism in Russia. Dr, Hahn received his BA and MA from Boston College, and his Ph.D. from Boston University.

Saudi Arabia
Leisel Bogan (2017 Edition)
Leisel Bogan works in the private sector on global strategy and cybersecurity. Leisel's career has focused on driving programs and initiatives across the international policy, technology, and national security sectors. Prior to her current role she was a Research Fellow at Stanford University's Hoover Institution where she focused on cybersecurity and international policy, and led the initial strategic outreach and coalition efforts of the Hoover Institution's Washington D.C. office. From 2009-the end of 2012 she worked for Dr. Condoleezza Rice in a variety of capacities including as her deputy and interim Chief of Staff, ending her tenure as Director of Research, while concurrently working for private clients in emerging markets at the boutique geostrategic consulting firm, RiceHadleyGates, LLC. Leisel has also worked on new media technologies and strategy at Warner Bros. Entertainment and business advisor strategy, communications, and philanthropy at Palantir Technologies. She has lived and worked in Germany, and conducted Fellowships in Georgia, Armenia, Azerbaijan, Japan, and Egypt. She holds a master's degree in Public Policy with concentrations in economics and international relations from Pepperdine University, and has guest lectured at the undergraduate school's study abroad program in Florence, Italy. Leisel began her career in television advertising as a child actor and trained professionally in ballet before teaching it for more than ten years. She is Term Member in the Council on Foreign Relations and is a 2016 Gabr Foundation Fellow.

Steve Miller (2011 and 2014 Editions)
Steve Miller is a Research Associate at the Foundation for Defense of Democracies (FDD) and co-author of Facebook Fatwa: Saudi Clerics, Wahhabi Islam and Social Media. He is fluent in Arabic and as part of his research at FDD; he monitors and analyzes the Arabic language press. He also conducts research related to extremism, ideology, and online media in Saudi Arabia. Prior to his time at the FDD, Mr. Miller was a policy analyst at the Institute for Gulf Affairs in Washington, DC. He received his BA in Economics and Near Eastern Languages and Cultures, including classical Arabic from Indiana University.

Somalia

J. Peter Pham (2011, 2014, and 2017 Editions)
J. Peter Pham is Vice President for Research and Regional Initiatives at the Atlantic Council as well as Director of the Council's Africa Center. He also serves as Vice President of the Association for the Study of the Middle East and Africa (ASMEA) and Editor-in-Chief of its refereed *Journal of the Middle East and Africa*.

South Africa
Anonymous (2017 Edition)
AFPC thanks our anonymous authors for their generous contributions to the *World Almanac of Islamism*.

Laura Grossman (2011 and 2014 Editions)
Laura Grossman is a Research Analyst for the Foundation for Defense of Democracies' Iran Energy Project. She co-authored *Homegrown Terrorists in the U.S. and the U.K.* and *Terrorism in the West 2008* with Daveed Gartenstein-Ross, in addition to *Iran's Energy Partners* and *Iran's Chinese Energy Partners* with Mark Dubowitz. She holds a BA in History from the University of Michigan and an MS in Global Affairs from New York University.

Spain
Margot van Loon (2014 and 2017 Editions)
Margot van Loon is a former Junior Fellow at the American Foreign Policy Council. She conducts research, editing, and analysis in support of multiple AFPC publications. She formerly served as the Project Coordinator for AFPC's World Almanac of Islamism. A graduate of American University, her research focuses on U.S. foreign policy and public diplomacy. Her commentary has appeared in *U.S. News and World Report*.

Rafael Bardaji (2011 Editions)
Rafael Bardaji is a member of the Atlantic Council's Strategic Advisors Group. He has published several books and multiple works for scholarly journals. He was the founder and Director of the Grupo de Estudios Estrategicos until 1996 when he served as the executive adviser to the Spanish Ministers of Defense Eduardo Serra and Federico Trillo. He is also a member of the IISS in London and the International Council of the Institute for Foreign Policy Analysis. Mr. Bardaji is a graduate in Political Sciences and Sociology from the Complutense University of Madrid.

Syria

Aymenn Jawad Al-Tamimi (2017 Edition)
Aymenn Jawad Al-Tamimi is a graduate from Brasenose College, Oxford University, and a Jihad-Intel Research Fellow at the Middle East Forum. Follow him on Twitter at @ajaltamimi.

Matt Brodsky (2011 and 2014 Editions)
Matt Brodsky is the Director of Policy for the Jewish Policy Center (JPC) and the editor for the JPC's journal, inFOCUS Quarterly. Prior to his work at the JPC, Mr. Brodsky was the Senior Geopolitical Analyst for IntelliWhiz LLC and a Legacy Heritage Fellow at the American Foreign Policy Council. He is an expert in Middle Eastern Affairs and Arab Politics, and has on multiple occasions has briefed and advised members of Congress, the Department of State, the Department of Defense and the National Security Council. Mr. Brodsky holds a MA in Middle East History from the Tel Aviv University.

Tajikistan
Svante E. Cornell and Julian Tucker (2017 Edition)
Svante E. Cornell joined the American Foreign Policy Council as Senior Fellow for Eurasia in January 2017. He also servs as the Director of the Central Asia-Caucasus Institute & Silk Road Studies Program, and a co-founder of the Institue for Security and Development Policy, Stockholm. His main areas of expertise are security issues, state-building, and transnational crime in Southwest and Central Asia, with a specific focus on the Caucasus and Turkey. He is the Editor of *The Central Asia-Caucasus Analyst*, the Joint Center's bi-weekly publication, and of the Joint Center's *Silk Road Papers* series of occasional papers.

Cornell is the author of four books, including *Small Nations and Great Powers*, the first comprehensive study of the post-Soviet conflicts in the Caucasus, and *Azerbaijan Since Independence*. Cornell is an Associate Research Professor at Johns Hopkins University's Paul H. Nitze School of Advanced International Studies. He was educated at the Middle East Technical University, received his Ph.D. in Peace and Conflict Studies from Uppsala University, and holds an honorary degree from the National Academy of Sciences of Azerbaijan. He is a member of the Swedish Royal Academy of Military Science, and a Research Associate with the W. Martens Center for European Studies in Brussels. Formerly, Cornell served as Associate Professor of Government at Uppsala University.

Mr. Julian Tucker is a Research Coordinator at the Stockholm China Center of the Institute for Security and Development Policy. He recently completed his Master of Arts in Central Asian Studies at the Humboldt University in Berlin, Germany. He also pursued Uzbek language and history courses at the Samarkand State Institute of Foreign Languages in Uzbekistan. He holds a BA in Anthropology and Middle Eastern Languages from McGill University in Montreal, Canada. Mr. Tucker's research interests include the implications of regional authority and security structures in Central Asia for international development efforts. At the China Centre his work will focus primarily on the One Belt One Road Initiative and Maritime Security in The South China Sea.

Tablighi Jama'at

Aaron Mannes (2017 Edition)
Aaron Mannes is a researcher at the University of Maryland's Laboratory for Computational Cultural Dynamics, a PhD candidate at the University of Maryland's School of Public Policy, and a co-author of *Computational Analysis of Terror Groups: Lashkar-e-Taiba* (Springer 2013) as well as numerous popular and scholarly articles on terrorism and international affairs. He can be reached through his website—www.aaronmannes.com.

Timothy R. Furnish (2011 and 2014 Editions)
Dr. Timothy R. Furnish works as an analyst and author specializing in Islamic eschatology, Mahdism and sects. He blogs on these topics at the History News Network as the Occidental Jihadist (http://hnn.us/blogs/78.html) and on his own site www.mahdiwatch.org. He is the author of *The Caliphate: Threat or Opportunity?*

Taliban

Javid Ahmad (2014 and 2017 Editions)
Javid Ahmad is a nonresident fellow with the Atlantic Council's South Asia Center and a senior intelligence manager at iJET International, a risk management firm, where he manages a fifteen-member team of intelligence analysts and provides analytical content and assessments to business and government clients. He is also a senior policy adviser to Afghanistan's minister of finance, focusing on devising policies and strategies on anti-money-laundering and counterterrorism financing issues. Additionally, he is a nonresident fellow at the Modern War Institute at West Point, where he researches and publishes on pressing security and counterterrorism issues in South Asia.

Previously, Javid worked on South Asia supporting the Pentagon's Afghanistan-

Pakistan Hands program and the US Naval Postgraduate School. He also worked as a program coordinator for Asia for the German Marshall Fund of the United States, a Washington-based think tank. In addition, he has worked for the NATO HQ in Brussels, the Voice of America, and the Afghan embassy in Washington. He has also worked on governance issues for organizations in Kabul. Javid's writing has appeared, *inter alia*, in *The New York Times, The Washington Post, The Financial Times, The Wall Street Journal, Foreign Policy, CNN.com, Foreign Affairs, The National Interest,* and *The Daily Beast*. He has a BA in international relations from Beloit College and an MA in security studies from Yale University.

Matt DuPee (2011 Edition)
Matt DuPee has studied political and security events in Afghanistan since 1999. His articles have been published in a variety of publications, including *The CTC Sentinel, World Politics Review, Himal SouthAsian Magazine, Asia Times, The Center for Conflict and Peace Studies,* and others. He holds an M.A. in Regional Security Studies (South Asia) from the Naval Postgraduate School, Monterey, California, and continues his research on Afghanistan's narcotics, politics, security, geography and human terrain issues for the U.S. Department of Defense.

Tanzania

Kelsey Lilley (2017 Edition)
Kelsey Lilley is associate director of the Atlantic Council's Africa Center. Her work focuses on emerging security threats and political developments in sub-Saharan Africa, with particular interest in East Africa and the Horn.
Prior to the Atlantic Council, Kelsey worked for the Society for International Development and the Africa Center for Strategic Studies. From 2012 to 2013, she lived in Addis Ababa, Ethiopia, where she was a Princeton in Africa fellow for the International Rescue Committee.

Harvey Glickman (2014 Edition)
A member of Haverford College's faculty since 1960, Glickman was the first director and campus co-ordinator of African Studies, part of the four college Consortium on African Studies, headquartered at University of Pennsylvania. He has served as visiting professor at universities in Tanzania, South Africa, Israel and in several states in the USA. He has authored, and edited and contributed to six books and numerous articles and reviews for a number of scholarly journals in political science and international relations. He is now a Fellow of the Foreign Policy Association, has served as Secretary of the American

Political Science Association, and continues to serve as manuscript reviewer and book reviewer for several publishers and scholarly journals. He also consults for several government agencies and non-governmental organization.

Thailand

Don Pathan (2017 Edition)
Don Pathan is a Thailand-based consultant/analyst with more than 20 years of experience in covering diplomacy, international relations, transnational crime and insurgency in mainland Southeast Asia. Pathan has been working closely with The Asia Foundation and the World Bank on development in the conflict affected region in southern Thailand. Pathan briefs the diplomatic community, international think tanks and INGOs on a regular basis on issues pertaining to security in Thailand and the region. Pathan co-wrote a chapter that appeared in *Promoting Conflict or Peace through Identity*, a UN University book published by Ashgate in 2008, and co-authored *Confronting Ghosts: Thailand's Shapeless Southern Insurgency* with Dr. Joseph Liow. Lowy Institute in Sydney, Australia, published the monograph in 2006. Pathan also wrote a chapter in the *Trouble in the Triangle: Opium and Conflict in Burma* in 2005 in which he examine the nexus between the United Wa State Army, the Thai government and the military regime o f Burma/Myanmar. Pathan is also one of the founding member of the Patani Forum, a civil society organization dedicated to promoting critical discussion on the conflict and insurgency in Thailand's Malay-speaking South He is an associate at Asia Conflict and Security Consulting, Ltd. (ACAS), a Hong Kong-based consultancy that work on the intersect of conflict, development and investment.

Imtiyaz Yusuf (2014 Edition)
Dr. Imtiyaz Yusuf is Assistant Professor, Lecturer and Director of the Center for Buddhist-Muslim Understanding in the College of Religious Studies at Mahidol University in Thailand. He specializes in Religion with a focus on Islam in Thailand and Southeast Asia and also Muslim-Buddhist dialogue. In 2009-2010, he was visiting Associate Professor and Malaysia Chair of Islam in Southeast Asia at ACMCU, Georgetown University, Washington DC, USA. Dr. Yusuf has contributed to the *Oxford Encyclopedia of Islamic World* (2009); *Oxford Dictionary of Islam* (2003); *Encyclopedia of Qur'an* (2002); and *Oxford Encyclopedia of Modern Islamic World* (1995). He was also the Special Editor of *The Muslim World - A Special Issue on Islam and Buddhism* Vol. 100, Nos 2-3 April/July 2010.

Zachary Abuza (2011 Edition)

Zachary Abuza is Professor of National Security Studies at the National War College and Professor of Political Science and International Relations at Simmons College. He is the author of four books on politics and security issues in Southeast Asia.

Tunisia

Chloe Thompson (2017 Edition)
Chloe Thompson is a Research Fellow and Program Officer at the American Foreign Policy Council. She serves as the Managing Editor of the *World Almanac of Islamism*. Her previous work with AFPC involved research on the military use and strategic implications of unmanned aerial vehicles, as well as militant groups in the Middle East and Latin America. Ms. Thompson joined AFPC in June 2016 after graduating with High Honors from Carnegie Mellon University.

Lawrence Velte (2011 and 2014 Editions)
Lawrence Velte is an Associate Professor at the Near East South Asia Center for Strategic Studies at the National Defense University, focusing on the Maghreb and the Levant. He previously served as Deputy Chief of the Middle East Division, Joint Chiefs of Staff, and, as a U.S. Army officer, Middle East specialist, with tours of duty in Tunisia, Jerusalem, and Jordan.

Turkey

Claire Berlinski (2017 Edition)
Claire Berlinski is a former Senior Fellow for Turkey at AFPC. Ms. Berlinski is a City Journal contributing editor, a freelance investigative journalist, traveler writer, biographer, and novelist who lives in Istanbul. She is the author of *Menace in Europe: Why the Continent's Crisis is America's, Too*, and *There is No Alternative: Why Margaret Thatcher Matters*.
Her journalism has been published in *The New York Times, The Washington Post, The Los Angeles Times, First Post, The Oxford International Review, The American, Asia Times, The Globe and Mail, The New York Sun, The Weekly Standard, National Review, Policy Review, Radio Free Europe*, and *World Affairs Journal*, among others. She is also author of two spy novels and frequent guest on local and international radio talk shows.

Aaron Mannes (2014 Edition)
Aaron Mannes is a researcher at the University of Maryland's Laboratory for Computational Cultural Dynamics, a PhD candidate at the University of Maryland's School of Public Policy, and a co-author of *Computational*

Analysis of Terror Groups: Lashkar-e-Taiba (Springer 2013) as well as numerous popular and scholarly articles on terrorism and international affairs. He can be reached through his website—www.aaronmannes.com.

Okan Altiparmak (2011 Edition)
Okan Altiparmak is an international consultant on business and political matters located in Istanbul, Turkey. He is the founder of Nimbus Productions, which provides consultation and production services for film production and media companies filming or seeking guidance in Turkey.

Turkmenistan
Cory Bender (2014 and 2017 Editions)
Cory Bender is the Program Officer for Central Asia at the Institute for Global Engagement. He received a bachelor's degree in Russian Studies and Political Science from the University of Massachusetts Amherst. Before coming to IGE, Bender worked at the American Foreign Policy Council, and conducted research on Central Asia at the Hudson Institute's Center for Political-Military Analysis. He also interned at the U.S. Embassy in Moscow, where he coordinated public affairs and consular programs. In 2011, Bender studied abroad at the American University of Central Asia in Bishkek, Kyrgyzstan, where he also worked as an Editorial Assistant at the Institute for Public Policy, a Bishkek-based think tank. He studied Russian in Kazan, Russia as a Critical Language Scholar and at Middlebury College, where he was a Kathryn Davis Fellow. He is originally from Chelmsford, Massachusetts and currently resides in Alexandria, Virginia.

Annette Bohr (2011 Edition)
Annette Bohr is an Associate Fellow of the Russia and Eurasia Programme at the Institute of International Affairs in London (Chatham House). She is the author or co-author of two monographs and numerous articles on Central Asian politics, contemporary history, and ethnic and language policies.

United Arab Emirates
Malcolm Peck (2011, 2014, and 2017 Editions)
Malcolm Peck has been a program officer at Meridian International Center for the past 30 years, where he helps to plan and implement professional study tours for participants in the State Department's International Visitor Leadership Program. Between 1981 and 1983, he was Arabian Peninsula analyst for the State Department's Bureau of Intelligence and Research and,

from 1970 to 1981, was the director of programs at the Middle East Institute. Earlier, he taught at the University of Tennessee, Chattanooga and was a postdoctoral fellow at the Harvard University Center for Middle Eastern Studies. Dr. Peck is a specialist on Gulf-Arabian Peninsula issues and has published three books, ten chapters, and numerous articles on the topic. He received an A.B. and A.M. from Harvard University and an M.A., M.A.L.D., and Ph.D. from the Fletcher School of Law and Diplomacy.

United Kingdom
Anonymous (2017 Edition)
AFPC thanks our anonymous authors for their generous contributions to the *World Almanac of Islamism*.

Robin Simcox (2014 Edition)
Robin Simcox is a Research Fellow at the Henry Jackson Society, where he studies al-Qaeda and al-Qaeda inspired terrorism. Simcox has testified in front of the House of Representative Homeland Security Committee, and briefed the White House, National Counterterrorism Center, British Parliament, U.S. Special Operations Command and the European Parliament. He has written terrorism analysis for *The Wall Street Journal, The Los Angeles Times, The Washington Times, The Atlantic, World Affairs, National Interest and The New Republic*, among others. He also regularly appears on the media for the likes of the *BBC, CNN, Sky News, Fox News* and *Al-Jazeera*.
Simcox has an MSc in U.S. Foreign Policy from the Institute for the Study of Americas, University of London, and a BA in History (International) from the University of Leeds, which included a year at the University of Newcastle, Australia.

Alexander Meleagrou-Hitchens (2011 Edition)
Alexander Meleagrou-Hitchens is a Research Fellow at the International Centre for the Study of Radicalisation, King's College, London, where he is also a PhD candidate. His main area of study is Islamism in the West, and Salafi-Jihadist messaging in the English language.

United States
Anonymous (2017 Edition)
AFPC thanks our anonymous authors for their generous contributions to the *World Almanac of Islamism*.

Ilan Berman (2014 Edition)

Ilan Berman is Vice President of the American Foreign Policy Council in Washington, DC. An expert on regional security in the Middle East, Central Asia, and the Russian Federation, he has consulted for both the U.S. Central Intelligence Agency and the U.S. Department of Defense, and provided assistance on foreign policy and national security issues to a range of governmental agencies and congressional offices. Berman is the author or editor of six books: *Tehran Rising: Iran's Challenge to the United States* (Rowman & Littlefield, 2005), *Dismantling Tyranny: Transitioning Beyond Totalitarian Regimes* (Rowman & Littlefield, 2005), *Taking on Tehran: Strategies for Confronting the Islamic Republic* (Rowman & Littlefield, 2007), *Winning the Long War: Retaking the Offensive Against Radical Islam* (Rowman & Littlefield, 2009), *Implosion: The End of Russia and What it Means for America* (Regnery Publishing, 2013), and *Iran's Deadly Ambition: The Islamic Republic's Quest for Global Power* (Encounter Books, 2015).

Ryan Evans (2011 Edition)
Ryan Evans is an Associate Fellow at the International Centre for the Study of Radicalisation and Political Violence, King's College London, where he previously worked as a project manager. In that capacity, he designed research projects and managed a U.S. government-funded study on the radicalization of Muslims in the West in collaboration with the National Consortium for the Study of Terrorism and Responses to Terrorism at the University of Maryland. From 2005 to 2008, he was a senior research analyst at the Washington-based Investigative Project on Terrorism.

Uzbekistan
Evgeuni Novikov (2014 and 2017 Editions)
Evgueni Novikov is an expert with extensive on-the-ground experience in Islam and considerable practical experience in the Central Asia and Persian Gulf regions. Dr. Novikov was one of top experts on Islamic affairs for the Soviet government. He is the author of a number of articles and of several books, including *Gorbachev and the Collapse of the Soviet Communist Party: The Historical and Theoretical Background* (Peter Lang, 1994) and *Central Asian Responses to Radical Islam* (AFPC, 2006).

Orozbek Moldaliev (2011 Edition)
Orozbek Moldaliev is one of the best-informed Central Asian experts on terrorism and radical Islam. Dr. Moldaliev is professor and head of the Department of World Politics and International Relations at the Diplomatic Academy of the Kyrgyz Republic. Both a faithful Muslim and an established

intellectual, he has published 36 books and articles on Islam, Islamic terrorism and problems of Central Asian national security.

Venezuela
Anonymous (2017 Edition)
AFPC thanks our anonymous authors for their generous contributions to the *World Almanac of Islamism*.

Pearse Rafael Marchner (2011 and 2014 Editions)
P.R. Marschner is a student of Latin American and Levantine synergies and has worked for the U.S. Departments of State and Defense. The views expressed are his own.

Yemen
Katherine Zimmerman (2017 Edition)
Katherine Zimmerman is a research fellow at the American Enterprise Institute (AEI) and the research manager for AEI's Critical Threats Project. As the senior analyst on al Qaeda, she studies how the terrorist network operates globally. Her work is also focused on al Qaeda's affiliates in the Gulf of Aden region and in western and northern Africa. She specializes in al Qaeda in the Arabian Peninsula, the Yemen-based al Qaeda faction, and in al Shabaab, al Qaeda's affiliate in Somalia.
Ms. Zimmerman has testified before Congress about the threats to US national security interests emanating from al Qaeda and its network. She has also briefed members of Congress, their staff, and members of the defense community. Her analyses have been widely published, including in *CNN. com*, *The Huffington Post*, *The Wall Street Journal*, and *The Washington Post*. She graduated with distinction from Yale University with a B.A. in political science and modern Middle East studies.

Adam Seitz (2011 and 2014 Editions)
Adam C. Seitz is the Senior Research Associate for Middle East Studies at Marine Corps University in Quantico, Virginia where he supports the University with his expertise on the Middle East, with a concentration on Iran and the Persian Gulf Region. Mr. Seitz is the co-author, with Anthony H. Cordesman (CSIS), of the book *Iranian Weapons of Mass Destruction: The Birth of a Regional Nuclear Arms Race?* (Praeger Security International, 2009). Mr. Seitz served in the U.S. Army as an Intelligence Analyst and is an Operation Iraqi Freedom Veteran, serving in Al-Anbar province in 2003 and 2004.